P9-CME-940

COLLINS
GERMAN
DICTIONARY

FULLY REVISED AND UPDATED—
AMERICAN ENGLISH USAGE

Contributors

Howard Atkinson
Stuart Fortey
Robin Sawers
Veronika Schnorr
Yvonne Stein
Karin Weindl

HARPER

An Imprint of HarperCollins*Publishers*

HARPER

An Imprint of HarperCollins*Publishers*
195 Broadway,
New York, N Y 10007.

© William Collins Sons & Co. Ltd. 1990
© HarperCollins Publishers 2000, 2007
ISBN: 978-0-06-126048-3
ISBN-10: 0-06-126048-7

First Harper paperback printing: September 2007

Visit Harper paperbacks on the World Wide Web at www.harper
collins.com

10 9 8 7

INHALT

CONTENTS

WARENZEICHEN

NOTE ON TRADEMARKS

EINFÜHRUNG

Wir freuen uns sehr, dass Sie sich zum Kauf eines Collins
Wörterbuchs Deutsch entschlossen haben. Wir wünschen Ihnen
viel Spaß beim Gebrauch in der Schule, zu Hause, im Urlaub und
im Beruf.

INTRODUCTION

We are delighted you have decided to buy the Collins German
Dictionary and hope you will enjoy and benefit from using it at
school, at home, on holiday or at work.

William Collins' dream of knowledge
for all began with the publication of his
first book in 1819. A self-educated mill
worker, he not only enriched millions
of lives, but also founded a flourishing
publishing house. Today, staying true to
this spirit, Collins books are packed with
inspiration, innovation, and practical
expertise. They place you at the centre
of a world of possibility and give you
exactly what you need to explore it.

Language is the key to this exploration,
and at the heart of Collins Dictionaries is
language as it is really used. New words,
phrases, and meanings spring up every
day, and all of them are captured and
analysed by the Collins Word Web.
Constantly updated, and with over 2.5
billion entries, this living language
resource is unique to our dictionaries.

Words are tools for life. And a Collins
Dictionary makes them work for you.

Collins. Do more

ABKÜRZUNGEN

ABBREVIATIONS

auch	*a.*	also
Abkürzung	*abk, abbr*	abbreviation
Akronym	*acr*	acronym
Adjektiv	*adj*	adjective
Adverb	*adv*	adverb
Landwirtschaft	*Agr*	agriculture
Akkusativ	*akk*	accusative
Akronym	*akr*	acronym
Anatomie	*Anat*	anatomy
Artikel	*art*	article
Bildende Künste	*Art*	fine arts
Astronomie, Astrologie	*Astr*	astronomy, astrology
Auto, Verkehr	*Auto*	automobiles, traffic
Luftfahrt	*Aviat*	aviation
Biologie	*Bio*	biology
Botanik	*Bot*	botany
britisch	*BRIT*	British
schweizerisch	*CH*	Swiss
Chemie	*Chem*	chemistry
Film	*Cine*	cinema
Wirtschaft	*Comm*	commerce
Konjunktion	*conj*	conjunction
Dativ	*dat*	dative
Eisenbahn	*Eisenb*	railways
Elektrizität	*Elek, Elec*	electricity
besonders	*esp*	especially
und so weiter	*etc*	et cetera
etwas	*etw*	
Femininum	*f*	feminine
umgangssprachlich	*fam*	familiar, informal
übertragen	*fig*	figurative
Finanzen, Börse	*Fin*	finance
Fotografie	*Foto*	photography
Gastronomie	*Gastr*	cooking, gastronomy
Genitiv	*gen*	genitive
Geographie, Geologie	*Geo*	geography, geology
Geschichte	*Hist*	history
Imperativ	*imper*	imperative
Imperfekt	*imperf*	past tense
Informatik und Computer	*Inform*	computing
Interjektion, Ausruf	*interj*	interjection
unveränderlich	*inv*	invariable
unregelmäßig	*irr*	irregular
jemand	*jd*	
jemandem	*jdm*	
jemanden	*jdn*	

jemandes	jds	
Rechtsprechung	Jur	law
Konjunktion	konj	conjunction
Bildende Künste	Kunst	fine arts
Sprachwissenschaft, Grammatik	Ling	linguistics, grammar
Maskulinum	m	masculine
Mathematik	Math	mathematics
Medizin	Med	medicine
Meteorologie	Meteo	meteorology
Maskulinum und Femininum	mf	masculine and feminine
Militär	Mil	military
Musik	Mus	music
Substantiv	n	noun
Seefahrt	Naut	nautical, naval
Neutrum	nt	neuter
Zahlwort	num	numeral
oder	o	or
pejorativ, abwertend	pej	pejorative
Physik	Phys	physics
Plural	pl	plural
Politik	Pol	politics
Partizip Perfekt	pp	past participle
Präfix	pref	prefix
Präposition	prep	preposition
Pronomen	pron	pronoun
1. Vergangenheit	pt	past tense
Warenzeichen	®	registered trademark
Radio	Radio	radio
Eisenbahn	Rail	railways
Religion	Rel	religion
siehe	s.	see
	sb	someone, somebody
schottisch	SCOT	Scottish
Singular	sing	singular
Skisport	Ski	skiing
Sport	Sport	sports
	sth	something
Technik	Tech	technology
Nachrichtentechnik	Tel	telecommunications
Theater	Theat	theatre
Fernsehen	TV	television
Typographie, Buchdruck	Typo	printing
unpersönlich	unpers	impersonal
(nord)amerikanisch	US	(North) American
Verb	vb	verb
Hilfsverb	vb aux	auxiliary verb
intransitives Verb	vi	intransitive verb
reflexives Verb	vr	reflexive verb

transitives Verb	*vt*	transitive verb
vulgär	*vulg*	vulgar
Zoologie	*Zool*	zoology
zwischen zwei Sprechern	-	change of speaker
ungefähre Entsprechung	≈	cultural equivalent
abtrennbares Präfix	|	separable prefix

LAUTSCHRIFT   PHONETIC SYMBOLS

[:] Längezeichen, length mark
['] Betonung, stress mark
[*] Bindungs-R, 'r' pronounced before a vowel

alle Vokallaute sind nur ungefähre Entsprechungen
all vowel sounds are approximate only

VOKALE UND DIPHTHONGE

plant, arm, father	[ɑ:]	Bahn
fiancé	[ɑ̃:]	Ensemble
life	[aɪ]	weit
house	[au]	Haut
man, sad	[æ]	
but, son	[ʌ]	Butler
get, bed	[e]	Metall
name, lame	[eɪ]	
ago, better	[ə]	bitte
bird, her	[ɜ:]	
there, care	[ɛə]	mehr
it, wish	[ɪ]	Bischof
bee, me, beat, belief	[i:]	viel
here	[ɪə]	Bier
no, low	[əu]	
not, long	[ɒ]	Post
law, all	[ɔ:]	Mond
boy, oil	[ɔɪ]	Heu
push, look	[ʊ]	Pult
you, do	[u:]	Hut
poor, sure	[ʊə]	

KONSONANTEN

been, blind	[b]	Ball
do, had	[d]	dann
jam, object	[dʒ]	
father, wolf	[f]	Fass
go, beg	[g]	Gast
house	[h]	Herr
youth, Indian	[j]	ja
keep, milk	[k]	kalt
lamp, oil, ill	[l]	Last
man, am	[m]	Mast
no, manner	[n]	Nuss
long, sing	[ŋ]	lang

El Niño	[ɲ]	El Niño
paper, happy	[p]	Pakt
red, dry	[r]	rot
stand, sand, yes	[s]	Rasse
ship, station	[ʃ]	Schal
tell, fat	[t]	Tal
thank, death	[θ]	
this, father	[ð]	
church, catch	[tʃ]	Rutsch
voice, live	[v]	was
water, we, which	[w]	
loch	[x]	Bach
zeal, these, gaze	[z]	Hase
pleasure	[ʒ]	Genie

Regular German noun endings

nominative		genitive	plural		nominative		genitive	plural
-ade	f	-ade	-aden		-ist	m	-isten	-isten
-ant	m	-anten	-anten		-ium	nt	-iums	-ien
-anz	f	-anz	-anzen		-ius	m	-ius	-iusse
-ar	m	-ars	-are		-ive	f	-ive	-iven
-är	m	-ärs	-äre		-keit	f	-keit	-keiten
-at	nt	-at(e)s	-ate		-lein	nt	-leins	-lein
-atte	f	-atte	-atten		-ling	m	-lings	-linge
-chen	nt	-chens	-chen		-ment	nt	-ments	-mente
-ei	f	-ei	-eien		-mus	m	-mus	-men
-elle	f	-elle	-ellen		-nis	f	-nis	-nisse
-ent	m	-enten	-enten		-nis	nt	-nisses	-nisse
-enz	f	-enz	-enzen		-nom	m	-nomen	-nomen
-ette	f	-ette	-etten		-rich	m	-richs	-riche
-eur	m	-eurs	-eure		-schaft	f	-schaft	-schaften
-euse	f	-euse	-eusen		-sel	nt	-sels	-sel
-heit	f	-heit	-heiten		-tät	f	-tät	-täten
-ie	f	-ie	-ien		-tiv	nt, m	-tivs	-tive
-ik	f	-ik	-iken		-tor	m	-tors	-toren
-in	f	-in	-innen		-tum	m, nt	-tums	-tümer
-ine	f	-ine	-inen		-ung	f	-ung	-ungen
-ion	f	-ion	-ionen		-ur	f	-ur	-uren

Substantive, die mit einem geklammerten 'r' oder 's' enden (z.B. **Ange-stellte(r)** *mf*, **Beamte(r)** *m*, **Gute(s)** *nt*) werden wie Adjektive dekliniert:

Nouns listed with an 'r' or an 's' in brackets (eg **Angestellte(r)** *mf*, **Beamte(r)** *m*, **Gute(s)** *nt*) take the same endings as adjectives:

der Angestellte *m*	**die Angestellte** *f*	**die Angestellten** *pl*
ein Angestellter *m*	**eine Angestellte** *f*	**Angestellte** *pl*
der Beamte *m*		**die Beamten** *pl*
ein Beamter *m*		**Beamte** *pl*
das Gute *nt*		
ein Gutes *nt*		

Unregelmäßige englische Verben

present	past tense	past participle	present	past tense	past participle
arise (arising)	arose	arisen	drink	drank	drunk
awake (awaking)	awoke	awaked	drive (driving)	drove	driven
be (am, is, are; being)	was, were	been	eat	ate	eaten
			fall	fell	fallen
bear	bore	born(e)	feed	fed	fed
beat	beat	beaten	feel	felt	felt
become (becoming)	became	become	fight	fought	fought
			find	found	found
begin (beginning)	began	begun	flee	fled	fled
			fling	flung	flung
bend	bent	bent	fly (flies)	flew	flown
bet (betting)	bet	bet	forbid (forbidding)	forbade	forbidden
bid (bidding)	bid	bid	foresee	foresaw	foreseen
bind	bound	bound	forget (forgetting)	forgot	forgotten
bite (biting)	bit	bitten			
bleed	bled	bled	forgive (forgiving)	forgave	forgiven
blow	blew	blown			
break	broke	broken	freeze (freezing)	froze	frozen
breed	bred	bred			
bring	brought	brought	get (getting)	got	got, (US) gotten
build	built	built			
burn	burnt (o burned)	burnt (o burned)	give (giving)	gave	given
burst	burst	burst	go (goes)	went	gone
buy	bought	bought	grind	ground	ground
can	could	(been able)	grow	grew	grown
cast	cast	cast	hang	hung (o hanged)	hung (o hanged)
catch	caught	caught			
choose (choosing)	chose	chosen	have (has; having)	had	had
cling	clung	clung	hear	heard	heard
come (coming)	came	come	hide (hiding)	hid	hidden
cost	cost	cost	hit (hitting)	hit	hit
creep	crept	crept	hold	held	held
cut (cutting)	cut	cut	hurt	hurt	hurt
deal	dealt	dealt	keep	kept	kept
dig (digging)	dug	dug	kneel	knelt (o kneeled)	knelt (o kneeled)
do (does)	did	done			
draw	drew	drawn	know	knew	known
dream	dreamed (o dreamt)	dreamed (o dreamt)	lay	laid	laid
			lead	led	led

present	past tense	past participle	present	past tense	past participle
lean	leant (o leaned)	leant (o leaned)	shoot	shot	shot
leap	leapt (o leaped)	leapt (o leaped)	show	showed	shown
learn	learnt (o learned)	learnt (o learned)	shrink	shrank	shrunk
			shut (shutting)	shut	shut
leave (leaving)	left	left	sing	sang	sung
lend	lent	lent	sink	sank	sunk
let (letting)	let	let	sit (sitting)	sat	sat
lie (lying)	lay	lain	sleep	slept	slept
light	lit (o lighted)	lit (o lighted)	slide (sliding)	slid	slid
lose (losing)	lost	lost	sling	slung	slung
make (making)	made	made	slit (slitting)	slit	slit
			smell	smelt (o smelled)	smelt (o smelled)
may	might	–	sow	sowed	sown (o sowed)
mean	meant	meant	speak	spoke	spoken
meet	met	met	speed	sped (o speeded)	sped (o speeded)
mow	mowed	mown (o mowed)	spell	spelt (o spelled)	spelt (o spelled)
must	(had to)	(had to)			
pay	paid	paid	spend	spent	spent
put (putting)	put	put	spin (spinning)	spun	spun
quit (quitting)	quit (o quitted)	quit (o quitted)	spit (spitting)	spat	spat
read	read	read	split (splitting)	split	split
rid (ridding)	rid	rid			
ride (riding)	rode	ridden	spoil	spoiled (o spoilt)	spoiled (o spoilt)
ring	rang	rung	spread	spread	spread
rise (rising)	rose	risen	spring	sprang	sprung
run (running)	ran	run	stand	stood	stood
saw	sawed	sawn	steal	stole	stolen
say	said	said	stick	stuck	stuck
see	saw	seen	sting	stung	stung
seek	sought	sought	stink	stank	stunk
sell	sold	sold	strike (striking)	struck	struck
send	sent	sent			
set (setting)	set	set	strive (striving)	strove	striven
shake (shaking)	shook	shaken			
			swear	swore	sworn
shall	should	–	sweep	swept	swept
shine (shining)	shone	shone	swell	swelled	swollen (o swelled)

present	past tense	past participle	present	past tense	past participle
swim (swimming)	swam	swum	wake (waking)	woke (o waked)	woken (o waked)
swing	swung	swung	wear	wore	worn
take (taking)	took	taken	weave (weaving)	wove (o weaved)	woven (o weaved)
teach	taught	taught	weep	wept	wept
tear	tore	torn	win (winning)	won	won
tell	told	told			
think	thought	thought	wind	wound	wound
throw	threw	thrown	write (writing)	wrote	written
thrust	thrust	thrust			
tread	trod	trodden			

GERMAN IRREGULAR VERBS

Infinitiv	Präsens 2., 3. Singular	Imperfekt	Partizip Perfekt
backen	bäckst, bäckt	backte o buk	gebacken
befehlen	befiehlst, befiehlt	befahl	befohlen
beginnen	beginnst, beginnt	begann	begonnen
beißen	beißt, beißt	biss	gebissen
bergen	birgst, birgt	barg	geborgen
betrügen	betrügst, betrügt	betrog	betrogen
biegen	biegst, biegt	bog	gebogen
bieten	bietest, bietet	bot	geboten
binden	bindest, bindet	band	gebunden
bitten	bittest, bittet	bat	gebeten
blasen	bläst, bläst	blies	geblasen
bleiben	bleibst, bleibt	blieb	geblieben
braten	brätst, brät	briet	gebraten
brechen	brichst, bricht	brach	gebrochen
brennen	brennst, brennt	brannte	gebrannt
bringen	bringst, bringt	brachte	gebracht
denken	denkst, denkt	dachte	gedacht
dringen	dringst, dringt	drang	gedrungen
dürfen	darfst, darf	durfte	gedurft
empfangen	empfängst, empfängt	empfing	empfangen
empfehlen	empfiehlst, empfiehlt	empfahl	empfohlen
empfinden	empfindest, empfindet	empfand	empfunden
erschrecken	erschrickst, erschrickt	erschrak	erschrocken
essen	isst, isst	aß	gegessen
fahren	fährst, fährt	fuhr	gefahren
fallen	fällst, fällt	fiel	gefallen
fangen	fängst, fängt	fing	gefangen
finden	findest, findet	fand	gefunden
flechten	flichtst, flicht	flocht	geflochten
fliegen	fliegst, fliegt	flog	geflogen
fließen	fließt, fließt	floss	geflossen
fressen	frisst, frisst	fraß	gefressen
frieren	frierst, friert	fror	gefroren
geben	gibst, gibt	gab	gegeben
gehen	gehst, geht	ging	gegangen
gelingen	–, gelingt	gelang	gelungen
gelten	giltst, gilt	galt	gegolten
genießen	genießt, genießt	genoss	genossen
geraten	gerätst, gerät	geriet	geraten
geschehen	–, geschieht	geschah	geschehen
gewinnen	gewinnst, gewinnt	gewann	gewonnen
gießen	gießt, gießt	goss	gegossen
gleichen	gleichst, gleicht	glich	geglichen
gleiten	gleitest, gleitet	glitt	geglitten

Infinitiv	Präsens 2., 3. Singular	Imperfekt	Partizip Perfekt
graben	gräbst, gräbt	grub	gegraben
greifen	greifst, greift	griff	gegriffen
haben	hast, hat	hatte	gehabt
halten	hältst, hält	hielt	gehalten
hängen	hängst, hängt	hing	gehangen
hauen	haust, haut	haute	gehauen
heben	hebst, hebt	hob	gehoben
heißen	heißt, heißt	hieß	geheißen
helfen	hilfst, hilft	half	geholfen
kennen	kennst, kennt	kannte	gekannt
klingen	klingst, klingt	klang	geklungen
kneifen	kneifst, kneift	kniff	gekniffen
kommen	kommst, kommt	kam	gekommen
können	kannst, kann	konnte	gekonnt
kriechen	kriechst, kriecht	kroch	gekrochen
laden	lädst, lädt	lud	geladen
lassen	lässt, lässt	ließ	gelassen
laufen	läufst, läuft	lief	gelaufen
leiden	leidest, leidet	litt	gelitten
leihen	leihst, leiht	lieh	geliehen
lesen	liest, liest	las	gelesen
liegen	liegst, liegt	lag	gelegen
lügen	lügst, lügt	log	gelogen
mahlen	mahlst, mahlt	mahlte	gemahlen
meiden	meidest, meidet	mied	gemieden
messen	misst, misst	maß	gemessen
misslingen	–, misslingt	misslang	misslungen
mögen	magst, mag	mochte	gemocht
müssen	musst, muss	musste	gemusst
nehmen	nimmst, nimmt	nahm	genommen
nennen	nennst, nennt	nannte	genannt
pfeifen	pfeifst, pfeift	pfiff	gepfiffen
quellen	quillst, quillt	quoll	gequollen
raten	rätst, rät	riet	geraten
reiben	reibst, reibt	rieb	gerieben
reißen	reißt, reißt	riss	gerissen
reiten	reitest, reitet	ritt	geritten
rennen	rennst, rennt	rannte	gerannt
riechen	riechst, riecht	roch	gerochen
ringen	ringst, ringt	rang	gerungen
rufen	rufst, ruft	rief	gerufen
salzen	salzt, salzt	salzte	gesalzen
saufen	säufst, säuft	soff	gesoffen
saugen	saugst, saugt	sog o saugte	gesogen o gesaugt
schaffen	schaffst, schafft	schuf	geschaffen
scheiden	scheidest, scheidet	schied	geschieden

Infinitiv	Präsens 2., 3. Singular	Imperfekt	Partizip Perfekt
scheinen	scheinst, scheint	schien	geschienen
scheißen	scheißt, scheißt	schiss	geschissen
schieben	schiebst, schiebt	schob	geschoben
schießen	schießt, schießt	schoss	geschossen
schlafen	schläfst, schläft	schlief	geschlafen
schlagen	schlägst, schlägt	schlug	geschlagen
schleichen	schleichst, schleicht	schlich	geschlichen
schleifen	schleifst, schleift	schliff	geschliffen
schließen	schließt, schließt	schloss	geschlossen
schmeißen	schmeißt, schmeißt	schmiss	geschmissen
schmelzen	schmilzt, schmilzt	schmolz	geschmolzen
schneiden	schneidest, schneidet	schnitt	geschnitten
schreiben	schreibst, schreibt	schrieb	geschrieben
schreien	schreist, schreit	schrie	geschrie(e)n
schweigen	schweigst, schweigt	schwieg	geschwiegen
schwellen	schwillst, schwillt	schwoll	geschwollen
schwimmen	schwimmst, schwimmt	schwamm	geschwommen
schwören	schwörst, schwört	schwor	geschworen
sehen	siehst, sieht	sah	gesehen
sein	bist, ist	war	gewesen
senden	sendest, sendet	sandte	gesandt
singen	singst, singt	sang	gesungen
sinken	sinkst, sinkt	sank	gesunken
sitzen	sitzt, sitzt	saß	gesessen
sollen	sollst, soll	sollte	gesollt
spinnen	spinnst, spinnt	spann	gesponnen
sprechen	sprichst, spricht	sprach	gesprochen
springen	springst, springt	sprang	gesprungen
stechen	stichst, sticht	stach	gestochen
stehen	stehst, steht	stand	gestanden
stehlen	stiehlst, stiehlt	stahl	gestohlen
steigen	steigst, steigt	stieg	gestiegen
sterben	stirbst, stirbt	starb	gestorben
stinken	stinkst, stinkt	stank	gestunken
stoßen	stößt, stößt	stieß	gestoßen
streichen	streichst, streicht	strich	gestrichen
streiten	streitest, streitet	stritt	gestritten
tragen	trägst, trägt	trug	getragen
treffen	triffst, trifft	traf	getroffen
treiben	treibst, treibt	trieb	getrieben
treten	trittst, tritt	trat	getreten
trinken	trinkst, trinkt	trank	getrunken
tun	tust, tut	tat	getan
verderben	verdirbst, verdirbt	verdarb	verdorben
vergessen	vergisst, vergisst	vergaß	vergessen
verlieren	verlierst, verliert	verlor	verloren

Infinitiv	Präsens 2., 3. Singular	Imperfekt	Partizip Perfekt
verschwinden	verschwindest, verschwindet	verschwand	verschwunden
verzeihen	verzeihst, verzeiht	verzieh	verziehen
wachsen	wächst, wächst	wuchs	gewachsen
waschen	wäschst, wäscht	wusch	gewaschen
weisen	weist, weist	wies	gewiesen
wenden	wendest, wendet	wandte	gewandt
werben	wirbst, wirbt	warb	geworben
werden	wirst, wird	wurde	geworden
werfen	wirfst, wirft	warf	geworfen
wiegen	wiegst, wiegt	wog	gewogen
wissen	weißt, weiß	wusste	gewusst
wollen	willst, will	wollte	gewollt
ziehen	ziehst, zieht	zog	gezogen
zwingen	zwingst, zwingt	zwang	gezwungen

a

à *prep* +*akk* at ... each; **4 Tickets ~ 8 Euro** 4 tickets at 8 euros each

A *abk* = **Autobahn** ≈ M (*Brit*), ≈ I (*US*)

Aal (*-(e)s, -e*) *m* eel

ab *präp* +*dat* from; **Kinder ab 12 Jahren** children from the age of 12; **ab morgen** from tomorrow; **ab sofort** as of now ▷ *adv* **1** off; **links ab** to the left; **der Knopf ist ab** the button has come off; **ab nach Hause!** off you go home

2 (*zeitlich*): **von da ab** from then on; **von heute ab** from today, as of today

3 (*auf Fahrplänen*): **München ab 12.20** leaving Munich 12.20

4: **ab und zu** *od* **an** now and then *od* again

ab|bauen *vt* (*Zelt*) to take down; (*verringern*) to reduce

ab|beißen *irr vt* to bite off

ab|bestellen *vt* to cancel

ab|biegen *irr vi* to turn off; (*Straße*) to bend; **nach links/rechts ~** to turn left/right; **Abbiegespur** *f* filter lane

Abbildung *f* illustration

ab|blasen *irr vt* (*fig*) to call off

ab|blenden *vt, vi* (*Auto*) (**die Scheinwerfer**) **~** to dip (*Brit*) (*o* to dim (*US*)) one's headlights; **Abblendlicht** *nt* dipped (*Brit*) (*o* dimmed (*US*)) headlights *pl*

ab|brechen *irr vt* to break off; (*Gebäude*) to pull down; (*aufhören*) to stop; (*Computerprogramm*) to abort

ab|bremsen *vi* to brake, to slow down

ab|bringen *irr vt* **jdn von einer Idee ~** to talk sb out of an idea; **jdn vom Thema ~** to get sb away from the subject; **davon lasse ich mich nicht ~** nothing will make me change my mind about it

ab|buchen *vt* to debit (*von* to)

ab|danken *vi* to resign

ab|drehen *vt* (*Gas, Wasser*) to turn off; (*Licht*) to switch off ▷ *vi* (*Schiff, Flugzeug*) to change course

Abend (*-s, -e*) *m* evening; **am ~** in the evening; **zu ~ essen** to have dinner; **heute/morgen/gestern ~** this/tomorrow/yesterday evening; **guten ~!** good evening; **Abendbrot** *nt* supper; **Abendessen** *nt* dinner; **Abendgarderobe** *f* evening dress (*o* gown); **Abendkasse** *f* box office; **Abendkleid** *nt* evening dress (*o* gown); **Abendkurs** *m* evening class; **Abendmahl** *nt* **das ~** (Holy) Communion; **abends** *adv* in the evening; **montags ~** on Monday evenings

Abenteuer (*-s, -*) *nt* adventure; **Abenteuerurlaub** *m* adventure holiday

aber *conj* but; (*jedoch*) however; **oder ~** alternatively; **~ ja!** (but) of course; **das ist ~ nett von Ihnen** that's really nice of you

abergläubisch *adj* superstitious

ab|fahren *irr vi* to leave (*o* to depart) (*nach* for); (*Ski*) to ski down; **Abfahrt** *f* departure; (*von Autobahn*) exit; (*Ski*) descent; (*Piste*) run; **Abfahrtslauf** *m* (*Ski*) downhill; **Abfahrtszeit** *f* departure time

Abfall *m* waste; (*Müll*) rubbish (*Brit*), garbage (*US*); **Abfalleimer** *m* rubbish bin (*Brit*), garbage can (*US*)

abfällig *adj* disparaging; **~ von jdm sprechen** to make disparaging remarks about sb

ab|färben *vi* (*Wäsche*) to run; (*fig*) to rub off

ab|fertigen vt (Pakete) to prepare for dispatch; (an der Grenze) to clear; **Abfertigungsschalter** m (am Flughafen) check-in desk

ab|finden irr vt to pay off ▷ vr **sich mit etw ~** to come to terms with sth; **Abfindung** f (Entschädigung) compensation; (von Angestellten) redundancy payment

ab|fliegen irr vi (Flugzeug) to take off; (Passagier a.) to fly off; **Abflug** m departure; (Start) takeoff; **Abflughalle** f departure lounge; **Abflugzeit** f departure time

Abfluss m drain; (am Waschbecken) plughole (Brit); **Abflussrohr** nt waste pipe; (außen) drainpipe

ab|fragen vt to test; (Inform) to call up

ab|führen vi (Med) to have a laxative effect ▷ vt (Steuern, Gebühren) to pay; **jdn ~ lassen** to take sb into custody; **Abführmittel** nt laxative

Abgabe f handing in; (von Ball) pass; (Steuer) tax; (einer Erklärung) making; **abgabenfrei** adj tax-free; **abgabenpflichtig** adj liable to tax

Abgase pl (Auto) exhaust fumes pl; **Abgas(sonder)untersuchung** f exhaust emission test

ab|geben irr vt (Gepäck, Schlüssel) to leave (bei with); (Schularbeit etc) to hand in; (Wärme) to give off; (Erklärung, Urteil) to make ▷ vr **sich mit jdm ~** to associate with sb; **sich mit etw ~** to bother with sth

abgebildet adj **wie oben ~** as shown above

ab|gehen irr vi (Post) to go; (Knopf etc) to come off; (abgezogen werden) to be taken off; (Straße) to branch off; **von der Schule ~** to leave school; **sie geht mir ab** I really miss her; **was geht denn hier ab?** (fam) what's going on here?

abgehetzt adj exhausted, shattered

abgelaufen adj (Pass) expired; (Zeit, Frist) up; **die Milch ist ~** the milk is past its sell-by date

abgelegen adj remote

abgemacht interj OK, it's a deal, that's settled, then

abgeneigt adj **einer Sache** (dat) **~ sein** to be averse to sth; **ich wäre nicht ~, das zu tun** I wouldn't mind doing that

Abgeordnete(r) mf Member of Parliament

abgepackt adj prepacked

abgerissen adj **der Knopf ist ~** the button has come off

abgesehen adj **es auf jdn/etw ~ haben** to be after sb/sth; **~ von** apart from

abgespannt adj (Person) exhausted, worn out

abgestanden adj stale; (Bier) flat

abgestorben adj (Pflanze) dead; (Finger) numb

abgestumpft adj (Person) insensitive

abgetragen adj (Kleidung) worn

ab|gewöhnen vt **jdm etw ~** to cure sb of sth; **sich etw ~** to give sth up

ab|haken vt to tick off; **das (Thema) ist schon abgehakt** that's been dealt with

ab|halten irr vt (Versammlung) to hold; **jdn von etw ~** (fernhalten) to keep sb away from sth; (hindern) to keep sb from sth

abhanden adj **~ kommen** to get lost

Abhang m slope

ab|hängen vt (Bild) to take down; (Anhänger) to uncouple; (Verfolger) to shake off ▷ irr vi **von jdm/etw ~** to depend on sb/sth; **das hängt davon ab, ob ...** it depends (on) whether ...; **abhängig** adj dependent (von on)

ab|hauen irr vt (abschlagen) to cut off ▷ vi (fam: verschwinden) to clear off; **hau ab!** get lost!, beat it!

ab|heben irr vt (Geld) to withdraw; (Telefonhörer, Spielkarte) to pick up ▷ vi (Flugzeug) to take off; (Rakete) to lift off; (Karten) to cut

ab|holen vt to collect; (am Bahnhof etc) to meet; (mit dem Auto) to pick up; **Abholmarkt** m cash and carry

ab|horchen vt (Med) to listen to

ab|hören vt (Vokabeln) to test; (Telefongespräch) to tap; (Tonband etc) to listen to

Abitur (-s, -e) nt German school-leaving examination, ≈ A-levels (Brit), ≈ High School Diploma (US)

● **Abitur**

●
● The **Abitur** is the German
● school-leaving examination which is
● taken at the age of 18 or 19 by pupils
● at a **Gymnasium**. It is taken in four
● subjects and is necessary for entry to
● university.

ab|kaufen vt jdm etw ~ to buy sth from sb; **das kauf ich dir nicht ab!** (fam: glauben) I don't believe you

ab|klingen irr vi (Schmerz) to ease; (Wirkung) to wear off

ab|kommen irr vi to get away; **von der Straße ~** to leave the road; **von einem Plan ~** to give up a plan; **vom Thema ~** to stray from the point

Abkommen (-s, -) nt agreement

ab|koppeln vt (Anhänger) to unhitch

ab|kratzen vt to scrape off ▷ vi (fam: sterben) to kick the bucket, to croak

ab|kühlen vi, vt to cool down ▷ vr **sich ~** to cool down

ab|kürzen vt (Wort) to abbreviate; **den Weg ~** to take a short cut; **Abkürzung** f (Wort) abbreviation; (Weg) short cut

ab|laden irr vt to unload

Ablage f (für Akten) tray; (Aktenordnung) filing system

Ablauf m (Abfluss) drain; (von Ereignissen) course; (einer Frist, Zeit) expiry; **ab|laufen** irr vi (abfließen) to drain away; (Ereignisse) to happen; (Frist, Zeit, Pass) to expire

ab|legen vt to put down; (Kleider) to take off; (Gewohnheit) to get out of; (Prüfung) to take, to sit; (Akten) to file away ▷ vi (Schiff) to cast off

ab|lehnen vt to reject; (Einladung) to decline; (missbilligen) to disapprove of; (Bewerber) to turn down ▷ vi to decline

ab|lenken vt to distract; **jdn von der Arbeit ~** to distract sb from their work; **vom Thema ~** to change the subject; **Ablenkung** f distraction

ab|lesen vt (Text, Rede) to read; **das Gas/den Strom ~** to read the gas/electricity meter

ab|liefern vt to deliver

ab|machen vt (entfernen) to take off; (vereinbaren) to agree; **Abmachung** f agreement

ab|melden vt (Zeitung) to cancel; (Auto) to take off the road ▷ vr **sich ~** to give notice of one's departure; (im Hotel) to check out; (vom Verein) to cancel one's membership

ab|messen irr vt to measure

ab|nehmen irr vt to take off, to remove; (Hörer) to pick up; (Führerschein) to take away; (Geld) to get (jdm out of sb); (kaufen, umg: glauben) to buy (jdm from sb) ▷ vi to decrease; (schlanker werden) to lose weight; (Tel) to pick up the phone; **fünf Kilo ~** to lose five kilos

Abneigung f dislike (gegen of); (stärker) aversion (gegen to)

ab|nutzen vt to wear out ▷ vr **sich ~** to wear out

Abonnement (-s, -s) nt subscription; **Abonnent(in)** m(f) subscriber; **abonnieren** vt to subscribe to

ab|raten irr vi jdm von etw ~ to advise sb against sth

ab|räumen vt **den Tisch ~** to clear the table; **das Geschirr ~** to clear away the dishes; (Preis etc) to walk off with

Abrechnung f settlement; (Rechnung) bill

ab|regen vr **sich ~** (fam) to calm (o to cool) down; **reg dich ab!** take it easy

Abreise f departure; **ab|reisen** vi to leave (nach for)

ab|reißen irr vt (Haus) to pull down; (Blatt) to tear off; **den Kontakt nicht ~ lassen** to stay in touch ▷ vi (Knopf etc) to come off

ab|runden vt **eine Zahl nach oben/unten ~** to round a number up/down

abrupt adj abrupt

ABS nt abk = **Antiblockiersystem** (Auto) ABS

Abs. abk = **Absender** from

ab|sagen vt to cancel, to call off; (Einladung) to turn down ▷ vi (ablehnen) to decline; **ich muss leider ~** I'm afraid I can't come

Absatz m (Comm) sales pl; (neuer Abschnitt) paragraph; (Schuh) heel

ab|schaffen vt to abolish, to do away with

ab|schalten vt, vi (a. fig) to switch off

ab|schätzen vt to estimate; (Lage) to assess; **jdn ~** to size sb up

abscheulich adj disgusting

ab|schicken vt to send off

ab|schieben irr vt (ausweisen) to deport

Abschied (-(e)s, -e) m parting; **~ nehmen** to say good-bye (von jdm to sb); **Abschiedsfeier** f farewell party

Abschlagszahlung f interim payment

Abschleppdienst m (Auto) breakdown service; **ab|schleppen** vt to tow; **Abschleppseil** nt towrope;

Abschleppwagen m breakdown truck (Brit), tow truck (US)

ab|schließen irr vt (Tür) to lock; (beenden) to conclude, to finish; (Vertrag, Handel) to conclude; **Abschluss** m (Beendigung) close, conclusion; (von Vertrag, Handel) conclusion

ab|schmecken vt (kosten) to taste; (würzen) to season

ab|schminken vr **sich ~** to take one's make-up off ▷ vt (fam) **sich** (dat) **etw ~** to get sth out of one's mind

ab|schnallen vr **sich ~** to undo one's seatbelt

ab|schneiden irr vt to cut off ▷ vi **gut/schlecht ~** to do well/badly

Abschnitt m (von Buch, Text) section; (Kontrollabschnitt) stub

ab|schrauben vt to unscrew

ab|schrecken vt to deter, to put off

ab|schreiben irr vt to copy (bei, von from, off); (verloren geben) to write off; (Comm: absetzen) to deduct

abschüssig adj steep

ab|schwächen vt to lessen; (Behauptung, Kritik) to tone down

ab|schwellen irr vi (Entzündung) to go down; (Lärm) to die down

absehbar adj foreseeable; **in ~er Zeit** in the foreseeable future; **ab|sehen** irr vt (Ende, Folgen) to foresee ▷ vi **von etw ~** to refrain from sth

abseits adv out of the way; (Sport) offside ▷ prep +gen away from; **Abseits** nt (Sport) offside; **Abseitsfalle** f (Sport) offside trap

ab|senden irr vt to send off; (Post) to post; **Absender(in)** (-s, -) m(f) sender

ab|setzen vt (Glas, Brille etc) to put down; (aussteigen lassen) to drop (off); (Comm) to sell; (Fin) to deduct; (streichen) to drop ▷ vr **sich ~** (sich entfernen) to clear off; (sich ablagern) to be deposited

Absicht f intention; **mit ~** on purpose; **absichtlich** adj intentional, deliberate

absolut adj absolute

ab|specken vi (fam) to lose weight

ab|speichern vt (Inform) to save

ab|sperren vt to block (o to close) off; (Tür) to lock; **Absperrung** f (Vorgang) blocking (o closing) off; (Sperre) barricade

ab|spielen vt (CD etc) to play ▷ vr **sich ~** to happen

ab|springen irr vi to jump down/off; (von etw Geplantem) to drop out (von of)

ab|spülen vt to rinse; (Geschirr) to wash (up)

Abstand m distance; (zeitlich) interval; **~ halten** to keep one's distance

ab|stauben vt, vi to dust; (fam: stehlen) to pinch

Abstecher (-s, -) m detour

ab|steigen irr vi (vom Rad etc) to get off, to dismount; (in Gasthof) to stay (in +dat at)

ab|stellen vt (niederstellen) to put down; (Auto) to park; (ausschalten) to turn (o to switch) off; (Missstand, Unsitte) to stop; **Abstellraum** m store room

Abstieg (-(e)s, -e) m (vom Berg) descent; (Sport) relegation

ab|stimmen vi to vote ▷ vt (Termine, Ziele) to fit in (auf +akk with); **Dinge aufeinander ~** to coordinate things ▷ vr **sich ~** to come to an agreement (o arrangement)

abstoßend adj repulsive

abstrakt adj abstract

ab|streiten irr vt to deny

Abstrich m (Med) smear; **~e machen** to cut back (an +dat on); (weniger erwarten) to lower one's sights

Absturz m fall; (Aviat, Inform) crash; **ab|stürzen** vi to fall; (Aviat, Inform) to crash

absurd adj absurd

Abszess (-es, -e) m abscess

ab|tauen vt, vi to thaw; (Kühlschrank) to defrost

Abtei (-, -en) f abbey

Abteil (-(e)s, -e) nt compartment

Abteilung f (in Firma, Kaufhaus) department; (in Krankenhaus) section

ab|treiben irr vt (Kind) to abort ▷ vi to be driven off course; (Med: Abtreibung vornehmen) to carry out an abortion; (Abtreibung vornehmen lassen) to have an abortion; **Abtreibung** f abortion

ab|trocknen vt to dry

ab|warten vt to wait for; **das bleibt abzuwarten** that remains to be seen ▷ vi to wait

abwärts adv down

Abwasch (-(e)s) m washing-up; **ab|waschen** irr vt (Schmutz) to wash off; (Geschirr) to wash (up)

Abwasser (-s, Abwässer) nt sewage

ab|wechseln vr **sich ~ to** alternate; **sich mit jdm ~** to take turns with sb; **abwechselnd** adv alternately; **Abwechslung** f change; **zur ~** for a change

ab|weisen irr vt to turn away; (Antrag) to turn down; **abweisend** adj unfriendly

abwesend adj absent; **Abwesenheit** f absence

ab|wiegen irr vt to weigh (out)

ab|wischen vt (Gesicht, Tisch etc) to wipe; (Schmutz) to wipe off

ab|zählen vt to count; (Geld) to count out

Abzeichen nt badge

ab|zeichnen vt to draw, to copy; (Dokument) to initial ▷ vr **sich ~** to stand out; (fig: bevorstehen) to loom

ab|ziehen irr vt to take off; (Bett) to strip; (Schlüssel) to take out; (subtrahieren) to take away, to subtract ▷ vi to go away

Abzug m (Foto) print; (Öffnung) vent; (Truppen) withdrawal; (Betrag) deduction; **nach ~ der Kosten** charges deducted; **abzüglich** prep +gen minus; **~ 20% Rabatt** less 20% discount

ab|zweigen vi to branch off ▷ vt to set aside; **Abzweigung** f junction

Accessoires pl accessories pl

ach interj oh; **~ so!** oh, I see; **~ was!** (Überraschung) really?; (Ärger) don't talk nonsense

Achse (-, -n) f axis; (Auto) axle

Achsel (-, -n) f shoulder; (Achselhöhle) armpit

acht num eight; **heute in ~ Tagen** in a week('s time), a week from today

Acht (-) f **sich in ~ nehmen** to be careful (vor +dat of), to watch out (vor +dat for); **~ geben** to take care (auf +akk of); **etw außer ~ lassen** to disregard sth

achte(r, s) adj eighth; siehe auch **dritte**; **Achtel** (-s, -) nt (Bruchteil) eighth; (Wein etc) eighth of a litre; (Glas Wein) ≈ small glass

achten vt to respect ▷ vi to pay attention (auf +akk to)

Achterbahn f big dipper, roller coaster

achthundert num eight hundred; **achtmal** adv eight times

Achtung f attention; (Ehrfurcht) respect ▷ interj look out

achtzehn num eighteen; **achtzehnte(r, s)** adj eighteenth; siehe auch **dritte**; **achtzig** num eighty; **in den ~er Jahren** in the eighties; **achtzigste(r, s)** adj eightieth

Acker (-s, Äcker) m field

Action (-, -s) f (fam) action; **Actionfilm** m action film

Adapter (-s, -) m adapter

addieren vt to add (up)

Adel (-s) m nobility; **adelig** adj noble

Ader (-, -n) f vein

Adjektiv nt adjective

Adler (-s, -) m eagle

adoptieren vt to adopt; **Adoption** f adoption; **Adoptiveltern** pl adoptive parents pl; **Adoptivkind** nt adopted child

Adrenalin (-s) nt adrenalin

Adressbuch nt directory; (persönliches) address book; **Adresse** (-, -n) f address; **adressieren** vt to address (an +akk to)

Advent (-s, -e) m Advent; **Adventskranz** m Advent wreath

Adverb nt adverb

Aerobic (-s) nt aerobics sing

Affäre (-, -n) f affair

Affe (-n, -n) m monkey

Afghanistan (-s) nt Afghanistan

Afrika (-s) nt Africa; **Afrikaner(in)** (-s, -) m(f) African; **afrikanisch** adj African

After (-s, -) m anus

Aftershave (-(s), -s) nt aftershave

AG (-, -s) f abk = **Aktiengesellschaft** plc (Brit), corp. (US)

Agent(in) m(f) agent; **Agentur** f agency

aggressiv adj aggressive

Ägypten (-s) nt Egypt

ah interj ah, ooh

äh interj (Sprechpause) er, um; (angeekelt) ugh

aha interj I see, aha

ähneln vi +dat to be like, to resemble ▷ vr **sich ~** to be alike (o similar)

ahnen vt to suspect; **du ahnst es nicht!** would you believe it?

ähnlich adj similar (dat to); **jdm ~ sehen** to look like sb; **Ähnlichkeit** f similarity

Ahnung f idea; (Vermutung) suspicion; **keine ~!** no idea; **ahnungslos** adj unsuspecting

Ahorn (-s, -e) m maple

Aids (-) nt Aids; **aidskrank** adj suffering

from Aids; **aidspositiv** adj tested positive
for Aids; **Aidstest** m Aids test
Airbag (-s, -s) m (Auto) airbag; **Airbus** m
airbus
Akademie (-, -n) f academy;
Akademiker(in) (-s, -) m(f) (university)
graduate
akklimatisieren vr **sich ~** to acclimatize
oneself
Akkordeon (-s, -s) nt accordion
Akku (-s, -s) m (storage) battery
Akkusativ m accusative (case)
Akne (-, -) f acne
Akrobat(in) (-s, -en) m(f) acrobat
Akt (-(e)s, -e) m act; (Kunst) nude
Akte (-, -n) f file; **etw zu den ~n legen** (a.
fig) to file sth away; **Aktenkoffer** m
briefcase
Aktie (-, -n) f share; **Aktiengesellschaft** f
public limited company (Brit), corporation
(US)
Aktion f (Kampagne) campaign; (Einsatz)
operation
Aktionär(in) (-s, -e) m(f) shareholder
aktiv adj active
aktualisieren vt to update; **aktuell** adj
(Thema) topical; (modern) up-to-date;
(Problem) current; **nicht mehr ~** no longer
relevant
Akupunktur f acupuncture
akustisch adj acoustic; **Akustik** f
acoustics sing
akut adj acute
AKW (-s, -s) nt abk = **Atomkraftwerk**
nuclear power station
Akzent (-(e)s, -e) m accent; (Betonung)
stress; **mit starkem schottischen ~** with
a strong Scottish accent
akzeptieren vt to accept
Alarm (-(e)s, -e) m alarm; **Alarmanlage**
f alarm system; **alarmieren** vt to
alarm; **die Polizei ~** to call the
police
Albanien (-s) nt Albania
Albatros (-ses, -se) m albatross
albern adj silly
Albtraum m nightmare
Album (-s, Alben) nt album
Algen pl algae pl; (Meeresalgen) seaweed
sing
Algerien (-s) nt Algeria
Alibi (-s, -s) nt alibi
Alimente pl maintenance sing

Alkohol (-s, -e) m alcohol; **alkoholfrei** adj
non-alcoholic; **~es Getränk** soft drink;
Alkoholiker(in) (-s, -) m(f) alcoholic;
alkoholisch adj alcoholic
All (-s) nt universe

⬤ **SCHLÜSSELWORT**

alle(r, s) adj **1** (sämtliche) all; **wir alle** all of
us; **alle Kinder waren da** all the children
were there; **alle Kinder mögen ...** all
children like ...; **alle beide** both of
us/them; **sie kamen alle** they all came;
alles Gute all the best; **alles in allem** all in
all
2 (mit Zeit- oder Maßangaben) every; **alle
vier Jahre** every four years; **alle fünf
Meter** every five metres
▷ pron everything; **alles was er
sagt** everything he says, all that he
says
▷ adv (zu Ende, aufgebraucht) finished; **die
Milch ist alle** the milk's all gone, there's no
milk left; **etw alle machen** to finish sth
up

Allee (-, -n) f avenue
allein adj, adv alone; (ohne Hilfe) on one's
own, by oneself; **nicht ~** (nicht nur) not
only; **~ erziehende Mutter** single mother;
~ stehend single, unmarried;
Alleinerziehende(r) mf single
mother/father/parent
allerbeste(r, s) adj very best
allerdings adv (zwar) admittedly; (gewiss)
certainly, sure (US)
allererste(r, s) adj very first; **zu
allererst** first of all
Allergie f allergy; **Allergiker(in)** (-s, -)
m(f) allergy sufferer; **allergisch** adj
allergic (gegen to)
allerhand adj inv (fam) all sorts of; **das ist
doch ~!** (Vorwurf) that's the limit; **~!**
(lobend) that's pretty good
Allerheiligen (-) nt All Saints' Day
allerhöchste(r, s) adj very highest;
allerhöchstens adv at the very most;
allerlei adj inv all sorts of; **allerletzte(r, s)**
adj very last; **allerwenigste(r, s)** adj very
least
alles pron everything; **~ in allem** all in all;
siehe auch **alle**
Alleskleber (-s, -) m all-purpose glue

allgemein *adj* general; **im Allgemeinen** in general

Alligator (-s, -en) *m* alligator

alljährlich *adj* annual

allmählich *adj* gradual ▷ *adv* gradually

Allradantrieb *m* all-wheel drive

Alltag *m* everyday life; **alltäglich** *adj* everyday; (*gewöhnlich*) ordinary; (*tagtäglich*) daily

allzu *adv* all too

Allzweckreiniger (-s, -) *m* multi-purpose cleaner

Alpen *pl* **die ~** the Alps *pl*

Alphabet (-(e)s, -e) *nt* alphabet; **alphabetisch** *adj* alphabetical

Alptraum *m siehe* **Albtraum**

als *konj* **1** (*zeitlich*) when; (*gleichzeitig*) as; **damals, als …** (in the days) when …; **gerade, als …** just as …

2 (*in der Eigenschaft*) than; **als Antwort** as an answer; **als Kind** as a child

3 (*bei Vergleichen*) than; **ich kam später als er** I came later than he (did) *od* later than him; **lieber … als …** rather … than …; **nichts als Ärger** nothing but trouble

4: **als ob/wenn** as if

also *conj* (*folglich*) so, therefore ▷ *adv, interj* so; **~ gut** (*o* **schön**)**!** okay then

alt *adj* old; **wie ~ sind Sie?** how old are you?; **28 Jahre ~** 28 years old; **vier Jahre älter** four years older

Altar (-(e)s, Altäre) *m* altar

Alter (-s, -) *nt* age; (*hohes*) old age; **im ~ von** at the age of; **er ist in meinem ~** he's my age

alternativ *adj* alternative; (*umweltbewusst*) ecologically minded; (*Landwirtschaft*) organic; **Alternative** *f* alternative

Altersheim *nt* old people's home

Altglas *nt* used glass; **Altglascontainer** *m* bottle bank; **altmodisch** *adj* old-fashioned; **Altöl** *nt* used (*o* waste) oil; **Altpapier** *nt* waste paper; **Altstadt** *f* old town

Alt-Taste *f* Alt key

Alufolie *f* tin (*o* kitchen) foil

Aluminium (-s) *nt* aluminium (*Brit*), aluminum (*US*)

Alzheimerkrankheit *f* Alzheimer's (disease)

am *kontr von* **an dem; ~ 2. Januar** on January 2(nd); **~ Morgen** in the morning; **~ Strand** on the beach; **~ Bahnhof** at the station; **was gefällt Ihnen ~ besten?** what do you like best?; **~ besten bleiben wir hier** it would be best if we stayed here

Amateur(in) *m(f)* amateur

ambulant *adj* outpatient; **kann ich ~ behandelt werden?** can I have it done as an outpatient?; **Ambulanz** *f* (*Krankenwagen*) ambulance; (*in der Klinik*) outpatients' department

Ameise (-, -n) *f* ant

amen *interj* amen

Amerika (-s) *nt* America; **Amerikaner(in)** (-s, -) *m(f)* American; **amerikanisch** *adj* American

Ampel (-, -n) *f* traffic lights *pl*

Amphitheater *nt* amphitheatre

Amsel (-, -n) *f* blackbird

Amt (-(e)s, Ämter) *nt* (*Dienststelle*) office, department; (*Posten*) post; **amtlich** *adj* official; **Amtszeichen** *nt* (*Tel*) dialling tone (*Brit*), dial tone (*US*)

amüsant *adj* amusing; **amüsieren** *vt* to amuse ▷ *vr* **sich ~** to enjoy oneself, to have a good time

an *präp* +*dat* **1** (*räumlich: wo?*) at; (*auf, bei*) on; (*nahe bei*) near; **an diesem Ort** at this place; **an der Wand** on the wall; **zu nahe an etw** too near to sth; **unten am Fluss** down by the river; **Köln liegt am Rhein** Cologne is on the Rhine

2 (*zeitlich: wann?*) on; **an diesem Tag** on this day; **an Ostern** at Easter

3: **arm an Fett** low in fat; **an etw sterben** to die of sth; **an (und für) sich** actually

▷ *präp* +*akk* **1** (*räumlich: wohin?*) to; **er ging ans Fenster** he went (over) to the window; **etw an die Wand hängen/ schreiben** to hang/write sth on the wall

2 (*zeitlich: woran?*) **an etw denken** to think of sth

3 (*gerichtet an*) to; **ein Gruß/eine Frage an dich** greetings/a question to you

▷ *adv* **1** (*ungefähr*) about; **an die hundert** about a hundred

2 (*auf Fahrplänen*): **Frankfurt an 18.30** arriving Frankfurt 18.30

3 (*ab*): **von dort/heute an** from there/today onwards

4 (*angeschaltet, angezogen*) on; **das Licht ist an** the light is on; **ohne etwas an** with nothing on; *siehe auch* **am**

anal *adj* anal

analog *adj* analogous; (*Inform*) analog

Analyse (*-, -n*) *f* analysis; **analysieren** *vt* to analyse

Ananas (*-, - o -se*) *f* pineapple

an|baggern *vt* (*fam*) to chat up (*Brit*), to come on to (*US*)

Anbau *m* (*Agr*) cultivation; (*Gebäude*) extension; **an|bauen** *vt* (*Agr*) to cultivate; (*Gebäudeteil*) to build on

an|behalten *irr vt* to keep on

anbei *adv* enclosed; **~ sende ich ...** please find enclosed ...

an|beten *vt* to worship

an|bieten *irr vt* to offer ▷ *vr* **sich ~** to volunteer

an|binden *irr vt* to tie up

Anblick *m* sight

an|braten *irr vt* to brown

an|brechen *irr vt* to start; (*Vorräte, Ersparnisse*) to break into; (*Flasche, Packung*) to open ▷ *vi* to start; (*Tag*) to break; (*Nacht*) to fall

an|brennen *irr vt, vi* to burn; **das Fleisch schmeckt angebrannt** the meat tastes burnt

an|bringen *irr vt* (*herbeibringen*) to bring; (*befestigen*) to fix, to attach

Andacht (*-, -en*) *f* devotion; (*Gottesdienst*) prayers *pl*

an|dauern *vi* to continue, to go on; **andauernd** *adj* continual

Andenken (*-s, -*) *nt* memory; (*Gegenstand*) souvenir

andere(r, s) *adj* (*weitere*) other; (*verschieden*) different; (*folgend*) next; **am ~n Tag** the next day; **von etw/jmd ~m sprechen** to talk about sth/sb else; **unter ~m** among other things; **andererseits** *adv* on the other hand

ändern *vt* to alter, to change ▷ *vr* **sich ~** to change

andernfalls *adv* otherwise

anders *adv* differently (*als* from); **jemand/irgendwo ~** someone/somewhere else; **sie ist ~ als ihre Schwester** she's not like her sister; **es geht nicht ~** there's no other way; **anders(he)rum** *adv* the other way round; **anderswo** *adv* somewhere else

anderthalb *num* one and a half

Änderung *f* change, alteration

an|deuten *vt* to indicate; (*Wink geben*) to hint at

Andorra (*-s*) *nt* Andorra

Andrang *m* **es herrschte großer ~** there was a huge crowd

an|drohen *vt* **jdm etw ~** to threaten sb with sth

aneinander *adv* at/on/to one another (*o* each other); **~ denken** think of each other; **~ geraten** to clash; **sich ~ gewöhnen** to get used to each other; **~ legen** to put together

Anemone (*-, -n*) *f* anemone

an|erkennen *irr vt* (*Staat, Zeugnis etc*) to recognize; (*würdigen*) to appreciate; **Anerkennung** *f* recognition; (*Würdigung*) appreciation

an|fahren *irr vt* (*fahren gegen*) to run into; (*Ort, Hafen*) to stop (*o* call) at; (*liefern*) to deliver; **jdn ~** (*fig: schimpfen*) to jump on sb ▷ *vi* to start; (*losfahren*) to drive off

Anfall *m* (*Med*) attack; **anfällig** *adj* delicate; (*Maschine*) temperamental; **~ für** prone to

Anfang (*-(e)s, Anfänge*) *m* beginning, start; **zu/am ~** to start with; **~ Mai** at the beginning of May; **sie ist ~ 20** she's in her early twenties; **an|fangen** *irr vt, vi* to begin, to start; **damit kann ich nichts ~** that's no use to me; **Anfänger(in)** (*-s, -*) *m(f)* beginner; **anfangs** *adv* at first; **Anfangsbuchstabe** *m* first (*o* initial) letter

an|fassen *vt* (*berühren*) to touch ▷ *vi* **kannst du mal mit ~?** can you give me a hand? ▷ *vr* **sich weich ~** to feel soft

Anflug *m* (*Aviat*) approach; (*Hauch*) trace

an|fordern *vt* to demand; **Anforderung** *f* request (*von* for); (*Anspruch*) demand

Anfrage *f* inquiry

an|freunden *vr* **sich mit jdm ~** to make (*o* to become) friends with sb

an|fühlen *vr* **sich ~** to feel; **es fühlt sich gut an** it feels good

Anführungszeichen *pl* quotation marks *pl*

Angabe *f* (*Tech*) specification; (*fam: Prahlerei*) showing off; (*Tennis*) serve; **~n** *pl* (*Auskunft*) particulars *pl*; **die ~n waren falsch** (*Info*) the information was wrong; **an|geben** *irr vt* (*Name, Grund*) to give; (*zeigen*) to indicate; (*bestimmen*) to set ▷ *vi* (*fam: prahlen*) to boast; (*Sport*) to serve; **Angeber(in)** (*-s, -*) *m(f)* (*fam*) show-off; **angeblich** *adj* alleged

angeboren *adj* inborn

Angebot *nt* offer; (*Comm*) supply (*an +dat* of); **~ und Nachfrage** supply and demand

angebracht *adj* appropriate

angebunden *adj* **kurz ~** curt

angeheitert *adj* tipsy

an|gehen *irr vt* to concern; **das geht dich nichts an** that's none of your business; **ein Problem ~** to tackle a problem; **was ihn angeht** as far as he's concerned, as for him ▷ *vi* (*Feuer*) to catch; (*fam: beginnen*) to begin; **angehend** *adj* prospective

Angehörige(r) *mf* relative

Angeklagte(r) *mf* accused, defendant

Angel (*-, -n*) *f* fishing rod; (*an der Tür*) hinge

Angelegenheit *f* affair, matter

Angelhaken *m* fish hook; **angeln** *vt* to catch ▷ *vi* to fish; **Angeln** (*-s*) *nt* angling, fishing; **Angelrute** (*-, -n*) *f* fishing rod

angemessen *adj* appropriate, suitable

angenehm *adj* pleasant; **~!** (*bei Vorstellung*) pleased to meet you; **das ist mir gar nicht ~** I don't like the idea of that

angenommen *adj* assumed ▷ *conj* **~, es regnet, was machen wir dann?** suppose it rains, what do we do then?

angesehen *adj* respected

angesichts *prep +gen* in view of, considering

Angestellte(r) *mf* employee

angetan *adj* **von jdm/etw ~ sein** to be impressed by (*o* taken with) sb/sth

angewiesen *adj* **auf jdn/etw ~ sein** to be dependent on sb/sth

an|gewöhnen *vt* **sich etw ~** to get used to doing sth; **Angewohnheit** *f* habit

Angina (*-, Anginen*) *f* tonsillitis; **Angina Pectoris** (*-*) *f* angina

Angler(in) (*-s, -*) *m(f)* angler

Angora (*-s*) *nt* angora

an|greifen *irr vt* to attack; (*anfassen*) to

touch; (*beschädigen*) to damage; **Angriff** *m* attack; **etw in ~ nehmen** to get started on sth

Angst (*-, Ängste*) *f* fear; **~ haben** to be afraid (*o* scared) (*vor +dat* of); **jdm ~ machen** to scare sb; **ängstigen** *vt* to frighten ▷ *vr* **sich ~** to worry (*um, wegen +dat* about); **ängstlich** *adj* nervous; (*besorgt*) worried

an|haben *irr vt* (*Kleidung*) to have on, to wear; (*Licht*) to have on

an|halten *irr vi* to stop; (*andauern*) to continue; **anhaltend** *adj* continuous; **Anhalter(in)** (*-s, -*) *m(f)* hitch-hiker; **per ~ fahren** to hitch-hike

anhand *prep +gen* with; **~ von** by means of

an|hängen *vt* to hang up; (*Eisenb: Wagen*) to couple; (*Zusatz*) to add (*on*); **jdm etw ~** (*fam: unterschieben*) to pin sth on sb; **Anhänger** (*-s, -*) *m* (*Auto*) trailer; (*am Koffer*) tag; (*Schmuck*) pendant; **Anhänger(in)** (*-s, -*) *m(f)* supporter; **Anhängerkupplung** *f* towbar; **anhänglich** *adj* affectionate; (*pej*) clinging

Anhieb *m* **auf ~** straight away; **das kann ich nicht auf ~ sagen** I can't say offhand

an|himmeln *vt* to worship, to idolize

an|hören *vt* to listen to ▷ *vr* **sich ~** to sound; **das hört sich gut an** that sounds good

Animateur(in) *m(f)* host/hostess

Anis (*-es, -e*) *m* aniseed

Anker (*-s, -*) *m* anchor; **ankern** *vt, vi* to anchor; **Ankerplatz** *m* anchorage

Ankleidekabine *f* changing cubicle

an|klicken *vt* (*Inform*) to click on

an|klopfen *vi* to knock (*an +akk* on)

an|kommen *irr vi* to arrive; **bei jdm gut ~** to go down well with sb; **es kommt darauf an** it depends (*ob* on whether); **darauf kommt es nicht an** that doesn't matter

an|kotzen *vt* (*vulg*) **es kotzt mich an** it makes me sick

an|kreuzen *vt* to mark with a cross

an|kündigen *vt* to announce

Ankunft (*-, Ankünfte*) *f* arrival; **Ankunftszeit** *f* arrival time

Anlage *f* (*Veranlagung*) disposition; (*Begabung*) talent; (*Park*) gardens *pl*, grounds *pl*; (*zu Brief etc*) enclosure; (*Stereoanlage*) stereo (system); (*Tech*) plant; (*Fin*) investment

Anlass (*-es, Anlässe*) m cause (*zu* for);
(*Ereignis*) occasion; **aus diesem ~** for this
reason; **an|lassen** *irr vt* (*Motor*) to start;
(*Licht, Kleidung*) to leave on; **Anlasser**
(*-s, -*) m (*Auto*) starter; **anlässlich** *prep*
+gen on the occasion of

Anlauf m run-up; **an|laufen** *irr vi* to
begin; (*Film*) to open; (*Fenster*) to mist up;
(*Metall*) to tarnish

an|legen *vt* to put (*an +akk* against/on);
(*Schmuck*) to put on; (*Garten*) to lay out;
(*Geld*) to invest; (*Gewehr*) to aim (*auf +akk*
at); **es auf etw** (*akk*) **~** to be out for sth
▷ *vi* (*Schiff*) to berth, to dock ▷ *vr* **sich mit**
jdm ~ (*fam*) to pick a quarrel with sb;
Anlegestelle f moorings *pl*

an|lehnen *vt* to lean (*an +akk* against);
(*Tür*) to leave ajar ▷ *vr* **sich ~** to lean (*an*
+akk against)

an|leiern *vt* **etw ~** (*fam*) to get sth going

Anleitung f instructions *pl*

Anliegen (*-s, -*) nt matter; (*Wunsch*)
request

Anlieger(in) (*-s, -*) m(f) resident; **~ frei**
residents only

an|lügen *irr vt* to lie to

an|machen *vt* (*befestigen*) to attach;
(*einschalten*) to switch on; (*Salat*) to dress;
(*fam: aufreizen*) to turn on; (*fam: ansprechen*)
to chat up (*Brit*), to come on to (*US*); (*fam:
beschimpfen*) to have a go at

Anmeldeformular nt application form;
(*bei Amt*) registration form; **an|melden** *vt*
(*Besuch etc*) to announce ▷ *vr* **sich ~** (*beim
Arzt etc*) to make an appointment; (*bei
Amt, für Kurs etc*) to register;
Anmeldeschluss m deadline for
applications, registration deadline;
Anmeldung f registration; (*Antrag*)
application

an|nähen *vt* **einen Knopf (an den**
Mantel) ~ to sew a button on (one's coat)

annähernd *adv* roughly; **nicht ~** nowhere
near

Annahme (*-, -n*) f acceptance;
(*Vermutung*) assumption; **annehmbar** *adj*
acceptable; **an|nehmen** *irr vt* to accept;
(*Namen*) to take; (*Kind*) to adopt;
(*vermuten*) to suppose, to assume

Annonce (*-, -n*) f advertisement

an|öden *vt* (*fam*) to bore stiff (*o silly*)

annullieren *vt* to cancel

anonym *adj* anonymous

Anorak (*-s, -s*) m anorak

an|packen *vt* (*Problem, Aufgabe*) to tackle;
mit ~ to lend a hand

an|passen *vt* (*fig*) to adapt (*dat* to) ▷ *vr*
sich ~ to adapt (*an +akk* to)

an|pfeifen *irr vt* (*Fußballspiel*) **das Spiel**
~ to start the game; **Anpfiff** m (*Sport*)
(starting) whistle; (*Beginn*) kick-off; (*fam:
Tadel*) roasting

an|probieren *vt* to try on

Anrede f form of address; **an|reden** *vt* to
address

an|regen *vt* to stimulate; **Anregung** f
stimulation; (*Vorschlag*) suggestion

Anreise f journey; **der Tag der ~** the day
of arrival; **an|reisen** *vi* to arrive

Anreiz m incentive

an|richten *vt* (*Speisen*) to prepare;
(*Schaden*) to cause

Anruf m call; **Anrufbeantworter** (*-s, -*) m
answering machine, answerphone;
an|rufen *irr vt* (*Tel*) to call, to phone, to
ring (*Brit*)

ans *kontr von* **an das**

Ansage f announcement; (*auf
Anrufbeantworter*) recorded message;
an|sagen *vt* to announce; **angesagt sein**
to be recommended; (*modisch sein*) to be
the in thing; **Spannung ist angesagt** we
are in for some excitement ▷ *vr* **er sagte**
sich an he said he would come

an|schaffen *vt* to buy

an|schauen *vt* to look at

Anschein m appearance; **dem** (*o allem*)
~ nach ... it looks as if ...; **den**
~ erwecken, hart zu arbeiten to give the
impression of working hard; **anscheinend**
adj apparent ▷ *adv* apparently

an|schieben *irr vt* **könnten Sie mich mal**
~? (*Auto*) could you give me a push?

Anschlag m notice; (*Attentat*) attack;
an|schlagen *irr vt* (*Plakat*) to put up;
(*beschädigen*) to chip ▷ *vi* (*wirken*) to take
effect; **mit etw an etw** (*akk*) **~** to bang sth
against sth

an|schließen *irr vt* (*Elek, Tech*) to connect
(*an +akk* to); (*mit Stecker*) to plug in ▷ *vi, vr*
(*sich*) **an etw** (*akk*) **~** (*Gebäude etc*) to
adjoin sth; (*zeitlich*) to follow sth ▷ *vr* **sich**
~ to join (*jdm/einer Gruppe* sb/a group);
anschließend *adj* adjacent; (*zeitlich*)
subsequent ▷ *adv* afterwards; **~ an** (*+akk*)
following; **Anschluss** m (*Elek, Eisenb*)

connection; (*von Wasser, Gas etc*) supply; **im ~ an** (+*akk*) following; **kein ~ unter dieser Nummer** (*Tel*) the number you have dialled has not been recognized; **Anschlussflug** *m* connecting flight

an|schnallen *vt* (*Skier*) to put on ▷ *vr* **sich ~** to fasten one's seat belt

Anschrift *f* address

an|schwellen *irr vi* to swell (up)

an|sehen *irr vt* to look at; (*bei etw zuschauen*) to watch; **jdn/etw als etw ~** to look on sb/sth as sth; **das sieht man ihm an** he looks it

an sein *irr vi siehe* **an**

an|setzen *vt* (*Termin*) to fix; (*zubereiten*) to prepare ▷ *vi* (*anfangen*) to start, to begin; **zu etw ~** to prepare to do sth

Ansicht *f* (*Meinung*) view, opinion; (*Anblick*) sight; **meiner ~ nach** in my opinion; **zur ~** on approval; **Ansichtskarte** *f* postcard

ansonsten *adv* otherwise

Anspiel *nt* (*Sport*) start of play; **anspielen** *vi* **auf etw** (*akk*) **~** to allude to sth; **Anspielung** *f* allusion (*auf* +*akk* to)

an|sprechen *irr vt* to speak to; (*gefallen*) to appeal to ▷ *vi* **auf etw** (*akk*) **~** (*Patient*) to respond to sth; **ansprechend** *adj* attractive; **Ansprechpartner(in)** *m(f)* contact

an|springen *irr vi* (*Auto*) to start

Anspruch *m* claim; (*Recht*) right (*auf* +*akk* to); **etw in ~ nehmen** to take advantage of sth; **~ auf etw haben** to be entitled to sth; **anspruchslos** *adj* undemanding; (*bescheiden*) modest; **anspruchsvoll** *adj* demanding

Anstalt (-, -*en*) *f* institution

Anstand *m* decency; **anständig** *adj* decent; (*fig, fam*) proper; (*groß*) considerable

an|starren *vt* to stare at

anstatt *prep* +*gen* instead of

an|stecken *vt* to pin on; (*Med*) to infect; **jdn mit einer Erkältung ~** to pass one's cold on to sb ▷ *vr* **ich habe mich bei ihm angesteckt** I caught it from him ▷ *vi* (*fig*) to be infectious; **ansteckend** *adj* infectious; **Ansteckungsgefahr** *f* danger of infection

an|stehen *irr vi* (*in Warteschlange*) to queue (*Brit*), to stand in line (*US*); (*erledigt werden müssen*) to be on the agenda

anstelle *prep* +*gen* instead of

an|stellen *vt* (*einschalten*) to turn on; (*Arbeit geben*) to employ; (*machen*) to do; **was hast du wieder angestellt?** what have you been up to now? ▷ *vr* **sich ~** to queue (*Brit*), to stand in line (*US*); (*fam*) **stell dich nicht so an!** stop making such a fuss

Anstoß *m* impetus; (*Sport*) kick-off; **an|stoßen** *irr vt* to push; (*mit Fuß*) to kick ▷ *vi* to knock, to bump; (*mit Gläsern*) to drink (a toast) (*auf* +*akk* to); **anstößig** *adj* offensive; (*Kleidung etc*) indecent

an|strengen *vt* to strain ▷ *vr* **sich ~** to make an effort; **anstrengend** *adj* tiring

Antarktis *f* Antarctic

Anteil *m* share (*an* +*dat* in); **~ nehmen an** (+*dat*) (*mitleidig*) to sympathize with; (*sich interessieren*) to take an interest in

Antenne (-, -*n*) *f* aerial

Antibabypille *f* **die ~** the pill; **Antibiotikum** (-*s*, *Antibiotika*) *nt* (*Med*) antibiotic

antik *adj* antique

Antilope (-, -*n*) *f* antelope

Antiquariat *nt* (*für Bücher*) second-hand bookshop

Antiquitäten *pl* antiques *pl*; **Antiquitätenhändler(in)** *m(f)* antique dealer

an|törnen *vt* (*fam*) to turn on

Antrag (-(*e*)*s*, *Anträge*) *m* proposal; (*Pol*) motion; (*Formular*) application form; **einen ~ stellen auf** (+*akk*) to make an application for

an|treffen *irr vt* to find

an|treiben *irr vt* (*Tech*) to drive; (*anschwemmen*) to wash up; **jdn zur Arbeit ~** to make sb work

an|treten *irr vt* **eine Reise ~** to set off on a journey

Antrieb *m* (*Tech*) drive; (*Motivation*) impetus

an|tun *irr vt* **jdm etwas ~** to do sth to sb; **sich** (*dat*) **etwas ~** (*Selbstmord begehen*) to kill oneself

Antwort (-, -*en*) *f* answer, reply; **um ~ wird gebeten** RSVP (*répondez s'il vous plaît*); **antworten** *vi* to answer, to reply; **jdm ~** to answer sb; **auf etw** (*akk*) **~** to answer sth

an|vertrauen *vt* **jdm etw ~** to entrust sb with sth

Anwalt (-s, *Anwälte*) m, **Anwältin** f lawyer

an|weisen irr vt (*anleiten*) to instruct; (*zuteilen*) to allocate (*jdm etw* sth to sb); **Anweisung** f instruction; (*von Geld*) money order

an|wenden irr vt to use; (*Gesetz, Regel*) to apply; **Anwender(in)** (-s, -) m(f) user; **Anwendung** f use; (*Inform*) application

anwesend adj present; **Anwesenheit** f presence

an|widern vt to disgust

Anwohner(in) (-s, -) m(f) resident

Anzahl f number (*an +dat* of); **an|zahlen** vt to pay a deposit on; **100 Euro ~** to pay 100 euros as a deposit; **Anzahlung** f deposit

Anzeichen nt sign; (*Med*) symptom

Anzeige (-, -n) f (*Werbung*) advertisement; (*elektronisch*) display; (*bei Polizei*) report; **an|zeigen** vt (*Temperatur, Zeit*) to indicate, to show; (*elektronisch*) to display; (*bekannt geben*) to announce; **jdn/einen Autodiebstahl bei der Polizei ~** to report sb/a stolen car to the police

an|ziehen irr vt to attract; (*Kleidung*) to put on; (*Schraube, Seil*) to tighten ▷ vr **sich ~** to get dressed; **anziehend** adj attractive

Anzug m suit

anzüglich adj suggestive

an|zünden vt to light; (*Haus etc*) to set fire to

an|zweifeln vt to doubt

Aperitif (-s, -s (*o -e*)) m aperitif

Apfel (-s, *Äpfel*) m apple; **Apfelbaum** m apple tree; **Apfelkuchen** m apple cake; **Apfelmus** nt apple purée; **Apfelsaft** m apple juice; **Apfelsine** f orange; **Apfelwein** m cider

Apostroph (-s, -e) m apostrophe

Apotheke (-, -n) f chemist's (shop) (*Brit*), pharmacy (*US*); **apothekenpflichtig** adj only available at the chemist's (*o* pharmacy); **Apotheker(in)** (-s, -) m(f) chemist (*Brit*), pharmacist (*US*)

Apparat (-(e)s, -e) m (piece of) apparatus; (*Tel*) telephone; (*Radio, Tv*) set; **am ~!** (*Tel*) speaking; **am ~ bleiben** (*Tel*) to hold the line

Appartement (-s, -s) nt studio flat (*Brit*) (*o* apartment (*US*))

Appetit (-(e)s, -e) m appetite; **guten ~!** bon appétit; **appetitlich** adj appetizing

Applaus (-es, -e) m applause

Aprikose (-, -n) f apricot

April (-(s), -e) m April; siehe auch **Juni ~, ~!** April fool!; **Aprilscherz** (-es, -e) m April fool's joke

apropos adv by the way; **~ Urlaub ...** while we're on the subject of holidays ...

Aquaplaning (-(s)) nt aquaplaning

Aquarell (-s, -e) nt watercolour

Aquarium nt aquarium

Äquator m equator

Araber(in) (-s, -) m(f) Arab; **arabisch** adj Arab; (*Ziffer, Sprache*) Arabic; (*Meer, Wüste*) Arabian

Arbeit (-, -en) f work; (*Stelle*) job; (*Erzeugnis*) piece of work; **arbeiten** vi to work; **Arbeiter(in)** (-s, -) m(f) worker; (*ungelernt*) labourer; **Arbeitgeber(in)** (-s, -) m(f) employer; **Arbeitnehmer(in)** (-s, -) m(f) employee; **Arbeitsamt** nt job centre (*Brit*), employment office (*US*); **Arbeitserlaubnis** f work permit; **arbeitslos** adj unemployed; **Arbeitslose(r)** mf unemployed person; **die ~n** pl the unemployed pl; **Arbeitslosengeld** nt (income-related) unemployment benefit, job-seeker's allowance (*Brit*); **Arbeitslosenhilfe** f (non-income related) unemployment benefit; **Arbeitslosigkeit** f unemployment; **Arbeitsplatz** m job; (*Ort*) workplace; **Arbeitsspeicher** m (*Inform*) main memory; **Arbeitszeit** f working hours pl; **gleitende ~** flexible working hours pl, flexitime; **Arbeitszimmer** nt study

Archäologe (-n, -n) m, **Archäologin** f archaeologist

Architekt(in) (-en, -en) m(f) architect; **Architektur** f architecture

Archiv (-s, -e) nt archives pl

arg adj bad; (*schrecklich*) awful ▷ adv (*sehr*) terribly

Argentinien (-s) nt Argentina

Ärger (-s) m annoyance; (*stärker*) anger; (*Unannehmlichkeiten*) trouble; **ärgerlich** adj (*zornig*) angry; (*lästig*) annoying; **ärgern** vt to annoy ▷ vr **sich ~** to get annoyed

Argument (-s, -e) nt argument

Arktis (-) f Arctic

arm *adj* poor

Arm (-(e)s, -e) *m* arm; (*Fluss*) branch

Armaturenbrett *nt* instrument panel; (*Auto*) dashboard

Armband *nt* bracelet; **Armbanduhr** *f* (wrist)watch

Armee (-, -n) *f* army

Ärmel (-s, -) *m* sleeve; **Ärmelkanal** *m* (English) Channel

Armut (-) *f* poverty

Aroma (-s, Aromen) *nt* aroma; **Aromatherapie** *f* aromatherapy

arrogant *adj* arrogant

Art (-, -en) *f* (*Weise*) way; (*Sorte*) kind, sort; (*bei Tieren*) species; **nach ~ des Hauses** à la maison; **auf diese ~ (und Weise)** in this way; **das ist nicht seine ~** that's not like him

Arterie (-, -n) *f* artery

artig *adj* good, well-behaved

Artikel (-s, -) *m* (*Ware*) article, item; (*Zeitung*) article

Artischocke (-, -n) *f* artichoke

Artist(in) (-en, -en) *m(f)* (circus) performer

Arznei *f* medicine; **Arzt** (-es, Ärzte) *m* doctor; **Arzthelfer(in)** *m(f)* doctor's assistant; **Ärztin** *f* (female) doctor; **ärztlich** *adj* medical; **sich ~ behandeln lassen** to undergo medical treatment

Asche (-, -n) *f* ashes *pl*; (*von Zigarette*) ash; **Aschenbecher** *m* ashtray; **Aschermittwoch** *m* Ash Wednesday

Asiat(in) (-en, -en) *m(f)* Asian; **asiatisch** *adj* Asian; **Asien** (-s) *nt* Asia

Aspekt (-(e)s, -e) *m* aspect

Asphalt (-(e)s, -e) *m* asphalt

Aspirin® (-s, -e) *nt* aspirin

aß *imperf von* **essen**

Ass (-es, -e) *nt* (*Karten, Tennis*) ace

Assistent(in) *m(f)* assistant

Ast (-(e)s, Äste) *m* branch

Asthma (-s) *nt* asthma

Astrologie *f* astrology; **Astronaut(in)** (-en, -en) *m(f)* astronaut; **Astronomie** *f* astronomy

ASU (-, -s) *f abk =* **Abgassonderuntersuchung** exhaust emission test

Asyl (-s, -e) *nt* asylum; (*Heim*) home; (*für Obdachlose*) shelter; **Asylant(in)** *m(f)*, **Asylbewerber(in)** *m(f)* asylum seeker

Atelier (-s, -s) *nt* studio

Atem (-s) *m* breath; **atemberaubend** *adj* breathtaking; **Atembeschwerden** *pl* breathing difficulties *pl*; **atemlos** *adj* breathless; **Atempause** *f* breather

Athen *nt* Athens

Äthiopien (-s) *nt* Ethiopia

Athlet(in) (-en, -en) *m(f)* athlete

Atlantik (-s) *m* Atlantic (Ocean)

Atlas (- *o* Atlasses, Atlanten) *m* atlas

atmen *vt, vi* to breathe; **Atmung** *f* breathing

Atom (-s, -e) *nt* atom; **Atombombe** *f* atom bomb; **Atomkraftwerk** *nt* nuclear power station; **Atommüll** *m* nuclear waste; **Atomwaffen** *pl* nuclear weapons *pl*

Attentat (-(e)s, -e) *nt* assassination (*auf +akk* of); (*Versuch*) assassination attempt

Attest (-(e)s, -e) *nt* certificate

attraktiv *adj* attractive

Attrappe (-, -n) *f* dummy

ätzend *adj* (*fam*) revolting; (*schlecht*) lousy

au *interj* ouch; **~ ja!** yeah

Aubergine (-, -n) *f* aubergine, eggplant (US)

🔘 **SCHLÜSSELWORT**

auch *adv* **1** (*ebenfalls*) also, too, as well; **das ist auch schön** that's nice too *od* as well; **er kommt — ich auch** he's coming — so am I me too; **auch nicht** not ... either; **ich auch nicht** nor I, me neither; **oder auch** or; **auch das noch!** not that as well!

2 (*selbst, sogar*) even; **auch wenn das Wetter schlecht ist** even if the weather is bad; **ohne auch nur zu fragen** without even asking

3 (*wirklich*) really; **du siehst müde aus — bin ich auch** you look tired — (so) I am; **so sieht es auch aus** it looks like it too

4 (*auch immer*); **wer auch** whoever; **was auch** whatever; **wie dem auch sei** be that as it may; **wie sehr er sich auch bemühte** however much he tried

audiovisuell *adj* audiovisual

○ SCHLÜSSELWORT

auf *präp* +dat (*wo?*) on; **auf dem Tisch** on the table; **auf der Reise** on the way; **auf der Post/dem Fest** at the post office/party; **auf der Straße** on the road; **auf dem Land/der ganzen Welt** in the country/the whole world

▷ *präp* +akk **1** (*wohin?*) on(to); **auf den Tisch** on(to) the table; **auf die Post gehen** go to the post office; **auf das Land** into the country; **etw auf einen Zettel schreiben** to write sth on a piece of paper

2: **auf Deutsch** in German; **auf Lebenszeit** for my/his lifetime; **bis auf ihn** except for him; **auf einmal** at once; **auf seinen Vorschlag (hin)** at his suggestion

▷ *adv* **1** (*offen*) open; **auf sein** (*umg*) (*Tür, Geschäft*) to be open; **das Fenster ist auf** the window is open

2 (*hinauf*) up; **auf und ab** up and down; **auf und davon** up and away; **auf!** (*los!*) come on!

3 (*aufgestanden*) up; **auf sein** to be up; **ist er schon auf?** is he up yet?

▷ *konj*: **auf dass** (so) that

auf|atmen *vi* to breathe a sigh of relief

auf|bauen *vt* (*errichten*) to put up; (*schaffen*) to build up; (*gestalten*) to construct; (*gründen*) to found, to base (*auf* +akk on); **sich eine Existenz ~** to make a life for oneself

auf|bewahren *vt* to keep, to store

auf|bleiben *irr vi* (*Tür, Laden etc*) to stay open; (*Mensch*) to stay up

auf|blenden *vi, vt* (**die Scheinwerfer**) **~** to put one's headlights on full beam

auf|brechen *irr vt* to break open ▷ *vi* to burst open; (*gehen*) to leave; (*abreisen*) to set off; **Aufbruch** *m* departure

auf|drängen *vt*: **jdm etw ~** to force sth on sb ▷ *vr*: **sich ~** to intrude (*jdm* on sb); **aufdringlich** *adj* pushy

aufeinander *adv* (*übereinander*) on top of each other; **~ achten** to look after each other; **~ schießen** to shoot at each other; **~ vertrauen** to trust each other; **~ folgen** to follow one another; **~ prallen** to crash into one another

Aufenthalt *m* stay; (*Zug*) stop; **Aufenthaltsgenehmigung** *f* residence permit; **Aufenthaltsraum** *m* lounge

auf|essen *irr vt* to eat up

auf|fahren *irr vi* (*Auto*) to run (*o* to crash) (*auf* +akk into); (*herankommen*) to drive up; **Auffahrt** *f* (*am Haus*) drive; (*Autobahn*) slip road (*Brit*), ramp (*US*); **Auffahrunfall** *m* rear-end collision; (*mehrere Fahrzeuge*) pile-up

auf|fallen *irr vi* to stand out; **jdm ~** to strike sb; **das fällt gar nicht auf** nobody will notice; **auffallend** *adj* striking; **auffällig** *adj* conspicuous; (*Kleidung, Farbe*) striking

auf|fangen *irr vt* (*Ball*) to catch; (*Stoß*) to cushion

auf|fassen *vt* to understand; **Auffassung** *f* view; (*Meinung*) opinion; (*Auslegung*) concept; (*Auffassungsgabe*) grasp

auf|fordern *vt* (*befehlen*) to call upon; (*bitten*) to ask

auf|frischen *vt* (*Kenntnisse*) to brush up

auf|führen *vt* (*Theat*) to perform; (*in einem Verzeichnis*) to list; (*Beispiel*) to give ▷ *vr*: **sich ~** (*sich benehmen*) to behave; **Aufführung** *f* (*Theat*) performance

Aufgabe *f* job, task; (*Schule*) exercise; (*Hausaufgabe*) homework

Aufgang *m* (*Treppe*) staircase

auf|geben *irr vt* (*verzichten auf*) to give up; (*Paket*) to post; (*Gepäck*) to check in; (*Bestellung*) to place; (*Inserat*) to insert; (*Rätsel, Problem*) to set ▷ *vi* to give up

auf|gehen *irr vi* (*Sonne, Teig*) to rise; (*sich öffnen*) to open; (*klar werden*) to dawn (*jdm* on sb)

aufgelegt *adj*: **gut/schlecht ~** in a good/bad mood

aufgeregt *adj* excited

aufgeschlossen *adj* open(minded)

aufgeschmissen *adj* (*fam*) in a fix

aufgrund, auf Grund *prep* +gen on the basis of; (*wegen*) because of

auf|haben *irr vt* (*Hut etc*) to have on; **viel ~** (*Schule*) to have a lot of homework to do ▷ *vi* (*Geschäft*) to be open

auf|halten *irr vt* (*jdn*) to detain; (*Entwicklung*) to stop; (*Tür, Hand*) to hold open; (*Augen*) to keep open ▷ *vr*: **sich ~** (*wohnen*) to live; (*vorübergehend*) to stay

auf|hängen *irr vt* to hang up
auf|heben *irr vt* (*vom Boden etc*) to pick up; (*aufbewahren*) to keep
auf|holen *vt* (*Zeit*) to make up ▷ *vi* to catch up
auf|hören *vi* to stop; **~, etw zu tun** to stop doing sth
auf|klären *vt* (*Geheimnis etc*) to clear up; **jdn ~** to enlighten sb; (*sexuell*) to tell sb the facts of life
Aufkleber (*-s, -*) *m* sticker
auf|kommen *irr vi* (*Wind*) to come up; (*Zweifel, Gefühl*) to arise; (*Mode etc*) to appear on the scene; **für den Schaden ~** to pay for the damage
auf|laden *irr vt* to load; (*Handy etc*) to charge; **Aufladegerät** *nt* charger
Auflage *f* edition; (*von Zeitung*) circulation; (*Bedingung*) condition
auf|lassen *vt* (*Hut, Brille*) to keep on; (*Tür*) to leave open
Auflauf *m* (*Menschen*) crowd; (*Speise*) bake
auf|legen *vt* (*CD, Schminke etc*) to put on; (*Hörer*) to put down ▷ *vi* (*Tel*) to hang up
auf|leuchten *vi* to light up
auf|lösen *vt* (*in Flüssigkeit*) to dissolve ▷ *vr* **sich ~** (*in Flüssigkeit*) to dissolve; **der Stau hat sich aufgelöst** traffic is back to normal; **Auflösung** *f* (*von Rätsel*) solution; (*von Bildschirm*) resolution
auf|machen *vt* to open; (*Kleidung*) to undo ▷ *vr* **sich ~** to set out (*nach for*)
aufmerksam *adj* attentive; **jdn auf etw** (*akk*) **~ machen** to draw sb's attention to sth; **Aufmerksamkeit** *f* attention; (*Konzentration*) attentiveness; (*Geschenk*) small token
auf|muntern *vt* (*ermutigen*) to encourage; (*aufheitern*) to cheer up
Aufnahme (*-, -n*) *f* (*Foto*) photo(graph); (*einzelne*) shot; (*in Verein, Krankenhaus etc*) admission; (*Beginn*) beginning; (*auf Tonband etc*) recording; **Aufnahmeprüfung** *f* entrance exam; **auf|nehmen** *irr vt* (*in Krankenhaus, Verein etc*) to admit; (*Musik*) to record; (*beginnen*) to take up; (*in Liste*) to include; (*begreifen*) to take in; **mit jdm Kontakt ~** to get in touch with sb
auf|passen *vi* (*aufmerksam sein*) to pay attention; (*vorsichtig sein*) to take care; **auf jdn/etw ~** to keep an eye on sb/sth

Aufprall (*-s, -e*) *m* impact; **auf|prallen** *vi* **auf etw** (*akk*) **~** to hit sth, to crash into sth
Aufpreis *m* extra charge
auf|pumpen *vt* to pump up
Aufputschmittel *nt* stimulant
auf|räumen *vt, vi* (*Dinge*) to clear away; (*Zimmer*) to tidy up
aufrecht *adj* upright
auf|regen *vt* to excite; (*ärgern*) to annoy ▷ *vr* **sich ~** to get worked up; **aufregend** *adj* exciting; **Aufregung** *f* excitement
auf|reißen *irr vt* (*Tüte*) to tear open; (*Tür*) to fling open; (*fam: Person*) to pick up
Aufruf *m* (*Aviat, Inform*) call; (*öffentlicher*) appeal; **auf|rufen** *irr vt* (*auffordern*) to call upon (*zu for*); (*Namen*) to call out; (*Aviat*) to call; (*Inform*) to call up
auf|runden *vt* (*Summe*) to round up
aufs *kontr von* **auf das**
Aufsatz *m* essay
auf|schieben *irr vt* (*verschieben*) to postpone; (*verzögern*) to put off; (*Tür*) to slide open
Aufschlag *m* (*auf Preis*) extra charge; (*Tennis*) service; **auf|schlagen** *irr vt* (*öffnen*) to open; (*verletzen*) to cut open; (*Zelt*) to pitch, to put up; (*Lager*) to set up ▷ *vi* (*Tennis*) to serve; **auf etw** (*+akk*) **~** (*aufprallen*) to hit sth
auf|schließen *irr vt* to unlock, to open up ▷ *vi* (*aufrücken*) to close up
auf|schneiden *irr vt* to cut open; (*in Scheiben*) to slice ▷ *vi* (*angeben*) to boast, to show off
Aufschnitt *m* (*slices pl of*) cold meat; (*bei Käse*) (assorted) sliced cheeses *pl*
auf|schreiben *irr vt* to write down
Aufschrift *f* inscription; (*Etikett*) label
Aufschub *m* (*Verzögerung*) delay; (*Vertagung*) postponement
Aufsehen (*-s*) *nt* stir; **großes ~ erregen** to cause a sensation; **Aufseher(in)** (*-s, -*) *m(f)* guard; (*im Betrieb*) supervisor; (*im Museum*) attendant; (*im Park*) keeper
auf sein *irr vi siehe* **auf**
auf|setzen *vt* to put on; (*Dokument*) to draw up ▷ *vi* (*Flugzeug*) to touch down
Aufsicht *f* supervision; (*bei Prüfung*) invigilation; **die ~ haben** to be in charge
auf|spannen *vt* (*Schirm*) to put up
auf|sperren *vt* (*Mund*) to open wide; (*aufschließen*) to unlock
auf|springen *irr vi* to jump (*auf +akk*

onto); (*hochspringen*) to jump up; (*sich öffnen*) to spring open

auf|stehen *irr vi* to get up; (*Tür*) to be open

auf|stellen *vt* (*aufrecht stellen*) to put up; (*aufreihen*) to line up; (*nominieren*) to put up; (*Liste, Programm*) to draw up; (*Rekord*) to set up

Aufstieg (-(e)s, -e) *m* (*auf Berg*) ascent; (*Fortschritt*) rise; (*beruflich, im Sport*) promotion

Aufstrich *m* spread

auf|tanken *vt, vi* (*Auto*) to tank up; (*Flugzeug*) to refuel

auf|tauchen *vi* to turn up; (*aus Wasser etc*) to surface; (*Frage, Problem*) to come up

auf|tauen *vt* (*Speisen*) to defrost ▷ *vi* to thaw; (*fig: Person*) to unbend

Auftrag (-(e)s, Aufträge) *m* (*Comm*) order; (*Arbeit*) job; (*Anweisung*) instructions *pl*; (*Aufgabe*) task; **im ~ von** on behalf of;

auf|tragen *irr vt* (*Salbe etc*) to apply; (*Essen*) to serve

auf|treten *irr vi* to appear; (*Problem*) to come up; (*sich verhalten*) to behave;

Auftritt *m* (*des Schauspielers*) entrance; (*fig: Szene*) scene

auf|wachen *vi* to wake up

auf|wachsen *irr vi* to grow up

Aufwand (-(e)s) *m* expenditure; (*Kosten a.*) expense; (*Anstrengung*) effort; **aufwändig** *adj* costly; **das ist zu ~** that's too much trouble

auf|wärmen *vt* to warm up ▷ *vr* **sich ~** to warm up

aufwärts *adv* upwards; **mit etw geht es ~** things are looking up for sth

auf|wecken *vt* to wake up

aufwendig *adj siehe* **aufwändig**

auf|wischen *vt* to wipe up; (*Fußboden*) to wipe

auf|zählen *vt* to list;

Aufzählungszeichen *nt* bullet

auf|zeichnen *vt* to sketch; (*schriftlich*) to jot down; (*auf Band etc*) to record;

Aufzeichnung *f* (*schriftlich*) note; (*Tonband etc*) recording; (*Film*) record

auf|ziehen *irr vt* (*öffnen*) to pull open; (*Uhr*) to wind (up); (*fam: necken*) to tease; (*Kinder*) to bring up; (*Tiere*) to rear ▷ *vi* (*Gewitter*) to come up

Aufzug *m* (*Fahrstuhl*) lift (*Brit*), elevator (*US*); (*Kleidung*) get-up; (*Theat*) act

Auge (-s, -n) *nt* eye; **jdm etw aufs ~ drücken** (*fam*) to force sth on sb; **ins ~ gehen** (*fam*) to go wrong; **unter vier ~n** in private; **etw im ~ behalten** to keep sth in mind; **Augenarzt** *m*, **Augenärztin** *f* eye specialist, eye doctor (*US*); **Augenblick** *m* moment; **im ~** at the moment; **Augenbraue** (-, -n) *f* eyebrow; **Augenbrauenstift** *m* eyebrow pencil; **Augenfarbe** *f* eye colour; **seine ~** the colour of his eyes; **Augenlid** *nt* eyelid; **Augenoptiker(in)** (-s, -) *m(f)* optician; **Augentropfen** *pl* eyedrops *pl*; **Augenzeuge** *m*, **Augenzeugin** *f* eyewitness

August (-(e)s o -, -e) *m* August; *siehe auch* **Juni**

Auktion *f* auction

SCHLÜSSELWORT

aus *präp +dat* **1** (*räumlich*) out of (*von ... her*) from; **er ist aus Berlin** he's from Berlin; **aus dem Fenster** out of the window

2 (*gemacht/hergestellt aus*) made of; **ein Herz aus Stein** a heart of stone

3 (*auf Ursache deutend*) out of; **aus Mitleid** out of sympathy; **aus Erfahrung** from experience; **aus Spaß** for fun

4: **aus ihr wird nie etwas** she'll never get anywhere

▷ *adv* **1** (*zu Ende*) finished, over; **aus sein** to be over; **aus und vorbei** over and done with

2 (*ausgeschaltet, ausgezogen*) out (*Aufschrift an Geräten*) off; **aus sein** (*nicht brennen*) to be out, (*abgeschaltet sein: Radio, Herd*) to be off; **Licht aus!** lights out!

3 (*nicht zu Hause*): **aus sein** to be out

4 (*in Verbindung mit von*): **von Rom aus** from Rome; **vom Fenster aus** out of the window; **von sich aus** (*selbstständig*) of one's own accord; **von ihm aus** as far as he's concerned

aus|atmen *vi* to breathe out

aus|bauen *vt* (*Haus, Straße*) to extend; (*Motor etc*) to remove

aus|bessern *vt* to repair; (*Kleidung*) to mend

aus|bilden *vt* to educate; (*Lehrling etc*) to train; (*Fähigkeiten*) to develop; **Ausbildung**

f education; (*von Lehrling etc*) training; (*von Fähigkeiten*) development
Ausblick m view; (*fig*) outlook
aus|brechen *irr vi* to break out; **in Tränen ~** to burst into tears; **in Gelächter ~** to burst out laughing
aus|breiten *vt* to spread (out); (*Arme*) to stretch out ▷ *vr* **sich ~** to spread
Ausbruch m (*Krieg, Seuche etc*) outbreak; (*Vulkan*) eruption; (*Gefühle*) outburst; (*von Gefangenen*) escape
aus|buhen *vt* to boo
Ausdauer f perseverance; (*Sport*) stamina
aus|dehnen *vt* to stretch; (*fig: Macht*) to extend
aus|denken *irr vt* **sich** (*dat*) **etw ~** to come up with sth
Ausdruck m (*Ausdrücke*) expression ▷ m (*Ausdrucke*) (*Computerausdruck*) print-out; **aus|drucken** *vt* (*Inform*) to print (out)
aus|drücken *vt* (*formulieren*) to express; (*Zigarette*) to put out; (*Zitrone etc*) to squeeze ▷ *vr* **sich ~** to express oneself; **ausdrücklich** *adj* express ▷ *adv* expressly
auseinander *adv* (*getrennt*) apart; **~ gehen** (*Menschen*) to separate; (*Meinungen*) to differ; (*Gegenstand*) to fall apart; **~ halten** to tell apart; **~ schreiben** to write as separate words; **~ setzen** (*erklären*) to explain; **sich ~ setzen** (*sich beschäftigen*) to look (*mit* at); (*sich streiten*) to argue (*mit* with); **Auseinandersetzung** f (*Streit*) argument; (*Diskussion*) debate
Ausfahrt f (*des Zuges etc*) departure; (*Autobahn, Garage etc*) exit
aus|fallen *irr vi* (*Haare*) to fall out; (*nicht stattfinden*) to be cancelled; (*nicht funktionieren*) to break down; (*Strom*) to be cut off; (*Resultat haben*) to turn out; **groß/klein ~** (*Kleidung, Schuhe*) to be too big/too small
ausfindig machen *vt* to discover
aus|flippen *vi* (*fam*) to freak out
Ausflug m excursion, outing; **Ausflugsziel** nt destination
Ausfluss m (*Med*) discharge
aus|fragen *vt* to question
Ausfuhr (*-, -en*) f export
aus|führen *vt* (*verwirklichen*) to carry

out; (*Person*) to take out; (*Comm*) to export; (*darlegen*) to explain
ausführlich *adj* detailed ▷ *adv* in detail
aus|füllen *vt* to fill up; (*Fragebogen etc*) to fill in (*o* out)
Ausgabe f (*Geld*) expenditure; (*Inform*) output; (*Buch*) edition; (*Nummer*) issue
Ausgang m way out, exit; (*Flugsteig*) gate; (*Ende*) end; (*Ergebnis*) result; **„kein ~"** 'no exit'
aus|geben *irr vt* (*Geld*) to spend; (*austeilen*) to distribute; **jdm etw ~** (*spendieren*) to buy sb sth ▷ *vr* **sich für etw/jdn ~** to pass oneself off as sth/sb
ausgebucht *adj* fully booked
ausgefallen *adj* (*ungewöhnlich*) unusual
aus|gehen *irr vi* (*abends etc*) to go out; (*Benzin, Kaffee etc*) to run out; (*Haare*) to fall out; (*Feuer, Licht etc*) to go out; (*Resultat haben*) to turn out; **davon ~, dass** to assume that; **ihm ging das Geld aus** he ran out of money
ausgelassen *adj* exuberant
ausgeleiert *adj* worn out
ausgenommen *conj, prep* +gen *o* dat except
ausgerechnet *adv* **~ du** you of all people; **~ heute** today of all days
ausgeschildert *adj* signposted
ausgeschlafen *adj* **bist du ~?** have you had enough sleep?
ausgeschlossen *adj* (*unmöglich*) impossible, out of the question
ausgesprochen *adj* (*absolut*) out-and-out; (*unverkennbar*) marked ▷ *adv* extremely; **~ gut** really good
ausgezeichnet *adj* excellent
ausgiebig *adj* (*Gebrauch*) thorough; (*Essen*) substantial
aus|gießen *irr vt* (*Getränk*) to pour out; (*Gefäß*) to empty
aus|gleichen *irr vt* to even out ▷ *vi* (*Sport*) to equalize
Ausguss m (*Spüle*) sink; (*Abfluss*) outlet
aus|halten *irr vt* to bear, to stand; **nicht auszuhalten sein** to be unbearable ▷ *vi* to hold out
aus|händigen *vt* **jdm etw ~** to hand sth over to sb
Aushang m notice
Aushilfe f temporary help; (*im Büro*) temp
aus|kennen *irr vr* **sich ~** to know a lot

(bei, mit about); *(an einem Ort)* to know one's way around

aus|kommen *irr vi* **gut/schlecht mit jdm ~** to get on well/badly with sb; **mit etw ~** to get by with sth

Auskunft (-, *Auskünfte*) *f* information; *(nähere)* details *pl*; *(Schalter)* information desk; *(Tel)* (directory) enquiries *sing (kein Artikel, Brit)*, information *(US)*

aus|lachen *vt* to laugh at

aus|laden *irr vt (Gepäck etc)* to unload; **jdn ~** *(Gast)* to tell sb not to come

Auslage *f* window display; **~n** *pl (Kosten)* expenses

Ausland *nt* foreign countries *pl*; **im/ins ~** abroad; **Ausländer(in)** (-s, -) *m(f)* foreigner; **ausländerfeindlich** *adj* hostile to foreigners, xenophobic; **ausländisch** *adj* foreign; **Auslandsgespräch** *nt* international call; **Auslandskrankenschein** *m* health insurance certificate for foreign countries, ≈ E111 *(Brit)*; **Auslandsschutzbrief** *m* international *(motor)* insurance cover *(documents pl)*

aus|lassen *irr vt* to leave out; *(Wort etc a.)* to omit; *(überspringen)* to skip; *(Wut, Ärger)* to vent *(an +dat* on) ▷ *vr* **sich über etw** *(akk)* **~** to speak one's mind about sth

aus|laufen *irr vi (Flüssigkeit)* to run out; *(Tank etc)* to leak; *(Schiff)* to leave port; *(Vertrag)* to expire

aus|legen *vt (Waren)* to display; *(Geld)* to lend; *(Text etc)* to interpret; *(technisch ausstatten)* to design *(für, auf +akk* for)

aus|leihen *irr vt (verleihen)* to lend; **sich** *(dat)* **etw ~** to borrow sth

aus|loggen *vi (Inform)* to log out *(o* off)

aus|lösen *vt (Explosion, Alarm)* to set off; *(hervorrufen)* to cause; **Auslöser** (-s, -) *m (Foto)* shutter release

aus|machen *vt (Licht, Radio)* to turn off; *(Feuer)* to put out; *(Termin, Preis)* to fix; *(vereinbaren)* to agree; *(Anteil darstellen, betragen)* to represent; *(bedeuten)* to matter; **macht es Ihnen etwas aus, wenn ...?** would you mind if ...?; **das macht mir nichts aus** I don't mind

Ausmaß *nt* extent

Ausnahme (-, -*n*) *f* exception; **ausnahmsweise** *adv* as an exception, just this once

aus|nutzen *vt (Zeit, Gelegenheit, Einfluss)* to use; *(jdn, Gutmütigkeit)* to take advantage of

aus|packen *vt* to unpack

aus|probieren *vt* to try (out)

Auspuff (-(e)s, -e) *m (Tech)* exhaust; **Auspuffrohr** *nt* exhaust (pipe); **Auspufftopf** *m (Auto)* silencer *(Brit)*, muffler *(US)*

aus|rauben *vt* to rob

aus|räumen *vt (Dinge)* to clear away; *(Schrank, Zimmer)* to empty; *(Bedenken)* to put aside

aus|rechnen *vt* to calculate, to work out

Ausrede *f* excuse

aus|reden *vi* to finish speaking ▷ *vt* **jdm etw ~** to talk sb out of sth

ausreichend *adj* sufficient, satisfactory; *(Schulnote)* ≈ D

Ausreise *f* departure; **bei der ~** on leaving the country; **Ausreiseerlaubnis** *f* exit visa; **aus|reisen** *vi* to leave the country

aus|reißen *irr vt* to tear out ▷ *vi* to come off; *(fam: davonlaufen)* to run away

aus|renken *vt* **sich** *(dat)* **den Arm ~** to dislocate one's arm

aus|richten *vt (Botschaft)* to deliver; *(Gruß)* to pass on; *(erreichen)* **ich konnte bei ihr nichts ~** I couldn't get anywhere with her; **jdm etw ~** to tell sb sth

aus|rufen *irr vt (über Lautsprecher)* to announce; **jdn ~ lassen** to page sb; **Ausrufezeichen** *nt* exclamation mark

aus|ruhen *vi* to rest ▷ *vr* **sich ~** to rest

Ausrüstung *f* equipment

aus|rutschen *vi* to slip

aus|schalten *vt* to switch off; *(fig)* to eliminate

Ausschau *f* **~ halten** to look out *(nach* for)

aus|scheiden *irr vt (Med)* to give off, to secrete ▷ *vi* to leave *(aus etw* sth); *(Sport)* to be eliminated

aus|schlafen *irr vi* to have a lie-in ▷ *vr* **sich ~** to have a lie-in ▷ *vt* to sleep off

Ausschlag *m (Med)* rash; **den ~ geben** *(fig)* to tip the balance; **aus|schlagen** *irr vt (Zahn)* to knock out; *(Einladung)* to turn down ▷ *vi (Pferd)* to kick out; **ausschlaggebend** *adj* decisive

aus|schließen *irr vt* to lock out; *(fig)* to exclude; **ausschließlich** *adv* exclusively ▷ *prep* +*gen* excluding

Ausschnitt m (Teil) section; (von Kleid) neckline; (aus Zeitung) cutting
Ausschreitungen pl riots pl
aus|schütten vt (Flüssigkeit) to pour out; (Gefäß) to empty
aus|sehen irr vi to look; **krank ~** to look ill; **gut ~** (Person) to be good-looking; (Sache) to be looking good; **es sieht nach Regen aus** it looks like rain; **es sieht schlecht aus** things look bad
aus sein irr vi siehe **aus**
außen adv outside; **nach ~** outwards; **von ~** from (the) outside; **Außenbordmotor** m outboard motor; **Außenminister(in)** m(f) foreign minister, Foreign Secretary (Brit); **Außenseite** f outside; **Außenseiter(in)** m(f) outsider; **Außenspiegel** m wing mirror (Brit), side mirror (US)
außer prep +dat (abgesehen von) except (for); **nichts ~** nothing but; **~ Betrieb** out of order; **~ sich sein** to be beside oneself (vor with); **~ Atem** out of breath ▷ conj (ausgenommen) except; **~ wenn** unless; **~ dass** except; **außerdem** conj besides
äußere(r, s) adj outer, external
außergewöhnlich adj unusual ▷ adv exceptionally; **~ kalt** exceptionally cold; **außerhalb** prep +gen outside
äußerlich adj external
äußern vt to express; (zeigen) to show ▷ vr **sich ~** to give one's opinion; (sich zeigen) to show itself
außerordentlich adj extraordinary; **außerplanmäßig** adj unscheduled
äußerst adv extremely; **äußerste(r, s)** adj utmost; (räumlich) farthest; (Termin) last possible
Äußerung f remark
aus|setzen vt (Kind, Tier) to abandon; (Belohnung) to offer; **ich habe nichts daran auszusetzen** I have no objection to it ▷ vi (aufhören) to stop; (Pause machen) to drop out; (beim Spiel) to miss a turn
Aussicht f (Blick) view; (Chance) prospect; **aussichtslos** adj hopeless; **Aussichtsplattform** f observation platform; **Aussichtsturm** m observation tower
Aussiedler(in) (-s, -) m(f) émigré (person of German descent from Eastern Europe)
aus|spannen vi (erholen) to relax ▷ vt **er hat ihm die Freundin ausgespannt** (fam) he's nicked his girlfriend

aus|sperren vt to lock out ▷ vr **sich ~** to lock oneself out
Aussprache f (von Wörtern) pronunciation; (Gespräch) (frank) discussion; **aus|sprechen** irr vt to pronounce; (äußern) to express ▷ vr **sich ~** to talk (über +akk about) ▷ vi (zu Ende sprechen) to finish speaking
aus|spülen vt to rinse (out)
Ausstattung f (Ausrüstung) equipment; (Einrichtung) furnishings pl; (von Auto) fittings pl
aus|stehen irr vt to endure; **ich kann ihn nicht ~** I can't stand him ▷ vi (noch nicht da sein) to be outstanding
aus|steigen irr vi to get out (aus of); **aus dem Bus/Zug ~** to get off the bus/train; **Aussteiger(in)** m(f) dropout
aus|stellen vt to display; (auf Messe, in Museum etc) to exhibit; (fam: ausschalten) to switch off; (Scheck etc) to make out; (Pass etc) to issue; **Ausstellung** f exhibition
aus|sterben irr vi to die out
aus|strahlen vt to radiate; (Programm) to broadcast; **Ausstrahlung** f (Radio, Tv) broadcast; (fig: von Person) charisma
aus|strecken vr **sich ~** to stretch out ▷ vt (Hand) to reach out (nach for)
aus|suchen vt to choose
Austausch m exchange; **aus|tauschen** vt to exchange (gegen for)
aus|teilen vt to distribute; (aushändigen) to hand out
Auster (-, -n) f oyster; **Austernpilz** m oyster mushroom
aus|tragen irr vt (Post) to deliver; (Wettkampf) to hold
Australien (-s) nt Australia; **Australier(in)** (-s, -) m(f) Australian; **australisch** adj Australian
aus|trinken irr vt (Glas) to drain; (Getränk) to drink up ▷ vi to finish one's drink
aus|trocknen vi to dry out; (Fluss) to dry up
aus|üben vt (Beruf, Sport) to practise; (Einfluss) to exert
Ausverkauf m sale; **ausverkauft** adj (Karten, Artikel) sold out
Auswahl f selection, choice (an +dat of); **aus|wählen** vt to select, to choose
aus|wandern vi to emigrate
auswärtig adj (nicht am/vom Ort) not

local; (ausländisch) foreign; **auswärts** adv
(außerhalb der Stadt) out of town; (Sport)
~ **spielen** to play away; **Auswärtsspiel** nt
away match

aus|wechseln vt to replace; (Sport) to
substitute

Ausweg m way out

aus|weichen irr vi to get out of the way;
jdm/einer Sache ~ to move aside for
sb/sth; (fig) to avoid sb/sth

Ausweis (-es, -e) m (Personalausweis)
identity card, ID; (für Bibliothek etc) card;
aus|weisen irr vt to expel ▷ vr **sich** ~ to
prove one's identity; **Ausweiskontrolle** f
ID check; **Ausweispapiere** pl
identification documents pl

auswendig adv by heart

aus|wuchten vt (Auto: Räder) to balance

aus|zahlen vt (Summe) to pay (out);
(Person) to pay off ▷ vr **sich** ~ to be worth
it

aus|zeichnen vt (ehren) to honour;
(Comm) to price ▷ vr **sich** ~ to distinguish
oneself

aus|ziehen irr vt (Kleidung) to take off ▷ vr
sich ~ to undress ▷ vi (aus Wohnung) to
move out

Auszubildende(r) mf trainee

Auto (-s, -s) nt car; ~ **fahren** to drive;
Autoatlas m road atlas; **Autobahn** f
motorway (Brit), freeway (US);
Autobahnauffahrt f motorway access
road (Brit), on-ramp (US);
Autobahnausfahrt f motorway exit (Brit),
off-ramp (US); **Autobahngebühr** f toll;
Autobahnkreuz nt motorway
interchange; **Autobahnring** m motorway
ring (Brit), beltway (US); **Autobombe** f car
bomb; **Autofähre** f car ferry;
Autofahrer(in) m(f) driver, motorist;
Autofahrt f drive

Autogramm (-s, -e) nt autograph

Automarke f make of car

Automat (-en, -en) m vending machine

Automatik (-, -en) f (Auto) automatic
transmission; **Automatikschaltung** f
automatic gear change (Brit) (o shift (US));
Automatikwagen m automatic

automatisch adj automatic ▷ adv
automatically

Automechaniker(in) m(f) car
mechanic; **Autonummer** f registration
(Brit) (o license (US)) number; **Autoradio**

nt car radio; **Autoreifen** m car tyre;
Autoreisezug m Motorail train® (Brit),
auto train (US); **Autorennen** nt motor
racing; (einzelnes Rennen) motor race;
Autoschlüssel m car key; **Autotelefon**
nt car phone; **Autounfall** m car accident;
Autoverleih m, **Autovermietung** f car
hire (Brit) (o rental (US)); (Firma) car hire
(Brit) (o rental (US)) company;
Autowaschanlage f car wash;
Autowerkstatt f car repair shop, garage;
Autozubehör nt car accessories pl

Avocado (-, -s) f avocado

Axt (-, Äxte) f axe

Azubi (-s, -s) m (-, -s) f akr =
Auszubildende trainee

swimming trunks *pl*; **Badekappe** *f* swimming cap; **Bademantel** *m* bathrobe; **Bademeister(in)** *m(f)* pool attendant; **Bademütze** *f* swimming cap

baden *vi* to have a bath; (*schwimmen*) to swim, to bathe (*Brit*) ▷ *vt* to bath (*Brit*), to bathe (*US*)

Baden-Württemberg (-*s*) *nt* Baden-Württemberg

Badeort *m* spa; **Badesachen** *pl* swimming things *pl*; **Badetuch** *nt* bath towel; **Badewanne** *f* bath (tub); **Badezimmer** *nt* bathroom

Badminton *nt* badminton

baff *adj* ~ **sein** (*fam*) to be flabbergasted (*o* gobsmacked)

Bagger (-*s*, -) *m* excavator; **Baggersee** *m* artificial lake in quarry etc, used for bathing

Bahamas *pl* **die** ~ the Bahamas *pl*

Bahn (-, -*en*) *f* (*Eisenbahn*) railway (*Brit*), railroad (*US*); (*Rennbahn*) track; (*für Läufer*) lane; (*Astr*) orbit; **bahnbrechend** *adj* groundbreaking; **BahnCard®** (-, -*s*) *f* rail card (*allowing 50% or 25% reduction on tickets*); **Bahnfahrt** *f* railway (*Brit*) (*o* railroad (*US*)) journey; **Bahnhof** *m* station; **am** (*o* **auf dem**) ~ at the station; **Bahnlinie** *f* railway (*Brit*) (*o* railroad (*US*)) line; **Bahnpolizei** *f* railway (*Brit*) (*o* railroad (*US*)) police; **Bahnsteig** (-(*e*)*s*, -*e*) *m* platform; **Bahnstrecke** *f* railway (*Brit*) (*o* railroad (*US*)) line; **Bahnübergang** *m* level crossing (*Brit*), grade crossing (*US*)

Bakterien *pl* bacteria *pl*, germs *pl*

bald *adv* (*zeitlich*) soon; (*beinahe*) almost; **bis ~!** see you soon (*o* later); **baldig** *adj* quick, speedy

Balkan (-*s*) *m* **der** ~ the Balkans *pl*

Balken (-*s*, -) *m* beam

Balkon (-*s*, -*s o* -*e*) *m* balcony

Ball (-(*e*)*s*, *Bälle*) *m* ball; (*Tanz*) dance, ball

Ballett (-*s*,) *nt* ballet

Ballon (-*s*, -*s*) *m* balloon

Ballspiel *nt* ball game

Ballungsgebiet *nt* conurbation

Baltikum (-*s*) *nt* **das** ~ the Baltic States *pl*

Bambus (-*ses*, -*se*) *m* bamboo; **Bambussprossen** *pl* bamboo shoots *pl*

banal *adj* banal; (*Frage, Bemerkung*) trite

Banane (-, -*n*) *f* banana

band *imperf von* **binden**

Band (-(*e*)*s*, *Bände*) *m* (*Buch*) volume ▷ (-(*e*)*s*, *Bänder*) *nt* (*aus Stoff*) ribbon, tape;

Baby (-*s*, -*s*) *nt* baby; **Babybett** *nt* cot (*Brit*), crib (*US*); **Babyfläschchen** *nt* baby's bottle; **Babynahrung** *f* baby food; **Babysitter(in)** *m(f)* babysitter; **Babysitz** *m* child seat; **Babywickelraum** *m* baby-changing room

Bach (-(*e*)*s*, *Bäche*) *m* stream

Backblech *nt* baking tray (*Brit*), cookie sheet (*US*)

Backbord *nt* port (side)

Backe (-, -*n*) *f* cheek

backen (*backte, gebacken*) *vt, vi* to bake

Backenzahn *m* molar

Bäcker(in) (-*s*, -) *m(f)* baker; **Bäckerei** *f* bakery; (*Laden*) baker's (shop)

Backofen *m* oven; **Backpulver** *nt* baking powder

Backspace-Taste *f* (*Inform*) backspace key

Backstein *m* brick

Backwaren *pl* bread, cakes and pastries *pl*

Bad (-(*e*)*s*, *Bäder*) *nt* bath; (*Schwimmen*) swim; (*Ort*) spa; **ein ~ nehmen** to have (*o* take) a bath; **Badeanzug** *m* swimsuit, swimming costume (*Brit*); **Badehose** *f*

(*Fließband*) production line; (*Tonband*) tape; (*Anat*) ligament; **etw auf ~ aufnehmen** to tape sth ▷ (-, -s) f (*Musikgruppe*) band
Bandage (-, -n) f bandage; **bandagieren** vt to bandage
Bande (-, -n) f (*Gruppe*) gang
Bänderriss m (*Med*) torn ligament
Bandscheibe f (*Anat*) disc; **Bandwurm** m tapeworm
Bank (-, *Bänke*) f (*Sitzbank*) bench ▷ (-, -en) f (*Fin*) bank
Bankautomat m cash dispenser; **Bankkarte** f bank card; **Bankkonto** nt bank account; **Bankleitzahl** f bank sort code; **Banknote** f banknote; **Bankverbindung** f (*Kontonummer etc*) banking (o account) details pl
bar adj **~es Geld** cash; **etw (in) ~ bezahlen** to pay sth (in) cash
Bar (-, -s) f bar
Bär (-en, -en) m bear
barfuß adj barefoot
barg imperf von **bergen**
Bargeld nt cash; **bargeldlos** adj non-cash
Barkeeper (-s, -) m, **Barmann** m barman, bartender (*US*)
barock adj baroque
Barometer (-s, -) m barometer
barsch adj brusque
Barsch (-(e)s, -e) m perch
Barscheck m open (o uncrossed) cheque
Bart (-(e)s, *Bärte*) m beard; **bärtig** adj bearded
Barzahlung f cash payment
Basar (-s, -e) m bazaar
Baseballmütze f baseball cap
Basel (-s) nt Basle
Basilikum (-s) nt basil
Basis (-, *Basen*) f basis
Baskenland nt Basque region
Basketball m basketball
Bass (-es, *Bässe*) m bass
basta interj **und damit ~!** and that's that
basteln vt to make ▷ vi to make things, to do handicrafts
bat imperf von **bitten**
Batterie f battery; **batteriebetrieben** adj battery-powered
Bau (-(e)s) m (*Bauen*) building, construction; (*Aufbau*) structure; (*Baustelle*) building site ▷ m (*Baue*) (*Tier*) burrow ▷ m (*Bauten*) (*Gebäude*) building;

Bauarbeiten pl construction work sing; (*Straßenbau*) roadworks pl (*Brit*), roadwork (*US*); **Bauarbeiter(in)** m(f) construction worker
Bauch (-(e)s, *Bäuche*) m stomach; **Bauchnabel** m navel; **Bauchredner(in)** m(f) ventriloquist; **Bauchschmerzen** pl stomach-ache sing; **Bauchspeicheldrüse** f pancreas; **Bauchtanz** m belly dance; (*das Tanzen*) belly dancing; **Bauchweh** (-s) nt stomach-ache
Baudenkmal nt monument
bauen vt, vi to build; (*Tech*) to construct
Bauer (-n o -s, -n) m farmer; (*Schach*) pawn; **Bäuerin** f farmer; (*Frau des Bauern*) farmer's wife; **Bauernhof** m farm
baufällig adj dilapidated; **Baujahr** adj year of construction; **der Wagen ist ~ 2002** the car is a 2002 model, the car was made in 2002
Baum (-(e)s, *Bäume*) m tree
Baumarkt m DIY centre
Baumwolle f cotton
Bauplatz m building site; **Baustein** m (*für Haus*) stone; (*Spielzeug*) brick; (*fig*) element; **elektronischer ~** chip; **Baustelle** f building site; (*bei Straßenbau*) roadworks pl (*Brit*), roadwork (*US*); **Bauteil** nt prefabricated part; **Bauunternehmer(in)** m(f) building contractor; **Bauwerk** nt building
Bayern (-s) nt Bavaria
beabsichtigen vt to intend
beachten vt (*Aufmerksamkeit schenken*) to pay attention to; (*Vorschrift etc*) to observe; **nicht ~** to ignore; **beachtlich** adj considerable
Beachvolleyball nt beach volleyball
Beamte(r) (-n, -n) m, **Beamtin** f official; (*Staatsbeamter*) civil servant
beanspruchen vt to claim; (*Zeit, Platz*) to take up; **jdn ~** to keep sb busy
beanstanden vt to complain about
beantragen vt to apply for
beantworten vt to answer
bearbeiten vt to work; (*Material, Daten*) to process; (*Chem*) to treat; (*Fall etc*) to deal with; (*Buch etc*) to revise; (*fam: beeinflussen wollen*) to work on; **Bearbeitungsgebühr** f handling (o service) charge
beatmen vt **jdn ~** to give sb artificial respiration

beaufsichtigen vt to supervise; (bei Prüfung) to invigilate

beauftragen vt to instruct; **jdn mit etw ~ to** give sb the job of doing sth

Becher (-s, -) m mug; (ohne Henkel) tumbler; (für Jogurt) pot; (aus Pappe) tub

Becken (-s, -) nt basin; (Spüle) sink; (zum Schwimmen) pool; (Mus) cymbal; (Anat) pelvis

bedanken vr **sich ~ to** say thank you; **sich bei jdm für etw ~ to** thank sb for sth

Bedarf (-(e)s) m need (an +dat for); (Comm) demand (an +dat for); **je nach ~** according to demand; **bei ~** if necessary; **Bedarfshaltestelle** f request stop, flag stop (US)

bedauerlich adj regrettable; **bedauern** vt to regret; (bemitleiden) to feel sorry for; **bedauernswert** adj (Zustände) regrettable; (Mensch) unfortunate

bedeckt adj covered; (Himmel) overcast

bedenken vt to consider; **Bedenken** (-s, -) nt (Überlegen) consideration; (Zweifel) doubt; (Skrupel) scruples pl; **bedenklich** adj dubious; (Zustand) serious

bedeuten vt to mean; **jdm nichts/viel ~ to** mean nothing/a lot to sb; **bedeutend** adj important; (beträchtlich) considerable; **Bedeutung** f meaning; (Wichtigkeit) importance

bedienen vt to serve; (Maschine) to operate ▷ vr **sich ~** (beim Essen) to help oneself; **Bedienung** f service; (Kellner/Kellnerin) waiter/waitress; (Verkäufer(in)) shop assistant; (Zuschlag) service (charge); **Bedienungsanleitung** f operating instructions pl; **Bedienungshandbuch** nt instruction manual; **Bedingung** f condition; **unter der ~, dass** on condition that; **unter diesen ~en** under these circumstances

bedrohen vt to threaten

Bedürfnis nt need

beeilen vr **sich ~ to** hurry

beeindrucken vt to impress

beeinflussen vt to influence

beeinträchtigen vt to affect

beenden vt to end; (fertigstellen) to finish

beerdigen vt to bury; **Beerdigung** f burial; (Feier) funeral

Beere (-, -n) f berry; (Traubenbeere) grape

Beet (-(e)s, -e) nt bed

befahl imperf von **befehlen**

befahrbar adj passable; (Naut) navigable; **befahren** irr vt (Straße) to use; (Pass) to drive over; (Fluss etc) to navigate ▷ adj **stark/wenig ~** busy/quiet

Befehl (-(e)s, -e) m order; (Inform) command; **befehlen** (befahl, befohlen) vt to order; **jdm ~, etw zu tun** to order sb to do sth ▷ vi to give orders

befestigen vt to fix; (mit Schnur, Seil) to attach; (mit Klebestoff) to stick

befeuchten vt to moisten

befinden irr vr **sich ~ to** be

befohlen pp von **befehlen**

befolgen vt (Rat etc) to follow

befördern vt (transportieren) to transport; (beruflich) to promote; **Beförderung** f transport; (beruflich) promotion; **Beförderungsbedingungen** pl conditions pl of carriage

Befragung f questioning; (Umfrage) opinion poll

befreundet adj friendly; **~ sein** to be friends (mit jdm with sb)

befriedigen vt to satisfy; **befriedigend** adj satisfactory; (Schulnote) ~ C; **Befriedigung** f satisfaction

befristet adj limited (auf +akk to)

befruchten vt to fertilize; (fig) to stimulate

Befund (-(e)s, -e) m findings pl; (Med) diagnosis

befürchten vt to fear

befürworten vt to support

begabt adj gifted, talented; **Begabung** f talent, gift

begann imperf von **beginnen**

begegnen vi to meet (jdm sb), to meet with (einer Sache dat sth)

begehen irr vt (Straftat) to commit; (Jubiläum etc) to celebrate

begehrt adj sought-after; (Junggeselle) eligible

begeistern vt to fill with enthusiasm; (inspirieren) to inspire ▷ vr **sich für etw ~ to** be/get enthusiastic about sth; **begeistert** adj enthusiastic

Beginn (-(e)s) m beginning; **zu ~** at the beginning; **beginnen** (begann, begonnen) vt, vi to start, to begin

beglaubigen vt to certify; **Beglaubigung** f certification

begleiten vt to accompany;

Begleiter(in) m(f) companion;
Begleitung f company; (Mus)
accompaniment
beglückwünschen vt to congratulate
(zu on)
begonnen pp von **beginnen**
begraben irr vt to bury; **Begräbnis** nt
burial; (Feier) funeral
begreifen irr vt to understand
Begrenzung f boundary; (fig) restriction
Begriff (-(e)s, -e) m concept; (Vorstellung)
idea; **im ~ sein, etw zu tun** to be on the
point of doing sth; **schwer von ~ sein** to
be slow on the uptake
begründen vt (rechtfertigen) to justify;
Begründung f explanation;
(Rechtfertigung) justification
begrüßen vt to greet; (willkommen heißen)
to welcome; **Begrüßung** f greeting;
(Empfang) welcome
behaart adj hairy
behalten irr vt to keep; (im Gedächtnis) to
remember; **etw für sich ~** to keep sth to
oneself
Behälter (-s, -) m container
behandeln vt to treat; **Behandlung** f
treatment
behaupten vt to claim, to maintain ▷ vr
sich ~ to assert oneself; **Behauptung** f
claim
beheizen vt to heat
behelfen irr vr **sich mit/ohne etw ~** to
make do with/without sth
beherbergen vt to accommodate
beherrschen vt (Situation, Gefühle) to
control; (Instrument) to master ▷ vr **sich
~** to control oneself; **Beherrschung** f
control (über +akk of); **die ~ verlieren** to
lose one's self-control
behilflich adj helpful; **jdm ~ sein** to help
sb (bei with)
behindern vt to hinder; (Verkehr, Sicht) to
obstruct; **Behinderte(r)** mf disabled
person; **behindertengerecht** adj suitable
for disabled people
Behörde (-, -n) f authority; **die ~n** pl the
authorities pl

◯ **SCHLÜSSELWORT**

bei präp +dat **1** (nahe bei) near; (zum
Aufenthalt) at, with; (unter, zwischen)
among; **bei München** near Munich; **bei**
uns at our place; **beim Friseur** at the
hairdresser's; **bei seinen Eltern wohnen**
to live with one's parents; **bei einer Firma
arbeiten** to work for a firm; **etw bei sich
haben** to have sth on one; **jdn bei sich
haben** to have sb with one; **bei Goethe** in
Goethe; **beim Militär** in the army
2 (zeitlich) at, on; (während) during
(Zustand, Umstand) in; **bei Nacht** at night;
bei Nebel in fog; **bei Regen** if it rains; **bei
solcher Hitze** in such heat; **bei meiner
Ankuft** on my arrival; **bei der Arbeit**
when I'm etc working; **beim Fahren** while
driving

bei|behalten irr vt to keep
Beiboot nt dinghy
bei|bringen irr vt **jdm etw ~** (mitteilen) to
break sth to sb; (lehren) to teach sb sth
beide(s) pron both; **meine ~n Brüder** my
two brothers, both my brothers; **wir
~** both (o the two) of us; **keiner von ~n**
neither of them; **alle ~** both (of them); **~s
ist sehr schön** both are very nice; **30
~** (beim Tennis) 30 all
beieinander adv together
Beifahrer(in) m(f) passenger;
Beifahrerairbag m passenger airbag;
Beifahrersitz m passenger seat
Beifall (-(e)s) m applause
beige adj inv beige
Beigeschmack m aftertaste
Beil (-(e)s, -e) nt axe
Beilage f (Gastr) side dish; (Gemüse)
vegetables pl; (zu Buch etc) supplement
beiläufig adj casual ▷ adv casually
Beileid nt condolences pl; **(mein)
herzliches ~** please accept my sincere
condolences
beiliegend adj enclosed
beim kontr von **bei dem**
Bein (-(e)s, -e) nt leg
beinah(e) adv almost, nearly
beinhalten vt to contain
Beipackzettel m instruction leaflet
beisammen adv together;
Beisammensein (-s) nt get-together
Beischlaf m sexual intercourse
beiseite adv aside; **etw ~ legen** (sparen) to
put sth by
Beispiel (-(e)s, -e) nt example; **sich** (dat)
an jdm/etw ein ~ nehmen to take sb/sth
as an example; **zum ~** for example

beißen (biss, gebissen) vt to bite ▷ vi to bite; (stechen: Rauch, Säure) to sting ▷ vr **sich ~** (Farben) to clash

Beitrag (-(e)s, Beiträge) m contribution; (für Mitgliedschaft) subscription; (Versicherung) premium; **bei|tragen** irr vt, vi to contribute (zu to)

bekannt adj well-known; (nicht fremd) familiar; **mit jdm ~ sein** to know sb; **~ geben** to announce; **jdn mit jdm ~ machen** to introduce sb to sb; **Bekannte(r)** mf friend; (entfernter) acquaintance; **bekanntlich** adv as everyone knows; **Bekanntschaft** f acquaintance

bekiffen vr **sich ~** (fam) to get stoned

beklagen vr **sich ~** to complain

Bekleidung f clothing

bekommen irr vt to get; (erhalten) to receive; (Kind) to have; (Zug, Grippe) to catch, to get; **wie viel ~ Sie dafür?** how much is that? ▷ vi **jdm ~** (Essen) to agree with sb; **wir ~ schon** (bedient werden) we're being served

beladen irr vt to load

Belag (-(e)s, Beläge) m coating; (auf Zähnen) plaque; (auf Zunge) fur

belasten vt to load; (Körper) to strain; (Umwelt) to pollute; (fig: mit Sorgen etc) to burden; (Comm: Konto) to debit; (Jur) to incriminate

belästigen vt to bother; (stärker) to pester; (sexuell) to harass; **Belästigung** f annoyance; **sexuelle ~** sexual harassment

belebt adj (Straße etc) busy

Beleg (-(e)s, -e) m (Comm) receipt; (Beweis) proof; **belegen** vt (Brot) to spread; (Platz) to reserve; (Kurs, Vorlesung) to register for; (beweisen) to prove

belegt adj (Tel) engaged (Brit), busy (US); (Hotel) full; (Zunge) coated; **~es Brötchen** sandwich; **der Platz ist ~** this seat is taken; **Belegtzeichen** nt (Tel) engaged tone (Brit), busy tone (US)

beleidigen vt to insult; (kränken) to offend; **Beleidigung** f insult; (Jur) slander; (schriftliche) libel

beleuchten vt to light; (bestrahlen) to illuminate; (fig) to examine; **Beleuchtung** f lighting; (Bestrahlung) illumination

Belgien (-s) nt Belgium; **Belgier(in)** (-s, -) m(f) Belgian; **belgisch** adj Belgian

belichten vt to expose; **Belichtung** f exposure; **Belichtungsmesser** (-s, -) m light meter

Belieben nt **(ganz) nach ~** (just) as you wish

beliebig adj **jedes ~e Muster** any pattern; **jeder ~e** anyone ▷ adv **~ lange** as long as you like; **~ viel** as many (o much) as you like

beliebt adj popular; **sich bei jdm ~ machen** to make oneself popular with sb

beliefern vt to supply

bellen vi to bark

Belohnung f reward

Belüftung f ventilation

belügen irr vt to lie to

bemerkbar adj noticeable; **sich ~ machen** (Mensch) to attract attention; (Zustand) to become noticeable; **bemerken** vt (wahrnehmen) to notice; (sagen) to remark; **bemerkenswert** adj remarkable; **Bemerkung** f remark

bemitleiden vt to pity

bemühen vr **sich ~** to try (hard), to make an effort; **Bemühung** f effort

bemuttern vt to mother

benachbart adj neighbouring

benachrichtigen vt to inform; **Benachrichtigung** f notification

benachteiligen vt to (put at a) disadvantage; (wegen Rasse etc) to discriminate against

benehmen irr vr **sich ~** to behave; **Benehmen** (-s) nt behaviour

beneiden vt to envy; **jdn um etw ~** to envy sb sth

Beneluxländer pl Benelux countries pl

benommen adj dazed

benötigen vt to need

benutzen vt to use; **Benutzer(in)** (-s, -) m(f) user; **benutzerfreundlich** adj user-friendly; **Benutzerhandbuch** nt user's guide; **Benutzerkennung** f user ID; **Benutzeroberfläche** f (Inform) user/system interface

Benzin (-s, -e) nt (Auto) petrol (Brit), gas (US); **Benzingutschein** m petrol (Brit) (o gas (US)) coupon; **Benzinkanister** m petrol (Brit) (o gas (US)) can; **Benzinpumpe** f petrol (Brit) (o gas (US)) pump; **Benzintank** m petrol (Brit) (o gas (US)) tank; **Benzinuhr** f fuel gauge

beobachten vt to observe;
Beobachtung f observation
bequem adj comfortable; (Ausrede)
convenient; (faul) lazy; **machen Sie es
sich ~** make yourself at home;
Bequemlichkeit f comfort; (Faulheit)
laziness
beraten irr vt to advise; (besprechen) to
discuss ▷ vr **sich ~** to consult; **Beratung** f
advice; (bei Arzt etc) consultation
berauben vt to rob
berechnen vt to calculate; (Comm) to
charge; **berechnend** adj (Mensch)
calculating
berechtigen vt to entitle (zu to); (fig) to
justify; **berechtigt** adj justified; **zu etw
~ sein** to be entitled to sth
bereden vt (besprechen) to discuss
Bereich (-(e)s, -e) m area; (Ressort, Gebiet)
field
bereisen vt to travel through
bereit adj ready; **zu etw ~ sein** to be
ready for sth; **sich ~ erklären, etw zu tun**
to agree to do sth
bereiten vt to prepare; (Kummer) to
cause; (Freude) to give
bereit|legen vt to lay out
bereit|machen vr **sich ~** to get ready
bereits adv already
Bereitschaft f readiness; **~ haben** (Arzt)
to be on call
bereit|stehen vi to be ready
bereuen vt to regret
Berg (-(e)s, -e) m mountain; (kleiner) hill; **in
die ~e fahren** to go to the mountains;
bergab adv downhill; **bergauf** adv uphill;
Bergbahn f mountain railway (Brit) (o
railroad (US))
bergen (barg, geborgen) vt (retten) to
rescue; (enthalten) to contain
Bergführer(in) m(f) mountain guide;
Berghütte f mountain hut; **bergig** adj
mountainous; **Bergkette** f mountain
range; **Bergschuh** m climbing boot;
Bergsteigen (-s) nt mountaineering;
Bergsteiger(in) (-s, -) m(f) mountaineer;
Bergtour f mountain hike
Bergung f (Rettung) rescue; (von Toten,
Fahrzeugen) recovery
Bergwacht (-, -en) f mountain rescue
service; **Bergwerk** nt mine
Bericht (-(e)s, -e) m report; **berichten** vt,
vi to report

berichtigen vt to correct
Bermudadreieck nt Bermuda triangle;
Bermudainseln pl Bermuda sing;
Bermudashorts pl Bermuda shorts pl
Bernstein m amber
berüchtigt adj notorious, infamous
berücksichtigen vt to take into
account; (Antrag, Bewerber) to consider
Beruf (-(e)s, -e) m occupation;
(akademischer) profession; (Gewerbe)
trade; **was sind Sie von ~?** what do you
do (for a living)?; **beruflich** adj
professional
Berufsausbildung f vocational training;
Berufsschule f vocational college;
berufstätig adj employed;
Berufsverkehr m commuter traffic
beruhigen vt to calm ▷ vr **sich ~** (Mensch,
Situation) to calm down; **beruhigend** adj
reassuring; **Beruhigungsmittel** nt
sedative
berühmt adj famous
berühren vt to touch; (gefühlsmäßig
bewegen) to move; (betreffen) to affect;
(flüchtig erwähnen) to mention, to touch on
▷ vr **sich ~** to touch
besaufen irr vr **sich ~** (fam) to get
plastered
beschädigen vt to damage
beschäftigen vt to occupy; (beruflich) to
employ ▷ vr **sich mit etw ~** to occupy
oneself with sth; (sich befassen) to deal
with sth; **beschäftigt** adj busy, occupied;
Beschäftigung f (Beruf) employment;
(Tätigkeit) occupation; (geistige)
preoccupation (mit with)
Bescheid (-(e)s, -e) m information;
~ wissen to be informed (o know) (über
+akk about); **ich weiß ~** I know; **jdm
~ geben** (o sagen) to let sb know
bescheiden adj modest
bescheinigen vt to certify; (bestätigen) to
acknowledge; **Bescheinigung** f
certificate; (Quittung) receipt
bescheißen irr vt (vulg) to cheat (um out
of)
beschimpfen vt (mit Kraftausdrücken) to
swear at
Beschiss (-es) m **das ist ~** (vulg) that's
a rip-off; **beschissen** adj (vulg)
shitty
beschlagnahmen vt to confiscate
Beschleunigung f acceleration;

Beschleunigungsspur f acceleration lane

beschließen irr vt to decide on; (beenden) to end; **Beschluss** m decision

beschränken vt to limit, to restrict (auf +akk to) ▷ vr **sich ~** to restrict oneself (auf +akk to); **Beschränkung** f limitation, restriction

beschreiben irr vt to describe; (Papier) to write on; **Beschreibung** f description

beschuldigen vt to accuse (gen of); **Beschuldigung** f accusation

beschummeln vt, vi (fam) to cheat (um out of)

beschützen vt to protect (vor +dat from)

Beschwerde (-, -n) f complaint; **~n** pl (Leiden) trouble sing; **beschweren** vt to weight down; (fig) to burden ▷ vr **sich ~** to complain

beschwipst adj tipsy

beseitigen vt to remove; (Problem) to get rid of; (Müll) to dispose of; **Beseitigung** f removal; (von Müll) disposal

Besen (-s, -) m broom

besetzen vt (Haus, Land) to occupy; (Platz) to take; (Posten) to fill; (Rolle) to cast; **besetzt** adj full; (Tel) engaged (Brit), busy (US); (Platz) taken; (WC) engaged; **Besetztzeichen** nt engaged tone (Brit), busy tone (US)

besichtigen vt (Museum) to visit; (Sehenswürdigkeit) to have a look at; (Stadt) to tour

besiegen vt to defeat

Besitz (-es) m possession; (Eigentum) property; **besitzen** irr vt to own; (Eigenschaft) to have; **Besitzer(in)** (-s, -) m(f) owner

besoffen adj (fam) plastered

besondere(r, s) adj special; (bestimmt) particular; (eigentümlich) peculiar; **nichts ~s** nothing special; **Besonderheit** f special feature; (besondere Eigenschaft) peculiarity; **besonders** adv especially, particularly; (getrennt) separately

besorgen vt (beschaffen) to get (jdm for sb); (kaufen a.) to purchase; (erledigen: Geschäfte) to deal with

besprechen irr vt to discuss; **Besprechung** f discussion; (Konferenz) meeting

besser adj better; **es geht ihm ~** he feels better; **~ gesagt** or rather; **~ werden** to

improve; bessern vt to improve ▷ vr **sich ~** to improve; (Mensch) to mend one's ways; **Besserung** f improvement; **gute ~!** get well soon

beständig adj constant; (Wetter) settled

Bestandteil m component

bestätigen vt to confirm; (Empfang, Brief) to acknowledge; **Bestätigung** f confirmation; (von Brief) acknowledgement

beste(r, s) adj best; **das ~ wäre, wir ...** it would be best if we ... ▷ adv **sie singt am ~n** she sings best; **so ist es am ~n** it's best that way; **am ~n gehst du gleich** you'd better go at once

bestechen irr vt to bribe; **Bestechung** f bribery

Besteck (-(e)s, -e) nt cutlery

bestehen irr vi to be, to exist; (andauern) to last; **~ auf** (+dat) to insist on; **~ aus** to consist of ▷ vt (Probe, Prüfung) to pass; (Kampf) to win

bestehlen irr vt to rob

bestellen vt to order; (reservieren) to book; (Grüße, Auftrag) to pass on (jdm to sb); (kommen lassen) to send for; **Bestellnummer** f order number; **Bestellung** f (Comm) order; (das Bestellen) ordering

bestens adv very well

bestimmen vt to determine; (Regeln) to lay down; (Tag, Ort) to fix; (ernennen) to appoint; (vorsehen) to mean (für for); **bestimmt** adj definite; (gewiss) certain; (entschlossen) firm ▷ adv definitely; (wissen) for sure; **Bestimmung** f (Verordnung) regulation; (Zweck) purpose

Best.-Nr. abk = **Bestellnummer** order number

bestrafen vt to punish

bestrahlen vt to illuminate; (Med) to treat with radiotherapy

bestreiten irr vt (leugnen) to deny

Bestseller (-s, -) m bestseller

bestürzt adj dismayed

Besuch (-(e)s, -e) m visit; (Mensch) visitor; **~ haben** to have visitors/a visitor; **besuchen** vt to visit; (Schule, Kino etc) to go to; **Besucher(in)** (-s, -) m(f) visitor; **Besuchszeit** f visiting hours pl

betäuben vt (Med) to anaesthetize; **Betäubungsmittel** nt anaesthetic

Bete (-, -n) f **Rote ~** beetroot

beteiligen vr **sich an etw** (dat) ~ to take part in sth, to participate in sth ▷ vt **jdn an etw** (dat) ~ to involve sb in sth; **Beteiligung** f participation; (Anteil) share; (Besucherzahl) attendance

beten vi to pray

Beton (-s, -s) m concrete

betonen vt to stress; (hervorheben) to emphasize; **Betonung** f stress; (fig) emphasis

Betr. abk = **Betreff** re

Betracht m **in ~ ziehen** to take into consideration; **in ~ kommen** to be a possibility; **nicht in ~ kommen** to be out of the question; **betrachten** vt to look at; **~ als** to regard as; **beträchtlich** adj considerable

Betrag (-(e)s, Beträge) m amount, sum; **betragen** irr vt to amount to (o come) to ▷ vr **sich ~** to behave

betreffen irr vt to concern; (Regelung etc) to affect; **was mich betrifft** as for me; **betreffend** adj relevant, in question

betreten irr vt to enter; (Bühne etc) to step onto; **„Betreten verboten"** 'keep off/out'

betreuen vt to look after; (Reisegruppe, Abteilung) to be in charge of; **Betreuer(in)** (-s, -) m(f) (Pfleger) carer; (von Kind) child minder; (von Reisegruppe) groupleader

Betrieb (-(e)s, -e) m (Firma) firm; (Anlage) plant; (Tätigkeit) operation; (Treiben) bustle; **außer ~ sein** to be out of order; **in ~ sein** to be in operation; **betriebsbereit** adj operational; **Betriebsrat** m (Gremium) works council; **Betriebssystem** nt (Inform) operating system

betrinken irr vr **sich ~** to get drunk

betroffen adj (bestürzt) shaken; **von etw ~ werden/sein** to be affected by sth

betrog imperf von **betrügen; betrogen** pp von **betrügen**

Betrug (-(e)s) m deception; (Jur) fraud; **betrügen** (betrog, betrogen) vt to deceive; (Jur) to defraud; (Partner) to cheat on; **Betrüger(in)** (-s, -) m(f) cheat

betrunken adj drunk

Bett (-(e)s, -en) nt bed; **ins** (o zu) **~ gehen** to go to bed; **das ~ machen** to make the bed; **Bettbezug** m duvet cover; **Bettdecke** f blanket

betteln vi to beg

Bettlaken nt sheet

Bettler(in) (-s, -) m(f) beggar

Bettsofa nt sofa bed; **Betttuch** nt sheet; **Bettwäsche** f bed linen; **Bettzeug** m bedding

beugen vt to bend ▷ vr **sich ~** to bend; (sich fügen) to submit (dat to)

Beule (-, -n) f (Schwellung) bump; (Delle) dent

beunruhigen vt to worry ▷ vr **sich ~** to worry

beurteilen vt to judge

Beute (-) f (von Dieb) booty, loot; (von Tier) prey

Beutel (-s, -) m bag

Bevölkerung f population

bevollmächtigt adj authorized (zu etw to do sth)

bevor conj before; **bevor|stehen** irr vi (Schwierigkeiten) to lie ahead; (Gefahr) to be imminent; **jdm ~** (Überraschung etc) to be in store for sb; **bevorstehend** adj forthcoming; **bevorzugen** vt to prefer

bewachen vt to guard; **bewacht** adj **~er Parkplatz** supervised car park (Brit), guarded parking lot (US)

bewegen vt to move; **jdn dazu ~, etw zu tun** to get sb to do sth ▷ vr **sich ~** to move; **es bewegt sich etwas** (fig) things are beginning to happen; **Bewegung** f movement; (Phys) motion; (innere) emotion; (körperlich) exercise; **Bewegungsmelder** (-s, -) m sensor (which reacts to movement)

Beweis (-es, -e) m proof; (Zeugnis) evidence; **beweisen** irr vt to prove; (zeigen) to show

bewerben irr vr **sich ~** to apply (um for); **Bewerbung** f application; **Bewerbungsunterlagen** pl application documents pl

bewilligen vt to allow; (Geld) to grant

bewirken vt to cause, to bring about

bewohnen vt to live in; **Bewohner(in)** (-s, -) m(f) inhabitant; (von Haus) resident

bewölkt adj cloudy, overcast; **Bewölkung** f clouds pl

bewundern vt to admire; **bewundernswert** adj admirable

bewusst adj conscious; (absichtlich) deliberate; **sich** (dat) **einer Sache** (gen) **~ sein** to be aware of sth ▷ adv consciously; (absichtlich) deliberately; **bewusstlos** adj unconscious; **Bewusstlosigkeit** f unconsciousness;

Bewusstsein (-s) nt consciousness; **bei ~ sein** conscious

bezahlen vt to pay; (Ware, Leistung) to pay for; **kann ich bar/mit Kreditkarte ~?** can I pay cash/by credit card?; **sich bezahlt machen** to be worth it; **Bezahlung** f payment

bezeichnen vt (kennzeichnen) to mark; (nennen) to call; (beschreiben) to describe; **Bezeichnung** f (Name) name; (Begriff) term

beziehen irr vt (Bett) to change; (Haus, Position) to move into; (erhalten) to receive; (Zeitung) to take; **einen Standpunkt ~** (fig) to take up a position ▷ vr **sich ~** to refer (auf +akk to); **Beziehung** f (Verbindung) connection; (Verhältnis) relationship; **~en haben** (vorteilhaft) to have connections (o contacts); **in dieser ~** in this respect; **beziehungsweise** adv or; (genauer gesagt) or rather

Bezirk (-(e)s, -e) m district

Bezug (-(e)s, Bezüge) m (Überzug) cover; (von Kopfkissen) pillowcase; **in ~ auf** (+akk) with regard to; **bezüglich** prep +gen concerning

bezweifeln vt to doubt

BH (-s, -s) m bra

Bhf. abk = **Bahnhof** station

Biathlon (-s, -s) m biathlon

Bibel (-, -n) f Bible

Biber (-s, -) m beaver

Bibliothek (-, -en) f library

biegen (bog, gebogen) vt to bend ▷ vr **sich ~** to bend ▷ vi to turn (in +akk into); **Biegung** f bend

Biene (-, -n) f bee

Bier (-(e)s, -e) nt beer; **helles ~** ≈ lager (Brit), beer (US); **dunkles ~** ≈ brown ale (Brit), dark beer (US); **zwei ~, bitte!** two beers, please; **Biergarten** m beer garden; **Bierzelt** nt beer tent

bieten (bot, geboten) vt to offer; (bei Versteigerung) bid; **sich** (dat) **etw ~ lassen** to put up with sth ▷ vr **sich ~** (Gelegenheit) to present itself (dat to)

Bikini (-s, -s) m bikini

Bild (-(e)s, -er) nt picture; (gedankliches) image; (Foto) photo

bilden vt to form; (geistig) to educate; (ausmachen) to constitute ▷ vr **sich ~** (entstehen) to form; (lernen) to educate oneself

Bilderbuch nt picture book

Bildhauer(in) (-s, -) m(f) sculptor

Bildschirm m screen; **Bildschirmschoner** (-s, -) m screen saver; **Bildschirmtext** m viewdata, videotext

Bildung f formation; (Wissen, Benehmen) education; **Bildungsurlaub** m educational holiday; (von Firma) study leave

Billard nt billiards sing

billig adj cheap; (gerecht) fair

Binde (-, -n) f bandage; (Armbinde) band; (Damenbinde) sanitary towel (Brit), sanitary napkin (US)

Bindehautentzündung f conjunctivitis

binden (band, gebunden) vt to tie; (Buch) to bind; (Soße) to thicken

Bindestrich m hyphen

Bindfaden m string

Bindung f bond, tie; (Skibindung) binding

Bio- in zW bio-; **Biokost** f health food

Bioladen

A **Bioladen** is a shop which specializes in selling environmentally friendly products such as phosphate-free washing powders, recycled paper and organically grown vegetables.

Biologie f biology; **biologisch** adj biological; (Anbau) organic

Birke (-, -n) f birch

Birne (-, -n) f (Obst) pear; (Elek) (light) bulb

○ SCHLÜSSELWORT

bis präp +akk, adv **1** (zeitlich) till, until; (bis spätestens) by; **Sie haben bis Dienstag Zeit** you have until od till Tuesday; **bis Dienstag muss es fertig sein** it must be ready by Tuesday; **bis auf weiteres** until further notice; **bis in die Nacht** into the night; **bis bald/gleich** see you later/soon

2 (räumlich) (up) to; **ich fahre bis Köln** I'm going to od I'm going as far as Cologne; **bis an unser Grundstück** (right od up) to our plot; **bis hierher** this far

3 (bei Zahlen) up to; **bis zu** up to

4: **bis auf etw** akk (außer) except sth (einschließlich) including sth

▷ *konj* **1** *(mit Zahlen)* to; **10 bis 20** 10 to 20

2 *(zeitlich)* till, until; **bis es dunkel wird** till *od* until it gets dark; **von ... bis ...** from ... to ...

Bischof *(-s, Bischöfe) m* bishop

bisher *adv* up to now, so far

Biskuit *(-(e)s, -s o -e) nt* sponge

biss *imperf von* **beißen**

Biss *(-es, -e) m* bite

bisschen *adj* **ein ~** a bit of; **ein ~ Salz/Liebe** a bit of salt/love; **ich habe kein ~ Hunger** I'm not a bit hungry ▷ *adv* **ein ~** a bit; **kein ~** not at all

bissig *adj (Hund)* vicious; *(Bemerkung)* cutting

Bit *(-s, -s) nt (Inform)* bit

bitte *interj* please; **(wie) ~?** (I beg your) pardon?; **~ (schön)!** *(als Antwort auf Dank)* you're welcome, that's alright; **hier, ~ here** you are; **Bitte** *(-, -n) f* request; **bitten** *(bat, gebeten) vt, vi* to ask *(um for)*

bitter *adj* bitter

Blähungen *pl (Med)* wind *sing*

blamieren *vr* **sich ~** to make a fool of oneself ▷ *vt* **jdn ~** to make sb look a fool

Blankoscheck *m* blank cheque

Blase *(-, -n) f* bubble; *(Med)* blister; *(Anat)* bladder

blasen *(blies, geblasen) vi* to blow; **jdm einen ~** *(vulg)* to give sb a blow job

Blasenentzündung *f* cystitis

blass *adj* pale

Blatt *(-(e)s, Blätter) nt* leaf; *(von Papier)* sheet; **blättern** *vi (Inform)* to scroll; **in etw** *(dat)* **~** to leaf through sth; **Blätterteig** *m* puff pastry; **Blattsalat** *m* green salad; **Blattspinat** *m* spinach

blau *adj* blue; *(fam: betrunken)* plastered; *(Gastr)* boiled; **~es Auge** black eye; **~er Fleck** bruise; **Blaubeere** *f* bilberry, blueberry; **Blaulicht** *nt* flashing blue light; **blau|machen** *vi* to skip work; *(in Schule)* to skip school; **Blauschimmelkäse** *m* blue cheese

Blazer *(-s, -) m* blazer

Blech *(-(e)s, -e) nt* sheet metal; *(Backblech)* baking tray *(Brit)*, cookie sheet *(US)*; **Blechschaden** *m (Auto)* damage to the bodywork

Blei *(-(e)s, -e) nt* lead

bleiben *(blieb, geblieben) vi* to stay; **lass das ~!** stop it; **das bleibt unter uns** that's (just) between ourselves; **mir bleibt keine andere Wahl** I have no other choice

bleich *adj* pale; **bleichen** *vt* to bleach

bleifrei *adj (Benzin)* unleaded; **bleihaltig** *adj (Benzin)* leaded

Bleistift *m* pencil

Blende *(-, -n) f (Foto)* aperture

Blick *(-(e)s, -e) m* look; *(kurz)* glance; *(Aussicht)* view; **auf den ersten ~** at first sight; **einen ~ auf etw** *(akk)* **werfen** to have a look at sth; **blicken** *vi* to look; **sich ~ lassen** to show up

blieb *imperf von* **bleiben**

blies *imperf von* **blasen**

blind *adj* blind; *(Glas etc)* dull; **Blinddarm** *m* appendix; **Blinddarmentzündung** *f* appendicitis; **Blinde(r)** *mf* blind person/man/woman; **die ~n** *pl* the blind *pl*; **Blindenhund** *m* guide dog; **Blindenschrift** *f* braille

blinken *vi (Stern, Lichter)* to twinkle; *(aufleuchten)* to flash; *(Auto)* to indicate; **Blinker** *(-s, -) m (Auto)* indicator *(Brit)*, turn signal *(US)*

blinzeln *vi (mit beiden Augen)* to blink; *(mit einem Auge)* to wink

Blitz *(-es, -e) m* (flash of) lightning; *(Foto)* flash; **blitzen** *vi (Foto)* to use a/the flash; **es blitzte und donnerte** there was thunder and lightning; **Blitzlicht** *nt* flash

Block *(-(e)s, Blöcke) m (a. fig)* block; *(von Papier)* pad; **Blockflöte** *f* recorder; **Blockhaus** *nt* log cabin; **blockieren** *vt* to block ▷ *vi* to jam; *(Räder)* to lock; **Blockschrift** *f* block letters *pl*

blöd *adj* stupid; **blödeln** *vi (fam)* to fool around

blond *adj* blond; *(Frau)* blonde

⊙ **SCHLÜSSELWORT**

bloß *adj* **1** *(unbedeckt)* bare *(nackt)* naked; **mit der bloßen Hand** with one's bare hand; **mit bloßem Auge** with the naked eye

2 *(alleinig, nur)* mere; **der bloße Gedanke** the very thought; **bloßer Neid** sheer envy

▷ *adv* only, merely; **lass das bloß!** just don't do that!; **wie ist das bloß passiert?** how on earth did that happen?

blühen vi to bloom; (*fig*) to flourish
Blume (-, -n) f flower; (*von Wein*) bouquet;
Blumenkohl m cauliflower;
Blumenladen m flower shop;
Blumenstrauß m bunch of flowers;
Blumentopf m flowerpot; **Blumenvase** f
vase
Bluse (-, -n) f blouse
Blut (-(e)s) nt blood; **Blutbild** nt blood
count; **Blutdruck** m blood pressure
Blüte (-, -n) f (*Pflanzenteil*) flower, bloom;
(*Baumblüte*) blossom; (*fig*) prime
bluten vi to bleed
Blütenstaub m pollen
Bluter (-s, -) m (*Med*) haemophiliac;
Bluterguss m haematoma; (*blauer Fleck*)
bruise; **Blutgruppe** f blood group; **blutig**
adj bloody; **Blutkonserve** f unit of stored
blood; **Blutprobe** f blood sample;
Blutspende f blood donation;
Bluttransfusion f blood transfusion;
Blutung f bleeding; **Blutvergiftung** f
blood poisoning; **Blutwurst** f black
pudding (*Brit*), blood sausage (*US*)
BLZ abk = **Bankleitzahl**
Bob (-s, -s) m bob(sleigh)
Bock (-(e)s, Böcke) m (*Reh*) buck; (*Schaf*)
ram; (*Gestell*) trestle; (*Sport*) vaulting
horse; **ich hab keinen ~ (drauf)** (*fam*) I
don't feel like it
Boden (-s, Böden) m ground; (*Fußboden*)
floor; (*von Meer, Fass*) bottom; (*Speicher*)
attic; **Bodennebel** m ground mist;
Bodenpersonal nt ground staff;
Bodenschätze pl mineral resources pl
Bodensee m der ~ Lake Constance
Body (-s, -s) m body; **Bodybuilding** (-s) nt
bodybuilding
bog imperf von **biegen**
Bogen (-s, -) m (*Biegung*) curve; (*in der
Architektur*) arch; (*Waffe, Instrument*) bow;
(*Papier*) sheet
Bohne (-, -n) f bean; **grüne ~n** pl green (o
French (*Brit*)) beans pl; **weiße ~n** pl haricot
beans pl; **Bohnenkaffee** m real coffee;
Bohnensprosse f bean sprout
bohren vt to drill; **Bohrer** (-s, -) m drill
Boiler (-s, -) m water heater
Boje (-, -n) f buoy
Bolivien (-s) nt Bolivia
Bombe (-, -n) f bomb
Bon (-s, -s) m (*Kassenzettel*) receipt;
(*Gutschein*) voucher, coupon

Bonbon (-s, -s) nt sweet (*Brit*), candy (*US*)
Bonus (- o -ses, -se o Boni) m bonus;
(*Punktvorteil*) bonus points pl;
(*Schadenfreiheitsrabatt*) no-claims bonus
Boot (-(e)s, -e) nt boat; **Bootsverleih** m
boat hire (*Brit*) (o rental (*US*))
Bord (-(e)s, -e) m **an ~ (eines Schiffes)** on
board (a ship); **an ~ gehen** (*Schiff*) to go on
board; (*Flugzeug*) to board; **von ~ gehen** to
disembark; **Bordcomputer** m dashboard
computer
Bordell (-s, -e) nt brothel
Bordkarte f boarding card
Bordstein m kerb (*Brit*), curb (*US*)
borgen vt to borrow; **jdm etw ~** to lend
sb sth; **sich** (*dat*) **etw ~** to borrow sth
Börse (-, -n) f stock exchange; (*Geldbörse*)
purse
bös adj siehe **böse**; **bösartig** adj
malicious; (*Med*) malignant
Böschung f slope; (*Uferböschung*)
embankment
böse adj bad; (*stärker*) evil; (*Wunde*) nasty;
(*zornig*) angry; **bist du mir ~?** are you
angry with me?
boshaft adj malicious
Bosnien (-s) nt Bosnia;
Bosnien-Herzegowina (-s) nt
Bosnia-Herzegovina
böswillig adj malicious
bot imperf von **bieten**
botanisch adj **~er Garten** botanical
gardens pl
Botschaft f message; (*Pol*) embassy;
Botschafter(in) m(f) ambassador
Botsuana (-s) nt Botswana
Bouillon (-, -s) f stock
Boutique (-, -n) f boutique
Bowle (-, -n) f punch
Box (-, -en) f (*Behälter, Pferdebox*) box;
(*Lautsprecher*) speaker; (*bei Autorennen*) pit
boxen vi to box; **Boxer** (-s, -) m (*Hund,
Sportler*) boxer; **Boxershorts** pl boxer
shorts pl; **Boxkampf** m boxing match
Boykott (-s, -e) m boycott
brach imperf von **brechen**
brachte imperf von **bringen**
Brainstorming (-s) nt brainstorming
Branchenverzeichnis nt yellow
pages® pl
Brand (-(e)s, Brände) m fire; **einen
~ haben** (*fam*) to be parched
Brandenburg (-s) nt Brandenburg

Brandsalbe f ointment for burns

Brandung f surf

Brandwunde f burn

brannte imperf von **brennen**

Brasilien (-s) nt Brazil

braten (briet, gebraten) vt to roast; (auf dem Rost) to grill; (in der Pfanne) to fry; **Braten** (-s, -) m roast; (roher) joint; **Bratensoße** f gravy; **Brathähnchen** nt roast chicken; **Bratkartoffeln** pl fried potatoes pl; **Bratpfanne** f frying pan; **Bratspieß** m spit; **Bratwurst** f fried sausage; (gegrillte) grilled sausage

Brauch (-s, Bräuche) m custom

brauchen vt (nötig haben) to need (für, zu for); (erfordern) to require; (Zeit) to take; (gebrauchen) to use; **wie lange wird er ~?** how long will it take him?; **du brauchst es nur zu sagen** you only need to say; **das braucht (seine) Zeit** it takes time; **ihr braucht es nicht zu tun** you don't have (o need) to do it; **sie hätte nicht zu kommen** – she needn't have come

brauen vt to brew; **Brauerei** f brewery

braun adj brown; (von Sonne) tanned; **Bräune** (-, -n) f brownness; (von Sonne) tan; **Bräunungsstudio** nt tanning studio

Brause (-, -n) f (Dusche) shower; (Getränk) fizzy drink (Brit), soda (US)

Braut (-, Bräute) f bride; **Bräutigam** (-s, -e) m bridegroom

brav adj (artig) good, well-behaved

bravo interj well done

BRD (-) f abk = **Bundesrepublik Deutschland** FRG

brechen (brach, gebrochen) vt to break; (erbrechen) to bring up; **sich** (dat) **den Arm** ~ to break one's arm ▷ vi to break; (erbrechen) to vomit, to be sick; **Brechreiz** m nausea

Brei (-(e)s, -e) m (Breimasse) mush, pulp; (Haferbrei) porridge; (für Kinder) pap

breit adj wide; (Schultern) broad; **zwei Meter** ~ two metres wide; **Breite** (-, -n) f breadth; (bei Maßangaben) width; (Geo) latitude; **der ~ nach** widthways; **Breitengrad** m (degree of) latitude

Bremen (-s) nt Bremen

Bremsbelag m brake lining; **Bremse** (-, -n) f brake; (Zool) horsefly; **bremsen** vi to brake ▷ vt (Auto) to slow down; (fig) to slow down; **Bremsflüssigkeit** f brake fluid; **Bremslicht** nt brake light; **Bremspedal** nt brake pedal; **Bremsspur** f tyre marks pl; **Bremsweg** m braking distance

brennen (brannte, gebrannt) vi to burn; (in Flammen stehen) to be on fire; **es brennt!** fire!; **mir ~ die Augen** my eyes are smarting; **das Licht ~ lassen** to leave the light on; **Brennholz** nt firewood; **Brennnessel** f stinging nettle; **Brennspiritus** m methylated spirits pl; **Brennstab** m fuel rod; **Brennstoff** m fuel

Brett (-(e)s, -er) nt board; (länger) plank; (Regal) shelf; (Spielbrett) board; **schwarzes** ~ notice board, bulletin board (US); **~er** pl (ski) skis pl; **Brettspiel** nt board game

Brezel (-, -n) f pretzel

Brief (-(e)s, -e) m letter; **Briefbombe** f letter bomb; **Brieffreund(in)** m(f) penfriend, pen pal; **Briefkasten** m letterbox (Brit), mailbox (US); **elektronischer** ~ electronic mailbox; **Briefmarke** f stamp; **Briefpapier** nt writing paper; **Brieftasche** f wallet; **Briefträger(in)** m(f) postman/-woman; **Briefumschlag** m envelope; **Briefwaage** f letter scales pl

brief imperf von **braten**

Brille (-, -n) f glasses pl; (Schutzbrille) goggles pl; **Brillenetui** nt glasses case

bringen (brachte, gebracht) vt (herbringen) to bring; (mitnehmen, vom Sprecher weg) to take; (holen, herbringen) to get, to fetch; (Theat, Cine) to show; (Radio, Tv) to broadcast; **~ Sie mir bitte noch ein Bier** could you bring me another beer, please?; **jdn nach Hause** ~ to take sb home; **jdn dazu** ~, **etw zu tun** to make sb do sth; **jdn auf eine Idee** ~ to give sb an idea

Brise (-, -n) f breeze

Brite (-n, -n) m, **Britin** f British person,

Briton; **er ist ~** he is British; **die ~n** the British; **britisch** adj British

Brocken (-s, -) m bit; (größer) lump, chunk

Brokkoli m broccoli

Brombeere f blackberry

Bronchitis (-) f bronchitis

Bronze (-, -n) f bronze

Brosche (-, -n) f brooch

Brot (-(e)s, -e) nt bread; (Laib) loaf; **Brotaufstrich** m spread; **Brötchen** nt roll; **Brotzeit** f (Pause) break; (Essen) snack; **~ machen** to have a snack

Browser (-s, -) m (Inform) browser

Bruch (-(e)s, Brüche) m (Brechen) breaking; (Bruchstelle; mit Partei, Tradition etc) break; (Med: Eingeweidebruch) rupture, hernia; (Knochenbruch) fracture; (Math) fraction; **brüchig** adj brittle

Brücke (-, -n) f bridge

Bruder (-s, Brüder) m brother

Brühe (-, -n) f (Suppe) (clear) soup; (Grundlage) stock; (pej: Getränk) muck; **Brühwürfel** m stock cube

brüllen vi to roar; (Stier) to bellow; (vor Schmerzen) to scream (with pain)

brummen vi (Bär, Mensch) to growl; (brummeln) to mutter; (Insekt) to buzz; (Motor, Radio) to drone ▷ vt to growl

brünett adj brunette

Brunnen (-s, -) m fountain; (tief) well; (natürlich) spring

Brust (-, Brüste) f breast; (beim Mann) chest; **Brustschwimmen** (-s) nt breaststroke; **Brustwarze** f nipple

brutal adj brutal

brutto adv gross

BSE (-) nt abk = bovine spongiforme Enzephalopathie BSE

Bube (-n, -n) m boy, lad; (Karten) jack

Buch (-(e)s, Bücher) nt book

Buche (-, -n) f beech (tree)

buchen vt to book; (Betrag) to enter

Bücherei f library

Buchfink m chaffinch

Buchhalter(in) m(f) accountant

Buchhandlung f bookshop

Büchse (-, -n) f tin (Brit), can; **Büchsenfleisch** nt tinned meat (Brit), canned meat; **Büchsenmilch** f tinned milk (Brit), canned milk; **Büchsenöffner** m tin opener (Brit), can opener

Buchstabe (-ns, -n) m letter; **buchstabieren** vt to spell

Bucht (-, -en) f bay

Buchung f booking; (Comm) entry

Buckel (-s, -) m hump

bücken vr **sich ~** to bend down

Buddhismus (-) m Buddhism

Bude (-, -en) f (auf Markt) stall; (fam: Wohnung) pad, place

Büfett (-s, -s) nt sideboard; **kaltes ~** cold buffet

Büffel (-s, -) m buffalo

Bügel (-s, -) m (Kleidung) hanger; (Steigbügel) stirrup; (Brille) sidepiece; (von Skilift) T-bar; **Bügelbrett** nt ironing board; **Bügeleisen** nt iron; **Bügelfalte** f crease; **bügelfrei** adj non-iron; **bügeln** vt, vi to iron

buh interj boo

Bühne (-, -n) f stage; **Bühnenbild** nt set

Bulgare (-n, -n) m, **Bulgarin** f Bulgarian; **Bulgarien** (-s) nt Bulgaria; **bulgarisch** adj Bulgarian; **Bulgarisch** nt Bulgarian

Bulimie f bulimia

Bulle (-n, -n) m bull; (fam: Polizist) cop

Bummel (-s, -) m stroll; **bummeln** vi to stroll; (trödeln) to dawdle; (faulenzen) to loaf around; **Bummelzug** m slow train

bums interj bang

bumsen vi (vulg) to screw

Bund (-(e)s, Bünde) m (von Hose, Rock) waistband; (Freundschaftsbund) bond; (Organisation) association; (Pol) confederation; **der ~** (fam: Bundeswehr) the army ▷ (-(e)s, -e) nt bunch; (von Stroh etc) bundle

Bundes- in zW Federal; (auf Deutschland bezogen a.) German; **Bundesbahn** f German railway company; **Bundeskanzler(in)** m(f) Chancellor; **Bundesland** nt state, Land; **Bundesliga** f **erste/zweite ~** First/Second Division; **Bundespräsident(in)** m(f) President; **Bundesrat** m (in Deutschland) Upper House (of the German Parliament); (in der Schweiz) Council of Ministers; **Bundesregierung** f Federal Government; **Bundesrepublik** f Federal Republic; **~ Deutschland** Federal Republic of Germany; **Bundesstraße** f = A road (Brit), = state highway (US); **Bundestag** m Lower House (of the German Parliament); **Bundeswehr** f (German) armed forces pl

● **Bundeswehr**

The **Bundeswehr** is the name for the
German armed forces. It was
established in 1955, first of all for
volunteers, but since 1956 there has
been compulsory military service for
all able-bodied young men of 18. In
peacetime the Defence Minister is
the head of the 'Bundeswehr', but in
wartime the **Bundeskanzler** takes over.
The 'Bundeswehr' comes under the
jurisdiction of NATO.

Bündnis *nt* alliance
Bungalow (-s, -s) *m* bungalow
Bungeejumping (-s) *nt* bungee jumping
bunt *adj* colourful; (*von Programm etc*)
varied; **~e Farben** bright colours ▷ *adv*
(*anstreichen*) in bright colours; **Buntstift** *m*
crayon, coloured pencil
Burg (-, *-en*) *f* castle
Bürger(in) (-s, -) *m(f)* citizen; **bürgerlich**
adj (*Rechte, Ehe etc*) civil; (*vom Mittelstand*)
middle-class; (*pej*) bourgeois; **Bürger-
meister(in)** *m(f)* mayor; **Bürgersteig**
(-(e)s, -e) *m* pavement (*Brit*), sidewalk (*US*)
Büro (-s, -s) *nt* office; **Büroklammer** *f*
paper clip
Bürokratie *f* bureaucracy
Bursche (-n, -n) *m* lad; (*Typ*) guy
Bürste (-, -n) *f* brush; **bürsten** *vt* to brush
Bus (-ses, -se) *m* bus; (*Reisebus*) coach (*Brit*),
bus; **Busbahnhof** *m* bus station
Busch (-(e)s, Büsche) *m* bush; (*Strauch*) shrub
Busen (-s, -) *m* breasts *pl*, bosom
Busfahrer(in) *m(f)* bus driver;
Bushaltestelle *f* bus stop
Businessclass (-) *f* business class
Busreise *f* coach tour (*Brit*), bus tour
Bußgeld *nt* fine
Büstenhalter (-s, -) *m* bra
Busverbindung *f* bus connection
Butter (-) *f* butter; **Butterbrot** *nt* slice of
bread and butter; **Butterkäse** *m* *type of
mild, full-fat cheese*; **Buttermilch** *f* butter-
milk; **Butterschmalz** *nt* clarified butter
Button (-s, -s) *m* badge (*Brit*), button (*US*)
b. w. *abk* = **bitte wenden** pto
Byte (-s, -s) *nt* byte
bzw. *adv abk* = **beziehungsweise**

C

ca. *adv abk* = **circa** approx
Cabrio (-s, -s) *nt* convertible
Café (-s, -s) *nt* café
Cafeteria (-, -s) *f* cafeteria
Call-Center (-s, -) *nt* call centre
campen *vi* to camp; **Camping** (-s) *nt* camping; **Campingbus** *m* camper; **Campingplatz** *m* campsite, camping ground (US)
Cappuccino (-s, -) *m* cappuccino
Carving (-s) *nt* (Ski) carving; **Carvingski** *m* carving ski
CD (-, -s) *f abk* = **Compact Disc** CD; **CD-Brenner** (-s, -) *m* CD burner, CD writer; **CD-Player** (-s, -) *m* CD player; **CD-ROM** (-, -s) *f abk* = **Compact Disc Read Only Memory** CD-ROM; **CD-ROM-Laufwerk** *nt* CD-ROM drive, **CD-Spieler** *m* CD player
Cello (-s, -s *o Celli) nt* cello
Celsius *nt* celsius; **20 Grad ~** 20 degrees Celsius, 68 degrees Fahrenheit
Cent (-, -s) *m* (von Dollar und Euro) cent
Chamäleon (-s, -s) *nt* chameleon
Champagner (-s, -) *m* champagne
Champignon (-s, -s) *m* mushroom

Champions League (-, -s) *f* Champions League
Chance (-, -n) *f* chance; **die ~n stehen gut** the prospects are good
Chaos (-) *nt* chaos; **Chaot(in)** (-en, -en) *m(f)* (fam) disorganized person, scatterbrain; **chaotisch** *adj* chaotic
Charakter (-s, -e) *m* character; **charakteristisch** *adj* characteristic (für of)
Charisma (-s, Charismen *o* Charismata) *nt* charisma
charmant *adj* charming
Charterflug *m* charter flight; **chartern** *vt* to charter
checken *vt* (überprüfen) to check; (fam: verstehen) to get
Check-in (-s, -s) *m* check-in; **Check-in-Schalter** *m* check-in desk
Chef(in) (-s, -s) *m(f)* boss; **Chefarzt** *m*, **Chefärztin** *f* senior consultant (Brit), medical director (US)
Chemie (-) *f* chemistry; **chemisch** *adj* chemical; **~e Reinigung** dry cleaning
Chemotherapie *f* chemotherapy
Chicoree (-s) *m* chicory
Chiffre (-, -n) *f* (Geheimzeichen) cipher; (in Zeitung) box number
Chile (-s) *nt* Chile
Chili (-s, -s) *m* chilli
China (-s) *nt* China; **Chinakohl** *m* Chinese leaves *pl* (Brit), bok choy (US); **Chinarestaurant** *nt* Chinese restaurant; **Chinese** (-n, -n) *m* Chinese; **Chinesin** (-, -nen) *f* Chinese (woman); **sie ist ~** she's Chinese; **chinesisch** *adj* Chinese; **Chinesisch** *nt* Chinese
Chip (-s, -s) *m* (Inform) chip; **Chipkarte** *f* smart card
Chips *pl* (Kartoffelchips) crisps *pl* (Brit), chips *pl* (US)
Chirurg(in) (-en, -en) *m(f)* surgeon
Chlor (-s) *nt* chlorine
Choke (-s, -s) *m* choke
Cholera (-) *f* cholera
Cholesterin (-s) *nt* cholesterol
Chor (-(e), Chöre) *m* choir; (Theat) chorus
Choreografie *f* choreography
Christ(in) (-en, -en) *m(f)* Christian; **Christbaum** *m* Christmas tree; **Christi Himmelfahrt** *f* the Ascension (of Christ); **Christkind** *nt* baby Jesus; (das Geschenke

bringt) ≈ Father Christmas, Santa Claus;
christlich *adj* Christian
Chrom *(-s) nt* chrome; *(Chem)* chromium
chronisch *adj* chronic
chronologisch *adj* chronological ▷ *adv*
in chronological order
Chrysantheme *(-, -n) f* chrysanthemum
circa *adv* about, approximately
City *(-) f* city centre, downtown *(US)*
Clementine *(-, -n) f* clementine
clever *adj* clever, smart
Clique *(-, -n) f* group; *(pej)* clique;
  David und seine ~ David and his lot *o*
  crowd
Clown *(-s, -s) m* clown
Club *(-s, -s) m* club; **Cluburlaub** *m* club
  holiday *(Brit)*, club vacation *(US)*
Cocktail *(-s, -s) m* cocktail;
  Cocktailtomate *f* cherry tomato
Cognac *(-s) m* cognac
Cola *(-, -s) f* Coke®, cola
Comic *(-s, -s) m* comic strip; *(Heft)* comic
Compact Disc *(-, -s) f* compact disc
Computer *(-s, -) m* computer;
  Computerfreak *m* computer nerd;
  computergesteuert *adj*
  computer-controlled; **Computergrafik** *f*
  computer graphics *pl*; **computerlesbar**
  adj machine-readable; **Computerspiel** *nt*
  computer game; **Computertomografie** *f*
  computer tomography, scan;
  Computervirus *m* computer virus
Container *(-s, -) m (zum Transport)*
  container; *(für Bauschutt etc)* skip
Control-Taste *f* control key
Cookie *(-s, -s) nt (Inform)* cookie
cool *adj (fam)* cool
Cornflakes *pl* cornflakes *pl*
Couch *(-, -en) f* couch; **Couchtisch** *m*
  coffee table
Coupé *(-s, -s) nt* coupé
Coupon *(-s, -s) m* coupon
Cousin *(-s, -s) m* cousin; **Cousine** *f*
  cousin
Crack *(-s) nt (Droge)* crack
Creme *(-, -s) f* cream; *(Gastr)* mousse
Creutzfeld-Jakob-Krankheit *f*
  Creutzfeld-Jakob disease, CJD
Croissant *(-s, -s) nt* croissant
Curry *(-s) m* curry powder ▷ *(-s) nt*
  (indisches Gericht) curry; **Currywurst** *f fried
  sausage with ketchup and curry powder*
Cursor *(-s, -) m (Inform)* cursor

Cybercafé *nt* cybercafé; **Cyberspace** *(-)*
  m cyberspace

d

ich bleibe dabei I'm not changing my mind

dabei|haben irr vt **er hat seine Schwester dabei** he's brought his sister; **ich habe kein Geld dabei** I haven't got any money on me

Dach (-(e)s, Dächer) nt roof; **Dachboden** m attic, loft; **Dachgepäckträger** m roofrack; **Dachrinne** f gutter

Dachs (-es, -e) m badger

dachte imperf von **denken**

Dackel (-s, -) m dachshund

dadurch adv (räumlich) through it; (durch diesen Umstand) in that way; (deshalb) because of that, for that reason ▷ conj **~, dass** because; **~, dass er hart arbeitete** (indem) by working hard

dafür adv for it; (anstatt) instead; **~ habe ich 50 Euro bezahlt** I paid 50 euros for it; **ich bin ~ zu bleiben** I'm for (o in favour of) staying; **~ ist er ja da** that's what he's there for; **er kann nichts ~** he can't help it

dagegen adv against it; (im Vergleich damit) in comparison; (bei Tausch) for it; **ich habe nichts ~** I don't mind

daheim adv at home

da adv **1** (örtlich) there (hier) here; **da draußen** out there; **da sein** to be there; **da bin ich** here I am; **da, wo** where; **ist noch Milch da?** is there any milk left? **2** (zeitlich) then; (folglich) so **3**: **da haben wir Glück gehabt** we were lucky there; **da kann man nichts machen** nothing can be done about it ▷ konj (weil) as since

dabei adv (räumlich) close to it; (zeitlich) at the same time; (obwohl, doch) though; **sie hörte Radio und rauchte ~** she was listening to the radio and smoking (at the same time); **~ fällt mir ein ...** that reminds me ...; **~ kam es zu einem Unfall** this led to an accident; **... und ~ hat er gar keine Ahnung** ... even though he has no idea; **ich finde nichts ~** I don't see anything wrong with it; **es bleibt ~** that's settled; **~ sein** (anwesend) to be present; (beteiligt) to be involved; **ich bin ~!** count me in; **er war gerade ~ zu gehen** he was just (o on the point of) leaving

dabei|bleiben irr vi to stick with it;

daher adv (räumlich) from there; (Ursache) that's why ▷ conj (deshalb) that's why

dahin adv (räumlich) there; (zeitlich) then; (vergangen) gone; **bis ~** (zeitlich) till then; (örtlich) up to there; **bis ~ muss die Arbeit fertig sein** the work must be finished by then

dahinter adv behind it; **~ kommen** to find out

dahinterkommen vi to find out

Dahlie f dahlia

Dalmatiner (-s, -) m dalmatian

damals adv at that time, then

Dame (-, -n) f lady; (Karten) queen; (Spiel) draughts sing (Brit), checkers sing (US); **Damenbinde** f sanitary towel (Brit), sanitary napkin (US); **Damenfriseur** m ladies' hairdresser; **Damenkleidung** f ladies' wear; **Damentoilette** f ladies' toilet (o restroom (US))

damit adv with it; (begründend) by that; **was meint er ~?** what does he mean by that?; **genug ~!** that's enough ▷ conj so that

Damm (-(e)s, Dämme) m dyke; (Staudamm) dam; (am Hafen) mole; (Bahn-, Straßendamm) embankment

Dämmerung f twilight; (am Morgen) dawn; (am Abend) dusk

Dampf (-(e)s, Dämpfe) m steam; (Dunst) vapour; **Dampfbad** nt Turkish bath; **Dampfbügeleisen** nt steam iron; **dampfen** vi to steam

dämpfen vt (Gastr) to steam; (Geräusch) to deaden; (Begeisterung) to dampen

Dampfer (-s, -) m steamer

Dampfkochtopf m pressure cooker

danach adv after that; (zeitlich a.) afterwards; (demgemäß) accordingly; **mir ist nicht ~** I don't feel like it; **~ sieht es aus** that's what it looks like

Däne (-n, -n) m Dane

daneben adv beside it; (im Vergleich) in comparison

Dänemark (-s) nt Denmark; **Dänin** f Dane, Danish woman/girl; **dänisch** adj Danish; **Dänisch** nt Danish

dank prep +dat o gen thanks to; **Dank** (-(e)s) m thanks pl; **vielen ~!** thank you very much; **jdm ~ sagen** to thank sb; **dankbar** adj grateful; (Aufgabe) rewarding; **danke** interj thank you, thanks; **nein ~!** no, thank you; **~, gerne!** yes, please; **~, gleichfalls!** thanks, and the same to you; **danken** vi jdm für etw ~ to thank sb for sth; **nichts zu ~!** you're welcome

dann adv then; **bis ~!** see you (later); **~ eben nicht** okay, forget it, suit yourself

daran adv (räumlich) on it; (befestigen) to it; (stoßen) against it; **es liegt ~, dass ...** it's because ...

darauf adv (räumlich) on it; (zielgerichtet) towards it; (danach) afterwards; **es kommt ganz ~ an, ob ...** it all depends whether ...; **ich freue mich ~** I'm looking forward to it; **am Tag ~** the next day; **~ folgend** (Tag, Jahr) next, following

darauffolgend adj (Tag, Jahr) next, following

daraus adv from it; **was ist ~ geworden?** what became of it?

darin adv in it; **das Problem liegt ~, dass ...** the basic problem is that ...

Darlehen (-s, -) nt loan

Darm (-(e)s, Därme) m intestine; (Wurstdarm) skin; **Darmgrippe** f gastroenteritis

dar|stellen vt to represent; (Theat) to play; (beschreiben) to describe;

Darsteller(in) m(f) actor/actress; **Darstellung** f representation; (Beschreibung) description

darüber adv (räumlich) above it, over it; (fahren) over it; (mehr) more; (währenddessen) meanwhile; (sprechen, streiten, sich freuen) about it

darum adv (deshalb) that's why; **es geht ~, dass ...** the point (o thing) is that ...

darunter adv (räumlich) under it; (dazwischen) among them; (weniger) less; **was verstehen Sie ~?** what do you understand by that?; **~ fallen** to be included

darunterfallen vi to be included

das art the; **~ Auto da** that car; **er hat sich ~ Bein gebrochen** he's broken his leg; **vier Euro ~ Kilo** four euros a kilo ▷ pron that (one), this (one); (relativ, Sache) that, which; (relativ, Person) who, that; (demonstrativ) this/that one; **~ Auto da** that car; **ich nehme ~ da** I'll take that one; **~ Auto, ~ er kaufte** the car (that (o which)) he bought; **~ Mädchen, ~ nebenan wohnt** the girl who (o that) lives next door; **~ heißt** that is; **~ sind Amerikaner** they're American

da sein irr vi siehe da

dass conj that; **so ~** so that; **es sei denn, ~** unless; **ohne ~ er grüßte** without saying hello

dasselbe pron the same

Datei f (Inform) file; **Dateimanager** m file manager

Daten pl data pl; **Datenbank** f database; **Datenmissbrauch** m misuse of data; **Datenschutz** m data protection; **Datenträger** m data carrier; **Datenverarbeitung** f data processing

datieren vt to date

Dativ m dative (case)

Dattel (-, -n) f date

Datum (-s, Daten) nt date

Dauer (-, -n) f duration; (Länge) length; **auf die ~** in the long run; **für die ~ von zwei Jahren** for (a period of) two years; **Dauerauftrag** m (Fin) standing order; **dauerhaft** adj lasting; (Material) durable; **Dauerkarte** f season ticket; **dauern** vi to last; (Zeit benötigen) to take; **es hat sehr lange gedauert, bis er ...** it took him a long time to ...; **wie lange dauert es denn noch?** how much longer will it be?; **das**

dauert mir zu lange I can't wait that
long; **dauernd** adj lasting; (ständig)
constant ▷ adv always, constantly; **er
lachte ~** he kept laughing; **unterbrich
mich nicht ~** stop interrupting me;
Dauerwelle f perm (Brit), permanent (US)

Daumen (-s, -) m thumb

Daunendecke f eiderdown

davon adv of it; (räumlich) away; (weg von)
from it; (Grund) because of it; **ich hätte
gerne ein Kilo ~** I'd like one kilo of that;
~ habe ich gehört I've heard of it;
(Geschehen) I've heard about it; **das
kommt ~, wenn ...** that's what happens
when ...; **was habe ich ~?** what's the
point?; **auf und ~** up and away;
davon|laufen irr vi to run away

davor adv (räumlich) in front of it; (zeitlich)
before; **ich habe Angst ~** I'm afraid of it

dazu adv (zusätzlich) on top of that, as
well; (zu diesem Zweck) for it, for that
purpose; **ich möchte Reis ~** I'd like rice
with it; **und ~ noch** in addition;
~ fähig sein, etw zu tun to be capable of
doing sth; **wie kam es ~?** how did it
happen?; **dazu|gehören** vi to belong to
it; **dazu|kommen** irr vi (zu jdm ~) to join
sb; **kommt noch etwas dazu?** anything
else?

dazwischen adv in between; (Unterschied
etc) between them; (in einer Gruppe) among
them

dazwischen|kommen irr vi **wenn
nichts dazwischenkommt** if all goes
well; **mir ist etwas
dazwischengekommen** something has
cropped up

DDR (-) f abk = **Deutsche Demokratische
Republik** (Hist) GDR

dealen vi (fam: mit Drogen) to deal in drugs;
Dealer(in) (-s, -) m(f) (fam) dealer, pusher

Deck (-(e)s, -s o -e) nt deck; **an ~** on
deck

Decke (-, -n) f cover; (für Bett) blanket; (für
Tisch) tablecloth; (von Zimmer) ceiling

Deckel (-s, -) m lid

decken vt to cover; (Tisch) to lay, to set
▷ vr **sich ~** (Interessen) to coincide;
(Aussagen) to correspond ▷ vi (den Tisch
decken) to lay (o set) the table

Decoder (-s, -) m decoder

defekt adj faulty; **Defekt** (-(e)s, -e) m
fault, defect

definieren vt to define; **Definition**
(-, -en) f definition

deftig adj (Preise) steep; **ein ~es Essen** a
good solid meal

dehnbar adj flexible, elastic; **dehnen** vt
to stretch ▷ vr **sich ~** to stretch

Deich (-(e)s, -e) m dyke

dein pron (adjektivisch) your; **deine(r, s)**
pron (substantivisch) yours, of you; **deiner**
pron gen von **du**; of you; **deinetwegen** adv
(wegen dir) because of you; (dir zuliebe) for
your sake; (um dich) about you

deinstallieren vt (Programm) to
uninstall

Dekolleté (-s, -s) nt low neckline

Dekoration f decoration; (in Laden)
window dressing; **dekorativ** adj
decorative; **dekorieren** vt to decorate;
(Schaufenster) to dress

Delfin (-s, -e) m dolphin

delikat adj (lecker) delicious; (heikel)
delicate

Delikatesse (-, -n) f delicacy

Delle (-, -en) f (fam) dent

Delphin (-s, -e) m dolphin

dem dat sing von **der/das**; **wie ~ auch sein
mag** be that as it may

demnächst adv shortly, soon

Demo (-, -s) f (fam) demo

Demokratie (-, -n) f democracy;
demokratisch adj democratic

demolieren vt to demolish

Demonstration f demonstration;
demonstrieren vt, vi to demonstrate

den art akk sing, dat pl von **der**; **sie hat sich
~ Arm gebrochen** she's broken her arm
▷ pron him; (Sache) that one; (relativ:
Person) who, that, whom; (relativ: Sache)
which, that; **~ hab ich schon ewig nicht
mehr gesehen** I haven't seen him in ages
▷ pron (Person) who, that, whom; (Sache)
which, that; **der Typ, auf ~ sie steht** the
guy (who) she fancies; **der Berg, auf ~ wir
geklettert sind** the mountain (that) we
climbed

denkbar adj **das ist ~** that's possible
▷ adv **~ einfach** extremely simple;
denken (dachte, gedacht) vt, vi to think
(über +akk about); **an jdn/etw ~** to think of
sb/sth; (sich erinnern, berücksichtigen) to
remember sb/sth; **woran denkst Du?**
what are you thinking about?; **denk an
den Kaffee!** don't forget the coffee ▷ vr

sich ~ (*sich vorstellen*) to imagine; **das kann ich mir ~** I can (well) imagine

Denkmal (-s, *Denkmäler*) *nt* monument; **Denkmalschutz** *m* monument preservation; **unter ~ stehen** to be listed

denn *conj* for, because ▷ *adv* then; (*nach Komparativ*) than; **was ist ~?** what's wrong?; **ist das ~ so schwierig?** is it really that difficult?

dennoch *conj* still, nevertheless

Deo (-s, -s) *nt*, **Deodorant** (-s, -s) *nt* deodorant; **Deoroller** *m* roll-on deodorant; **Deospray** *m o nt* deodorant spray

Deponie (-, -n) *f* waste disposal site, tip

Depressionen *pl* **an ~ leiden** to suffer from depression *sing*; **deprimieren** *vt* to depress

◯ **SCHLÜSSELWORT**

der (*f* **die**, *nt* **das**, *gen* **des, der, des**, *dat* **dem, der, dem**, *akk* **den, die, das**, *pl* **die**) *def art* the; **der Rhein** the Rhine; **der Klaus** (*umg*) Klaus; **die Frau** (*im Allgemeinen*) women; **der Tod/das Leben** death/life; **der Fuß des Berges** the foot of the hill; **gib es der Frau** give it to the woman; **er hat sich die Hand verletzt** he has hurt his hand ▷ *relativ pron* (*bei Menschen*) who, that (*bei Tieren, Sachen*) which, that; **der Mann, den ich gesehen habe** the man who *od* whom *od* that I saw ▷ *demonstrativ pron* he/she/it (*jener, dieser*) that, (*pl*) those; **der/die war es** it was him/her; **der mit der Brille** the one with glasses; **ich will den (da)** I want that one

derart *adv* so; (*solcher Art*) such; **derartig** *adj* **ein ~er Fehler** such a mistake, a mistake like that

deren *gen von* **die** ▷ *pron* (*Person*) her; (*Sache*) its; (*Plural*) their ▷ *pron* (*Person*) whose; (*Sache*) of which; **meine Freundin und ~ Mutter** my friend and her mother; **das sind ~ Sachen** that's their stuff; **die Frau, ~ Tochter ...** the woman whose daughter ...; **ich bin mir ~ bewusst** I'm aware of that

dergleichen *pron* **und ~ mehr** and the like, and so on; **nichts ~** no such thing

derjenige *pron* the one; **~, der** (*relativ*) the one who (*o that*)

dermaßen *adv* so much; (*mit Adj*) so

derselbe *pron* the same (person/thing)

deshalb *adv* therefore; **~ frage ich ja** that's why I'm asking

Design (-s, -s) *nt* design; **Designer(in)** (-s, -) *m(f)* designer

Desinfektionsmittel *nt* disinfectant; **desinfizieren** *vt* to disinfect

dessen *gen von* **der, das** ▷ *pron* (*Person*) his; (*Sache*) its; **ich bin mir ~** I'm aware of that ▷ *pron* (*Person*) whose; (*Sache*) of which; **mein Freund und ~ Mutter** my friend and his mother; **der Mann, ~ Tochter ...** the man whose daughter ...; **ich bin mir ~ bewusst** I'm aware of that

Dessert (-s, -s) *nt* dessert; **zum** (*o als*) **~** for dessert

destilliert *adj* distilled

desto *adv* **je eher, ~ besser** the sooner, the better

deswegen *conj* therefore

Detail (-s, -s) *nt* detail; **ins ~ gehen** to go into detail

Detektiv(in) (-s, -e) *m(f)* detective

deutlich *adj* clear; (*Unterschied*) distinct

deutsch *adj* German; **Deutsch** *nt* German; **auf ~** in German; **ins ~e übersetzen** to translate into German; **Deutsche(r)** *mf* German; **Deutschland** *nt* Germany

Devise (-, -n) *f* motto; **~n** *pl* (*Fin*) foreign currency *sing*; **Devisenkurs** *m* exchange rate

Dezember (-(s), -) *m* December; *siehe auch* **Juni**

dezent *adj* discreet

d.h. *abk von* **das heißt** i.e. (*gesprochen: i.e. oder that is*)

Dia (-s, -s) *nt* slide

Diabetes (-, -) *m* (*Med*) diabetes; **Diabetiker(in)** (-s, -) *m(f)* diabetic

Diagnose (-, -n) *f* diagnosis

diagonal *adj* diagonal

Dialekt (-(e)s, -e) *m* dialect

Dialog (-(e)s, -e) *m* dialogue; (*Inform*) dialog

Dialyse (-, -n) *f* (*Med*) dialysis

Diamant *m* diamond

Diaprojektor *m* slide projector

Diät (-, -en) *f* diet; **eine ~ machen** to be on a diet; (*anfangen*) to go on a diet

dich *pron* *akk von* **du** you; **~ (selbst)**

(reflexiv) yourself; **pass auf ~ auf** look after yourself; **reg ~ nicht auf** don't get upset

dicht *adj* dense; *(Nebel)* thick; *(Gewebe)* close; *(wasserdicht)* watertight; *(Verkehr)* heavy ▷ *adv* **~ an/bei** close to; **~ bevölkert** densely populated

Dichter(in) *(-s, -) m(f)* poet; *(Autor)* writer

Dichtung *f (Auto)* gasket; *(Dichtungsring)* washer; *(Gedichte)* poetry

Dichtungsring *m (Tech)* washer

dick *adj* thick; *(Person)* fat; **jdn ~ haben** to be sick of sb; **Dickdarm** *m* colon; **Dickkopf** *m* stubborn (o pig-headed) person; **Dickmilch** *f* sour milk

die *art* the; **~ arme Sarah** poor Sarah ▷ *pron (sing, Person, als Subjekt)* she; *(Person, als Subjekt, Plural)* they; *(Person, als Objekt)* her; *(Person, als Objekt, Plural)* them; *(Sache)* that (one), this (one); *(Plural)* those (ones); *(Sache, Plural)* those (ones); *(relativ, auf Person)* who, that; *(relativ, auf Sache)* which, that; **~ mit den langen Haaren** the one (o her) with the long hair; **sie war ~ erste, ~ es erfuhr** she was the first to know; **ich nehme ~ da** I'll take that one/those ▷ *pl vor* **der, die, das**

Dieb(in) *(-(e)s, -e) m(f)* thief; **Diebstahl** *(-(e)s, Diebstähle) m* theft; **Diebstahlsicherung** *f* burglar alarm

diejenige *pron* the one; **~, die** *(relativ)* the one who (o that); **~n** *pl* those *pl*, the ones

Diele *(-, -n) f* hall

Dienst *(-(e)s, -e) m* service; **außer ~** retired; **~ haben** to be on duty; **der ~ habende Arzt** the doctor on duty

Dienstag *m* Tuesday; *siehe auch* **Mittwoch**; **dienstags** *adv* on Tuesdays; *siehe auch* **mittwochs**

Dienstbereitschaft *f* **~ haben** *(Arzt)* to be on call; **Dienstleistung** *f* service; **dienstlich** *adj* official; **er ist ~ unterwegs** he's away on business; **Dienstreise** *f* business trip; **Dienststelle** *f* department; **Dienstwagen** *m* company car; **Dienstzeit** *f* office hours *pl*; *(Mil)* period of service

diesbezüglich *adj (formell)* on this matter

diese(r, s) *pron* this (one); *pl* these; **~ Frau** this woman; **~r Mann** this man; **~s Mädchen** this girl; **~ Leute** these people; **ich nehme ~/~n/~s** *(hier)* I'll take this one; *(dort)* I'll take that one; **ich nehme ~** *pl*

(hier) I'll take these (ones); *(dort)* I'll take those (ones)

Diesel *(-s, -) m (Auto)* diesel

dieselbe *pron* the same; **es sind immer ~n** it's always the same people

Dieselmotor *m* diesel engine; **Dieselöl** *nt* diesel (oil)

diesig *adj* hazy, misty

diesmal *adv* this time

Dietrich *(-s, -e) m* skeleton key

Differenz *(-, -en) f* difference

digital *adj* digital; **Digital-** *in zW (Kamera, Anzeige etc)* digital

Diktat *(-(e)s, -e) nt* dictation

Diktatur *f* dictatorship

Dill *(-s) m* dill

DIN *abk* = **Deutsche Industrienorm** DIN; **~ A4** A4

Ding *(-(e)s, -e) nt* thing; **vor allen ~en** above all; **der Stand der ~e** the state of affairs; **das ist nicht mein ~** *(fam)* it's not my sort of thing (o cup of tea); **Dingsbums** *(-) nt (fam)* thingy, thingummybob

Dinosaurier *m* dinosaur

Diphtherie *f* diphtheria

Diplom *(-(e)s, -e) nt* diploma

Diplomat(in) *(-en, -en) m(f)* diplomat

dir *pron dat von* **du** (to) you; **hat er ~ geholfen?** did he help you?; **ich werde es ~ erklären** I'll explain it to you; *(reflexiv)* **wasch ~ die Hände** go and wash your hands; **ein Freund von ~** a friend of yours

direkt *adj* direct; *(Frage)* straight; **~e Verbindung** through service ▷ *adv* directly; *(sofort)* immediately; **~ am Bahnhof** right next to the station; **Direktflug** *m* direct flight

Direktor(in) *m(f)* director; *(Schule)* headmaster/-mistress *(Brit)*, principal *(US)*

Direktübertragung *f* live broadcast

Dirigent(in) *m(f)* conductor; **dirigieren** *vt* to direct; *(Mus)* to conduct

Discman® *(-s, -s) m* Discman®

Diskette *f* disk, diskette; **Diskettenlaufwerk** *nt* disk drive

Diskjockey *(-s, -s) m* disc jockey; **Disko** *(-, -s) f (fam)* disco, club; **Diskothek** *(-, -en) f* discotheque, club

diskret *adj* discreet

diskriminieren *vt* to discriminate against

Diskussion f discussion; **diskutieren** vt, vi to discuss

Display (-s, -s) nt display

disqualifizieren vt to disqualify

Distanz f distance

Distel (-, -n) f thistle

Disziplin (-, -en) f discipline

divers adj various

dividieren vt to divide (durch by); **8 dividiert durch 2 ist 4** 8 divided by 2 is 4

DJ (-s, -s) m abk = **Diskjockey** DJ

◯ SCHLÜSSELWORT

doch adv **1** (dennoch) after all (sowieso) anyway; **er kam doch noch** he came after all; **du weißt es ja doch besser** you know better than I do anyway; **und doch ...** and yet ...

2 (als bejahende Antwort) yes I do/it does etc; **das ist nicht wahr — doch!** that's not true — yes it is!

3 (auffordernd): **komm doch** do come; **lass ihn doch** just leave him; **nicht doch!** oh no!

4: **sie ist doch noch so jung** but she's still so young; **Sie wissen doch, wie das ist** you know how it is(, don't you?); **wenn doch** if only

▷ konj (aber) but (trotzdem) all the same; **und doch hat er es getan** but still he did it

Doktor(in) m(f) doctor

Dokument nt document; **Dokumentarfilm** m documentary (film); **dokumentieren** vt to document; **Dokumentvorlage** f (Inform) document template

Dolch (-(e)s, -e) m dagger

Dollar (-(s), -s) m dollar

dolmetschen vt, vi to interpret; **Dolmetscher(in)** (-s, -) m(f) interpreter

Dolomiten pl Dolomites pl

Dom (-(e)s, -e) m cathedral

Domäne (-, -n) f domain, province; (Inform: Domain) domain

Dominikanische Republik f Dominican Republic

Domino (-s, -s) nt dominoes sing

Donau (-) f Danube

Döner (-s, -) m, **Döner Kebab** (-(s), -s) m doner kebab

Donner (-s, -) m thunder; **donnern** vi **es donnert** it's thundering

Donnerstag m Thursday; siehe auch **Mittwoch**; **donnerstags** adv on Thursdays; siehe auch **mittwochs**

doof adj (fam) stupid

dopen vt to dope; **Doping** (-s) nt doping; **Dopingkontrolle** f drugs test

Doppel (-s, -) nt duplicate; (Sport) doubles sing; **Doppelbett** nt double bed; **Doppeldecker** m double-decker; **Doppelhaushälfte** f semi-detached house (Brit), duplex (US); **doppelklicken** vi to double-click; **Doppelname** m double-barrelled name; **Doppelpunkt** m colon; **Doppelstecker** m two-way adaptor; **doppelt** adj double; **in ~er Ausführung** in duplicate; **Doppelzimmer** nt double room

Dorf (-(e)s, Dörfer) nt village

Dorn (-(e)s, -en) m (Bot) thorn

Dörrobst nt dried fruit

Dorsch (-(e)s, -e) m cod

dort adv there; **~ drüben** over there; **dorther** adv from there

Dose (-, -n) f box; (Blechdose) tin (Brit), can; (Bierdose) can

dösen vi to doze

Dosenbier nt canned beer; **Dosenmilch** f canned milk, tinned milk (Brit); **Dosenöffner** m tin opener (Brit), can opener

Dotter (-s, -) m (egg) yolk

downloaden vt to download

Downsyndrom (-(e)s, -e) nt (Med) Down's syndrome

Dozent(in) m(f) lecturer

Dr. abk = **Doktor**

Drache (-n, -n) m dragon; **Drachen** (-s, -) m (Spielzeug) kite; (Sport) hang-glider; **Drachenfliegen** (-s) nt hang-gliding; **Drachenflieger(in)** (-s, -) m(f) hang-glider

Draht (-(e)s, Drähte) m wire; **Drahtseilbahn** f cable railway

Drama (-s, Dramen) nt drama; **dramatisch** adj dramatic

dran adv (fam) kontr von **daran**; **gut ~ sein** (reich) to be well-off; (glücklich) to be fortunate; (gesundheitlich) to be well; **schlecht ~ sein** to be in a bad way; **wer ist ~?** whose turn is it?; **ich bin ~** it's my turn; **bleib ~!** (Tel) hang on

drang imperf von **dringen**

Drang (-(e)s, *Dränge*) m (*Trieb*) urge (*nach* for); (*Druck*) pressure

drängeln vt, vi to push

drängen vt (*schieben*) to push; (*antreiben*) to urge ▷ vi (*eilig sein*) to be urgent; (*Zeit*) to press; **auf etw** (*akk*) **~** to press for sth

dran|kommen irr vi **wer kommt dran?** who's turn is it?, who's next?

drauf (*fam*) kontr von **darauf; gut/schlecht ~ sein** to be in a good/bad mood

Draufgänger(in) (-s, -) m(f) daredevil

drauf|kommen irr vi to remember; **ich komme nicht drauf** I can't think of it

drauf|machen vi (*fam*) **einen ~** to go on a binge

draußen adv outside

Dreck (-(e)s) m dirt, filth; **dreckig** adj dirty, filthy

drehen vt, vi to turn; (*Zigaretten*) to roll; (*Film*) to shoot ▷ vr **sich ~** to turn; (*um Achse*) to rotate; **sich ~ um** (*handeln von*) to be about

Drehstrom m three-phase current; **Drehtür** f revolving door; **Drehzahlmesser** m rev counter

drei num three; **~ viertel voll** three-quarters full; **es ist ~ viertel neun** it's a quarter to nine; **Drei** (-, -en) f three; (*Schulnote*) ≈ C; **Dreieck** nt triangle; **dreieckig** adj triangular; **dreifach** adj triple ▷ adv three times; **dreihundert** num three hundred; **Dreikönigstag** m Epiphany; **dreimal** adv three times; **Dreirad** nt tricycle; **dreispurig** adj three-lane

dreißig num thirty; **dreißigste(r, s)** adj thirtieth; *siehe auch* **dritte**

Dreiviertelstunde f **eine ~** three quarters of an hour

dreizehn num thirteen; **dreizehnte(r, s)** adj thirteenth; *siehe auch* **dritte**

dressieren vt to train

Dressing (-s, -s) nt (salad) dressing

Dressman (-s, *Dressmen*) m (male) model

Dressur (-, -en) f training

drin (*fam*) kontr von **darin** in it; **mehr war nicht ~** that was the best I could do

dringen (*drang, gedrungen*) vi (*Wasser, Licht, Kälte*) to penetrate (*durch* through, *in* +akk into); **auf etw** (*akk*) **~** to insist on sth; **dringend, dringlich** adj urgent

drinnen adv inside

dritt adv **wir sind zu ~** there are three of us; **dritte(r, s)** adj third; **die Dritte Welt** the Third World; **7. Juni** 7(th) June (*gesprochen: the seventh of June*); **am 7. Juni** on 7(th) June, on June 7(th) (*gesprochen: on the seventh of June*); **München, den 7. Juni** Munich, June 7(th); **Drittel** (-s, -) nt (*Bruchteil*) third; **drittens** adv thirdly

Droge (-, -n) f drug; **drogenabhängig, drogensüchtig** adj addicted to drugs

Drogerie f chemist's (*Brit*), drugstore (*US*); **Drogeriemarkt** m discount chemist's (*Brit*) (o drugstore (*US*))

● **Drogerie**

● The **Drogerie** as opposed to the
● **Apotheke** sells medicines not
● requiring a prescription. It tends to
● be cheaper and also sells cosmetics,
● perfume and toiletries.

drohen vi to threaten (*jdm* sb); **mit etw ~** to threaten to do sth

dröhnen vi (*Motor*) to roar; (*Stimme, Musik*) to boom; (*Raum*) to resound

Drohung f threat

Drossel (-, -n) f thrush

drüben adv over there; (*auf der anderen Seite*) on the other side

drüber (*fam*) kontr von **darüber**

Druck (-(e)s, *Drücke*) m (*Phys*) pressure; (*fig: Belastung*) stress; **jdn unter ~ setzen** to put sb under pressure ▷ (-(e)s, -e) m (*Typo: Vorgang*) printing; (*Produkt, Schriftart*) print; **Druckbuchstabe** m block letter; **in ~n schreiben** to print; **drucken** vt, vi to print

drücken vt, vi (*Knopf, Hand*) to press; (*zu eng sein*) to pinch; (*fig: Preise*) to keep down; **jdm etw in die Hand ~** to press sth into sb's hand ▷ vr **sich vor etw** (*dat*) **~** to get out of sth; **drückend** adj oppressive

Drucker (-s, -) m (*Inform*) printer; **Druckertreiber** m printer driver

Druckknopf m press stud (*Brit*), snap fastener (*US*); **Drucksache** f printed matter; **Druckschrift** f block letters pl

drunten adv down there

drunter (*fam*) kontr von **darunter**

Drüse (-, -n) f gland

Dschungel (-s, -) m jungle

du *pron* you; **bist ~ es?** is it you?; **wir sind per ~** we're on first-name terms

Dübel (-s, -) *m* Rawlplug®

ducken *vt* to duck ▷ *vr* **sich ~** to duck

Dudelsack *m* bagpipes *pl*

Duett (-s, -e) *nt* duet

Duft (-(e)s, Düfte) *m* scent; **duften** *vi* to smell nice; **es duftet nach ...** it smells of ...

dulden *vt* to tolerate

dumm *adj* stupid; **Dummheit** *f* stupidity; (*Tat*) stupid thing; **Dummkopf** *m* idiot

dumpf *adj* (*Ton*) muffled; (*Erinnerung*) vague; (*Schmerz*) dull

Düne (-, -n) *f* dune

Dünger (-s, -) *m* fertilizer

dunkel *adj* dark; (*Stimme*) deep; (*Ahnung*) vague; (*rätselhaft*) obscure; (*verdächtig*) dubious; **im Dunkeln tappen** (*fig*) to be in the dark; **dunkelblau** *adj* dark blue; **dunkelblond** *adj* light brown; **dunkelhaarig** *adj* dark-haired; **Dunkelheit** *f* darkness

dünn *adj* thin; (*Kaffee*) weak

Dunst (-es, Dünste) *m* haze; (*leichter Nebel*) mist; (*Chem*) vapour

dünsten *vt* (*Gastr*) to steam

Duo (-s, -s) *nt* duo

Dur (-) *nt* (*Mus*) major (key); **in G-~** in G major

SCHLÜSSELWORT

durch *präp* +akk **1** (*hindurch*) through; **durch den Urwald** through the jungle; **durch die ganze Welt reisen** to travel all over the world

2 (*mittels*) through, by (means of) (*aufgrund*) due to, owing to; **Tod durch Herzschlag/den Strang** death from a heart attack/by hanging; **durch die Post** by post; **durch seine Bemühungen** through his efforts

▷ *adv* **1** (*hindurch*) through; **die ganze Nacht durch** all through the night; **den Sommer durch** during the summer; **8 Uhr durch** past 8 o'clock; **durch und durch** completely

2 (*durchgebraten etc*): **(gut) durch** well-done

durchaus *adv* absolutely; **~ nicht** not at all

Durchblick *m* view; **den ~ haben** (*fig*) to know what's going on; **durch|blicken** *vi* to look through; (*fam: verstehen*) to understand (*bei etw* sth); **etw ~ lassen** (*fig*) to hint at sth

Durchblutung *f* circulation

durch|brennen *irr vi* (*Sicherung*) to blow; (*Draht*) to burn through; (*fam: davonlaufen*) to run away

durchdacht *adj* gut **~** well thought-out

durch|drehen *vt* (*Fleisch*) to mince ▷ *vi* (*Räder*) to spin; (*fam: nervlich*) to crack up

durcheinander *adv* in a mess; (*fam: verwirrt*) confused; **~ bringen** to mess up; (*verwirren*) to confuse; **~ reden** to talk all at the same time; **~ trinken** to mix one's drinks; **Durcheinander** (-s) *nt* (*Verwirrung*) confusion; (*Unordnung*) mess

Durchfahrt *f* way through; **„~ verboten!"** 'no thoroughfare'

Durchfall *m* (*Med*) diarrhoea

durch|fallen *irr vi* to fall through; (*in Prüfung*) to fail

durch|fragen *vr* **sich ~** to ask one's way

durch|führen *vt* to carry out

Durchgang *m* passage; (*Sport*) round; (*bei Wahl*) ballot; **Durchgangsverkehr** *m* through traffic

durchgebraten *adj* well done

durchgefroren *adj* frozen to the bone

durch|gehen *irr vi* to go through (*durch etw* sth); (*ausreißen: Pferd*) to break loose; (*Mensch*) to run away; **durchgehend** *adj* (*Zug*) through; **~ geöffnet** open all day

durch|halten *irr vi* to hold out ▷ *vt* (*Tempo*) to keep up; **etw ~** (*bis zum Schluss*) to see sth through

durch|kommen *irr vi* to get through; (*Patient*) to pull through

durch|lassen *irr vt* (*jdn*) to let through; (*Wasser*) to let in

Durchlauf(wasser)erhitzer (-s, -) *m* instantaneous water heater

durch|lesen *irr vt* to read through

durchleuchten *vt* to X-ray

durch|machen *vt* to go through; (*Entwicklung*) to undergo; **die Nacht ~** to make a night of it, to have an all-nighter

Durchmesser (-s, -) *m* diameter

Durchreise *f* journey through; **auf der ~** passing through; (*Güter*) in transit; **Durchreisevisum** nt transit visa

durch|reißen irr vt, vi to tear (in two)

durchs kontr von **durch das**

Durchsage (-, -n) f announcement

durchschauen vt (jdn, Lüge) to see through

durch|schlagen irr vr **sich ~** to struggle through

durch|schneiden irr vt to cut (in two)

Durchschnitt m (Mittelwert) average; **im ~** on average; **durchschnittlich** adj average ▷ adv (im Durchschnitt) on average; **Durchschnittsgeschwindigkeit** f average speed

durch|setzen vt to get through ▷ vr **sich ~** (Erfolg haben) to succeed; (sich behaupten) to get one's way

durchsichtig adj transparent, see-through

durch|stellen vt (Tel) to put through

durch|streichen irr vt to cross out

durchsuchen vt to search (nach for); **Durchsuchung** f search

durchwachsen adj (Speck) streaky; (fig: mittelmäßig) so-so

Durchwahl f direct dialling; (Nummer) extension

durch|ziehen irr vt (Plan) to carry through

Durchzug m draught

◯ SCHLÜSSELWORT

dürfen unreg vi **1** (Erlaubnis haben) to be allowed to; **ich darf das** I'm allowed to (do that); **darf ich?** may I?; **darf ich ins Kino?** can od may I go to the cinema?; **es darf geraucht werden** you may smoke

2 (in Verneinungen); **er darf das nicht** he's not allowed to (do that); **das darf nicht geschehen** that must not happen; **da darf sie sich nicht wundern** that shouldn't surprise her

3 (in Höflichkeitsformeln): **darf ich Sie bitten, das zu tun?** may od could I ask you to do that?; **was darf es sein?** what can I do for you?

4 (können): **das dürfen Sie mir glauben** you can believe me

5 (Möglichkeit): **das dürfte genug sein** that should be enough; **es dürfte Ihnen**

bekannt sein, dass ... as you will probably know ...

dürftig adj (ärmlich) poor; (unzulänglich) inadequate

dürr adj dried-up; (Land) arid; (mager) skinny

Durst (-(e)s) m thirst; **~ haben** to be thirsty; **durstig** adj thirsty

Dusche (-, -n) f shower; **duschen** vi to have a shower ▷ vr **sich ~** to have a shower; **Duschgel** nt shower gel; **Duschvorhang** m shower curtain

Düse (-, -n) f nozzle; (Tech) jet; **Düsenflugzeug** nt jet (aircraft)

Dussel (-s, -) m (fam) dope; **duss(e)lig** adj (fam) stupid

düster adj dark; (Gedanken, Zukunft) gloomy

Dutyfreeshop (-s, -s) m duty-free shop

Dutzend (-s, -e) nt dozen

duzen vt to address as 'du' ▷ vr **sich ~ (mit jdm)** to address each other as 'du', to be on first-name terms

DVD (-, -s) f abk = **Digital Versatile Disk** DVD

dynamisch adj dynamic

Dynamo (-s, -s) m dynamo

D-Zug m fast train

e

mir ~ I don't care, it's all the same to me; **~ wie teuer** no matter how expensive

egoistisch *adj* selfish

ehe *conj* before

Ehe (-, -n) *f* marriage; **Ehefrau** *f* wife; (*verheiratete Frau*) married woman; **Eheleute** *pl* married couple *sing*

ehemalig *adj* former; **ehemals** *adv* formerly

Ehemann *m* husband; (*verheirateter Mann*) married man; **Ehepaar** *nt* married couple

eher *adv* (*früher*) sooner; (*lieber*) rather, sooner; (*mehr*) more; **je ~, desto besser** the sooner the better

Ehering *m* wedding ring

eheste(r, s) *adj* (*früheste*) first ▷ *adv* **am ~n** (*am wahrscheinlichsten*) most likely

Ehre (-, -n) *f* honour; **ehren** *vt* to honour; **ehrenamtlich** *adj* voluntary; **Ehrengast** *m* guest of honour; **Ehrenwort** *nt* word of honour; **~!** I promise; **ich gebe dir mein ~** I give you my word

ehrgeizig *adj* ambitious

ehrlich *adj* honest

Ei (-(e)s, -er) *nt* egg; **hart gekochtes/weiches ~** hard-boiled/soft-boiled egg

Eiche (-, -n) *f* oak (tree); **Eichel** (-, -n) *f* acorn

Eichhörnchen *nt* squirrel

Eid (-(e)s, -e) *m* oath

Eidechse (-, -n) *f* lizard

Eierbecher *m* eggcup; **Eierstock** *m* ovary; **Eieruhr** *f* egg timer

Eifersucht *f* jealousy; **eifersüchtig** *adj* jealous (*auf +akk* of)

Eigelb (-(e)s, -) *nt* egg yolk

eigen *adj* own; (*typisch*) characteristic (*jdm* of sb); (*eigenartig*) peculiar; **eigenartig** *adj* peculiar; **Eigenschaft** *f* quality; (*Chem, Phys*) property; (*Merkmal*) characteristic

eigentlich *adj* actual, real ▷ *adv* actually, really; **was denken Sie sich ~ dabei?** what on earth do you think you're doing?

Eigentum *nt* property; **Eigentümer(in)** *m(f)* owner; **Eigentumswohnung** *f* owner-occupied flat (*Brit*), condominium (*US*)

eignen *vr* **sich ~ für** to be suited for; **er würde sich als Lehrer ~** he'd make a good teacher

Eilbrief *m* express letter, special-delivery

Ebbe (-, -n) *f* low tide

eben *adj* level; (*glatt*) smooth ▷ *adv* just; (*bestätigend*) exactly

Ebene (-, -n) *f* plain; (*fig*) level

ebenfalls *adv* also, as well; (*Antwort: gleichfalls!*) you too; **ebenso** *adv* just as; **~ gut** just as well; **~ viel** just as much

Eber (-s, -) *m* boar

EC (-, -s) *m abk* = **Eurocityzug**

Echo (-s, -s) *nt* echo

echt *adj* (*Leder, Gold*) real, genuine; **ein ~er Verlust** a real loss

EC-Karte *f* = debit card

Ecke (-, -n) *f* corner; (*Math*) angle; **an der ~** at the corner; **gleich um die ~** just round the corner; **eckig** *adj* rectangular; **Eckzahn** *m* canine

Economyclass (-) *f* coach (class), economy class

Ecstasy (-) *f* (*Droge*) ecstasy

edel *adj* noble; **Edelstein** *m* precious stone

EDV (-) *f abk* = **elektronische Datenverarbeitung** EDP

Efeu (-s) *m* ivy

Effekt (-s, -e) *m* effect

egal *adj* **das ist ~** it doesn't matter; **das ist**

letter; **Eile** (-) f hurry; **eilen** vi (dringend sein) to be urgent; **es eilt nicht** there's no hurry; **eilig** adj hurried; (dringlich) urgent; **es ~ haben** to be in a hurry

Eimer (-s, -) m bucket

ein adv **nicht ~ noch aus wissen** not to know what to do; **~ - aus** (Schalter) on - off

ein(e) art a; (vor gesprochenem Vokal) an; **~ Mann** a man; **~ Apfel** an apple; **~e Stunde** an hour; **~ Haus** a house; **~ (gewisser) Herr Miller** a (certain) Mr Miller; **~es Tages** one day

einander pron one another, each other

ein|arbeiten vt to train ▷ vr **sich ~** to get used to the work

ein|atmen vt, vi to breathe in

Einbahnstraße f one-way street

ein|bauen vt to build in; (Motor etc) to install, to fit; **Einbauküche** f fitted kitchen

ein|biegen irr vi to turn (in +akk into)

ein|bilden vt **sich** (dat) **etw ~** to imagine sth

ein|brechen irr vi (in Haus) to break in; (Dach etc) to fall in, to collapse; **Einbrecher(in)** (-s, -) m(f) burglar

ein|bringen irr vt (Ernte) to bring in; (Gewinn) to yield; **jdm etw ~** to bring (o earn) sb sth ▷ vr **sich in** (akk) **etw ~** to make a contribution to sth

Einbruch m (Haus) break-in, burglary; **bei ~ der Nacht** at nightfall

Einbürgerung f naturalization

ein|checken vt to check in

ein|cremen vt to put some cream on ▷ vr **sich ~** to put some cream on

eindeutig adj clear, obvious ▷ adv clearly; **~ falsch** clearly wrong

ein|dringen irr vi (gewaltsam) to force one's way in (in +akk -to); (in Haus) to break in (in +akk -to); (Gas, Wasser) to get in (in +akk -to)

Eindruck m impression; **großen ~ auf jdn machen** to make a big impression on sb

eine(r, s) pron one; (jemand) someone; **~r meiner Freunde** one of my friends; **~r nach dem andern** one after the other

eineiig adj (Zwillinge) identical

eineinhalb num one and a half

einerseits adv on the one hand

einfach adj (nicht kompliziert) simple; (Mensch) ordinary; (Essen) plain; (nicht mehrfach) single; **~e Fahrkarte** single

ticket (Brit), one-way ticket (US) ▷ adv simply; (nicht mehrfach) once

Einfahrt f (Vorgang) driving in; (eines Zuges) arrival; (Ort) entrance

Einfall m (Idee) idea; **ein|fallen** irr vi (Licht etc) to fall in; (einstürzen) to collapse; **ihm fiel ein, dass ...** it occurred to him that ...; **ich werde mir etwas ~ lassen** I'll think of something; **was fällt Ihnen ein!** what do you think you're doing?

Einfamilienhaus nt detached house

einfarbig adj all one colour; (Stoff etc) self-coloured

Einfluss m influence

ein|frieren irr vt, vi to freeze

ein|fügen vt to fit in; (zusätzlich) to add; (Inform) to insert; **Einfügetaste** f (Inform) insert key

Einfuhr (-, -en) f import; **Einfuhrbestimmungen** pl import regulations pl

ein|führen vt to introduce; (Ware) to import; **Einführung** f introduction

Eingabe f (Dateneingabe) input; **Eingabetaste** f (Inform) return (o enter) key

Eingang m entrance; **Eingangshalle** f entrance hall, lobby (US)

ein|geben irr vt (Daten etc) to enter, to key in

eingebildet adj imaginary; (eitel) arrogant

Eingeborene(r) mf native

ein|gehen irr vi (Sendung, Geld) to come in, to arrive; (Tier, Pflanze) to die; (Stoff) to shrink; **auf etw** (akk) **~** to agree to sth; **auf jdn ~** to respond to sb ▷ vt (Vertrag) to enter into; (Wette) to make; (Risiko) to take

eingelegt adj (in Essig) pickled

eingeschaltet adj (switched) on

eingeschlossen adj locked in; (inklusive) included

ein|gewöhnen vr **sich ~** to settle in

ein|gießen irr vt to pour

ein|greifen irr vi to intervene; **Eingriff** m intervention; (Operation) operation

ein|halten irr vt (Versprechen etc) to keep

ein|hängen vt (Telefon) (**den Hörer**) **~** to hang up

einheimisch adj (Produkt, Mannschaft) local; **Einheimische(r)** mf local

Einheit f (Geschlossenheit) unity; (Maß) unit; **einheitlich** adj uniform

ein|holen vt (Vorsprung aufholen) to catch

up with; (*Verspätung*) to make up for; (*Rat, Erlaubnis*) to ask for

Einhorn *nt* unicorn

einhundert *num* one (*o* a) hundred

einig *adj* (*vereint*) united; **sich** (*dat*) **~ sein** to agree

einige *pron pl* some; (*mehrere*) several ▷ *adj* some; **nach ~er Zeit** after some time; **~e hundert Euro** some hundred euros

einigen *vr* **sich ~** to agree (*auf +akk* on)

einigermaßen *adv* fairly, quite; (*leidlich*) reasonably

einiges *pron* something; (*ziemlich viel*) quite a bit; (*mehreres*) a few things; **es gibt noch ~ zu tun** there's still a fair bit to do

Einkauf *m* purchase; **Einkäufe (machen)** (to do one's) shopping; **ein|kaufen** *vt* to buy ▷ *vi* to go shopping;
Einkaufsbummel *m* shopping trip;
Einkaufstasche *f*, **Einkaufstüte** *f* shopping bag; **Einkaufswagen** *m* shopping trolley (*Brit*) (*o* cart (*US*));
Einkaufszentrum *nt* shopping centre (*Brit*) (*o* mall (*US*))

ein|klemmen *vt* to jam; **er hat sich** (*dat*) **den Finger eingeklemmt** he got his finger caught

Einkommen (*-s, -*) *nt* income

ein|laden *irr vt* (*jdn*) to invite; (*Gegenstände*) to load; **jdn zum Essen ~** to take sb out for a meal; **ich lade dich ein** (*bezahle*) it's my treat; **Einladung** *f* invitation

Einlass (*-es, Einlässe*) *m* admittance; **~ ab 18 Uhr** doors open at 6 pm; **ein|lassen** *irr vr* **sich mit jdm/auf etw** (*akk*) **~** to get involved with sb/sth

ein|leben *vr* **sich ~** to settle down

ein|legen *vt* (*Film etc*) to put in; (*marinieren*) to marinate; **eine Pause ~** to take a break

ein|leiten *vt* to start; (*Maßnahmen*) to introduce; (*Geburt*) to induce;
Einleitung *f* introduction; (*von Geburt*) induction

ein|leuchten *vi* **jdm ~** to be (*o* become) clear to sb; **einleuchtend** *adj* clear

ein|loggen *vi* (*Inform*) to log on (*o* in)

ein|lösen *vt* (*Scheck*) to cash; (*Gutschein*) to redeem; (*Versprechen*) to keep

einmal *adv* once; (*früher*) before; (*in Zukunft*) some day; (*erstens*) first; **~ im Jahr** once a year; **noch ~** once more, again; **ich war schon ~ hier** I've been here before; **warst du schon ~ in London?** have you ever been to London?; **nicht ~** not even; **auf ~** suddenly; (*gleichzeitig*) at once; **einmalig** *adj* unique; (*einmal geschehend*) single; (*prima*) fantastic

ein|mischen *vr* **sich ~** to interfere (*in +akk* with)

Einnahme (*-, -n*) *f* (*Geld*) takings *pl*; (*von Medizin*) taking; **ein|nehmen** *irr vt* (*Medizin*) to take; (*Geld*) to take in; (*Standpunkt, Raum*) to take up; **jdn für sich ~** to win sb over

ein|ordnen *vt* to put in order; (*klassifizieren*) to classify; (*Akten*) to file ▷ *vr* **sich ~** (*Auto*) to get in lane; **sich rechts/links ~** to get into the right/left lane

ein|packen *vt* to pack (up)

ein|parken *vt, vi* to park

ein|planen *vt* to allow for

ein|prägen *vt* **sich** (*dat*) **etw ~** to remember (*o* memorize) sth

ein|räumen *vt* (*Bücher, Geschirr*) to put away; (*Schrank*) to put things in

ein|reden *vt* **jdm/sich etw ~** to talk sb/oneself into (believing) sth

ein|reiben *irr vt* **sich mit etw ~** to rub sth into one's skin

ein|reichen *vt* to hand in; (*Antrag*) to submit

Einreise *f* entry; **Einreisebestimmungen** *pl* entry regulations *pl*; **Einreiseerlaubnis** *f*, **Einreisegenehmigung** *f* entry permit; **ein|reisen** *vi* to enter (*in ein Land* a country); **Einreisevisum** *nt* entry visa

ein|renken *vt* (*Arm, Bein*) to set

ein|richten *vt* (*Wohnung*) to furnish; (*gründen*) to establish, to set up; (*arrangieren*) to arrange ▷ *vr* **sich ~** (*in Haus*) to furnish one's home; (*sich vorbereiten*) to prepare oneself (*auf +akk* for); (*sich anpassen*) to adapt (*auf +akk* to); **Einrichtung** *f* (*Wohnung*) furnishings *pl*; (*öffentliche Anstalt*) institution; (*Schwimmbad etc*) facility

eins *num* one; **Eins** (*-, -en*) *f* one; (*Schulnote*) ≈ A

einsam *adj* lonely

ein|sammeln *vt* to collect

Einsatz *m* (*Teil*) insert; (*Verwendung*) use;

(Spieleinsatz) stake; *(Risiko)* risk; *(Mus)* entry

ein|schalten vt *(Elek)* to switch on

ein|schätzen vt to estimate, to assess

ein|schenken vt to pour

ein|schiffen vr **sich ~** to embark *(nach for)*

ein|schlafen irr vi to fall asleep, to drop off; **mir ist der Arm eingeschlafen** my arm's gone to sleep

ein|schlagen irr vt *(Fenster)* to smash; *(Zähne, Schädel)* to smash in; *(Weg, Richtung)* to take ▷ vi to hit *(in etw akk sth, auf jdn sb)*; *(Blitz)* to strike; *(Anklang finden)* to be a success

ein|schließen irr vt *(jdn)* to lock in; *(Gegenstand)* to lock away; *(umgeben)* to surround; *(fig: beinhalten)* to include; **einschließlich** adv inclusive ▷ prep +gen including; **von Montag bis ~ Freitag** from Monday up to and including Friday, Monday through Friday *(US)*

ein|schränken vt to limit, to restrict; *(verringern)* to cut down on ▷ vr **sich ~** to cut down (on expenditure)

ein|schreiben irr vr **sich ~** to register; *(Schule)* to enrol; **Einschreiben** *(-s, -)* nt registered letter; **etw per ~ schicken** to send sth by special delivery

ein|schüchtern vt to intimidate

ein|sehen irr vt *(verstehen)* to see; *(Fehler)* to recognize; *(Akten)* to have a look at

einseitig adj one-sided

ein|senden irr vt to send in

ein|setzen vt to put in; *(in Amt)* to appoint; *(Geld)* to stake; *(verwenden)* to use ▷ vi *(beginnen)* to set in; *(Mus)* to enter, to come in ▷ vr **sich ~** to work hard; **sich für jdn/etw ~** to support sb/sth

Einsicht f insight; **zu der ~ kommen, dass ...** to come to realize that ...

ein|sperren vt to lock up

ein|spielen vt *(Geld)* to bring in

ein|springen irr vi *(aushelfen)* to step in *(für for)*

Einspruch m objection *(gegen to)*

einspurig adj single-lane

Einstand m *(Tennis)* deuce

ein|stecken vt to pocket; *(Elek: Stecker)* to plug in; *(Brief)* to post, to mail *(US)*; *(mitnehmen)* to take; *(hinnehmen)* to swallow

ein|steigen irr vi *(in Auto)* to get in; *(in*

Bus, Zug, Flugzeug) to get on; *(sich beteiligen)* to get involved

ein|stellen vt *(beenden)* to stop; *(Geräte)* to adjust; *(Kamera)* to focus; *(Sender, Radio)* to tune in; *(unterstellen)* to put; *(in Firma)* to employ, to take on ▷ vr **sich auf jdn/etw ~** to adapt to sb/prepare oneself for sth; **Einstellung** f *(von Gerät)* adjustment; *(von Kamera)* focusing; *(von Arbeiter)* taking on; *(Meinung)* attitude

ein|stürzen vi to collapse

eintägig adj one-day

ein|tauschen vt to exchange *(gegen for)*

eintausend num one (o a) thousand

ein|teilen vt *(in Teile)* to divide (up) *(in +akk into)*; *(Zeit)* to organize

eintönig adj monotonous

Eintopf m stew

ein|tragen irr vt *(in eine Liste)* to put down, to enter ▷ vr **sich ~** to put one's name down, to register

ein|treffen irr vi to happen; *(ankommen)* to arrive

ein|treten irr vi *(hineingehen)* to enter *(in etw akk sth)*; *(in Klub, Partei)* to join *(in etw akk sth)*; *(sich ereignen)* to occur; **~ für** to support; **Eintritt** m admission; **„~ frei"** 'admission free'; **Eintrittskarte** f *(entrance)* ticket; **Eintrittspreis** m admission charge

einverstanden interj okay, all right ▷ adj **mit etwas ~ sein** to agree to sth, to accept sth

Einwanderer m, **Einwanderin** f immigrant; **ein|wandern** vi to immigrate

einwandfrei adj perfect, flawless

Einwegflasche f non-returnable bottle; **Einwegwaschlappen** m disposable flannel *(Brit)* (o washcloth *(US)*)

ein|weichen vt to soak

ein|weihen vt *(Gebäude)* to inaugurate, to open; **jdn in etw** *(akk)* **~** to let sb in on sth; **Einweihungsparty** f housewarming party

ein|werfen irr vt *(Ball, Bemerkung etc)* to throw in; *(Brief)* to post, to mail *(US)*; *(Geld)* to put in, to insert; *(Fenster)* to smash

ein|wickeln vt to wrap up; *(fig)* **jdn ~** to take sb in

Einwohner(in) *(-s, -)* m(f) inhabitant; **Einwohnermeldeamt** nt registration office for residents

Einwurf m *(Öffnung)* slot; *(Sport)* throw-in

Einzahl f singular
ein|zahlen vt to pay in (auf ein Konto -to an account)
Einzel (-s, -) nt (Tennis) singles sing; **Einzelbett** nt single bed; **Einzelfahrschein** m single ticket (Brit), one-way ticket (US); **Einzelgänger(in)** m(f) loner; **Einzelhandel** m retail trade; **Einzelkind** nt only child
einzeln adj individual; (getrennt) separate; (einzig) single; **~e ...** several ..., some ...; **der/die Einzelne** the individual; **im Einzelnen** in detail ▷ adv separately; (verpacken, aufführen) individually; **~ angeben** to specify; **~ eintreten** to enter one by one
Einzelzimmer nt single room; **Einzelzimmerzuschlag** m single-room supplement
ein|ziehen irr vt **den Kopf ~** to duck ▷ vi (in ein Haus) to move in
einzig adj only; (einzeln) single; (einzigartig) unique; **kein ~er Fehler** not a single mistake; **das Einzige** the only thing; **der/die Einzige** the only person ▷ adv only; **die ~ richtige Lösung** the only correct solution; **einzigartig** adj unique
Eis (-es, -) nt ice; (Speiseeis) ice-cream; **~ laufen** to skate; **Eisbahn** f ice(skating) rink; **Eisbär** m polar bear; **Eisbecher** m (ice-cream) sundae; **Eisberg** m iceberg; **Eiscafé** nt, **Eisdiele** f ice-cream parlour
Eisen (-s, -) nt iron; **Eisenbahn** f railway (Brit), railroad (US); **eisern** adj iron
eisgekühlt adj chilled; **Eishockey** nt ice hockey; **Eiskaffee** m iced coffee; **eiskalt** adj ice-cold; (Temperatur) freezing; **Eiskunstlauf** m figure skating; **Eissalat** m iceberg lettuce; **Eisschokolade** f iced chocolate; **Eisschrank** m fridge, ice-box (US); **Eistee** m iced tea; **Eiswürfel** m ice cube; **Eiszapfen** m icicle
eitel adj vain
Eiter (-s) m pus
Eiweiß (-es, -e) nt egg white; (Chem, Bio) protein
ekelhaft, ek(e)lig adj disgusting, revolting; **ekeln** vr **sich ~** to be disgusted (vor +dat at)
EKG (-s, -s) nt abk = **Elektrokardiogramm** ECG
Ekzem (-s, -e) nt (Med) eczema

Elastikbinde f elastic bandage; **elastisch** adj elastic
Elch (-(e)s, -e) m elk; (nordamerikanischer) moose
Elefant m elephant
elegant adj elegant
Elektriker(in) (-s, -) m(f) electrician; **elektrisch** adj electric; **Elektrizität** f electricity; **Elektroauto** nt electric car; **Elektrogerät** nt electrical appliance; **Elektrogeschäft** nt electrical shop; **Elektroherd** m electric cooker; **Elektromotor** m electric motor; **Elektronik** f electronics sing; **elektronisch** adj electronic; **Elektrorasierer** (-s, -) m electric razor
Element (-s, -e) nt element
elend adj miserable; **Elend** (-(e)s) nt misery
elf num eleven; **Elf** (-, -en) f (Sport) eleven
Elfenbein nt ivory
Elfmeter m (Sport) penalty (kick)
elfte(r, s) adj eleventh; siehe auch **dritte**
Ell(en)bogen m elbow
Elster (-, -n) f magpie
Eltern pl parents pl
EM f abk = **Europameisterschaft** European Championship(s)
Email (-s, -s) nt enamel
E-Mail (-, -s) f (Inform) e-mail; **jdm eine ~ schicken** to e-mail sb, to send sb an e-mail; **jdm etwas per ~ schicken** to e-mail sth to sb; **E-Mail-Adresse** f e-mail address; **e-mailen** vt to e-mail
Emoticon (-s, -s) nt emoticon
emotional adj emotional
empfahl imperf von **empfehlen**
empfand imperf von **empfinden**
Empfang (-(e)s, Empfänge) m (Rezeption; Veranstaltung) reception; (Erhalten) receipt; **in ~ nehmen** to receive; **empfangen** (empfing, empfangen) vt to receive; **Empfänger(in)** (-s, -) m(f) recipient; (Adressat) addressee ▷ m (Tech) receiver; **Empfängnisverhütung** f contraception; **Empfangshalle** f reception area
empfehlen (empfahl, empfohlen) vt to recommend; **Empfehlung** f recommendation
empfinden (empfand, empfunden) vt to feel; **empfindlich** adj (Mensch) sensitive; (Stelle) sore; (reizbar) touchy; (Material) delicate

empfing imperf von **empfangen**
empfohlen pp von **empfehlen**
empfunden pp von **empfinden**
empört adj indignant (über +akk at)
Ende (-s, -n) nt end; (Film, Roman) ending; **am ~** at the end; (schließlich) in the end; **~ Mai** at the end of May; **~ der Achtzigerjahre** in the late eighties; **sie ist ~ zwanzig** she's in her late twenties; **zu ~** over, finished; **enden** vi to end; **der Zug endet hier** this service (o train) terminates here; **endgültig** adj final; (Beweis) conclusive
Endivie f endive
endlich adv at last, finally; (am Ende) eventually; **Endspiel** nt final; (Endrunde) finals pl; **Endstation** f terminus; **Endung** f ending
Energie f energy; **~ sparend** energy-saving; **Energiebedarf** m energy requirement; **Energieverbrauch** m energy consumption
energisch adj (entschlossen) forceful
eng adj narrow; (Kleidung) tight; (fig: Freundschaft, Verhältnis) close; **das wird ~** (fam: zeitlich) we're running out of time, it's getting tight ▷ adv **~ befreundet sein** to be close friends
engagieren vt to engage ▷ vr **sich ~** to commit oneself, to be committed (für to)
Engel (-s, -) m angel
England nt England; **Engländer(in)** (-s, -) m(f) Englishman/ -woman; **die ~** pl the English pl; **englisch** adj English; (Gastr) rare; **Englisch** nt English; **ins ~e übersetzen** to translate into English
Enkel (-s, -) m grandson; **Enkelin** f granddaughter
enorm adj enormous; (fig) tremendous
Entbindung f (Med) delivery
entdecken vt to discover; **Entdeckung** f discovery
Ente (-, -n) f duck
Enter-Taste f (Inform) enter (o return) key
entfernen vt to remove; (Inform) to delete ▷ vr **sich ~** to go away; **entfernt** adj distant; **15 km von X ~** 15 km away from X; **20 km voneinander ~** 20 km apart; **Entfernung** f distance; **aus der ~** from a distance
entführen vt to kidnap; **Entführer(in)** m(f) kidnapper; **Entführung** f kidnapping

entgegen prep +dat contrary to ▷ adv towards; **dem Wind ~** against the wind; **entgegengesetzt** adj (Richtung) opposite; (Meinung) opposing; **entgegen|kommen** irr vi **jdm ~** to come to meet sb; (fig) to accommodate sb; **entgegenkommend** adj (Verkehr) oncoming; (fig) obliging
entgegnen vt to reply (auf +akk to)
entgehen irr vi **jdm ~** to escape sb's notice; **sich** (dat) **etw ~ lassen** to miss sth
entgleisen vi (Eisenb) to be derailed; (fig: Mensch) to misbehave
Enthaarungscreme f hair remover
enthalten irr vt (Behälter) to contain; (Preis) to include ▷ vr **sich ~** to abstain (gen from)
entkoffeiniert adj decaffeinated
entkommen irr vi to escape
entkorken vt to uncork
entlang prep +akk o dat **~ dem Fluss, den Fluss ~** along the river; **entlang|gehen** irr vi to walk along
entlassen irr vt (Patient) to discharge; (Arbeiter) to dismiss
entlasten vt **jdn ~** (Arbeit abnehmen) to relieve sb of some of his/her work
entmutigen vt to discourage
entnehmen vt to take (dat from)
entrahmt adj (Milch) skimmed
entschädigen vt to compensate; **Entschädigung** f compensation
entscheiden irr vt, vi to decide ▷ vr **sich ~** to decide; **sich für/gegen etw ~** to decide on/against sth; **wir haben uns entschieden, nicht zu gehen** we decided not to go; **das entscheidet sich morgen** that'll be decided tomorrow; **entscheidend** adj decisive; (Stimme) casting; (Frage, Problem) crucial; **Entscheidung** f decision
entschließen irr vr **sich ~** to decide (zu, für on), to make up one's mind; **Entschluss** m decision
entschuldigen vt to excuse ▷ vr **sich ~** to apologize; **sich bei jdm für etw ~** to apologize to sb for sth ▷ vi **entschuldige!, ~ Sie!** (vor einer Frage) excuse me; (Verzeihung!) (I'm) sorry, excuse me (US); **Entschuldigung** f apology; (Grund) excuse; **jdn um ~ bitten** to apologize to sb; **~!** (bei Zusammenstoß) (I'm) sorry, excuse me (US); (vor einer Frage)

excuse me; (*wenn man etw nicht verstanden hat*) (I beg your) pardon?

entsetzlich *adj* dreadful, appalling

entsorgen *vt* to dispose of

entspannen *vt* (*Körper*) to relax; (*Pol: Lage*) to ease ▷ *vr* **sich ~** to relax; (*fam*) to chill out; **Entspannung** *f* relaxation

entsprechen *irr vi* +*dat* to correspond to; (*Anforderungen, Wünschen etc*) to comply with; **entsprechend** *adj* appropriate ▷ *adv* accordingly ▷ *prep* +*dat* according to, in accordance with

entstehen *vi* (*Schwierigkeiten*) to arise; (*gebaut werden*) to be built; (*hergestellt werden*) to be created

enttäuschen *vt* to disappoint; **Enttäuschung** *f* disappointment

entweder *conj* **~ ... oder ...** either ... or ...; **~ oder!** take it or leave it

entwerfen *irr vt* (*Möbel, Kleider*) to design; (*Plan, Vertrag*) to draft

entwerten *vt* to devalue; (*Fahrschein*) to cancel; **Entwerter** (*-s, -*) *m* ticket-cancelling machine

entwickeln *vt* (*a. Foto*) to develop; (*Mut, Energie*) to show, to display ▷ *vr* **sich ~** to develop; **Entwicklung** *f* development; (*Foto*) developing; **Entwicklungshelfer(in)** (*-s, -*) *m(f)* development worker; **Entwicklungsland** *nt* developing country

Entwurf *m* outline; (*Design*) design; (*Vertragsentwurf, Konzept*) draft

entzückend *adj* delightful, charming

Entzug *m* withdrawal; (*Behandlung*) detox; **Entzugserscheinung** *f* withdrawal symptom

entzünden *vr* **sich ~** to catch fire; (*Med*) to become inflamed; **Entzündung** *f* (*Med*) inflammation

Epidemie *f* epidemic

Epilepsie *f* epilepsy

er *pron* (*Person*) he; (*Sache*) it; **er ists** it's him; **wo ist mein Mantel? - ~ ist ...** where's my coat? - it's ...

Erbe (*-n, -n*) *m* heir ▷ (*-s*) *nt* inheritance; (*fig*) heritage; **erben** *vt* to inherit; **Erbin** *f* heiress; **erblich** *adj* hereditary

erbrechen *irr vt* to vomit ▷ *vr* **sich ~** to vomit; **Erbrechen** *nt* vomiting

Erbschaft *f* inheritance

Erbse (*-, -n*) *f* pea

Erdapfel *m* potato; **Erdbeben** *nt* earthquake; **Erdbeere** *f* strawberry; **Erde** (*-, -n*) *f* (*Planet*) earth; (*Boden*) ground; **Erdgas** *nt* natural gas; **Erdgeschoss** *nt* ground floor (Brit), first floor (US); **Erdkunde** *f* geography; **Erdnuss** *f* peanut; **Erdöl** *nt* (mineral) oil; **Erdrutsch** *m* landslide; **Erdteil** *m* continent

ereignen *vr* **sich ~** to happen, to take place; **Ereignis** *nt* event

erfahren *irr vt* to learn, to find out; (*erleben*) to experience ▷ *adj* experienced; **Erfahrung** *f* experience

erfinden *irr vt* to invent; **erfinderisch** *adj* inventive, creative; **Erfindung** *f* invention

Erfolg (*-(e)s, -e*) *m* success; (*Folge*) result; **~ versprechend** promising; **viel ~!** good luck; **erfolglos** *adj* unsuccessful; **erfolgreich** *adj* successful

erforderlich *adj* necessary

erforschen *vt* to explore; (*untersuchen*) investigate

erfreulich *adj* pleasing, pleasant; (*Nachricht*) good; **erfreulicherweise** *adv* fortunately

erfrieren *irr vi* to freeze to death; (*Pflanzen*) to be killed by frost

Erfrischung *f* refreshment

erfüllen *vt* (*Raum*) to fill; (*Bitte, Wunsch etc*) to fulfil ▷ *vr* **sich ~** to come true

ergänzen *vt* (*hinzufügen*) to add; (*vervollständigen*) to complete ▷ *vr* **sich ~** to complement one another; **Ergänzung** *f* completion; (*Zusatz*) supplement

ergeben *irr vt* (*Betrag*) to come to; (*zum Ergebnis haben*) to result in ▷ *irr vr* **sich ~** to surrender; (*folgen*) to result (*aus* from) ▷ *adj* devoted; (*demütig*) humble

Ergebnis *nt* result

ergreifen *irr vt* to seize; (*Beruf*) to take up; (*Maßnahme, Gelegenheit*) to take; (*rühren*) to move

erhalten *irr vt* (*bekommen*) to receive; (*bewahren*) to preserve; **gut ~ sein** to be in good condition; **erhältlich** *adj* available

erheblich *adj* considerable

erhitzen *vt* to heat (up)

erhöhen *vt* to raise; (*verstärken*) to increase ▷ *vr* **sich ~** to increase

erholen *vr* **sich ~** to recover; (*sich ausruhen*) to have a rest; **erholsam** *adj*

restful; **Erholung** f recovery;
(*Entspannung*) relaxation, rest

erinnern vt to remind (*an* +akk of) ▷ vr
sich ~ to remember (*an etw akk* sth);
Erinnerung f memory; (*Andenken*)
souvenir; (*Mahnung*) reminder

erkälten vr **sich ~** to catch a cold;
erkältet adj (**stark**) **~ sein** to have a (bad)
cold; **Erkältung** f cold

erkennen irr vt to recognize; (*sehen,
verstehen*) to see; **~, dass ...** to realize that
...; **erkenntlich** adj **sich ~ zeigen** to show
one's appreciation

Erker (*-s, -*) m bay

erklären vt to explain; (*kundtun*) to
declare; **Erklärung** f explanation;
(*Aussage*) declaration

erkundigen vr **sich ~** to enquire (*nach*
about)

erlauben vt to allow, to permit; **jdm ~,
etw zu tun** to allow (o permit) sb to do
sth; **sich** (*dat*) **etw ~** to permit oneself sth;
~ Sie(, dass ich rauche)? do you mind (if I
smoke)?; **was ~ Sie sich?** what do you
think you're doing?; **Erlaubnis** f
permission

Erläuterung f explanation; (*zu Text*)
comment

erleben vt to experience; (*schöne Tage etc*)
to have; (*Schlimmes*) to go through;
(*miterleben*) to witness; (*noch miterleben*) to
live to see; **Erlebnis** nt experience

erledigen vt (*Angelegenheit, Aufgabe*) to
deal with; (*fam: ruinieren*) to finish;
erledigt adj (*beendet*) finished; (*gelöst*)
dealt with; (*fam: erschöpft*) whacked,
knackered (*Brit*)

erleichtert adj relieved

Erlös (*-es, -e*) m proceeds pl

ermahnen vt (*warnend*) to warn

ermäßigt adj reduced; **Ermäßigung** f
reduction

ermitteln vt to find out; (*Täter*) to trace
▷ vi (*Jur*) to investigate

ermöglichen vt to make possible (*dat* for)

ermorden vt to murder

ermüdend adj tiring

ermutigen vt to encourage

ernähren vt to feed; (*Familie*) to support
▷ vr **sich ~** to support oneself; **sich ~ von**
to live on; **Ernährung** f (*Essen*) food;
Ernährungsberater(in) m(f) nutritional
(o dietary) adviser

erneuern vt to renew; (*restaurieren*) to
restore; (*renovieren*) to renovate;
(*auswechseln*) to replace

ernst adj serious ▷ adv **jdn/etw
~ nehmen** take sb/sth seriously; **Ernst**
(*-es*) m seriousness; **das ist mein ~** I'm
quite serious; **im ~?** seriously?; **ernsthaft**
adj serious ▷ adv seriously

Ernte (*-, -n*) f harvest; **Erntedankfest** nt
harvest festival (*Brit*), Thanksgiving (Day)
(*US: 4. Donnerstag im November*); **ernten** vt
to harvest; (*Lob etc*) to earn

erobern vt to conquer

eröffnen vt to open; **Eröffnung** f opening

erogen adj erogenous

erotisch adj erotic

erpressen vt (*jdn*) to blackmail; (*Geld etc*)
to extort; **Erpressung** f blackmail; (*von
Geld*) extortion

erraten irr vt to guess

erregen vt to excite; (*sexuell*) to arouse;
(*ärgern*) to annoy; (*hervorrufen*) to arouse
▷ vr **sich ~** to get worked up; **Erreger**
(*-s, -*) m (*Med*) germ; (*Virus*) virus

erreichbar adj **~ sein** to be within reach;
(*Person*) to be available; **das
Stadtzentrum ist zu Fuß/mit dem
Wagen leicht ~** the city centre is within
easy walking/driving distance; **erreichen**
vt to reach; (*Zug etc*) to catch

Ersatz (*-es*) m replacement; (*auf Zeit*)
substitute; (*Ausgleich*) compensation;
Ersatzreifen m (*Auto*) spare tyre;
Ersatzteil nt spare (part)

erscheinen irr vi to appear; (*wirken*) to
seem

erschöpft adj exhausted; **Erschöpfung** f
exhaustion

erschrecken vt to frighten ▷ (*erschrak,
erschrocken*) vi to get a fright;
erschreckend adj alarming; **erschrocken**
adj frightened

erschwinglich adj affordable

ersetzen vt to replace; (*Auslagen*) to
reimburse

⊙ **SCHLÜSSELWORT**

erst adv **1** first; **mach erst mal die Arbeit
fertig** finish your work first; **wenn du
das erst mal hinter dir hast** once you've
got that behind you
2 (*nicht früher als, nur*) only; (*nicht bis*) not

till; **erst gestern** only yesterday; **erst morgen** not until tomorrow; **erst als** only when not until; **wir fahren erst später** we're not going until later; **er ist (gerade) erst angekommen** he's only just arrived
3: **wäre er doch erst zurück!** if only he were back!

erstatten vt (Kosten) to refund; **Bericht ~ to** report (über +akk on); **Anzeige gegen jdn ~** to report sb to the police

erstaunlich adj astonishing; **erstaunt** adj surprised

erstbeste(r, s) adj **das ~ Hotel** any old hotel; **der Erstbeste** just anyone

erste(r, s) adj first; siehe auch **dritte zum ~n Mal** for the first time; **er wurde Erster** he came first; **auf den ~n Blick** at first sight

erstens adv first(ly), in the first place

ersticken vi (Mensch) to suffocate; **in Arbeit ~** to be snowed under with work

erstklassig adj first-class; **erstmals** adv for the first time

erstrecken vr **sich ~** to extend, to stretch (auf +akk to; über +akk over)

ertappen vt to catch

erteilen vt (Rat, Erlaubnis) to give

Ertrag (-(e)s, Erträge) m yield; (Gewinn) proceeds pl; **ertragen** irr vt (Schmerzen) to bear, to stand; (dulden) to put up with; **erträglich** adj bearable; (nicht zu schlecht) tolerable

ertrinken irr vi to drown

erwachsen adj grown-up; **~ werden** to grow up; **Erwachsene(r)** mf adult, grown-up

erwähnen vt to mention

erwarten vt to expect; (warten auf) to wait for; **ich kann den Sommer kaum ~** I can hardly wait for the summer

erwerbstätig adj employed

erwidern vt to reply; (Gruß, Besuch) to return

erwischen vt (fam) to catch (bei etw doing sth)

erwünscht adj desired; (willkommen) welcome

Erz (-es, -e) nt ore

erzählen vt to tell (jdm etw sb sth); **Erzählung** f story, tale

erzeugen vt to produce; (Strom) to generate; **Erzeugnis** nt product

erziehen irr vt to bring up; (geistig) to educate; (Tier) to train; **Erzieher(in)** (-s, -) m(f) educator; (Kindergarten) (nursery school) teacher; **Erziehung** f upbringing; (Bildung) education

es pron (Sache, im Nom und Akk) it; (Baby, Tier) he/she; **ich bin ~** it's me; **~ ist kalt** it's cold; **~ gibt ...** there is .../there are ...; **ich hoffe ~** I hope so; **ich kann ~** I can do it

Escape-Taste f (Inform) escape key

Esel (-s, -) m donkey

Espresso (-s, -) m espresso

essbar adj edible; **essen** (aß, gegessen) vt, vi to eat; **zu Mittag/Abend ~** to have lunch/dinner; **was gibt's zu ~?** what's for lunch/dinner?; **~ gehen** to eat out; **gegessen sein** (fig, fam) to be history; **Essen** (-s, -) nt (Mahlzeit) meal; (Nahrung) food

Essig (-s, -e) m vinegar; **Essiggurke** f gherkin

Esslöffel m dessert spoon; **Esszimmer** nt dining room

Estland nt Estonia

Etage (-, -n) f floor, storey; **in** (o **auf**) **der ersten ~** on the first (Brit) (o second (US)) floor; **Etagenbett** nt bunk bed

Etappe (-, -n) f stage

ethnisch adj ethnic

Etikett (-(e)s, -e) nt label

etliche pron pl several, quite a few; **etliches** pron quite a lot

etwa adv (ungefähr) about; (vielleicht) perhaps; (beispielsweise) for instance

etwas pron something; (verneinend, fragend) anything; (ein wenig) a little; **~ Neues** something/anything new; **~ zu essen** something to eat; **~ Salz** some salt; **wenn ich noch ~ tun kann ...** if I can do anything else ... ▷ adv a bit, a little; **~ mehr** a little more

EU (-) f abk = **Europäische Union** EU

euch pron akk, dat von **ihr;** you, (to) you; **~ (selbst)** (reflexiv) yourselves; **wo kann ich ~ treffen?** where can I meet you?; **sie schickt es ~** she'll send it to you; **ein Freund von ~** a friend of yours; **setzt ~ bitte** please sit down; **habt ihr ~ amüsiert?** did you enjoy yourselves?

euer pron (adjektivisch) your; **~ David** (am

Briefende) Yours, David ▷ *pron gen von* **ihr**; of you; **euere(r, s)** *pron siehe* **eure**

Eule (-, -n) *f* owl

eure(r, s) *pron (substantivisch)* yours; **das ist ~** that's yours; **euretwegen** *adv (wegen euch)* because of you; *(euch zuliebe)* for your sake; *(um euch)* about you

Euro (-, -) *m (Währung)* euro; **Eurocent** *m* eurocent; **Eurocity** (-(s), -s) *m*, **Eurocityzug** *m* Eurocity Intercity train; **Europa** (-s) *nt* Europe; **Europäer(in)** (-s, -) *m(f)* European; **europäisch** *adj* European; **Europäische Union** European Union; **Europameister(in)** *m(f)* European champion; *(Mannschaft)* European champions *pl*; **Europaparlament** *nt* European Parliament

Euter (-s, -) *nt* udder

evangelisch *adj* Protestant

eventuell *adj* possible ▷ *adv* possibly, perhaps

ewig *adj* eternal; **er hat ~ gebraucht** it took him ages; **Ewigkeit** *f* eternity

Ex- *in zW* ex-, former; **~frau** ex-wife; **~minister** former minister

exakt *adj* precise

Examen (-s, -) *nt* exam

Exemplar (-s, -e) *nt* specimen; *(Buch)* copy

Exil (-s, -e) *nt* exile

Existenz *f* existence; *(Unterhalt)* livelihood, living; **existieren** *vi* to exist

exklusiv *adj* exclusive; **exklusive** *adv*, *prep +gen* excluding

exotisch *adj* exotic

Experte (-n, -n) *m*, **Expertin** *f* expert

explodieren *vi* to explode; **Explosion** *f* explosion

Export (-(e)s, -e) *m* export; **exportieren** *vt* to export

Express (-es) *m*, **Expresszug** *m* express (train)

extra *adj inv (fam: gesondert)* separate; *(zusätzlich)* extra ▷ *adv (gesondert)* separately; *(speziell)* specially; *(absichtlich)* on purpose; **Extra** (-s, -s) *nt* extra

extrem *adj* extreme ▷ *adv* extremely; **~ kalt** extremely cold

exzellent *adj* excellent

Eyeliner (-s, -) *m* eyeliner

f

fabelhaft adj fabulous, marvellous

Fabrik f factory

Fach (-(e)s, Fächer) nt compartment; (Schulfach, Sachgebiet) subject; **Facharzt** m, **Fachärztin** f specialist; **Fachausdruck** (-s, Fachausdrücke) m technical term

Fächer (-s, -) m fan

Fachfrau f specialist, expert; **Fachmann** (-leute) m specialist, expert; **Fachwerkhaus** nt half-timbered house

Fackel (-, -n) f torch

fad(e) adj (Essen) bland; (langweilig) dull

Faden (-s, Fäden) m thread

fähig adj capable (zu, gen of); **Fähigkeit** f ability

Fahndung f search

Fahne (-, -n) f flag

Fahrausweis m ticket; **Fahrausweisautomat** m ticket machine; **Fahrausweiskontrolle** f ticket inspection

Fahrbahn f road; (Spur) lane

Fähre (-, -n) f ferry

fahren (fuhr, gefahren) vt to drive; (Rad) to ride; (befördern) to drive, to take; **50 km/h ~** to drive at (o do) 50 kph ▷ vi (sich bewegen) to go; (Autofahrer) to drive; (Schiff) to sail; (abfahren) to leave; **mit dem Auto/Zug ~** to go by car/train; **rechts ~!** keep to the right; **Fahrer(in)** (-s, -) m(f) driver; **Fahrerairbag** m driver airbag; **Fahrerflucht** f **~ begehen** to fail to stop after an accident; **Fahrersitz** m driver's seat

Fahrgast m passenger; **Fahrgeld** nt fare; **Fahrgemeinschaft** f car pool; **Fahrkarte** f ticket; **Fahrkartenautomat** m ticket machine; **Fahrkartenschalter** m ticket office

fahrlässig adj negligent

Fahrlehrer(in) m(f) driving instructor; **Fahrplan** m timetable; **Fahrplanauszug** m individual timetable; **fahrplanmäßig** adj (Eisenb) scheduled; **Fahrpreis** m fare; **Fahrpreisermäßigung** f fare reduction; **Fahrrad** nt bicycle; **Fahrradschlauch** m bicycle tube; **Fahrradschloss** nt bicycle lock; **Fahrradverleih** m cycle hire (Brit) (o rental (US)); **Fahrradweg** m cycle path; **Fahrschein** m ticket; **Fahrscheinautomat** m ticket machine; **Fahrscheinentwerter** m ticket-cancelling machine; **Fahrschule** f driving school; **Fahrschüler(in)** m(f) learner (driver) (Brit), student driver (US); **Fahrspur** f lane; **Fahrstreifen** m lane; **Fahrstuhl** m lift (Brit), elevator (US)

Fahrt (-, -en) f journey; (kurz) trip; (Auto) drive; **auf der ~ nach London** on the way to London; **nach drei Stunden ~** after travelling for three hours; **gute ~!** have a good trip; **Fahrtkosten** pl travelling expenses pl; **Fahrtrichtung** f direction of travel

fahrtüchtig f (Person) fit to drive; (Fahrzeug) roadworthy

Fahrtunterbrechung f break in the journey, stop

Fahrverbot nt **~ erhalten/haben** to be banned from driving; **Fahrzeug** nt vehicle; **Fahrzeugbrief** m (vehicle) registration document; **Fahrzeughalter(in)** m(f) registered owner; **Fahrzeugpapiere** pl vehicle documents pl

fair adj fair

Fakultät f faculty

Falke (-n, -n) m falcon

Fall (-(e)s, Fälle) m (Sturz) fall; (Sachverhalt, juristisch) case; **auf jeden ~, auf alle Fälle**

in any case; (*bestimmt*) definitely; **auf keinen ~** on no account; **für den ~, dass ...** in case ...

Falle (*-, -n*) *f* trap

fallen (*fiel, gefallen*) *vi* to fall; **etw ~ lassen** to drop sth

fällig *adj* due

falls *adv* if; (*für den Fall, dass*) in case

Fallschirm *m* parachute; **Fallschirmspringen** *nt* parachuting, parachute jumping; **Fallschirmspringer(in)** *m(f)* parachutist

falsch *adj* (*unrichtig*) wrong; (*unehrlich, unecht*) false; (*Schmuck*) fake; **~ verbunden** sorry, wrong number; **fälschen** *vt* to forge; **Falschfahrer(in)** *m(f)* *person driving the wrong way on the motorway*; **Falschgeld** *nt* counterfeit money; **Fälschung** *f* forgery, fake

Faltblatt *nt* leaflet

Falte (*-, -n*) *f* (*Knick*) fold; (*Haut*) wrinkle; (*Rock*) pleat; (*Bügel*) crease; **falten** *vt* to fold; **faltig** *adj* (*zerknittert*) creased; (*Haut, Gesicht*) wrinkled

Familie *f* family; **Familienangehörige(r)** *mf* family member; **Familienname** *m* surname; **Familienstand** *m* marital status

Fan (*-s, -s*) *m* fan

fand *imperf von* **finden**

fangen (*fing, gefangen*) *vt* to catch ▷ *vr* **sich ~** (*nicht fallen*) to steady oneself; (*fig*) to compose oneself

Fantasie *f* imagination

fantastisch *adj* fantastic

Farbbild *nt* colour photograph; **Farbdrucker** *m* colour printer; **Farbe** (*-, -n*) *f* colour; (*zum Malen etc*) paint; (*für Stoff*) dye; **farbecht** *adj* colourfast; **färben** *vt* to colour; (*Stoff, Haar*) to dye; **Farbfernsehen** *nt* colour television; **Farbfilm** *m* colour film; **Farbfoto** *nt* colour photo; **farbig** *adj* coloured; **Farbkopierer** *m* colour copier; **farblos** *adj* colourless; **Farbstoff** *m* dye; (*für Lebensmittel*) colouring

Farn (*-(e)s, -e*) *m* fern

Fasan (*-(e)s, -e(n)*) *m* pheasant

Fasching (*-s, -e*) *m* carnival, Mardi Gras (US); **Faschingsdienstag** (*-s, -e*) *m* Shrove Tuesday, Mardi Gras (US)

Faschismus *m* fascism

Faser (*-, -n*) *f* fibre

Fass (*-es, Fässer*) *nt* barrel; (*Öl*) drum

fassen *vt* (*ergreifen*) to grasp; (*enthalten*) to hold; (*Entschluss*) to take; (*verstehen*) to understand; **nicht zu ~!** unbelievable ▷ *vr* **sich ~** to compose oneself; **Fassung** *f* (*Umrahmung*) mount; (*Brille*) frame; (*Lampe*) socket; (*Wortlaut*) version; (*Beherrschung*) composure; **jdn aus der ~ bringen** to throw sb; **die ~ verlieren** to lose one's cool

fast *adv* almost, nearly

fasten *vi* to fast; **Fastenzeit** *f* **die ~** (*christlich*) Lent; (*muslimisch*) Ramadan

Fast Food (*-s*) *nt* fast food

Fastnacht *f* (*Fasching*) carnival

fatal *adj* (*verhängnisvoll*) disastrous; (*peinlich*) embarrassing

faul *adj* (*Obst, Gemüse*) rotten; (*Mensch*) lazy; (*Ausreden*) lame; **faulen** *vi* to rot

faulenzen *vi* to do nothing, to hang around; **Faulheit** *f* laziness

faulig *adj* rotten; (*Geruch, Geschmack*) foul

Faust (*-, Fäuste*) *f* fist; **Fausthandschuh** *m* mitten

Fax (*-, -(e)*) *nt* fax; **faxen** *vi, vt* to fax; **Faxgerät** *nt* fax machine; **Faxnummer** *f* fax number

FCKW (*-, -s*) *nt* *abk* = **Fluorchlorkohlenwasserstoff** CFC

Februar (*-(s), -e*) *m* February; *siehe auch* **Juni**

Fechten *nt* fencing

Feder (*-, -n*) *f* feather; (*Schreibfeder*) (*pen-*)nib; (*Tech*) spring; **Federball** *m* (*Ball*) shuttlecock; (*Spiel*) badminton; **Federung** *f* suspension

Fee (*-, -n*) *f* fairy

fegen *vi, vt* to sweep

fehl *adj* **~ am Platz** (*o Ort*) out of place

fehlen *vi* (*abwesend sein*) to be absent; **etw fehlt jdm** sb lacks sth; **was fehlt ihm?** what's wrong with him?; **du fehlst mir** I miss you; **es fehlt an ...** there's no...

Fehler (*-s, -*) *m* mistake, error; (*Mangel, Schwäche*) fault; **Fehlermeldung** *f* (*Inform*) error message

Fehlzündung *f* (*Auto*) misfire

Feier (*-, -n*) *f* celebration; (*Party*) party; **Feierabend** *m* *end of the working day*; **~ haben** to finish work; **nach ~** after work; **feierlich** *adj* solemn; **feiern** *vt, vi* to celebrate, to have a party; **Feiertag** *m*

holiday; **gesetzlicher ~** public (o bank (Brit) o legal (US)) holiday

feig(e) adj cowardly

Feige (-, -n) f fig

Feigling m coward

Feile (-, -n) f file

fein adj fine; (vornehm) refined; **~!** great!; **das schmeckt ~** that tastes delicious

Feind(in) (-(e)s, -e) m(f) enemy; **feindlich** adj hostile

Feinkost (-) f delicacies pl; **Feinkostladen** m delicatessen; **Feinschmecker(in)** (-s, -) m(f) gourmet

Feinwaschmittel nt washing powder for delicate fabrics

Feld (-(e)s, -er) nt field; (Schach) square; (Sport) pitch; **Feldsalat** m lamb's lettuce; **Feldweg** m path across the fields

Felge (-, -n) f (wheel) rim

Fell (-(e)s, -e) nt fur; (von Schaf) fleece

Fels (-en, -en) m, **Felsen** (-s, -) m rock; (Klippe) cliff; **felsig** adj rocky

feminin adj feminine; **Femininum** (-s, Feminina) nt (Ling) feminine noun

feministisch adj feminist

Fenchel (-s, -) m fennel

Fenster (-s, -) nt window; **Fensterbrett** nt windowsill; **Fensterladen** m shutter; **Fensterplatz** m windowseat; **Fensterscheibe** f windowpane

Ferien pl holidays pl (Brit), vacation sing (US); **~ haben/machen** to be/go on holiday (Brit) (o vacation (US)); **Ferienhaus** nt holiday (Brit) (o vacation (US)) home; **Ferienkurs** m holiday (Brit) (o vacation (US)) course; **Ferienlager** nt holiday camp (Brit), vacation camp (US); (für Kinder im Sommer) summer camp; **Ferienort** m holiday (Brit) (o vacation (US)) resort; **Ferienwohnung** f holiday flat (Brit), vacation apartment (US)

Ferkel (-s, -) nt piglet

fern adj distant, far-off; **von ~** from a distance; **Fernabfrage** f remote-control access; **Fernbedienung** f remote control; **Ferne** f distance; **aus der ~** from a distance

ferner adj, adv further; (außerdem) besides

Fernflug m long-distance flight; **Ferngespräch** nt long-distance call; **ferngesteuert** adj remote-controlled; **Fernglas** nt binoculars pl; **Fernlicht** nt full beam (Brit), high beam (US)

Fernsehapparat m TV (set); **fern|sehen** irr vi to watch television; **Fernsehen** nt television; **im ~** on television; **Fernseher** m TV (set); **Fernsehkanal** m TV channel; **Fernsehprogramm** nt (Sendung) TV programme; (Zeitschrift) TV guide; **Fernsehserie** f TV series sing; **Fernsehturm** m TV tower; **Fernsehzeitschrift** f TV guide

Fernstraße f major road; **Ferntourismus** m long-haul tourism; **Fernverkehr** m long-distance traffic

Ferse (-, -n) f heel

fertig adj (bereit) ready; (beendet) finished; (gebrauchsfertig) ready-made; **~ machen** (beenden) to finish; **jdn ~ machen** (kritisieren) to give sb hell; (zur Verzweiflung bringen) to drive sb mad; (deprimieren) to get sb down; **sich ~ machen** to get ready; **mit etw ~ werden** to be able to cope with sth; **auf die Plätze, ~, los!** on your marks, get set, go!; **Fertiggericht** nt ready meal

fest adj firm; (Nahrung) solid; (Gehalt) regular; (Schuhe) sturdy; (Schlaf) sound

Fest (-(e)s, -e) nt party; (Rel) festival

Festbetrag m fixed amount

fest|binden irr vt to tie (an +dat to); **fest|halten** irr vt to hold onto ▷ vr **sich ~** to hold on (an +dat to)

Festiger (-s, -) m setting lotion

Festival (-s, -s) nt festival

Festland nt mainland; **das europäische ~** the (European) continent

fest|legen vt to fix ▷ vr **sich ~** to commit oneself

festlich adj festive

fest|machen vt to fasten; (Termin etc) to fix; **fest|nehmen** irr vt to arrest; **Festnetz** nt (Tel) fixed-line network; **Festplatte** f (Inform) hard disk

fest|setzen vt to fix

Festspiele pl festival sing

fest|stehen irr vi to be fixed

fest|stellen vt to establish; (sagen) to remark

Feststelltaste f shift lock

Festung f fortress

Festzelt nt marquee

Fete (-, -n) f party

fett adj (dick) fat; (Essen etc) greasy; (Schrift) bold; **Fett** (-(e)s, -e) nt fat; (Tech) grease; **fettarm** adj low-fat; **fettig** adj fatty; (schmierig) greasy

fetzig adj (fam: Musik) funky

feucht adj damp; (Luft) humid; **Feuchtigkeit** f dampness; (Luftfeuchtigkeit) humidity; **Feuchtigkeitscreme** f moisturizing cream

Feuer (-s, -) nt fire; **haben Sie ~?** have you got a light?; **Feueralarm** m fire alarm; **feuerfest** adj fireproof; **feuergefährlich** adj inflammable; **Feuerlöscher** (-s, -) m fire extinguisher; **Feuermelder** (-s, -) m fire alarm; **Feuertreppe** f fire escape; **Feuerwehr** (-, -en) f fire brigade; **Feuerwehrfrau** f firewoman, fire fighter; **Feuerwehrmann** m fireman, fire fighter; **Feuerwerk** nt fireworks pl; **Feuerzeug** nt (cigarette) lighter

Fichte (-, -n) f spruce

ficken vt, vi (vulg) to fuck

Fieber (-s, -) nt temperature, fever; **~ haben** to have a high temperature; **Fieberthermometer** nt thermometer

fiel imperf von **fallen**

fies adj (fam) nasty

Figur (-, -en) f figure; (im Schach) piece

Filet (-s, -s) nt fillet; **filetieren** vt to fillet; **Filetsteak** nt fillet steak

Filiale (-, -n) f (Comm) branch

Film (-(e)s, -e) m film, movie; **filmen** vt, vi to film

Filter (-s, -) m filter; **Filterkaffee** m filter coffee; **filtern** vt to filter; **Filterpapier** nt filter paper

Filz (-es, -e) m felt; **Filzschreiber** m, **Filzstift** m felt(-tip) pen, felt-tip

Finale (-s, -) nt (Sport) final

Finanzamt nt tax office; **finanziell** adj financial; **finanzieren** vt to finance

finden (fand, gefunden) vt to find; (meinen) to think; **ich finde nichts dabei, wenn ...** I don't see what's wrong if ...; **ich finde es gut/schlecht** I like/don't like it ▷ vr **es fanden sich nur wenige Helfer** there were only a few helpers

fing imperf von **fangen**

Finger (-s, -) m finger; **Fingerabdruck** m fingerprint; **Fingerhandschuh** m glove; **Fingernagel** m fingernail

Fink (-en, -en) m finch

Finne (-n, -n) m, **Finnin** f Finn, Finnish man/woman; **finnisch** adj Finnish; **Finnisch** nt Finnish; **Finnland** nt Finland

finster adj dark; (verdächtig) dubious; (verdrossen) grim; (Gedanke) dark; **Finsternis** f darkness

Firewall (-, -s) f (Inform) firewall

Firma (-, Firmen) f firm

Fisch (-(e)s, -e) m fish; **~e** pl (Astr) Pisces sing; **fischen** vt, vi to fish; **Fischer(in)** (-s, -) m(f) fisherman/-woman; **Fischerboot** nt fishing boat; **Fischgericht** nt fish dish; **Fischhändler(in)** m(f) fishmonger; **Fischstäbchen** nt fish finger (Brit) (o stick (US))

Fisole (-, -n) f French bean

fit adj fit; **Fitness** (-) f fitness; **Fitnesscenter** (-s, -) nt fitness centre

fix adj (schnell) quick; **~ und fertig** exhausted

fixen vi (fam) to shoot up; **Fixer(in)** (-s, -) m(f) (fam) junkie

FKK f abk = **Freikörperkultur** nudism; **FKK-Strand** m nudist beach

flach adj flat; (Gewässer, Teller) shallow; **~er Absatz** low heel; **Flachbildschirm** m flat screen

Fläche (-, -n) f area; (Oberfläche) surface

Flagge (-, -n) f flag

flambiert adj flambé(ed)

Flamme (-, -n) f flame

Flanell (-s) m flannel

Flasche (-, -n) f bottle; **eine ~ sein** (fam) to be useless; **Flaschenbier** nt bottled beer; **Flaschenöffner** m bottle opener; **Flaschenpfand** nt deposit; **Flaschentomate** f plum tomato

flatterhaft adj fickle; **flattern** vi to flutter

flauschig adj fluffy

Flausen pl (fam) daft ideas pl

Flaute (-, -n) f calm; (Comm) recession

Flechte (-, -n) f plait; (Med) scab; (Bot) lichen; **flechten** (flocht, geflochten) vt to plait; (Kranz) to bind

Fleck (-(e)s, -e) m, **Flecken** (-s, -) m spot; (Schmutz) stain; (Stoff~) patch; (Makel) blemish; **Fleckentferner** (-s, -) m stain remover; **fleckig** adj spotted; (mit Schmutzflecken) stained

Fledermaus f bat

Fleisch (-(e)s) nt flesh; (Essen) meat; **Fleischbrühe** f meat stock; **Fleischer(in)** (-s, -) m(f) butcher; **Fleischerei** f butcher's (shop); **Fleischtomate** f beef tomato

fleißig adj diligent, hard-working

flexibel adj flexible

flicken vt to mend; **Flickzeug** nt repair kit

Flieder (-s, -) m lilac

Fliege (-, -n) f fly; (Krawatte) bow tie

fliegen (flog, geflogen) vt, vi to fly

Fliese (-, -n) f tile

Fließband nt conveyor belt; (als Einrichtung) production (o assembly) line; **fließen** (floss, geflossen) vi to flow; **fließend** adj (Rede, Deutsch) fluent; (Übergänge) smooth; **~(es) Wasser** running water

Flipper (-s, -) m pinball machine; **flippern** vi to play pinball

flippig adj (fam) eccentric

flirten vi to flirt

Flitterwochen pl honeymoon sing

flocht imperf von **flechten**

Flocke (-, -n) f flake

flog imperf von **fliegen**

Floh (-(e)s, Flöhe) m flea; **Flohmarkt** m flea market

Flop (-s, -s) m flop

Floskei (-, -n) f empty phrase

floss imperf von **fließen**

Floß (-es, Flöße) nt raft

Flosse (-, -n) f fin; (Schwimmflosse) flipper

Flöte (-, -n) f flute; (Blockflöte) recorder

flott adj lively; (elegant) smart; (Naut) afloat

Fluch (-(e)s, Flüche) m curse; **fluchen** vi to swear, to curse

Flucht (-, -en) f flight; **flüchten** vi to flee (vor +dat from); **flüchtig** adj **ich kenne ihn nur ~** I don't know him very well at all; **Flüchtling** m refugee

Flug (-(e)s, Flüge) m flight; **Flugbegleiter(in)** (-s, -) m(f) flight attendant; **Flugblatt** nt leaflet

Flügel (-s, -) m wing; (Mus) grand piano

Fluggast m passenger (on a plane); **Fluggesellschaft** f airline; **Flughafen** m airport; **Fluglotse** m air-traffic controller; **Flugnummer** f flight number; **Flugplan** m flight schedule; **Flugplatz** m airport; (klein) airfield; **Flugschein** m plane ticket; **Flugschreiber** m flight recorder, black box; **Flugsteig** (-s, -e) m gate; **Flugstrecke** f air route; **Flugticket** nt plane ticket; **Flugverbindung** f flight connection; **Flugverkehr** m air traffic; **Flugzeit** f flying time; **Flugzeug** nt plane; **Flugzeugentführung** f hijacking

Flunder (-, -n) f flounder

Fluor (-s) nt fluorine

Flur (-(e)s, -e) m hall

Fluss (-es, Flüsse) m river; (Fließen) flow

flüssig adj liquid; **Flüssigkeit** f liquid

flüstern vt, vi to whisper

Flut (-, -en) f (a. fig) flood; (Gezeiten) high tide; **Flutlicht** nt floodlight

Fohlen (-s, -) nt foal

Föhn (-(e)s, -e) m hairdryer; (Wind) foehn; **föhnen** vt to dry; (beim Friseur) to blow-dry

Folge (-, -n) f (Reihe, Serie) series sing; (Aufeinanderfolge) sequence; (Fortsetzung eines Romans) instalment; (Fortsetzung einer Fernsehserie) episode; (Auswirkung) result; **etw zur ~ haben** to result in sth; **~n haben** to have consequences; **folgen** vi to follow (jdm sb); (gehorchen) to obey (jdm sb); **jdm ~ können** (fig) to be able to follow sb; **folgend** adj following; **folgendermaßen** adv as follows; **folglich** adv consequently

Folie f foil; (für Projektor) transparency

Fön® m siehe **Föhn**

Fondue (-s, -s) nt fondue

fönen vt siehe **föhnen**

fordern vt to demand

fördern vt to promote; (unterstützen) to help

Forderung f demand

Forelle f trout

Form (-, -en) f form; (Gestalt) shape; (Gussform) mould; (Backform) baking tin (Brit) (o pan (US)); **in ~ sein** to be in good form; **Formalität** f formality; **Format** nt format; **von internationalem ~** of international standing; **formatieren** vt (Diskette) to format; (Text) to edit

Formblatt nt form; **formen** vt to form, to shape; **förmlich** adj formal; (buchstäblich) real; **formlos** adj informal; **Formular** (-s, -e) nt form; **formulieren** vt to formulate

forschen vi to search (nach for); (wissenschaftlich) to (do) research; **Forscher(in)** m(f) researcher; **Forschung** f research

Förster(in) (-s, -) m(f) forester; (für Wild) gamekeeper

fort adv away; (verschwunden) gone; **fort|bewegen** vt to move away ▷ vr **sich ~** to move; **Fortbildung** f further

education; (*im Beruf*) further training;
fort|fahren *irr vi* to go away;
(*weitermachen*) to continue; **fort|gehen** *irr*
vi to go away; **fortgeschritten** *adj*
advanced; **Fortpflanzung** *f* reproduction
Fortschritt *m* progress; **~e machen** to
make progress; **fortschrittlich** *adj*
progressive
fort|setzen *vt* to continue; **Fortsetzung**
f continuation; (*folgender Teil*) instalment;
~ folgt to be continued
Foto (*-s, -s*) *nt* photo ▷ (*-s, -s*) *m*
(*Fotoapparat*) camera; **Fotograf(in)** (*-en,
-en*) *m(f)* photographer; **Fotografie** *f*
photography; (*Bild*) photograph;
fotografieren *vt* to photograph ▷ *vi* to
take photographs; **Fotokopie** *f*
photocopy; **fotokopieren** *vt* to
photocopy
Foul (*-s, -s*) *nt* foul
Foyer (*-s, -s*) *nt* foyer
Fr. *f abk=***Frau** Mrs; (*unverheiratet, neutral*) Ms
Fracht (*-, -en*) *f* freight; (*Naut*) cargo; (*Preis*)
carriage; **Frachter** (*-s, -*) *m* freighter
Frack (*-(e)s, Fräcke*) *m* tails *pl*
Frage (*-, -n*) *f* question; **das ist eine ~ der
Zeit** that's a matter (*o* question) of time;
das kommt nicht in ~ that's out of the
question; **Fragebogen** *m* questionnaire;
fragen *vt, vi* to ask; **Fragezeichen** *nt*
question mark; **fragwürdig** *adj* dubious
Franken (*-s, -*) *m* (*Schweizer Währung*)
Swiss franc ▷ (*-s*) *nt* (*Land*) Franconia
frankieren *vt* to stamp; (*maschinell*) to
frank
Frankreich (*-s*) *nt* France; **Franzose** (*-n,
-n*) *m*, **Französin** *f* Frenchman/-woman;
die ~n *pl* the French *pl*; **französisch** *adj*
French; **Französisch** *nt* French
fraß *imperf von* **fressen**
Frau (*-, -en*) *f* woman; (*Ehefrau*) wife;
(*Anrede*) Mrs; (*unverheiratet, neutral*) Ms;
Frauenarzt *m*, **Frauenärztin** *f*
gynaecologist; **Frauenbewegung** *f*
women's movement; **frauenfeindlich** *adj*
misogynous; **Frauenhaus** *nt* refuge (for
battered women)
Fräulein *nt* (*junge Dame*) young lady;
(*veraltet als Anrede*) Miss
Freak (*-s, -s*) *m* (*fam*) freak
frech *adj* cheeky; **Frechheit** *f* cheek; **so
eine ~!** what a cheek
Freeclimbing (*-s*) *nt* free climbing

frei *adj* free; (*Straße*) clear; (*Mitarbeiter*)
freelance; **ein ~er Tag** a day off; **~e
Arbeitsstelle** vacancy; **Zimmer ~** room(s)
to let (*Brit*), room(s) for rent (*US*); **im
Freien** in the open air; **Freibad** *nt*
open-air (swimming) pool; **freiberuflich**
adj freelance; **freig(i)ebig** *adj* generous;
Freiheit *f* freedom; **Freikarte** *f* free
ticket; **frei|lassen** *irr vt* to (set) free
freilich *adv* of course
Freilichtbühne *f* open-air theatre;
frei|machen *vr* **sich ~** to undress;
frei|nehmen *irr vt* **sich** (*dat*) **einen
Tag ~** to take a day off; **Freisprechanlage**
f hands-free phone; **Freistoß** *m* free
kick
Freitag *m* Friday; *siehe auch* **Mittwoch**;
freitags *adv* on Fridays; *siehe auch*
mittwochs
freiwillig *adj* voluntary
Freizeichen *nt* (*Tel*) ringing tone
Freizeit *f* spare (*o* free) time;
Freizeithemd *nt* sports shirt;
Freizeitkleidung *f* leisure wear;
Freizeitpark *m* leisure park
fremd *adj* (*nicht vertraut*) strange;
(*ausländisch*) foreign; (*nicht eigen*) someone
else's; **Fremde(r)** *mf* (*Unbekannter*)
stranger; (*Ausländer*) foreigner;
fremdenfeindlich *adj* anti-foreigner,
xenophobic; **Fremdenführer(in)** *m(f)*
(tourist) guide; **Fremdenverkehr** *m*
tourism; **Fremdenverkehrsamt** *nt*
tourist information office;
Fremdenzimmer *nt* (guest) room;
Fremdsprache *f* foreign language;
Fremdsprachenkenntnisse *pl*
knowledge *sing* of foreign languages;
Fremdwort *nt* foreign word
Frequenz *f* (*Radio*) frequency
fressen (*fraß, gefressen*) *vt, vi* (*Tier*) to eat;
(*Mensch*) to guzzle
Freude (*-, -n*) *f* joy, delight; **freuen** *vt* to
please; **es freut mich, dass ...** I'm pleased
that ... ▷ *vr* **sich ~** to be pleased (*über +akk*
about); **sich auf etw** (*akk*) **~** to look
forward to sth
Freund (*-(e)s, -e*) *m* friend; (*in Beziehung*)
boyfriend; **Freundin** *f* friend; (*in
Beziehung*) girlfriend; **freundlich** *adj*
friendly; (*liebenswürdig*) kind;
freundlicherweise *adv* kindly;
Freundlichkeit *f* friendliness;

(*Liebenswürdigkeit*) kindness;
Freundschaft f friendship
Frieden (-s, -) m peace; **Friedhof** m
cemetery; **friedlich** adj peaceful
frieren (*fror, gefroren*) vt, vi to freeze; **ich
friere, es friert mich** I'm freezing
Frikadelle f rissole
Frisbeescheibe® f frisbee®
frisch adj fresh; (*lebhaft*) lively;
„~ gestrichen" 'wet paint'; **sich ~ machen**
to freshen up; **Frischhaltefolie** f
clingfilm® (*Brit*), plastic wrap (*US*);
Frischkäse m cream cheese
Friseur m, **Friseuse** f hairdresser;
frisieren vt jdn ~ to do sb's hair ▷ vr **sich
~** to do one's hair; **Frisör** (-s, -e) m,
Frisöse (-, -n) f hairdresser
Frist (-, -en) f period; (*Zeitpunkt*) deadline;
**innerhalb einer ~ von zehn
Tagen** within a ten-day period; **eine
~ einhalten** to meet a deadline; **die ~ ist
abgelaufen** the deadline has expired;
fristgerecht adj, adv within the specified
time; **fristlos** adj **~e Entlassung**
dismissal without notice
Frisur f hairdo, hairstyle
frittieren vt to deep-fry
Frl. f abk = **Fräulein** Miss
froh adj happy; **~e Weihnachten!** Merry
Christmas
fröhlich adj happy, cheerful
Fronleichnam (-(e)s) m Corpus Christi
frontal adj frontal;
Frontalzusammenstoß m head-on
collision
fror imperf von **frieren**
Frosch (-(e)s, Frösche) m frog
Frost (-(e)s, Fröste) m frost; **bei ~** in frosty
weather; **Frostschutzmittel** nt
anti-freeze
Frottee nt terry(cloth); **frottieren** vt
to rub down; **Frottier(hand)tuch** nt
towel
Frucht (-, Früchte) f (a. fig) fruit; (*Getreide*)
corn; **Fruchteis** nt fruit-flavoured
ice-cream; **Früchtetee** m fruit tea;
fruchtig adj fruity; **Fruchtpresse** f
juicer; **Fruchtsaft** m fruit juice;
Fruchtsalat m fruit salad
früh adj, adv early; **heute ~** this morning;
um fünf Uhr ~ at five (o'clock) in the
morning; **~ genug** soon enough; **früher**
adj earlier; (*ehemalig*) former ▷ adv

formerly, in the past; **frühestens** adv at
the earliest
Frühjahr nt, **Frühling** m spring;
Frühlingsrolle f spring roll;
Frühlingszwiebel f spring onion (*Brit*),
scallion (*US*)
frühmorgens adv early in the morning
Frühschicht f **~ haben** to be on the early
shift
Frühstück nt breakfast; **frühstücken** vi
to have breakfast; **Frühstücksbüfett** nt
breakfast buffet; **Frühstücksfernsehen**
nt breakfast television; **Frühstücksspeck**
m bacon
frühzeitig adj early
Frust (-s) m (*fam*) frustration; **frustrieren**
vt to frustrate
Fuchs (-es, Füchse) m fox
fühlen vt, vi to feel ▷ vr **sich ~** to feel
fuhr imperf von **fahren**
führen vt to lead; (*Geschäft*) to run; (*Name*)
to bear; (*Buch*) to keep ▷ vi to lead, to be
in the lead ▷ vr **sich ~** to behave;
Führerschein m driving licence (*Brit*),
driver's license (*US*); **Führung** f
leadership; (*eines Unternehmens*)
management; (*Mil*) command; (*in Museum,
Stadt*) guided tour; **in ~ liegen** to be in the
lead
füllen vt to fill; (*Gastr*) to stuff ▷ vr **sich
~** to fill
Füller (-s, -) m, **Füllfederhalter** (-s, -) m
fountain pen
Füllung f filling
Fund (-(e)s, -e) m find; **Fundbüro** nt lost
property office (*Brit*), lost and found (*US*);
Fundsachen pl lost property sing
fünf num five; **Fünf** (-, -en) f five;
(*Schulnote*) = E; **fünfhundert** num five
hundred; **fünfmal** adv five times;
fünfte(r, s) adj fifth; siehe auch **dritte**;
Fünftel (-s, -) nt (*Bruchteil*) fifth; **fünfzehn**
num fifteen; **fünfzehnte(r, s)** adj
fifteenth; siehe auch **dritte**; **fünfzig** num
fifty; **fünfzigste(r, s)** adj fiftieth
Funk (-s) m radio; **über ~** by radio
Funke (-ns, -n) m spark; **funkeln** vi to
sparkle
Funkgerät nt radio set; **Funktaxi** nt
radio taxi, radio cab
Funktion f function; **funktionieren** vi to
work, to function; **Funktionstaste** f
(*Inform*) function key

für *prep +akk* for; **was ~ (ein) ...?** what kind
(o sort) of ...?; **Tag ~ Tag** day after day

Furcht (-) *f* fear; **furchtbar** *adj* terrible;
fürchten *vt* to be afraid of, to fear ▷ *vr*
sich ~ to be afraid (vor +dat of);
fürchterlich *adj* awful

füreinander *adv* for each other

fürs *kontr von* **für das**

Fürst(in) (-en, -en) *m(f)* prince/princess;
Fürstentum *nt* principality; **fürstlich** *adj*
(*fig*) splendid

Furunkel (-s, -) *nt* boil

Furz (-es, -e) *m* (*vulg*) fart; **furzen** *vi* (*vulg*)
to fart

Fuß (-es, Füße) *m* foot; (von Glas, Säule etc)
base; (von Möbel) leg; **zu ~** on foot; **zu
~ gehen** to walk; **Fußball** *m* football (*Brit*),
soccer; **Fußballmannschaft** *f* football
(*Brit*) (o soccer) team; **Fußballplatz** *m*
football pitch (*Brit*), soccer field (*US*);
Fußballspiel *nt* football (*Brit*) (o soccer)
match; **Fußballspieler(in)** *m(f)*
footballer (*Brit*), soccer player; **Fußboden**
m floor; **Fußgänger(in)** (-s, -) *m(f)*
pedestrian; **Fußgängerüberweg** *m*
pedestrian crossing (*Brit*), crosswalk (*US*);
Fußgängerzone *f* pedestrian precinct
(*Brit*) (o zone (*US*)); **Fußgelenk** *nt* ankle;
Fußpilz *m* athlete's foot; **Fußtritt** *m*
kick; **jdm einen ~ geben** to give sb a kick,
to kick sb; **Fußweg** *m* footpath

Futon (-s, -s) *m* futon

futsch *adj* (*fam: kaputt*) broken;
(zerschlagen) smashed; (weg, verloren) gone

Futter (-s, -) *nt* feed; (Heu etc) fodder;
(Stoff) lining; **füttern** *vt* to feed; (Kleidung)
to line

Futur (-s, -e) *nt* (*Ling*) future (tense)

Fuzzi (-s, -s) *m* (*fam*) guy

g

gab imperf von **geben**

Gabe (-, -n) f gift

Gabel (-, -n) f fork; **Gabelung** f fork

gaffen vi to gape

Gage (-, -n) f fee

gähnen vi to yawn

Galerie f gallery

Galle (-, -n) f gall; (Organ) gall bladder; **Gallenstein** m gallstone

Galopp (-s) m gallop; **galoppieren** vi to gallop

galt imperf von **gelten**

Gameboy® (-s, -s) m Gameboy®

gammeln vi to loaf (o hang) around; **Gammler(in)** (-s, -) m(f) layabout

gang adj ~ **und gäbe sein** to be quite normal

Gang (-(e)s, Gänge) m walk; (im Flugzeug) aisle; (Essen, Ablauf) course; (Flur etc) corridor; (Durchgang) passage; (Auto) gear; **den zweiten ~ einlegen** to change into second (gear); **etw in ~ bringen** to get sth going; **Gangschaltung** f gears pl; **Gangway** (-, -s) f (Aviat) steps pl; (Naut) gangway

Gans (-, Gänse) f goose; **Gänseblümchen** nt daisy; **Gänsehaut** f goose pimples pl (Brit), goose bumps pl (US)

ganz adj whole; (vollständig) complete; ~ **Europa** all of Europe; **sein ~es Geld** all his money; **den ~en Tag** all day; **die ~e Zeit** all the time ▷ adv quite; (völlig) completely; **es hat mir ~ gut gefallen** I quite liked it; ~ **schön viel** quite a lot; ~ **und gar nicht** not at all; **das ist etwas ~ anderes** that's a completely different matter; **ganztägig** adj all-day; (Arbeit, Stelle) full-time

gar adj done, cooked ▷ adv at all; ~ **nicht/nichts/keiner** not/nothing/nobody at all; ~ **nicht schlecht** not bad at all

Garage (-, -n) f garage

Garantie f guarantee; **garantieren** vt to guarantee

Garderobe (-, -n) f (Kleidung) wardrobe; (Abgabe) cloakroom

Gardine f curtain

Garn (-(e)s, -e) nt thread

Garnele (-, -n) f shrimp

garnieren vt to decorate; (Speisen) to garnish

Garten (-s, Gärten) m garden; **Gärtner(in)** (-s, -) m(f) gardener; **Gärtnerei** f nursery; (Gemüsegärtnerei) market garden (Brit), truck farm (US)

Garzeit f cooking time

Gas (-es, -e) nt gas; ~ **geben** (Auto) to accelerate; (fig) to get a move on; **Gasanzünder** m gas lighter; **Gasbrenner** m gas burner; **Gasflasche** f gas bottle; **Gasheizung** f gas heating; **Gasherd** m gas stove, gas cooker (Brit); **Gaskocher** m camping stove; **Gaspedal** nt accelerator, gas pedal (US)

Gasse (-, -n) f alley

Gast (-es, Gäste) m guest; **Gäste haben** to have guests; **Gastarbeiter(in)** m(f) foreign worker; **Gästebett** nt spare bed; **Gästebuch** nt visitors' book; **Gästehaus** nt guest house; **Gästezimmer** nt guest room; **gastfreundlich** adj hospitable; **Gastgeber(in)** (-s, -) m(f) host/hostess; **Gasthaus** nt, **Gasthof** m inn; **Gastland** nt host country

Gastritis (-) f gastritis

Gastronomie f (Gewerbe) catering trade

Gastspiel nt (Sport) away game; **Gaststätte** f restaurant; (Trinklokal) pub

(Brit), bar; **Gastwirt(in)** m(f) landlord/
-lady

GAU (-s, -s) m akr = **größter anzunehmender Unfall** MCA

Gaumen (-s, -) m palate

Gaze (-, -n) f gauze

geb. adj abk = **geboren** b. ▷ adj abk = **geborene** née; siehe **geboren**

Gebäck (-(e)s, -e) nt pastries pl; (Kekse) biscuits pl (Brit), cookies pl (US)

gebacken pp von **backen**

Gebärdensprache f sign language

Gebärmutter f womb

Gebäude (-s, -) nt building

geben (gab, gegeben) vt, vi to give (jdm etw sb sth, sth to sb); (Karten) to deal; **lass dir eine Quittung ~** ask for a receipt ▷ vt impers **es gibt** there is/are; (in Zukunft) there will be; **das gibt's nicht** I don't believe it ▷ vr **sich ~** (sich verhalten) to behave, to act; **das gibt sich wieder** it'll sort itself out

Gebet (-(e)s, -e) nt prayer

gebeten pp von **bitten**

Gebiet (-(e)s, -e) nt area; (Hoheitsgebiet) territory; (fig) field

gebildet adj educated; (belesen) well-read

Gebirge (-s, -) nt mountains pl; **gebirgig** adj mountainous

Gebiss (-es, -e) nt teeth pl; (künstlich) dentures pl; **gebissen** pp von **beißen**; **Gebissreiniger** m denture tablets pl

Gebläse (-s, -) nt fan, blower

geblasen pp von **blasen**

geblieben pp von **bleiben**

gebogen pp von **biegen**

geboren pp von **gebären** ▷ adj born; **Andrea Jordan, ~e Christian** Andrea Jordan, née Christian

geborgen pp von **bergen** ▷ adj secure, safe

geboten pp von **bieten**

gebracht pp von **bringen**

gebrannt pp von **brennen**

gebraten pp von **braten**

gebrauchen vt to use; **Gebrauchsanweisung** f directions pl for use; **gebrauchsfertig** adj ready to use; **gebraucht** adj used; **etw ~ kaufen** to buy sth secondhand; **Gebrauchtwagen** m secondhand (o used) car

gebräunt adj tanned

gebrochen pp von **brechen**

Gebühr (-, -en) f charge; (Maut) toll; (Honorar) fee; **Gebühreneinheit** f (Tel) unit; **gebührenfrei** adj free of charge; (Telefonnummer) freefone® (Brit), toll-free (US); **gebührenpflichtig** adj subject to charges; **~e Straße** toll road

gebunden pp von **binden**

Geburt (-, -en) f birth; **gebürtig** adj **er ist ~er Schweizer** he is Swiss by birth; **Geburtsdatum** nt date of birth; **Geburtsjahr** nt year of birth; **Geburtsname** m birth name; (einer Frau) maiden name; **Geburtsort** m birthplace; **Geburtstag** m birthday; **herzlichen Glückwunsch zum ~!** Happy Birthday; **Geburtsurkunde** f birth certificate

Gebüsch (-(e)s, -e) nt bushes pl

gedacht pp von **denken**

Gedächtnis nt memory; **im ~ behalten** to remember

Gedanke (-ns, -n) m thought; **sich** (dat) **über etw** (akk) **~n machen** to think about sth; (besorgt) to be worried about sth; **Gedankenstrich** m dash

Gedeck (-(e)s, -e) nt place setting; (Speisenfolge) set meal

Gedenkstätte f memorial; **Gedenktafel** f commemorative plaque

Gedicht (-(e)s, -e) nt poem

Gedränge (-s) nt crush, crowd

gedrungen pp von **dringen**

Geduld (-) f patience; **geduldig** adj patient

gedurft pp von **dürfen**

geehrt adj **Sehr ~er Herr Young** Dear Mr Young

geeignet adj suitable

Gefahr (-, -en) f danger; **auf eigene ~** at one's own risk; **außer ~** out of danger; **gefährden** vt to endanger

gefahren pp von **fahren**

gefährlich adj dangerous

Gefälle (-s, -) nt gradient, slope

gefallen pp von **fallen** ▷ irr vi **jdm ~** to please sb; **er/es gefällt mir** I like him/it; **sich** (dat) **etw ~ lassen** to put up with sth

Gefallen (-s, -) m favour; **jdm einen ~ tun** to do sb a favour

gefälligst adv ..., will you!; **sei ~ still!** be quiet, will you!

gefangen pp von **fangen**

Gefängnis nt prison

Gefäß (-es, -e) nt (Behälter) container, receptacle; (Anat, Bot) vessel

gefasst adj composed, calm; **auf etw (akk) ~ sein** to be prepared (o ready) for sth

geflochten pp von **flechten**

geflogen pp von **fliegen**

geflossen pp von **fließen**

Geflügel (-s) nt poultry

gefragt adj in demand

gefressen pp von **fressen**

Gefrierbeutel m freezer bag; **gefrieren** irr vi to freeze; **Gefrierfach** nt freezer compartment; **Gefrierschrank** m (upright) freezer; **Gefriertruhe** f (chest) freezer

gefroren pp von **frieren**

Gefühl (-(e)s, -e) nt feeling

gefunden pp von **finden**

gegangen pp von **gehen**

gegeben pp von **geben**; **gegebenenfalls** adv if need be

⊙ SCHLÜSSELWORT

gegen präp +akk **1** against; **nichts gegen jdn haben** to have nothing against sb; **X gegen Y** (Sport, Jur) X versus Y; **ein Mittel gegen Schnupfen** something for colds

2 (in Richtung auf) towards; **gegen Osten** to(wards) the east; **gegen Abend** towards evening; **gegen einen Baum fahren** to drive into a tree

3 (ungefähr) round about; **gegen 3 Uhr** around 3 o'clock

4 (gegenüber) towards (ungefähr) around; **gerecht gegen alle** fair to all

5 (im Austausch für) for; **gegen bar** for cash; **gegen Quittung** against a receipt

6 (verglichen mit) compared with

Gegend (-, -en) f area; **hier in der ~** around here

gegeneinander adv against one another

Gegenfahrbahn f opposite lane; **Gegenmittel** nt remedy (gegen for); **Gegenrichtung** f opposite direction; **Gegensatz** m contrast; **im ~ zu** in contrast to; **gegensätzlich** adj conflicting; **gegenseitig** adj mutual; **sich ~ helfen** to help each other

Gegenstand m object; (Thema) subject

Gegenteil nt opposite; **im ~** on the contrary; **gegenteilig** adj opposite, contrary

gegenüber prep +dat opposite; (zu jdm) to(wards); (angesichts) in the face of ▷ adv opposite; **gegenüber|stehen** vt to face; (Problemen) to be faced with; **gegenüber|stellen** vt to confront (dat with); (fig) compare (dat with)

Gegenverkehr m oncoming traffic; **Gegenwart** (-) f present (tense)

Gegenwind m headwind

gegessen pp von **essen**

geglichen pp von **gleichen**

geglitten pp von **gleiten**

Gegner(in) (-s, -) m(f) opponent

gegolten pp von **gelten**

gegossen pp von **gießen**

gegraben pp von **graben**

gegriffen pp von **greifen**

gehabt pp von **haben**

Gehackte(s) nt mince(d meat) (Brit), ground meat (US)

Gehalt (-(e)s, -e) m content ▷ (-(e)s, Gehälter) nt salary

gehalten pp von **halten**

gehangen pp von **hängen**

gehässig adj spiteful, nasty

gehauen pp von **hauen**

gehbehindert adj **sie ist ~** she can't walk properly

geheim adj secret; **etw ~ halten** to keep sth secret; **Geheimnis** nt secret; (rätselhaft) mystery; **geheimnisvoll** adj mysterious; **Geheimnummer** f, **Geheimzahl** f (von Kreditkarte) PIN number

geheißen pp von **heißen**

gehen (ging, gegangen) vt, vi to go; (zu Fuß) to walk; (funktionieren) to work; **über die Straße ~** to cross the street; **~ nach** (Fenster) to face

▷ vi impers **wie geht es (dir)?** how are you (o things)?; **mir/ihm geht es gut** I'm/he's (doing) fine; **geht das?** is that possible?; **geht's noch?** can you still manage?; **es geht** not too bad, OK; **das geht nicht** that's not on; **es geht um ...** it's about ...

Gehirn (-(e)s, -e) nt brain; **Gehirnerschütterung** f concussion

gehoben pp von **heben**

geholfen pp von **helfen**

Gehör (-(e)s) nt hearing

gehorchen vi to obey (jdm sb)

gehören vi to belong (jdm to sb); **wem gehört das Buch?** whose book is this?; **gehört es dir?** is it yours? ▷ vr impers **das gehört sich nicht** it's not done

gehörlos adj deaf

gehorsam adj obedient

Gehsteig m

Gehweg (-(e)s, -e) m pavement (Brit), sidewalk (US)

Geier (-s, -) m vulture

Geige (-, -n) f violin

geil adj randy (Brit), horny (US); (fam: toll) fantastic

Geisel (-, -n) f hostage

Geist (-(e)s, -er) m spirit; (Gespenst) ghost; (Verstand) mind; **Geisterbahn** f ghost train, tunnel of horror (US); **Geisterfahrer(in)** m(f) person driving the wrong way on the motorway

geizig adj stingy

gekannt pp von **kennen**

geklungen pp von **klingen**

geknickt adj (fig) dejected

gekniffen pp von **kneifen**

gekommen pp von **kommen**

gekonnt pp von **können** ▷ adj skilful

gekrochen pp von **kriechen**

Gel (-s, -s) nt gel

Gelächter (-s, -) nt laughter

geladen pp von **laden** ▷ adj loaded; (Elek) live; (fig) furious

gelähmt adj paralysed

Gelände (-s, -) nt land, terrain; (Fabrik, Sportgelände) grounds pl; (Baugelände) site

Geländer (-s, -) nt railing; (Treppengeländer) banister

Geländewagen m off-road vehicle

gelang imperf von **gelingen**

gelassen pp von **lassen** ▷ adj calm, composed

Gelatine f gelatine

gelaufen pp von **laufen**

gelaunt adj **gut/schlecht ~** in a good/bad mood

gelb adj yellow; (Ampel) amber, yellow (US); **gelblich** adj yellowish; **Gelbsucht** f jaundice

Geld (-(e)s, -er) nt money; **Geldautomat** m cash machine (o dispenser (Brit)), ATM (US); **Geldbeutel** m, **Geldbörse** f purse;

Geldbuße f fine; **Geldschein** m (bank)note (Brit), bill (US); **Geldstrafe** f fine; **Geldstück** nt coin; **Geldwechsel** m exchange of money; (Ort) bureau de change; **Geldwechselautomat** m, **Geldwechsler** (-s, -) m change machine

Gelee (-s, -s) nt jelly

gelegen pp von **liegen** ▷ adj situated; (passend) convenient; **etw kommt jdm ~** sth is convenient for sb

Gelegenheit f opportunity; (Anlass) occasion

gelegentlich adj occasional ▷ adv occasionally; (bei Gelegenheit) some time (or other)

Gelenk (-(e)s, -e) nt joint

gelernt adj skilled

gelesen pp von **lesen**

geliehen pp von **leihen**

gelingen (gelang, gelungen) vi to succeed; **es ist mir gelungen, ihn zu erreichen** I managed to get hold of him

gelitten pp von **leiden**

gelockt adj curly

gelogen pp von **lügen**

gelten (galt, gegolten) vt (wert sein) to be worth; **jdm viel/wenig ~** to mean a lot/not to mean much to sb ▷ vi (gültig sein) to be valid; (erlaubt sein) to be allowed; **jdm ~** (gemünzt sein auf) to be meant for (o aimed at) sb; **etw ~ lassen** to accept sth; **als etw ~** to be considered to be sth; **Geltungsdauer** f **eine ~ von fünf Tagen haben** to be valid for five days

gelungen pp von **gelingen**

gemahlen pp von **mahlen**

Gemälde (-s, -) nt painting, picture

gemäß prep +dat in accordance with ▷ adj appropriate (dat to)

gemein adj (niederträchtig) mean, nasty; (gewöhnlich) common

Gemeinde (-, -n) f district, community; (Pfarrgemeinde) parish; (Kirchengemeinde) congregation

gemeinsam adj joint, common ▷ adv together, jointly; **das Haus gehört uns beiden ~** the house belongs to both of us

Gemeinschaft f community; **~ Unabhängiger Staaten** Commonwealth of Independent States

gemeint pp von **meinen**; **das war nicht so ~** I didn't mean it like that

gemessen pp von **messen**

gemieden pp von **meiden**

gemischt adj mixed

gemocht pp von **mögen**

Gemüse (-s, -) nt vegetables pl; **Gemüsehändler(in)** m(f) greengrocer

gemusst pp von **müssen**

gemustert adj patterned

gemütlich adj comfortable, cosy; (Mensch) good-natured, easy-going; **mach es dir ~** make yourself at home

genannt pp von **nennen**

genau adj exact, precise ▷ adv exactly, precisely; **~ in der Mitte** right in the middle; **es mit etw ~ nehmen** to be particular about sth; **~ genommen** strictly speaking; **ich weiß es ~** I know for certain (o for sure); **genauso** adv exactly the same (way); **~ gut/viel/viele Leute** just as well/much/many people (wie as)

genehmigen vt to approve; **sich** (dat) **etw ~** to indulge in sth; **Genehmigung** f approval

Generalkonsulat nt consulate general

Generation f generation

Genf (-s) nt Geneva; **~er See** Lake Geneva

genial adj brilliant

Genick (-(e)s, -e) nt (back of the) neck

Genie (-s, -s) nt genius

genieren vr **sich ~** to feel awkward; **ich geniere mich vor ihm** he makes me feel embarrassed

genießen (genoss, genossen) vt to enjoy

Genitiv m genitive (case)

genommen pp von **nehmen**

genoss imperf von **genießen**

genossen pp von **genießen**

genug adv enough

genügen vi to be enough (jdm for sb); **danke, das genügt** thanks, that's enough (o that will do)

Genuss (-es, Genüsse) m pleasure; (Zusichnehmen) consumption

geöffnet adj (Geschäft etc) open

Geografie f geography

Geologie f geology

Georgien (-s) nt Georgia

Gepäck (-(e)s) nt luggage (Brit), baggage; **Gepäckabfertigung** f luggage (Brit) (o baggage) check-in; **Gepäckablage** f luggage (Brit) (o baggage) rack; **Gepäckannahme** f (zur Beförderung) luggage (Brit) (o baggage) office; (zur Aufbewahrung) left-luggage office (Brit), baggage checkroom (US); **Gepäckaufbewahrung** f left-luggage office (Brit), baggage checkroom (US); **Gepäckausgabe** f luggage (Brit) (o baggage) office; (am Flughafen) baggage reclaim; **Gepäckband** nt luggage (Brit) (o baggage) conveyor; **Gepäckkontrolle** f luggage (Brit) (o baggage) check; **Gepäckstück** nt item of luggage (Brit) (o baggage (US)); **Gepäckträger** m porter; (an Fahrrad) carrier; **Gepäckversicherung** f luggage (Brit) (o baggage) insurance; **Gepäckwagen** m luggage van (Brit), baggage car (US)

gepfiffen pp von **pfeifen**

gepflegt adj well-groomed; (Park) well looked after

gequollen pp von **quellen**

⬤ SCHLÜSSELWORT

gerade adj straight (aufrecht) upright; **eine gerade Zahl** an even number ▷ adv **1** (genau) just exactly; (speziell) especially; **gerade deshalb** that's just od exactly why; **das ist es ja gerade!** that's just it!; **gerade du** you especially; **warum gerade ich?** why me (of all people)?; **jetzt gerade nicht!** not now!; **gerade neben** right next to

2 (eben, soeben) just; **er wollte gerade aufstehen** he was just about to get up; **gerade erst** only just; **gerade noch** (only) just

gerannt pp von **rennen**

geraspelt adj grated

Gerät (-(e)s, -e) nt device, gadget; (Werkzeug) tool; (Radio, Fernseher) set; (Zubehör) equipment

geraten pp von **raten** ▷ irr vi to turn out; **gut/schlecht ~** to turn out well/badly; **an jdn ~** to come across sb; **in etw** (akk) **~** to get into sth

geräuchert adj smoked

geräumig adj roomy

Geräusch (-(e)s, -e) nt sound; (unangenehm) noise

gerecht adj fair; (Strafe, Belohnung) just; **jdm/einer Sache ~ werden** to do justice to sb/sth

gereizt adj irritable

Gericht (-(e)s, -e) nt (Jur) court; (Essen) dish

gerieben pp von **reiben**

gering adj small; (unbedeutend) slight; (niedrig) low; (Zeit) short; **geringfügig** adj slight, minor ▷ adv slightly

gerissen pp von **reißen**

geritten pp von **reiten**

gern(e) adv willingly, gladly; **~ haben, ~ mögen** to like; **etw ~ tun** to like doing sth; **~ geschehen** you're welcome

gerochen pp von **riechen**

Gerste (-, -n) f barley; **Gerstenkorn** nt (im Auge) stye

Geruch (-(e)s, Gerüche) m smell

Gerücht (-(e)s, -e) nt rumour

gerufen pp von **rufen**

Gerümpel (-s) nt junk

gerungen pp von **ringen**

Gerüst (-(e)s, -e) nt (auf Bau) scaffolding; (Gestell) trestle; (fig) framework (zu of)

gesalzen pp von **salzen**

gesamt adj whole, entire; (Kosten) total; (Werke) complete; **Gesamtschule** f = comprehensive school

gesandt pp von **senden**

Gesäß (-es, -e) nt bottom

geschaffen pp von **schaffen**

Geschäft (-(e)s, -e) nt business; (Laden) shop; (Geschäftsabschluss) deal; **geschäftlich** adj commercial ▷ adv on business; **Geschäftsfrau** f businesswoman; **Geschäftsführer(in)** m(f) managing director; (von Laden) manager; **Geschäftsmann** m businessman; **Geschäftsreise** f business trip; **Geschäftsstraße** f shopping street; **Geschäftszeiten** pl business (o opening) hours pl

geschehen (geschah, geschehen) vi to happen

Geschenk (-(e)s, -e) nt present, gift; **Geschenkgutschein** m gift voucher; **Geschenkpapier** nt gift-wrapping paper, giftwrap

Geschichte (-, -n) f story; (Sache) affair; (Hist) history

geschickt adj skilful

geschieden pp von **scheiden** ▷ adj divorced

geschienen pp von **scheinen**

Geschirr (-(e)s, -e) nt crockery; (zum Kochen) pots and pans pl; (von Pferd) harness; **~ spülen** to do (o wash) the dishes, to do the washing-up (Brit); **Geschirrspülmaschine** f dishwasher; **Geschirrspülmittel** nt washing-up liquid (Brit), dishwashing liquid (US); **Geschirrtuch** nt tea towel (Brit), dish towel (US)

geschissen pp von **scheißen**

geschlafen pp von **schlafen**

geschlagen pp von **schlagen**

Geschlecht (-(e)s, -er) nt sex; (Ling) gender; **Geschlechtskrankheit** f sexually transmitted disease, STD; **Geschlechtsorgan** nt sexual organ; **Geschlechtsverkehr** m sexual intercourse

geschlichen pp von **schleichen**

geschliffen pp von **schleifen**

geschlossen adj closed

Geschmack (-(e)s, Geschmäcke) m taste; **geschmacklos** adj tasteless; **Geschmack(s)sache** f das ist **~** that's a matter of taste; **geschmackvoll** adj tasteful

geschmissen pp von **schmeißen**

geschmolzen pp von **schmelzen**

geschnitten pp von **schneiden**

geschoben pp von **schieben**

Geschoss (-es, -e) nt (Stockwerk) floor

geschossen pp von **schießen**

Geschrei (-s) nt cries pl; (fig) fuss

geschrieben pp von **schreiben**

geschrie(e)n pp von **schreien**

geschützt adj protected

Geschwätz (-es) nt chatter; (Klatsch) gossip; **geschwätzig** adj talkative, gossipy

geschweige adv **~ (denn)** let alone

geschwiegen pp von **schweigen**

Geschwindigkeit f speed; (Phys) velocity; **Geschwindigkeitsbegrenzung** f speed limit

Geschwister (-s) pl brothers and sisters pl

geschwollen adj (angeschwollen) swollen; (Rede) pompous

geschwommen pp von **schwimmen**

geschworen pp von **schwören**

Geschwulst (-, Geschwülste) f growth

Geschwür (-(e)s, -e) nt ulcer

gesehen pp von **sehen**

gesellig adj sociable; **Gesellschaft** f society; (Begleitung) company; (Abend~) party; **~ mit beschränkter Haftung**

limited company (Brit), limited corporation (US)

gesessen pp von **sitzen**

Gesetz (-es, -e) nt law; **gesetzlich** adj legal; **~er Feiertag** public (o bank (Brit) o legal (US)) holiday; **gesetzwidrig** adj illegal

Gesicht (-(e)s, -er) nt face; (Miene) expression; **mach doch nicht so ein ~!** stop pulling such a face; **Gesichtscreme** f face cream; **Gesichtswasser** nt toner

gesoffen pp von **saufen**

gesogen pp von **saugen**

gespannt adj tense; (begierig) eager; **ich bin ~, ob ...** I wonder if ...; **auf etw/jdn ~ sein** to look forward to sth/to seeing sb

Gespenst (-(e)s, -er) nt ghost

gesperrt adj closed

gesponnen pp von **spinnen**

Gespräch (-(e)s, -e) nt talk, conversation; (Diskussion) discussion; (Anruf) call

gesprochen pp von **sprechen**

gesprungen pp von **springen**

Gestalt (-, -en) f form, shape; (Mensch) figure

gestanden pp von **stehen, gestehen**

Gestank (-(e)s) m stench

gestatten vt to permit, to allow; **~ Sie?** may I?

Geste (-, -n) f gesture

gestehen irr vt to confess

gestern adv yesterday; **~ Abend/Morgen** yesterday evening/morning

gestiegen pp von **steigen**

gestochen pp von **stechen**

gestohlen pp von **stehlen**

gestorben pp von **sterben**

gestört adj disturbed; (Empfang) poor

gestoßen pp von **stoßen**

gestreift adj striped

gestrichen pp von **streichen**

gestritten pp von **streiten**

gestunken pp von **stinken**

gesund adj healthy; **wieder ~ werden** to get better; **Gesundheit** f health; **~!** bless you!; **gesundheitsschädlich** adj unhealthy

gesungen pp von **singen**

gesunken pp von **sinken**

getan pp von **tun**

getragen pp von **tragen**

Getränk (-(e)s, -e) nt drink;

Getränkeautomat m drinks machine; **Getränkekarte** f list of drinks

Getreide (-s, -) nt cereals pl, grain

getrennt adj separate; **~ leben** to live apart; **~ zahlen** to pay separately

getreten pp von **treten**

Getriebe (-s, -) nt (Auto) gearbox

getrieben pp von **treiben**

Getriebeschaden m gearbox damage

getroffen pp von **treffen**

getrunken pp von **trinken**

Getue nt fuss

geübt adj experienced

gewachsen pp von **wachsen** ▷ adj **jdm/einer Sache ~ sein** to be a match for sb/up to sth

Gewähr (-) f guarantee; **keine ~ übernehmen für** to accept no responsibility for

Gewalt (-, -en) f (Macht) power; (Kontrolle) control; (große Kraft) force; (~taten) violence; **mit aller ~** with all one's might; **gewaltig** adj tremendous; (Irrtum) huge

gewandt pp von **wenden** ▷ adj (flink) nimble; (geschickt) skilful

gewann imperf von **gewinnen**

gewaschen pp von **waschen**

Gewebe (-s, -) nt (Stoff) fabric; (Bio) tissue

Gewehr (-(e)s, -e) nt rifle, gun

Geweih (-(e)s, -e) nt antlers pl

gewellt adj (Haare) wavy

gewendet pp von **wenden**

Gewerbe (-s, -) nt trade; **Gewerbegebiet** nt industrial estate (Brit) (o park (US)); **gewerblich** adj commercial

Gewerkschaft f trade union

gewesen pp von **sein**

Gewicht (-(e)s, -e) nt weight; (fig) importance

gewiesen pp von **weisen**

Gewinn (-(e)s, -e) m profit; (bei Spiel) winnings pl; **gewinnen** (gewann, gewonnen) vt to win; (erwerben) to gain; (Kohle, Öl) to extract ▷ vi to win; (profitieren) to gain; **Gewinner(in)** (-s, -) m(f) winner

gewiss adj certain ▷ adv certainly

Gewissen (-s, -) nt conscience; **ein gutes/schlechtes ~ haben** to have a clear/bad conscience

Gewitter (-s, -) nt thunderstorm; **gewittern** vi impers **es gewittert** it's thundering

gewogen pp von **wiegen**

gewöhnen vt jdn an etw (akk) ~ to accustom sb to sth ▷ vr **sich an jdn/etw** ~ to get used (o accustomed) to sb/sth; **Gewohnheit** f habit; (Brauch) custom; **gewöhnlich** adj usual; (durchschnittlich) ordinary; (pej) common; **wie** ~ as usual; **gewohnt** adj usual; **etw** ~ **sein** to be used to sth

Gewölbe (-s, -) nt (Deckengewölbe) vault

gewonnen pp von **gewinnen**

geworben pp von **werben**

geworden pp von **werden**

geworfen pp von **werfen**

Gewürz (-es, -e) nt spice; **Gewürznelke** f clove; **gewürzt** adj seasoned

gewusst pp von **wissen**

Gezeiten pl tides pl

gezogen pp von **ziehen**

gezwungen pp von **zwingen**

Gibraltar (-s) nt Gibraltar

Gicht (-) f gout

Giebel (-s, -) m gable

gierig adj greedy

gießen (goss, gegossen) vt to pour; (Blumen) to water; (Metall) to cast; **Gießkanne** f watering can

Gift (-(e)s, -e) nt poison; **giftig** adj poisonous

Gigabyte nt gigabyte

Gin (-s, -s) m gin

ging imperf von **gehen**; **Gin Tonic** (-(s), -s) m gin and tonic

Gipfel (-s, -) m summit, peak; (Pol) summit; (fig: Höhepunkt) height

Gips (-es, -e) m (a. Med) plaster; **Gipsbein** nt **sie hat ein** ~ she's got her leg in plaster; **Gipsverband** m plaster cast

Giraffe (-, -n) f giraffe

Girokonto nt current account (Brit), checking account (US)

Gitarre (-, -n) f guitar

Gitter (-s, -) nt bars pl

glänzen vi (a. fig) to shine; **glänzend** adj shining; (fig) brilliant

Glas (-es, Gläser) nt glass; (Marmelade) jar; **zwei** ~ **Wein** two glasses of wine; **Glascontainer** m bottle bank; **Glaser(in)** m(f) glazier; **Glasscheibe** f pane (of glass); **Glassplitter** m splinter of glass

Glasur f glaze; (Gastr) icing

glatt adj smooth; (rutschig) slippery; (Lüge) downright; **Glatteis** nt (black) ice

Glatze (-, -n) f bald head; (fam: Skinhead) skinhead

glauben vt, vi to believe (an +akk in); (meinen) to think; **jdm** ~ to believe sb

gleich adj equal; (identisch) same, identical; **alle Menschen sind** ~ all people are the same; **es ist mir** ~ it's all the same to me ▷ adv equally; (sofort) straight away; (bald) in a minute; ~ **groß/alt** the same size/age; ~ **nach/an** right after/at; **Gleichberechtigung** f equal rights pl; **gleichen** (glich, geglichen) vi **jdm/einer Sache** ~ to be like sb/sth ▷ vr **sich** ~ to be alike; **gleichfalls** adv likewise; **danke** ~! thanks, and the same to you; **gleichgültig** adj indifferent; **gleichmäßig** adj regular; (Verteilung) even, equal; **gleichzeitig** adj simultaneous ▷ adv at the same time

Gleis (-es, -e) nt track, rails pl; (Bahnsteig) platform

gleiten (glitt, geglitten) vi to glide; (rutschen) to slide; **Gleitschirmfliegen** (-s) nt paragliding

Gletscher (-s, -) m glacier; **Gletscherskifahren** nt glacier skiing; **Gletscherspalte** f crevasse

glich imperf von **gleichen**

Glied (-(e)s, -er) nt (Arm, Bein) limb; (von Kette) link; (Penis) penis; **Gliedmaßen** pl limbs pl

glitschig adj slippery

glitt imperf von **gleiten**

glitzern vi to glitter; (Sterne) to twinkle

Glocke (-, -n) f bell; **Glockenspiel** nt chimes pl

Glotze (-, -n) f (fam: TV) box; **glotzen** vi (fam) to stare

Glück (-(e)s) nt luck; (Freude) happiness; ~ **haben** to be lucky; **viel** ~! good luck; **zum** ~ fortunately; **glücklich** adj lucky; (froh) happy; **glücklicherweise** adj fortunately; **Glückwunsch** m congratulations pl; **herzlichen** ~ **zur bestandenen Prüfung** congratulations on passing your exam; **herzlichen** ~ **zum Geburtstag!** Happy Birthday

Glühbirne f light bulb; **glühen** vi to glow; **Glühwein** m mulled wine

GmbH (-, -s) f abk = **Gesellschaft mit beschränkter Haftung** ≈ Ltd (Brit), ≈ Inc (US)

Gokart (-(s), -s) m go-kart

Gold (-(e)s) nt gold; **golden** adj gold; (fig) golden; **Goldfisch** m goldfish; **Goldmedaille** f gold medal; **Goldschmied(in)** m(f) goldsmith

Golf (-(e)s, -e) m gulf; **der ~ von Biskaya** the Bay of Biscay ▷ (-s) nt golf; **Golfplatz** m golf course; **Golfschläger** m golf club

Gondel (-, -n) f gondola; (Seilbahn) cable-car

gönnen vt **ich gönne es ihm** I'm really pleased for him; **sich** (dat) **etw ~** to allow oneself sth

goss imperf von **gießen**

gotisch adj Gothic

Gott (-es, Götter) m God; (Gottheit) god; **Gottesdienst** m service; **Göttin** f goddess

Grab (-(e)s, Gräber) nt grave

graben (grub, gegraben) vt to dig; **Graben** (-s, Gräben) m ditch

Grabstein m gravestone

Grad (-(e)s, -e) m degree; **wir haben 30 ~ Celsius** it's 30 degrees Celsius, it's 86 degrees Fahrenheit; **bis zu einem gewissen ~** up to a certain extent

Graf (-en, -en) m count; (in Großbritannien) earl

Graffiti pl graffiti sing

Grafik (-, -en) f graph; (Kunstwerk) graphic; (Illustration) diagram; **Grafikkarte** f (Inform) graphics card; **Grafikprogramm** nt (Inform) graphics software

Gräfin (-, -nen) f countess

Gramm (-s) nt gram(me)

Grammatik f grammar

Grapefruit (-, -s) f grapefruit

Graphik f siehe **Grafik**

Gras (-es, Gräser) nt grass

grässlich adj horrible

Gräte (-, -n) f (fish)bone

gratis adj, adv free (of charge)

gratulieren vi **jdm (zu etw) ~** to congratulate sb (on sth); **(ich) gratuliere!** congratulations!

grau adj grey, gray (US); **grauhaarig** adj grey-haired

grausam adj cruel

gravierend adj (Fehler) serious

greifen (griff, gegriffen) vt to seize; **zu etw ~** (fig) to resort to sth ▷ vi (Regel etc) to have an effect (bei on)

grell adj harsh

Grenze (-, -n) f boundary; (Staat) border;

(Schranke) limit; **grenzen** vi to border (an +akk on); **Grenzkontrolle** f border control; **Grenzübergang** m border crossing point; **Grenzverkehr** m border traffic

Grieche (-n, -n) m Greek; **Griechenland** nt Greece; **Griechin** f Greek; **griechisch** adj Greek; **Griechisch** nt Greek

griesgrämig adj grumpy

Grieß (-es, -e) m (Gastr) semolina

griff imperf von **greifen**

Griff (-(e)s, -e) m grip; (Tür etc) handle; **griffbereit** adj handy

Grill (-s, -s) m grill; (im Freien) barbecue

Grille (-, -n) f cricket

grillen vt to grill ▷ vi to have a barbecue; **Grillfest** nt, **Grillfete** f barbecue; **Grillkohle** f charcoal

grinsen vi to grin; (höhnisch) to sneer

Grippe (-, -n) f flu; **Grippeschutzimpfung** f flu vaccination

grob adj coarse; (Fehler, Verstoß) gross; (Einschätzung) rough

Grönland (-s) nt Greenland

groß adj big, large; (hoch) tall; (fig) great; (Buchstabe) capital; (erwachsen) grown-up; **im Großen und Ganzen** on the whole ▷ adv greatly; **großartig** adj wonderful

Großbritannien (-s) nt (Great) Britain

Großbuchstabe m capital letter

Größe (-, -n) f size; (Länge) height; (fig) greatness; **welche ~ haben Sie?** what size do you take?

Großeltern pl grandparents pl; **Großhandel** m wholesale trade; **Großmarkt** m hypermarket; **Großmutter** f grandmother; **Großraum** m **der ~ Manchester** Greater Manchester; **groß|schreiben** irr vt to write with a capital letter; **Großstadt** f city; **Großvater** m grandfather; **großzügig** adj generous; (Planung) on a large scale

Grotte (-, -n) f grotto

grub imperf von **graben**

Grübchen nt dimple

Grube (-, -n) f pit

grüezi interj (schweizerisch) hello

Gruft -, -en vault

grün adj green; **~er Salat** lettuce; **~e Bohnen** French beans; **die Bananen sind noch zu ~** the bananas aren't ripe yet; **der ~e Punkt** symbol for recyclable packaging; **im ~en Bereich** hunky-dory

grüner Punkt

The **grüner Punkt** is the green spot symbol which appears on packaging, indicating that the packaging should not be thrown into the normal household refuse but kept separate to be recycled through the **DSD** (Duales System Deutschland) system. The recycling is financed by licences bought by the manufacturer from the 'DSD' and the cost of this is often passed on to the consumer.

Grünanlage f park
Grund (-(e)s, Gründe) m (Ursache) reason; (Erdboden) ground; (See, Gefäß) bottom; (Grundbesitz) land, property; **aus gesundheitlichen Gründen** for health reasons; **im ~e** basically; **aus diesem ~** for this reason
gründen vt to found; **Gründer(in)** m(f) founder
Grundgebühr f basic charge; **Grundgesetz** nt (German) Constitution
gründlich adj thorough
Gründonnerstag m Maundy Thursday
grundsätzlich adj fundamental, basic; **sie kommt ~ zu spät** she's always late; **Grundschule** f primary school; **Grundstück** nt plot; (Anwesen) estate; (Baugrundstück) site; **Grundwasser** nt ground water
Grüne(r) mf (Pol) Green; **die ~n** the Green Party
Gruppe (-, -n) f group; **Gruppenermäßigung** f group discount; **Gruppenreise** f group tour
Gruß (-es, Grüße) m greeting; **viele Grüße** best wishes; **Grüße an** (+akk) regards to; **mit freundlichen Grüßen** Yours sincerely (Brit), Sincerely yours (US); **sag ihm einen schönen ~ von mir** give him my regards; **grüßen** vt to greet; **grüß deine Mutter von mir** give your mother my regards; **Julia lässt (euch) ~** Julia sends (you) her regards
gucken vi to look
Gulasch (-(e)s, -e) nt goulash
gültig adj valid
Gummi (-s, -s) m o nt rubber; **Gummiband** nt rubber (o elastic (Brit)) band; **Gummibärchen** pl gums pl (in the shape of

a bear) (Brit), gumdrops pl (in the shape of a bear) (US); **Gummihandschuhe** pl rubber gloves pl; **Gummistiefel** m wellington (boot) (Brit), rubber boot (US)
günstig adj favourable; (Preis) good
gurgeln vi to gurgle; (im Mund) to gargle
Gurke (-, -n) f cucumber; **saure ~** gherkin
Gurt (-(e)s, -e) m belt
Gürtel (-s, -) m belt; (Geo) zone; **Gürtelrose** f shingles sing
GUS (-) f akr = **Gemeinschaft Unabhängiger Staaten** CIS

SCHLÜSSELWORT

gut adj good; **alles Gute** all the best; **also gut** all right then
▷ adv well; **gut gehen** to work, to come off; **es geht jdm gut** sb's doing fine; **gut gemeint** well meant; **gut schmecken** to taste good; **jdm gut tun** to do sb good; **gut, aber ...** OK, but ...; **(na) gut, ich komme** all right, I'll come; **gut drei Stunden** a good three hours; **das kann gut sein** that may well be; **lass es gut sein** that'll do

Gutachten (-s, -) nt report; **Gutachter(in)** (-s, -) m(f) expert
gutartig adj (Med) benign
Güter pl goods pl; **Güterbahnhof** m goods station; **Güterzug** m goods train
gutgläubig adj trusting; **Guthaben** (-s) nt (credit) balance
gutmütig adj good-natured
Gutschein m voucher; **Gutschrift** f credit
Gymnasium nt ≈ grammar school (Brit), ≈ high school (US)
Gymnastik f exercises pl, keep-fit
Gynäkologe m, **Gynäkologin** f gynaecologist
Gyros (-, -) nt doner kebab

h

Haar (-(e)s, -e) nt hair; **um ein ~** nearly; **sich** (dat) **die ~e schneiden lassen** to have one's hair cut; **Haarbürste** f hairbrush; **Haarfestiger** m setting lotion; **Haargel** nt hair gel; **haarig** adj hairy; (fig) nasty; **Haarschnitt** m haircut; **Haarspange** f hair slide (Brit), barrette (US); **Haarspliss** m split ends pl; **Haarspray** nt hair spray; **Haartrockner** (-s, -) m hairdryer; **Haarwaschmittel** nt shampoo; **Haarwasser** nt hair tonic

haben (hatte, gehabt) vt, vaux to have; **Hunger/Angst ~** to be hungry/afraid; **Ferien ~** to be on holiday (Brit) (o vacation (US)); **welches Datum ~ wir heute?** what's the date today?; **ich hätte gerne ...** I'd like ...; **hätten Sie etwas dagegen, wenn ...?** would you mind if ...?; **was hast du denn?** what's the matter (with you)?

Haben nt (Comm) credit

Habicht (-(e)s, -e) m hawk

Hacke (-, -n) f (im Garten) hoe; (Ferse) heel; **hacken** vt to chop; (Loch) to hack; (Erde) to hoe; **Hacker(in)** (-s, -) m(f) (Inform) hacker; **Hackfleisch** nt mince(d meat) (Brit), ground meat (US)

Hafen (-s, Häfen) m harbour; (großer) port; **Hafenstadt** f port

Hafer (-s, -) m oats pl; **Haferflocken** pl rolled oats pl

Haft (-) f custody; **haftbar** adj liable, responsible; **haften** vi to stick; **~ für** to be liable (o responsible) for; **Haftnotiz** f Post-it®; **Haftpflichtversicherung** f third party insurance; **Haftung** f liability

Hagebutte (-, -n) f rose hip

Hagel (-s) m hail; **hageln** vi impers to hail

Hahn (-(e)s, Hähne) m cock; (Wasserhahn) tap (Brit), faucet (US); **Hähnchen** nt cockerel; (Gastr) chicken

Hai(fisch) (-(e)s, -e) m shark

häkeln vi, vt to crochet; **Häkelnadel** f crochet hook

Haken (-s, -) m hook; (Zeichen) tick

halb adj half; **~ eins** half past twelve; (fam) half twelve; **eine ~e Stunde** half an hour; **~ offen** half-open; **Halbfinale** nt semifinal; **halbieren** vt to halve; **Halbinsel** f peninsula; **Halbjahr** nt half-year; **halbjährlich** adj half-yearly; **Halbmond** m (Astr) half-moon; (Symbol) crescent; **Halbpension** f half board; **halbseitig** adj **~ gelähmt** paralyzed on one side; **halbtags** adv (arbeiten) part-time; **halbwegs** adv (leidlich) reasonably; **Halbzeit** f half; (Pause) half-time

half imperf von **helfen**; **Hälfte** (-, -n) f half

Halle (-, -n) f hall; **Hallenbad** nt indoor (swimming) pool

hallo interj hello, hi

Halogenlampe f halogen lamp; **Halogenscheinwerfer** m halogen headlight

Hals (-es, Hälse) m neck; (Kehle) throat; **Halsband** nt (für Tiere) collar; **Halsentzündung** f sore throat; **Halskette** f necklace; **Hals-Nasen-Ohren-Arzt** m, **Hals-Nasen-Ohren-Ärztin** f ear, nose and throat specialist; **Halsschmerzen** pl sore throat sing; **Halstuch** nt scarf

halt interj stop ▷ adv **das ist ~ so** that's just the way it is; **Halt** (-(e)s, -e) m stop; (fester) hold; (innerer) stability

haltbar adj durable; (Lebensmittel) non-perishable; **Haltbarkeitsdatum** nt best-before date

halten (hielt, gehalten) vt to keep; (festhalten) to hold; **~ für** to regard as; **~ von** to think of; **den Elfmeter ~** to save the penalty; **eine Rede ~** to give (o make) a speech ▷ vi to hold; (frisch bleiben) to keep; (stoppen) to stop; **zu jdm ~** to stand by sb ▷ vr **sich ~** (frisch bleiben) to keep; (sich behaupten) to hold out

Haltestelle f stop; **Halteverbot** nt **hier ist ~** you can't stop here

Haltung f (Körper) posture; (fig) attitude; (Selbstbeherrschung) composure; **~ bewahren** to keep one's composure

Hamburg (-s) nt Hamburg; **Hamburger** (-s, -) m (Gastr) hamburger

Hammelfleisch nt mutton

Hammer (-s, Hämmer) m hammer; (fig, fam: Fehler) howler; **das ist der ~** (unerhört) that's a bit much

Hämorr(ho)iden pl haemorrhoids pl, piles pl

Hamster (-s, -) m hamster

Hand (-, Hände) f hand; **jdm die ~ geben** to shake hands with sb; **jdn bei der ~ nehmen** to take sb by the hand; **eine ~ voll Reis/Leute** a handful of rice/people; **zu Händen von** attention; **Handarbeit** f (Schulfach) handicraft; **~ sein** to be handmade; **Handball** m handball; **Handbremse** f handbrake; **Handbuch** nt handbook, manual; **Handcreme** f hand cream; **Händedruck** m handshake

Handel (-s) m trade; (Geschäft) transaction; **handeln** vi to act; (Comm) to trade; **~ von** to be about ▷ vr impers **sich ~ um** to be about; **es handelt sich um ...** it's about ...; **Handelskammer** f chamber of commerce; **Handelsschule** f business school

Handfeger (-s, -) m brush; **Handfläche** f palm; **Handgelenk** nt wrist; **handgemacht** adj handmade; **Handgepäck** nt hand luggage (Brit) (o baggage)

Händler(in) (-s, -) m(f) dealer

handlich adj handy

Handlung f act, action; (von Roman, Film) plot

Handschellen pl handcuffs pl; **Handschrift** f handwriting; **Handschuh** m glove; **Handschuhfach** nt glove compartment; **Handtasche** f handbag, purse (US); **Handtuch** nt towel;

Handwerk nt trade; (Kunst~) craft; **Handwerker** (-s, -) m workman

Handy (-s, -s) nt mobile (phone), cell phone (US)

Hanf (-(e)s) m hemp

Hang (-(e)s, Hänge) m (Abhang) slope; (fig) tendency

Hängebrücke f suspension bridge; **Hängematte** f hammock

hängen (hing, gehangen) vi to hang; **an der Wand/an der Decke ~** to hang on the wall/from the ceiling; **an jdm ~** (fig) to be attached to sb; **~ bleiben** to get caught (an +dat on); (fig) to get stuck ▷ vt to hang (an +akk on)

Hantel (-, -n) f dumbbell

Hardware (-, -s) f (Inform) hardware

Harfe (-, -n) f harp

harmlos adj harmless

harmonisch adj harmonious

Harn (-(e)s, -e) m urine; **Harnblase** f bladder

Harpune (-, -n) f harpoon

hart adj hard; (fig) harsh; **zu jdm ~ sein** to be hard on sb; **~ gekocht** (Ei) hard-boiled; **hartnäckig** adj stubborn

Haschee (-s, -s) nt hash

Haschisch (-) nt hashish

Hase (-n, -n) m hare

Haselnuss f hazelnut

Hasenscharte f (Med) harelip

Hass (-es) m hatred (auf, gegen +akk of), hate; **einen ~ kriegen** (fam) to see red; **hassen** vt to hate

hässlich adj ugly; (gemein) nasty

Hast (-) f haste, hurry; **hastig** adj hasty

hatte imperf von **haben**

Haube (-, -n) f hood; (Mütze) cap; (Auto) bonnet (Brit), hood (US)

Hauch (-(e)s, -e) m breath; (Luft~) breeze; (fig) trace; **hauchdünn** adj (Schicht, Scheibe) wafer-thin

hauen (haute, gehauen) vt to hit

Haufen (-s, -) m pile; **ein ~ Geld** (viel Geld) a lot of money

häufig adj frequent ▷ adv frequently, often

Haupt- in zW main; **Hauptbahnhof** m central (o main) station; **Hauptdarsteller(in)** m(f) leading actor/lady; **Haupteingang** m main entrance; **Hauptgericht** nt main course;

Hauptgeschäftszeiten pl peak shopping hours pl; **Hauptgewinn** m first prize
Häuptling m chief
Hauptquartier nt headquarters pl; **Hauptreisezeit** f peak tourist season; **Hauptrolle** f leading role; **Hauptsache** f main thing; **hauptsächlich** adv mainly, chiefly; **Hauptsaison** f high (o peak) season; **Hauptsatz** m main clause; **Hauptschule** f ≈ secondary school (Brit), ≈ junior high school (US); **Hauptspeicher** m (Inform) main storage (o memory); **Hauptstadt** f capital; **Hauptstraße** f main road; (im Stadtzentrum) main street; **Hauptverkehrszeit** f rush hour
Haus (-es, Häuser) nt house; **nach ~e** home; **zu ~e** at home; **jdn nach ~e bringen** to take sb home; **bei uns zu ~e** (Heimat) where we come from; (Familie) in my family; (Haus) at our place; **Hausarbeit** f housework; **Hausaufgabe** f (Schule) homework; **~n** pl homework sing; **Hausbesitzer(in)** (-s, -) m(f) house owner; (Vermieter) landlord/-lady; **Hausbesuch** m home visit; **Hausbewohner(in)** (-s, -) m(f) occupant; **Hausflur** m hall; **Hausfrau** f housewife; **hausgemacht** adj homemade; **Haushalt** m household; (Pol) budget; **Hausherr(in)** m(f) host/hostess; (Vermieter) landlord/-lady
häuslich adj domestic
Hausmann m house-husband; **Hausmannskost** f good plain cooking; **Hausmeister(in)** m(f) caretaker (Brit), janitor (US); **Hausnummer** f house number; **Hausordnung** f (house) rules pl; **Hausschlüssel** m front-door key; **Hausschuh** m slipper; **Haustier** nt pet; **Haustür** f front door
Haut (-, Häute) f skin; (Tier) hide; **Hautarzt** m, **Hautärztin** f dermatologist; **Hautausschlag** m skin rash; **Hautcreme** f skin cream; **Hautfarbe** f skin colour; **Hautkrankheit** f skin disease
Hawaii (-s) nt Hawaii
Hbf. abk = **Hauptbahnhof** central station
Hebamme (-, -n) f midwife
Hebel (-s, -) m lever
heben (hob, gehoben) vt to raise, to lift
Hebräisch (-) nt Hebrew
Hecht (-(e)s, -e) m pike
Heck (-(e)s, -e) nt (von Boot) stern; (von Auto) rear; **Heckantrieb** m rear-wheel drive

Hecke (-, -n) f hedge
Heckklappe f tailgate; **Hecklicht** nt tail-light; **Heckscheibe** f rear window; **Heckscheibenheizung** f rear-window defroster
Hefe (-, -n) f yeast
Heft (-(e)s, -e) nt notebook, exercise book; (Ausgabe) issue
heftig adj violent; (Kritik, Streit) fierce
Heftklammer f paper clip; **Heftpflaster** nt plaster (Brit), Band-Aid® (US)
Heide (-, -n) f heath, moor; **Heidekraut** nt heather
Heidelbeere f bilberry, blueberry
heidnisch adj (Brauch) pagan
heikel adj (Angelegenheit) awkward; (wählerisch) fussy
heil adj (Sache) in one piece, intact; (Person) unhurt; **heilbar** adj curable
Heilbutt (-(e)s, -e) m halibut
heilen vt to cure ▷ vi to heal
heilig adj holy; **Heiligabend** m Christmas Eve; **Heilige(r)** mf saint
Heilmittel n remedy, cure (gegen for); **Heilpraktiker(in)** (-s, -) m(f) non-medical practitioner
heim adv home; **Heim** (-(e), -e) nt home
Heimat (-, -en) f home (town/country); **Heimatland** nt home country
heim|fahren irr vi to drive home; **Heimfahrt** f journey home; **heimisch** adj (Bevölkerung, Brauchtum) local; (Tiere, Pflanzen) native; **heim|kommen** irr vi to come (o return) home
heimlich adj secret
Heimreise f journey home; **Heimspiel** nt (Sport) home game; **Heimvorteil** m (Sport) home advantage; **Heimweg** m way home; **Heimweh** (-s) nt homesickness; **~ haben** to be homesick; **Heimwerker(in)** m(f) DIY enthusiast
Heirat (-, -en) f marriage; **heiraten** vi to get married ▷ vt to marry; **Heiratsantrag** m proposal; **er hat ihr einen ~ gemacht** he proposed to her
heiser adj hoarse
heiß adj hot; (Diskussion) heated; **mir ist ~** I'm hot
heißen (hieß, geheißen) vi to be called; (bedeuten) to mean; **ich heiße Tom** my name is Tom; **wie ~ Sie?** what's your name?; **wie heißt sie mit Nachnamen?** what's her surname?; **wie heißt das auf**

Englisch? what's that in English? ▷ vi impers **es heißt** (man sagt) it is said; **es heißt in dem Brief ...** it says in the letter ...; **das heißt** that is

Heißluftherd m fan-assisted oven

heiter adj cheerful; (Wetter) bright

heizen vt to heat; **Heizkissen** m (Med) heated pad; **Heizkörper** m radiator; **Heizöl** nt fuel oil; **Heizung** f heating

Hektar (-s, -) nt hectare

Hektik (-, -en) f **nur keine ~!** take it easy; **hektisch** adj hectic

Held (-en, -en) m hero; **Heldin** f heroine

helfen (half, geholfen) vi to help (jdm bei etw sb with sth); (nützen) to be of use; **sie weiß sich** (dat) **zu ~** she can manage ▷ vi impers **es hilft nichts, du musst ...** it's no use, you have to ...; **Helfer(in)** m(f) helper; (Mitarbeiter) assistant

Helikopter-Skiing (-s) nt heliskiing, helicopter skiing

hell adj bright; (Farbe) light; (Hautfarbe) fair; **hellblau** adj light blue; **hellblond** adj ash-blond; **hellgelb** adj pale yellow; **hellgrün** adj light green; **Hellseher(in)** m(f) clairvoyant

Helm (-(e)s, -e) m helmet; **Helmpflicht** f compulsory wearing of helmets

Hemd (-(e)s, -en) nt shirt; (Unter~) vest

hemmen vt to check; (behindern) to hamper; **gehemmt sein** to be inhibited; **Hemmung** f (psychisch) inhibition; **sie hatte keine ~, ihn zu betrügen** she had no scruples about deceiving him; (moralisch) scruple

Henkel (-s, -) m handle

Henna (-s) nt henna

Henne (-, -n) f hen

Hepatitis (-, Hepatitiden) f hepatitis

○ **SCHLÜSSELWORT**

her adv **1** (Richtung): **komm her zu mir** come here (to me); **von England her** from England; **von weit her** from a long way away; **her damit!** hand it over!; **wo hat er das her?** where did he get that from?; **wo bist du her?** where do you come from?

2 (Blickpunkt): **von der Form her** as far as the form is concerned

3 (zeitlich): **das ist 5 Jahre her** that was 5 years ago; **ich kenne ihn von früher her** I know him from before

herab adv down; **herablassend** adj (Bemerkung) condescending; **herab|sehen** irr vt **auf jdn ~** to look down on sb; **herab|setzen** vt to reduce; (fig) to disparage

heran adv **näher ~!** come closer; **heran|kommen** irr vi to approach; **~ an** (+akk) to be able to get at; (fig) to be able to get hold of; **heran|wachsen** irr vi to grow up

herauf adv up; **herauf|beschwören** irr vt to evoke; (verursachen) to cause; **herauf|ziehen** irr vt to pull up ▷ vi to approach; (Sturm) to gather

heraus adv out; **heraus|bekommen** irr vt (Geheimnis) to find out; (Rätsel) to solve; **ich bekomme noch zwei Euro heraus** I've got two euros change to come; **heraus|bringen** irr vt to bring out; **heraus|finden** irr vt to find out; **heraus|fordern** vt to challenge; **Herausforderung** f challenge; **heraus|geben** irr vt (Buch) to edit; (veröffentlichen) to publish; **jdm zwei Euro ~** to give sb two euros change; **geben Sie mir bitte auf 20 Euro heraus** could you give me change for 20 euros, please?; **heraus|holen** vt to get out (aus of); **heraus|kommen** irr vi to come out; **dabei kommt nichts heraus** nothing will come of it; **heraus|stellen** vt **sich ~** to turn out (als to be); **heraus|ziehen** irr vt to pull out

Herbst (-(e)s, -e) m autumn, fall (US)

Herd (-(e)s, -e) m cooker, stove

Herde (-, -n) f herd; (Schafe) flock

herein adv in; **~!** come in; **herein|fallen** irr vi **wir sind auf einen Betrüger hereingefallen** we were taken in by a swindler; **herein|legen** vt **jdn ~** (fig) to take sb for a ride

Herfahrt f journey here; **auf der ~** on the way here

Hergang m course (of events); **schildern Sie mir den ~** tell me what happened

Hering (-s, -e) m herring

her|kommen irr vi to come; **wo kommt sie her?** where does she come from?

Heroin (-s) nt heroin

Herpes (-) m (Med) herpes

Herr (-(e)n, -en) m (vor Namen) Mr; (Mann) gentleman; (Adliger, Gott) Lord; **mein ~!** sir; **meine ~en!** gentlemen; **Sehr geehrte Damen und ~en** Dear Sir or Madam; **herrenlos** adj (Gepäckstück) abandoned; (Tier) stray; **Herrentoilette** f men's toilet, gents

her|richten vt to prepare

herrlich adj marvellous, splendid

Herrschaft f rule; (Macht) power; **meine ~en!** ladies and gentlemen!

herrschen vi to rule; (bestehen) to be

her|stellen vt to make; (industriell) to manufacture; **Hersteller(in)** m(f) manufacturer; **Herstellung** f production

herüber adv over

herum adv around; (im Kreis) round; **um etw ~** around sth; **du hast den Pulli falsch ~ an** you're wearing your sweater inside out; **anders ~** the other way round; **herum|fahren** irr vi to drive around; **herum|führen** vt **jdn in der Stadt ~** to show sb around the town ▷ vi **die Straße führt um das Zentrum herum** the road goes around the city centre; **herum|kommen** irr vi **sie ist viel in der Welt herumgekommen** she's been around the world; **um etw ~** (vermeiden) to get out of sth; **herum|kriegen** vt to talk round; **herum|treiben** irr vr **sich ~** to hang around

herunter adv down; **heruntergekommen** adj (Gebäude, Gegend) run-down; (Person) down-at-heel; **herunter|handeln** vt to get down; **herunter|holen** vt to bring down; **herunter|kommen** irr vi to come down; **herunter|laden** irr vt (Inform) to download

hervor adv out; **hervor|bringen** irr vt to produce; (Wort) to utter; **hervor|heben** irr vt to emphasize, to stress; **hervorragend** adj excellent; **hervor|rufen** irr vt to cause, to give rise to

Herz (-ens, -en) nt heart; (Karten) hearts pl; **von ganzem ~en** wholeheartedly; **sich** (dat) **etw zu ~en nehmen** to take sth to heart; **Herzanfall** m heart attack; **Herzbeschwerden** pl heart trouble sing; **Herzfehler** m heart defect; **herzhaft** adj (Essen) substantial; **~ lachen** to have a good laugh; **Herzinfarkt** m heart attack; **Herzklopfen** (-s) nt (Med) palpitations pl;

ich hatte ~ (vor Aufregung) my heart was pounding (with excitement); **herzkrank** adj **sie ist ~** she's got a heart condition; **herzlich** adj (Empfang, Mensch) warm; **~en Glückwunsch** congratulations

Herzog(in) (-s, Herzöge) m(f) duke/duchess

Herzschlag m heartbeat; (Herzversagen) heart failure; **Herzschrittmacher** m pacemaker; **Herzstillstand** m cardiac arrest

Hessen (-s) nt Hessen

heterosexuell adj heterosexual; **Heterosexuelle(r)** mf heterosexual

Hetze (-, -n) f (Eile) rush; **hetzen** vt to rush ▷ vr **sich ~** to rush

Heu (-(e)s) nt hay

heuer adv this year

heulen vi to howl; (weinen) to cry

Heuschnupfen m hay fever; **Heuschrecke** (-, -n) f grasshopper; (größer) locust

heute adv today; **~ Abend/früh** this evening/morning; **~ Nacht** tonight; (letzte Nacht) last night; **~ in acht Tagen** a week (from) today; **sie hat bis ~ nicht bezahlt** she hasn't paid to this day; **heutig** adj **die ~e Zeitung/Generation** today's paper/generation; **heutzutage** adv nowadays

Hexe (-, -n) f witch; **Hexenschuss** m lumbago

hielt imperf von **halten**

hier adv here; **~ entlang** this way; **~ bleiben** to stay here; **~ lassen** to leave here; **ich bin auch hier von ~** I'm a stranger here myself; **hierher** adv here; **das gehört nicht ~** that doesn't belong here; **hiermit** adv with this; **hierzulande, hier zu Lande** adv in this country

hiesig adj local

hieß imperf von **heißen**

Hi-Fi-Anlage f hi-fi (system)

high adj (fam) high; **Highlife** (-s) nt high life; **~ machen** to live it up; **Hightech** (-s) nt high tech

Hilfe (-, -n) f help; (für Notleidende, finanziell) aid; **~!** help!; **erste ~ leisten** to give first aid; **um ~ bitten** to ask for help; **hilflos** adj helpless; **hilfsbereit** adj helpful; **Hilfsmittel** nt aid

Himbeere f raspberry

Himmel (-s, -) m sky; (Rel) heaven;
  Himmelfahrt f Ascension;
  Himmelsrichtung f direction;
  himmlisch adj heavenly

○ **SCHLÜSSELWORT**

hin adv **1** Richtung): **hin und zurück** there
and back; **hin und her** to and fro; **bis zur
Mauer hin** up to the wall; **wo ist er hin?**
where has he gone?; **Geld hin, Geld her**
money or no money
  2 (auf … hin): **auf meine Bitte hin** at my
request; **auf seinen Rat hin** on the basis
of his advice
  3: **mein Glück ist hin** my happiness has
gone

hinab adv down; **hinab|gehen** irr vi to go
down
hinauf adv up; **hinauf|gehen** irr vi, vt
to go up; **hinauf|steigen** irr vi to climb
(up)
hinaus adv out; **hinaus|gehen** irr vi to go
out; **das Zimmer geht auf den See
hinaus** the room looks out onto the lake;
  ~ über (+akk) to exceed; **hinaus|laufen** irr
vi to run out; **~ auf** (+akk) to come to, to
amount to; **hinaus|schieben** irr vi to put
off, to postpone; **hinaus|werfen** irr vt to
throw out; (aus Firma) to fire, to sack
(Brit); **hinaus|zögern** vr **sich ~** to take
longer than expected
Hinblick m **in** (o **im**) **~ auf** (+akk) with
regard to; (wegen) in view of
hin|bringen irr vt **ich bringe Sie hin** I'll
take you there
hindern vt to prevent; **jdn daran ~, etw
zu tun** to stop (o prevent) sb from doing
sth; **Hindernis** nt obstacle
Hinduismus m Hinduism
hindurch adv through; **das ganze Jahr
~** throughout the year, all year round; **die
ganze Nacht ~** all night (long)
hinein adv in; **hinein|gehen** irr vi to go
in; **~ in** (+akk) to go into, to enter;
hinein|passen vi to fit in; **~ in** (+akk) to
fit into
hin|fahren irr vi to go there ▷ vt to take
there; **Hinfahrt** f outward journey
hin|fallen irr vi to fall (down)
Hinflug m outward flight
hing imperf von **hängen**

hin|gehen irr vi to go there; (Zeit) to pass;
hin|halten irr vt to hold out; (warten
lassen) to put off
hinken vi to limp; **der Vergleich hinkt**
the comparison doesn't work
hin|knien vr **sich ~** to kneel down;
hin|legen vt to put down ▷ vr **sich ~** to
lie down; **hin|nehmen** irr vt (fig) to put
up with, to take; **Hinreise** f outward
journey; **hin|setzen** vr **sich ~** to sit down;
hinsichtlich prep +gen with regard to;
hin|stellen vt to put (down) ▷ vr **sich
~** to stand
hinten adv at the back; (im Auto) in the
back; (dahinter) behind
hinter prep +dat o akk behind; (nach) after;
  ~ jdm her sein to be after sb; **etw ~ sich**
(akk) **bringen** to get sth over (and done)
with; **Hinterachse** f rear axle;
Hinterausgang m rear exit; **Hinterbein** nt
hind leg; **Hinterbliebene(r)** mf
dependant; **hintere(r, s)** adj rear, back;
hintereinander adv (in einer Reihe) one
behind the other; (hintereinander her) one
after the other; **drei Tage ~** three days
running (o in a row); **Hintereingang** m
rear entrance; **Hintergedanke** m ulterior
motive; **hintergehen** irr vt to deceive;
Hintergrund m background; **hinterher**
adv (zeitlich) afterwards; **los, ~!** come on,
after him/her/them; **Hinterkopf** m back
of the head; **hinterlassen** vt to leave;
jdm eine Nachricht ~ to leave a
message for sb; **hinterlegen** vt to leave
(bei with)
Hintern (-, -) m (fam) backside, bum
Hinterradantrieb m (Auto) rear-wheel
drive; **Hinterteil** nt back (part); (Hintern)
behind; **Hintertür** f back door
hinüber adv over; **~ sein** (fam: kaputt) to
be ruined; (verdorben) to have gone bad;
hinüber|gehen irr vi to go over
hinunter adv down; **hinunter|gehen** irr
vi, vt to go down; **hinunter|schlucken** vt
(a. fig) to swallow
Hinweg m outward journey
hinweg|setzen vr **sich über etw** (akk)
~ to ignore sth
Hinweis (-es, -e) m (Andeutung) hint;
(Anweisung) instruction; (Verweis)
reference; **hin|weisen** irr vi **jdn auf etw**
(acc) **~** to point sth out to sb; **jdn nochmal
auf etw ~** to remind sb of sth

hinzu *adv* in addition; **hinzu|fügen** *vt* to add; **hinzu|kommen** *irr vi* **zu jdm ~** to join sb; **es war kalt, hinzu kam, dass es auch noch regnete** it was cold, and on top of that it was raining

Hirn *(-(e)s, -e) nt* brain; *(Verstand)* brains *pl*; **Hirnhautentzündung** *f* meningitis; **hirnverbrannt** *adj* crazy

Hirsch *(-(e)s, -e) m* deer; *(als Speise)* venison

Hirse *(-, -n) f* millet

Hirte *(-n, -n) m* shepherd

historisch *adj* historical

Hit *(-s, -s) m* (fig, Mus, Inform) hit; **Hitliste** *f*, **Hitparade** *f* charts *pl*

Hitze *(-) f* heat; **hitzebeständig** *adj* heat-resistant; **Hitzewelle** *f* heatwave; **hitzig** *adj* hot-tempered; *(Debatte)* heated; **Hitzschlag** *m* heatstroke

HIV *(-(s), -(s)) nt abk = Human Immunodeficiency Virus* HIV; **HIV-negativ** *adj* HIV-negative; **HIV-positiv** *adj* HIV-positive

H-Milch *f* long-life milk

hob *imperf von* **heben**

Hobby *(-s, -s) nt* hobby

Hobel *(-s, -) m* plane

hoch *adj* high; *(Baum, Haus)* tall; *(Schnee)* deep; **der Zaun ist drei Meter ~** the fence is three metres high; **~ auflösend** high-resolution; **~ begabt** extremely gifted; **das ist mir zu ~** that's above my head; **~ soll sie leben!, sie lebe ~!** three cheers for her; **4 ~ 2 ist 16** 4 squared is 16; **4 ~ 5** 4 to the power of 5

Hoch *(-s, -s) nt* (Ruf) cheer; *(Meteo)* high; **hochachtungsvoll** *adv* (in Briefen) Yours faithfully; **Hochbetrieb** *m* **es herrscht ~** they/we are extremely busy; **Hochdeutsch** *nt* High German; **Hochgebirge** *nt* high mountains *pl*; **Hochgeschwindigkeitszug** *m* high-speed train; **Hochhaus** *nt* high rise; **hoch|heben** *irr vt* to lift (up); **hochprozentig** *adj* (Alkohol) high-proof; **Hochsaison** *f* high season; **Hochschule** *f* college; *(Universität)* university; **hochschwanger** *adj* heavily pregnant; **Hochsommer** *m* midsummer; **Hochspannung** *f* great tension; *(Elek)* high voltage; **Hochsprung** *m* high jump

höchst *adv* highly, extremely; **höchste(r, s)** *adj* highest; *(äußerste)* extreme; **höchstens**

adv at the most; **Höchstgeschwindigkeit** *f* maximum speed; **Höchstparkdauer** *f* maximum stay

Hochstuhl *m* high chair

höchstwahrscheinlich *adv* very probably

Hochwasser *nt* high water; *(Überschwemmung)* floods *pl*; **hochwertig** *adj* high-quality

Hochzeit *(-, -en) f* wedding; **Hochzeitsnacht** *f* wedding night; **Hochzeitsreise** *f* honeymoon; **Hochzeitstag** *m* wedding day; *(Jahrestag)* wedding anniversary

hocken *vi* to squat, to crouch

Hocker *(-s, -) m* stool

Hockey *(-s) nt* hockey

Hoden *(-s, -) m* testicle

Hof *(-(e)s, Höfe) m* (Hinterhof) yard; *(Innenhof)* courtyard; *(Bauernhof)* farm; *(Königshof)* court

hoffen *vi* to hope (auf +akk for); **ich hoffe es** I hope so; **hoffentlich** *adv* hopefully; **~ nicht** I hope not; **Hoffnung** *f* hope; **hoffnungslos** *adj* hopeless

höflich *adj* polite; **Höflichkeit** *f* politeness

hohe(r, s) *adj siehe* **hoch**

Höhe *(-, -n) f* height; *(Anhöhe)* hill; *(einer Summe)* amount; **in einer ~ von 5000 Metern** at an altitude of 5,000 metres; *(Flughöhe)* altitude; **Höhenangst** *f* vertigo; **Höhensonne** *f* sun lamp

Höhepunkt *m* (einer Reise) high point; *(einer Veranstaltung)* highlight; *(eines Films, sexuell)* climax

höher *adj, adv* higher

hohl *adj* hollow

Höhle *(-, -n) f* cave

holen *vt* to get, to fetch; *(abholen)* to pick up; *(Atem)* to catch; **die Polizei ~** to call the police; **jdn/etw ~ lassen** to send for sb/sth

Holland *nt* Holland; **Holländer(in)** *(-s, -) m(f)* Dutchman/-woman; **holländisch** *adj* Dutch

Hölle *(-, -n) f* hell

Hologramm *nt* hologram

holperig *adj* bumpy

Holunder *(-s, -) m* elder

Holz *(-es, Hölzer) nt* wood; **Holzboden** *m* wooden floor; **hölzern** *adj* wooden; **holzig** *adj* (Stängel) woody; **Holzkohle** *f* charcoal

Homebanking (-s) nt home banking, online banking; **Homepage** (-, -s) f home page; **Hometrainer** m exercise machine

homöopathisch adj homeopathic

homosexuell adj homosexual; **Homosexuelle(r)** mf homosexual

Honig (-s, -e) m honey; **Honigmelone** f honeydew melon

Honorar (-s, -e) nt fee

Hopfen (-s, -) m (Bot) hop; (beim Brauen) hops pl

hoppla interj whoops, oops

horchen vi to listen (auf+akk to); (an der Tür) to eavesdrop

hören vt, vi (passiv, mitbekommen) to hear; (zufällig) to overhear; (aufmerksam zuhören; Radio, Musik) to listen to; **ich habe schon viel von Ihnen gehört** I've heard a lot about you; **Hörer** m (Tel) receiver; **Hörer(in)** m(f) listener; **Hörgerät** nt hearing aid

Horizont (-(e)s, -e) m horizon; **das geht über meinen ~** that's beyond me

Hormon (-s, -e) nt hormone

Hornhaut f hard skin; (des Auges) cornea

Hornisse (-, -n) f hornet

Horoskop (-s, -e) nt horoscope

Hörsaal m lecture hall; **Hörsturz** m acute hearing loss; **Hörweite** f in/außer ~ within/out of earshot

Höschenwindel (-, -n) f nappy (Brit), diaper (US)

Hose (-, -n) f trousers pl (Brit), pants pl (US); (Unterhose) (under)pants pl; **eine ~ a** pair of trousers/pants; **kurze ~** (pair of) shorts pl; **Hosenanzug** m trouser suit (Brit), pantsuit (US); **Hosenschlitz** m fly, flies (Brit); **Hosentasche** f trouser pocket (Brit), pant pocket (US); **Hosenträger** m braces pl (Brit), suspenders pl (US)

Hospital (-s, Hospitäler) nt hospital

Hotdog (-s, -s) nt o m hot dog

Hotel (-s, -s) nt hotel; **in welchem ~ seid ihr?** which hotel are you staying at?; **Hoteldirektor(in)** m(f) hotel manager; **Hotelkette** f hotel chain; **Hotelzimmer** nt hotel room

Hotline (-, -s) f hot line

Hubraum m cubic capacity

hübsch adj (Mädchen, Kind, Kleid) pretty; (gutaussehend; Mann, Frau) good-looking, cute

Hubschrauber (-s, -) m helicopter

Huf (-(e)s, -e) m hoof; **Hufeisen** nt horseshoe

Hüfte (-, -n) f hip

Hügel (-s, -) m hill; **hügelig** adj hilly

Huhn (-(e)s, Hühner) nt hen; (Gastr) chicken; **Hühnchen** nt chicken; **Hühnerauge** nt corn; **Hühnerbrühe** f chicken broth

Hülle (-, -n) f cover; (für Ausweis) case; (Zellophan) wrapping

Hummel (-, -n) f bumblebee

Hummer (-s, -) m lobster; **Hummerkrabbe** f king prawn

Humor (-s) m humour; **~ haben** to have a sense of humour; **humorvoll** adj humorous

humpeln vi hobble

Hund (-(e)s, -e) m dog; **Hundeleine** f dog lead (Brit), dog leash (US)

hundert num hundred; **Hundertjahrfeier** f centenary; **hundertprozentig** adj, adv one hundred per cent; **hundertste(r, s)** adj hundredth

Hündin f bitch

Hunger (-s) m hunger; **~ haben/bekommen** to be/get hungry; **hungern** vi to go hungry; (ernsthaft, dauernd) to starve

Hupe (-, -n) f horn; **hupen** vi to sound one's horn

Hüpfburg f bouncy castle®; **hüpfen** vi to hop; (springen) to jump

Hürde (-, -n) f hurdle

Hure (-, -n) f whore

hurra interj hooray

husten vi to cough; **Husten** (-s) m cough; **Hustenbonbon** nt cough sweet; **Hustensaft** m cough mixture

Hut (-(e)s, Hüte) m hat

hüten vt to look after ▷ vr **sich ~** to watch out; **sich ~, etw zu tun** to take care not to do sth; **sich ~ vor** (+dat) to beware of

Hütte (-, -n) f hut, cottage; **Hüttenkäse** m cottage cheese

Hyäne (-, -n) f hyena

Hydrant m hydrant

hygienisch adj hygienic

Hyperlink (-s, -s) m hyperlink

Hypnose (-, -n) f hypnosis; **Hypnotiseur(in)** m(f) hypnotist; **hypnotisieren** vt to hypnotize

Hypothek (-, -en) f mortgage

hysterisch adj hysterical

ihnen pron dat pl von **sie**; (to) them; **wie geht es ~?** how are they?; **ein Freund von ~** a friend of theirs

Ihnen pron dat sing u pl von **Sie**; (to) you; **wie geht es ~?** how are you?; **ein Freund von ~** a friend of yours

 SCHLÜSSELWORT

ihr pron **1** (nom pl) you; **ihr seid es** it's you

2 (dat von sie) to her; **gib es ihr** give it to her; **er steht neben ihr** he is standing beside her

▷ possessiv pron **1** (sg) her; (bei Tieren, Dingen) its; **ihr Mann** her husband

2 (pl) their; **die Bäume und ihre Blätter** the trees and their leaves

Ihr pron von **Sie**; (adjektivisch) your; **~(e) XY** (am Briefende) Yours, XY

ihre(r, s) pron (substantivisch, sing) hers; (pl) theirs; **das ist ~/~r/ihr(e)s** that's hers; (pl) that's theirs

Ihre(r, s) pron (substantivisch) yours; **das ist ~/~r/Ihr(e)s** that's yours

ihretwegen adv (wegen ihr) because of her; (ihr zuliebe) for her sake; (um sie) about her; (von ihr aus) as far as she is concerned ▷ adv (wegen ihnen) because of them; (ihnen zuliebe) for their sake; (um sie) about them; (von ihnen aus) as far as they are concerned; **Ihretwegen** adv (wegen Ihnen) because of you; (Ihnen zuliebe) for your sake; (um Sie) about you; (von Ihnen aus) as far as you are concerned

Ikone (-, -n) f icon

illegal adj illegal

Illusion f illusion; **sich** (dat) **~en machen** to delude oneself; **illusorisch** adj illusory

Illustration f illustration

Illustrierte (-n, -n) f (glossy) magazine

im kontr von **in dem**; **~ Bett** in bed; **~ Fernsehen** on TV; **~ Radio** on the radio; **~ Bus/Zug** on the bus/train; **~ Januar** in January; **~ Stehen** (while) standing up

Imbiss (-es, -e) m snack; **Imbissbude** f, **Imbissstube** f snack bar

Imbussschlüssel m hex key

immer adv always; **~ mehr** more and more; **~ wieder** again and again; **~ noch** still; **~ noch nicht** still not; **für ~** forever; **~ wenn ich ...** every time I ...;

---

i. A. abk = **im Auftrag** pp

IC (-, -s) m abk = **Intercityzug** Intercity (train)

ICE (-, -s) m abk = **Intercityexpresszug** German high-speed train

ich pron I; **~ bin's** it's me; **~ nicht** not me; **du und ~** you and me; **hier bin ~!** here I am; **~ Idiot!** stupid me

Icon (-s, -s) nt (Inform) icon

IC-Zuschlag m Intercity supplement

ideal adj ideal; **Ideal** (-s, -e) nt ideal

Idee (-, -n) f idea

identifizieren vt to identify ▷ vr **sich mit jdm/etw ~** to identify with sb/sth

identisch adj identical

Idiot(in) (-en, -en) m(f) idiot; **idiotisch** adj idiotic

Idol (-s, -e) nt idol

Idylle f idyll; **idyllisch** adj idyllic

Igel (-s, -) m hedgehog

ignorieren vt to ignore

ihm pron dat sing von **er/es**; (to) him, (to) it; **wie geht es ~?** how is he?; **ein Freund von ~** a friend of his ▷ pron dat von **es**; (to) it

ihn pron akk sing von **er**; (Person) him; (Sache) it

~ **schöner/trauriger** more and more beautiful/sadder and sadder; **was/wer/ wo/wann (auch)** ~ whatever/whoever/wherever/whenever; **immerhin** adv after all; **immerzu** adv all the time

Immigrant(in) m(f) immigrant

Immobilien pl property sing, real estate sing; **Immobilienmakler(in)** m(f) estate agent (Brit), realtor (US)

immun adj immune (gegen to); **Immunschwäche** f immunodeficiency; **Immunschwächekrankheit** f immune deficiency syndrome; **Immunsystem** nt immune system

impfen vt to vaccinate; **ich muss mich gegen Pocken ~ lassen** I've got to get myself vaccinated against smallpox; **Impfpass** m vaccination card; **Impfstoff** m vaccine; **Impfung** f vaccination

imponieren vi to impress (jdm sb)

Import (-(e)s, -e) m import; **importieren** vt to import

impotent adj impotent

imstande adj ~ **sein** to be in a position; (fähig) to be able

○ SCHLÜSSELWORT

in präp +akk **1** (räumlich: wohin?) in, into; **in die Stadt** into town; **in die Schule gehen** to go to school

2 (zeitlich): **bis ins 20. Jahrhundert** into od up to the 20th century

▷ präp +dat ~ **1** (räumlich: wo) in; **in der Stadt** in town; **in der Schule sein** to be at school

2 (zeitlich: wann); **in diesem Jahr** this year (in jenem Jahr) in that year; **heute in zwei Wochen** two weeks today

inbegriffen adj included

indem conj **sie gewann, ~ sie mogelte** she won by cheating

Inder(in) (-s, -) m(f) Indian

Indianer(in) (-s, -) m(f) American Indian, Native American; **indianisch** adj American Indian, Native American

Indien (-s) nt India

indirekt adj indirect

indisch adj Indian

indiskret adj indiscreet

individuell adj individual

Indonesien (-s) nt Indonesia

Industrie f industry; **Industrie-** in zW industrial; **Industriegebiet** nt industrial area; **industriell** adj industrial

ineinander adv in(to) one another (o each other)

Infarkt (-(e)s, -e) m (Herzinfarkt) heart attack

Infektion f infection; **Infektionskrankheit** f infectious disease; **infizieren** vt to infect ▷ vr **sich ~** to be infected

Info (-, -s) f (fam) info

infolge prep +gen as a result of, owing to; **infolgedessen** adv consequently

Informatik f computer science; **Informatiker(in)** (-s, -) m(f) computer scientist

Information f information; **Informationsschalter** m information desk; **informieren** vt to inform; **falsch ~** to misinform ▷ vr **sich ~** to find out (über +akk about)

infrage adv **das kommt nicht ~** that's out of the question; **etw ~ stellen** to question sth

Infrastruktur f infrastructure

Infusion f infusion

Ingenieur(in) m(f) engineer

Ingwer (-s) m ginger

Inhaber(in) (-s, -) m(f) owner; (Haus~) occupier; (von Lizenz) holder; (Fin) bearer

Inhalt (-(e)s, -e) m contents pl; (eines Buchs etc) content; (Math) volume; (Flächeninhalt) area; **Inhaltsangabe** f summary; **Inhaltsverzeichnis** nt table of contents

Initiative f initiative; **die ~ ergreifen** to take the initiative

Injektion f injection

inklusive adv, prep inclusive (gen of)

inkonsequent adj inconsistent

Inland nt (Pol, Comm) home; **im ~** at home; (Geo) inland; **inländisch** adj domestic; **Inlandsflug** m domestic flight; **Inlandsgespräch** nt national call

Inlineskates pl Rollerblades® pl, inline skates pl

innen adv inside; **Innenarchitekt(in)** m(f) interior designer; **Innenhof** m (inner) courtyard; **Innenminister(in)** m(f) minister of the interior, Home Secretary (Brit); **Innenseite** f inside; **Innenspiegel**

m rearview mirror; **Innenstadt** *f* town centre; *(von Großstadt)* city centre

innere(r, s) *adj* inner; *(im Körper, inländisch)* internal; **Innere(s)** *nt* inside; *(Mitte)* centre; *(fig)* heart

Innereien *pl* innards *pl*

innerhalb *adv, prep +gen* within; *(räumlich)* inside

innerlich *adj* internal; *(geistig)* inner

innerste(r, s) *adj* innermost

Innovation *f* innovation; **innovativ** *adj* innovative

inoffiziell *adj* unofficial; *(zwanglos)* informal

ins *kontr von* **in das**

Insasse (-n, -n) *m*, **Insassin** *f* *(Auto)* passenger; *(Anstalt)* inmate

insbesondere *adv* particularly, in particular

Inschrift *f* inscription

Insekt (-(e)s, -en) *nt* insect, bug *(US)*; **Insektenschutzmittel** *nt* insect repellent; **Insektenstich** *m* insect bite

Insel (-, -n) *f* island

Inserat *nt* advertisement

insgesamt *adv* altogether, all in all

Insider(in) (-s, -) *m(f)* insider

insofern *adv* in that respect; *(deshalb)* (and) so ▷ *conj* if; **~ als** in so far as

Installateur(in) *m(f)* *(Klempner)* plumber; *(Elektroinstallateur)* electrician; **installieren** *vt* *(Inform)* to install

Instinkt (-(e)s, -e) *m* instinct

Institut (-(e)s, -e) *nt* institute

Institution *f* institution

Instrument *nt* instrument

Insulin (-s) *nt* insulin

Inszenierung *f* production

intakt *adj* intact

intellektuell *adj* intellectual

intelligent *adj* intelligent; **Intelligenz** *f* intelligence

intensiv *adj* *(gründlich)* intensive; *(Gefühl, Schmerz)* intense; **Intensivkurs** *m* crash course; **Intensivstation** *f* intensive care unit

interaktiv *adj* interactive

Intercityexpress(zug) *m* German high-speed train; **Intercityzug** *m* Intercity (train); **Intercityzuschlag** *m* Intercity supplement

interessant *adj* interesting; **Interesse** (-s, -n) *nt* interest; **~ haben an** (+*dat*) to be

interested in; **interessieren** *vt* to interest ▷ *vr* **sich ~** to be interested *(für in)*

Interface (-, -s) *nt* *(Inform)* interface

Internat *nt* boarding school

international *adj* international

Internet (-s) *nt* Internet, Net; **im ~** on the Internet; **im ~ surfen** to surf the Net; **Internetcafé** *nt* Internetcafé, cybercafé; **Internetfirma** *f* dotcom company; **Internethandel** *m* e-commerce; **Internetseite** *f* web page

interpretieren *vt* to interpret *(als as)*

Interpunktion *f* punctuation

Interregio (-s, -s) *m* regional train

Interview (-s, -s) *nt* interview; **interviewen** *vt* to interview

intim *adj* intimate

intolerant *adj* intolerant

investieren *vt* to invest

inwiefern *adv* in what way; *(in welchem Ausmaß)* to what extent; **inwieweit** *adv* to what extent

inzwischen *adv* meanwhile

Irak (-(s)) *m* **(der) ~** Iraq

Iran (-(s)) *m* **(der) ~** Iran

Ire (-n, -n) *m* Irishman

irgend *adv* **~ so ein Idiot** some idiot; **wenn ~ möglich** if at all possible; **irgendein** *pron*, **irgendeine(r, s)** *adj* some; *(fragend, im Bedingungssatz; beliebig)* any; **irgendetwas** *pron* something; *(fragend, im Bedingungssatz)* anything; **irgendjemand** *pron* somebody; *(fragend, im Bedingungssatz)* anybody; **irgendwann** *adv* sometime; *(zu beliebiger Zeit)* any time; **irgendwie** *adv* somehow; **irgendwo** *adv* somewhere; *(fragend, im Bedingungssatz)* anywhere

Irin *f* Irishwoman; **irisch** *adj* Irish; **Irland** *nt* Ireland

ironisch *adj* ironic

irre *adj* crazy, mad; *(toll)* terrific; **Irre(r)** *mf* lunatic; **irreführen** *irr vt* to mislead; **irremachen** *vt* to confuse; **irren** *vi* to be mistaken; *(umherirren)* to wander ▷ *vr* **sich ~** to be mistaken; **wenn ich mich nicht irre** if I'm not mistaken; **sich in der Nummer ~** *(Telefon)* to get the wrong number; **irrsinnig** *adj* mad, crazy; **Irrtum** (-s, -tümer) *m* mistake, error; **irrtümlich** *adj* mistaken ▷ *adv* by mistake

ISBN (-) *nt abk = industrial standard business network* ISBN ▷ (-) *f abk =*

Internationale Standard Buchnummer
ISBN

Ischias (-) *m* sciatica

ISDN (-) *nt abk* = **integrated services digital network** ISDN

Islam (-s) *m* Islam; **islamisch** *adj* Islamic

Island *nt* Iceland; **Isländer(in)** (-s, -) *m(f)* Icelander; **isländisch** *adj* Icelandic; **Isländisch** *nt* Icelandic

Isolierband *nt* insulating tape; **isolieren** *vt* to isolate; (*Elek*) to insulate

Isomatte *f* thermomat, karrymat®

Israel (-s) *nt* Israel; **Israeli** (-(s), -(s)) *m* (-, -(s)) *f* Israeli; **israelisch** *adj* Israeli

IT (-) *f abk* = **Informationstechnologie** IT

Italien (-s) *nt* Italy; **Italiener(in)** (-s, -) *m(f)* Italian; **italienisch** *adj* Italian; **Italienisch** *nt* Italian

j

Jahreszeit f season; **Jahrgang** m (Wein) year, vintage; **der ~ 1989** (Personen) those born in 1989; **Jahrhundert** (-s, -e) nt century; **jährlich** adj yearly, annual; **Jahrmarkt** m fair; **Jahrtausend** nt millennium; **Jahrzehnt** nt decade
jähzornig adj hot-tempered
Jakobsmuschel f scallop
Jalousie f (venetian) blind
Jamaika (-s) nt Jamaica
jämmerlich adj pathetic
jammern vi to moan
Januar (-(s), -e) m January; siehe auch **Juni**
Japan (-s) nt Japan; **Japaner(in)** (-s, -) m(f) Japanese; **japanisch** adj Japanese; **Japanisch** nt Japanese
jaulen vi to howl
jawohl adv yes (of course)
Jazz (-) m jazz

je adv 1 (jemals) ever; **hast du so was je gesehen?** did you ever see anything like it?

2 (jeweils) every each; **sie zahlten je 3 Euro** they paid 3 euros each

▷ konj 1: **je nach** depending on; **je nachdem** it depends; **je nachdem, ob ...** depending on whether ...

2: **je eher, desto** od **umso besser** the sooner the better

Jeans (-, -) f jeans pl
jede(r, s) unbest Zahlwort (insgesamt gesehen) every; (einzeln gesehen) each; (jede(r, s) beliebige) any; **~s Mal** every time, each time; **~n zweiten Tag** every other day; **sie hat an ~m Finger einen Ring** she's got a ring on each finger; **~r Computer reicht aus** any computer will do; **bei ~m Wetter** in any weather ▷ pron everybody; (jeder Einzelne) each; **~r von euch/uns** each of you/us; **jedenfalls** adv in any case; **jederzeit** adv at any time; **jedesmal** adv every time
jedoch adv however
jemals adv ever
jemand pron somebody; (in Frage und Verneinung) anybody
Jemen (-(s)) m Yemen
jene(r, s) adj that, those pl ▷ pron that (one), those pl

ja adv 1 yes; **haben Sie das gesehen? — ja** did you see it? — yes(, I did); **ich glaube ja** (yes,) I think so

2 (fragend) really?; **ich habe gekündigt — ja?** I've quit — have you?; **du kommst, ja?** you're coming, aren't you?

3: **sei ja vorsichtig** do be careful; **Sie wissen ja, dass ...** as you know, ...; **tu das ja nicht!** don't do that!; **ich habe es ja gewusst** I just knew it; **ja, also ...** well you see ...

Jacht (-, -en) f yacht; **Jachthafen** m marina
Jacke (-, -n) f jacket; (Wolljacke) cardigan
Jackett (-s, -s o -e) nt jacket
Jagd (-, -en) f hunt; (Jagen) hunting; **jagen** vi to hunt ▷ vt to hunt; (verfolgen) to chase; **Jäger(in)** m(f) hunter
Jaguar (-s, -e) m jaguar
Jahr (-(e)s, -e) nt year; **ein halbes ~** six months pl; **Anfang der neunziger ~e** in the early nineties; **mit sechzehn ~en** at (the age of) sixteen; **Jahrestag** m anniversary; **Jahreszahl** f date, year;

jenseits adv on the other side ▷ prep +gen on the other side of; (fig) beyond

Jetlag (-s) m jet lag

jetzig adj present

jetzt adv now; **erst ~** only now; **~ gleich** right now; **bis ~** so far, up to now; **von ~ an** from now on

jeweils adv **~ zwei zusammen** two at a time; **zu ~ 5 Euro** at 5 euros each

Job (-s, -s) m job; **jobben** vi (fam) to work, to have a job

Jod (-(e)s) nt iodine

Joga (-s) nt yoga

joggen vi to jog; **Jogging** (-s) nt jogging; **Jogginganzug** m jogging suit, tracksuit; **Jogginghose** f jogging pants pl

Jog(h)urt (-s, -s) m o nt yoghurt

Johannisbeere f **Schwarze ~** blackcurrant; **Rote ~** redcurrant

Joint (-s, -s) m (fam) joint

jonglieren vi to juggle

Jordanien (-s) nt Jordan

Joule (-(s), -) nt joule

Journalist(in) m(f) journalist

Joystick (-s, -s) m (Inform) joystick

jubeln vi to cheer

Jubiläum (-s, Jubiläen) nt jubilee; (Jahrestag) anniversary

jucken vi to itch ▷ vt **es juckt mich am Arm** my arm is itching; **das juckt mich nicht** (fam) I couldn't care less; **Juckreiz** m itch

Jude (-n, -n) m, **Jüdin** f Jew; **sie ist Jüdin** she's Jewish; **jüdisch** adj Jewish

Judo (-(s)) nt judo

Jugend (-) f youth; **jugendfrei** adj **ein ~er Film** a U-rated film (Brit), a G-rated film (US); **ein nicht ~er Film** an X-rated film; **Jugendherberge** (-, -n) f youth hostel; **jugendlich** adj youthful; **Jugendliche(r)** mf young person; **Jugendstil** m art nouveau; **Jugendzentrum** nt youth centre

Jugoslawien (-s) nt (Hist) Yugoslavia; **das ehemalige ~** the former Yugoslavia

Juli (-(s), -s) m July; siehe auch **Juni**

jung adj young

Junge (-n, -n) m boy

Junge(s) (-n, -n) nt young animal; **die ~n** pl the young pl

Jungfrau f virgin; (Astr) Virgo

Junggeselle (-n, -n) m bachelor; **Junggesellin** f single woman

Juni (-(s), -s) m June; **im ~** in June; **am 4. ~** on 4(th) June, on June 4(th) (gesprochen: on the fourth of June); **Anfang/Mitte/Ende ~** at the beginning/in the middle/at the end of June; **letzten/nächsten ~** last/next June

Jupiter (-s) m Jupiter

Jura ohne Artikel (Studienfach) law; **~ studieren** to study law; **Jurist(in)** m(f) lawyer; **juristisch** adj legal

Justiz (-) f justice; **Justizminister(in)** m(f) minister of justice

Juwel (-s, -en) nt jewel; **Juwelier(in)** (-s, -e) m(f) jeweller

Jux (-es, -e) m joke, lark

K

Kabel (-s, -) nt (Elek) wire; (stark) cable; **Kabelfernsehen** nt cable television

Kabeljau (-s, -e o -s) m cod

Kabine f cabin; (im Schwimmbad) cubicle

Kabrio (-s, -s) nt convertible

Kachel (-, -n) f tile; **Kachelofen** m tiled stove

Käfer (-s, -) m beetle, bug (US)

Kaff (-s, -s) nt dump, hole

Kaffee (-s, -s) m coffee; ~ **kochen** to make some coffee; **Kaffeefilter** m coffee filter; **Kaffeekanne** f coffeepot; **Kaffeeklatsch** (-(e)s, -e) m chat over coffee and cakes, coffee klatch (US); **Kaffeelöffel** m coffee spoon; **Kaffeemaschine** f coffee maker (o machine); **Kaffeetasse** f coffee cup

Käfig (-s, -e) m cage

kahl adj (Mensch, Kopf) bald; (Baum, Wand) bare

Kahn (-(e)s, Kähne) m boat; (Lastkahn) barge

Kai (-s, -e o -s) m quay

Kaiser (-s, -) m emperor; **Kaiserin** f empress; **Kaiserschnitt** m (Med) caesarean (section)

Kajak (-s, -s) nt kayak

Kajal (-s) m kohl

Kajüte (-, -n) f cabin

Kakao (-s, -s) m cocoa; (Getränk) (hot) chocolate

Kakerlake (-, -n) f cockroach

Kaki (-, -s) f kaki

Kaktee (-, -n) f, **Kaktus** (-, -se) m cactus

Kalb (-(e)s, Kälber) nt calf; **Kalbfleisch** nt veal; **Kalbsbraten** m roast veal; **Kalbsschnitzel** nt veal cutlet; (paniert) escalope of veal

Kalender (-s, -) m calendar; (Taschenkalender) diary

Kalk (-(e)s, -e) m lime; (in Knochen) calcium

Kalorie f calorie; **kalorienarm** adj low-calorie

kalt adj cold; **mir ist (es) ~** I'm cold; **kaltblütig** adj cold-blooded; **Kälte** (-) f cold; (fig) coldness

kam imperf von **kommen**

Kambodscha (-s) nt Cambodia

Kamel (-(e)s, -e) nt camel

Kamera (-, -s) f camera

Kamerad(in) (-en, -en) m(f) friend; (als Begleiter) companion

Kamerafrau f, **Kameramann** m camerawoman/-man

Kamille (-, -n) f camomile; **Kamillentee** m camomile tea

Kamin (-s, -e) m (außen) chimney; (innen) fireplace

Kamm (-(e)s, Kämme) m comb; (Berg) ridge; (Hahn) crest; **kämmen** vr **sich ~, sich** (dat) **die Haare ~** to comb one's hair; **Kammermusik** f chamber music

Kampf (-(e)s, Kämpfe) m fight; (Schlacht) battle; (Wettbewerb) contest; (fig: Anstrengung) struggle; **kämpfen** vi to fight (für, um for); **Kampfsport** m martial art

Kanada (-s) nt Canada; **Kanadier(in)** (-s, -) m(f) Canadian; **kanadisch** adj Canadian

Kanal (-s, Kanäle) m (Fluss) canal; (Rinne, TV) channel; (für Abfluss) drain; **der ~** (Ärmelkanal) the (English) Channel; **Kanalinseln** pl Channel Islands pl; **Kanalisation** f sewerage system; **Kanaltunnel** m Channel Tunnel

Kanarienvogel m canary

Kandidat(in) (-en, -en) m(f) candidate

Kandis(zucker) (-) m rock candy

Känguru (-s, -s) nt kangaroo

Kaninchen nt rabbit

Kanister (-s, -) m can

Kännchen nt pot; **ein ~ Kaffee/Tee** a pot

of coffee/tea; **Kanne** (-, -n) f (Krug) jug;
(Kaffeekanne) pot; (Milchkanne) churn;
(Gießkanne) can

kannte imperf von **kennen**

Kante (-, -n) f edge

Kantine f canteen

Kanton (-s, -e) m canton

Kanu (-s, -s) nt canoe

Kanzler(in) (-s, -) m(f) chancellor

Kap (-s, -s) nt cape

Kapazität f capacity; (Fachmann)
authority

Kapelle f (Gebäude) chapel; (Mus) band

Kaper (-, -n) f caper

kapieren vi, vt (fam) to understand;
kapiert? got it?

Kapital (-s, -e o -ien) nt capital

Kapitän (-s, -e) m captain

Kapitel (-s, -) nt chapter

Kappe (-, -n) f cap

Kapsel (-, -n) f capsule

kaputt adj (fam) broken; (Mensch)
exhausted; **kaputt|gehen** irr vi to break;
(Schuhe) to fall apart; (Firma) to go bust;
(Stoff) to wear out; **kaputt|machen** vt to
break; (jdn) to wear out

Kapuze (-, -n) f hood

Kap Verde (-s) nt Cape Verde

Karaffe (-, -n) f carafe; (mit Stöpsel)
decanter

Karambole (-, -n) f star fruit, carambola

Karamell (-s) m caramel, toffee

Karaoke (-(s)) nt karaoke

Karat (-s, -e) nt carat

Karate (-s) nt karate

Kardinal (-s, Kardinäle) m cardinal

Karfreitag m Good Friday

kariert adj checked; (Papier) squared

Karies (-) f (tooth) decay

Karikatur f caricature

Karneval (-s, -e o -s) m carnival

> **Karneval**
>
> **Karneval** is the name given to the days
> immediately before Lent when
> people gather to sing, dance, eat,
> drink and generally make merry
> before the fasting begins.
> **Rosenmontag**, the day before Shrove
> Tuesday, is the most important day
> of 'Karneval' on the Rhine. Most
> firms take a day's holiday on that day

> to enjoy the parades and revelry. In
> South Germany 'Karneval' is called
> **Fasching**.

Kärnten (-s) nt Carinthia

Karo (-s, -s) nt square; (Karten) diamonds
pl

Karosserie f (Auto) body(work)

Karotte (-, -n) f carrot

Karpfen (-s, -) m carp

Karriere (-, -n) f career

Karte (-, -n) f card; (Landkarte) map;
(Speisekarte) menu; (Eintrittskarte,
Fahrkarte) ticket; **mit ~ bezahlen** to pay by
credit card; **~n spielen** to play cards; **die
~n mischen/geben** to shuffle/deal the
cards

Kartei f card index; **Karteikarte** f index
card

Kartenspiel nt card game;
Kartentelefon nt cardphone;
Kartenvorverkauf m advance booking

Kartoffel (-, -n) f potato; **Kartoffelbrei** m
mashed potatoes pl; **Kartoffelchips** pl
crisps pl (Brit), chips pl (US);
Kartoffelpuffer m potato cake (made
from grated potatoes); **Kartoffelpüree** nt
mashed potatoes pl; **Kartoffelsalat** m
potato salad

Karton (-s, -s) m cardboard; (Schachtel)
(cardboard) box

Kartusche (-, -n) f cartridge

Karussell (-s, -s) nt roundabout (Brit),
merry-go-round

Kaschmir (-s, e) m (Stoff) cashmere

Käse (-s, -) m cheese; **Käsekuchen**
m cheesecake; **Käseplatte** f
cheeseboard

Kasino (-s, -s) nt (Spielkasino) casino

Kaskoversicherung f comprehensive
insurance

Kasper(l) (-s, -) m Punch; (fig) clown;
Kasperl(e)theater nt (Vorstellung) Punch
and Judy show; (Gebäude) Punch and Judy
theatre

Kasse (-, -n) f (in Geschäft) till, cash
register; (im Supermarkt) checkout;
(Geldkasten) cashbox; (Theater) box office;
(Kino) ticket office; (Krankenkasse) health
insurance; (Spar~) savings bank;
Kassenbon (-s, -s) m, **Kassenzettel** m
receipt; **Kassenzettel** m receipt

Kassette f (small) box; (Tonband)

cassette; **Kassettenrekorder** m cassette recorder

kassieren vt to take ▷ vi **darf ich ~?** would you like to pay now?; **Kassierer(in)** m(f) cashier

Kastanie f chestnut

Kasten (-s, Kästen) m (Behälter) box; (Getränkekasten) crate

Kat m abk = **Katalysator**

Katalog (-(e)s, -e) m catalogue

Katalysator m (Auto) catalytic converter; (Phys) catalyst

Katar (-s) nt Qatar

Katarr(h) (-s, -e) m catarrh

Katastrophe (-, -n) f catastrophe, disaster

Kategorie (-, -n) f category

Kater (-s, -) m tomcat; (fam: nach zu viel Alkohol) hangover

Kathedrale (-, -n) f cathedral

Katholik(in) m(f) Catholic; **katholisch** adj Catholic

Katze (-, -n) f cat

Kauderwelsch (-(s)) nt (unverständlich) gibberish; (Fachjargon) jargon

kauen vt, vi to chew

Kauf (-(e)s, Käufe) m purchase; (Kaufen) buying; **ein guter ~** a bargain; **etw in ~ nehmen** to put up with sth; **kaufen** vt to buy; **Käufer(in)** m(f) buyer; **Kauffrau** f businesswoman; **Kaufhaus** nt department store; **Kaufmann** m businessman; (im Einzelhandel) shopkeeper (Brit), storekeeper (US); **Kaufpreis** m purchase price; **Kaufvertrag** m purchase agreement

Kaugummi m chewing gum

Kaulquappe (-, -n) f tadpole

kaum adv hardly, scarcely

Kaution f deposit; (Jur) bail

Kaviar m caviar

KB (-, -) nt, **Kbyte** (-, -) nt abk = **Kilobyte** KB

Kebab (-(s), -s) m kebab

Kegel (-s, -) m skittle; (beim Bowling) pin; (Math) cone; **Kegelbahn** f bowling alley; **kegeln** vi to play skittles; (bowlen) to bowl

Kehle (-, -n) f throat; **Kehlkopf** m larynx

Kehre (-, -n) f sharp bend

kehren vt (fegen) to sweep

Keilriemen m (Auto) fan belt

kein pron no, not ... any; **ich habe ~ Geld** I have no money, I don't have money; **~ Mensch** no one; **du bist ~ Kind mehr**

you're not a child any more; **keine(r, s)** pron (Person) no one, nobody; (Sache) not ... any, none; **~r von ihnen** none of them; (bei zwei Personen/Sachen) neither of them; **ich will keins von beiden** I don't want either (of them); **keinesfalls** adv on no account, under no circumstances

Keks (-es, -e) m biscuit (Brit), cookie (US); **jdm auf den ~ gehen** (fam) to get on sb's nerves

Keller (-s, -) m cellar; (Geschoss) basement

Kellner (-s, -) m waiter; **Kellnerin** f waitress

Kenia (-s) nt Kenya

kennen (kannte, gekannt) vt to know; **wir ~ uns seit 1990** we've known each other since 1990; **wir ~ uns schon** we've already met; **kennst du mich noch?** do you remember me?; **~ lernen** to get to know; **sich ~ lernen** to get to know each other; (zum ersten Mal) to meet

Kenntnis f knowledge; **seine ~se** his knowledge

Kennwort nt (a. Inform) password; **Kennzeichen** nt mark, sign; (Auto) number plate (Brit), license plate (US); **besondere ~** distinguishing marks

Kerl (-s, -e) m guy, bloke (Brit)

Kern (-(e)s, -e) m (Obst) pip; (Pfirsich, Kirsche etc) stone; (Nuss) kernel; (Atomkern) nucleus; (fig) heart, core

Kernenergie f nuclear energy; **Kernkraft** f nuclear power; **Kernkraftwerk** nt nuclear power station

Kerze (-, -n) f candle; (Zündkerze) plug

Ket(s)chup (-(s), -s) m o nt ketchup

Kette (-, -n) f chain; (Halskette) necklace

keuchen vi to pant; **Keuchhusten** m whooping cough

Keule (-, -n) f club; (Gastr) leg; (von Hähnchen a.) drumstick

Keyboard (-s, -s) nt (Mus) keyboard

Kfz nt abk = **Kraftfahrzeug**

Kfz-Brief m ≈ logbook

Kfz-Steuer f ≈ road tax (Brit), vehicle tax (US)

KG (-, -s) f abk = **Kommanditgesellschaft** limited partnership

Kichererbse f chick pea

kichern vi to giggle

Kickboard® (-s, -s) nt micro scooter

Kicker (-s, -) m (Spiel) table football (Brit), foosball (US)

kidnappen vt to kidnap

Kidney-Bohne f kidney bean

Kiefer (-s, -) m jaw ▷ (-, -n) f pine

Kieme (-, -n) f gill

Kies (-es, -e) m gravel; **Kiesel** (-s, -) m, **Kieselstein** m pebble

kiffen vi (fam) to smoke pot

Kilo (-s, -(s)) nt kilo; **Kilobyte** nt kilobyte; **Kilogramm** nt kilogram; **Kilojoule** nt kilojoule; **Kilometer** m kilometre; **Kilometerstand** m ≈ mileage; **Kilometerzähler** m ≈ mileometer; **Kilowatt** nt kilowatt

Kind (-(e)s, -er) nt child; **sie bekommt ein ~** she's having a baby; **Kinderarzt** m, **Kinderärztin** f paediatrician; **Kinderbetreuung** f childcare; **Kinderbett** nt cot (Brit), crib (US); **Kinderfahrkarte** f child's ticket; **Kindergarten** m nursery school, kindergarten; **Kindergärtnerin** f nursery-school teacher; **Kindergeld** nt child benefit; **Kinderkrankheit** f children's illness; **Kinderkrippe** f crèche (Brit), daycare center (US); **Kinderlähmung** f polio; **Kindermädchen** nt nanny (Brit), nurse(maid); **kindersicher** adj childproof; **Kindersicherung** f childproof safety catch; (an Flasche) childproof cap; **Kindersitz** m child seat; **Kindertagesstätte** nt day nursery; **Kinderteller** m (im Restaurant) children's portion; **Kinderwagen** m pram (Brit), baby carriage (US); **Kinderzimmer** nt children's (bed)room; **Kindheit** f childhood; **kindisch** adj childish; **kindlich** adj childlike

Kinn (-(e)s, -e) nt chin

Kino (-s, -s) nt cinema (Brit), movie theater (US); **ins ~ gehen** to go to the cinema (Brit) (o to the movies (US))

Kiosk (-(e)s, -e) m kiosk

Kippe f (fam: Zigarettenstummel) cigarette end, fag end (Brit)

kippen vi to tip over ▷ vt to tilt; (Regierung, Minister) to topple

Kirche (-, -n) f church; **Kirchturm** m church tower; (mit Spitze) steeple

Kirmes (-, -sen) f fair

Kirsche (-, -n) f cherry; **Kirschtomate** f cherry tomato

Kissen (-s, -) nt cushion; (Kopfkissen) pillow; **Kissenbezug** m cushion cover; (für Kopfkissen) pillowcase

Kiste (-, -n) f box; (Truhe) chest

kitschig adj kitschy, cheesy

kitzelig adj (a. fig) ticklish; **kitzeln** vt, vi to tickle

Kiwi (-, -s) f (Frucht) kiwi (fruit)

Klage (-, -n) f complaint; (Jur) lawsuit; **klagen** vi to complain (über +akk about, bei to); **kläglich** adj wretched

Klammer (-, -n) f (in Text) bracket; (Büroklammer) clip; (Wäscheklammer) peg (Brit), clothespin (US); (Zahnklammer) brace; **Klammeraffe** m (fam) at-sign, @; **klammern** vr **sich ~** to cling (an +akk to)

klang imperf von **klingen**

Klang (-(e)s, Klänge) m sound

Klappbett nt folding bed

klappen vi impers (gelingen) to work; **es hat gut geklappt** it went well

klappern vi to rattle; (Geschirr) to clatter; **Klapperschlange** f rattlesnake

Klappfahrad nt folding bicycle; **Klappstuhl** m folding chair

klar adj clear; **sich** (dat) **im Klaren sein** to be clear (über +akk about); **alles ~?** everything okay?

klären vt (Flüssigkeit) to purify; (Probleme, Frage) to clarify ▷ vr **sich ~** to clear itself up

Klarinette (-, -n) f clarinet

klar|kommen irr vi **mit etw ~** to cope with something; **kommst du klar?** are you managing all right?; **mit jdm ~** to get along with sb; **klar|machen** vt **jdm etw ~** to make sth clear to sb; **Klarsichtfolie** f clingfilm (Brit), plastic wrap (US); **klar|stellen** vt to clarify

Klärung f (von Frage, Problem) clarification

klasse adj inv (fam) great, brilliant

Klasse (-, -n) f class; (Schuljahr) form (Brit), grade (US); **erster ~ reisen** to travel first class; **in welche ~ gehst du?** which form (Brit) (o grade (US)) are you in?; **Klassenarbeit** f test; **Klassenlehrer(in)** m(f) class teacher; **Klassenzimmer** nt classroom

Klassik f (Zeit) classical period; (Musik) classical music

Klatsch (-(e)s, -e) m (Gerede) gossip; **klatschen** vi (schlagen) to smack; (Beifall) to applaud, to clap; (reden) to gossip; **Klatschmohn** m (corn) poppy; **klatschnass** adj soaking (wet)

Klaue (-, -n) f claw; (fam: Schrift) scrawl; **klauen** vt (fam) to pinch

Klavier (-s, -e) nt piano

Klebeband nt adhesive tape; **kleben** vt to stick (an +akk to) ▷ vi (klebrig sein) to be sticky; **klebrig** adj sticky; **Klebstoff** m glue; **Klebstreifen** m adhesive tape

Klecks (-es, -e) m blob; (Tinte) blot

Klee (-s) m clover

Kleid (-(e)s, -er) nt (Frauen~) dress; **~er** pl (Kleidung) clothes pl; **Kleiderbügel** m coat hanger; **Kleiderschrank** m wardrobe (Brit), closet (US); **Kleidung** f clothing

klein adj small, little; (Finger) little; **mein ~er Bruder** my little (o younger) brother; **als ich noch ~ war** when I was a little boy/girl; **etw ~ schneiden** to chop sth up; **etw ~ schreiben** to write sth with a small letter; **Kleinanzeige** f classified ad; **Kleinbuchstabe** m small letter; **Kleinbus** m minibus; **Kleingeld** nt change; **Kleinigkeit** f trifle; (Zwischenmahlzeit) snack; **Kleinkind** nt toddler; **klein|schreiben** vt to write with a small letter; **Kleinstadt** f small town

Kleister (-s, -) m paste

Klempner(in) m(f) plumber

klettern vi to climb

Klettverschluss m Velcro® fastening

klicken vi (a. Inform) to click

Klient(in) (-en, -en) m(f) client

Klima (-s, -s) nt climate; **Klimaanlage** f air conditioning; **klimatisiert** adj air-conditioned

Klinge (-, -n) f blade

Klingel (-, -n) f bell; **klingeln** vi to ring

klingen (klang, geklungen) vi to sound

Klinik f clinic; (Krankenhaus) hospital

Klinke (-, -n) f handle

Klippe (-, -n) f cliff; (im Meer) reef; (fig) hurdle

Klischee (-s, -s) nt (fig) cliché

Klo (-s, -s) nt (fam) loo (Brit), john (US); **Klobrille** f toilet seat; **Klopapier** nt toilet paper

klopfen vt, vi to knock; (Herz) to thump

Kloß (-es, Klöße) m (im Hals) lump; (Gastr) dumpling

Kloster (-s, Klöster) nt (für Männer) monastery; (für Frauen) convent

Klub (-s, -s) m club

klug adj clever

knabbern vt, vi to nibble

Knäckebrot nt crispbread

knacken vt, vi to crack

Knall (-(e)s, -e) m bang; **Knallbonbon** nt cracker; **knallen** vi to bang

knapp adj (kaum ausreichend) scarce; (Sieg) narrow; **~ bei Kasse sein** to be short of money; **~ zwei Stunden** just under two hours

Knauf (-s, Knäufe) m knob

Knautschzone f (Auto) crumple zone

kneifen (kniff, gekniffen) vt, vi to pinch; (sich drücken) to back out (vor +dat of); **Kneifzange** f pincers pl

Kneipe (-, -n) f (fam) pub (Brit), bar

Knete (-) f (fam: Geld) dough; **kneten** vt to knead; (formen) to mould

knicken vt, vi (brechen) to break; (Papier) to fold; **geknickt sein** (fig) to be downcast

Knie (-s, -) nt knee; **in die ~ gehen** to bend one's knees; **Kniebeuge** f knee bend; **Kniegelenk** nt knee joint; **Kniekehle** f back of the knee; **knien** vi to kneel; **Kniescheibe** f kneecap; **Knieschoner** (-s, -) m, **Knieschützer** (-s, -) m knee pad; **Kniestrumpf** m knee-length sock

kniff imperf von **kneifen**

knipsen vt to punch; (Foto) to snap ▷ vi (Foto) to take snaps

knirschen vi to crunch; **mit den Zähnen ~** to grind one's teeth

knitterfrei adj non-crease; **knittern** vi to crease

Knoblauch m garlic; **Knoblauchbrot** nt garlic bread; **Knoblauchzehe** f clove of garlic

Knöchel (-s, -) m (Finger) knuckle; (Fuß) ankle

Knochen (-s, -) m bone; **Knochenbruch** m fracture; **Knochenmark** nt marrow

Knödel (-s, -) m dumpling

Knollensellerie m celeriac

Knopf (-(e)s, Knöpfe) m button; **Knopfdruck** m **auf ~** at the touch of a button; **Knopfloch** nt buttonhole

Knospe (-, -n) f bud

knoten vt to knot; **Knoten** (-s, -) m knot; (Med) lump

Know-how (-(s)) nt know-how, expertise

knurren vi (Hund) to growl; (Magen) to rumble; (Mensch) to grumble

knusprig adj crisp; (Keks) crunchy

knutschen vi (fam) to smooch

k. o. adj inv (Sport) knocked out; (fig) knackered

Koalition f coalition

Koch (-(e)s, Köche) m cook; **Kochbuch** nt cookery book, cookbook; **kochen** vt, vi to cook; (Wasser) to boil; (Kaffee, Tee) to make; **Köchin** f cook; **Kochlöffel** m wooden spoon; **Kochnische** f kitchenette; **Kochplatte** f hotplate; **Kochrezept** nt recipe; **Kochtopf** m saucepan

Kode (-s, -s) m code

Köder (-s, -) m bait

Koffein (-s) nt caffeine; **koffeinfrei** adj decaffeinated

Koffer (-s, -) m (suit)case; **Kofferraum** m (Auto) boot (Brit), trunk (US)

Kognak (-s, -s) m brandy

Kohl (-(e)s, -e) m cabbage

Kohle (-, -n) f coal; (Holzkohle) charcoal; (Chem) carbon; (fam: Geld) cash, dough; **Kohlehydrat** nt carbohydrate; **Kohlendioxid** nt carbon dioxide; **Kohlensäure** f (in Getränken) fizz; **ohne ~** still, non-carbonated (US); **mit ~** sparkling, carbonated (US); **Kohletablette** f charcoal tablet

Kohlrabi (-(s), -(s)) m kohlrabi

Kohlrübe f swede (Brit), rutabaga (US)

Koje (-, -n) f cabin; (Bett) bunk

Kokain (-s) nt cocaine

Kokosnuss f coconut

Kolben (-s, -) m (Tech) piston; (Mais~) cob

Kolik (-, -en) f colic

Kollaps (-es, -e) m collapse

Kollege (-n, -n) m, **Kollegin** f colleague

Köln (-s) nt Cologne

Kolonne (-, -n) f convoy; **in ~ fahren** to drive in convoy

Kölsch (-, -) nt (Bier) (strong) lager (from the Cologne region)

Kolumbien (-s) nt Columbia

Koma (-s, -s) nt coma

Kombi (-(s), -s) m estate (car) (Brit), station wagon (US); **Kombination** f combination; (Folgerung) deduction; (Hemdhose) combinations pl; (Aviat) flying suit; **kombinieren** vt to combine ▷ vi to reason; (vermuten) to guess; **Kombizange** f (pair of) pliers pl

Komfort (-s) m conveniences pl; (Bequemlichkeit) comfort

Komiker(in) m(f) comedian, comic; **komisch** adj funny

Komma (-s, -s) nt comma

Kommanditgesellschaft f limited partnership

kommen (kam, gekommen) vi to come; (näher kommen) to approach; (passieren) to happen; (gelangen, geraten) to get; (erscheinen) to appear; (in die Schule, das Gefängnis etc) to go; **~ lassen** to send for; **zu sich ~** to come round (o to); **zu etw ~ (bekommen)** to acquire sth; (Zeit dazu finden) to get round to sth; **wer kommt zuerst?** who's first?; **kommend** adj coming; **~e Woche** next week; **in den ~en Jahren** in the years to come

Kommentar m commentary; **kein ~** no comment

Kommilitone (-n, -n) m, **Kommilitonin** f fellow student

Kommissar(in) m(f) inspector

Kommode (-, -n) f chest of drawers

Kommunikation f communication

Kommunion f (Rel) communion

Kommunismus m communism

Komödie f comedy

kompakt adj compact

Kompass (-es, -e) m compass

kompatibel adj compatible

kompetent adj competent

komplett adj complete

Kompliment nt compliment; **jdm ein ~ machen** to pay sb a compliment; **~!** congratulations

Komplize (-n, -n) m accomplice

kompliziert adj complicated

Komponist(in) m(f) composer

Kompost (-(e)s, -e) m compost; **Komposthaufen** m compost heap; **kompostierbar** adj biodegradable

Kompott (-(e)s, -e) nt stewed fruit

Kompresse (-, -n) f compress

Kompromiss (-es, -e) m compromise

Kondensmilch f condensed milk, evaporated milk

Kondition f (Leistungsfähigkeit) condition; **sie hat eine gute ~** she's in good shape

Konditorei f cake shop; (mit Café) café

Kondom (-s, -e) nt condom

Konfektionsgröße f size

Konferenz f conference

Konfession f religion; (christlich) denomination

Konfetti (-(s)) nt confetti

Konfirmation f (Rel) confirmation
Konfitüre (-, -n) f jam
Konflikt (-(e)s, -e) m conflict
konfrontieren vt to confront
Kongo (-s) m Congo
Kongress (-es, -e) m conference; **der ~** (Parlament der USA) Congress
König (-(e)s, -e) m king; **Königin** f queen; **Königinpastete** f vol-au-vent; **königlich** adj royal; **Königreich** nt kingdom
Konkurrenz f competition

SCHLÜSSELWORT

können (pt **konnte**, pp **gekonnt** od (als Hilfsverb) **können**) vt, vi **1** to be able to; **ich kann es machen** I can do it, I am able to do it,; **ich kann es nicht machen** I can't do it, I'm not able to do it; **ich kann nicht … ** I can't …, I cannot …; **ich kann nicht mehr** I can't go on
2 (wissen, beherrschen) to know; **können Sie Deutsch?** can you speak German?; **er kann gut Englisch** he speaks English well; **sie kann keine Mathematik** she can't do mathematics
3 (dürfen) to be allowed to; **kann ich gehen?** can I go?; **könnte ich …?** could I …?; **kann ich mit?** (umg) can I come with you?
4 (möglich sein): **Sie könnten Recht haben** you may be right; **das kann sein** that's possible; **kann sein** maybe

konsequent adj consistent; **Konsequenz** f consequence
konservativ adj conservative
Konserven pl tinned food sing (Brit), canned food sing; **Konservendose** f tin (Brit), can
konservieren vt to preserve; **Konservierungsmittel** nt preservative
Konsonant m consonant
Konsul(in) (-s, -n) m(f) consul; **Konsulat** nt consulate
Kontakt (-(e)s, -e) m contact; **kontaktarm** adj **er ist ~** he lacks contact with other people; **kontaktfreudig** adj sociable; **Kontaktlinsen** pl contact lenses pl
Kontinent m continent
Konto (-s, Konten) nt account;

Kontoauszug m (bank) statement; **Kontoauszugsdrucker** m bank-statement machine; **Kontoinhaber(in)** m(f) account holder; **Kontonummer** f account number; **Kontostand** m balance
Kontrabass m double bass
Kontrast (-(e)s, -e) m contrast
Kontrolle (-, -n) f control; (Aufsicht) supervision; (Passkontrolle) passport control; **kontrollieren** vt to control; (nachprüfen) to check
Konzentration f concentration; **Konzentrationslager** nt (Hist) concentration camp; **konzentrieren** vt to concentrate ▷ vr **sich ~** to concentrate
Konzept (-(e)s, -e) nt rough draft; **jdn aus dem ~ bringen** to put sb off
Konzert (-(e)s, -e) nt concert; (Stück) concerto; **Konzertsaal** m concert hall
koordinieren vt to coordinate
Kopf (-(e)s, Köpfe) m head; **pro ~** per person; **sich den ~ zerbrechen** to rack one's brains; **Kopfhörer** m headphones pl; **Kopfkissen** nt pillow; **Kopfsalat** m lettuce; **Kopfschmerzen** pl headache sing; **Kopfstütze** f headrest; **Kopftuch** nt headscarf; **kopfüber** adv headfirst
Kopie f copy; **kopieren** vt (a. Inform) to copy; **Kopierer** (-s, -) m, **Kopiergerät** nt copier
Kopilot(in) m(f) co-pilot
Koralle (-, -n) f coral
Koran (-s) m (Rel) Koran
Korb (-(e)s, Körbe) m basket; **jdm einen ~ geben** (fig) to turn sb down
Kord (-(e)s, -e) m corduroy
Kordel (-, -n) f cord
Korinthe (-e, -n) f currant
Kork (-(e)s, -e) m cork; **Korken** (-s, -) m cork; **Korkenzieher** (-s, -) m corkscrew
Korn (-(e)s, Körner) nt grain; **Kornblume** f cornflower
Körper (-s, -) m body; **Körperbau** m build; **körperbehindert** adj disabled; **Körpergeruch** m body odour; **Körpergröße** f height; **körperlich** adj physical; **Körperteil** m part of the body; **Körperverletzung** f physical injury
korrekt adj correct
Korrespondent(in) m(f) correspondent; **Korrespondenz** f correspondence
korrigieren vt to correct
Kosmetik f cosmetics pl;

Kosmetikkoffer m vanity case;
Kosmetiksalon m beauty parlour;
Kosmetiktuch nt paper tissue
Kost (-) f (Nahrung) food; (Verpflegung)
board
kostbar adj precious; (teuer) costly,
expensive
kosten vt to cost ▷ vt, vi (versuchen) to
taste; **Kosten** pl costs pl, cost; (Ausgaben)
expenses pl; **auf ~ von** at the expense of;
kostenlos adj free (of charge);
Kostenvoranschlag m estimate
köstlich adj (Essen) delicious; (Einfall)
delightful; **sich ~ amüsieren** to have a
marvellous time
Kostprobe f taster; (fig) sample;
kostspielig adj expensive
Kostüm (-s, -e) nt costume;
(Damenkostüm) suit
Kot (-(e)s) m excrement
Kotelett (-(e)s, -e o -s) nt chop, cutlet
Koteletten pl sideboards pl (Brit),
sideburns pl (US)
Kotflügel m (Auto) wing
Krabbe (-, -n) f shrimp; (größer) prawn;
(Krebs) crab
krabbeln vi to crawl
Krach (-(e)s, -s o -e) m crash; (andauernd)
noise; (fam: Streit) row
Kraft (-, Kräfte) f strength; (Pol, Phys)
force; (Fähigkeit) power; (Arbeits~) worker;
in ~ treten to come into effect;
Kraftausdruck m swearword;
Kraftfahrzeug nt motor vehicle;
Kraftfahrzeugbrief m ≈ logbook;
Kraftfahrzeugschein m vehicle
registration document;
Kraftfahrzeugsteuer f ≈ road tax (Brit),
vehicle tax (US);
Kraftfahrzeugversicherung f car
insurance; **kräftig** adj strong; (gesund)
healthy; (Farben) intense, strong;
Kraftstoff m fuel; **Kraftwerk** nt power
station
Kragen (-s, -) m collar
Krähe (-, -n) f crow
Kralle (-, -n) f claw; (Parkkralle) wheel
clamp
Kram (-(e)s) m stuff
Krampf (-(e)s, Krämpfe) m cramp;
(zuckend) spasm; **Krampfader** f varicose
vein
Kran (-(e)s, Kräne) m crane

Kranich (-s, -e) m (Zool) crane
krank adj ill, sick
kränken vt to hurt
Krankengymnastik f physiotherapy;
Krankenhaus nt hospital;
Krankenkasse f health insurance;
Krankenpfleger (-s, -) m (male) nurse;
Krankenschein m health insurance
certificate; **Krankenschwester** f nurse;
Krankenversicherung f health
insurance; **Krankenwagen** m
ambulance; **Krankheit** f illness; (durch
Infektion hervorgerufen) disease
Kränkung f insult
Kranz (-es, Kränze) m wreath
krass adj crass; (fam: toll) wicked
kratzen vt, vi to scratch; **Kratzer** (-s, -) m
scratch
kraulen vi (schwimmen) to do the crawl
▷ vt (streicheln) to pet
Kraut (-(e)s, Kräuter) nt plant; (Gewürz)
herb; (Gemüse) cabbage; **Kräuter** pl herbs
pl; **Kräuterbutter** f herb butter;
Kräutertee m herbal tea; **Krautsalat** m
coleslaw
Krawatte f tie
kreativ adj creative
Krebs (-es, -e) m (Zool) crab; (Med) cancer;
(Astr) Cancer
Kredit (-(e)s, -e) m credit; **auf ~** on credit;
einen ~ aufnehmen to take out a loan;
Kreditkarte f credit card
Kreide (-, -n) f chalk
Kreis (-es, -e) m circle; (Bezirk) district
kreischen vi to shriek; (Bremsen, Säge) to
screech
Kreisel (-s, -) m (Spielzeug) top;
(Verkehrskreisel) roundabout (Brit), traffic
circle (US)
Kreislauf m (Med) circulation; (fig: der
Natur etc) cycle; **Kreislaufstörungen** pl
(Med) **ich habe ~** I've got problems with
my circulation; **Kreisverkehr** m
roundabout (Brit), traffic circle (US),
rotary (US)
Kren (-s) m horseradish
Kresse (-, -n) f cress
Kreuz (-es, -e) nt cross; (Anat) small of the
back; (Karten) clubs pl; **mir tut das ~ weh**
I've got backache; **Kreuzband** m cruciate
ligament; **kreuzen** vt to cross ▷ vr **sich
~** to cross ▷ vi (Naut) to cruise;
Kreuzfahrt f cruise; **Kreuzgang** m

cloisters pl; **Kreuzotter** (-, -n) f adder; **Kreuzschlitzschraubenzieher** m Phillips® screwdriver; **Kreuzschlüssel** m (Auto) wheel brace; **Kreuzschmerzen** pl backache sing; **Kreuzung** f (Verkehrskreuzung) crossroads sing, intersection; (Züchtung) cross; **Kreuzworträtsel** nt crossword (puzzle)

kriechen (kroch, gekrochen) vi to crawl; (unauffällig) to creep; (fig, pej) **(vor jdm)** ~ to crawl (to sb); **Kriechspur** f crawler lane

Krieg (-(e)s, -e) m war

kriegen vt (fam) to get; (erwischen) to catch; **sie kriegt ein Kind** she's having a baby; **ich kriege noch Geld von dir** you still owe me some money

Krimi (-s, -s) m (fam) thriller; **Kriminalität** f criminality; **Kriminalpolizei** f detective force, ≈ CID (Brit), ≈ FBI (US); **Kriminalroman** m detective novel; **kriminell** adj criminal

Krippe (-, -n) f (Futterkrippe) manger; (Weihnachtskrippe) crib (Brit), crèche (US); (Kinderkrippe) crèche (Brit), daycare center (US)

Krise (-, -n) f crisis

Kristall (-s, -e) m crystal ▷ (-s) nt (Glas) crystal

Kritik f criticism; (Rezension) review; **Kritiker(in)** m(f) critic; **kritisch** adj critical

kritzeln vt, vi to scribble, to scrawl

Kroate (-n, -n) m Croat; **Kroatien** (-s) nt Croatia; **Kroatin** f Croat; **kroatisch** adj Croatian; **Kroatisch** nt Croatian

kroch imperf von **kriechen**

Krokodil (-s, -e) nt crocodile

Krokus (-, -o -se) m crocus

Krone (-, -n) f crown; **Kronleuchter** m chandelier

Kropf (-(e)s, Kröpfe) m (Med) goitre; (von Vogel) crop

Kröte (-, -n) f toad

Krücke (-, -n) f crutch

Krug (-(e)s, Krüge) m jug; (Bierkrug) mug

Krümel (-s, -) m crumb

krumm adj crooked

Krüppel (-s, -) m cripple

Kruste (-, -n) f crust

Kruzifix (-es, -e) nt crucifix

Kuba (-s) nt Cuba

Kübel (-s, -) m tub; (Eimer) bucket

Kubikmeter m cubic metre

Küche (-, -n) f kitchen; (Kochen) cooking

Kuchen (-s, -) m cake; (mit Teigdeckel) pie; **Kuchengabel** f cake fork

Küchenmaschine f food processor; **Küchenpapier** nt kitchen roll; **Küchenschrank** m (kitchen) cupboard

Kuckuck (-s, -e) m cuckoo

Kugel (-, -n) f ball; (Math) sphere; (Mil) bullet; (Weihnachtskugel) bauble; **Kugellager** nt ball bearing; **Kugelschreiber** m (ball-point) pen, biro® (Brit); **Kugelstoßen** (-s) nt shot put

Kuh (-, Kühe) f cow

kühl adj cool; **Kühlakku** (-s, -s) m ice pack; **Kühlbox** f cool box; **kühlen** vt to cool; **Kühler** (-s, -) m (Auto) radiator; **Kühlerhaube** f (Auto) bonnet (Brit), hood (US); **Kühlschrank** m fridge, refrigerator; **Kühltasche** f cool bag; **Kühltruhe** f freezer; **Kühlwasser** nt (Auto) radiator water

Kuhstall m cowshed

Küken (-s, -) nt chick

Kuli (-s, -s) m (fam: Kugelschreiber) pen, biro® (Brit)

Kulisse (-, -n) f scenery

Kult (-s, -e) m cult; **Kultfigur** f cult figure

Kultur f culture; (Lebensform) civilization; **Kulturbeutel** m toilet bag (Brit), washbag; **kulturell** adj cultural

Kümmel (-s, -) m caraway seeds pl

Kummer (-s) m grief, sorrow

kümmern vr **sich um jdn** ~ to look after sb; **sich um etw** ~ to see to sth ▷ vt to concern; **das kümmert mich nicht** that doesn't worry me

Kumpel (-s, -) m (fam) mate, pal

Kunde (-n, -n) m customer; **Kundendienst** m after-sales (o customer) service; **Kunden(kredit)karte** f storecard, chargecard; **Kundennummer** f customer number

kündigen vi to hand in one's notice; (Mieter) to give notice that one is moving out; **jdm** ~ to give sb his/her notice; (Vermieter) to give sb notice to quit ▷ vt to cancel; (Vertrag) to terminate; **jdm die Stellung** ~ to give sb his/her notice; **jdm die Wohnung** ~ to give sb notice to quit; **Kündigung** f (Arbeitsverhältnis) dismissal; (Vertrag) termination; (Abonnement)

cancellation; (Frist) notice;
Kündigungsfrist f period of notice
Kundin f customer; **Kundschaft** f
customers pl
künftig adj future
Kunst (-, Künste) f art; (Können) skill;
Kunstausstellung f art exhibition;
Kunstgewerbe nt arts and crafts pl;
Künstler(in) (-s, -) m(f) artist;
künstlerisch adj artistic
künstlich adj artificial
Kunststoff m synthetic material;
Kunststück nt trick; **Kunstwerk** nt
work of art
Kupfer (-s, -) nt copper
Kuppel (-, -n) f dome
kuppeln vi (Auto) to operate the clutch;
Kupplung f coupling; (Auto) clutch
Kur (-, -en) f course of treatment; (am
Kurort) cure
Kür (-, -en) f (Sport) free programme
Kurbel (-, -n) f crank; (von Rollo, Fenster)
winder
Kürbis (-ses, -se) m pumpkin
Kurierdienst m courier service
kurieren vt to cure
Kurort m health resort
Kurs (-es, -e) m course; (Fin) rate;
(Wechselkurs) exchange rate
kursiv adj italic ▷ adv in italics
Kursleiter(in) m(f) course tutor;
Kursteilnehmer(in) m(f) (course)
participant; **Kurswagen** m (Eisenb)
through carriage
Kurve (-, -n) f curve; (Straßenkurve) bend;
kurvenreich adj (Straße) winding
kurz adj short; (zeitlich a.) brief;
~ **vorher/darauf** shortly before/after;
kannst du ~ kommen? could you come
here for a minute?; ~ **gesagt** in short;
kurzärmelig adj short-sleeved; **kürzen**
vt to cut short; (in der Länge) to shorten;
(Gehalt) to reduce; **kurzerhand** adv on the
spot; **kurzfristig** adj short-term; **das
Konzert wurde ~ abgesagt** the concert
was called off at short notice;
Kurzgeschichte f short story;
kurzhaarig adj short-haired; **kürzlich**
adv recently; **Kurznachrichten** pl news
summary sing; **Kurzparkzone** f
short-stay (Brit) (o short-term (US))
parking zone; **Kurzschluss** m (Elek) short
circuit; **kurzsichtig** adj short-sighted;

Kurzurlaub m short holiday (Brit), short
vacation (US); **Kurzwelle** f short wave
Kusine f cousin
Kuss (-es, Küsse) m kiss; **küssen** vt to kiss
▷ vr **sich ~** to kiss
Küste (-, -n) f coast; (Ufer) shore;
Küstenwache f coastguard
Kutsche (-, -n) f carriage; (geschlossene)
coach
Kuvert (-s, -s) nt envelope
Kuvertüre (-, -n) f coating
Kuwait (-s) nt Kuwait
KZ (-s, -s) nt abk = **Konzentrationslager**
(Hist) concentration camp

Labor (-s, -e o -s) nt lab

Labyrinth (-s, -e) nt maze

Lache (-, -n) f (Pfütze) puddle; (Blut~, Öl~) pool

lächeln vi to smile; **Lächeln** (-s) nt smile; **lachen** vi to laugh; **lächerlich** adj ridiculous

Lachs (-es, -e) m salmon

Lack (-(e)s, -e) m varnish; (Farblack) lacquer; (an Auto) paint; **lackieren** vt to varnish; (Auto) to spray; **Lackschaden** m scratch (on the paintwork)

Ladegerät nt (battery) charger; **laden** (lud, geladen) vt (a. Inform) to load; (einladen) to invite; (Handy etc) to charge

Laden (-s, Läden) m shop; (Fensterladen) shutter; **Ladendieb(in)** m(f) shoplifter; **Ladendiebstahl** m shoplifting; **Ladenschluss** m closing time

Ladung f load; (Naut, Aviat) cargo; (Jur) summons sing

lag imperf von **liegen**

Lage (-, -n) f position, situation; (Schicht) layer; **in der ~ sein zu** to be in a position to

Lager (-s, -) nt camp; (Comm) warehouse; (Tech) bearing; **Lagerfeuer** nt campfire; **lagern** vi (Dinge) to be stored; (Menschen) to camp ▷ vt to store

Lagune f lagoon

lahm adj lame; (langweilig) dull; **lähmen** vt to paralyse; **Lähmung** f paralysis

Laib (-s, -e) m loaf

Laie (-n, -n) m layman

Laken (-s, -) nt sheet

Lakritze (-, -n) f liquorice

Lamm (-(e)s, Lämmer) nt (a. Lammfleisch) lamb

Lampe (-, -n) f lamp; (Glühbirne) bulb; **Lampenfieber** nt stage fright; **Lampenschirm** m lampshade

Lampion (-s, -s) m Chinese lantern

Land (-(e)s, Länder) nt (Gelände) land; (Nation) country; (Bundesland) state, Land; **auf dem ~(e)** in the country

Land

A **Land** (plural **Länder**) is a member state of the **BRD**. There are 16 **Länder**, namely Baden-Württemberg, Bayern, Berlin, Brandenburg, Bremen, Hamburg, Hessen, Mecklenburg-Vorpommern, Niedersachsen, Nordrhein-Westfalen, Rheinland-Pfalz, Saarland, Sachsen, Sachsen-Anhalt, Schleswig-Holstein and Thüringen. Each 'Land' has its own parliament and constitution.

Landebahn f runway; **landen** vt, vi to land; (Schiff) to dock

Länderspiel nt international (match)

Landesgrenze f national border, frontier; **Landesinnere** nt interior; **landesüblich** adj customary; **Landeswährung** f national currency; **landesweit** adj nationwide

Landhaus nt country house; **Landkarte** f map; **Landkreis** m administrative region, ≈ district

ländlich adj rural

Landschaft f countryside; (schöne) scenery; (Kunst) landscape; **Landstraße** f country road, B road (Brit)

Landung f landing; **Landungsbrücke** f, **Landungssteg** m gangway

Landwirt(in) m(f) farmer;

Landwirtschaft f agriculture, farming;
landwirtschaftlich adj agricultural

lang adj long; (Mensch) tall; **ein zwei
Meter ~er Tisch** a table two metres long;
den ganzen Tag ~ all day long; **die Straße
~** along the street; **langärmelig** adj
long-sleeved; **lange** adv (for) a long time;
ich musste ~ warten I had to wait (for) a
long time; **ich bleibe nicht ~** I won't stay
long; **es ist ~ her, dass wir uns gesehen
haben** it's a long time since we saw each
other; **Länge** (-, -n) f length; (Geo)
longitude

langen vi (fam: ausreichen) to be enough;
(fam: fassen) to reach (nach for); **mir
langt's** I've had enough

Langeweile f boredom

langfristig adj long-term ▷ adv in the
long term

Langlauf m cross-country skiing

längs prep +gen **die Bäume ~ der Straße**
the trees along(side) the road ▷ adv **die
Streifen laufen ~ über das Hemd** the
stripes run lengthways down the shirt

langsam adj slow ▷ adv slowly

Langschläfer(in) (-s, -) m(f) late riser

längst adv **das ist ~ fertig** that was
finished a long time ago; **sie sollte ~ da
sein** she should have been here long ago;
als sie kam, waren wir ~ weg when she
arrived we had long since left

Langstreckenflug m long-haul flight

Languste (-, -n) f crayfish, crawfish
(US)

langweilen vt to bore; **ich langweile
mich** I'm bored; **langweilig** adj boring;
Langwelle f long wave

Laos (-) nt Laos

Lappen (-s, -) m cloth, rag; (Staublappen)
duster

läppisch adj silly; (Summe) ridiculous

Laptop (-s, -s) m laptop

Lärche (-, -n) f larch

Lärm (-(e)s) m noise

las imperf von lesen

Lasche (-, -n) f flap

Laser (-s, -) m laser; **Laserdrucker** m
laser printer

○ **SCHLÜSSELWORT**

lassen (pt **ließ**, pp **gelassen** od (als
Hilfsverb) **lassen**) vt 1 (unterlassen) to stop

(momentan) to leave; **lass das (sein)!** don't
(do it)!; (hör auf!) stop it!; **lass mich!** leave
me alone; **lassen wir das!** let's leave it; **er
kann das Trinken nicht lassen** he can't
stop drinking

2 (zurücklassen) to leave; **etw lassen, wie
es ist** to leave sth (just) as it is

3 (überlassen): **jdn ins Haus lassen** to let
sb into the house

▷ vi: **lass mal, ich mache das schon**
leave it, I'll do it

▷ Hilfsverb 1 (veranlassen): **etw machen
lassen** to have od get sth done; **sich** dat
etw schicken lassen to have sth sent (to one)

2 (zulassen): **jdn etw wissen lassen** to let
sb know sth; **das Licht brennen lassen** to
leave the light on; **jdn warten lassen** to
keep sb waiting; **das lässt sich machen**
that can be done

3: **lass uns gehen** let's go

lässig adj casual

Last (-, -en) f load; (Bürde) burden; (Naut,
Aviat) cargo

Laster (-s, -) nt vice; (fam) truck, lorry
(Brit)

lästern vi **über jdn/etw ~** to make nasty
remarks about sb/sth

lästig adj annoying; (Person) tiresome

Last-Minute-Flug m last-minute flight;
Last-Minute-Ticket nt last-minute ticket

Lastwagen m truck, lorry (Brit)

Latein (-s) nt Latin

Laterne (-, -n) f lantern; (Straßenlaterne)
streetlight

Latte (-, -n) f slat; (Sport) bar

Latz (-es, Lätze) m bib; **Lätzchen** nt bib;
Latzhose f dungarees pl

lau adj (Wind, Luft) mild

Laub (-(e)s) nt foliage; **Laubfrosch** m tree
frog; **Laubsäge** f fretsaw

Lauch (-(e)s, -e) m leeks pl; **eine Stange
~ laufen** a leek; **Lauchzwiebel** f spring onions pl
(Brit), scallions pl (US)

Lauf (-(e)s, Läufe) m run; (Wettlauf) race;
(Entwicklung) course; (von Gewehr) barrel;
Laufbahn f career; **laufen** (lief, gelaufen) vi,
vt to run; (gehen) to walk; (funktionieren) to
work; **mir läuft die Nase** my nose is
running; **was läuft im Kino?** what's on at
the cinema?; **wie läuft's so?** how are
things?; **laufend** adj running; (Monat,
Ausgaben) current; **auf dem Laufenden**

sein/halten to be/to keep up-to-date; **Läufer** (-s, -) m (Teppich) rug; (Schach) bishop; **Läufer(in)** m(f) (Sport) runner; **Laufmasche** f ladder (Brit), run (US); **Laufwerk** nt (Inform) drive

Laune (-, -n) f mood; **gute/schlechte ~ haben** to be in a good/bad mood; **launisch** adj moody

Laus (-, Läuse) f louse

lauschen vi to listen; (heimlich) to eavesdrop

laut adj loud ▷ adv loudly; (lesen) aloud ▷ prep +gen o dat according to

läuten vt, vi to ring

lauter adv (fam: nichts als) nothing but

Lautsprecher m loudspeaker; **Lautstärke** f loudness; (Radio, Tv) volume

lauwarm adj lukewarm

Lava (-, Laven) f lava

Lavendel (-s, -) m lavender

Lawine f avalanche

LCD-Anzeige f LCD-display

leasen vt to lease; **Leasing** (-s) nt leasing

leben vt, vi to live; (am Leben sein) to be alive; **wie lange ~ Sie schon hier?** how long have you been living here?; **von ... ~** (Nahrungsmittel etc) to live on ...; (Beruf, Beschäftigung) to make one's living from ...; **Leben** (-s, -) nt life; **lebend** adj living; **lebendig** adj alive; (lebhaft) lively; **lebensgefährlich** adj very dangerous; (Verletzung) critical; **Lebensgefährte** m, **Lebensgefährtin** f partner; **Lebenshaltungskosten** pl cost sing of living; **lebenslänglich** adj for life; **~ bekommen** to get life; **Lebenslauf** m curriculum vitae (Brit), CV (Brit), resumé (US); **Lebensmittel** pl food sing; **Lebensmittelgeschäft** nt grocer's (shop); **Lebensmittelvergiftung** f food poisoning; **lebensnotwendig** adj vital; **Lebensretter(in)** m(f) rescuer; **Lebensstandard** m standard of living; **Lebensunterhalt** m livelihood; **Lebensversicherung** f life insurance (o assurance (Brit)); **Lebenszeichen** nt sign of life

Leber (-, -n) f liver; **Leberfleck** m mole; **Leberpastete** f liver pâté

Lebewesen nt living being

lebhaft adj lively; (Erinnerung, Eindruck) vivid; **Lebkuchen** m gingerbread; **ein ~** a piece of gingerbread; **leblos** adj lifeless

Leck nt leak

lecken vi (Loch haben) to leak ▷ vt, vi (schlecken) to lick

lecker adj delicious, tasty

Leder (-s, -) nt leather

ledig adj single

leer adj empty; (Seite) blank; (Batterie) dead; **leeren** vt to empty ▷ vr **sich ~** to empty; **Leerlauf** m (Gang) neutral; **Leertaste** f space bar; **Leerung** f emptying; (Briefkasten) collection; **Leerzeichen** nt blank, space

legal adj legal, lawful

legen vt to put, to place; (Eier) to lay ▷ vr **sich ~** to lie down; (Sturm, Begeisterung) to die down; (Schmerz, Gefühl) to wear off

Legende (-, -n) f legend

leger adj casual

Lehm (-(e)s, -e) m loam; (Ton) clay

Lehne (-, -n) f arm(rest); (Rückenlehne) back(rest); **lehnen** vt to lean ▷ vr **sich ~** to lean (an/gegen +akk against); **Lehnstuhl** m armchair

Lehrbuch nt textbook; **Lehre** (-, -n) f teaching; (beruflich) apprenticeship; (moralisch) lesson; **lehren** vt to teach; **Lehrer(in)** (-s, -) m(f) teacher; **Lehrgang** m course; **Lehrling** m apprentice; **lehrreich** adj instructive

Leib (-(e)s, -er) m body; **Leibgericht** nt, **Leibspeise** f favourite dish; **Leibwächter(in)** m(f) bodyguard

Leiche (-, -n) f corpse; **Leichenhalle** f mortuary; **Leichenwagen** m hearse

leicht adj light; (einfach) easy, simple; (Erkrankung) slight; **jdm ~ fallen** to be easy for sb; **es sich** (dat) **~ machen** to take the easy way out ▷ adv (mühelos, schnell) easily; (geringfügig) slightly; **Leichtathletik** f athletics sing; **leichtsinnig** adj careless; (stärker) reckless

leid adj **jdn/etw ~ sein** to be tired of sb/sth; **Leid** (-(e)s) nt grief, sorrow; **es tut mir/ihm ~** I'm/he's sorry; **er tut mir ~** I'm sorry for him; **~ tun**; siehe auch **leidtun**; **leiden** (litt, gelitten) vi, vt to suffer (an, unter +dat from); **ich kann ihn/es nicht ~** I can't stand him/it; **Leiden** (-s, -) nt suffering; (Krankheit) illness

Leidenschaft f passion; **leidenschaftlich** adj passionate

leider adv unfortunately; **wir müssen**

jetzt ~ gehen I'm afraid we have to go now; ~ ja/nein I'm afraid so/not

leidtun vi **es tut mir/ihm ~** I'm/he's sorry; **er tut mir ~** I'm sorry for him

Leihbücherei f lending library

leihen (lieh, geliehen) vt **jdm etw ~** to lend sb sth; **sich** (dat) **etw von jdm ~** to borrow sth from sb; **Leihfrist** f lending period; **Leihgebühr** f hire charge; (für Buch) lending charge; **Leihwagen** m hire car (Brit), rental car (US)

Leim (-(e)s, -e) m glue

Leine (-, -n) f cord; (für Wäsche) line; (Hundeleine) lead (Brit), leash (US)

Leinen (-s, -) nt linen; **Leintuch** nt (für Bett) sheet; **Leinwand** f (Kunst) canvas; (Cine) screen

leise adj quiet; (sanft) soft ▷ adv quietly

Leiste (-, -n) f ledge; (Zierleiste) strip; (Anat) groin

leisten vt (Arbeit) to do; (vollbringen) to achieve; **jdm Gesellschaft ~** to keep sb company; **sich** (dat) **etw ~** (gönnen) to treat oneself to sth; **ich kann es mir nicht ~** I can't afford it

Leistenbruch m hernia

Leistung f performance; (gute) achievement

Leitartikel m leading article (Brit), editorial (US)

leiten vt to lead; (Firma) to run; (in eine Richtung) to direct; (Elek) to conduct

Leiter (-, -n) f ladder

Leiter(in) (-s, -) m(f) (von Geschäft) manager

Leitplanke (-, -n) f crash barrier

Leitung f (Führung) direction; (Tel) line; (von Firma) management; (Wasserleitung) pipe; (Kabel) cable; **eine lange ~ haben** to be slow on the uptake; **Leitungswasser** nt tap water

Lektion f lesson

Lektüre (-, -n) f (Lesen) reading; (Lesestoff) reading matter

Lende (-, -n) f (Speise) loin; (vom Rind) sirloin; **die ~n** pl (Med) the lumbar region sing

lenken vt to steer; (Blick) to direct (auf +akk towards); **jds Aufmerksamkeit auf etw** (akk) **~** to draw sb's attention to sth; **Lenker** m (von Fahrrad, Motorrad) handlebars pl; **Lenkrad** nt steering

wheel; **Lenkradschloss** nt steering lock; **Lenkstange** f handlebars pl

Leopard (-en, -en) m leopard

Lepra (-) f leprosy

Lerche (-, -n) f lark

lernen vt, vi to learn; (für eine Prüfung) to study, to revise

lesbisch adj lesbian

Lesebuch nt reader; **lesen** (las, gelesen) vi, vt to read; (ernten) to pick; **Leser(in)** m(f) reader; **Leserbrief** m letter to the editor; **leserlich** adj legible; **Lesezeichen** nt bookmark

Lettland nt Latvia

letzte(r, s) adj last; (neueste) latest; (endgültig) final; **zum ~n Mal** for the last time; **am ~n Montag** last Monday; **in ~r Zeit** lately, recently; **letztens** adv (vor kurzem) recently; **letztere(r, s)** adj the latter

Leuchtanzeige f illuminated display; **Leuchte** (-, -n) f lamp, light; **leuchten** vi to shine; (Feuer, Zifferblatt) to glow; **Leuchter** (-s, -) m candlestick; **Leuchtfarbe** f fluorescent colour; (Anstrichfarbe) luminous paint; **Leuchtreklame** f neon sign; **Leuchtstift** m highlighter; **Leuchtstoffröhre** f strip light; **Leuchtturm** m lighthouse

leugnen vt to deny ▷ vi to deny everything

Leukämie f leukaemia (Brit), leukemia (US)

Leukoplast® (-(e)s, -e) nt Elastoplast® (Brit), Band-Aid® (US)

Leute pl people pl

Lexikon (-s, Lexika) nt encyclopaedia (Brit), encyclopedia (US); (Wörterbuch) dictionary

Libanon (-s) m **der ~** Lebanon

Libelle f dragonfly

liberal adj liberal

Libyen (-s) nt Libya

Licht (-(e)s, -er) nt light; **Lichtblick** m ray of hope; **lichtempfindlich** adj sensitive to light; **Lichempfindlichkeit** f (Foto) speed; **Lichthupe** f **die ~ betätigen** to flash one's lights; **Lichtjahr** nt light year; **Lichtmaschine** f dynamo; **Lichtschalter** m light switch; **Lichtschranke** f light barrier; **Lichtschutzfaktor** m sun protection factor, SPF

Lichtung f clearing

Lid (-(e)s, -er) nt eyelid; **Lidschatten** m eyeshadow

lieb adj (nett) nice; (teuer, geliebt) dear; (liebenswert) sweet; **das ist ~ von dir** that's nice of you; **Lieber Herr X** Dear Mr X; **Liebe** (-, -n) f love; **lieben** vt to love; (sexuell) to make love to; **liebenswürdig** adj kind; **lieber** adv rather; **ich möchte ~ nicht** I'd rather not; **welches ist dir ~?** which one do you prefer?; siehe auch **gern**, **lieb**; **Liebesbrief** m love letter; **Liebeskummer** m ~ **haben** to be lovesick; **Liebespaar** nt lovers pl; **liebevoll** adj loving; **Liebhaber(in)** (-s, -) m(f) lover; **lieblich** adj lovely; (Wein) sweet; **Liebling** m darling; (Günstling) favourite; **Lieblings-** in zW favourite; **liebste(r, s)** adj favourite; **liebsten** adv **am ~ esse ich ...** my favourite food is ...; **am ~ würde ich bleiben** I'd really like to stay

Liechtenstein (-s) nt Liechtenstein

Lied (-(e)s, -er) nt song; (Rel) hymn

lief imperf von **laufen**

Lieferant(in) m(f) supplier

lieferbar adj available

liefern vt to deliver; (beschaffen) to supply

Lieferschein m delivery note; **Lieferung** f delivery; **Lieferwagen** m delivery van

Liege (-, -n) f (beim Arzt) couch; (Notbett) campbed; (Gartenliege) lounger; **liegen** (lag, gelegen) vi to lie; (sich befinden) to be; **mir liegt nichts/viel daran** it doesn't matter to me/it matters a lot to me; **woran liegt es nur, dass ...?** why is it that ...?; **~ bleiben** (Mensch) to stay lying down; (im Bett) to stay in bed; (Ding) to be left (behind); **~ lassen** (vergessen) to leave behind; **Liegestuhl** m deck chair; **Liegestütz** m press-up (Brit), push-up (US); **Liegewagen** m (Eisenb) couchette car

lieh imperf von **leihen**

ließ imperf von **lassen**

Lift (-(e)s, -e o -s) m lift, elevator (US)

Liga (-, Ligen) f league, division

light adj (Cola) diet; (fettarm) low-fat; (kalorienarm) low-calorie; (Zigaretten) mild

Likör (-s, -e) m liqueur

lila adj inv purple

Lilie f lily

Limette (-, -n) f lime

Limo (-, -s) f (fam) fizzy drink (Brit), soda

(US); **Limonade** f fizzy drink (Brit), soda (US); (mit Zitronengeschmack) lemonade

Limone (-, -n) f lime

Limousine (-, -n) f saloon (car) (Brit), sedan (US); (fam) limo

Linde (-, -n) f lime tree

lindern vt to relieve, to soothe

Lineal (-s, -e) nt ruler

Linie f line; **Linienflug** m scheduled flight; **Linienrichter** m linesman; **liniert** adj ruled, lined

Linke (-n, -n) f left-hand side; (Hand) left hand; (Pol) left (wing); **linke(r, s)** adj left; **auf der ~n Seite** on the left, on the left-hand side; **links** adv on the left; **~ abbiegen** to turn left; **~ von** to the left of; **~ oben** at the top left; **Linksaußen** m left winger; **Linkshänder(in)** (-s, -) m(f) left-hander; **linksherum** adv anticlockwise; **Linksverkehr** m driving on the left

Linse (-, -n) f lentil; (optisch) lens; **Linsensuppe** f lentil soup

Lippe (-, -n) f lip; **Lipgloss** nt lip gloss; **Lippenstift** m lipstick

lispeln vi to lisp

List (-, -en) f cunning; (Trick) trick

Liste (-, -n) f list

Litauen (-s) nt Lithuania

Liter (-s, -) m o nt litre

literarisch adj literary; **Literatur** f literature

Litschi (-, -s) f lychee, litchi

litt imperf von **leiden**

live adv (Radio, TV) live

Lizenz f licence

Lkw (-(s), -(s)) m abk = **Lastkraftwagen** truck, lorry (Brit)

Lob (-(e)s) nt praise; **loben** vt to praise

Loch (-(e)s, Löcher) nt hole; **lochen** vt to punch; **Locher** (-s, -) m (hole) punch

Locke (-, -n) f curl; **locken** vt (anlocken) to lure; (Haare) to curl; **Lockenstab** m curling tongs pl (Brit), curling irons pl (US); **Lockenwickler** (-s, -) m curler

locker adj (Schraube, Zahn) loose; (Haltung) relaxed; (Person) easy-going; **das schaffe ich ~** (fam) I'll manage it, no problem; **lockern** vt to loosen ▷ vr **sich ~** to loosen

lockig adj curly

Löffel (-s, -) m spoon; **einen ~ Mehl zugeben** add a spoonful of flour; **Löffelbiskuit** (-s, -s) m sponge finger

log imperf von **lügen**

Loge (-, -n) f (Theat) box

logisch adj logical

Logo (-s, -s) nt logo

Lohn (-(e)s, Löhne) m reward; (Arbeitslohn) pay, wages pl

lohnen vr **sich ~** to be worth it; **es lohnt sich nicht zu warten** it's no use waiting

Lohnerhöhung f pay rise (Brit), pay raise (US); **Lohnsteuer** f income tax

Lokal (-(e)s, -e) nt (Gaststätte) restaurant; (Kneipe) pub (Brit), bar

Lokomotive f locomotive

London (-s) nt London

Lorbeer (-s, -en) m laurel; **Lorbeerblatt** nt (Gastr) bay leaf

los adj loose; **~!** go on!; **jdn/etw ~ sein** to be rid of sb/sth; **was ist ~?** what's the matter?, what's up?; **dort ist nichts/viel ~** there's nothing/a lot going on there

Los (-es, -e) nt (Schicksal) lot, fate; (Lotterie etc) ticket

los|binden irr vt to untie

löschen vt (Feuer, Licht) to put out, to extinguish; (Durst) to quench; (Tonband) to erase; (Daten, Zeile) to delete; **Löschtaste** f delete key

lose adj loose

Lösegeld nt ransom

losen vi to draw lots

lösen vt (lockern) to loosen; (Rätsel) to solve; (Chem) to dissolve; (Fahrkarte) to buy ▷ vr **sich ~** (abgehen) to come off; (Zucker etc) to dissolve; (Problem, Schwierigkeit) to (re)solve itself

los|fahren irr vi to leave; **los|gehen** irr vi to set out; (anfangen) to start; **los|lassen** irr vt to let go

löslich adj soluble

Lösung f (eines Rätsels, Problems, Flüssigkeit) solution

los|werden irr vt to get rid of

Lotterie f lottery; **Lotto** (-s) nt National Lottery; **~ spielen** to play the lottery

Löwe (-n, -n) m (Zool) lion; (Astr) Leo; **Löwenzahn** m dandelion

Luchs (-es, -e) m lynx

Lücke (-, -n) f gap; **Lückenbüßer(in)** (-s, -) m(f) stopgap

lud imperf von **laden**

Luft (-, Lüfte) f air; (Atem) breath; **Luftballon** m balloon; **Luftblase** f (air) bubble; **luftdicht** adj airtight; **Luftdruck** m (Meteo) atmospheric pressure; (in Reifen) air pressure

lüften vt to air; (Geheimnis) to reveal

Luftfahrt f aviation; **Luftfeuchtigkeit** f humidity; **Luftfilter** m air filter; **Luftfracht** f air freight; **Luftkissenfahrzeug** nt hovercraft; **Luftlinie** f **10 km ~** 10 km as the crow flies; **Luftmatratze** f airbed; **Luftpirat(in)** m(f) hijacker; **Luftpost** f airmail; **Luftpumpe** f (bicycle) pump; **Luftröhre** f windpipe

Lüftung f ventilation

Luftveränderung f change of air; **Luftverschmutzung** f air pollution; **Luftwaffe** f air force; **Luftzug** m draught (Brit), draft (US)

Lüge (-, -n) f lie; **lügen** (log, gelogen) vi to lie; **Lügner(in)** (-s, -) m(f) liar

Luke (-, -n) f hatch

Lumpen (-s, -) m rag

Lunchpaket nt packed lunch

Lunge (-, -n) f lungs pl; **Lungenentzündung** f pneumonia

Lupe (-, -n) f magnifying glass; **etw unter die ~ nehmen** (fig) to have a close look at sth

Lust (-, Lüste) f joy, delight; (Neigung) desire; **~ auf etw** (akk) **haben** to feel like sth; **~ haben, etw zu tun** to feel like doing sth

lustig adj (komisch) amusing, funny; (fröhlich) cheerful

lutschen vt to suck ▷ vi **~ an** (+dat) to suck; **Lutscher** (-s, -) m lollipop

Luxemburg (-s) nt Luxembourg

luxuriös adj luxurious

Luxus (-) m luxury

Lymphdrüse f lymph gland; **Lymphknoten** m lymph node

Lyrik (-) f poetry

m

machbar adj feasible

machen vt **1** to do; (*herstellen, zubereiten*) to make; **was machst du da?** what are you doing (there)?; **das ist nicht zu machen** that can't be done; **das Radio leiser machen** to turn the radio down; **aus Holz gemacht** made of wood

2 (*verursachen, bewirken*) to make; **jdm Angst machen** to make sb afraid; **das macht die Kälte** it's the cold that does that

3 (*ausmachen*) to matter; **das macht nichts** that doesn't matter; **die Kälte macht mir nichts** I don't mind the cold

4 (*kosten, ergeben*) to be; **3 und 5 macht 8** 3 and 5 is o are 8; **was o wie viel macht das?** how much does that make?

5: was macht die Arbeit? how's the work going?; **was macht dein Bruder?** how is your brother doing?; **das Auto machen lassen** to have the car done; **machs gut!** take care!; (*viel Glück*) good luck!

▷ vi: **mach schnell!** hurry up!; **Schluss machen** to finish (off); **mach schon!** come on!; **das macht müde** it makes you tired; **in etw** *dat* **machen** to be o deal in sth

▷ vr to come along (nicely); **sich an etw** *akk* **machen** to set about sth; **sich verständlich machen** to make o.s. understood; **sich** *dat* **viel aus jdm/etw machen** to like sb/sth

Macho (-s, -s) m (*fam*) macho (type)
Macht (-, *Mächte*) f power; **mächtig** adj powerful; (*fam: ungeheuer*) enormous; **machtlos** adj powerless; **da ist man ~** there's nothing you can do (about it)
Mädchen nt girl; **Mädchenname** m maiden name
Made (-, -n) f maggot
Magazin (-s, -e) nt magazine
Magen (-s, - o *Mägen*) m stomach; **Magenbeschwerden** pl stomach trouble sing; **Magen-Darm-Infektion** f gastroenteritis; **Magengeschwür** nt stomach ulcer; **Magenschmerzen** pl stomachache sing
mager adj (*Fleisch, Wurst*) lean; (*Person*) thin; (*Käse, Joghurt*) low-fat; **Magermilch** f skimmed milk; **Magersucht** f anorexia; **magersüchtig** adj anorexic
magisch adj magical
Magnet (-s o -en, -en) m magnet
mähen vt, vi to mow
mahlen (*mahlte, gemahlen*) vt to grind
Mahlzeit f meal; (*für Baby*) feed ▷ interj (*guten Appetit*) enjoy your meal
Mähne (-, -n) f mane
mahnen vt to urge; **jdn schriftlich ~** to send sb a reminder; **Mahngebühr** f fine; **Mahnung** f (*schriftlich*) reminder
Mai (-(s), -e) m May; *siehe auch* **Juni**; **Maifeiertag** m May Day; **Maiglöckchen** nt lily of the valley; **Maikäfer** m cockchafer
Mail (-, -s) f e-mail; **Mailbox** f (*Inform*) mailbox; **mailen** vi, vt to e-mail
Mais (-es, -e) m maize, corn (US); **Maiskolben** m corn cob; (*Gastr*) corn on the cob
Majestät (-, -en) f Majesty
Majonäse (-, -n) f mayonnaise
Majoran (-s, -e) m marjoram
makaber adj macabre
Make-up (-s, -s) nt make-up

Makler(in) (-s, -) m(f) broker; (Immobilienmakler) estate agent (Brit), realtor (US)

Makrele (-, -n) f mackerel

Makro (-s, -s) nt (Inform) macro

Makrone (-, -n) f macaroon

mal adv (beim Rechnen) times, multiplied by; (beim Messen) by; (fam: einmal = früher) once; (einmal = zukünftig) some day; **4 ~ 3 ist 12** 4 times 3 is (o equals) twelve; **da habe ich ~ gewohnt** I used to live there; **irgendwann ~ werde ich dort hinfahren** I'll go there one day; **das ist nun ~ so** well, that's just the way it is (o goes); **Mal** (-(e)s, -e) nt (Zeitpunkt) time; (Markierung) mark; **jedes ~** every time; **ein paar ~** a few times; **ein einziges ~** just once

Malaria (-) f malaria

Malaysia (-s) nt Malaysia

Malbuch nt colouring book

Malediven pl Maldives pl

malen vt, vi to paint; **Maler(in)** (-s, -) m(f) painter; **Malerei** f painting; **malerisch** adj picturesque

Mallorca (-s) nt Majorca, Mallorca

mal|nehmen irr vt to multiply (mit by)

Malta (-s) nt Malta

Malventee m mallow tea

Malz (-es) nt malt; **Malzbier** nt malt beer

Mama (-, -s) f mum(my) (Brit), mom(my) (US)

man pron you; (förmlich) one; (jemand) someone, somebody; (die Leute) they, people pl; **wie schreibt ~ das?** how do you spell that?; **~ hat ihr das Fahrrad gestohlen** someone stole her bike; **~ sagt, dass ...** they (o people) say that ...

managen vt (fam) to manage; **Manager(in)** (-s, -) m(f) manager

manche(r, s) adj many a; (mit pl) a number of, some ⊳ pron (einige) some; (viele) many; **~ Politiker** many politicians pl, many a politician; **manchmal** adv sometimes

Mandant(in) m(f) client

Mandarine f mandarin, tangerine

Mandel (-, -n) f almond; **~n** (Anat) tonsils pl; **Mandelentzündung** f tonsillitis

Manege (-, -n) f ring

Mangel (-s, Mängel) m (Fehlen) lack; (Knappheit) shortage (an +dat of); (Fehler) defect, fault; **mangelhaft** adj (Ware) faulty; (Schulnote) ≈ E

Mango (-, -s) f mango

Mangold (-s) m mangel(wurzel)

Manieren pl manners pl

Maniküre (-, -n) f manicure

manipulieren vt to manipulate

Manko (-s, -s) nt deficiency

Mann (-(e)s, Männer) m man; (Ehemann) husband; **Männchen** nt **es ist ein ~** (Tier) it's a he; **männlich** adj masculine; (Bio) male

Mannschaft f (Sport, fig) team; (Naut, Aviat) crew

Mansarde (-, -n) f attic

Manschettenknopf m cufflink

Mantel (-s, Mäntel) m coat; (Tech) casing, jacket

Mappe (-, -n) f briefcase; (Aktenmappe) folder

Maracuja (-, -s) f passion fruit

Marathon (-s, -s) m marathon

Märchen nt fairy tale

Marder (-s, -) m marten

Margarine f margarine

Marienkäfer m ladybird (Brit), ladybug (US)

Marihuana (-s) nt marijuana

Marille (-, -n) f apricot

Marinade f marinade

Marine f navy

marinieren vt to marinate

Marionette f puppet

Mark (-(e)s) nt (Knochenmark) marrow; (Fruchtmark) pulp

Marke (-, -n) f (Warensorte) brand; (Fabrikat) make; (Briefmarke) stamp; (Essenmarke) voucher, ticket; (aus Metall etc) disc; (Messpunkt) mark; **Markenartikel** m branded item, brand name product; **Markenzeichen** nt trademark

markieren vt to mark; **Markierung** f marking; (Zeichen) mark

Markise (-, -n) f awning

Markt (-(e)s, Märkte) m market; **auf den ~ bringen** to launch; **Markthalle** f covered market; **Marktlücke** f gap in the market; **Marktplatz** m market place; **Marktwirtschaft** f market economy

Marmelade f jam; (Orangenmarmelade) marmalade

Marmor (-s, -e) m marble; **Marmorkuchen** m marble cake

Marokko (-s) nt Morocco
Marone (-, -n) f chestnut
Mars (-) m Mars
Marsch (-(e)s, Märsche) m march
Märtyrer(in) (-s, -) m(f) martyr
März (-(es), -e) m March; siehe auch **Juni**
Marzipan (-s, -e) nt marzipan
Maschine f machine; (Motor) engine;
  maschinell adj mechanical, machine-;
  Maschinenbau m mechanical
  engineering
Masern pl (Med) measles sing
Maske (-, -n) f mask; **Maskenball** m
  fancy-dress ball; **maskieren** vr sich
  ~ (Maske aufsetzen) to put on a mask;
  (verkleiden) to dress up
Maskottchen nt mascot
maß imperf von **messen**
Maß (-es, -e) nt measure; (Mäßigung)
  moderation; (Grad) degree, extent; **~e**
  (Person) measurements; (Raum)
  dimensions; **in gewissem/hohem ~e** to a
  certain/high degree; **in zunehmendem**
  ~e increasingly
Mass (-, -(en)) f (Bier) litre of beer
Massage (-, -n) f massage
Masse (-, -n) f mass; (von Menschen)
  crowd; (Großteil) majority; **massenhaft**
  adv masses (o loads) of; **am See sind**
  ~ Mücken there are masses of
  mosquitoes at the lake;
  Massenkarambolage f pile-up;
  Massenmedien pl mass media pl;
  Massenproduktion f mass production;
  Massentourismus m mass tourism
Masseur(in) m(f) masseur/masseuse
maßgeschneidert adj (Kleidung)
  made-to-measure
massieren vt to massage
mäßig adj moderate
massiv adj solid; (fig) massive
maßlos adj extreme
Maßnahme (-, -n) f measure, step
Maßstab m rule, measure; (fig) standard;
  im ~ von 1:5 on a scale of 1:5
Mast (-(e)s, -e(n)) m mast; (Elek) pylon
Material (-s, -ien) nt material;
  (Arbeitsmaterial) materials pl;
  materialistisch adj materialistic
Materie f matter; **materiell** adj material
Mathematik f mathematics sing;
  Mathematiker(in) m(f) mathematician
Matinee (-, -n) f ≈ matinee

Matratze (-, -n) f mattress
Matrose (-n, -n) m sailor
Matsch (-(e)s) m mud; (Schnee) slush;
  matschig adj (Boden) muddy; (Schnee)
  slushy; (Obst) mushy
matt adj weak; (glanzlos) dull; (Foto) matt;
  (Schach) mate
Matte (-, -n) f mat
Matura (-) f Austrian school-leaving
  examination; ≈ A-levels (Brit), ≈ High School
  Diploma (US)
Mauer (-, -n) f wall
Maul (-(e)s, Mäuler) nt mouth; (fam) gob;
  halt's ~! shut your face (o gob);
  Maulbeere f mulberry; **Maulesel** m
  mule; **Maulkorb** m muzzle; **Maul- und**
  Klauenseuche f foot-and-mouth
  disease; **Maulwurf** m mole
Maurer(in) (-s, -) m(f) bricklayer
Mauritius (-) nt Mauritius
Maus (-, Mäuse) f mouse; **Mausefalle** f
  mousetrap; **Mausklick** (-s, -s) m mouse
  click; **Mauspad** (-s, -s) nt mouse mat (o
  pad); **Maustaste** f mouse key (o button)
Maut (-, -en) f toll; **Mautgebühr** f toll;
  mautpflichtig adj **~e Straße** toll road,
  turnpike (US); **Mautstelle** f tollbooth,
  tollgate; **Mautstraße** f toll road,
  turnpike (US)
maximal adv **ihr habt ~ zwei Stunden**
  Zeit you've got two hours at the (the) most;
  ~ vier Leute a maximum of four people
Mayonnaise f siehe **Majonäse**
Mazedonien (-s) nt Macedonia
MB (-, -) nt, **Mbyte** (-, -) nt abk =
  Megabyte MB
Mechanik f mechanics sing; (Getriebe)
  mechanics pl; **Mechaniker(in)** (-s, -) m(f)
  mechanic; **mechanisch** adj mechanical;
  Mechanismus m mechanism
meckern vi (Ziege) to bleat; (fam:
  schimpfen) to moan
Mecklenburg-Vorpommern (-s) nt
  Mecklenburg-Western Pomerania
Medaille (-, -n) f medal
Medien pl media pl
Medikament nt medicine
Meditation f meditation; **meditieren** vi
  to meditate
medium adj (Steak) medium
Medizin (-, -en) f medicine (gegen for);
  medizinisch adj medical
Meer (-(e)s, -e) nt sea; **am ~** by the sea;

Meerenge f straits pl; **Meeresfrüchte** pl
seafood sing; **Meeresspiegel** m sea level;
Meerrettich m horseradish;
Meerschweinchen nt guinea pig;
Meerwasser nt seawater
Megabyte nt megabyte; **Megahertz** nt
megahertz
Mehl (-(e)s, -e) nt flour; **Mehlspeise** f
sweet dish made from flour, eggs and milk
mehr pron, adv more; **~ will ich nicht
ausgeben** I don't want to spend any
more, that's as much as I want to spend;
was willst du ~? what more do you want?
▷ adv **immer ~ (Leute)** more and more
(people); **~ als fünf Minuten** more than
five minutes; **je ~ ..., desto besser** the
more ..., the better; **ich kann nicht
~ stehen** I can't stand any more (o longer);
es ist kein Brot ~ da there's no bread left;
nie ~ never again; **mehrdeutig** adj
ambiguous; **mehrere** pron several;
mehreres pron several things; **mehrfach**
adj multiple; (wiederholt) repeated;
Mehrfachstecker m multiple plug;
Mehrheit f majority; **mehrmals** adv
repeatedly; **mehrsprachig** adj
multilingual; **Mehrwegflasche** f
returnable bottle, deposit bottle;
Mehrwertsteuer f value added tax,
VAT; **Mehrzahl** f majority; (Plural)
plural
meiden (mied, gemieden) vt to avoid
Meile (-, -n) f mile
mein pron (adjektivisch) my; **meine(r, s)**
pron (substantivisch) mine
meinen vt, vi (glauben, der Ansicht sein) to
think; (sagen) to say; (sagen wollen,
beabsichtigen) to mean; **das war nicht so
gemeint** I didn't mean it like that
meinetwegen adv (wegen mir) because of
me; (mir zuliebe) for my sake; (von mir aus)
as far as I'm concerned
Meinung f opinion; **meiner ~ nach** in my
opinion; **Meinungsumfrage** f opinion
poll; **Meinungsverschiedenheit** f
disagreement (über +akk about)
Meise (-, -n) f tit; **eine ~ haben** (fam) to be
crazy
Meißel (-s, -) m chisel
meist adv mostly; **meiste(r, s)** pron
(adjektivisch) most; **die ~n (Leute)** most
people; **die ~ Zeit** most of the time; **das
~ (davon)** most of it; **die ~n von ihnen**

most of them; (substantivisch) most of
them; **am ~n** (the) most; **meistens** adv
mostly; (zum größten Teil) for the most part
Meister(in) (-s, -) m(f) master; (Sport)
champion; **Meisterschaft** f
championship; **Meisterwerk** nt
masterpiece
melden vt to report ▷ vr **sich ~** to report
(bei to); (Schule) to put one's hand up;
(freiwillig) to volunteer; (auf etw, am Telefon)
to answer; **Meldung** f announcement;
(Bericht) report; (Inform) message
Melodie f tune, melody
Melone (-, -n) f melon
Memoiren pl memoirs pl
Menge (-, -n) f quantity; (Menschen)
crowd; **eine ~ (große Anzahl)** a lot (gen of);
Mengenrabatt m bulk discount
Meniskus (-, Menisken) m meniscus
Mensa (-, Mensen) f canteen, cafeteria (US)
Mensch (-en, -en) m human being, man;
(Person) person; **kein ~** nobody; **~!**
(bewundernd) wow!; (verärgert) bloody hell!;
Menschenmenge f crowd;
Menschenrechte pl human rights pl;
Menschenverstand m **gesunder
~** common sense; **Menschheit** f
humanity, mankind; **menschlich** adj
human; (human) humane
Menstruation f menstruation
Mentalität f mentality, mindset
Menthol (-s) nt menthol
Menü (-s, -s) nt set meal; (Inform) menu;
Menüleiste f (Inform) menu bar
Merkblatt nt leaflet; **merken** vt
(bemerken) to notice; **sich** (dat) **etw ~** to
remember sth; **Merkmal** nt feature
Merkur (-s) m Mercury
merkwürdig adj odd
Messbecher m measuring jug
Messe (-, -n) f fair; (Rel) mass;
Messebesucher(in) m(f) visitor to a/the
fair; **Messegelände** nt exhibition site
messen (maß, gemessen) vt to measure;
(Temperatur, Puls) to take ▷ vr **sich ~** to
compete; **sie kann sich mit ihm nicht
~** she's no match for him
Messer (-s, -) nt knife
Messgerät nt measuring device, gauge
Messing (-s) nt brass
Metall (-s, -e) nt metal
Meteorologe m, **Meteorologin** f
meteorologist

Meter (-s, -) m o nt metre; **Metermaß** nt tape measure

Methode (-, -n) f method

Metzger(in) (-s, -) m(f) butcher; **Metzgerei** f butcher's (shop)

Mexiko (-s) nt Mexico

MEZ f abk = **mitteleuropäische Zeit** CET

miau interj miaow

mich pron akk von **ich** me; **~ (selbst)** (reflexiv) myself; **stell dich hinter ~** stand behind me; **ich fühle ~ wohl** I feel fine

mied imperf von **meiden**

Miene (-, -n) f look, expression

mies adj (fam) lousy

Miesmuschel f mussel

Mietauto nt siehe **Mietwagen**; **Miete** (-, -n) f rent; **mieten** vt to rent; (Auto) to hire (Brit), to rent (US); **Mieter(in)** (-s, -) m(f) tenant; **Mietshaus** nt block of flats (Brit), apartment house (US); **Mietvertrag** m rental agreement; **Mietwagen** m hire car (Brit), rental car (US); **einen ~ nehmen** to hire (Brit) (o rent (US)) a car

Migräne (-, -n) f migraine

Mikrofon (-s, -e) nt microphone

Mikrowelle (-, -n) f, **Mikrowellenherd** m microwave (oven)

Milch (-) f milk; **Milcheis** nt ice-cream (made with milk); **Milchglas** nt (dickes, trübes Glas) frosted glass; **Milchkaffee** m milky coffee; **Milchprodukte** pl dairy products pl; **Milchpulver** nt powdered milk; **Milchreis** m rice pudding; **Milchshake** m milk shake; **Milchstraße** f Milky Way

mild adj mild; (Richter) lenient; (freundlich) kind

Militär (-s) nt military, army

Milliarde (-, -n) f billion; **Milligramm** nt milligram; **Milliliter** m millilitre; **Millimeter** m millimetre; **Million** f million; **Millionär(in)** m(f) millionaire

Milz (-, -en) f spleen

Mimik f facial expression(s)

Minderheit f minority

minderjährig adj underage

minderwertig adj inferior; **Minderwertigkeitskomplex** m inferiority complex

Mindest- in zW minimum; **mindeste(r, s)** adj least; **mindestens** adv at least; **Mindesthaltbarkeitsdatum** nt best-before date, sell-by date (Brit)

Mine (-, -n) f mine; (Bleistift) lead; (Kugelschreiber) refill

Mineralwasser nt mineral water

Minibar f minibar; **Minigolf** nt miniature golf, crazy golf (Brit)

minimal adj minimal

Minimum (-s, Minima) nt minimum

Minirock m miniskirt

Minister(in) (-s, -) m(f) minister; **Ministerium** nt ministry; **Ministerpräsident(in)** m(f) (von Bundesland) Minister President (Prime Minister of a Bundesland)

minus adv minus; **Minus** (-, -) nt deficit; **im ~ sein** to be in the red; (Konto) to be overdrawn

Minute (-, -n) f minute

Minze (-, -n) f mint

Mio. nt abk von **Million(en)** m

mir pron dat von **ich** (to) me; **kannst du ~ helfen?** can you help me?; **kannst du es ~ erklären?** can you explain it to me?; **ich habe ~ einen neuen Rechner gekauft** I bought (myself) a new computer; **ein Freund von ~** a friend of mine

Mirabelle (-, -n) f mirabelle (small yellow plum)

mischen vt to mix; (Karten) to shuffle; **Mischmasch** m (fam) hotchpotch; **Mischung** f mixture (aus of)

missachten vt to ignore; **Missbrauch** m abuse; (falscher Gebrauch) misuse; **missbrauchen** vt to misuse (zu for); (sexuell) to abuse; **Misserfolg** m failure; **Missgeschick** nt (Panne) mishap; **misshandeln** vt to ill-treat

Mission f mission

misslingen (misslang, misslungen) vi to fail; **der Versuch ist mir misslungen** my attempt failed; **misstrauen** vt +dat to distrust; **Misstrauen** (-s) nt mistrust, suspicion (gegenüber of); **misstrauisch** adj distrustful; (argwöhnisch) suspicious; **Missverständnis** nt misunderstanding; **missverstehen** irr vt to misunderstand

Mist (-(e)s) m (fam) rubbish; (von Kühen) dung; (als Dünger) manure

Mistel (-, -n) f mistletoe

mit prep +dat with; (mittels) by; **~ der Bahn** by train; **~ der Kreditkarte bezahlen** to pay by credit card; **~ 10 Jahren** at the age of 10; **wie wärs ~ ...?** how about ...? ▷ adv along, too; **wollen Sie ~?** do you want to come along?

Mitarbeiter(in) m(f) (Angestellter) employee; (an Projekt) collaborator; (freier) freelancer

mit|bekommen irr vt (fam: aufschnappen) to catch; (hören) to hear; (verstehen) to get

mit|benutzen vt to share

Mitbewohner(in) m(f) (in Wohnung) flatmate (Brit), roommate (US)

mit|bringen irr vt to bring along; **Mitbringsel** (-s, -) nt small present

miteinander adv with one another; (gemeinsam) together

mit|erleben vt to see (with one's own eyes)

Mitesser (-s, -) m blackhead

Mitfahrgelegenheit f ≈ lift, ride (US); **Mitfahrzentrale** f agency for arranging lifts

mit|geben irr vt jdm etw ~ to give sb sth (to take along)

Mitgefühl nt sympathy

mit|gehen irr vi to go/come along

mitgenommen adj worn out, exhausted

Mitglied nt member

mithilfe prep +gen ~ von with the help of

mit|kommen irr vi to come along; (verstehen) to follow

Mitleid nt pity; ~ haben mit to feel sorry for

mit|machen vt to take part in ▷ vi to take part

mit|nehmen irr vt to take along; (anstrengen) to wear out, to exhaust

mit|schreiben irr vi to take notes ▷ vt to take down

Mitschüler(in) m(f) schoolmate

mit|spielen vi (in Mannschaft) to play; (bei Spiel) to join in; **in einem Film/Stück ~** to act in a film/play

Mittag m midday; **gestern ~** at midday yesterday, yesterday lunchtime; **über ~ geschlossen** closed at lunchtime; **zu ~ essen** to have lunch; **Mittagessen** nt lunch; **mittags** adv at lunchtime, at midday; **Mittagspause** f lunch break

Mitte (-, -n) f middle; **~ Juni** in the middle of June; **sie ist ~ zwanzig** she's in her mid-twenties

mit|teilen vt jdm etw ~ to inform sb of sth; **Mitteilung** f notification

Mittel (-s -) nt means sing; (Maßnahme, Methode) method; (Med) remedy (gegen

for); **das ist ein gutes ~, (um) junge Leute zu erreichen** that's a good way of engaging with young people

Mittelalter nt Middle Ages pl; **mittelalterlich** adj medieval; **Mittelamerika** nt Central America; **Mitteleuropa** nt Central Europe; **Mittelfeld** nt midfield; **Mittelfinger** m middle finger; **mittelmäßig** adj mediocre; **Mittelmeer** nt Mediterranean (Sea); **Mittelohrentzündung** f inflammation of the middle ear; **Mittelpunkt** m centre; **im ~ stehen** to be the centre of attention

mittels prep +gen by means of

Mittelstreifen m central reservation (Brit), median (US); **Mittelstürmer(in)** m(f) striker, centre-forward; **Mittelwelle** f medium wave

mitten adv in the middle; **~ auf der Straße/in der Nacht** in the middle of the street/night

Mitternacht f midnight

mittlere(r, s) adj middle; (durchschnittlich) average

mittlerweile adv meanwhile

Mittwoch (-s, -e) m Wednesday; **(am) ~** on Wednesday; **(am) ~ Morgen/Nachmittag/Abend** (on) Wednesday morning/afternoon/evening; **diesen/letzten/nächsten ~** this/last/next Wednesday; **jeden ~** every Wednesday; **~ in einer Woche** a week on Wednesday, Wednesday week; **mittwochs** adv on Wednesdays; **~ abends** (jeden Mittwochabend) on Wednesday evenings

mixen vt to mix; **Mixer** (-s, -) m (Küchengerät) blender

MKS f abk = Maul- und Klauenseuche FMD

mobben vt to harass (o to bully) (at work)

Mobbing (-s) nt workplace bullying (o harassment)

Möbel (-s, -) nt piece of furniture; **die ~** pl the furniture sing; **Möbelwagen** m removal van

mobil adj mobile

Mobilfunknetz nt cellular network; **Mobiltelefon** nt mobile phone

möblieren vt to furnish

mochte imperf von **mögen**

Mode (-, -n) f fashion
Model (-s, -s) nt model
Modell (-s, -e) nt model
Modem (-s, -s) nt (Inform) modem
Mode(n)schau f fashion show
Moderator(in) m(f) presenter
modern adj modern; (modisch)
fashionable
Modeschmuck m costume jewellery;
modisch adj fashionable
Modus (-, Modi) m (Inform) mode; (fig) way
Mofa (-s, -s) nt moped
mogeln vi to cheat

⊙ **SCHLÜSSELWORT**

mögen (pt **mochte**, pp **gemocht** od (als
Hilfsverb) **mögen**) vt, vi to like; **magst
du/mögen Sie ihn?** do you like him?; **ich
möchte …** I would like … I'd like …; **er
möchte in die Stadt** he'd like to go into
town; **ich möchte nicht, dass du …** I
wouldn't like you to …; **ich mag nicht
mehr** I've had enough
▷ Hilfsverb to like to (wollen) to want;
möchtest du etwas essen? would you
like something to eat?; **sie mag nicht
bleiben** she doesn't want to stay; **das
mag wohl sein** that may well be; **was
mag das heißen?** what might that
mean?; **Sie möchten zu Hause anrufen**
could you please call home?

möglich adj possible; **so bald wie ~** as
soon as possible; **möglicherweise** adv
possibly; **Möglichkeit** f possibility;
möglichst adv as … as possible
Mohn (-(e)s, -e) m (Blume) poppy; (Samen)
poppy seed
Möhre (-, -n) f, **Mohrrübe** f carrot
Mokka (-s, -s) m mocha
Moldawien (-s) nt Moldova
Molkerei (-, -en) f dairy
Moll (-) nt minor (key); **a~** A minor
mollig adj cosy; (dicklich) plump
Moment (-(e)s, -e) m moment; **im ~** at the
moment; **einen ~ bitte!** just a minute;
momentan adj momentary ▷ adv at the
moment
Monaco (-s) nt Monaco
Monarchie f monarchy
Monat (-(e)s, -e) m month; **sie ist im
dritten ~** (schwanger) she's three months

pregnant; **monatlich** adj, adv monthly;
~ 100 Euro zahlen to pay 100 euros a
month (o every month); **Monatskarte** f
monthly season ticket
Mönch (-s, -e) m monk
Mond (-(e)s, -e) m moon; **Mondfinsternis**
f lunar eclipse
Mongolei (-) f **die ~** Mongolia
Monitor m (Inform) monitor
monoton adj monotonous
Monsun (-s, -e) m monsoon
Montag m Monday; siehe auch **Mittwoch**;
montags adv on Mondays; siehe auch
mittwochs
Montenegro (-s) nt Montenegro
Monteur(in) (-s, -e) m(f) fitter;
montieren vt to assemble, to set up
Monument nt monument
Moor (-(e)s, -e) nt moor
Moos (-es, -e) nt moss
Moped (-s, -s) nt moped
Moral (-) f (Werte) morals pl; (einer
Geschichte) moral; **moralisch** adj moral
Mord (-(e)s, -e) m murder; **Mörder(in)**
(-s, -) m(f) murderer/murderess
morgen adv tomorrow; **~ früh** tomorrow
morning
Morgen (-s, -) m morning; **am ~** in the
morning; **Morgenmantel** m,
Morgenrock m dressing gown;
Morgenmuffel m er ist ein ~ he's not a
morning person; **morgens** adv in the
morning; **um 3 Uhr ~** at 3 (o'clock) in the
morning, at 3 am
Morphium (-s) nt morphine
morsch adj rotten
Mosaik (-s, -e(n)) nt mosaic
Mosambik (-s) nt Mozambique
Moschee (-, -n) f mosque
Moskau (-s) nt Moscow
Moskito (-s, -s) m mosquito;
Moskitonetz nt mosquito net
Moslem (-s, -s) m, **Moslime** (-, -n) f
Muslim
Most (-(e)s, -e) m (unfermented) fruit
juice; (Apfelwein) cider
Motel (-s, -s) nt motel
motivieren vt to motivate
Motor m engine; (Elek) motor;
Motorboot nt motorboat; **Motorenöl** nt
engine oil; **Motorhaube** f bonnet (Brit),
hood (US); **Motorrad** nt motorbike,
motorcycle; **Motorradfahrer(in)** m(f)

motorcyclist; **Motorroller** m (motor)
scooter; **Motorschaden** m engine
trouble
Motte (-, -n) f moth
Motto (-s, -s) nt motto
Mountainbike (-s, -s) nt mountain bike
Möwe (-, -n) f (sea)gull
Mrd. f abk = **Milliarde(n)**
MS (-) f abk = **multiple Sklerose** MS
Mücke (-, -n) f midge; (tropische)
mosquito; **Mückenstich** m mosquito bite
müde adj tired
muffig adj (Geruch) musty; (Gesicht,
Mensch) grumpy
Mühe (-, -n) f trouble, pains pl; **sich** (dat)
große ~ geben to go to a lot of trouble
muhen vi to moo
Mühle (-, -n) f mill; (Kaffeemühle) grinder
Mull (-(e)s, -e) m muslin; (Med) gauze
Müll (-(e)s) m rubbish (Brit), garbage (US);
Müllabfuhr f rubbish (Brit) (o garbage
(US)) disposal
Mullbinde f gauze bandage
Müllcontainer m waste container;
Mülldeponie f rubbish (Brit) (o garbage
(US)) dump; **Mülleimer** m rubbish bin
(Brit), garbage can (US); **Mülltonne** f
dustbin (Brit), garbage can (US);
Mülltrennung f sorting and collecting
household waste according to type of material;
Müllverbrennungsanlage f incineration
plant; **Müllwagen** m dustcart (Brit),
garbage truck (US)
multikulturell adj multicultural
Multimedia- in zW multimedia
Multiple-Choice-Verfahren nt
multiple choice
multiple Sklerose (-n, -) f multiple
sclerosis
Multiplexkino nt multiplex (cinema)
multiplizieren vt to multiply (mit by)
Mumie f mummy
Mumps (-) m mumps sing
München (-s) nt Munich
Mund (-(e)s, Münder) m mouth; **halt den ~!**
shut up; **Mundart** f dialect;
Munddusche f dental water jet
münden vi to flow (in +akk into)
Mundgeruch m bad breath;
Mundharmonika (-, -s) f mouth organ
mündlich adj oral
Mundschutz m mask; **Mundwasser** nt
mouthwash

Munition f ammunition
Münster (-s, -) nt minster, cathedral
munter adj lively
Münzautomat m vending machine;
Münze (-, -n) f coin; **Münzeinwurf** m
slot; **Münzrückgabe** f coin return;
Münztelefon nt pay phone;
Münzwechsler m change machine
murmeln vt, vi to murmur, to mutter
Murmeltier nt marmot
mürrisch adj sullen, grumpy
Mus (-es, -e) nt puree
Muschel (-, -n) f mussel; (~schale) shell
Museum (-s, Museen) nt museum
Musical (-s, -s) nt musical
Musik f music; **musikalisch** adj musical;
Musiker(in) (-s, -) m(f) musician;
Musikinstrument nt musical
instrument; **musizieren** vi to play music
Muskat (-(e)s) m nutmeg
Muskel (-s, -n) m muscle; **Muskelkater** m
~ haben to be stiff; **Muskelriss** m torn
muscle; **Muskelzerrung** f pulled muscle;
muskulös adj muscular
Müsli (-s, -) nt muesli
Muslim(in) (-s, -s) m(f) Muslim
Muss (-) nt must

◯ SCHLÜSSELWORT

müssen (pt musste, pp gemusst od (als
Hilfsverb) müssen) vi **1** (Zwang) must; (nur
im Präsens) to have to; **ich muss es tun** I
must do it, I have to do it; **ich musste es
tun** I had to do it; **er muss es nicht tun** he
doesn't have to do it; **muss ich?** must I?,
do I have to?; **wann müsst ihr zur Schule?**
when do you have to go to school?; **er hat
gehen müssen** he (has) had to go; **muss
das sein?** is that really necessary?; **ich
muss mal** (umg) I need the toilet
2 (sollen): **das musst du nicht tun!** you
oughtn't to od shouldn't do that; **Sie
hätten ihn fragen müssen** you should
have asked him
3: **es muss geregnet haben** it must have
rained; **es muss nicht wahr sein** it
needn't be true

Muster (-s, -) nt (Dessin) pattern, design;
(Probe) sample; (Vorbild) model; **mustern**
vt to have a close look at; **jdn ~** to look sb
up and down

Mut (-(e)s) m courage; **jdm ~ machen** to encourage sb; **mutig** adj brave, courageous

Mutter (-, Mütter) f mother ▷ (-, -n) f (Schraubenmutter) nut; **Muttersprache** f mother tongue; **Muttertag** m Mother's Day; **Mutti** f mum(my) (Brit), mom(my) (US)

mutwillig adj deliberate

Mütze (-, -n) f cap

MwSt. abk = **Mehrwertsteuer** VAT

Myanmar (-s) nt Myanmar

n

N *abk* = **Nord** N

na *interj* **~ also!, ~ bitte!** see?, what did I tell you?; **~ ja** well; **~ und?** so what?

Nabel (-s, -) *m* navel

○ SCHLÜSSELWORT

nach *präp* +dat **1** (*örtlich*) to; **nach Berlin** to Berlin; **nach links/rechts** (to the) left/right; **nach oben/hinten** up/back

2 (*zeitlich*) after; **einer nach dem anderen** one after the other; **nach Ihnen!** after you!; **zehn (Minuten) nach drei** ten (minutes) past three

3 (*gemäß*) according to; **nach dem Gesetz** according to the law; **dem Namen nach** judging by his/her name; **nach allem, was ich weiß** as far as I know

▷ *adv*: **ihm nach!** after him!; **nach und nach** gradually little by little; **nach wie vor** still

Nachbar(in) (-n, -n) *m(f)* neighbour; **Nachbarschaft** *f* neighbourhood

nach|bestellen *vt* to order some more

nachdem *conj* after; (*weil*) since; **je ~ (ob/wie)** depending on (whether/how)

nach|denken *irr vi* to think (**über** +*akk* about); **nachdenklich** *adj* thoughtful

nacheinander *adv* one after another (o the other)

Nachfolger(in) (-s, -) *m(f)* successor

nach|forschen *vt* to investigate

Nachfrage *f* inquiry; (*Comm*) demand; **nach|fragen** *vi* to inquire

Nachfüllpack *m* refill pack

nach|geben *irr vi* to give in (**jdm** to sb)

Nachgebühr *f* surcharge; (*für Briefe etc*) excess postage

nach|gehen *irr vi* to follow (**jdm** sb); (*erforschen*) to inquire (**einer Sache** *dat* into sth); **die Uhr geht (zehn Minuten) nach** this watch is (ten minutes) slow

nachher *adv* afterwards; **bis ~!** see you later

Nachhilfe *f* extra tuition

nach|holen *vt* to catch up with; (*Versäumtes*) to make up for

nach|kommen *irr vi* to follow; **einer Verpflichtung** (*dat*) **~** to fulfil an obligation

nach|lassen *irr vt* (*Summe*) to take off ▷ *vi* to decrease, to ease off; (*schlechter werden*) to deteriorate; **nachlässig** *adj* negligent, careless

nach|laufen *irr vi* to run after, to chase (**jdm** sb)

nach|lösen *vt* **eine Fahrkarte ~** to buy a ticket on the bus/train

nach|machen *vt* to imitate, to copy (**jdm etw** sth from sb); (*fälschen*) to counterfeit

Nachmittag *m* afternoon; **heute ~** this afternoon; **am ~** in the afternoon; **nachmittags** *adv* in the afternoon; **um 3 Uhr ~** at 3 (o'clock) in the afternoon, at 3 pm

Nachnahme (-, -n) *f* cash on delivery; **per ~** COD

Nachname *m* surname

Nachporto *nt* excess postage

nach|prüfen *vt* to check

nach|rechnen *vt* to check

Nachricht (-, -en) *f* (piece of) news *sing*; (*Mitteilung*) message; **Nachrichten** *pl* news *sing*

Nachsaison *f* off-season

nach|schauen vi **jdm ~** to gaze after sb
▷ vt (prüfen) to check
nach|schicken vt to forward
nach|schlagen irr vt to look up
nach|sehen irr vt (prüfen) to check
nach|senden irr vt to forward
Nachspeise f dessert
nächstbeste(r, s) adj **der ~ Zug/Job** the
first train/job that comes along;
nächste(r, s) adj next; (nächstgelegen)
nearest
Nacht (-, Nächte) f night; **in der ~** during
the night; (bei Nacht) at night; **Nachtclub**
m nightclub; **Nachtdienst** m night duty;
~ haben (Apotheke) to be open all night
Nachteil m disadvantage
Nachtflug m night flight; **Nachtfrost** m
overnight frost; **Nachthemd** nt (für
Damen) nightdress; (für Herren)
nightshirt
Nachtigall (-, -en) f nightingale
Nachtisch m dessert, sweet (Brit),
pudding (Brit); **Nachtleben** nt nightlife
nach|tragen irr vt **jdm etw ~** (übel
nehmen) to hold sth against sb
nachträglich adv **~ alles Gute zum**
Geburtstag! Happy belated birthday
nachts adv at night; **um 11 Uhr ~** at 11
(o'clock) at night, at 11 pm; **um 2 Uhr ~** at 2
(o'clock) in the morning, at 2 am;
Nachtschicht f night shift; **Nachttarif** m
off-peak rate; **Nachttisch** m bedside
table; **Nachtzug** m night train
Nachweis (-es, -e) m proof
Nachwirkung f after-effect
nach|zahlen vi to pay extra ▷ vt **20 Euro**
~ to pay 20 euros extra
nach|zählen vt to check
Nacken (-s, -) m (nape of the) neck
nackt adj naked; (Tatsachen) plain, bare;
Nacktbadestrand m nudist beach
Nadel (-, -n) f needle; (Stecknadel) pin;
Nadelstreifen pl pinstripes pl
Nagel (-s, Nägel) m nail; **Nagelfeile** f
nail-file; **Nagellack** m nail varnish (o
polish); **Nagellackentferner** (-s, -) m
nail-varnish (o nail-polish) remover;
Nagelschere f nail scissors pl
nah(e) adj, adv (räumlich) near(by);
(zeitlich) near; (Verwandte, Freunde) close;
jdm ~e gehen to upset sb; **jdm etw ~e**
legen to suggest sth to sb; **~e liegen** to be
obvious ▷ prep +dat near (to), close to;

Nähe (-) f (Umgebung) vicinity; **in der**
~ nearby; **in der ~ von** near to
nähen vt, vi to sew
nähere(r, s) adj (Erklärung, Erkundigung)
more detailed; **die ~ Umgebung** the
immediate area; **Nähere(s)** nt details pl;
nähern vr **sich ~** to approach
nahezu adv virtually, almost
nahm imperf von **nehmen**
Nähmaschine f sewing machine;
Nähnadel f (sewing) needle
nahrhaft adj nourishing, nutritious;
Nahrung f food; **Nahrungsmittel** nt
food
Naht (-, Nähte) f seam; (Med) stitches pl,
suture; (Tech) join
Nahverkehr m local traffic;
Nahverkehrszug m local train
Nähzeug nt sewing kit
naiv adj naive
Name (-ns, -n) m name
nämlich adv that is to say, namely; (denn)
since
nannte imperf von **nennen**
Napf (-(e)s, Näpfe) m bowl, dish
Narbe (-, -n) f scar
Narkose (-, -n) f anaesthetic
Narzisse (-, -n) f narcissus
naschen vt, vi to nibble; **Naschkatze** f
(fam) nibbler; **eine ~ sein** to have a sweet
tooth
Nase (-, -n) f nose; **Nasenbluten** (-s) nt
nosebleed; **~ haben** to have a nosebleed;
Nasenloch nt nostril; **Nasentropfen** pl
nose drops pl
Nashorn nt rhinoceros
nass adj wet; **Nässe** (-) f wetness;
nässen vi (Wunde) to weep
Nation (-, -en) f nation; **national** adj
national; **Nationalfeiertag** m national
holiday; **Nationalhymne** (-, -n) f national
anthem; **Nationalität** f nationality;
Nationalmannschaft f national team;
Nationalspieler(in) m(f) international
(player)
NATO (-) f abk = **North Atlantic Treaty**
Organization NATO, Nato
Natur f nature; **Naturkost** f health food;
natürlich adj natural ▷ adv naturally;
(selbstverständlich) of course; **Naturpark** m
nature reserve; **naturrein** adj natural,
pure; **Naturschutz** m conservation;
Naturschutzgebiet nt nature reserve;

Naturwissenschaft f (natural) science;
Naturwissenschaftler(in) m(f) scientist
Navigationssystem nt (Auto)
navigation system
n. Chr. abk = **nach Christus** AD
Nebel (-s, -) m fog, mist; **nebelig** adj
foggy, misty; **Nebelscheinwerfer** m
foglamp; **Nebelschlussleuchte** f (Auto)
rear foglight
neben prep +akk o dat next to; (außer)
apart from, besides; **nebenan** adv next
door; **Nebenausgang** m side exit;
nebenbei adv at the same time;
(außerdem) additionally; (beiläufig)
incidentally; **nebeneinander** adv side by
side; **Nebeneingang** m side entrance;
Nebenfach nt subsidiary subject
nebenher adv (zusätzlich) besides;
(gleichzeitig) at the same time; (daneben)
alongside
Nebenkosten pl extra charges pl, extras
pl; **Nebensache** f minor matter;
nebensächlich adj minor; **Nebensaison**
f low season; **Nebenstelle** f (Geschäft)
branch; (Telefon) extension; **Nebenstraße**
f side street; **Nebenwirkung** f side effect
neblig adj foggy, misty
necken vt to tease
Neffe (-n, -n) m nephew
negativ adj negative; **Negativ** nt (Foto)
negative
nehmen (nahm, genommen) vt to take;
jdm etw ~ to take sth (away) from sb; **wie
man's nimmt** it depends on how you look
at it; **den Bus/Zug ~** to take the
bus/train; **jdn/etw ernst ~** to take sb/sth
seriously; **etw zu sich ~** to eat sth; **jdn
zu sich ~** to have sb come and live with
one; **jdn an die Hand ~** to take sb by the
hand
neidisch adj envious
neigen vi **zu etw ~** to tend towards sth;
Neigung f (des Geländes) slope; (Tendenz)
inclination; (Vorliebe) liking
nein adv no
Nektarine f nectarine
Nelke (-, -n) f carnation; (Gewürz) clove
nennen (nannte, genannt) vt to name; (mit
Namen) to call
Neonazi (-s, -s) m neo-Nazi
Neonlicht nt neon light; **Neonröhre** f
neon tube
Nepal (-s) nt Nepal

Neptun (-s) m Neptune
Nerv (-s, -en) m nerve; **jdm auf die ~en
gehen** to get on sb's nerves; **nerven** vt
jdn ~ (fam) to get on sb's nerves;
Nervenzusammenbruch m nervous
breakdown; **nervös** adj nervous
Nest (-(e)s, -er) nt nest; (pej: Ort) dump
nett adj nice; (freundlich) kind; **sei so ~ und
...** do me a favour and ...
netto adv net
Netz (-es, -e) nt net; (für Einkauf) string
bag; (System) network; (Stromnetz) mains,
power (US); **Netzanschluss** m mains
connection; **Netzbetreiber(in)** m(f)
network operator; (Inform) Internet (o
Net) operator; **Netzgerät** nt power pack;
Netzkarte f season ticket; **Netzwerk** nt
(Inform) network; **Netzwerkkarte** f
network card
neu adj new; (Sprache, Geschichte) modern;
die ~esten Nachrichten the latest news;
Neubau m new building; **neuerdings** adv
recently; **Neueröffnung** f (Geschäft) new
business; **Neuerung** f innovation;
(Reform) reform
Neugier f curiosity; **neugierig** adj
curious (auf +akk about); **ich bin ~, ob ...** I
wonder whether (o if) ...; **ich bin ~ , was
du dazu sagst** I'll be interested to hear
what you have to say about it
Neuheit f novelty; **Neuigkeit** f news
sing; **eine ~** a piece of news; **Neujahr** nt
New Year; **prosit ~!** Happy New Year;
neulich adv recently, the other day;
Neumond m new moon
neun num nine; **neunhundert** num nine
hundred; **neunmal** adv nine times;
neunte(r, s) adj ninth; siehe auch **dritte**;
Neuntel (-s, -) nt ninth; **neunzehn** num
nineteen; **neunzehnte(r, s)** adj
nineteenth; siehe auch **dritte**; **neunzig** num
ninety; **in den ~er Jahren** in the nineties;
Neunzigerjahre pl nineties pl;
neunzigste(r, s) adj ninetieth
neureich adj nouveau riche
Neurologe m, **Neurologin** f neurologist;
Neurose (-, -n) f neurosis; **neurotisch** adj
neurotic
Neuseeland nt New Zealand
Neustart m (Inform) restart, reboot
neutral adj neutral
neuwertig adj nearly new
Nicaragua (-s) nt Nicaragua

○ SCHLÜSSELWORT

nicht adv **1** (Verneinung) not; **er ist es nicht** it's not him it isn't him; **er raucht nicht** (gerade) he isn't smoking (gewöhnlich) he doesn't smoke; **ich kann das nicht — ich auch nicht** I can't do it — neither od nor can I; **es regnet nicht mehr** it's not raining any more; **nicht rostend** stainless

2 (Bitte, Verbot): **nicht!** don't!, no!; **nicht berühren!** do not touch!; **nicht doch!** don't!

3 (rhetorisch): **du bist müde, nicht (wahr)?** you're tired, aren't you?; **das ist schön, nicht (wahr)?** it's nice, isn't it?

4: **was du nicht sagst!** the things you say!

Nichte (-, -n) f niece
Nichtraucher(in) m(f) non-smoker; **Nichtraucherabteil** nt non-smoking compartment; **Nichtraucherzone** f non-smoking area
nichts pron nothing; **für ~ und wieder ~** for nothing at all; **ich habe ~ gesagt** I didn't say anything; **~ sagend** meaningless; **macht ~** never mind
Nichtschwimmer(in) m(f) non-swimmer
nicken vi to nod
Nickerchen nt nap
nie adv never; **~ wieder** (o mehr) never again; **fast ~** hardly ever
nieder adj (niedrig) low; (gering) inferior ▷ adv down; **niedergeschlagen** adj depressed; **Niederlage** f defeat
Niederlande pl Netherlands pl; **Niederländer(in)** m(f) Dutchman/Dutchwoman; **niederländisch** adj Dutch; **Niederländisch** nt Dutch
Niederlassung f branch
Niederösterreich nt Lower Austria; **Niedersachsen** nt Lower Saxony
Niederschlag m (Meteo) precipitation; (Regen) rainfall
niedlich adj sweet, cute
niedrig adj low; (Qualität) inferior
niemals adv never
niemand pron nobody, no one; **ich habe**

~en gesehen I haven't seen anyone; **~ von ihnen** none of them
Niere (-, -n) f kidney; **Nierenentzündung** f kidney infection; **Nierensteine** pl kidney stones pl
nieseln vi impers to drizzle; **Nieselregen** m drizzle
niesen vi to sneeze
Niete (-, -n) f (Los) blank; (Reinfall) flop; (pej: Mensch) failure; (Tech) rivet
Nigeria (-s) nt Nigeria
Nikotin (-s) nt nicotine; **nikotinarm** adj low in nicotine
Nilpferd nt hippopotamus
nippen vi to sip; **an etw** (dat) **~** to sip sth
nirgends adv nowhere
Nische (-, -n) f niche
Nitrat nt nitrate
Niveau (-s, -s) nt level; **sie hat ~** she's got class
nobel adj (großzügig) generous; (fam: luxuriös) classy, posh; **Nobelpreis** m Nobel Prize

○ SCHLÜSSELWORT

noch adv **1** (weiterhin) still; **noch nicht** not yet; **noch nie** never (yet); **noch immer** od **immer noch** still; **bleiben Sie doch noch** stay a bit longer

2 (in Zukunft) still, yet; **das kann noch passieren** that might still happen; **er wird noch kommen** he'll come (yet)

3 (nicht später als): **noch vor einer Woche** only a week ago; **noch am selben Tag** the very same day; **noch im 19. Jahrhundert** as late as the 19th century; **noch heute** today

4 (zusätzlich): **wer war noch da?** who else was there?; **noch einmal** once more again; **noch dreimal** three more times; **noch einer** another one

5 (bei Vergleichen): **noch größer** even bigger; **das ist noch besser** that's better still; **und wenn es noch so schwer ist** however hard it is

6: **Geld noch und noch** heaps (and heaps) of money; **sie hat noch und noch versucht, ...** she tried again and again to ...
▷ konj: **weder A noch B** neither A nor B

Nominativ m nominative (case)
Nonne (-, -n) f nun
Non-Stop-Flug m nonstop flight
Nord north; **Nordamerika** nt North
America; **Norddeutschland** nt Northern
Germany; **Norden** (-s) m north; **im
~ Deutschlands** in the north of Germany;
Nordeuropa nt Northern Europe;
Nordirland nt Northern Ireland;
nordisch adj (Völker, Sprache) Nordic;
Nordkorea (-s) nt North Korea; **nördlich**
adj northern; (Kurs, Richtung) northerly;
Nordost(en) m northeast; **Nordpol** m
North Pole; **Nordrhein-Westfalen** (-s) nt
North Rhine-Westphalia; **Nordsee** f
North Sea; **nordwärts** adv north,
northwards; **Nordwest(en)** m
northwest; **Nordwind** m north wind
nörgeln vi to grumble
Norm (-, -en) f norm; (Größenvorschrift)
standard
normal adj normal; **Normalbenzin** nt
regular (petrol (Brit) o gas (US));
normalerweise adv normally
normen vt to standardize
Norwegen (-s) nt Norway; **Norweger(in)**
m(f) Norwegian; **norwegisch** adj
Norwegian; **Norwegisch** nt Norwegian
Not (-, Nöte) f need; (Armut) poverty;
(Elend) hardship; (Bedrängnis) trouble;
(Mangel) want; (Mühe) trouble; (Zwang)
necessity; **zur ~** if necessary; (gerade noch)
just about
Notar(in) m(f) public notary; **notariell**
adj **~ beglaubigt** attested by a notary
Notarzt m, **Notärztin** f emergency
doctor; **Notarztwagen** m emergency
ambulance; **Notausgang** m emergency
exit; **Notbremse** f emergency brake;
Notdienst m emergency service,
after-hours service; **notdürftig** adj
scanty; (behelfsmäßig) makeshift
Note (-, -n) f note; (in Schule) mark, grade
(US); (Mus) note
Notebook (-(s), -s) nt (Inform) notebook
Notfall m emergency; **notfalls** adv if
necessary
notieren vt to note down
nötig adj necessary; **etw ~ haben** to need
sth
Notiz (-, -en) f note; (Zeitungs~) item;
Notizblock m notepad; **Notizbuch** nt
notebook

Notlage f crisis; (Elend) plight;
notlanden vi to make a forced
(o emergency) landing; **Notruf**
m emergency call; **Notrufnummer**
f emergency number;
Notrufsäule f emergency telephone
notwendig adj necessary
Nougat (-s, -s) m od nt nougat
November (-(s), -) m November; siehe
auch **Juni**
Nr. abk = **Nummer** No., no.
Nu m **im ~** in no time
nüchtern adj sober; (Magen) empty
Nudel (-, -n) f noodle; **~n** pl (italienische)
pasta sing; **Nudelsuppe** f noodle
soup
null num zero; (Tel) O (Brit), zero (US);
~ Fehler no mistakes; **~ Uhr** midnight;
Null (-, -en) f nought, zero; (pej: Mensch)
dead loss; **Nulltarif** m **zum ~** free of
charge
Numerus clausus (-) m restriction on the
number of students allowed to study a
particular subject
Nummer (-, -n) f number; **nummerieren**
vt to number; **Nummernschild** nt (Auto)
number plate (Brit), license plate (US)
nun adv now; **von ~ an** from now on
▷ interj well; **~ gut!** all right, then; **es ist
~ mal so** that's the way it is
nur adv only; **nicht ~ ..., sondern auch ...**
not only ..., but also ...; **~ Anna nicht**
except Anna
Nürnberg (-s) nt Nuremberg
Nuss (-, Nüsse) f nut; **Nussknacker** (-s, -)
m nutcracker; **Nuss-Nougat-Creme** f
chocolate nut cream
Nutte (-, -n) f (fam) tart
nutz, nütze adj **zu nichts ~ sein** to be
useless; **nutzen, nützen** vt to use (zu etw
for sth); **was nützt es?** what use is it? ▷ vi
to be of use; **das nützt nicht viel** that
doesn't help much; **es nützt nichts(, es
zu tun)** it's no use (doing it); **Nutzen** (-s, -)
m usefulness; (Gewinn) profit; **nützlich**
adj useful
Nylon (-s) nt nylon

O

o *interj* oh

O *abk* = **Ost** E

Oase (-, -n) *f* oasis

ob *conj* if, whether; **so als ~** as if; **er tut so, als ~ er krank wäre** he's pretending to be sick; **und ~!** you bet

obdachlos *adj* homeless

oben *adv* (*am oberen Ende*) at the top; (*obenauf*) on (the) top; (*im Haus*) upstairs; (*in einem Text*) above; **~ erwähnt** (*o genannt*) above-mentioned; **mit dem Gesicht nach ~** face up; **da ~** up there; **von ~ bis unten** from top to bottom; **siehe ~** see above

Ober (-s, -) *m* waiter

obere(r, s) *adj* upper, top

Oberfläche *f* surface; **oberflächlich** *adj* superficial; **Obergeschoss** *nt* upper floor

oberhalb *adv*, *prep* +*gen* above

Oberhemd *nt* shirt; **Oberkörper** *m* upper body; **Oberlippe** *f* upper lip; **Oberösterreich** *nt* Upper Austria; **Oberschenkel** *m* thigh

oberste(r, s) *adj* very top, topmost

Oberteil *nt* top; **Oberweite** *f* bust/chest measurement

obig *adj* above(-mentioned)

Objekt (-(e)s, -e) *nt* object

objektiv *adj* objective; **Objektiv** *nt* lens

obligatorisch *adj* compulsory, obligatory

Oboe (-, -n) *f* oboe

Observatorium *nt* observatory

Obst (-(e)s) *nt* fruit; **Obstkuchen** *m* fruit tart; **Obstsalat** *m* fruit salad

obszön *adj* obscene

obwohl *conj* although

Ochse (-n, -n) *m* ox; **Ochsenschwanzsuppe** *f* oxtail soup

ocker *adj* ochre

öd(e) *adj* waste; (*unbebaut*) barren; (*fig*) dull

oder *conj* or; **~ aber** or else; **er kommt doch, ~?** he's coming, isn't he?

Ofen (-s, Öfen) *m* oven; (*Heizofen*) heater; (*Kohleofen*) stove; (*Herd*) cooker, stove; **Ofenkartoffel** *f* baked (*ö* jacket) potato

offen *adj* open; (*aufrichtig*) frank; (*Stelle*) vacant ▷ *adv* frankly; **~ gesagt** to be honest

offenbar *adj* obvious; **offensichtlich** *adj* evident, obvious

öffentlich *adj* public; **Öffentlichkeit** *f* (*Leute*) public; (*einer Versammlung etc*) public nature

offiziell *adj* official

offline *adv* (*Inform*) offline

öffnen *vt* to open ▷ *vr* **sich ~** to open; **Öffner** (-s, -) *m* opener; **Öffnung** *f* opening; **Öffnungszeiten** *pl* opening times *pl*

oft *adv* often; **schon ~** many times; **öfter** *adv* more often (*o frequently*); **öfters** *adv* often, frequently

ohne *conj*, *prep* +*akk* without; **~ weiteres** without a second thought; (*sofort*) immediately; **~ ein Wort zu sagen** without saying a word; **~ mich** count me out

Ohnmacht (-*machten*) *f* unconsciousness; (*Hilflosigkeit*) helplessness; **in ~ fallen** to faint; **ohnmächtig** *adj* unconscious; **sie ist ~** she has fainted

Ohr (-(e)s, -en) *nt* ear; (*Gehör*) hearing

Öhr (-(e)s, -e) *nt* eye

Ohrenarzt *m*, **Ohrenärztin** *f* ear specialist; **Ohrenschmerzen** *pl* earache; **Ohrentropfen** *pl* ear drops *pl*; **Ohrfeige** *f*

slap (in the face); **Ohrläppchen** nt
earlobe; **Ohrringe** pl earrings pl
oje interj oh dear
okay interj OK, okay
Ökoladen m health food store;
ökologisch adj ecological; **-e
Landwirtschaft** organic farming
ökonomisch adj economic; (sparsam)
economical
Ökosystem nt ecosystem
Oktanzahl f (bei Benzin) octane rating
Oktober (-(s), -) m October; siehe auch **Juni**

> **Oktoberfest**
>
> The annual October beer festival, the
> **Oktoberfest**, takes place in Munich on
> a huge field where beer tents, roller
> coasters and many other
> amusements are set up. People sit at
> long wooden tables, drink beer from
> enormous litre beer mugs, eat
> pretzels and listen to brass bands. It
> is a great attraction for tourists and
> locals alike.

Öl (-(e)s, -e) nt oil; **Ölbaum** m olive tree;
ölen vt to oil; (Tech) to lubricate; **Ölfarbe**
f oil paint; **Ölfilter** m oil filter;
Ölgemälde nt oil painting; **Ölheizung** f
oil-fired central heating; **ölig** adj oily
oliv adj inv olive-green; **Olive** (-, -n) f
olive; **Olivenöl** nt olive oil
Ölmessstab m dipstick; **Ölofen** m oil
stove; **Ölpest** f oil pollution; **Ölsardine** f
sardine in oil; **Ölstandanzeiger** m (Auto)
oil gauge; **Ölteppich** m oil slick;
Ölwechsel m oil change
Olympiade f Olympic Games pl;
olympisch adj Olympic
Oma f, **Omi** (-s, -s) f grandma, gran(ny)
Omelett (-(e)s, -s) nt, **Omelette** f
omelette
Omnibus m bus
onanieren vi to masturbate
Onkel (-s, -) m uncle
online adv (Inform) online; **Onlinedienst**
m (Inform) online service
OP (-s, -s) m abk = **Operationssaal**
operating theatre (Brit) (o room (US))
Opa m, **Opi** (-s, -s) m grandpa, grandad
Openairkonzert nt open-air concert
Oper (-, -n) f opera; (Gebäude) opera house

Operation f operation
Operette f operetta
operieren vi to operate ▷ vt to operate
on
Opernsänger(in) m(f) opera singer
Opfer (-s, -) nt sacrifice; (Mensch) victim;
ein ~ bringen to make a sacrifice
Opium (-s) nt opium
Opposition f opposition
Optiker(in) (-s, -) m(f) optician
optimal adj optimal, optimum
optimistisch adj optimistic
oral adj oral; **Oralverkehr** m oral sex
orange adj inv orange; **Orange** (-, -n) f
orange; **Orangenmarmelade** f
marmalade; **Orangensaft** m orange juice
Orchester (-s, -) nt orchestra
Orchidee (-, -n) f orchid
Orden (-s, -) m (Rel) order; (Mil) decoration
ordentlich adj (anständig) respectable;
(geordnet) tidy, neat; (fam: annehmbar) not
bad; (fam: tüchtig) proper ▷ adv properly
ordinär adj common, vulgar; (Witz) dirty
ordnen vt to sort out; **Ordner** (-s, -) m
(bei Veranstaltung) steward; (Aktenordner)
file; **Ordnung** f order; (Geordnetsein)
tidiness; (**geht**) **in ~!** (that's) all right; **mit
dem Drucker ist etwas nicht in ~** there's
something wrong with the printer
Oregano (-s) m oregano
Organ (-s, -e) nt organ; (Stimme) voice
Organisation f organization;
organisieren vt to organize; (fam:
beschaffen) to get hold of ▷ vr **sich ~** to
organize
Organismus m organism
Orgasmus m orgasm
Orgel (-, -n) f organ
Orgie f orgy
orientalisch adj oriental
orientieren vr **sich ~** to get one's
bearings; **Orientierung** f orientation;
Orientierungssinn m sense of direction
original adj original; (echt) genuine;
Original (-s, -e) nt original;
Originalfassung f original version
originell adj original; (komisch) witty
Orkan (-(e)s, -e) m hurricane
Ort (-(e)s, -e) m place; (Dorf) village; **an
~ und Stelle, vor ~** on the spot
Orthopäde (-n, -n) m, **Orthopädin** f
orthopaedist
örtlich adj local; **Ortschaft** f village,

small town; **Ortsgespräch** nt local call;
Ortstarif m local rate; **Ortszeit** f local
time

● **Ossi**

● **Ossi** is a colloquial and rather
● derogatory word used to describe a
● German from the former **DDR**.

Ost east; **Ostdeutschland** nt (als
Landesteil) Eastern Germany; (Hist) East
Germany; **Osten** (-s) m east
Osterei nt Easter egg; **Osterglocke** f
daffodil; **Osterhase** m Easter bunny;
Ostermontag m Easter Monday; **Ostern**
(-, -) nt Easter; **an** (o zu) ~ at Easter; **frohe**
~ Happy Easter
Österreich (-s) nt Austria;
Österreicher(in) (-s, -) m(f) Austrian;
österreichisch adj Austrian
Ostersonntag m Easter Sunday
Osteuropa nt Eastern Europe; **Ostküste**
f east coast; **östlich** adj eastern; (Kurs,
Richtung) easterly; **Ostsee** f **die** ~ the
Baltic (Sea); **Ostwind** m east(erly) wind
OSZE (-) f abk = **Organisation für
Sicherheit und Zusammenarbeit in
Europa** OSCE
Otter (-s, -) m otter
out adj (fam) out; **outen** vt to out
oval adj oval
Overheadprojektor m overhead
projector
Ozean (-s, -e) m ocean; **der Stille** ~ the
Pacific (Ocean)
Ozon (-s) nt ozone; **Ozonbelastung** f
ozone level; **Ozonloch** nt hole in the
ozone layer; **Ozonschicht** f ozone layer;
Ozonwerte pl ozone levels pl

P

paar adj inv **ein ~** a few; **ein ~ Mal** a few times; **ein ~ Äpfel** some apples

Paar (-(e)s, -e) nt pair; (Ehepaar) couple; **ein ~ Socken** a pair of socks

pachten vt to lease

Päckchen nt package; (Zigaretten) packet; (zum Verschicken) small parcel; **packen** vt to pack; (fassen) to grasp, to seize; (fam: schaffen) to manage; (fig: fesseln) to grip; **Packpapier** nt brown paper; **Packung** f packet, pack (US); **Packungsbeilage** f package insert, patient information leaflet

Pädagoge (-n, -n) m, **Pädagogin** f teacher; **pädagogisch** adj educational; **~e Hochschule** college of education

Paddel (-s, -) nt paddle; **Paddelboot** nt canoe; **paddeln** vi to paddle

Paket (-(e)s, -e) nt packet; (Postpaket) parcel; (Inform) package; **Paketbombe** f parcel bomb; **Paketkarte** f dispatch form (to be filled in with details of the sender and the addressee when handing in a parcel at the post office)

Pakistan (-s) nt Pakistan

Palast (-es, Paläste) m palace

Palästina (-s) nt Palestine; **Palästinenser(in)** (-s, -) m(f) Palestinian

Palatschinken pl filled pancakes pl

Palette f (von Maler) palette; (Ladepalette) pallet; (Vielfalt) range

Palme (-, -n) f palm (tree); **Palmsonntag** m Palm Sunday

Pampelmuse (-, -n) f grapefruit

pampig adj (fam: frech) cheeky; (breiig) gooey

Panda(bär) (-s, -s) m panda

panieren vt (Gastr) to coat with breadcrumbs; **paniert** adj breaded

Panik f panic

Panne (-, -n) f (Auto) breakdown; (Missgeschick) slip; **Pannendienst** m, **Pannenhilfe** f breakdown (o rescue) service

Pant(h)er (-s, -) m panther

Pantoffel (-s, -n) m slipper

Pantomime (-, -n) f mime

Panzer (-s, -) m (Panzerung) armour (plating); (Mil) tank

Papa (-s, -s) m dad(dy), pa (US)

Papagei (-s, -en) m parrot

Papaya (-, -s) f papaya

Papier (-s, -e) nt paper; **~e** pl (Ausweispapiere) papers pl; (Dokumente, Urkunden) papers pl, documents pl; **Papiercontainer** m paper bank; **Papierformat** nt paper size; **Papiergeld** nt paper money; **Papierkorb** m wastepaper basket; (Inform) recycle bin; **Papiertaschentuch** nt (paper) tissue; **Papiertonne** f paper bank

Pappbecher m paper cup; **Pappe** (-, -n) f cardboard; **Pappkarton** m cardboard box; **Pappteller** m paper plate

Paprika (-s, -s) m (Gewürz) paprika; (Schote) pepper

Papst (-(e)s, Päpste) m pope

Paradeiser (-s, -) m tomato

Paradies (-es, -e) nt paradise

Paragliding (-s) nt paragliding

Paragraph (-en, -en) m paragraph; (Jur) section

parallel adj parallel

Paranuss f Brazil nut

Parasit (-en, -en) m parasite

parat adj ready; **etw ~ haben** to have sth ready

Pärchen nt couple

Parfüm (-s, -s o -e) nt perfume; **Parfümerie** f perfumery; **parfümieren** vt to scent, to perfume

Pariser (-s, -) m (fam: Kondom) rubber

Park (-s, -s) m park

Park-and-ride-System nt park-and-ride system; **Parkanlage** f park; (um Gebäude) grounds pl; **Parkbank** f park bench; **Parkdeck** nt parking level; **parken** vt, vi to park

Parkett (-s, -e) nt parquet flooring; (Theat) stalls pl (Brit), parquet (US)

Parkhaus nt multi-storey car park (Brit), parking garage (US)

parkinsonsche Krankheit f Parkinson's disease

Parkkralle f (Auto) wheel clamp; **Parklicht** nt parking light; **Parklücke** f parking space; **Parkplatz** m (für ein Auto) parking space; (für mehrere Autos) car park (Brit), parking lot (US); **Parkscheibe** f parking disc; **Parkscheinautomat** m pay point; (Parkscheinausgabegerät) ticket machine; **Parkuhr** f parking meter; **Parkverbot** nt (Stelle) no-parking zone; **hier ist ~** you can't park here

Parlament nt parliament

Parmesan (-s) m Parmesan (cheese)

Partei f party

Parterre (-s, -s) nt ground floor (Brit), first floor (US)

Partie f part; (Spiel) game; (Mann, Frau) catch; **mit von der ~ sein** to be in on it

Partitur f (Mus) score

Partizip (-s, -ien) nt participle

Partner(in) (-s, -) m(f) partner; **Partnerschaft** f partnership; **eingetragene ~** civil partnership; **Partnerstadt** f twin town

Party (-, -s) f party; **Partymuffel** (-s, -) m party pooper; **Partyservice** m catering service

Pass (-es, Pässe) m pass; (Ausweis) passport

passabel adj reasonable

Passagier (-s, -e) m passenger

Passamt nt passport office

Passant(in) m(f) passer-by; **Passbild** nt passport photo

passen vi (Größe) to fit; (Farbe, Stil) to go (zu with); (auf Frage) to pass; **passt (es) dir morgen?** does tomorrow suit you?; **das passt mir gut** that suits me fine; **passend** adj suitable; (zusammenpassend) matching; (angebracht) fitting; (Zeit) convenient; **haben Sie es nicht ~?** (Kleingeld) have you got the right change?

passieren vi to happen

passiv adj passive

Passkontrolle f passport control

Passwort nt password

Paste (-, -n) f paste

Pastellfarbe f pastel colour

Pastete (-, -n) f (warmes Gericht) pie; (Pastetchen) vol-au-vent; (ohne Teig) pâté

Pastor(in) (-s, -en) m(f) minister, vicar

Pate (-n, -n) m godfather; **Patenkind** nt godchild

Patient(in) m(f) patient

Patin f godmother

Patrone (-, -n) f cartridge

patsch interj splat; **Patsche** (-, -n) f (Fliegen~) swat; (Bedrängnis) mess; **patschnass** adj soaking wet

pauschal adj (Kosten) inclusive; (Urteil) sweeping; **Pauschale** (-, -n) f, **Pauschalgebühr** f flat rate (charge); **Pauschalpreis** m flat rate; (für Hotel, Reise) all-inclusive price; **Pauschalreise** f package tour

Pause (-, -n) f break; (Theat) interval; (Kino etc) intermission; (Innehalten) pause

Pavian (-s, -e) m baboon

Pavillon (-s, -s) m pavilion

Pay-TV (-s) nt pay-per-view television, pay TV

Pazifik (-s) m Pacific (Ocean)

PC (-s, -s) m abk = **Personalcomputer** PC

Pech (-s, -e) nt (fig) bad luck; **~ haben** to be unlucky; **~ gehabt!** tough (luck)

Pedal (-s, -e) nt pedal

Pediküre (-, -en) f pedicure

Peeling (-s, -s) nt (facial/body) scrub

peinlich adj (unangenehm) embarrassing, awkward; (genau) painstaking; **es war mir sehr ~** I was totally embarrassed

Peitsche (-, -n) f whip

Pelikan (-s, -e) m pelican

Pellkartoffeln pl potatoes pl boiled in their skins

Pelz (-es, -e) m fur; **pelzig** adj (Zunge) furred

pendeln vi (Zug, Bus) to shuttle; (Mensch) to commute; **Pendelverkehr** m shuttle traffic; (für Pendler) commuter traffic; **Pendler(in)** (-s, -) m(f) commuter

penetrant adj sharp; (Mensch) pushy

Penis (-, -se) m penis

Pension f (Geld) pension; (Ruhestand) retirement; (für Gäste) guesthouse, B&B;

pensioniert adj retired; **Pensionsgast** m guest (in a guesthouse)
Peperoni (-, -) f chilli
per prep +akk by, per; (pro) per; (bis) by
perfekt adj perfect
Pergamentpapier nt greaseproof paper
Periode (-, -n) f period
Perle (-, -n) f (a. fig) pearl
perplex adj dumbfounded
Person (-, -en) f person; **ein Tisch für drei ~en** a table for three; **Personal** (-s) nt staff, personnel; (Bedienung) servants pl; **Personalausweis** m identity card; **Personalien** pl particulars pl; **Personenschaden** m injury to persons; **Personenwaage** f (bathroom) scales pl; **Personenzug** m passenger train; **persönlich** adj personal; (auf Briefen) private ▷ adv personally; (selbst) in person; **Persönlichkeit** f personality
Peru (-s) nt Peru
Perücke (-, -n) f wig
pervers adj perverted
pessimistisch adj pessimistic
Pest (-) f plague
Petersilie f parsley
Petroleum (-s) nt paraffin (Brit), kerosene (US)
Pfad (-(e)s, -e) m path; **Pfadfinder** (-s, -) m boy scout; **Pfadfinderin** f girl guide
Pfahl (-(e)s, Pfähle) m post, stake
Pfand (-(e)s, Pfänder) nt security; (Flaschenpfand) deposit; (im Spiel) forfeit; **Pfandflasche** f returnable bottle
Pfanne (-, -n) f (frying) pan
Pfannkuchen m pancake
Pfarrei f parish; **Pfarrer(in)** (-s, -) m(f) priest
Pfau (-(e)s, -en) m peacock
Pfeffer (-s, -) m pepper; **Pfefferkuchen** m gingerbread; **Pfefferminze** (-e) f peppermint; **Pfefferminztee** m peppermint tea; **Pfeffermühle** f pepper mill; **pfeffern** vt to put pepper on/in; **Pfefferstreuer** (-s, -) m pepper pot
Pfeife (-, -n) f whistle; (für Tabak, von Orgel) pipe; **pfeifen** (pfiff, gepfiffen) vt, vi to whistle
Pfeil (-(e)s, -e) m arrow
Pfeiltaste f (Inform) arrow key
Pferd (-(e)s, -e) nt horse; **Pferdeschwanz** m (Frisur) ponytail; **Pferdestall** m stable; **Pferdestärke** f horsepower

pfiff imperf von **pfeifen**
Pfifferling m chanterelle
Pfingsten (-, -) nt Whitsun, Pentecost (US); **Pfingstmontag** m Whit Monday; **Pfingstsonntag** m Whit Sunday, Pentecost (US); **Pfingstrose** f peony
Pfirsich (-s, -e) m peach
Pflanze (-, -n) f plant; **pflanzen** vt to plant; **Pflanzenfett** nt vegetable fat
Pflaster (-s, -) nt (für Wunde) plaster, Band Aid® (US); (Straßenpflaster) road surface, pavement (US)
Pflaume (-, -n) f plum
Pflege (-, -n) f care; (Krankenpflege) nursing; (von Autos, Maschinen) maintenance; **pflegebedürftig** adj in need of care; **pflegeleicht** adj easy-care; (fig) easy to handle; **pflegen** vt to look after; (Kranke) to nurse; (Beziehungen) to foster; (Fingernägel, Gesicht) to take care of; (Daten) to maintain; **Pflegepersonal** nt nursing staff; **Pflegeversicherung** f long-term care insurance
Pflicht (-, -en) f duty; (Sport) compulsory section; **pflichtbewusst** adj conscientious; **Pflichtfach** nt (Schule) compulsory subject; **Pflichtversicherung** f compulsory insurance
pflücken vt to pick
Pforte (-, -n) f gate; **Pförtner(in)** (-s, -) m(f) porter
Pfosten (-s, -) m post
Pfote (-, -n) f paw
pfui interj ugh
Pfund (-(e)s, -e) nt pound
pfuschen vi (fam) to be sloppy
Pfütze (-, -n) f puddle
Phantasie f siehe **Fantasie**; **phantastisch** adj siehe **fantastisch**
Phase (-, -n) f phase
Philippinen pl Philippines pl
Philosophie f philosophy
Photo nt siehe **Foto**
pH-neutral adj pH-balanced; **pH-Wert** m pH-value
Physalis (-, Physalen) f physalis
Physik f physics sing
physisch adj physical
Pianist(in) (-en, -en) m(f) pianist
Pickel (-s, -) m pimple; (Werkzeug) pickaxe; (Berg~) ice-axe
Picknick (-s, -e o -s) nt picnic; **ein ~ machen** to have a picnic

piepsen vi to chirp

piercen vt **sich die Nase ~ lassen** to have one's nose pierced; **Piercing** (-s) nt (body) piercing

pieseln vi (fam) to pee

Pik (-, -) nt (Karten) spades pl

pikant adj spicy

Pilger(in) m(f) pilgrim; **Pilgerfahrt** f pilgrimage

Pille (-, -n) f pill; **sie nimmt die ~** she's on the pill

Pilot(in) (-en, -en) m(f) pilot

Pilz (-es, -e) m (essbar) mushroom; (giftig) toadstool; (Med) fungus

PIN (-, -s) f PIN (number)

pingelig adj (fam) fussy

Pinguin (-s, -e) m penguin

Pinie f pine; **Pinienkern** m pine nut

pink adj shocking pink

pinkeln vi (fam) to pee

Pinsel (-s, -) m (paint)brush

Pinzette f tweezers pl

Pistazie f pistachio

Piste (-, -n) f (Ski) piste; (Aviat) runway

Pistole (-, -n) f pistol

Pixel (-s) nt (Inform) pixel

Pizza (-, -s) f pizza; **Pizzaservice** m pizza delivery service; **Pizzeria** (-, Pizzerien) f pizzeria

Pkw (-(s), -(s)) m abk = **Personenkraftwagen** car

Plakat nt poster

Plakette f (Schildchen) badge; (Aufkleber) sticker

Plan (-(e)s, Pläne) m plan; (Karte) map; **planen** vt to plan

Planet (-en, -en) m planet; **Planetarium** nt planetarium

planmäßig adj scheduled

Plan(t)schbecken nt paddling pool; **plan(t)schen** vi to splash around

Planung f planning

Plastik f sculpture ▷ (-s) nt (Kunststoff) plastic; **Plastikfolie** f plastic film; **Plastiktüte** f plastic bag

Platin (-s) nt platinum

platsch interj splash

platt adj flat; (fam: überrascht) flabbergasted; (fig: geistlos) flat, boring

Platte (-, -n) f (Foto, Tech, Gastr) plate; (Steinplatte) flag; (Schallplatte) record; **Plattenspieler** m record player

Plattform f platform; **Plattfuß** m flat foot; (Reifen) flat (tyre)

Platz (-es, Plätze) m place; (Sitzplatz) seat; (freier Raum) space, room; (in Stadt) square; (Sportplatz) playing field; **nehmen Sie ~** please sit down, take a seat; **ist dieser ~ frei?** is this seat taken?; **Platzanweiser(in)** m(f) usher/usherette

Plätzchen nt spot; (Gebäck) biscuit

platzen vi to burst; (Bombe) to explode

Platzkarte f seat reservation; **Platzreservierung** f seat reservation; **Platzverweis** m **er erhielt einen ~** he was sent off; **Platzwunde** f laceration, cut

plaudern vi to chat, to talk

pleite adj (fam) broke; **Pleite** (-, -n) f (Bankrott) bankruptcy; (fam: Reinfall) flop

Plombe (-, -n) f lead seal; (Zahnplombe) filling; **plombieren** vt (Zahn) to fill

plötzlich adj sudden ▷ adv suddenly, all at once

plump adj clumsy; (Hände) ungainly; (Körper) shapeless

plumps interj thud; (in Flüssigkeit) plop

Plural (-s, -e) m plural

plus adv plus; **fünf ~ sieben ist zwölf** five plus seven is (o are) twelve; **zehn Grad ~** ten degrees above zero; **Plus** (-, -) nt plus; (Fin) profit; (Vorteil) advantage

Plüsch (-(e)s, -e) m plush

Pluto (-) m Pluto

PLZ abk = **Postleitzahl** postcode (Brit), zip code (US)

Po (-s, -s) m (fam) bottom, bum

Pocken pl smallpox sing

poetisch adj poetic

Pointe (-, -n) f punch line

Pokal (-s, -e) m goblet; (Sport) cup

pökeln vt to pickle

Pol (-s, -e) m pole

Pole (-n, -n) m Pole; **Polen** (-s) nt Poland

Police (-, -n) f (insurance) policy

polieren vt to polish

Polin f Pole, Polish woman

Politik f politics sing; (eine bestimmte) policy; **Politiker(in)** m(f) politician; **politisch** adj political

Politur f polish

Polizei f police pl; **Polizeibeamte(r)** m, **Polizeibeamtin** f police officer; **polizeilich** adj police; **sie wird ~ gesucht** the police are looking for her;

Polizeirevier nt, **Polizeiwache** f police station; **Polizeistunde** f closing time; **Polizeiwache** f police station; **Polizist(in)** m(f) policeman/-woman

Pollen (-s, -) m pollen; **Pollenflug** (-s) m pollen count

polnisch adj Polish; **Polnisch** nt Polish

Polo (-s) nt polo; **Polohemd** nt polo shirt

Polster (-s, -) nt cushion; (Polsterung) upholstery; (in Kleidung) padding; (fig: Geld) reserves pl; **Polstergarnitur** f living-room suite; **Polstermöbel** pl upholstered furniture sing; **polstern** vt to upholster; (Kleidung) to pad

Polterabend m party prior to a wedding, at which old crockery is smashed to bring good luck

poltern vi (Krach machen) to crash; (schimpfen) to rant

Polyester (-s, -) m polyester

Polypen pl (Med) adenoids pl

Pommes frites pl chips pl (Brit), French fries pl (US)

Pony (-s, -s) m (Frisur) fringe (Brit), bangs pl (US) ▷ (-s, -s) nt (Pferd) pony

Popcorn (-s) nt popcorn

Popmusik f pop (music)

populär adj popular

Pore (-, -n) f pore

Pornografie f pornography

Porree (-s, -s) m leeks pl; **eine Stange ~** a leek

Portemonnaie, Portmonee (-s, -s) nt purse

Portier (-s, -s) m porter; siehe auch **Pförtner**

Portion f portion, helping

Porto (-s, -s) nt postage

Portrait, Porträt (-s, -s) nt portrait

Portugal (-s) nt Portugal; **Portugiese** (-n, -n) m Portuguese; **Portugiesin** (-, -nen) f Portuguese; **portugiesisch** adj Portuguese; **Portugiesisch** nt Portuguese

Portwein (-s, -e) m port

Porzellan (-s, -e) nt china

Posaune (-, -n) f trombone

Position f position

positiv adj positive

Post® (-, -en) f post office; (Briefe) post (Brit), mail; **Postamt** nt post office; **Postanweisung** f postal order (Brit), money order (US); **Postbank** f German post office bank; **Postbote** m, **-botin** f postman/-woman

Posten (-s, -) m post, position; (Comm) item; (auf Liste) entry

Poster (-s, -) nt poster

Postfach nt post-office box, PO box; **Postkarte** f postcard; **postlagernd** adv poste restante; **Postleitzahl** f postcode (Brit), zip code (US)

postmodern adj postmodern

Postsparkasse f post office savings bank; **Poststempel** m postmark; **Postweg** m **auf dem ~** by mail

Potenz f (Math) power; (eines Mannes) potency

PR (-, -s) f abk = **Public Relations** PR

prächtig adj splendid

prahlen vi to boast, to brag

Praktikant(in) m(f) trainee; **Praktikum** (-s, Praktika) nt practical training; **praktisch** adj practical; **-er Arzt** general practitioner

Praline f chocolate

Prämie f (bei Versicherung) premium; (Belohnung) reward; (von Arbeitgeber) bonus

Präparat nt (Med) medicine; (Bio) preparation

Präservativ nt condom

Präsident(in) m(f) president

Praxis (-, Praxen) f practice; (Behandlungsraum) surgery; (von Anwalt) office

präzise adj precise, exact

predigen vt, vi to preach; **Predigt** (-, -en) f sermon

Preis (-es, -e) m (zu zahlen) price; (bei Sieg) prize; **den ersten ~ gewinnen** to win first prize; **Preisausschreiben** nt competition

Preiselbeere f cranberry

preisgünstig adj inexpensive; **Preislage** f price range; **Preisliste** f price list; **Preisschild** nt price tag; **Preisträger(in)** m(f) prizewinner; **preiswert** adj inexpensive

Prellung f bruise

Premiere (-, -n) f premiere, first night

Premierminister(in) m(f) prime minister, premier

Presse (-, -n) f press

pressen vt to press

prickeln vi to tingle

Priester(in) (-s, -) m(f) priest/(woman) priest

Primel (-, -n) f primrose
primitiv adj primitive
Prinz (-en, -en) m prince; **Prinzessin** f princess
Prinzip (-s, -ien) nt principle; **im ~ basically; aus ~** on principle
Priorität f priority
privat adj private; **Privatfernsehen** nt commercial television; **Privatgrundstück** nt private property; **privatisieren** vt to privatize; **Privatquartier** nt private accommodation
pro prep +akk per; **5 Euro ~ Stück/Person** 5 euros each/per person; **Pro** (-s) nt pro
Probe (-, -n) f test; (Teststück) sample; (Theat) rehearsal; **Probefahrt** f test drive; **eine ~ machen** to go for a test drive; **Probezeit** f trial period; **probieren** vt, vi to try; (Wein, Speise) to taste, to sample
Problem (-s, -e) nt problem
Produkt (-(e)s, -e) nt product; **Produktion** f production; (produzierte Menge) output; **produzieren** vt to produce
Professor(in) (-s, -en) m(f) professor
Profi (-s, -s) m pro
Profil (-s, -e) nt profile; (von Reifen, Schuhsohle) tread
Profit (-(e)s, -e) m profit; **profitieren** vi to profit (von from)
Prognose (-, -n) f prediction; (Wetter) forecast
Programm (-s, -e) nt programme; (Inform) program; (TV) channel; **Programmheft** nt programme; **programmieren** vt to program; **Programmierer(in)** (-s, -) m(f) programmer; **Programmkino** nt arts (o repertory (US)) cinema
Projekt (-(e)s, -e) nt project
Projektor m projector
Promenade (-, -n) f promenade
Promille (-(s), -) nt (blood) alcohol level; **0,8 ~** 0,08 per cent; **Promillegrenze** f legal alcohol limit
prominent adj prominent; **Prominenz** f VIPs pl, prominent figures pl; (fam: Stars) the glitterati pl
Propeller (-s, -) m propeller
prosit interj cheers
Prospekt (-(e)s, -e) m leaflet, brochure
prost interj cheers
Prostituierte(r) mf prostitute
Protest (-(e)s, -e) m protest

Protestant(in) m(f) Protestant; **protestantisch** adj Protestant
protestieren vi to protest (gegen against)
Prothese (-, -n) f artificial arm/leg; (Gebiss) dentures pl
Protokoll (-s, -e) nt (bei Sitzung) minutes pl; (diplomatisch) (Inform) protocol; (bei Polizei) statement
protzen vi to show off; **protzig** adj flashy
Proviant (-s, -e) m provisions pl
Provider (-s, -) m (Inform) (service) provider
Provinz (-, -en) f province
Provision f (Comm) commission
provisorisch adj provisional
provozieren vt to provoke
Prozent (-(e)s, -e) nt per cent
Prozess (-es, -e) m (Vorgang) process; (Jur) trial; (Rechtsfall) (court) case; **prozessieren** vi to go to law (mit against)
Prozession f procession
Prozessor (-s, -en) m (Inform) processor
prüde adj prudish
prüfen vt to test; (nachprüfen) to check; **Prüfung** f (Schule) exam; (Überprüfung) check; **eine ~ machen** (Schule) to take an exam
Prügelei f fight; **prügeln** vt to beat ▷ vr **sich ~** to fight
PS abk = **Pferdestärke** hp ▷ abk = **Postskript(um)** PS
pseudo- präf pseudo; **Pseudokrupp** (-s) m (Med) pseudocroup; **Pseudonym** (-s, -e) nt pseudonym
pst interj ssh
Psychiater(in) (-s, -) m(f) psychiatrist; **psychisch** adj psychological; (Krankheit) mental; **Psychoanalyse** f psychoanalysis; **Psychologe** (-n, -n) m, **Psychologin** f psychologist; **Psychologie** f psychology
Psychopharmaka pl mind-affecting drugs pl, psychotropic drugs pl; **psychosomatisch** adj psychosomatic; **Psychoterror** m psychological intimidation; **Psychotherapie** f psychotherapy
Pubertät f puberty
Publikum (-s) nt audience; (Sport) crowd
Pudding (-s, -e o -s) m blancmange
Pudel (-s, -) m poodle

Puder (-s, -) m powder; **Puderzucker** m icing sugar

Puerto Rico (-s) nt Puerto Rico

Pulli (-s, -s) m, **Pullover** (-s, -) m sweater, pullover, jumper (Brit)

Puls (-es, -e) m pulse

Pulver (-s, -) nt powder; **Pulverkaffee** m instant coffee; **Pulverschnee** m powder snow

pummelig adj chubby

Pumpe (-, -n) f pump; **pumpen** vt to pump; (fam: verleihen) to lend; (fam: sich ausleihen) to borrow

Pumps pl court shoes pl (Brit), pumps pl (US)

Punk (-s, -s) m (Musik, Mensch) punk

Punkt (-(e)s, -e) m point; (bei Muster) dot; (Satzzeichen) full stop (Brit), period (US); **~ zwei Uhr** at two o'clock sharp

pünktlich adj punctual, on time; **Pünktlichkeit** f punctuality

Punsch (-(e)s, -e) m punch

Pupille (-, -n) f pupil

Puppe (-, -n) f doll

pur adj pure; (völlig) sheer; (Whisky) neat

Püree (-s, -s) nt puree; (Kartoffelpüree) mashed potatoes pl

Puste (-) f (fam) puff; **außer ~ sein** to be puffed

Pustel (-, -n) f pustule; (Pickel) pimple; **pusten** vi to blow; (keuchen) to puff

Pute (-, -n) f turkey; **Putenschnitzel** nt turkey escalope

Putsch (-es, -e) m putsch

Putz (-es) m (Mörtel) plaster

putzen vt to clean; **sich** (dat) **die Nase ~** to blow one's nose; **sich** (dat) **die Zähne ~** to brush one's teeth; **Putzfrau** f cleaner; **Putzlappen** m cloth, **Putzmann** m cleaner; **Putzmittel** nt cleaning agent, cleaner

Puzzle (-s, -s) nt jigsaw (puzzle)

Pyjama (-s, -s) m pyjamas pl

Pyramide (-, -n) f pyramid

Python (-s, -s) m python

q

(*rechtwinklig*) at right angles; **~ über die Straße** straight across the street; **querfeldein** *adv* across country; **Querflöte** *f* flute; **Querschnitt** *m* cross section; **querschnittsgelähmt** *adj* paraplegic; **Querstraße** *f* side street
quetschen *vt* to squash, to crush; (*Med*) to bruise; **Quetschung** *f* bruise
Queue (*-s, -s*) *m* (billiard) cue
quietschen *vi* to squeal; (*Tür, Bett*) to squeak; (*Bremsen*) to screech
Quirl (*-s, -e*) *m* whisk
quitt *adj* quits, even
Quitte (*-, -n*) *f* quince
Quittung *f* receipt
Quiz (*-, -*) *nt* quiz
Quote (*-, -n*) *f* rate; (*Comm*) quota

Quadrat *nt* square; **quadratisch** *adj* square; **Quadratmeter** *m* square metre
quaken *vi* (*Frosch*) to croak; (*Ente*) to quack
Qual (*-, -en*) *f* pain, agony; (*seelisch*) anguish; **quälen** *vt* to torment ▷ *vr* **sich ~** to struggle; (*geistig*) to torment oneself; **Quälerei** *f* torture, torment
qualifizieren *vt* to qualify; (*einstufen*) to label ▷ *vr* **sich ~** to qualify
Qualität *f* quality
Qualle (*-, -n*) *f* jellyfish
Qualm (*-(e)s*) *m* thick smoke; **qualmen** *vt, vi* to smoke
Quantität *f* quantity
Quarantäne (*-, -n*) *f* quarantine
Quark (*-s*) *m* quark; (*fam: Unsinn*) rubbish
Quartett (*-s, -e*) *nt* quartet; (*Kartenspiel*) happy families *sing*
Quartier (*-s, -e*) *nt* accommodation
quasi *adv* more or less
Quatsch (*-es*) *m* (*fam*) rubbish; **quatschen** *vi* (*fam*) to chat
Quecksilber *nt* mercury
Quelle (*-, -n*) *f* spring; (*eines Flusses*) source
quellen *vi* to pour
quer *adv* crossways, diagonally;

r

Rabatt (-(e)s, -e) m discount
Rabbi (-(s), -s) m rabbi; **Rabbiner** (-s, -) m rabbi
Rabe (-n, -n) m raven
Rache (-) f revenge, vengeance
Rachen (-s, -) m throat
rächen vt to avenge ▷ vr **sich ~** to take (one's) revenge (an +dat on)
Rad (-(e)s, Räder) nt wheel; (Fahrrad) bike; **~ fahren** to cycle; **mit dem ~ fahren** to go by bike
Radar (-s) m o nt radar; **Radarfalle** f speed trap; **Radarkontrolle** f radar speed check
radeln vi (fam) to cycle; **Radfahrer(in)** m(f) cyclist; **Radfahrweg** m cycle track (o path)
Radicchio (-s) m (Salatsorte) radicchio
radieren vt to rub out, to erase; **Radiergummi** m rubber (Brit), eraser; **Radierung** f (Kunst) etching
Radieschen nt radish
radikal adj radical
Radio (-s, -s) nt radio; **im ~** on the radio
radioaktiv adj radioactive
Radiologe (-n, -n) m, **Radiologin** f radiologist

Radiorekorder m radio cassette recorder; **Radiosender** m radio station; **Radiowecker** m radio alarm (clock)
Radkappe f (Auto) hub cap
Radler(in) (-s, -) m(f) cyclist
Radler (-s, -) nt = shandy
Radlerhose f cycling shorts pl; **Radrennen** nt cycle racing; (einzelnes Rennen) cycle race; **Radtour** f cycling tour; **Radweg** m cycle track (o path)
raffiniert adj crafty, cunning; (Zucker) refined
Rafting (-s) nt white water rafting
Ragout (-s, -s) nt ragout
Rahm (-s) m cream
rahmen vt to frame; **Rahmen** (-s, -) m frame
Rakete (-, -n) f rocket
rammen vt to ram
Rampe (-, -n) f ramp
ramponieren vt (fam) to damage, to batter
Ramsch (-(e)s, -e) m junk
ran (fam) kontr von **heran**
Rand (-(e)s, Ränder) m edge; (von Brille, Tasse etc) rim; (auf Papier) margin; (Schmutzrand, unter Augen) ring; (fig) verge, brink
randalieren vi to (go on the) rampage; **Randalierer(in)** (-s, -) m(f) hooligan
Randstein m kerb (Brit), curb (US); **Randstreifen** m shoulder
rang imperf von **ringen**
Rang (-(e)s, Ränge) m rank; (in Wettbewerb) place; (Theat) circle
rannte imperf von **rennen**
ranzig adj rancid
Rap (-(s), -s) m (Mus) rap; **rappen** vi (Mus) to rap; **Rapper(in)** (-s, -) m(f) (Mus) rapper
rar adj rare, scarce
rasant adj quick, rapid
rasch adj quick
rascheln vi to rustle
rasen vi (sich schnell bewegen) to race; (toben) to rave; **gegen einen Baum ~** to crash into a tree
Rasen (-s, -) m lawn
rasend adj (vor Wut) furious
Rasenmäher (-s, -) m lawnmower
Rasierapparat m razor; (elektrischer) shaver; **Rasiercreme** f shaving cream;

rasieren vt to shave ▷ vr **sich ~** to shave;
Rasierer m shaver; **Rasiergel** nt shaving
gel; **Rasierklinge** f razor blade;
Rasiermesser nt (cutthroat) razor;
Rasierpinsel m shaving brush;
Rasierschaum m shaving foam
Rasse (-, -n) f race; (Tiere) breed
Rassismus m racism; **Rassist(in)** m(f)
racist; **rassistisch** adj racist
Rast (-, -en) f rest, break; **~ machen** to
have a rest (o break); **rasten** vi to rest;
Rastplatz m (Auto) rest area; **Raststätte**
f (Auto) service area; (Gaststätte)
motorway (Brit) (o highway (US))
restaurant
Rasur f shave
Rat (-(e)s, Ratschläge) m (piece of) advice;
sie hat mir einen ~ gegeben she gave me
some advice; **um ~ fragen** to ask for
advice
Rate (-, -n) f instalment; **etw auf ~n
kaufen** to buy sth in instalments (Brit), to
buy sth on the instalment plan (US)
raten (riet, geraten) vt, vi to guess;
(empfehlen) to advise (jdm sb)
Rathaus nt town hall
Ration f ration
ratlos adj at a loss, helpless; **ratsam** adj
advisable
Rätsel (-s, -) nt puzzle; (Worträtsel) riddle;
das ist mir ein ~ it's a mystery to me;
rätselhaft adj mysterious
Ratte (-, -n) f rat
rau adj rough, coarse; (Wetter) harsh
Raub (-(e)s) m robbery; (Beute) loot, booty;
rauben vt to steal; **jdm etw ~** to rob sb of
sth; **Räuber(in)** (-s, -) m(f) robber;
Raubfisch m predatory fish; **Raubkopie**
f pirate copy; **Raubmord** m robbery with
murder; **Raubtier** nt predator;
Raubüberfall m mugging; **Raubvogel** m
bird of prey
Rauch (-(e)s) m smoke; (Abgase) fumes pl;
rauchen vt, vi to smoke; **Raucher(in)**
(-s, -) m(f) smoker; **Raucherabteil** nt
smoking compartment
Räucherlachs m smoked salmon;
räuchern vt to smoke
rauchig adj smoky; **Rauchmelder** m
smoke detector; **Rauchverbot** nt
smoking ban; **hier ist ~** there's no
smoking here
rauf (fam) kontr von **herauf**

rauh adj siehe **rau**; **Rauhreif** m siehe
Raureif
Raum (-(e)s, Räume) m space; (Zimmer,
Platz) room; (Gebiet) area
räumen vt to clear; (Wohnung, Platz) to
vacate; (wegbringen) to shift, to move; (in
Schrank etc) to put away
Raumfähre f space shuttle; **Raumfahrt**
f space travel; **Raumschiff** nt spacecraft,
spaceship; **Raumsonde** f space probe;
Raumstation f space station
Raumtemperatur f room temperature
Räumungsverkauf m clearance sale,
closing-down sale
Raupe (-, -n) f caterpillar
Raureif m hoarfrost
raus (fam) kontr von **heraus, hinaus**; **~!**
(get) out!
Rausch (-(e)s, Räusche) m intoxication;
einen ~ haben/kriegen to be/get drunk
rauschen vi (Wasser) to rush; (Baum) to
rustle; (Radio etc) to hiss; **Rauschgift** nt
drug; **Rauschgiftsüchtige(r)** mf drug
addict
raus|fliegen irr vi (fam) to be kicked out
raus|halten irr vr (fam) **halt du dich da
raus!** (you) just keep out of it
räuspern vr **sich ~** to clear one's throat
raus|schmeißen irr vt (fam) to throw out
Razzia (-, Razzien) f raid
reagieren vi to react (auf +akk to);
Reaktion f reaction
real adj real; **realisieren** vt (merken) to
realize; (verwirklichen) to implement;
realistisch adj realistic; **Realität** (-, -en) f
reality; **Reality-TV** (-s) nt reality TV
Realschule f ≈ secondary school, junior
high (school) (US)
Rebe (-, -n) f vine
rebellieren vi to rebel
Rebhuhn nt partridge
rechnen vt, vi to calculate; **~ mit** to
expect; (bauen auf) to count on ▷ vr **sich
~** to pay off, to turn out to be profitable;
Rechner (-s, -) m calculator; (Computer)
computer; **Rechnung** f calculation(s);
(Comm) bill (Brit), check (US); **die ~, bitte!**
can I have the bill, please?; **das geht auf
meine ~** this is on me
recht adj (richtig, passend) right; **mir soll's
~ sein** it's alright by me; **mir ist es ~** I
don't mind ▷ adv really, quite; (richtig)
right(ly); **ich weiß nicht ~** I don't really

know; **es geschieht ihm ~** it serves him right

Recht (-(e)s, -e) nt right; (Jur) law; **~ haben** to be right; **jdm ~ geben** to agree with sb

Rechte (-n, -n) f right-hand side; (Hand) right hand; (Pol) right (wing); **rechte(r, s)** adj right; **auf der ~n Seite** on the right, on the right-hand side; **Rechte(s)** nt right thing; **etwas/nichts ~s** something/nothing proper

Rechteck (-s, -e) nt rectangle; **rechteckig** adj rectangular

rechtfertigen vt to justify ▷ vr **sich ~** to justify oneself

rechtlich adj legal; **rechtmäßig** adj legal, lawful

rechts adv on the right; **~ abbiegen** to turn right; **~ von** to the right of; **~ oben** at the top right

Rechtsanwalt m, **-anwältin** f lawyer

Rechtschreibung f spelling

Rechtshänder(in) (-s, -) m(f) right-hander; **rechtsherum** adv to the right, clockwise; **rechtsradikal** adj (Pol) extreme right-wing

Rechtsschutzversicherung f legal costs insurance

Rechtsverkehr m driving on the right

rechtswidrig adj illegal

rechtwinklig adj right-angled; **rechtzeitig** adj timely ▷ adv in time

recycelbar adj recyclable; **recyceln** vt to recycle; **Recycling** (-s) nt recycling; **Recyclingpapier** nt recycled paper

Redakteur(in) m(f) editor; **Redaktion** f editing; (Leute) editorial staff; (Büro) editorial office(s)

Rede (-, -n) f speech; (Gespräch) talk; **eine ~ halten** to make a speech; **reden** vi to talk, to speak ▷ vt to say; (Unsinn etc) to talk; **Redewendung** f idiom; **Redner(in)** m(f) speaker

reduzieren vt to reduce

Referat (-s, -e) nt paper; **ein ~ halten** to give a paper (über +akk on)

reflektieren vt to reflect

Reform (-, -en) f reform; **Reformhaus** nt health food shop; **reformieren** vt to reform

Regal (-s, -e) nt shelf; (Möbelstück) shelves pl

Regel (-, -n) f rule; (Med) period; **regelmäßig** adj regular; **regeln** vt to regulate, to control; (Angelegenheit) to settle ▷ vr **sich von selbst ~** to sort itself out; **Regelung** f regulation

Regen (-s, -) m rain; **Regenbogen** m rainbow; **Regenmantel** m raincoat; **Regenrinne** f gutter; **Regenschauer** m shower; **Regenschirm** m umbrella; **Regenwald** m rainforest; **Regenwurm** m earthworm

Regie f direction

regieren vt, vi to govern, to rule; **Regierung** f government; (von Monarch) reign

Region f region; **regional** adj regional

Regisseur(in) m(f) director

registrieren vt to register; (bemerken) to notice

regnen vi impers to rain; **regnerisch** adj rainy

regulär adj regular; **regulieren** vt to regulate, to adjust

Reh (-(e)s, -e) nt deer; (Fleisch) venison

Rehabilitationszentrum nt (Med) rehabilitation centre

Reibe (-, -n) f, **Reibeisen** nt grater; **reiben** (rieb, gerieben) vt to rub; (Gastr) to grate; **reibungslos** adj smooth

reich adj rich

Reich (-(e)s, -e) nt empire; (eines Königs) kingdom

reichen vi to reach; (genügen) to be enough, to be sufficient (jdm for sb) ▷ vt to hold out; (geben) to pass, to hand; (anbieten) to offer

reichhaltig adj ample, rich; **reichlich** adj (Trinkgeld) generous; (Essen) ample; **~ Zeit** plenty of time; **Reichtum** (-s, -tümer) m wealth

reif adj ripe; (Mensch, Urteil) mature

Reif (-(e)s) m (Raureif) hoarfrost ▷ (-(e)s, -e) m (Ring) ring, hoop

reifen vi to mature; (Obst) to ripen

Reifen (-s, -) m ring, hoop; (von Auto) tyre; **Reifendruck** m tyre pressure; **Reifenpanne** f puncture; **Reifenwechsel** m tyre change

Reihe (-, -n) f row; (von Tagen etc, fam: Anzahl) series sing; **der ~ nach** one after the other; **er ist an der ~** it's his turn; **Reihenfolge** f order, sequence; **Reihenhaus** nt terraced house (Brit), row house (US)

Reiher (-s, -) m heron
rein (fam) kontr von **herein, hinein** ▷ adj pure; (sauber) clean
Reinfall m (fam) letdown; **rein|fallen** irr vi (fam) **auf etw** (akk) **~** to fall for sth
reinigen vt to clean; **Reinigung** f cleaning; (Geschäft) (dry) cleaner's; **Reinigungsmittel** nt cleaning agent, cleaner
rein|legen vt jdn **~** to take sb for a ride
Reis (-es, -e) m rice
Reise (-, -n) f journey; (auf Schiff) voyage; **Reiseapotheke** f first-aid kit; **Reisebüro** nt travel agent's; **Reisebus** m coach; **Reiseführer(in)** m(f) (Mensch) courier; (Buch) guide(book); **Reisegepäck** nt luggage (Brit), baggage; **Reisegesellschaft** f (Veranstalter) tour operator; **Reiseleiter(in)** m(f) courier; **reisen** vi to travel; **~ nach** to go to; **Reisende(r)** mf traveller; **Reisepass** m passport; **Reiseroute** f route, itinerary; **Reiserücktrittversicherung** f holiday cancellation insurance; **Reisescheck** m traveller's cheque; **Reisetasche** f holdall (Brit), carryall (US); **Reiseveranstalter** m tour operator; **Reiseverkehr** m holiday traffic; **Reiseversicherung** f travel insurance; **Reiseziel** nt destination
reißen (riss, gerissen) vt, vi to tear; (ziehen) to pull, to drag; (Witz) to crack
Reißnagel m drawing pin (Brit), thumbtack (US); **Reißverschluss** m zip (Brit), zipper (US); **Reißzwecke** f drawing pin (Brit), thumbtack (US)
reiten (ritt, geritten) vt, vi to ride; **Reiter(in)** m(f) rider; **Reithose** f riding breeches pl; **Reitsport** m riding; **Reitstiefel** m riding boot
Reiz (-es, -e) m stimulus; (angenehm) charm; (Verlockung) attraction; **reizen** vt to stimulate; (unangenehm) to annoy; (verlocken) to appeal to, to attract; **reizend** adj charming; **Reizgas** nt irritant gas; **Reizung** f irritation
Reklamation f complaint
Reklame (-, -n) f advertising; (Einzelwerbung) advertisement; (im Fernsehen) commercial
reklamieren vi to complain (wegen about)
Rekord (-(e)s, -e) m record
relativ adj relative ▷ adv relatively

relaxen vi to relax, to chill out
Religion f religion; **religiös** adj religious
Remoulade (-, -n) f tartar sauce
Renaissance f renaissance, revival; (Hist) Renaissance
Rennbahn f racecourse; (Auto) racetrack; **rennen** (rannte, gerannt) vt, vi to run; **Rennen** (-s, -) nt running; (Wettbewerb) race; **Rennfahrer(in)** m(f) racing driver; **Rennrad** nt racing bike; **Rennwagen** m racing car
renommiert adj famous, noted (wegen, für for)
renovieren vt to renovate; **Renovierung** f renovation
rentabel adj profitable
Rente (-, -n) f pension; **Rentenversicherung** f pension scheme
Rentier nt reindeer
rentieren vr **sich ~** to pay, to be profitable
Rentner(in) (-s, -) m(f) pensioner, senior citizen
Reparatur f repair; **Reparaturwerkstatt** f repair shop; (Auto) garage; **reparieren** vt to repair
Reportage f report; **Reporter(in)** (-s, -) m(f) reporter
Reptil (-s, -ien) nt reptile
Republik f republic
Reservat (-s, -e) nt nature reserve; (für Ureinwohner) reservation; **Reserve** (-, -n) f reserve; **Reservekanister** m spare can; **Reserverad** nt (Auto) spare wheel; **Reservespieler(in)** m(f) reserve; **reservieren** vt to reserve; **Reservierung** f reservation
resignieren vi to give up; **resigniert** adj resigned
Respekt (-(e)s) m respect; **respektieren** vt to respect
Rest (-(e)s, -e) m rest, remainder; (Überreste) remains pl; **der ~ ist für Sie** (zur Bedienung) keep the change
Restaurant (-s, -s) nt restaurant
restaurieren vt to restore
Restbetrag m balance; **restlich** adj remaining; **restlos** adj complete
Resultat nt result
retten vt to save, to rescue
Rettich (-s, -e) m radish (large white or red variety)
Rettung f rescue; (Hilfe) help;

(*Rettungsdienst*) ambulance service;
Rettungsboot nt lifeboat;
Rettungshubschrauber m rescue
helicopter; **Rettungsring** m lifebelt, life
preserver (US); **Rettungswagen** m
ambulance

Reue (-) f remorse; (*Bedauern*) regret;
reuen vt **es reut ihn** he regrets it

revanchieren vr **sich ~** (*sich rächen*)
to get one's own back, to get one's
revenge; (*für Hilfe etc*) to return the
favour

Revolution f revolution

Rezept (-(e)s, -e) nt (*Gastr*) recipe; (*Med*)
prescription; **rezeptfrei** adj
over-the-counter, non-prescription

Rezeption f (*im Hotel*) reception

rezeptpflichtig adj available only on
prescription

R-Gespräch nt reverse-charge (*Brit*)
(o collect (US)) call

Rhabarber (-s) m rhubarb

Rhein (-s) m Rhine; **Rheinland-Pfalz** (-)
nt Rhineland-Palatinate

Rheuma (-s) nt rheumatism

Rhythmus m rhythm

richten vt (*lenken*) to direct (*auf +akk* to);
(*Waffe, Kamera*) to point (*auf +akk* at); (*Brief,
Anfrage*) to address (*an +akk* to); (*einstellen*)
to adjust; (*instand setzen*) to repair;
(*zurechtmachen*) to prepare ▷ vr **sich
~ nach** (*Regel etc*) to keep to; (*Mode,
Beispiel*) to follow; (*abhängen von*) to
depend on

Richter(in) (-s, -) m(f) judge

Richtgeschwindigkeit f recommended
speed

richtig adj right, correct; (*echt*) proper;
etw ~ stellen to correct sth ▷ adv (*fam:
sehr*) really

Richtlinie f guideline

Richtung f direction; (*Tendenz*) tendency

rieb imperf von **reiben**

riechen (roch, gerochen) vt, vi to smell;
nach etw ~ to smell of sth; **an etw** (*dat*)
~ to smell sth

rief imperf von **rufen**

Riegel (-s, -) m bolt; (*Gastr*) bar

Riemen (-s, -) m strap; (*Gürtel*) belt

Riese (-n, -n) m giant; **Riesengarnele** f
king prawn; **riesengroß** adj gigantic,
huge; **Riesenrad** nt big wheel; **riesig** adj
enormous, huge

riet imperf von **raten**

Riff (-(e)s, -e) nt reef

Rind (-(e)s, -er) nt cow; (*Bulle*) bull; (*Gastr*)
beef; **~er** pl cattle pl

Rinde (-, -n) f (*Baum*) bark; (*Käse*) rind;
(*Brot*) crust

Rinderbraten m roast beef;
Rinderwahn(sinn) m mad cow disease;
Rindfleisch nt beef

Ring (-(e)s, -e) m ring; (*Straße*) ring road;
Ringbuch nt ring binder

ringen (rang, gerungen) vi to wrestle;
Ringer(in) m(f) wrestler; **Ringfinger** m
ring finger; **Ringkampf** m wrestling
match; **ringsherum** adv round about

Rippe (-, -n) f rib; **Rippenfellentzündung**
f pleurisy

Risiko (-s, -s o Risiken) nt risk; **auf eigenes
~** at one's own risk; **riskant** adj risky;
riskieren vt to risk

riss imperf von **reißen**

Riss (-es, -e) m tear; (*in Mauer, Tasse
etc*) crack; **rissig** adj cracked; (*Haut*)
chapped

ritt imperf von **reiten**

Ritter (-s, -) m knight

Rivale (-n, -n) m, **Rivalin** f rival

Rizinusöl nt castor oil

Robbe (-, -n) f seal

Roboter (-s, -) m robot

robust adj robust

roch imperf von **riechen**

Rock (-(e)s, Röcke) m skirt

Rockband f (*Musikgruppe*) rock band;
Rockmusik f rock (music)

Rodelbahn f toboggan run; **rodeln** vi to
toboggan

Roggen (-s, -) m rye; **Roggenbrot** nt rye
bread

roh adj raw; (*Mensch*) coarse, crude;
Rohkost f raw vegetables and fruit pl

Rohr (-(e)s, -e) nt pipe; (*Bot*) cane; (*Schilf*)
reed; **Röhre** (-, -n) f tube; (*Leitung*) pipe;
(*Elek*) valve; (*Backröhre*) oven; **Rohrzucker**
m cane sugar

Rohstoff m raw material

Rokoko (-s) nt rococo

Rolle (-, -n) f (*etw Zusammengerolltes*) roll;
(*Theat*) role

rollen vt, vi to roll

Roller (-s, -) m scooter

Rollerblades® pl Rollerblades® pl;
Rollerskates pl roller skates pl

Rollkragenpullover m polo-neck (Brit) (o turtleneck (US)) sweater; **Rollladen** m, **Rollo** (-s, -s) m (roller) shutters pl; **Rollschuh** m roller skate; **Rollstuhl** m wheelchair; **rollstuhlgerecht** adj suitable for wheelchairs; **Rolltreppe** f escalator

Roman (-s, -e) m novel

Romantik f romance; **romantisch** adj romantic

römisch-katholisch adj Roman Catholic

röntgen vt to X-ray; **Röntgenaufnahme** f, **Röntgenbild** nt X-ray; **Röntgenstrahlen** pl X-rays pl

rosa adj inv pink

Rose (-, -n) f rose

Rosenkohl m (Brussels) sprouts pl

Rosé(wein) m rosé (wine)

rosig adj rosy

Rosine f raisin

Rosmarin (-s) m rosemary

Rosskastanie f horse chestnut

Rost (-(e)s, -e) m rust; (zum Braten) grill, gridiron; **Rostbratwurst** f grilled sausage; **rosten** vi to rust; **rösten** vt to roast, to grill; (Brot) to toast; **rostfrei** adj rustproof; (Stahl) stainless; **rostig** adj rusty; **Rostschutz** m rustproofing

rot adj red; ~ **werden** to blush; ~**e Karte** red card; ~**e Be(e)te** beetroot; **bei Rot über die Ampel fahren** to jump the lights; **das Rote Kreuz** the Red Cross

Röteln pl German measles sing

röten vt to redden ▷ vr **sich** ~ to redden

rothaarig adj red-haired

rotieren vi to rotate; **am Rotieren sein** (fam) to be rushing around like a mad thing

Rotkehlchen nt robin; **Rotkohl** m, **Rotkraut** nt red cabbage; **Rotlichtviertel** nt red-light district; **Rotwein** m red wine

Rouge (-s, -s) nt rouge

Route (-, -n) f route

Routine f experience; (Trott) routine

Rubbellos nt scratchcard; **rubbeln** vt to rub

Rübe (-, -n) f turnip; **Gelbe** ~ carrot; **Rote** ~ beetroot

rüber (fam) kontr von **herüber, hinüber**

Rubin (-s, -e) m ruby

rücken vt, vi to move; **könntest du ein bisschen** ~? could you move over a bit?

Rücken (-s, -) m back; **Rückenlehne** f

back(rest); **Rückenmark** nt spinal cord; **Rückenschmerzen** pl backache sing; **Rückenschwimmen** (-s) nt backstroke; **Rückenwind** m tailwind

Rückerstattung f refund; **Rückfahrkarte** f return ticket (Brit), round-trip ticket (US); **Rückfahrt** f return journey; **Rückfall** m relapse; **Rückflug** m return flight; **Rückgabe** f return; **rückgängig** adj etw ~ **machen** to cancel sth; **Rückgrat** (-(e)s, -e) nt spine, backbone; **Rückkehr** (-, -en) f return; **Rücklicht** nt rear light; **Rückreise** f return journey; **auf der** ~ on the way back

Rucksack m rucksack, backpack; **Rucksacktourist(in)** m(f) backpacker

Rückschritt m step back; **Rückseite** f back; (hinterer Teil) rear; **siehe** ~ see overleaf; **Rücksicht** f consideration; ~ **nehmen auf** (+akk) to show consideration for; **rücksichtslos** adj inconsiderate; (Fahren) reckless; (unbarmherzig) ruthless; **rücksichtsvoll** adj considerate; **Rücksitz** m back seat; **Rückspiegel** m (Auto) rear-view mirror; **Rückstand** m sie sind zwei Tore im ~ they're two goals down; **im** ~ **sein mit** (Arbeit, Miete) to be behind with; **Rücktaste** f backspace key; **Rückvergütung** f refund; **rückwärts** adv backwards, back; **Rückwärtsgang** m (Auto) reverse (gear); **Rückweg** m return journey, way back; **Rückzahlung** f repayment; **Rückzieher** m einen ~ **machen** to back out

Ruder (-s, -) nt oar; (Steuer) rudder; **Ruderboot** nt rowing boat (Brit), rowboat (US); **rudern** vt, vi to row

Ruf (-(e)s, -e) m call, cry; (Ansehen) reputation; **rufen** (rief, gerufen) vt, vi to call; (schreien) to cry; **Rufnummer** f telephone number

Ruhe (-) f rest; (Ungestörtheit) peace, quiet; (Gelassenheit, Stille) calm; (Schweigen) silence; **lass mich in** ~! leave me alone; **ruhen** vi to rest; **Ruhestand** m retirement; **im** ~ **sein** to be retired; **Ruhestörung** f disturbance of the peace; **Ruhetag** m closing day; **montags** ~ **haben** to be closed on Mondays

ruhig adj quiet; (bewegungslos) still; (Hand) steady; (gelassen) calm

Ruhm (-(e)s) *m* fame, glory

Rührei *nt* scrambled egg(s); **rühren** *vt* to move; (*umrühren*) to stir ▷ *vr* **sich ~** to move; (*sich bemerkbar machen*) to say something; **rührend** *adj* touching, moving; **Rührung** *f* emotion

Ruine (-, -n) *f* ruin; **ruinieren** *vt* to ruin

rülpsen *vi* to burp, to belch

rum (*fam*) *kontr von* **herum**

Rum (-s, -s) *m* rum

Rumänien (-s) *nt* Romania

Rummel (-s) *m* (*Trubel*) hustle and bustle; (*Jahrmarkt*) fair; (*Medienrummel*) hype; **Rummelplatz** *m* fairground

rumoren *vi* **es rumort in meinem Bauch/Kopf** my stomach is rumbling/my head is spinning

Rumpf (-(e)s, Rümpfe) *m* (*Anat*) trunk; (*Aviat*) fuselage; (*Naut*) hull

rümpfen *vt* **die Nase ~** to turn one's nose up (*über at*)

Rumpsteak *nt* rump steak

rund *adj* round ▷ *adv* (*etwa*) around; **~ um etw** (a)round sth; **Runde** (-, -n) *f* round; (*in Rennen*) lap; **Rundfahrt** *f* tour (*durch of*); **Rundfunk** *m* broadcasting; (*Rundfunkanstalt*) broadcasting service; **im ~** on the radio; **Rundgang** *m* tour (*durch of*); (*von Wächter*) round

rundlich *adj* plump; **Rundreise** *f* tour (*durch of*)

runter (*fam*) *kontr von* **herunter, hinunter**; **runterscrollen** *vt* (*Inform*) to scroll down

runzeln *vt* **die Stirn ~** to frown; **runzelig** *adj* wrinkled

ruppig *adj* gruff

Rüsche (-, -n) *f* frill

Ruß (-es) *m* soot

Russe (-n, -n) *m* Russian

Rüssel (-s, -) *m* (*Elefant*) trunk; (*Schwein*) snout

Russin *f* Russian; **russisch** *adj* Russian; **Russisch** *nt* Russian; **Russland** *nt* Russia

Rüstung *f* (*mit Waffen*) arming; (*Ritterrüstung*) armour; (*Waffen*) armaments *pl*

Rutsch (-(e)s, -e) *m* **guten ~ (ins neue Jahr)!** Happy New Year; **Rutschbahn** *f*, **Rutsche** *f* slide; **rutschen** *vi* to slide; (*ausrutschen*) to slip; **rutschig** *adj* slippery

rütteln *vt, vi* to shake

S

S *abk* = **Süd** S

s. *abk* = **siehe** see; **S.** *abk* = **Seite** p.

Saal (-(e)s, Säle) *m* hall; (für Sitzungen) room

Saarland *nt* Saarland

sabotieren *vt* to sabotage

Sache (-, -n) *f* thing; (Angelegenheit) affair, business; (Frage) matter; **bei der ~ bleiben** to keep to the point; **sachkundig** *adj* competent; **Sachlage** *f* situation; **sachlich** *adj* (objektiv) objective; (nüchtern) matter-of-fact; (inhaltlich) factual; **sächlich** *adj* (Ling) neuter; **Sachschaden** *m* material damage

Sachsen (-s) *nt* Saxony; **Sachsen-Anhalt** (-s) *nt* Saxony-Anhalt

sacht(e) *adv* softly, gently

Sachverständige(r) *mf* expert

Sack (-(e)s, Säcke) *m* sack; (pej: Mensch) bastard, bugger; **Sackgasse** *f* dead end, cul-de-sac

Safe (-s, -s) *m* safe

Safer Sex *m* safe sex

Safran (-s, -e) *m* saffron

Saft (-(e)s, Säfte) *m* juice; **saftig** *adj* juicy

Sage (-, -n) *f* legend

Säge (-, -n) *f* saw; **Sägemehl** *nt* sawdust

sagen *vt, vi* to say (jdm to sb), to tell (jdm

sb); **wie sagt man ... auf Englisch?** what's ... in English?; **ich will dir mal was ~** let me tell you something

sägen *vt, vi* to saw

sagenhaft *adj* legendary; (fam: großartig) fantastic

sah *imperf von* **sehen**

Sahne (-) *f* cream; **Sahnetorte** *f* gateau

Saison (-, -s) *f* season; **außerhalb der ~** out of season

Saite (-, -n) *f* string

Sakko (-s, -s) *nt* jacket

Salami (-, -s) *f* salami

Salat (-(e)s, -e) *m* salad; (Kopfsalat) lettuce; **Salatbar** *f* salad bar; **Salatschüssel** *f* salad bowl; **Salatsoße** *f* salad dressing

Salbe (-, -n) *f* ointment

Salbei (-s) *m* sage

Salmonellenvergiftung *f* salmonella (poisoning)

salopp *adj* (Kleidung) casual; (Sprache) slangy

Salsamusik *f* salsa (music)

Salto (-s, -s) *m* somersault

Salz (-es, -e) *nt* salt; **salzarm** *adj* low-salt; **salzen** (salzte, gesalzen) *vt* to salt; **Salzgurke** *f* pickled gherkin; **Salzhering** *m* pickled herring; **salzig** *adj* salty; **Salzkartoffeln** *pl* boiled potatoes *pl*; **Salzstange** *f* pretzel stick; **Salzstreuer** *m* salt cellar (Brit) (o shaker (US)); **Salzwasser** *nt* salt water

Samba (-, -s) *f* samba

Samen (-s, -) *m* seed; (Sperma) sperm

sammeln *vt* to collect; **Sammler(in)** *m(f)* collector; **Sammlung** *f* collection; (Ansammlung, Konzentration) concentration

Samstag *m* Saturday; siehe auch **Mittwoch**; **samstags** *adv* on Saturdays; siehe auch **mittwochs**

samt *prep +dat* (along) with, together with

Samt (-(e)s, -e) *m* velvet

sämtliche(r, s) *adj* all (the)

Sanatorium (-s, Sanatorien) *nt* sanatorium (Brit), sanitarium (US)

Sand (-(e)s, -e) *m* sand

Sandale (-, -n) *f* sandal

sandig *adj* sandy; **Sandkasten** *m* sandpit (Brit), sandbox (US); **Sandpapier** *nt* sandpaper; **Sandstrand** *m* sandy beach

sandte *imperf von* **senden**

sanft *adj* soft, gentle

sang *imperf von* **singen**; **Sänger(in)** (-s, -) *m(f)* singer

Sangria (-, -s) *f* sangria

sanieren *vt* to redevelop; *(Gebäude)* to renovate; *(Betrieb)* to restore to profitability

sanitär *adj* sanitary; **~e Anlagen** *pl* sanitation

Sanitäter(in) (-s, -) *m(f)* ambulance man/woman, paramedic

sank *imperf von* **sinken**

Sankt Gallen (-s) *nt* St Gallen

Saphir (-s, -e) *m* sapphire

Sardelle *f* anchovy

Sardine *f* sardine

Sarg (-(e)s, Särge) *m* coffin

saß *imperf von* **sitzen**

Satellit (-en, -en) *m* satellite; **Satellitenfernsehen** *nt* satellite TV; **Satellitenschüssel** *f (fam)* satellite dish

Satire (-, -n) *f* satire *(auf +akk* on)

satt *adj* full; *(Farbe)* rich, deep; **~ sein** *(gesättigt)* to be full; **~ machen** to be filling; **jdn/etw ~ sein** *(o haben)* to be fed up with sb/sth

Sattel (-s, Sättel) *m* saddle

Saturn (-s) *m* Saturn

Satz (-es, Sätze) *m (Ling)* sentence; *(Mus)* movement; *(Tennis)* set; *(Kaffee)* grounds *pl*; *(Comm)* rate; *(Sprung)* jump; *(Comm)* rate

Satzzeichen *nt* punctuation mark

Sau (-, Säue) *f* sow; *(pej: Mensch)* dirty bugger

sauber *adj* clean; *(ironisch)* fine; **~ machen** to clean; **Sauberkeit** *f* cleanness; *(von Person)* cleanliness; **säubern** *vt* to clean

saublöd *adj (fam)* really stupid, dumb

Sauce (-, -n) *f* sauce; *(zu Braten)* gravy

Saudi-Arabien (-s) *nt* Saudi Arabia

sauer *adj* sour; *(Chem)* acid; *(fam: verärgert)* cross; **saurer Regen** acid rain; **Sauerkirsche** *f* sour cherry; **Sauerkraut** *nt* sauerkraut; **säuerlich** *adj* slightly sour; **Sauermilch** *f* sour milk; **Sauerrahm** *m* sour cream; **Sauerstoff** *m* oxygen

saufen *(soff, gesoffen) vt* to drink; *(fam: Mensch)* to knock back ▷ *vi* to drink; *(fam: Mensch)* to booze

saugen *(sog o saugte, gesogen o gesaugt) vt, vi* to suck; *(mit Staubsauger)* to vacuum, to hoover *(Brit)*; **Sauger** (-s, -) *m (auf Flasche)*

teat; **Säugetier** *nt* mammal; **Säugling** *m* infant, baby

Säule (-, -n) *f* column, pillar

Saum (-s, Säume) *m* hem; *(Naht)* seam

Sauna (-, -s) *f* sauna

Säure (-, -n) *f* acid

sausen *vi (Ohren)* to buzz; *(Wind)* to howl; *(Mensch)* to rush

Saustall *m* pigsty; **Sauwetter** *nt* **was für ein ~** *(fam)* what lousy weather

Saxophon (-s, -e) *nt* saxophone

S-Bahn *f* suburban railway; **S-Bahn-Haltestelle** *f*, **S-Bahnhof** *m* suburban (train) station

scannen *vt* to scan; **Scanner** (-s, -) *m* scanner

schäbig *adj* shabby

Schach (-(e)s, -s) *nt* chess; *(Stellung)* check; **Schachbrett** *nt* chessboard; **Schachfigur** *f* chess piece; **schachmatt** *adj* checkmate

Schacht (-(e)s, Schächte) *m* shaft

Schachtel (-, -n) *f* box

schade *interj* what a pity

Schädel (-s, -) *m* skull; **Schädelbruch** *m* fractured skull

schaden *vi* to damage, to harm *(jdm* sb); **das schadet nichts** it won't do any harm; **Schaden** (-s, Schäden) *m* damage; *(Verletzung)* injury; *(Nachteil)* disadvantage; **einen ~ verursachen** to cause damage; **Schadenersatz** *m* compensation, damages *pl*; **schadhaft** *adj* faulty; *(beschädigt)* damaged; **schädigen** *vt* to damage; *(jdn)* to do harm to, to harm; **schädlich** *adj* harmful *(für* to); **Schadstoff** *m* harmful substance; **schadstoffarm** *adj* low-emission

Schaf (-(e)s, -e) *nt* sheep; **Schafbock** *m* ram; **Schäfer** (-s, -) *m* shepherd; **Schäferhund** *m* Alsatian *(Brit)*, German shepherd; **Schäferin** *f* shepherdess

schaffen *(schuf, geschaffen) vt* to create; *(Platz)* to make ▷ *vt (erreichen)* to manage, to do; *(erledigen)* to finish; *(Prüfung)* to pass; *(transportieren)* to take; **jdm zu ~ machen** to cause sb trouble

Schaffner(in) (-s, -) *m(f) (in Bus)* conductor/conductress; *(Eisenb)* guard

Schafskäse *m* sheep's (milk) cheese

schal *adj (Getränk)* flat

Schal (-s, -e *o* -s) *m* scarf

Schälchen nt (small) bowl

Schale (-, -n) f skin; (abgeschält) peel; (Nuss, Muschel, Ei) shell; (Geschirr) bowl, dish

schälen vt to peel; (Tomate, Mandel) to skin; (Erbsen, Eier, Nüsse) to shell; (Getreide) to husk ▷ vr **sich ~** to peel

Schall (-(e)s, -e) m sound; **Schalldämpfer** (-s, -) m (Auto) silencer (Brit), muffler (US); **Schallplatte** f record

Schalotte (-, -n) f shallot

schalten vt to switch ▷ vi (Auto) to change gear; (fam: begreifen) to catch on; **Schalter** (-s, -) m (auf Post, Bank) counter; (an Gerät) switch; **Schalterhalle** f main hall; **Schalteröffnungszeiten** pl business hours pl

Schaltfläche f (Inform) button; **Schalthebel** m gear lever (Brit) (o shift (US)); **Schaltjahr** nt leap year; **Schaltknüppel** m gear lever (Brit) (o shift (US)); **Schaltung** f gear change (Brit), gearshift (US)

Scham (-) f shame; (Schamgefühl) modesty; **schämen** vr **sich ~** to be ashamed

Schande (-) f disgrace

Schanze (-, -n) f ski jump

Schar (-, -en) f (von Vögeln) flock; (Menge) crowd; **in ~en** in droves

scharf adj (Messer, Kritik) sharp; (Essen) hot; **auf etw** (akk) **~ sein** (fam) to be keen on sth

Schärfe (-, -n) f sharpness; (Strenge) rigour; (Foto) focus

Scharlach (-s) m (Med) scarlet fever

Scharnier (-s, -e) nt hinge

Schaschlik (-s, -s) m o nt (shish) kebab

Schatten (-s, -) m shadow; **30 Grad im ~** 30 degrees in the shade; **schattig** adj shady

Schatz (-es, Schätze) m treasure; (Mensch) love

schätzen vt (abschätzen) to estimate; (Gegenstand) to value; (würdigen) to value, to esteem; (vermuten) to reckon; **Schätzung** f estimate; (das Schätzen) estimation; (von Wertgegenstand) valuation; **schätzungsweise** adv roughly, approximately

Schau (-, -en) f show; (Ausstellung) exhibition

schauen vi to look; **ich schau mal, ob ...** I'll go and have a look whether ...; **schau, dass ...** see (to it) that ...

Schauer (-s, -) m (Regen) shower; (Schreck) shudder

Schaufel (-, -n) f shovel; **~ und Besen** dustpan and brush; **schaufeln** vt to shovel; **Schnee ~** to clear the snow away

Schaufenster nt shop window; **Schaufensterbummel** m window-shopping expedition

Schaukel (-, -n) f swing; **schaukeln** vi to rock; (mit Schaukel) to swing; **Schaukelstuhl** m rocking chair

Schaulustige(r) mf gawper (Brit), rubbernecker (US)

Schaum (-(e)s, Schäume) m foam; (Seifenschaum) lather; (Bierschaum) froth; **Schaumbad** nt bubble bath; **schäumen** vi to foam; **Schaumfestiger** (-s, -) m styling mousse; **Schaumgummi** m foam (rubber); **Schaumwein** m sparkling wine

Schauplatz m scene; **Schauspiel** nt spectacle; (Theat) play; **Schauspieler(in)** m(f) actor/actress

Scheck (-s, -s) m cheque; **Scheckheft** nt chequebook; **Scheckkarte** f cheque card

Scheibe (-, -n) f disc; (von Brot, Käse etc) slice; (Glasscheibe) pane; **Scheibenbremse** f (Auto) disc brake; **Scheibenwaschanlage** f (Auto) windscreen (Brit) (o windshield (US)) washer unit; **Scheibenwischer** (-s, -) m (Auto) windscreen (Brit) (o windshield (US)) wiper

Scheich (-s, -s) m sheik(h)

Scheide (-, -n) f (Anat) vagina

scheiden (schied, geschieden) vt (trennen) to separate; (Ehe) to dissolve; **sich ~ lassen** to get a divorce; **sie hat sich von ihm ~ lassen** she divorced him; **Scheidung** f divorce

Schein (-(e)s, -e) m light; (Anschein) appearance; (Geld) (bank)note; **scheinbar** adj apparent; **scheinen** (schien, geschienen) vi (Sonne) to shine; (den Anschein haben) to seem; **Scheinwerfer** (-s, -) m floodlight; (Theat) spotlight; (Auto) headlight

Scheiß- in zW (vulg) damned, bloody (Brit); **Scheiße** (-) f (vulg) shit, crap; **scheißegal** adj (vulg) **das ist mir ~** I don't give a damn (o toss); **scheißen** (schiss, geschissen) vi (vulg) to shit

Scheitel (-s, -) m parting (Brit), part (US)
scheitern vi to fail (an +dat because of)
Schellfisch m haddock
Schema (-s, -s o Schemata) nt scheme,
plan; (Darstellung) diagram
Schenkel (-s, -) m thigh
schenken vt to give; **er hat es mir
geschenkt** he gave it to me (as a present);
sich (dat) **etw ~** (fam: weglassen) to skip
sth
Scherbe (-, -n) f broken piece, fragment
Schere (-, -n) f scissors pl; (groß) shears pl;
eine ~ a pair of scissors/shears
Scherz (-es, -e) m joke
scheu adj shy
scheuen vr **sich ~ vor** (+dat) to be afraid
of, to shrink from ▷ vt to shun ▷ vi (Pferd)
to shy
scheuern vt to scrub; **jdm eine ~** (fam) to
slap sb in the face
Scheune (-, -n) f barn
scheußlich adj dreadful
Schi (-s, -er) m siehe **Ski**
Schicht (-, -en) f layer; (in Gesellschaft)
class; (in Fabrik etc) shift
schick adj stylish, chic
schicken vt to send ▷ vr **sich ~** (sich
beeilen) to hurry up
Schickimicki (-(s), -s) m (fam) trendy
Schicksal (-s, -e) nt fate
Schiebedach nt (Auto) sunroof; **schieben**
(schob, geschoben) vt, vi to push; **die Schuld
auf jdn ~** to put the blame on sb;
Schiebetür f sliding door
schied imperf von **scheiden**
Schiedsrichter(in) m(f) referee; (Tennis)
umpire; (Schlichter) arbitrator
schief adj crooked; (Blick) funny ▷ adv
crooked(ly); **~ gehen** (fam) to go wrong
schielen vi to squint
schien imperf von **scheinen**
Schienbein nt shin
Schiene (-, -n) f rail; (Med) splint
schier adj pure; (fig) sheer ▷ adv nearly,
almost
schießen (schoss, geschossen) vt to shoot;
(Ball) to kick; (Tor) to score; (Foto) to take
▷ vi to shoot (auf +akk at)
Schiff (-(e)s, -e) nt ship; (in Kirche) nave;
Schifffahrt f shipping; **Schiffsreise** f
voyage
schikanieren vt to harass; (Schule) to
bully

Schild (-(e)s, -e) m (Schutz) shield ▷ (-(e)s,
-er) nt sign; **was steht auf dem ~?** what
does the sign say?
Schilddrüse f thyroid gland
schildern vt to describe
Schildkröte f tortoise; (Wasserschildkröte)
turtle
Schimmel (-s, -) m mould; (Pferd) white
horse; **schimmeln** vi to go mouldy
schimpfen vt to tell off ▷ vi (sich
beklagen) to complain; **mit jdm ~** to tell sb
off; **Schimpfwort** nt swearword
Schinken (-s, -) m ham
Schirm (-(e)s, -e) m (Regenschirm)
umbrella; (Sonnenschirm) parasol,
sunshade
schiss imperf von **scheißen**
Schlacht (-, -en) f battle; **schlachten** vt to
slaughter; **Schlachter(in)** (-s, -) m(f)
butcher; **Schlachtfeld** nt battlefield
Schlaf (-(e)s) m sleep; **Schlafanzug** m
pyjamas pl; **Schlafcouch** f bed settee
Schläfe (-, -n) f temple
schlafen (schlief, geschlafen) vi to sleep;
schlaf gut! sleep well; **hast du gut
geschlafen?** did you sleep all right?; **er
schläft noch** he's still asleep; **~ gehen** to
go to bed
schlaff adj slack; (kraftlos) limp; (erschöpft)
exhausted
Schlafgelegenheit f place to sleep;
Schlaflosigkeit f sleeplessness;
Schlafmittel nt sleeping pill; **schläfrig**
adj sleepy
Schlafsaal m dormitory; **Schlafsack** m
sleeping bag; **Schlaftablette** f sleeping
pill; **er ist eine richtige ~** (fam: langweilig)
he's such a bore; **Schlafwagen** m
sleeping car, sleeper; **Schlafzimmer** nt
bedroom
Schlag (-(e)s, Schläge) m blow; (Puls) beat;
(Elek) shock; (fam: Portion) helping; (Art)
kind, type; **Schlagader** f artery;
Schlaganfall m (Med) stroke; **schlagartig**
adj sudden; **Schlagbohrmaschine** f
hammer drill
schlagen (schlug, geschlagen) vt to hit;
(besiegen) to beat; (Sahne) to whip; **jdn zu
Boden ~** to knock sb down ▷ vi (Herz) to
beat; (Uhr) to strike; **mit dem Kopf gegen
etw ~** to bang one's head against sth ▷ vr
sich ~ to fight
Schläger (-s, -) m (Sport) bat; (Tennis)

racket; (Golf) (golf) club; (Hockey) hockey stick; (Mensch) brawler; **Schlägerei** f fight, brawl

schlagfertig adj quick-witted; **Schlagloch** nt pothole; **Schlagsahne** f whipping cream; (geschlagen) whipped cream; **Schlagzeile** f headline; **Schlagzeug** nt drums pl; (in Orchester) percussion

Schlamm (-(e)s, -e) m mud

schlampig adj (fam) sloppy

schlang imperf von **schlingen**

Schlange (-, -n) f snake; (von Menschen) queue (Brit), line (US); **~ stehen** to queue (Brit), to stand in line (US); **Schlangenlinie** f wavy line; **in ~n fahren** to swerve about

schlank adj slim

schlapp adj limp; (locker) slack

Schlappe (-, -n) f (fam) setback

schlau adj clever, smart; (raffiniert) crafty, cunning

Schlauch (-(e)s, Schläuche) m hose; (in Reifen) inner tube; **Schlauchboot** nt rubber dinghy

schlecht adj bad; **mir ist ~** I feel sick; **jdn ~ machen** to run sb down; **die Milch ist ~** the milk has gone off ▷ adv badly; **es geht ihm ~** he's having a hard time; (gesundheitlich) he's not feeling well; (finanziell) he's pretty hard up

schleichen (schlich, geschlichen) vi to creep

Schleier (-s, -) m veil

Schleife (-, -n) f (Inform, Aviat, Elek) loop; (Band) bow

schleifen vt (ziehen, schleppen) to drag ▷ (schliff, geschliffen) vt (schärfen) to grind; (Edelstein) to cut

Schleim (-(e)s, -e) m slime; (Med) mucus; **Schleimer** (-s, -) m (fam) creep; **Schleimhaut** f mucous membrane

schlendern vi to stroll

schleppen vt to drag; (Auto, Schiff) to tow; (tragen) to lug; **Schlepplift** m ski tow

Schleswig-Holstein (-s) nt Schleswig-Holstein

Schleuder (-, -n) f catapult; (für Wäsche) spin-dryer; **schleudern** vt to hurl; (Wäsche) to spin-dry ▷ vi (Auto) to skid; **Schleudersitz** m ejector seat

schleunigst adv straight away

schlich imperf von **schleichen**

schlicht adj simple, plain

schlichten vt (Streit) to settle

schlief imperf von **schlafen**

schließen (schloss, geschlossen) vt, vi to close, to shut; (beenden) to close; (Freundschaft, Ehe) to enter into; (folgern) to infer (aus from) ▷ vr **sich ~** to close, to shut; **Schließfach** nt locker

schließlich adv finally; (schließlich doch) after all

schliff imperf von **schleifen**

schlimm adj bad; **schlimmer** adj worse; **schlimmste(r, s)** adj worst; **schlimmstenfalls** adv at (the) worst

Schlinge (-, -n) f loop; (Med) sling

Schlips (-es, -e) m tie

Schlitten (-s, -) m sledge, toboggan; (mit Pferden) sleigh; **Schlittenfahren** (-s) nt tobogganing

Schlittschuh m ice skate; **~ laufen** to ice-skate

Schlitz (-es, -e) m slit; (für Münze) slot; (an Hose) flies pl

schloss imperf von **schließen**

Schloss (-es, Schlösser) nt lock; (Burg) castle

Schlosser(in) m(f) mechanic

Schlucht (-, -en) f gorge, ravine

schluchzen vi to sob

Schluck (-(e)s, -e) m swallow; **Schluckauf** (-s) m hiccups pl; **schlucken** vt, vi to swallow

schludern vi (fam) to do sloppy work

schlug imperf von **schlagen**

Schlüpfer (-s, -) m panties pl

schlüpfrig adj slippery; (fig) lewd; (Witz) risqué

schlürfen vt, vi to slurp

Schluss (-es, Schlüsse) m end; (Schlussfolgerung) conclusion; **am ~** at the end; **mit jdm ~ machen** to finish (o split up) with sb

Schlüssel (-s, -) m (a. fig) key; **Schlüsselbein** nt collarbone; **Schlüsselblume** f cowslip; **Schlüsselbund** m bunch of keys; **Schlüsseldienst** m key-cutting service; **Schlüsselloch** nt keyhole

Schlussfolgerung f conclusion; **Schlusslicht** nt tail-light; (fig) tail-ender; **Schlusspfiff** m final whistle; **Schlussverkauf** m clearance sale

schmächtig adj frail

schmal adj narrow; (Mensch, Buch etc) slim; (karg) meagre

Schmalz (-es, -e) nt dripping, lard; (fig: Sentimentalitäten) schmaltz

schmatzen vi to eat noisily

schmecken vt, vi to taste (nach of); **es schmeckt ihm** he likes it; **lass es dir ~!** bon appétit

Schmeichelei f flattery; **schmeichelhaft** adj flattering; **schmeicheln** vi **jdm ~** to flatter sb

schmeißen (schmiss, geschmissen) vt (fam) to chuck, to throw

schmelzen (schmolz, geschmolzen) vt, vi to melt; (Metall, Erz) to smelt; **Schmelzkäse** m cheese spread

Schmerz (-es, -en) m pain; (Trauer) grief; **~en haben** to be in pain; **~en im Rücken haben** to have a pain in one's back; **schmerzen** vt, vi to hurt; **Schmerzensgeld** nt compensation; **schmerzhaft, schmerzlich** adj painful; **schmerzlos** adj painless; **Schmerzmittel** nt painkiller; **schmerzstillend** adj painkilling; **Schmerztablette** f painkiller

Schmetterling m butterfly

Schmied(in) (-(e)s, -e) m(f) blacksmith; **schmieden** vt to forge; (Pläne) to make

schmieren vt to smear; (ölen) to lubricate, to grease; (bestechen) to bribe ▷ vt, vi (unsauber schreiben) to scrawl; **Schmiergeld** nt (fam) bribe; **schmierig** adj greasy; **Schmiermittel** nt lubricant; **Schmierpapier** nt scrap paper; **Schmierseife** f soft soap

Schminke (-, -n) f make-up; **schminken** vr **sich ~** to put one's make-up on

schmiss imperf von **schmeißen**

schmollen vi to sulk; **schmollend** adj sulky

schmolz imperf von **schmelzen**

Schmuck (-(e)s, -e) m jewellery (Brit), jewelry (US); (Verzierung) decoration; **schmücken** vt to decorate

schmuggeln vt, vi to smuggle

schmunzeln vi to smile

schmusen vi to (kiss and) cuddle

Schmutz (-es) m dirt, filth; **schmutzig** adj dirty

Schnabel (-s, Schnäbel) m beak, bill; (Ausguss) spout

Schnake (-, -n) f mosquito

Schnalle (-, -n) f buckle

Schnäppchen nt (fam) bargain; **schnappen** vt (fangen) to catch ▷ vi **nach**

Luft ~ to gasp for breath; **Schnappschuss** m (Foto) snap(shot)

Schnaps (-es, Schnäpse) m schnapps

schnarchen vi to snore

schnaufen vi to puff, to pant

Schnauzbart m moustache; **Schnauze** (-, -n) f snout, muzzle; (Ausguss) spout; (fam: Mund) trap; **die ~ voll haben** to have had enough

schnäuzen vr **sich ~** to blow one's nose

Schnecke (-, -n) f snail; **Schneckenhaus** nt snail's shell

Schnee (-s) m snow; **Schneeball** m snowball; **Schneebob** m snowmobile; **Schneebrille** f snow goggles pl; **Schneeflocke** f snowflake; **Schneegestöber** (-s, -) nt snow flurry; **Schneeglöckchen** nt snowdrop; **Schneegrenze** f snowline; **Schneekanone** f snow thrower; **Schneekette** f (Auto) snow chain; **Schneemann** m snowman; **Schneematsch** m slush; **Schneepflug** m snowplough; **Schneeregen** m sleet; **Schneeschmelze** f thaw; **Schneesturm** m snowstorm, blizzard; **Schneetreiben** nt light blizzards pl; **Schneewehe** f snowdrift

Schneide (-, -n) f edge; (Klinge) blade; **schneiden** (schnitt, geschnitten) vt to cut; **sich** (dat) **die Haare ~ lassen** to have one's hair cut ▷ vr **sich ~** to cut oneself; **Schneider(in)** (-s, -) m(f) tailor; (für Damenmode) dressmaker; **Schneiderin** f dressmaker; **Schneidezahn** m incisor

schneien vi impers to snow

schnell adj quick, fast ▷ adv quickly, fast; **mach ~!** hurry up; **Schnelldienst** m express service; **Schnellhefter** m loose-leaf binder; **Schnellimbiss** m snack bar; **Schnellkochtopf** m pressure cooker; **Schnellreinigung** f express dry cleaning; (Geschäft) express (dry) cleaner's; **Schnellstraße** f expressway; **Schnellzug** m fast train

schneuzen vr siehe **schnäuzen**

schnitt imperf von **schneiden**

Schnitt (-(e)s, -e) m cut; (Schnittpunkt) intersection; (Querschnitt) (cross) section; (Durchschnitt) average; (eines Kleides) style; **Schnittblume** f cut flower; **Schnitte**

(-, -n) f slice; (belegt) sandwich;
Schnittkäse m cheese slices pl;
Schnittlauch m chives pl; **Schnittmuster**
nt pattern; **Schnittstelle** f (Inform, fig)
interface; **Schnittwunde** f cut, gash
Schnitzel (-s, -) nt (Papier) scrap; (Gastr)
escalope
schnitzen vt to carve
Schnorchel (-s, -) m snorkel;
schnorcheln vi to go snorkelling, to
snorkel; **Schnorcheln** (-s) nt snorkelling
schnüffeln vi to sniff
Schnuller (-s, -) m dummy (Brit), pacifier
(US)
Schnulze (-, -n) f (Film, Roman) weepie
Schnupfen (-s, -) m cold
schnuppern vi to sniff
Schnur (-, Schnüre) f string, cord; (Elek)
lead; **schnurlos** adj (Telefon) cordless
Schnurrbart m moustache
schnurren vi to purr
Schnürschuh m lace-up (shoe);
Schnürsenkel (-s, -) m shoelace
schob imperf von **schieben**
Schock (-(e)s, -e) m shock; **unter ~ stehen**
to be in a state of shock; **schockieren** vt
to shock
Schokolade f chocolate; **Schokoriegel**
m chocolate bar
Scholle (-, -n) f (Fisch) plaice; (Eis) ice floe

🔵 SCHLÜSSELWORT

schon adv 1 (bereits) already; **er ist schon
da** he's there already, he's already there;
ist er schon da? is he there yet?; **warst du
schon einmal da?** have you ever been
there?; **ich war schon einmal da** I've been
there before; **das war schon immer so**
so that has always been the case; **schon oft**
often; **hast du schon gehört?** have you
heard?
2 (bestimmt) all right; **du wirst schon
sehen** you'll see (all right); **das wird
schon noch gut** that'll be OK
3 (bloß) just; **allein schon das Gefühl ...**
just the very feeling ...; **schon der
Gedanke** the very thought; **wenn ich
das schon höre** I only have to hear
that
4 (einschränkend): **ja schon, aber ...** yes
(well), but ...
5: **schon möglich** possible; **schon gut!**

OK!; **du weißt schon** you know; **komm
schon!** come on!

schön adj beautiful; (nett) nice; (Frau)
beautiful, pretty; (Mann) beautiful,
handsome; (Wetter) fine; **~e Grüße** best
wishes; **~es Wochenende** have a nice
weekend
schonen vt (pfleglich behandeln) to look
after ▷ vr **sich** ~ to take it easy
Schönheit f beauty
Schonkost f light diet
schöpfen vt to scoop; (mit Kelle) to ladle;
Schöpfkelle f, **Schöpflöffel** m ladle
Schöpfung f creation
Schoppen (-s, -) m glass (of wine)
Schorf (-(e)s, -e) m scab
Schorle (-, -n) f spritzer
Schornstein m chimney;
Schornsteinfeger(in) (-s, -) m(f) chimney
sweep
schoss imperf von **schießen**
Schoß (-es, Schöße) m lap
Schotte (-n, -n) m Scot, Scotsman;
Schottin f Scot, Scotswoman;
schottisch adj Scottish, Scots;
Schottland nt Scotland
schräg adj slanting; (Dach) sloping; (Linie)
diagonal; (fam: unkonventionell) wacky
Schrank (-(e)s, Schränke) m cupboard;
(Kleiderschrank) wardrobe (Brit), closet
(US)
Schranke (-, -n) f barrier
Schrankwand f wall unit
Schraube (-, -n) f screw; **schrauben** vt to
screw; **Schraubendreher** (-s, -) m
screwdriver; **Schraubenschlüssel** m
spanner; **Schraubenzieher** (-s, -) m
screwdriver; **Schraubverschluss** m
screw top, screw cap
Schreck (-(e)s, -e) m, **Schrecken** (-s, -) m
terror; (Angst) fright; **jdm einen
~ einjagen** to give sb a fright;
schreckhaft adj jumpy; **schrecklich** adj
terrible, dreadful
Schrei (-(e)s, -e) m scream; (Ruf) shout
Schreibblock m writing pad; **schreiben**
(schrieb, geschrieben) vt, vi to write;
(buchstabieren) to spell; **wie schreibt man
...?** how do you spell ...?; **Schreiben** (-s, -)
nt writing; (Brief) letter; **Schreibfehler** m
spelling mistake; **schreibgeschützt** adj
(Diskette) write-protected; **Schreibtisch**

m desk; **Schreibwaren** *pl* stationery *sing*;
Schreibwarenladen *m* stationer's
schreien (schrie, geschrie(e)n) *vt, vi* to
scream; (rufen) to shout
Schreiner(in) *m(f)* joiner; **Schreinerei** *f*
joiner's workshop
schrie *imperf von* **schreien**
schrieb *imperf von* **schreiben**
Schrift (-, -en) *f* writing; (Handschrift)
handwriting; (Schriftart) typeface;
(Schrifttyp) font; **schriftlich** *adj* written
▷ *adv* in writing; **würden Sie uns das
bitte ~ geben?** could we have that in
writing, please?; **Schriftsteller(in)** (-s, -)
m(f) writer
Schritt (-(e)s, -e) *m* step; **~ für ~** step by
step; **~e gegen etw unternehmen** to take
steps against sth;
Schrittgeschwindigkeit *f* walking
speed; **Schrittmacher** *m* (Med)
pacemaker
Schrott (-(e)s, -e) *m* scrap metal; (fig)
rubbish
schrubben *vi, vt* to scrub; **Schrubber**
(-s, -) *m* scrubbing brush
schrumpfen *vi* to shrink
Schubkarren (-s, -) *m* wheelbarrow;
Schublade *f* drawer
schubsen *vt* to shove, to push
schüchtern *adj* shy
schuf *imperf von* **schaffen**
Schuh (-(e)s, -e) *m* shoe; **Schuhcreme** *f*
shoe polish; **Schuhgeschäft** *nt* shoe
shop; **Schuhgröße** *f* shoe size;
Schuhlöffel *m* shoehorn; **Schuhsohle** *f*
sole
Schulabschluss *m* school-leaving
qualification
schuld *adj* **wer ist ~ daran?** whose fault is
it?; **er ist ~** it's his fault, he's to blame;
Schuld (-) *f* guilt; (Verschulden) fault;
~ haben to be to blame (an +dat for); **er
hat ~** it's his fault; **sie gibt mir die ~ an
dem Unfall** she blames me for the
accident; **schulden** *vt* to owe (jdm etw sb
sth), **Schulden** *pl* debts *pl*; **~ haben** to be
in debt; **~ machen** to run up debts; **seine
~ zahlen** to pay off one's debts;
schuldig *adj* guilty (an +dat of);
(gebührend) due; **jdm etw ~ sein** to owe sb
sth
Schule (-, -n) *f* school; **in der ~** at school;
in die ~ gehen to go to school;

Schüler(in) (-s, -) *m(f)* (jüngerer) pupil;
(älterer) student; **Schüleraustausch** *m*
school exchange; **Schulfach** *nt* subject;
Schulferien *pl* school holidays *pl* (Brit) (o
vacation (US)); **schulfrei** *adj* **morgen ist
~** there's no school tomorrow;
Schulfreund(in) *m(f)* schoolmate;
Schuljahr *nt* school year;
Schulkenntnisse *pl* **~ in Französisch**
school(-level) French; **Schulklasse** *f* class;
Schulleiter(in) *m(f)*
headmaster/headmistress (Brit), principal
(US)
Schulter (-, -n) *f* shoulder; **Schulterblatt**
nt shoulder blade
Schulung *f* training; (Veranstaltung)
training course
Schund (-(e)s) *m* trash
Schuppe (-, -n) *f* (von Fisch) scale;
schuppen *vt* to scale ▷ *vr* **sich ~** to peel;
Schuppen *pl* (im Haar) dandruff *sing*
Schürfwunde *f* graze
Schürze (-, -n) *f* apron
Schuss (-es, Schüsse) *m* shot; **mit einem
~ Wodka** with a dash of vodka
Schüssel (-, -n) *f* bowl
Schuster(in) (-s, -) *m(f)* shoemaker
Schutt (-(e)s) *m* rubble
Schüttelfrost *m* shivering fit; **schütteln**
vt to shake ▷ *vr* **sich ~** to shake
schütten *vt* to pour; (Zucker, Kies etc) to tip
▷ *vi impers* to pour (down)
Schutz (-es) *m* protection (gegen, vor
against, from); (Unterschlupf) shelter; **jdn
in ~ nehmen** to stand up for sb;
Schutzblech *nt* mudguard; **Schutzbrief**
m travel insurance document for drivers;
Schutzbrille *f* (safety) goggles *pl*
Schütze (-n, -n) *m* (beim Fußball) scorer;
(Astr) Sagittarius
schützen *vt* **jdn gegen/vor etw ~** to
protect sb against/from sth;
Schutzimpfung *f* inoculation,
vaccination
schwach *adj* weak; **~e Augen** poor
eyesight *sing*; **Schwäche** (-, -n) *f*
weakness; **Schwachstelle** *f* weak point;
Schwachstrom *m* low-voltage current
Schwager (-s, Schwäger) *m*
brother-in-law; **Schwägerin** *f*
sister-in-law
Schwalbe (-, -n) *f* swallow; (beim Fußball)
dive

schwamm *imperf von* **schwimmen**

Schwamm (-(e)s, Schwämme) *m* sponge;
~ **drüber!** (fam) let's forget it!

Schwan (-(e)s, Schwäne) *m* swan

schwanger *adj* pregnant; **im vierten
Monat ~ sein** to be four months
pregnant; **Schwangerschaft** *f*
pregnancy; **Schwangerschaftsabbruch**
m abortion; **Schwangerschaftstest** *m*
pregnancy test

schwanken *vi* to sway; (Preise, Zahlen) to
fluctuate; (zögern) to hesitate; (taumeln) to
stagger; **ich schwanke zwischen A und B**
I can't decide between A and B

Schwanz (-es, Schwänze) *m* tail; (vulg:
Penis) cock

Schwarm (-(e)s, Schwärme) *m* swarm;
(fam: angehimmelte Person) heartthrob;
schwärmen *vi* to swarm; ~ **für** to be mad
about

schwarz *adj* black; ~ **sehen** (fam) to be
pessimistic (für about); **mir wurde ~ vor
Augen** everything went black;
Schwarzarbeit *f* illicit work; **Schwarzbrot**
nt black bread; **schwarz|fahren** *irr vi* to
travel without a ticket; (ohne Führerschein)
to drive without a licence;
Schwarzfahrer(in) *m(f)* fare-dodger;
Schwarzmarkt *m* black market;
Schwarzwald *m* Black Forest;
schwarzweiß *adj* black and white;
Schwarzwurzel *f* black salsify

schwatzen *vi* to chatter; **Schwätzer(in)**
(-s, -) *m(f)* chatterbox; (Schwafler) gasbag;
(Klatschmaul) gossip

Schwebebahn *f* suspension railway;
schweben *vi* to float; (hoch) to soar

Schwede (-n, -n) *m* Swede; **Schweden**
(-s) *nt* Sweden; **Schwedin** *f* Swede;
schwedisch *adj* Swedish; **Schwedisch** *nt*
Swedish

Schwefel (-s) *m* sulphur

schweigen (schwieg, geschwiegen) *vi* to be
silent; (nicht mehr reden) to stop talking;
Schweigen (-s) *nt* silence;
Schweigepflicht *f* duty of
confidentiality; **die ärztliche ~** medical
confidentiality

Schwein (-(e)s, -e) *nt* pig; (fam: Glück) luck;
(fam: gemeiner Mensch) swine;
Schweinebraten *m* roast pork;
Schweinefleisch *nt* pork; **Schweinerei** *f*
mess; (Gemeinheit) dirty trick

Schweiß (-es) *m* sweat

schweißen *vt, vi* to weld

Schweißfüße *pl* sweaty feet *pl*

Schweiz (-) *f* **die ~** Switzerland;
Schweizer(in) (-s, -) *m(f)* Swiss;
Schweizerdeutsch *nt* Swiss German;
schweizerisch *adj* Swiss

Schwelle (-, -n) *f* doorstep; (a. fig)
threshold

schwellen *vi* to swell (up); **Schwellung** *f*
swelling

schwer *adj* heavy; (schwierig) difficult,
hard; (schlimm) serious, bad; **er ist ~ zu
verstehen** it's difficult to understand
what he's saying ▷ *adv* (sehr) really;
(verletzt etc) seriously, badly; **jdm ~ fallen**
to be difficult for sb; **etw ~ nehmen** to
take sth hard; **Schwerbehinderte(r)** *mf*
severely disabled person; **schwerhörig**
adj hard of hearing

Schwert (-(e)s, -er) *nt* sword; **Schwertlilie**
f iris

Schwester (-, -n) *f* sister; (Med) nurse

schwieg *imperf von* **schweigen**

Schwiegereltern *pl* parents-in-law *pl*;
Schwiegermutter *f* mother-in-law;
Schwiegersohn *m* son-in-law;
Schwiegertochter *f* daughter-in-law;
Schwiegervater *m* father-in-law

schwierig *adj* difficult, hard;
Schwierigkeit *f* difficulty; **in ~en
kommen** to get into trouble; **jdm ~en
machen** to make things difficult for sb

Schwimmbad *nt* swimming pool;
Schwimmbecken *nt* swimming pool;
schwimmen (schwamm, geschwommen) *vi*
to swim; (treiben) to float; (fig: unsicher
sein) to be all at sea; **Schwimmer(in)** *m(f)*
swimmer; **Schwimmflosse** *f* flipper;
Schwimmflügel *m* water wing;
Schwimmreifen *m* rubber ring;
Schwimmweste *f* life jacket

Schwindel (-s) *m* dizziness; (Anfall) dizzy
spell; (Betrug) swindle; **schwindelfrei** *adj*
nicht ~ sein to suffer from vertigo; ~ **sein**
to have a head for heights; **schwindlig** *adj*
dizzy; **mir ist ~** I feel dizzy

Schwips *m* **einen ~ haben** to be tipsy

schwitzen *vi* to sweat

schwoll *imperf von* **schwellen**

schwor *imperf von* **schwören**

schwören (schwor, geschworen) *vt, vi* to
swear; **einen Eid ~** to take an oath

schwul adj gay

schwül adj close

Schwung (-(e)s, Schwünge) m swing; (Triebkraft) momentum; (fig: Energie) energy; (fam: Menge) batch; **in ~ kommen** to get going

Schwur (-s, Schwüre) m oath

scrollen vi (Inform) to scroll

sechs num six; **Sechs** (-, -en) f six; (Schulnote) ≈ F; **Sechserpack** m sixpack; **sechshundert** num six hundred; **sechsmal** adv six times; **sechste(r, s)** adj sixth; siehe auch **dritte; Sechstel** (-s, -) nt sixth; **sechzehn** num sixteen; **sechzehnte(r, s)** adj sixteenth; siehe auch **dritte; sechzig** num sixty; **in den ~er Jahren** in the sixties; **sechzigste(r, s)** adj sixtieth

Secondhandladen m secondhand shop

See (-, -n) f sea; **an der ~** by the sea ▷ (-s, -n) m lake; **am ~** by the lake; **Seegang** m waves; **hoher/schwerer/leichter ~** rough/heavy/calm seas pl; **Seehund** m seal; **Seeigel** m sea urchin; **seekrank** adj seasick

Seele (-, -n) f soul

Seeleute pl seamen pl, sailors pl

seelisch adj mental, psychological

Seelöwe m sea lion; **Seemann** m sailor, seaman; **Seemeile** f nautical mile; **Seemöwe** f seagull; **Seenot** f distress (at sea); **Seepferdchen** nt sea horse; **Seerose** f water lily; **Seestern** m starfish; **Seezunge** f sole

Segel (-s, -) nt sail; **Segelboot** nt yacht; **Segelfliegen** (-s) nt gliding; **Segelflugzeug** nt glider; **segeln** vt, vi to sail; **Segelschiff** nt sailing ship

sehbehindert adj partially sighted

sehen (sah, gesehen) vt, vi to see; (in bestimmte Richtung) to look; **gut/schlecht ~** to have good/bad eyesight; **auf die Uhr ~** to look at one's watch; **kann ich das mal ~?** can I have a look at it?; **wir ~ uns morgen!** see you tomorrow!; **ich kenne sie nur vom Sehen** I only know her by sight; **Sehenswürdigkeiten** pl sights pl

Sehne (-, -n) f tendon; (an Bogen) string

sehnen vr **sich ~** to long (nach for)

Sehnenscheidenentzündung f (Med) tendovaginitis; **Sehnenzerrung** f (Med) pulled tendon

Sehnsucht f longing; **sehnsüchtig** adj longing

sehr adv (vor Adjektiv, Adverb) very; (mit Verben) a lot, very much; **zu ~** too much

seicht adj shallow

Seide (-, -n) f silk

Seife (-, -n) f soap; **Seifenoper** f soap (opera); **Seifenschale** f soap dish

Seil (-(e)s, -e) nt rope; (Kabel) cable; **Seilbahn** f cable railway

○ **SCHLÜSSELWORT**

sein (pt **war**, pp **gewesen**) vi **1** to be; **ich bin** I am; **du bist** you are; **er/sie/es ist** he/she/it is; **wir sind/ihr seid/sie sind** we/you/they are; **wir waren** we were; **wir sind gewesen** we have been

2: seien Sie nicht böse don't be angry; **sei so gut und ...** be so kind as to ...; **das wäre gut** that would od that'd be a good thing; **wenn ich Sie wäre** if I were od was you; **das wärs** that's all, that's it; **morgen bin ich in Rom** tomorrow I'll od I will od I shall be in Rome; **waren Sie mal in Rom?** have you ever been to Rome?

3: wie ist das zu verstehen? how is that to be understood?; **er ist nicht zu ersetzen** he cannot be replaced; **mit ihr ist nicht zu reden** you can't talk to her

4: mir ist kalt I'm cold; **was ist?** what's the matter?, what is it?; **ist was?** is something the matter?; **es sei denn, dass ...** unless ...; **wie dem auch sei** be that as it may; **wie wäre es mit ...?** how od what about ...?; **lass das sein!** stop that!

seit conj (bei Zeitpunkt) since; (bei Zeitraum) for; **er ist ~ Montag hier** he's been here since Monday; **er ist ~ einer Woche hier** he's been here for a week; **~ langem** for a long time; **seitdem** adv, conj since

Seite (-, -n) f side; (in Buch) page; **zur ~ gehen** to step aside; **Seitenairbag** m side-impact airbag; **Seitenaufprallschutz** m (Auto) side-impact protection; **Seitensprung** m affair; **Seitenstechen** (-s) nt **~ haben/bekommen** to have/get a stitch; **Seitenstraße** f side street; **Seitenstreifen** m hard shoulder (Brit), shoulder (US); **seitenverkehrt** adj the wrong way round; **Seitenwind** m crosswind

seither adv since (then)

seitlich adj side

Sekretär(in) m(f) secretary

Sekt (-(e)s, -e) m sparkling wine (similar to champagne)

Sekte (-, -n) f sect

Sekunde (-, -n) f second;
Sekundenkleber (-s, -) m superglue;
Sekundenschnelle f **es geschah alles in ~** it was all over in a matter of seconds

○ **SCHLÜSSELWORT**

selbst pron **1**: **ich/er/wir selbst** I myself/he himself/we ourselves; **sie ist die Tugend selbst** she's virtue itself; **er braut sein Bier selbst** he brews his own beer; **wie gehts? — gut, und selbst?** how are things? — fine, and yourself?
2 (ohne Hilfe) alone on my/his/one's etc own; **von selbst** by itself; **er kam von selbst** he came of his own accord; **selbst gemacht** home-made
▷ adv even; **selbst wenn** even if; **selbst Gott** even God (himself)

selbständig adj siehe **selbstständig**
Selbstauslöser (-s, -) m (Foto) self-timer;
Selbstbedienung f self-service;
Selbstbefriedigung f masturbation;
Selbstbeherrschung f self-control;
Selbstbeteiligung f (einer Versicherung) excess; **selbstbewusst** adj (self-)confident; **Selbstbräuner** (-s, -) m self-tanning lotion; **selbstgemacht** adj self-made; **Selbstgespräch** nt **~e führen** to talk to oneself; **selbstklebend** adj self-adhesive; **Selbstkostenpreis** m cost price; **Selbstlaut** m vowel; **Selbstmord** m suicide; **selbstsicher** adj self-assured; **selbstständig** adj independent; (arbeitend) self-employed;
Selbstverpflegung f self-catering;
selbstverständlich adj obvious; **ich halte das für ~** I take that for granted ▷ adv naturally; **Selbstvertrauen** nt self-confidence

Sellerie (-s, -(s)) m (-, -n) f (Knollensellerie) celeriac; (Stangensellerie) celery

selten adj rare ▷ adv seldom, rarely

seltsam adj strange;

~ schmecken/riechen to taste/smell strange

Semester (-s, -) nt semester;
Semesterferien pl vacation sing

Semikolon (-s, Semikola) nt semicolon

Seminar (-s, -e) nt seminar

Semmel (-, -n) f roll; **Semmelbrösel** pl breadcrumbs

Senat (-(e)s, -e) m senate

senden (sandte, gesandt) vt to send ▷ vt, vi (Radio, Tv) to broadcast; **Sender** (-s, -) m (TV) channel; (Radio) station; (Anlage) transmitter; **Sendung** f (Radio, Tv) broadcasting; (Programm) programme

Senf (-(e)s, -e) m mustard

Senior(in) m(f) senior citizen;
Seniorenpass m senior citizen's travel pass

senken vt to lower ▷ vr **sich ~** to sink

senkrecht adj vertical

Sensation (-, -en) f sensation

sensibel adj sensitive

sentimental adj sentimental

separat adj separate

September (-(s), -) m September; siehe auch **Juni**

Serbien (-s) nt Serbia

Serie f series sing

seriös adj (ernsthaft) serious; (anständig) respectable

Serpentine f hairpin (bend)

Serum (-s, Seren) nt serum

Server (-s, -) m (Inform) server

Service (-(s), -) nt (Geschirr) service ▷ (-, -s) m service

servieren vt, vi to serve

Serviette f napkin, serviette

Servolenkung f (Auto) power steering

Sesam (-s, -s) m sesame seeds pl

Sessel (-s, -) m armchair; **Sessellift** m chairlift

Set (-s, -s) m o nt set; (Tischset) tablemat

setzen vt to put; (Baum etc) to plant; (Segel) to set ▷ vr **sich ~** to settle; (hinsetzen) to sit down; **~ Sie sich doch** please sit down

Seuche (-, -n) f epidemic

seufzen vt, vi to sigh

Sex (-(es)) m sex; **Sexismus** m sexism; **sexistisch** adj sexist; **Sextourismus** m sex tourism; **Sexualität** f sexuality; **sexuell** adj sexual

Seychellen pl Seychelles pl
sfr abk = **Schweizer Franken** Swiss
franc(s)
Shampoo (-s, -s) nt shampoo
Shareware (-, -s) f (Inform) shareware
Shorts pl shorts pl
Shuttlebus m shuttle bus

○ SCHLÜSSELWORT

sich pron 1 (akk): **er/sie/es ... sich**
he/she/it ... himself/herself/itself; **sie**
pl/**man ... sich** they/one ...
themselves/oneself; **Sie ... sich** you ...
yourself/yourselves pl; **sich wiederholen**
to repeat oneself/itself
2 (dat): **er/sie/es ... sich** he/she/it ... to
himself/herself/itself; **sie** pl/**man ... sich**
they/one ... to themselves/oneself; **Sie ...
sich** you ... to yourself/yourselves pl; **sie
hat sich einen Pullover gekauft** she
bought herself a jumper; **sich die Haare
waschen** to wash one's hair
3 (mit Präposition): **haben Sie Ihren
Ausweis bei sich?** do you have your
pass on you?; **er hat nichts bei sich** he's
got nothing on him; **sie bleiben gern
unter sich** they keep themselves to
themselves
4 (einander) each other one another; **sie
bekämpfen sich** they fight each other od
one another
5: **dieses Auto fährt sich gut** this car
drives well; **hier sitzt es sich gut** it's good
to sit here

sicher adj safe (vor +dat from); (gewiss)
certain (gen of); (zuverlässig) reliable;
(selbstsicher) confident; **aber ~!** of course,
sure; **Sicherheit** f safety; (Aufgabe von
Sicherheitsbeamten) (Fin) security;
(Gewissheit) certainty; (Selbstsicherheit)
confidence; **mit ~** definitely;
Sicherheitsabstand m safe distance;
Sicherheitsgurt m seat belt;
sicherheitshalber adv just to be on the
safe side; **Sicherheitsnadel** f safety pin;
Sicherheitsvorkehrung f safety
precaution; **sicherlich** adv certainly;
(wahrscheinlich) probably
sichern vt to secure (gegen against);
(schützen) to protect; (Daten) to back up;
Sicherung f (Sichern) securing;

(Vorrichtung) safety device; (an Waffen)
safety catch; (Elek) fuse; (Inform) backup;
die ~ ist durchgebrannt the fuse has
blown
Sicht (-) f sight; (Aussicht) view; **sichtbar**
adj visible; **sichtlich** adj evident, obvious;
Sichtverhältnisse pl visibility sing;
Sichtweite f **in/außer ~** within/out of
sight
sie pron (3. Person sing) she; (3. Person pl)
they; (akk von sing) her; (akk von pl) them;
(für eine Sache) it; **da ist ~ ja** there she is; **da
sind ~ ja** there they are; **ich kenne ~** (Frau)
I know her; (mehrere Personen) I know
them; **~ lag gerade noch hier** (meine Jacke,
Uhr) it was here just a minute ago; **ich hab
~ gefunden** (meine Jacke, Uhr) I've found it;
**hast du meine Brille/Hose gesehen? -
ich kann ~ nirgends finden** have you
seen my glasses/trousers? - I can't find
them anywhere
Sie pron (Höflichkeitsform, Nom und Akk) you
Sieb (-(e)s, -e) nt sieve; (Teesieb) strainer
sieben num seven; **siebenhundert** num
seven hundred; **siebenmal** adv seven
times; **siebte(r, s)** adj seventh; siehe auch
dritte; **Siebtel** (-s, -) nt seventh; **siebzehn**
num seventeen; **siebzehnte(r, s)** adj
seventeenth; siehe auch **dritte**; **siebzig**
num seventy; **in den ~er Jahren** in the
seventies; **siebzigste(r, s)** adj seventieth
Siedlung (-, -en) f (Wohngebiet) housing
estate (Brit) (o development (US))
Sieg (-(e)s, -e) m victory; **siegen** vi to win;
Sieger(in) (-s, -) m(f) winner;
Siegerehrung f presentation ceremony
siehe imper see
siezen vt to address as 'Sie'
Signal (-s, -e) nt signal
Silbe (-, -n) f syllable
Silber (-s) nt silver; **Silberhochzeit** f
silver wedding; **Silbermedaille** f silver
medal
Silikon (-s, -e) nt silicone
Silvester (-s, -) nt, **Silvesterabend** m
New Year's Eve, Hogmanay (SCOT)

● **Silvester**
●
● **Silvester** is the German name for New
● Year's Eve. Although not an official
● holiday, most businesses close early
● and shops shut at midday. Most

Germans celebrate in the evening and at midnight they let off fireworks and rockets; the revelry usually lasts until the early hours of the morning.

Simbabwe (-s) *nt* Zimbabwe
simpel *adj* simple
simultan *adj* simultaneous
simsen *vt, vi* (*fam*) to text
Sinfonie (-, -n) *f* symphony;
Sinfonieorchester *nt* symphony orchestra
Singapur (-s) *nt* Singapore
singen (*sang, gesungen*) *vt, vi* to sing; **richtig/falsch ~** to sing in tune/out of tune
Single (-, -s) *f* (*CD*) single ▷ (-s, -s) *m* (*Mensch*) single
Singular *m* singular
sinken (*sank, gesunken*) *vi* to sink; (*Preise etc*) to fall, to go down
Sinn (-(e)s, -e) *m* (*Denken*) mind; (*Wahrnehmung*) sense; (*Bedeutung*) sense, meaning; **~ machen** to make sense; **das hat keinen ~** it's no use; **sinnlich** *adj* sensuous; (*erotisch*) sensual; (*Wahrnehmung*) sensory; **sinnlos** *adj* (*unsinnig*) stupid; (*Verhalten*) senseless; (*zwecklos*) pointless; (*bedeutungslos*) meaningless; **sinnvoll** *adj* meaningful; (*vernünftig*) sensible
Sirup (-s, -e) *m* syrup
Sitte (-, -n) *f* custom
Situation *f* situation
Sitz (-es, -e) *m* seat; **sitzen** (*saß, gesessen*) *vi* to sit; (*Bemerkung, Schlag*) to strike home; (*Gelerntes*) to have sunk in; **der Rock sitzt gut** the skirt is a good fit; **Sitzgelegenheit** *f* place to sit down; **Sitzplatz** *m* seat; **Sitzung** *f* meeting
Sizilien (-s) *nt* Sicily
Skandal (-s, -e) *m* scandal
Skandinavien (-s) *nt* Scandinavia
Skateboard (-s, -s) *nt* skateboard; **Skateboardfahrer(in)** *m(f)* skateboarder
Skelett (-s, -e) *nt* skeleton
skeptisch *adj* sceptical
Ski (-s, -er) *m* ski; **~ laufen** (*o fahren*) to ski; **Skianzug** *m* ski suit; **Skibrille** *f* ski goggles *pl*; **Skifahren** (-s) *nt* skiing; **Skigebiet** (-s, -e) *nt* skiing area; **Skihose** *f* skiing trousers *pl*; **Skikurs** *m* skiing course;

Skilanglauf *m* cross-country skiing; **Skiläufer(in)** *m(f)* skier; **Skilehrer(in)** *m(f)* ski instructor; **Skilift** *m* ski-lift
Skinhead (-s, -s) *m* skinhead
Skipiste *f* ski run; **Skischanze** (-, -n) *f* ski jump; **Skischuh** *m* ski boot; **Skischule** *f* ski school; **Skispringen** (-s, -n) *nt* ski jumping; **Skistiefel** (-s, -) *m* ski boot; **Skistock** *m* ski pole; **Skiträger** *m* ski rack; **Skiurlaub** *m* skiing holiday (*Brit*) (*o* vacation (*US*))
Skizze (-, -n) *f* sketch
Skonto (-s, -s) *m o nt* discount
Skorpion (-s, -e) *m* (*Zool*) scorpion; (*Astr*) Scorpio
Skulptur (-, -en) *f* sculpture
S-Kurve *f* double bend
Slalom (-s, -s) *m* slalom
Slip (-s, -s) *m* (pair of) briefs *pl*; **Slipeinlage** *f* panty liner
Slowakei (-) *f* Slovakia; **slowakisch** *adj* Slovakian; **Slowakische Republik** Slovak Republic; **Slowakisch** *nt* Slovakian
Slowenien (-s) *nt* Slovenia; **slowenisch** *adj* Slovenian; **Slowenisch** *nt* Slovenian
Smiley (-s, -s) *m* smiley
Smog (-s) *m* smog; **Smogalarm** *m* smog alert
Smoking (-s, -s) *m* dinner jacket (*Brit*), tuxedo (*US*)
SMS *nt abk* = **Short Message Service** ▷ *f* (*Nachricht*) text message; **ich schicke dir eine ~** I'll text you, I'll send you a text (message)
Snowboard (-s, -s) *nt* snowboard; **Snowboardfahren** (-s) *nt* snowboarding; **Snowboardfahrer(in)** *m(f)* snowboarder

🔵 **SCHLÜSSELWORT**

so *adv* **1** (*so sehr*) so; **so groß/schön** *etc* so big/nice *etc*; **so groß/schön wie ...** as big/nice as ...; **so viel (wie)** as much as; **rede nicht so viel** don't talk so much; **so weit sein** to be ready; **so weit wie** *od* **als möglich** as far as possible; **ich bin so weit zufrieden** by and large I'm quite satisfied; **so wenig (wie)** as little (as); **das hat ihn so geärgert, dass ...** that annoyed him so much that ...; **so einer wie ich** somebody like me; **na so was!** well, well!

2 (*auf diese Weise*) like this; **mach es nicht**

so don't do it like that; **so oder so** in one way or the other; **und so weiter** and so on; **... oder so was** ... or something like that; **das ist gut so** that's fine; **so gennant** so-called

3 (umg: umsonst); **ich habe es so bekommen** I got it for nothing

▷ konj: **so dass**; **sodass** so that; **so wie es jetzt ist** as things are at the moment

▷ excl: **so?** really?; **so, das wärs** so, that's it then

s. o. abk = **siehe oben** see above

sobald conj as soon as

Socke (-, -n) f sock

Sodbrennen (-s) nt heartburn

Sofa (-s, -s) nt sofa

sofern conj if, provided (that)

sofort adv immediately, at once; **Sofortbildkamera** f instant camera

Softeis nt soft ice-cream

Software (-, -s) f software

sog imperf von **saugen**

sogar adv even; **kalt, ~ sehr kalt** cold, in fact very cold

Sohle (-, -n) f sole

Sohn (-(e)s, Söhne) m son

Soja (-, Sojen) f soya; **Sojasprossen** pl bean sprouts pl

solang(e) conj as long as

Solarium nt solarium

Solarzelle f solar cell

solche(r, s) pron such; **eine ~ Frau, solch eine Frau** such a woman, a woman like that; **~ Sachen** things like that, such things; **ich habe ~ Kopfschmerzen** I've got such a headache; **ich habe ~n Hunger** I'm so hungry

Soldat(in) (-en, -en) m(f) soldier

solidarisch adj showing solidarity; **sich ~ erklären mit** to declare one's solidarity with

solid(e) adj solid; (Leben, Mensch) respectable

Soll (-(s), -(s)) nt (Fin) debit; (Arbeitsmenge) quota, target

SCHLÜSSELWORT

sollen (pt **sollte**, pp **gesollt** od (als Hilfsverb) **sollen**) Hilfsverb **1** (Pflicht, Befehl) to be

supposed to; **du hättest nicht gehen sollen** you shouldn't have gone, you oughtn't to have gone, **soll ich?** shall I?; **soll ich dir helfen?** shall I help you?; **sag ihm, er soll warten** tell him he's to wait; **was soll ich machen?** what should I do?

2 (Vermutung): **sie soll verheiratet sein** she's said to be married; **was soll das heißen?** what's that supposed to mean?; **man sollte glauben, dass ...** you would think that ...; **sollte das passieren, ...** if that should happen ...

▷ vt, vi: **was soll das?** what's all this?; **das sollst du nicht** you shouldn't do that; **was solls?** what the hell!

Solo (-s, -) nt solo

Sommer (-s, -) m summer; **Sommerfahrplan** m summer timetable; **Sommerferien** pl summer holidays pl (Brit) (o vacation sing (US)); **sommerlich** adj summery; (Sommer-) summer; **Sommerreifen** m normal tyre; **Sommersprossen** pl freckles pl; **Sommerzeit** f summertime; (Uhrzeit) daylight saving time

Sonderangebot nt special offer; **sonderbar** adj strange, odd; **Sondermarke** f special stamp; **Sondermaschine** f special plane; **Sondermüll** m hazardous waste

sondern conj but; **nicht nur ..., ~ auch** not only ..., but also

Sonderpreis m special price; **Sonderschule** f special school; **Sonderzeichen** nt (Inform) special character; **Sonderzug** m special train

Song (-s, -s) m song

Sonnabend m Saturday; siehe auch **Mittwoch**; **sonnabends** adv on Saturdays; **~ morgens** on Saturday mornings; siehe auch **mittwochs**

Sonne (-, -n) f sun; **sonnen** vr **sich ~** to sunbathe; **Sonnenallergie** f sun allergy; **Sonnenaufgang** m sunrise; **Sonnenblume** f sunflower; **Sonnenblumenkern** m sunflower seed; **Sonnenbrand** m sunburn; **Sonnenbrille** f sunglasses pl, shades pl; **Sonnencreme** f sun cream; **Sonnendach** nt (an Haus) awning; (Auto) sunroof; **Sonnendeck** nt sun deck; **Sonnenmilch** f suntan lotion;

Sonnenöl nt suntan oil; **Sonnenschein** m sunshine; **Sonnenschirm** m parasol, sunshade; **Sonnenschutzcreme** f sunscreen; **Sonnenstich** m sunstroke; **Sonnenstudio** nt solarium; **Sonnenuhr** f sundial; **Sonnenuntergang** m sunset; **sonnig** adj sunny

Sonntag m Sunday; siehe auch **Mittwoch**; **sonntags** adv on Sundays; siehe auch **mittwochs**

sonst adv, conj (außerdem) else; (andernfalls) otherwise, (or) else; (mit Pron, in Fragen) else; (normalerweise) normally, usually; **~ noch etwas?** anything else?; **~ nichts** nothing else

sooft conj whenever

Sopran (-s, -e) m soprano

Sorge (-, -n) f worry; (Fürsorge) care; **sich** (dat) **um jdn ~n machen** to be worried about sb; **sorgen** vi **für jdn ~** to look after sb; **für etw ~** to take care of sth, to see to sth ▷ vr **sich ~** to worry (um about); **sorgfältig** adj careful

sortieren vt to sort (out)

Sortiment nt assortment

sosehr conj however much

Soße (-, -n) f sauce; (zu Braten) gravy

Soundkarte f (Inform) sound card

Souvenir (-s, -s) nt souvenir

soviel conj as far as

soweit conj as far as

sowie conj (wie auch) as well as; (sobald) as soon as

sowohl conj **~ ... als** (o **wie**) **auch** both ... and

sozial adj social; **Sozialhilfe** f income support (Brit), welfare (aid) (US); **Sozialismus** m socialism; **Sozialversicherung** f social security; **Sozialwohnung** f council flat (Brit), state-subsidized apartment (US)

Soziologie f sociology

sozusagen adv so to speak

Spachtel (-s, -) m spatula

Spag(h)etti pl spaghetti sing

Spalte (-, -n) f crack; (Gletscher) crevasse; (in Text) column

spalten vt to split ▷ vr **sich ~** to split

Spange (-, -n) f clasp; (Haarspange) hair slide (Brit), barrette (US)

Spanien (-s) nt Spain; **Spanier(in)** (-s, -) m(f) Spaniard; **spanisch** adj Spanish; **Spanisch** nt Spanish

spann imperf von **spinnen**

spannen vt (straffen) to tighten; (befestigen) to brace ▷ vi to be tight

spannend adj exciting, gripping; **Spannung** f tension; (Elek) voltage; (fig) suspense

Sparbuch nt savings book; (Konto) savings account; **sparen** vt, vi to save

Spargel (-s, -) m asparagus; **Spargelsuppe** f asparagus soup

Sparkasse f savings bank; **Sparkonto** f savings account

spärlich adj meagre; (Bekleidung) scanty

sparsam adj economical; **Sparschwein** nt piggy bank

Spaß (-es, Späße) m joke; (Freude) fun; **es macht mir ~** I enjoy it, it's (great) fun; **viel ~!** I have fun

spät adj, adv late; **zu ~ kommen** to be late

Spaten (-s, -) m spade

später adj, adv later; **spätestens** adv at the latest; **Spätlese** f late vintage (wine); **Spätvorstellung** f late-night performance

Spatz (-en, -en) m sparrow

spazieren vi to stroll, to walk; **~ gehen** to go for a walk; **Spaziergang** m walk

Specht (-(e)s, -e) m woodpecker

Speck (-(e)s, -e) m bacon fat; (durchwachsen) bacon

Spedition f (für Umzug) removal firm

Speiche (-, -n) f spoke

Speichel (-s) m saliva

Speicher (-s, -) m storehouse; (Dachboden) attic; (Inform) memory; **speichern** vt (Inform) to store; (sichern) to save

Speise (-, -n) f food; (Gericht) dish; **Speisekarte** f menu; **Speiseröhre** f gullet, oesophagus; **Speisesaal** m dining hall; **Speisewagen** m dining car

Spende (-, -n) f donation; **spenden** vt to donate, to give

spendieren vt **jdm etw ~** to treat sb to sth

Sperre (-, -n) f barrier; (Verbot) ban; **sperren** vt (Sport) to block; (Sport) to suspend; (verbieten) to ban

Sperrgepäck m bulky luggage; **Sperrmüll** m bulky refuse; **Sperrstunde** f closing time; **Sperrung** f closing

Spesen pl expenses pl

spezialisieren vr **sich ~** to specialize (auf

+*akk* in); **Spezialist(in)** *m(f)* specialist;
Spezialität *f* speciality (*Brit*), specialty
(*US*); **speziell** *adj* special ▷ *adv* especially
Spiegel (*-s, -*) *m* mirror; **Spiegelei** *nt* fried
egg (sunny-side up (*US*)); **spiegelglatt** *adj*
very slippery; **Spiegelreflexkamera** *f*
reflex camera
Spiel (*-(e)s, -e*) *nt* game; (*Tätigkeit*)
play(ing); (*Karten*) pack, deck; (*Tech*) (free)
play; **Spielautomat** *m* (*ohne Geldgewinn*)
gaming machine; (*mit Geldgewinn*) slot
machine; **spielen** *vt, vi* to play; (*um Geld*) to
gamble; (*Theat*) to perform, to act; **Klavier**
~ to play the piano; **spielend** *adv* easily;
Spieler(in) (*-s, -*) *m(f)* player; (*um Geld*)
gambler; **Spielfeld** *nt* (*für Fußball, Hockey*)
field; (*für Basketball*) court; **Spielfilm** *m*
feature film; **Spielkasino** *nt* casino;
Spielplatz *m* playground; **Spielraum** *m*
room to manoeuvre; **Spielregel** *f* rule;
sich an die ~n halten to stick to the rules;
Spielsachen *pl* toys *pl*; **Spielverderber(in)**
(*-s, -*) *m(f)* spoilsport; **Spielzeug** *nt* toys
pl; (*einzelnes*) toy
Spieß (*-es, -e*) *m* spear; (*Bratspieß*) spit;
Spießer(in) (*-s, -*) *m(f)* square, stuffy type;
spießig *adj* square, uncool
Spikes *pl* (*Sport*) spikes *pl*; (*Auto*) studs *pl*
Spinat (*-(e)s, -e*) *m* spinach
Spinne (*-, -n*) *f* spider; **spinnen** (*spann,
gesponnen*) *vt, vi* to spin; (*fam: Unsinn reden*)
to talk rubbish; (*verrückt sein*) to be crazy;
du spinnst! you must be mad; **Spinnwebe**
(*-, -n*) *f* cobweb
Spion(in) (*-s, -e*) *m(f)* spy; **spionieren** *vi*
to spy; (*fig*) to snoop around
Spirale (*-, -n*) *f* spiral; (*Med*) coil
Spirituosen *pl* spirits *pl*, liquor *sing* (*US*)
Spiritus (*-, -se*) *m* spirit
spitz *adj* (*Nase, Kinn*) pointed; (*Bleistift,
Messer*) sharp; (*Winkel*) acute; **Spitze** (*-, -n*)
f point; (*von Finger, Nase*) tip; (*Bemerkung*)
taunt, dig; (*erster Platz*) lead; (*Gewebe*) lace;
Spitzengeschwindigkeit *f* top speed;
Spitzer (*-s, -*) *m* pencil sharpener;
Spitzname *m* nickname
Spliss (*-*) *m* split ends *pl*
sponsern *vt* to sponsor; **Sponsor(in)**
(*-s, -en*) *m(f)* sponsor
spontan *adj* spontaneous
Sport (*-(e)s, -e*) *m* sport; ~ **treiben** to do
sport; **Sportanlage** *f* sports grounds *pl*;
Sportart *f* sport; **Sportbekleidung** *f*

sportswear; **Sportgeschäft** *nt* sports
shop; **Sporthalle** *f* gymnasium, gym;
Sportlehrer(in) (*-s, -*) *m(f)* sports
instructor; (*Schule*) PE teacher;
Sportler(in) (*-s, -*) *m(f)* sportsman/
-woman; **sportlich** *adj* sporting; (*Mensch*)
sporty; **Sportplatz** *m* playing field;
Sporttauchen *nt* (skin-)diving; (*mit
Gerät*) scuba-diving; **Sportverein** *m*
sports club; **Sportwagen** *m* sports car
sprach *imperf von* **sprechen**
Sprache (*-, -n*) *f* language; (*Sprechen*)
speech; **Sprachschule** *f* language
school; **Sprachführer** *m* phrasebook;
Sprachkenntnisse *pl* knowledge *sing* of
languages; **gute englische ~ haben** to
have a good knowledge of English;
Sprachkurs *m* language course;
Sprachunterricht *m* language
teaching
sprang *imperf von* **springen**
Spray (*-s, -s*) *m o nt* spray
Sprechanlage *f* intercom; **sprechen**
(*sprach, gesprochen*) *vt, vi* to speak (*jdn, mit
jdm* to sb); (*sich unterhalten*) to talk (*mit* to,
über, von about); ~ **Sie Deutsch?** do you
speak German?; **kann ich bitte mit David
~?** (*am Telefon*) can I speak to David,
please?; **Sprecher(in)** *m(f)* speaker;
(*Ansager*) announcer; **Sprechstunde** *f*
consultation; (*Arzt*) surgery hours *pl*;
(*Anwalt etc*) office hours *pl*;
Sprechzimmer *nt* consulting room
Sprengstoff *m* explosive
Sprichwort *nt* proverb
Springbrunnen *m* fountain
springen (*sprang, gesprungen*) *vi* to jump;
(*Glas*) to crack; (*mit Kopfsprung*) to dive
Sprit (*-(e)s, -e*) *m* (*fam: Benzin*) petrol (*Brit*),
gas (*US*)
Spritze (*-, -n*) *f* (*Gegenstand*) syringe;
(*Injektion*) injection; (*an Schlauch*) nozzle;
spritzen *vt* to spray; (*Med*) to inject ▷ *vi*
to splash; (*Med*) to give injections
Spruch (*-(e)s, Sprüche*) *m* saying
Sprudel (*-s, -*) *m* sparkling mineral water;
(*süßer*) fizzy drink (*Brit*), soda (*US*);
sprudeln *vi* to bubble
Sprühdose *f* aerosol (can); **sprühen** *vt, vi*
to spray; (*fig*) to sparkle; **Sprühregen** *m*
drizzle
Sprung (*-(e)s, Sprünge*) *m* jump; (*Riss*)
crack; **Sprungbrett** *nt* springboard;

Sprungschanze f ski jump; **Sprungturm** m diving platforms pl

Spucke (-) f spit; **spucken** vt, vi to spit; (fam: sich erbrechen) to vomit; **Spucktüte** f sick bag

spuken vi (Geist) to walk; **hier spukt es** this place is haunted

Spülbecken nt sink

Spule (-, -n) f spool; (Elek) coil

Spüle (-, -n) f sink; **spülen** vt, vi to rinse; (Geschirr) to wash up; (Toilette) to flush; **Spülmaschine** f dishwasher; **Spülmittel** nt washing-up liquid (Brit), dishwashing liquid (US); **Spültuch** nt dishcloth; **Spülung** f (von WC) flush

Spur (-, -en) f trace; (Fußspur, Radspur) track; (Fährte) trail; (Fahrspur) lane; **die ~ wechseln** to change lanes pl

spüren vt to feel; (merken) to notice; **Spürhund** m sniffer dog

Squash (-) nt squash; **Squashschläger** m squash racket

Sri Lanka (-s) nt Sri Lanka

Staat (-(e)s, -en) m state; **staatlich** adj state(-); (vom Staat betrieben) state-run; **Staatsangehörigkeit** f nationality; **Staatsanwalt** m, **-anwältin** f prosecuting counsel (Brit), district attorney (US); **Staatsbürger(in)** m(f) citizen; **Staatsbürgerschaft** f nationality; **doppelte ~** dual nationality; **Staatsexamen** nt final exam taken by trainee teachers, medical and law students

Stab (-(e)s, Stäbe) m rod; (Gitter) bar; **Stäbchen** nt (Essstäbchen) chopstick; **Stabhochsprung** m pole vault

stabil adj stable; (Möbel) sturdy

stach imperf von stechen

Stachel (-s, -n) m spike; (von Tier) spine; (von Insekten) sting; **Stachelbeere** f gooseberry; **Stacheldraht** m barbed wire; **stachelig** adj prickly

Stadion (-s, Stadien) nt stadium

Stadt (-, Städte) f town; (groß) city; **in der ~** in town; **Stadtautobahn** f urban motorway (Brit) (o expressway (US)); **Stadtbummel** (-s, -) m **einen ~ machen** to go round town; **Städtepartnerschaft** f twinning; **Stadtführer** m (Heft) city guide; **Stadtführung** f city sightseeing tour; **Stadthalle** f municipal hall; **städtisch** adj municipal; **Stadtmauer** f city wall(s); **Stadtmitte** f town/city

centre, downtown (US); **Stadtplan** m (street) map; **Stadtrand** m outskirts pl; **Stadtrundfahrt** f city tour; **Stadtteil** m, **Stadtviertel** nt district, part of town; **Stadtzentrum** nt town/city centre, downtown (US)

stahl imperf von stehlen

Stahl (-(e)s, Stähle) m steel

Stall (-(e)s, Ställe) m stable; (Kaninchen) hutch; (Schweine) pigsty; (Hühner) henhouse

Stamm (-(e)s, Stämme) m (Baum) trunk; (von Menschen) tribe; **stammen** vi **~ aus** to come from; **Stammgast** m regular (guest); **Stammkunde** m, **Stammkundin** f regular (customer); **Stammtisch** m table reserved for regulars

stampfen vt, vi to stamp; (mit Werkzeug) to pound; (stapfen) to tramp

stand imperf von stehen

Stand (-(e)s, Stände) m (Wasser, Benzin) level; (Stehen) standing position; (Zustand) state; (Spielstand) score; (auf Messe etc) stand; (Klasse) class; **im ~e sein** to be in a position; (fähig) to be able

Standby-Betrieb m stand-by; **Standby-Ticket** nt stand-by ticket

Ständer (-s, -) m (Gestell) stand; (fam: Erektion) hard-on

Standesamt nt registry office

ständig adj permanent; (ununterbrochen) constant, continual

Standlicht nt sidelights pl (Brit), parking lights pl (US); **Standort** m position; **Standpunkt** m standpoint; **Standspur** f (Auto) hard shoulder (Brit), shoulder (US)

Stange (-, -n) f stick; (Stab) pole; (Metall) bar; (Zigaretten) carton; **Stangenbohne** f runner (Brit) (o string (US)) bean; **Stangenbrot** nt French stick; **Stangensellerie** m celery

stank imperf von stinken

Stapel (-s, -) m pile

Star (-(e)s, -e) m (Vogel) starling; (Med) cataract ▷ (-s, -s) m (in Film etc) star

starb imperf von sterben

stark adj strong; (heftig, groß) heavy; (Maßangabe) thick; **Stärke** (-, -n) f strength; (Dicke) thickness; (Wäschestärke, Speisestärke) starch; **stärken** vt to strengthen; (Wäsche) to starch; **Starkstrom** m high-voltage current;

Stärkung f strengthening; (*Essen*) refreshment

starr adj stiff; (*unnachgiebig*) rigid; (*Blick*) staring

starren vi to stare

Start (-(e)s, -e) m start; (*Aviat*) takeoff; **Startautomatik** f automatic choke; **Startbahn** f runway; **starten** vt, vi to start; (*Aviat*) to take off; **Starthilfekabel** nt jump leads pl (Brit), jumper cables pl (US); **Startmenü** nt (*Inform*) start menu

Station f (*Haltestelle*) stop; (*Bahnhof*) station; (*im Krankenhaus*) ward; **stationär** adj stationary; **~e Behandlung** in-patient treatment; **jdn ~ behandeln** to treat sb as an in-patient

Statistik f statistics pl

Stativ nt tripod

statt conj, prep +gen o dat instead of; **~ zu arbeiten** instead of working

statt|finden irr vi to take place

Statue (-, -n) f statue

Statusleiste f, **Statuszeile** f (*Inform*) status bar

Stau (-(e)s, -e) m (*im Verkehr*) (traffic) jam; **im ~ stehen** to be stuck in a traffic jam

Staub (-(e)s) m dust; **~ wischen** to dust; **staubig** adj dusty; **staubsaugen** vt, vi to vacuum, to hoover (Brit); **Staubsauger** m vacuum cleaner, hoover® (Brit); **Staubtuch** nt duster

Staudamm m dam

staunen vi to be astonished (*über +akk* at)

Stausee m reservoir; **Stauung** f (*von Wasser*) damming-up; (*von Blut, Verkehr*) congestion; **Stauwarnung** f traffic report

Std. abk = **Stunde** h

Steak (-s, -s) nt steak

stechen (*stach, gestochen*) vt, vi (*mit Nadel etc*) to prick; (*mit Messer*) to stab; (*mit Finger*) to poke; (*Biene*) to sting; (*Mücke*) to bite; (*Sonne*) to burn; (*Kartenspiel*) to trump; **Stechen** (-s, -) nt sharp pain, stabbing pain; **Stechmücke** f mosquito

Steckdose f socket; **stecken** vt to put; (*Nadel*) to stick; (*beim Nähen*) to pin ▷ vi (*festsitzen*) to be stuck; (*Nadeln*) to be (sticking); **der Schlüssel steckt** the key is in the door; **Stecker** (-s, -) m plug; **Stecknadel** f pin; **Steckrübe** f swede (Brit), rutabaga (US)

Steg (-s, -e) m bridge

stehen (*stand, gestanden*) vi to stand (*zu* by); (*sich befinden*) to be; (*stillstehen*) to have stopped; **was steht im Brief?** what does it say in the letter?; **jdm (gut) ~ to** suit sb; **~ bleiben** (*Uhr*) to stop; **~ lassen** to leave ▷ vi impers **wie steht's?** (*Sport*) what's the score?; **Stehlampe** f standard lamp (Brit), floor lamp (US)

stehlen (*stahl, gestohlen*) vt to steal

Stehplatz m (*im Konzert etc*) standing ticket

Steiermark (-) f Styria

steif adj stiff

steigen (*stieg, gestiegen*) vi (*Preise, Temperatur*) to rise; (*klettern*) to climb; **~ in/auf** (+akk) to get in/on

steigern vt to increase ▷ vr **sich ~** to increase

Steigung f incline, gradient

steil adj steep; **Steilhang** m steep slope; **Steilküste** f steep coast

Stein (-(e)s, -e) m stone; **Steinbock** m (*Zool*) ibex; (*Astr*) Capricorn; **Steinbutt** (-s, -e) m turbot; **steinig** adj stony; **Steinschlag** m falling rocks pl

Stelle (-, -n) f place, spot; (*Arbeit*) post, job; (*Amt*) office; **ich an deiner ~** if I were you; **auf der ~** straightaway; **stellen** vt to put; (*Uhr etc*) to set (*auf +akk* to); (*zur Verfügung stellen*) to provide ▷ vr **sich ~** (*bei Polizei*) to give oneself up; **sich schlafend ~ to** pretend to be asleep; **Stellenangebot** nt job offer, vacancy; **stellenweise** adv in places; **Stellenwert** m (*fig*) status; **einen hohen ~ haben** to play an important role; **Stellplatz** m parking space; **Stellung** f position; **zu etw ~ nehmen** to comment on sth; **Stellvertreter(in)** m(f) representative; (*amtlich*) deputy; (*von Arzt*) locum (Brit), locum tenens (US)

Stempel (-s, -) m stamp; **stempeln** vt to stamp; (*Briefmarke*) to cancel

sterben (*starb, gestorben*) vi to die

Stereoanlage f stereo (system)

steril adj sterile; **sterilisieren** vt to sterilize

Stern (-(e)s, -e) m star; **ein Hotel mit vier ~en** a four-star hotel; **Sternbild** nt constellation; (*Sternzeichen*) star sign, sign of the zodiac; **Sternfrucht** f star fruit; **Sternschnuppe** (-, -n) f shooting star; **Sternwarte** (-e, -n) f observatory; **Sternzeichen** nt star sign, sign of the zodiac; **welches ~ bist du?** what's your star sign?

stets *adv* always

Steuer (-s, -) *nt* (*Auto*) steering wheel ▷ (-, -n) *f* tax; **Steuerberater(in)** *m(f)* tax adviser; **Steuerbord** *nt* starboard; **Steuererklärung** *f* tax declaration; **steuerfrei** *adj* tax-free; (*Waren*) duty-free; **Steuerknüppel** *m* control column; (*Aviat, Inform*) joystick; **steuern** *vt, vi* to steer; (*Flugzeug*) to pilot; (*Entwicklung, Tonstärke*) (*Inform*) to control; **steuerpflichtig** *adj* taxable; **Steuerung** *f* (*Auto*) steering; (*Vorrichtung*) controls *pl*; (*Aviat*) piloting; (*fig*) control; **Steuerungstaste** *f* (*Inform*) control key

Stich (-(e)s, -e) *m* (*von Insekt*) sting; (*von Mücke*) bite; (*durch Messer*) stab; (*beim Nähen*) stitch; (*Färbung*) tinge; (*Kartenspiel*) trick; (*Kunst*) engraving; **Stichprobe** *f* spot check

sticken *vt, vi* to embroider

Sticker (-s, -) *m* sticker

Stickerei *f* embroidery

stickig *adj* stuffy, close

Stiefbruder *m* stepbrother

Stiefel (-s, -) *m* boot

Stiefmutter *f* stepmother

Stiefmütterchen *nt* pansy

Stiefschwester *f* stepsister; **Stiefsohn** *m* stepson; **Stieftochter** *f* stepdaughter; **Stiefvater** *m* stepfather

stieg *imperf von* **steigen**

Stiege (-, -n) *f* steps *pl*

Stiel (-(e)s, -e) *m* handle; (*Bot*) stalk; **ein Eis am ~** an ice lolly (*Brit*), a Popsicle® (*US*)

Stier (-(e)s, -e) *m* (*Zool*) bull; (*Astr*) Taurus; **Stierkampf** *m* bullfight; **Stierkämpfer(in)** *m(f)* bullfighter

stieß *imperf von* **stoßen**

Stift (-(e)s, -e) *m* (*aus Holz*) peg; (*Nagel*) tack; (*zum Schreiben*) pen; (*Farbstift*) crayon; (*Bleistift*) pencil

Stil (-s, -e) *m* style

still *adj* quiet; (*unbewegt*) still

stillen *vt* (*Säugling*) to breast-feed

still|halten *irr vi* to keep still; **Stillleben** *nt* still life; **still|stehen** *irr vi* to stand still

Stimme (-, -n) *f* voice; (*bei Wahl*) vote

stimmen *vi* to be right; **stimmt!** that's right; **hier stimmt was nicht** there's something wrong here; **stimmt so!** (*beim Bezahlen*) keep the change

Stimmung *f* mood; (*Atmosphäre*) atmosphere

Stinkefinger *m* (*fam*) **jdm den ~ zeigen** to give sb the finger (*o bird* (*US*))

stinken (stank, gestunken) *vi* to stink (*nach* of)

Stipendium *nt* scholarship; (*als Unterstützung*) grant

Stirn (-, -en) *f* forehead; **Stirnhöhle** *f* sinus

Stock (-(e)s, Stöcke) *m* stick; (*Bot*) stock ▷ *m* (*Stockwerke*) floor, storey; **Stockbett** *nt* bunk bed; **Stöckelschuhe** *pl* high-heels; **Stockwerk** *nt* floor; **im ersten ~** on the first floor (*Brit*), on the second floor (*US*)

Stoff (-(e)s, -e) *m* (*Gewebe*) material; (*Materie*) matter; (*von Buch etc*) subject (matter); (*fam: Rauschgift*) stuff

stöhnen *vi* to groan (*vor* with)

stolpern *vi* to stumble, to trip

stolz *adj* proud

stopp *interj* hold it; (*Moment mal!*) hang on a minute; **stoppen** *vt, vi* to stop; (*mit Uhr*) to time; **Stoppschild** *nt* stop sign; **Stoppuhr** *f* stopwatch

Stöpsel (-s, -) *m* plug; (*für Flaschen*) stopper

Storch (-(e)s, Störche) *m* stork

stören *vt* to disturb; (*behindern*) to interfere with; **darf ich dich kurz ~?** can I trouble you for a minute?; **stört es dich, wenn ...?** do you mind if ...?

stornieren *vt* to cancel; **Stornogebühr** *f* cancellation fee

Störung *f* disturbance; (*in der Leitung*) fault

Stoß (-es, Stöße) *m* (*Schub*) push; (*Schlag*) blow; (*mit Fuß*) kick; (*Haufen*) pile; **Stoßdämpfer** (-s, -) *m* shock absorber

stoßen (stieß, gestoßen) *vt* (*mit Druck*) to shove, to push; (*mit Schlag*) to knock; (*mit Fuß*) to kick; (*anstoßen*) to bump; (*zerkleinern*) to pulverize ▷ *vr* **sich ~** to bang oneself; **sich ~ an** (+*dat*) (*fig*) to take exception to

Stoßstange *f* (*Auto*) bumper

stottern *vt, vi* to stutter

Str. *abk von* **Straße** St, Rd

Strafe (-, -n) *f* punishment; (*Sport*) penalty; (*Gefängnisstrafe*) sentence; (*Geldstrafe*) fine; **strafen** *vt* to punish; **Strafraum** *m* penalty area; **Strafstoß** *m* penalty kick; **Straftat** *f* (criminal) offence; **Strafzettel** *m* ticket

Strahl (-s, -en) m ray, beam; (Wasser) jet; **strahlen** vi to radiate; (fig) to beam

Strähne (-, -n) f strand; (weiß, gefärbt) streak

Strand (-(e)s, Strände) m beach; **am ~** on the beach; **Strandcafé** nt beach café; **Strandkorb** m wicker beach chair with a hood; **Strandpromenade** f promenade

strapazieren vt (Material) to be hard on; (Mensch, Kräfte) to be a strain on

Straße (-, -n) f road; (in der Stadt) street; **Straßenarbeiten** pl roadworks pl (Brit), road repairs pl (US); **Straßenbahn** f tram (Brit), streetcar (US); **Straßencafé** nt pavement café (Brit), sidewalk café (US); **Straßenfest** nt street party; **Straßenglätte** f slippery roads pl; **Straßenkarte** f road map; **Straßenrand** m **am ~** at the roadside; **Straßenschild** nt street sign; **Straßensperre** f roadblock; **Straßenverhältnisse** pl road conditions pl

Strategie (-, -n) f strategy

Strauch (-(e)s, Sträucher) m bush, shrub; **Strauchtomate** f vine-ripened tomato

Strauß (-es, Sträuße) m bunch; (als Geschenk) bouquet ▷ m (Strauße) (Vogel) ostrich

Strecke (-, -n) f route; (Entfernung) distance; (Eisenb) line

strecken vt to stretch ▷ vr **sich ~** to stretch

streckenweise adv (teilweise) in parts; (zeitweise) at times

Streich (-(e)s, -e) m trick, prank

streicheln vt to stroke

streichen (strich, gestrichen) vt (anmalen) to paint; (berühren) to stroke; (auftragen) to spread; (durchstreichen) to delete; (nicht genehmigen) to cancel

Streichholz nt match; **Streichholzschachtel** f matchbox; **Streichkäse** m cheese spread

Streifen (-s, -) m (Linie) stripe; (Stück) strip; (Film) film

Streifenwagen m patrol car

Streik (-(e)s, -s) m strike; **streiken** vi to be on strike

Streit (-(e)s, -e) m argument (um, wegen about, over); **streiten** (stritt, gestritten) vi to argue (um, wegen about, over) ▷ vr **sich ~** to argue (um, wegen about, over)

streng adj (Blick) severe; (Lehrer) strict; (Geruch) sharp

Stress (-es) m stress; **stressen** vt to stress (out); **stressig** adj (fam) stressful

Stretching (-s) nt (Sport) stretching exercises pl

streuen vt to scatter; **die Straßen ~** to grit the roads; (mit Salz) to put salt down on the roads; **Streufahrzeug** nt gritter lorry (Brit), salt truck (US)

strich imperf von **streichen**

Strich (-(e)s, -e) m (Linie) line; **Stricher** m (fam: Strichjunge) rent boy (Brit), boy prostitute; **Strichkode** (-s, -s) m bar code; **Stricherin** f (fam: Strichmädchen) hooker; **Strichpunkt** m semicolon

Strick (-(e)s, -e) m rope

stricken vt, vi to knit; **Strickjacke** f cardigan; **Stricknadel** f knitting needle

Stripper(in) m(f) stripper; **Striptease** (-) m striptease

stritt imperf von **streiten**

Stroh (-(e)s) nt straw; **Strohdach** nt thatched roof; **Strohhalm** m (drinking) straw; **Strohhut** m straw hat

Strom (-(e)s, Ströme) m river; (fig) stream; (Elek) current; **Stromanschluss** m connection; **Stromausfall** m power failure

strömen vi to stream, to pour; **Strömung** f current

Stromverbrauch m power consumption; **Stromzähler** m electricity meter

Strophe (-, -n) f verse

Strudel (-s, -) m (in Fluss) whirlpool; (Gebäck) strudel

Struktur f structure; (von Material) texture

Strumpf (-(e)s, Strümpfe) m (Damenstrumpf) stocking; (Socke) sock; **Strumpfhose** f (pair of) tights pl (Brit), pantyhose (US)

Stück (-(e)s, -e) nt piece; (von Zucker) lump; (etwas) bit; (Zucker) lump; (Theat) play; **ein ~ Käse** a piece of cheese

Student(in) m(f) student; **Studentenausweis** m student card; **Studentenwohnheim** nt hall of residence (Brit), dormitory (US); **Studienabschluss** m qualification (at the end of a course of higher education); **Studienfahrt** f study trip; **Studienplatz** m university/college place; **studieren** vt, *vi* to study; **Studium** *nt* studies *pl*; **während seines ~s** while he is/was studying

Stufe (-, -n) *f* step; (*Entwicklungsstufe*) stage

Stuhl (-(e)s, Stühle) *m* chair

stumm *adj* silent; (*Med*) dumb

stumpf *adj* blunt; (*teilnahmslos, glanzlos*) dull; **stumpfsinnig** *adj* dull

Stunde (-, -n) *f* hour; (*Unterricht*) lesson; **eine halbe ~** half an hour; **Stundenkilometer** *m* 80 ~ 80 kilometres an hour; **stundenlang** *adv* for hours; **Stundenlohn** *m* hourly wage; **Stundenplan** *m* timetable; **stündlich** *adj* hourly

Stuntman (-s, Stuntmen) *m* stuntman; **Stuntwoman** (-, Stuntwomen) *f* stuntwoman

stur *adj* stubborn; (*stärker*) pigheaded

Sturm (-(e)s, Stürme) *m* storm; **stürmen** *vi* (*Wind*) to blow hard; (*rennen*) to storm; **Stürmer(in)** *m(f)* striker, forward; **Sturmflut** *f* storm tide; **stürmisch** *adj* stormy; (*fig*) tempestuous; (*Zeit*) turbulent; (*Liebhaber*) passionate; (*Beifall, Begrüßung*) tumultuous; **Sturmwarnung** *f* gale warning

Sturz (-es, Stürze) *m* fall; (*Pol*) overthrow; **stürzen** *vt* (*werfen*) to hurl; (*Pol*) to overthrow; (*umkehren*) to overturn ▷ *vi* to fall; (*rennen*) to dash; **Sturzhelm** *m* crash helmet

Stute (-, -n) *f* mare

Stütze (-, -n) *f* support; (*Hilfe*) help; (*fam: Arbeitslosenunterstützung*) dole (*Brit*), welfare (*US*)

stützen *vt* to support; (*Ellbogen*) to prop

stutzig *adj* perplexed, puzzled; (*misstrauisch*) suspicious

Styropor® (-s) *nt* polystyrene (*Brit*), styrofoam (*US*)

subjektiv *adj* subjective

Substanz (-, -en) *f* substance

subtrahieren *vt* to subtract

Subvention *f* subsidy; **subventionieren** *vt* to subsidize

Suche *f* search (*nach* for); **auf der ~ nach etw sein** to be looking for sth; **suchen** *vt* to look for; (*Inform*) to search ▷ *vi* to look, to search (*nach* for); **Suchmaschine** *f* (*Inform*) search engine

Sucht (-, Süchte) *f* mania; (*Med*) addiction;

süchtig *adj* addicted; **Süchtige(r)** *mf* addict

Süd south; **Südafrika** *nt* South Africa; **Südamerika** *nt* South America; **Süddeutschland** *nt* Southern Germany; **Süden** (-s) *m* south; **im ~ Deutschlands** in the south of Germany; **Südeuropa** *nt* Southern Europe; **Südkorea** (-s) *nt* South Korea; **südlich** *adj* southern; (*Kurs, Richtung*) southerly; **Verkehr in ~er Richtung** southbound traffic; **Südost(en)** *m* southeast; **Südpol** *m* South Pole; **Südstaaten** *pl* (*der USA*) the Southern States *pl*, the South *sing*; **südwärts** *adv* south, southwards; **Südwest(en)** *m* southwest; **Südwind** *m* south wind

Sultanine *f* sultana

Sülze (-, -n) *f* jellied meat

Summe (-, -n) *f* sum; (*Gesamtsumme*) total

summen *vi, vt* to hum; (*Insekt*) to buzz

Sumpf (-(e)s, Sümpfe) *m* marsh; (*subtropischer*) swamp; **sumpfig** *adj* marshy

Sünde (-, -n) *f* sin

super *adj* (*fam*) super, great; **Super** (-s) *nt* (*Benzin*) four star (petrol) (*Brit*), premium (*US*); **Supermarkt** *m* supermarket

Suppe (-, -n) *f* soup; **Suppengrün** *nt* bunch of herbs and vegetables for flavouring soup; **Suppenlöffel** *m* soup spoon; **Suppenschüssel** *f* soup tureen; **Suppentasse** *f* soup cup; **Suppenteller** *m* soup plate; **Suppenwürfel** *m* stock cube

Surfbrett *nt* surfboard; **surfen** *vi* to surf; **im Internet ~** to surf the Internet; **Surfer(in)** (-s, -) *m(f)* surfer

Surrealismus *m* surrealism

süß *adj* sweet; **süßen** *vt* to sweeten; **Süßigkeit** *f* (*Bonbon etc*) sweet (*Brit*), candy (*US*); **Süßkartoffel** *f* sweet potato, yam (*US*); **süßsauer** *adj* sweet-and-sour; **Süßspeise** *f* dessert; **Süßstoff** *m* sweetener; **Süßwasser** *nt* fresh water

Sweatshirt (-s, -s) *nt* sweatshirt

Swimmingpool (-s, -s) *m* (swimming) pool

Sylvester *nt siehe* Silvester

Symbol (-s, -e) *nt* symbol; **Symbolleiste** *f* (*Inform*) toolbar

Symmetrie (-, -n) *f* symmetry; **symmetrisch** *adj* symmetrical

sympathisch *adj* nice; **jdn ~ finden** to
 like sb
Symphonie (-, -*n*) *f* symphony
Symptom (-*s*, -*e*) *nt* symptom (*für* of)
Synagoge (-, -*n*) *f* synagogue
synchronisiert *adj* (*Film*) dubbed;
 Synchronstimme *f* dubbing voice
Synthesizer (-*s*, -) *m* (*Mus*) synthesizer
Synthetik (-, -*en*) *f* synthetic (fibre);
 synthetisch *adj* synthetic
Syrien (-*s*) *nt* Syria
System (-*s*, -*e*) *nt* system; **systematisch**
 adj systematic; **Systemsteuerung** *f*
 (*Inform*) control panel
Szene (-, -*n*) *f* scene

t

Tabak (-s, -e) *m* tobacco; **Tabakladen** *m* tobacconist's

Tabelle *f* table

Tablett (-s, -s) *nt* tray

Tablette *f* tablet, pill

Tabulator *m* tabulator, tab

Tacho(meter) (-s, -) *m* (*Auto*) speedometer

Tafel (-, -n) *f* (*a. Math*) table; (*Anschlagtafel*) board; (*Wandtafel*) blackboard; (*Schiefer~*) slate; (*Gedenktafel*) plaque; **eine ~ Schokolade** a bar of chocolate; **Tafelwasser** *nt* table water; **Tafelwein** *m* table wine

Tag (-(e)s, -e) *m* day; (*Tageslicht*) daylight; **guten ~!** good morning/afternoon; **am ~ during the day; sie hat ihre ~e** she's got her period; **eines ~es** one day; **~ der Arbeit** Labour Day; **Tagebuch** *nt* diary; **tagelang** *adj* for days (on end); **Tagesanbruch** *m* daybreak; **Tagesausflug** *m* day trip; **Tagescreme** *f* day cream; **Tagesdecke** *f* bedspread; **Tagesgericht** *nt* dish of the day; **Tageskarte** *f* (*Fahrkarte*) day ticket; **die ~ (Speisekarte)** today's menu; **Tageslicht** *nt* daylight; **Tagesmutter** *f* child minder;

Tagesordnung *f* agenda; **Tagestour** *f* day trip; **Tageszeitung** *f* daily newspaper; **täglich** *adj, adv* daily; **tags(über)** *adv* during the day; **Tagung** *f* conference

Tai Chi (-) *nt* tai chi

Taille (-, -n) *f* waist; **tailliert** *adj* fitted

Taiwan (-s) *nt* Taiwan

Takt (-(e)s, -e) *m* (*Taktgefühl*) tact; (*Mus*) time

Taktik (-, -en) *f* tactics *pl*

taktlos *adj* tactless; **taktvoll** *adj* tactful

Tal (-(e)s, Täler) *nt* valley

Talent (-(e)s, -e) *nt* talent; **talentiert** *adj* talented

Talkmaster(in) (-s, -) *m(f)* talk-show host; **Talkshow** (-, -s) *f* talkshow

Tampon (-s, -s) *m* tampon

Tandem (-s, -s) *nt* tandem

Tang (-s, -e) *m* seaweed

Tank (-s, -s) *m* tank; **Tankanzeige** *f* fuel gauge; **Tankdeckel** *m* fuel cap; **tanken** *vi* to get some petrol (*Brit*) (*o* gas (*US*)); (*Aviat*) to refuel; **Tanker** (-s, -) *m* (oil) tanker; **Tankstelle** *f* petrol station (*Brit*), gas station (*US*); **Tankwart(in)** (-s, -e) *m(f)* petrol pump attendant (*Brit*), gas station attendant (*US*)

Tanne (-, -n) *f* fir; **Tannenzapfen** *m* fir cone

Tansania (-s) *nt* Tanzania

Tante (-, -n) *f* aunt; **Tante-Emma-Laden** *m* corner shop (*Brit*), grocery store (*US*)

Tanz (-es, Tänze) *m* dance; **tanzen** *vt, vi* to dance; **Tänzer(in)** *m(f)* dancer; **Tanzfläche** *f* dance floor; **Tanzkurs** *m* dancing course; **Tanzlehrer(in)** *m(f)* dancing instructor; **Tanzstunde** *f* dancing lesson

Tapete (-, -n) *f* wallpaper; **tapezieren** *vt, vi* to wallpaper

Tarantel (-, -n) *f* tarantula

Tarif (-s, -e) *m* tariff, (scale of) fares/charges *pl*

Tasche (-, -n) *f* bag; (*Hosentasche*) pocket; (*Handtasche*) bag (*Brit*), purse (*US*); **Taschen-** in *zW* pocket; **Taschenbuch** *nt* paperback; **Taschendieb(in)** *m(f)* pickpocket; **Taschengeld** *nt* pocket money; **Taschenlampe** *f* torch (*Brit*), flashlight (*US*); **Taschenmesser** *nt* penknife; **Taschenrechner** *m* pocket calculator; **Taschentuch** *nt* handkerchief

Tasse (-, -n) f cup; **eine ~ Kaffee** a cup of coffee

Tastatur f keyboard; **Taste** (-, -n) f button; (von Klavier, Computer) key; **Tastenkombination** f (Inform) shortcut; **Tastentelefon** nt push-button telephone

tat imperf von **tun**

Tat (-, -en) f action

Tatar (-s, -s) nt raw minced beef

Täter(in) (-s, -) m(f) culprit

tätig adj active; **in einer Firma ~ sein** to work for a firm; **Tätigkeit** f activity; (Beruf) occupation

tätowieren vt to tattoo; **Tätowierung** f tattoo (an +dat on)

Tatsache f fact; **tatsächlich** adj actual ▷ adv really

Tau (-(e)s, -e) nt (Seil) rope ▷ (-(e)s) m dew

taub adj deaf; (Füße etc) numb (vor Kälte with cold)

Taube (-, -n) f pigeon; (Turtel~, fig: Friedenssymbol) dove

taubstumm adj deaf-and-dumb; **Taubstumme(r)** mf deaf-mute

tauchen vt to dip ▷ vi to dive; (Naut) to submerge; **Tauchen** (-s) nt diving; **Taucher(in)** (-s, -) m(f) diver; **Taucheranzug** m diving (o wet) suit; **Taucherbrille** f diving goggles pl; **Tauchermaske** f diving mask; **Tauchkurs** m diving course; **Tauchsieder** (-s, -) m portable immersion coil for heating water

tauen vi impers to thaw

Taufe (-, -n) f baptism; **taufen** vt to baptize; (nennen) to christen

taugen vi to be suitable (für for); **nichts ~** to be no good

Tausch (-(e)s, -e) m exchange; **tauschen** vt to exchange, to swap

täuschen vt to deceive ▷ vi to be deceptive ▷ vr **sich ~** to be wrong; **täuschend** adj deceptive; **Täuschung** f deception; (optisch) illusion

tausend num a thousand; **vier~** four thousand; **~ Dank!** thanks a lot; **tausendmal** adv a thousand times; **tausendste(r, s)** adj thousandth; **Tausendstel** (-s, -) nt (Bruchteil) thousandth

Tauwetter nt thaw

Taxi nt taxi; **Taxifahrer(in)** m(f) taxi driver; **Taxistand** m taxi rank (Brit), taxi stand (US)

Team (-s, -s) nt team; **Teamarbeit** f team work; **teamfähig** adj able to work in a team

Technik f technology; (angewandte) engineering; (Methode) technique; **Techniker(in)** (-s, -) m(f) engineer; (Sport, Mus) technician; **technisch** adj technical

Techno (-s) m (Mus) techno

Teddybär m teddy bear

Tee (-s, -s) m tea; **Teebeutel** m teabag; **Teekanne** f teapot; **Teelöffel** m teaspoon

Teer (-(e)s, -e) m tar

Teesieb nt tea strainer; **Teetasse** f teacup

Teich (-(e)s, -e) m pond

Teig (-(e)s, -e) m dough; **Teigwaren** pl pasta sing

Teil (-(e)s, -e) m part; (Anteil) share; **zum ~** partly ▷ (-(e)s, -e) nt part; (Bestandteil) component; **teilen** vt to divide; (mit jdm) to share (mit with); **20 durch 4 ~** to divide 20 by 4 ▷ vr **sich ~** to divide

Teilkaskoversicherung f third party, fire and theft insurance

teilmöbliert adj partly furnished

Teilnahme (-, -n) f participation (an +dat in); **teil|nehmen** irr vi to take part (an +dat in); **Teilnehmer(in)** (-s, -) m(f) participant

teils adv partly; **teilweise** adv partially, in part; **Teilzeit** f **~ arbeiten** to work part-time

Teint (-s, -s) m complexion

Tel. abk von **Telefon** tel.

Telefon (-s, -e) nt telephone; **Telefonanruf** m, **Telefonat** nt (tele)phone call; **Telefonanschluss** m telephone connection; **Telefonauskunft** f directory enquiries pl (Brit), directory assistance (US); **Telefonbuch** nt telephone directory; **Telefongebühren** pl telephone charges pl; **Telefongespräch** nt telephone conversation; **telefonieren** vi **ich telefoniere gerade (mit ...)** I'm on the phone (to ...); **telefonisch** adj telephone; (Benachrichtigung) by telephone; **Telefonkarte** f phonecard; **Telefonnummer** f (tele)phone number; **Telefonrechnung** f phone bill; **Telefonverbindung** f telephone connection; **Telefonzelle** f phone box (Brit), phone booth; **Telefonzentrale** f

switchboard; **über die ~** through the
switchboard
Telegramm nt telegram; **Teleobjektiv**
nt telephoto lens; **Teleshopping** (-s) nt
teleshopping; **Teleskop** (-s, -e) nt
telescope
Teller (-s, -) m plate
Tempel (-s, -) m temple
Temperament nt temperament;
(Schwung) liveliness; **temperamentvoll**
adj lively
Temperatur f temperature; **bei ~en von
30 Grad** at temperatures of 30 degrees;
~ haben to have a temperature; **~ bei jdm
messen** to take sb's temperature
Tempo (-s, -s) nt (Geschwindigkeit) speed;
Tempolimit (-s, -s) nt speed limit
Tempotaschentuch® nt
(Papiertaschentuch) (paper) tissue, ≈
Kleenex®
Tendenz f tendency; (Absicht) intention
Tennis (-) nt tennis; **Tennisball** m tennis
ball; **Tennisplatz** m tennis court;
Tennisschläger m tennis racket;
Tennisspieler(in) m(f) tennis player;
Tennisturnier nt tennis tournament
Tenor (-s, Tenöre) m tenor
Teppich (-s, -e) m carpet; **Teppichboden**
m (wall-to-wall) carpet
Termin (-s, -e) m (Zeitpunkt) date; (Frist)
deadline; (Arzttermin etc) appointment
Terminal (-s, -s) nt (Inform, Aviat) terminal
Terminkalender m diary; **Terminplaner**
m (in Buchform) personal organizer,
Filofax®; (Taschencomputer) personal
digital assistant, PDA
Terpentin (-s, -e) nt turpentine, turps sing
Terrasse (-, -n) f terrace; (hinter einem
Haus) patio
Terror (-s) m terror; **Terroranschlag** m
terrorist attack; **terrorisieren** vt to
terrorize; **Terrorismus** m terrorism;
Terrorist(in) m(f) terrorist
Tesafilm® m ≈ sellotape® (Brit), ≈ Scotch
tape® (US)
Test (-s, -s) m test
Testament nt will; **das Alte/Neue ~** the
Old/New Testament
testen vt to test; **Testergebnis** nt test
results pl
Tetanus (-) m tetanus; **Tetanusimpfung**
f (anti-)tetanus injection
teuer adj expensive, dear (Brit)

Teufel (-s, -) m devil; **was/wo zum
~** what/where the devil; **Teufelskreis** m
vicious circle
Text (-(e)s, -e) m text; (Liedertext) words pl,
lyrics pl; **Textmarker** (-s, -) m highlighter;
Textverarbeitung f word processing;
Textverarbeitungsprogramm nt word
processing program
Thailand nt Thailand
Theater (-s, -) nt theatre; (fam) fuss; **ins
~ gehen** to go to the theatre;
Theaterkasse f box office;
Theaterstück nt (stage) play;
Theatervorstellung f (stage)
performance
Theke (-, -n) f (Schanktisch) bar;
(Ladentisch) counter
Thema (-s, Themen) nt subject, topic; **kein
~!** no problem
Themse (-) f Thames
Theologie f theology
theoretisch adj theoretical; **~ stimmt
das** that's right in theory; **Theorie** f
theory
Therapeut(in) m(f) therapist; **Therapie**
f therapy; **eine ~ machen** to undergo
therapy
Thermalbad nt thermal bath; (Ort)
thermal spa; **Thermometer** (-s, -) nt
thermometer
Thermosflasche® f, **Thermoskanne®** f
Thermos® (flask); **Thermostat** (-(e)s, -e) m
thermostat
These (-, -n) f theory
Thron (-(e)s, -e) m throne
Thunfisch m tuna
Thüringen (-s) nt Thuringia
Thymian (-s, -e) m thyme
Tick (-(e)s, -s) m tic; (Eigenart) quirk;
(Fimmel) craze; **ticken** vi to tick; **er
tickt nicht ganz richtig** he's off his
rocker
Ticket (-s, -s) nt (plane) ticket
Tiebreak (-s, -s) m (Sport: Tennis) tie
break(er)
tief adj deep; (Ausschnitt, Ton, Sonne) low; **2
Meter ~** 2 metres deep; **Tief** (-s, -s) nt
(Meteo) low; (seelisch) depression;
Tiefdruck m (Meteo) low pressure; **Tiefe**
(-, -n) f depth; **Tiefgarage** f underground
car park (Brit) (o garage (US)); **tiefgekühlt**
adj frozen; **Tiefkühlfach** nt freezer
compartment; **Tiefkühlkost** f frozen

food; **Tiefkühltruhe** f freezer; **Tiefpunkt** m low

Tier (-(e)s, -e) nt animal; **Tierarzt** m, **Tierärztin** f vet; **Tiergarten** m zoo; **Tierhandlung** f pet shop; **Tierheim** nt animal shelter; **tierisch** adj animal ▷ adv (fam) really; ~ **ernst** deadly serious; **ich hatte ~ Angst** I was dead scared; **Tierkreiszeichen** nt sign of the zodiac; **Tierpark** m zoo; **Tierquälerei** f cruelty to animals; **Tierschützer(in)** (-s, -) m(f) animal rights campaigner; **Tierversuch** m animal experiment

Tiger (-s, -) m tiger

timen vt to time; **Timing** (-s) nt timing

Tinte (-, -n) f ink; **Tintenfisch** m cuttlefish; (klein) squid; (achtarmig) octopus; **Tintenschringe** pl calamari pl; **Tintenstrahldrucker** m ink-jet printer

Tipp (-s, -s) m tip; **tippen** vt, vi to tap; (fam: schreiben) to type; (fam: raten) to guess

Tirol (-s) nt Tyrol

Tisch (-(e)s, -e) m table; **Tischdecke** f tablecloth; **Tischlerei** f joiner's workshop; (Arbeit) joinery; **Tischtennis** nt table tennis; **Tischtennisschläger** m table-tennis bat

Titel (-s, -) m title; **Titelbild** nt cover picture; **Titelmusik** f theme music; **Titelverteidiger(in)** m(f) defending champion

Toast (-(e)s, -s) m toast; **toasten** vt to toast; **Toaster** (-s, -) m toaster

Tochter (-, Töchter) f daughter

Tod (-(e)s, -e) m death; **Todesopfer** nt casualty; **Todesstrafe** f death penalty; **todkrank** adj terminally ill; (sehr krank) seriously ill; **tödlich** adj deadly, fatal; **er ist ~ verunglückt** he was killed in an accident; **todmüde** adj (fam) dead tired; **todsicher** adj (fam) dead certain

Tofu (-(s)) m tofu, bean curd

Toilette f toilet, restroom (US); **Toilettenpapier** nt toilet paper

toi, toi, toi interj good luck

tolerant adj tolerant (gegen of)

toll adj mad; (Treiben) wild; (fam: großartig) great; **Tollkirsche** f deadly nightshade; **Tollwut** f rabies sing

Tomate (-, -n) f tomato; **Tomatenmark** nt tomato purée (Brit) (o paste (US)); **Tomatensaft** m tomato juice

Tombola (-, -s) f raffle, tombola (Brit)

Ton (-(e)s, -e) m (Erde) clay ▷ m (Töne) (Laut) sound; (Mus) note; (Redeweise) tone; (Farbton, Nuance) shade; **Tonband** nt tape; **Tonbandgerät** nt tape recorder

tönen vi to sound ▷ vt to shade; (Haare) to tint

Toner (-s, -) m toner; **Tonerkassette** f toner cartridge

Tonne (-, -n) f (Fass) barrel; (Gewicht) tonne, metric ton

Tontechniker(in) m(f) sound engineer

Tönung f hue; (für Haar) rinse

Top (-s, -s) nt top

Topf (-(e)s, Töpfe) m pot

Töpfer(in) (-s, -) m(f) potter; **Töpferei** f pottery; (Gegenstand) piece of pottery

Tor (-(e)s, -e) nt gate; (Sport) goal; **ein ~ schießen** to score a goal; **Torhüter(in)** m(f) goalkeeper

torkeln vi to stagger

Torlinie f goal line

Tornado (-s, -s) m tornado

Torpfosten m goalpost; **Torschütze** m, **Torschützin** f (goal)scorer

Torte (-, -n) f cake; (Obsttorte) flan; (Sahnetorte) gateau

Torwart(in) (-s, -e) m(f) goalkeeper

tot adj dead; ~**er Winkel** blind spot

total adj total, complete; **Totalschaden** m complete write-off

Tote(r) mf dead man/woman; (Leiche) corpse; **töten** vt, vi to kill; **Totenkopf** m skull

tot|lachen vr **sich ~** to kill oneself laughing

Toto (-s, -s) m o nt pools pl

tot|schlagen irr vt to beat to death; **die Zeit ~** to kill time

Touchscreen (-s, -s) m touch screen

Toupet (-s, -s) nt toupee

Tour (-, -en) f trip; (Rundfahrt) tour; **eine ~ nach York machen** to go on a trip to York; **Tourenski** m touring ski

Tourismus m tourism; **Tourist(in)** m(f) tourist; **Touristenklasse** f tourist class; **touristisch** adj tourist; (pej) touristy

traben vi to trot

Tournee (-, -n) f tour

Tracht (-, -en) f (Kleidung) traditional costume

Trackball (-s, -s) m (Inform) trackball
Tradition f tradition; **traditionell** adj
traditional
traf imperf von **treffen**
Trafik (-, -en) f tobacconist's
Tragbahre (-, -n) f stretcher
tragbar adj portable
träge adj sluggish, slow
tragen (trug, getragen) vt to carry;
(Kleidung, Brille, Haare) to wear; (Namen,
Früchte) to bear; **Träger** (-s, -) m (an
Kleidung) strap; (Hosen~) braces pl (Brit),
suspenders pl (US); (in der Architektur)
beam; (Stahl~, Eisen~) girder
Tragfläche f wing; **Tragflügelboot** nt
hydrofoil
tragisch adj tragic; **Tragödie** f tragedy
Trainer(in) (-s, -) m(f) trainer, coach;
trainieren vt, vi to train; (jdn a.) to
coach; (Übung) to practise; **Training**
(-s, -s) nt training; **Trainingsanzug** m
tracksuit
Traktor m tractor
Trambahn f tram (Brit), streetcar (US)
trampen vi to hitchhike; **Tramper(in)**
m(f) hitchhiker
Träne (-, -n) f tear; **tränen** vi to water;
Tränengas nt teargas
trank imperf von **trinken**
Transfusion f transfusion
Transitverkehr m transit traffic;
Transitvisum nt transit visa
Transplantation f transplant;
(Hauttransplantation) graft
Transport (-(e)s, -e) m transport;
transportieren vt to transport;
Transportmittel nt means sing of
transport; **Transportunternehmen** nt
haulage firm
Transvestit (-en, -en) m transvestite
trat imperf von **treten**
Traube (-, -n) f (einzelne Beere) grape;
(ganze Frucht) bunch of grapes;
Traubensaft m grape juice;
Traubenzucker m glucose
trauen vi jdm/einer Sache ~ to trust
sb/sth; **ich traute meinen Ohren nicht** I
couldn't believe my ears ▷ vr **sich ~** to
dare ▷ vt to marry; **sich ~ lassen** to get
married
Trauer (-) f sorrow; (für Verstorbenen)
mourning
Traum (-(e)s, Träume) m dream; **träumen**

vt, vi to dream (von of, about); **traumhaft**
adj dreamlike; (fig) wonderful
traurig adj sad (über +akk about)
Trauschein m marriage certificate;
Trauung f wedding ceremony;
Trauzeuge m, **Trauzeugin** f witness (at
wedding ceremony), ≈ best man/maid of
honour
Travellerscheck m traveller's cheque
treffen (traf, getroffen) vr **sich ~** to meet
▷ vt, vi to hit; (Bemerkung) to hurt;
(begegnen) to meet; (Entscheidung) to
make; (Maßnahmen) to take; **Treffen** (-s, -)
nt meeting; **Treffer** (-s, -) m (Tor) goal;
Treffpunkt m meeting place
treiben (trieb, getrieben) vt to drive; (Sport)
to do ▷ vi (im Wasser) to drift; (Pflanzen) to
sprout; (Tee, Kaffee) to be diuretic; **Treiber**
(-s, -) m (Inform) driver
Treibgas nt propellant; **Treibhaus** nt
greenhouse; **Treibstoff** m fuel
trennen vt to separate; (teilen) to divide
▷ vr **sich ~** to separate; **sich von jdm ~** to
leave sb; **sich von etw ~** to part with sth;
Trennung f separation
Treppe (-, -n) f stairs pl; (im Freien) steps pl;
Treppengeländer nt banister;
Treppenhaus nt staircase
Tresen (-s, -) m (in Kneipe) bar; (in Laden)
counter
Tresor (-s, -e) m safe
Tretboot nt pedal boat; **treten** (trat,
getreten) vi to step; **~ nach** to kick at; **mit
jdm in Verbindung ~** to get in contact
with sb ▷ vt to kick; (nieder~) to tread
treu adj (gegenüber Partner) faithful; (Kunde,
Fan) loyal; **Treue** (-) f (eheliche)
faithfulness; (von Kunde, Fan) loyalty
Triathlon (-s, -s) m triathlon
Tribüne (-, -n) f stand; (Rednertribüne)
platform
Trick (-s, -e o -s) m trick; **Trickfilm** m
cartoon
trieb imperf von **treiben**
Trieb (-(e)s, -e) m urge; (Instinkt) drive;
(Neigung) inclination; (an Baum etc) shoot;
Triebwerk nt engine
Trikot (-s, -s) nt shirt, jersey
Trimm-Dich-Pfad m fitness trail
trinkbar adj drinkable; **trinken** (trank,
getrunken) vt, vi to drink; **einen ~ gehen** to
go out for a drink; **Trinkgeld** nt tip;
Trinkhalm m (drinking) straw;

Trinkschokolade f drinking chocolate; **Trinkwasser** nt drinking water

Trio (-s, -s) nt trio

Tripper (-s, -) m gonorrhoea

Tritt (-(e)s, -e) m (Schritt) step; (Fußtritt) kick; **Trittbrett** nt running board

Triumph (-(e)s, -e) m triumph; **triumphieren** vi to triumph (über +akk over)

trivial adj trivial

trocken adj dry; **Trockenhaube** f hair-dryer; **Trockenheit** f dryness; **trocken|legen** vt (Baby) to change; **trocknen** vt, vi to dry; **Trockner** (-s, -) m dryer

Trödel (-s) m (fam) junk; **Trödelmarkt** m flea market

trödeln vi (fam) to dawdle

Trommel (-, -n) f drum; **Trommelfell** nt eardrum; **trommeln** vt, vi to drum

Trompete (-, -n) f trumpet

Tropen pl tropics pl

Tropf (-(e)s, -e) m (Med) drip; **am ~ hängen** to be on a drip; **tröpfeln** vi to drip; **es tröpfelt** it's drizzling; **tropfen** vt, vi to drip; **Tropfen** (-s, -) m drop; **tropfenweise** adv drop by drop; **tropfnass** adj dripping wet; **Tropfsteinhöhle** f stalactite cave

tropisch adj tropical

Trost (-es) m consolation, comfort; **trösten** vt to console, to comfort; **trostlos** adj bleak; (Verhältnisse) wretched; **Trostpreis** m consolation prize

Trottoir (-s, -s) nt pavement (Brit), sidewalk (US)

trotz prep +gen o dat in spite of; **Trotz** (-es) m defiance; **trotzdem** adv nevertheless ▷ conj although; **trotzig** adj defiant

trüb adj dull; (Flüssigkeit, Glas) cloudy; (fig) gloomy

Trüffel (-, -n) f truffle

trug imperf von **tragen**

trügerisch adj deceptive

Truhe (-, -n) f chest

Trümmer pl wreckage sing; (Bau~) ruins pl

Trumpf (-(e)s, Trümpfe) m trump

Trunkenheit f intoxication; **~ am Steuer** drink driving (Brit), drunk driving (US)

Truthahn m turkey

Tscheche (-n, -n) m, **Tschechin** f Czech; **Tschechien** (-s) nt Czech Republic; **tschechisch** adj Czech; **Tschechische**

Republik Czech Republic; **Tschechisch** nt Czech

Tschetschenien (-s) nt Chechnya

tschüs(s) interj bye

T-Shirt (-s, -s) nt T-shirt

Tube (-, -n) f tube

Tuberkulose (-, -n) f tuberculosis, TB

Tuch (-(e)s, Tücher) nt cloth; (Halstuch) scarf; (Kopftuch) headscarf

tüchtig adj competent; (fleißig) efficient; (fam: kräftig) good

Tugend (-, -en) f virtue; **tugendhaft** adj virtuous

Tulpe (-, -n) f tulip

Tumor (-s, -en) m tumour

Tümpel (-s, -) m pond

tun (tat, getan) vt (machen) to do; (legen) to put; **was tust du da?** what are you doing?; **das tut man nicht** you shouldn't do that; **jdm etw ~** (antun) to do sth to sb; **das tut es auch** that'll do ▷ vi to act; **so ~, als ob** to act as if ▷ vr impers **es tut sich etwas/viel** something/a lot is happening

Tuner (-s, -) m tuner

Tunesien (-s) nt Tunisia

Tunfisch m siehe **Thunfisch** tuna

Tunnel (-s, -s o -) m tunnel

Tunte (-, -n) f (pej, fam) fairy

tupfen vt, vi to dab; (mit Farbe) to dot; **Tupfen** (-s, -) m dot

Tür (-, -en) f door; **vor/an der ~** at the door; **an die ~ gehen** to answer the door

Türke (-n, -n) m Turk; **Türkei** (-) f **die ~** Turkey; **Türkin** f Turk

Türkis (-es, -e) m turquoise

türkisch adj Turkish; **Türkisch** nt Turkish

Turm (-(e)s, Türme) m tower; (spitzer Kirchturm) steeple; (Sprung~) diving platform; (Schach) rook, castle

turnen vi to do gymnastics; **Turnen** (-s) nt gymnastics sing; (Schule) physical education, PE; **Turner(in)** m(f) gymnast; **Turnhalle** f gym(nasium); **Turnhose** f gym shorts pl

Turnier (-s, -e) nt tournament

Turnschuh m gym shoe, sneaker (US)

Türschild nt doorplate; **Türschloss** nt lock

tuscheln vt, vi to whisper

Tussi (-, -s) f (pej, fam) chick

Tüte (-, -n) f bag

TÜV (-s, -s) m akr = Technischer Überwachungsverein

TÜV

The **TÜV** is the organization
responsible for checking the safety of
machinery, particularly vehicles. Cars
over three years old have to be
examined every two years for their
safety and for their exhaust
emissions. **TÜV** is also the name
given to the test itself.

TÜV-Plakette *f badge attached to a vehicle's
numberplate, indicating that it has passed the
'TÜV'*
Tweed (-s, -s) *m* tweed
Typ (-s, -en) *m* type; (*Auto*) model; (*Mann*)
guy, bloke
Typhus (-) *m* typhoid
typisch *adj* typical (*für of*); **ein ~er Fehler**
a common mistake; **~ Marcus!** that's just
like Marcus; **~ amerikanisch!** that's so
American

u

u. *abk* = **und**

u. a. *abk* = **und andere(s)** and others; = **unter anderem, unter anderen** among other things

u. A. w. g. *abk* = **um Antwort wird gebeten** RSVP

U-Bahn *f* underground (*Brit*), subway (*US*)

übel *adj* bad; (*moralisch*) wicked; **mir ist ~** I feel sick; **diese Bemerkung hat er mir ~ genommen** he took offence at my remark; **Übelkeit** *f* nausea

üben *vt, vi* to practise

⊙ SCHLÜSSELWORT

über *präp* +dat **1** (*räumlich*) over above; **zwei Grad über null** two degrees above zero

2 (*zeitlich*) over; **über der Arbeit einschlafen** to fall asleep over one's work

▷ *präp* +akk

1 (*räumlich*) over; (*hoch über auch*) above; (*quer über auch*) across

2 (*zeitlich*) over; **über Weihnachten** over Christmas; **über kurz oder lang** sooner or later

3 (*mit Zahlen*): **Kinder über 12 Jahren** children over *od* above 12 years of age; **ein Scheck über 200 Euro** a cheque for 200 euros

4 (*auf dem Wege*) via; **nach Köln über Aachen** to Cologne via Aachen; **ich habe es über die Auskunft erfahren** I found out from information

5 (*betreffend*) about; **ein Buch über ...** a book about *od* on ...; **über jdn/etw lachen** to laugh about *od* at sb/sth

6: **Macht über jdn haben** to have power over sb; **sie liebt ihn über alles** she loves him more than everything

▷ *adv* over; **über und über** over and over; **den ganzen Tag über** all day long; **jdm in etw** *dat* **über sein** to be superior to sb in sth

überall *adv* everywhere

überanstrengen *vr* **sich ~** to overexert oneself

überbacken *adj* (**mit Käse**) **~** au gratin; **überbelichten** *vt* (*Foto*) to overexpose; **überbieten** *irr vt* to outbid; (*übertreffen*) to surpass; (*Rekord*) to break

Überbleibsel (**-s, -**) *nt* remnant

Überblick *m* overview; (*fig: in Darstellung*) survey; (*Fähigkeit zu verstehen*) grasp (**über** +akk **of**)

überbuchen *vt* to overbook; **Überbuchung** *f* overbooking

überdurchschnittlich *adj* above average

übereinander *adv* on top of each other; (*sprechen etc*) about each other

überein|stimmen *vi* to agree (**mit** with)

überempfindlich *adj* hypersensitive

überfahren *irr vt* (*Auto*) to run over; **Überfahrt** *f* crossing

Überfall *m* (*Banküberfall*) robbery; (*Mil*) raid; (*auf jdn*) assault; **überfallen** *irr vt* to attack; (*Bank*) to raid

überfällig *adj* overdue

überfliegen *irr vt* to fly over; (*Buch*) to skim through

Überfluss *m* overabundance, excess (**an** +dat **of**); **überflüssig** *adj* superfluous

überfordern *vt* to demand too much of; (*Kräfte*) to overtax; **da bin ich überfordert** (*bei Antwort*) you've got me there

Überführung *f* (*Brücke*) flyover (*Brit*), overpass (*US*)

überfüllt *adj* overcrowded

Übergabe f handover
Übergang m crossing; (Wandel, Überleitung) transition; **Übergangslösung** f temporary solution, stopgap
übergeben irr vt to hand over ▷ vr **sich ~** to be sick, to vomit
Übergepäck nt excess baggage
Übergewicht nt excess weight; (10 Kilo) **~ haben** to be (10 kilos) overweight
überglücklich adj overjoyed; (fam) over the moon
Übergröße f outsize
überhaupt adv at all; (im Allgemeinen) in general; (besonders) especially; **was willst du ~?** what is it you want?
überheblich adj arrogant
überholen vt to overtake; (Tech) to overhaul; **Überholspur** f overtaking (Brit) (o passing (US)) lane; **überholt** adj outdated
Überholverbot nt **hier herrscht ~** you can't overtake here
überhören vt to miss, not to catch; (absichtlich) to ignore; **überladen** irr vt to overload ▷ adj (fig) cluttered; **überlassen** irr vt **jdm etw ~** to leave sth to sb; **über|laufen** irr vi (Flüssigkeit) to overflow
überleben vt, vi to survive; **Überlebende(r)** mf survivor
überlegen vt to consider; **sich** (dat) **etw ~** to think about sth; **er hat es sich** (dat) **anders überlegt** he's changed his mind ▷ adj superior (dat to); **Überlegung** f consideration
überm kontr von **über dem**
übermäßig adj excessive
übermorgen adv the day after tomorrow
übernächste(r, s) adj **~ Woche** the week after next
übernachten vi to spend the night (bei jdm at sb's place); **übernächtigt** adj bleary-eyed, very tired; **Übernachtung** f overnight stay; **~ mit Frühstück** bed and breakfast
übernehmen irr vt to take on; (Amt, Geschäft) to take over ▷ vr **sich ~** to take on too much
überprüfen vt to check; **Überprüfung** f check; (Überprüfen) checking
überqueren vt to cross
überraschen vt to surprise; **Überraschung** f surprise

überreden vt to persuade; **er hat mich überredet** he talked me into it
überreichen vt to hand over
übers kontr von **über das**
überschätzen vt to overestimate; **überschlagen** irr vt (berechnen) to estimate; (auslassen: Seite) to skip ▷ vr **sich ~** to somersault; (Auto) to overturn; (Stimme) to crack; **überschneiden** irr vr **sich ~** (Linien etc) to intersect; (Termine) to clash
Überschrift f heading
Überschwemmung f flood
Übersee f **nach/in ~** overseas
übersehen irr vt (Gelände) to look (out) over; (nicht beachten) to overlook
übersetzen vt to translate (aus from, in +akk into); **Übersetzer(in)** (-s, -) m(f) translator; **Übersetzung** f translation
Übersicht f overall view; (Darstellung) survey; **übersichtlich** adj clear
überstehen irr vt (durchstehen) to get over; (Winter etc) to get through
Überstunden pl overtime sing
überstürzt adj hasty
überteuert adj overpriced
übertragbar adj transferable; (Med) infectious; **übertragen** irr vt to transfer (auf +akk to); (Radio) to broadcast; (Krankheit) to transmit ▷ vr to spread (auf +akk to) ▷ adj figurative; **Übertragung** f (Radio) broadcast; (von Daten) transmission
übertreffen irr vt to surpass
übertreiben irr vt, vi to exaggerate, to overdo; **Übertreibung** f exaggeration; **übertrieben** adj exaggerated, overdone
überwachen vt to supervise; (Verdächtigen) to keep under surveillance
überwand imperf von **überwinden**
überweisen irr vt to transfer; (Patienten) to refer (an +akk to); **Überweisung** f transfer; (von Patienten) referral
überwiegend adv mainly
überwinden (überwand, überwunden) vt to overcome ▷ vr **sich ~** to make an effort, to force oneself; **überwunden** pp von **überwinden**
Überzelt nt flysheet
überzeugen vt to convince; **Überzeugung** f conviction
überziehen irr vt (bedecken) to cover; (Jacke etc) to put on; (Konto) to overdraw;

die Betten frisch ~ to change the
sheets; **Überziehungskredit** m overdraft
facility
üblich adj usual
übrig adj remaining; **ist noch Saft ~?** is
there any juice left?; **für jdn etwas
~ haben** (fam) to have a soft spot for sb;
die Übrigen pl the rest pl; **im Übrigen**
besides; **~ bleiben** to be left (over); **mir
blieb nichts anderes ~(, als zu gehen)** I
had no other choice (but to go);
übrigens adv besides; (nebenbei bemerkt)
by the way
Übung f practice; (im Sport, Aufgabe etc)
exercise
Ufer (-s, -) nt (Fluss) bank; (Meer, See) shore;
am ~ on the bank/shore
Ufo (-(s), -s) nt akr = **unbekanntes
Flugobjekt** UFO
Uhr (-, -en) f clock; (am Arm) watch; **wie
viel ~ ist es?** what time is it?; **1 ~** 1 o'clock;
20 ~ 8 o'clock, 8 pm; **Uhrzeigersinn** m **im
~** clockwise; **gegen den ~** anticlockwise
(Brit), counterclockwise (US); **Uhrzeit** f
time (of day)
Ukraine (-) f **die ~** the Ukraine
UKW abk = **Ultrakurzwelle** VHF
Ulme (-, -n) f elm
Ultrakurzwelle f very high frequency;
Ultraschallaufnahme f (Med) scan

⊙ SCHLÜSSELWORT

um präp +akk **1** (um herum) (a)round; **um
Weihnachten** around Christmas; **er
schlug um sich** he hit about him
2 (mit Zeitangabe) at; **um acht (Uhr)** at
eight (o'clock)
3 (mit Größenangabe) by; **etw um 4 cm
kürzen** to shorten sth by 4 cm; **um 10%
teurer** 10% more expensive; **um vieles
besser** better by far; **um so besser** so
much the better
4: **der Kampf um den Titel** the battle for
the title; **um Geld spielen** to play for
money; **Stunde um Stunde** hour after
hour; **Auge um Auge** an eye for an eye
▷ präp +gen: **um ... willen** for the sake of
...; **um Gottes willen** for goodness' od
(stärker) God's sake
▷ konj: **um ... zu** (in order) to ...; **zu klug,
um zu ...** too clever to ...; siehe **umso**
▷ adv **1** (ungefähr) about; **um (die) 30**

Leute about od around 30 people
2 (vorbei): **die 2 Stunden sind um** the two
hours are up

umarmen vt to embrace
Umbau m rebuilding; (zu etwas)
conversion (zu into); **um|bauen** vt to
rebuild; (zu etwas) to convert (zu into)
um|blättern vt, vi to turn over
um|bringen irr vt to kill
um|buchen vi to change one's
reservation/flight
um|drehen vt to turn (round); (obere Seite
nach unten) to turn over ▷ vr **sich ~** to turn
(round); **Umdrehung** f turn; (Phys, Auto)
revolution
um|fahren irr vt to knock down
um|fallen irr vi to fall over
Umfang m (Ausmaß) extent; (von Buch)
size; (Reichweite) range; (Math)
circumference; **umfangreich** adj
extensive
Umfeld nt environment
Umfrage f survey
Umgang m company; (mit jdm) dealings
pl; **umgänglich** adj sociable;
Umgangssprache f colloquial language,
slang
Umgebung f surroundings pl; (Milieu)
environment; (Personen) people around one
umgehen irr vi (Gerücht) to go round;
~ (können) mit (know how to) handle
▷ irr vt to avoid; (Schwierigkeit, Verbot) to
get round
um|gehen irr vi **mit etw ~** to handle sth;
Umgehungsstraße f bypass
umgekehrt adj reverse; (gegenteilig)
opposite ▷ adv the other way round; **und
~** and vice versa
um|hören vr **sich ~** to ask around;
um|kehren vi to turn back ▷ vt to
reverse; (Kleidungsstück) to turn inside out;
um|kippen vt to tip over ▷ vi to
overturn; (fig) to change one's mind; (fam:
ohnmächtig werden) to pass out
Umkleidekabine f changing cubicle
(Brit), dressing room (US); **Umkleideraum**
m changing room
Umkreis m neighbourhood; **im ~ von**
within a radius of
um|leiten vt to divert; **Umleitung** f
diversion
um|rechnen vt to convert (in +akk into);

Umrechnung f conversion;
Umrechnungskurs m rate of exchange
Umriss m outline
um|rühren vi, vt to stir
ums kontr von **um das**
Umsatz m turnover
um|schalten vi to turn over
Umschlag m cover; (Buch) jacket; (Med) compress; (Brief) envelope
Umschulung f retraining
um|sehen irr vr **sich ~** to look around; (suchen) to look out (nach for)
umso adv all the; **~ mehr** all the more; **~ besser** so much the better
umsonst adv (vergeblich) in vain; (gratis) for nothing
Umstand m circumstance; **Umstände** (pl) (fig) fuss; **in anderen Umständen sein** to be pregnant; **jdm Umstände machen** to cause sb a lot of trouble; **machen Sie bitte keine Umstände** please, don't put yourself out; **unter diesen/keinen Umständen** under these/no circumstances; **unter Umständen** possibly; **umständlich** adj (Methode) complicated; (Ausdrucksweise) long-winded; (Mensch) ponderous; **Umstandsmode** f maternity wear
um|steigen irr vi to change (trains/buses)
um|stellen vt (an anderen Ort) to change round; (Tech) to convert ▷ vr **sich ~** to adapt (auf +akk to); **Umstellung** f change; (Umgewöhnung) adjustment; (Tech) conversion
Umtausch m exchange; **um|tauschen** vt to change; (Währung) to change
Umweg m detour
Umwelt f environment;
Umweltbelastung f ecological damage;
umweltbewusst adj environmentally aware; **umweltfreundlich** adj environment-friendly; **Umweltpapier** nt recycled paper; **umweltschädlich** adj harmful to the environment;
Umweltschutz m environmental protection; **Umweltschützer(in)** (-s, -) m(f) environmentalist;
Umweltverschmutzung f pollution;
umweltverträglich adj environment-friendly
um|werfen irr vt to knock over; (fig:

ändern) to upset; (fig, fam: jdn) to flabbergast
um|ziehen irr vt to change ▷ vr **sich ~** to change ▷ vi to move (house); **Umzug** m (Straßenumzug) procession; (Wohnungsumzug) move
unabhängig adj independent;
Unabhängigkeitstag m Independence Day, Fourth of July (US)
unabsichtlich adv unintentionally
unangenehm adj unpleasant;
Unannehmlichkeit f inconvenience; **~en** pl trouble sing
unanständig adj indecent;
unappetitlich adj (Essen) unappetizing; (abstoßend) off-putting; **unbeabsichtigt** adj unintentional; **unbedeutend** adj insignificant, unimportant; (Fehler) slight
unbedingt adj unconditional ▷ adv absolutely
unbefriedigend adj unsatisfactory;
unbegrenzt adj unlimited; **unbekannt** adj unknown; **unbeliebt** adj unpopular;
unbemerkt adj unnoticed; **unbequem** adj (Stuhl, Mensch) uncomfortable; (Regelung) inconvenient; **unbeständig** adj (Wetter) unsettled; (Lage) unstable; (Mensch) unreliable; **unbestimmt** adj indefinite; **unbeteiligt** adj (nicht dazugehörig) uninvolved; (innerlich nicht berührt) indifferent, unconcerned;
unbewacht adj unguarded; **unbewusst** adj unconscious; **unbezahlt** adj unpaid;
unbrauchbar adj useless
und conj and; **~ so weiter** and so on; **na ~?** so what?
undankbar adj (Person) ungrateful; (Aufgabe) thankless; **undenkbar** adj inconceivable; **undeutlich** adj indistinct; **undicht** adj leaky; **uneben** adj uneven; **unecht** adj (Schmuck etc) fake; **unehelich** adj (Kind) illegitimate; **unendlich** adj endless; (Math) infinite; **unentbehrlich** adj indispensable; **unentgeltlich** adj free (of charge)
unentschieden adj undecided; **~ enden** (Sport) to end in a draw
unerfreulich adj unpleasant
unerhört adj unheard-of; (Bitte) outrageous; **unerlässlich** adj indispensable; **unerträglich** adj unbearable; **unerwartet** adj unexpected

unerwünscht adj unwelcome; (Eigenschaften) undesirable; **unfähig** adj incompetent; **~ sein, etw zu tun** to be incapable of doing sth; **unfair** adj unfair

Unfall m accident; **Unfallbericht** m accident report; **Unfallflucht** f failure to stop after an accident; **Unfallhergang** m **den ~ schildern** to give details of the accident; **Unfallstation** f casualty ward; **Unfallstelle** f scene of the accident; **Unfallversicherung** f accident insurance

unfreundlich adj unfriendly

Ungarn (-s) nt Hungary

Ungeduld f impatience; **ungeduldig** adj impatient

ungeeignet adj unsuitable

ungefähr adj approximate ▷ adv approximately; **~ 10 Kilometer** about 10 kilometres; **wann ~?** about what time?; **wo ~?** whereabouts?

ungefährlich adj harmless; (sicher) safe

ungeheuer adj huge ▷ adv (fam) enormously; **Ungeheuer** (-s, -) nt monster

ungehorsam adj disobedient (gegenüber to)

ungelegen adj inconvenient; **ungemütlich** adj unpleasant; (Mensch) disagreeable; **ungenießbar** adj inedible; (Getränk) undrinkable; **ungenügend** adj unsatisfactory; (Schulnote) ≈ F; **ungepflegt** adj (Garten) untended; (Aussehen) unkempt; (Hände) neglected; **ungerade** adj odd

ungerecht adj unjust; **ungerechtfertigt** adj unjustified; **Ungerechtigkeit** f injustice, unfairness

ungern adv reluctantly; **ungeschickt** adj clumsy; **ungeschminkt** adj without make-up; **ungesund** adj unhealthy; **ungewiss** adj uncertain; **ungewöhnlich** adj unusual

Ungeziefer (-s) nt vermin pl

ungezogen adj ill-mannered

ungezwungen adj relaxed

ungiftig adj non-toxic

unglaublich adj incredible

Unglück (-(e)s, -e) nt (Unheil) misfortune; (Pech) bad luck; (Unglücksfall) disaster; (Verkehrs~) accident; **das bringt ~** that's unlucky; **unglücklich** adj unhappy; (erfolglos) unlucky; (unerfreulich)

unfortunate; **unglücklicherweise** adv unfortunately

ungültig adj invalid

ungünstig adj inconvenient

unheilbar adj incurable; **~ krank sein** to be terminally ill

unheimlich adj eerie ▷ adv (fam) incredibly

unhöflich adj impolite

uni adj plain

Uni (-, -s) f uni

Uniform (-, -en) f uniform

Universität f university

Unkenntnis f ignorance

unklar adj unclear

Unkosten pl expenses pl; **Unkostenbeitrag** m contribution (towards expenses)

Unkraut nt weeds pl, ~art, weed

unlogisch adj illogical

unmissverständlich adj unambiguous

unmittelbar adj immediate; **~ darauf** immediately afterwards

unmöbliert adj unfurnished

unmöglich adj impossible

unnahbar adj unapproachable

unnötig adj unnecessary

UNO (-) f akr = **United Nations Organization** UN

unordentlich adj untidy; **Unordnung** f disorder

unpassend adj inappropriate; (Zeit) inconvenient; **unpersönlich** adj impersonal; **unpraktisch** adj impractical

Unrecht nt wrong; **zu ~** wrongly; **~ haben, im ~ sein** to be wrong

unregelmäßig adj irregular; **unreif** adj unripe; **unruhig** adj restless; **~ schlafen** to have a bad night

uns pron akk, dat von **wir**; us, (to) us; **~ (selbst)** (reflexiv) ourselves; **sehen Sie ~?** can you see us?; **er schickte es ~** he sent it to us; **lasst ~ in Ruhe** leave us alone; **ein Freund von ~** a friend of ours; **wir haben ~ hingesetzt** we sat down; **wir haben ~ amüsiert** we enjoyed ourselves; **wir mögen ~** we like each other

unscharf adj (Foto) blurred, out of focus

unscheinbar adj insignificant; (Aussehen) unprepossessing

unschlüssig adj undecided

unschuldig adj innocent

unser *pron (adjektivisch)* our ▷ *pron gen von* **wir**; of us; **unsere(r, s)** *pron (substantivisch)* ours; **unseretwegen** *adv (wegen uns)* because of us; *(uns zuliebe)* for our sake; *(um uns)* about us; *(von uns aus)* as far as we are concerned

unseriös *adj* dubious; **unsicher** *adj (ungewiss)* uncertain; *(Person, Job)* insecure

Unsinn *m* nonsense

unsterblich *adj* immortal; **~ verliebt** madly in love

unsympathisch *adj* unpleasant; **er ist mir ~** I don't like him

unten *adv* below; *(im Haus)* downstairs; *(an der Treppe etc)* at the bottom; **nach ~** down; **unter** *prep +akk o dat* under, below; *(bei Menschen)* among; *(während)* during

⊙ SCHLÜSSELWORT

unter *präp +dat* **1** *(räumlich, mit Zahlen)* under; *(drunter)* underneath, below; **unter 18 Jahren** under 18 years
2 *(zwischen)* among(st); **sie waren unter sich** they were by themselves; **einer unter ihnen** one of them; **unter anderem** among other things
▷ *präp +akk* under below

Unterarm *m* forearm
unterbelichtet *adj (Foto)* underexposed
Unterbewusstsein *nt* subconscious
unterbrechen *irr vt* to interrupt; **Unterbrechung** *f* interruption; **ohne ~** nonstop
unterdrücken *vt* to suppress; *(Leute)* to oppress
unterdurchschnittlich *adj* below average
untere(r, s) *adj* lower
untereinander *adv (räumlich)* one below the other; *(gegenseitig)* each other; *(miteinander)* among themselves/yourselves/ourselves
Unterführung *f* underpass
unter|gehen *irr vi* to go down; *(Sonne)* to set; *(Volk)* to perish; *(Welt)* to come to an end; *(im Lärm)* to be drowned out
Untergeschoss *nt* basement; **Untergewicht** *nt* **(3 Kilo) ~ haben** to be (3 kilos) underweight; **Untergrund** *m* foundation; *(Pol)* underground;

Untergrundbahn *f* underground (Brit), subway (US)
unterhalb *adv, prep +gen* below; **~ von** below
Unterhalt *m* maintenance; **unterhalten** *irr vt* to maintain; *(belustigen)* to entertain ▷ *vr* **sich ~** to talk; *(sich belustigen)* to enjoy oneself; **Unterhaltung** *f (Belustigung)* entertainment; *(Gespräch)* talk, conversation
Unterhemd *nt* vest (Brit), undershirt (US); **Unterhose** *f* underpants *pl*; *(für Damen)* briefs *pl*
unterirdisch *adj* underground
Unterkiefer *m* lower jaw
Unterkunft *(-, -künfte)* *f* accommodation
Unterlage *f (Beleg)* document; *(Schreibunterlage)* pad
unterlassen *irr vt* **es ~, etw zu tun** *(versäumen)* to fail to do sth; *(bleiben lassen)* to refrain from doing sth
unterlegen *adj* inferior *(dat* to); *(besiegt)* defeated
Unterleib *m* abdomen
Unterlippe *f* lower lip
Untermiete *f* **zur ~ wohnen** to be a subtenant; **Untermieter(in)** *m(f)* subtenant
unternehmen *irr vt (Reise)* to go on; *(Versuch)* to make; **etwas ~** to do something *(gegen* about); **Unternehmen** *(-s, -)* *nt* undertaking; *(Comm)* company; **Unternehmensberater(in)** *(-s, -)* *m(f)* management consultant; **Unternehmer(in)** *(-s, -)* *m(f)* entrepreneur
Unterricht *(-(e)s, -e)* *m* lessons *pl*; **unterrichten** *vt* to teach
unterschätzen *vt* to underestimate
unterscheiden *irr vt* to distinguish *(von* from, *zwischen +dat* between) ▷ *vr* **sich ~** to differ *(von* from)
Unterschenkel *m* lower leg
Unterschied *(-(e)s, -e)* *m* difference; **im ~ zu dir** unlike you; **unterschiedlich** *adj* different
unterschreiben *irr vt* to sign; **Unterschrift** *f* signature
Untersetzer *(-s, -)* *m* tablemat; *(für Gläser)* coaster
unterste(r, s) *adj* lowest, bottom
unter|stellen *vr* **sich ~** to take shelter
unterstellen *vt (rangmäßig)* to

subordinate (*dat* to); (*fig*) to impute (*jdm etw* sth to sb)
unterstreichen *irr vt* (*a. fig*) to underline
Unterstrich *m* (*Inform*) underscore
unterstützen *vt* to support;
  Unterstützung *f* support
untersuchen *vt* (*Med*) to examine;
  (*Polizei*) to investigate; **Untersuchung** *f*
  examination; (*polizeiliche*) investigation
untertags *adv* during the day
Untertasse *f* saucer
Unterteil *nt* lower part, bottom
Untertitel *m* subtitle
untervermieten *vt* to sublet
Unterwäsche *f* underwear
unterwegs *adv* on the way
unterzeichnen *vt* to sign
untreu *adj* unfaithful
untröstlich *adj* inconsolable; **unüberlegt**
  adj ill-considered ▷ *adv* without thinking;
  unüblich *adj* unusual; **unverantwortlich**
  adj irresponsible; (*unentschuldbar*)
  inexcusable
unverbindlich *adj* not binding; (*Antwort*)
  noncommittal ▷ *adv* (*Comm*) without
  obligation
unverbleit *adj* unleaded; **unverheiratet**
  adj unmarried, single; **unvermeidlich** *adj*
  unavoidable; **unvernünftig** *adj* silly;
  unverschämt *adj* impudent;
  unverständlich *adj* incomprehensible;
  unverträglich *adj* (*Person*) quarrelsome;
  (*Essen*) indigestible
unverwüstlich *adj* indestructible;
  (*Mensch*) irrepressible
unverzeihlich *adj* unpardonable;
  unverzüglich *adj* immediate;
  unvollständig *adj* incomplete;
  unvorsichtig *adj* careless
unwahrscheinlich *adj* improbable,
  unlikely ▷ *adv* (*fam*) incredibly
Unwetter *nt* thunderstorm
unwichtig *adj* unimportant
unwiderstehlich *adj* irresistible
unwillkürlich *adj* involuntary ▷ *adv*
  instinctively; **ich musste ~ lachen** I
  couldn't help laughing
unwohl *adj* unwell, ill
unzählig *adj* innumerable, countless
unzerbrechlich *adj* unbreakable;
  unzertrennlich *adj* inseparable;
  unzufrieden *adj* dissatisfied;
  unzugänglich *adj* inaccessible;

unzumutbar *adj* unacceptable
unzusammenhängend *adj*
  disconnected; (*Äußerung*) incoherent;
  unzutreffend *adj* inapplicable;
  (*unwahr*) incorrect; **unzuverlässig** *adj*
  unreliable
Update (*-s, -s*) *nt* (*Inform*) update
üppig *adj* (*Essen*) lavish; (*Vegetation*) lush
uralt *adj* ancient, very old
Uran (*-s*) *nt* uranium
Uranus (*-*) *m* Uranus
Uraufführung *f* premiere
Urenkel *m* great-grandson; **Urenkelin** *f*
  great-granddaughter; **Urgroßeltern** *pl*
  great-grandparents *pl*; **Urgroßmutter** *f*
  great-grandmother; **Urgroßvater** *m*
  great-grandfather
Urheber(in) (*-s, -*) *m(f)* originator; (*Autor*)
  author
Urin (*-s, -e*) *m* urine; **Urinprobe** *f* urine
  specimen
Urkunde (*-, -n*) *f* document
Urlaub (*-(e)s, -e*) *m* holiday (*Brit*), vacation
  (*US*); **im ~** on holiday (*Brit*), on vacation
  (*US*); **in ~ fahren** to go on holiday (*Brit*)
  (*o vacation* (*US*)); **Urlauber(in)** (*-s, -*) *m(f)*
  holiday-maker (*Brit*), vacationer (*US*);
  Urlaubsort *m* holiday resort; **urlaubsreif**
  adj ready for a holiday (*Brit*) (*o vacation*
  (*US*)); **Urlaubszeit** *f* holiday season (*Brit*),
  vacation period (*US*)
Urne (*-, -n*) *f* urn
Urologe *m*, **Urologin** *f* urologist
Ursache *f* cause (*für* of); **keine ~!** not at
  all; (*bei Entschuldigung*) that's all right
Ursprung *m* origin; (*von Fluss*) source;
  ursprünglich *adj* original ▷ *adv*
  originally; **Ursprungsland** *adj* country of
  origin
Urteil (*-s, -e*) *nt* (*Meinung*) opinion; (*Jur*)
  verdict; (*Strafmaß*) sentence; **urteilen** *vi*
  to judge
Uruguay (*-s*) *nt* Uruguay
Urwald *m* jungle
USA *pl* USA *sing*
User(in) (*-s, -*) *m(f)* (*Inform*) user
usw. *abk* = **und so weiter** etc
Utensilien *pl* utensils *pl*

vage adj vague

Vagina (-, Vaginen) f vagina

vakuumverpackt adj vacuum-packed

Valentinstag m St Valentine's Day

Vandalismus m vandalism

Vanille (-) f vanilla

variieren vt, vi to vary

Vase (-, -n) f vase

Vaseline (-) f Vaseline®

Vater (-s, Väter) m father; **väterlich** adj paternal; **Vaterschaft** f fatherhood; (Jur) paternity; **Vatertag** m Father's Day; **Vaterunser** nt **das ~ (beten)** (to say) the Lord's Prayer

V-Ausschnitt m V-neck

v. Chr. abk = **vor Christus** BC

Veganer(in) (-s, -) m(f) vegan; **Vegetarier(in)** (-s, -) m(f) vegetarian; **vegetarisch** adj vegetarian

Veilchen nt violet

Velo (-s, -s) nt (schweizerisch) bicycle

Vene (-, -n) f vein

Venedig (-s) nt Venice

Venezuela (-s) nt Venezuela

Ventil (-s, -e) nt valve

Ventilator m ventilator

Venus (-) f Venus

Venusmuschel f clam

verabreden vt to arrange ▷ vr **sich ~** to arrange to meet (mit jdm sb); **ich bin schon verabredet** I'm already meeting someone; **Verabredung** f arrangement; (Termin) appointment; (zum Ausgehen) date

verabschieden vt (Gäste) to say goodbye to; (Gesetz) to pass ▷ vr **sich ~** to say goodbye

verachten vt to despise; **verächtlich** adj contemptuous; (verachtenswert) contemptible; **Verachtung** f contempt

verallgemeinern vt to generalize

Veranda (-, Veranden) f veranda, porch (US)

veränderlich adj changeable; **verändern** vt to change ▷ vr **sich ~** to change; **Veränderung** f change

veranlassen vt to cause

veranstalten vt to organize; **Veranstalter(in)** (-s, -) m(f) organizer; **Veranstaltung** f event; **Veranstaltungsort** m venue

verantworten vt to take responsibility for ▷ vr **sich für etw ~** to answer for sth; **verantwortlich** adj responsible (für for); **Verantwortung** f responsibility (für for)

verärgern vt to annoy

verarschen vt (fam) to take the piss out of (Brit), to make a sucker out of (US)

Verb (-s, -en) nt verb

Verband m (Med) bandage; (Bund) association; **Verband(s)kasten** m first-aid box; **Verband(s)zeug** nt dressing material

verbergen irr vt to hide (vor +dat from) ▷ vr **sich ~** to hide (vor +dat from)

verbessern vt to improve; (berichtigen) to correct ▷ vr **sich ~** to improve; (berichtigen) to correct oneself; **Verbesserung** f improvement; (Berichtigung) correction

verbiegen irr vi to bend ▷ vr **sich ~** to bend

verbieten irr vt to forbid; **jdm ~, etw zu tun** to forbid sb to do sth

verbilligt adj reduced

verbinden irr vt to connect; (kombinieren) to combine; (Med) to bandage; **können Sie mich mit ... ~?** (Tel) can you put me through to ...?; **ich verbinde** (Tel) I'm putting you through ▷ vr (Chem) **sich ~** to combine

verbindlich adj binding; (freundlich) friendly; **Verbindung** f connection

verbleit adj leaded

verblüffen vt to amaze

verblühen vi to fade

verborgen adj hidden

Verbot (-(e)s, -e) nt ban (für, von on); **verboten** adj forbidden; **es ist ~** it's not allowed; **es ist ~, hier zu parken** you're not allowed to park here; **Rauchen ~** no smoking

verbrannt adj burnt

Verbrauch (-(e)s) m consumption; **verbrauchen** vt to use up; **Verbraucher(in)** (-s, -) m(f) consumer

Verbrechen (-s, -) nt crime; **Verbrecher(in)** (-s, -) m(f) criminal

verbreiten vt to spread ▷ vr **sich ~** to spread

verbrennen irr vt to burn; **Verbrennung** f burning; (in Motor) combustion

verbringen irr vt to spend

verbunden adj **falsch ~** sorry, wrong number

Verdacht (-(e)s) m suspicion; **verdächtig** adj suspicious; **verdächtigen** vt to suspect

verdammt interj (fam) damn

verdanken vt **jdm etw ~** to owe sth to sb

verdarb imperf von **verderben**

verdauen vt (a. fig) to digest; **verdaulich** adj digestible; **das ist schwer ~** that is hard to digest; **Verdauung** f digestion

Verdeck (-(e)s, -e) nt top

verderben (verdarb, verdorben) vt to spoil; (schädigen) to ruin; (moralisch) to corrupt; **es sich** (dat) **mit jdm ~** to get into sb's bad books; **ich habe mir den Magen verdorben** I've got an upset stomach ▷ vi (Lebensmittel) to go off

verdienen vt to earn; (moralisch) to deserve; **Verdienst** (-(e)s, -e) m earnings pl ▷ (-(e)s, -e) nt merit; (Leistung) service (um to)

verdoppeln vt to double

verdorben pp von **verderben** ▷ adj spoilt; (geschädigt) ruined; (moralisch) corrupt

verdrehen vt to twist; (Augen) to roll; **jdm den Kopf ~** (fig) to turn sb's head

verdünnen vt to dilute

verdunsten vi to evaporate

verdursten vi to die of thirst

verehren vt to admire; (Rel) to worship; **Verehrer(in)** (-s, -) m(f) admirer

Verein (-(e)s, -e) m association; (Klub) club

vereinbar adj compatible

vereinbaren vt to arrange; **Vereinbarung** f agreement, arrangement

vereinigen vt to unite ▷ vr **sich ~** to unite; **Vereinigtes Königreich** nt United Kingdom; **Vereinigte Staaten (von Amerika)** pl United States sing (of America); **Vereinigung** f union; (Verein) association; **Vereinte Nationen** pl United Nations pl

vereisen vi (Straße) to freeze over; (Fenster) to ice up ▷ vt (Med) to freeze

vererben vt **jdm etw ~** to leave sth to sb; (Bio) to pass sth on to sb ▷ vr **sich ~** to be hereditary; **vererblich** adj hereditary

verfahren irr vi to proceed ▷ vr **sich ~** to get lost; **Verfahren** (-s, -) nt procedure; (Tech) method; (Jur) proceedings pl

verfallen irr vi to decline; (Haus) to be falling apart; (Fin) to lapse; (Fahrkarte etc) to expire; **~ in** (+akk) to lapse into; **Verfallsdatum** nt expiry (Brit) (o expiration (US)) date; (von Lebensmitteln) best-before date

verfärben vr **sich ~** to change colour; (Wäsche) to discolour

Verfasser(in) (-s, -) m(f) author, writer; **Verfassung** f (gesundheitlich) condition; (Pol) constitution

verfaulen vi to rot

verfehlen vt to miss

verfeinern vt to refine

Verfilmung f film (o screen) version

verfluchen vt to curse

verfolgen vt to pursue; (Pol) to persecute

verfügbar adj available; **verfügen** vi **über etw** (akk) **~** to have sth at one's disposal; **Verfügung** f order; **jdm zur ~ stehen** to be at sb's disposal; **jdm etw zur ~ stellen** to put sth at sb's disposal

verführen vt to tempt; (sexuell) to seduce; **verführerisch** adj seductive

vergangen adj past; **~e Woche** last week; **Vergangenheit** f past

Vergaser (-s, -) m (Auto) carburettor

vergaß imperf von **vergessen**

vergeben irr vt to forgive (jdm etw sb for sth); (weggeben) to award, to allocate;

vergebens adv in vain; **vergeblich** adv in vain ▷ adj vain, futile
vergehen irr vi to pass ▷ vr **sich an jdm ~** to indecently assault sb; **Vergehen** (-s, -) nt offence
Vergeltung f retaliation
vergessen (vergaß, vergessen) vt to forget; **vergesslich** adj forgetful
vergeuden vt to squander, to waste
vergewaltigen vt to rape; **Vergewaltigung** f rape
vergewissern vr **sich ~** to make sure
vergiften vt to poison; **Vergiftung** f poisoning
Vergissmeinnicht (-(e)s, -e) nt forget-me-not
Vergleich (-(e)s, -e) m comparison; (Jur) settlement; **im ~ zu** compared to (o with); **vergleichen** irr vt to compare (mit to, with)
Vergnügen (-s, -) nt pleasure; **viel ~!** enjoy yourself; **vergnügt** adj cheerful; **Vergnügungspark** m amusement park
vergoldet adj gold-plated
vergriffen adj (Buch) out of print; (Ware) out of stock
vergrößern vt to enlarge; (Menge) to increase; (mit Lupe) to magnify; **Vergrößerung** f enlargement; (Menge) increase; (mit Lupe) magnification; **Vergrößerungsglas** nt magnifying glass
verh. adj abk = **verheiratet** married
verhaften vt to arrest
verhalten irr vr **sich ~** (sich benehmen) to behave; (Sache) to be; **Verhalten** (-s) nt behaviour
Verhältnis nt relationship (zu with); (Math) ratio; **-se** pl circumstances pl, conditions pl; **im ~ von 1 zu 2** in a ratio of 1 to 2; **verhältnismäßig** adj relative ▷ adv relatively
verhandeln vi to negotiate (über etw akk sth); **Verhandlung** f negotiation
verheimlichen vt to keep secret (jdm from sb)
verheiratet adj married
verhindern vt to prevent; **sie ist verhindert** she can't make it
Verhör (-(e)s, -e) nt interrogation; (gerichtlich) examination; **verhören** vt to interrogate; (bei Gericht) to examine ▷ vr **sich ~** to mishear
verhungern vi to starve to death

verhüten vt to prevent; **Verhütung** f prevention; (mit Pille, Kondom etc) contraception; **Verhütungsmittel** nt contraceptive
verirren vr **sich ~** to get lost
Verkauf m sale; **verkaufen** vt to sell; **zu ~** for sale; **Verkäufer(in)** m(f) seller; (beruflich) salesperson; (in Laden) shop assistant (Brit), salesperson (US); **verkäuflich** adj for sale
Verkehr (-s, -e) m traffic; (Sex) intercourse; (Umlauf) circulation; **verkehren** vi (Bus etc) to run; **~ in** to frequent; **~ mit** to associate (o mix) with; **Verkehrsampel** f traffic lights pl; **Verkehrsamt** nt tourist information office; **verkehrsfrei** adj traffic-free; **Verkehrsfunk** m traffic news sing; **Verkehrsinsel** f traffic island; **Verkehrsmeldung** f traffic report; **Verkehrsmittel** nt means sing of transport; **öffentliche ~** pl public transport sing; **Verkehrsschild** nt traffic sign; **Verkehrstote(r)** mf road casualty; **die Zahl der ~n** the number of deaths on the road; **Verkehrsunfall** m road accident; **Verkehrszeichen** nt traffic sign
verkehrt adj wrong; (verkehrt herum) the wrong way round; (Pullover etc) inside out; **du machst es ~** you're doing it wrong
verklagen vt to take to court
verkleiden vt to dress up (als as) ▷ vr **sich ~** to dress up (als as); (um unerkannt zu bleiben) to disguise oneself; **Verkleidung** f (Karneval) fancy dress; (um nicht erkannt zu werden) disguise
verkleinern vt to reduce; (Zimmer, Gebiet etc) to make smaller
verkneifen irr vr **sich** (dat) **etw ~** (Lachen) to stifle sth; (Schmerz) to hide sth; (sich versagen) to do without sth; **verkommen** irr vi to deteriorate; (Mensch) to go downhill ▷ adj (Haus) dilapidated; (moralisch) depraved; **verkraften** vt to cope with
verkratzt adj scratched
verkühlen vr **sich ~** to get a chill
verkürzen vt to shorten
Verlag (-(e)s, -e) m publishing company
verlangen vt (fordern) to demand; (wollen) to want; (Preis) to ask; (Qualifikation) to require; (erwarten) to ask (von of); (fragen

nach) to ask for; (*Pass etc*) to ask to see; **~ Sie Herrn X** ask for Mr X ▷ *vi* **~ nach** to ask for

verlängern *vt* to extend; (*Pass, Erlaubnis*) renew; **Verlängerung** *f* extension; (*Sport*) extra time; (*von Pass, Erlaubnis*) renewal; **Verlängerungsschnur** *f* extension cable; **Verlängerungswoche** *f* extra week

verlassen *irr vt* to leave ▷ *irr vr* **sich ~** to rely (*auf +akk* on) ▷ *adj* desolate; (*Mensch*) abandoned; **verlässlich** *adj* reliable

Verlauf *m* course; **verlaufen** *irr vi* (*Weg, Grenze*) to run (*entlang* along); (*zeitlich*) to pass; (*Farben*) to run ▷ *vr* **sich ~** to get lost; (*Menschenmenge*) to disperse

verlegen *vt* to move; (*verlieren*) to mislay; (*Buch*) to publish ▷ *adj* embarrassed; **Verlegenheit** *f* embarrassment; (*Situation*) difficulty

Verleih (*-(e)s, -e*) *m* (*Firma*) hire company (*Brit*), rental company (*US*); **verleihen** *irr vt* to lend; (*vermieten*) to hire (out) (*Brit*), to rent (out) (*US*); (*Preis, Medaille*) to award

verleiten *vt* **jdn dazu ~, etw zu tun** to induce sb to do sth

verlernen *vt* to forget

verletzen *vt* to injure; (*fig*) to hurt; **Verletzte(r)** *mf* injured person; **Verletzung** *f* injury; (*Verstoß*) violation

verlieben *vr* **sich ~** to fall in love (*in jdn* with sb); **verliebt** *adj* in love

verlieren (*verlor, verloren*) *vt, vi* to lose

verloben *vr* **sich ~** to get engaged (*mit* to); **Verlobte(r)** *mf* fiancé/fiancée; **Verlobung** *f* engagement

verlor *imperf von* **verlieren**

verloren *pp von* **verlieren** ▷ *adj* lost; (*Eier*) poached; **~ gehen** to go missing

verlosen *vt* to raffle; **Verlosung** *f* raffle

Verlust (*-(e)s, -e*) *m* loss

vermehren *vt* to multiply; (*Menge*) to increase ▷ *vr* **sich ~** to multiply; (*Menge*) to increase

vermeiden *irr vt* to avoid

vermeintlich *adj* supposed

vermieten *vt* to rent (out), to let (out) (*Brit*), (*Auto*) to hire (out) (*Brit*), to rent (out) (*US*); **Vermieter(in)** *m(f)* landlord/-lady

vermischen *vt* to mix ▷ *vr* **sich ~** to mix

vermissen *vt* to miss; **vermisst** *adj*

missing; **jdn als ~ melden** to report sb missing

Vermittlung *f* (*bei Streit*) mediation; (*Herbeiführung*) arranging; (*Stelle*) agency

Vermögen (*-s, -*) *nt* fortune

vermuten *vt* to suppose; (*argwöhnen*) to suspect; **vermutlich** *adj* probable ▷ *adv* probably; **Vermutung** *f* supposition; (*Verdacht*) suspicion

vernachlässigen *vt* to neglect

vernichten *vt* to destroy; **vernichtend** *adj* (*fig*) crushing; (*Blick*) withering; (*Kritik*) scathing

Vernunft (*-*) *f* reason; **ich kann ihn nicht zur ~ bringen** I can't make him see reason; **vernünftig** *adj* sensible; (*Preis*) reasonable

veröffentlichen *vt* to publish

verordnen *vt* (*Med*) to prescribe; **Verordnung** *f* order; (*Med*) prescription

verpachten *vt* to lease (out) (*an +akk* to)

verpacken *vt* to pack; (*einwickeln*) to wrap up

Verpackung *f* packaging; **Verpackungskosten** *pl* packing charges *pl*

verpassen *vt* to miss

verpflegen *vt* to feed; **Verpflegung** *f* feeding; (*Kost*) food; (*in Hotel*) board

verpflichten *vt* to oblige; (*anstellen*) to engage ▷ *vr* **sich ~** to commit oneself (*etw zu tun* to doing sth)

verpfuschen *vt* (*fam*) to make a mess of; (*vulg*) to fuck up

verprügeln *vt* to beat up

verraten *irr vt* to betray; (*Geheimnis*) to divulge; **aber nicht ~!** but don't tell anyone ▷ *vr* **sich ~** to give oneself away

verrechnen *vt* **~ mit** to set off against ▷ *vr* **sich ~** to miscalculate; **Verrechnungsscheck** *m* crossed cheque (*Brit*), check for deposit only (*US*)

verregnet *adj* rainy

verreisen *vi* to go away (*nach* to); **sie ist (geschäftlich) verreist** she's away (on business); **verrenken** *vt* to contort; (*Med*) to dislocate; **sich** (*dat*) **den Knöchel ~** to sprain (*o* twist) one's ankle; **verringern** *vt* to reduce

verrostet *adj* rusty

verrückt *adj* mad, crazy; **es macht mich ~** it's driving me mad

versagen vi to fail; **Versagen** (-s) nt
failure; **Versager(in)** (-s, -) m(f) failure
versalzen irr vt to put too much salt in/on
versammeln vt to assemble, to gather
▷ vr **sich ~** to assemble, to gather;
Versammlung f meeting
Versand (-(e)s) m dispatch; (Abteilung)
dispatch department; **Versandhaus** nt
mail-order company
versäumen vt to miss; (unterlassen) to
neglect; **~, etw zu tun** to fail to do sth
verschätzen vr **sich ~** to miscalculate
verschenken vt to give away; (Chance) to
waste
verschicken vt to send off
verschieben vt irr (auf später) to postpone,
to put off; (an anderen Ort) to move
verschieden adj (unterschiedlich)
different; (mehrere) various; **sie sind
~ groß** they are of different sizes;
Verschiedene pl various people/things pl;
Verschiedenes various things pl
verschimmelt adj mouldy
verschlafen irr vt to sleep through; (fig)
to miss ▷ vi to oversleep
verschlechtern vr **sich ~** to deteriorate,
to get worse; **Verschlechterung** f
deterioration
Verschleiß (-es) m wear and tear
verschließbar adj lockable;
verschließen irr vt to close; (mit Schlüssel)
to lock
verschlimmern vt to make worse ▷ vr
sich ~ to get worse
verschlossen adj locked; (fig) reserved
verschlucken vt to swallow ▷ vr **sich
~** to choke (an +dat on)
Verschluss m lock; (von Kleid) fastener;
(Foto) shutter; (Stöpsel) stopper
verschmutzen vt to get dirty; (Umwelt)
to pollute
verschnaufen vi **ich muss mal ~** I need
to get my breath back
verschneit adj snow-covered
verschnupft adj **~ sein** to have a cold;
(fam: beleidigt) to be peeved
verschonen vt to spare (jdn mit etw sb sth)
verschreiben irr vt (Med) to prescribe;
verschreibungspflichtig adj available
only on prescription
verschwand imperf von **verschwinden**
verschweigen irr vt to keep secret; **jdm
etw ~** to keep sth from sb

verschwenden vt to waste;
Verschwendung f waste
verschwiegen adj discreet; (Ort)
secluded
verschwinden (verschwand, verschwunden)
vi to disappear, to vanish; **verschwinde!**
get lost!; **verschwunden** pp von
verschwinden
Versehen (-s, -) nt **aus ~** by mistake;
versehentlich adv by mistake
versenden irr vt to send off
versessen adj **~ auf** (+akk) mad about
versetzen vt to transfer; (verpfänden) to
pawn; (fam: bei Verabredung) to stand up
▷ vr **sich in jdn** (o **jds Lage) ~** to put
oneself in sb's place
verseuchen vt to contaminate
versichern vt to insure; (bestätigen) to
assure; **versichert sein** to be insured;
Versichertenkarte f health-insurance
card; **Versicherung** f insurance;
Versicherungskarte f **grüne ~** green card
(Brit), insurance document for driving abroad;
Versicherungspolice f insurance policy
versilbert adj silver-plated
versinken irr vi to sink
Version f version
versöhnen vt to reconcile ▷ vr **sich ~** to
become reconciled
versorgen vt to provide, to supply (mit
with); (Familie) to look after ▷ vr **sich ~** to
look after oneself; **Versorgung** f
provision; (Unterhalt) maintenance; (für
Alter etc) benefit
verspäten vr **sich ~** to be late; **verspätet**
adj late; **Verspätung** f delay; (eine
Stunde) **~ haben** to be (an hour) late
versprechen irr vt to promise ▷ vr **ich
habe mich versprochen** I didn't mean to
say that
Verstand m mind; (Vernunft) (common)
sense; **den ~ verlieren** to lose one's mind;
verständigen vt to inform ▷ vr **sich ~** to
communicate; (sich einigen) to come to an
understanding; **Verständigung** f
communication; **verständlich** adj
understandable; **Verständnis** nt
understanding (für of); (Mitgefühl)
sympathy; **verständnisvoll** adj
understanding
Verstärker (-s, -) m amplifier
verstauchen vt to sprain
Versteck (-(e)s, -e) nt hiding place;

~ spielen to play hide-and-seek;
verstecken vt to hide (vor +dat from) ⊳ vr
sich **~** to hide (vor +dat from)
verstehen irr vt to understand; **falsch
~** to misunderstand ⊳ vr **sich ~** to get on
(mit with)
Versteigerung f auction
verstellbar adj adjustable; **verstellen** vt
to move; (Uhr) to adjust; (versperren) to
block; (Stimme, Handschrift) to disguise ⊳ vr
sich ~ to pretend, to put on an act
verstopfen vt to block up; (Med) to
constipate; **Verstopfung** f obstruction;
(Med) constipation
Verstoß m infringement, violation (gegen
of)
Versuch (-(e)s, -e) m attempt;
(wissenschaftlich) experiment; **versuchen**
vt to try
vertauschen vt to exchange;
(versehentlich) to mix up
verteidigen vt to defend;
Verteidiger(in) (-s, -) m(f) (Sport)
defender; (Jur) defence counsel;
Verteidigung f defence
verteilen vt to distribute
Vertrag (-(e)s, Verträge) m contract; (Pol)
treaty
vertragen irr vt to stand, to bear ⊳ vr
sich ~ to get along (with each other); (sich
aussöhnen) to make it up
verträglich adj (Mensch) good-natured;
(Speisen) digestible
vertrauen vi jdm/einer Sache **~** to trust
sb/sth; **Vertrauen** (-s) nt trust (in +akk in,
zu in); **ich habe kein ~ zu ihm** I don't trust
him; **ich hab's ihm im ~ gesagt** I told him
in confidence; **vertraulich** adj (geheim)
confidential; **vertraut** adj **sich mit etw
~ machen** to familiarize oneself with
sth
vertreten irr vt to represent; (Ansicht) to
hold; **Vertreter(in)** (-s, -) m(f)
representative
Vertrieb (-(e)s, -e) m (Abteilung) sales
department
vertrocknen vi to dry up
vertun irr vr **sich ~** to make a mistake
vertuschen vt to cover up
verunglücken vi to have an accident;
tödlich ~ to be killed in an accident
verunsichern vt to make uneasy
verursachen vt to cause

verurteilen vt to condemn
vervielfältigen vt to make copies of
verwackeln vt (Foto) to blur
verwählen vr **sich ~** to dial the wrong
number
verwalten vt to manage; (behördlich) to
administer; **Verwalter(in)** (-s, -) m(f)
manager; (Vermögens~) trustee;
Verwaltung f management; (amtlich)
administration
verwandt adj related (mit to);
Verwandte(r) mf relative, relation;
Verwandtschaft f relationship;
(Menschen) relations pl
verwarnen vt to warn; (Sport) to
caution
verwechseln vt to confuse (mit with);
(halten für) to mistake (mit for)
verweigern vt to refuse
verwenden vt to use; (Zeit) to spend;
Mühe auf etw (akk) ~ to take trouble over
sth; **Verwendung** f use
verwirklichen vt to realize; **sich selbst
~** to fulfil oneself
verwirren vt to confuse; **Verwirrung** f
confusion
verwitwet adj widowed
verwöhnen vt to spoil
verwunderlich adj surprising;
Verwunderung f astonishment
verwüsten vt to devastate
verzählen vr **sich ~** to miscount
verzehren vt to consume
Verzeichnis nt (Liste) list; (Katalog) catalogue; (in Buch) index; (Inform) directory
verzeihen (verzieh, verziehen) vt, vi to
forgive (jdm etw sb for sth); **~ Sie bitte, ...**
(vor Frage etc) excuse me, ...; **~ Sie die
Störung** sorry to disturb you; **Verzeihung**
f **~!** sorry; **~, ...** (vor Frage etc) excuse me,
...; **(jdn) um ~ bitten** to apologize (to sb)
verzichten vi **auf etw (akk) ~** to do
without sth; (aufgeben) to give sth up
verzieh imperf von **verzeihen**
verziehen pp von **verzeihen**
verziehen irr vt (Kind) to spoil; **das
Gesicht ~** to pull a face ⊳ vr **sich ~** to go
out of shape; (Gesicht) to contort;
(verschwinden) to disappear
verzieren vt to decorate
verzögern vt to delay ⊳ vr **sich ~** to be
delayed; **Verzögerung** f delay
verzweifeln vi to despair (an +dat of);

verzweifelt adj desperate; **Verzweiflung** f despair

Veterinär(in) (-s, -e) m(f) veterinary surgeon (Brit), veterinarian (US)

Vetter (-s, -n) m cousin

vgl. abk = **vergleiche** cf

Viagra® (-s) nt Viagra®

Vibrator (-s, -en) m vibrator; **vibrieren** vi to vibrate

Video (-s, -s) nt video; **auf ~ aufnehmen** to video; **Videoclip** (-s, -s) m video clip; **Videofilm** m video; **Videogerät** nt video (recorder); **Videokamera** f video camera; **Videokassette** f video (cassette); **Videorekorder** m video recorder; **Videospiel** nt video game; **Videothek** (-, -en) f video library

Vieh (-(e)s) nt cattle

viel pron a lot (of), lots of; **~ Arbeit** a lot of work, lots of work; **~e Leute** a lot of people, lots of people, many people; **zu ~** too much; **zu ~e** too many; **sehr ~** a great deal of; **sehr ~e** a great many; **ziemlich ~/~e** quite a lot of; **nicht ~** not much, not a lot of; **nicht ~e** not many, not a lot of ▷ pron a lot; **sie sagt nicht ~** she doesn't say a lot; **nicht ~** not much, not a lot of; **nicht ~e** not many, not a lot of; **gibt es ~?** is there much?, is there a lot?; **gibt es ~e?** are there many?, are there a lot? ▷ adv a lot; **er geht ~ ins Kino** he goes a lot to the cinema; **sehr ~** a great deal; **ziemlich ~** quite a lot; **~ besser** much better; **~ teurer** much more expensive; **~ zu ~** far too much

vielleicht adv perhaps; **~ ist sie krank** perhaps she's ill, she might be ill; **weißt du ~, wo er ist?** do you know where he is (by any chance)?

vielmal(s) adv many times; **danke ~s** many thanks; **vielmehr** adv rather; **vielseitig** adj very varied; (Mensch, Gerät) versatile

vier num four; **auf allen ~en** on all fours; **unter ~ Augen** in private, privately; **Vier** (-, -en) f four; (Schulnote) ≈ D; **Vierbettzimmer** nt four-bed room; **Viereck** (-(e)s, -e) nt four-sided figure; (Quadrat) square; **viereckig** adj four-sided; (quadratisch) square; **vierfach** adj **die ~e Menge** four times the amount; **vierhundert** num four hundred; **viermal** adv four times; **vierspurig** adj four-lane

viert adv **wir sind zu ~** there are four of us; **vierte(r, s)** adj fourth; siehe auch **dritte**

Viertel (-s, -) nt (Stadtviertel) quarter, district; (Bruchteil) quarter; (Viertelliter) quarter-litre; (Uhrzeit) quarter; **~ vor/nach drei** a quarter to/past three; **viertel drei** a quarter past two; **drei viertel drei** a quarter to three; **Viertelfinale** nt quarter-final; **vierteljährlich** adj quarterly; **Viertelstunde** f quarter of an hour

vierzehn num fourteen; **in ~ Tagen** in two weeks, in a fortnight (Brit); **vierzehntägig** adj two-week, fortnightly (Brit); **vierzehnte(r, s)** adj fourteenth; siehe auch **dritte**; **vierzig** num forty; **vierzigste(r, s)** adj fortieth

Vietnam (-s) nt Vietnam

Vignette f (Autobahn~) motorway (Brit) (o freeway (US)) permit

Villa (-, Villen) f villa

violett adj purple

Violine f violin

Virus (-, Viren) m o nt virus

Visitenkarte f card

Visum (-s, Visa o Visen) nt visa

Vitamin (-s, -e) nt vitamin

Vitrine (-, -n) f (glass) cabinet; (Schaukasten) display case

Vogel (-s, Vögel) m bird; **vögeln** vi, vt (vulg) to screw

Voicemail (-, -s) f voice mail

Vokal (-s, -e) m vowel

Volk (-(e)s, Völker) nt people pl; (Nation) nation; **Volksfest** nt festival; (Jahrmarkt) funfair; **Volkshochschule** f adult education centre; **Volkslied** nt folksong; **Volksmusik** f folk music; **volkstümlich** adj (einfach und beliebt) popular; (herkömmlich) traditional; (Kunst) folk

voll adj full (von of); **~ machen** to fill (up); **~ tanken** to fill up

Vollbart m beard; **Vollbremsung** f **eine ~ machen** to slam on the brakes; **vollends** adv completely

Volleyball m volleyball

Vollgas nt **mit ~** at full throttle; **~ geben** to step on it

völlig adj complete ▷ adv completely

volljährig adj of age; **Vollkaskoversicherung** f fully comprehensive insurance;

vollklimatisiert adj fully air-conditioned; **vollkommen** adj perfect; **~er Unsinn** complete rubbish ▷ adv completely

Vollkornbrot nt wholemeal (Brit) (o whole wheat (US)) bread

Vollmacht (-, -en) f authority; (Urkunde) power of attorney

Vollmilch f full-fat milk (Brit), whole milk (US); **Vollmilchschokolade** f milk chocolate; **Vollmond** m full moon; **Vollnarkose** f general anaesthetic; **Vollpension** f full board

vollständig adj complete

Volltreffer m direct hit; **Vollwaschmittel** nt all-purpose washing powder; **Vollwertkost** f wholefood; **vollzählig** adj complete

Volt (-, -) nt volt

Volumen (-s, -) nt volume

vom kontr von **von dem** (räumlich, zeitlich, Ursache) from; **ich kenne sie nur ~ Sehen** I only know her by sight

○ SCHLÜSSELWORT

von präp +dat **1** (Ausgangspunkt) from; **von ... bis** from ... to; **von morgens bis abends** from morning till night; **von ... nach ...** from ... to ...; **von ... an** from ...; **von ... aus** from ...; **von dort aus** from there; **etw von sich aus tun** to do sth of one's own accord; **von mir aus** (umg) if you like I don't mind; **von wo/wann ...?** where/when ... from?

2 (Ursache, im Passiv) by; **ein Gedicht von Schiller** a poem by Schiller; **von etw müde** tired from sth

3 (als Genitiv) of; **ein Freund von mir** a friend of mine; **nett von dir** nice of you; **jeweils zwei von zehn** two out of every ten

4 (über) about; **er erzählte vom Urlaub** he talked about his holiday

5: **von wegen!** (umg) no way!

○ SCHLÜSSELWORT

vor präp +dat **1** (räumlich) in front of; **vor der Kirche links abbiegen** turn left before the church

2 (zeitlich) before; **ich war vor ihm da** I was there before him; **vor 2 Tagen** 2 days ago; **5 (Minuten) vor 4** 5 (minutes) to 4;
vor kurzem a little while ago

3 (Ursache) with; **vor Wut/Liebe** with rage/love; **vor Hunger sterben** to die of hunger; **vor lauter Arbeit** because of work

4: **vor allem, vor allen Dingen** most of all
▷ präp +akk (räumlich) in front of
▷ adv: **vor und zurück** backwards and forwards

voran|gehen irr vi to go ahead; **einer Sache** (dat) **~** to precede sth; **voran|kommen** irr vi to make progress

Vorarlberg (-s) nt Vorarlberg

voraus adv **jdm ~ sein** to be ahead of sb; **im Voraus** in advance; **voraus|fahren** irr vi to drive on ahead; **vorausgesetzt** conj provided (that); **Voraussage** f prediction; (Wetter) forecast; **voraus|sagen** vt to predict; **voraus|sehen** irr vt to foresee; **voraus|setzen** vt to assume; **Voraussetzung** f requirement, prerequisite; **voraussichtlich** adj expected ▷ adv probably; **voraus|zahlen** vt to pay in advance

Vorbehalt (-(e)s, -e) m reservation; **vor|behalten** irr vt **sich/jdm etw ~** to reserve sth (for oneself)/for sb

vorbei adv past, over, finished; **vorbei|bringen** irr vt to drop by (o in); **vorbei|fahren** irr vi to drive past; **vorbei|gehen** irr vi to pass by, to go past; (verstreichen, aufhören) to pass; **vorbei|kommen** irr vi to drop by; **vorbei|lassen** irr vt **kannst du die Leute ~?** would you let these people pass?; **lässt du mich bitte mal vorbei?** can I get past, please?; **vorbei|reden** vi **aneinander ~** to talk at cross-purposes

vor|bereiten vt to prepare ▷ vr **sich ~** to get ready (auf +akk, für for); **Vorbereitung** f preparation

vor|bestellen vt to book in advance; (Essen) to order in advance; **Vorbestellung** f booking, reservation

vor|beugen vi to prevent (dat sth); **vorbeugend** adj preventive; **Vorbeugung** f prevention

Vorbild nt (role) model; **vorbildlich** adj model, ideal

Vorderachse f front axle; **vordere(r, s)** adj front; **Vordergrund** m foreground; **Vorderradantrieb** m (Auto) front-wheel drive; **Vorderseite** f front; **Vordersitz** m front seat; **Vorderteil** m o nt front (part)

vor|drängen vr **sich ~** to push forward

Vordruck m form

voreilig adj hasty, rash; **~e Schlüsse ziehen** to jump to conclusions; **voreingenommen** adj biased

vor|enthalten irr vt **jdm etw ~** to withhold sth from sb

vorerst adv for the moment

vor|fahren irr vi (vorausfahren) to drive on ahead; **vor das Haus ~** to drive up to the house; **fahren Sie bis zur Ampel vor** drive as far as the traffic lights

Vorfahrt f (Auto) right of way; **~ achten** give way (Brit), yield (US); **Vorfahrtsschild** nt give way (Brit) (o yield (US)) sign; **Vorfahrtsstraße** f major road

Vorfall m incident

vor|führen vt to demonstrate; (Film) to show; (Theaterstück, Trick) to perform

Vorgänger(in) m(f) predecessor

vor|gehen irr vi (vorausgehen) to go on ahead; (nach vorn) to go forward; (handeln) to act, to proceed; (Uhr) to be fast; (Vorrang haben) to take precedence; (passieren) to go on; **Vorgehen** (-s) nt procedure

Vorgesetzte(r) mf superior

vorgestern adv the day before yesterday

vor|haben irr vt to plan; **hast du schon was vor?** have you got anything on?; **ich habe vor, nach Rom zu fahren** I'm planning to go to Rome

vor|halten irr vt **jdm etw ~** to accuse sb of sth

Vorhand f forehand

vorhanden adj existing; (erhältlich) available

Vorhang m curtain

Vorhängeschloss nt padlock

Vorhaut f foreskin

vorher adv before; **zwei Tage ~** two days before; **~ essen wir** we'll eat first; **Vorhersage** f forecast; **vorher|sehen** irr vt to foresee

vorhin adv just now, a moment ago

vorig adj previous; (Woche etc) last

Vorkenntnisse pl previous knowledge sing

vor|kommen irr vi (nach vorne kommen) to come forward; (geschehen) to happen; (sich finden) to occur; (scheinen) to seem (to be); **sich** (dat) **dumm ~** to feel stupid

Vorlage f model

vor|lassen irr vt **jdn ~** to let sb go first

vorläufig adj temporary

vor|lesen irr vt to read out

Vorlesung f lecture

vorletzte(r, s) adj last but one; **am ~n Samstag** (on) the Saturday before last

Vorliebe f preference

vor|machen vt **kannst du es mir ~?** can you show me how to do it?; **jdm etwas ~** (fig: täuschen) to fool sb

vor|merken vt to note down; (Plätze) to book

Vormittag m morning; **am ~** in the morning; **heute ~** this morning; **vormittags** adv in the morning; **um 9 Uhr ~** at 9 (o'clock) in the morning, at 9 am

vorn(e) adv in front; **von ~ anfangen** to start at the beginning; **nach ~** to the front; **weiter ~** further up; **von ~ bis hinten** from beginning to end

Vorname m first name; **wie heißt du mit ~** what's your first name?

vornehm adj (von Rang) distinguished; (Benehmen) refined; (fein, elegant) elegant

vor|nehmen irr vt **sich** (dat) **etw ~** to start on sth; **sich** (dat) **~, etw zu tun** (beschließen) to decide to do sth

vornherein adv **von ~** from the start

Vorort m suburb

vorrangig adj priority

Vorrat m stock, supply; **vorrätig** adj in stock; **Vorratskammer** f pantry

Vorrecht nt privilege

Vorruhestand m early retirement

Vorsaison f early season

Vorsatz m intention; (Jur) intent; **vorsätzlich** adj intentional; (Jur) premeditated

Vorschau f preview; (Film) trailer

Vorschlag m suggestion, proposal; **vorschlagen** irr vt to suggest, to propose; **ich schlage vor, dass wir gehen** I suggest we go

vor|schreiben irr vt (befehlen) to stipulate; **jdm etw ~** to dictate sth to sb

Vorschrift f regulation, rule; (Anweisung) instruction; **vorschriftsmäßig** adj correct

Vorschule f nursery school, pre-school (US)

Vorsicht f care; ~! look out; (Schild) caution; ~ **Stufe!** mind the step; **vorsichtig** adj careful; **vorsichtshalber** adv just in case

Vorsorge f precaution; (Vorbeugung) prevention; **Vorsorgeuntersuchung** f checkup; **vorsorglich** adv as a precaution

Vorspann (-(e)s, -e) m credits pl

Vorspeise f starter

Vorsprung m projection; (Abstand) lead

vor|stellen vt (bekannt machen) to introduce; (Uhr) to put forward; (vor etw) to put in front; **sich** (dat) **etw ~** to imagine sth; **Vorstellung** f (Bekanntmachen) introduction; (Theat) performance; (Gedanke) idea; **Vorstellungsgespräch** nt interview

vor|täuschen vt to feign

Vorteil m advantage (gegenüber over); **die Vor- und Nachteile** the pros and cons; **vorteilhaft** adj advantageous

Vortrag (-(e)s, Vorträge) m talk (über +akk on); (akademisch) lecture; **einen ~ halten** to give a talk

vorüber adv over; **vorüber|gehen** irr vi to pass; **vorübergehend** adj temporary ▷ adv temporarily, for the time being

Vorurteil nt prejudice

Vorverkauf m advance booking

vor|verlegen vt to bring forward

Vorwahl f (Tel) dialling code (Brit), area code (US)

Vorwand (-(e)s, Vorwände) m pretext, excuse; **unter dem ~, dass** with the excuse that

vorwärts adv forward; **~ gehen** (fig) to progress; **Vorwärtsgang** m (Auto) forward gear

vorweg adv in advance; **vorweg|nehmen** irr vt to anticipate

Vorweihnachtszeit f pre-Christmas period, run-up to Christmas (Brit)

vor|werfen irr vt **jdm etw ~** to accuse sb of sth

vorwiegend adv mainly

Vorwort nt preface

Vorwurf m reproach; **sich** (dat) **Vorwürfe machen** to reproach oneself; **jdm**

Vorwürfe machen to accuse sb; **vorwurfsvoll** adj reproachful

vor|zeigen vt to show

vorzeitig adj premature, early

vor|ziehen irr vt (lieber haben) to prefer

Vorzug m preference; (gute Eigenschaft) merit; (Vorteil) advantage

vorzüglich adj excellent

vulgär adj vulgar

Vulkan (-s, -e) m volcano; **Vulkanausbruch** m volcanic eruption

W

W *abk* = **West** W

Waage (-, -n) *f* scales *pl*; (*Astr*) Libra;
waagerecht *adj* horizontal

wach *adj* awake; **~ werden** to wake up;
Wache (-, -n) *f* guard

Wachs (-es, -e) *nt* wax

wachsen (wuchs, gewachsen) *vi* to grow

wachsen *vt* (*Skier*) to wax

Wachstum *nt* growth

Wachtel (-, -n) *f* quail

Wächter(in) (-s, -) *m(f)* guard; (*auf Parkplatz*) attendant

wackelig *adj* wobbly; (*fig*) shaky;
Wackelkontakt *m* loose connection;
wackeln *vi* (*Stuhl*) to be wobbly; (*Zahn, Schraube*) to be loose; **mit dem Kopf ~** to waggle one's head

Wade (-, -n) *f* (*Anat*) calf

Waffe (-, -n) *f* weapon

Waffel (-, -n) *f* waffle; (*Keks, Eiswaffel*) wafer

wagen *vt* to risk; **es ~, etw zu tun** to dare to do sth

Wagen (-s, -) *m* (*Auto*) car; (*Eisenb*) carriage; **Wagenheber** (-s, -) *m* jack;
Wagentyp *m* model, make

Wahl (-, -en) *f* choice; (*Pol*) election

wählen *vt* to choose; (*Tel*) to dial; (*Pol*) to vote for; (*durch Wahl ermitteln*) to elect ▷ *vi* to choose; (*Tel*) to dial; (*Pol*) to vote;
Wähler(in) (-s, -) *m(f)* voter; **wählerisch** *adj* choosy

Wahlkampf *m* election campaign;
wahllos *adv* at random;
Wahlwiederholung *f* redial

Wahnsinn *m* madness; **~!** amazing!;
wahnsinnig *adj* insane, mad ▷ *adv* (*fam*) incredibly

wahr *adj* true; **das darf doch nicht ~ sein!** I don't believe it; **nicht ~?** that's right, isn't it?

während *prep* +*gen* during ▷ *conj* while;
währenddessen *adv* meanwhile, in the meantime

Wahrheit *f* truth

wahrnehmbar *adj* noticeable, perceptible; **wahr|nehmen** *irr vt* to perceive

Wahrsager(in) (-s, -) *m(f)* fortune-teller

wahrscheinlich *adj* probable, likely ▷ *adv* probably; **ich komme ~ zu spät** I'll probably be late; **Wahrscheinlichkeit** *f* probability

Währung *f* currency

Wahrzeichen *nt* symbol

Waise (-, -n) *f* orphan

Wal (-(e)s, -e) *m* whale

Wald (-(e)s, *Wälder*) *m* wood; (*groß*) forest;
Waldbrand *m* forest fire; **Waldlauf** *m* cross-country run; **Waldsterben** (-s) *nt* forest dieback

Wales (-) *nt* Wales; **Waliser(in)** *m(f)* Welshman/Welshwoman; **walisisch** *adj* Welsh; **Walisisch** *nt* Welsh

Walkie-Talkie (-(s), -s) *nt* walkie-talkie

Walkman® (-s, -s) *m* walkman®, personal stereo

Wall (-(e)s, *Wälle*) *m* embankment

Wallfahrt *f* pilgrimage; **Wallfahrtsort** *m* place of pilgrimage

Walnuss *f* walnut

Walross (-es, -e) *nt* walrus

wälzen *vt* to roll; (*Bücher*) to pore over; (*Probleme*) to deliberate on ▷ *vr* **sich ~** to wallow; (*vor Schmerzen*) to roll about; (*im Bett*) to toss and turn

Walzer (-s, -) *m* waltz

Wand (-, *Wände*) *f* wall; (*Trenn~*) partition; (*Berg~*) (rock) face

Wandel (-s) *m* change; **wandeln** *vt* to change ▷ *vr* **sich ~** to change

Wanderer (-s, -) m, **Wanderin** f hiker; **Wanderkarte** f hiking map; **wandern** vi to hike; (Blick) to wander; (Gedanken) to stray; **Wanderschuh** m walking shoe; **Wanderstiefel** m hiking boot; **Wanderung** f hike; **eine ~ machen** to go on a hike; **Wanderweg** m walking (o hiking) trail

Wandleuchte f wall lamp; **Wandmalerei** f mural; **Wandschrank** m built-in cupboard (Brit), closet (US)

wandte imperf von **wenden**

Wange (-, -n) f cheek

wann adv when; **seit ~ ist sie da?** how long has she been here?; **bis ~ bleibt ihr?** how long are you staying?

Wanne (-, -n) f (bath) tub

Wappen (-s, -) nt coat of arms

war imperf von **sein**

warb imperf von **werben**

Ware (-, -n) f product; **~n** goods pl; **Warenhaus** nt department store; **Warenprobe** f sample; **Warensendung** f consignment; **Warenzeichen** nt trademark

warf imperf von **werfen**

warm adj warm; (Essen) hot; **~ laufen** to warm up; **mir ist es zu ~** I'm too warm; **Wärme** (-, -n) f warmth; **wärmen** vt to warm; (Essen) to warm (o to heat) up ▷ vi (Kleidung, Sonne) to be warm ▷ vr **sich ~** to warm up; (gegenseitig) to keep each other warm; **Wärmflasche** f hot-water bottle; **Warmstart** m (Inform) warm start

Warnblinkanlage f (Auto) warning flasher; **Warndreieck** nt (Auto) warning triangle; **warnen** vt to warn (vor +dat about, of); **Warnung** f warning

Warteliste f waiting list; **warten** vi to wait (auf +akk for); **warte mal!** wait (o hang on) a minute ▷ vt (Tech) to service

Wärter(in) m(f) attendant

Wartesaal m, **Wartezimmer** nt waiting room

Wartung f service; (das Warten) servicing

warum adv why

Warze (-, -n) f wart

was pron what; (fam: etwas) something; **~ kostet das?** what does it cost? how much is it?; **~ für ein Auto ist das?** what kind of car is that?; **~ für eine Farbe/Größe?** what colour/size?; **~?** (fam: wie bitte?) what?; **~ ist/gibt's?** what is it?

what's up? **du weißt, ~ ich meine** you know what I mean; **~ (auch) immer** whatever; **soll ich dir ~ mitbringen?** do you want me to bring you anything?; **alles, ~ er hat** everything he's got

Waschanlage f (Auto) car wash; **waschbar** adj washable; **Waschbär** m raccoon; **Waschbecken** nt washbasin

Wäsche (-, -n) f washing; (schmutzig) laundry; (Bettwäsche) linen; (Unterwäsche) underwear; **in der ~** in the wash; **Wäscheklammer** f clothes peg (Brit) (o pin (US)); **Wäscheleine** f clothesline

waschen (wusch, gewaschen) vt, vi to wash; **Waschen und Legen** shampoo and set ▷ vr **sich ~** to (have a) wash; **sich** (dat) **die Haare ~** to wash one's hair

Wäscherei f laundry; **Wäscheschleuder** f spin-drier; **Wäscheständer** m clothes horse; **Wäschetrockner** m tumble-drier

Waschgelegenheit f washing facilities pl; **Waschlappen** m flannel (Brit), washcloth (US); (fam: Mensch) wet blanket; **Waschmaschine** f washing machine; **Waschmittel** nt, **Waschpulver** nt washing powder; **Waschraum** m washroom; **Waschsalon** (-s, -s) m launderette (Brit), laundromat (US); **Waschstraße** f car wash

Wasser (-s, -) nt water; **fließendes ~** running water; **Wasserball** m (Sport) water polo; **Wasserbob** m jet ski; **wasserdicht** adj watertight; (Uhr etc) waterproof; **Wasserfall** m waterfall; **Wasserfarbe** f watercolour; **wasserfest** adj watertight, waterproof; **Wasserhahn** m tap (Brit), faucet (US); **wässerig** adj watery; **Wasserkessel** m kettle; **Wasserkocher** m electric kettle; **Wasserleitung** f water pipe; **wasserlöslich** adj water-soluble; **Wassermann** m (Astr) Aquarius; **Wassermelone** f water melon; **Wasserrutschbahn** f water chute; **Wasserschaden** m water damage; **wasserscheu** adj scared of water; **Wasserski** nt water-skiing; **Wasserspiegel** m surface of the water; (Wasserstand) water level; **Wassersport** m water sports pl; **Wasserspülung** f flush; **wasserundurchlässig** adj watertight, waterproof; **Wasserverbrauch** m water consumption; **Wasserversorgung** f water supply; **Wasserwaage** f spirit level; **Wasserwerk** nt waterworks pl

waten vi to wade

Watt (-(e)s, -en) nt (Geo) mud flats pl ▷ (-s, -) nt (Elek) watt

Watte (-, -n) f cotton wool; **Wattepad** (-s, -s) m cotton pad; **Wattestäbchen** nt cotton bud, Q-tip® (US)

WC (-s, -s) nt toilet, restroom (US); **WC-Reiniger** m toilet cleaner

Web (-s) nt (Inform) Web; **Webseite** f (Inform) web page

Wechsel (-s, -) m change; (Spieler~) (Sport) substitution; **Wechselgeld** nt change; **wechselhaft** adj (Wetter) changeable; **Wechseljahre** pl menopause sing; **Wechselkurs** m exchange rate; **wechseln** vt to change; (Blicke) to exchange; **Geld ~** to change some money; (in Kleingeld) to get some change; **Euro in Pfund ~** to change euros into pounds ▷ vi to change; **kannst du ~?** can you change this?; **Wechselstrom** m alternating current, AC; **Wechselstube** f bureau de change

Weckdienst m wake-up call service; **wecken** vt to wake (up); **Wecker** (-s, -) m alarm clock; **Weckruf** m wake-up call

wedeln vi (Ski) to wedel; **mit etw ~** to wave sth; **mit dem Schwanz ~** to wag its tail; **der Hund wedelte mit dem Schwanz** the dog wagged its tail

weder conj **~ ... noch ...** neither ... nor ...

weg adv (entfernt, verreist) away; (los, ab) off; **er war schon ~** he had already left (o gone); **Hände ~!** hands off!; **weit ~** a long way away (o off)

Weg (-(e)s, -e) m way; (Pfad) path; (Route) route; **jdn nach dem ~ fragen** to ask sb the way; **auf dem ~ sein** to be on the way

weg|bleiben irr vi to stay away; **weg|bringen** irr vt to take away

wegen prep +gen o dat because of

weg|fahren irr vi to drive away; (abfahren) to leave; (in Urlaub) to go away; **Wegfahrsperre** f (Auto) (engine) immobilizer; **weg|gehen** irr vi to go away; **weg|kommen** irr vi to get away; (fig) **gut/schlecht ~** to come off well/badly; **weg|lassen** irr vt to leave out; **weg|laufen** irr vi to run away; **weg|legen** vt to put aside; **weg|machen**

vt (fam) to get rid of; **weg|müssen** irr vi **ich muss weg** I've got to go; **weg|nehmen** irr vt to take away; **weg|räumen** vt to clear away; **weg|rennen** irr vi to run away; **weg|schicken** vt to send away; **weg|schmeißen** irr vt to throw away; **weg|sehen** irr vi to look away; **weg|tun** irr vt to put away

Wegweiser (-s, -) m signpost

weg|werfen irr vt to throw away; **Wegwerfflasche** f non-returnable bottle; **weg|wischen** vt to wipe off; **weg|ziehen** irr vi to move (away)

weh adj sore; siehe auch **wehtun**

wehen vt, vi to blow; (Fahne) to flutter

Wehen pl labour pains pl

Wehrdienst m military service

wehren vr **sich ~** to defend oneself

weh|tun irr vi to hurt; **jdm/sich ~** to hurt sb/oneself

Weibchen nt **es ist ein ~** (Tier) it's a she; **weiblich** adj feminine; (Bio) female

weich adj soft; **~ gekocht** (Ei) soft-boiled

Weichkäse m soft cheese; (Streichkäse) cheese spread; **weichlich** adj soft; (körperlich) weak; **Weichspüler** (-s, -) m (für Wäsche) (fabric) softener

Weide (-, -n) f (Baum) willow; (Grasfläche) meadow

weigern vr **sich ~** to refuse; **Weigerung** f refusal

Weiher (-s, -) m pond

Weihnachten (-, -) nt Christmas; **Weihnachtsabend** m Christmas Eve; **Weihnachtsbaum** m Christmas tree; **Weihnachtsfeier** f Christmas party; **Weihnachtsferien** pl Christmas holidays pl (Brit), Christmas vacation sing (US); **Weihnachtsgeschenk** nt Christmas present; **Weihnachtslied** nt Christmas carol; **Weihnachtsmann** m Father Christmas, Santa (Claus)

Weihnachtsmarkt

The **Weihnachtsmarkt** is a market held in most large towns in Germany in the weeks prior to Christmas. People visit it to buy presents, toys and Christmas decorations, and to enjoy the festive atmosphere. Food and drink associated with the Christmas

- festivities can also be eaten and
- drunk there, for example,
- gingerbread and mulled wine.

Weihnachtsstern m (Bot) poinsettia;
Weihnachtstag m **erster ~** Christmas
Day; **zweiter ~** Boxing Day;
Weihnachtszeit f Christmas season
weil conj because
Weile (-) f while; short time; **es kann
noch eine ~ dauern** it could take some
time
Wein (-(e)s, -e) m wine; (Pflanze) vine;
Weinbeere f grape; **Weinberg** m
vineyard; **Weinbergschnecke** f snail;
Weinbrand m brandy
weinen vt, vi to cry
Weinglas nt wine glass; **Weinkarte** f
wine list; **Weinkeller** m wine cellar;
Weinlese (-, -n) f vintage; **Weinprobe** f
wine tasting; **Weintraube** f grape
weise adj wise
Weise (-, -n) f manner, way; **auf diese
(Art und) ~** this way
weisen (wies, gewiesen) vt to show
Weisheit f wisdom; **Weisheitszahn** m
wisdom tooth
weiß adj white; **Weißbier** nt ≈ wheat
beer; **Weißbrot** nt white bread;
weißhaarig adj white-haired; **Weißkohl**
m, **Weißkraut** nt (white) cabbage;
Weißwein m white wine
weit adj wide; (Begriff) broad; (Reise, Wurf)
long; (Kleid) loose; **wie ~ ist es ...?** how
far is it ...?; **so ~ sein** to be ready ▷ adv
far; **~ verbreitet** widespread; **~ gereist**
widely travelled; **~ offen** wide open; **das
geht zu ~** that's going too far, that's
pushing it
weiter adj wider; (~ weg) farther (away);
(zusätzlich) further; **~e Informationen**
further information sing ▷ adv further; **~!**
go on; (weitergehen!) keep moving;
~ nichts/niemand nothing/nobody else;
und so ~ and so on; **weiter|arbeiten** vi to
carry on working; **Weiterbildung** f
further training (o education);
weiter|empfehlen irr vt to recommend;
weiter|erzählen vt **nicht ~!** don't tell
anyone; **weiter|fahren** irr vi to go on
(nach to, bis as far as); **weiter|geben** irr vt
to pass on; **weiter|gehen** irr vi to go on;
weiter|helfen irr vi jdm **~** to help sb;

weiterhin adv etw **~ tun** to go on doing
sth; **weiter|machen** vt, vi to continue;
weiter|reisen vi to continue one's
journey
weitgehend adj considerable ▷ adv
largely; **weitsichtig** adj long-sighted; (fig)
far-sighted; **Weitspringer(in)** m(f) long
jumper; **Weitsprung** m long jump;
Weitwinkelobjektiv nt (Foto) wide-angle
lens
Weizen (-s, -) m wheat; **Weizenbier** nt ≈
wheat beer

○ **SCHLÜSSELWORT**

welche(r, s) interrogativ pron which;
welcher von beiden? which (one) of the
two?; **welchen hast du genommen?**
which (one) did you take?; **welche eine
...!** what a ...!; **welche Freude!** what joy!
▷ indef pron some; (in Fragen) any; **ich habe
welche** I have some, **haben Sie welche?**
do you have any?
▷ relativ pron (bei Menschen) who (bei Sachen)
which that; **welche(r, s) auch immer**
whoever/whichever/whatever

welk adj withered; **welken** vi to wither
Welle (-, -n) f wave; **Wellengang** m
waves pl; **starker ~** heavy seas pl;
Wellenlänge f (a. fig) wavelength;
Wellenreiten nt surfing; **Wellensittich**
(-s, -e) m budgerigar, budgie; **wellig** adj
wavy
Welpe (-n, -n) m puppy
Welt (-, -en) f world; **auf der ~** in the
world; **auf die ~ kommen** to be born;
Weltall nt universe; **weltbekannt**,
weltberühmt adj world-famous;
Weltkrieg m world war; **Weltmacht** f
world power; **Weltmeister(in)** m(f)
world champion; **Weltmeisterschaft** f
world championship; (im Fußball) World
Cup; **Weltraum** m space; **Weltreise** f
trip round the world; **Weltrekord** m
world record; **Weltstadt** f metropolis;
weltweit adj worldwide, global
wem pron dat von **wer** who ... to, (to)
whom; **~ hast du's gegeben?** who did you
give it to?; **~ gehört es?** who does it
belong to?, whose is it?; **~ auch immer es
gehört** whoever it belongs to
wen pron akk von **wer** who, whom; **~ hast**

du besucht? who did you visit?;
~ möchten Sie sprechen? who would you
like to speak to?; **~ auch immer du
gesprochen hast** whoever you talked
to
Wende (-, -n) f turning point;
(*Veränderung*) change; **die ~** (*Hist*) the fall
of the Berlin Wall; **Wendekreis** m (*Auto*)
turning circle
Wendeltreppe f spiral staircase
wenden (*wendete o wandte, gewendet o
gewandt*) vt, vi to turn (round); (*um 180°*)
to make a U-turn; **sich an jdn ~** to turn
to sb; **bitte ~!** please turn over, PTO
▷ vr **sich ~** to turn; **sich an jdn ~** to turn
to sb
wenig pron, adv little; **~(e)** pl few; **(nur) ein
(klein) ~** (just) a little (bit); **ein ~ Zucker** a
little bit of sugar, a little sugar; **wir haben
~ Zeit** we haven't got much time; **zu ~** too
little; pl too few; **nur ~ wissen** only a few
know ▷ adv **er spricht ~** he doesn't talk
much; **~ bekannt** little known; **wenige**
pron pl few pl; **wenigste(r, s)** adj least;
wenigstens adv at least

wenn konj **1** (*falls, bei Wünschen*) if; **wenn
auch ..., selbst wenn ...** even if ...; **wenn
ich doch ...** if only I ...
2 (*zeitlich*) when; **immer wenn** whenever

wer pron who; **~ war das?** who was that?;
~ von euch? which (one) of you? ▷ pron
**~ das glaubt,
ist dumm** anyone who believes that is
stupid; **~ auch immer** whoever ▷ pron
somebody, someone; (*in Fragen*)
anybody, anyone; **ist da ~?** is (there)
anybody there?
Werbefernsehen nt TV commercials pl;
Werbegeschenk nt promotional gift;
werben (*warb, geworben*) vt to win;
(*Mitglied*) to recruit ▷ vi to advertise;
Werbespot (-s, -s) m commercial;
Werbung f advertising

werden (pt **wurde**, pp **geworden** od (*bei
Passiv*) **worden**) vi to become; **was ist aus
ihm/aus der Sache geworden?** what

became of him/it?; **es ist nichts/gut
geworden** it came to nothing/turned out
well; **es wird Nacht/Tag** it's getting
dark/light; **mir wird kalt** I'm getting cold;
mir wird schlecht I feel ill; **Erster werden**
to come od be first; **das muss anders
werden** that'll have to change; **rot/zu Eis
werden** to turn red/to ice; **was willst du
(mal) werden?** what do you want to be?;
die Fotos sind gut geworden the photos
have come out nicely
▷ als Hilfsverb **1** (*bei Futur*): **er wird es tun**
he will od he'll do it; **er wird das nicht tun**
he will not od he won't do it; **es wird
gleich regnen** it's going to rain
2 (*bei Konjunktiv*): **ich würde ...** I would ...;
er würde gern ... he would od he'd like to
...; **ich würde lieber ...** I would od I'd
rather ...
3 (*bei Vermutung*): **sie wird in der Küche
sein** she will be in the kitchen
4 (*bei Passiv*): **gebraucht werden** to be
used; **er ist erschossen worden** he has od
he's been shot; **mir wurde gesagt, dass
...** I was told that ...

werfen (*warf, geworfen*) vt to throw
Werft (-, -en) f shipyard, dockyard
Werk (-(e)s, -e) nt (*Kunstwerk, Buch etc*)
work; (*Fabrik*) factory; (*Mechanismus*)
works pl; **Werkstatt** (-, -stätten) f
workshop; (*Auto*) garage; **Werktag** m
working day; **werktags** adv on weekdays,
during the week; **Werkzeug** nt tool;
Werkzeugkasten m toolbox
wert adj worth; **es ist etwa 50 Euro ~** it's
worth about 50 euros; **das ist nichts ~** it's
worthless; **Wert** (-(e)s, -e) m worth;
(*Zahlen~*) (*Fin*) value; **~ legen auf** (+akk) to
attach importance to; **es hat doch
keinen ~** (*Sinn*) it's pointless; **Wertangabe**
f declaration of value; **Wertbrief** m
insured letter; **Wertgegenstand** m
valuable object; **wertlos** adj worthless;
Wertmarke f token; **Wertpapiere** pl
securities pl; **Wertsachen** pl valuables pl;
Wertstoff m recyclable waste; **wertvoll**
adj valuable
Wesen (-s, -) nt being; (*Natur, Charakter*)
nature
wesentlich adj significant; (*beträchtlich*)
considerable ▷ adv considerably
weshalb adv why

Wespe (-, -n) f wasp; **Wespenstich** m wasp sting

wessen pron gen von **wer**; whose

> **Wessi**
>
> A **Wessi** is a colloquial and often derogatory word used to describe a German from the former West Germany. The expression 'Besserwessi' is used by East Germans to describe a West German who is considered to be a know-all.

West west; **Westdeutschland** nt (als Landesteil) Western Germany; (Hist) West Germany
Weste (-, -n) f waistcoat (Brit), vest (US); (Wollweste) cardigan
Westen (-s) m west; **im ~ Englands** in the west of England; **der Wilde ~** the Wild West; **Westeuropa** nt Western Europe; **Westküste** f west coast; **westlich** adj western; (Kurs, Richtung) westerly; **Westwind** m west(erly) wind
weswegen adv why
Wettbewerb m competition; **Wettbüro** nt betting office; **Wette** (-, -n) f bet; **eine ~ abschließen** to make a bet; **die ~ gilt!** you're on; **wetten** vt, vi to bet (auf+akk on); **ich habe mit ihm gewettet, dass ...** I bet him that ...; **ich wette mit dir um 50 Euro** I'll bet you 50 euros; **~, dass?** wanna bet?
Wetter (-s, -) nt weather; **Wetterbericht** m, **Wettervorhersage** f weather forecast; **Wetterkarte** f weather map; **Wetterlage** f weather situation; **Wettervorhersage** f weather forecast
Wettkampf m contest; **Wettlauf** m race; **Wettrennen** nt race
WG (-, -s) f abk = **Wohngemeinschaft**
Whirlpool® (-s, -s) m jacuzzi®
Whisky (-s, -s) m (schottisch) whisky; (irisch, amerikanisch) whiskey
wichtig adj important
wickeln vt (Schnur) to wind (um round); (Schal, Decke) to wrap (um round); **ein Baby ~** to change a baby's nappy (Brit) (o diaper (US)); **Wickelraum** m baby-changing room; **Wickeltisch** m baby-changing table
Widder (-s, -) m (Zool) ram; (Astr) Aries sing

wider prep +akk against
widerlich adj disgusting
widerrufen irr vt to withdraw; (Auftrag, Befehl etc) to cancel
widersprechen irr vi to contradict (jdm sb); **Widerspruch** m contradiction
Widerstand m resistance; **widerstandsfähig** adj resistant (gegen to)
widerwärtig adj disgusting
widerwillig adj unwilling, reluctant
widmen vt to dedicate ▷ vr **sich jdm/etw ~** to devote oneself to sb/sth; **Widmung** f dedication

🔵 SCHLÜSSELWORT

wie adv how; **wie groß/schnell?** how big/fast?; **wie wärs?** how about it?; **wie ist er?** what's he like?; **wie gut du das kannst!** you're very good at it; **wie bitte?** pardon?; (entrüstet) I beg your pardon!; **und wie!** and how!; **wie viel** how much; **wie viel Menschen** how many people; **wie weit** to what extent
▷ konj **1** (bei Vergleichen); **so schön wie ...** as beautiful as ...; **wie ich schon sagte** as I said; **wie du** like you; **singen wie ein ...** to sing like a ...; **wie (zum Beispiel)** such as (for example)
2 (zeitlich): **wie er das hörte, ging er** when he heard that he left; **er hörte, wie der Regen fiel** he heard the rain falling

wieder adv again; **~ ein(e) ...** another ...; **~ erkennen** to recognize; **etw ~ gutmachen** to make up for sth; **~ verwerten** to recycle
wieder|bekommen irr vt to get back
wiederholen vt to repeat; **Wiederholung** f repetition
Wiederhören nt (Tel) **auf ~** goodbye
wieder|kommen irr vi to come back
wieder|sehen irr vt to see again; (wieder treffen) to meet again; **Wiedersehen** (-s) nt reunion; **auf ~!** goodbye
Wiedervereinigung f reunification
Wiege (-, -n) f cradle; **wiegen** (wog, gewogen) vt, vi (Gewicht) to weigh
Wien (-s) nt Vienna
wies imperf von **weisen**
Wiese (-, -n) f meadow
Wiesel (-s, -) nt weasel
wieso adv why

wievielmal adv how often; **wievielte(r, s)** adj **zum ~n Mal?** how many times?; **den Wievielten haben wir heute?** what's the date today?; **am Wievielten hast du Geburtstag?** which day is your birthday?

wieweit conj to what extent

wild adj wild

Wild (-(e)s) nt game

wildfremd adj (fam) **ein ~er Mensch** a complete (o total) stranger; **Wildleder** nt suede; **Wildpark** m game park; **Wildschwein** nt (wild) boar; **Wildwasserfahren** (-s) nt whitewater canoeing (o rafting)

Wille (-ns, -n) m will

willen prep +gen **um ... ~** for the sake of ...; **um Himmels ~!** (vorwurfsvoll) for heaven's sake; (betroffen) goodness me

willkommen adj welcome

Wimper (-, -n) f eyelash; **Wimperntusche** f mascara

Wind (-(e)s, -e) m wind

Windei (-, -n) f nappy (Brit), diaper (US)

windgeschützt adj sheltered from the wind; **windig** adj windy; (fig) dubious; **Windjacke** f windcheater; **Windmühle** f windmill; **Windpocken** pl chickenpox sing; **Windschutzscheibe** f (Auto) windscreen (Brit), windshield (US); **Windstärke** f wind force; **Windsurfen** (-s) nt windsurfing; **Windsurfer(in)** m(f) windsurfer

Winkel (-s, -) m (Math) angle; (Gerät) set square; (in Raum) corner; **im rechten ~ zu** at right angles to

winken vt, vi to wave

Winter (-s, -) m winter; **Winterausrüstung** f (Auto) winter equipment; **Winterfahrplan** m winter timetable; **winterlich** adj wintry; **Wintermantel** m winter coat; **Winterreifen** m winter tyre; **Winterschlussverkauf** m winter sales pl; **Wintersport** m winter sports pl

Winterzeit f (Uhrzeit) winter time (Brit), standard time (US)

winzig adj tiny

wir pron we; **~ selbst** we ourselves; **~ alle** all of us; **~ drei** the three of us; **~ sind's** it's us; **~ nicht** not us

Wirbel (-s, -) m whirl; (Trubel) hurly-burly; (Aufsehen) fuss; (Anat) vertebra; **Wirbelsäule** f spine

wirken vi to be effective; (erfolgreich sein) to work; (scheinen) to seem

wirklich adj real; **Wirklichkeit** f reality

wirksam adj effective; **Wirkung** f effect

wirr adj confused; **Wirrwarr** (-s) m confusion

Wirsing (-s) m savoy cabbage

Wirt (-(e)s, -e) m landlord; **Wirtin** f landlady

Wirtschaft f (Comm) economy; (Gaststätte) pub; **wirtschaftlich** adj (Pol, Comm) economic; (sparsam) economical

Wirtshaus nt pub

wischen vt, vi to wipe; **Wischer** (-s, -) m wiper; **Wischlappen** m cloth

wissen (wusste, gewusst) vt to know; **weißt du schon, ...?** did you know ...?; **woher weißt du das?** how do you know?; **das musst du selbst ~** that's up to you; **Wissen** (-s) nt knowledge

Wissenschaft f science; **Wissenschaftler(in)** (-s, -) m(f) scientist; (Geisteswissenschaftler) academic; **wissenschaftlich** adj scientific; (geisteswissenschaftlich) academic

Witwe (-, -n) f widow; **Witwer** (-s, -) m widower

Witz (-(e)s, -e) m joke; **mach keine ~e!** you're kidding!; **das soll wohl ein ~ sein** you've got to be joking; **witzig** adj funny

wo adv where; **zu einer Zeit, ~ ...** at a time when ...; **überall, ~ ich hingehe** wherever I go ▷ conj **jetzt, ~ du da bist** now that you're here; **~ ich dich gerade spreche** while I'm talking to you; **woanders** adv somewhere else

wobei adv **~ mir einfällt ...** which reminds me ...

Woche (-, -n) f week; **während** (o **unter**) **der ~** during the week; **einmal die ~** once a week; **Wochenende** nt weekend; **am ~ at** (Brit) (o **on** (US)) the weekend; **wir fahren übers ~ weg** we're going away for the weekend; **Wochenendhaus** nt weekend cottage; **Wochenkarte** f weekly (season) ticket; **wochenlang** adv for weeks (on end); **Wochenmarkt** m weekly market; **Wochentag** m weekday; **wöchentlich** adj, adv weekly

Wodka (-s, -s) m vodka

wodurch adv **~ unterscheiden sie sich?** what's the difference between them?;

~ hast du es gemerkt? how did you notice?; **wofür** adv (relativ) for which; (Frage) what ... for; **~ brauchst du das?** what do you need that for?

wog imperf von **wiegen**

woher adv where ... from; **wohin** adv where ... to

○ SCHLÜSSELWORT

wohl adv **1**: **sich wohl fühlen** (zufrieden) to feel happy; (gesundheitlich) to feel well; **jdm wohl tun** to do sb good; **wohl oder übel** whether one likes it or not

2 (wahrscheinlich) probably; (gewiss) certainly; (vielleicht) perhaps; **sie ist wohl zu Hause** she's probably at home; **das ist doch wohl nicht dein Ernst!** surely you're not serious!; **das mag wohl sein** that may well be; **ob das wohl stimmt?** I wonder if that's true; **er weiß das sehr wohl** he knows that perfectly well

Wohlwollen (-s) nt goodwill

Wohnblock m block of flats (Brit), apartment house (US); **wohnen** vi to live; **Wohngemeinschaft** f shared flat (Brit) (o apartment (US)); **ich wohne in einer ~** I share a flat (o apartment); **wohnhaft** adj resident; **Wohnküche** f kitchen-cum-living-room; **Wohnmobil** (-s, -e) nt camper, RV (US); **Wohnort** m place of residence; **Wohnsitz** m place of residence; **Wohnung** f flat (Brit), apartment (US); **Wohnungstür** f front door; **Wohnwagen** m caravan; **Wohnzimmer** nt living room

Wolf (-(e)s, **Wölfe**) m wolf

Wolke (-, -n) f cloud; **Wolkenkratzer** m skyscraper; **wolkenlos** adj cloudless; **wolkig** adj cloudy

Wolldecke f (woollen) blanket; **Wolle** (-, -n) f wool

○ SCHLÜSSELWORT

wollen (pt **wollte**, pp **gewollt** od (als Hilfsverb) **wollen**) vt, vi to want; **ich will nach Hause** I want to go home; **er will nicht** he doesn't want to; **er wollte das nicht** he didn't want it; **wenn du willst** if you like; **ich will, dass du mir zuhörst** I want you to listen to me

▷ Hilfsverb: **er will ein Haus kaufen** he wants to buy a house; **ich wollte, ich wäre ...** I wish I were ...; **etw gerade tun wollen** to be going to do sth

Wolljacke f cardigan

womit adv what ... with; **~ habe ich das verdient?** what have I done to deserve that?

womöglich adv possibly

woran adv **~ denkst du?** what are you thinking of?; **~ ist er gestorben?** what did he die of?; **~ sieht man das?** how can you tell?

worauf adv **~ wartest du?** what are you waiting for?

woraus adv **~ ist das gemacht?** what is it made of?

Workshop (-s, -s) m workshop

World Wide Web nt World Wide Web

Wort (-(e)s, **Wörter**) nt (Vokabel) word ▷ (-(e)s, -e) nt (Äußerung) word; **mit anderen ~en** in other words; **jdn beim ~ nehmen** to take sb at his/her word; **Wörterbuch** nt dictionary; **wörtlich** adj literal

worüber adv **~ redet sie?** what is she talking about?

worum adv **~ gehts?** what is it about?

worunter adv **~ leidet er?** what is he suffering from?

wovon adv (relativ) from which; **~ redest du?** what are you talking about?; **wozu** adv (relativ) to/for which; (interrogativ) what ... for/to; (warum) why; **~?** what for?; **~ brauchst du das?** what do you need it for?; **~ soll das gut sein?** what's it for?; **~ hast du Lust?** what do you feel like doing?

Wrack (-(e)s, -s) nt wreck

Wucher (-s) m profiteering; **das ist ~!** that's daylight robbery!

wuchs imperf von **wachsen**

wühlen vi to rummage; (Tier) to root; (Maulwurf) to burrow

Wühltisch m bargain counter

wund adj sore; **Wunde** (-, -n) f wound

Wunder (-s, -) nt miracle; **es ist kein ~** it's no wonder; **wunderbar** adj wonderful, marvellous; **Wunderkerze** f sparkler; **Wundermittel** nt wonder cure; **wundern** vr **sich ~** to be surprised (über +akk at) ▷ vt

to surprise; **wunderschön** adj beautiful;
wundervoll adj wonderful

Wundsalbe f antiseptic ointment;
Wundstarrkrampf m tetanus

Wunsch (-(e)s, Wünsche) m wish (nach for);
wünschen vt to wish; **sich** (dat) **etw ~** to
want sth; **ich wünsche dir alles Gute** I
wish you all the best; **wünschenswert**
adj desirable

wurde imperf von **werden**

Wurf (-s, Würfe) m throw; (Zool) litter

Würfel (-s, -) m dice; (Math) cube;
würfeln vi to throw (the dice); (Würfel
spielen) to play dice ▷ vt (Zahl) to throw;
(Gastr) to dice; **Würfelzucker** m lump
sugar

Wurm (-(e)s, Würmer) m worm

Wurst (-, Würste) f sausage; **das ist mir
~** (fam) I couldn't care less

Würstchen nt frankfurter

Würze (-, -n) f seasoning, spice

Wurzel (-, -n) f root

würzen vt to season, to spice; **würzig** adj
spicy

wusch imperf von **waschen**

wusste imperf von **wissen**

wüst adj (unordentlich) chaotic;
(ausschweifend) wild; (öde) desolate; (fam:
heftig) terrible

Wüste (-, -n) f desert

Wut (-) f rage, fury; **ich habe eine ~ auf
ihn** I'm really mad at him; **wütend** adj
furious

WWW (-) nt abk = **World Wide Web**
WWW

X-Beine *pl* knock-knees *pl*; **x-beinig** *adj*
knock-kneed
x-beliebig *adj* **ein ~es Buch** any book
(you like)
x-mal *adv* umpteen times
Xylophon (-s, -e) *nt* xylophone

Yacht *(-, -en)* f yacht
Yoga *(-(s))* m o nt yoga
Yuppie *(-s, -s)* m *(-, -s)* f yuppie

Zacke (-, -n) f point; (*Säge, Kamm*) tooth; (*Gabel*) prong; **zackig** adj (*Linie etc*) jagged; (*fam: Tempo*) brisk

zaghaft adj timid

zäh adj tough; (*Flüssigkeit*) thick

Zahl (-, -en) f number; **zahlbar** adj payable; **zahlen** vt, vi to pay; **~ bitte!** could I have the bill (*Brit*) (*o* check (*US*)) please?; **bar ~** to pay cash; **zählen** vt, vi to count (*auf+akk* on); **~ zu** to be one of; **Zahlenschloss** nt combination lock; **Zähler** (-s, -) m (*Gerät*) counter; (*für Strom, Wasser*) meter; **zahlreich** adj numerous; **Zahlung** f payment; **Zahlungsanweisung** f money order; **Zahlungsbedingungen** pl terms pl of payment

zahm adj tame; **zähmen** vt to tame

Zahn (-(e)s, Zähne) m tooth; **Zahnarzt** m, **Zahnärztin** f dentist; **Zahnbürste** f toothbrush; **Zahncreme** f toothpaste; **Zahnersatz** m dentures pl; **Zahnfleisch** nt gums pl; **Zahnfleischbluten** nt bleeding gums pl; **Zahnfüllung** f filling; **Zahnklammer** f brace; **Zahnpasta** f, **Zahnpaste** f toothpaste; **Zahnradbahn** f rack railway (*Brit*) (*o* railroad (*US*));

Zahnschmerzen pl toothache sing; **Zahnseide** f dental floss; **Zahnspange** f brace; **Zahnstocher** (-s, -) m toothpick

Zange (-, -n) f pliers pl; (*Zuckerzange*) tongs pl; (*Beißzange, Zool*) pincers pl; (*Med*) forceps pl

zanken vi to quarrel ▷ vr **sich ~** to quarrel

Zäpfchen nt (*Anat*) uvula; (*Med*) suppository

zapfen vt (*Bier*) to pull; **Zapfsäule** f petrol (*Brit*) (*o* gas (*US*)) pump

zappeln vi to wriggle; (*unruhig sein*) to fidget

zappen vi to zap, to channel-hop

zart adj (*weich, leise*) soft; (*Braten etc*) tender; (*fein, schwächlich*) delicate; **zartbitter** adj (*Schokolade*) plain, dark

zärtlich adj tender, affectionate; **Zärtlichkeit** f tenderness; **~en** pl hugs and kisses pl

Zauber (-s, -) m magic; (*Bann*) spell; **Zauberei** f magic; **Zauberer** (-s, -) m magician; (*Künstler*) conjuror; **Zauberformel** f (magic) spell; **zauberhaft** adj enchanting; **Zauberin** f sorceress; **Zauberkünstler(in)** m(f) magician, conjuror; **Zaubermittel** nt magic cure; **zaubern** vi to do magic; (*Künstler*) to do conjuring tricks; **Zauberspruch** m (magic) spell

Zaun (-(e)s, Zäune) m fence

z. B. abk = **zum Beispiel** e.g., eg

Zebra (-s, -s) nt zebra; **Zebrastreifen** m zebra crossing (*Brit*), crosswalk (*US*)

Zechtour f pub crawl

Zecke (-, -n) f tick

Zehe (-, -n) f toe; (*Knoblauch*) clove; **Zehennagel** m toenail; **Zehenspitze** f tip of the toes

zehn num ten; **Zehnerkarte** f ticket valid for ten trips; **Zehnkampf** m decathlon; **Zehnkämpfer(in)** m(f) decathlete; **zehnmal** adv ten times; **zehntausend** num ten thousand; **zehnte(r, s)** adj tenth; siehe auch **dritte**; **Zehntel** (-s, -) nt (*Bruchteil*) tenth; **Zehntelsekunde** f tenth of a second

Zeichen (-s, -) nt sign; (*Schriftzeichen*) character; **Zeichenblock** m sketch pad; **Zeichenerklärung** f key; **Zeichensetzung** f punctuation; **Zeichensprache** f sign language; **Zeichentrickfilm** m cartoon

zeichnen vt, vi to draw; **Zeichnung** f drawing

Zeigefinger m index finger; **zeigen** vt to show; **sie zeigte uns die Stadt** she showed us around the town; **zeig mal!** let me see ▷ vi to point (*auf +akk* to, at) ▷ vr **sich ~** to show oneself; **es wird sich ~** time will tell; **Zeiger** (*-s, -*) m pointer; (*Uhr*) hand

Zeile (*-, -n*) f line

Zeit (*-, -en*) f time; **ich habe keine ~** I haven't got time; **lass dir ~** take your time; **das hat ~** there's no rush; **von ~ zu ~** from time to time; **Zeitansage** f (*Tel*) speaking clock (*Brit*), correct time (*US*); **Zeitarbeit** f temporary work; **zeitgenössisch** adj contemporary, modern; **zeitgleich** adj simultaneous ▷ adv at exactly the same time; **zeitig** adj early; **Zeitkarte** f season ticket; **zeitlich** adj (*Reihenfolge*) chronological; **es passt ~ nicht** it isn't a convenient time; **ich schaff es ~ nicht** I'm not going to make it; **Zeitlupe** f slow motion; **Zeitplan** m schedule; **Zeitpunkt** m point in time; **Zeitraum** m period (of time); **Zeitschrift** f magazine; (*wissenschaftliche*) periodical

Zeitung f newspaper; **es steht in der ~** it's in the paper(s); **Zeitungsanzeige** f newspaper advertisement; **Zeitungsartikel** m newspaper article; **Zeitungskiosk** m, **Zeitungsstand** m newsstand

Zeitunterschied m time difference; **Zeitverschiebung** f time lag; **Zeitvertreib** (*-(e)s, -e*) m **zum ~** to pass the time; **zeitweise** adv occasionally; **Zeitzone** f time zone

Zelle (*-, -n*) f cell

Zellophan® (*-s*) nt cellophane®

Zelt (*-(e)s, -e*) nt tent; **zelten** vi to camp, to go camping; **Zeltplatz** m campsite, camping site

Zement (*-(e)s, -e*) m cement

Zentimeter m o nt centimetre

Zentner (*-s, -*) m (metric) hundredweight; (*in Deutschland*) fifty kilos; (*in Österreich und der Schweiz*) one hundred kilos

zentral adj central; **Zentrale** (*-, -n*) f central office; (*Tel*) exchange; **Zentralheizung** f central heating;

Zentralverriegelung f (*Auto*) central locking; **Zentrum** (*-s, Zentren*) nt centre

zerbrechen irr vt, vi to break; **zerbrechlich** adj fragile

Zeremonie (*-, -n*) f ceremony

zergehen irr vi to dissolve; (*schmelzen*) to melt

zerkleinern vt to cut up; (*zerhacken*) to chop (up); **zerkratzen** vt to scratch; **zerlegen** vt to take to pieces; (*Fleisch*) to carve; (*Gerät, Maschine*) to dismantle; **zerquetschen** vt to squash; **zerreißen** irr vt to tear to pieces ▷ vi to tear

zerren vt to drag; **sich** (*dat*) **einen Muskel ~** to pull a muscle ▷ vi to tug (*an +dat* at); **Zerrung** f (*Med*) pulled muscle

zerschlagen irr vt to smash ▷ vr **sich ~** to come to nothing

zerschneiden irr vt to cut up

Zerstäuber (*-s, -*) m atomizer

zerstören vt to destroy; **Zerstörung** f destruction

zerstreuen vt to scatter; (*Menge*) to disperse; (*Zweifel etc*) to dispel ▷ vr **sich ~** (*Menge*) to disperse; **zerstreut** adj scattered; (*Mensch*) absent-minded; (*kurzfristig*) distracted

zerteilen vt to split up

Zertifikat (*-(e)s, -e*) nt certificate

Zettel (*-s, -*) m piece of paper; (*Notizzettel*) note

Zeug (*-(e)s, -e*) nt (*fam*) stuff; (*Ausrüstung*) gear; **dummes ~** nonsense

Zeuge (*-n, -n*) m, **Zeugin** f witness

Zeugnis nt certificate; (*Schule*) report; (*Referenz*) reference

z. H(d). abk = **zu Händen von** attn

zickig adj (*fam*) touchy, bitchy

Zickzack (*-(e)s, -e*) m **im ~ fahren** to zigzag (across the road)

Ziege (*-, -n*) f goat

Ziegel (*-s, -*) m brick; (*Dach*) tile

Ziegenkäse m goat's cheese; **Ziegenpeter** m mumps

ziehen (*zog, gezogen*) vt to draw; (*zerren*) to pull; (*Spielfigur*) to move; (*züchten*) to rear ▷ vi (*zerren*) to pull; (*sich bewegen*) to move; (*Rauch, Wolke etc*) to drift; **den Tee ~ lassen** to let the tea stand ▷ vi impers **es zieht** there's a draught ▷ vr **sich ~** (*Treffen, Rede*) to drag on

Ziel (*-(e)s, -e*) nt (*Reise*) destination; (*Sport*) finish; (*Absicht*) goal, aim; **zielen** vi to aim (*auf* +akk at); **Zielgruppe** *f* target group; **ziellos** *adj* aimless; **Zielscheibe** *f* target

ziemlich *adj* considerable; **ein ~es Durcheinander** quite a mess; **mit ~er Sicherheit** with some certainty ▷ *adv* rather, quite; **~ viel** quite a lot

zierlich *adj* dainty; (*Frau*) petite

Ziffer (-, -n) *f* figure; **arabische/römische ~n** *pl* Arabic/Roman numerals *pl*; **Zifferblatt** *nt* dial, face

zig *adj* (*fam*) umpteen

Zigarette *f* cigarette; **Zigarettenautomat** *m* cigarette machine; **Zigarettenpapier** *nt* cigarette paper; **Zigarettenschachtel** *f* cigarette packet; **Zigarettenstummel** *m* cigarette end; **Zigarillo** (-s, -s) *m* cigarillo; **Zigarre** (-, -n) *f* cigar

Zigeuner(in) (-s, -) *m(f)* gipsy

Zimmer (-s, -) *nt* room; **haben Sie ein ~ für zwei Personen?** do you have a room for two?; **Zimmerlautstärke** *f* reasonable volume; **Zimmermädchen** *nt* chambermaid; **Zimmermann** *m* carpenter; **Zimmerpflanze** *f* house plant; **Zimmerschlüssel** *m* room key; **Zimmerservice** *m* room service; **Zimmervermittlung** *f* accommodation agency

Zimt (-(e)s, -e) *m* cinnamon; **Zimtstange** *f* cinnamon stick

Zink (-(e)s) *nt* zinc

Zinn (-(e)s) *nt* (*Element*) tin; (*legiertes*) pewter

Zinsen *pl* interest *sing*

Zipfel (-s, -) *m* corner; (*spitz*) tip; (*Hemd*) tail; (*Wurst*) end; (*fam: Penis*) willy; **Zipfelmütze** *f* pointed hat

zirka *adv* about, approximately

Zirkel (-s, -) *m* (*Math*) (pair of) compasses *pl*

Zirkus (-, -se) *m* circus

zischen *vi* to hiss

Zitat (-(e)s, -e) *nt* quotation (*aus* from); **zitieren** *vt* to quote

Zitronat *nt* candied lemon peel; **Zitrone** (-, -n) *f* lemon; **Zitronenlimonade** *f* lemonade; **Zitronensaft** *m* lemon juice

zittern *vi* to tremble (*vor* +dat with)

zivil *adj* civilian; (*Preis*) reasonable; **Zivil** (-s) *nt* plain clothes *pl*; (*Mil*) civilian clothes *pl*; **Zivildienst** *m* community service (*for conscientious objectors*)

zocken *vi* (*fam*) to gamble

Zoff (-s) *m* (*fam*) trouble

zog *imperf von* **ziehen**

zögerlich *adj* hesitant; **zögern** *vi* to hesitate

Zoll (-(e)s, Zölle) *m* customs *pl*; (*Abgabe*) duty; **Zollabfertigung** *f* customs clearance; **Zollamt** *nt* customs office; **Zollbeamte(r)** *m*, **-beamtin** *f* customs official; **Zollerklärung** *f* customs declaration; **zollfrei** *adj* duty-free; **Zollgebühren** *pl* customs duties *pl*; **Zollkontrolle** *f* customs check; **Zöllner(in)** *m(f)* customs officer; **zollpflichtig** *adj* liable to duty

Zombie (-s, -s) *m* zombie

Zone (-, -n) *f* zone

Zoo (-s, -s) *m* zoo

Zoom (-s, -s) *nt* zoom (shot); (*Objektiv*) zoom (lens)

Zopf (-(e)s, Zöpfe) *m* plait (*Brit*), braid (*US*)

Zorn (-(e)s) *m* anger; **zornig** *adj* angry (*über etw akk* about sth, *auf jdn* with sb)

🔵 **SCHLÜSSELWORT**

zu *präp* +dat **1** (*örtlich*) to; **zum Bahnhof/ Arzt gehen** to go to the station/doctor; **zur Schule/Kirche gehen** to go to school/church; **sollen wir zu euch gehen?** shall we go to your place?; **sie sah zu ihm hin** she looked towards him; **zum Fenster herein** through the window; **zu meiner Linken** to *od* on my left

2 (*zeitlich*) at; **zu Ostern** at Easter; **bis zum 1. Mai** until May 1st; (*nicht später als*) by May 1st; **zu meiner Zeit** in my time

3 (*Zusatz*) with; **Wein zum Essen trinken** to drink wine with one's meal; **sich zu jdm setzen** to sit down beside sb; **setz dich doch zu uns** (come and) sit down with us; **Anmerkungen zu etw** notes on sth

4 (*Zweck*) for; **Wasser zum Waschen** water for washing; **Papier zum Schreiben** paper to write on; **etw zum Geburtstag bekommen** to get sth for one's birthday

5 (*Veränderung*) into; **zu etw werden** to turn into sth; **jdn zu etw machen** to make sb (into) sth; **zu Asche verbrennen** to burn to ashes

6 (*mit Zahlen*); **3 zu 2** (*Sport*) 3-2; **das Stück zu 5 Euro** at 5 euros each; **zum ersten Mal** for the first time
7: **zu meiner Freude** *etc* to my joy *etc*; **zum Glück** luckily; **zu Fuß** on foot; **es ist zum Weinen** it's enough to make you cry ▷ *konj* to; **etw zu essen** sth to eat; **um besser sehen zu können** in order to see better; **ohne es zu wissen** without knowing it; **noch zu bezahlende Rechnungen** bills that are still to be paid ▷ *adv* **1** (*allzu*) too; **zu sehr** too much; **zu viel** too much; **zu wenig** too little
2 (*örtlich*) toward(s); **er kam auf mich zu** he came up to me
3 (*geschlossen*) shut, closed; **die Geschäfte haben zu** the shops are closed; „**auf/zu**" (*Wasserhahn etc*) "on/off"
4 (*umg: los*): **nur zu!** just keep on!; **mach zu!** hurry up!

zuallererst *adv* first of all; **zuallerletzt** *adv* last of all
Zubehör (*-(e)s, -e*) *nt* accessories *pl*
zu|bereiten *vt* to prepare; **Zubereitung** *f* preparation
zu|binden *irr vt* to do (*o* tie) up
Zucchini *pl* courgettes *pl* (*Brit*), zucchini *pl* (*US*)
züchten *vt* (*Tiere*) to breed; (*Pflanzen*) to grow
zucken *vi* to jerk; (*krampfhaft*) to twitch; (*Strahl etc*) to flicker; **mit den Schultern ~** to shrug (one's shoulders)
Zucker (*-s, -*) *m* sugar; (*Med*) diabetes *sing*; **Zuckerdose** *f* sugar bowl; **zuckerkrank** *adj* diabetic; **Zuckerrohr** *nt* sugar cane; **Zuckerrübe** *f* sugar beet; **Zuckerwatte** *f* candy-floss (*Brit*), cotton candy (*US*)
zu|decken *vt* to cover up
zu|drehen *vt* to turn off
zueinander *adv* to one other; (*mit Verb*) together; **~ halten** to stick together
zuerst *adv* first; (*zu Anfang*) at first; **~ einmal** first of all
Zufahrt *f* access; (*Einfahrt*) drive(way); **Zufahrtsstraße** *f* access road; (*Autobahn*) slip road (*Brit*), ramp (*US*)
Zufall *m* chance; (*Ereignis*) coincidence; **durch ~** by accident; **so ein ~!** what a coincidence; **zufällig** *adj* chance ▷ *adv* by chance; **weißt du ~, ob ...?** do you happen to know whether ...?

zufrieden *adj* content(ed); (*befriedigt*) satisfied; **sich mit etw ~ geben** to settle for sth; **lass sie ~** leave her alone (*o* in peace); **sie ist schwer ~ zu stellen** she is hard to please; **Zufriedenheit** *f* contentment; (*Befriedigtsein*) satisfaction
zu|fügen *vt* to add (*dat* to); **jdm Schaden/Schmerzen ~** to cause sb harm/pain
Zug (*-(e)s, Züge*) *m* (*Eisenb*) train; (*Luft*) draught; (*Ziehen*) pull; (*Gesichtszug*) feature; (*Schach*) move; (*Charakterzug*) trait; (*an Zigarette*) puff, drag; (*Schluck*) gulp
Zugabe *f* extra; (*in Konzert etc*) encore
Zugabteil *nt* train compartment
Zugang *m* access; „**kein ~!**" 'no entry!'
Zugauskunft *f* (*Stelle*) train information office/desk; **Zugbegleiter(in)** *m(f)* guard (*Brit*), conductor (*US*)
zu|geben *irr vt* (*zugestehen*) admit; **zugegeben** *adv* admittedly
zu|gehen *irr vi* (*schließen*) to shut; **auf jdn/etw ~** to walk towards sb/sth; **dem Ende ~** to be coming to a close ▷ *vi impers* (*sich ereignen*) to happen; **es ging lustig zu** we/they had a lot of fun; **dort geht es streng zu** it's strict there
Zügel (*-s, -*) *m* rein
Zugführer(in) *m(f)* guard (*Brit*), conductor (*US*)
zugig *adj* draughty
zügig *adj* speedy
Zugluft *f* draught
Zugpersonal *nt* train staff
zu|greifen *irr vi* (*fig*) to seize the opportunity; (*beim Essen*) to help oneself; **~ auf** (*+akk*) (*Inform*) to access
Zugrestauraunt *nt* dining car, diner (*US*)
Zugriffsberechtigung *f* (*Inform*) access right
zugrunde *adv* **~ gehen** to perish; **~ gehen an** (*+dat*) (*sterben*) to die of
Zugschaffner(in) *m(f)* ticket inspector; **Zugunglück** *nt* train crash
zugunsten *prep* +*gen* o *dat* in favour of
Zugverbindung *f* train connection
zu|haben *irr vi* to be closed
zu|halten *irr vt* **sich** (*dat*) **die Nase ~** to hold one's nose; **sich** (*dat*) **die Ohren ~** to hold one's hands over one's ears; **die Tür ~** to hold the door shut
Zuhause (*-s*) *nt* home

zu|hören vi to listen (dat to); **Zuhörer(in)** m(f) listener
zu|kleben vt to seal
zu|kommen irr vi to come up (auf +akk to); **jdm etw ~ lassen** to give/send sb sth; **etw auf sich** (akk) **~ lassen** to take sth as it comes
zu|kriegen vt **ich krieg den Koffer nicht zu** I can't shut the case
Zukunft (-, Zukünfte) f future; **zukünftig** adj future ▷ adv in future
zu|lassen irr vt (hereinlassen) to admit; (erlauben) to permit; (Auto) to license; (fam: nicht öffnen) to keep shut; **zulässig** adj permissible, permitted
zuletzt adv finally, at last
zuliebe adv **jdm ~** for sb's sake
zum kontr von **zu dem**; **~ dritten Mal** for the third time; **~ Scherz** as a joke; **~ Trinken** for drinking
zu|machen vt to shut; (Kleidung) to do up ▷ vi to shut
zumindest adv at least
zu|muten vt **jdm etw ~** to expect sth of sb ▷ vr **sich** (dat) **zu viel ~** to overdo things
zunächst adv first of all; **~ einmal** to start with
Zunahme (-, -n) f increase
Zuname m surname, last name
zünden vt, vi (Auto) to ignite, to fire; **Zündholz** nt match; **Zündkabel** f (Auto) ignition cable; **Zündkerze** f (Auto) spark plug; **Zündschloss** nt ignition lock; **Zündschlüssel** m ignition key; **Zündung** f ignition
zu|nehmen irr vi to increase; (Mensch) to put on weight ▷ vt **5 Kilo ~** to put on 5 kilos
Zunge (-, -n) f tongue
Zungenkuss m French kiss
zunichte adv **~ machen** to ruin
zunutze adv **sich** (dat) **etw ~ machen** to make use of sth
zu|parken vt to block
zur kontr von **zu der**
zurecht|finden irr vr **sich ~** to find one's way around; **zurecht|kommen** irr vi to cope (mit etw with sth); **zurecht|machen** vt to prepare ▷ vr **sich ~** to get ready
Zürich (-s) nt Zurich
zurück adv back
zurück|bekommen irr vt to get back;

zurück|blicken vi to look back (auf +akk at); **zurück|bringen** irr vt (hierhin) to bring back; (woandershin) to take back; **zurück|erstatten** vt to refund; **zurück|fahren** irr vi to go back; **zurück|geben** irr vt to give back; (antworten) to answer; **zurück|gehen** irr vi to go back; (zeitlich) to date back (auf +akk to)
zurück|halten irr vt to hold back; (hindern) to prevent ▷ vr **sich ~** to hold back; **zurückhaltend** adj reserved
zurück|holen vt to fetch back; **zurück|kommen** irr vi to come back; **auf etw** (akk) **~** to return (o get back) to sth; **zurück|lassen** irr vt to leave behind; **zurück|legen** irr vt to put back; (Geld) to put by; (reservieren) to keep back; (Strecke) to cover; **zurück|nehmen** irr vt to take back; **zurück|rufen** irr vt to call back; **zurück|schicken** vt to send back; **zurück|stellen** vt to put back; **zurück|treten** irr vi to step back; (von Amt) to retire; **zurück|verlangen** vt **etw ~** to ask for sth back; **zurück|zahlen** vt to pay back
zurzeit adv at present
Zusage f promise; (Annahme) acceptance; **zu|sagen** vt to promise ▷ vi to accept; **jdm ~** (gefallen) to appeal to sb
zusammen adv together
Zusammenarbeit f collaboration; **zusammen|arbeiten** vi to work together
zusammen|brechen irr vi to collapse; (psychisch) to break down; **Zusammenbruch** m collapse; (psychischer) breakdown
zusammen|fassen vt to summarize; (vereinigen) to unite; **zusammenfassend** adj summarizing ▷ adv to summarize; **Zusammenfassung** f summary
zusammen|gehören vi to belong together; **zusammen|halten** irr vi to stick together
Zusammenhang m connection; **im/aus dem ~** in/out of context; **zusammen|hängen** vi to be connected; **zusammenhängend** adj coherent; **zusammenhang(s)los** adj incoherent
zusammen|klappen vi, vt to fold up
zusammen|knüllen vt to screw up
zusammen|kommen irr vi to meet;

(sich ereignen) to happen together;
zusammen|legen *vt* to fold up ▷ *vi (Geld sammeln)* to club together;
zusammen|nehmen *irr vt* to summon up; **alles zusammengenommen** all in all ▷ *vr* **sich ~** to pull oneself together; *(fam)* to get a grip, to get one's act together;
zusammen|passen *vi* to go together; *(Personen)* to be suited;
zusammen|rechnen *vt* to add up
Zusammensein *(-s) nt* get-together
zusammen|setzen *vt* to put together ▷ *vr* **sich ~ aus** to be composed of; **Zusammensetzung** *f* composition
Zusammenstoß *m* crash, collision; **zusammen|stoßen** *irr vi* to crash *(mit into)*
zusammen|zählen *vt* to add up
zusammen|ziehen *irr vi (in Wohnung etc)* to move in together
Zusatz *m* addition; **Zusatzgerät** *nt* attachment; *(Inform)* add-on; **zusätzlich** *adj* additional ▷ *adv* in addition
zu|schauen *vi* to watch; **Zuschauer(in)** *(-s, -) m(f)* spectator; **die ~** *(pl) (Theat)* the audience *sing;* **Zuschauertribüne** *f* stand
zu|schicken *vt* to send
Zuschlag *m* extra charge; *(Fahrkarte)* supplement
zuschlagpflichtig *adj* subject to an extra charge; *(Eisenb)* subject to a supplement
zu|schließen *irr vt* to lock up
zu|sehen *irr vi* to watch *(jdm sb)*; **~, dass** *(dafür sorgen)* to make sure that
zu|sichern *vt* **jdm etw ~** to assure sb of sth
Zustand *m* state, condition; **sie bekommt Zustände, wenn sie das sieht** *(fam)* she'll have a fit if she sees that
zustande *adv* **~ bringen** to bring about; **~ kommen** to come about
zuständig *adj (Behörde)* relevant; **~ für** responsible for
Zustellung *f* delivery
zu|stimmen *vi* to agree *(einer Sache dat to sth, jdm with sb)*; **Zustimmung** *f* approval
zu|stoßen *irr vi (fig)* to happen *(jdm to sb)*
Zutaten *pl* ingredients *pl*
zu|trauen *vt* **jdm etw ~** to think sb is capable of sth; **das hätte ich ihm nie zugetraut** I'd never have thought he was capable of it; **ich würde es ihr ~** *(etw*

Negatives) I wouldn't put it past her;
Zutrauen *(-s) nt* confidence *(zu in)*;
zutraulich *adj* trusting; *(Tier)* friendly
zu|treffen *irr vi* to be correct; **~ auf** *(+akk)* to apply to; **Zutreffendes bitte streichen** please delete as applicable
Zutritt *m* entry; *(Zugang)* access; **~ verboten!** no entry
zuverlässig *adj* reliable; **Zuverlässigkeit** *f* reliability
Zuversicht *f* confidence; **zuversichtlich** *adj* confident
zuvor *adv* before; *(zunächst)* first; **zuvor|kommen** *irr vi* **jdm ~** to beat sb to it; **zuvorkommend** *adj* obliging
Zuwachs *(-es, Zuwächse) m* increase, growth; *(fam: Baby)* addition to the family
zuwider *adv* **es ist mir ~** I hate *(o detest)* it
zuzüglich *prep +gen* plus
zwang *imperf von* **zwingen**
Zwang *(-(e)s, Zwänge) m (innerer)* compulsion; *(Gewalt)* force
zwängen *vt* to squeeze *(in +akk into)* ▷ *vr* **sich ~** to squeeze *(in +akk into)*
zwanglos *adj* informal
zwanzig *num* twenty; **zwanzigste(r, s)** *adj* twentieth; *siehe auch* **dritte**
zwar *adv* **und ~ ...** *(genauer)* ..., to be precise; **das ist ~ schön, aber ...** it is nice, but ...; **ich kenne ihn ~, aber ...** I know him all right, but ...
Zweck *(-(e)s, -e) m* purpose; **zwecklos** *adj* pointless
zwei *num* two; **Zwei** *(-, -en) f* two; *(Schulnote)* ≈ B; **Zweibettzimmer** *nt* twin room; **zweideutig** *adj* ambiguous; *(unanständig)* suggestive; **zweifach** *adj, adv* double
Zweifel *(-s, -) m* doubt; **zweifellos** *adv* undoubtedly; **zweifeln** *vi* to doubt *(an etw dat sth)*; **Zweifelsfall** *m* **im ~** in case of doubt
Zweig *(-(e)s, -e) m* branch
Zweigstelle *f* branch
zweihundert *num* two hundred; **zweimal** *adv* twice; **zweisprachig** *adj* bilingual; **zweispurig** *adj (Auto)* two-lane; **zweit** *adv* **wir sind zu ~** there are two of us; **zweite(r, s)** *adj* second; *siehe auch* **dritte eine ~ Portion** a second helping; **zweitens** *adv* secondly; *(bei Aufzählungen)*

second; **zweitgrößte(r, s)** *adj* second
largest; **Zweitschlüssel** *m* spare key
Zwerchfell *nt* diaphragm
Zwerg(in) *(-(e)s, -e) m(f)* dwarf
Zwetschge *(-, -n) f* plum
zwicken *vt* to pinch
Zwieback *(-(e)s, -e) m* rusk
Zwiebel *(-, -n) f* onion; *(von Blume)* bulb;
  Zwiebelsuppe *f* onion soup
Zwilling *(-s, -e) m* twin; **~e** *(pl) (Astr)*
  Gemini *sing*
zwingen *(zwang, gezwungen) vt* to force
zwinkern *vi* to blink; *(absichtlich)* to wink
zwischen *prep +akk o dat* between
Zwischenablage *f (Inform)* clipboard
zwischendurch *adv* in between
Zwischenfall *m* incident
Zwischenlandung *f* stopover
zwischenmenschlich *adj* interpersonal
Zwischenraum *m* space
Zwischenstopp *(-s, -s) m* stopover
Zwischensumme *f* subtotal
Zwischenzeit *f* **in der ~** in the meantime
zwitschern *vt, vi* to twitter, to chirp
zwölf *num* twelve; **zwölfte(r, s)** *adj*
  twelfth; *siehe auch* **dritte**
Zylinder *(-s, -) m* cylinder; *(Hut)* top hat;
  Zylinderkopfdichtung *f* cylinder-head
  gasket
zynisch *adj* cynical
Zypern *(-s) nt* Cyprus
Zyste *(-, -n) f* cyst

a

a [eɪ, ə] (before vowel or silent h: an) indef art **1** ein; eine; **a woman** eine Frau; **a book** ein Buch; **an eagle** ein Adler; **she's a doctor** sie ist Ärztin
2 (instead of the number "one") ein, eine; **a year ago** vor einem Jahr; **a hundred/thousand** etc **pounds** (ein) hundert/(ein) tausend etc Pfund
3 (in expressing ratios, prices etc) pro; **3 a day/week** 3 pro Tag/Woche 3 am Tag/in der Woche; **10 km an hour** 10 km pro Stunde/in der Stunde

AA abbr = **Automobile Association** britischer Automobilklub, ≈ ADAC m
aback adv **taken ~** erstaunt
abandon [ə'bændən] vt (desert) verlassen; (give up) aufgeben
abbey ['æbɪ] n Abtei f
abbreviate [əbri:'vɪ'eɪt] vt abkürzen; **abbreviation** [əbri:vɪ'eɪʃən] n Abkürzung f
ABC ['eɪbi:'si:] n (a. fig) Abc nt
abdicate ['æbdɪkeɪt] vi (king) abdanken; **abdication** [æbdɪ'keɪʃən] n Abdankung f

abdomen ['æbdəmən] n Unterleib m
ability [ə'bɪlɪtɪ] n Fähigkeit f; **able** ['eɪbl] adj fähig; **to be ~ to do sth** etw tun können
abnormal [æb'nɔ:ml] adj anormal
aboard [ə'bɔ:d] adv, prep an Bord +gen
abolish [ə'bɒlɪʃ] vt abschaffen
aborigine [æbə'rɪdʒɪni:] n Ureinwohner(in) m(f) (Australiens)
abort [ə'bɔ:t] vt (Med: foetus) abtreiben; (Space: mission) abbrechen; **abortion** [ə'bɔ:ʃən] n Abtreibung f

about [ə'baʊt] adv **1** (approximately) etwa, ungefähr; **about a hundred/thousand** etc etwa hundert/tausend etc; **at about 2 o'clock** etwa um 2 Uhr; **I've just about finished** ich bin gerade fertig
2 (referring to place) herum, umher; **to leave things lying about** Sachen herumliegen lassen; **to run/walk** etc **about** herumrennen/gehen etc
3: **to be about to do sth** im Begriff sein, etw zu tun; **he was about to go to bed** er wollte gerade ins Bett gehen
▷ prep **1** (relating to) über +acc; **a book about London** ein Buch über London; **what is it about?** worum geht es?; (book etc) wovon handelt es?; **we talked about it** wir haben darüber geredet; **what or how about doing this?** wollen wir das machen?
2 (referring to place) um (… herum); **to walk about the town** in der Stadt herumgehen; **her clothes were scattered about the room** ihre Kleider waren über das ganze Zimmer verstreut

above [ə'bʌv] adv oben; **children aged 8 and ~** Kinder ab 8 Jahren; **on the floor ~** ein Stockwerk höher ▷ prep über; **~ 40 degrees** über 40 Grad; **~ all** vor allem ▷ adj obig
abroad [ə'brɔ:d] adv im Ausland; **to go ~** ins Ausland gehen
abrupt [ə'brʌpt] adj (sudden) plötzlich, abrupt
abscess ['æbsɪs] n Geschwür nt
absence ['æbsəns] n Abwesenheit f; **absent** ['æbsənt] adj abwesend; **to be ~ fehlen**; **absent-minded** adj zerstreut

absolute ['æbsəlu:t] adj absolut; (power)
unumschränkt; (rubbish) vollkommen,
total; **absolutely** adv absolut;
(true, stupid) vollkommen; **~!** genau!;
you're ~ right du hast/Sie haben völlig
Recht

absorb [əb'zɔ:b] vt absorbieren; (fig:
information) in sich aufnehmen; **absorbed**
adj **~ in sth** in etw vertieft; **absorbent** adj
absorbierend; **~ cotton** (US) Watte f;
absorbing adj (fig) faszinierend,
fesselnd

abstain [əb'steɪn] vi **to ~ (from voting)**
sich (der Stimme) enthalten

abstract ['æbstrækt] adj abstrakt

absurd [əb'sз:d] adj absurd

abundance [ə'bʌndəns] n Reichtum m (of
an +dat)

abuse [ə'bju:s] n (rude language)
Beschimpfungen pl; (mistreatment)
Missbrauch m ▷ [ə'bju:z] vt (misuse)
missbrauchen; (insult) beschimpfen,
beleidigend; **abusive** [ə'bju:sɪv] adj

AC abbr = **alternating current**
Wechselstrom m ▷ abbr = **air
conditioning** Klimaanlage

a/c abbr = **account** Kto.

academic [ækə'demɪk] n
Wissenschaftler(in) m(f) ▷ adj
akademisch, wissenschaftlich

accelerate [æk'seləreɪt] vi (car etc)
beschleunigen; (driver) Gas geben;
acceleration [əkselə'reɪʃən] n
Beschleunigung f; **accelerator**
[ək'seləreɪtə*] n Gas(pedal) nt

accent ['æksənt] n Akzent m

accept [ək'sept] vt annehmen; (agree to)
akzeptieren; (responsibility) übernehmen;
acceptable [ək'septəbl] adj annehmbar

access ['ækses] n Zugang m; (Inform)
Zugriff m; **accessible** [æk'sesəbl] adj
(leicht) zugänglich/erreichbar; (place)
(leicht) erreichbar

accessory [æk'sesərɪ] n Zubehörteil nt

access road n Zufahrtsstraße f

accident ['æksɪdənt] n Unfall m; **by
~** zufällig; **accidental** [æksɪ'dentl] adj
unbeabsichtigt; (meeting) zufällig; (death)
durch Unfall; **~ damage** Unfallschaden m;
accident-prone adj vom Pech verfolgt

acclimatize [ə'klaɪmətaɪz] vt **to
~ oneself** sich gewöhnen (to an +akk)

accommodate [ə'kɒmədeɪt] vt

unterbringen; **accommodation(s)**
[əkɒmə'deɪʃən(z)] n Unterkunft f

accompany [ə'kʌmpənɪ] vt begleiten

accomplish [ə'kʌmplɪʃ] vt erreichen

accord [ə'kɔ:d] n **of one's own
~** freiwillig; **according to** prep nach, laut
+dat

account [ə'kaʊnt] n (in bank etc) Konto nt;
(narrative) Bericht m; **on ~ of** wegen; **on no
~** auf keinen Fall; **to take into
~** berücksichtigen, in Betracht ziehen;
accountant [ə'kaʊntənt] n
Buchhalter(in) m(f); **account for** vt
(explain) erklären; (expenditure)
Rechenschaft ablegen für; **account
number** n Kontonummer f

accumulate [ə'kju:mjʊleɪt] vt
ansammeln ▷ vi sich ansammeln

accuracy ['ækjʊrəsɪ] n Genauigkeit f;
accurate ['ækjʊrɪt] adj genau

accusation [ækjʊ'zeɪʃən] n Anklage f,
Beschuldigung f

accusative [ə'kju:zətɪv] n Akkusativ m

accuse [ə'kju:z] vt beschuldigen; (Jur)
anklagen (of wegen +gen); **~ sb of doing
sth** jdn beschuldigen, etw getan zu
haben; **accused** n (Jur) Angeklagte(r) mf

accustom [ə'kʌstəm] vt gewöhnen (to an
+akk); **accustomed** adj gewohnt; **to get
~ to sth** sich an etw akk gewöhnen

ace [eɪs] n Ass nt ▷ adj Star-

ache [eɪk] n Schmerz m ▷ vi wehtun

achieve [ə'tʃi:v] vt erreichen;
achievement n Leistung f

acid ['æsɪd] n Säure f ▷ adj sauer; **~ rain**
saurer Regen

acknowledge [ək'nɒlɪdʒ] vt (recognize)
anerkennen; (admit) zugeben; (receipt of
letter etc) bestätigen; **acknowledgement**
n Anerkennung f, (of letter)
Empfangsbestätigung f

acne ['æknɪ] n Akne f

acorn ['eɪkɔ:n] n Eichel f

acoustic [ə'ku:stɪk] adj akustisch;
acoustics [ə'ku:stɪks] npl Akustik f

acquaintance [ə'kweɪntəns] n (person)
Bekannte(r) mf

acquire [ə'kwaɪə*] vt erwerben, sich
aneignen; **acquisition** [ækwɪ'zɪʃn] n (of
skills etc) Erwerb m; (object) Anschaffung f

acrobat ['ækrəbæt] n Akrobat(in) m(f)

across [ə'krɒs] prep über +akk; **he lives
~ the street** er wohnt auf der anderen

Seite der Straße ▷ *adv* hinüber, herüber;
100m ~ 100m breit

act [ækt] *n (deed)* Tat *f; (Jur: law)* Gesetz *nt;
(Theat)* Akt *m; (fig: pretence)* Schau *f;* **it's all
an ~** es ist alles nur Theater; **to be in the
~ of doing sth** gerade dabei sein, etw zu
tun ▷ *vi (take action)* handeln; *(behave)* sich
verhalten; *(Theat)* spielen; **to ~ as** *(person)*
fungieren als; *(thing)* dienen als ▷ *vt (a
part)* spielen

action ['ækʃən] *n (of play, novel etc)*
Handlung *f; (in film etc)* Action *f; (Mil)*
Kampf *m;* **to take ~** etwas unternehmen;
out of ~ *(machine)* außer Betrieb; **to put a
plan into ~** einen Plan in die Tat
umsetzen; **action replay** *n (Sport, Tv)*
Wiederholung *f*

active ['æktɪv] *adj* aktiv; *(child)* lebhaft;
activity [æk'tɪvɪtɪ] *n* Aktivität *f;*
(occupation) Beschäftigung *f; (organized
event)* Veranstaltung *f*

actor ['æktə*] *n* Schauspieler(in) *m(f);*
actress ['æktrɪs] *n* Schauspielerin *f*

actual ['æktjʊəl] *adj* wirklich; **actually**
adv eigentlich; *(said in surprise)* tatsächlich

acupuncture ['ækjʊpʌŋktʃə*] *n*
Akupunktur *f*

acute [ə'kjuːt] *adj (pain)* akut; *(sense of
smell)* fein; *(Math: angle)* spitz

ad [æd] *abbr* = **advertisement**

AD *abbr* = **Anno Domini** nach Christi, n.
Chr.

adapt [ə'dæpt] *vi* sich anpassen *(to +dat)*
▷ *vt* anpassen *(to +dat); (rewrite)*
bearbeiten *(for* für); **adaptable** *adj*
anpassungsfähig; **adaptation** *n (of book
etc)* Bearbeitung *f;* **adapter** *n (Elec)*
Zwischenstecker *m,* Adapter *m*

add [æd] *vt (ingredient)* hinzufügen;
(numbers) addieren; **add up** *vi (make sense)*
stimmen ▷ *vt (numbers)* addieren

addict ['ædɪkt] *n* Süchtige(r) *mf;* **addicted**
[ə'dɪktɪd] *adj* **~ to alcohol/drugs**
alkohol-/drogensüchtig

addition [ə'dɪʃən] *n* Zusatz *m; (to bill)*
Aufschlag *m; (Math)* Addition *f;* **in
~ außerdem, zusätzlich *(to* zu); **additional**
adj zusätzlich, weiter; **additive** ['ædɪtɪv]
n Zusatz *m;* **add-on** ['ædɒn] *n*
Zusatzgerät *nt*

address [ə'dres] *n* Adresse *f* ▷ *vt (letter)*
adressieren; *(person)* anreden

adequate ['ædɪkwɪt] *adj (appropriate)*

angemessen; *(sufficient)* ausreichend;
(time) genügend

adhesive [əd'hiːsɪv] *n* Klebstoff *m;*
adhesive tape *n* Klebstreifen *m*

adjacent [ə'dʒeɪsənt] *adj* benachbart

adjective ['ædʒəktɪv] *n* Adjektiv *nt*

adjoining [ə'dʒɔɪnɪŋ] *adj* benachbart,
Neben-

adjust [ə'dʒʌst] *vt* einstellen; *(put right
also)* richtig stellen; *(speed, flow)*
regulieren; *(in position)* verstellen ▷ *vi* sich
anpassen *(to +dat);* **adjustable** *adj*
verstellbar

admin [əd'mɪn] *n (fam)* Verwaltung *f;*
administration [ədmɪnɪs'treɪʃən] *n*
Verwaltung *f; (Pol)* Regierung *f*

admirable ['ædmərəbl] *adj*
bewundernswert; **admiration**
[ædmɪ'reɪʃən] *n* Bewunderung *f,* **admire**
[əd'maɪə*] *vt* bewundern

admission [əd'mɪʃən] *n (entrance)* Zutritt
m; (to university etc) Zulassung *f; (fee)*
Eintritt *m; (confession)* Eingeständnis *nt;*
admission charge, admission fee *n*
Eintrittspreis *m;* **admit** [əd'mɪt] *vt (let in)*
hereinlassen *(to* in *+akk); (to university etc)*
zulassen; *(confess)* zugeben, gestehen; **to
be ~ted to hospital** ins Krankenhaus
eingeliefert werden

adolescent [ædə'lesnt] *n* Jugendliche(r)
mf

adopt [ə'dɒpt] *vt (child)* adoptieren;
(idea) übernehmen; **adoption** [ə'dɒptʃn]
n (of child) Adoption *f; (of idea)* Übernahme
f

adorable [ə'dɔːrəbl] *adj* entzückend;
adore [ə'dɔː*] *vt* anbeten; *(person)* über
alles lieben, vergöttern

adult ['ædʌlt] *adj (person)* erwachsen;
(film etc) für Erwachsene ▷ *n*
Erwachsene(r) *mf*

adultery [ə'dʌltərɪ] *n* Ehebruch *m*

advance [əd'vɑːns] *n (money)* Vorschuss
m; (progress) Fortschritt *m;* **in ~** im Voraus;
to book in ~ vorbestellen ▷ *vi (move
forward)* vorrücken ▷ *vt (money)*
vorschießen; **advance booking** *n*
Reservierung *f; (Theat)* Vorverkauf *m;*
advanced *adj (modern)* fortschrittlich;
(course, study) für Fortgeschrittene;
advance payment *n* Vorauszahlung *f*

advantage [əd'vɑːntɪdʒ] *n* Vorteil *m;* **to
take ~ of** *(exploit)* ausnutzen; *(profit from)*

Nutzen ziehen aus; **it's to your ~** es ist in deinem/Ihrem Interesse

adventure [əd'ventʃə*] n Abenteuer nt; **adventure holiday** n Abenteuerurlaub m; **adventure playground** n Abenteuerspielplatz m; **adventurous** [əd'ventʃərəs] adj (person) abenteuerlustig

adverb ['ædvɜ:b] n Adverb nt

adverse ['ædvɜ:s] adj (conditions etc) ungünstig; (effect, comment etc) negativ

advert ['ædvɜ:t] n Anzeige f; **advertise** ['ædvətaiz] vt werben für; (in newspaper) inserieren; (job) ausschreiben ▷ vi Reklame machen; (in newspaper) annoncieren (for für); **advertisement** [əd'vɜ:tismənt] n Werbung f; (announcement) Anzeige f; **advertising** n Werbung f

advice [əd'vais] n Rat(schlag) m; **word** o **piece of ~** Ratschlag m; **take my ~** hör auf mich; **advisable** [əd'vaizəbl] adj ratsam; **advise** [əd'vaiz] vt raten (sb jdm): **to ~ sb to do sth/not to do sth** jdm zuraten/abraten, etw zu tun

Aegean [i:'dʒi:ən] n **the ~ (Sea)** die Ägäis

aerial ['εəriəl] n Antenne f ▷ adj Luft-

aerobatics [εərəʊ'bætiks] npl Kunstfliegen nt

aerobics [εə'rəʊbiks] nsing Aerobic nt

aeroplane ['εərəplein] n Flugzeug nt

afaik abbr = **as far as I know**; (SMS) ≈ soweit ich weiß

affair [ə'fεə*] n (matter, business) Sache f, Angelegenheit f; (scandal) Affäre f; (love affair) Verhältnis nt

affect [ə'fekt] vt (influence) (ein)wirken auf +akk; (health, organ) angreifen; (move deeply) berühren; (concern) betreffen; **affection** [ə'fekʃən] n Zuneigung f; **affectionate** [ə'fekʃənit] adj liebevoll

affluent ['æfluənt] adj wohlhabend

afford [ə'fɔ:d] vt sich leisten; **I can't ~ it** ich kann es mir nicht leisten; **affordable** [ə'fɔ:dəbl] adj erschwinglich

Afghanistan [æf'gænistæn] n Afghanistan nt

aforementioned [əfɔ:'menʃənd] adj oben genannt

afraid [ə'freid] adj **to be ~** Angst haben (of vor +dat); **to be ~ that ...** fürchten, dass ...; **I'm ~ I don't know** das weiß ich leider nicht

Africa ['æfrikə] n Afrika nt; **African** adj afrikanisch ▷ n Afrikaner(in) m(f); **African American**, **Afro-American** n Afroamerikaner(in) m(f)

after ['ɑ:ftə*] prep nach; **ten ~ five** (US) zehn nach fünf; **to be ~ sb/sth** (following, seeking) hinter jdm/etw her sein; **~ all** schließlich; (in spite of everything) (schließlich) doch ▷ conj nachdem ▷ adv **soon ~** bald danach; **aftercare** n Nachbehandlung f; **after-effect** n Nachwirkung f

afternoon n Nachmittag m; **~, good ~** guten Tag!; **in the ~** nachmittags

afters npl Nachtisch m; **after-sales service** n Kundendienst m; **after-shave (lotion)** n Rasierwasser nt; **after-sun lotion** n After-Sun-Lotion f; **afterwards** adv nachher; (after that) danach

again [ə'gen] adv wieder; (one more time) noch einmal; **not ~!** (nicht) schon wieder; **~ and ~** immer wieder; **the same ~ please** das Gleiche noch mal bitte

against [ə'genst] prep gegen; **~ my will** wider Willen; **~ the law** unrechtmäßig, illegal

age [eidʒ] n Alter nt; (period of history) Zeitalter nt; **at the ~ of four** im Alter von vier (Jahren); **what ~ is she?, what is her ~?** wie alt ist sie?; **to come of ~** volljährig werden; **under ~** minderjährig ▷ vi altern, alt werden; **aged** adj **~ thirty** dreißig Jahre alt; **a son ~ twenty** ein zwanzigjähriger Sohn ▷ adj ['eidʒid] (elderly) betagt; **age group** n Altersgruppe f; **ageism** n Diskriminierung f aufgrund des Alters; **age limit** n Altersgrenze f

agency ['eidʒənsi] n Agentur f

agenda [ə'dʒendə] n Tagesordnung f

agent ['eidʒənt] n (Comm) Vertreter(in) m(f); (for writer, actor etc) Agent(in) m(f)

aggression [ə'greʃn] n Aggression f; **aggressive** [ə'gresiv] adj aggressiv

agitated adj aufgeregt; **to get ~** sich aufregen

AGM abbr = **Annual General Meeting** JHV f

ago [ə'gəʊ] adv **two days ~** heute vor zwei Tagen; **not long ~** (erst) vor kurzem

agonize ['ægənaiz] vi sich den Kopf zerbrechen (over über dat); **agonizing** adj qualvoll; **agony** ['ægəni] n Qual f

agree [ə'gri:] vt (date, price etc)

vereinbaren; **to ~ to do sth** sich bereit erklären, etw zu tun; **to ~ that ...** sich *dat* einig sein, dass ...; *(decide)* beschließen, dass ...; *(admit)* zugeben, dass ... ▷ *vi (have same opinion, correspond)* übereinstimmen (with mit); *(consent)* zustimmen; *(come to an agreement)* sich einigen *(about, on* auf +*akk); (food)* **not to ~ with sb** jdm nicht bekommen; **agreement** *n (agreeing)* Übereinstimmung *f; (contract)* Abkommen *nt*, Vereinbarung *f*

agricultural [æɡrɪˈkʌltʃərəl] *adj* landwirtschaftlich, Landwirtschafts-; **agriculture** [ˈæɡrɪkʌltʃəʳ] *n* Landwirtschaft *f*

ahead [əˈhed] *adv* **to be ~** führen, vorne liegen; **~ of** vor +*dat*; **to be ~ of sb** *(person)* jdm voraus sein; *(thing)* vor jdm liegen; **to be 3 metres ~** 3 Meter Vorsprung haben

aid [eɪd] *n* Hilfe *f*; **in ~ of** zugunsten +*gen*; **with the ~ of** mithilfe +*gen* ▷ *vt* helfen +*dat*; *(support)* unterstützen

Aids [eɪdz] *n acr* = **acquired immune deficiency syndrome** Aids *nt*

aim [eɪm] *vt (gun, camera)* richten *(at* auf +*akk)* ▷ *vi* **to ~ at** *(with gun etc)* zielen auf +*akk; (fig)* abzielen auf +*akk*; **to ~ to do sth** beabsichtigen, etw zu tun ▷ *n* Ziel *nt*

air [ɛəʳ] *n* Luft *f*; **in the open ~** im Freien; *(Radio, TV)* **to be on the ~** *(programme)* auf Sendung sein; *(station)* senden ▷ *vt* lüften; **airbag** *n (Auto)* Airbag *m*; **air-conditioned** *adj* mit Klimaanlage; **air-conditioning** *n* Klimaanlage *f*; **aircraft** *n* Flugzeug *nt*; **airfield** *n* Flugplatz *m*; **air force** *n* Luftwaffe *f*; **airgun** *n* Luftgewehr *nt*; **airline** *n* Fluggesellschaft *f*; **airmail** *n* Luftpost *f*; **by ~** mit Luftpost; **airplane** *n (US)* Flugzeug *nt*; **air pollution** *n* Luftverschmutzung *f*; **airport** *n* Flughafen *m*; **airsick** *adj* luftkrank; **airtight** *adj* luftdicht; **air-traffic controller** *n* Fluglotse *m*, Fluglotsin *f*; **airy** *adj* luftig; *(manner)* lässig

aisle [aɪl] *n* Gang *m*; *(in church)* Seitenschiff *nt*; **~ seat** Sitz *m* am Gang

ajar [əˈdʒɑːʳ] *adj (door)* angelehnt

alarm [əˈlɑːm] *n (warning)* Alarm *m*; *(bell etc)* Alarmanlage *f* ▷ *vt* beunruhigen; **alarm clock** *n* Wecker *m*; **alarmed** *adj (protected)* alarmgesichert; **alarming** *adj* beunruhigend

Albania [ælˈbeɪnɪə] *n* Albanien *nt*; **Albanian** *adj* albanisch ▷ *n (person)* Albaner(in) *m(f); (language)* Albanisch *nt*

album [ˈælbəm] *n* Album *nt*

alcohol [ˈælkəhɒl] *n* Alkohol *m*; **alcohol-free** *adj* alkoholfrei; **alcoholic** [ælkəˈhɒlɪk] *adj (drink)* alkoholisch ▷ *n* Alkoholiker(in) *m(f)*; **alcoholism** *n* Alkoholismus *m*

ale [eɪl] *n* Ale *nt (helles englisches Bier)*

alert [əˈlɜːt] *adj* wachsam ▷ *n* Alarm *m* ▷ *vt* warnen *(to* vor +*dat)*

algebra [ˈældʒɪbrə] *n* Algebra *f*

Algeria [ælˈdʒɪərɪə] *n* Algerien *nt*

alibi [ˈælɪbaɪ] *n* Alibi *nt*

alien [ˈeɪlɪən] *n (foreigner)* Ausländer(in) *m(f); (from space)* Außerirdische(r) *mf*

align [əˈlaɪn] *vt* ausrichten *(with* auf +*akk)*

alike [əˈlaɪk] *adj, adv* gleich; *(similar)* ähnlich

alive [əˈlaɪv] *adj* lebendig; **to keep sth ~** etw am Leben erhalten; **he's still ~** er lebt noch

⊙ **KEYWORD**

all [ɔːl] *adj* alle (r, s); **all day/night** den ganzen Tag/die ganze Nacht; **all men are equal** alle Menschen sind gleich; **all five came** alle fünf kamen; **all the books/food** die ganzen Bücher/das ganze Essen; **all the time** die ganze Zeit (über); **all his life** sein ganzes Leben (lang)
▷ *pron* **1** alles; **I ate it all, I ate all of it** ich habe alles gegessen; **all of us/the boys went** wir gingen alle/alle Jungen gingen; **we all sat down** wir setzten uns alle
2 *(in phrases)*: **above all** vor allem; **after all** schließlich; **at all**: **not at all** *(in answer to question)* überhaupt nicht; *(in answer to thanks)* gern geschehen; **I'm not at all tired** ich bin überhaupt nicht müde; **anything at all will do** es ist egal, welche(r, s); **all in all** alles in allem
▷ *adv* ganz; **all alone** ganz allein; **it's not as hard as all that** so schwer ist es nun auch wieder nicht; **all the more/the better** umso mehr/besser; **all but** fast; **the score is 2 all** es steht 2 zu 2

allegation [ælɪˈɡeɪʃən] *n* Behauptung *f*; **alleged** *adj* angeblich

allergic [ə'lə:dʒɪk] adj allergisch (to gegen); **allergy** ['ælədʒɪ] n Allergie f

alleviate [ə'li:vɪeɪt] vt (pain) lindern

alley ['ælɪ] n (enge) Gasse; (passage) Durchgang m; (bowling) Bahn f

alliance [ə'laɪəns] n Bündnis nt

alligator ['ælɪgeɪtə*] n Alligator m

all-night adj (café, cinema) die ganze Nacht geöffnet

allocate ['æləkeɪt] vt zuweisen, zuteilen (to dat)

allotment n (plot) Schrebergarten m

allow [ə'laʊ] vt (permit) erlauben (sb jdm); (grant) bewilligen; (time) einplanen; **allow for** vt berücksichtigen; (cost etc) einkalkulieren; **allowance** n (from state) Beihilfe f; (from parent) Unterhaltsgeld nt

all right ['ɔ:l'raɪt] adj okay, in Ordnung; **I'm ~** mir geht's gut ▷ adv (satisfactorily) ganz gut ▷ interj okay

all-time adj (record, high) aller Zeiten

allusion [ə'lu:ʒn] n Anspielung f (to auf +akk)

all-wheel drive ['ɔ:lwi:l'draɪv] n (Auto) Allradantrieb m

ally ['ælaɪ] n Verbündete(r) mf; (Hist) Alliierte(r) mf

almond ['ɑ:mənd] n Mandel f

almost ['ɔ:lməʊst] adv fast

alone [ə'ləʊn] adj, adv allein

along [ə'lɒŋ] prep entlang +akk; **~ the river** den Fluss entlang; (position) am Fluss entlang ▷ adv (onward) weiter; **~ with** zusammen mit; **all ~** die ganze Zeit; **alongside** prep neben +dat ▷ adv (walk) nebenher

aloud [ə'laʊd] adv laut

alphabet ['ælfəbet] n Alphabet nt

alpine ['ælpaɪn] adj alpin; **Alps** [ælps] npl **the ~** die Alpen

already [ɔ:l'redɪ] adv schon, bereits

Alsace ['ælsæs] n Elsass nt; **Alsatian** [æl'seɪʃən] adj elsässisch ▷ n Elsässer(in) m(f); (Brit: dog) Schäferhund m

also ['ɔ:lsəʊ] adv auch

altar ['ɔ:ltə*] n Altar m

alter ['ɔ:ltə*] vt ändern; **alteration** [ɔ:ltə'reɪʃən] n Änderung f; **~s** (to building) Umbau m

alternate [ɔ:l'tɜ:nət] adj abwechselnd ▷ ['ɔ:ltəneɪt] vi abwechseln (with mit); **alternating current** n Wechselstrom m

alternative [ɔ:l'tɜ:nətɪv] adj Alternativ- ▷ n Alternative f

although [ɔ:l'ðəʊ] conj obwohl

altitude ['æltɪtju:d] n Höhe f

altogether [ɔ:ltə'geðə*] adv (in total) insgesamt; (entirely) ganz und gar

aluminium, aluminum (US) [ælju'mɪnɪəm, ə'lu:mɪnəm] n Aluminium nt

always ['ɔ:lweɪz] adv immer

am [æm] present of **be**; bin

am, a.m. abbr = **ante meridiem** vormittags, vorm.

amateur ['æmətə*] n Amateur(in) m(f) ▷ adj Amateur-; (theatre, choir) Laien-

amaze [ə'meɪz] vt erstaunen; **amazed** adj erstaunt (at über +akk); **amazing** adj erstaunlich

Amazon ['æməzən] n **~ (river)** Amazonas m

ambassador [æm'bæsədə*] n Botschafter m

amber ['æmbə*] n Bernstein m

ambiguity [æmbɪ'gjuɪtɪ] n Zweideutigkeit f; **ambiguous** [æm'bɪgjʊəs] adj zweideutig

ambition [æm'bɪʃən] n Ambition f; (ambitious nature) Ehrgeiz m; **ambitious** [æm'bɪʃəs] adj ehrgeizig

ambulance ['æmbjʊləns] n Krankenwagen m

amend [ə'mend] vt (law etc) ändern

America [ə'merɪkə] n Amerika nt; **American** adj amerikanisch ▷ n Amerikaner(in) m(f); **native ~** Indianer(in) m(f)

amiable ['eɪmɪəbl] adj liebenswürdig

amicable ['æmɪkəbl] adj freundlich; (relations) freundschaftlich; (Jur: settlement) gütlich

amnesia [æm'ni:zɪə] n Gedächtnisverlust m

among(st) [ə'mʌŋ(st)] prep unter +dat

amount [ə'maʊnt] n (quantity) Menge f; (of money) Betrag m; **a large/small ~ of ...** ziemlich viel/wenig ... ▷ vi **to ~ to** (total) sich belaufen auf +akk

amp, ampere [æmp, 'æmpeə*] n Ampere nt

amplifier ['æmplɪfaɪə*] n Verstärker m

amputate ['æmpjʊteɪt] vt amputieren

Amtrak® ['æmtræk] n amerikanische Eisenbahngesellschaft

amuse [əˈmjuːz] vt amüsieren; (entertain) unterhalten; **amused** adj **I'm not ~** das finde ich gar nicht lustig; **amusement** n (enjoyment) Vergnügen nt; (recreation) Unterhaltung f; **amusement arcade** n Spielhalle f; **amusement park** n Vergnügungspark m; **amusing** adj amüsant

an [æn, ən] art ein(e)

anaemic [əˈniːmɪk] adj blutarm

anaesthetic [ænɪsˈθetɪk] n Narkose f; (substance) Narkosemittel nt

analyse, analyze [ˈænəlaɪz] vt analysieren; **analysis** [əˈnælɪsɪs] n Analyse f

anatomy [əˈnætəmɪ] n Anatomie f; (structure) Körperbau m

ancestor [ˈænsestə*] n Vorfahr m

anchor [ˈæŋkə*] n Anker m ▷ vt verankern; **anchorage** n Ankerplatz m

anchovy [ˈæntʃəvɪ] n Sardelle f

ancient [ˈeɪnʃənt] adj alt; (fam: person, clothes etc) uralt

and [ænd, ənd] conj und

Andorra [ænˈdɔːrə] n Andorra nt

anemic adj (US) see **anaemic**

anesthetic n (US) see **anaesthetic**

angel [ˈeɪndʒəl] n Engel m

anger [ˈæŋgə*] n Zorn m ▷ vt ärgern

angina, angina pectoris [ænˈdʒaɪnə(ˈpektərɪs)] n Angina Pectoris f

angle [ˈæŋgl] n Winkel m; (fig) Standpunkt m

angler [ˈæŋglə*] n Angler(in) m(f); **angling** [ˈæŋglɪŋ] n Angeln nt

angry [ˈæŋgrɪ] adj verärgert; (stronger) zornig; **to be ~ with sb** auf jdn böse sein

angular [ˈæŋgjʊlə*] adj eckig; (face) kantig

animal [ˈænɪməl] n Tier nt; **animal rights** npl Tierrechte pl

animated [ˈænɪmeɪtɪd] adj lebhaft; **~ film** Zeichentrickfilm m

aniseed [ˈænɪsiːd] n Anis m

ankle [ˈæŋkl] n (Fuß)knöchel m

annex [ˈæneks] n Anbau m

anniversary [ænɪˈvɜːsərɪ] n Jahrestag m

announce [əˈnaʊns] vt bekannt geben; (officially) bekannt machen; (on radio, TV etc) (Radio, TV) ansagen; **announcement** n Bekanntgabe f; (official) Bekanntmachung f; (Radio, TV) Ansage f;

announcer n (Radio, TV) Ansager(in) m(f)

annoy [əˈnɔɪ] vt ärgern; **annoyance** n Ärger m; **annoyed** adj ärgerlich; **to be ~ with sb (about sth)** sich über jdn (über etw) ärgern; **annoying** adj ärgerlich; (person) lästig, nervig

annual [ˈænjʊəl] adj jährlich ▷ n Jahrbuch nt

anonymous [əˈnɒnɪməs] adj anonym

anorak [ˈænəræk] n Anorak m; (Brit fam: pej) Freak m

anorexia [ænəˈreksɪə] n Magersucht f; **anorexic** adj magersüchtig

another [əˈnʌðə*] adj, pron (different) ein(e) andere(r, s); (additional) noch eine(r, s); **let me put it ~ way** lass es mich anders sagen

answer [ˈɑːnsə*] n Antwort f (to auf +akk); (solution) Lösung f +gen ▷ vi antworten; (on phone) sich melden ▷ vt (person) antworten +dat; (letter, question) beantworten; (telephone) gehen an +akk, abnehmen; (door) öffnen; **answer back** vi widersprechen; **answering machine**, **answerphone** n Anrufbeantworter m

ant [ænt] n Ameise f

Antarctic [æntˈɑːktɪk] n Antarktis f; **Antarctic Circle** n südlicher Polarkreis

antelope [ˈæntɪləʊp] n Antilope f

antenna [ænˈtenə] (pl **antennae**) n (Zool) Fühler m; (Radio) Antenne f

anti- [ˈæntɪ] pref Anti-, anti-; **antibiotic** [ˈæntɪbaɪˈɒtɪk] n Antibiotikum nt

anticipate [ænˈtɪsɪpeɪt] vt (expect: trouble, question) erwarten, rechnen mit; **anticipation** [æntɪsɪˈpeɪʃən] n Erwartung f

anticlimax [æntɪˈklaɪmæks] n Enttäuschung f; **anticlockwise** [æntɪˈklɒkwaɪz] adv entgegen dem Uhrzeigersinn

antidote [ˈæntɪdəʊt] n Gegenmittel nt; **antifreeze** n Frostschutzmittel nt

Antipodes [ænˈtɪpədiːz] npl Australien und Neuseeland

antiquarian [æntɪˈkwɛərɪən] adj **~ bookshop** Antiquariat nt

antique [ænˈtiːk] n Antiquität f ▷ adj antik; **antique shop** n Antiquitätengeschäft nt

anti-Semitism [ˌæntɪˈsemɪtɪzm] *n*
Antisemitismus *m*; **antiseptic**
[ˌæntɪˈseptɪk] *n* Antiseptikum *nt* ▷ *adj*
antiseptisch; **antisocial** *adj* (*person*)
ungesellig; (*behaviour*) unsozial,
asozial

antlers [ˈæntləz] *npl* Geweih *nt*

anxiety [æŋˈzaɪətɪ] *n* Sorge *f* (*about* um);
anxious [ˈæŋkʃəs] *adj* besorgt (*about* um);
(*apprehensive*) ängstlich

⊘ **KEYWORD**

any [ˈenɪ] *adj* **1** (*in questions etc*): **have you
any butter?** haben Sie (etwas) Butter?;
have you any children? haben Sie
Kinder?; **if there are any tickets left** falls
noch Karten da sind
2 (*with negative*): **I haven't any
money/books** ich habe kein Geld/keine
Bücher
3 (*no matter which*) jede(r, s) (beliebige): **any
colour (at all)** jede beliebige Farbe;
choose any book you like nehmen Sie ein
beliebiges Buch
4 (*in phrases*): **in any case** in jedem Fall;
any day now jeden Tag; **at any
moment** jeden Moment; **at any rate**
auf jeden Fall
▷ *pron* **1** (*in questions etc*): **have you got
any?** haben Sie welche?; **can any of you
sing?** kann (irgend)einer von euch singen?
2 (*with negative*): **I haven't any (of them)**
ich habe keinen/keines (davon)
3 (*no matter which one(s)*): **take any of
those books (you like)** nehmen Sie
irgendeines dieser Bücher
▷ *adv* **1** (*in questions etc*): **do you want any
more soup/sandwiches?** möchten Sie
noch Suppe/Brote?; **are you feeling any
better?** fühlen Sie sich etwas besser?
2 (*with negative*): **I can't hear him any
more** ich kann ihn nicht mehr hören

⊘ **KEYWORD**

anything [ˈenɪθɪŋ] *pron* **1** (*in questions etc*)
(irgend)etwas; **can you see anything?**
können Sie etwas sehen?
2 (*with negative*): **I can't see anything** ich
kann nichts sehen
3 (*no matter what*): **you can say anything**

you like Sie können sagen, was Sie
wollen; **anything will do**
irgendetwas(, wird genügen)
irgendeine(r, s) (wird genügen); **he'll eat
anything** er ißt alles

apart [əˈpɑːt] *adv* auseinander; **~ from**
außer; **live ~** getrennt leben
apartment [əˈpɑːtmənt] *n* (*esp US*)
Wohnung *f*; **apartment block** *n* (*esp US*)
Wohnblock *m*
ape [eɪp] *n* (Menschen)affe *m*
aperitif [əˈperɪtɪf] *n* Aperitif *m*
aperture [ˈæpətjuə*] *n* Öffnung *f*; (*Foto*)
Blende *f*
apologize [əˈpɒlədʒaɪz] *vi* sich
entschuldigen; **apology** *n*
Entschuldigung *f*
apostrophe [əˈpɒstrəfɪ] *n* Apostroph *m*
appalled [əˈpɔːld] *adj* entsetzt (*at* über
+*akk*); **appalling** *adj* entsetzlich
apparatus [ˌæpəˈreɪtəs] *n* Apparat *m*;
(*piece of apparatus*) Gerät *nt*
apparent [əˈpærənt] *adj* (*obvious*)
offensichtlich (*to* für); (*seeming*) scheinbar;
apparently *adv* anscheinend
appeal [əˈpiːl] *vi* (dringend) bitten (*for*
um, *to* +*akk*); (*Jur*) Berufung einlegen; **to
~ to sb** (*be attractive*) jdm zusagen ▷ *n*
Aufruf *m* (*to* an +*akk*); (*Jur*) Berufung *f*;
(*attraction*) Reiz *m*; **appealing** *adj*
ansprechend, attraktiv
appear [əˈpɪə*] *vi* erscheinen; (*Theat*)
auftreten; (*seem*) scheinen; **appearance** *n*
Erscheinen *nt*; (*Theat*) Auftritt *m*; (*look*)
Aussehen *nt*
appendicitis [əpendɪˈsaɪtɪs] *n*
Blinddarmentzündung *f*; **appendix**
[əˈpendɪks] *n* Blinddarm *m*; (*to book*)
Anhang *m*
appetite [ˈæpɪtaɪt] *n* Appetit *m*; (*fig:
desire*) Verlangen *nt*; (*sexual*) Lust *f*;
appetizing [ˈæpɪtaɪzɪŋ] *adj* appetitlich,
appetitanregend
applause [əˈplɔːz] *n* Beifall *m*, Applaus *m*
apple [ˈæpl] *n* Apfel *m*; **apple crumble** *n*
mit Streuseln bestreutes Apfeldessert; **apple
juice** *n* Apfelsaft *m*; **apple pie** *n*
gedeckter Apfelkuchen *m*; **apple puree** *n*
apple sauce *n* Apfelmus *nt*; **apple tart** *n*
Apfelkuchen *m*; **apple tree** *n* Apfelbaum *m*
appliance [əˈplaɪəns] *n* Gerät *nt*;
applicable [əˈplɪkəbl] *adj* anwendbar; (*on*

forms) zutreffend; **applicant** ['æplɪkənt] n
Bewerber(in) m(f); **application**
[æplɪ'keɪʃən] n (request) Antrag m (for auf
+akk); (for job) Bewerbung f (for um);
application form n Anmeldeformular nt;
apply [ə'plaɪ] vi (be relevant) zutreffen
(to auf +akk); (for job etc) sich bewerben
(for um) ▷ vt (cream, paint etc) auftragen;
(put into practice) anwenden; (brakes)
betätigen
appoint [ə'pɔɪnt] vt (to post) ernennen;
appointment n Verabredung f; (at doctor,
hairdresser etc, in business) Termin m; **by**
~ nach Vereinbarung
appreciate [ə'priːʃɪeɪt] vt (value) zu
schätzen wissen; (understand) einsehen; **to**
be much ~d richtig gewürdigt werden ▷ vi
(increase in value) im Wert steigen;
appreciation [əpriːʃɪ'eɪʃən] n (esteem)
Anerkennung f, Würdigung f; (of person
also) Wertschätzung f
apprehensive [æprɪ'hensɪv] adj
ängstlich
apprentice [ə'prentɪs] n Lehrling m
approach [ə'prəʊtʃ] vi sich nähern ▷ vt
(place) sich nähern +dat; (person)
herantreten an +akk; (problem) angehen
appropriate [ə'prəʊprɪət] adj passend;
(to occasion) angemessen; (remark)
treffend; **appropriately** adv passend;
(expressed) treffend
approval [ə'pruːvəl] n (show of
satisfaction) Anerkennung f; (permission)
Zustimmung f (of zu); **approve** [ə'pruːv]
vt billigen ▷ vi **to ~ of sth/sb** etw
billigen/von jdm etwas halten; **I don't**
~ ich missbillige das
approx [ə'prɒks] abbr = **approximately**
ca.; **approximate** [ə'prɒksɪmɪt] adj
ungefähr; **approximately** adv ungefähr,
circa
apricot ['eɪprɪkɒt] n Aprikose f
April ['eɪprəl] n April m; see also
September
apron ['eɪprən] n Schürze f
aptitude [æptɪtjuːd] n Begabung f
aquaplaning ['ækwəpleɪnɪŋ] n (Auto)
Aquaplaning nt
aquarium [ə'kweərɪəm] n Aquarium nt
Aquarius [ə'kweərɪəs] n (Astr)
Wassermann m
Arab ['ærəb] n Araber(in) m(f); (horse)
Araber m; **Arabian** [ə'reɪbɪən] adj

arabisch; **Arabic** ['ærəbɪk] n (language)
Arabisch nt ▷ adj arabisch
arbitrary ['ɑːbɪtrərɪ] adj willkürlich
arcade [ɑː'keɪd] n Arkade f; (shopping
arcade) Einkaufspassage f
arch [ɑːtʃ] n Bogen m
archaeologist, archeologist (US)
[ɑːkɪ'ɒlədʒɪst] n Archäologe m,
Archäologin f; **archaeology, archeology**
(US) [ɑːkɪ'ɒlədʒɪ] n Archäologie f
archaic [ɑː'keɪɪk] adj veraltet
archbishop [ɑːtʃ'bɪʃəp] n Erzbischof m
archery ['ɑːtʃərɪ] n Bogenschießen nt
architect ['ɑːkɪtekt] n Architekt(in)
m(f); **architecture** ['ɑːkɪtektʃə] n
Architektur f
archive(s) ['ɑːkaɪv(z)] n(pl) Archiv nt
archway ['ɑːtʃweɪ] n Torbogen m
Arctic ['ɑːktɪk] n Arktis f; **Arctic Circle** n
nördlicher Polarkreis
are [ə], unstressed [ɑː*] present of **be**
area ['eərɪə] n (region, district) Gebiet nt,
Gegend f; (amount of space) Fläche f;
(part of building etc) Bereich m, Zone f; (fig:
field) Bereich m; **the London ~** der
Londoner Raum; **area code** n (US)
Vorwahl f
aren't [ɑːnt] contr of **are not**
Argentina [ɑːdʒən'tiːnə] n Argentinien
nt
argue ['ɑːgjuː] vi streiten (about, over über
+akk); **to ~ that ...** behaupten, dass ...; **to**
~ for/against ... sprechen für/gegen ...;
argument n (reasons) Argument nt;
(quarrel) Streit m; **to have an ~** sich
streiten
Aries ['eəriːz] nsing (Astr) Widder m
arise [ə'raɪz] (**arose, arisen**) vi sich
ergeben, entstehen; (problem, question,
wind) aufkommen
aristocracy [ærɪs'tɒkrəsɪ] n (class) Adel
m; **aristocrat** ['ærɪstəkræt] n Adlige(r)
mf; **aristocratic** [ærɪstə'krætɪk] adj
aristokratisch, adlig
arm [ɑːm] n Arm m; (sleeve) Ärmel m; (of
armchair) Armlehne f ▷ vt bewaffnen;
armchair ['ɑːmtʃeə*] n Lehnstuhl m
armed [ɑːmd] adj bewaffnet
armpit ['ɑːmpɪt] n Achselhöhle f
arms [ɑːmz] npl Waffen pl
army ['ɑːmɪ] n Armee f, Heer nt
A road ['eɪrəʊd] n (Brit) ≈ Bundesstraße f
aroma [ə'rəʊmə] n Duft m, Aroma nt;

aromatherapy [ərəʊmə'θerəpɪ] n
Aromatherapie f

arose [ə'rəʊz] pt of **arise**

around [ə'raʊnd] adv herum, umher;
(present) hier (irgendwo); (approximately)
ungefähr; (with time) gegen; **he's
~ somewhere** er ist hier irgendwo in der
Nähe ▷ prep (surrounding) um ... (herum);
(about in) in ... herum

arr. abbr = **arrival, arrives** Ank.

arrange [ə'reɪndʒ] vt (put in order)
(an)ordnen; (alphabetically) ordnen;
(artistically) arrangieren; (agree to: meeting
etc) vereinbaren, festsetzen; (holidays)
festlegen; (organize) planen; **to ~ that ...**
es so einrichten, dass ...; **we ~d to meet
at eight o'clock** wir haben uns für acht
Uhr verabredet; **it's all ~d** es ist alles
arrangiert; **arrangement** n (layout)
Anordnung f; (agreement) Vereinbarung
f, Plan m; **make ~s** Vorbereitungen
treffen

arrest [ə'rest] vt (person) verhaften ▷ n
Verhaftung f; **under ~** verhaftet

arrival [ə'raɪvəl] n Ankunft f; **new
~** (person) Neuankömmling m; **arrivals** n
(airport) Ankunftshalle f; **arrive** [ə'raɪv] vi
ankommen (at bei, in +dat); **to ~ at a
solution** eine Lösung finden

arrogant ['ærəgənt] adj arrogant

arrow ['ærəʊ] n (=weapon, sign) Pfeil m

art [ɑːt] n Kunst f, **~s** (pl)
Geisteswissenschaften pl

artery ['ɑːtərɪ] n (Med) Schlagader f,
Arterie f

art gallery n Kunstgalerie f,
Kunstmuseum nt

arthritis [ɑː'θraɪtɪs] n Arthritis f

artichoke ['ɑːtɪtʃəʊk] n Artischocke f

article ['ɑːtɪkl] n Artikel m; (object)
Gegenstand m

artificial [ɑːtɪ'fɪʃəl] adj künstlich, Kunst-;
(smile etc) gekünstelt

artist ['ɑːtɪst] n Künstler(in) m(f); **artistic**
[ɑː'tɪstɪk] adj künstlerisch

○ KEYWORD

as [æz] conj **1** (referring to time) als; **as
the years went by** mit den Jahren; **he
came in as I was leaving** als er
hereinkam, ging ich gerade; **as from
tomorrow** ab morgen

2 (in comparisons): **as big as** so groß wie;
twice as big as zweimal so groß wie; **as
much/many as** so viel/so viele wie; **as
soon as** sobald

3 (since, because) da; **he left early as he
had to be home by 10** er ging früher, da er
um 10 zu Hause sein musste

4 (referring to manner, way) wie; **do as you
wish** mach was du willst; **as she said** wie
sie sagte

5 (concerning): **as for or to that** was das
betrifft or angeht

6: **as if** or **though** als ob
▷ prep als; see also **long**; **he works as a
driver** er arbeitet als Fahrer; see also
such; **he gave it to me as a present** er
hat es mir als Geschenk gegeben; see also
well

asap [eɪeseɪ'piː, 'eɪsæp] acr = **as soon as
possible** möglichst bald

ascertain [æsə'teɪn] vt feststellen

ash [æʃ] n (dust) Asche f; (tree)
Esche f

ashamed [ə'ʃeɪmd] adj beschämt; **to
be ~ (of sb/sth)** sich (für jdn/etw)
schämen

ashore [ə'ʃɔː*] adv an Land

ashtray ['æʃtreɪ] n Aschenbecher m

Asia ['eɪʃə] n Asien nt; **Asian** adj asiatisch
▷ n Asiat(in) m(f)

aside [ə'saɪd] adv beiseite, zur Seite;
~ from (esp US) außer

ask [ɑːsk] vt, vi fragen; (question) stellen;
(request) bitten um; (invite) einladen; **to
~ sb the way** jdn nach dem Weg fragen;
to ~ sb to do sth jdn darum bitten, etw zu
tun; **ask for** vt bitten um

asleep [ə'sliːp] adj, adv **to be ~** schlafen;
to fall ~ einschlafen

asparagus [əs'pærəgəs] n Spargel m

aspect ['æspekt] n Aspekt m

aspirin ['æsprɪn] n Aspirin® nt

ass [æs] n (a. fig) Esel m

assassinate [ə'sæsɪneɪt] vt ermorden;
assassination [ə'sæsɪneɪʃn] n
Ermordung f; **~ attempt** Attentat nt

assault [ə'sɔːlt] n (Jur)
Körperverletzung f ▷ vt überfallen,
herfallen über +akk

assemble [ə'sembl] vt (parts)
zusammensetzen; (people)
zusammenrufen ▷ vi sich versammeln;

assembly [əˈsemblɪ] n (of people)
Versammlung f; (putting together)
Zusammensetzen nt; **assembly hall** n
Aula f

assert [əˈsɜːt] vt behaupten; **assertion**
[əˈsɜːʃən] n Behauptung f

assess [əˈses] vt einschätzen;
assessment n Einschätzung f

asset [ˈæset] n Vermögenswert m; (fig)
Vorteil m; **~s** pl Vermögen nt

assign [əˈsaɪn] vt zuweisen; **assignment**
n Aufgabe f; (mission) Auftrag m

assist [əˈsɪst] vt helfen +dat; **assistance** n
Hilfe f; **assistant** n Assistent(in) m(f),
Mitarbeiter(in) m(f); (in shop) Verkäufer(in)
m(f)

associate [əˈsəʊʃɪət] n (partner)
Partner(in) m(f), Teilhaber(in) m(f)
▷ [əˈsəʊʃɪeɪt] vt verbinden (with mit);
association [əsəʊsɪˈeɪʃən] n (organization)
Verband m, Vereinigung f; **in ~ with ...** in
Zusammenarbeit mit ...

assorted [əˈsɔːtɪd] adj gemischt;
assortment n Auswahl f (of an +dat); (of
sweets) Mischung f

assume [əˈsjuːm] vt annehmen (that
... dass ...); (role, responsibility)
übernehmen; **assumption** [əˈsʌmpʃən] n
Annahme f

assurance [əˈʃʊərəns] n Versicherung f;
(confidence) Zuversicht f; **assure** [əˈʃʊə*] vt
(say confidently) versichern +dat; **to ~ sb of**
sth jdm etw zusichern; **to be ~d of sth**
einer Sache sicher sein

asterisk [ˈæstərɪsk] n Sternchen nt

asthma [ˈæsmə] n Asthma nt

astonish [əˈstɒnɪʃ] vt erstaunen;
astonished adj erstaunt (at über);
astonishing adj erstaunlich;
astonishment n Erstaunen nt

astound [əˈstaʊnd] vt sehr erstaunen;
astounding adj erstaunlich

astray [əˈstreɪ] adv **to go ~** (letter etc)
verloren gehen; (person) vom Weg
abkommen; **to lead ~** irreführen, verführen

astrology [əsˈtrɒlədʒɪ] n Astrologie f

astronaut [ˈæstrənɔːt] n Astronaut(in)
m(f)

astronomy [əsˈtrɒnəmɪ] n Astronomie
f

asylum [əˈsaɪləm] n (home) Anstalt f;
(political asylum) Asyl nt; **asylum seeker** n
Asylbewerber(in) m(f)

○ **KEYWORD**

at [æt] prep **1** (referring to position, direction)
an +dat, bei +dat; (with place) in +dat; **at the**
top an der Spitze; **at home/school** zu
Hause, zuhause (österreichisch,
schweizerisch)/in der Schule; **at the**
baker's beim Bäcker; **to look at sth** auf
etw acc blicken; **to throw sth at sb** etw
nach jdm werfen
2 (referring to time): **at 4 o'clock** um 4 Uhr;
at night bei Nacht; **at Christmas** zu
Weihnachten; **at times** manchmal
3 (referring to rates, speed etc): **at £1 a kilo** zu £1
pro Kilo; **two at a time** zwei auf einmal;
at 50 km/h mit 50 km/h
4 (referring to manner): **at a stroke** mit
einem Schlag; **at peace** in Frieden
5 (referring to activity): **to be at work** bei
der Arbeit sein; **to play at cowboys**
Cowboy spielen; **to be good at sth** gut in
etw dat sein
6 (referring to cause): **shocked/surprised/**
annoyed at sth schockiert/überrascht/
verärgert über etw acc; **I went at his**
suggestion ich ging auf seinen Vorschlag
hin

ate [et, eɪt] pt of **eat**

athlete [ˈæθliːt] n Athlet(in) m(f); (track
and field) Leichtathlet(in) m(f); (sportsman)
Sportler(in) m(f); **~'s foot** Fußpilz m;
athletic [æθˈletɪk] adj sportlich; (build)
athletisch; **athletics** npl Leichtathletik f

Atlantic [ətˈlæntɪk] n **the ~ (Ocean)** der
Atlantik

atlas [ˈætləs] n Atlas m

ATM abbr = **automated teller machine**
Geldautomat m

atmosphere [ˈætməsfɪə*] n Atmosphäre
f; (fig) Stimmung f

atom [ˈætəm] n Atom nt; **atom(ic) bomb**
n Atombombe f; **atomic** [əˈtɒmɪk] adj
Atom-; **~ energy** Atomenergie f; **~ power**
Atomkraft f

A to Z® [ˈeɪtəˈzed] n Stadtplan m (in
Buchform)

atrocious [əˈtrəʊʃəs] adj grauenhaft;
atrocity [əˈtrɒsɪtɪ] n Grausamkeit f;
(deed) Gräueltat f

attach [əˈtætʃ] vt befestigen, anheften (to
an +dat); **to ~ importance to sth** Wert auf

etw *akk* legen; **to be ~ed to sb/sth** an jdm/etw hängen; **attachment** [əˈtætʃmənt] *n* (*affection*) Zuneigung *f*; (*Inform*) Attachment *nt*, Anhang *m*, Anlage *f*

attack [əˈtæk] *vt, vi* angreifen ▷ *n* Angriff *+akk* (*on* auf *m*); (*Med*) Anfall *m*

attempt [əˈtempt] *n* Versuch *m*; **to make an ~ to do sth** versuchen, etw zu tun ▷ *vt* versuchen

attend [əˈtend] *vt* (*go to*) teilnehmen an *+dat*; (*lectures, school*) besuchen ▷ *vi* (*be present*) anwesend sein; **attend to** *vt* sich kümmern um; (*customer*) bedienen; **attendance** *n* (*presence*) Anwesenheit *f*; (*people present*) Teilnehmerzahl *f*; **attendant** *n* (*in car park etc*) Wächter(in) *m(f)*; (*in museum*) Aufseher(in) *m(f)*

attention [əˈtenʃən] *n* Aufmerksamkeit *f*; (**your**) **~ please** Achtung!; **to pay ~ to sth** etw beachten; **to pay ~ to sb** jdm aufmerksam zuhören; (*listen*) jdm/etw aufmerksam zuhören; **for the ~ of ...** zu Händen von ...; **attentive** [əˈtentɪv] *adj* aufmerksam

attic [ˈætɪk] *n* Dachboden *m*; (*lived in*) Mansarde *f*

attitude [ˈætɪtjuːd] *n* (*mental*) Einstellung *f* (*to, towards* zu); (*more general, physical*) Haltung *f*

attorney [əˈtɜːnɪ] *n* (*US: lawyer*) Rechtsanwalt *m*, Rechtsanwältin *f*

attract [əˈtrækt] *vt* anziehen; (*attention*) erregen; **to be ~ed to or by sb** sich zu jdm hingezogen fühlen; **attraction** [əˈtrækʃən] *n* Anziehungskraft *f*; (*thing*) Attraktion *f*; **attractive** *adj* attraktiv; (*thing, idea*) reizvoll

aubergine [ˈəʊbəʒiːn] *n* Aubergine *f*

auction [ˈɔːkʃən] *n* Versteigerung *f*, Auktion *f* ▷ *vt* versteigern

audible [ˈɔːdɪbl] *adj* hörbar

audience [ˈɔːdɪəns] *n* Publikum *nt*; (*Radio*) Zuhörer *pl*; (*Tv*) Zuschauer *pl*

audio [ˈɔːdɪəʊ] *adj* Ton-

audition [ɔːˈdɪʃən] *n* Probe *f* ▷ *vi* (*Theat*) vorspielen, vorsingen

auditorium [ɔːdɪˈtɔːrɪəm] *n* Zuschauerraum *m*

Aug *abbr* = **August**

August [ˈɔːgəst] *n* August *m*; *see also* **September**

aunt [ɑːnt] *n* Tante *f*

au pair [əʊˈpɛə*] *n* Aupairmädchen *nt*, Aupairjunge *m*

Australia [ɒˈstreɪlɪə] *n* Australien *nt*; **Australian** *adj* australisch ▷ *n* Australier(in) *m(f)*

Austria [ˈɒstrɪə] *n* Österreich *nt*; **Austrian** *adj* österreichisch ▷ *n* Österreicher(in) *m(f)*

authentic [ɔːˈθentɪk] *adj* echt; (*signature*) authentisch; **authenticity** [ɔːθenˈtɪsɪtɪ] *n* Echtheit *f*

author [ˈɔːθə*] *n* Autor(in) *m(f)*; (*of report etc*) Verfasser(in) *m(f)*

authority [ɔːˈθɒrɪtɪ] *n* (*power, expert*) Autorität *f*; **an ~ on sth** eine Autorität auf dem Gebiet einer Sache; **the authorities** (*pl*) die Behörden *pl*; **authorize** [ˈɔːθəraɪz] *vt* (*permit*) genehmigen; **to be ~d to do sth** offiziell berechtigt sein, etw zu tun

auto [ˈɔːtəʊ] (*pl* **-s**) *n* (*US*) Auto *nt*

autobiography [ɔːtəʊbaɪˈɒgrəfɪ] *n* Autobiographie *f*; **autograph** [ˈɔːtəgrɑːf] *n* Autogramm *nt*

automatic [ɔːtəˈmætɪk] *adj* automatisch; **~ gear change** (*Brit*), **~ gear shift** (*US*) Automatikschaltung *f* ▷ *n* (*car*) Automatikwagen *m*

automobile [ˈɔːtəməbiːl] *n* (*US*) Auto(mobil) *nt*; **autotrain** [ˈɔːtəʊtreɪn] *n* (*US*) Autoreisezug *m*

autumn [ˈɔːtəm] *n* (*Brit*) Herbst *m*

auxiliary [ɔːgˈzɪlɪərɪ] *adj* Hilfs-; **~ verb** Hilfsverb *nt* ▷ *n* Hilfskraft *f*

availability [əveɪləˈbɪlɪtɪ] *n* (*of product*) Lieferbarkeit *f*; (*of resources*) Verfügbarkeit *f*; **available** *adj* erhältlich; (*existing*) vorhanden; (*product*) lieferbar; (*person*) erreichbar; **to be/make ~ to sb** jdm zur Verfügung stehen/stellen; **they're only ~ in black** es gibt sie nur in Schwarz, sie sind nur in Schwarz erhältlich

avalanche [ˈævəlɑːnʃ] *n* Lawine *f*

Ave *abbr* = **avenue**

avenue [ˈævənjuː] *n* Allee *f*

average [ˈævrɪdʒ] *n* Durchschnitt *m*; **on ~** im Durchschnitt ▷ *adj* durchschnittlich; **~ speed** Durchschnittsgeschwindigkeit *f*; **of ~ height** von mittlerer Größe

aviation [eɪvɪˈeɪʃən] *n* Luftfahrt *f*

avocado [ævəˈkɑːdəʊ] (*pl* **-s**) *n* Avocado *f*

avoid [əˈvɔɪd] *vt* vermeiden; **to ~ sb** jdm aus dem Weg gehen; **avoidable** *adj* vermeidbar

awake [əˈweɪk] **(awoke, awoken)** vi
aufwachen ▷ adj wach

award [əˈwɔːd] n (prize) Preis m; (for
bravery etc) Auszeichnung f ▷ vt
zuerkennen (to sb jdm); (present) verleihen
(to sb jdm)

aware [əˈwɛə*] adj bewusst; **to be ~ of
sth** sich dat einer Sache gen bewusst sein; **I
was not ~ that ...** es war mir nicht klar,
dass ...

away [əˈweɪ] adv weg; **to look
~** wegsehen; **he's ~** er ist nicht da; (on a
trip) er ist verreist; (from school, work) er
fehlt; (Sport) **they are (playing) ~** sie
spielen auswärts; (with distance) **three
miles ~** drei Meilen (von hier) entfernt; **to
work ~** drauflos arbeiten

awful [ˈɔːfʊl] adj schrecklich, furchtbar;
awfully adv furchtbar

awkward [ˈɔːkwəd] adj (clumsy)
ungeschickt; (embarrassing) peinlich;
(difficult) schwierig

awning [ˈɔːnɪŋ] n Markise f

awoke [əˈwəʊk] pt of **awake**; **awoken**
[əˈwəʊkən] pp of **awake**

ax (US), **axe** [æks] n Axt f

axle [ˈæksl] n (Tech) Achse f

BA *abbr* = **Bachelor of Arts**

BSc *abbr* = **Bachelor of Science**

babe [beɪb] *n* (*fam*) Baby *nt*; (*fam: affectionate*) Schatz *m*, Kleine(r) *mf*

baby ['beɪbɪ] *n* Baby *nt*; (*of animal*) Junge(s) *nt*; (*fam: affectionate*) Schatz *m*, Kleine(r) *mf*; **to have a ~** ein Kind bekommen; **it's your ~** (*fam: responsibility*) das ist dein Bier; **baby carriage** *n* (*US*) Kinderwagen *m*; **baby food** *n* Babynahrung *f*; **babyish** *adj* kindisch; **baby shower** *n* (*US*) Party für die werdende Mutter; **baby-sit** *irr vi* babysitten; **baby-sitter** *n* Babysitter(in) *m(f)*

bachelor ['bætʃələ*] *n* Junggeselle *m*; **Bachelor of Arts/Science** *erster akademischer Grad*, ≈ Magister/Diplom; **bachelorette** *n* Junggesellin *f*; **bachelorette party** *n* (*US*) Junggesellinnenabschied; **bachelor party** *n* (*US*) Junggesellenabschied

back [bæk] *n* (*of person, animal*) Rücken *m*; (*of house, coin etc*) Rückseite *f*; (*of chair*) Rückenlehne *f*; (*of car*) Rücksitz *m*; (*of train*) Ende *nt*; (*Sport: defender*) Verteidiger(in) *m(f)*; **at the ~ of ...**, (*US*) **in ~ of** (*inside*) hinten in ...; (*outside*) hinter ...; **~ to front** verkehrt herum ▷ *vt* (*support*) unterstützen; (*car*) rückwärts fahren ▷ *vi* (*go backwards*) rückwärts gehen o fahren ▷ *adj* Hinter-; **~ wheel** Hinterrad *nt* ▷ *adv* zurück; **they're ~** sie sind wieder da; **back away** *vi* sich zurückziehen; **back down** *vi* nachgeben; **back up** *vi* (*car etc*) zurücksetzen ▷ *vt* (*support*) unterstützen; (*Inform*) sichern; (*car*) zurückfahren

backache *n* Rückenschmerzen *pl*; **backbone** *n* Rückgrat *nt*; **backdate** *vt* zurückdatieren; **backdoor** *n* Hintertür *f*; **backfire** *vi* (*plan*) fehlschlagen; (*Auto*) fehlzünden; **background** *n* Hintergrund *m*; **backhand** *n* (*Sport*) Rückhand *f*; **backlog** *n* (*of work*) Rückstand *m*; **backpack** *n* (*US*) Rucksack *m*; **backpacker** *n* Rucksacktourist(in) *m(f)*; **backpacking** *n* Rucksacktourismus *m*; **back seat** *n* Rücksitz *m*; **backside** *n* (*fam*) Po *m*; **back street** *n* Seitensträßchen *nt*; **backstroke** *n* Rückenschwimmen *nt*; **back-up** *n* (*support*) Unterstützung *f*; **~ (copy)** (*Inform*) Sicherungskopie *f*; **backward** *adj* (*child*) zurückgeblieben; (*region*) rückständig; **~ movement** Rückwärtsbewegung *f*; **backwards** *adv* rückwärts; **backyard** *n* Hinterhof *m*

bacon ['beɪkən] *n* Frühstücksspeck *m*

bacteria [bæk'tɪərɪə] *npl* Bakterien *pl*

bad [bæd] (**worse, worst**) *adj* schlecht, schlimm; (*smell*) übel; **I have a ~ back** mir tut der Rücken weh; **I'm ~ at maths/sport** ich bin schlecht in Mathe/Sport; **to go ~** schlecht werden, verderben

badge [bædʒ] *n* Abzeichen *nt*

badger ['bædʒə*] *n* Dachs *m*

badly ['bædlɪ] *adv* schlecht; **~ wounded** schwer verwundet; **to need sth ~** etw dringend brauchen; **bad-tempered** ['bæd'tempəd] *adj* schlecht gelaunt

bag [bæg] *n* (*small*) Tüte *f*; (*larger*) Beutel *m*; (*handbag*) Tasche *f*; **my ~s** (*luggage*) mein Gepäck; **it's not my ~** (*fam*) das ist nicht mein Ding

baggage ['bægɪdʒ] *n* Gepäck *nt*; **baggage allowance** *n* Freigepäck *nt*; **baggage (re)claim** *n* Gepäckrückgabe *f*

baggy ['bægɪ] *adj* (*zu*) weit; (*trousers, suit*) ausgebeult

bag lady ['bæglɛɪdɪ] *n* Stadtstreicherin *f*

bagpipes ['bægpaɪps] *npl* Dudelsack *m*

Bahamas [bəˈhɑːməz] *npl* **the ~** die
Bahamas *pl*
bail [beɪl] *n (money)* Kaution *f*
bait [beɪt] *n* Köder *m*
bake [beɪk] *vt, vi* backen; **baked beans**
npl weiße Bohnen in Tomatensoße; **baked
potato** *(pl* **-es)** *n* in der Schale gebackene
Kartoffel, Ofenkartoffel *f;* **baker** *n*
Bäcker(in) *m(f);* **bakery** [ˈbeɪkərɪ] *n*
Bäckerei *f;* **baking powder** *n* Backpulver
nt
balance [ˈbæləns] *n (equilibrium)*
Gleichgewicht *nt* ▷ *vt (make up for)*
ausgleichen; **balanced** *adj* ausgeglichen;
balance sheet *n* Bilanz *f*
balcony [ˈbælkənɪ] *n* Balkon *m*
bald [bɔːld] *adj* kahl; **to be ~** eine Glatze
haben
Balkans [ˈbɔːlkənz] *npl* **the ~** der Balkan,
die Balkanländer *pl*
ball [bɔːl] *n* Ball *m;* **to have a ~** *(fam)* sich
prima amüsieren
ballet [ˈbæleɪ] *n* Ballett *nt;* **ballet dancer**
n Balletttänzer(in) *m(f)*
balloon [bəˈluːn] *n* (Luft)ballon *m*
ballot [ˈbælət] *n* (geheime) Abstimmung;
ballot box *n* Wahlurne *f;* **ballot paper** *n*
Stimmzettel *m*
ballpoint (pen) [ˈbɔːlpɔɪnt] *n*
Kugelschreiber *m*
ballroom [ˈbɔːlruːm] *n* Tanzsaal *m*
Baltic [ˈbɔːltɪk] *adj* **~ Sea** Ostsee *f;* **the
~ States** die baltischen Staaten
bamboo [bæmˈbuː] *n* Bambus *m;*
bamboo shoots *npl* Bambussprossen *pl*
ban [bæn] *n* Verbot *nt* ▷ *vt* verbieten
banana [bəˈnɑːnə] *n* Banane *f;* **he's ~s** er
ist völlig durchgeknallt; **banana split** *n*
Bananensplit *nt*
band [bænd] *n (group)* Gruppe *f; (of
criminals)* Bande *f; (Mus)* Kapelle *f; (pop, rock
etc)* Band *f; (strip)* Band *nt*
bandage [ˈbændɪdʒ] *n* Verband *m;*
(elastic) Bandage *f* ▷ *vt* verbinden
B & B *abbr* = **bed and breakfast**
bang [bæŋ] *n (noise)* Knall *m; (blow)* Schlag
m ▷ *vt, vi* knallen; *(door)* zuschlagen,
zuknallen; **banger** [bæŋə*] *n (Brit fam:
firework)* Knallkörper *m; (sausage)*
Würstchen *nt; (fam: old car)* Klapperkiste
f
bangs [bæŋz] *npl (US: of hair)* Pony *m*
banish [ˈbænɪʃ] *vt* verbannen

banister(s) [ˈbænɪstə*] *n*
(Treppen)geländer *nt*
bank [bæŋk] *n (Fin)* Bank *f; (of river etc)*
Ufer *nt;* **bank account** *n* Bankkonto *nt;*
bank balance *n* Kontostand *m;* **bank
card** *n* Bankkarte *f;* **bank code** *n*
Bankleitzahl *f;* **bank holiday** *n*
gesetzlicher Feiertag

bank holiday

Als **bank holiday** wird in
Großbritannien ein gesetzlicher
Feiertag bezeichnet, an dem die
Banken geschlossen sind. Die
meisten dieser Feiertage, abgesehen
von Weihnachten und Ostern, fallen
auf Montage im Mai und August. An
diesen langen Wochenenden (bank
holiday weekends) fahren viele
Briten in Urlaub, so dass dann auf
den Straßen, Flughäfen und bei der
Bahn sehr viel Betrieb ist.

bank manager *n* Filialleiter(in) *m(f);*
banknote *n* Banknote *f*
bankrupt *vt* ruinieren; **to go ~** Pleite
gehen
bank statement *n* Kontoauszug *m*
baptism [ˈbæptɪzəm] *n* Taufe *f;* **baptize**
[ˈbæptaɪz] *vt* taufen
bar [bɑː*] *n (for drinks)* Bar *f; (less smart)*
Lokal *nt; (rod)* Stange *f; (of chocolate etc)*
Riegel *m,* Tafel *f; (of soap)* Stück *nt;*
(counter) Theke *f* ▷ *prep* außer; **~ none**
ohne Ausnahme
barbecue [ˈbɑːbɪkjuː] *n (device)* Grill *m;*
(party) Barbecue *nt,* Grillfete *f;* **to have a
~** grillen
barbed wire [ˈbɑːbdwaɪə*] *n*
Stacheldraht *m*
barber [ˈbɑːbə*] *n* (Herren)friseur *m*
bar code [ˈbɑːkəʊd] *n* Strichkode *m*
bare [bɛə*] *adj* nackt; **~ patch** kahle
Stelle; **barefoot** *adj, adv* barfuß;
bareheaded *adj, adv* ohne
Kopfbedeckung; **barely** *adv* kaum; *(with
age)* knapp
bargain [ˈbɑːgɪn] *n (cheap offer)* günstiges
Angebot, Schnäppchen *nt; (transaction)*
Geschäft *nt;* **what a ~** das ist aber günstig!
▷ *vi* (ver)handeln

barge [bɑ:dʒ] n (for freight) Lastkahn m; (unpowered) Schleppkahn m

bark [bɑ:k] n (of tree) Rinde f; (of dog) Bellen nt ▷ vi (dog) bellen

barley [ˈbɑ:lɪ] n Gerste f

barmaid [ˈbɑ:meɪd] n Bardame f; **barman** [ˈbɑ:mən] (pl **-men**) n Barkeeper m

barn [bɑ:n] n Scheune f

barometer [bəˈrɒmɪtə*] n Barometer nt

baroque [bəˈrɒk] adj barock, Barock-

barracks [ˈbærəks] npl Kaserne f

barrel [ˈbærəl] n Fass nt; **barrel organ** n Drehorgel f

barricade [bærɪˈkeɪd] n Barrikade f

barrier [ˈbærɪə*] n (obstruction) Absperrung f, Barriere f; (across road etc) Schranke f

barrow [ˈbærəʊ] n (cart) Schubkarren m

bartender [ˈbɑ:tendə*] n (US) Barkeeper m

base [beɪs] n Basis f; (of lamp, pillar etc) Fuß m; (Mil) Stützpunkt m ▷ vt gründen (on auf +akk); **to be ~d on sth** auf etw dat basieren; **baseball** n Baseball m; **baseball cap** n Baseballmütze f; **basement** n Kellergeschoss nt

bash [bæʃ] (fam) n Schlag m; (fam) Party f ▷ vt hauen

basic [ˈbeɪsɪk] adj einfach; (fundamental) Grund-; (importance, difference) grundlegend; (in principle) grundsätzlich; **the accomodation is very ~** die Unterkunft ist sehr bescheiden; **basically** adv im Grunde; **basics** npl **the ~** das Wesentliche

basil [ˈbæzl] n Basilikum nt

basin [ˈbeɪsn] n (for washing, valley) (Wasch)becken nt

basis [ˈbeɪsɪs] n Basis f; **on the ~ of** aufgrund +gen; **on a monthly ~** monatlich

basket [ˈbɑ:skɪt] n Korb m; **basketball** n Basketball m

Basque [bæsk] n (person) Baske m, Baskin f; (language) Baskisch nt ▷ adj baskisch

bass [beɪs] n (Mus) Bass m; (Zool) Barsch m ▷ adj (Mus) Bass-

bastard [ˈbɑ:stəd] n (vulg: awful person) Arschloch nt

bat [bæt] n (Zool) Fledermaus f; (Sport: cricket, baseball) Schlagholz nt; (table tennis) Schläger m

batch [bætʃ] n Schwung m; (fam: of letters, books etc) Stoß m

bath [bɑ:θ] n Bad nt; (tub) Badewanne f; **to have a ~** baden ▷ vt (child etc) baden

bathe [beɪð] vt, vi (wound etc) baden; **bathing cap** n Badekappe f; **bathing costume, bathing suit** (US) n Badeanzug m

bathmat [ˈbɑ:θmæt] n Badevorleger m; **bathrobe** n Bademantel m; **bathroom** n Bad(ezimmer) nt; **baths** [bɑ:ðz] npl (Schwimm)bad nt; **bath towel** n Badetuch nt; **bathtub** n Badewanne f

baton [ˈbætən] n (Mus) Taktstock m; (police) Schlagstock m

batter [ˈbætə*] n Teig m ▷ vt heftig schlagen; **battered** adj übel zugerichtet; (hat, car) verbeult; (wife, baby) misshandelt

battery [ˈbætərɪ] n (Elec) Batterie f; **battery charger** n Ladegerät nt

battle [ˈbætl] n Schlacht f; (fig) Kampf m (for um +akk); **battlefield** n Schlachtfeld nt; **battlements** npl Zinnen pl

Bavaria [bəˈvɛərɪə] n Bayern nt; **Bavarian** adj bay(e)risch ▷ n Bayer(in) m(f)

bay [beɪ] n (of sea) Bucht f; (on house) Erker m; (tree) Lorbeerbaum m; **bay leaf** n Lorbeerblatt nt; **bay window** n Erkerfenster nt

BBC abbr = **British Broadcasting Corporation** BBC f

BC abbr = **before Christ** vor Christi Geburt, v. Chr.

◯ **KEYWORD**

be [bi:] (pt **was, were**, pp **been**) aux vb **1** (with present participle: forming continuous tenses); **what are you doing?** was machst du (gerade)?; **it is raining** es regnet; **I've been waiting for you for hours** ich warte schon seit Stunden auf dich

2 (with pp: forming passives): **to be killed** getötet werden; **the thief was nowhere to be seen** der Dieb war nirgendwo zu sehen

3 (in tag questions): **it was fun, wasn't it?** es hat Spaß gemacht, nicht wahr?

4 (+to +infin): **the house is to be sold** das Haus soll verkauft werden; **he's not to open it** er darf es nicht öffnen

▷ vb +complement 1 (usu) sein; **I'm tired** ich bin müde; **I'm hot/cold** mir ist heiß/kalt; **he's a doctor** er ist Arzt; **2 and 2 are 4** 2 und 2 ist or sind 4; **she's tall/pretty** sie ist groß/hübsch; **be careful/quiet** sei vorsichtig/ruhig
2 (of health): **how are you?** wie geht es dir?; **he's very ill** er ist sehr krank; **I'm fine now** jetzt geht es mir gut
3 (of age): **how old are you?** wie alt bist du?; **I'm sixteen (years old)** ich bin sechzehn (Jahre alt)
4 (cost): **how much was the meal?** was or wie viel hat das Essen gekostet?; **that'll be £5.75, please** das macht £5.75, bitte
▷ vi 1 (exist, occur etc) sein; **is there a God?** gibt es einen Gott?; **be that as it may** wie dem auch sei; **so be it** also gut
2 (referring to place): **I won't be here tomorrow** iche werde morgen nicht hier sein
3 (referring to movement): **where have you been?** wo bist du gewesen?; **I've been in the garden** ich war im Garten
▷ impers vb 1 (referring to time, distance, weather) sein; **it's 5 o'clock** es ist 5 Uhr; **it's 10 km to the village** es sind 10 km bis zum Dorf; **it's too hot/cold** es ist zu heiß/kalt
2 (emphatic): **it's me** ich bins; **it's the postman** es ist der Briefträger

beach [biːtʃ] n Strand m; **beachwear** n Strandkleidung f
bead [biːd] n (of glass, wood etc) Perle f; (drop) Tropfen m
beak [biːk] n Schnabel m
beam [biːm] n (of wood etc) Balken m; (of light) Strahl m ▷ vi (smile etc) strahlen
bean [biːn] n Bohne f; **bean curd** n Tofu m
bear [bɛə*] n (carry) tragen; (tolerate) ertragen ▷ n Bär m; **bearable** adj erträglich
beard [biəd] n Bart m
beast [biːst] n Tier nt; (brutal person) Bestie f; (disliked person) Biest nt
beat [biːt] n (beat, beaten) vt schlagen; (as punishment) prügeln; **to ~ sb at tennis** jdn im Tennis schlagen ▷ n (of heart, drum etc) Schlag m; (Mus) Takt m; (type of music) Beat m; **beat up** vt zusammenschlagen
beaten ['biːtn] pp of beat; **of the ~ track** abgelegen
beautiful ['bjuːtɪful] adj schön; (splendid)

herrlich; **beauty** ['bjuːtɪ] n Schönheit f; **beauty spot** n (place) lohnendes Ausflugsziel
beaver ['biːvə*] n Biber m
became [bɪˈkeɪm] pt of become
because [bɪˈkɒz] adv, conj weil ▷ prep **~ of** wegen +gen o dat
become [bɪˈkʌm] (became, become) vt werden; **what's ~ of him?** was ist aus ihm geworden?
bed [bed] n Bett nt; (in garden) Beet nt; **bed and breakfast** n Übernachtung f mit Frühstück; **bedclothes** npl Bettwäsche f; **bedding** n Bettzeug nt; **bed linen** n Bettwäsche f; **bedroom** n Schlafzimmer nt; **bed-sit(ter)** n (fam) möblierte Einzimmerwohnung; **bedspread** n Tagesdecke f; **bedtime** n Schlafenszeit f
bee [biː] n Biene f
beech [biːtʃ] n Buche f
beef [biːf] n Rindfleisch nt; **beefburger** n Hamburger m; **beef tomato** (pl -es) n Fleischtomate f
beehive ['biːhaɪv] n Bienenstock m
been [biːn] pp of be
beer [bɪə*] n Bier nt; **beer garden** n Biergarten m
beetle ['biːtl] n Käfer m
beetroot ['biːtruːt] n Rote Bete
before [bɪˈfɔː*] prep vor; **the year ~ last** vorletztes Jahr; **the day ~ yesterday** vorgestern ▷ conj bevor ▷ adv (of time) vorher; **have you been there ~?** waren Sie/warst du schon einmal dort?; **beforehand** adv vorher
beg [beg] vt **to ~ sb to do sth** jdn inständig bitten, etw zu tun ▷ vi (beggar) betteln (for um +akk)
began [bɪˈgæn] pt of begin
beggar ['begə*] n Bettler(in) m(f)
begin [bɪˈgɪn] (began, begun) vt, vi anfangen, beginnen; **to ~ to do sth** anfangen, etw zu tun; **beginner** n Anfänger(in) m(f); **beginning** n Anfang m
begun [bɪˈgʌn] pp of begin
behalf [bɪˈhɑːf] n **on ~ of, in ~ of** (US) im Namen/Auftrag von; **on my ~** für mich
behave [bɪˈheɪv] vi sich benehmen; **~ yourself!** benimm dich!; **behavior** (US), **behaviour** [bɪˈheɪvjə*] n Benehmen nt
behind [bɪˈhaɪnd] prep hinter; **to be ~ time** Verspätung haben ▷ adv hinten; **to be ~ with one's work** mit seiner Arbeit

im Rückstand sein ▷ n (fam) Hinterteil nt

beige [beɪʒ] adj beige

being ['biːɪŋ] n (existence) Dasein nt; (person) Wesen nt

Belarus [belə'rʊs] n Weißrussland nt

belch [beltʃ] n Rülpser m ▷ vi rülpsen

belfry ['belfrɪ] n Glockenturm m

Belgian ['beldʒən] adj belgisch ▷ n Belgier(in) m(f); **Belgium** ['beldʒəm] n Belgien nt

belief [bɪ'liːf] n Glaube m (in an +akk); (conviction) Überzeugung f; **it's my ~ that ...** ich bin der Überzeugung, dass ...;

believe [bɪ'liːv] vt glauben; **believe in** vi glauben an +akk; **believer** n (Rel) Gläubige(r) mf

bell [bel] n (church) Glocke f; (bicycle, door) Klingel f; **bellboy** ['belbɔɪ] n (esp US) Page m

bellows ['beləʊz] npl (for fire) Blasebalg m

belly ['belɪ] n Bauch m; **bellyache** n Bauchweh nt ▷ vi (fam) meckern; **belly button** n (fam) Bauchnabel m; **bellyflop** n (fam) Bauchklatscher m

belong [bɪ'lɒŋ] vi gehören (to sb jdm); (to club) angehören +dat; **belongings** npl Habe f

below [bɪ'ləʊ] prep unter ▷ adv unten

belt [belt] n (round waist) Gürtel m; (safety belt) Gurt m; **below the ~** unter der Gürtellinie ▷ vi (fam: go fast) rasen, düsen; **beltway** n (US) Umgehungsstraße f

bench [bentʃ] n Bank f

bend [bend] n Biegung f; (in road) Kurve f ▷ vt (bent, bent) (curve) biegen; (head, arm) beugen ▷ vi sich biegen; (person) sich beugen; **bend down** vi sich bücken

beneath [bɪ'niːθ] prep unter ▷ adv darunter

beneficial [benɪ'fɪʃl] adj gut, nützlich (to für); **benefit** ['benɪfɪt] n (advantage) Vorteil m; (profit) Nutzen m; **for your/his ~** deinetwegen/seinetwegen; **unemployment ~** Arbeitslosengeld nt ▷ vt gut tun +dat ▷ vi Nutzen ziehen (from aus)

Benelux ['benɪlʌks] n Beneluxländer pl

benign [bɪ'naɪn] adj (person) gütig; (climate) mild; (Med) gutartig

bent [bent] pt, pp of **bend** ▷ adj krumm; (fam) korrupt

beret ['bereɪ] n Baskenmütze f

Bermuda [bə'mjuːdə] n **the ~s** pl die Bermudas pl ▷ adj **~ shorts** pl Bermudashorts pl; **the ~ triangle** das Bermudadreieck

berry ['berɪ] n Beere f

berth [bɜːθ] n (for ship) Ankerplatz m; (in ship) Koje f; (in train) Bett nt ▷ vt am Kai festmachen ▷ vi anlegen

beside [bɪ'saɪd] prep neben; **~ the sea/lake** am Meer/See; **besides** [bɪ'saɪdz] prep außer ▷ adv außerdem

besiege [bɪ'siːdʒ] vt belagern

best [best] adj beste(r, s); **my ~ friend** mein bester o engster Freund; **the ~ thing (to do) would be to ...** das Beste wäre zu ...; (on food packaging) **~ before ...** mindestens haltbar bis ... ▷ n der/die/das Beste; **all the ~** alles Gute; **to make the ~ of it** das Beste daraus machen ▷ adv am besten; **I like this ~** das mag ich am liebsten; **best-before date** n Mindesthaltbarkeitsdatum nt; **best man** ['best'mæn] (pl **men**) n Trauzeuge m; **bestseller** ['bestselə*] n Bestseller m

bet [bet] (**bet, bet**) vt, vi wetten (on auf +akk); **I ~ him £5 that ...** ich habe mit ihm um 5 Pfund gewettet, dass ...; **you ~** (fam) und ob!; **I ~ he'll be late** er kommt mit Sicherheit zu spät ▷ n Wette f

betray [bɪ'treɪ] vt verraten; **betrayal** n Verrat m

better ['betə*] adj, adv besser; **to get ~** (healthwise) sich erholen, wieder gesund werden; (improve) sich verbessern; **I'm much ~ today** es geht mir heute viel besser; **you'd ~ go** du solltest lieber gehen; **a change for the ~** eine Wendung zum Guten

betting ['betɪŋ] n Wetten nt; **betting shop** n Wettbüro nt

between [bɪ'twiːn] prep zwischen; (among) unter; **~ you and me, ...** unter uns gesagt, ... ▷ adv (in) dazwischen

beverage ['bevərɪdʒ] n (formal) Getränk nt

beware [bɪ'weə*] vt **to ~ of sth** sich vor etw +dat hüten; **'~ of the dog'** „Vorsicht, bissiger Hund!"

bewildered [bɪ'wɪldəd] adj verwirrt

beyond [bɪ'jɒnd] prep (place) jenseits +gen; (time) über ... hinaus; (out of reach) außerhalb +gen; **it's ~ me** da habe ich keine Ahnung, da bin ich überfragt ▷ adv darüber hinaus

bias ['baɪəs] n (prejudice) Vorurteil nt,
Voreingenommenheit f
bias(s)ed adj voreingenommen
bib [bɪb] n Latz m
Bible ['baɪbl] n Bibel f
bicycle ['baɪsɪkl] n Fahrrad nt
bid [bɪd] n (bid, bid) vt (offer) bieten ▷ n
(attempt) Versuch m; (offer) Gebot nt
big [bɪg] adj groß; **it's no ~ deal** (fam) es
ist nichts Besonderes; **big dipper** n (Brit)
Achterbahn f; **bigheaded** [bɪg'hedɪd] adj
eingebildet
bike [baɪk] n (fam) Rad nt
bikini [bɪ'kiːnɪ] n Bikini m
bilberry ['bɪlbərɪ] n Heidelbeere f
bilingual [baɪ'lɪŋgwəl] adj
zweisprachig
bill [bɪl] n (account) Rechnung f; (US:
banknote) Banknote f; (Pol) Gesetzentwurf
m; (Zool) Schnabel m; **billfold** ['bɪlfəʊld] n
(US) Brieftasche f
billiards ['bɪlɪədz] nsing Billard nt; **billiard
table** Billardtisch m
billion ['bɪlɪən] n Milliarde f
bin [bɪn] n Behälter m; (rubbish bin)
(Müll)eimer m; (for paper) Papierkorb m
bind [baɪnd] (bound, bound) vt binden;
(bind together) zusammenbinden; (wound)
verbinden; **binding** n (ski) Bindung f;
(book) Einband m
binge [bɪndʒ] n (fam: drinking) Sauferei f;
to go on a ~ auf Sauftour gehen
bingo ['bɪŋgəʊ] n Bingo nt
binoculars [bɪ'nɒkjʊləz] npl Fernglas nt
biodegradable ['baɪəʊdɪ'greɪdəbl] adj
biologisch abbaubar
biography [baɪ'ɒgrəfɪ] n Biografie f
biological [baɪə'lɒdʒɪkəl] adj biologisch;
biology [baɪ'blədʒɪ] n Biologie f
birch [bɜːtʃ] n Birke f
bird [bɜːd] n Vogel m; (Brit fam: girl,
girlfriend) Tussi f; **bird watcher** n
Vogelbeobachter(in) m(f)
birth [bɜːθ] n Geburt f; **birth certificate**
n Geburtsurkunde f; **birth control** n
Geburtenkontrolle f; **birthday** n
Geburtstag m; **happy ~** herzlichen
Glückwunsch zum Geburtstag; **birthday
card** n Geburtstagskarte f; **birthday
party** n Geburtstagsfeier f; **birthplace** n
Geburtsort m
biscuit ['bɪskɪt] n (Brit) Keks m
bisexual [baɪ'seksjʊəl] adj bisexuell

bishop ['bɪʃəp] n Bischof m; (in chess)
Läufer m
bit [bɪt] pt of **bite** ▷ n (piece) Stück(chen)
nt; (Inform) Bit nt; **a ~ (of ...)** (small amount)
ein bisschen ...; **a ~ tired** etwas müde;
~ by ~ allmählich; (time) **for a ~** ein
Weilchen; **quite a ~** (a lot) ganz schön viel
bitch [bɪtʃ] n (dog) Hündin f; **bitchy** adj
gemein, zickig
bite [baɪt] (bit, bitten) vt, vi beißen ▷ n
Biss m; (mouthful) Bissen m; (insect) Stich
m; **to have a ~** eine Kleinigkeit essen;
bitten pp of **bite**
bitter ['bɪtə*] adj bitter; (memory etc)
schmerzlich ▷ n (Brit: beer) halbdunkles
Bier; **bitter lemon** n Bitter Lemon nt
bizarre [bɪ'zɑː*] adj bizarr
black [blæk] adj schwarz; **blackberry** n
Brombeere f; **blackbird** n Amsel f;
blackboard n (Wand)tafel f; **black box** n
(Aviat) Flugschreiber m; **blackcurrant** n
Schwarze Johannisbeere; **black eye** n
blaues Auge; **Black Forest** n
Schwarzwald m; **Black Forest gateau** n
Schwarzwälder Kirschtorte f; **blackmail** n
Erpressung f ▷ vt erpressen; **black
market** n Schwarzmarkt m; **blackout** n
(Med) Ohnmacht f; **to have a
~** ohnmächtig werden; **black pudding** n
≈ Blutwurst f; **Black Sea** n **the ~** das
Schwarze Meer; **blacksmith** n
Schmied(in) m(f); **black tie** n
Abendanzug m, Smoking m; **is it ~?**
ist/besteht da Smokingzwang?
bladder ['blædə*] n Blase f
blade [bleɪd] n (of knife) Klinge f; (of
propeller) Blatt nt; (of grass) Halm m
blame [bleɪm] n Schuld f ▷ vt **to ~ sth on
sb** jdm die Schuld an etw dat geben; **he is
to ~** er ist daran schuld
bland [blænd] adj (taste) fade; (comment)
nichts sagend
blank [blæŋk] adj (page, space) leer,
unbeschrieben; (look) ausdruckslos;
~ cheque Blankoscheck m
blanket ['blæŋkɪt] n (Woll)decke f
blast [blɑːst] n (of wind) Windstoß m;
(of explosion) Druckwelle f ▷ vt (blow
up) sprengen; **~!** (fam) Mist!,
verdammt!
blatant ['bleɪtənt] adj (undisguised) offen;
(obvious) offensichtlich
blaze [bleɪz] vi lodern; (sun) brennen ▷ n

(building) Brand m; (other fire) Feuer nt; **a ~ of colour** eine Farbenpracht

blazer ['bleɪzə*] n Blazer m

bleach [bliːtʃ] n Bleichmittel nt ▷ vt bleichen

bleak [bliːk] adj öde, düster; (future) trostlos

bleary ['blɪərɪ] adj (eyes) trübe, verschlafen

bleed [bliːd] (**bled, bled**) vi bluten

bleep [bliːp] n Piepton m ▷ vi piepen; **bleeper** n (fam) Piepser m

blend [blend] n Mischung f ▷ vt mischen ▷ vi sich mischen; **blender** n Mixer m

bless [bles] vt segnen; **~ you!** Gesundheit!; **blessing** n Segen m

blew [bluː] pt of **blow**

blind [blaɪnd] adj blind; (corner) unübersichtlich; **to turn a ~ eye to sth** bei etw ein Auge zudrücken ▷ n (for window) Rollo nt ▷ vt blenden; **blind alley** n Sackgasse f; **blind spot** n (Auto) toter Winkel; (fig) schwacher Punkt

blink [blɪŋk] vi blinzeln; (light) blinken

bliss [blɪs] n (Glück)seligkeit f

blister ['blɪstə*] n Blase f

blizzard ['blɪzəd] n Schneesturm m

bloated ['bləʊtɪd] adj aufgedunsen

block [blɒk] n (of wood, stone, ice) Block m, Klotz m; (of buildings) Häuserblock m; **~ of flats** (Brit) Wohnblock m ▷ vt (road etc) blockieren; (pipe, nose) verstopfen; **blockage** ['blɒkɪdʒ] n Verstopfung f; **blockbuster** ['blɒkbʌstə*] n Knüller m; **block letters** npl Blockschrift f

bloke [bləʊk] n (Brit fam) Kerl m, Typ m

blonde [blɒnd] adj blond ▷ n (person) Blondine f, blonder Typ

blood [blʌd] n Blut nt; **blood count** n Blutbild nt; **blood donor** n Blutspender(in) m(f); **blood group** n Blutgruppe f; **blood poisoning** n Blutvergiftung f; **blood pressure** n Blutdruck m; **blood sample** n Blutprobe f; **bloodsports** npl Sportarten, bei denen Tiere getötet werden; **bloodthirsty** adj blutrünstig; **bloody** adj (Brit fam) verdammt, Scheiß-; (literal sense) blutig

bloom [bluːm] n Blüte f ▷ vi blühen

blossom ['blɒsəm] n Blüte f ▷ vi blühen

blot [blɒt] n (of ink) Klecks m; (fig) Fleck m

blouse [blaʊz] n Bluse f; **big girl's ~** (fam) Schwächling m, femininer Typ

blow [bləʊ] n Schlag m ▷ vi, vt (**blew, blown**) (wind) wehen, blasen; (person: trumpet etc) blasen; **to ~ one's nose** sich dat die Nase putzen; **blow out** vt (candle etc) ausblasen; **blow up** vi explodieren ▷ vt sprengen; (balloon, tyre) aufblasen; (Foto: enlarge) vergrößern; **blow-dry** vt föhnen; **blowjob** n (fam) **to give sb a ~** jdm einen blasen; **blown** [bləʊn] pp of **blow**; **blow-out** n (Auto) geplatzter Reifen

BLT n abbr = **bacon, lettuce and tomato sandwich** mit Frühstücksspeck, Kopfsalat und Tomaten belegtes Sandwich

blue [bluː] adj blau; (fam: unhappy) trübsinnig, niedergeschlagen; (film) pornografisch; (joke) anzüglich; (language) derb; **bluebell** n Glockenblume f; **blueberry** n Blaubeere f; **blue cheese** n Blauschimmelkäse m; **blues** npl **the ~** (Mus) der Blues; **to have the ~** (fam) niedergeschlagen sein

blunder ['blʌndə*] n Schnitzer m

blunt [blʌnt] adj (knife) stumpf; (fig) unverblümt; **bluntly** adv geradeheraus

blurred [blɜːd] adj verschwommen, unklar

blush [blʌʃ] vi erröten

board [bɔːd] n (of wood) Brett nt; (committee) Ausschuss m; (of firm) Vorstand m; **~ and lodging** Unterkunft und Verpflegung; **on ~** an Bord ▷ vt (train, bus) einsteigen in +akk; (ship) an Bord +gen gehen; **boarder** n Pensionsgast m; (school) Internatsschüler(in) m(f); **board game** n Brettspiel nt; **boarding card**, **boarding pass** n Bordkarte f, Einsteigekarte f; **boarding school** n Internat nt; **board meeting** n Vorstandssitzung f; **boardroom** n Sitzungssaal m (des Vorstands)

boast [bəʊst] vi prahlen (about mit) ▷ n Prahlerei f

boat [bəʊt] n Boot nt; (ship) Schiff nt; **boatman** n (hirer) Bootsverleiher m; **boat race** n Regatta f; **boat train** n Zug m mit Schiffsanschluss

bob(sleigh) ['bɒbsleɪ] n Bob m

bodily ['bɒdɪlɪ] adj körperlich ▷ adv (forcibly) gewaltsam; **body** ['bɒdɪ] n Körper m; (dead) Leiche f; (of car) Karosserie

f; **bodybuilding** n Bodybuilding nt;
bodyguard n Leibwächter m; (group)
Leibwache f; **body jewellery** n
Intimschmuck m; **body odour** n
Körpergeruch m; **body piercing** n
Piercing nt; **bodywork** n Karosserie f

boil [bɔɪl] vt, vi kochen ▷ n (Med)
Geschwür nt; **boiler** n Boiler m; **boiling**
adj (water etc) kochend (heiß); **I was ~** (hot)
mir war fürchterlich heiß; (with rage) ich
kochte vor Wut; **boiling point** n
Siedepunkt m

bold [bəʊld] adj kühn, mutig; (colours)
kräftig; (type) fett

Bolivia [bə'lɪvɪə] n Bolivien nt

bolt [bəʊlt] n (lock) Riegel m; (screw)
Bolzen m ▷ vt verriegeln

bomb [bɒm] n Bombe f ▷ vt
bombardieren

bond [bɒnd] n (link) Bindung f; (Fin)
Obligation f

bone [bəʊn] n Knochen m; (of fish) Gräte
f; **boner** n (US fam) Schnitzer m; (erection)
Ständer m

bonfire ['bɒnfaɪə*] n Feuer nt (im Freien)

bonnet ['bɒnɪt] n (Brit Auto) Haube f; (for
baby) Häubchen nt

bonny ['bɒnɪ] adj (esp Scottish) hübsch

bonus ['bəʊnəs] n Bonus m, Prämie f

boo [bu:] vt auspfeifen, ausbuhen ▷ vi
buhen ▷ n Buhruf m

book [bʊk] n Buch nt; (of tickets, stamps)
Heft nt ▷ vt (ticket etc) bestellen; (hotel,
flight etc) buchen; (Sport) verwarnen; **fully
~ed (up)** ausgebucht; (performance)
ausverkauft; **book in** vt eintragen; **to be
~ed in at a hotel** ein Zimmer in einem
Hotel bestellt haben; **bookable** adj im
Vorverkauf erhältlich; **bookcase** n
Bücherregal nt; **booking** n Buchung f;
booking office n (Rail)
Fahrkartenschalter m; (Theat)
Vorverkaufsstelle f; **book-keeping** n
Buchhaltung f; **booklet** n Broschüre f;
bookmark n (a. Inform) Lesezeichen nt;
bookshelf n Bücherbord nt; **bookshelves**
Bücherregal nt; **bookshop**, **bookstore** n
(esp US) Buchhandlung f

boom [bu:m] n (of business) Boom m;
(noise) Dröhnen nt ▷ vi (business) boomen;
(fam) florieren; (voice etc) dröhnen

boomerang ['bu:məræŋ] n Bumerang m

boost [bu:st] n Auftrieb m ▷ vt

(production, sales) ankurbeln; (power, profits
etc) steigern; **booster (injection)** n
Wiederholungsimpfung f

boot [bu:t] n Stiefel m; (Brit Auto)
Kofferraum m ▷ vt (Inform) laden, booten

booth [bu:ð] n (at fair etc) Bude f; (at trade
fair etc) Stand m

booze [bu:z] n (fam) Alkohol m ▷ vi (fam)
saufen

border ['bɔ:də*] n Grenze f; (edge) Rand m;
north/south of the Border in
Schottland/England; **borderline** n
Grenze f

bore [bɔ:*] pt of bear ▷ vt (hole etc)
bohren; (person) langweilen ▷ n (person)
Langweiler(in) m(f), langweiliger Mensch;
(thing) langweilige Sache; **bored** adj **to be
~** sich langweilen; **boredom** n
Langeweile f; **boring** adj langweilig

born [bɔ:n] adj **he was ~ in London** er ist
in London geboren

borne [bɔ:n] pp of bear

borough ['bʌrə] n Stadtbezirk m

borrow ['bɒrəʊ] vt borgen

Bosnia-Herzegovina
['bɒznɪəhɜ:tsəgəʊ'vi:nə] n
Bosnien-Herzegowina nt; **Bosnian**
['bɒznɪən] adj bosnisch ▷ n Bosnier(in)
m(f)

boss [bɒs] n Chef(in) m(f), Boss m; **boss
around** vt herumkommandieren; **bossy**
adj herrisch

botanical [bə'tænɪkəl] adj botanisch;
~ garden(s) botanischer Garten

both [bəʊθ] adj beide; **~ the books** beide
Bücher ▷ pron (people) beide; (things)
beides; **~ (of) the boys** beide Jungs; **I like
~ of them** ich mag sie (alle) beide ▷ adv
~ X and Y sowohl X als auch Y

bother ['bɒðə*] vt ärgern, belästigen; **it
doesn't ~ me** das stört mich nicht; **he
can't be ~ed with details** mit Details gibt
er sich nicht ab; **I'm not ~ed** das ist mir
egal ▷ vi sich kümmern (about um); **don't
~** (das ist) nicht nötig, lass es! ▷ n (trouble)
Mühe f; (annoyance) Ärger m

bottle ['bɒtl] n Flasche f ▷ vt (in
Flaschen) abfüllen; **bottle out** vi (fam)
den Mut verlieren, aufgeben; **bottle bank**
n Altglascontainer m; **bottled** adj in
Flaschen; **~ beer** Flaschenbier nt;
bottleneck n (fig) Engpass m; **bottle
opener** n Flaschenöffner m

bottom ['bɒtəm] n (of container) Boden m; (underside) Unterseite f; (fam: of person) Po m; **at the ~ of the sea/table/page** auf dem Meeresgrund/am Tabellenende/unten auf der Seite ▷ adj unterste(r, s); **to be ~ of the class/league** Klassenletzte(r)/Tabellenletzte(r) sein; **~ gear** (Auto) erster Gang

bought [bɔ:t] pt, pp of **buy**

bounce [baʊns] vi (ball) springen, aufprallen; (cheque) platzen; **~ up and down** (person) herumhüpfen; **bouncy** adj (ball) gut springend; (person) munter; **bouncy castle®** n Hüpfburg f

bound [baʊnd] pt, pp of **bind** ▷ adj (tied up) gebunden; (obliged) verpflichtet; **to be ~ to do sth** (sure to) etw bestimmt tun (werden); (have to) etw tun müssen; **it's ~ to happen** es muss so kommen; **to be ~ for ...** auf dem Weg nach ... sein; **boundary** ['baʊndərɪ] n Grenze f

bouquet [bʊ'keɪ] n (flowers) Strauß m; (of wine) Blume f

boutique [bu:'ti:k] n Boutique f

bow [baʊ] n (ribbon) Schleife f; (instrument, weapon) Bogen m ▷ [baʊ] vi sich verbeugen ▷ [baʊ] n (with head) Verbeugung f; (of ship) Bug m

bowels ['baʊəlz] npl Darm m

bowl [bəʊl] n (basin) Schüssel f; (shallow) Schale f; (for animal) Napf m ▷ vt, vi (in cricket) werfen

bowler ['bəʊlə*] n (in cricket) Werfer(in) m(f); (hat) Melone f

bowling ['bəʊlɪŋ] n Kegeln nt; **bowling alley** n Kegelbahn f; **bowling green** n Rasen m zum Bowling-Spiel; **bowls** [bəʊlz] nsing (game) Bowling-Spiel nt

bow tie [bəʊ'taɪ] n Fliege f

box [bɒks] n Schachtel f; (cardboard) Karton m; (bigger) Kasten m; (space on form) Kästchen nt; (Theat) Loge f; **boxer** Boxer(in) m(f); **boxers, boxer shorts** npl Boxershorts pl; **boxing** n (Sport) Boxen nt; **Boxing Day** n zweiter Weihnachtsfeiertag

Boxing Day

Boxing Day ist ein Feiertag in Großbritannien. Fällt Weihnachten auf ein Wochenende, wird der Feiertag am nächsten Wochentag

nachgeholt. Der Name geht auf einen alten Brauch zurück: früher erhielten Händler und Lieferanten an diesem Tag ein Geschenk, die so genannte Christmas Box.

boxing gloves npl Boxhandschuhe pl; **boxing ring** n Boxring m

box number n Chiffre f

box office n Kasse f

boy [bɔɪ] n Junge m

boycott ['bɔɪkɒt] n Boykott m ▷ vt boykottieren

boyfriend ['bɔɪfrend] n (fester) Freund m; **boy scout** n Pfadfinder m

bra [brɑ:] n BH m

brace [breɪs] n (Tech) Strebe f; (on teeth) Spange f

bracelet ['breɪslɪt] n Armband nt

braces ['breɪsɪz] npl (Brit) Hosenträger pl

bracket ['brækɪt] n (in text) Klammer f; (Tech) Träger m ▷ vt einklammern

brag [bræg] vi angeben

Braille [breɪl] n Blindenschrift f

brain [breɪn] n (Anat) Gehirn nt; (mind) Verstand m; **~s** (pl) (intelligence) Grips m; **brainwave** n Geistesblitz m; **brainy** adj schlau, clever

braise [breɪz] vt schmoren

brake [breɪk] n Bremse f ▷ vi bremsen; **brake fluid** n Bremsflüssigkeit f; **brake light** n Bremslicht nt; **brake pedal** n Bremspedal nt

branch [brɑ:ntʃ] n (of tree) Ast m; (of family, subject) Zweig m; (of firm) Filiale f, Zweigstelle f; **branch off** vi (road) abzweigen

brand [brænd] n (Comm) Marke f

brand-new ['brænd'nju:] adj (funkel)nagelneu

brandy ['brændɪ] n Weinbrand m

brass [brɑ:s] n Messing nt; (Brit fam: money) Knete f; **brass band** n Blaskapelle f

brat [bræt] n (pej, fam) Gör nt

brave [breɪv] adj tapfer, mutig; **bravery** ['breɪvərɪ] n Mut m

brawl [brɔ:l] n Schlägerei f

brawn [brɔ:n] n (strength) Muskelkraft f; (Gastr) Sülze f; **brawny** adj muskulös

Brazil [brə'zɪl] n Brasilien nt; **Brazilian** adj brasilianisch ▷ n Brasilianer(in) m(f); **brazil nut** n Paranuss f

bread [bred] n Brot nt; **breadbin** (Brit),

breadbox (US) n Brotkasten m;
breadcrumbs npl Brotkrumen pl; (Gastr)
Paniermehl nt; **breaded** adj paniert;
breadknife n Brotmesser nt
breadth [bredθ] n Breite f
break [breɪk] n (fracture) Bruch m; (rest)
Pause f; (short holiday) Kurzurlaub m; **give
me a ~** gib mir eine Chance, hör auf
damit! ▷ vt (**broke, broken**) (fracture)
brechen; (in pieces) zerbrechen; (toy, device)
kaputtmachen; (promise) nicht halten;
(silence) brechen; (law) verletzen; (journey)
unterbrechen; (news) mitteilen (to sb jdm);
I broke my leg ich habe mir das Bein
gebrochen; **he broke it to her gently** er
hat es ihr schonend beigebracht ▷ vi
(come apart) (auseinander) brechen; (in
pieces) zerbrechen; (toy, device)
kaputtgehen; (person) zusammenbrechen;
(day, dawn) anbrechen; (news) bekannt
werden; **break down** vi (car) eine Panne
haben; (machine) versagen; (person)
zusammenbrechen; **break in** vi (burglar)
einbrechen; **break into** vt einbrechen in
+akk; **break off** vi, vt abbrechen; **break
out** vi ausbrechen; **to ~ in a rash** einen
Ausschlag bekommen; **break up** vi
aufbrechen; (meeting, organisation) sich
auflösen; (marriage) in die Brüche gehen;
(couple) sich trennen; **school breaks up on
Friday** am Freitag beginnen die Ferien
▷ vt aufbrechen; (marriage) zerstören;
(meeting) auflösen; **breakable** adj
zerbrechlich; **breakage** n Bruch m;
breakdown n (of car) Panne f; (of machine)
Störung f; (of person, relations, system)
Zusammenbruch m; **breakdown service**
n Pannendienst m; **breakdown truck** n
Abschleppwagen m
breakfast ['brekfəst] n Frühstück nt; **to
have ~** frühstücken; **breakfast cereal** n
Cornflakes, Muesli etc; **breakfast television**
n Frühstücksfernsehen nt
break-in ['breɪkɪn] n Einbruch m;
breakup ['breɪkʌp] n (of meeting,
organization) Auflösung f; (of marriage)
Zerrüttung f
breast [brest] n Brust f; **breastfeed** vt
stillen; **breaststroke** n Brustschwimmen
nt
breath [breθ] n Atem m; **out of ~** außer
Atem; **breathalyse, breathalyze**
['breθəlaɪz] vt (ins Röhrchen) blasen

lassen; **breathalyser, breathalyzer** n
Promillemesser m; **breathe** [briːð] vt, vi
atmen; **breathe in** vt, vi einatmen;
breathe out vt, vi ausatmen;
breathless ['breθlɪs] adj atemlos;
breath-taking ['breθteɪkɪŋ] adj
atemberaubend
bred [bred] pt, pp of **breed**
breed [briːd] n (race) Rasse f ▷ vi (**bred,
bred**) sich vermehren ▷ vt züchten;
breeder n Züchter(in) m(f); (fam) Hetero
m; **breeding** n (of animals) Züchtung f; (of
person) (gute) Erziehung
breeze [briːz] n Brise f
brevity ['brevɪtɪ] n Kürze f
brew [bruː] vt (beer) brauen; (tea) kochen;
brewery n Brauerei f
bribe ['braɪb] n Bestechungsgeld nt ▷ vt
bestechen; **bribery** ['braɪbərɪ] n
Bestechung f
brick [brɪk] n Backstein m; **bricklayer** n
Maurer(in) m(f)
bride [braɪd] n Braut f; **bridegroom** n
Bräutigam m; **bridesmaid** n Brautjungfer
f
bridge [brɪdʒ] n Brücke f; (cards) Bridge nt
brief [briːf] adj kurz ▷ vt instruieren (on
über +akk); **briefcase** n Aktentasche f,
briefs npl Slip m
bright [braɪt] adj hell; (colour) leuchtend;
(cheerful) heiter; (intelligent) intelligent;
(idea) glänzend; **brighten up** vt aufhellen;
(person) aufheitern ▷ vi sich aufheitern;
(person) fröhlicher werden
brilliant ['brɪljənt] adj (sunshine, colour)
strahlend; (person) brillant; (idea)
glänzend; (Brit fam) **it was ~** es war
fantastisch
brim [brɪm] n Rand m
bring [brɪŋ] (**brought, brought**) vt
bringen; (with one) mitbringen; **bring
about** vt herbeiführen, bewirken; **bring
back** vt zurückbringen; (memories)
wecken; **bring down** vt (reduce) senken;
(government etc) zu Fall bringen; **bring in** vt
hereinbringen; (introduce) einführen; **bring
out** vt herausbringen; **bring round**,
bring to vt wieder zu sich bringen; **bring
up** vt (child) aufziehen; (question) zur
Sprache bringen
brisk [brɪsk] adj (trade) lebhaft; (wind)
frisch
bristle ['brɪsl] n Borste f

Brit [brɪt] n (fam) Brite m, Britin f; **Britain** ['brɪtn] n Großbritannien nt; **British** ['brɪtɪʃ] adj britisch; **the ~ Isles** (pl) die Britischen Inseln pl ▷ n **the ~** (pl) die Briten pl

Brittany ['brɪtənɪ] n die Bretagne

brittle ['brɪtl] adj spröde

broad [brɔːd] adj breit; (accent) stark; **in ~ daylight** am helllichten Tag ▷ (US fam) Frau f

B road ['biːrəʊd] ≈ Landstraße f

broadcast ['brɔːdkɑːst] n Sendung f ▷ irr vt, vi senden; (event) übertragen

broaden ['brɔːdn] vt **to ~ the mind** den Horizont erweitern; **broad-minded** adj tolerant

broccoli ['brɒkəlɪ] n Brokkoli pl

brochure ['brəʊʃʊə*] n Prospekt m, Broschüre f

broke [brəʊk] pt of **break** ▷ adj (Brit fam) pleite; **broken** ['brəʊkən] pp of **break**; **broken-hearted** adj untröstlich

broker ['brəʊkə*] n Makler(in) m(f)

brolly ['brɒlɪ] n (Brit fam) Schirm m

bronchitis [brɒŋ'kaɪtɪs] n Bronchitis f

bronze [brɒnz] n Bronze f

brooch [brəʊtʃ] n Brosche f

broom [bruːm] n Besen m

Bros [brɒs] abbr = **brothers** Gebr.

broth [brɒθ] n Fleischbrühe f

brothel ['brɒθl] n Bordell nt

brother ['brʌðə*] n Bruder m; **~s** (pl) (Comm) Gebrüder pl; **brother-in-law** (pl **brothers-in-law**) n Schwager m

brought [brɔːt] pt, pp of **bring**

brow [braʊ] n (eyebrow) (Augen)braue f; (forehead) Stirn f

brown [braʊn] adj braun; **brown bread** n Mischbrot nt; (wholemeal) Vollkornbrot nt; **brownie** ['braʊnɪ] n (Gastr) Brownie m; (Brit) junge Pfadfinderin; **brown paper** n Packpapier nt; **brown rice** n Naturreis m; **brown sugar** n brauner Zucker

browse [braʊz] vi (in book) blättern; (in shop) schmökern, herumschauen; **browser** n (Inform) Browser m

bruise [bruːz] n blauer Fleck ▷ vt **to ~ one's arm** sich dat einen blauen Fleck (am Arm) holen

brunette [brʊ'nɛt] n Brünette f

brush [brʌʃ] n Bürste f; (for sweeping) Handbesen m; (for painting) Pinsel m ▷ vt bürsten; (sweep) fegen; **to ~ one's teeth**

sich dat die Zähne putzen; **brush up** vt (French etc) auffrischen

Brussels sprouts [brʌsl'spraʊts] npl Rosenkohl m, Kohlsprossen pl

brutal ['bruːtl] adj brutal; **brutality** [bruː'tælɪtɪ] n Brutalität f

BSE abbr = **bovine spongiform encephalopathy** BSE f

bubble ['bʌbl] n Blase f; **bubble bath** n Schaumbad nt; **bubbly** ['bʌblɪ] adj sprudelnd; (person) temperamentvoll ▷ n (fam) Schampus m

buck [bʌk] n (animal) Bock m; (US fam) Dollar m

bucket ['bʌkɪt] n Eimer m

Buckingham Palace

Der **Buckingham Palace** ist die offizielle Londoner Residenz der britischen Monarchen und liegt am St James's Park. Der Palast wurde 1703 für den Herzog von Buckingham erbaut, 1762 von George III gekauft, zwischen 1821 und 1836 von John Nash umgebaut, und Anfang des 20. Jahrhunderts teilweise neu gestaltet. Teile des Buckingham Palace sind heute der Öffentlichkeit zugänglich.

buckle ['bʌkl] n Schnalle f ▷ vi (Tech) sich verbiegen ▷ vt zuschnallen

bud [bʌd] n Knospe f

Buddhism ['bʊdɪzəm] n Buddhismus m; **Buddhist** adj buddhistisch ▷ n Buddhist(in) m(f)

buddy ['bʌdɪ] n (fam) Kumpel m

budget ['bʌdʒɪt] n Budget nt

budgie ['bʌdʒɪ] n (fam) Wellensittich m

buff [bʌf] adj (US) muskulös; **in the ~** nackt ▷ n (enthusiast) Fan m

buffalo ['bʌfələʊ] (pl **-es**) n Büffel m

buffer ['bʌfə*] n (a. Inform) Puffer m

buffet ['bʊfeɪ] n (food) (kaltes) Büfett nt

bug [bʌg] n (Inform) Bug m, Programmfehler m; (listening device) Wanze f; (US: insect) Insekt nt; (fam: illness) Infektion f ▷ vt (fam) nerven

bugger ['bʌgə*] n (vulg) Scheißkerl m ▷ interj (vulg) Scheiße f; **bugger off** vi (vulg) abhauen, Leine ziehen

buggy® ['bʌgɪ] n (for baby) Buggy® m; (US: pram) Kinderwagen m

build [bɪld] **(built, built)** *vt* bauen; **build up** *vt* aufbauen; **builder** *n* Bauunternehmer(in) *m(f)*; **building** *n* Gebäude *nt*; **building site** *n* Baustelle *f*; **building society** *n* Bausparkasse *f*

built *pt, pp of* **build**; **built-in** *adj* (*cupboard*) Einbau-, eingebaut

bulb [bʌlb] *n* (*Bot*) (Blumen)zwiebel *f*; (*Elec*) Glühbirne *f*

Bulgaria [bʌlˈgɛərɪə] *n* Bulgarien *nt*; **Bulgarian** *adj* bulgarisch ▷ *n* (*person*) Bulgare *m*, Bulgarin *f*; (*language*) Bulgarisch *nt*

bulimia [bəˈlɪmɪə] *n* Bulimie *f*

bulk [bʌlk] *n* (*size*) Größe *f*; (*greater part*) Großteil *m* (*of +gen*): **in ~** en gros; **bulky** *adj* (*goods*) sperrig; (*person*) stämmig

bull [bʊl] *n* Stier *m*; **bulldog** *n* Bulldogge *f*; **bulldoze** [ˈbʊldəʊz] *vt* planieren; **bulldozer** *n* Planierraupe *f*

bullet [ˈbʊlɪt] *n* Kugel *f*

bulletin [ˈbʊlɪtɪn] *n* Bulletin *nt*; (*announcement*) Bekanntmachung *f*; (*Med*) Krankenbericht *m*; **bulletin board** *n* (*US: Inform*) schwarzes Brett

bullfight [ˈbʊlfaɪt] *n* Stierkampf *m*; **bullshit** *n* (*fam*) Scheiß *m*

bully [ˈbʊlɪ] *n* Tyrann *m*

bum [bʌm] *n* (*Brit fam: backside*) Po *m*; (*US: vagrant*) Penner *m*; (*worthless person*) Rumtreiber *m*; **bum around** *vi* herumgammeln

bumblebee [ˈbʌmblbiː] *n* Hummel *f*

bump [bʌmp] *n* (*fam: swelling*) Beule *f*; (*road*) Unebenheit *f*; (*blow*) Stoß *m* ▷ *vt* stoßen; **to ~ one's head** sich *dat* den Kopf anschlagen (*on* an +*dat*): **bump into** *vt* stoßen gegen; (*fam: meet*) (zufällig) begegnen +*dat*; **bumper** *n* (*Auto*) Stoßstange *f* ▷ *adj* (*edition etc*) Riesen-; (*crop etc*) Rekord-; **bumpy** [ˈbʌmpɪ] *adj* holp(e)rig

bun [bʌn] *n* süßes Brötchen

bunch [bʌntʃ] *n* (*of flowers*) Strauß *m*; (*fam: of people*) Haufen *m*; **~ of keys** Schlüsselbund *m*; **~ of grapes** Weintraube *f*

bundle [ˈbʌndl] *n* Bündel *nt*

bungalow [ˈbʌŋgələʊ] *n* Bungalow *m*

bungee jumping [ˈbʌndʒɪdʒʌmpɪŋ] *n* Bungeejumping *nt*

bunk [bʌŋk] *n* Koje *f*; **bunk bed(s)** *n(pl)* Etagenbett *nt*

bunker [ˈbʌŋkə*] *n* (*Mil*) Bunker *m*

bunny [ˈbʌnɪ] *n* Häschen *nt*

buoy [bɔɪ] *n* Boje *f*; **buoyant** [ˈbɔɪənt] *adj* (*floating*) schwimmend

BUPA [ˈbuːpə] *abbr* (*Brit*) *private Krankenkasse*

burden [ˈbɜːdn] *n* Last *f*

bureau [ˈbjʊərəʊ] *n* Büro *nt*; (*government department*) Amt *nt*; **bureaucracy** [bjʊˈrɒkrəsɪ] *n* Bürokratie *f*; **bureaucratic** [bjʊərəˈkrætɪk] *adj* bürokratisch; **bureau de change** [ˈbjuːrəʊ də ˈʃɒnʒ] *n* Wechselstube *f*

burger [ˈbɜːgə*] *n* Hamburger *m*

burglar [ˈbɜːglə*] *n* Einbrecher(in) *m(f)*; **burglar alarm** *n* Alarmanlage *f*; **burglarize** *vt* (*US*) einbrechen in +*akk*; **burglary** *n* Einbruch *m*; **burgle** [ˈbɜːgl] *vt* einbrechen in +*akk*

burial [ˈberɪəl] *n* Beerdigung *f*

burn [bɜːn] **(burnt** *o* **burned, burnt** *o* **burned)** *vt* verbrennen; (*food, slightly*) anbrennen; **to ~ one's hand** sich *dat* die Hand verbrennen ▷ *vi* brennen ▷ *n* (*injury*) Brandwunde *f*; (*on material*) verbrannte Stelle; **burn down** *vt, vi* abbrennen

burp [bɜːp] *vi* rülpsen ▷ *vt* (*baby*) aufstoßen lassen

bursary [ˈbɜːsərɪ] *n* Stipendium *nt*

burst [bɜːst] **(burst, burst)** *vt* platzen lassen ▷ *vi* platzen; **to ~ into tears** in Tränen ausbrechen

bury [ˈberɪ] *vt* begraben; (*in grave*) beerdigen; (*hide*) vergraben

bus [bʌs] *n* Bus *m*; **bus driver** *n* Busfahrer(in) *m(f)*

bush [bʊʃ] *n* Busch *m*

business [ˈbɪznɪs] *n* Geschäft *nt*; (*enterprise*) Unternehmen *nt*; (*concern, affair*) Sache *f*; **I'm here on ~** ich bin geschäftlich hier; **it's none of your ~** das geht dich nichts an; **business card** *n* Visitenkarte *f*; **business class** *n* (*Aviat*) Businessclass *f*; **business hours** *npl* Geschäftsstunden *pl*; **businessman** (*pl* **-men**) *n* Geschäftsmann *m*; **business studies** *npl* Betriebswirtschaftslehre *f*; **businesswoman** (*pl* **-women**) *n* Geschäftsfrau *f*

bus service *n* Busverbindung *f*; **bus shelter** *n* Wartehäuschen *nt*; **bus station** *n* Busbahnhof *m*; **bus stop** *n* Bushaltestelle *f*

bust [bʌst] n Büste f ▷ adj (broken)
kaputt; **to go ~** Pleite gehen; **bust-up** n
(fam) Krach m

busy ['bɪzɪ] adj beschäftigt; (street, place)
belebt; (esp US: telephone) besetzt; **~ signal**
(US) Besetztzeichen nt

⭕ **KEYWORD**

but [bʌt] conj **1** (yet) aber; **not X but Y**
nicht X sondern Y

2 (however): **I'd love to come, but I'm
busy** ich würde gern kommen, bin aber
beschäftigt

3 (showing disagreement, surprise etc): **but
that's fantastic!** (aber) das ist ja
fantastisch!

▷ prep (apart from, except); **nothing but
trouble** nichts als Ärger; **no-one but
him can do it** niemand außer ihn kann es
machen; **but for you/your help** ohne
dich/deine Hilfe; **anything but that** alles,
nur das nicht

▷ adv (just, only): **she's but a child** sie ist
noch ein Kind; **had I but known** wenn ich
es nur gewusst hätte; **I can but try** ich
kann es immerhin versuchen; **all but
finished** so gut wie fertig

butcher ['bʊtʃə*] n Fleischer(in) m(f),
Metzger(in) m(f)
butler ['bʌtlə*] n Butler m
butter ['bʌtə*] n Butter f ▷ vt buttern;
buttercup n Butterblume f; **butterfly** n
Schmetterling m
buttocks ['bʌtəks] npl Gesäß nt
button ['bʌtn] n Knopf m; (badge) Button
m ▷ vt zuknöpfen; **buttonhole** n
Knopfloch nt
buy [baɪ] n Kauf m ▷ vt (bought, bought)
kaufen (from von); **he bought me a ring** er
hat mir einen Ring gekauft; **buyer** n
Käufer(in) m(f)
buzz [bʌz] n Summen nt; **to give sb a
~** (fam) jdn anrufen ▷ vi summen; **buzzer**
['bʌzə*] n Summer m; **buzz word** n (fam)
Modewort nt

⭕ **KEYWORD**

by [baɪ] prep **1** (referring to cause, agent) von
durch; **killed by lightning** vom Blitz
getötet; **a painting by Picasso** ein
Gemälde von Picasso

2 (referring to method, manner): **by
bus/car/train** mit dem
Bus/Auto/Zug; **to pay by cheque** per
Scheck bezahlen; **by moonlight** bei
Mondschein; **by saving hard, he ...** indem
er eisern sparte, ... er ...

3 (via, through) über +acc; **he came in by
the back door** er kam durch die Hintertür
herein

4 (close to, past) bei an +dat; **a holiday by
the sea** ein Urlaub am Meer; **she rushed
by me** sie eilte an mir vorbei

5 (not later than): **by 4 o'clock** bis 4 Uhr; **by
this time tomorrow** morgen um diese
Zeit; **by the time I got here it was too
late** als ich hier ankam, war es zu spät

6 (during): **by day** bei Tag

7 (amount): **by the kilo/metre**
kiloweise/meterweise; **paid by the hour**
stundenweise bezahlt

8 (Math, measure): **to divide by 3** durch 3
teilen; **to multiply by 3** mit 3 malnehmen;
a room 3 metres by 4 ein Zimmer 3 mal 4
Meter; **it's broader by a metre** es ist (um)
einem Meter breiter

9 (according to) nach; **it's all right by me**
von mir aus gern

10: **(all) by oneself** etc ganz allein

11: **by the way** übrigens

▷ adv **1**: see **go**, **pass** etc

2: **by and by** irgendwann; (with past tenses)
nach einiger Zeit; **by and large** (on the
whole) im Großen und Ganzen

bye-bye ['baɪ'baɪ] interj (fam)
Wiedersehen, tschüss
by-election n Nachwahl f; **bypass** n
Umgehungsstraße f; (Med) Bypass m;
byproduct n Nebenprodukt nt; **byroad** n
Nebenstraße f; **bystander** n
Zuschauer(in) m(f)
byte [baɪt] n Byte nt

C

C [siː] *abbr* = **Celsius** C

c *abbr* = **circa** ca

cab [kæb] *n* Taxi *nt*

cabbage ['kæbɪdʒ] *n* Kohl *m*

cabin ['kæbɪn] *n* (*Naut*) Kajüte *f*; (*Aviat*) Passagierraum *m*; (*wooden house*) Hütte *f*; **cabin crew** *n* Flugbegleitpersonal *nt*; **cabin cruiser** *n* Kajütboot *nt*

cabinet ['kæbɪnɪt] *n* Schrank *m*; (*for display*) Vitrine *f*; (*Pol*) Kabinett *nt*

cable ['keɪbl] *n* (*Elec*) Kabel *nt*; **cable-car** *n* Seilbahn *f*; **cable railway** *n* Drahtseilbahn *f*; **cable television**, **cablevision** (*US*) *n* Kabelfernsehen *nt*

cactus ['kæktəs] *n* Kaktus *m*

CAD *abbr* = **computer-aided design** CAD *nt*

Caesarean [siːˈzeərɪən] *adj* ~ (**section**) Kaiserschnitt *m*

café ['kæfeɪ] *n* Café *nt*; **cafeteria** [kæfɪˈtɪərɪə] *n* Cafeteria *f*; **cafetiere** [kæfəˈtjɛə*] *n* Kaffeebereiter *m*

caffein(e) ['kæfiːn] *n* Koffein *nt*

cage [keɪdʒ] *n* Käfig *m*

Cairo ['kaɪərəʊ] *n* Kairo *nt*

cake [keɪk] *n* Kuchen *m*; **cake shop** *n* Konditorei *f*

calamity [kəˈlæmɪtɪ] *n* Katastrophe *f*

calculate ['kælkjʊleɪt] *vt* berechnen; (*estimate*) kalkulieren; **calculating** *adj* berechnend; **calculation** [kælkjʊˈleɪʃən] *n* Berechnung *f*, (*estimate*) Kalkulation *f*; **calculator** ['kælkjʊleɪtə*] *n* Taschenrechner *m*

calendar ['kælɪndə*] *n* Kalender *m*

calf [kɑːf] (*pl* **calves**) *n* Kalb *nt*; (*Anat*) Wade *f*

California [kælɪˈfɔːnɪə] *n* Kalifornien *nt*

call [kɔːl] *vt* rufen; (*name, describe as*) nennen; (*Tel*) anrufen; (*Inform, Aviat*) aufrufen; **what's this ~ed?** wie heißt das?; **that's what I ~ service** das nenne ich guten Service ▷ *vi* (*shout*) rufen (*for help* um Hilfe); (*visit*) vorbeikommen; **to ~ at the doctor's** beim Arzt vorbeigehen; (*of train*) **to ~ at ...** in ... halten ▷ *n* (*shout*) Ruf *m*; (*Tel*) Anruf *m*; (*Inform, Aviat*) Aufruf *m*; **to make a ~** telefonieren; **to give sb a ~** jdn anrufen; **to be on ~** Bereitschaftsdienst haben; **call back** *vt, vi* zurückrufen; **call for** *vt* (*come to pick up*) abholen; (*demand, require*) verlangen; **call off** *vt* absagen

call centre *n* Callcenter *nt*; **caller** *n* Besucher(in) *m(f)*; (*Tel*) Anrufer(in) *m(f)*

calm [kɑːm] *n* Stille *f*; (*also of person*) Ruhe *f*; (*of sea*) Flaute *f* ▷ *vt* beruhigen ▷ *adj* ruhig; **calm down** *vi* sich beruhigen

calorie ['kælərɪ] *n* Kalorie *f*

calves [kɑːvz] *pl of* **calf**

Cambodia [kæmˈbəʊdɪə] *n* Kambodscha *nt*

camcorder ['kæmkɔːdə*] *n* Camcorder *m*

came [keɪm] *pt of* **come**

camel ['kæməl] *n* Kamel *nt*

camera ['kæmərə] *n* Fotoapparat *m*, Kamera *f*

camomile ['kæməmaɪl] *n* Kamille *f*

camouflage ['kæməflɑːʒ] *n* Tarnung *f*

camp [kæmp] *n* Lager *nt*; (*camping place*) Zeltplatz *m* ▷ *vi* zelten, campen ▷ *adj* (*fam*) theatralisch, tuntig

campaign [kæmˈpeɪn] *n* Kampagne *f*, (*Pol*) Wahlkampf *m* ▷ *vi* sich einsetzen (*for/against* für/gegen)

campbed ['kæmpbed] *n* Campingliege *f*, **camper** ['kæmpə*] *n* (*person*) Camper(in) *m(f)*; (*van*) Wohnmobil *nt*; **camping** ['kæmpɪŋ] *n* Zelten *nt*, Camping *nt*; **campsite** ['kæmpsaɪt] *n* Zeltplatz *m*, Campingplatz *m*

campus ['kæmpəs] n (of university)
Universitätsgelände nt, Campus m
can¹ [kæn] (**could, been able**) vb aux (be
able) können; (permission) dürfen; **I ~not** o
~'t see ich kann nichts sehen; **~ I go now?**
darf ich jetzt gehen? ▷ n (for food, beer)
Dose f; (for water, milk) Kanne f

⊙ **KEYWORD**

can² [kæn] (negative **cannot, can't**,
conditional **could**) aux vb **1** (be able to, know
how to) können; **I can see you tomorrow,
if you like** ich könnte Sie morgen sehen,
wenn Sie wollen; **I can swim** ich kann
schwimmen; **can you speak German?**
sprechen Sie Deutsch?
2 (may) können dürfen; **could I have a
word with you?** könnte ich Sie kurz
sprechen?

Canada ['kænədə] n Kanada nt;
Canadian [kə'neɪdɪən] adj kanadisch ▷ n
Kanadier(in) m(f)
canal [kə'næl] n Kanal m
canary [kə'nɛərɪ] n Kanarienvogel m
cancel ['kænsəl] vt (plans) aufgeben;
(meeting, event) absagen; (Comm: order etc)
stornieren; (contract) kündigen; (Inform)
löschen; (Aviat: flight) streichen; **to be ~led**
(event, train, bus) ausfallen; **cancellation**
[kænsə'leɪʃən] n Absage f, (Comm)
Stornierung f, (Aviat) gestrichener Flug
cancer ['kænsə*] n (Med) Krebs m; **Cancer**
n (Astr) Krebs m
candid ['kændɪd] adj (person, conversation)
offen
candidate ['kændɪdət] n (for post)
Bewerber(in) m(f); (Pol) Kandidat(in) m(f)
candle ['kændl] n Kerze f; **candlelight** n
Kerzenlicht nt; **candlestick** n
Kerzenhalter m
candy ['kændɪ] n (US) Bonbon nt;
(quantity) Süßigkeiten pl; **candy-floss** n
(Brit) Zuckerwatte f
cane [keɪn] n Rohr nt; (stick) Stock
m
cannabis ['kænəbɪs] n Cannabis m
canned [kænd] adj Dosen-
cannot ['kænɒt] contr of **can not**
canny ['kænɪ] adj (shrewd) schlau
canoe [kə'nuː] n Kanu nt; **canoeing** n
Kanufahren nt

canopener ['kænəʊpnə*] n Dosenöffner m
canopy ['kænəpɪ] n Baldachin m; (awning)
Markise f; (over entrance) Vordach nt
can't [kɑːnt] contr of **can not**
canteen [kæn'tiːn] n (in factory) Kantine
f; (in university) Mensa f
canvas ['kænvəs] n (for sails, shoes)
Segeltuch nt; (for tent) Zeltstoff m; (for
painting) Leinwand f
canvass ['kænvəs] vi um Stimmen
werben (for für)
canyon ['kænjən] n Felsenschlucht f,
canyoning ['kænjənɪŋ] n Canyoning nt
cap [kæp] n Mütze f; (lid) Verschluss m,
Deckel m
capability [keɪpə'bɪlɪtɪ] n Fähigkeit f,
capable ['keɪpəbl] adj fähig; **to be ~ of
sth** zu etw fähig (o imstande) sein; **to be
~ of doing sth** etw tun können
capacity [kə'pæsɪtɪ] n (of building,
container) Fassungsvermögen nt; (ability)
Fähigkeit f; (function) **in his ~ as ...** in
seiner Eigenschaft als ...
cape [keɪp] n (garment) Cape nt, Umhang
m; (Geo) Kap nt
caper ['keɪpə*] n (for cooking) Kaper f
capital ['kæpɪtl] n (Fin) Kapital nt; (letter)
Großbuchstabe m; **~ (city)** Hauptstadt f,
capitalism n Kapitalismus m; **capital
punishment** n die Todesstrafe
Capricorn ['kæprɪkɔːn] n (Astr) Steinbock
m
capsize [kæp'saɪz] vi kentern
capsule ['kæpsjuːl] n Kapsel f
captain ['kæptɪn] n Kapitän m; (army)
Hauptmann m
caption ['kæpʃən] n Bildunterschrift f
captive ['kæptɪv] n Gefangene(r) mf;
capture ['kæptʃə*] vt (person) fassen,
gefangen nehmen; (town etc) einnehmen;
(Inform: data) erfassen ▷ n
Gefangennahme f; (Inform) Erfassung f
car [kɑː*] n Auto nt; (US Rail) Wagen m
carafe [kə'ræf] n Karaffe f
carambola [kærəm'bəʊlə] n Sternfrucht f
caramel ['kærəmɛl] n Karamelle f
caravan ['kærəvæn] n Wohnwagen m;
caravan site n Campingplatz m für
Wohnwagen
caraway (seed) ['kærəweɪ] n Kümmel m
carbohydrate [kɑːbəʊ'haɪdreɪt] n
Kohle(n)hydrat nt
car bomb n Autobombe f

carbon ['kɑːbən] n Kohlenstoff m
car boot sale n auf einem Parkplatz stattfindender Flohmarkt
carburettor, carburetor (US) ['kɑːbjʊretə*] n Vergaser m
card [kɑːd] n Karte f; (material) Pappe f; **cardboard** n Pappe f; **~ (box)** Karton m; (smaller) Pappschachtel f; **card game** n Kartenspiel nt
cardiac ['kɑːdɪæk] adj Herz-
cardigan ['kɑːdɪgən] n Strickjacke f
card index n Kartei f; **cardphone** ['kɑːdfəʊn] n Kartentelefon nt
care [keə*] n (worry) Sorge f; (carefulness) Sorgfalt f; (looking after things, people) Pflege f; **with ~** sorgfältig; (cautiously) vorsichtig; **to take ~** (watch out) vorsichtig sein; (in address) **~ of** bei; **to take ~ of** sorgen für, sich kümmern um ▷ vi **I don't ~** es ist mir egal; **to ~ about sth** Wert auf etw akk legen; **he ~s about her** sie liegt ihm am Herzen; **care for** vt (look after) sorgen für, sich kümmern um; (like) mögen
career [kə'rɪə*] n Karriere f, Laufbahn f; **career woman** (pl **women**) n Karrierefrau f; **careers adviser** n Berufsberater(in) m(f)
carefree ['keəfriː] adj sorgenfrei; **careful**, **carefully** adj, adv sorgfältig; (cautious, cautiously) vorsichtig; **careless, carelessly** adj, adv nachlässig; (driving etc) leichtsinnig; (remark) unvorsichtig; **carer** ['keərə*] n Betreuer(in) m(f), Pfleger(in) m(f); **caretaker** ['keəteɪkə*] n Hausmeister(in) m(f); **careworker** n Pfleger(in) m(f)
car-ferry ['kɑːferɪ] n Autofähre f
cargo ['kɑːgəʊ] (pl **-(e)s**) n Ladung f
car hire, car hire company n Autovermietung f
Caribbean [kærɪ'biːən] n Karibik f ▷ adj karibisch
caring ['keərɪŋ] adj mitfühlend; (parent, partner) liebevoll; (looking after sb) fürsorglich
car insurance n Kraftfahrzeugversicherung f
carnation [kɑː'neɪʃən] n Nelke f
carnival ['kɑːnɪvəl] n Volksfest nt; (before Lent) Karneval m
carol ['kærəl] n Weihnachtslied nt
carp [kɑːp] n (fish) Karpfen m

car park n (Brit) Parkplatz m; (multi-storey car park) Parkhaus nt
carpenter ['kɑːpəntə*] n Zimmermann m; **carpet** ['kɑːpɪt] n Teppich m
car phone n Autotelefon nt; **carpool** n Fahrgemeinschaft f; (vehicles) Fuhrpark m ▷ vi eine Fahrgemeinschaft bilden; **car rental** n Autovermietung f
carriage ['kærɪdʒ] n (Brit Rail: coach) Wagen m; (compartment) Abteil nt; (horse-drawn) Kutsche f; (transport) Beförderung f; **carriageway** n (Brit: on road) Fahrbahn f
carrier ['kærɪə*] n (Comm) Spediteur(in) m(f); **carrier bag** n Tragetasche f
carrot ['kærət] n Karotte f
carry ['kærɪ] vt tragen; (in vehicle) befördern; (have on one) bei sich haben; **carry on** vi (continue) weitermachen; (fam: make a scene) ein Theater machen ▷ vt (continue) fortführen; **to ~ on working** weiter arbeiten; **carry out** vt (orders, plan) ausführen, durchführen
carrycot n Babytragetasche f
carsick ['kɑːsɪk] adj **he gets ~** ihm wird beim Autofahren übel
cart [kɑːt] n Wagen m, Karren m; (US: shopping trolley) Einkaufswagen m
carton ['kɑːtən] n (Papp)karton m; (of cigarettes) Stange f
cartoon [kɑː'tuːn] n Cartoon m o nt; (one drawing) Karikatur f; (film) (Zeichen)trickfilm m
cartridge ['kɑːtrɪdʒ] n (for film) Kassette f; (for gun, pen, printer) Patrone f; (for copier) Kartusche f
carve [kɑːv] vt, vi (wood) schnitzen; (stone) meißeln; (meat) schneiden, tranchieren; **carving** n (in wood) Schnitzerei f; (in stone) Skulptur f; (Ski) Carving nt
car wash n Autowaschanlage f
case [keɪs] n (crate) Kiste f; (box) Schachtel f; (for jewels) Schatulle f; (for spectacles) Etui nt; (Jur, matter) Fall m; **in ~** falls; **in that ~** in dem Fall; **in ~ of fire** bei Brand; **it's a ~ of ...** es handelt sich hier um ...
cash [kæʃ] n Bargeld nt; **in ~** bar; **~ on delivery** per Nachnahme ▷ vt (cheque) einlösen; **cash desk** n Kasse f; **cash dispenser** n Geldautomat m; **cashier** [kæ'ʃɪə*] n Kassierer(in) m(f); **cash machine** n (Brit) Geldautomat m

cashmere ['kæʃmɪə*] n Kaschmirwolle f
cash payment n Barzahlung f;
  cashpoint n (Brit) Geldautomat m
casing ['keɪsɪŋ] n Gehäuse nt
casino [kə'si:nəʊ] (pl -s) n Kasino nt
cask [kɑ:sk] n Fass nt
casserole ['kæsərəʊl] n Kasserole f; (food)
  Schmortopf m
cassette [kæ'set] n Kassette f; **cassette
  recorder** n Kassettenrekorder m
cast [kɑ:st] (**cast, cast**) vt (throw) werfen;
  (Theat, Cine) besetzen; (roles) verteilen ▷ n
  (Theat, Cine) Besetzung f; (Med)
  Gipsverband m; **cast off** vi (Naut)
  losmachen
caster ['kɑ:stə*] n ~ **sugar** Streuzucker
  m
castle ['kɑ:sl] n Burg f
castrate [kæs'treɪt] vt kastrieren
casual ['kæʒjʊəl] adj (arrangement, remark)
  beiläufig; (attitude, manner) (nach)lässig,
  zwanglos; (dress) leger; (work, earnings)
  Gelegenheits-; (look, glance) flüchtig;
  ~ **wear** Freizeitkleidung f; ~ **sex**
  Gelegenheitssex m; **casually** adv (remark,
  say) beiläufig; (meet) zwanglos; (dressed)
  leger
casualty ['kæʒjʊəltɪ] n Verletzte(r) mf;
  (dead) Tote(r) mf; (department in hospital)
  Notaufnahme f
cat [kæt] n Katze f; (male) Kater m
catalog (US), **catalogue** ['kætəlɒg] n
  Katalog m ▷ vt katalogisieren
cataract ['kætərækt] n Wasserfall m;
  (Med) grauer Star
catarrh [kə'tɑ:*] n Katarr(h) m
catastrophe [kə'tæstrəfɪ] n Katastrophe
  f
catch [kætʃ] n (fish etc) Fang m ▷ vt
  (**caught, caught**) fangen; (thief) fassen;
  (train, bus etc) nehmen; (not miss)
  erreichen; **to ~ a cold** sich erkälten; **to
  ~ fire** Feuer fangen; **I didn't ~ that** das
  habe ich nicht mitgekriegt; **catch on** vi
  (become popular) Anklang finden; **catch up**
  vt, vi **to ~ with sb** jdn einholen; **to ~ on
  sth** etw nachholen; **catching** adj
  ansteckend
category ['kætɪgərɪ] n Kategorie f
cater ['keɪtə*] vi die Speisen und Getränke
  liefern (for für); **cater for** vt (have facilities
  for) eingestellt sein auf +akk; **catering** n
  Versorgung f mit Speisen und Getränken,

Gastronomie f; **catering service** n
  Partyservice m
caterpillar ['kætəpɪlə*] n Raupe f
cathedral [kə'θi:drəl] n Kathedrale f,
  Dom m
Catholic ['kæθəlɪk] adj katholisch
  ▷ Katholik(in) m(f)
cat nap n (Brit) kurzer Schlaf; **cat's eyes**
  ['kætsaɪz] npl (in road) Katzenaugen pl,
  Reflektoren pl
catsup ['kætsəp] n (US) Ketchup nt o m
cattle ['kætl] npl Vieh nt
caught [kɔ:t] pt, pp of **catch**
cauliflower ['kɒlɪflaʊə*] n Blumenkohl m;
  cauliflower cheese n Blumenkohl m in
  Käsesoße
cause [kɔ:z] n (origin) Ursache f (of für);
  .(reason) Grund m (for zu); (purpose) Sache f;
  for a good ~ für wohltätige Zwecke; **no
  ~ for alarm/complaint** kein Grund zur
  Aufregung/Klage ▷ vt verursachen
causeway ['kɔ:zweɪ] n Damm m
caution ['kɔ:ʃən] n Vorsicht f; (Jur, Sport)
  Verwarnung f ▷ vt (ver)warnen; **cautious**
  ['kɔ:ʃəs] adj vorsichtig
cave [keɪv] n Höhle f; **cave in** vi
  einstürzen
cavity ['kævɪtɪ] n Hohlraum m; (in tooth)
  Loch nt
cayenne (pepper) [keɪ'en] n
  Cayennepfeffer m
CCTV abbr = **closed circuit television**
  Videoüberwachungsanlage f
CD abbr = **Compact Disc** CD f; **CD player** n
  CD-Spieler m; **CD-ROM** abbr = **Compact
  Disc Read Only Memory** CD-ROM f;
CD-RW abbr = **Compact Disc Rewritable**
  CD-RW f
cease [si:s] vi aufhören ▷ vt beenden; **to
  ~ doing sth** aufhören, etw zu tun; **cease
  fire** n Waffenstillstand m
ceiling ['si:lɪŋ] n Decke f
celebrate ['selɪbreɪt] vt, vi feiern;
  celebrated adj gefeiert; **celebration**
  [selɪ'breɪʃən] n Feier f; **celebrity**
  [sɪ'lebrɪtɪ] n Berühmtheit f, Star m
celeriac [sə'lerɪæk] n (Knollen)sellerie m
  o f; **celery** ['selərɪ] n (Stangen)sellerie m
  o f
cell [sel] n Zelle f; (US) see **cellphone**
cellar ['selə*] n Keller m
cello ['tʃeləʊ] (pl -s) n Cello nt
cellphone ['selfəʊn], **cellular phone**

['seljʊlə* 'fəʊn] n Mobiltelefon nt, Handy nt

Celt [kelt] n Kelte m, Keltin f; **Celtic** ['keltɪk] adj keltisch ▷ n (language) Keltisch nt

cement [sɪ'ment] n Zement m

cemetery ['semɪtrɪ] n Friedhof m

censorship ['sensəʃɪp] n Zensur f

cent [sent] n (of dollar, euro etc) Cent m

center n (US) see **centre**

centiliter (US), **centilitre** ['sentɪliːtə*] n Zentiliter m; **centimeter** (US), **centimetre** ['sentɪmiːtə*] n Zentimeter m

central ['sentrəl] adj zentral; **Central America** n Mittelamerika nt; **Central Europe** n Mitteleuropa nt; **central heating** n Zentralheizung f; **centralize** vt zentralisieren; **central locking** n (Auto) Zentralverriegelung f; **central reservation** n (Brit) Mittelstreifen m; **central station** n Hauptbahnhof m

centre ['sentə*] n Mitte f; (building, of city) Zentrum nt ▷ vt zentrieren; **centre forward** n (Sport) Mittelstürmer m

century ['sentjʊrɪ] n Jahrhundert nt

ceramic [sɪ'ræmɪk] adj keramisch

cereal ['sɪərɪəl] n (any grain) Getreide nt; (breakfast cereal) Frühstücksflocken pl

ceremony ['serɪmənɪ] n Feier f, Zeremonie f

certain ['sɜːtən] adj sicher (of +gen); (particular) bestimmt; **for ~** mit Sicherheit; **certainly** adv sicher; (without doubt) bestimmt; **~!** aber sicher!; **~ not** ganz bestimmt nicht!

certificate [sə'tɪfɪkɪt] n Bescheinigung f; (in school, of qualification) Zeugnis nt; **certify** ['sɜːtɪfaɪ] vt, vi bescheinigen

cervical smear ['sɜː'vɪkəl smɪə*] n Abstrich m

CFC abbr = **chlorofluorocarbon** FCKW nt

chain [tʃeɪn] n Kette f ▷ vt **to ~ (up)** anketten; **chain reaction** n Kettenreaktion f; **chain store** n Kettenladen m

chair [tʃeə*] n Stuhl m; (university) Lehrstuhl m; (armchair) Sessel m; (chairperson) Vorsitzende(r) mf; **chairlift** n Sessellift m; **chairman** (pl **-men**) n Vorsitzende(r) m; (of firm) Präsident m; **chairperson** n Vorsitzende(r) mf; (of firm) Präsident(in) m(f); **chairwoman** (pl

-women) n Vorsitzende f; (of firm) Präsidentin f

chalet ['ʃæleɪ] n (in mountains) Berghütte f; (holiday dwelling) Ferienhäuschen nt

chalk ['tʃɔːk] n Kreide f

challenge ['tʃælɪndʒ] n Herausforderung f ▷ vt (person) herausfordern; (statement) bestreiten

chambermaid ['tʃeɪmbə*meɪd] n Zimmermädchen nt

chamois leather ['ʃæmwɑː'leðə*] n (for windows) Fensterleder nt

champagne [ʃæm'peɪn] n Champagner m

champion ['tʃæmpɪən] n (Sport) Meister(in) m(f); **championship** n Meisterschaft f; **Champions League** n Champions League f

chance [tʃɑːns] n (fate) Zufall m; (possibility) Möglichkeit f; (opportunity) Gelegenheit f; (risk) Risiko nt; **by ~** zufällig; **he doesn't stand a ~ (of winning)** er hat keinerlei Chance(, zu gewinnen)

chancellor ['tʃɑːnsələ*] n Kanzler(in) m(f)

chandelier [ʃændɪ'lɪə*] n Kronleuchter m

change [tʃeɪndʒ] vt verändern; (alter) ändern; (money, wheel, nappy) wechseln; (exchange) (um)tauschen; **to ~ one's clothes** sich umziehen; **to ~ trains** umsteigen; **to ~ gear** (Auto) schalten ▷ vi sich ändern; (esp outwardly) sich verändern; (get changed) sich umziehen ▷ n Veränderung f; (alteration) Änderung f; (money) Wechselgeld nt; (coins) Kleingeld nt; **for a ~** zur Abwechslung; **can you give me ~ for £10?** können Sie mir auf 10 Pfund herausgeben?; **change down** vi (Brit Auto) herunterschalten; **change over** vi sich umstellen (to auf +akk); **change up** vi (Brit Auto) hochschalten

changeable adj (weather) veränderlich, wechselhaft; **change machine** n Geldwechsler m; **changing room** n Umkleideraum m

channel ['tʃænl] n Kanal m; (Radio, Tv) Kanal m, Sender m; **the (English) Channel** der Ärmelkanal; **the Channel Islands** die Kanalinseln; **the Channel Tunnel** der Kanaltunnel; **channel-hopping** n Zappen nt

chaos ['keɪɒs] n Chaos nt; **chaotic** [keɪ'ɒtɪk] adj chaotisch

chap [tʃæp] n (Brit fam) Bursche m, Kerl m

chapel ['tʃæpəl] n Kapelle f
chapped ['tʃæpt] adj (lips) aufgesprungen
chapter ['tʃæptə*] n Kapitel nt
character ['kærəktə*] n Charakter m,
Wesen nt; (in a play, novel etc) Figur f; (Typo)
Zeichen nt; **he's a real ~** er ist ein echtes
Original; **characteristic** [kærəktə'rɪstɪk]
n typisches Merkmal
charcoal ['tʃɑː.kəʊl] n Holzkohle f
charge [tʃɑːdʒ] n (cost) Gebühr f; (Jur)
Anklage f; **free of ~** gratis, kostenlos; **to be
in ~ of** verantwortlich sein für ▷ vt
(money) verlangen; (Jur) anklagen; (battery)
laden; **charge card** n Kundenkreditkarte f
charity ['tʃærɪtɪ] n (institution) wohltätige
Organisation f; **a collection for ~** eine
Sammlung für wohltätige Zwecke;
charity shop n Geschäft einer 'charity', in
dem freiwillige Helfer gebrauchte Kleidung,
Bücher etc verkaufen
charm [tʃɑːm] n Charme m ▷ vt
bezaubern; **charming** adj reizend,
charmant
chart [tʃɑːt] n Diagramm nt; (map) Karte
f; **the ~s** pl die Charts, die Hitliste
charter ['tʃɑːtə*] n Urkunde f ▷ vt (Naut,
Aviat) chartern; **charter flight** n
Charterflug m
chase [tʃeɪs] vt jagen, verfolgen ▷ n
Verfolgungsjagd f; (hunt) Jagd f
chassis ['ʃæsɪ] n (Auto) Fahrgestell nt
chat [tʃæt] vi plaudern; (Inform) chatten
▷ n Plauderei f; **chat up** vt anmachen,
anbaggern; **chatroom** n (Inform)
Chatroom m; **chat show** n Talkshow f;
chatty adj geschwätzig
chauffeur ['ʃəʊfə*] n Chauffeur(in) m(f),
Fahrer(in) m(f)
cheap [tʃiːp] adj billig; (of poor quality)
minderwertig
cheat [tʃiːt] vt, vi betrügen; (in school,
game) mogeln
Chechen ['tʃetʃen] adj tschetschenisch
▷ n Tschetschene m, Tschetschenin f;
Chechnya ['tʃetʃnɪə] n Tschetschenien nt
check [tʃek] vt (examine) überprüfen (for
auf +akk); (Tech: adjustment etc)
kontrollieren; (US: tick) abhaken; (Aviat:
luggage) einchecken; (US: coat) abgeben
▷ n (examination, restraint) Kontrolle f; (US:
restaurant bill) Rechnung f; (pattern)
Karo(muster) nt; (US) see cheque; **check in**
vt, vi (Aviat) einchecken; (into hotel) sich

anmelden; **check out** vi sich abmelden,
auschecken; **check up** vi nachprüfen; **to
~ on sb** Nachforschungen über jdn
anstellen
checkers ['tʃekəz] nsing (US) Damespiel nt
check-in ['tʃekɪn] n (airport) Check-in m;
(hotel) Anmeldung f; **check-in desk** n
Abfertigungsschalter m; **checking
account** n (US) Scheckkonto nt; **check
list** n Kontrollliste f; **checkout** n
(supermarket) Kasse f; **checkout time** n
(hotel) Abreise(zeit) f; **checkpoint** n
Kontrollpunkt m; **checkroom** n (US)
Gepäckaufbewahrung f; **checkup** n (Med)
(ärztliche) Untersuchung f
cheddar ['tʃedə*] n Cheddarkäse m
cheek [tʃiːk] n Backe f, Wange f;
(insolence) Frechheit f; **what a ~** so eine
Frechheit!; **cheekbone** n Backenknochen
m; **cheeky** adj frech
cheer [tʃɪə*] n Beifallsruf m; **~s** (when
drinking) prost!; (Brit fam: thanks) danke;
(Brit: goodbye) tschüs ▷ vt zujubeln +dat
▷ vi jubeln; **cheer up** vt aufmuntern ▷ vi
fröhlicher werden; **~!** Kopf hoch!; **cheerful**
['tʃɪəfʊl] adj fröhlich
cheese [tʃiːz] n Käse m; **cheeseboard** n
Käsebrett nt; (as course) (gemischte)
Käseplatte; **cheesecake** n Käsekuchen m
chef [ʃef] n Koch m; (in charge of kitchen)
Küchenchef(in) m(f)
chemical ['kemɪkəl] adj chemisch
▷ Chemikalie f; **chemist** ['kemɪst] n
(pharmacist) Apotheker(in) m(f); (industrial
chemist) Chemiker(in) m(f); **~'s (shop)**
Apotheke f; **chemistry** n Chemie f
cheque [tʃek] n (Brit) Scheck m; **cheque
account** n (Brit) Girokonto nt; **cheque
book** n (Brit) Scheckheft nt; **cheque card**
n (Brit) Scheckkarte f
chequered ['tʃekəd] adj kariert
cherish ['tʃerɪʃ] vt (look after) liebevoll
sorgen für; (hope) hegen; (memory)
bewahren
cherry ['tʃerɪ] n Kirsche f; **cherry tomato**
(pl **-es**) n Kirschtomate f
chess [tʃes] n Schach nt; **chessboard** n
Schachbrett nt
chest [tʃest] n Brust f; (box) Kiste f; **~ of
drawers** Kommode f
chestnut ['tʃesnʌt] n Kastanie f
chew [tʃuː] vt, vi kauen; **chewing gum** n
Kaugummi m

chick [tʃɪk] n Küken nt; **chicken** n Huhn nt; (food: roast) Hähnchen nt; (coward) Feigling m; **chicken breast** n Hühnerbrust f; **chicken Kiev** n paniertes Hähnchen, mit Knoblauchbutter gefüllt; **chickenpox** n Windpocken pl; **chickpea** n Kichererbse f

chicory ['tʃɪkəri] n Chicorée f

chief [tʃi:f] n (of department etc) Leiter(in) m(f); (boss) Chef(in) m(f); (of tribe) Häuptling m ▷ adj Haupt-; **chiefly** adv hauptsächlich

child [tʃaɪld] (pl **children**) n Kind nt; **child abuse** n Kindesmisshandlung f; **child allowance**, **child benefit** (Brit) n Kindergeld nt; **childbirth** n Geburt f, Entbindung f; **childhood** n Kindheit f; **childish** adj kindisch; **child lock** n Kindersicherung f; **childproof** adj kindersicher; **children** ['tʃɪldrən] pl of **child**; **child seat** n Kindersitz m

Chile ['tʃɪli] n Chile nt

chill [tʃɪl] n Kühle f; (Med) Erkältung f ▷ vt (wine) kühlen; **chill out** vi (fam) relaxen; **chilled** adj gekühlt

chilli ['tʃɪli] n Pepperoni pl; (spice) Chili m; **chilli con carne** ['tʃɪlɪkɒn'kɑːnɪ] n Chili con carne nt

chilly ['tʃɪli] adj kühl, frostig

chimney ['tʃɪmnɪ] n Schornstein m; **chimneysweep** n Schornsteinfeger(in) m(f)

chimpanzee [tʃɪmpæn'ziː] n Schimpanse m

chin [tʃɪn] n Kinn nt

china ['tʃaɪnə] n Porzellan nt

China ['tʃaɪnə] n China nt; **Chinese** [tʃaɪ'niːz] adj chinesisch ▷ n (person) Chinese m, Chinesin f; (language) Chinesisch nt; **Chinese leaves** npl Chinakohl m

chip [tʃɪp] n (of wood etc) Splitter m; (damage) angeschlagene Stelle; (Inform) Chip m; **~s** (Brit: potatoes) Pommes frites pl; (US: crisps) Kartoffelchips pl ▷ vt anschlagen, beschädigen; **chippie** (fam), **chip shop** n Frittenbude f

chiropodist [kɪ'rɒpədɪst] n Fußpfleger(in) m(f)

chirp [tʃɜːp] vi zwitschern

chisel ['tʃɪzl] n Meißel m

chitchat ['tʃɪttʃæt] n Gerede nt

chives [tʃaɪvz] npl Schnittlauch m

chlorine ['klɔːriːn] n Chlor nt

chocaholic, **chocoholic** [tʃɒkə'hɒlɪk] n Schokoladenfreak m; **choc-ice** ['tʃɒkaɪs] n Eis nt mit Schokoladenüberzug; **chocolate** ['tʃɒklɪt] n Schokolade f; (chocolate-coated sweet) Praline f; **a bar of ~** eine Tafel Schokolade; **a box of ~s** eine Schachtel Pralinen; **chocolate cake** n Schokoladenkuchen m; **chocolate sauce** n Schokoladensoße f

choice [tʃɔɪs] n Wahl f; (selection) Auswahl f ▷ adj auserlesen; (product) Qualitäts-

choir ['kwaɪə*] n Chor m

choke [tʃəʊk] vi sich verschlucken; (Sport) die Nerven verlieren ▷ vt erdrosseln ▷ n (Auto) Choke m

cholera ['kɒlərə] n Cholera f

cholesterol [kə'lestərəl] n Cholesterin nt

choose [tʃuːz] (**chose**, **chosen**) vt wählen; (pick out) sich aussuchen; **there are three to ~ from** es stehen drei zur Auswahl

chop [tʃɒp] vt (zer)hacken; (meat etc) klein schneiden ▷ n (meat) Kotelett nt; **to get the ~** gefeuert werden; **chopper** n Hackbeil nt; (fam: helicopter) Hubschrauber m; **chopsticks** npl Essstäbchen pl

chorus ['kɔːrəs] n Chor m; (in song) Refrain m

chose, **chosen** [tʃəʊz, 'tʃəʊzn] pt, pp of **choose**

chowder ['tʃaʊdə*] n (US) dicke Suppe mit Meeresfrüchten

christen ['krɪsn] vt taufen; **christening** n Taufe f; **Christian** ['krɪstɪən] adj christlich ▷ n Christ(in) m(f); **Christian name** n (Brit) Vorname m

Christmas ['krɪsməs] n Weihnachten pl; **Christmas card** n Weihnachtskarte f; **Christmas carol** n Weihnachtslied nt; **Christmas Day** n der erste Weihnachtstag; **Christmas Eve** n Heiligabend m; **Christmas pudding** n Plumpudding m; **Christmas tree** n Weihnachtsbaum m

chronic ['krɒnɪk] adj (Med, fig) chronisch; (fam: very bad) miserabel

chrysanthemum [krɪ'sænθɪməm] n Chrysantheme f

chubby ['tʃʌbɪ] adj (child) pummelig; (adult) rundlich

chuck [tʃʌk] vt (fam) schmeißen; **chuck in** vt (fam: job) hinschmeißen; **chuck out** vt (fam) rausschmeißen; **chuck up** vi (fam) kotzen

chunk [tʃʌŋk] n Klumpen m; (of bread) Brocken m; (of meat) Batzen m; **chunky** adj (person) stämmig

Chunnel ['tʃʌnəl] n (fam) Kanaltunnel m

church [tʃɜːtʃ] n Kirche f; **churchyard** n Kirchhof m

chute [ʃuːt] n Rutsche f

chutney ['tʃʌtnɪ] n Chutney m

CIA abbr = **Central Intelligence Agency** (US) CIA f

CID abbr = **Criminal Investigation Department** (Brit) ≈ Kripo f

cider ['saɪdə*] n ≈ Apfelmost m

cigar [sɪ'gaː*] n Zigarre f; **cigarette** [sɪɡə'ret] n Zigarette f

cinema ['sɪnəmə] n Kino nt

cinnamon ['sɪnəmən] n Zimt m

circa ['sɜːkə] prep zirka

circle ['sɜːkl] n Kreis m ▷ vi kreisen; **circuit** ['sɜːkɪt] n Rundfahrt f; (on foot) Rundgang m; (for racing) Rennstrecke f; (Elec) Stromkreis m; **circular** ['sɜːkjʊlə*] adj (kreis)rund, kreisförmig ▷ n Rundschreiben nt; **circulation** [sɜːkjʊ'leɪʃən] n (of blood) Kreislauf m; (of newspaper) Auflage f

circumstances ['sɜːkəmstənsəz] npl (facts) Umstände pl; (financial condition) Verhältnisse pl; **in/under the ~** unter den Umständen; **under no ~** auf keinen Fall

circus ['sɜːkəs] n Zirkus m

cissy ['sɪsɪ] n (fam) Weichling m

cistern ['sɪstən] n Zisterne f; (of WC) Spülkasten m

cite [saɪt] vt zitieren

citizen ['sɪtɪzn] n Bürger(in) m(f); (of nation) Staatsangehörige(r) mf; **citizenship** n Staatsangehörigkeit f

city ['sɪtɪ] n Stadt f; (large) Großstadt f; **the ~** (London's financial centre) die (Londoner) City; **city centre** n Innenstadt f, Zentrum nt

civil ['sɪvɪl] adj (of town) Bürger-; (of state) staatsbürgerlich; (not military) zivil; **civil ceremony** n standesamtliche Hochzeit; **civil engineering** n Hoch- und Tiefbau m, Bauingenieurwesen nt; **civilian** [sɪ'vɪljən] n Zivilist(in) m(f); **civilization** [sɪvɪlaɪ'zeɪʃən] n Zivilisation f, Kultur f;

civilized ['sɪvɪlaɪzd] adj zivilisiert, kultiviert; **civil partnership** n eingetragene Partnerschaft; **civil rights** npl Bürgerrechte pl; **civil servant** n (Staats)beamte(r) m, (Staats)beamtin f; **civil service** n Staatsdienst m; **civil war** n Bürgerkrieg m

CJD abbr = **Creutzfeld-Jakob disease** Creutzfeld-Jakob-Krankheit f

cl abbr = **centilitre(s)** cl

claim [kleɪm] vt beanspruchen; (apply for) beantragen; (demand) fordern; (assert) behaupten (that dass) ▷ n (demand) Forderung f (for für); (right) Anspruch m (to auf +akk); **~ for damages** Schadenersatzforderung f; **to make** o **put in a ~** (insurance) Ansprüche geltend machen; **claimant** n Antragsteller(in) m(f)

clam [klæm] n Venusmuschel f; **clam chowder** n (US) dicke Muschelsuppe (mit Sellerie, Zwiebeln etc)

clap [klæp] vi (Beifall) klatschen

claret ['klærɪt] n roter Bordeaux(wein)

clarify ['klærɪfaɪ] vt klären

clarinet [klærɪ'net] n Klarinette f

clarity ['klærɪtɪ] n Klarheit f

clash [klæʃ] vi (physically) zusammenstoßen (with mit); (argue) sich auseinandersetzen (with mit); (fig: colours) sich beißen ▷ n Zusammenstoß m; (argument) Auseinandersetzung f

clasp [klɑːsp] n (on belt) Schnalle f

class [klɑːs] n Klasse f ▷ vt einordnen, einstufen

classic ['klæsɪk] adj (mistake, example etc) klassisch ▷ n Klassiker m; **classical** ['klæsɪkəl] adj (music, ballet etc) klassisch

classification [klæsɪfɪ'keɪʃn] n Klassifizierung f; **classify** ['klæsɪfaɪ] vt klassifizieren; **classified advertisement** Kleinanzeige f

classroom ['klɑːsrʊm] n Klassenzimmer nt

classy ['klɑːsɪ] adj (fam) nobel, exklusiv

clatter ['klætə*] vi klappern

clause [klɔːz] n (Ling) Satz m; (Jur) Klausel f

claw [klɔː] n Kralle f

clay [kleɪ] n Lehm m; (for pottery) Ton m

clean [kliːn] adj sauber; **~ driving licence** Führerschein ohne Strafpunkte ▷ adv (completely) glatt ▷ vt sauber machen;

(carpet etc) reinigen; *(window, shoes, vegetables)* putzen; *(wound)* säubern; **clean up** vt sauber machen ▷ vi aufräumen; **cleaner** n *(person)* Putzmann m, Putzfrau f; *(substance)* Putzmittel nt; **~'s** *(firm)* Reinigung f

cleanse [klenz] vt reinigen; *(wound)* säubern; **cleanser** n Reinigungsmittel nt

clear ['klɪə*] adj klar; *(distinct)* deutlich; *(conscience)* rein; *(free, road etc)* frei; **to be ~ about sth** sich über etw im Klaren sein ▷ adv **to stand ~** zurücktreten ▷ vt *(road, room etc)* räumen; *(table)* abräumen; *(Jur: find innocent)* freisprechen *(of von)* ▷ vi *(fog, mist)* sich verziehen; *(weather)* aufklaren; **clear away** vt wegräumen; *(dishes)* abräumen; **clear off** vi *(fam)* abhauen; **clear up** vi *(tidy up)* aufräumen; *(weather)* sich aufklären ▷ vt *(room)* aufräumen; *(litter)* wegräumen; *(matter)* klären

clearance sale n Räumungsverkauf m; **clearing** n Lichtung f; **clearly** adv klar; *(speak, remember)* deutlich; *(obviously)* eindeutig; **clearout** n Entrümpelungsaktion f; **clearway** n *(Brit)* Straße f mit Halteverbot nt

clench [klentʃ] vt *(fist)* ballen; *(teeth)* zusammenbeißen

clergyman ['klɜːdʒɪmæn] *(pl -men)* n Geistliche(r) m

clerk [klɑːk], *(US)* [klɜːk] n *(in office)* Büroangestellte(r) mf; *(US: salesperson)* Verkäufer(in) m(f)

clever ['klevə*] adj schlau, klug; *(idea)* clever

cliché ['kliːʃeɪ] n Klischee nt

click [klɪk] n Klicken nt; *(Inform)* Mausklick m ▷ vi klicken; **to ~ on sth** *(Inform)* etw anklicken; **it ~ed** *(fam)* ich hab's/er hat's etc geschnallt, es hat gefunkt, es hat Klick gemacht; **they ~ed** sie haben sich gleich verstanden; **click on** vt *(Inform)* anklicken

client ['klaɪənt] n Kunde m, Kundin f; *(Jur)* Mandant(in) m(f)

cliff [klɪf] n Klippe f

climate ['klaɪmɪt] n Klima nt

climax ['klaɪmæks] n Höhepunkt m

climb [klaɪm] vi *(person)* klettern; *(aircraft, sun)* steigen; *(road)* ansteigen ▷ vt *(mountain)* besteigen; *(tree etc)* klettern auf +akk ▷ n Aufstieg m; **climber** n *(mountaineer)* Bergsteiger(in) m(f);

climbing n Klettern nt, Bergsteigen nt; **climbing frame** n Klettergerüst nt

cling [klɪŋ] *(clung, clung)* vi sich klammern *(to an +akk)*; **cling film®** n Frischhaltefolie f

clinic ['klɪnɪk] n Klinik f; **clinical** adj klinisch

clip [klɪp] n Klammer f ▷ vt *(fix)* anklemmen *(to an +akk)*; *(fingernails)* schneiden; **clipboard** n Klemmbrett nt; **clippers** npl Schere f; *(for nails)* Zwicker m

cloak [kləʊk] n Umhang m; **cloakroom** n *(for coats)* Garderobe f

clock [klɒk] n Uhr f; *(Auto: fam)* Tacho m; **round the ~** rund um die Uhr; **clockwise** adv im Uhrzeigersinn; **clockwork** n Uhrwerk nt

clog [klɒg] n Holzschuh m ▷ vt verstopfen

cloister ['klɔɪstə*] n Kreuzgang m

clone [kləʊn] n Klon m ▷ vt klonen

close [kləʊs] adj nahe *(to +dat)*; *(friend, contact)* eng; *(resemblance)* groß; **~ to the beach** in der Nähe des Strandes; **~ win** knapper Sieg; **on ~r examination** bei näherer o genauerer Untersuchung ▷ adv [kləʊs] dicht; **he lives ~ by** er wohnt ganz in der Nähe ▷ vt [kləʊz] schließen; *(road)* sperren; *(discussion, matter)* abschließen ▷ vi [kləʊz] schließen; n [kləʊz] Ende nt; **close down** vi schließen; *(factory)* stillgelegt werden ▷ vt *(shop)* schließen; *(factory)* stilllegen; **closed** adj *(road)* gesperrt; *(shop etc)* geschlossen; **closed circuit television** n Videoüberwachungsanlage f; **closely** adv *(related)* eng, nah; *(packed, follow)* dicht; *(attentively)* genau

closet ['klɒzɪt] n *(esp US)* Schrank m

close-up ['kləʊsʌp] n Nahaufnahme f

closing ['kləʊzɪŋ] adj **~ date** letzter Termin; *(for competition)* Einsendeschluss m; **~ time** *(of shop)* Ladenschluss m; *(Brit: of pub)* Polizeistunde f

clot [klɒt] n *(blood)* **~** Blutgerinnsel nt; *(fam: idiot)* Trottel m ▷ vi *(blood)* gerinnen

cloth [klɒθ] n *(material)* Tuch nt; *(for cleaning)* Lappen m

clothe [kləʊð] vt kleiden; **clothes** npl Kleider pl, Kleidung f; **clothes line** n Wäscheleine f; **clothes peg, clothespin** *(US)* n Wäscheklammer f; **clothing** ['kləʊðɪŋ] n Kleidung f

clotted ['klɒtɪd] *adj* ~ **cream** dicke Sahne *f* (aus erhitzter Milch)

cloud [klaʊd] *n* Wolke *f*; **cloudy** *adj* (sky) bewölkt; (liquid) trüb

clove [kləʊv] *n* Gewürznelke *f*; ~ **of garlic** Knoblauchzehe *f*

clover ['kləʊvə*] *n* Klee *m*; **cloverleaf** (pl -**leaves**) *n* Kleeblatt *nt*

clown [klaʊn] *n* Clown *m*

club [klʌb] *n* (weapon) Knüppel *m*; (society) Klub *m*, Verein *m*; (nightclub) Disko *f*; (golf club) Golfschläger *m*; ~**s** (Cards) Kreuz *nt*; **clubbing** *n* **to go** ~ in die Disko gehen; **club class** *n* (Aviat) Businessclass *f*

clue [kluː] *n* Anhaltspunkt *m*, Hinweis *m*; **he hasn't a** ~ er hat keine Ahnung

clumsy ['klʌmzɪ] *adj* unbeholfen, ungeschickt

clung [klʌŋ] *pt, pp of* **cling**

clutch [klʌtʃ] *n* (Auto) Kupplung *f* ▷ *vt* umklammern; (book etc) an sich *akk* klammern

cm *abbr* = **centimetre(s)** cm

c/o *abbr* = **care of** bei

Co *abbr* = **company** Co

coach [kəʊtʃ] *n* (Brit: bus) Reisebus *m*; (Rail) (Personen)wagen *m*; (Sport: trainer) Trainer(in) *m(f)* ▷ *vt* Nachhilfeunterricht geben +dat; (Sport) trainieren; **coach (class)** *n* (Aviat) Economyclass *f*; **coach driver** *n* Busfahrer(in) *m(f)*; **coach station** *n* Busbahnhof *m*; **coach trip** *n* Busfahrt *f*; (tour) Busreise *f*

coal [kəʊl] *n* Kohle *f*

coalition [kəʊə'lɪʃən] *n* (Pol) Koalition *f*

coalmine ['kəʊlmaɪn] *n* Kohlenbergwerk *nt*; **coalminer** *n* Bergarbeiter *m*

coast [kəʊst] *n* Küste *f*; **coastguard** *n* Küstenwache *f*; **coastline** *n* Küste *f*

coat [kəʊt] *n* Mantel *m*; (jacket) Jacke *f*; (on animals) Fell *nt*, Pelz *m*; (of paint) Schicht *f*; ~ **of arms** Wappen *nt*; **coathanger** *n* Kleiderbügel *m*; **coating** *n* Überzug *m*; (layer) Schicht *f*

cobble(stone)s ['kɒbl(stəʊn)z] *npl* Kopfsteine *pl*; (surface) Kopfsteinpflaster *nt*

cobweb ['kɒbweb] *n* Spinnennetz *nt*

cocaine [kə'keɪn] *n* Kokain *nt*

cock [kɒk] *n* Hahn *m*; (vulg: penis) Schwanz *m*; **cockerel** ['kɒkərəl] *n* junger Hahn

cockle ['kɒkl] *n* Herzmuschel *f*

cockpit ['kɒkpɪt] *n* (in plane, racing car) Cockpit *nt*; **cockroach** ['kɒkrəʊtʃ] *n* Kakerlake *f*; **cocksure** *adj* todsicher; **cocktail** ['kɒkteɪl] *n* Cocktail *m*; **cock-up** *n* (Brit fam) **to make a** ~ **of sth** bei etw Mist bauen; **cocky** ['kɒkɪ] *adj* großspurig, von sich selbst überzeugt

cocoa ['kəʊkəʊ] *n* Kakao *m*

coconut ['kəʊkənʌt] *n* Kokosnuss *f*

cod [kɒd] *n* Kabeljau *m*

COD *abbr* = **cash on delivery** per Nachnahme

code [kəʊd] *n* Kode *m*

coeducational [kəʊedjʊ'keɪʃənl] *adj* (school) gemischt

coffee ['kɒfɪ] *n* Kaffee *m*; **coffee bar** *n* Café *nt*; **coffee break** *n* Kaffeepause *f*; **coffee maker** *n* Kaffeemaschine *f*; **coffee pot** *n* Kaffeekanne *f*; **coffee shop** *n* Café *nt*; **coffee table** *n* Couchtisch *m*

coffin ['kɒfɪn] *n* Sarg *m*

coil [kɔɪl] *n* Rolle *f*; (Elec) Spule *f*; (Med) Spirale *f*

coin [kɔɪn] *n* Münze *f*

coincide [kəʊɪn'saɪd] *vi* (happen together) zusammenfallen (with mit); **coincidence** [kəʊ'ɪnsɪdəns] *n* Zufall *m*

coke [kəʊk] *n* Koks *m*; **Coke®** Cola *f*

cola ['kəʊlə] *n* Cola *f*

cold [kəʊld] *adj* kalt; **I'm** ~ mir ist kalt, ich friere ▷ *n* Kälte *f*; (illness) Erkältung *f*, Schnupfen *m*; **to catch a** ~ sich erkälten; **cold box** *n* Kühlbox *f*; **coldness** *n* Kälte *f*; **cold sore** *n* Herpes *m*; **cold turkey** *n* (fam) Totalentzug *m*; (symptoms) Entzugserscheinungen *pl*

coleslaw ['kəʊlslɔː] *n* Krautsalat *m*

collaborate [kə'læbəreɪt] *vi* zusammenarbeiten (with mit); **collaboration** [kəlæbə'reɪʃən] *n* Zusammenarbeit *f*; (of one party) Mitarbeit *f*

collapse [kə'læps] *vi* zusammenbrechen; (building etc) einstürzen ▷ *n* Zusammenbruch *m*; (of building) Einsturz *m*; **collapsible** [kə'læpsəbl] *adj* zusammenklappbar, Klapp-

collar ['kɒlə*] *n* Kragen *m*; (for dog, cat) Halsband *nt*; **collarbone** *n* Schlüsselbein *nt*

colleague ['kɒliːg] *n* Kollege *m*, Kollegin *f*

collect [kə'lekt] *vt* sammeln; (fetch) abholen ▷ *vi* sich sammeln; **collect call** *n*

(US) R-Gespräch *nt*; **collected** *adj (works)* gesammelt; *(person)* gefasst; **collector** *n* Sammler(in) *m(f)*; **collection** [kə'lekʃən] *n* Sammlung *f*; *(Rel)* Kollekte *f*; *(from postbox)* Leerung *f*

college ['kɒlɪdʒ] *n (residential)* College *nt*; *(specialist)* Fachhochschule *f*; *(vocational)* Berufsschule *f*; *(US: university)* Universität *f*; **to go to ~** *(US)* studieren

collide [kə'laɪd] *vi* zusammenstoßen; **collision** [kə'lɪʒən] *n* Zusammenstoß *m*

colloquial [kə'ləʊkwɪəl] *adj* umgangssprachlich

Cologne [kə'ləʊn] *n* Köln *nt*

colon ['kəʊlən] *n (punctuation mark)* Doppelpunkt *m*

colonial [kə'ləʊnɪəl] *adj* Kolonial-; **colonize** ['kɒlənaɪz] *vt* kolonisieren; **colony** ['kɒlənɪ] *n* Kolonie *f*

color *n (US)*, **colour** ['kʌlə*] *n* Farbe *f*; *(of skin)* Hautfarbe *f* ▷ *vt* anmalen; *(bias)* färben; **colour-blind** *adj* farbenblind; **coloured** *adj* farbig; *(biased)* gefärbt; **colour film** *n* Farbfilm *m*; **colourful** *adj (lit, fig)* bunt; *(life, past)* bewegt; **colouring** *n (in food etc)* Farbstoff *m*; *(complexion)* Gesichtsfarbe *f*; **colourless** *adj (lit, fig)* farblos; **colour photo(graph)** *n* Farbfoto *nt*; **colour television** *n* Farbfernsehen *nt*

column ['kɒləm] *n* Säule *f*; *(of print)* Spalte *f*

comb [kəʊm] *n* Kamm *m* ▷ *vt* kämmen; **to ~ one's hair** sich kämmen

combination [kɒmbɪ'neɪʃən] *n* Kombination *f*; *(mixture)* Mischung *f (of aus)*; **combine** [kəm'baɪn] *vt* verbinden *(with mit)*; *(two things)* kombinieren

come [kʌm] *(came, come)* *vi* kommen; *(arrive)* ankommen; *(on list, in order)* stehen; *(with adjective: become)* werden; **~ and see us** besuchen Sie uns mal; **coming** ich komm ja schon!; **to ~ first/second** erster/zweiter werden; **to ~ true** wahr werden; **to ~ loose** sich lockern; **the years to ~** die kommenden Jahre; **there's one more to ~** es kommt noch eins/noch einer; **how ~ ...?** *(fam)* wie kommt es, dass ...?; **~ to think of it** *(fam)* wo es mir gerade einfällt; **come across** *vt (find)* stoßen auf *+akk*; **come back** *vi* zurückkommen; **I'll ~ to that** ich komme darauf zurück; **come down** *vi* herunterkommen; *(rain, snow, price)* fallen;

come from *vt (result)* kommen von; **where do you ~?** wo kommen Sie her?; **I ~ London** ich komme aus London; **come in** *vi* hereinkommen; *(arrive)* ankommen; *(in race)* **to ~ fourth** Vierter werden; **come off** *vi (button, handle etc)* abgehen; *(succeed)* gelingen; **to ~ well/badly** gut/schlecht wegkommen; **come on** *vi (progress)* vorankommen; **~!** komm!; *(hurry)* beeil dich!; *(encouraging)* los!; **come out** *vi* herauskommen; *(photo)* was werden; *(homosexual)* sich outen; **come round** *vi (visit)* vorbeikommen; *(regain consciousness)* wieder zu sich kommen; **come to** *vi (regain consciousness)* wieder zu sich kommen ▷ *vt (sum)* sich belaufen auf *+akk*; **when it comes to ...** wenn es um ... geht; **come up** *vi* hochkommen; *(sun, moon)* aufgehen; **to ~ (for discussion)** zur Sprache kommen; **come up to** *vt (approach)* zukommen auf *+akk*; *(water)* reichen bis zu; *(expectations)* entsprechen *+dat*; **come up with** *vt (idea)* haben; *(solution, answer)* kommen auf *+akk*; **to ~ a suggestion** einen Vorschlag machen

comedian [kə'miːdɪən] *n* Komiker(in) *m(f)*

comedown ['kʌmdaʊn] *n* Abstieg *m*

comedy ['kɒmədɪ] *n* Komödie *f*

come-on ['kʌmɒn] *n* **to give sb the ~** *(fam)* jdn anmachen

comfort ['kʌmfət] *n* Komfort *m*; *(consolation)* Trost *m* ▷ *vt* trösten; **comfortable** *adj* bequem; *(income)* ausreichend; *(temperature, life)* angenehm; **comfort station** *n (US)* Toilette *f*; **comforting** *adj* tröstlich

comic ['kɒmɪk] *n (magazine)* Comic(heft) *nt*; *(comedian)* Komiker(in) *m(f)* ▷ *adj* komisch

coming ['kʌmɪŋ] *adj* kommend; *(event)* bevorstehend

comma ['kɒmə] *n* Komma *nt*

command [kə'mɑːnd] *n* Befehl *m*; *(control)* Führung *f*; *(Mil)* Kommando *nt* ▷ *vt* befehlen *+dat*

commemorate [kə'meməreɪt] *vt* gedenken *+gen*; **commemoration** [kəmemə'reɪʃən] *n* **in ~ of** in Gedenken an *+akk*

comment ['kɒment] *n (remark)* Bemerkung *f*; *(note)* Anmerkung *f*; *(official)* Kommentar *m (on zu)*; **no ~** kein

Kommentar ▷ *vi* sich äußern (*on* zu);
commentary ['kɒməntrɪ] *n* Kommentar
m (*on* zu); (*Tv, Sport*) Livereportage *f*;
commentator ['kɒmənteɪtə*] *n*
Kommentator(in) *m(f)*; (*Tv, Sport*)
Reporter(in) *m(f)*
commerce ['kɒmɜːs] *n* Handel *m*;
commercial [kə'mɜːʃəl] *adj* kommerziell;
(*training*) kaufmännisch; **~ break**
Werbepause *f*; **~ vehicle** Lieferwagen *m*
▷ *n* (*Tv*) Werbespot *m*
commission [kə'mɪʃən] *n* Auftrag *m*; (*fee*)
Provision *f*; (*reporting body*) Kommission *f*
▷ *vt* beauftragen
commit [kə'mɪt] *vt* (*crime*) begehen ▷ *vr*
to ~ oneself (*undertake*) sich verpflichten
(*to* zu); **commitment** *n* Verpflichtung *f*;
(*Pol*) Engagement *nt*
committee [kə'mɪtɪ] *n* Ausschuss *m*,
Komitee *nt*
commodity [kə'mɒdɪtɪ] *n* Ware *f*
common ['kɒmən] *adj* (*experience*)
allgemein, alltäglich; (*shared*) gemeinsam;
(*widespread, frequent*) häufig; (*pej*)
gewöhnlich, ordinär; **to have sth in ~** etw
gemein haben ▷ *n* (*Brit: land*)
Gemeindewiese *f*; **commonly** *adv* häufig,
allgemein; **commonplace** *adj* alltäglich;
(*pej*) banal; **commonroom** *n*
Gemeinschaftsraum *m*; **Commons** *n* (*Brit
Pol*) **the (House of) ~** das Unterhaus;
common sense *n* gesunder
Menschenverstand; **Commonwealth** *n*
Commonwealth *nt*; **~ of Independent
States** Gemeinschaft *f* Unabhängiger
Staaten
communal ['kɒmjʊnl] *adj* gemeinsam;
(*of a community*) Gemeinschafts-,
Gemeinde-
communicate [kə'mjuːnɪkeɪt] *vi*
kommunizieren (*with* mit);
communication [kəmjuːnɪ'keɪʃən] *n*
Kommunikation *f*, Verständigung *f*;
communications satellite *n*
Nachrichtensatellit *m*;
communications technology *n*
Nachrichtentechnik *f*; **communicative**
adj gesprächig
communion [kə'mjuːnɪən] *n* (*Holy*)
Communion Heiliges Abendmahl;
(*Catholic*) Kommunion *f*
communism ['kɒmjʊnɪzəm] *n*
Kommunismus *m*; **communist**

['kɒmjʊnɪst] *adj* kommunistisch ▷ *n*
Kommunist(in) *m(f)*
community [kə'mjuːnɪtɪ] *n*
Gemeinschaft *f*; **community centre** *n*
Gemeindezentrum *nt*; **community
service** *n* (*Jur*) Sozialdienst *m*
commutation ticket [kɒmjʊ'teɪʃəntɪkɪt]
n (*US*) Zeitkarte *f*; **commute** [kə'mjuːt] *vi*
pendeln; **commuter** *n* Pendler(in) *m(f)*
compact [kəm'pækt] *adj* kompakt
▷ ['kɒmpækt] *n* (*for make-up*) Puderdose *f*;
(*US: car*) ≈ Mittelklassewagen *m*; **compact
camera** *n* Kompaktkamera *f*; **compact
disc** *n* Compact Disc *f*, CD *f*
companion [kəm'pænɪən] *n*
Begleiter(in) *m(f)*
company ['kʌmpənɪ] *n* Gesellschaft *f*;
(*Comm*) Firma *f*; **to keep sb ~** jdm
Gesellschaft leisten; **company car** *n*
Firmenauto *nt*
comparable ['kɒmpərəbl] *adj*
vergleichbar (*with, to* mit)
comparative [kəm'pærətɪv] *adj* relativ
▷ *n* (*Ling*) Komparativ *m*; **comparatively**
adv verhältnismäßig
compare [kəm'peə*] *vt* vergleichen (*with,
to* mit); **~d with** *o* **to** im Vergleich zu;
beyond ~ unvergleichlich; **comparison**
[kəm'pærɪsn] *n* Vergleich *m*; **in ~ with** im
Vergleich mit (*o* zu)
compartment [kəm'pɑːtmənt] *n* (*Rail*)
Abteil *nt*; (*in desk etc*) Fach *nt*
compass ['kʌmpəs] *n* Kompass *m*; **~es** *pl*
Zirkel *m*
compassion [kəm'pæʃən] *n* Mitgefühl *nt*
compatible [kəm'pætɪbl] *adj* vereinbar
(*with* mit); (*Inform*) kompatibel; **we're not
~** wir passen nicht zueinander
compensate ['kɒmpenseɪt] *vt* (*person*)
entschädigen (*for* für) ▷ *vi* **to ~ for sth**
Ersatz für etw leisten; (*make up for*) etw
ausgleichen; **compensation**
[kɒmpen'seɪʃən] *n* Entschädigung *f*;
(*money*) Schadenersatz *m*; (*Jur*) Abfindung *f*
compete [kəm'piːt] *vi* konkurrieren (*for*
um); (*Sport*) kämpfen (*for* um); (*take part*)
teilnehmen (*in an* +*dat*)
competence ['kɒmpɪtəns] *n* Fähigkeit *f*;
(*Jur*) Zuständigkeit *f*; **competent** *adj*
fähig; (*Jur*) zuständig
competition [kɒmpɪ'tɪʃən] *n* (*contest*)
Wettbewerb *m*; (*Comm*) Konkurrenz *f* (*for*
um); **competitive** [kəm'petɪtɪv] *adj* (*firm*,

price, product) konkurrenzfähig;
competitor [kəm'petɪtə*] *n (Comm)*
Konkurrent(in) *m(f)*; *(Sport)* Teilnehmer(in)
m(f)
complain [kəm'pleɪn] *vi* klagen; *(formally)*
sich beschweren *(about über +akk)*;
complaint *n* Klage *f*; *(formal)* Beschwerde
f; *(Med)* Leiden *nt*
complement *vt* ergänzen
complete [kəm'pliːt] *adj* vollständig;
(finished) fertig; *(failure, disaster)* total;
(happiness) vollkommen; **are we ~?** sind
wir vollzählig? ▷ *vt* vervollständigen;
(finish) beenden; *(form)* ausfüllen;
completely *adv* völlig; **not ~ ...** nicht
ganz ...
complex ['kɒmpleks] *adj* komplex; *(task,
theory etc)* kompliziert ▷ *n* Komplex *m*
complexion [kəm'plekʃən] *n*
Gesichtsfarbe *f*, Teint *m*
complicated ['kɒmplɪkeɪtɪd] *adj*
kompliziert; **complication**
['kɒmplɪkeɪʃən] *n* Komplikation *f*
compliment ['kɒmplɪmənt] *n*
Kompliment *nt*; **complimentary**
[kɒmplɪ'mentərɪ] *adj* lobend; *(free of
charge)* Gratis-; **~ ticket** Freikarte *f*
comply [kəm'plaɪ] *vi* **to ~ with the
regulations** den Vorschriften
entsprechen
component [kəm'pəʊnənt] *n*
Bestandteil *m*
compose [kəm'pəʊz] *vt (music)*
komponieren; **to ~ oneself** sich
zusammennehmen; **composed** *adj*
gefasst; **to be ~ of** bestehen aus;
composer *n* Komponist(in) *m(f)*;
composition [kɒmpə'zɪʃən] *n (of a group)*
Zusammensetzung *f*; *(Mus)* Komposition *f*
comprehend [kɒmprɪ'hend] *vt*
verstehen; **comprehension**
[kɒmprɪ'henʃən] *n* Verständnis *nt*
comprehensive [kɒmprɪ'hensɪv] *adj*
umfassend; **~ school** Gesamtschule *f*
compress [kəm'pres] *vt* komprimieren
comprise [kəm'praɪz] *vt* umfassen,
bestehen aus
compromise ['kɒmprəmaɪz] *n*
Kompromiss *m* ▷ *vi* einen Kompromiss
schließen
compulsory [kəm'pʌlsərɪ] *adj*
obligatorisch; **~ subject** Pflichtfach *nt*
computer [kəm'pjuːtə*] *n* Computer *m*;

computer aided *adj* computergestützt;
computer-controlled *adj*
rechnergesteuert; **computer game** *n*
Computerspiel *nt*; **computer-literate** *adj*
to be ~ mit dem Computer umgehen
können; **computer scientist** *n*
Informatiker(in) *m(f)*; **computing** *n*
(subject) Informatik *f*
con [kɒn] *(fam)* *n* Schwindel *m* ▷ *vt*
betrügen *(out of um)*
conceal [kən'siːl] *vt* verbergen *(from vor
+dat)*
conceivable [kən'siːvəbl] *adj* denkbar,
vorstellbar; **conceive** [kən'siːv] *vt*
(imagine) sich vorstellen; *(child)*
empfangen
concentrate ['kɒnsəntreɪt] *vi* sich
konzentrieren *(on auf +akk)*;
concentration [kɒnsən'treɪʃən] *n*
Konzentration *f*
concept ['kɒnsept] *n* Begriff *m*
concern [kən'sɜːn] *n (affair)*
Angelegenheit *f*, *(worry)* Sorge *f*;
(Comm: firm) Unternehmen *nt*; **it's not my
~** das geht mich nichts an; **there's
no cause for ~** kein Grund zur
Beunruhigung ▷ *vt (affect)* angehen;
(have connection with) betreffen; *(be
about)* handeln von; **those ~ed** die
Betroffenen; **as far as I'm ~ed** was
mich betrifft; **concerned** *adj (anxious)*
besorgt; **concerning** *prep* bezüglich,
hinsichtlich +*gen*
concert ['kɒnsət] *n* Konzert *nt*; **~ hall**
Konzertsaal *m*
concession [kən'seʃən] *n* Zugeständnis
nt; *(reduction)* Ermäßigung *f*
concise [kən'saɪs] *adj* knapp gefasst,
prägnant
conclude [kən'kluːd] *vt (end)* beenden,
(ab)schließen; *(infer)* folgern *(from aus)*; **to
~ that ...** zu dem Schluss kommen, dass
...; **conclusion** [kən'kluːʒən] *n* Schluss *m*,
Schlussfolgerung *f*
concrete ['kɒnkriːt] *n* Beton *m* ▷ *adj*
konkret
concussion [kən'kʌʃən] *n*
Gehirnerschütterung *f*
condemn [kən'dem] *vt* verdammen; *(esp
Jur)* verurteilen
condensed milk *n* Kondensmilch *f*,
Dosenmilch *f*
condition [kən'dɪʃən] *n (state)* Zustand *m*;

(*requirement*) Bedingung *f*; **on ~ that ...**
unter der Bedingung, dass ...; **~s ...**
(*circumstances, weather*) Verhältnisse *pl*;
conditional *adj* bedingt; (*Ling*)
Konditional-; **conditioner** *n* Weichspüler
m; (*for hair*) Pflegespülung *f*

condo ['kɒndəʊ] (*pl* **-s**) *n see*
condominium

condolences [kən'dəʊlənsɪz] *npl* Beileid
nt

condom ['kɒndəm] *n* Kondom *nt*

condominium [kɒndə'mɪnɪəm] *n* (*US:
apartment*) Eigentumswohnung *f*

conduct ['kɒndʌkt] *n* (*behaviour*)
Verhalten *nt* ▷ [kən'dʌkt] *vt* führen, leiten;
(*orchestra*) dirigieren; **conductor**
[kən'dʌktə*] *n* (*of orchestra*) Dirigent(in)
m(f); (*in bus*) Schaffner(in) *m(f)*; (*US: on
train*) Zugführer(in) *m(f)*

cone [kəʊn] *n* Kegel *m*; (*for ice cream*)
Waffeltüte *f*; (*fir cone*) (Tannen)zapfen *m*

conference ['kɒnfərəns] *n* Konferenz *f*

confess [kən'fes] *vt*, *vi* **to ~ that ...**
gestehen, dass ...; **confession** [kən'feʃən]
n Geständnis *nt*; (*Rel*) Beichte *f*

confetti [kən'fetɪ] *n* Konfetti *nt*

confidence ['kɒnfɪdəns] *n* Vertrauen *nt*
(*in zu*); (*assurance*) Selbstvertrauen *nt*;
confident *adj* (*sure*) zuversichtlich (*that ...*
dass ...), überzeugt (*of von*); (*self-assured*)
selbstsicher; **confidential** [kɒnfɪ'denʃəl]
adj vertraulich

confine [kən'faɪn] *vt* beschränken (*to auf
+akk*)

confirm [kən'fɜːm] *vt* bestätigen;
confirmation [kɒnfə'meɪʃən] *n*
Bestätigung *f*; (*Rel*) Konfirmation *f*;
confirmed *adj* überzeugt; (*bachelor*)
eingefleischt

confiscate ['kɒnfɪskeɪt] *vt*
beschlagnahmen, konfiszieren

conflict ['kɒnflɪkt] *n* Konflikt *m*

confuse [kən'fjuːz] *vt* verwirren; (*sth with
sth*) verwechseln (*with mit*); (*several things*)
durcheinanderbringen; **confused** *adj*
(*person*) konfus, verwirrt; (*account*)
verworren; **confusing** *adj* verwirrend;
confusion [kən'fjuːʒən] *n* Verwirrung *f*;
(*of two things*) Verwechslung *f*; (*muddle*)
Chaos *nt*

congested [kən'dʒestɪd] *adj* verstopft;
(*overcrowded*) überfüllt; **congestion**
[kən'dʒestʃən] *n* Stau *m*

congratulate [kən'grætjʊleɪt] *vt*
gratulieren (*on zu*); **congratulations**
[kəngrætjʊ'leɪʃənz] *npl* Glückwünsche *pl*;
~! gratuliere!, herzlichen Glückwunsch!

congregation [kɒngrɪ'geɪʃən] *n* (*Rel*)
Gemeinde *f*

congress ['kɒŋgres] *n* Kongress *m*; (*US*)
Congress der Kongress; **congressman** (*pl*
-men), **congresswoman** (*pl* **-women**) *n*
(*US*) Mitglied *nt* des
Repräsentantenhauses

conifer ['kɒnɪfə*] *n* Nadelbaum *m*

conjunction [kən'dʒʌŋkʃən] *n* (*Ling*)
Konjunktion *f*; **in ~ with** in Verbindung
mit

conk out [kɒŋk 'aʊt] *vi* (*fam: appliance,
car*) den Geist aufgeben, streiken; (*person:
die*) ins Gras beißen

connect [kə'nekt] *vt* verbinden (*with, to
mit*); (*Elec, Tech: appliance etc*) anschließen
(*to an +akk*) ▷ *vi* (*train, plane*) Anschluss
haben (*with an +akk*); **~ing flight**
Anschlussflug *m*; **~ing train** Anschlusszug
m; **connection** [kə'nekʃən] *n* Verbindung
f; (*link*) Zusammenhang *m*; (*for train, plane,
electrical appliance*) Anschluss *m* (*with, to an
+akk*); (*business etc*) Beziehung *f*; **in ~ with**
in Zusammenhang mit; **bad ~** (*Tel*)
schlechte Verbindung; (*Elec*)
Wackelkontakt *m*; **connector** *n* (*Inform:
computer*) Stecker *m*

conscience ['kɒnʃəns] *n* Gewissen *nt*;
conscientious [kɒnʃɪ'enʃəs] *adj*
gewissenhaft

conscious ['kɒnʃəs] *adj* (*act*) bewusst;
(*Med*) bei Bewusstsein; **to be ~** bei
Bewusstsein sein; **consciousness** *n*
Bewusstsein *nt*

consecutive [kən'sekjʊtɪv] *adj*
aufeinander folgend

consent [kən'sent] *n* Zustimmung *f* ▷ *vi*
zustimmen (*to dat*)

consequence ['kɒnsɪkwəns] *n* Folge *f*,
Konsequenz *f*; **consequently**
['kɒnsɪkwəntlɪ] *adv* folglich

conservation [kɒnsə'veɪʃən] *n* Erhaltung
f; (*of buildings*) Denkmalschutz *m*; (*nature
conservation*) Naturschutz *m*;
conservation area *n* Naturschutzgebiet
nt; (*in town*) unter Denkmalschutz
stehendes Gebiet

Conservative [kən'sɜːvətɪv] *adj* (*Pol*)
konservativ

conservatory [kən'sɜːvətri] n
(greenhouse) Gewächshaus nt; (room)
Wintergarten m
consider [kən'sɪdə*] vt (reflect on)
nachdenken über, sich überlegen; (take
into account) in Betracht ziehen; (regard)
halten für; **he is ~ed (to be)** ... er gilt als
...; **considerable** [kən'sɪdərəbl] adj
beträchtlich; **considerate** [kən'sɪdərɪt]
adj aufmerksam, rücksichtsvoll;
consideration [kənsɪdə'reɪʃən] n
(thoughtfulness) Rücksicht f; (thought)
Überlegung f; **to take sth into ~** etw in
Betracht ziehen; **considering**
[kən'sɪdərɪŋ] prep in Anbetracht +gen
▷ conj da
consist [kən'sɪst] vi **to ~ of ...** bestehen
aus ...
consistent [kən'sɪstənt] adj (behaviour,
process etc) konsequent; (statements)
übereinstimmend; (argument) folgerichtig;
(performance, results) beständig
consolation [kɒnsə'leɪʃən] n Trost m;
console [kən'səʊl] vt trösten
consolidate [kən'sɒlɪdeɪt] vt festigen
consonant ['kɒnsənənt] n Konsonant m
conspicuous [kən'spɪkjʊəs] adj auffällig,
auffallend
conspiracy [kən'spɪrəsɪ] n Komplott nt;
conspire [kən'spaɪə*] vi sich
verschwören (against gegen)
constable ['kʌnstəbl] n (Brit) Polizist(in)
m(f)
Constance ['kɒnstəns] n Konstanz nt;
Lake ~ der Bodensee
constant ['kɒnstənt] adj (continual)
ständig, dauernd; (unchanging: temperature
etc) gleich bleibend; **constantly** adv
dauernd
consternation [kɒnstə'neɪʃən] n
(dismay) Bestürzung f
constituency [kən'stɪtjʊənsɪ] n
Wahlkreis m
constitution [kɒnstɪ'tjuːʃən] n
Verfassung f; (of person) Konstitution f
construct [kən'strʌkt] vt bauen;
construction [kən'strʌkʃən] n (process,
result) Bau m; (method) Bauweise f; **under
~** im Bau befindlich; **construction site** n
Baustelle f; **construction worker** n
Bauarbeiter(in) m(f)
consulate ['kɒnsjʊlət] n Konsulat nt
consult [kən'sʌlt] vt um Rat fragen;

(doctor) konsultieren; (book) nachschlagen
in +dat; **consultant** n (Med) Facharzt m,
Fachärztin f; **consultation** [kɒnsəl'teɪʃən]
n Beratung f; (Med) Konsultation f
consume [kən'sjuːm] vt verbrauchen;
(food) konsumieren; **consumer** n
Verbraucher(in) m(f); **consumer-friendly**
adj verbraucherfreundlich
contact ['kɒntækt] n (touch) Berührung f;
(communication) Kontakt m; (person)
Kontaktperson f; **to be/keep in ~ (with
sb)** (mit jdm) in Kontakt sein/bleiben ▷ vt
sich in Verbindung setzen mit; **contact
lenses** npl Kontaktlinsen pl
contagious [kən'teɪdʒəs] adj ansteckend
contain [kən'teɪn] vt enthalten;
container n Behälter m; (for transport)
Container m
contaminate [kən'tæmɪneɪt] vt
verunreinigen; (chemically) verseuchen; **~d
by radiation** strahlenverseucht,
verstrahlt; **contamination**
[kəntæmɪ'neɪʃən] n Verunreinigung f; (by
radiation) Verseuchung f
contemporary [kən'tempərərɪ] adj
zeitgenössisch
contempt [kən'tempt] n Verachtung f;
contemptuous adj verächtlich; **to be
~** voller Verachtung sein (of für)
content [kən'tent] adj zufrieden
content(s) ['kɒntent(s)] n pl Inhalt m
contest ['kɒntest] n (Wett)kampf m (for
um); (competition) Wettbewerb m
▷ [kən'test] vt kämpfen um +akk; (dispute)
bestreiten; **contestant** [kən'testənt] n
Teilnehmer(in) m(f)
context ['kɒntekst] n Zusammenhang m;
out of ~ aus dem Zusammenhang
gerissen
continent ['kɒntɪnənt] n Kontinent m,
Festland nt; **the Continent** (Brit) das
europäische Festland, der Kontinent;
continental [kɒntɪ'nentl] adj
kontinental; **~ breakfast** kleines
Frühstück mit Brötchen und Marmelade, Kaffee
oder Tee
continual [kən'tɪnjʊəl] adj (endless)
ununterbrochen; (constant) dauernd,
ständig; **continually** adv dauernd; (again
and again) immer wieder; **continuation**
[kəntɪnjʊ'eɪʃən] n Fortsetzung f;
continue [kən'tɪnjuː] vi weitermachen
(with mit); (esp talking) fortfahren (with

mit); (*travelling*) weiterfahren; (*state, conditions*) fortdauern, anhalten ▷ *vt* fortsetzen; **to be ~d** Fortsetzung folgt; **continuous** [kən'tɪnjʊəs] *adj* (*endless*) ununterbrochen; (*constant*) ständig

contraceptive [kɒntrə'septɪv] *n* Verhütungsmittel *nt*

contract ['kɒntrækt] *n* Vertrag *m*

contradict [kɒntrə'dɪkt] *vt* widersprechen +*dat*; **contradiction** [kɒntrə'dɪkʃən] *n* Widerspruch *m*

contrary ['kɒntrəri] *n* Gegenteil *nt*; **on the ~** im Gegenteil ▷ *adj* **~ to** entgegen +*dat*

contrast ['kɒntrɑːst] *n* Kontrast *m*, Gegensatz *m*; **in ~ to** im Gegensatz zu ▷ [kən'trɑːst] *vt* entgegensetzen

contribute [kən'trɪbjuːt] *vt, vi* beitragen (*to* zu); (*money*) spenden (*to* für); **contribution** [kɒntrɪ'bjuːʃən] *n* Beitrag *m*

control [kən'trəʊl] *vt* (*master*) beherrschen; (*temper etc*) im Griff haben; (*esp Tech*) steuern; **to ~ oneself** sich beherrschen ▷ *n* Kontrolle *f*; (*mastery*) Beherrschung *f*; (*of business*) Leitung *f*; (*esp Tech*) Steuerung *f*; **~s** *pl* (*knobs, switches etc*) Bedienungselemente *pl*; (*collectively*) Steuerung *f*; **to be out of ~** außer Kontrolle sein; **control knob** *n* Bedienungsknopf *m*; **control panel** *n* Schalttafel *f*

controversial [kɒntrə'vɜːʃəl] *adj* umstritten

convalesce [kɒnvə'les] *vi* gesund werden; **convalescence** *n* Genesung *f*

convenience [kən'viːnɪəns] *n* (*quality, thing*) Annehmlichkeit *f*; **at your ~** wann es Ihnen passt; **with all modern ~s** mit allem Komfort; **convenience food** *n* Fertiggericht *nt*; **convenient** *adj* günstig, passend

convent ['kɒnvənt] *n* Kloster *nt*

convention [kən'venʃən] *n* (*custom*) Konvention *f*; (*meeting*) Konferenz *f*; **the Geneva Convention** die Genfer Konvention; **conventional** *adj* herkömmlich, konventionell

conversation [kɒnvə'seɪʃən] *n* Gespräch *nt*, Unterhaltung *f*

conversion [kən'vɜːʃən] *n* Umwandlung *f* (*into* in +*akk*); (*of building*) Umbau *m* (*into* zu); (*calculation*) Umrechnung *f*;

conversion table *n* Umrechnungstabelle *f*; **convert** [kən'vɜːt] *vt* umwandeln; (*person*) bekehren; (*Inform*) konvertieren; **to ~ into Euros** in Euro umrechnen; **convertible** *n* (*Auto*) Kabrio *nt* ▷ *adj* umwandelbar

convey [kən'veɪ] *vt* (*carry*) befördern; (*feelings*) vermitteln; **conveyor belt** *n* Förderband *nt*, Fließband *nt*

convict [kən'vɪkt] *vt* verurteilen (*of* wegen) ▷ ['kɒnvɪkt] *n* Strafgefangene(r) *mf*; **conviction** *n* (*Jur*) Verurteilung *f*; (*strong belief*) Überzeugung *f*

convince [kən'vɪns] *vt* überzeugen (*of* von); **convincing** *adj* überzeugend

cook [kʊk] *vt, vi* kochen ▷ *n* Koch *m*, Köchin *f*; **cookbook** *n* Kochbuch *nt*; **cooker** *n* Herd *m*; **cookery** *n* Kochkunst *f*; **~ book** Kochbuch *nt*; **cookie** *n* (*US*) Keks *m*; **cooking** *n* Kochen *nt*; (*style of cooking*) Küche *f*

cool [kuːl] *adj* kühl, gelassen; (*fam: brilliant*) cool, stark *p*; **~ it** (*ab*)kühlen; **~ it** reg dich ab! ▷ *n* **to keep/lose one's ~** (*fam*) ruhig bleiben/durchdrehen; **cool down** *vi* abkühlen; (*calm down*) sich beruhigen

cooperate [kəʊ'ɒpəreɪt] *vi* zusammenarbeiten, kooperieren; **cooperation** [kəʊɒpə'reɪʃən] *n* Zusammenarbeit *f*, Kooperation *f*; **cooperative** [kəʊ'ɒpərətɪv] *adj* hilfsbereit ▷ *n* Genossenschaft *f*

coordinate [kəʊ'ɔːdɪneɪt] *vt* koordinieren

cop [kɒp] *n* (*fam: policeman*) Bulle *m*

cope [kəʊp] *vi* zurechtkommen, fertig werden (*with* mit)

Copenhagen [kəʊpən'heɪgən] *n* Kopenhagen *nt*

copier ['kɒpɪə*] *n* Kopierer *m*

copper ['kɒpə*] *n* Kupfer *nt*; (*Brit fam: policeman*) Bulle *m*; (*fam: coin*) Kupfermünze *f*; **~s** Kleingeld *nt*

copy ['kɒpɪ] *n* Kopie *f*; (*of book*) Exemplar *nt* ▷ *vt* kopieren; (*imitate*) nachahmen; **copyright** *n* Urheberrecht *nt*

coral ['kɒrəl] *n* Koralle *f*

cord [kɔːd] *n* Schnur *f*; (*material*) Kordsamt *m*

cordial ['kɔːdɪəl] *adj* freundlich

cordless ['kɔːdlɪs] *adj* (*phone*) schnurlos

core [kɔː*] *n* (*a. fig*) Kern *m*; (*of apple, pear*)

Kerngehäuse nt; **core business** n
Kerngeschäft nt

cork [kɔːk] n (material) Kork m; (stopper)
Korken m; **corkscrew** ['kɔːkskruː] n
Korkenzieher m

corn [kɔːn] n Getreide nt, Korn nt; (US:
maize) Mais m; (on foot) Hühnerauge nt;
~ on the cob (gekochter) Maiskolben;
corned beef n Cornedbeef nt

corner ['kɔːnə*] n Ecke f; (on road) Kurve f;
(Sport) Eckstoß m ▷ vt in die Enge treiben;
corner shop n Laden m an der Ecke

cornflakes ['kɔːfleɪks] npl Cornflakes pl;
cornflour ['kɔːnflaʊə*] (Brit), **cornstarch**
['kɔːnstaːtʃ] (US) n Maismehl nt

Cornish ['kɔːnɪʃ] adj kornisch; **~ pasty** mit
Fleisch und Kartoffeln gefüllte Pastete;
Cornwall ['kɔːnwəl] n Cornwall nt

coronary ['kɒrənərɪ] n (Med) Herzinfarkt
m

coronation [kɒrə'neɪʃən] n Krönung f

corporation [kɔːpə'reɪʃən] n (US Comm)
Aktiengesellschaft f

corpse [kɔːps] n Leiche f

correct [kə'rekt] adj (accurate) richtig;
(proper) korrekt ▷ vt korrigieren,
verbessern; **correction** n (esp written)
Korrektur f

correspond [kɒrɪ'spɒnd] vi entsprechen
(to dat); (two things) übereinstimmen;
(exchange letters) korrespondieren;
corresponding adj entsprechend

corridor ['kɒrɪdɔː*] n (in building) Flur m;
(in train) Gang m

corrupt [kə'rʌpt] adj korrupt

cosmetic [kɒz'metɪk] adj kosmetisch;
cosmetics npl Kosmetika pl; **cosmetic
surgeon** n Schönheitschirurg(in) m(f);
cosmetic surgery n Schönheitschirurgie f

cosmopolitan [kɒzmə'pɒlɪtən] adj
international; (attitude) weltoffen

cost [kɒst] (cost, cost) vt kosten ▷ n
Kosten pl; **at all ~s, at any ~** um jeden
Preis; **~ of living** Lebenshaltungskosten
pl; **costly** adj kostspielig

costume ['kɒstjuːm] n (Theat) Kostüm nt

cosy ['kəʊzɪ] adj gemütlich

cot [kɒt] n (Brit) Kinderbett nt; (US)
Campingliege f

cottage ['kɒtɪdʒ] n kleines Haus; (country
cottage) Landhäuschen nt; **cottage cheese**
n Hüttenkäse m; **cottage pie** n
Hackfleisch mit Kartoffelbrei überbacken

cotton ['kɒtn] n Baumwolle f; **cotton
candy** n (US) Zuckerwatte f; **cotton wool**
n (Brit) Watte f

couch [kaʊtʃ] n Couch f; (sofa) Sofa nt;
couchette [kuː'ʃet] n Liegewagen(platz)
m

cough [kɒf] vi husten ▷ n Husten m;
cough mixture n Hustensaft m; **cough
sweet** n Hustenbonbon nt

could [kʊd] pt of **can** konnte; conditional
könnte; **~ you come earlier?** könntest du
früher kommen?

couldn't contr of **could not**

council ['kaʊnsl] n (Pol) Rat m; (local ~)
Gemeinderat m; (town ~) Stadtrat m;
council estate n Siedlung f des sozialen
Wohnungsbaus; **council house** n
Sozialwohnung f; **councillor** ['kaʊnsɪlə*]
n Gemeinderat m, Gemeinderätin f;
council tax n Gemeindesteuer f

count [kaʊnt] vt, vi zählen; (include)
mitrechnen ▷ n Zählung f; (noble) Graf m;
count on vt (rely on) sich verlassen auf
+akk; (expect) rechnen mit

counter ['kaʊntə*] n (in shop) Ladentisch m;
(in café) Theke f; (in bank, post office)
Schalter m; **counter attack** n
Gegenangriff m ▷ vi zurückschlagen;
counter-clockwise adv (US) entgegen
dem Uhrzeigersinn

counterfoil ['kaʊntəfɔɪl] n
(Kontroll)abschnitt m

counterpart ['kaʊntəpɑːt] n Gegenstück
nt (of zu)

countess n Gräfin f

countless ['kaʊntlɪs] adj zahllos,
unzählig

country ['kʌntrɪ] n Land nt; **in the ~** auf
dem Land(e); **in this ~** hierzulande;
country cousin n (fam) Landei nt;
country dancing n Volkstanz m;
country house n Landhaus nt;
countryman n (compatriot) Landsmann
m; **country music** n Countrymusic f;
country road n Landstraße f;
countryside n Landschaft f; (rural area)
Land nt

county ['kaʊntɪ] n (Brit) Grafschaft f; (US)
Verwaltungsbezirk m; **county town** n
(Brit) ~ Kreisstadt f

couple ['kʌpl] n Paar nt; **a ~ of** ein paar

coupon ['kuːpɒn] n (voucher) Gutschein
m

courage ['kʌrɪdʒ] n Mut m; **courageous** [kə'reɪdʒəs] adj mutig

courgette [kuə'ʒet] n (Brit) Zucchini f

courier ['kurɪə*] n (for tourists) Reiseleiter(in) m(f); (messenger) Kurier m

course [kɔ:s] n (of study) Kurs m; (for race) Strecke f; (Naut, Aviat) Kurs m; (at university) Studiengang m; (in meal) Gang m; **of ~** natürlich; **in the ~ of** während

court [kɔ:t] n (Sport) Platz m; (Jur) Gericht nt

courteous ['kɜ:tɪəs] adj höflich; **courtesy** ['kɜ:təsɪ] n Höflichkeit f; **~ bus/coach** (gebührenfreier) Zubringerbus

courthouse ['kɔ:thaʊs] n (US) Gerichtsgebäude nt; **court order** n Gerichtsbeschluss m; **courtroom** n Gerichtssaal m

courtyard ['kɔ:tjɑ:d] n Hof m

cousin ['kʌzn] n (male) Cousin m; (female) Cousine f

cover ['kʌvə*] vt bedecken (in, with mit); (distance) zurücklegen; (loan, costs) decken ▷ n (for bed etc) Decke f; (of cushion) Bezug m; (lid) Deckel m; (of book) Umschlag m; (insurance) ~ Versicherungsschutz m; **cover up** vt zudecken; (error etc) vertuschen; **coverage** n Berichterstattung f (of über +akk); **cover charge** n Kosten pl für ein Gedeck; **covering** n Decke f; **covering letter** n Begleitbrief m; **cover story** n (newspaper) Titelgeschichte f

cow [kaʊ] n Kuh f

coward ['kaʊəd] n Feigling m; **cowardly** adj feig(e)

cowboy ['kaʊbɔɪ] n Cowboy m

coy [kɔɪ] adj gespielt schüchtern, kokett

cozy ['kəʊzɪ] adj (US) gemütlich

CPU abbr = **central processing unit** Zentraleinheit f

crab [kræb] n Krabbe f

crabby ['kræbɪ] adj mürrisch, reizbar

crack [kræk] n Riss m; (in pottery, glass) Sprung m; (drug) Crack nt; **to have a ~ at sth** etw ausprobieren ▷ vi (pottery, glass) einen Sprung bekommen; (wood, ice etc) einen Riss bekommen; **to get ~ing** (fam) loslegen ▷ vt (bone) anbrechen; (nut, code) knacken

cracker ['krækə*] n (biscuit) Kräcker m; (Christmas ~) Knallbonbon nt; **crackers** adj (fam) verrückt, bekloppt; **he's ~** er hat nicht alle Tassen im Schrank

crackle ['krækl] vi knistern; (telephone, radio) knacken; **crackling** n (Gastr) Kruste f (des Schweinebratens)

cradle ['kreɪdl] n Wiege f

craft [krɑ:ft] n Handwerk nt; (art) Kunsthandwerk nt; (Naut) Boot nt; **craftsman** (pl **-men**) n Handwerker m; **craftsmanship** n Handwerkskunst f; (ability) handwerkliches Können

crafty ['krɑ:ftɪ] adj schlau

cram [kræm] vt stopfen (into in +akk); **to be ~med with ...** mit ... voll gestopft sein ▷ vi (revise for exam) pauken (for für)

cramp [kræmp] n Krampf m

cranberry ['krænbərɪ] n Preiselbeere f

crane [kreɪn] n (machine) Kran m; (bird) Kranich m

crash [kræʃ] vi einen Unfall haben; (two vehicles) zusammenstoßen; (plane, computer) abstürzen; (economy) zusammenbrechen; **to ~ into sth** gegen etw knallen ▷ vt einen Unfall haben mit ▷ n (car) Unfall m; (train) Unglück nt; (collision) Zusammenstoß m; (Aviat, Inform) Absturz m; (noise) Krachen nt; **crash barrier** n Leitplanke f; **crash course** n Intensivkurs m; **crash helmet** n Sturzhelm m; **crash landing** n Bruchlandung f

crate [kreɪt] n Kiste f; (of beer) Kasten m

crater ['kreɪtə*] n Krater m

craving ['kreɪvɪŋ] n starkes Verlangen, Bedürfnis nt

crawl [krɔ:l] vi kriechen; (baby) krabbeln ▷ n (swimming) Kraul nt; **crawler lane** n Kriechspur f

crayfish ['kreɪfɪʃ] n Languste f

crayon ['kreɪən] n Buntstift m

crazy ['kreɪzɪ] adj verrückt (about nach)

cream [kri:m] n (from milk) Sahne f, Rahm m; (polish, cosmetic) Creme f ▷ adj cremefarben; **cream cake** n (small) Sahnetörtchen nt; (big) Sahnetorte f; **cream cheese** n Frischkäse m; **creamer** n Kaffeeweißer m; **cream tea** n (Brit) Nachmittagstee mit Törtchen, Marmelade und Schlagsahne; **creamy** adj sahnig

crease [kri:s] n Falte f ▷ vt falten; (untidy) zerknittern

create [kri'eit] vt schaffen; (cause) verursachen; **creative** [kri:'eitiv] adj schöpferisch; (person) kreativ; **creature** ['kri:tʃə] n Geschöpf nt

crèche [kreiʃ] n Kinderkrippe f

credible ['kredibl] adj (person) glaubwürdig; **credibility** n Glaubwürdigkeit f

credit ['kredit] n (Fin: amount allowed) Kredit m; (amount possessed) Guthaben nt; (recognition) Anerkennung f; **~s** (of film) Abspann m; **credit card** n Kreditkarte f

creep [kri:p] vi kriechen; **creeps** n **he gives me the ~** er ist mir nicht ganz geheuer; **creepy** ['kri:pi] adj (frightening) gruselig, unheimlich

crept [krept] pt, pp of **creep**

cress [kres] n Kresse f

crest [krest] n Kamm m; (coat of arms) Wappen nt

crew [kru:] n Besatzung f, Mannschaft f

crib [krib] n (US) Kinderbett nt

cricket ['krikit] n (insect) Grille f; (game) Kricket nt

crime [kraim] n Verbrechen nt; **criminal** ['kriminl] n Verbrecher(in) m(f) ▷ adj kriminell, strafbar

cripple ['kripl] n Krüppel m ▷ vt verkrüppeln, lähmen

crisis ['kraisis] n (pl **crises**) Krise f

crisp [krisp] adj knusprig; **crisps** npl (Brit) Chips pl; **crispbread** n Knäckebrot nt

criterion [krai'tiəriən] n Kriterium nt; **critic** ['kritik] n Kritiker(in) m(f); **critical** adj kritisch; **critically** adv kritisch; **~ ill/injured** schwer krank/verletzt; **criticism** ['kritisizəm] n Kritik f; **criticize** ['kritisaiz] vt kritisieren

Croat ['krəuæt] n Kroate m, Kroatin f; **Croatia** [krəu'eiʃə] n Kroatien nt; **Croatian** [krəu'eiʃən] adj kroatisch

crockery ['krɒkəri] n Geschirr nt

crocodile ['krɒkədail] n Krokodil nt

crocus ['krəukəs] n Krokus m

crop [krɒp] n (harvest) Ernte f; **crops** npl Getreide nt; **crop up** vi auftauchen

croquette [krə'ket] n Krokette f

cross [krɒs] n Kreuz nt; **to mark sth with a ~** etw ankreuzen ▷ vt (road, river etc) überqueren; (legs) übereinander schlagen; **it ~ed my mind** es fiel mir ein; **to ~ one's**

fingers die Daumen drücken ▷ adj ärgerlich, böse; **cross out** vt durchstreichen

crossbar n (of bicycle) Stange f; (Sport) Querlatte f; **cross-country** adj **~ running** Geländelauf m; **~ skiing** Langlauf m; **cross-examination** n Kreuzverhör nt; **cross-eyed** adj **to be ~** schielen; **crossing** n (crossroads) (Straßen)kreuzung f; (for pedestrians) Fußgängerüberweg m; (on ship) Überfahrt f; **crossroads** nsing o pl Straßenkreuzung f; **cross section** n Querschnitt m; **crosswalk** n (US) Fußgängerüberweg m; **crossword (puzzle)** n Kreuzworträtsel nt

crouch [krautʃ] vi hocken

crouton ['kru:tɒn] n Croûton m

crow [krəu] n Krähe f

crowbar [krəuba:*] n Brecheisen nt

crowd [kraud] n Menge f ▷ vi sich drängen (into in +akk; round um); **crowded** adj überfüllt

crown [kraun] n Krone f ▷ vt krönen; (fam) **and to ~ it all ...** und als Krönung ...; **crown jewels** npl Kronjuwelen pl

crucial ['kru:ʃəl] adj entscheidend

crude [kru:d] adj primitiv; (humour, behaviour) derb, ordinär ▷ n **~ (oil)** Rohöl nt

cruel ['kruəl] adj grausam (to zu, gegen); (unfeeling) gefühllos; **cruelty** n Grausamkeit f; **~ to animals** Tierquälerei f

cruise [kru:z] n Kreuzfahrt f ▷ vi (ship) kreuzen; (car) mit Reisegeschwindigkeit fahren; **cruise liner** n Kreuzfahrtschiff nt; **cruise missile** n Marschflugkörper m; **cruising speed** n Reisegeschwindigkeit f

crumb [krʌm] n Krume f

crumble ['krʌmbl] vt, vi zerbröckeln ▷ n mit Streuseln überbackenes Kompott

crumpet ['krʌmpit] n weiches Hefegebäck zum Toasten; (fam: attractive woman) Schnecke f

crumple ['krʌmpl] vt zerknittern; **crumple zone** n (Auto) Knautschzone f

crunchy ['krʌntʃi] adj (Brit) knusprig

crusade [kru:'seid] n Kreuzzug m

crush [krʌʃ] vt zerdrücken; (finger etc) quetschen; (spices, stone) zerstoßen ▷ n **to have a ~ on sb** in jdn verknallt sein; **crushing** adj (defeat, remark) vernichtend

crust [krʌst] n Kruste f; **crusty** adj knusprig

crutch [krʌtʃ] *n* Krücke *f*

cry [kraɪ] *vi* (*call*) rufen; (*scream*) schreien; (*weep*) weinen ▷ *n* (*call*) Ruf *m*; (*louder*) Schrei *m*

crypt [krɪpt] *n* Krypta *f*

crystal [ˈkrɪstl] *n* Kristall *m*

cu *abbr* = **see you** (*SMS, E-Mail*) bis bald

cub [kʌb] *n* (*animal*) Junge(s) *nt*

Cuba [ˈkjuːbə] *n* Kuba *nt*

cube [kjuːb] *n* Würfel *m*

cubic [ˈkjuːbɪk] *adj* Kubik-

cubicle [ˈkjuːbɪkl] *n* Kabine *f*

cuckoo [ˈkʊkuː] *n* Kuckuck *m*

cucumber [ˈkjuːkʌmbə*] *n* Salatgurke *f*

cuddle [ˈkʌdl] *vt* in den Arm nehmen; (*amorously*) schmusen mit ▷ *n* Liebkosung *f*, Umarmung *f*; **to have a ~** schmusen; **cuddly** *adj* verschmust; **cuddly toy** *n* Plüschtier *nt*

cuff [kʌf] *n* Manschette *f*; (*US: trouser ~*) Aufschlag *m*; **off the ~** aus dem Stegreif; **cufflink** *n* Manschettenknopf *m*

cuisine [kwɪˈziːn] *n* Kochkunst *f*, Küche *f*

cul-de-sac [ˈkʌldəsæk] *n* (*Brit*) Sackgasse *f*

culprit [ˈkʌlprɪt] *n* Schuldige(r) *mf*; (*fig*) Übeltäter(in) *m(f)*

cult [kʌlt] *n* Kult *m*

cultivate [ˈkʌltɪveɪt] *vt* (*Agr: land*) bebauen; (*crop*) anbauen; **cultivated** *adj* (*person*) kultiviert, gebildet

cultural [ˈkʌltʃərəl] *adj* kulturell, Kultur-; **culture** [ˈkʌltʃə*] *n* Kultur *f*; **cultured** *adj* gebildet, kultiviert; **culture vulture** (*Brit fam*) *n* Kulturfanatiker(in) *m(f)*

cumbersome [ˈkʌmbəsəm] *adj* (*object*) unhandlich

cumin [ˈkʌmɪn] *n* Kreuzkümmel *m*

cunning [ˈkʌnɪŋ] *adj* schlau; (*person a.*) gerissen

cup [kʌp] *n* Tasse *f*; (*prize*) Pokal *m*; **it's not his ~ of tea** das ist nicht sein Fall; **cupboard** [ˈkʌbəd] *n* Schrank *m*; **cup final** *n* Pokalendspiel *nt*; **cup tie** *n* Pokalspiel *nt*

cupola [ˈkjuːpələ] *n* Kuppel *f*

curable [ˈkjʊərəbl] *adj* heilbar

curb [kɜːb] *n* (*US*) *see* **kerb**

curd [kɜːd] *n* **~ cheese, ~s** ≈ Quark *m*

cure [kjʊə*] *n* Heilmittel *nt* (*for* gegen); (*process*) Heilung *f* ▷ *vt* heilen; (*Gastr*) pökeln; (*smoke*) räuchern

curious [ˈkjʊərɪəs] *adj* neugierig; (*strange*) seltsam

curl [kɜːl] *n* Locke *f* ▷ *vi* sich kräuseln; **curly** *adj* lockig

currant [ˈkʌrənt] *n* (*dried*) Korinthe *f*; (*red, black*) Johannisbeere *f*

currency [ˈkʌrənsɪ] *n* Währung *f*; **foreign ~** Devisen *pl*

current [ˈkʌrənt] *n* (*in water*) Strömung *f*; (*electric ~*) Strom *m* ▷ *adj* (*issue, affairs*) aktuell, gegenwärtig; (*expression*) gängig; **current account** *n* Girokonto *nt*; **currently** *adv* zur Zeit

curriculum [kəˈrɪkjʊləm] *n* Lehrplan *m*; **curriculum vitae** [kəˈrɪkjʊləmˈviːtaɪ] *n* (*Brit*) Lebenslauf *m*

curry [ˈkʌrɪ] *n* Currygericht *nt*; **curry powder** *n* Curry(pulver) *nt*

curse [kɜːs] *vi* (*swear*) fluchen (*at* auf +*akk*) ▷ *n* Fluch *m*

cursor [ˈkɜːsə*] *n* (*Inform*) Cursor *m*

curt [kɜːt] *adj* schroff, kurz angebunden

curtain [ˈkɜːtn] *n* Vorhang *m*; **it was ~s for Benny** für Benny war alles vorbei

curve [kɜːv] *n* Kurve *f* ▷ *vi* einen Bogen machen; **curved** *adj* gebogen

cushion [ˈkʊʃən] *n* Kissen *nt*

custard [ˈkʌstəd] *n* dicke Vanillesoße, die warm oder kalt zu vielen englischen Nachspeisen gegessen wird

custom [ˈkʌstəm] *n* Brauch *m*; (*habit*) Gewohnheit *f*; **customary** [ˈkʌstəmrɪ] *adj* üblich; **custom-built** *adj* nach Kundenangaben gefertigt; **customer** [ˈkʌstəmə*] *n* Kunde *m*, Kundin *f*; **customer loyalty card** *n* Kundenkarte *f*; **customer service** *n* Kundendienst *m*

customs [ˈkʌstəmz] *npl* (*organization, location*) Zoll *m*; **to pass through ~** durch den Zoll gehen; **customs officer** *n* Zollbeamte(r) *m*, Zollbeamtin *f*

cut [kʌt] (*cut, cut*) *vt* schneiden; (*cake*) anschneiden; (*wages, benefits*) kürzen; (*prices*) heruntersetzen; **I ~ my finger** ich habe mir in den Finger geschnitten ▷ *n* Schnitt *m*; (*wound*) Schnittwunde *f*; (*reduction*) Kürzung *f* (*in gen*); **price/tax ~** Preissenkung/Steuersenkung *f*; **to be a ~ above the rest** eine Klasse besser als die anderen sein; **cut back** *vt* (*workforce etc*) reduzieren; **cut down** *vt* (*tree*) fällen; **to ~ on sth** etwas einschränken; **cut in** *vi* (*Auto*) scharf einscheren; **to ~ on sb** jdn schneiden; **cut off** *vt* abschneiden; (*gas,*

electricity) abdrehen, abstellen; (*Tel*) **I was**
~ ich wurde unterbrochen

cutback *n* Kürzung *f*

cute [kju:t] *adj* putzig, niedlich; (*US:*
shrewd) clever

cutlery ['kʌtlərɪ] *n* Besteck *nt*

cutlet ['kʌtlɪt] *n* (*pork*) Kotelett *nt*; (*veal*)
Schnitzel *nt*

cut-price *adj* verbilligt

cutting ['kʌtɪŋ] *n* (*from paper*) Ausschnitt
m; (*of plant*) Ableger *m* ▷ *adj* (*comment*)
verletzend

CV *abbr* = **curriculum vitae**

cwt *abbr* = **hundredweight** = Zentner, Ztr.

cybercafé [saɪbə'kæfeɪ] *n* Internetcafé *nt*;
cyberspace *n* Cyberspace *m*

cyclamen ['sɪkləmən] *n* Alpenveilchen *nt*

cycle ['saɪkl] *n* Fahrrad *nt* ▷ *vi* Rad
fahren; **cycle lane, cycle path** *n* Radweg
m; **cycling** *n* Radfahren *nt*; **cyclist**
['saɪklɪst] *n* Radfahrer(in) *m(f)*

cylinder ['sɪlɪndə*] *n* Zylinder *m*

cynical ['sɪnɪkəl] *adj* zynisch

cypress ['saɪprɪs] *n* Zypresse *f*

Cypriot ['sɪprɪət] *adj* zypriotisch ▷ *n*
Zypriote *m*, Zypriotin *f*; **Cyprus** ['saɪprəs]
n Zypern *nt*

czar [zɑ:*] *n* Zar *m*; **czarina** [zɑ'ri:nə] *n*
Zarin *f*

Czech [tʃek] *adj* tschechisch ▷ *n* (*person*)
Tscheche *m*, Tschechin *f*; (*language*)
Tschechisch *nt*; **Czech Republic** *n*
Tschechische Republik, Tschechien *nt*

d

dab [dæb] vt (wound, nose etc) betupfen (with mit)

dachshund ['dækshʊnd] n Dackel m

dad(dy) ['dæd(ɪ)] n Papa m, Vati m; **daddy-longlegs** nsing (Brit) Schnake; (US) Weberknecht m

daffodil ['dæfədɪl] n Osterglocke f

daft [dɑːft] adj (fam) blöd, doof

dahlia ['deɪlɪə] n Dahlie f

daily ['deɪlɪ] adj, adv täglich ▷ n (paper) Tageszeitung f

dairy ['dɛərɪ] n (on farm) Molkerei f; **dairy products** npl Milchprodukte pl

daisy ['deɪzɪ] n Gänseblümchen nt

dam [dæm] n Staudamm m ▷ vt stauen

damage ['dæmɪdʒ] n Schaden m; **~s** pl (Jur) Schadenersatz m ▷ vt beschädigen; (reputation, health) schädigen, schaden +dat

damn [dæm] adj (fam) verdammt ▷ vt (condemn) verurteilen; **~ (it)!** verflucht! ▷ n **he doesn't give a ~** es ist ihm völlig egal

damp [dæmp] adj feucht ▷ n Feuchtigkeit f; **dampen** ['dæmpən] vt befeuchten

dance [dɑːns] n Tanz m; (event) Tanzveranstaltung f ▷ vi tanzen; **dance floor** n Tanzfläche f; **dancer** n Tänzer(in) m(f); **dancing** n Tanzen nt

dandelion ['dændɪlaɪən] n Löwenzahn m

dandruff ['dændrəf] n Schuppen pl

Dane [deɪn] n Däne m, Dänin f

danger ['deɪndʒə*] n Gefahr f; **~ (sign)** Achtung!; **to be in ~** in Gefahr sein; **dangerous** adj gefährlich

Danish ['deɪnɪʃ] adj dänisch ▷ n (language) Dänisch nt; **the ~** pl die Dänen; **Danish pastry** n Plundergebäck nt

Danube ['dænjuːb] n Donau f

dare [dɛə*] vi **to ~ (to) do sth** es wagen, etw zu tun; **I didn't ~ ask** ich traute mich nicht, zu fragen; **how ~ you** was fällt dir ein!; **daring** adj (person) mutig; (film, clothes etc) gewagt

dark [dɑːk] adj dunkel; (gloomy) düster, trübe; (sinister) finster; **~ chocolate** Bitterschokolade f; **~ green/blue** dunkelgrün/dunkelblau ▷ n Dunkelheit f; **in the ~** im Dunkeln; **dark glasses** npl Sonnenbrille f; **darkness** n Dunkelheit nt

darling ['dɑːlɪŋ] n Schatz m; (also favourite) Liebling m

dart [dɑːts] n Wurfpfeil m; **darts** nsing (game) Darts nt

dash [dæʃ] vi stürzen, rennen ▷ vt **to ~ hopes** Hoffnungen zerstören ▷ n (in text) Gedankenstrich m; (of liquid) Schuss m; **dashboard** n Armaturenbrett nt

data ['deɪtə] npl Daten pl; **data bank**, **data base** n Datenbank f; **data capture** n Datenerfassung f; **data processing** n Datenverarbeitung f; **data protection** n Datenschutz m

date [deɪt] n Datum nt; (for meeting, delivery etc) Termin m; (with person) Verabredung f; (with girlfriend etc) Date nt; (fruit) Dattel f; **what's the ~ (today)?** der Wievielte ist heute?; **out of ~** adj veraltet; **up to ~** adj (news) aktuell; (fashion) zeitgemäß ▷ vt (letter etc) datieren; (person) gehen mit; **dated** adj altmodisch; **date of birth** n Geburtsdatum nt; **dating agency** n Partnervermittlung f

dative ['deɪtɪv] n Dativ m

daughter ['dɔːtə*] n Tochter f; **daughter-in-law** (pl **daughters-in-law**) n Schwiegertöchter f

dawn [dɔːn] n Morgendämmerung f ▷ vi

dämmern; **it ~ed on me** mir ging ein Licht auf

day [deɪ] *n* Tag *m*; **one ~** eines Tages; **by ~** bei Tage; **~ after ~, ~ by ~** Tag für Tag; **the ~ after/before** am Tag danach/zuvor; **the ~ before yesterday** vorgestern; **the ~ after tomorrow** übermorgen; **these ~s** heutzutage; **in those ~s** damals; **let's call it a ~** Schluss für heute!; **daybreak** *n* Tagesanbruch *m*; **daydream** *n* Tagtraum *m* ▷ *vi* (mit offenen Augen) träumen; **daylight** *n* Tageslicht *nt*; **in ~** bei Tage; **daylight saving time** *n* Sommerzeit *f*; **day nursery** *n* Kindertagesstätte *f*; **day return** *n* (*Brit Rail*) Tagesrückfahrkarte *f*; **daytime** *n* **in the ~** bei Tage, tagsüber; **daytrip** *n* Tagesausflug *m*

dazed [deɪzd] *adj* benommen

dazzle ['dæzl] *vt* blenden; **dazzling** *adj* blendend, glänzend

dead [ded] *adj* tot; (*limb*) abgestorben ▷ *adv* genau; (*fam*) total, völlig; **~ tired** *adj* todmüde; **~ slow** (*sign*) Schritt fahren; **dead end** *n* Sackgasse *f*; **deadline** *n* Termin *m*; (*period*) Frist *f*; **~ for applications** Anmeldeschluss *m*; **deadly** *adj* tödlich ▷ *adv* **~ dull** todlangweilig

deaf [def] *adj* taub; **deafen** *vt* taub machen; **deafening** *adj* ohrenbetäubend

deal [di:l] (**dealt, dealt**) *vt, vi* (*cards*) geben, austeilen ▷ *n* (*business ~*) Geschäft *nt*; (*agreement*) Abmachung *f*; **it's a ~** abgemacht!; **a good/great ~ of** ziemlich/sehr viel; **deal in** *vt* handeln mit; **deal with** *vt* (*matter*) sich beschäftigen mit; (*book, film*) behandeln; (*successfully: person, problem*) fertig werden mit; (*matter*) erledigen; **dealer** *n* (*Comm*) Händler(in) *m(f)*; (*drugs*) Dealer(in) *m(f)*; **dealings** *npl* (*Comm*) Geschäfte *pl*

dealt [delt] *pt, pp of* **deal**

dear [dɪə*] *adj* lieb, teuer; **Dear Sir or Madam** Sehr geehrte Damen und Herren; **Dear David** Lieber David ▷ *n* Schatz *m*; (*as address*) mein Schatz, Liebling; **dearly** *adv* (*love*) (heiß und) innig; (*pay*) teuer

death [deθ] *n* Tod *m*; (*of project, hopes*) Ende *nt*; **~s** *pl* Todesfälle; (*in accident*) Todesopfer; **death certificate** *n* Totenschein *m*; **death penalty** *n* Todesstrafe *f*; **death toll** *n* Zahl *f* der

Todesopfer; **death trap** *n* Todesfalle *f*

debatable [dɪ'beɪtəbl] *adj* fraglich; (*question*) strittig; **debate** [dɪ'beɪt] *n* Debatte *f* ▷ *vt* debattieren

debauched [dɪ'bɔ:tʃt] *adj* ausschweifend

debit ['debɪt] *n* Soll *nt* ▷ *vt* (*account*) belasten; **debit card** *n* Geldkarte *f*

debris ['debri:] *n* Trümmer *pl*

debt [det] *n* Schuld *f*; **to be in ~** verschuldet sein

decade ['dekeɪd] *n* Jahrzehnt *nt*

decadent ['dekədənt] *adj* dekadent

decaff ['di:kæf] *n* (*fam*) koffeinfreier Kaffee; **decaffeinated** [di:'kæfɪneɪtɪd] *adj* koffeinfrei

decanter [dɪ'kæntə*] *n* Dekanter *m*, Karaffe *f*

decay [dɪ'keɪ] *n* Verfall *m*; (*rotting*) Verwesung *f*; (*of tooth*) Fäule *f* ▷ *vi* verfallen; (*rot*) verwesen; (*wood*) vermodern; (*teeth*) faulen; (*leaves*) verrotten

deceased [dɪ'si:st] *n* **the ~** der/die Verstorbene

deceit [dɪ'si:t] *n* Betrug *m*; **deceive** [dɪ'si:v] *vt* täuschen

December [dɪ'sembə*] *n* Dezember *m*; *see also* **September**

decent ['di:sənt] *adj* anständig

deception [dɪ'sepʃən] *n* Betrug *m*; **deceptive** [dɪ'septɪv] *adj* täuschend, irreführend

decide [dɪ'saɪd] *vt* (*question*) entscheiden; (*body of people*) beschließen; **I can't ~ what to do** ich kann mich nicht entscheiden, was ich tun soll ▷ *vi* sich entscheiden; **to ~ on sth** (*in favour of sth*) sich für etw entscheiden, sich zu etw entschließen; **decided** *adj* entschieden; (*clear*) deutlich; **decidedly** *adv* entschieden

decimal ['desɪml] *adj* Dezimal-; **decimal system** *n* Dezimalsystem *nt*

decipher [dɪ'saɪfə*] *vt* entziffern

decision [dɪ'sɪʒən] *n* Entscheidung *f* (*on* über +*akk*); (*of committee, jury etc*) Beschluss *m*; **to make a ~** eine Entscheidung treffen; **decisive** [dɪ'saɪsɪv] *adj* entscheidend; (*person*) entscheidungsfreudig

deck [dek] *n* (*Naut*) Deck *nt*; (*of cards*) Blatt *nt*; **deckchair** *n* Liegestuhl *m*

declaration [deklə'reɪʃən] *n* Erklärung *f*; **declare** [dɪ'kleə*] *vt* erklären; (*state*) behaupten (*that* dass); (*at customs*) **have**

you anything to ~? haben Sie etwas zu verzollen?

decline [dɪˈklaɪn] n Rückgang m ▷ vt (invitation, offer) ablehnen ▷ vi (become less) sinken, abnehmen; (health) sich verschlechtern

decode [diːˈkəʊd] vt entschlüsseln

decompose [diːkəmˈpəʊz] vi sich zersetzen

decontaminate [diːkənˈtæmɪneɪt] vt entgiften; (from radioactivity) entseuchen

decorate [ˈdekəreɪt] vt (aus)schmücken; (wallpaper) tapezieren; (paint) anstreichen; **decoration** [dekəˈreɪʃən] n Schmuck m; (process) Schmücken nt; (wallpapering) Tapezieren nt; (painting) Anstreichen nt; **Christmas ~s** Weihnachtsschmuck m; **decorator** n Maler(in) m(f)

decrease [ˈdiːkriːs] n Abnahme f ▷ [diːˈkriːs] vi abnehmen

dedicate [ˈdedɪkeɪt] vt widmen (to sb jdm); **dedicated** adj (person) engagiert; **dedication** [dedɪˈkeɪʃən] n Widmung f; (commitment) Hingabe f, Engagement nt

deduce [dɪˈdjuːs] vt folgern, schließen (from aus, that dass)

deduct [dɪˈdʌkt] vt abziehen (from von); **deduction** [dɪˈdʌkʃən] n (of money) Abzug m; (conclusion) (Schluss)folgerung f

deed [diːd] n Tat f

deep [diːp] adj tief; **deepen** vt vertiefen; **deep-freeze** n Tiefkühltruhe f; (upright) Gefrierschrank m; **deep-fry** vt frittieren

deer [dɪə*] n Reh nt; (with stag) Hirsch m

defeat [dɪˈfiːt] n Niederlage f; **to admit ~** sich geschlagen geben ▷ vt besiegen

defect [ˈdiːfekt] n Defekt m, Fehler m; **defective** [dɪˈfektɪv] adj fehlerhaft

defence [dɪˈfens] n Verteidigung f; **defend** [dɪˈfend] vt verteidigen; **defendant** [dɪˈfendənt] n (Jur) Angeklagte(r) mf; **defender** n (Sport) Verteidiger(in) m(f); **defensive** [dɪˈfensɪv] adj defensiv

deficiency [dɪˈfɪʃənsɪ] n Mangel m; **deficient** adj mangelhaft; **deficit** [ˈdefɪsɪt] n Defizit nt

define [dɪˈfaɪn] vt (word) definieren; (duties, powers) bestimmen; **definite** [ˈdefɪnɪt] adj (clear) klar, eindeutig; (certain) sicher; **it's ~** es steht fest; **definitely** adv bestimmt; **definition** [defɪˈnɪʃən] n Definition f; (Foto) Schärfe f

deflate [diːˈfleɪt] vt die Luft ablassen aus

defrost [diːˈfrɒst] vt (fridge) abtauen; (food) auftauen

degrading [dɪˈɡreɪdɪŋ] adj erniedrigend

degree [dɪˈɡriː] n Grad m; (at university) akademischer Grad; **a certain/high ~ of** ein gewisses/hohes Maß an +dat; **to a certain ~** einigermaßen; **I have a ~ in chemistry** ≈ ich habe Chemie studiert

dehydrated [diːhaɪˈdreɪtɪd] adj (food) getrocknet, Trocken-; (person) ausgetrocknet

de-ice [diːˈaɪs] vt enteisen

delay [dɪˈleɪ] vt (postpone) verschieben, aufschieben; **to be ~ed** (event) sich verzögern; **the train/flight was ~ed** der Zug/die Maschine hatte Verspätung ▷ vi warten; (hesitate) zögern ▷ n Verzögerung f; (of train etc) Verspätung f; **without ~** unverzüglich; **delayed** adj (train etc) verspätet

delegate n [ˈdelɪɡət] Delegierte(r) mf ▷ [ˈdelɪɡeɪt] vt delegieren; **delegation** [delɪˈɡeɪʃən] n Abordnung f; (foreign) Delegation f

delete [dɪˈliːt] vt (aus)streichen; (Inform) löschen; **deletion** n Streichung f; (Inform) Löschung f

deli [ˈdelɪ] n (fam) Feinkostgeschäft nt

deliberate [dɪˈlɪbərət] adj (intentional) absichtlich; **deliberately** adv mit Absicht, extra

delicate [ˈdelɪkɪt] adj (fine) fein; (fragile) zart; (a. Med) empfindlich; (situation) heikel

delicatessen [delɪkəˈtesn] nsing Feinkostgeschäft nt

delicious [dɪˈlɪʃəs] adj köstlich, lecker

delight [dɪˈlaɪt] n Freude f ▷ vt entzücken; **delighted** adj sehr erfreut (with über +akk); **delightful** adj entzückend; (weather, meal etc) herrlich

deliver [dɪˈlɪvə*] vt (goods) liefern (to sb jdm); (letter, parcel) zustellen; (speech) halten; (baby) entbinden; **delivery** n Lieferung f; (of letter, parcel) Zustellung f; (of baby) Entbindung f; **delivery van** n Lieferwagen m

delude [dɪˈluːd] vt täuschen; **don't ~ yourself** mach dir nichts vor; **delusion** n Irrglaube m

de luxe [dɪˈlʌks] adj Luxus-

demand [dɪˈmɑːnd] vt verlangen (from

von); (*time, patience etc*) erfordern ▷ *n*
(*request*) Forderung *f*, Verlangen *nt* (*for
nach*); (*Comm: for goods*) Nachfrage *f*; **on
~ auf Wunsch; very much in ~** sehr
gefragt; **demanding** *adj* anspruchsvoll
demented [dɪˈmentɪd] *adj* wahnsinnig
demerara [deməˈrεərə] *n* **~ (sugar)**
brauner Zucker
demister *n* Defroster *m*
demo [ˈdeməʊ] (*pl* **-s**) *n* (*fam*) Demo *f*
democracy [dɪˈmɒkrəsɪ] *n* Demokratie *f*;
democrat, Democrat (*US Pol*)
[ˈdeməkræt] Demokrat(in) *m(f)*;
democratic *adj* demokratisch; **the
Democratic Party** (*US Pol*) die
Demokratische Partei
demolish [dɪˈmɒlɪʃ] *vt* abreißen; (*fig*)
zerstören; **demolition** [deməˈlɪʃən] *n*
Abbruch *m*
demonstrate [ˈdemənstreɪt] *vt, vi*
demonstrieren, beweisen;
demonstration *n* Demonstration *f*
demoralize [dɪˈmɒrəlaɪz] *vt*
demoralisieren
denationalization [ˈdiːnæʃnəlaɪˈzeɪʃən]
n Privatisierung *f*
denial [dɪˈnaɪəl] *n* Leugnung *f*; (*official ~*)
Dementi *nt*
denim [ˈdenɪm] *n* Jeansstoff *m*; **denim
jacket** *n* Jeansjacke *f*; **denims** *npl*
Bluejeans *pl*
Denmark [ˈdenmɑːk] *n* Dänemark *nt*
denomination [dɪnɒmɪˈneɪʃən] *n* (*Rel*)
Konfession *f*; (*Comm*) Nennwert *m*
dense [dens] *adj* dicht; (*fam: stupid*)
schwer von Begriff; **density** [ˈdensɪtɪ] *n*
Dichte *f*
dent [dent] *n* Beule *f*, Delle *f* ▷ *vt*
einbeulen
dental [ˈdentl] *adj* Zahn-; **~ care**
Zahnpflege *f*; **~ floss** Zahnseide *f*; **dentist**
[ˈdentɪst] *n* Zahnarzt *m*, Zahnärztin;
dentures [ˈdentʃəz] *npl* Zahnprothese *f*;
(*full*) Gebiss *nt*
deny [dɪˈnaɪ] *vt* leugnen, bestreiten;
(*refuse*) ablehnen
deodorant [diːˈəʊdərənt] *n* Deo(dorant)
nt; **~ spray** Deospray *nt o m*
depart [dɪˈpɑːt] *vi* abreisen; (*bus, train*)
abfahren (*for nach, from von*); (*plane*)
abfliegen (*for nach, from von*)
department [dɪˈpɑːtmənt] *n* Abteilung *f*;
(*at university*) Institut *nt*; (*Pol: ministry*)

Ministerium *nt*; **department store** *n*
Kaufhaus *nt*
departure [dɪˈpɑːtʃə*] *n* (*of person*)
Weggang *m*; (*on journey*) Abreise *f* (*for
nach*); (*of train etc*) Abfahrt *f* (*for nach*); (*of
plane*) Abflug *m* (*for nach*); **departure
lounge** (*Aviat*) Abflughalle *f*;
departure time *n* Abfahrtzeit *f*; (*Aviat*)
Abflugzeit *f*
depend [dɪˈpend] *vi* **it ~s** es kommt
darauf an (*whether, if ob*); **depend on** *vt*
(*thing*) abhängen von; (*person: rely on*) sich
verlassen auf +*akk*; (*person, area etc*)
angewiesen sein auf +*akk*; **it ~s on the
weather** es kommt auf das Wetter an;
dependable *adj* zuverlässig;
dependence *n* Abhängigkeit *f* (*on von*);
dependent *adj* abhängig (*on von*)
deplorable [dɪˈplɔːrəbl] *adj* bedauerlich;
deplore *vt* bedauern
deport [dɪˈpɔːt] *vt* ausweisen,
abschieben; **deportation** [diːpɔːˈteɪʃən] *n*
Abschiebung *f*
deposit [dɪˈpɒzɪt] *n* (*down payment*)
Anzahlung *f*; (*security*) Kaution *f*; (*for bottle*)
Pfand *nt*; (*to bank account*) Einzahlung *f*; (*in
river etc*) Ablagerung *f* ▷ *vt* (*put down*)
abstellen, absetzen; (*to bank account*)
einzahlen; (*sth valuable*) deponieren;
deposit account *n* Sparkonto *nt*
depot [ˈdepəʊ] *n* Depot *nt*
depreciate [dɪˈpriːʃɪeɪt] *vi* an Wert
verlieren
depress [dɪˈpres] *vt* (*in mood*)
deprimieren; **depressed** *adj* (*person*)
niedergeschlagen, deprimiert; **~ area**
Notstandsgebiet *nt*; **depressing** *adj*
deprimierend; **depression** [dɪˈpreʃən] *n*
(*mood*) Depression *f*; (*Meteo*) Tief *nt*
deprive [dɪˈpraɪv] *vt* **to ~ sb of sth** jdn
einer Sache berauben; **deprived** *adj*
(*child*) (sozial) benachteiligt
dept *abbr* = **department** Abt.
depth [depθ] *n* Tiefe *f*
deputy [ˈdepjʊtɪ] *adj* stellvertretend,
Vize- ▷ *n* Stellvertreter(in) *m(f)*; (*US Pol*)
Abgeordnete(r) *mf*
derail [dɪˈreɪl] *vt* entgleisen lassen; **to be
~ed** entgleisen
deranged [dɪˈreɪndʒd] *adj* geistesgestört
derivation [derɪˈveɪʃən] *n* Ableitung *f*;
derive [dɪˈraɪv] *vt* ableiten (*from von*)
▷ abstammen (*from von*)

dermatitis [də:mə'taɪtɪs] n
Hautentzündung f

derogatory [dɪ'rɒgətərɪ] adj abfällig

descend [dɪ'send] vt, vi hinabsteigen,
hinuntergehen; (person) **to ~ o be ~ed
from** abstammen von; **descendant** n
Nachkomme m; **descent** [dɪ'sent] n
(coming down) Abstieg m; (origin)
Abstammung f

describe [dɪs'kraɪb] vt beschreiben;
description [dɪ'skrɪpʃən] n Beschreibung
f

desert ['dezət] n Wüste f ▷ [dɪ'zɜ:t] vt
verlassen; (abandon) im Stich lassen;
deserted adj verlassen; (empty)
menschenleer

deserve [dɪ'zɜ:v] vt verdienen

design [dɪ'zaɪn] n (plan) Entwurf m; (of
vehicle, machine) Konstruktion f; (of object)
Design nt; (planning) Gestaltung f ▷ vt
entwerfen; (machine etc) konstruieren; **~ed
for sb/sth** (intended) für jdn/etw
konzipiert

designate ['dezɪgneɪt] vt bestimmen

designer [dɪ'zaɪnə*] n Designer(in) m(f);
(Tech) Konstrukteur(in) m(f); **designer
drug** n Designerdroge f

desirable [dɪ'zaɪərəbl] n wünschenswert;
(person) begehrenswert; **desire** [dɪ'zaɪə*]
n Wunsch m (for nach); (esp sexual)
Begierde f (for nach) ▷ vt wünschen; (ask
for) verlangen; **if ~d** auf Wunsch

desk [desk] n Schreibtisch m; (reception ~)
Empfang m; (at airport etc) Schalter m;
desktop publishing n Desktoppublishing
nt

desolate ['desəlɪt] adj trostlos

despair [dɪs'peə*] n Verzweiflung f (at
über +akk) ▷ vi verzweifeln (of an +dat)

despatch [dɪs'spætʃ] see **dispatch**

desperate ['despərɪt] adj verzweifelt;
(situation) hoffnungslos; **to be ~ for sth**
etw dringend brauchen, unbedingt
wollen; **desperation** [despə'reɪʃən] n
Verzweiflung f

despicable [dɪ'spɪkəbl] adj
verachtenswert; **despise** [dɪ'spaɪz] vt
verachten

despite [dɪ'spaɪt] prep trotz +gen

dessert [dɪ'zɜ:t] n Nachtisch m;
dessertspoon n Dessertlöffel m

destination [destɪ'neɪʃən] n (of person)
(Reise)ziel nt; (of goods) Bestimmungsort

m; **destine** vt **we're ~d for Hull** wir sind
auf dem Weg nach Hull; **he was ~d to die
young** er sollte früh sterben; **destiny**
['destɪnɪ] n Schicksal nt

destroy [dɪ'strɔɪ] vt zerstören;
(completely) vernichten; **destruction**
[dɪ'strʌkʃən] n Zerstörung f; (complete)
Vernichtung f; **destructive** [dɪ'strʌktɪv]
adj zerstörerisch; (esp fig) destruktiv

detach [dɪ'tætʃ] vt abnehmen; (from form
etc) abtrennen; (free) lösen (from von);
detachable adj abnehmbar; (from form
etc) abtrennbar; **detached** adj (attitude)
distanziert, objektiv; **~ house** Einzelhaus
nt

detail ['di:teɪl,] (US) [dɪ:'teɪl] n Einzelheit
f, Detail nt; (**further**) **~s from …** Näheres
erfahren Sie bei …; **to go into ~** ins Detail
gehen; **in ~** ausführlich; **detailed** adj
detailliert, ausführlich

detain [dɪ'teɪn] vt aufhalten; (police) in
Haft nehmen

detect [dɪ'tekt] vt entdecken; (notice)
wahrnehmen; **detective** [dɪ'tektɪv] n
Detektiv(in) m(f); **detective story** n
Detektivroman, Krimi m

detention [dɪ'tenʃən] n Haft f, (Sch)
Nachsitzen nt

deter [dɪ'tɜ:*] vt abschrecken (from
von)

detergent [dɪ'tɜ:dʒənt] n
Reinigungsmittel nt; (soap powder)
Waschmittel nt

deteriorate [dɪ'tɪərɪəreɪt] vi sich
verschlechtern

determination [dɪtɜ:mɪ'neɪʃən] n
Entschlossenheit f; **determine** [dɪ'tɜ:mɪn]
vt bestimmen; **determined** adj (fest)
entschlossen

deterrent [dɪ'terənt] n
Abschreckungsmittel nt

detest [dɪ'test] vt verabscheuen;
detestable adj abscheulich

detour ['di:tuə*] n Umweg m; (of traffic)
Umleitung f

deuce [dju:s] n (Tennis) Einstand m

devalue [di:'vælju:] vt abwerten

devastate ['devəsteɪt] vt verwüsten;
devastating ['devəsteɪtɪŋ] adj
verheerend

develop [dɪ'veləp] vt entwickeln; (illness)
bekommen ▷ vi sich entwickeln;
developing country n Entwicklungsland

nt; **development** *n* Entwicklung *f*; *(of land)* Erschließung *f*

device [dɪ'vaɪs] *n* Vorrichtung *f*, Gerät *nt*

devil ['devl] *n* Teufel *m*; **devilish** *adj* teuflisch

devote [dɪ'vəʊt] *vt* widmen *(to dat)*; **devoted** *adj* liebend; *(servant etc)* treu ergeben; **devotion** *n* Hingabe *f*

devour [dɪ'vaʊə*] *vt* verschlingen

dew [dju:] *n* Tau *m*

diabetes [daɪə'bi:ti:z] *n* Diabetes *m*, Zuckerkrankheit *f*; **diabetic** [daɪə'betɪk] *adj* zuckerkrank, für Diabetiker ▷ *n* Diabetiker(in) *m(f)*

diagnosis *(diagnoses)* [daɪəg'nəʊsɪs] *(pl* **diagnoses)** *n* Diagnose *f*

diagonal [daɪ'ægənl] *adj* diagonal

diagram ['daɪəgræm] *n* Diagramm *nt*

dial ['daɪəl] *n* Skala *f*; *(of clock)* Zifferblatt *nt* ▷ *vt* *(Tel)* wählen; **dial code** *n* *(US)* Vorwahl *f*

dialect ['daɪəlekt] *n* Dialekt *m*

dialling code *n* *(Brit)* Vorwahl *f*; **dialling tone** *n* *(Brit)* Amtszeichen *nt*

dialogue, dialog *(US)* ['daɪəlɒg] *n* Dialog *m*

dial tone *n* *(US)* Amtszeichen *nt*

dialysis [daɪ'æləsɪs] *n* *(Med)* Dialyse *f*

diameter [daɪ'æmɪtə*] *n* Durchmesser *m*

diamond ['daɪəmənd] *n* Diamant *m*; *(Cards)* Karo *nt*

diaper ['daɪpə*] *n* *(US)* Windel *f*

diarrhoea [daɪə'ri:ə] *n* Durchfall *m*

diary ['daɪərɪ] *n* (Taschen)kalender *m*; *(account)* Tagebuch *nt*

dice [daɪs] *npl* Würfel *pl*; **diced** *adj* in Würfel geschnitten

dictate [dɪk'teɪt] *vt* diktieren; **dictation** [dɪk'teɪʃən] *n* Diktat *nt*

dictator [dɪk'teɪtə*] *n* Diktator(in) *m(f)*; **dictatorship** [dɪk'teɪtəʃɪp] *n* Diktatur *f*

dictionary ['dɪkʃənrɪ] *n* Wörterbuch *nt*

did [dɪd] *pt of* **do**

didn't ['dɪdnt] *contr of* **did not**

die [daɪ] *vi* sterben *(of an +dat)*; *(plant, animal)* eingehen; *(engine)* absterben; **to be dying to do sth** darauf brennen, etw zu tun; **I'm dying for a drink** ich brauche unbedingt was zu trinken; **die away** *vi* schwächer werden; *(wind)* sich legen; **die down** *vi* nachlassen; **die out** *vi* aussterben

diesel ['di:zəl] *n* *(fuel, car)* Diesel *m*; **~ engine** Dieselmotor *m*

diet ['daɪət] *n* Kost *f*; *(special food)* Diät *f* ▷ *vi* eine Diät machen

differ ['dɪfə*] *vi* *(be different)* sich unterscheiden; *(disagree)* anderer Meinung sein; **difference** ['dɪfrəns] *n* Unterschied *m*; **it makes no ~ (to me)** es ist (mir) egal; **it makes a big ~** es macht viel aus; **different** *adj* andere(r, s); *(with pl)* verschieden; **to be quite ~** ganz anders sein *(from als)*; *(two people, things)* völlig verschieden sein; **a ~ person** ein anderer Mensch; **differentiate** [dɪfə'renʃɪeɪt] *vt, vi* unterscheiden; **differently** ['dɪfrəntlɪ] *adv* anders *(from als)*; *(from one another)* unterschiedlich

difficult ['dɪfɪkəlt] *adj* schwierig; **I find it ~** es fällt mir schwer; **difficulty** *n* Schwierigkeit *f*; **with ~** nur schwer; **to have ~ in doing sth** etw nur mit Mühe machen können

dig [dɪg] *(dug, dug)* *vt, vi* *(hole)* graben; **dig in** *vi* *(fam: to food)* reinhauen; **~!** greif(t) zu!; **dig up** *vt* ausgraben

digest [daɪ'dʒest] *vt* *(a. fig)* verdauen; **digestible** [dɪ'dʒestəbl] *adj* verdaulich; **digestion** [dɪ'dʒestʃən] *n* Verdauung *f*; **digestive** [dɪ'dʒestɪv] *adj* **~ biscuit** *(Brit)* Vollkornkeks *m*

digit ['dɪdʒɪt] *n* Ziffer *f*; **digital** ['dɪdʒɪtəl] *adj* digital; **~ computer** Digitalrechner *m*; **~ watch/clock** Digitaluhr *f*; **digital camera** *n* Digitalkamera *f*

dignified ['dɪgnɪfaɪd] *adj* würdevoll; **dignity** ['dɪgnɪtɪ] *n* Würde *f*

dilapidated [dɪ'læpɪdeɪtɪd] *adj* baufällig

dilemma [daɪ'lemə] *n* Dilemma *nt*

dill [dɪl] *n* Dill *m*

dilute [daɪ'lu:t] *vt* verdünnen

dim [dɪm] *adj* *(light)* schwach; *(outline)* undeutlich; *(stupid)* schwer von Begriff ▷ *vt* verdunkeln; *(US Auto)* abblenden; **~med headlights** *(US)* Abblendlicht *nt*

dime [daɪm] *n* *(US)* Zehncentstück *nt*

dimension [daɪ'menʃən] *n* Dimension *f*; **~s** *pl* Maße *pl*

diminish [dɪ'mɪnɪʃ] *vt* verringern ▷ *vi* sich verringern

dimple ['dɪmpl] *n* Grübchen *nt*

dine [daɪn] *vi* speisen; **dine out** *vi* außer Haus essen; **diner** *n* Gast *m*; *(Rail)* Speisewagen *m*; *(US)* Speiselokal *nt*

dinghy ['dɪŋgɪ] n Ding(h)i nt; (inflatable) Schlauchboot nt

dingy ['dɪndʒɪ] adj düster; (dirty) schmuddelig

dining car ['daɪnɪŋkɑ:*] n Speisewagen m; **dining room** n Esszimmer nt; (in hotel) Speiseraum m; **dining table** n Esstisch m

dinner ['dɪnə*] n Abendessen nt; (lunch) Mittagessen nt; (public) Diner nt; **to be at ~** beim Essen sein; **to have ~** zu Abend/Mittag essen; **dinner jacket** n Smoking m; **dinner party** n Abendgesellschaft f (mit Essen); **dinnertime** n Essenszeit f

dinosaur ['daɪnəsɔ:*] n Dinosaurier m

dip [dɪp] vt tauchen (in in +akk); **to ~ (one's headlights)** (Brit Auto) abblenden; **~ped headlights** Abblendlicht nt ▷ n (in ground) Bodensenke f; (sauce) Dip m

diploma [dɪ'pləʊmə] n Diplom nt

diplomat ['dɪpləmæt] n Diplomat(in) m(f); **diplomatic** [dɪplə'mætɪk] adj diplomatisch

dipstick ['dɪpstɪk] n Ölmessstab m

direct [daɪ'rekt] adj direkt; (cause, consequence) unmittelbar; **~ debit** (mandate) Einzugsermächtigung f; (transaction) Abbuchung f im Lastschriftverfahren; **~ train** durchgehender Zug ▷ vt (aim, send) richten (at, to an +akk); (film) die Regie führen bei; (traffic) regeln; **direct current** n (Elec) Gleichstrom m

direction [dɪ'rekʃən] n (course) Richtung f; (Cine) Regie f; **in the ~ of ...** in Richtung ...; **~s** pl **for use** Gebrauchsanweisung f; **~s** pl (to a place) Wegbeschreibung f

directly [dɪ'rektlɪ] adv direkt; (at once) sofort

director [dɪ'rektə*] n Direktor(in) m(f), Leiter(in) m(f); (of film) Regisseur(in) m(f)

directory [dɪ'rektərɪ] n Adressbuch nt; (Tel) Telefonbuch nt; **~ enquiries** o (US) **assistance** (Tel) Auskunft f

dirt [dɜ:t] n Schmutz m, Dreck m; **dirt cheap** adj spottbillig; **dirt road** n unbefestigte Straße; **dirty** adj schmutzig

disability [dɪsə'bɪlɪtɪ] n Behinderung f; **disabled** [dɪs'eɪbld] adj behindert, Behinderten- ▷ npl **the ~** die Behinderten

disadvantage [dɪsəd'vɑ:ntɪdʒ] n Nachteil m; **at a ~** benachteiligt;

disadvantageous [dɪsædvɑ:n'teɪdʒəs] adj nachteilig, ungünstig

disagree [dɪsə'gri:] vi anderer Meinung sein; (two people) sich nicht einig sein; (two reports etc) nicht übereinstimmen; **to ~ with sb** mit jdm nicht übereinstimmen; (food) jdm nicht bekommen; **disagreeable** adj unangenehm; (person) unsympathisch; **disagreement** n Meinungsverschiedenheit f

disappear [dɪsə'pɪə*] vi verschwinden; **disappearance** n Verschwinden nt

disappoint [dɪsə'pɔɪnt] vt enttäuschen; **disappointing** adj enttäuschend; **disappointment** n Enttäuschung f

disapproval [dɪsə'pru:vl] n Missbilligung f; **disapprove** [dɪsə'pru:v] vi missbilligen (of akk)

disarm [dɪs'ɑ:m] vt entwaffnen ▷ vi (Pol) abrüsten; **disarmament** n Abrüstung f; **disarming** adj (smile, look) gewinnend

disaster [dɪ'zɑ:stə*] n Katastrophe f; **disastrous** [dɪ'zɑ:strəs] adj katastrophal

disbelief [dɪsbə'li:f] n Ungläubigkeit f

disc [dɪsk] n Scheibe f, CD f; see also **disk** (Anat) Bandscheibe f; **disc brake** n Scheibenbremse f

discharge ['dɪstʃɑ:dʒ] n (Med) Ausfluss m ▷ [dɪs'tʃɑ:dʒ] vt (person) entlassen; (emit) ausstoßen; (Med) ausscheiden

discipline ['dɪsɪplɪn] n Disziplin f

disc jockey ['dɪskdʒɒkɪ] n Diskjockey m

disclose [dɪs'kləʊz] vt bekannt geben; (secret) enthüllen

disco ['dɪskəʊ] n (pl **-s**) n Disko f, Diskomusik f

discomfort [dɪs'kʌmfət] n (slight pain) leichte Schmerzen pl; (unease) Unbehagen nt

disconnect [dɪskə'nekt] vt (electricity, gas, phone) abstellen; (unplug) **to ~ the TV (from the mains)** den Stecker des Fernsehers herausziehen; (Tel) **I've been ~ed** das Gespräch ist unterbrochen worden

discontent [dɪskən'tent] n Unzufriedenheit f; **discontented** adj unzufrieden

discontinue [dɪskən'tɪnju:] vt einstellen; (product) auslaufen lassen

discotheque ['dɪskəʊtek] n Diskothek f

discount ['dɪskaʊnt] n Rabatt m

discover [dɪs'kʌvə*] vt entdecken;
  discovery n Entdeckung f
discredit [dɪs'kredɪt] vt in Verruf bringen
  ▷ n Misskredit m
discreet [dɪs'kriːt] adj diskret
discrepancy [dɪs'krepənsɪ] n
  Unstimmigkeit f, Diskrepanz f
discriminate [dɪs'krɪmɪneɪt] vi
  unterscheiden; **to ~ against sb** jdn
  diskriminieren; **discrimination**
  [dɪskrɪmɪ'neɪʃən] n (different treatment)
  Diskriminierung f
discus ['dɪskəs] n Diskus m
discuss [dɪs'kʌs] vt diskutieren,
  besprechen; **discussion** [dɪs'kʌʃən] n
  Diskussion f
disease [dɪ'ziːz] n Krankheit f
disembark [dɪsɪm'bɑːk] vi von Bord
  gehen
disentangle ['dɪsɪn'tæŋgl] vt entwirren
disgrace [dɪs'greɪs] n Schande f ▷ vt
  Schande machen +dat; (family etc) Schande
  bringen über +akk; (less strong) blamieren;
  disgraceful adj skandalös; **it's ~** es ist
  eine Schande
disguise [dɪs'gaɪz] vt verkleiden; (voice)
  verstellen ▷ n Verkleidung f; **in
  ~** verkleidet
disgust [dɪs'gʌst] n Abscheu m; (physical)
  Ekel m ▷ vt anekeln, anwidern;
  disgusting adj widerlich; (physically)
  ekelhaft
dish [dɪʃ] n Schüssel f; (food) Gericht nt;
  ~es pl (crockery) Geschirr nt; **to do/wash
  the ~es** abwaschen; **dishcloth** n (for
  washing) Spültuch nt; (for drying)
  Geschirrtuch nt
dishearten [dɪs'hɑːtən] vt entmutigen;
  don't be ~ed lass den Kopf nicht
  hängen!
dishonest [dɪs'ɒnɪst] adj unehrlich
dishonour [dɪs'ɒnə*] n Schande f
dish towel n (US) Geschirrtuch nt; **dish
  washer** n Geschirrspülmaschine f
dishy ['dɪʃɪ] adj (Brit fam) klasse, attraktiv
disillusioned [dɪsɪ'luːʒənd] adj
  desillusioniert
disinfect [dɪsɪn'fekt] vt desinfizieren;
  disinfectant n Desinfektionsmittel nt
disintegrate [dɪs'ɪntɪgreɪt] vi zerfallen;
  (group) sich auflösen
disjointed [dɪs'dʒɔɪntɪd] adj
  unzusammenhängend

disk [dɪsk] n (Inform: floppy) Diskette f;
  disk drive n Diskettenlaufwerk nt;
  diskette [dɪ'sket] n Diskette f
dislike [dɪs'laɪk] n Abneigung f ▷ vt nicht
  mögen; **to ~ doing sth** etw ungern tun
dislocate ['dɪsləʊkeɪt] vt (Med)
  verrenken, ausrenken
dismal ['dɪzməl] adj trostlos
dismantle [dɪs'mæntl] vt auseinander
  nehmen; (machine) demontieren
dismay [dɪs'meɪ] n Bestürzung f;
  dismayed adj bestürzt
dismiss [dɪs'mɪs] vt (employee) entlassen;
  dismissal n Entlassung f
disobedience [dɪsə'biːdɪəns] n
  Ungehorsam m; **disobedient** adj
  ungehorsam; **disobey** [dɪsə'beɪ] vt nicht
  gehorchen +dat
disorder [dɪs'ɔːdə*] n (mess) Unordnung
  f; (riot) Aufruhr m; (Med) Störung f, Leiden
  nt
disorganized [dɪs'ɔːgənaɪzd] adj
  chaotisch
disparaging adj geringschätzig
dispatch [dɪ'spætʃ] vt abschicken,
  abfertigen
dispensable [dɪ'spensəbl] adj
  entbehrlich; **dispense** vt verteilen;
  dispense with vt verzichten auf +akk;
  dispenser n Automat m
disperse [dɪ'spɜːs] vi sich zerstreuen
display [dɪ'spleɪ] n (exhibition)
  Ausstellung f, Show f; (of goods) Auslage f;
  (Tech) Anzeige f, Display nt ▷ vt zeigen;
  (goods) ausstellen
disposable [dɪ'spəʊzəbl] adj (container,
  razor etc) Wegwerf-; **~ nappy**
  Wegwerfwindel f; **disposal** [dɪ'spəʊzəl] n
  Loswerden nt; (of waste) Beseitigung f; **to be
  at sb's ~** jdm zur Verfügung stehen; **dispose
  of** vt loswerden; (waste etc) beseitigen
dispute [dɪ'spjuːt] n Streit m; (industrial)
  Auseinandersetzung f ▷ vt bestreiten
disqualification [dɪskwɒlɪfɪ'keɪʃən] n
  Disqualifikation f; **disqualify**
  [dɪs'kwɒlɪfaɪ] vt disqualifizieren
disregard [dɪsrɪ'gɑːd] vt nicht beachten
disreputable [dɪs'repjʊtəbl] adj verrufen
disrespect [dɪsrɪ'spekt] n
  Respektlosigkeit f
disrupt [dɪs'rʌpt] vt stören; (interrupt)
  unterbrechen; **disruption** [dɪs'rʌpʃən] n
  Störung f; (interruption) Unterbrechung f

dissatisfied [dɪsˈsætɪsfaɪd] adj
unzufrieden

dissent [dɪˈsent] n Widerspruch m

dissolve [dɪˈzɒlv] vt auflösen ▷ vi sich
auflösen

dissuade [dɪˈsweɪd] vt (davon abbringen)
to ~ sb from doing sth jdn davon
abbringen, etw zu tun

distance [ˈdɪstəns] n Entfernung f; **in
the/from a ~** in/aus der Ferne; **distant**
adj (a. in time) fern; (relative etc) entfernt;
(person) distanziert

distaste [dɪsˈteɪst] n Abneigung f (for
gegen)

distil [dɪsˈtɪl] vt destillieren; **distillery** n
Brennerei f

distinct [dɪsˈtɪŋkt] adj verschieden; (clear)
klar, deutlich; **distinction** [dɪsˈtɪŋkʃən] n
(difference) Unterschied m; (in exam etc)
Auszeichnung f; **distinctive** adj
unverkennbar; **distinctly** adv deutlich

distinguish [dɪsˈtɪŋgwɪʃ] vt
unterscheiden (sth from sth etw von
etw)

distort [dɪsˈtɔːt] vt verzerren; (truth)
verdrehen

distract [dɪsˈtrækt] vt ablenken;
distraction [dɪsˈtrækʃən] n Ablenkung f;
(diversion) Zerstreuung f

distress [dɪsˈtres] n (need, danger) Not f;
(suffering) Leiden nt; (mental) Qual f; (worry)
Kummer m ▷ vt mitnehmen, erschüttern;
distressed area n Notstandsgebiet nt;
distress signal n Notsignal nt

distribute [dɪsˈtrɪbjuːt] vt verteilen;
(Comm: goods) vertreiben; **distribution**
[dɪstrɪˈbjuːʃən] n Verteilung f; (Comm: of
goods) Vertrieb m; **distributor**
[dɪsˈtrɪbjʊtə*] n (Auto) Verteiler m; (Comm)
Händler(in) m(f)

district [ˈdɪstrɪkt] n Gegend f;
(administrative) Bezirk m; **district attorney**
n (US) Staatsanwalt m, Staatsanwältin f

distrust [dɪsˈtrʌst] vt misstrauen +dat ▷ n
Misstrauen nt

disturb [dɪsˈtɜːb] vt stören; (worry)
beunruhigen; **disturbance** n Störung f;
disturbing adj beunruhigend

ditch [dɪtʃ] n Graben m ▷ vt (fam: person)
den Laufpass geben +dat; (plan etc)
verwerfen

ditto [ˈdɪtəʊ] n dito, ebenfalls

dive [daɪv] n (into water) Kopfsprung m;

(Aviat) Sturzflug m; (fam) zwielichtiges
Lokal ▷ vi (under water) tauchen; **diver** n
Taucher(in) m(f)

diverse [daɪˈvɜːs] adj verschieden;
diversion [daɪˈvɜːʃən] n (of traffic)
Umleitung f; (distraction) Ablenkung f;
divert [daɪˈvɜːt] vt ablenken; (traffic)
umleiten

divide [dɪˈvaɪd] vt teilen; (in several parts,
between people) aufteilen ▷ vi sich teilen;
dividend [ˈdɪvɪdend] n Dividende f

divine [dɪˈvaɪn] adj göttlich

diving [ˈdaɪvɪŋ] n (Sport) tauchen nt;
(jumping in) Springen nt; (Sport: from board)
Kunstspringen nt; **diving board** n
Sprungbrett nt; **diving goggles** npl
Taucherbrille f; **diving mask** n
Tauchmaske f

division [dɪˈvɪʒən] n Teilung f; (Math)
Division f; (department) Abteilung f; (Sport)
Liga f

divorce [dɪˈvɔːs] n Scheidung f ▷ vt sich
scheiden lassen von; **divorced** adj
geschieden; **to get ~** sich scheiden lassen;
divorcee [dɪvɔːˈsiː] n Geschiedene(r) mf

DIY [diːaɪˈwaɪ] abbr = **do-it-yourself**; **DIY
centre** n Baumarkt m

dizzy [ˈdɪzɪ] adj schwindlig

DJ [diːˈdʒeɪ] abbr = **dinner jacket** Smoking
m ▷ abbr = **disc jockey** Diskjockey m, DJ m

DNA abbr = **desoxyribonucleic acid** DNS f

KEYWORD

do [duː] (pt **did**, pp **done**) n (inf: party etc)
Fete f
▷ aux vb **1** (in negative constructions and
questions): **I don't understand** ich
verstehe nicht; **didn't you know?**
wusstest du das nicht?; **what do you
think?** was meinen Sie?
2 (for emphasis, in polite phrases): **she does
seem rather tired** sie scheint wirklich
sehr müde zu sein; **do sit down/help
yourself** setzen Sie sich doch hin/greifen
Sie doch zu
3 (used to avoid repeating vb): **she swims
better than I do** sie schwimmt besser als
ich; **she lives in Glasgow — so do I** sie
wohnt in Glasgow — ich auch
4 (in tag questions): **you like him, don't
you?** du magst ihn doch, oder?
▷ vt **1** (carry out, perform etc) tun machen;

what are you doing tonight? was macht du heute Abend?; **I've got nothing to do** ich habe nichts zu tun; **to do one's hair/nails** sich die Haare/Nägel machen
2 (Aut etc) fahren
▷ vi **1** (act, behave): **do as I do** mach es wie ich
2 (get on, fare): **he's doing well/badly at school** er ist gut/schlecht in der Schule; **how do you do?** guten Tag
3 (be suitable) gehen (be sufficient) reichen; **to make do (with)** auskommen mit;
do away with vt (kill) umbringen (abolish) (law etc) abschaffen;
do up vt (laces, dress, buttons) zumachen (renovate) (room, house) renovieren;
do with vt (need) brauchen (be connected) zu tun haben mit;
do without vt, vi auskommen ohne

dock [dɒk] n Dock nt; (Jur) Anklagebank f; **docker** n Hafenarbeiter m; **dockyard** n Werft f
doctor ['dɒktə*] n Arzt m, Ärztin; (in title, also academic) Doktor m
document ['dɒkjʊmənt] n Dokument nt; **documentary** [dɒkjʊ'mentərɪ] n Dokumentarfilm m; **documentation** [dɒkjʊmen'teɪʃən] n Dokumentation f
docusoap ['dɒkjʊsəʊp] n Reality-Serie f, Dokusoap f
doddery ['dɒdərɪ] adj tatterig
dodgem ['dɒdʒəm] n Autoskooter m
dodgy ['dɒdʒɪ] adj nicht ganz in Ordnung; (dishonest, unreliable) zwielichtig; **he has a ~ stomach** er hat sich den Magen verdorben
dog [dɒg] n Hund m; **dog food** n Hundefutter nt; **doggie bag** ['dɒgɪ'bæg] n Tüte oder Box, in der Essensreste aus dem Restaurant mit nach Hause genommen werden können
do-it-yourself ['duːɪtjə'self] n Heimwerken nt, Do-it-yourself nt ▷ adj Heimwerker-; **do-it-yourselfer** n Bastler(in) m(f), Heimwerker(in) m(f)
doll [dɒl] n Puppe f
dollar ['dɒlə*] n Dollar m
dolphin ['dɒlfɪn] n Delphin m
domain n Domäne f; (Inform) Domain f
dome [dəʊm] n Kuppel f
domestic [də'mestɪk] adj häuslich;

(within country) Innen-, Binnen-; **domestic animal** n Haustier nt; **domesticated** [də'mestɪkeɪtɪd] adj (person) häuslich; (animal) zahm; **domestic flight** n Inlandsflug m
domicile ['dɒmɪsaɪl] n (ständiger) Wohnsitz
dominant ['dɒmɪnənt] adj dominierend, vorherrschend; **dominate** ['dɒmɪneɪt] vt beherrschen
dominoes ['dɒmɪnəʊz] npl Domino(spiel) nt
donate [dəʊ'neɪt] vt spenden; **donation** n Spende f
done [dʌn] pp of **do** ▷ adj (cooked) gar; **well ~** durchgebraten
doner (kebab) ['dɒnəkə'bæb] n Döner (Kebab) m
donkey ['dɒŋkɪ] n Esel m
donor ['dəʊnə] n Spender(in) m(f)
don't [dəʊnt] contr of **do not**
doom [duːm] n Schicksal nt; (downfall) Verderben nt
door [dɔː*] n Tür f; **doorbell** n Türklingel f; **door handle** n Türklinke f; **doorknob** n Türknauf m; **doormat** n Fußabtreter m; **doorstep** n Türstufe f; **right on our ~** direkt vor unserer Haustür
dope [dəʊp] (Sport) n (for athlete) Aufputschmittel nt ▷ vt dopen; **dopey** adj (fam) bekloppt; (from drugs) benebelt; (sleepy) benommen
dormitory ['dɔːmɪtrɪ] n Schlafsaal m; (US) Studentenwohnheim nt
dosage ['dəʊsɪdʒ] n Dosierung f; **dose** [dəʊs] n Dosis f ▷ vt dosieren
dot [dɒt] n Punkt m; **on the ~** auf die Minute genau, pünktlich
dotcom ['dɒtkɒm] n **~ (company)** Internetfirma f, Dotcom-Unternehmen nt
dote on [dəʊt ɒn] vt abgöttisch lieben
dotted line n punktierte Linie
double ['dʌbl] adj, adv doppelt; **~ the quantity** die zweifache Menge, doppelt so viel ▷ vt verdoppeln ▷ n (person) Doppelgänger(in) m(f); (Cine) Double nt; **double bass** n Kontrabass m; **double bed** n Doppelbett nt; **double-click** vt (Inform) doppelklicken; **double cream** n Sahne mit hohem Fettgehalt; **doubledecker** n Doppeldecker m; **double glazing** n Doppelverglasung f; **double-park** vi in zweiter Reihe parken; **double room** n

Doppelzimmer nt; **doubles** npl (Sport: also match) Doppel nt

doubt [daʊt] n Zweifel m; **no ~** ohne Zweifel, zweifellos, wahrscheinlich; **to have one's ~s** Bedenken haben ▷ vt bezweifeln; (statement, word) anzweifeln; **I ~ it** das bezweifle ich; **doubtful** adj zweifelhaft, zweifelnd; **it is ~ whether ...** es ist fraglich, ob ...; **doubtless** adv ohne Zweifel, sicherlich

dough [dəʊ] n Teig m; **doughnut** n Donut m (rundes Hefegebäck)

dove [dʌv] n Taube f

down [daʊn] n Daunen pl; (fluff) Flaum m ▷ adv unten; (motion) nach unten; (towards speaker) herunter; (away from speaker) hinunter; **~ here/there** hier/dort unten; (downstairs) **they came ~ for breakfast** sie kamen zum Frühstück herunter; (southwards) **he came ~ from Scotland** er kam von Schottland herunter ▷ prep (towards speaker) herunter; (away from speaker) hinunter; **to drive ~ the hill/road** den Berg/die Straße hinunter fahren; (along) **to walk ~ the street** die Straße entlang gehen; **he's ~ the pub** (fam) er ist in der Kneipe ▷ vt (fam: drink) runterkippen ▷ adj niedergeschlagen, deprimiert

down-and-out adj heruntergekommen ▷ n Obdachlose(r) mf, Penner(in) m(f); **downcast** adj niedergeschlagen; **downfall** n Sturz m; **down-hearted** adj entmutigt; **downhill** adv bergab; **he's going ~** (fig) mit ihm geht es bergab

download ['daʊnləʊd] vt downloaden, herunterladen; **downmarket** adj für den Massenmarkt; **down payment** n Anzahlung f; **downpour** n Platzregen m; **downs** npl Hügelland nt; **downsize** vt

(business) verkleinern ▷ vi sich verkleinern

Down's syndrome ['daʊnz'sɪndrəʊm] n (Med) Downsyndrom nt

downstairs [daʊn'steəz] adv unten; (motion) nach unten; **downstream** adv flussabwärts; **downtime** n Ausfallzeit f; **downtown** adv (be, work etc) in der Innenstadt; (go) in die Innenstadt ▷ adv (US) in der Innenstadt; **~ Chicago** die Innenstadt von Chicago; **down under** adv (fam: in/to Australia) in/nach Australien; (in/to New Zealand) in/nach Neuseeland; **downwards** adv, adj nach unten; (movement, trend) Abwärts-

doze [dəʊz] vi dösen ▷ n Nickerchen nt

dozen ['dʌzn] n Dutzend nt; **two ~ eggs** zwei Dutzend Eier; **~s of times** x-mal

DP abbr = **data processing** DV f

drab [dræb] adj trist; (colour) düster

draft [drɑːft] n (outline) Entwurf m; (US Mil) Einberufung f

drag [dræg] vt schleppen ▷ n (fam) **to be a ~** (boring) stinklangweilig sein; (laborious) ein ziemlicher Schlauch sein; **drag on** vi sich in die Länge ziehen

dragon ['drægən] n Drache m; **dragonfly** n Libelle f

drain [dreɪn] n Abfluss m ▷ vt (water, oil) ablassen; (vegetables etc) abgießen; (land) entwässern, trockenlegen ▷ vi (of water) abfließen; **drainpipe** n Abflussrohr nt

drama ['drɑːmə] n (a. fig) Drama nt; **dramatic** [drə'mætɪk] adj dramatisch

drank [dræŋk] pt of **drink**

drapes [dreɪps] npl (US) Vorhänge pl

drastic ['dræstɪk] adj drastisch

draught [drɑːft] n (Luft)zug m; **there's a ~** es zieht; **on ~** (beer) vom Fass; **draughts** nsing Damespiel nt; **draughty** adj zugig

draw [drɔː] (drew, drawn) vt (pull) ziehen; (crowd) anlocken, anziehen; (picture) zeichnen ▷ vi (Sport) unentschieden spielen ▷ n (Sport) Unentschieden nt; (attraction) Attraktion f; (for lottery) Ziehung f; **draw out** vt herausziehen; (money) abheben; **draw up** vt (formulate) entwerfen; (list) erstellen ▷ vi (car) anhalten; **drawback** n Nachteil m; **drawbridge** n Zugbrücke f

drawer ['drɔː*] n Schublade f

drawing ['drɔːɪŋ] n Zeichnung f; **drawing pin** n Reißzwecke f

drawn [drɔːn] *pp of* **draw**

dread [dred] *n* Furcht *f (of* vor *+dat)* ▷ *vt* sich fürchten vor *+dat;* **dreadful** *adj* furchtbar; **dreadlocks** *npl* Rastalocken *pl*

dream [driːm] *(dreamed o dreamt, dreamed o dreamt) vt, vi* träumen *(about* von) ▷ *n* Traum *m;* **dreamt** [dremt] *pt, pp of* **dream**

dreary ['drɪərɪ] *adj (weather, place)* trostlos; *(book etc)* langweilig

drench [drentʃ] *vt* durchnässen

dress [dres] *n* Kleidung *f; (garment)* Kleid *nt* ▷ *vt* anziehen; *(Med: wound)* verbinden; **to get ~ed** sich anziehen; **dress up** *vi* sich fein machen; *(in costume)* sich verkleiden *(as* als); **dress circle** *n (Theat)* erster Rang; **dresser** *n* Anrichte *f, (US: dressing table)* (Frisier)kommode *f;* **dressing** *n (Gastr)* Dressing *nt,* Soße *f; (Med)* Verband *m;* **dressing gown** *n* Morgenmantel *m;* **dressing room** *n (Sport)* Umkleideraum *m; (Theat)* Künstlergarderobe *f;* **dressing table** *n* Frisierkommode *f;* **dress rehearsal** *n (Theat)* Generalprobe *f*

drew [druː] *pt of* **draw**

dried [draɪd] *adj* getrocknet; *(milk, flowers)* Trocken-; **~ fruit** Dörrobst *nt;* **drier** ['draɪə*] *n see* **dryer**

drift [drɪft] *vi* treiben ▷ *n (of snow)* Verwehung *f; (fig)* Tendenz *f;* **if you get my ~** wenn du mich richtig verstehst

drill [drɪl] *n* Bohrer *m* ▷ *vt, vi* bohren

drink [drɪŋk] **(drank, drunk)** *vt, vi* trinken ▷ *n* Getränk *nt; (alcoholic)* Drink *m;* **drink-driving** *n (Brit)* Trunkenheit *f* am Steuer; **drinking water** *n* Trinkwasser *nt*

drip [drɪp] *n* Tropfen *m* ▷ *vi* tropfen; **drip-dry** *adj* bügelfrei; **dripping** *n* Bratenfett *nt* ▷ *adj* **~ (wet)** tropfnass

drive [draɪv] **(drove, driven)** *vt (car, person in car)* fahren; *(force: person, animal)* treiben; *(Tech)* antreiben; **to ~ sb mad** jdn verrückt machen ▷ *vi* fahren ▷ *n* Fahrt *f; (entrance)* Einfahrt *f,* Auffahrt *f; (Inform)* Laufwerk *nt;* **to go for a ~** spazieren fahren; **drive away, drive off** *vi* wegfahren ▷ *vt* vertreiben

drive-in *adj* Drive-in-; **~ cinema** *(US)* Autokino *nt*

driven ['drɪvn] *pp of* **drive**

driver ['draɪvə*] *n* Fahrer(in) *m(f); (Inform)* Treiber *m;* **~'s license** *(US)* Führerschein *m;*

~'s seat Fahrersitz *m;* **driving** ['draɪvɪŋ] *n* (Auto)fahren *nt;* **he likes ~** er fährt gern Auto; **driving lesson** *n* Fahrstunde *f;* **driving licence** *n (Brit)* Führerschein *m;* **driving school** *n* Fahrschule *f;* **driving seat** *n (Brit)* Fahrersitz *m;* **to be in the ~** alles im Griff haben; **driving test** *n* Fahrprüfung *f*

drizzle ['drɪzl] *n* Nieselregen *m* ▷ *vi* nieseln

drop [drɒp] *n (of liquid)* Tropfen *m; (fall in price etc)* Rückgang *m* ▷ *vt (a. fig: give up)* fallen lassen ▷ *vi (fall)* herunterfallen; *(figures, temperature)* sinken, zurückgehen; **drop by, drop in** *vi* vorbeikommen; **drop off** *vi (to sleep)* einnicken; **drop out** *vi (withdraw)* aussteigen; *(university)* das Studium abbrechen; **dropout** *n* Aussteiger(in) *m(f)*

drought [draʊt] *n* Dürre *f*

drove [drəʊv] *pt of* **drive**

drown [draʊn] *vi* ertrinken ▷ *vt* ertränken

drowsy ['draʊzɪ] *adj* schläfrig

drug [drʌg] *n (Med)* Medikament *nt,* Arznei *f; (addictive)* Droge *f; (narcotic)* Rauschgift *nt;* **to be on ~s** drogensüchtig sein ▷ *vt* (mit Medikamenten) betäuben; **drug addict** *n* Rauschgiftsüchtige(r) *mf;* **drug dealer** *n* Drogenhändler(in) *m(f);* **druggist** *n (US)* Drogist(in) *m(f);* **drugstore** *n (US)* Drogerie *f*

drum [drʌm] *n* Trommel *f;* **~s** *pl* Schlagzeug *nt;* **drummer** *n* Schlagzeuger(in) *m(f)*

drunk [drʌŋk] *pp of* **drink** ▷ *adj* betrunken; **to get ~** sich betrinken ▷ *n* Betrunkene(r) *mf; (alcoholic)* Trinker(in) *m(f);* **drunk-driving** *n (US)* Trunkenheit *f* am Steuer; **drunken** *adj* betrunken, besoffen

dry [draɪ] *adj* trocken ▷ *vt* trocknen; *(dishes, oneself, one's hands etc)* abtrocknen ▷ *vi* trocknen, trocken werden; **dry out** *vi* trocknen; **dry up** *vi* austrocknen; **dry-clean** *vt* chemisch reinigen; **dry-cleaning** *n* chemische Reinigung; **dryer** *n* Trockner *m; (for hair)* Föhn *m; (over head)* Trockenhaube *f*

DTP *abbr* = **desktop publishing** DTP *nt*

dual ['djʊəl] *adj* doppelt; **~ carriageway** *(Brit)* zweispurige Schnellstraße *f,* **~ nationality** doppelte

Staatsangehörigkeit; **dual-purpose** adj Mehrzweck-

dubbed [dʌbd] adj (film) synchronisiert

dubious ['dju:bɪəs] adj zweifelhaft

duchess ['dʌtʃəs] n Herzogin f

duck [dʌk] n Ente f

dude [du:d] n (US fam) Typ m; **a cool ~** ein cooler Typ

due [dju:] adj (time) fällig; (fitting) angemessen; **in ~ course** zu gegebener Zeit; **~ to** infolge +gen, wegen +gen ▷ adv **~ south/north etc** direkt nach Norden/Süden etc

dug [dʌg] pt, pp of **dig**

duke [dju:k] n Herzog m

dull [dʌl] adj (colour, light, weather) trübe; (boring) langweilig

duly ['dju:lɪ] adv ordnungsgemäß; (as expected) wie erwartet

dumb [dʌm] adj stumm; (fam: stupid) doof, blöde

dumb-bell ['dʌmbel] n Hantel f

dummy ['dʌmɪ] n (sham) Attrappe f; (in shop) Schaufensterpuppe f; (Brit: teat) Schnuller m; (fam: person) Dummkopf m ▷ adj unecht, Schein-; **~ run** Testlauf m

dump [dʌmp] n Abfallhaufen m; (fam: place) Kaff nt ▷ vt (lit, fig) abladen; (fam) **he ~ed her** er hat mir ihr Schluss gemacht

dumpling ['dʌmplɪŋ] n Kloß m, Knödel m

dune [dju:n] n Düne f

dung [dʌŋ] n Dung m; (manure) Mist m

dungarees [dʌŋgə'ri:z] npl Latzhose f

dungeon ['dʌndʒən] n Kerker m

duplex ['dju:pleks] n zweistöckige Wohnung; (US) Doppelhaushälfte f

duplicate ['dju:plɪkɪt] n Duplikat nt ▷ ['dju:plɪkeɪt] vt (make copies of) kopieren; (repeat) wiederholen

durable ['djʊərəbl] adj haltbar; **duration** [djʊə'reɪʃən] n Dauer f

during ['djʊərɪŋ] prep (time) während +gen

dusk [dʌsk] n Abenddämmerung f

dust [dʌst] n Staub m ▷ vt abstauben; **dustbin** n (Brit) Mülleimer m; **dustcart** n (Brit) Müllwagen m; **duster** n Staubtuch nt; **dust jacket** n Schutzumschlag m; **dustman** n (Brit) Müllmann m; **dustpan** n Kehrschaufel f; **dusty** adj staubig

Dutch [dʌtʃ] adj holländisch ▷ n (language) Holländisch nt; **to speak/talk double ~** (fam) Quatsch reden; **the ~** pl die Holländer; **Dutchman** (pl **-men**) n

Holländer m; **Dutchwoman** (pl **-women**) n Holländerin f

duty ['dju:tɪ] n Pflicht f; (task) Aufgabe f; (tax) Zoll m; **on/off ~** im Dienst/nicht im Dienst; **to be on ~** Dienst haben; **duty-free** adj zollfrei; **~ shop** Dutyfreeshop m

duvet ['du:veɪ] n Federbett nt

DVD n abbr = **digital versatile disk** DVD f

dwarf [dwɔ:f] (pl **dwarves**) n Zwerg(in) m(f)

dwelling ['dwelɪŋ] n Wohnung f

dwindle ['dwɪndl] vi schwinden

dye [daɪ] n Farbstoff m ▷ vt färben

dynamic [daɪ'næmɪk] adj dynamisch

dynamo ['daɪnəməʊ] n Dynamo m

dyslexia [dɪs'leksɪə] n Legasthenie f; **dyslexic** adj legasthenisch; **to be ~** Legastheniker(in) sein

dyspepsia [dɪs'pepsɪə] n Verdauungsstörung f

e

E [i:] *abbr* = **east** O

E111 form *n* ≈ Auslandskrankenschein *m*

each [i:tʃ] *adj* jeder/jede/jedes ▷ *pron*
jeder/jede/jedes; **I'll have one of ~** ich
nehme von jedem eins; **they ~ have a car**
jeder von ihnen hat ein Auto; **~ other**
einander, sich; **for/against ~ other**
füreinander/gegeneinander ▷ *adv* je;
they cost 10 euros ~ sie kosten je 10 Euro,
sie kosten 10 Euro das Stück

eager ['i:gə*] *adj* eifrig; **to be ~ to do sth**
darauf brennen, etw zu tun

eagle ['i:gl] *n* Adler *m*

ear [ɪə*] *n* Ohr *nt*; **earache** *n*
Ohrenschmerzen *pl*; **eardrum** *n*
Trommelfell *nt*

earl [ɜ:l] *n* Graf *m*

early ['ɜ:lɪ] *adj, adv* früh; **to be 10 minutes
~** 10 Minuten zu früh kommen; **at the
earliest** frühestens; **in ~ June/2008**
Anfang Juni/2008; **~ retirement**
vorzeitiger Ruhestand; **~ warning
system** Frühwarnsystem *nt*

earn [ɜ:n] *vt* verdienen

earnest ['ɜ:nɪst] *adj* ernst; **in ~** im Ernst

earnings ['ɜ:nɪŋz] *npl* Verdienst *m*,
Einkommen *nt*

earphones ['ɪəfəʊnz] *npl* Kopfhörer *m*;
earplug *n* Ohrenstöpsel *m*, Ohropax® *nt*;
earring *n* Ohrring *m*

earth [ɜ:θ] *n* Erde *f*; **what on ~ ...?** was
in aller Welt ...? ▷ *vt* erden; **earthenware**
n Tonwaren *pl*; **earthquake** *n* Erdbeben
nt

earwig ['ɪəwɪg] *n* Ohrwurm *m*

ease [i:z] *vt* (*pain*) lindern; (*burden*)
erleichtern ▷ *n* (*easiness*) Leichtigkeit *f*; **to
feel at ~** sich wohl fühlen; **to feel ill at
~** sich nicht wohl fühlen; **easily** ['i:zɪlɪ]
adv leicht; **he is ~ the best** er ist mit
Abstand der Beste

east [i:st] *n* Osten *m*; **to the ~ of** östlich
von ▷ *adv* (*go, face*) nach Osten ▷ *adj*
Ost-; **~ wind** Ostwind *m*; **eastbound** *adj*
(in) Richtung Osten

Easter ['i:stə*] *n* Ostern *nt*; **at ~** zu
Ostern; **Easter egg** *n* Osterei *nt*; **Easter
Sunday** *n* Ostersonntag *m*

eastern ['i:stən] *adj* Ost-, östlich;
Eastern Europe Osteuropa *nt*; **East
Germany** *n* Ostdeutschland *nt*; **former
~** die ehemalige DDR, die neuen
Bundesländer; **eastwards** ['i:stwədz] *adv*
nach Osten

easy ['i:zɪ] *adj* leicht; (*task, solution*)
einfach; (*life*) bequem; (*manner*)
ungezwungen; **easy-care** *adj*
pflegeleicht; **easy-going** *adj* gelassen

eat [i:t] (ate, eaten) *vt* essen; (*animal*)
fressen; **eat out** *vi* zum Essen ausgehen;
eat up *vt* aufessen; (*animal*) auffressen

eaten ['i:tn] *pp of* **eat**

eavesdrop ['i:vzdrɒp] *vi* (heimlich)
lauschen; **to ~ on sb** jdn belauschen

eccentric [ɪk'sentrɪk] *adj* exzentrisch

echo ['ekəʊ] (*pl* -**es**) *n* Echo *nt* ▷ *vi*
widerhallen

ecological [i:kə'lɒdʒɪkl] *adj* ökologisch;
~ disaster Umweltkatastrophe *f*; **ecology**
[ɪ'kɒlədʒɪ] *n* Ökologie *f*

economic [i:kə'nɒmɪk] *adj*
wirtschaftlich, Wirtschafts-; **~ aid**
Wirtschaftshilfe *f*; **economical** *adj*
wirtschaftlich; (*person*) sparsam;
economics *nsing of pl*
Wirtschaftswissenschaft *f*; **economist**
[ɪ'kɒnəmɪst] *n*
Wirtschaftswissenschaftler(in) *m(f)*;
economize [ɪ'kɒnəmaɪz] *vi* sparen (*on an*
+*dat*); **economy** [ɪ'kɒnəmɪ] *n* (*of state*)

Wirtschaft f; (thrift) Sparsamkeit f;
economy class n (Aviat) Economyclass f
ecstasy ['ekstəsɪ] n Ekstase f; (drug)
Ecstasy f
eczema ['eksɪmə] n Ekzem nt
edge [edʒ] n Rand m; (of knife) Schneide f;
on ~ nervös; **edgy** ['edʒɪ] adj nervös
edible ['edɪbl] adj essbar
Edinburgh ['edɪnbərə] n Edinburg nt
edit ['edɪt] vt (series, newspaper etc)
herausgeben; (text) redigieren; (film)
schneiden; (Inform) editieren; **edition**
['dɪʃən] n Ausgabe f; **editor** n
Redakteur(in) m(f); (of series etc)
Herausgeber(in) m(f); **editorial**
[edɪ'tɔ:rɪəl] adj Redaktions- ▷ n
Leitartikel m
educate ['edjukeɪt] vt (child) erziehen; (at
school, university) ausbilden; (public)
aufklären; **educated** adj gebildet;
education [edju'keɪʃən] n Erziehung f;
(studies, training) Ausbildung f; (subject of
study) Pädagogik f; (system) Schulwesen nt;
(knowledge) Bildung f; **educational** adj
pädagogisch; (instructive) lehrreich;
~ television Schulfernsehen nt
eel [i:l] n Aal m
eerie ['ɪərɪ] adj unheimlich
effect [ɪ'fekt] n Wirkung f (on auf +akk); **to
come into ~** in Kraft treten; **effective** adj
wirksam, effektiv
effeminate [ɪ'femɪnət] adj (of man)
tuntig
efficiency [ɪ'fɪʃənsɪ] n Leistungsfähigkeit
f; (of method) Wirksamkeit f; **efficient** adj
(Tech) leistungsfähig; (method) wirksam,
effizient
effort ['efət] n Anstrengung f; (attempt)
Versuch m; **to make an ~** sich anstrengen;
effortless adj mühelos
eg abbr = **exempli gratia (for example)** z.
B.
egg [eg] n Ei nt; **eggcup** n Eierbecher m;
eggplant n (US) Aubergine f; **eggshell** n
Eierschale f
ego ['i:gəʊ] (pl **-s**) n Ich nt; (self-esteem)
Selbstbewusstsein nt; **ego(t)ist**
['egəʊ(t)ɪst] n Egozentriker(in) m(f)
Egypt ['i:dʒɪpt] n Ägypten nt; **Egyptian**
[ɪ'dʒɪpʃən] adj ägyptisch ▷ n Ägypter(in)
m(f)
eiderdown ['aɪdədaʊn] n Daunendecke f
eight [eɪt] num acht; **at the age of ~** im

Alter von acht Jahren; **it's ~ (o'clock)** es ist
acht Uhr ▷ n (a. bus etc) Acht f; (boat)
Achter m; **eighteen** [eɪ'ti:n] num
achtzehn ▷ n Achtzehn f; see also **eight**;
eighteenth adj achtzehnte(r, s); see also
eighth; **eighth** [eɪtθ] adj achte(r, s); **the
~ of June** der achte Juni ▷ n (fraction)
Achtel nt; **an ~ of a litre** ein Achtelliter;
eightieth ['eɪtɪəθ] adj achtzigste(r, s); see
also **eighth**; **eighty** ['eɪtɪ] num achtzig
▷ n Achtzig f; see also **eight**
Eire ['eərə] n die Republik Irland
either ['aɪðə*] conj **~ ... or** entweder ...
oder ▷ pron **~ of the two** eine(r, s) von
beiden ▷ adj **on ~ side** auf beiden Seiten
▷ adv **I won't go ~** ich gehe auch nicht
eject [ɪ'dʒekt] vt ausstoßen; (person)
vertreiben
elaborate [ɪ'læbərət] adj (complex)
kompliziert; (plan) ausgeklügelt;
(decoration) kunstvoll ▷ vi [ɪ'læbəreɪt]
could you ~ on that? könntest du mehr
darüber sagen?
elastic [ɪ'læstɪk] adj elastisch; **~ band**
Gummiband nt
elbow ['elbəʊ] n Ellbogen m
elder ['eldə*] adj (of two) älter ▷ n
Ältere(r) mf; (Bot) Holunder m; **elderly** adj
ältere(r, s) ▷ n **the ~** die älteren Leute;
eldest ['eldɪst] adj älteste(r, s)
elect [ɪ'lekt] vt wählen; **he was ~ed
chairman** er wurde zum Vorsitzenden
gewählt; **election** [ɪ'lekʃən] n Wahl f;
election campaign n Wahlkampf m;
electioneering [ɪlekʃə'nɪərɪŋ] n
Wahlpropaganda f; **electorate** [ɪ'lektərɪt]
n Wähler pl
electric [ɪ'lektrɪk] adj elektrisch; (car,
motor, razor etc) Elektro-; **~ blanket**
Heizdecke f; **~ cooker** Elektroherd m;
~ current elektrischer Strom; **~ shock**
Stromschlag m; **electrical** adj elektrisch;
~ goods/appliances Elektrogeräte;
electrician [ɪlek'trɪʃən] n Elektriker(in)
m(f); **electricity** [ɪlek'trɪsɪtɪ] n
Elektrizität f; **electrocute** [ɪ'lektrəʊkju:t]
vt durch einen Stromschlag töten;
electronic [ɪlek'trɒnɪk] adj elektronisch
elegance ['elɪgəns] n Eleganz f; **elegant**
adj elegant
element ['elɪmənt] n Element nt; **an ~ of
truth** ein Körnchen Wahrheit;
elementary [elɪ'mentərɪ] adj einfach;

(*basic*) grundlegend; **~ stage**
Anfangsstadium *nt*; **~ school** (*US*)
Grundschule *f*; **~ maths/French**
Grundkenntnisse in
Mathematik/Französisch

elephant ['elɪfənt] *n* Elefant *m*

elevator ['elɪveɪtə*] *n* (*US*) Fahrstuhl *m*

eleven [ɪ'levn] *num* elf ▷ *n* (*team, bus etc*)
Elf *f see* **eight**; **eleventh** [ɪ'levnθ] *adj*
elfte(r, s) ▷ *n* (*fraction*) Elftel *nt see* **eighth**

eligible ['elɪdʒəbl] *adj* in Frage kommend;
(*for grant etc*) berechtigt; **~ for a**
pension/competition
pensions-/teilnahmeberechtigt;
~ bachelor begehrter Junggeselle

eliminate [ɪ'lɪmɪneɪt] *vt* ausschließen
(*from aus*), ausschalten; (*problem etc*)
beseitigen; **elimination** *n* Ausschluss *m*
(*from aus*); (*of problem etc*) Beseitigung *f*

elm [elm] *n* Ulme *f*

elope [ɪ'ləʊp] *vi* durchbrennen (*with sb mit*
jdm)

eloquent ['eləkwənt] *adj* redegewandt

else [els] *adv* **anybody/anything ~** (*in*
addition) sonst (noch) jemand/etwas;
(*other*) ein anderer/etwas anderes;
somebody ~ jemand anders; **everyone**
~ alle anderen; **or ~** sonst; **elsewhere** *adv*
anderswo, woanders; (*direction*)
woandershin

ELT *abbr* = **English Language Teaching**

e-mail, E-mail ['i:meɪl] *vi, vt* mailen (*sth*
to sb jdm etw) ▷ *n* E-Mail *f*; **e-mail**
address *n* E-Mail-Adresse *f*

emancipated [ɪ'mænsɪpeɪtɪd] *adj*
emanzipiert

embankment [ɪm'bæŋkmənt] *n*
Böschung *f*; (*for railway*) Bahndamm *m*

embargo [ɪm'bɑːgəʊ] (*pl* **-es**) *n* Embargo
nt

embark [ɪm'bɑːk] *vi* an Bord gehen

embarrass [ɪm'bærəs] *vt* in Verlegenheit
bringen; **embarrassed** *adj* verlegen;
embarrassing *adj* peinlich

embassy ['embəsɪ] *n* Botschaft *f*

embrace [ɪm'breɪs] *vt* umarmen ▷ *n*
Umarmung *f*

embroider [ɪm'brɔɪdə*] *vt* besticken;
embroidery *n* Stickerei *f*

embryo ['embrɪəʊ] (*pl* **-s**) *n* Embryo *m*

emerald ['emərəld] *n* Smaragd *m*

emerge [ɪ'mɜːdʒ] *vi* auftauchen; **it ~d**
that ... es stellte sich heraus, dass ...

emergency [ɪ'mɜːdʒənsɪ] *n* Notfall *m*
▷ *adj* Not-; **~ exit** Notausgang *m*; **~ room**
(*US*) Unfallstation *f*; **~ service** Notdienst
m; **~ stop** Vollbremsung *f*

emigrate ['emɪgreɪt] *vi* auswandern

emit [ɪ'mɪt] *vt* ausstoßen; (*heat*) abgeben

emotion [ɪ'məʊʃən] *n* Emotion *f*, Gefühl
nt; **emotional** *adj* (*person*) emotional;
(*experience, moment, scene*) ergreifend

emperor ['empərə*] *n* Kaiser *m*

emphasis ['emfəsɪs] *n* Betonung *f*;
emphasize ['emfəsaɪz] *vt* betonen;
emphatic, emphatically [ɪm'fætɪk, -lɪ]
adj, adv nachdrücklich

empire ['empaɪə*] *n* Reich *nt*

employ [ɪm'plɔɪ] *vt* beschäftigen; (*hire*)
anstellen; (*use*) anwenden; **employee**
[emplɔɪ'iː] *n* Angestellte(r) *mf*; **employer**
n Arbeitgeber(in) *m(f)*; **employment** *n*
Beschäftigung *f*; (*position*) Stellung *f*;
employment agency *n*
Stellenvermittlung *f*

empress ['emprɪs] *n* Kaiserin *f*

empty ['emptɪ] *adj* leer ▷ *vt* (*contents*)
leeren; (*container*) ausleeren

enable [ɪ'neɪbl] *vt* **to ~ sb to do sth** es
jdm ermöglichen, etw zu tun

enamel [ɪ'næməl] *n* Email *nt*; (*of teeth*)
Zahnschmelz *m*

enchanting [ɪn'tʃɑːntɪŋ] *adj* bezaubernd

enclose [ɪn'kləʊz] *vt* einschließen; (*in*
letter) beilegen (*in, with dat*); **enclosure**
[ɪn'kləʊʒə*] *n* (*for animals*) Gehege *nt*; (*in*
letter) Anlage *f*

encore ['ɒŋkɔː*] *n* Zugabe *f*

encounter [ɪn'kaʊntə*] *n* Begegnung *f*
▷ *vt* (*person*) begegnen +*dat*; (*difficulties*)
stoßen auf +*akk*

encourage [ɪn'kʌrɪdʒ] *vt* ermutigen;
encouragement *n* Ermutigung *f*

encyclopaedia [ensaɪkləʊ'piːdɪə] *n*
Lexikon *nt*, Enzyklopädie *f*

end [end] *n* Ende *nt*; (*of film, play etc*)
Schluss *m*; (*purpose*) Zweck *m*; **at the ~ of**
May Ende Mai; **in the ~** schließlich; **to**
come to an ~ zu Ende gehen ▷ *vt*
beenden ▷ *vi* enden; **end up** *vi* enden

endanger [ɪn'deɪndʒə*] *vt* gefährden;
~ed species vom Aussterben bedrohte Art

endeavour [ɪn'devə*] *n* Bemühung *f* ▷ *vt*
sich bemühen (*to do sth* etw zu tun)

ending ['endɪŋ] *n* (*of book*) Ausgang *m*;
(*last part*) Schluss *m*; (*of word*) Endung *f*

endive ['endaɪv] n Endiviensalat m

endless ['endlɪs] adj endlos; (possibilities) unendlich

endurance [ɪn'djʊərəns] n Ausdauer f; **endure** [ɪn'djʊə*] vt ertragen

enemy ['enɪmɪ] n Feind(in) m(f) ⊳ adj feindlich

energetic [enə'dʒetɪk] adj energiegeladen; (active) aktiv; **energy** ['enədʒɪ] n Energie f

enforce [ɪn'fɔ:s] vt durchsetzen; (obedience) erzwingen

engage [ɪn'geɪdʒ] vt (employ) einstellen; (singer, performer) engagieren; **engaged** adj verlobt; (toilet, telephone line) besetzt; **to get ~** sich verloben (to mit); **engaged tone** n (Brit Tel) Belegtzeichen nt; **engagement** n (to marry) Verlobung f; **~ ring** Verlobungsring m; **engaging** adj gewinnend

engine ['endʒɪn] n (Auto) Motor m; (Rail) Lokomotive f; **~ failure** (Auto) Motorschaden m; **~ trouble** (Auto) Defekt m am Motor; **engineer** [endʒɪ'nɪə*] n Ingenieur(in) m(f); (US Rail) Lokomotivführer(in) m(f); **engineering** [endʒɪ'nɪərɪŋ] n Technik f; (mechanical ~) Maschinenbau m; (subject) Ingenieurwesen nt; **engine immobilizer** n (Auto) Wegfahrsperre f

England ['ɪŋglənd] n England nt; **English** adj englisch; **he's ~** er ist Engländer; **the ~ Channel** der Ärmelkanal ⊳ n (language) Englisch nt; **in ~** auf Englisch; **to translate into ~** ins Englische übersetzen; (people) **the ~** pl die Engländer; **Englishman** (pl -men) n Engländer m; **Englishwoman** (pl -women) n Engländerin f

engrave [ɪn'greɪv] vt eingravieren; **engraving** n Stich m

engrossed [ɪn'grəʊst] adj vertieft (in sth in etw akk)

enigma [ɪ'nɪgmə] n Rätsel nt

enjoy [ɪn'dʒɔɪ] vt genießen; **I ~ reading** ich lese gern; **he ~s teasing her** es macht ihm Spaß, sie aufzuziehen; **did you ~ the film?** hat dir der Film gefallen?; **enjoyable** adj angenehm; (entertaining) unterhaltsam; **enjoyment** n Vergnügen nt; (stronger) Freude f (of an +dat)

enlarge [ɪn'lɑːdʒ] vt vergrößern; (expand) erweitern; **enlargement** n Vergrößerung f

enormous, enormously [ɪ'nɔ:məs, -lɪ] adj, adv riesig, ungeheuer

enough [ɪ'nʌf] adj genug; **that's ~** das reicht!; (stop it) Schluss damit!; **I've had ~** das hat mir gereicht; (to eat) ich bin satt ⊳ adv genug, genügend

enquire [ɪn'kwaɪə*] vi sich erkundigen (about nach); **enquiry** [ɪn'kwaɪərɪ] n (question) Anfrage f; (for information) Erkundigung f (about über +akk); (investigation) Untersuchung f; **'Enquiries'** „Auskunft"

enrol [ɪn'rəʊl] vi sich einschreiben; (for course, school) sich anmelden; **enrolment** n Einschreibung f, Anmeldung f

en suite [ɒn'swiːt] adj, n **room with ~ (bathroom)** Zimmer nt mit eigenem Bad

ensure [ɪn'ʃʊə*] vt sicherstellen

enter ['entə*] vt eintreten in +akk, betreten; (drive into) einfahren in +akk; (country) einreisen in +akk; (in list) eintragen; (Inform) eingeben; (race, contest) teilnehmen an +dat ⊳ vi (towards speaker) hereinkommen; (away from speaker) hineingehen

enterprise ['entəpraɪz] n (Comm) Unternehmen nt

entertain [entə'teɪn] vt (guest) bewirten; (amuse) unterhalten; **entertaining** adj unterhaltsam; **entertainment** n (amusement) Unterhaltung f

enthusiasm [ɪn'θjuːzɪæzəm] n Begeisterung f; **enthusiastic** [ɪnθjuːzɪ'æstɪk] adj begeistert (about von)

entice [ɪn'taɪs] vt locken; (lead astray) verleiten

entire, entirely [ɪn'taɪə*, -lɪ] adj, adv ganz

entitle [ɪn'taɪtl] vt (qualify) berechtigen (to zu); (name) betiteln

entrance ['entrəns] n Eingang m; (for vehicles) Einfahrt f; (entering) Eintritt m; (Theat) Auftritt m; **entrance exam** n Aufnahmeprüfung f; **entrance fee** n Eintrittsgeld nt

entrust [ɪn'trʌst] vt **to ~ sb with sth** jdm etw anvertrauen

entry ['entrɪ] n (way in) Eingang m; (entering) Eintritt m; (in vehicle) Einfahrt f; (into country) Einreise f; (admission) Zutritt m; (in diary, accounts) Eintrag m; **'no ~'** „Eintritt verboten"; (for vehicles) „Einfahrt verboten"; **entry phone** n Türsprechanlage f

E-number n (food additive) E-Nummer f

envelope ['envələʊp] n (Brief)umschlag m

enviable ['enviəbl] adj beneidenswert; **envious** ['enviəs] adj neidisch

environment [in'vaiərənmənt] n Umgebung f; (ecology) Umwelt f; **environmental** [invaiərən'məntəl] adj Umwelt-; **~ pollution** Umweltverschmutzung f; **environmentalist** n Umweltschützer(in) m(f)

envy ['envi] n Neid m (of auf +akk) ▷ vt beneiden (sb sth jdn um etw)

epic ['epik] n Epos nt; (film) Monumentalfilm m

epidemic [epi'demik] n Epidemie f

epilepsy [epi'lepsi] n Epilepsie f; **epileptic** [epi'leptik] adj epileptisch

episode ['episəʊd] n Episode f; (Tv) Fortsetzung f, Folge f

epoch ['i:pɒk] n Zeitalter nt, Epoche f

equal ['i:kwl] adj gleich (to +dat) ▷ n Gleichgestellte(r) mf ▷ vt gleichen; (match) gleichkommen +dat; **two times two ~s four** zwei mal zwei ist gleich vier; **equality** [i'kwɒliti] n Gleichheit f; (equal rights) Gleichberechtigung f; **equalize** vi (Sport) ausgleichen; **equalizer** n (Sport) Ausgleichstreffer m; **equally** adv gleich; (on the other hand) andererseits; **equation** [i'kweiʒən] n (Math) Gleichung f

equator [i'kweitə*] n Äquator m

equilibrium [i:kwi'libriəm] n Gleichgewicht nt

equip [i'kwip] vt ausrüsten; (kitchen) ausstatten; **equipment** n Ausrüstung f; (for kitchen) Ausstattung f; **electrical ~** Elektrogeräte pl

equivalent [i'kwivələnt] adj gleichwertig (to dat); (corresponding) entsprechend (to dat) ▷ n Äquivalent nt; (amount) gleiche Menge; (in money) Gegenwert m

era ['iərə] n Ära f, Zeitalter nt

erase [i'reiz] vt ausradieren; (tape, disk) löschen; **eraser** n Radiergummi m

erect [i'rekt] adj aufrecht ▷ vt (building, monument) errichten; (tent) aufstellen; **erection** n Errichtung f; (Anat) Erektion f

erode [i'rəʊd] vt zerfressen; (land) auswaschen; (rights, power) aushöhlen; **erosion** [i'rəʊʒən] n Erosion f

erotic [i'rɒtik] adj erotisch

err [ɜ:*] vi sich irren

errand ['erənd] n Besorgung f

erratic [i'rætik] adj (behaviour) unberechenbar; (bus link etc) unregelmäßig; (performance) unbeständig

error ['erə*] n Fehler m; **in ~** irrtümlicherweise; **error message** n (Inform) Fehlermeldung f

erupt [i'rʌpt] vi ausbrechen

escalator ['eskəleitə*] n Rolltreppe f

escalope ['eskələp] n Schnitzel nt

escape [i'skeip] n Flucht f; (from prison etc) Ausbruch m; **to have a narrow ~** gerade noch davonkommen; **there's no ~** (fig) es gibt keinen Ausweg ▷ vt (pursuers) entkommen +dat; (punishment etc) entgehen +dat ▷ vi (from pursuers) entkommen (from dat); (from prison etc) ausbrechen (from dat); (leak: gas) ausströmen; (water) auslaufen

escort ['eskɔ:t] n (companion) Begleiter(in) m(f); (guard) Eskorte f ▷ vt [i'skɔ:t] (lady) begleiten

especially [i'speʃəli] adv besonders

espionage ['espiənɑ:ʒ] n Spionage f

Esquire [i'skwaiə*] n (Brit: in address) **J. Brown, Esq** Herrn J. Brown

essay ['esei] n Aufsatz m; (literary) Essay m

essential [i'senʃəl] adj (necessary) unentbehrlich, unverzichtbar; (basic) wesentlich ▷ n **the ~s** pl das Wesentliche; **essentially** adv im Wesentlichen

establish [i'stæbliʃ] vt (set up) gründen; (introduce) einführen; (relations) aufnehmen; (prove) nachweisen; **to ~ that ...** feststellen, dass ...; **establishment** n Institution f; (business) Unternehmen nt

estate [i'steit] n Gut nt; (of deceased) Nachlass m; (housing ~) Siedlung f; (country house) Landsitz m; **estate agent** n (Brit) Grundstücksmakler(in) m(f), Immobilienmakler(in) m(f); **estate car** n (Brit) Kombiwagen m

estimate ['estimət] n Schätzung f; (Comm: of price) Kostenvoranschlag m ▷ ['estimeit] vt schätzen

estuary ['estjʊəri] n Mündung f

etching ['etʃiŋ] n Radierung f

eternal, eternally [i'tɜ:nl, -nəli] adj, adv ewig; **eternity** n Ewigkeit f

ethical ['eθɪkəl] adj ethisch; **ethics** ['eθɪks] npl Ethik f

Ethiopia [i:θɪ'əʊpɪə] n Äthiopien nt

ethnic ['eθnɪk] adj ethnisch; (clothes etc) landesüblich; **~ minority** ethnische Minderheit

EU abbr = **European Union** EU f

euphemism ['ju:fɪmɪzəm] n Euphemismus m

euro ['jʊərəʊ] (pl **-s**) (Fin) Euro m; **~ symbol** Eurozeichen nt; **Eurocheque** ['jʊərəʊtʃek] n Euroscheck m; **Europe** ['jʊərəp] n Europa nt; **European** [jʊərə'pi:ən] adj europäisch; **~ Parliament** Europäisches Parlament; **~ Union** Europäische Union ▷ n Europäer(in) m(f); **Eurosceptic** ['jʊərəʊskeptɪk] n Euroskeptiker(in) m(f); **Eurotunnel** n Eurotunnel m

evacuate [ɪ'vækjʊeɪt] vt (place) räumen; (people) evakuieren

evade [ɪ'veɪd] vt ausweichen +dat; (pursuers) sich entziehen +dat

evaluate [ɪ'væljʊeɪt] vt auswerten

evaporate [ɪ'væpəreɪt] vi verdampfen; (fig) verschwinden; **~d milk** Kondensmilch f

even ['i:vən] adj (flat) eben; (regular) gleichmäßig; (equal) gleich; (number) gerade; **the score is ~** es steht unentschieden ▷ adv sogar; **~ you** selbst (o sogar) du; **~ if** selbst wenn, wenn auch; **~ though** obwohl; **not ~** nicht einmal; **~ better** noch besser; **even out** vi (prices) sich einpendeln

evening ['i:vnɪŋ] n Abend m; **in the ~** abends, am Abend; **this ~** heute Abend; **evening class** n Abendkurs m; **evening dress** n (generally) Abendkleidung f; (woman's) Abendkleid nt

evenly ['i:vənlɪ] adv gleichmäßig

event [ɪ'vent] n Ereignis nt; (organized) Veranstaltung f; (Sport: discipline) Disziplin f; **in the ~ of** im Falle +gen; **eventful** adj ereignisreich

eventual [ɪ'ventʃʊəl] adj (final) letztendlich; **eventually** [ɪ'ventʃʊəlɪ] adv (at last) am Ende; (given time) schließlich

ever ['evə*] adv (at any time) je(mals); **don't ~ do that again** tu das ja nie wieder; **he's the best ~** er ist der Beste, den es je gegeben hat; **have you ~ been to the States?** bist du schon einmal in den

Staaten gewesen?; **for ~** (für) immer; **for ~ and ~** auf immer und ewig; **~ so ...** (fam) äußerst ...; **~ so drunk** ganz schön betrunken

every ['evrɪ] adj jeder/jede/jedes; **~ day** jeden Tag; **~ other day** jeden zweiten Tag; **~ five days** alle fünf Tage; **I have ~ reason to believe that ...** ich habe allen Grund anzunehmen, dass ...; **everybody** pron jeder, alle pl; **everyday** adj (commonplace) alltäglich; (clothes, language etc) Alltags-; **everyone** pron jeder, alle pl; **everything** pron alles; **everywhere** adv überall; (with direction) überallhin

evidence ['evɪdəns] n Beweise pl; (single piece) Beweis m; (testimony) Aussage f; (signs) Spuren pl; **evident, evidently** adj, adv offensichtlich

evil ['i:vl] adj böse ▷ n Böse(s) nt; **an ~** ein Übel

evolution [i:və'lu:ʃən] n Entwicklung f; (of life) Evolution f; **evolve** [ɪ'vɒlv] vi sich entwickeln

ex- [eks] pref Ex-, ehemalig; **~wife** frühere Frau, Exfrau f; **ex** n (fam) Verflossene(r) mf, Ex mf

exact [ɪg'zækt] adj genau; **exactly** adv genau; **not ~ fast** nicht gerade schnell

exaggerate [ɪg'zædʒəreɪt] vt, vi übertreiben; **exaggerated** adj übertreiben; **exaggeration** n Übertreibung f

exam [ɪg'zæm] n Prüfung f; **examination** [ɪgzæmɪ'neɪʃən] n (Med etc) Untersuchung f, Prüfung f; (at university) Examen nt; (at customs etc) Kontrolle f; **examine** [ɪg'zæmɪn] vt untersuchen (for auf +akk); (check) kontrollieren, prüfen; **examiner** n Prüfer(in) m(f)

example [ɪg'zɑ:mpl] n Beispiel nt; **for ~** zum Beispiel

excavation [ekskə'veɪʃən] n Ausgrabung f

exceed [ɪk'si:d] vt überschreiten, übertreffen; **exceedingly** adv äußerst

excel [ɪk'sel] vt übertreffen; **he ~led himself** er hat sich selbst übertroffen ▷ vi sich auszeichnen (in in +dat, at bei); **excellent, excellently** ['eksələnt, -lɪ] adj, adv ausgezeichnet

except [ɪk'sept] prep **~ for** außer +dat; **~ for** abgesehen von ▷ vt ausnehmen; **exception** [ɪk'sepʃən] n Ausnahme f;

exceptional, exceptionally [ɪk'sepʃənl, -nəlɪ] *adj, adv* außergewöhnlich

excess [ek'ses] *n* Übermaß *nt* (*of* an +*dat*); **excess baggage** *n* Übergepäck *nt*; **excesses** *npl* Exzesse *pl*; (*drink, sex*) Ausschweifungen *pl*; **excess fare** *n* Nachlösegebühr *f*; **excessive, excessively** *adj, adv* übermäßig; **excess weight** *n* Übergewicht *nt*

exchange [ɪks'tʃeɪndʒ] *n* Austausch *m* (*for* gegen); (*of bought items*) Umtausch *m* (*for* gegen); (*Fin*) Wechsel *m*; (*Tel*) Vermittlung *f*, Zentrale *f* ▷ *vt* austauschen; (*goods*) tauschen; (*bought items*) umtauschen (*for* gegen); (*money, blows*) wechseln; **exchange rate** *n* Wechselkurs *m*

excite [ɪk'saɪt] *vt* erregen; **excited** *adj* aufgeregt; **to get ~** sich aufregen; **exciting** *adj* aufregend; (*book, film*) spannend

exclamation [eksklə'meɪʃən] *n* Ausruf *m*; **exclamation mark, exclamation point** (*US*) *n* Ausrufezeichen *nt*

exclude [ɪks'kluːd] *vt* ausschließen; **exclusion** [ɪks'kluːʒən] *n* Ausschluss *m*; **exclusive** [ɪks'kluːsɪv] *adj* (*select*) exklusiv; (*sole*) ausschließlich; **exclusively** *adv* ausschließlich

excrement ['ekskrɪmənt] *n* Kot *m*, Exkremente *pl*

excruciating [ɪks'kruːʃieɪtɪŋ] *adj* fürchterlich, entsetzlich

excursion [ɪks'kɜːʃən] *n* Ausflug *m*

excusable [ɪks'kjuːzəbl] *adj* entschuldbar; **excuse** [ɪks'kjuːz] *vt* entschuldigen; **~ me** Entschuldigung!; **to ~ sb for sth** jdm etw verzeihen; **to ~ sb from sth** jdn von etw befreien ▷ [ɪks'kjuːs] *n* Entschuldigung *f*, Ausrede *f*

ex-directory [eksdɪ'rektərɪ] *adj* **to be ~** (*Brit Tel*) nicht im Telefonbuch stehen

execute ['eksɪkjuːt] *vt* (*carry out*) ausführen; (*kill*) hinrichten; **execution** *n* (*killing*) Hinrichtung *f*; (*carrying out*) Ausführung *f*; **executive** [ɪg'zekjʊtɪv] *n* (*Comm*) leitender Angestellter, leitende Angestellte

exemplary [ɪg'zemplərɪ] *adj* beispielhaft

exempt [ɪg'zempt] *adj* befreit (*from* von) ▷ *vt* befreien

exercise ['eksəsaɪz] *n* (*in school, sports*) Übung *f*; (*movement*) Bewegung *f*; **to get more ~** mehr Sport treiben; **exercise bike** *n* Heimtrainer *m*; **exercise book** *n* Heft *nt*

exert [ɪg'zɜːt] *vt* (*influence*) ausüben

exhaust [ɪg'zɔːst] *n* (*fumes*) Abgase *pl*; (*Auto*) Auspuff *m*; **exhausted** *adj* erschöpft; **exhausting** *adj* anstrengend

exhibit [ɪg'zɪbɪt] *n* (*in exhibition*) Ausstellungsstück *nt*; **exhibition** [eksɪ'bɪʃən] *n* Ausstellung *f*; **exhibitor** *n* Aussteller(in) *m(f)*

exhilarating [ɪg'zɪləreɪtɪŋ] *adj* belebend, erregend

exile ['eksaɪl] *n* Exil *nt*; (*person*) Verbannte(r) *mf* ▷ *vt* verbannen

exist [ɪg'zɪst] *vi* existieren; (*live*) leben (*on* von); **existence** *n* Existenz *f*; **to come into ~** entstehen; **existing** *adj* bestehend

exit ['eksɪt] *n* Ausgang *m*; (*for vehicles*) Ausfahrt *f*; **exit poll** *n* Umfrage direkt nach dem Wahlgang

exorbitant [ɪg'zɔːbɪtənt] *adj* astronomisch

exotic [ɪg'zɒtɪk] *adj* exotisch

expand [ɪks'pænd] *vt* ausdehnen, erweitern ▷ *vi* sich ausdehnen; **expansion** [ɪks'pænʃən] *n* Expansion *f*, Erweiterung *f*

expect [ɪk'spekt] *vt* erwarten; (*suppose*) annehmen; **he ~s me to do it** er erwartet, dass ich es mache; **I ~ it'll rain** es wird wohl regnen; **I ~ so** ich denke schon ▷ *vi* **to be ~ing** ein Kind erwarten

expedition [ekspɪ'dɪʃən] *n* Expedition *f*

expenditure [ɪk'spendɪtʃə*] *n* Ausgaben *pl*

expense [ɪk'spens] *n* Kosten *pl*; (*single cost*) Ausgabe *f*; (**business**) **~s** *pl* Spesen *pl*; **at sb's ~** auf jds Kosten; **expensive** [ɪk'spensɪv] *adj* teuer

experience [ɪk'spɪərɪəns] *n* Erfahrung *f*; (*particular incident*) Erlebnis *nt*; **by/from ~** aus Erfahrung ▷ *vt* erfahren, erleben; (*hardship*) durchmachen; **experienced** *adj* erfahren

experiment [ɪk'sperɪmənt] *n* Versuch *m*, Experiment *nt* ▷ *vi* experimentieren

expert ['ekspɜːt] *n* Experte *m*, Expertin *f*; (*professional*) Fachmann *m*, Fachfrau *f*; (*Jur*) Sachverständige(r) *mf* ▷ *adj* fachmännisch; **expertise** [ekspə'tiːz] *n* Sachkenntnis *f*

expire [ɪk'spaɪə*] *vi* (*end*) ablaufen; **expiry date** [ɪk'spaɪərɪdeɪt] *n* Verfallsdatum *nt*

explain [ɪk'spleɪn] vt erklären (sth to sb jdm etw); **explanation** [eksplə'neɪʃən] n Erklärung f

explicit [ɪk'splɪsɪt] adj ausdrücklich, deutlich

explode [ɪk'spləʊd] vi explodieren

exploit [ɪk'splɔɪt] vt ausbeuten

explore [ɪk'splɔ:*] vt erforschen

explosion [ɪk'spləʊʒən] n Explosion f; **explosive** [ɪk'spləʊsɪv] adj explosiv ▷ n Sprengstoff m

export [ek'spɔ:t] vt, vi exportieren ▷ ['ekspɔ:t] n Export m ▷ adj (trade) Export-

expose [ɪk'spəʊz] vt (to danger etc) aussetzen (to dat); (uncover) freilegen; (imposter) entlarven; **exposed** adj (position) ungeschützt; **exposure** [ɪk'spəʊʒə*] n (Med) Unterkühlung f; (Foto: time) Belichtung(szeit) f; **24 ~s** 24 Aufnahmen

express [ɪk'spres] adj (speedy) Express-, Schnell-; **~ delivery** Eilzustellung f ▷ n (Rail) Schnellzug m ▷ vt ausdrücken ▷ vr **to ~ oneself** sich ausdrücken; **expression** [ɪk'spreʃən] n (phrase) Ausdruck m; (look) Gesichtsausdruck m; **expressive** adj ausdrucksvoll; **expressway** n (US) Schnellstraße f

extend [ɪk'stend] vt (arms) ausstrecken; (lengthen) verlängern; (building) vergrößern, ausbauen; (business, limits) erweitern; **extension** [ɪk'stenʃən] n (lengthening) Verlängerung f; (of building) Anbau m; (Tel) Anschluss m; (of business, limits) Erweiterung f; **extensive** [ɪk'stensɪv] adj (knowledge) umfangreich; (use) häufig; **extent** [ɪk'stent] n (length) Länge f; (size) Ausdehnung f; (scope) Umfang m, Ausmaß nt; **to a certain/large ~** in gewissem/hohem Maße

exterior [ek'stɪərɪə*] n Äußere(s) nt

external [ek'stɜ:nl] adj äußere(r, s), Außen-; **externally** adv äußerlich

extinct [ɪk'stɪŋkt] adj (species) ausgestorben

extinguish [ɪk'stɪŋgwɪʃ] vt löschen; **extinguisher** n Löschgerät nt

extra ['ekstrə] adj zusätzlich; **~ charge** Zuschlag m; **~ time** (Sport) Verlängerung f ▷ adv besonders; **~ large** (clothing) übergroß ▷ npl **~s** zusätzliche Kosten pl;

(food) Beilagen pl; (accessories) Zubehör nt; (for car etc) Extras pl

extract [ɪk'strækt] vt herausziehen (from aus); (tooth) ziehen ▷ ['ekstrækt] n (from book etc) Auszug m

extraordinary [ɪk'strɔ:dnrɪ] adj außerordentlich; (unusual) ungewöhnlich; (amazing) erstaunlich

extreme [ɪk'stri:m] adj äußerste(r, s); (drastic) extrem ▷ n Extrem nt; **extremely** adv äußerst, höchst; **extreme sports** npl Extremsportarten pl; **extremist** [ɪk'stri:mɪst] adj extremistisch ▷ n Extremist m

extricate ['ekstrɪkeɪt] vt befreien (from aus)

extrovert ['ekstrəʊvɜ:t] adj extrovertiert

exuberance [ɪg'zu:bərəns] n Überschwang m; **exuberant** adj überschwänglich

exultation [egzʌl'teɪʃən] n Jubel m

eye [aɪ] n Auge nt; **to keep an ~ on sb/sth** auf jdn/etw aufpassen ▷ vt mustern; **eyebrow** n Augenbraue f; **eyelash** n Wimper f; **eyelid** n Augenlid nt; **eyeliner** n Eyeliner m; **eyeopener** n **that was an ~** das hat mir die Augen geöffnet; **eyeshadow** n Lidschatten m; **eyesight** n Sehkraft f; **eyesore** n Schandfleck m; **eye witness** n Augenzeuge m, Augenzeugin f

f

fabric ['fæbrɪk] *n* Stoff *m*

fabulous ['fæbjʊləs] *adj* sagenhaft

façade [fə'sɑːd] *n* (*a. fig*) Fassade *f*

face [feɪs] *n* Gesicht *nt*; (*of clock*) Zifferblatt *nt*; (*of mountain*) Wand *f*, **in the ~ of** trotz +*gen*; **to be ~ to ~** (*people*) einander gegenüberstehen ▷ *vt, vi* (*person*) gegenüberstehen +*dat*; (*at table*) gegenübersitzen +*dat*; **to ~ north** nach Norden gehen; **to ~ (up to) the facts** den Tatsachen ins Auge sehen; **to be ~d with sth** mit etw konfrontiert sein; **face cream** *n* Gesichtscreme *f*; **face lift** *n* Gesichtsstraffung *f*; (*fig*) Verschönerung *f*; **face powder** *n* Gesichtspuder *m*

facet ['fæsɪt] *n* (*fig*) Aspekt *m*

face value *n* Nennwert *m*

facial ['feɪʃəl] *adj* Gesichts- ▷ *n* (*fam*) (kosmetische) Gesichtsbehandlung

facilitate [fə'sɪlɪteɪt] *vt* erleichtern

facility [fə'sɪlɪtɪ] *n* (*building etc to be used*) Einrichtung *f*, Möglichkeit *f*; (*installation*) Anlage *f*; (*skill*) Gewandtheit *f*

fact [fækt] *n* Tatsache *f*; **as a matter of ~, in ~** eigentlich, tatsächlich

factor ['fæktə*] *n* Faktor *m*

factory ['fæktərɪ] *n* Fabrik *f*; **factory outlet** *n* Fabrikverkauf *m*

factual ['fæktjʊəl] *adj* sachlich

faculty ['fækəltɪ] *n* Fähigkeit *f*; (*at university*) Fakultät *f*; (*US: teaching staff*) Lehrkörper *m*

fade [feɪd] *vi* (*a. fig*) verblassen; **faded** *adj* verblasst, verblichen

faff about ['fæfəbaʊt] *vi* (*Brit fam*) herumwursteln

fag [fæg] *n* (*Brit fam: cigarette*) Kippe *f*; (*US fam pej*) Schwule(r) *m*

Fahrenheit ['færənhaɪt] *n* Fahrenheit

fail [feɪl] *vt* (*exam*) nicht bestehen ▷ *vi* versagen; (*plan, marriage*) scheitern; (*student*) durchfallen; (*eyesight*) nachlassen; **words ~ me** ich bin sprachlos; **failing** *n* Schwäche *f*; **failure** ['feɪljə*] *n* (*person*) Versager(in) *m(f)*; (*act*) (*a. Tech*) Versagen *nt*; (*of engine etc*) Ausfall *m*; (*of plan, marriage*) Scheitern *nt*

faint [feɪnt] *adj* schwach; (*sound*) leise; (*fam*) **I haven't the ~est (idea)** ich habe keine Ahnung ▷ *vi* ohnmächtig werden (*with* vor +*dat*); **faintness** *n* (*Med*) Schwächegefühl *nt*

fair [feə*] *adj* (*hair*) blond; (*skin*) hell; (*just*) gerecht, fair; (*reasonable*) ganz ordentlich; (*in school*) befriedigend; (*weather*) schön; (*wind*) günstig; **a ~ number/amount of** ziemlich viele/viel ▷ *adv* **to play ~** fair spielen; (*fig*) fair sein; **~ enough** in Ordnung! ▷ *n* (*fun~*) Jahrmarkt *m*; (*Comm*) Messe *f*; **fair-haired** *adj* blond; **fairly** *adv* (*honestly*) fair; (*rather*) ziemlich

fairy ['feərɪ] *n* Fee *f*; **fairy tale** *n* Märchen *nt*

faith [feɪθ] *n* (*trust*) Vertrauen *nt* (*in sb zu* jdm); (*Rel*) Glaube *m*; **faithful, faithfully** *adj, adv* treu; **Yours ~ly** Hochachtungsvoll

fake [feɪk] *n* (*thing*) Fälschung *f* ▷ *adj* vorgetäuscht ▷ *vt* fälschen

falcon ['fɔːlkən] *n* Falke *m*

fall [fɔːl] (*fell, fallen*) *vi* fallen; (*from a height, badly*) stürzen; **to ~ ill** krank werden; **to ~ asleep** einschlafen; **to ~ in love** sich verlieben ▷ *n* Fall *m*; (*accident, fig: of regime*) Sturz *m*; (*decrease*) Sinken *nt* (*in* +*gen*); (*US: autumn*) Herbst *m*; **fall apart** *vi* auseinanderfallen; **fall behind** *vi* zurückbleiben; (*with work, rent*) in Rückstand geraten; **fall down** *vi* (*person*) hinfallen; **fall off** *vi* herunterfallen;

(decrease) zurückgehen; **fall out** vi
herausfallen; (quarrel) sich streiten; **fall
over** vi hinfallen; **fall through** vi (plan
etc) ins Wasser fallen

fallen ['fɔ:lən] pp of **fall**

fallout ['fɔ:laʊt] n radioaktiver
Niederschlag, Fall-out m

false [fɔ:ls] adj falsch; (artificial)
künstlich; **false alarm** n blinder Alarm;
false start n (Sport) Fehlstart m; **false
teeth** npl (künstliches) Gebiss

fame [feɪm] n Ruhm m

familiar [fə'mɪlɪə*] adj vertraut, bekannt;
to be ~ with vertraut sein mit, gut
kennen; **familiarity** [fəmɪlɪ'ærɪtɪ] n
Vertrautheit f

family ['fæmɪlɪ] n Familie f; (including
relations) Verwandtschaft f; **family man** n
Familienvater m; **family name** n
Familienname m, Nachname m

famine ['fæmɪn] n Hungersnot f;
famished ['fæmɪʃt] adj (fam)
ausgehungert

famous ['feɪməs] adj berühmt

fan [fæn] n (hand-held) Fächer m; (Elec)
Ventilator m; (admirer) Fan m

fanatic [fə'nætɪk] n Fanatiker(in) m(f)

fancy ['fænsɪ] adj (elaborate) kunstvoll;
(unusual) ausgefallen ⊳ vt (like) gern
haben; **he fancies her** er steht auf sie;
~ that stell dir vor!, so was!; **fancy dress**
n Kostüm nt, Verkleidung f

fan heater ['fænhi:tə*] n Heizlüfter m;
fanlight n Oberlicht nt

fan mail n Fanpost f

fantasise ['fæntəsaɪz] vi träumen (about
von); **fantastic** [fæn'tæstɪk] adj (a. fam)
fantastisch; **that's ~** (fam) das ist ja toll!;
fantasy ['fæntəzɪ] n Fantasie f

far [fɑ:*] (**further** o **farther, furthest** o
farthest) adj weit; **the ~ end of the room**
das andere Ende des Zimmers; **the Far
East** der Ferne Osten ⊳ adv weit; **~ better**
viel besser; **by ~ the best** bei weitem
der/die/das Beste; **as ~ as ...** bis zum o zur
...; (with place name) bis nach ...; **as ~ as I'm
concerned** was mich betrifft, von mir aus;
so ~ soweit, bisher; **faraway** adj weit
entfernt; (look) verträumt

fare [feə*] n Fahrpreis m; (money) Fahrgeld
nt

farm [fɑ:m] n Bauernhof m, Farm f;
farmer n Bauer m, Bäuerin f,

Landwirt(in) m(f); **farmhouse** n
Bauernhaus nt; **farming** n
Landwirtschaft f; **farmland** n Ackerland
nt; **farmyard** n Hof m

far-reaching ['fɑ:ri:tʃɪŋ] adj weit
reichend; **far-sighted** adj weitsichtig;
(fig) weitblickend

farther ['fɑ:ðə*] adj, adv comparative of
far; see **further**

farthest ['fɑ:ðɪst] adj, adv superlative of
far; see **furthest**

fascinating ['fæsɪneɪtɪŋ] adj
faszinierend; **fascination** n Faszination f

fascism ['fæʃɪzəm] n Faschismus m;
fascist ['fæʃɪst] adj faschistisch
⊳ n Faschist(in) m(f)

fashion ['fæʃən] n (clothes) Mode f;
(manner) Art (und Weise) f; **to be in ~** (in)
Mode sein; **out of ~** unmodisch;
fashionable, fashionably adj, adv
(clothes, person) modisch; (author, pub etc) in
Mode

fast [fɑ:st] adj schnell; (dye) waschecht;
to be ~ (clock) vorgehen ⊳ adv schnell;
(firmly) fest; **to be ~ asleep** fest schlafen
⊳ n Fasten nt ⊳ vi fasten; **fastback** n
(Auto) Fließheck nt

fasten ['fɑ:sn] vt (attach) befestigen (to
an +dat); (do up) zumachen; **~ your
seatbelts** bitte anschnallen; **fastener,
fastening** n Verschluss m

fast food n Fast Food nt; **fast forward** n
(for tape) Schnellvorlauf m; **fast lane** n
Überholspur f

fat [fæt] adj dick; (meat) fett ⊳ n (Anat,
Gastr, Chem) Fett nt

fatal ['feɪtl] adj tödlich

fate [feɪt] n Schicksal nt

fat-free adj (food) fettfrei

father ['fɑ:ðə*] n Vater m; (priest) Pfarrer
m ⊳ vt (child) zeugen; **Father Christmas**
n der Weihnachtsmann; **father-in-law** (pl
fathers-in-law) n Schwiegervater m

fatigue [fə'ti:g] n Ermüdung f

fattening ['fætnɪŋ] adj **to be ~** dick
machen; **fatty** ['fætɪ] adj (food) fettig

faucet ['fɔ:sɪt] n (US) Wasserhahn m

fault [fɔ:lt] n Fehler m; (Tech) Defekt m;
(Elec) Störung f; (blame) Schuld f; **it's your
~** du bist daran schuld; **faulty** adj
fehlerhaft; (Tech) defekt

favor (US), **favour** ['feɪvə*] n (approval)
Gunst f; (kindness) Gefallen m; **in ~ of** für;

I'm in ~ (of going) ich bin dafür(, dass wir gehen); **to do sb a ~** jdm einen Gefallen tun ▷ vt (prefer) vorziehen; **favourable** adj günstig (to, for für); **favourite** ['feɪvərɪt] n Liebling m, Favorit(in) m(f) ▷ adj Lieblings-

fax [fæks] vt faxen ▷ n Fax nt; **fax number** n Faxnummer f

faze [feɪz] vt (fam) aus der Fassung bringen

FBI abbr = **Federal Bureau of Investigation** FBI nt

fear [fɪə*] n Angst f (of vor +dat) ▷ vt befürchten; **I ~ that most** davor habe ich am meisten Angst; **fearful** adj (timid) ängstlich, furchtsam; (terrible) fürchterlich; **fearless** adj furchtlos

feasible ['fi:zəbl] adj machbar

feast [fi:st] n Festessen nt

feather ['feðə*] n Feder f

feature ['fi:tʃə*] n (facial) (Gesichts)zug m; (characteristic) Merkmal nt; (of car etc) Ausstattungsmerkmal nt; (in the press) (Cine) Feature nt ▷ vt bringen, (als Besonderheit) zeigen; **feature film** n Spielfilm m

February ['februərɪ] n Februar m; see also **September**

fed [fed] pt, pp of **feed**

federal ['fedərəl] adj Bundes-; **the Federal Republic of Germany** die Bundesrepublik Deutschland

fed-up ['fedʌp] adj **to be ~ with sth** etw satt haben; **I'm ~** ich habe die Nase voll

fee [fi:] n Gebühr f; (of doctor, lawyer) Honorar nt

feeble ['fi:bl] adj schwach

feed [fi:d] (**fed, fed**) vt (baby, animal) füttern; (support) ernähren ▷ n (for baby) Mahlzeit f; (for animals) Futter nt; (Inform: paper ~) Zufuhr f; **feed in** vt (information) eingeben; **feedback** n (information) Feed-back nt

feel [fi:l] (**felt, felt**) vt (sense) fühlen; (pain) empfinden; (touch) anfassen; (think) meinen ▷ vi (person) sich fühlen; **I ~ cold** mir ist kalt; **do you ~ like a walk?** hast du Lust, spazieren zu gehen?; **feeling** n Gefühl nt

feet [fi:t] pl of **foot**

fell [fel] pt of **fall** ▷ vt (tree) fällen

fellow ['felau] n Kerl m, Typ m; **~ citizen** Mitbürger(in) m(f); **~ countryman**

Landsmann m; **~ worker** Mitarbeiter(in) m(f)

felt [felt] pt, pp of **feel** ▷ n Filz m; **felt tip, felt-tip pen** n Filzstift m

female ['fi:meɪl] n (of animals) Weibchen nt ▷ adj weiblich; **~ doctor** Ärztin f; **~ dog** Hündin f; **feminine** ['femɪnɪn] adj weiblich; **feminist** ['femɪnɪst] n Feminist(in) m(f) ▷ adj feministisch

fence [fens] n Zaun m

fencing n (Sport) Fechten nt

fender ['fendə*] n (US Auto) Kotflügel m

fennel ['fenl] n Fenchel m

fern [fɜ:n] n Farn m

ferocious [fə'rəʊʃəs] adj wild

ferry ['ferɪ] n Fähre f ▷ vt übersetzen

fertile ['fɜ:taɪl] adj fruchtbar; **fertility** [fə'tɪlɪtɪ] n Fruchtbarkeit f; **fertilize** ['fɜ:tɪlaɪz] vt (Bio) befruchten; (Agr: land) düngen; **fertilizer** n Dünger m

festival ['festɪvəl] n (Rel) Fest nt; (Art, Mus) Festspiele pl; (pop music) Festival nt; **festive** ['festɪv] adj festlich; **festivities** [fe'stɪvɪtɪz] n Feierlichkeiten pl

fetch [fetʃ] vt holen; (collect) abholen; (in sale, money) einbringen; **fetching** adj reizend

fetish ['fetɪʃ] n Fetisch m

fetus ['fi:təs] n (US) Fötus m

fever ['fi:və*] n Fieber nt; **feverish** adj (Med) fiebrig; (fig) fieberhaft

few [fju:] adj, pron pl wenige pl; **a ~** pl ein paar; **fewer** adj weniger; **fewest** adj wenigste(r, s)

fiancé [fɪ'ɑ:nseɪ] n Verlobte(r) m; **fiancée** n Verlobte f

fiasco [fɪ'æskəʊ] (pl **-s** o US **-es**) n Fiasko nt

fiber (US), **fibre** ['faɪbə*] n Faser f; (material) Faserstoff m

fickle ['fɪkl] adj unbeständig

fiction ['fɪkʃən] n (novels) Prosaliteratur f; **fictional, fictitious** [fɪk'tɪʃəs] adj erfunden

fiddle ['fɪdl] n Geige f; (trick) Betrug m ▷ vt (accounts, results) frisieren; **fiddle with** vt herumfummeln an +dat; **fiddly** adj knifflig

fidelity [fɪ'delɪtɪ] n Treue f

fidget ['fɪdʒɪt] vi zappeln; **fidgety** adj zappelig

field [fi:ld] n Feld nt; (grass-covered) Wiese f; (fig: of work) (Arbeits)gebiet nt

fierce [fɪəs] *adj* heftig; (*animal, appearance*) wild; (*criticism, competition*) scharf

fifteen [fɪfˈtiːn] *num* fünfzehn ▷ *n* Fünfzehn *f*; *see also* **eight**; **fifteenth** *adj* fünfzehnte(r, s); *see also* **eighth**; **fifth** [fɪfθ] *adj* fünfte(r, s) ▷ *n* (*fraction*) Fünftel *nt*; *see also* **eighth**; **fifty** [ˈfɪftɪ] *num* fünfzig ▷ *n* Fünfzig *f*; *see also* **eight**; **fiftieth** *adj* fünfzigste(r, s); *see also* **eighth**

fig [fɪg] *n* Feige *f*

fight [faɪt] (**fought, fought**) *vi* kämpfen (*with, against* gegen, *for, over* um) ▷ *vt* (*person*) kämpfen mit; (*fig: disease, fire etc*) bekämpfen ▷ *n* Kampf *m*; (*brawl*) Schlägerei *f*; (*argument*) Streit *m*; **fight back** *vi* zurückschlagen; **fight off** *vt* abwehren; **fighter** *n* Kämpfer(in) *m(f)*

figurative [ˈfɪgərətɪv] *adj* übertragen

figure [ˈfɪgə*] *n* (*person*) Gestalt *f*; (*of person*) Figur *f*; (*number*) Zahl *f*, Ziffer *f*; (*amount*) Betrag *m*; **a four-figure sum** eine vierstellige Summe ▷ *vt* (*US: think*) glauben ▷ *vi* (*appear*) erscheinen; **figure out** *vt* (*work out*) herausbekommen; **I can't figure him out** ich werde aus ihm nicht schlau; **figure skating** *n* Eiskunstlauf *m*

file [faɪl] *n* (*tool*) Feile *f*; (*dossier*) Akte *f*; (*Inform*) Datei *f*; (*folder*) Aktenordner *m*; **on ~** in den Akten ▷ *vt* (*metal, nails*) feilen; (*papers*) ablegen (*under* unter) ▷ *vi* **to ~ in/out** hintereinander hereinkommen/hinausgehen; **filing cabinet** *n* Aktenschrank *m*

fill [fɪl] *vt* füllen; (*tooth*) plombieren; (*post*) besetzen; **fill in** *vt* (*hole*) auffüllen; (*form*) ausfüllen; (*tell*) informieren (*on* über); **fill out** *vt* (*form*) ausfüllen; **fill up** *vi* (*Auto*) voll tanken

fillet [ˈfɪlɪt] *n* Filet *nt*

filling [ˈfɪlɪŋ] *n* (*Gastr*) Füllung *f*; (*for tooth*) Plombe *f*; **filling station** *n* Tankstelle *f*

film [fɪlm] *n* Film *m* ▷ *vt* (*scene*) filmen; **film star** *n* Filmstar *m*; **film studio** *n* Filmstudio *nt*

filter [ˈfɪltə*] *n* Filter *m*; (*traffic lane*) Abbiegespur *f* ▷ *vt* filtern

filth [fɪlθ] *n* Dreck *m*; **filthy** *adj* dreckig

fin [fɪn] *n* Flosse *f*

final [ˈfaɪnl] *adj* letzte(r, s); (*stage, round*) End-; (*decision, version*) endgültig; **~ score** Schlussstand *m* ▷ *n* (*Sport*) Endspiel *nt*; (*competition*) Finale *nt*; **~s** *pl* Abschlussexamen *nt*; **finalize** *vt* die endgültige Form geben +*dat*; **finally** *adv* (*lastly*) zuletzt; (*eventually*) schließlich, endlich

finance [faɪˈnæns] *n* Finanzwesen *nt*; **~s** *pl* Finanzen *pl* ▷ *vt* finanzieren; **financial** [faɪˈnænʃəl] *adj* finanziell; (*adviser, crisis, policy etc*) Finanz-

find [faɪnd] (**found, found**) *vt* finden; **he was found dead** er wurde tot aufgefunden; **I ~ myself in difficulties** ich befinde mich in Schwierigkeiten; **she ~s it difficult/easy** es fällt ihr schwer/leicht; **find out** *vt* herausfinden; **findings** *npl* (*Jur*) Ermittlungsergebnis *nt*; (*of report, Med*) Befund *m*

fine [faɪn] *adj* (*thin*) dünn, fein; (*good*) gut; (*splendid*) herrlich; (*clothes*) elegant; (*weather*) schön; **I'm ~** es geht mir gut; **that's ~** das ist OK ▷ *adv* (*well*) gut ▷ *n* (*Jur*) Geldstrafe *f* ▷ *vt* (*Jur*) mit einer Geldstrafe belegen; **fine arts** *npl* **the ~** die schönen Künste *pl*; **finely** *adv* (*cut*) dünn; (*ground*) fein

finger [ˈfɪŋgə*] *n* Finger *m* ▷ *vt* herumfingern an +*dat*; **fingernail** *n* Fingernagel *m*; **fingerprint** *n* Fingerabdruck *m*; **fingertip** *n* Fingerspitze *f*

finicky [ˈfɪnɪkɪ] *adj* (*person*) pingelig; (*work*) knifflig

finish [ˈfɪnɪʃ] *n* Ende *nt*; (*Sport*) Finish *nt*; (*line*) Ziel *nt*; (*of product*) Verarbeitung *f* ▷ *vt* beenden; (*book etc*) zu Ende lesen; (*food*) aufessen; (*drink*) austrinken ▷ *vi* zu Ende gehen; (*song, story*) enden; (*person*) fertig sein; (*stop*) aufhören; **have you ~ed?** bist du fertig?; **to ~ first/second** (*Sport*) als erster/zweiter durchs Ziel gehen; **finishing line** *n* Ziellinie *f*

Finland [ˈfɪnlənd] *n* Finnland *nt*; **Finn** *n* Finne *m*, Finnin *f*; **Finnish** *adj* finnisch ▷ *n* (*language*) Finnisch *nt*

fir [fɜː*] *n* Tanne *f*

fire [faɪə*] *n* Feuer *nt*; (*house etc*) Brand *m*; **to set ~ to sth** etw in Brand stecken; **to be on ~** brennen ▷ *vt* (*bullets, rockets*) abfeuern; (*fam: dismiss*) feuern ▷ *vi* (*Auto: engine*) zünden; **to ~ at sb** auf jdn schießen; **fire alarm** *n* Feuermelder *m*; **fire brigade** *n* Feuerwehr *f*; **fire engine**

n Feuerwehrauto *nt*; **fire escape** *n* Feuerleiter *f*; **fire extinguisher** *n* Feuerlöscher *m*; **firefighter** *n* Feuerwehrmann *m*, Feuerwehrfrau *f*; **fireman** *n* Feuerwehrmann *m*; **fireplace** *n* (offener) Kamin; **fireproof** *adj* feuerfest; **fire station** *n* Feuerwache *f*; **firewood** *n* Brennholz *nt*; **fireworks** *npl* Feuerwerk *nt*

firm [fɜːm] *adj* fest; (*person*) **to be ~** entschlossen auftreten ▷ *n* Firma *f*

first [fɜːst] *adj* erste(r, s) ▷ *adv* (*at first*) zuerst; (*firstly*) erstens; (*arrive, finish*) als erste(r); (*happen*) zum ersten Mal; **~ of all** zuallererst ▷ *n* (*person*) Erste(r) *mf*; (*Auto: gear*) erster Gang; **at ~** zuerst, anfangs; **first aid** *n* erste Hilfe; **first-class** *adj* erstklassig; (*compartment, ticket*) erster Klasse; **~ mail** (*Brit*) bevorzugt beförderte Post ▷ *adv* (*travel*) erster Klasse; **first floor** *n* (*Brit*) erster Stock; (*US*) Erdgeschoss *nt*; **first lady** *n* (*US*) Frau *f* des Präsidenten; **firstly** *adv* erstens; **first name** *n* Vorname *m*; **first night** *n* (*Theat*) Premiere *f*; **first-rate** *adj* erstklassig

fir tree *n* Tannenbaum *m*

fish [fɪʃ] *n* Fisch *m*; **~ and chips** (*Brit*) frittierter Fisch mit Pommes frites ▷ *vi* fischen; (*with rod*) angeln; **to go ~ing** fischen/angeln gehen; **fishbone** *n* Gräte *f*; **fishcake** *n* Fischfrikadelle *f*; **fish farm** *n* Fischzucht *f*; **fish finger** *n* (*Brit*) Fischstäbchen *nt*; **fishing** ['fɪʃɪŋ] *n* Fischen *nt*; (*with rod*) Angeln *nt*; (*as industry*) Fischerei *f*; **fishing boat** *n* Fischerboot *nt*; **fishing line** *n* Angelschnur *f*; **fishing rod** *n* Angelrute *f*; **fishing village** *n* Fischerdorf *nt*; **fishmonger** ['fɪʃmʌŋɡə*] *n* Fischhändler(in) *m(f)*; **fish stick** *n* (*US*) Fischstäbchen *nt*; **fish tank** *n* Aquarium *nt*

fishy ['fɪʃɪ] *adj* (*fam: suspicious*) faul

fist [fɪst] *n* Faust *f*

fit [fɪt] *adj* (*Med*) gesund; (*Sport*) in Form, fit; (*suitable*) geeignet; **to keep ~** sich in Form halten ▷ *vt* passen +*dat*; (*attach*) anbringen (*to* an +*dat*); (*install*) einbauen (*in* in +*akk*) ▷ *vi* passen; (*in space, gap*) hineinpassen ▷ *n* (*of clothes*) Sitz *m*; (*Med*) Anfall *m*; **it's a good ~** es passt gut; **fit in** *vt* (*accommodate*) unterbringen; (*find time for*) einschieben ▷ *vi* (*in space*)

hineinpassen; (*plans, ideas*) passen; **he doesn't ~ (here)** er passt nicht hierher; **to ~ with sb's plans** sich mit jds Plänen vereinbaren lassen; **fitness** *n* (*Med*) Gesundheit *f*; (*Sport*) Fitness *f*; **fitted carpet** *n* Teppichboden *m*; **fitted kitchen** *n* Einbauküche *f*; **fitting** *adj* passend ▷ *n* (*of dress*) Anprobe *f*; **~s** *pl* Ausstattung *f*

five [faɪv] *num* fünf ▷ *n* Fünf *f*; *see also* **eight**; **fiver** *n* (*Brit fam*) Fünfpfundschein *m*

fix [fɪks] *vt* befestigen (*to* an +*dat*); (*settle*) festsetzen; (*place, time*) ausmachen; (*repair*) reparieren; **fixer** *n* (*drug addict*) Fixer(in) *m(f)*; **fixture** ['fɪkstʃə*] *n* (*Sport*) Veranstaltung *f*; (*match*) Spiel *nt*; (*in building*) Installationsteil *nt*; **~s (and fittings)** *pl* Ausstattung *f*

fizzy ['fɪzɪ] *adj* sprudelnd; **~ drink** Limo *f*

flabbergasted ['flæbəɡɑːstɪd] *adj* (*fam*) platt

flabby ['flæbɪ] *adj* (*fat*) wabbelig

flag [flæɡ] *n* Fahne *f*; **flagstone** *n* Steinplatte *f*

flake [fleɪk] *n* Flocke *f* ▷ *vi* **to ~ (off)** abblättern

flamboyant [flæm'bɔɪənt] *adj* extravagant

flame [fleɪm] *n* Flamme *f*; (*person*) **an old ~** eine alte Liebe

flan [flæn] *n* (*fruit ~*) Obstkuchen *m*

flannel ['flænl] *n* Flanell *m*; (*Brit: face ~*) Waschlappen *m*; (*fam: waffle*) Geschwafel *nt* ▷ *vi* herumlabern

flap [flæp] *n* Klappe *f*; (*fam*) **to be in a ~** rotieren ▷ *vt* (*wings*) schlagen mit ▷ *vi* flattern

flared [fleəd] *adj* (*trousers*) mit Schlag; **flares** *npl* Schlaghose *f*

flash [flæʃ] *n* Blitz *m*; (*news ~*) Kurzmeldung *f*; (*Foto*) Blitzlicht *nt*; **in a ~** im Nu ▷ *vt* **to ~ one's (head)lights** die Lichthupe betätigen ▷ *vi* aufblinken; (*brightly*) aufblitzen; **flashback** *n* Rückblende *f*, Flashback *m*; **flashlight** ['flæʃlaɪt] *n* (*Photo*) Blitzlicht *nt*; (*US: torch*) Taschenlampe *f*; **flashy** *adj* grell, schrill; (*pej*) protzig

flat [flæt] *adj* flach; (*surface*) eben; (*drink*) abgestanden; (*tyre*) platt; (*battery*) leer; (*refusal*) glatt ▷ *n* (*Brit: rooms*) Wohnung *f*; (*Auto*) Reifenpanne *f*; **flat screen** *n*

(*Inform*) Flachbildschirm m; **flatten** vt platt machen, einebnen

flatter ['flætə*] vt schmeicheln +dat; **flattering** adj schmeichelhaft

flatware ['flætweə] n (US) Besteck nt

flavor (US), **flavour** ['fleɪvə*] n Geschmack m ▷ vt Geschmack geben +dat; (*with spices*) würzen; **flavouring** n Aroma nt

flaw [flɔː] n Fehler m; **flawless** adj fehlerlos; (*complexion*) makellos

flea [fliː] n Floh m

fled [fled] pt, pp of **flee**

flee [fliː] (**fled, fled**) vi fliehen

fleece [fliːs] n (*of sheep*) Vlies nt; (*soft material*) Fleece m; (*jacket*) Fleecejacke f

fleet [fliːt] n Flotte f

Flemish ['flemɪʃ] adj flämisch ▷ n (*language*) Flämisch nt

flesh [fleʃ] n Fleisch nt

flew [fluː] pt of **fly**

flex [fleks] n (*Brit Elec*) Schnur f

flexibility [fleksɪ'bɪlɪtɪ] n Biegsamkeit f; (*fig*) Flexibilität f; **flexible** ['fleksɪbl] adj biegsam; (*plans, person*) flexibel; **flexitime** n gleitende Arbeitszeit, Gleitzeit f

flicker ['flɪkə*] vi flackern; (*Tv*) flimmern

flies [flaɪz] pl of **fly** ▷ n

flight [flaɪt] n Flug m; (*escape*) Flucht f; **~ of stairs** Treppe f; **flight attendant** n Flugbegleiter(in) m(f); **flight recorder** n Flugschreiber m

flimsy ['flɪmzɪ] adj leicht gebaut, nicht stabil; (*thin*) hauchdünn; (*excuse*) fadenscheinig

fling [flɪŋ] (**flung, flung**) vt schleudern ▷ n **to have a ~** eine (kurze) Affäre haben

flint [flɪnt] n Feuerstein m

flip [flɪp] vt schnippen; **to ~ a coin** eine Münze werfen; **flip through** vt (*book*) durchblättern; **flipchart** n Flipchart nt

flipper ['flɪpə*] n Flosse f

flirt [flɜːt] vi flirten

float [fləʊt] n (*for fishing*) Schwimmer m; (*in procession*) Festwagen m; (*money*) Wechselgeld nt ▷ vi schwimmen; (*in air*) schweben

flock [flɒk] n (*of sheep*) (*Rel*) Herde f; (*of birds*) Schwarm m; (*of people*) Schar f

flog [flɒg] vt auspeitschen; (*Brit fam*) verscheuern

flood [flʌd] n Hochwasser nt, Überschwemmung f; (*fig*) Flut f ▷ vt überschwemmen; **floodlight** n Flutlicht nt; **floodlit** adj (*building*) angestrahlt

floor [flɔː*] n Fußboden m; (*storey*) Stock m; **ground ~** (*Brit*), **first ~** (*US*) Erdgeschoss nt; **first ~** (*Brit*), **second ~** (*US*) erster Stock; **floorboard** n Diele f

flop [flɒp] n (*fam: failure*) Reinfall m, Flop m ▷ vi misslingen, floppen

floppy disk ['flɒpɪ'dɪsk] n Diskette f

Florence ['flɒrəns] n Florenz nt

florist ['flɒrɪst] n Blumenhändler(in) m(f)

flounder ['flaʊndə*] n (*fish*) Flunder f

flour ['flaʊə*] n Mehl nt

flourish ['flʌrɪʃ] vi gedeihen; (*business*) gut laufen; (*boom*) florieren ▷ vt (*wave about*) schwenken; **flourishing** adj blühend

flow [fləʊ] n Fluss m; **to go with the ~** mit dem Strom schwimmen ▷ vi fließen

flower ['flaʊə*] n Blume f ▷ vi blühen; **flower bed** n Blumenbeet nt; **flowerpot** n Blumentopf m

flown [fləʊn] pp of **fly**

flu [fluː] n (*fam*) Grippe f

fluent adj (*Italian etc*) fließend; **to be ~ in German** fließend Deutsch sprechen

fluid ['fluːɪd] n Flüssigkeit f ▷ adj flüssig

flung [flʌŋ] pt, pp of **fling**

fluorescent [flʊə'resnt] adj fluoreszierend, Leucht-

flush [flʌʃ] n (*lavatory*) Wasserspülung f; (*blush*) Röte f ▷ vt (*lavatory*) spülen

flute [fluːt] n Flöte f

fly [flaɪ] (**flew, flown**) vt, vi fliegen; **how time flies** wie die Zeit vergeht! ▷ n (*insect*) Fliege f; **~/flies** (*pl*) (*on trousers*) Hosenschlitz m; **fly-drive** n Urlaub m mit Flug und Mietwagen; **flyover** n (*Brit*) Straßenüberführung f, Eisenbahnüberführung f; **flysheet** n Überzelt nt

FM abbr = **frequency modulation** ≈ UKW

FO abbr = **Foreign Office** ≈ AA nt

foal [fəʊl] n Fohlen nt

foam [fəʊm] n Schaum m ▷ vi schäumen

fob off [fɒb ɒf] vt **to fob sb off with sth** jdm etw andrehen

focus ['fəʊkəs] n Brennpunkt m; **in/out of ~** (*photo*) scharf/unscharf; (*camera*) scharf/unscharf eingestellt ▷ vt (*camera*) scharf stellen ▷ vi sich konzentrieren (*on auf +akk*)

foetus ['fiːtəs] n Fötus m

fog [fɒg] n Nebel m; **foggy** adj neblig; **fog**

light n (Auto: at rear) Nebelschlussleuchte f

foil [fɔɪl] vt vereiteln ▷ n Folie f

fold [fəʊld] vt falten ▷ vi (fam: business) eingehen ▷ n Falte f; **fold up** vt (map etc) zusammenfalten; (chair etc) zusammenklappen ▷ vi (fam: business) eingehen; **folder** n (portfolio) Aktenmappe f; (pamphlet) Broschüre f; (Inform) Ordner m; **folding** adj zusammenklappbar; (bicycle, chair) Klapp-

folk [fəʊk] n Leute pl; (Mus) Folk m; **my ~s** pl (fam) meine Leute ▷ adj Volks-

follow ['fɒləʊ] vt folgen +dat; (pursue) verfolgen; (understand) folgen können +dat; (career, news etc) verfolgen; **as ~s** wie folgt ▷ vi folgen; (result) sich ergeben (from aus); **follow up** vt (request, rumour) nachgehen +dat, weiter verfolgen; **follower** n Anhänger(in) m(f); **following** adj folgend; **the ~ day** am (darauf)folgenden Tag ▷ prep nach; **follow up** n (event, book etc) Fortsetzung f

fond [fɒnd] adj **to be ~ of** gern haben; **fondly** adv (with love) liebevoll; **fondness** n Vorliebe f, (for people) Zuneigung f

fondue ['fɒndu:] n Fondue nt

font [fɒnt] n Taufbecken nt; (Typo) Schriftart f

food [fu:d] n Essen nt, Lebensmittel pl; (for animals) Futter nt; (groceries) Lebensmittel pl; **food poisoning** n Lebensmittelvergiftung f; **food processor** n Küchenmaschine f; **foodstuff** n Lebensmittel nt

fool [fu:l] n Idiot m, Narr m; **to make a ~ of oneself** sich blamieren ▷ vt (deceive) hereinlegen ▷ vi **to ~ around** herumalbern; (waste time) herumtrödeln; **foolish** adj dumm; **foolproof** adj idiotensicher

foot [fʊt] (pl **feet**) n [fi:t] Fuß m; (measure) Fuß m (30,48 cm); **on ~** zu Fuß ▷ vt (bill) bezahlen; **foot-and-mouth disease** n Maul- und Klauenseuche f; **football** n Fußball m; (US: American ~) Football m; **footballer** n Fußballspieler(in) m(f); **footbridge** n Fußgängerbrücke f; **footing** n (hold) Halt m; **footlights** npl Rampenlicht nt; **footnote** n Fußnote f; **footpath** n Fußweg m;

footprint n Fußabdruck m; **footwear** n Schuhwerk nt

○ KEYWORD

for [fɔ:*] prep **1** für; **is this for me?** ist das für mich?; **the train for London** der Zug nach London; **he went for the paper** er ging die Zeitung holen; **give it to me — what for?** gib es mir — warum?
2 (because of) wegen; **for this reason** aus diesem Grunde
3 (referring to distance); **there are roadworks for 5 km** die Baustelle ist 5 km lang; **we walked for miles** wir sind meilenweit gegangen
4 (referring to time) seit; (: with future sense) für; **he was away for 2 years** er war zwei Jahre lang weg
5 (+infin clauses): **it is not for me to decide** das kann ich nicht entscheiden; **for this to be possible ...** damit dies möglich wird/wurde ...
6 (in spite of) trotz +gen or (inf) dat; **for all his complaints** obwohl er sich ständig beschwert
▷ conj denn

forbade [fə'bæd] pt of **forbid**

forbid [fə'bɪd] (**forbade, forbidden**) vt verbieten

force [fɔ:s] n Kraft f; (compulsion) Zwang m, Gewalt; **to come into ~** in Kraft treten; **the Forces** pl die Streitkräfte ▷ vt zwingen; **forced** adj (smile) gezwungen; **~ landing** Notlandung f; **forceful** adj kraftvoll

forceps ['fɔ:seps] npl Zange f

forearm ['fɔ:rɑ:m] n Unterarm m

forecast ['fɔ:kɑ:st] vt voraussagen; (weather) vorhersagen ▷ n Vorhersage f

forefinger ['fɔ:fɪŋɡə*] n Zeigefinger m

foreground ['fɔ:ɡraʊnd] n Vordergrund m

forehand ['fɔ:hænd] n (Sport) Vorhand f

forehead ['fɔ:hed, 'fɒrɪd] n Stirn f

foreign ['fɒrən] adj ausländisch; **foreigner** n Ausländer(in) m(f); **foreign exchange** n Devisen pl; **foreign language** n Fremdsprache f; **foreign minister, foreign secretary** n Außenminister(in) m(f); **foreign policy** n Außenpolitik f

foremost ['fɔ:məʊst] *adj* erste(r, s); *(leading)* führend

forerunner ['fɔ:rʌnə*] *n* Vorläufer(in) *m(f)*

foresee [fɔ:'si:] *irr vt* vorhersehen; **foreseeable** *adj* absehbar

forest ['fɒrɪst] *n* Wald *m*; **forestry** ['fɒrɪstrɪ] *n* Forstwirtschaft *f*

forever [fə'revə*] *adv* für immer

forgave [fə'geɪv] *pt of* **forgive**

forge [fɔ:dʒ] *n* Schmiede *f* ▷ *vt* schmieden; *(fake)* fälschen; **forger** *n* Fälscher(in) *m(f)*; **forgery** *n* Fälschung *f*

forget [fə'get] *(forgot, forgotten) vt, vi* vergessen; **to ~ about sth** etw vergessen; **forgetful** *adj* vergesslich; **forgetfulness** *n* Vergesslichkeit *f*; **forget-me-not** *n* Vergissmeinnicht *nt*

forgive [fə'gɪv] *(forgave, forgiven) irr vt* verzeihen; **to ~ sb for sth** jdm etw verzeihen

forgot [fə'gɒt] *pt of* **forget**

forgotten [fə'gɒtn] *pp of* **forget**

fork [fɔ:k] *n* Gabel *f*; *(in road)* Gabelung *f* ▷ *vi (road)* sich gabeln

form [fɔ:m] *n (shape)* Form *f*, Klasse *f*; *(document)* Formular *nt*; *(person)* **to be in (good) ~** in Form sein ▷ *vt* bilden

formal ['fɔ:məl] *adj* förmlich, formell; **formality** [fɔ:'mælɪtɪ] *n* Formalität *f*

format ['fɔ:mæt] *n* Format *nt* ▷ *vt (Inform)* formatieren

former ['fɔ:mə*] *adj* frühere(r, s); *(opposite of latter)* erstere(r, s); **formerly** *adv* früher

formidable ['fɔ:mɪdəbl] *adj* gewaltig; *(opponent)* stark

formula ['fɔ:mjʊlə] *n* Formel *f*

formulate ['fɔ:mjʊleɪt] *vt* formulieren

forth [fɔ:θ] *adv* **and so ~** und so weiter; **forthcoming** [fɔ:θ'kʌmɪŋ] *adj* kommend, bevorstehend

fortify ['fɔ:tɪfaɪ] *vt* verstärken; *(for protection)* befestigen

fortieth ['fɔ:tɪəθ] *adj* vierzigste(r, s); *see also* **eighth**

fortnight ['fɔ:tnaɪt] *n* vierzehn Tage *pl*

fortress ['fɔ:trɪs] *n* Festung *f*

fortunate ['fɔ:tʃənɪt] *adj* glücklich; **I was ~** ich hatte Glück; **fortunately** *adv* zum Glück; **fortune** ['fɔ:tʃən] *n (money)* Vermögen *nt*; **good ~** Glück *nt*; **fortune-teller** *n* Wahrsager(in) *m(f)*

forty ['fɔ:tɪ] *num* vierzig ▷ *n* Vierzig *f*; *see also* **eight**

forward ['fɔ:wəd] *adv* vorwärts ▷ *n (Sport)* Stürmer(in) *m(f)* ▷ *vt (send on)* nachsenden; *(inform)* weiterleiten; **forwards** *adv* vorwärts

foster child ['fɒstətʃaɪld] *n* Pflegekind *nt*; **foster parents** *npl* Pflegeeltern *pl*

fought [fɔ:t] *pt, pp of* **fight**

foul [faʊl] *adj (weather)* schlecht; *(smell)* übel ▷ *n (Sport)* Foul *nt*

found [faʊnd] *pt, pp of* **find** ▷ *vt (establish)* gründen; **foundations** [faʊn'deɪʃənz] *npl* Fundament *nt*

fountain ['faʊntɪn] *n* Springbrunnen *m*; **fountain pen** *n* Füller *m*

four [fɔ:*] *num* vier ▷ *n* Vier *f*; *see also* **eight**; **fourteen** ['fɔ:'ti:n] *num* vierzehn ▷ *n* Vierzehn *f*; *see also* **eight**; **fourteenth** *adj* vierzehnte(r, s); *see also* **eighth**; **fourth** [fɔ:θ] *adj* vierte(r, s); *see also* **eighth**

four-wheel drive *n* Allradantrieb *m*; *(car)* Geländewagen *m*

fowl [faʊl] *n* Geflügel *nt*

fox [fɒks] *n (a. fig)* Fuchs *m*

fraction ['frækʃən] *n (Math)* Bruch *m*; *(part)* Bruchteil *m*; **fracture** ['fræktʃə*] *n (Med)* Bruch *m* ▷ *vt* brechen

fragile ['frædʒaɪl] *adj* zerbrechlich

fragment ['frægmənt] *n* Bruchstück *nt*

fragrance ['freɪɡrəns] *n* Duft *m*; **fragrant** *adj* duftend

frail [freɪl] *adj* gebrechlich

frame [freɪm] *n* Rahmen *m*; *(of spectacles)* Gestell *nt*; **~ of mind** Verfassung *f* ▷ *vt* einrahmen; **to ~ sb** *(fam: incriminate)* jdm etwas anhängen; **framework** *n* Rahmen *m*, Struktur *f*

France [frɑ:ns] *n* Frankreich *nt*

frank [fræŋk] *adj* offen

frankfurter ['fræŋkfə:tə*] *n* (Frankfurter) Würstchen *nt*

frankly ['fræŋklɪ] *adv* offen gesagt; **quite ~** ganz ehrlich; **frankness** *n* Offenheit *f*

frantic ['fræntɪk] *adj (activity)* hektisch; *(effort)* verzweifelt; **~ with worry** außer sich vor Sorge

fraud [frɔ:d] *n (trickery)* Betrug *m*; *(person)* Schwindler(in) *m(f)*

freak [fri:k] *n* Anomalie *f*; *(animal, person)* Missgeburt *f*; *(fam: fan)* Fan *m*, Freak *m* ▷ *adj (conditions)* außergewöhnlich, seltsam; **freak out** vi (fam) ausflippen

freckle ['frekl] n Sommersprosse f

free [fri:] adj, adv frei; (without payment) gratis, kostenlos; **for ~** umsonst ▷ vt befreien; **freebie** ['fri:bɪ] n (fam) Werbegeschenk nt; **it was a ~** es war gratis; **freedom** ['fri:dəm] n Freiheit f; **freefone** ['fri:fəʊn] adj **a ~ number** eine gebührenfreie Nummer; **free kick** n (Sport) Freistoß m

freelance ['fri:lɑ:ns] adj freiberuflich tätig; (artist) freischaffend ▷ n Freiberufler(in) m(f)

free-range ['fri:reɪndʒ] adj (hen) frei laufend; **~ eggs** pl Freilandeier pl

freeway ['fri:weɪ] n (US) (gebührenfreie) Autobahn

freeze [fri:z] (froze, frozen) vi (feel cold) frieren; (of lake etc) zufrieren; (water etc) gefrieren ▷ vt einfrieren; **freezer** n Tiefkühltruhe f; (in fridge) Gefrierfach nt; **freezing** adj eiskalt; **I'm ~** mir ist eiskalt; **freezing point** n Gefrierpunkt m

freight [freɪt] n (goods) Fracht f; (money charged) Frachtgebühr f; **freight car** n (US) Güterwagen m; **freight train** n (US) Güterzug m

French [frentʃ] adj französisch ▷ n (language) Französisch nt; **the ~** pl die Franzosen; **French bean** n grüne Bohne; **French bread** n Baguette f; **French dressing** n Vinaigrette f; **French fries** (US) npl Pommes frites pl; **French kiss** n Zungenkuss m; **Frenchman** (pl **-men**) n Franzose m; **French toast** n (US) in Ei und Milch getunktes gebratenes Brot; **French window(s)** n(pl) Balkontür f, Terrassentür f; **Frenchwoman** (pl **-women**) n Französin f

frequency ['fri:kwənsɪ] n Häufigkeit f; (Phys) Frequenz f; **frequent** ['fri:kwənt] adj häufig; **frequently** adv häufig

fresco ['freskəʊ] (pl **-es**) n Fresko nt

fresh [freʃ] adj frisch; (new) neu; **freshen** vi **to ~ (up)** (person) sich frisch machen; **freshman** (pl **-men**) n Erstsemester nt; **freshwater fish** n Süßwasserfisch m

Fri abbr = **Friday** Fr

friction ['frɪkʃən] n (a. fig) Reibung f

Friday ['fraɪdeɪ] n Freitag m; see also **Tuesday**

fridge [frɪdʒ] n Kühlschrank m

fried [fraɪd] adj gebraten; **~ potatoes** Bratkartoffeln pl; **~ egg** Spiegelei nt; **~ rice** gebratener Reis

friend [frend] n Freund(in) m(f); (less close) Bekannte(r) mf; **to make ~s with sb** sich mit jdm anfreunden; **we're good ~s** wir sind gut befreundet; **friendly** adj freundlich; **to be ~ with sb** mit jdm befreundet sein ▷ n (Sport) Freundschaftsspiel nt; **friendship** ['frendʃɪp] n Freundschaft f

fright [fraɪt] n Schrecken m; **frighten** vt erschrecken; **to be ~ed** Angst haben; **frightening** adj beängstigend

frill [frɪl] n Rüsche f; **~s** (fam) Schnickschnack

fringe [frɪndʒ] n (edge) Rand m; (on shawl etc) Fransen pl; (hair) Pony m

frivolous ['frɪvələs] adj leichtsinnig; (remark) frivol

frizzy ['frɪzɪ] adj kraus

frog [frɒg] n Frosch m

○ **KEYWORD**

from [frɒm] prep **1** (indicating starting place) von; (indicating origin etc) aus +dat; **a letter/telephone call from my sister** ein Brief/Anruf von meiner Schwester; **where do you come from?** woher kommen Sie?; **to drink from the bottle** aus der Flasche trinken

2 (indicating time) von ... an; (:past) seit; **from one o'clock to or until or till two** von ein Uhr bis zwei; **from January (on)** ab Januar

3 (indicating distance) von ... (entfernt)

4 (indicating price, number etc) ab +dat; **from £10** ab £10; **there were from 20 to 30 people there** es waren zwischen 20 und 30 Leute da

5 (indicating difference): **he can't tell red from green** er kann nicht zwischen Rot und Grün unterscheiden; **to be different from sb/sth** anders sein als jd/etw

6 (because of, based on): **from what he says** aus dem, was er sagt; **weak from hunger** schwach vor Hunger

front [frʌnt] n Vorderseite f; (of house) Fassade f; (in war, of weather) Front f; (at *seaside)* Promenade *f;* **in ~, at the ~** vorne; **in ~ of** vor; **up ~** *(in advance)* vorher, im Voraus ▷ *adj* vordere(r, s), Vorder-; *(first)* vorderste(r, s); **~ door** Haustür *f;* **~ page** Titelseite *f;* **~ seat** Vordersitz *m;* **~ wheel** Vorderrad *nt*

frontier ['frʌntɪə*] *n* Grenze *f*

front-wheel drive *n (Auto)* Frontantrieb *m*

frost [frɒst] *n* Frost *m; (white ~)* Reif *m;* **frosting** *n (US)* Zuckerguss *m;* **frosty** *adj* frostig

froth [frɒθ] *n* Schaum *m;* **frothy** *adj* schaumig

frown [fraʊn] *vi* die Stirn runzeln

froze [frəʊz] *pt of* **freeze**

frozen [frəʊzn] *pp of* **freeze** ▷ *adj (food)* tiefgekühlt, Tiefkühl-

fruit [fruːt] *n (as collective, a. type)* Obst *nt; (single ~, a. fig)* Frucht *f;* **fruit machine** *n* Spielautomat *m;* **fruit salad** *n* Obstsalat *m*

frustrated [frʌ'streɪtɪd] *adj* frustriert; **frustratration** *n* Frustration *f,* Frust *m*

fry [fraɪ] *vt* braten; **frying pan** *n* Bratpfanne *f*

fuchsia ['fjuːʃə] *n* Fuchsie *f*

fuck [fʌk] *vt (vulg)* ficken; **~ off** verpiss dich!; **fucking** *adj (vulg)* Scheiß-

fudge [fʌdʒ] *n* weiche Karamellsüßigkeit

fuel [fjʊəl] *n* Kraftstoff *m; (for heating)* Brennstoff *m;* **fuel consumption** *n* Kraftstoffverbrauch *m;* **fuel gauge** *n* Benzinuhr *f;* **fuel oil** *n* Gasöl *nt;* **fuel rod** *n* Brennstab *m;* **fuel tank** *n* Tank *m; (for oil)* Öltank *m*

fugitive ['fjuːdʒɪtɪv] *n* Flüchtling *m*

fulfil [fʊl'fɪl] *vt* erfüllen

full [fʊl] *adj* voll; *(person: satisfied)* satt; *(member, employment)* Voll(zeit)-; *(complete)* vollständig; **~ of ...** voller ... *gen;* **full beam** *n (Auto)* Fernlicht *nt;* **full moon** *n* Vollmond *m;* **full stop** *n* Punkt *m;* **full-time** *adj* **~ job** Ganztagsarbeit *f;* **fully** *adv* völlig; *(recover)* voll und ganz; *(discuss)* ausführlich

fumble ['fʌmbl] *vi* herumfummeln *(with, at* an *+dat)*

fumes [fjuːmz] *npl* Dämpfe *pl; (of car)* Abgase *pl*

fun [fʌn] *n* Spaß *m;* **for ~** zum Spaß; **it's ~** es macht Spaß; **to make ~ of** sich lustig machen über *+akk*

function ['fʌŋkʃən] *n* Funktion *f; (event)*

Feier *f; (reception)* Empfang *m* ▷ *vi* funktionieren; **function key** *n (Inform)* Funktionstaste *f*

fund [fʌnd] *n* Fonds *m;* **~s** *pl* Geldmittel *pl*

fundamental [fʌndə'mentl] *adj* grundlegend; **fundamentally** *adv* im Grunde

funding ['fʌndɪŋ] *n* finanzielle Unterstützung

funeral ['fjuːnərəl] *n* Beerdigung *f*

funfair ['fʌnfeə*] *n* Jahrmarkt *m*

fungus ['fʌŋgəs] *(pl* **fungi** *o* **funguses)** *n* Pilz *m*

funicular [fjuː'nɪkjʊlə*] *n* Seilbahn *f*

funnel ['fʌnl] *n* Trichter *m; (of steamer)* Schornstein *m*

funny ['fʌnɪ] *adj (amusing)* komisch, lustig; *(strange)* seltsam

fur [fɜː*] *n* Pelz *m; (of animal)* Fell *nt*

furious ['fjʊərɪəs] *adj* wütend *(with sb* auf jdn)

furnished ['fɜːnɪʃd] *adj* möbliert; **furniture** ['fɜːnɪtʃə*] *n* Möbel *pl;* **piece of ~** Möbelstück *nt*

further ['fɜːðə*] *comparative of* **far** ▷ *adj* weitere(r, s); **~ education** Weiterbildung *f;* **until ~ notice** bis auf weiteres ▷ *adv* weiter; **furthest** ['fɜːðɪst] *superlative of* **far** ▷ *adj* am weitesten entfernt ▷ *adv* am weitesten

fury ['fjʊərɪ] *n* Wut *f*

fuse [fjuːz] *n (Elec)* Sicherung *f* ▷ *vi (Elec)* durchbrennen; **fuse box** *n* Sicherungskasten *m*

fuss [fʌs] *n* Theater *nt;* **to make a ~** ein Theater machen; **fussy** *adj (difficult)* schwierig, kompliziert; *(attentive to detail)* pingelig

future ['fjuːtʃə*] *adj* künftig ▷ *n* Zukunft *f*

fuze *(US) see* **fuse**

fuzzy ['fʌzɪ] *adj (indistinct)* verschwommen; *(hair)* kraus

g

gable ['geɪbl] n Giebel m

gadget ['gædʒɪt] n Vorrichtung f, Gerät nt

Gaelic ['geɪlɪk] adj gälisch ▷ n (language) Gälisch nt

gain [geɪn] vt (obtain, win) gewinnen; (advantage, respect) sich verschaffen; (wealth) erwerben; (weight) zunehmen ▷ vi (improve) gewinnen (in an +dat); (clock) vorgehen ▷ n Gewinn m (in an +dat)

gale [geɪl] n Sturm m

gall bladder ['gɔ:lblædə*] n Gallenblase f

gallery ['gælərɪ] n Galerie f, Museum nt

gallon ['gælən] n Gallone f; ((Brit) 4,546 l, (US) 3,79 l)

gallop ['gæləp] n Galopp m ▷ vi galoppieren

gallstone ['gɔ:lstəʊn] n Gallenstein m

Gambia ['gæmbɪə] n Gambia nt

gamble ['gæmbl] vi um Geld spielen, wetten ▷ n **it's a ~** es ist riskant; **gambling** n Glücksspiel nt

game [geɪm] n Spiel nt; (animals) Wild nt; **a ~ of chess** eine Partie Schach; **~s** (in school) Sport m; **game show** n (TV) Gameshow f

gammon ['gæmən] n geräucherter Schinken

gang [gæŋ] n (of criminals, youths) Bande f, Gang f, Clique f ▷ vt **to ~ up on** sich verschwören gegen

gangster ['gæŋstə*] n Gangster m

gangway ['gæŋweɪ] n (for ship) Gangway f; (Brit: aisle) Gang m, Gangway f

gap [gæp] n (hole) Lücke f; (in time) Pause f; (in age) Unterschied m

gape [geɪp] vi (mit offenem Mund) starren

gap year n Jahr zwischen Schulabschluss und Studium, das oft zu Auslandsaufenthalten genutzt wird

garage ['gærɑ:ʒ] n Garage f; (for repair) (Auto)werkstatt f; (for fuel) Tankstelle f

garbage ['gɑ:bɪdʒ] n (US) Müll m; (fam: nonsense) Quatsch m; **garbage can** n (US) Mülleimer m; (outside) Mülltonne f; **garbage truck** n (US) Müllwagen m

garbled ['gɑ:bld] adj (story) verdreht

garden ['gɑ:dn] n Garten m; **(public) ~s** Park m; **garden centre** n Gartencenter nt; **gardener** n Gärtner(in) m(f); **gardening** n Gartenarbeit f

gargle ['gɑ:gl] vi gurgeln

gargoyle ['gɑ:gɔɪl] n Wasserspeier m

garlic ['gɑ:lɪk] n Knoblauch m; **garlic bread** n Knoblauchbrot nt; **garlic butter** n Knoblauchbutter f

gas [gæs] n Gas nt; (US: petrol) Benzin nt; **to step on the ~** Gas geben; **gas cooker** n Gasherd m; **gas cylinder** n Gasflasche f; **gas fire** n Gasofen m

gasket ['gæskɪt] n Dichtung f

gas lighter n (for cigarettes) Gasfeuerzeug nt; **gas mask** n Gasmaske f; **gas meter** n Gaszähler m

gasoline ['gæsəli:n] n (US) Benzin nt

gasp [gɑ:sp] vi keuchen; (in surprise) nach Luft schnappen

gas pedal n (US) Gaspedal nt; **gas pump** n (US) Zapfsäule f; **gas station** n (US) Tankstelle f; **gas tank** n (US) Benzintank m

gastric ['gæstrɪk] adj Magen-; **~ flu** Magen-Darm-Grippe f; **~ ulcer** Magengeschwür nt

gasworks ['gæswɜ:ks] n Gaswerk nt

gate [geɪt] n Tor nt; (barrier) Schranke f; (Aviat) Gate nt, Flugsteig m

gateau ['gætəʊ] n Torte f

gateway n Tor nt

gather ['gæðə*] vt (collect) sammeln; **to ~ speed** beschleunigen ▷ vi (assemble) sich versammeln; (understand) schließen (from aus); **gathering** n Versammlung f

gauge [geɪdʒ] n Meßgerät nt

gauze [gɔ:z] n Gaze f; (for bandages) Mull m

gave [geɪv] pt of **give**

gay [geɪ] adj (homosexual) schwul

gaze [geɪz] n Blick m ▷ vi starren

GCSE abbr = **general certificate of secondary education** (school) Abschlussprüfung f der Sekundarstufe, ≈ mittlere Reife

gear [gɪə*] n (Auto) Gang m; (equipment) Ausrüstung f; (clothes) Klamotten pl; **to change ~** schalten; **gearbox** n Getriebe nt; **gear change**, **gear shift** (US) n Gangschaltung f; **gear lever**, **gear stick** (US) n Schalthebel m

geese [gi:s] pl of **goose**

gel [dʒel] n Gel nt ▷ vi gelieren; **they really ~led** sie verstanden sich auf Anhieb

gelatine ['dʒeləti:n] n Gelatine f

gem [dʒem] n Edelstein m; (fig) Juwel nt

Gemini ['dʒemɪni:] nsing (Astr) Zwillinge pl

gender ['dʒendə*] n Geschlecht nt

gene [dʒi:n] n Gen nt

general ['dʒenərəl] adj allgemein; **~ knowledge** Allgemeinbildung f; **~ election** Parlamentswahlen pl; **generalize** ['dʒenrəlaɪz] vi verallgemeinern; **generally** ['dʒenrəli] adv im Allgemeinen

generation [dʒenə'reɪʃən] n Generation f; **generation gap** n Generationsunterschied m

generator ['dʒenəreɪtə*] n Generator m

generosity [dʒenə'rɔsɪti] n Großzügigkeit f; **generous** ['dʒenərəs] adj großzügig; (portion) reichlich

genetic [dʒɪ'netɪk] adj genetisch; **genetically modified** adj gentechnisch verändert, genmanipuliert; see also **GM**

Geneva [dʒɪ'ni:və] n Genf nt; **Lake ~** der Genfer See

genitals ['dʒenɪtlz] npl Geschlechtsteile pl

genitive ['dʒenɪtɪv] n Genitiv m

genius ['dʒi:nɪəs] n Genie nt

gentle ['dʒentl] adj sanft; (touch) zart;

gentleman (pl **-men**) n Herr m; (polite man) Gentleman m

gents [dʒents] n **'~'** (lavatory) „Herren"; **the ~** pl die Herrentoilette

genuine ['dʒenjuɪn] adj echt

geographical [dʒɪə'græfɪkəl] adj geografisch; **geography** [dʒɪ'ɒgrəfɪ] n Geografie f; (at school) Erdkunde f

geological [dʒɪəʊ'lɒdʒɪkəl] adj geologisch; **geology** [dʒɪ'ɒlədʒɪ] n Geologie f

geometry [dʒɪ'ɒmɪtrɪ] n Geometrie f

geranium [dʒɪ'reɪnɪəm] n Geranie f

germ [dʒɜ:m] n Keim m; (Med) Bazillus m

German ['dʒɜ:mən] adj deutsch; **she's ~** sie ist Deutsche; **~ shepherd** Deutscher Schäferhund ▷ n (person) Deutsche(r) mf; (language) Deutsch nt; **in ~** auf Deutsch; **German measles** n sing Röteln pl; **Germany** ['dʒɜ:mənɪ] n Deutschland nt

gesture ['dʒestʃə*] n Geste f

◯ **KEYWORD**

get [get] (pt, pp **got**, pp **gotten** (US)) vi
1 (become, be) werden; **to get old/tired** alt/müde werden; **to get married** heiraten
2 (go) (an)kommen gehen
3 (begin): **to get to know sb** jdn kennen lernen; **let's get going or started!** fangen wir an!
4 (modal aux vb): **you've got to do it** du musst es tun
▷ vt **1**: **to get sth done** (do) etw machen; (have done) etw machen lassen; **to get sth going or to go** etw in Gang bringen or bekommen; **to get sb to do sth** jdn dazu bringen, etw zu tun
2 (obtain: money, permission, results) erhalten; (find: job, flat) finden; (fetch: person, object) holen; **to get sth for sb** jdm etw besorgen; **get me Mr Jones, please** (Tel) verbinden Sie mich bitte mit Mr Jones
3 (receive: present, letter) bekommen kriegen; (acquire: reputation etc) erwerben
4 (catch) bekommen kriegen; (hit: target etc) treffen erwischen; **get him!** (to dog) fass!
5 (take, move) bringen; **to get sth to sb** jdm etw bringen

6 (*understand*) verstehen; (*hear*) mitbekommen; **I've got it!** ich habs!
7 (*have, possess*): **to have got sth** etw haben
get about vi herumkommen; (*news*) sich verbreiten
get along vi (*people*) (gut) zurechtkommen; (*depart*) sich acc auf den Weg machen
get at vt (*facts*) herausbekommen; **to get at sb** (*nag*) an jdm herumnörgeln
get away vi (*leave*) sich acc davonmachen; (*escape*); **to get away from sth** von etw dat entkommen; **to get away with sth** mit etw durchkommen
get back vi (*return*) zurückkommen ▷ vt zurückbekommen
get by vi (*pass*) vorbeikommen; (*manage*) zurechtkommen
get down vi (her)untergehen ▷ vt (*depress*) fertig machen; **to get down to** in Angriff nehmen (*find time to do*) kommen zu
get in vi (*train*) ankommen; (*arrive home*) heimkommen
get into vt (*enter*) hinein-/hereinkommen in +acc; (: *car, train etc*) einsteigen in +acc; (*clothes*) anziehen
get off vi (*from train etc*) aussteigen; (*from horse*) absteigen ▷ vt aussteigen aus; absteigen von
get on vi (*progress*) vorankommen; (*be friends*) auskommen; (*age*) alt werden; (*onto train etc*) einsteigen; (*onto horse*) aufsteigen ▷ vt einsteigen in +acc; auf etw acc aufsteigen
get out vi (*of house*) herauskommen; (*of vehicle*) aussteigen ▷ vt (*take out*) herausholen
get out of vt (*duty etc*) herumkommen um
get over vt (*illness*) sich acc erholen von; (*surprise*) verkraften; (*news*) fassen; (*loss*) sich abfinden mit ·
get round vt herumkommen; (*fig: person*) herumkriegen
get through to vt (*Tel*) durchkommen zu
get together vi zusammenkommen
get up vi aufstehen ▷ vt hinaufbringen; (*go up*) hinaufgehen; (*organize*) auf die Beine stellen
get up to vt (*reach*) erreichen; (*prank etc*) anstellen

Ghana ['gɑːnə] n Ghana nt
gherkin ['gɜːkɪn] n Gewürzgurke f
ghetto ['getəʊ] (pl **-es**) n Ghetto nt
ghost [gəʊst] n Gespenst nt; (*of sb*) Geist m
giant ['dʒaɪənt] n Riese m ▷ adj riesig
giblets ['dʒɪblɪts] npl Geflügelinnereien pl
Gibraltar [dʒɪˈbrɔːltə*] n Gibraltar nt
giddy ['gɪdɪ] adj schwindlig
gift [gɪft] n Geschenk nt; (*talent*) Begabung f; **gifted** adj begabt; **giftwrap** vt als Geschenk verpacken
gigantic [dʒaɪˈgæntɪk] adj riesig
giggle ['gɪgl] vi kichern ▷ n Gekicher nt
gill [gɪl] n (*of fish*) Kieme f
gimmick ['gɪmɪk] n (*for sales, publicity*) Gag m
gin [dʒɪn] n Gin m
ginger ['dʒɪndʒə*] n Ingwer m ▷ adj (*colour*) kupferrot; (*cat*) rötlichgelb; **ginger ale** n Gingerale nt; **ginger beer** n Ingwerlimonade f; **gingerbread** n Lebkuchen m (*mit Ingwergeschmack*); **ginger(-haired)** adj rotblond; **gingerly** adv (*move*) vorsichtig
gipsy ['dʒɪpsɪ] n Zigeuner(in) m(f)
giraffe [dʒɪˈrɑːf] n Giraffe f
girl [gɜːl] n Mädchen nt; **girlfriend** n (*feste*) Freundin f; **girl guide** n (*Brit*), **girl scout** (*US*) Pfadfinderin f
gist [dʒɪst] n **to get the ~ (of it)** das Wesentliche verstehen
give [gɪv] (**gave, given**) vt geben; (*as present*) schenken (*to sb* jdm); (*state: name etc*) angeben; (*speech*) halten; (*blood*) spenden; **to ~ sb sth** jdm etw geben/schenken ▷ vi (*yield*) nachgeben; **give away** vt (*give free*) verschenken; (*secret*) verraten; **give back** vt zurückgeben; **give in** vi aufgeben; **give up** vt, vi aufgeben; **give way** vi (*collapse*, *yield*) nachgeben; (*traffic*) die Vorfahrt beachten
given ['gɪvn] pp of **give** ▷ adj (*fixed*) festgesetzt; (*certain*) bestimmt; **~ name** (*US*) Vorname m ▷ conj **~ that ...** angesichts der Tatsache, dass ...
glacier ['glæsɪə*] n Gletscher m
glad [glæd] adj froh (*about* über); **I was ~ (to hear) that ...** es hat mich gefreut, dass ...; **gladly** ['glædlɪ] adv gerne
glance [glɑːns] n Blick m ▷ vi einen Blick werfen (*at* auf +akk)

gland [glænd] n Drüse f; **glandular fever** n Drüsenfieber nt

glare [gleə*] n grelles Licht; (stare) stechender Blick ▷ vi (angrily) **to ~ at sb** jdn böse anstarren; **glaring** adj (mistake) krass

glass [glɑ:s] n Glas nt; **~es** pl Brille f

glen [glen] n (SCOT) (enges) Bergtal nt

glide [glaɪd] vi gleiten; (hover) schweben; **glider** n Segelflugzeug nt; **gliding** n Segelfliegen nt

glimmer ['glɪmə*] n (of hope) Schimmer m

glimpse [glɪmps] n flüchtiger Blick

glitter ['glɪtə*] vi glitzern; (eyes) funkeln

glitzy [glɪtsɪ] adj (fam) glanzvoll, Schickimicki-

global ['gləʊbəl] adj global, Welt-; **~ warming** n die Erwärmung der Erdatmosphäre; **globe** [gləʊb] n (sphere) Kugel f; (world) Erdball m; (map) Globus m

gloomily ['glu:mɪlɪ], **gloomy** adv, adj düster

glorious ['glɔ:rɪəs] adj (victory, past) ruhmreich; (weather, day) herrlich; **glory** ['glɔ:rɪ] n Herrlichkeit f

gloss [glɒs] n (shine) Glanz m

glossary ['glɒsərɪ] n Glossar nt

glossy ['glɒsɪ] adj (surface) glänzend ▷ n (magazine) Hochglanzmagazin nt

glove [glʌv] n Handschuh m; **glove compartment** n Handschuhfach nt

glow [gləʊ] vi glühen

glucose ['glu:kəʊs] n Traubenzucker m

glue [glu:] n Klebstoff m ▷ vt kleben

glutton ['glʌtn] n Vielfraß m; **a ~ for punishment** (fam) Masochist m

GM abbr = **genetically modified** Gen-; **~ foods** gentechnisch veränderte Lebensmittel

GMT abbr = **Greenwich Mean Time** WEZ f

go [gəʊ] (**went, gone**) vi gehen; (in vehicle, travel) fahren; (plane) fliegen; (road) führen (to nach); (depart: train, bus) (ab)fahren; (person) (fort)gehen; (disappear) verschwinden; (time) vergehen; (function) gehen, funktionieren; (machine, engine) laufen; (fit, suit) passen (with zu); (fail) nachlassen; **I have to ~ to the doctor/to London** ich muss zum Arzt/nach London; **to ~ shopping** einkaufen gehen; **to ~ for a walk/swim** spazieren/schwimmen gehen; **has he gone yet?** ist er schon weg?; **the wine ~es in the cupboard** der Wein kommt in den Schrank; **to get sth ~ing** etw in Gang setzen; **to keep ~ing** weitermachen; (machine etc) weiterlaufen; **how's the job ~ing?** was macht der Job?; **his memory/eyesight is going** sein Gedächtnis lässt nach/seine Augen werden schwach; **to ~ deaf/mad/grey** taub/verrückt/grau werden ▷ vb aux **to be ~ing to do sth** etw tun werden; **I was ~ing to do it** ich wollte es tun ▷ n (pl **~es**) (attempt) Versuch m; **can I have another ~?** darf ich noch mal (probieren)?; **it's my ~** ich bin dran; **in one ~** auf einen Schlag; (drink) in einem Zug; **go after** vt nachlaufen +dat; (in vehicle) nachfahren +dat; **go ahead** vi (in front) vorausgehen; (start) anfangen; **go away** vi weggehen; (on holiday, business) verreisen; **go back** vi (return) zurückgehen; **we ~ a long way** (fam) wir kennen uns schon ewig; **go by** vi vorbeigehen; (vehicle) vorbeifahren; (years, time) vergehen ▷ vt (judge by) gehen nach; **go down** vi (sun, ship) untergehen; (flood, temperature) zurückgehen; (price) sinken; **to ~ well/badly** gut/schlecht ankommen; **go in** vi hineingehen; **go into** vt (enter) hineingehen in +akk; (crash) fahren gegen, hineinfahren in +akk; **to ~ teaching/politics/the army** Lehrer werden/in die Politik gehen/zum Militär gehen; **go off** vi (depart) weggehen; (in vehicle) wegfahren; (lights) ausgehen; (milk etc) sauer werden; (gun, bomb, alarm) losgehen ▷ vt (dislike) nicht mehr mögen; **go on** vi (continue) weitergehen; (lights) angehen; **to ~ with** o **doing sth** etw weitermachen; **go out** vi (leave house) hinausgehen; (fire, light, person socially) ausgehen; **to ~ for a meal** essen gehen; **go up** vi (temperature, price) steigen; (lift) hochfahren; **go without** vt verzichten auf +akk; (food, sleep) auskommen ohne

go-ahead ['gəʊəhed] adj (progressive) fortschrittlich ▷ n grünes Licht

goal [gəʊl] n (aim) Ziel nt; (Sport) Tor nt; **goalie, goalkeeper** n Torwart m, Torfrau f; **goalpost** n Torpfosten m

goat [gəʊt] n Ziege f

gob [gɒb] n (Brit fam) Maul nt; **shut your ~** halt's Maul ▷ vi spucken; **gobsmacked** (fam: surprised) platt

god [gɒd] n Gott m; **thank God** Gott sei Dank; **godchild** (pl **-children**) n

Patenkind nt; **goddaughter** n
Patentochter f; **goddess** ['gɒdes] n
Göttin f; **godfather** n Pate m;
godmother n Patin f; **godson** n
Patensohn m

goggles npl Schutzbrille f; (for skiing)
Skibrille f; (for diving) Taucherbrille f

going ['gəʊɪŋ] adj (rate) üblich; **goings-on**
npl Vorgänge pl

go-kart ['gəʊkɑːt] n Gokart m

gold [gəʊld] n Gold nt ▷ adj golden;
goldfish n Goldfisch m; **gold-plated** adj
vergoldet

golf [gɒlf] n Golf nt; **golf ball** n Golfball
m; **golf club** n Golfschläger m;
(association) Golfklub m; **golf course** n
Golfplatz m; **golfer** n Golfspieler(in) m(f)

gone [gɒn] pp of **go**; **he's ~** er ist weg
▷ prep **just – three** gerade drei Uhr vorbei

good [gʊd] n (benefit) Wohl nt; (morally
good things) Gute(s) nt; **for the ~ of** zum
Wohle +gen; **it's for your own ~** es ist zu
deinem Besten o Vorteil; **it's no ~** (doing
sth) es hat keinen Sinn o Zweck; (thing) es
taugt nichts; **for ~** für immer ▷ adj
(**better, best**) gut; (suitable) passend;
(thorough) gründlich; (well-behaved) brav;
(kind) nett, lieb; **to be ~ at sport/maths**
gut in Sport/Mathe sein; **to be no ~ at
sport/maths** schlecht in Sport/Mathe
sein; **it's ~ for you** es tut dir gut; **this is
~ for colds** das ist gut gegen Erkältungen;
too ~ to be true zu schön, um wahr zu
sein; **this is just not ~ enough** so geht das
nicht; **a ~ three hours** gute drei Stunden;
~ morning/evening guten
Morgen/Abend; **~ night** gute Nacht; **to
have a ~ time** sich gut amüsieren

goodbye [gʊdˈbaɪ] interj auf Wiedersehen

Good Friday n Karfreitag m

good-looking adj gut aussehend

goods [gʊdz] npl Waren pl, Güter pl;
goods train n (Brit) Güterzug m

goodwill [gʊdˈwɪl] n Wohlwollen nt

goose [guːs] (pl **geese**) n Gans f ▷ vt
(fam) **to – s.o.** jdn in den Arsch kneifen;
gooseberry ['gʊzbərɪ] n Stachelbeere f;
goose bumps n, **goose pimples** npl
Gänsehaut f

gorge [gɔːdʒ] n Schlucht f

gorgeous ['gɔːdʒəs] adj wunderschön;
he's ~ er sieht toll aus

gorilla [gəˈrɪlə] n Gorilla m

gossip ['gɒsɪp] n (talk) Klatsch m; (person)
Klatschtante f ▷ vi klatschen, tratschen

got [gɒt] pt, pp of **get**

gotten ['gɒtn] (US) pp of **get**

govern ['gʌvən] vt regieren; (province etc)
verwalten; **government** n Regierung f;
governor n Gouverneur(in) m(f); **govt**
abbr = **government** Regierung f

gown [gaʊn] n Abendkleid nt; (academic)
Robe f

GP abbr = **General Practitioner**
praktischer Arzt

GPS n abbr = **global positioning system**
GPS nt

grab [græb] vt packen; (person)
schnappen

grace [greɪs] n Anmut f; (prayer)
Tischgebet nt; **5 days' ~** 5 Tage Aufschub;
graceful adj anmutig

grade [greɪd] n Niveau nt; (of goods)
Güteklasse f; (mark) Note f; (US: year)
Klasse f; **to make the ~** es schaffen; **grade
crossing** n (US) Bahnübergang m; **grade
school** n (US) Grundschule f

gradient ['greɪdɪənt] n (upward) Steigung
f; (downward) Gefälle nt

gradual, gradually ['grædjʊəl, -lɪ] adj, adv
allmählich

graduate ['grædjʊɪt] n Uniabsolvent(in)
m(f), Akademiker(in) m(f),
Hochschulabsolvent(in) m(f)
▷ ['grædjʊeɪt] vi einen akademischen
Grad erwerben

grain [greɪn] n (cereals) Getreide nt;
(of corn, sand) Korn nt; (in wood) Maserung
f

gram [græm] n Gramm nt

grammar ['græmə*] n Grammatik f;
grammar school n (Brit) ≈ Gymnasium nt

gran [græn] n (fam) Oma f

grand [grænd] adj (pej) hochnäsig; (posh)
vornehm ▷ n (fam) 1000 Pfund bzw. 1000
Dollar

grand(d)ad n (fam) Opa m;
granddaughter n Enkelin f; **grandfather**
n Großvater m; **grandma** n (fam) Oma f;
grandmother n Großmutter f; **grandpa**
n (fam) Opa m; **grandparents** npl
Großeltern pl; **grandson** n Enkel m

grandstand n (Sport) Tribüne f

granny ['grænɪ] n (fam) Oma f

grant [grɑːnt] vt gewähren (sb sth jdm
etw); **to take sb/sth for ~ed** jdn/etw als

selbstverständlich hinnehmen ▷ *n* Subvention *f*, finanzielle Unterstützung *f*; *(for university)* Stipendium *nt*

grape [greɪp] *n* Weintraube *f*; **grapefruit** *n* Grapefruit *f*; **grape juice** *n* Traubensaft *m*

graph [grɑːf] *n* Diagramm *nt*; **graphic** ['græfɪk] *adj* grafisch; *(description)* anschaulich

grasp [grɑːsp] *vt* ergreifen; *(understand)* begreifen

grass [grɑːs] *n* Gras *nt*; *(lawn)* Rasen *m*; **grasshopper** *n* Heuschrecke *f*

grate [greɪt] *n* Feuerrost *m* ▷ *vi* kratzen ▷ *vt* *(cheese)* reiben

grateful, gratefully ['greɪtfʊl, -fəlɪ] *adj, adv* dankbar

grater ['greɪtə*] *n* Reibe *f*

gratifying ['grætɪfaɪɪŋ] *adj* erfreulich

gratitude ['grætɪtjuːd] *n* Dankbarkeit *f*

grave [greɪv] *n* Grab *nt* ▷ *adj* ernst; *(mistake)* schwer

gravel ['grævəl] *n* Kies *m*

graveyard ['greɪvjɑːd] *n* Friedhof *m*

gravity ['grævɪtɪ] *n* Schwerkraft *f*; *(seriousness)* Ernst *m*

gravy ['greɪvɪ] *n* Bratensoße *f*

gray [greɪ] *adj* *(US)* grau

graze [greɪz] *vi* *(of animals)* grasen ▷ *vt* *(touch)* streifen; *(Med)* abschürfen ▷ *n* *(Med)* Abschürfung *f*

grease [griːs] *n* *(fat)* Fett *nt*; *(lubricant)* Schmiere *f* ▷ *vt* einfetten; *(Tech)* schmieren; **greasy** ['griːsɪ] *adj* fettig; *(hands, tools)* schmierig; *(fam: person)* schleimig

great [greɪt] *adj* groß; *(fam: good)* großartig, super; **a ~ deal of** viel; **Great Britain** ['greɪt'brɪtn] *n* Großbritannien *nt*; **great-grandfather** *n* Urgroßvater *m*; **great-grandmother** *n* Urgroßmutter *f*; **greatly** *adv* sehr; **~ disappointed** zutiefst enttäuscht

Greece [griːs] *n* Griechenland *nt*

greed [griːd] *n* Gier *f* *(for nach)*; *(for food)* Gefräßigkeit *f*; **greedy** *adj* gierig; *(for food)* gefräßig

Greek [griːk] *adj* griechisch ▷ *n* *(person)* Grieche *m*, Griechin *f*; *(language)* Griechisch *nt*

green [griːn] *adj* grün ▷ *n* *(colour, for golf)* Grün *nt*; *(village ~)* Dorfwiese *f*; **~s** *(vegetables)* grünes Gemüse; **the Greens,**

the Green Party *(Pol)* die Grünen; **green card** *n* *(US: work permit)* Arbeitserlaubnis *f*; *(Brit: for car)* grüne Versicherungskarte; **greengage** *n* Reneklode *f*; **greengrocer** *n* Obst- und Gemüsehändler(in) *m(f)*; **greenhouse** *n* Gewächshaus *nt*; **~ effect** Treibhauseffekt *m*; **Greenland** *n* Grönland *nt*; **green pepper** *n* grüner Paprika; **green salad** *n* grüner Salat

Greenwich Mean Time ['grenɪdʒ'miːntaɪm] *n* westeuropäische Zeit

greet [griːt] *vt* grüßen; **greeting** *n* Gruß *m*

grew [gruː] *pt of* **grow**

grey [greɪ] *adj* grau; **grey-haired** *adj* grauhaarig; **greyhound** *n* Windhund *m*

grid [grɪd] *n* Gitter *nt*; **gridlock** *n* Verkehrsinfarkt *m*; **gridlocked** *adj* *(roads)* völlig verstopft; *(talks)* festgefahren

grief [griːf] *n* Kummer *m*; *(over loss)* Trauer *f*

grievance ['griːvəns] *n* Beschwerde *f*

grieve [griːv] *vi* trauern *(for um)*

grill [grɪl] *n* *(on cooker)* Grill *m* ▷ *vt* grillen

grim [grɪm] *adj* *(face, humour)* grimmig; *(situation, prospects)* trostlos

grin [grɪn] *n* Grinsen *nt* ▷ *vi* grinsen

grind [graɪnd] *(ground, ground)* *vt* mahlen; *(sharpen)* schleifen; *(US: meat)* durchdrehen, hacken

grip [grɪp] *n* Griff *m*; **get a ~** nimm dich zusammen!; **to get to ~s with sth** etw in den Griff bekommen ▷ *vt* packen; **gripping** *adj* *(exciting)* spannend

gristle ['grɪsl] *n* Knorpel *m*

groan [grəʊn] *vi* stöhnen *(with vor +dat)*

grocer ['grəʊsə*] *n* Lebensmittelhändler(in) *m(f)*; **groceries** *npl* Lebensmittel *pl*

groin [grɔɪn] *n* *(Anat)* Leiste *f*; **groin strain** *n* *(Med)* Leistenbruch *m*

groom [gruːm] *n* Bräutigam *m* ▷ *vt* **well ~ed** gepflegt

groovy ['gruːvɪ] *adj* *(fam)* cool

grope [grəʊp] *vi* tasten ▷ *vt* *(sexually harrass)* befummeln

gross [grəʊs] *adj* *(coarse)* derb; *(extreme: negligence, error)* grob; *(disgusting)* ekelhaft; *(Comm)* brutto; **~ national product** Bruttosozialprodukt *nt*; **~ salary** Bruttogehalt *nt*

grotty ['grɒtɪ] *adj* *(fam)* mies, vergammelt

ground [graʊnd] *pt, pp of* **grind** ▷ *n*
Boden *m*, Erde *f*; (*Sport*) Platz *m*; **~s** *pl*
(*around house*) (Garten)anlagen *pl*; (*reasons*)
Gründe *pl*; (*of coffee*) Satz *m*; **on (the) ~s of**
aufgrund von; **ground floor** *n* (*Brit*)
Erdgeschoss *nt*; **ground meat** *n* (*US*)
Hackfleisch *nt*

group [gruːp] *n* Gruppe *f* ▷ *vt*
gruppieren

grouse [graʊs] (*pl* **-**) *n* (*bird*) Schottisches
Moorhuhn; (*complaint*) Nörgelei *f*

grow [grəʊ] (**grew, grown**) *vi* wachsen;
(*increase*) zunehmen (*in an*); (*become*)
werden; **to ~ old** alt werden; **to ~ into ...**
sich entwickeln zu ... ▷ *vt* (*crop, plant*)
ziehen; (*commercially*) anbauen; **I'm ~ing a
beard** ich lasse mir einen Bart wachsen;
grow up *vi* aufwachsen; (*mature*)
erwachsen werden; **growing** *adj*
wachsend; **a ~ number of people** immer
mehr Leute

growl [graʊl] *vi* knurren

grown [grəʊn] *pp of* **grow**

grown-up [grəʊnˈʌp] *adj* erwachsen ▷ *n*
Erwachsene(r) *mf*; **growth** [grəʊθ] *n*
Wachstum *nt*; (*increase*) Zunahme *f*; (*Med*)
Wucherung *f*

grubby [ˈgrʌbɪ] *adj* schmuddelig

grudge [grʌdʒ] *n* Abneigung *f* (*against*
gegen) ▷ *vt* **to ~ sb sth** jdm etw nicht
gönnen

gruelling [ˈgruːəlɪŋ] *adj* aufreibend; (*pace*)
mörderisch

gruesome [ˈgruːsəm] *adj* grausig

grumble [ˈgrʌmbl] *vi* murren (*about über
+akk*)

grumpy [ˈgrʌmpɪ] *adj* (*fam*) mürrisch,
grantig

grunt [grʌnt] *vi* grunzen

G-string [ˈdʒiːstrɪŋ] *n* ≈ Tanga *m*

guarantee [gærənˈtiː] *n* Garantie *f* (*of*
für); **it's still under ~** es ist noch Garantie
darauf ▷ *vt* garantieren

guard [gɑːd] *n* (*sentry*) Wache *f*; (*in prison*)
Wärter(in) *m(f)*; (*Brit Rail*) Schaffner(in)
m(f) ▷ *vt* bewachen; **a closely ~ed secret**
ein streng gehütetes Geheimnis

guardian [ˈgɑːdɪən] *n* Vormund *m*;
~ angel Schutzengel *m*

guess [ges] *n* Vermutung *f*; (*estimate*)
Schätzung *f*; **have a ~** rate mal! ▷ *vt, vi*
raten; (*estimate*) schätzen; **I ~ you're right**
du hast wohl recht; **I ~ so** ich glaube

schon; **guesstimate** [ˈgestɪmɪt] *n* (*fam*)
grobe Schätzung

guest [gest] *n* Gast *m*; **be my ~** nur zu!;
guest-house *n* Pension *f*; **guest room** *n*
Gästezimmer *nt*

guidance [ˈgaɪdəns] *n* (*direction*) Leitung
f; (*advice*) Rat *m*; (*counselling*) Beratung *f*;
for your ~ zu Ihrer Orientierung; **guide**
[gaɪd] *n* (*person*) Führer(in) *m(f)*; (*tour*)
Reiseleiter(in) *m(f)*; (*book*) Führer *m*; (*girl ~*)
Pfadfinderin *f* ▷ *vt* führen; **guidebook** *n*
Reiseführer *m*; **guide dog** *n* Blindenhund
m; **guided tour** *n* Führung *f* (*of durch*);
guidelines *npl* Richtlinien *pl*

guilt [gɪlt] *n* Schuld *f*; **guilty** *adj* schuldig
(*of gen*); (*look*) schuldbewusst; **to have a
~ conscience** ein schlechtes Gewissen
haben

guinea pig [ˈgɪnɪ pɪg] *n*
Meerschweinchen *nt*; (*person*)
Versuchskaninchen *nt*

guitar [gɪˈtɑː*] *n* Gitarre *f*

gulf [gʌlf] *n* Golf *m*; (*gap*) Kluft *f*; **Gulf
States** *npl* Golfstaaten *pl*

gull [gʌl] *n* Möwe *f*

gullible [ˈgʌlɪbl] *adj* leichtgläubig

gulp [gʌlp] *n* (kräftiger) Schluck ▷ *vi*
schlucken

gum [gʌm] *n* (*around teeth, usu pl*)
Zahnfleisch *nt*; (*chewing ~*) Kaugummi *m*

gun [gʌn] *n* Schusswaffe *f*; (*rifle*) Gewehr
nt; (*pistol*) Pistole *f*; **gunfire** *n* Schüsse *pl*,
Geschützfeuer *nt*; **gunpowder** ·*n*
Schießpulver *nt*; **gunshot** *n* Schuss *m*

gush [gʌʃ] *vi* (heraus)strömen (*from aus*)

gut [gʌt] *n* Darm *m*; **~s** *pl* (*intestines*)
Eingeweide; (*courage*) Mumm *m*

gutter [ˈgʌtə*] *n* (*for roof*) Dachrinne *f*; (*in
street*) Rinnstein *m*, Gosse *f*; **gutter press**
n Skandalpresse *f*

guy [gaɪ] *n* (*man*) Typ *m*, Kerl *m*; **~s** *pl* (*US*)
Leute *pl*

gym [dʒɪm] *n* Turnhalle *f*; (*for working out*)
Fitnesscenter *nt*; **gymnasium**
[dʒɪmˈneɪzɪəm] *n* Turnhalle *f*; **gymnastics**
[dʒɪmˈnæstɪks] *nsing* Turnen *nt*;
gym-toned *adj* durchtrainiert

gynaecologist [gaɪnɪˈkɒlədʒɪst] *n*
Frauenarzt *m*, Frauenärztin *f*, Gynäkologe
m, Gynäkologin *f*; **gynaecology** *n*
Gynäkologie *f*, Frauenheilkunde *f*

gypsy [ˈdʒɪpsɪ] *n* Zigeuner(in) *m(f)*

h

habit ['hæbɪt] n Gewohnheit f; **habitual** [hə'bɪtjʊəl] adj gewohnt; (drinker, liar) gewohnheitsmäßig

hack [hæk] vt hacken; **hacker** n (Inform) Hacker(in) m(f)

had [hæd] pt, pp of **have**

haddock ['hædək] n Schellfisch m

hadn't ['hædnt] contr of **had not**

haemophiliac, **hemophiliac** (US) [hi:mə'fɪliæk] n Bluter(in) m(f); **haemorrhage**, **hemorrhage** (US) ['hemərɪdʒ] n Blutung f ▷ vi bluten; **haemorrhoids**, **hemorrhoids** (US) ['hemərɔɪdz] npl Hämorrhoiden pl

haggis ['hægɪs] n (Scot) mit gehackten Schafsinnereien und Haferschrot gefüllter Schafsmagen

Hague [heɪg] n **the ~** Den Haag

hail [heɪl] n Hagel m ▷ vi hageln ▷ vt to **~ sb as sth** jdn als etw feiern; **hailstone** n Hagelkorn nt; **hailstorm** n Hagelschauer m

hair [hεə*] n Haar nt, Haare pl; **to do one's ~** sich frisieren; **to get one's ~ cut** sich dat die Haare schneiden lassen; **hairbrush** n Haarbürste f; **hair conditioner** n Haarspülung f; **haircut** n Haarschnitt m; **to have a ~** sich dat die Haare schneiden lassen; **hairdo** (pl **-s**) n Frisur f; **hairdresser** n Friseur m, Friseuse f; **hairdryer** n Haartrockner m; (hand-held) Fön® m; (over head) Trockenhaube f; **hair gel** n Haargel nt; **hairpin** n Haarnadel f; **hair remover** n Enthaarungsmittel nt; **hair spray** n Haarspray nt; **hair style** n Frisur f; **hairy** adj haarig, behaart; (fam: dangerous) brenzlig

hake [heɪk] n Seehecht m

half [hɑ:f] (pl **halves**) n Hälfte f; (Sport: of game) Halbzeit f; **to cut in ~** halbieren ▷ adj halb; **three and a ~ pounds** dreieinhalb Pfund; **~ an hour, a ~ hour** eine halbe Stunde; **one and a ~** eineinhalb, anderthalb ▷ adv halb, zur Hälfte; **~ past three, ~ three** halb vier; **at ~ past** um halb; **~ asleep** fast eingeschlafen; **she's ~ German** sie ist zur Hälfte Deutsche; **~ as big (as)** halb so groß (wie); **half board** n Halbpension f; **half fare** n halber Fahrpreis; **half-hearted** adj halbherzig; **half-hour** n halbe Stunde; **half moon** n Halbmond m; **half pint** n ≈ Viertelliter m o nt; **half price** n (**at**) **~** zum halben Preis; **half-term** n (at school) Ferien pl in der Mitte des Trimesters; **half-time** n Halbzeit f; **halfway** adv auf halbem Wege; **halfwit** n (fam) Trottel m

halibut ['hælɪbət] n Heilbutt m

hall [hɔ:l] n (building) Halle f; (for audience) Saal m; (entrance ~) Flur m; (large) Diele f; **~ of residence** (Brit) Studentenwohnheim nt

hallmark ['hɔ:lmɑ:k] n Stempel m; (fig) Kennzeichen nt

hallo [hʌ'ləʊ] interj hallo

Hallowe'en [hæləʊ'i:n] n Halloween nt (Tag vor Allerheiligen, an dem sich Kinder verkleiden und von Tür zu Tür gehen)

Hallowe'en

Hallowe'en ist der 31. Oktober, der Vorabend von Allerheiligen und nach altem Glauben der Abend, an dem man Geister und Hexen sehen kann. In Großbritannien und vor allem in den USA feiern die Kinder Hallowe'en, indem sie sich verkleiden und mit selbst gemachten

Laternen aus Kürbissen von Tür zu
Tür ziehen.

halo ['heɪləʊ] (pl **-es**) n (of saint)
Heiligenschein m

halt [hɔ:lt] n Pause f, Halt m; **to come to
a ~** zum Stillstand kommen ▷ vt, vi
anhalten

halve [hɑ:v] vt halbieren

ham [hæm] n Schinken m; **~ and eggs**
Schinken mit Spiegelei

hamburger ['hæmbɜ:gə*] n (Gastr)
Hamburger m

hammer ['hæmə*] n Hammer m ▷ vt, vi
hämmern

hammock ['hæmək] n Hängematte f

hamper ['hæmpə*] vt behindern ▷ n (as
gift) Geschenkkorb m; (for picnic)
Picknickkkorb m

hamster ['hæmstə*] n Hamster m

hand [hænd] n Hand f; (of clock,
instrument) Zeiger m; (in card game) Blatt nt;
to be made by ~ Handarbeit sein; **~s up!**
Hände hoch!; (at school) meldet euch!; **~s
off!** Finger weg!; **on the one ~ ..., on the
other ~...** einerseits ..., andererseits ...; **to
give sb a ~** jdm helfen (with bei); **it's in his
~s** er hat es in der Hand; **to be in good ~s**
gut aufgehoben sein; **to get out of
~** außer Kontrolle geraten ▷ vt (pass)
reichen (to sb jdm); **hand down** vt
(tradition) überliefern; (heirloom) vererben;
hand in vt einreichen; (at school, university
etc) abgeben; **hand out** vt verteilen; .
hand over vt übergeben

handbag n Handtasche f; **handbook** n
Handbuch m; **handbrake** n (Brit)
Handbremse f; **hand cream** n
Handcreme f; **handcuffs** npl
Handschellen pl; **handful** n Handvoll f;
handheld PC n Handheld m

handicap ['hændɪkæp] n Behinderung f,
Handikap nt ▷ vt benachteiligen;
handicapped adj behindert; **the ~** die
Behinderten

handicraft ['hændɪkrɑ:ft] n
Kunsthandwerk nt

handkerchief ['hæŋkətʃɪf] n
Taschentuch nt

handle ['hændl] n. Griff m; (of door) Klinke
f; (of cup etc) Henkel m; (for winding) Kurbel f
▷ vt (touch) anfassen; (deal with: matter)
sich befassen mit; (people, machine etc)

umgehen mit; (situation, problem) fertig
werden mit; **handlebars** npl Lenkstange f

hand luggage ['hændlʌgɪdʒ] n
Handgepäck nt; **handmade** adj
handgefertigt; **to be ~** Handarbeit sein;
handout n (sheet) Handout nt,
Thesenpapier nt; **handset** n Hörer m;
please replace the ~ bitte legen Sie auf;
hands-free phone n Freisprechanlage f;
handshake n Händedruck m

handsome ['hænsəm] adj (man) gut
aussehend

hands-on [hændz'ɒn] adj
praxisorientiert; **~ experience** praktische
Erfahrung

handwriting ['hændraɪtɪŋ] n
Handschrift f

handy ['hændɪ] adj (useful) praktisch

hang [hæŋ] (**hung, hung**) vt
(auf)hängen; (execute: hanged, hanged)
hängen; **to ~ sth on sth** etw an etw akk
hängen ▷ vi hängen; **he's got the ~ of
it** er hat den Dreh raus; **hang about** vi
sich herumtreiben, rumhängen; **hang on**
vi sich festhalten (to an +dat); (fam: wait)
warten; **to ~ to sth** etw behalten; **hang
up** vi (Tel) auflegen ▷ vt aufhängen

hangar ['hæŋə*] n Flugzeughalle f

hanger ['hæŋə*] n Kleiderbügel m

hang glider ['hæŋglaɪdə*] n
(Flug)drachen m; (person)
Drachenflieger(in) m(f); **hang-gliding** n
Drachenfliegen nt

hangover ['hæŋəʊvə*] n (bad head) Kater
m; (relic) Überbleibsel nt

hankie ['hæŋkɪ] n (fam) Taschentuch nt

happen ['hæpən] vi geschehen; (sth
strange, unpleasant) passieren; **if anything
should ~ to me** wenn mir etwas passieren
sollte; **it won't ~ again** es wird nicht
wieder vorkommen; **I ~ed to be passing**
ich kam zufällig vorbei; **happening** n
Ereignis nt, Happening nt

happily ['hæpɪlɪ] adv fröhlich, glücklich;
(luckily) glücklicherweise; **happiness**
['hæpɪnɪs] n Glück nt; **happy** ['hæpɪ] adj
glücklich; (satisfied) **~ with sth** mit etw
zufrieden; (willing) **to be ~ to do sth** etw
gerne tun; **Happy Christmas** fröhliche
Weihnachten!; **Happy New Year** ein
glückliches Neues Jahr!; **Happy Birthday**
herzlichen Glückwunsch zum
Geburtstag!; **happy hour** n Happy Hour f

(Zeit, in der man in Bars Getränke zu günstigeren Preisen bekommt)

harass ['hærəs] vt (ständig) belästigen; **harassment** n Belästigung f; (at work) Mobbing nt; **sexual ~** sexuelle Belästigung

harbor (US), **harbour** ['hɑ:bə*] n Hafen m

hard [hɑ:d] adj hart; (difficult) schwer, schwierig; (harsh) hart(herzig); **don't be ~ on him** sei nicht zu streng zu ihm; **it's ~ to believe** es ist kaum zu glauben ▷ adv (work) schwer; (run) schnell; (rain, snow) stark; **to try ~/-er** sich dat große/mehr Mühe geben; **hardback** n gebundene Ausgabe; **hard-boiled** adj (egg) hart gekocht; **hard copy** n (Inform) Ausdruck m; **hard disk** n (Inform) Festplatte f; **harden** vt hart werden ▷ vi hart werden; **hardened** adj (person) abgehärtet (to gegen); **hard-hearted** adj hartherzig; **hardliner** n Hardliner(in) m(f); **hardly** ['hɑ:dlı] adv kaum; **~ ever** fast nie; **hardship** ['hɑ:dʃıp] n Not f; **hard shoulder** n (Brit) Standspur f; **hardware** n (Inform) Hardware f, Haushalts- und Eisenwaren pl; **hard-working** adj fleißig, tüchtig

hare [heə*] n Hase m

harm [hɑ:m] n Schaden m; (bodily) Verletzung f; **it wouldn't do any ~** es würde nicht schaden ▷ vt schaden +dat; (person) verletzen; **harmful** adj schädlich; **harmless** adj harmlos

harp [hɑ:p] n Harfe f

harsh [hɑ:ʃ] adj (climate, voice) rau; (light, sound) grell; (severe) hart, streng

harvest ['hɑ:vıst] n Ernte f; (time) Erntezeit f ▷ vt ernten

has [hæz] pres of **have**

hash [hæʃ] n (Gastr) Haschee nt; (fam: hashish) Haschisch nt; **to make a ~ of sth** etw vermasseln; **hash browns** npl (US) = Kartoffelpuffer pl

hassle ['hæsl] n Ärger m; (fuss) Theater nt; **no ~** kein Problem ▷ vt bedrängen

hasn't ['hæznt] contr of **has not**

haste [heıst] n Eile f; **hastily, hasty** adv, adj hastig; (rash) vorschnell

hat [hæt] n Hut m

hatch [hætʃ] n (Naut) Luke f; (in house) Durchreiche f; **hatchback** ['hætʃbæk] n (car) Wagen m mit Hecktür

hate [heıt] vt hassen; **I ~ doing this** ich mache das sehr ungern ▷ n Hass m (of auf +akk)

haul [hɔ:l] vt ziehen, schleppen ▷ n (booty) Beute f; **haulage** ['hɔ:lıdʒ] n Transport m; (trade) Spedition f; **haunted** adj **a ~ house** ein Haus, in dem es spukt

🅚 **KEYWORD**

have [hæv] (pt, pp **had**) aux vb **1** haben (esp with vbs of motion) sein; **to have arrived/slept** angekommen sein/geschlafen haben; **to have been** gewesen sein; **having eaten** or **when he had eaten, he left** nachdem er gegessen hatte, ging er

2 (in tag questions): **you've done it, haven't you?** du hast es doch gemacht, oder nicht?

3 (in short answers and questions): **you've made a mistake — so I have/no I haven't** du hast einen Fehler gemacht — ja, stimmt/nein; **we haven't paid — yes we have!** wir haben nicht bezahlt — doch; **I've been there before, have you?** ich war schon einmal da, du auch?

▷ modal aux vb (be obliged): **to have (got) to do sth** etw tun müssen; **you haven't to tell her** du darfst es ihr nicht erzählen

▷ vt **1** (possess) haben; **he has (got) blue eyes** er hat blaue Augen; **I have (got) an idea** ich habe eine Idee

2 (referring to meals etc): **to have breakfast/a cigarette** frühstücken/eine Zigarette rauchen

3 (receive, obtain etc) haben; **may I have your address?** kann ich Ihre Adresse haben?; **to have a baby** ein Kind bekommen

4 (maintain, allow): **he will have it that he is right** er besteht darauf, dass er Recht hat; **I won't have it** das lasse ich mir nicht bieten

5: **to have sth done** etw machen lassen; **to have sb do sth** jdn etw machen lassen; **he soon had them all laughing** er brachte sie alle zum Lachen

6 (experience, suffer): **she had her bag stolen** man hat ihr die Tasche gestohlen; **he had his arm broken** er hat sich den Arm gebrochen

7 (+*noun: take, hold etc*); **to have a walk/rest** spazieren gehen/sich ausruhen; **to have a meeting/party** eine Besprechung/Party haben
have out *vt*: **to have it out with sb** (*settle problem*) etw mit jdm bereden

Hawaii [hə'waii:] *n* Hawaii *nt*
hawk [hɔ:k] *n* Habicht *m*
hay [heɪ] *n* Heu *nt*; **hay fever** *n* Heuschnupfen *m*
hazard ['hæzəd] *n* Gefahr *f*; (*risk*) Risiko *nt*; **hazardous** *adj* gefährlich; **~ waste** Sondermüll *m*; **hazard warning lights** *npl* Warnblinkanlage *f*
haze [heɪz] *n* Dunst *m*
hazelnut ['heɪzlnʌt] *n* Haselnuss *f*
hazy ['heɪzɪ] *adj* (*misty*) dunstig; (*vague*) verschwommen
he [hi:] *pron* er
head [hed] *n* Kopf *m*; (*leader*) Leiter(in) *m(f)*; (*at school*) Schulleiter(in) *m(f)*; **~ of state** Staatsoberhaupt *nt*; **at the ~ of** an der Spitze von; (*tossing coin*) **~s or tails?** Kopf oder Zahl? ▷ *adj* (*leading*) Ober-; **~ boy** Schulsprecher *m*; **~ girl** Schulsprecherin *f* ▷ *vt* anführen; (*organization*) leiten; **head for** *vt* zusteuern auf +*akk*; **he's heading for trouble** er wird Ärger bekommen
headache ['hedeɪk] *n* Kopfschmerzen *pl*, Kopfweh *nt*; **header** *n* (*football*) Kopfball *m*; (*dive*) Kopfsprung *m*; **headfirst** *adj* kopfüber; **headhunt** *vt* (*Comm*) abwerben; **heading** *n* Überschrift *f*; **headlamp, headlight** *n* Scheinwerfer *m*; **headline** *n* Schlagzeile *f*; **headmaster** *n* Schulleiter *m*; **headmistress** *n* Schulleiterin *f*; **head-on collision** *adj* Frontalzusammenstoß *m*; **headphones** *npl* Kopfhörer *m*; **headquarters** *npl* (*of firm*) Zentrale *f*; **headrest, head restraint** *n* Kopfstütze *f*; **headscarf** (*pl* **-scarves**) *n* Kopftuch *nt*; **head teacher** *n* Schulleiter(in) *m(f)*
heal [hi:l] *vt, vi* heilen
health [helθ] *n* Gesundheit *f*; **good/bad for one's ~** gesund/ungesund; **your ~!** zum Wohl!; **health centre** *n* Ärztezentrum *nt*; **health club** *n* Fitnesscenter *nt*; **health food** *n* Reformkost *f*; **~ store** Bioladen *m*; **health insurance** *n* Krankenversicherung *f*;

health service *n* Gesundheitswesen *nt*; **healthy** *adj* gesund
heap [hi:p] *n* Haufen *m*; **~s of** (*fam*) jede Menge ▷ *vt, vi* häufen
hear [hɪə*] (**heard, heard**) *vt, vi* hören; **to ~ about sth** von etw erfahren; **I've ~d of it/him** ich habe schon davon/von ihm gehört; **hearing** *n* Gehör *nt*; (*Jur*) Verhandlung *f*; **hearing aid** *n* Hörgerät *nt*; **hearsay** *n* **from ~** vom Hörensagen
heart [hɑ:t] *n* Herz *nt*; **to loose/take ~** den Mut verlieren/Mut fassen; **to learn by ~** auswendig lernen; (*cards*) **~s** Herz *nt*; **queen of ~s** Herzdame *f*; **heart attack** *n* Herzanfall *m*; **heartbeat** *n* Herzschlag *m*; **heartbreaking** *adj* herzzerreißend; **heartbroken** *adj* todunglücklich, untröstlich; **heartburn** *n* Sodbrennen *nt*; **heart failure** *n* Herzversagen *nt*; **heartfelt** *adj* tief empfunden; **heartless** *adj* herzlos; **heart-throb** *n* (*fam*) Schwarm *m*; **heart-to-heart** *n* offene Aussprache; **hearty** ['hɑ:tɪ] *adj* (*meal, appetite*) herzhaft; (*welcome*) herzlich
heat [hi:t] *n* Hitze *f*; (*pleasant*) Wärme *f*; (*temperature*) Temperatur *f*; (*Sport*) Vorlauf *m* ▷ *vt* (*house, room*) heizen; **heat up** *vi* warm werden ▷ *vt* aufwärmen; **heated** *adj* beheizt; (*fig*) hitzig; **heater** *n* Heizofen *m*; (*Auto*) Heizung *f*
heath [hi:θ] *n* (*Brit*) Heide *f*; **heather** ['heðə*] *n* Heidekraut *nt*
heating ['hi:tɪŋ] *n* Heizung *f*; **heat resistant** *adj* hitzebeständig; **heatstroke** *n* Hitzschlag *m*; **heatwave** *n* Hitzewelle *f*
heaven ['hevn] *n* Himmel *m*; **heavenly** *adj* himmlisch
heavily ['hevɪlɪ] *adv* (*rain, drink etc*) stark; **heavy** ['hevɪ] *adj* schwer; (*rain, traffic, smoker etc*) stark; **heavy goods vehicle** *n* Lastkraftwagen *m*
Hebrew ['hi:bru:] *adj* hebräisch ▷ *n* (*language*) Hebräisch *nt*
hectic ['hektɪk] *adj* hektisch
he'd [hi:d] *contr of* **he had**; **he would**
hedge [hedʒ] *n* Hecke *f*
hedgehog ['hedʒhɒg] *n* Igel *m*
heel [hi:l] *n* (*Anat*) Ferse *f*; (*of shoe*) Absatz *m*
hefty ['heftɪ] *adj* schwer; (*person*) stämmig; (*fine, amount*) saftig
height [haɪt] *n* Höhe *f*, (*of person*) Größe *f*

heir [ɛə*] n Erbe m; **heiress** ['ɛərɪs] n
Erbin f

held [held] pt, pp of **hold**

helicopter ['helɪkɒptə*] n Hubschrauber
m; **heliport** ['helɪpɔ:t] n
Hubschrauberlandeplatz m

hell [hel] n Hölle f; **go to ~** scher dich zum
Teufel ▷ interj verdammt; **that's a ~ of a
lot of money** das ist verdammt viel Geld

he'll [hi:l] contr of **he will; he shall**

hello [hʌ'ləʊ] interj hallo

helmet ['helmɪt] n Helm m

help [help] n Hilfe f ▷ vt, vi helfen +dat
(with bei); **to ~ sb (to) do sth** jdm helfen,
etw zu tun; **can I ~?** kann ich (Ihnen)
behilflich sein?; **I couldn't ~ laughing** ich
musste einfach lachen; **I can't ~ it** ich
kann nichts dafür; **~ yourself** bedienen Sie
sich; **helpful** adj (person) hilfsbereit;
(useful) nützlich; **helping** n Portion f;
helpless adj hilflos

hem [hem] n Saum m

hemophiliac [hi:məʊ'fɪliæk] n (US)
Bluter m; **hemorrhage** ['hemərɪdʒ] n (US)
Blutung f; **hemorrhoids** ['hemərɔɪdz] npl
(US) Hämorrhoiden pl

hen [hen] n Henne f

hen night n (Brit)
Junggesellinnenabschied m

hence [hens] adv (reason) daher

henpecked ['henpekt] adj **to be ~** unter
dem Pantoffel stehen

hepatitis [hepə'taɪtɪs] n Hepatitis f

her [hɜ:*] adj ihr; **she's hurt ~ leg** sie hat
sich dat das Bein verletzt ▷ pron (direct
object) sie; (indirect object) ihr; **do you
know ~?** kennst du sie?; **can you help ~?**
kannst du ihr helfen?; **it's ~** sie ist's

herb [hɜ:b] n Kraut nt

herbal medicine ['hɜ:bəl-] n
Pflanzenheilkunde f; **herbal tea** n
Kräutertee m

herd [hɜ:d] n Herde f; **herd instinct** n
Herdentrieb m

here [hɪə*] adv hier; (to this place) hierher;
come ~ komm her; **I won't be ~ for lunch**
ich bin zum Mittagessen nicht da; **~ and
there** hier und da, da und dort

hereditary [hɪ'redɪtərɪ] adj erblich;
hereditary disease n Erbkrankheit f;
heritage ['herɪtɪdʒ] n Erbe nt

hernia ['hɜ:nɪə] n Leistenbruch m,
Eingeweidebruch m

hero ['hɪərəʊ] (pl -es) n Held m

heroin ['herəʊɪn] n Heroin nt

heroine ['herəʊɪn] n Heldin f; **heroism**
['herəʊɪzəm] n Heldentum nt

herring ['herɪŋ] n Hering m

hers [hɜ:z] pron ihr; **this is ~** das
gehört ihr; **a friend of ~** ein Freund von ihr

herself [hɜ:'self] pron (reflexive) sich; **she's
bought ~ a flat** sie hat sich eine Wohnung
gekauft; **she needs it for ~** sie braucht es
für sich (selbst); (emphatic) **she did it ~** sie
hat es selbst gemacht; **(all) by ~** allein

he's [hi:z] contr of **he is; he has**

hesitant ['hezɪtənt] adj zögernd;
hesitate ['hezɪteɪt] vi zögern; **don't ~ to
ask** fragen Sie ruhig; **hesitation** n Zögern
nt; **without ~** ohne zu zögern

heterosexual [hetərəʊ'seksjʊəl] adj
heterosexuell ▷ n Heterosexuelle(r) mf

HGV abbr = **heavy goods vehicle** LKW m

hi [haɪ] interj hi, hallo

hiccup ['hɪkʌp] n Schluckauf m; (minor
problem) Problemchen nt; **to have (the) ~s**
Schluckauf haben

hid [hɪd] pt of **hide**

hidden ['hɪdn] pp of **hide**

hide [haɪd] (**hid, hidden**) vt verstecken
(from vor +dat); (feelings, truth) verbergen;
(cover) verdecken ▷ vi sich verstecken
(from vor +dat)

hideous ['hɪdɪəs] adj scheußlich

hiding ['haɪdɪŋ] n (beating) Tracht f
Prügel; (concealment) **to be in ~** sich
versteckt halten; **hiding place** n Versteck
nt

hi-fi ['haɪfaɪ] n Hi-Fi nt; (system)
Hi-Fi-Anlage f

high [haɪ] adj hoch; (wind) stark; (living)
im großen Stil; (on drugs) high ▷ adv hoch
▷ n (Meteo) Hoch nt; **highchair** n
Hochstuhl m; **higher** adj höher; **higher
education** n Hochschulbildung f; **high
flier** n Hochbegabte(r) (m)f; **high heels**
npl Stöckelschuhe pl; **high jump** n
Hochsprung m; **Highlands** npl
(schottisches) Hochland nt; **highlight** n
(in hair) Strähnchen nt; (fig) Höhepunkt m
▷ vt (with pen) hervorheben; **highlighter**
n Textmarker m; **highly** adj hoch, sehr;
~ paid hoch bezahlt; **I think ~ of him** ich
habe eine hohe Meinung von ihm;
high-performance adj Hochleistungs-;
high pressure n Hochdruck m; **high**

school n (US) Highschool f, ≈ Gymnasium nt; **high-speed** adj Schnell-; **~ train** Hochgeschwindigkeitszug m; **high street** n Hauptstraße f; **high tech** adj Hightech- ▷ n Hightech nt; **high tide** n Flut f; **highway** n (US) ≈ Autobahn f; (Brit) Landstraße f

hijack ['haɪdʒæk] vt entführen, hijacken; **hijacker** n Entführer(in) m(f), Hijacker m

hike [haɪk] vi wandern ▷ n Wanderung f; **hiker** n Wanderer m, Wanderin f; **hiking** n Wandern nt

hilarious [hɪ'lɛərɪəs] adj zum Schreien komisch

hill [hɪl] n Hügel m; (higher) Berg m; **hilly** adj hügelig

him [hɪm] pron (direct object) ihn; (indirect object) ihm; (can you help ~? kannst du ihm helfen?; **it's ~** er ist's; **~ too** er auch

himself [hɪm'self] pron (reflexive) sich; **he's bought ~ a flat** er hat sich eine Wohnung gekauft; **he needs it for ~** er braucht es für sich (selbst); (emphatic) **he did it ~** er hat es selbst gemacht; **(all) by ~** allein

hinder ['hɪndə*] vt behindern; **hindrance** ['hɪndrəns] n Behinderung f

Hindu ['hɪnduː] adj hinduistisch ▷ n Hindu m; **Hinduism** ['hɪnduːɪzəm] n Hinduismus m

hinge [hɪndʒ] n Scharnier nt; (on door) Angel f

hint [hɪnt] n Wink m, Andeutung f; (trace) Spur f ▷ vi andeuten (at akk)

hip [hɪp] n Hüfte f ▷ adj (trend) hip, trendy

hippopotamus [hɪpə'pɒtəməs] n Nilpferd nt

hire ['haɪə*] vt (worker) anstellen; (car, bike etc) mieten ▷ n Miete f; **for ~** (taxi) frei; **hire(d) car** n Mietwagen m; **hire purchase** n Ratenkauf m

his [hɪz] adj sein; **he's hurt ~ leg** er hat sich dat das Bein verletzt ▷ pron seine(r, s); **it's ~** es gehört ihm; **a friend of ~** ein Freund von ihm

historic [hɪ'stɒrɪk] adj (significant) historisch; **historical** adj (monument etc) historisch; (studies etc) geschichtlich; **history** ['hɪstərɪ] n Geschichte f

hit [hɪt] n (blow) Schlag m; (on target) Treffer m; (success) Erfolg m; (Mus) Hit m ▷ vt (**hit, hit**) schlagen; (bullet, stone etc)

treffen; **the car ~ the tree** das Auto fuhr gegen einen Baum; **to ~ one's head on sth** sich dat den Kopf an etw dat stoßen; **hit (up)on** vt stoßen auf +akk; **hit-and-run** adj **~ accident** Unfall m mit Fahrerflucht

hitch [hɪtʃ] vt (pull up) hochziehen ▷ n Schwierigkeit f; **without a ~** reibungslos

hitch-hike ['hɪtʃhaɪk] vi trampen; **hitch-hiker** n Tramper(in) m(f); **hitchhiking** n Trampen nt

HIV abbr = **human immunodeficiency virus** HIV nt; **~ positive/negative** HIV-positiv/negativ

hive [haɪv] n Bienenstock m

HM abbr = His/Her Majesty

HMS abbr = His/Her Majesty's Ship

hoarse [hɔːs] adj heiser

hoax [həʊks] n Streich m, Jux m; (false alarm) blinder Alarm

hob [hɒb] n (of cooker) Kochfeld nt

hobble ['hɒbl] vi humpeln

hobby ['hɒbɪ] n Hobby nt

hobo ['həʊbəʊ] (pl **-es**) n (US) Penner(in) m(f)

hockey ['hɒkɪ] n Hockey nt

hold [həʊld] (**held, held**) vt halten; (contain) enthalten; (be able to contain) fassen; (post, office) innehaben; (value) behalten; (meeting) abhalten; (person as prisoner) gefangen halten; **to ~ one's breath** den Atem anhalten; **to ~ hands** Händchen halten; **~ the line** (Tel) bleiben Sie am Apparat ▷ vi halten; (weather) sich halten ▷ n (grasp) Halt m; (of ship, aircraft) Laderaum m; **hold back** vt zurückhalten; (keep secret) verheimlichen; **hold on** vi sich festhalten; (wait) warten; (Tel) dranbleiben; **to ~ to sth** etw festhalten; **hold out** vt ausstrecken; (offer) hinhalten; (offer) bieten ▷ vi durchhalten; **hold up** vt hochhalten; (support) stützen; (delay) aufhalten; **holdall** n Reisetasche f; **holder** n (person) Inhaber(in) m(f); **holdup** n (in traffic) Stau m; (robbery) Überfall m

hole [həʊl] n Loch nt; (of fox, rabbit) Bau m; **~ in the wall** (cash dispenser) Geldautomat m

holiday ['hɒlɪdeɪ] n (day off) freier Tag; (public ~) Feiertag m; (vacation) Urlaub m; (at school) Ferien pl; **on ~** im Urlaub; **to go on ~** Urlaub machen; **holiday camp** n Ferienlager nt; **holiday home**

Ferienhaus nt; (flat) Ferienwohnung f;
holidaymaker n Urlauber(in) m(f);
holiday resort n Ferienort m
Holland ['hɒlənd] n Holland nt
hollow ['hɒləʊ] adj hohl; (words) leer ▷ n
Vertiefung f
holly ['hɒlɪ] n Stechpalme f
holy ['həʊlɪ] adj heilig; **Holy Week** n
Karwoche f
home [həʊm] n Zuhause nt; (area, country)
Heimat f; (institution) Heim nt; **at ~** zu
Hause; **to make oneself at ~** es sich dat
bequem machen; **away from ~** verreist
▷ adv **to go ~** nach Hause gehen/fahren;
home address n Heimatadresse f; **home
country** n Heimatland nt; **home game** n
(Sport) Heimspiel nt; **homeless** adj
obdachlos; **homely** adj häuslich; (US:
ugly) unscheinbar; **home-made** adj selbst
gemacht; **home movie** n Amateurfilm
m; **Home Office** n (Brit)
Innenministerium nt
homeopathic adj (US) see
homoeopathic
home page ['həʊmpeɪdʒ] n (Inform)
Homepage f; **Home Secretary** n (Brit)
Innenminister(in) m(f); **homesick** adj **to
be ~** Heimweh haben; **home town** n
Heimatstadt f; **homework** n
Hausaufgaben pl
homicide ['hɒmɪsaɪd] n (US) Totschlag m
homoeopathic [həʊmɪəʊ'pæθɪk] adj
homöopathisch
homosexual [hɒməʊ'sekʃʊəl] adj
homosexuell ▷ n Homosexuelle(r) mf
Honduras [hɒn'djʊərəs] n Honduras nt
honest ['ɒnɪst] adj ehrlich; **honesty** n
Ehrlichkeit f
honey ['hʌnɪ] n Honig m; **honeycomb** n
Honigwabe f; **honeydew melon** n
Honigmelone f; **honeymoon** n
Flitterwochen pl
Hong Kong [hɒŋ'kɒŋ] n Hongkong nt
honor (US) see **honour**; **honorary**
['ɒnərərɪ] adj (member, title etc) Ehren-,
ehrenamtlich; **honour** ['ɒnə*] vt ehren;
(cheque) einlösen; (contract) einhalten ▷ n
Ehre f; **in ~ of** zu Ehren von; **honourable**
adj ehrenhaft; **honours degree** n
akademischer Grad mit Prüfung im
Spezialfach
hood [hʊd] n Kapuze f; (Auto) Verdeck nt;
(US Auto) Kühlerhaube f

hoof [hu:f] (pl **hooves**) n Huf m
hook [hʊk] n Haken m; **hooked** adj (keen)
besessen (on von); (drugs) abhängig sein
(on von)
hooligan ['hu:lɪgən] n Hooligan m
hoot [hu:t] vi (Auto) hupen
Hoover® ['hu:və] n Staubsauger m;
hoover vi, vt staubsaugen
hop [hɒp] vi hüpfen ▷ n (Bot) Hopfen m
hope [həʊp] vi, vt hoffen (for auf +akk); **I
~ so/~ not** hoffentlich/hoffentlich nicht; **I
~ (that) we'll meet** ich hoffe, dass wir uns
sehen werden ▷ n Hoffnung f; **there's no
~** es ist aussichtslos; **hopeful** adj
hoffnungsvoll; **hopefully** adv (full of hope)
hoffnungsvoll; (I hope so) hoffentlich;
hopeless adj hoffnungslos; (incompetent)
miserabel
horizon [hə'raɪzn] n Horizont m;
horizontal [hɒrɪ'zɒntl] adj horizontal
hormone ['hɔ:məʊn] n Hormon nt
horn [hɔ:n] n Horn nt; (Auto) Hupe f
hornet ['hɔ:nɪt] n Hornisse f
horny ['hɔ:nɪ] adj (fam) geil
horoscope ['hɒrəskəʊp] n Horoskop nt
horrible, horribly ['hɒrɪbl, -blɪ] adj, adv
schrecklich; **horrid, horridly** ['hɒrɪd, -lɪ]
adj, adv abscheulich; **horrify** ['hɒrɪfaɪ] vt
entsetzen; **horror** ['hɒrə*] n Entsetzen
nt; **~s** (things) Schrecken pl
hors d'œuvre [ɔ:'dɜ:vr] n Vorspeise f
horse [hɔ:s] n Pferd nt; **horse chestnut** n
Rosskastanie f; **horsepower** n
Pferdestärke f, PS nt; **horse racing** n
Pferderennen nt; **horseradish** n
Meerrettich m; **horse riding** n Reiten nt;
horseshoe n Hufeisen nt
horticulture ['hɔ:tɪkʌltʃə*] n Gartenbau
m
hose, hosepipe [həʊz, 'həʊzpaɪp] n
Schlauch m
hospitable [hɒ'spɪtəbl] adj
gastfreundlich
hospital ['hɒspɪtl] n Krankenhaus nt
hospitality [hɒspɪ'tælɪtɪ] n
Gastfreundschaft f
host [həʊst] n Gastgeber m; (Tv: of show)
Moderator(in) m(f), Talkmaster(in) m(f)
▷ vt (party) geben; (TV show)
moderieren
hostage ['hɒstɪdʒ] n Geisel f
hostel ['hɒstəl] n Wohnheim nt; (youth ~)
Jugendherberge f

hostess ['həʊstɪs] n (of a party)
Gastgeberin f
hostile ['hɒstaɪl] adj feindlich; **hostility**
[hɒsˈtɪlɪtɪ] n. Feindseligkeit f
hot [hɒt] adj heiß; (drink, food, water)
warm; (spiced) scharf; **I'm (feeling)** ~ mir
ist heiß; **hot cross bun** n Rosinenbrötchen
mit einem Kreuz darauf, hauptsächlich zu
Ostern gegessen; **hot dog** n Hotdog nt
hotel [həʊˈtel] n Hotel nt; **hotel room** n
Hotelzimmer nt
hothouse n Treibhaus nt; **hotline** n
Hotline f; **hotplate** n Kochplatte f;
hotpot n Fleischeintopf mit Kartoffeleinlage;
hot-water bottle n Wärmflasche f
hour ['aʊə*] n Stunde f; **to wait for ~s**
stundenlang warten; **~s** pl (of shops etc)
Geschäftszeiten pl; **hourly** adj stündlich
house [haʊs] (pl **houses**) n Haus nt; **at
my ~** bei mir (zu Hause); **to my ~** zu mir
(nach Hause); **on the ~** auf Kosten des
Hauses; **the House of Commons/Lords**
das britische Unterhaus/Oberhaus; **the
Houses of Parliament** das britische
Parlamentsgebäude ▷ [haʊz] vt
unterbringen; **houseboat** n Hausboot nt;
household n Haushalt m; ~ **appliance**
Haushaltsgerät nt; **house-husband** n
Hausmann m; **housekeeping** n
Haushaltung f; (money) Haushaltsgeld nt;
house-trained adj stubenrein;
house-warming (party) n Einzugsparty
f; **housewife** (pl **-wives**) n Hausfrau f;
house wine n Hauswein m; **housework**
n Hausarbeit f
housing ['haʊzɪŋ] n (houses) Wohnungen
pl; (house building) Wohnungsbau m;
housing benefit n Wohngeld nt;
housing development, housing estate
(Brit) n Wohnsiedlung f
hover ['hɒvə*] vi schweben; **hovercraft** n
Luftkissenboot nt
how [haʊ] adv wie; ~ **many** wie viele;
~ **much** wie viel; ~ **are you?** wie geht es
Ihnen?; ~ **are things?** wie geht's?; ~**'s
work?** was macht die Arbeit?; ~ **about ...?**
wie wäre es mit ...?; **however** [haʊˈevə*]
conj (but) jedoch, aber ▷ adv (no matter
how) wie ... auch; ~ **much it costs** wie viel
es auch kostet; ~ **you do it** wie man es
auch macht
howl [haʊl] vi heulen; **howler** ['haʊlə*] n
(fam) grober Schnitzer

HP, hp n (Brit) abbr = **hire purchase**
Ratenkauf m ▷ abbr = **horsepower** PS
HQ abbr = **headquarters**
hubcap ['hʌbkæp] n Radkappe f
hug [hʌg] vt umarmen ▷ n Umarmung f
huge [hju:dʒ] adj riesig
hum [hʌm] vi, vt summen
human ['hju:mən] adj menschlich;
~ **rights** Menschenrechte pl ▷ n ~ **(being)**
Mensch m; **humanitarian**
[hju:mænɪˈtɛərɪən] adj humanitär;
humanity [hju:ˈmænɪtɪ] n Menschheit f;
(kindliness) Menschlichkeit f; **humanities**
Geisteswissenschaften pl
humble ['hʌmbl] adj demütig; (modest)
bescheiden
humid ['hju:mɪd] adj feucht; **humidity**
[hju:ˈmɪdɪtɪ] n (Luft)feuchtigkeit f
humiliate [hju:ˈmɪlɪeɪt] vt demütigen;
humiliation [hju:mɪlɪˈeɪʃn] n
Erniedrigung f, Demütigung f
humor (US) see **humour**; **humorous**
['hju:mərəs] adj humorvoll; (story) lustig,
witzig; **humour** ['hju:mə*] n Humor m;
sense of ~ Sinn m für Humor
hump [hʌmp] n Buckel m
hunch [hʌntʃ] n Gefühl nt, Ahnung f ▷ vt
(back) krümmen; **hunchback** n
Bucklige(r) mf
hundred ['hʌndrəd] num **one** ~, **a**
~ (ein)hundert; **a** ~ **and one**
hundert(und)eins; **two** ~ zweihundert;
hundredth adj hundertste(r, s) ▷ n
(fraction) Hundertstel nt; **hundredweight**
n Zentner m (50,8 kg)
hung [hʌŋ] pt, pp of **hang**
Hungarian [hʌŋˈgɛərɪən] adj ungarisch
▷ n (person) Ungar(in) m(f); (language)
Ungarisch nt; **Hungary** ['hʌŋgərɪ] n
Ungarn nt
hunger ['hʌŋgə*] n Hunger m; **hungry**
['hʌŋgrɪ] adj hungrig; **to be** ~ Hunger
haben
hunk [hʌŋk] n (fam) gut aussehender
Mann
hunt [hʌnt] n Jagd f; (search) Suche f (for
nach) ▷ vt, vi jagen; (search) suchen (for
nach); **hunting** n Jagen nt, Jagd f
hurdle ['hɜ:dl] n (a. fig) Hürde f; **the
400m ~s** der 400m-Hürdenlauf
hurl [hɜ:l] vt schleudern
hurray [hʊˈreɪ] interj hurra
hurricane ['hʌrɪkən] n Orkan m

hurried ['hʌrɪd] *adj* eilig; **hurry** ['hʌrɪ] *n*
Eile *f*; **to be in a ~** es eilig haben; **there's
no ~** es eilt nicht ▷ *vi* sich beeilen; **~ (up)**
mach schnell! ▷ *vt* antreiben

hurt [hɜːt] (**hurt, hurt**) *vt* wehtun +*dat*;
(*wound: person, feelings*) verletzen; **I've
~ my arm** ich habe mir am Arm wehgetan
▷ *vi* wehtun; **my arm ~s** mir tut der Arm
weh

husband ['hʌzbənd] *n* Ehemann *m*

husky ['hʌskɪ] *adj* rau ▷ *n* Schlittenhund
m

hut [hʌt] *n* Hütte *f*

hyacinth ['haɪəsɪnθ] *n* Hyazinthe *f*

hybrid ['haɪbrɪd] *n* Kreuzung *f*

hydroelectric ['haɪdrəʊɪ'lektrɪk] *adj*
~ power station Wasserkraftwerk *nt*

hydrofoil ['haɪdrəʊfɔɪl] *n*
Tragflächenboot *nt*

hydrogen ['haɪdrədʒən] *n* Wasserstoff *m*

hygiene ['haɪdʒiːn] *n* Hygiene *f*; **hygienic**
[haɪ'dʒiːnɪk] *adj* hygienisch

hymn [hɪm] *n* Kirchenlied *nt*

hypermarket ['haɪpəmɑːkɪt] *n*
Großmarkt *m*; **hypersensitive** *adj*
überempfindlich

hyphen ['haɪfən] *n* Bindestrich *m*

hypnosis [hɪp'nəʊsɪs] *n* Hypnose *f*;
hypnotize ['hɪpnətaɪz] *vt* hypnotisieren

hypochondriac [haɪpəʊ'kɒndrɪæk] *n*
eingebildete(r) Kranke(r), eingebildete
Kranke

hypocrisy ['hɪ'pəkrəsɪ] *n* Heuchelei *f*;
hypocrite ['hɪpəkrɪt] *n* Heuchler(in) *m(f)*

hypodermic [haɪpə'dɜːmɪk] *adj, n*
~ (needle) Spritze *f*

hypothetical [haɪpəʊ'θetɪkəl] *adj*
hypothetisch

hysteria [hɪ'stɪərɪə] *n* Hysterie *f*;
hysterical [hɪ'sterɪkəl] *adj* hysterisch;
(*amusing*) zum Totlachen

I

I [aɪ] pron ich

ice [aɪs] n Eis nt ▷ vt (cake) glasieren;
iceberg n Eisberg m; **iceberg lettuce** n
Eisbergsalat m; **icebox** n (US)
Kühlschrank m; **icecold** adj eiskalt;
ice cream n Eis nt; **ice cube** n
Eiswürfel m; **iced** adj eisgekühlt; (coffee,
tea) Eis-; (cake) glasiert; **ice hockey** n
Eishockey nt

Iceland ['aɪslənd] n Island nt; **Icelander** n
Isländer(in) m(f); **Icelandic** [aɪs'lændɪk]
adj isländisch ▷ n (language) Isländisch nt

ice lolly ['aɪslɒlɪ] n (Brit) Eis nt am Stiel;
ice rink n Kunsteisbahn f; **ice skating** n
Schlittschuhlaufen nt

icing ['aɪsɪŋ] n (on cake) Zuckerguss m

icon ['aɪkɒn] n Ikone f; (Inform) Icon nt,
Programmsymbol nt

icy ['aɪsɪ] adj (slippery) vereist; (cold) eisig

I'd [aɪd] contr of **I would**; **I had**

ID abbr = **identification** Ausweis m

idea [aɪ'dɪə] n Idee f; (**I've**) **no ~** (ich habe)
keine Ahnung; **that's my ~ of ...** so stelle
ich mir ... vor

ideal [aɪ'dɪəl] n Ideal nt ▷ adj ideal;
ideally adv ideal; (before statement)
idealerweise

identical [aɪ'dentɪkəl] adj identisch;
~ twins eineiige Zwillinge
identify [aɪ'dentɪfaɪ] vt identifizieren;
identity [aɪ'dentɪtɪ] n Identität f;
identity card n Personalausweis m
idiom ['ɪdɪəm] n Redewendung f;
idiomatic adj idiomatisch
idiot ['ɪdɪət] n Idiot(in) m(f)
idle ['aɪdl] adj (doing nothing) untätig;
(worker) unbeschäftigt; (machines) außer
Betrieb; (lazy) faul; (promise, threat) leer
idol ['aɪdl] n Idol nt; **idolize** ['aɪdəlaɪz] vt
vergöttern
idyllic [ɪ'dɪlɪk] adj idyllisch
i.e. abbr = **id est** d.h.

if [ɪf] conj **1** wenn (in case also) falls; **if I
were you** wenn ich Sie wäre
2 (although): **(even) if** (selbst or auch)
wenn
3 (whether) ob
4: **if so/not** wenn ja/nicht; **if only ...**
wenn ... doch nur ...; **if only I could** wenn
ich doch nur könnte; see also **as**

ignition [ɪg'nɪʃən] n Zündung f; **ignition
key** n (Auto) Zündschlüssel m
ignorance ['ɪgnərəns] n Unwissenheit f;
ignorant adj unwissend; **ignore** [ɪg'nɔː*]
vt ignorieren, nicht beachten
I'll [aɪl] contr of **I will**; **I shall**
ill [ɪl] adj krank; **~ at ease** unbehaglich
illegal [ɪ'liːgəl] adj illegal
illegitimate [ɪlɪ'dʒɪtɪmət] adj unzulässig;
(child) unehelich
illiterate [ɪ'lɪtərət] adj **to be
~** Analphabet(in) sein
illness ['ɪlnəs] n Krankheit f
illuminate [ɪ'luːmɪneɪt] vt beleuchten;
illuminating adj (remark)
aufschlussreich
illusion [ɪ'luːʒən] n Illusion f; **to be under
the ~ that ...** sich einbilden, dass ...
illustrate ['ɪləstreɪt] vt illustrieren;
illustration n Abbildung f, Bild nt
I'm [aɪm] contr of **I am**
image ['ɪmɪdʒ] n Bild nt; (public ~) Image
nt; **imaginable** [ɪ'mædʒɪnəbl] adj
denkbar; **imaginary** [ɪ'mædʒɪnərɪ] adj
eingebildet; **~ world** Fantasiewelt f;
imagination [ɪmædʒɪ'neɪʃən] n Fantasie

f. (*mistaken*) Einbildung *f;* **imaginative**
[ɪ'mædʒɪnətɪv] *adj* fantasievoll; **imagine**
[ɪ'mædʒɪn] *vt* sich vorstellen; (*wrongly*)
sich einbilden; **~!** stell dir vor!
imbecile ['ɪmbəsiːl] *n* Trottel *m*
imitate ['ɪmɪteɪt] *vt* nachahmen,
nachmachen; **imitation** *n* Nachahmung *f*
▷ *adj* imitiert; **~ leather** Kunstleder *nt*
immaculate [ɪ'mækjʊlɪt] *adj* tadellos;
(*spotless*) makellos
immature [ɪmə'tjʊə*] *adj* unreif
immediate [ɪ'miːdɪət] *adj* unmittelbar;
(*instant*) sofortig; (*reply*) umgehend;
immediately *adv* sofort
immense, immensely [ɪ'mens, -lɪ] *adj,
adv* riesig, enorm
immersion heater [ɪ'mɜːʃn hiːtə] *n*
Boiler *m*
immigrant ['ɪmɪgrənt] *n* Einwanderer *m*,
Einwanderin *f;* **immigration** [ɪmɪ'greɪʃən]
n Einwanderung *f;* (*facility*)
Einwanderungskontrolle *f*
immobilize [ɪ'məʊbɪlaɪz] *vt* lähmen;
immobilizer *n* (*Auto*) Wegfahrsperre *f*
immoral [ɪ'mɒrəl] *adj* unmoralisch
immortal [ɪ'mɔːtl] *adj* unsterblich
immune [ɪ'mjuːn] *adj* (*Med*) immun (*from,
to* gegen); **immune system** *n*
Immunsystem *nt*
impact ['ɪmpækt] *n* Aufprall *m;* (*effect*)
Auswirkung *f* (*on* auf +*akk*)
impatience [ɪm'peɪʃəns] *n* Ungeduld *f;*
impatient, impatiently *adj, adv*
ungeduldig
impeccable [ɪm'pekəbl] *adj* tadellos
impede [ɪm'piːd] *vt* behindern
imperative [ɪm'perətɪv] *adj* unbedingt
erforderlich ▷ *n* (*Ling*) Imperativ *m*
imperfect [ɪm'pɜːfɪkt] *adj*
unvollkommen; (*goods*) fehlerhaft ▷ *n*
(*Ling*) Imperfekt *nt;* **imperfection**
[ɪmpə'fekʃən] *n* Unvollkommenheit *f;*
(*fault*) Fehler *m*
imperial [ɪm'pɪərɪəl] *adj* kaiserlich,
Reichs-; **imperialism** *n* Imperialismus *m*
impertinence [ɪm'pɜːtɪnəns] *n*
Unverschämtheit *f,* Zumutung *f;*
impertinent *adj* unverschämt
implant ['ɪmplɑːnt] *n* (*Med*) Implantat *nt*
implausible [ɪm'plɔːzəbl] *adj*
unglaubwürdig
implement ['ɪmplɪmənt] *n* Werkzeug *nt,*
Gerät *nt* ▷ [ɪmplɪ'ment] *vt* durchführen

implication [ɪmplɪ'keɪʃən] *n* Folge *f,*
Auswirkung *f;* (*logical*) Schlussfolgerung *f;*
implicit [ɪm'plɪsɪt] *adj* implizit,
unausgesprochen; **imply** [ɪm'plaɪ] *vt*
(*indicate*) andeuten; (*mean*) bedeuten; **are
you ~ing that ...** wollen Sie damit sagen,
dass ...
impolite [ɪmpə'laɪt] *adj* unhöflich
import [ɪm'pɔːt] *vt* einführen,
importieren ▷ *n* ['ɪmpɔːt] Einfuhr *f,*
Import *m*
importance [ɪm'pɔːtəns] *n* Bedeutung *f;*
of no ~ unwichtig; **important** *adj* wichtig
(*to sb* für jdn); (*significant*) bedeutend;
(*influential*) einflussreich
import duty ['ɪmpɔːtdjuːtɪ] *n*
Einfuhrzoll *m;* **import licence** *n*
Einfuhrgenehmigung *f*
impose [ɪm'pəʊz] *vt* (*conditions*)
auferlegen (*on dat*); (*penalty, sanctions*)
verhängen (*on gegen*); **imposing**
[ɪm'pəʊzɪŋ] *adj* eindrucksvoll, imposant
impossible [ɪm'pɒsəbl] *adj.* unmöglich
impotence ['ɪmpətəns] *n* Machtlosigkeit
f; (*sexual*) Impotenz *f;* **impotent** *adj*
machtlos; (*sexually*) impotent
impractical [ɪm'præktɪkəl] *adj*
unpraktisch; (*plan*) undurchführbar
impress [ɪm'pres] *vt* beeindrucken;
impression [ɪm'preʃən] *n* Eindruck *m;*
impressive *adj* eindrucksvoll
imprison [ɪm'prɪzn] *vt* inhaftieren;
imprisonment *n* Inhaftierung *f*
improbability [ɪmprɒbə'bɪlɪtɪ] *n*
Unwahrscheinlichkeit *f;* **improbable**
[ɪm'prɒbəbl] *adj* unwahrscheinlich
improper [ɪm'prɒpə*] *adj* (*indecent*)
unanständig; (*use*) unsachgemäß
improve [ɪm'pruːv] *vt* verbessern ▷ *vi*
sich verbessern, besser werden; (*patient*)
Fortschritte machen; **improvement** *n*
Verbesserung *f* (*in* +*gen; on* gegenüber); (*in
appearance*) Verschönerung *f*
improvise ['ɪmprəvaɪz] *vt, vi*
improvisieren
impulse ['ɪmpʌls] *n* Impuls *m;* **impulsive**
[ɪm'pʌlsɪv] *adj* impulsiv

○ **KEYWORD**

in [ɪn] *prep* **1** (*indicating place, position*) in
+*dat;* (*with motion*) in +*acc;* **in here/there**
hier/dort; **in London** in London; **in the**

United States in den Vereinigten
Staaten
2 (*indicating time: during*) in +*dat*; **in
summer** im Sommer; **in 1988** (im Jahre)
1988; **in the afternoon** nachmittags, am
Nachmittag
3 (*indicating time: in the space of*)
innerhalb von; **I'll see you in 2 weeks** or
in 2 weeks' time ich sehe Sie in zwei
Wochen
4 (*indicating manner, circumstances, state etc*)
in +*dat*; **in the sun/rain** in der Sonne/im
Regen; **in English/French** auf
Englisch/Französisch; **in a loud/soft
voice** mit lauter/leiser Stimme
5 (*with ratios, numbers*): **1 in 10** jeder
Zehnte; **20 pence in the pound** 20 Pence
pro Pfund; **they lined up in twos** sie
stellten sich in Zweierreihe auf
6 (*referring to people, works*): **the disease is
common in children** die Krankheit ist bei
Kindern häufig; **in Dickens** bei Dickens;
we have a loyal friend in him er ist uns
ein treuer Freund
7 (*indicating profession etc*): **to be in
teaching/the army** Lehrer in/beim
Militär sein; **to be in publishing** im
Verlagswesen arbeiten
8 (*with present participle*): **in saying this, I
...** wenn ich das sage, ... ich; **in accepting
this view, he ...** weil er diese Meinung
akzeptierte, ... er
▷ *adv*; **to be in** (*person: at home, work*) da
sein (*train, ship, plane*) angekommen sein
(*in fashion*) in sein: **to ask sb in** jdn
hereinbitten; **to run/limp** *etc* **in**
hereingerannt/gehumpelt *etc* kommen
▷ *n*; **the ins and outs** (*of proposal,
situation etc*) die Feinheiten

inability [ɪnəˈbɪlɪtɪ] *n* Unfähigkeit *f*
inaccessible [ɪnækˈsesəbl] *adj* (*a. fig*)
unzugänglich
inaccurate [ɪnˈækjʊrɪt] *adj* ungenau
inadequate [ɪnˈædɪkwət] *adj*
unzulänglich
inapplicable [ɪnəˈplɪkəbl] *adj*
unzutreffend
inappropriate [ɪnəˈprəʊprɪət] *adj*
unpassend; (*clothing*) ungeeignet; (*remark*)
unangebracht
inborn [ɪnˈbɔːn] *adj* angeboren
incapable [ɪnˈkeɪpəbl] *adj* unfähig (*of* zu);

to be ~ of doing sth nicht imstande sein,
etw zu tun
incense [ˈɪnsens] *n* Weihrauch *m*
incentive [ɪnˈsentɪv] *n* Anreiz *m*
incessant, incessantly [ɪnˈsesnt, -lɪ] *adj,
adv* unaufhörlich
incest [ˈɪnsest] *n* Inzest *m*
inch [ɪntʃ] *n* Zoll *m* (2,54 cm)
incident [ˈɪnsɪdənt] *n* Vorfall *m*;
(*disturbance*) Zwischenfall *m*; **incidentally**
[ɪnsɪˈdentlɪ] *adv* nebenbei bemerkt,
übrigens
inclination [ɪnklɪˈneɪʃən] *n* Neigung *f*;
inclined [ɪnˈklaɪnd] *adj* **to be ~ to do sth**
dazu neigen, etw zu tun
include [ɪnˈkluːd] *vt* einschließen; (*on list,
in group*) aufnehmen; **including** *prep*
einschließlich (+*gen*); **not ~ service**
Bedienung nicht inbegriffen; **inclusive**
[ɪnˈkluːsɪv] *adj* einschließlich (*of* +*gen*);
(*price*) Pauschal-
incoherent [ɪnkəʊˈhɪərənt] *adj*
zusammenhanglos
income [ˈɪnkʌm] *n* Einkommen *nt*; (*from
business*) Einkünfte *pl*; **income tax** *n*
Einkommensteuer *f*; (*on wages, salary*)
Lohnsteuer *f*; **incoming** [ˈɪnkʌmɪn] *adj*
ankommend; (*mail*) eingehend
incompatible [ɪnkəmˈpætəbl] *adj*
unvereinbar; (*people*) unverträglich;
(*Inform*) nicht kompatibel
incompetent [ɪnˈkɒmpɪtənt] *adj* unfähig
incomplete [ɪnkəmˈpliːt] *adj*
unvollständig
incomprehensible [ɪnkɒmprɪˈhensəbl]
adj unverständlich
inconceivable [ɪnkənˈsiːvəbl] *adj*
unvorstellbar
inconsiderate [ɪnkənˈsɪdərət] *adj*
rücksichtslos
inconsistency [ɪnkənˈsɪstənsɪ] *n*
Inkonsequenz *f*; (*contradictory*)
Widersprüchlichkeit *f*; **inconsistent** *adj*
inkonsequent; (*contradictory*)
widersprüchlich; (*work*) unbeständig
inconvenience [ɪnkənˈviːnɪəns] *n*
Unannehmlichkeit *f*; (*trouble*) Umstände
pl; **inconvenient** *adj* ungünstig,
unbequem; (*time*) **it's ~ for me** es kommt
mir ungelegen; **if it's not too ~ for you**
wenn es dir passt
incorporate [ɪnˈkɔːpəreɪt] *vt* aufnehmen
(*into* in +*akk*); (*include*) enthalten

incorrect [ɪnˈkərekt] *adj* falsch; (*improper*) inkorrekt

increase [ˈɪnkriːs] *n* Zunahme *f* (*in an* +dat); (*in amount, speed*) Erhöhung *f* (*in* +gen); **~ in size** Vergrößerung *f* ▷ [ɪnˈkriːs] *vt* (*price, taxes, salary, speed etc*) erhöhen; (*wealth*) vermehren; (*number*) vergrößern; (*business*) erweitern ▷ *vi* zunehmen (*in an* +dat); (*prices*) steigen; (*in size*) größer werden; (*in number*) sich vermehren; **increasingly** [ɪnˈkriːsɪŋlɪ] *adv* zunehmend

incredible, incredibly [ɪnˈkredəbl, -blɪ] *adj, adv* unglaublich; (*very good*) fantastisch

incredulous [ɪnˈkredjʊləs] *adj* ungläubig, skeptisch

incriminate [ɪnˈkrɪmɪneɪt] *vt* belasten

incubator [ˈɪnkjʊbeɪtə*] *n* Brutkasten *m*

incurable [ɪnˈkjʊərəbl] *adj* unheilbar

indecent [ɪnˈdiːsnt] *adj* unanständig

indecisive [ɪndɪˈsaɪsɪv] *adj* (*person*) unentschlossen; (*result*) nicht entscheidend

indeed [ɪnˈdiːd] *adv* tatsächlich; (*as answer*) allerdings; **very hot ~** wirklich sehr heiß

indefinite [ɪnˈdefɪnɪt] *adj* unbestimmt; **indefinitely** *adv* endlos; (*postpone*) auf unbestimmte Zeit

independence [ɪndɪˈpendəns] *n* Unabhängigkeit *f*

Independence Day

Der **Independence Day**, der 4. Juli, ist in den USA ein gesetzlicher Feiertag zum Gedenken an die Unabhängigkeitserklärung am 4. Juli 1776, mit der die 13 amerikanischen Kolonien ihre Freiheit und Unabhängigkeit von Großbritannien erklärten.

independent [ɪndɪˈpendənt] *adj* unabhängig (*of* von); (*person*) selbstständig

indescribable [ɪndɪˈskraɪbəbl] *adj* unbeschreiblich

index [ˈɪndeks] *n* Index *m*, Verzeichnis *nt*; **index finger** *n* Zeigefinger *m*

India [ˈɪndɪə] *n* Indien *nt*; **Indian** [ˈɪndɪən] *adj* indisch; (*Native American*) indianisch

▷ *n* Inder(in) *m(f)*; (*Native American*) Indianer(in) *m(f)*; **Indian Ocean** *n* Indischer Ozean; **Indian summer** *n* Spätsommer *m*, Altweibersommer *m*

indicate [ˈɪndɪkeɪt] *vt* (*show*) zeigen; (*instrument*) anzeigen; (*suggest*) hinweisen auf +akk ▷ *vi* (*Auto*) blinken; **indication** [ɪndɪˈkeɪʃn] *n* (*sign*) Anzeichen *nt* (*of* für); **indicator** [ˈɪndɪkeɪtə*] *n* (*Auto*) Blinker *m*

indifferent [ɪnˈdɪfrənt] *adj* (*not caring*) gleichgültig (*to, towards* gegenüber); (*mediocre*) mittelmäßig

indigestible [ɪndɪˈdʒestəbl] *adj* unverdaulich; **indigestion** [ɪndɪˈdʒestʃən] *n* Verdauungsstörung *f*

indignity [ɪnˈdɪgnɪtɪ] *n* Demütigung *f*

indirect, indirectly [ɪndɪˈrekt, -lɪ] *adj, adv* indirekt

indiscreet [ɪndɪˈskriːt] *adj* indiskret

indispensable [ɪndɪˈspensəbl] *adj* unentbehrlich

indisposed [ɪndɪˈspəʊzd] *adj* unwohl

indisputable [ɪndɪˈspjuːtəbl] *adj* unbestreitbar; (*evidence*) unanfechtbar

individual [ɪndɪˈvɪdjʊəl] *n* Einzelne(r) *mf* ▷ *adj* einzeln; (*distinctive*) eigen, individuell; **~ case** Einzelfall *m*; **individually** *adv* (*separately*) einzeln

Indonesia [ɪndəʊˈniːzjə] *n* Indonesien *nt*

indoor [ˈɪndɔː*] *adj* (*shoes*) Haus-; (*plant, games*) Zimmer-; (*Sport: football, championship, record etc*) Hallen-; **indoors** *adv* drinnen, im Haus

indulge [ɪnˈdʌldʒ] *vi* **~ to ~ in sth** sich *dat* etw gönnen; **indulgence** *n* Nachsicht *f*; (*enjoyment*) (übermäßiger) Genuss; (*luxury*) Luxus *m*; **indulgent** *adj* nachsichtig (*with* gegenüber)

industrial [ɪnˈdʌstrɪəl] *adj* Industrie-, industriell; **~ estate** Industriegebiet *nt*; **industry** [ˈɪndəstrɪ] *n* Industrie *f*

inedible [ɪnˈedɪbl] *adj* nicht essbar, ungenießbar

ineffective [ɪnɪˈfektɪv] *adj* unwirksam, wirkungslos; **inefficient** *adj* unwirksam; (*use, machine*) unwirtschaftlich; (*method etc*) unrationell

ineligible [ɪnˈelɪdʒəbl] *adj* nicht berechtigt (*for* zu)

inequality [ɪnɪˈkwɒlɪtɪ] *n* Ungleichheit *f*

inevitable [ɪnˈevɪtəbl] *adj* unvermeidlich; **inevitably** *adv* zwangsläufig

inexcusable [ɪnɪksˈkjuːzəbl] adj
unverzeihlich; **that's ~** das kann man
nicht verzeihen

inexpensive [ɪnɪksˈpensɪv] adj
preisgünstig

inexperience [ɪnɪksˈpɪəriəns] n
Unerfahrenheit f; **inexperienced** adj
unerfahren

inexplicable [ɪnɪksˈplɪkəbl] adj
unerklärlich

infallible [ɪnˈfæləbl] adj unfehlbar

infamous ['ɪnfəməs] adj (person)
berüchtigt (for wegen); (deed)
niederträchtig

infancy ['ɪnfənsɪ] n frühe Kindheit;
infant ['ɪnfənt] n Säugling m; (small child)
Kleinkind nt; **infant school** n Vorschule f

infatuated [ɪnˈfætʃueɪtɪd] adj vernarrt
(with in +akk), verknallt (with in +akk)

infect [ɪnˈfekt] vt (person) anstecken;
(wound) infizieren; **infection** [ɪnˈfekʃən] n
Infektion f; **infectious** [ɪnˈfekʃəs] adj
ansteckend

inferior [ɪnˈfɪərɪə*] adj (in quality)
minderwertig; (in rank) untergeordnet;
inferiority [ɪnfɪərɪˈɒrɪtɪ] n
Minderwertigkeit f; **~ complex**
Minderwertigkeitskomplex m

infertile [ɪnˈfɜːtaɪl] adj unfruchtbar

infidelity [ɪnfɪˈdelɪtɪ] n Untreue f

infinite ['ɪnfɪnɪt] adj unendlich

infinitive [ɪnˈfɪnɪtɪv] n (Ling) Infinitiv m

infinity [ɪnˈfɪnɪtɪ] n Unendlichkeit f

infirmary [ɪnˈfɜːmərɪ] n Krankenhaus nt

inflame [ɪnˈfleɪm] vt (Med) entzünden;
inflammation [ɪnfləˈmeɪʃən] n (Med)
Entzündung f

inflatable [ɪnˈfleɪtəbl] adj aufblasbar;
~ dinghy Schlauchboot nt; **inflate** [ɪnˈfleɪt]
vt aufpumpen; (by blowing) aufblasen;
(prices) hochtreiben

inflation [ɪnˈfleɪʃən] n Inflation f

inflexible [ɪnˈfleksəbl] adj unflexibel

inflict [ɪnˈflɪkt] vt **to ~ sth on sb** jdm etw
zufügen; (punishment) jdm etw auferlegen;
(wound) jdm etw beibringen

in-flight [ɪnˈflaɪt] adj (catering, magazine)
Bord-; **~ entertainment** Bordprogramm
nt

influence ['ɪnfluəns] n Einfluss m (on auf
+akk) ▷ vt beeinflussen; **influential**
[ɪnfluˈenʃəl] adj einflussreich

influenza [ɪnfluˈenzə] n Grippe f

inform [ɪnˈfɔːm] vt informieren (of, about
über +akk); **to keep sb ~ed** jdn auf dem
Laufenden halten

informal [ɪnˈfɔːməl] adj zwanglos,
ungezwungen

information [ɪnfəˈmeɪʃən] n Auskunft f,
Informationen pl; **for your ~** zu Ihrer
Information; **further ~** weitere
Informationen, weiteres; **information
desk** n Auskunftsschalter m;
information technology n
Informationstechnik f; **informative**
[ɪnˈfɔːmətɪv] adj aufschlussreich

infra-red [ɪnfrəˈred] adj infrarot

infrastructure n Infrastruktur f

infuriate [ɪnˈfjuərɪeɪt] vt wütend
machen; **infuriating** adj äußerst
ärgerlich

infusion [ɪnˈfjuːʒən] n (herbal tea)
Aufguss m; (Med) Infusion f

ingenious [ɪnˈdʒiːnɪəs] adj (person)
erfinderisch; (device) raffiniert; (idea)
genial

ingredient [ɪnˈɡriːdɪənt] n (Gastr) Zutat f

inhabit [ɪnˈhæbɪt] vt bewohnen;
inhabitant n Einwohner(in) m(f)

inhale [ɪnˈheɪl] vt einatmen; (cigarettes,
Med) inhalieren; **inhaler** n
Inhalationsgerät nt

inherit [ɪnˈherɪt] vt erben; **inheritance** n
Erbe nt

inhibited [ɪnˈhɪbɪtɪd] adj gehemmt;
inhibition [ɪnhɪˈbɪʃən] n Hemmung f

in-house ['ɪnhaʊs] adj intern

inhuman [ɪnˈhjuːmən] adj unmenschlich

initial [ɪˈnɪʃəl] adj anfänglich; **~ stage**
Anfangsstadium nt ▷ vt mit Initialen
unterschreiben; **initially** adv anfangs;
initials npl Initialen pl

initiative [ɪˈnɪʃətɪv] n Initiative f

inject [ɪnˈdʒekt] vt (drug etc) einspritzen;
to ~ sb with sth jdm etw (ein)spritzen;
injection n Spritze f, Injektion f

in-joke ['ɪndʒəʊk] n Insiderwitz m

injure ['ɪndʒə*] vt verletzen; **to ~ one's
leg** sich dat das Bein verletzen; **injury**
['ɪndʒərɪ] n Verletzung f

injustice [ɪnˈdʒʌstɪs] n Ungerechtigkeit f

ink [ɪŋk] n Tinte f; **ink-jet printer** n
Tintenstrahldrucker m

inland ['ɪnlənd] adj Binnen- ▷ adv
landeinwärts; **inland revenue** n (Brit)
Finanzamt nt

in-laws ['ɪnlɔːz] npl (fam) Schwiegereltern pl

inline skates ['ɪnlaɪnskeɪts] npl Inlineskates pl, Inliner pl

inmate ['ɪnmeɪt] n Insasse m

inn [ɪn] n Gasthaus nt

innate [ɪ'neɪt] adj angeboren

inner ['ɪnə*] adj innere(r, s); **~ city** Innenstadt f

innocence ['ɪnəsns] n Unschuld f; **innocent** adj unschuldig

innovation [ɪnəʊ'veɪʃən] n Neuerung f

innumerable [ɪ'njuːmərəbl] adj unzählig

inoculate [ɪ'nɒkjʊleɪt] vt impfen (against gegen); **inoculation** [ɪnɒkjʊ'leɪʃən] n Impfung f

in-patient ['ɪnpeɪʃənt] n stationärer Patient, stationäre Patientin

input ['ɪnpʊt] n (contribution) Beitrag m; (Inform) Eingabe f

inquest ['ɪnkwest] n gerichtliche Untersuchung (einer Todesursache)

inquire [ɪn'kwaɪə*] see enquire; **inquiry** [ɪn'kwaɪərɪ] see enquiry

insane [ɪn'seɪn] adj wahnsinnig; (Med) geisteskrank; **insanity** [ɪn'sænɪtɪ] n Wahnsinn m

insatiable [ɪn'seɪʃəbl] adj unersättlich

inscription [ɪn'skrɪpʃən] n (on stone etc) Inschrift f

insect ['ɪnsekt] n Insekt nt; **insecticide** [ɪn'sektɪsaɪd] n Insektenbekämpfungsmittel nt; **insect repellent** n Insektenschutzmittel nt

insecure [ɪnsɪ'kjʊə*] adj (person) unsicher; (shelves) instabil

insensitive [ɪn'sensɪtɪv] adj unempfindlich (to gegen); (unfeeling) gefühllos; **insensitivity** [ɪnsensɪ'tɪvɪtɪ] n Unempfindlichkeit f (to gegen); (unfeeling nature) Gefühllosigkeit f

inseparable [ɪn'sepərəbl] adj unzertrennlich

insert [ɪn'sɜːt] vt einfügen; (coin) einwerfen; (key etc) hineinstecken ▷ n (in magazine) Beilage f; **insertion** n (in text) Einfügen n

inside ['ɪn'saɪd] n the ~ das Innere; (surface) die Innenseite; **from the ~** von innen ▷ adj innere(r, s), Innen-; **~ lane** (Auto) Innenspur f; (Sport) Innenbahn f ▷ adv (place) innen; (direction) hinein; **to**

go ~ hineingehen ▷ prep (place) in +dat; (into) in +akk ... hinein; (time, within) innerhalb +gen; **inside out** adv verkehrt herum; (know) in- und auswendig; **insider** n Eingeweihte(r) mf, Insider(in) m(f)

insight ['ɪnsaɪt] n Einblick m (into in +akk)

insignificant [ɪnsɪɡ'nɪfɪkənt] adj unbedeutend

insincere [ɪnsɪn'sɪə*] adj unaufrichtig, falsch

insinuate [ɪn'sɪnjʊeɪt] vt andeuten; **insinuation** [ɪnsɪnjʊ'eɪʃən] n Andeutung f

insist [ɪn'sɪst] vi darauf bestehen; **to ~ on sth** auf etw dat bestehen; **insistent** adj hartnäckig

insoluble [ɪn'sɒljʊbl] adj unlösbar

insomnia [ɪn'sɒmnɪə] n Schlaflosigkeit f

inspect [ɪn'spekt] vt prüfen, kontrollieren; **inspection** n Prüfung f; (check) Kontrolle f; **inspector** n (police ~) Inspektor(in) m(f); (senior) Kommissar(in) m(f); (on bus etc) Kontrolleur(in) m(f)

inspiration [ɪnspɪ'reɪʃən] n Inspiration f; **inspire** [ɪn'spaɪə*] vt (respect) einflößen (in dat); (person) inspirieren

install [ɪn'stɔːl] vt (software) installieren; (furnishings) einbauen

installment, instalment [ɪn'stɔːlmənt] n Rate f; (of story) Folge f; **to pay in ~s** auf Raten zahlen; **installment plan** n (US) Ratenkauf m

instance ['ɪnstəns] n (of discrimination) Fall m; (example) Beispiel nt; **for ~** zum Beispiel

instant ['ɪnstənt] n Augenblick m ▷ adj sofortig; **instant coffee** n Instantkaffee m; **instantly** adv sofort

instead [ɪn'sted] adv stattdessen; **instead of** prep (an)statt +gen; **~ of me** an meiner Stelle; **~ of going** (an)statt zu gehen

instinct ['ɪnstɪŋkt] n Instinkt m; **instinctive, instinctively** [ɪn'stɪŋktɪv, -lɪ] adj, adv instinktiv

institute ['ɪnstɪtjuːt] n Institut nt; **institution** [ɪnstɪ'tjuːʃən] n (organisation) Institution f, Einrichtung f; (home) Anstalt f

instruct [ɪn'strʌkt] vt anweisen; **instruction** [ɪn'strʌkʃən] n (teaching) Unterricht m; (command) Anweisung f; **~s for use** Gebrauchsanweisung f.

instructor n Lehrer(in) m(f); (US) Dozent(in) m(f)

instrument ['ɪnstrʊmənt] n Instrument nt; **instrument panel** n Armaturenbrett nt

insufficient [ɪnsə'fɪʃənt] adj ungenügend

insulate ['ɪnsjʊleɪt] vt (Elec) isolieren; **insulating tape** n Isolierband nt; **insulation** [ɪnsjʊ'leɪʃən] n Isolierung f

insulin ['ɪnsjʊlɪn] n Insulin nt

insult ['ɪnsʌlt] n Beleidigung f ▷ [ɪn'sʌlt] vt beleidigen; **insulting** [ɪn'sʌltɪŋ] adj beleidigend

insurance [ɪn'ʃʊərəns] n Versicherung f; ~ **company** Versicherungsgesellschaft f; ~ **policy** Versicherungspolice f; **insure** [ɪn'ʃʊə*] vt versichern (against gegen)

intact [ɪn'tækt] adj intakt

intake ['ɪnteɪk] n Aufnahme f

integrate [ɪntɪ'greɪt] vt integrieren (into in +akk); **integration** n Integration f

integrity [ɪn'tegrətɪ] n Integrität f, Ehrlichkeit f

intellect ['ɪntɪlekt] n Intellekt m; **intellectual** [ɪntɪ'lektjʊəl] adj intellektuell; (interests etc) geistig

intelligence [ɪn'telɪdʒəns] n (understanding) Intelligenz f; **intelligent** adj intelligent

intend [ɪn'tend] vt beabsichtigen; **to ~ to do sth** vorhaben, etw zu tun

intense [ɪn'tens] adj intensiv; (pressure) enorm; (competition) heftig; **intensity** n Intensität f; **intensive** adj intensiv; **intensive care unit** n Intensivstation f; **intensive course** n Intensivkurs m

intent [ɪn'tent] adj **to be ~ on doing sth** fest entschlossen sein, etw zu tun; **intention** [ɪn'tenʃən] n Absicht f; **intentional, intentionally** adj, adv absichtlich

interact [ɪntər'ækt] vi aufeinander einwirken; **interaction** n Interaktion f, Wechselwirkung f; **interactive** adj interaktiv

interchange ['ɪntətʃeɪndʒ] n (of motorways) Autobahnkreuz nt; **interchangeable** [ɪntə'tʃeɪndʒəbl] adj austauschbar

intercity [ɪntə'sɪtɪ] n Intercityzug m, IC m

intercom ['ɪntəkɒm] n (Gegen)sprechanlage f

intercourse ['ɪntəkɔːs] n (sexual) Geschlechtsverkehr m

interest ['ɪntrest] n Interesse nt; (Fin: on money) Zinsen pl; (Comm: share) Anteil m; **to be of** ~ von Interesse sein (to für) ▷ vt interessieren; **interested** adj interessiert (in an +dat); **to be ~ed in** sich interessieren für; **are you ~ in coming?** hast du Lust, mitzukommen?; **interest-free** adj zinsfrei; **interesting** adj interessant; **interest rate** n Zinssatz m

interface ['ɪntəfeɪs] n (Inform) Schnittstelle f

interfere [ɪntə'fɪə*] vi (meddle) sich einmischen (with, in in +akk); **interference** n Einmischung f; (Tv, Radio) Störung f

interior [ɪn'tɪərɪə*] adj Innen- ▷ n Innere(s) nt; (of car) Innenraum m; (of house) Innenausstattung f

intermediate [ɪntə'miːdɪət] adj Zwischen-; ~ **stage** Zwischenstadium nt

intermission [ɪntə'mɪʃən] n Pause f

intern [ɪn'tɜːn] n Assistent(in) m(f)

internal [ɪn'tɜːnl] adj innere(r, s); (flight) Inlands-; ~ **revenue** (US) Finanzamt nt; **internally** adv innen; (in body) innerlich

international [ɪntə'næʃnəl] adj international; ~ **match** Länderspiel nt; ~ **flight** Auslandsflug m ▷ n (Sport: player) Nationalspieler(in) m(f)

Internet ['ɪntənet] n (Inform) Internet nt; **Internet banking** n Onlinebanking nt; **Internet café** n Internetcafé nt; **Internet provider** n Internetprovider m

interpret [ɪn'tɜːprɪt] vi, vt (translate) dolmetschen; (explain) interpretieren; **interpretation** [ɪntɜːprɪ'teɪʃən] n Interpretation f; **interpreter** [ɪn'tɜːprɪtə*] n Dolmetscher(in) m(f)

interrogate [ɪn'terəgeɪt] vt verhören; **interrogation** n Verhör nt

interrupt [ɪntə'rʌpt] vt unterbrechen; **interruption** [ɪntə'rʌpʃən] n Unterbrechung f

intersection [ɪntə'sekʃən] n (of roads) Kreuzung f

interstate [ɪntə'steɪt] n (US) zwischenstaatlich; ~ **highway** ≈ Bundesautobahn f

interval ['ɪntəvəl] n (space, time) Abstand m; (theatre etc) Pause f

intervene [ɪntə'viːn] vi eingreifen (in in);

intervention [ɪntəˈvenʃən] n Eingreifen nt; (Pol) Intervention f

interview [ˈɪntəvjuː] n Interview nt; (for job) Vorstellungsgespräch nt ▷ vt interviewen; (job applicant) ein Vorstellungsgespräch führen mit; **interviewer** n Interviewer(in) m(f)

intestine [ɪnˈtestɪn] n Darm m; **~s** pl Eingeweide pl

intimate [ˈɪntɪmət] adj (friends) vertraut, eng; (atmosphere) gemütlich; (sexually) intim

intimidate [ɪnˈtɪmɪdeɪt] vt einschüchtern; **intimidation** n Einschüchterung f

into [ˈɪntʊ] prep in +akk; (crash) gegen; **to change ~ sth** (turn ~) zu etw werden; (put on) sich dat etw anziehen; **to translate ~ French** ins Französische übersetzen; **to be ~ sth** (fam) auf etw akk stehen

intolerable [ɪnˈtɒlərəbl] adj unerträglich

intolerant [ɪnˈtɒlərənt] adj intolerant

intoxicated [ɪnˈtɒksɪkeɪtɪd] adj betrunken; (fig) berauscht

intricate [ˈɪntrɪkət] adj kompliziert

intrigue [ɪnˈtriːg] vt faszinieren; **intriguing** adj faszinierend, fesselnd

introduce [ɪntrəˈdjuːs] vt (person) vorstellen (to sb jdm); (sth new) einführen (to in +akk); **introduction** [ɪntrəˈdʌkʃən] n Einführung f (to in +akk); (to book) Einleitung f (to zu); (to person) Vorstellung f

introvert [ˈɪntrəʊvɜːt] n Introvertierte(r) mf

intuition [ɪntjuːˈɪʃn] n Intuition f

invade [ɪnˈveɪd] vt einfallen in +akk

invalid [ˈɪnvəlɪd] n Kranke(r) mf; (disabled) Invalide m ▷ adj [ɪnˈvælɪd] (not valid) ungültig

invaluable [ɪnˈvæljʊəbl] adj äußerst wertvoll, unschätzbar

invariably [ɪnˈveərɪəblɪ] adv ständig; (every time) jedes Mal, ohne Ausnahme

invasion [ɪnˈveɪʒən] n Invasion f (of in +akk), Einfall m (of in +akk)

invent [ɪnˈvent] vt erfinden; **invention** [ɪnˈvenʃən] n Erfindung f; **inventor** n Erfinder(in) m(f)

inverted commas [ɪnˈvɜːtɪd ˈkɒməz] npl Anführungszeichen pl

invest [ɪnˈvest] vt, vi investieren (in in +akk)

investigate [ɪnˈvestɪgeɪt] vt untersuchen; **investigation** [ɪnvestɪˈgeɪʃən] n Untersuchung f (into +gen)

investment [ɪnˈvestmənt] n Investition f; **it's a good ~** es ist eine gute Anlage; (it'll be useful) es macht sich bezahlt

invigorating [ɪnˈvɪgəreɪtɪŋ] adj erfrischend, belebend; (tonic) stärkend

invisible [ɪnˈvɪzəbl] adj unsichtbar

invitation [ɪnvɪˈteɪʃən] n Einladung f; **invite** [ɪnˈvaɪt] vt einladen

invoice [ˈɪnvɔɪs] n (bill) Rechnung f

involuntary [ɪnˈvɒləntərɪ] adj unbeabsichtigt

involve [ɪnˈvɒlv] vt verwickeln (in sth in etw akk); (entail) zur Folge haben; **to be ~d in sth** (participate in) an etw dat beteiligt sein; **I'm not ~d** (affected) ich bin nicht betroffen

inward [ˈɪnwəd] adj innere(r, s); **inwardly** adv innerlich; **inwards** adv nach innen

iodine [ˈaɪədiːn] n Jod nt

IOU [aɪəʊˈjuː] abbr = **I owe you** Schuldschein m

IQ abbr = **intelligence quotient** IQ m

Iran [ɪˈrɑːn] n der Iran

Iraq [ɪˈrɑːk] n der Irak

Ireland [ˈaɪələnd] n Irland nt

iris [ˈaɪrɪs] n (flower) Schwertlilie f; (of eye) Iris f

Irish [ˈaɪrɪʃ] adj irisch; **~ coffee** Irishcoffee m; **~ Sea** die Irische See ▷ n (language) Irisch nt; **the ~** pl die Iren pl; **Irishman** (pl **-men**) n Ire m; **Irishwoman** (pl **-women**) n Irin f

iron [ˈaɪən] n Eisen nt; (for ironing) Bügeleisen nt ▷ adj eisern ▷ vt bügeln

ironic(al) [aɪˈrɒnɪk(əl)] adj ironisch

ironing board n Bügelbrett nt

irony [ˈaɪrənɪ] n Ironie f

irrational [ɪˈræʃənl] adj irrational

irregular [ɪˈregjʊlə*] adj unregelmäßig; (shape) ungleichmäßig

irrelevant [ɪˈreləvənt] adj belanglos, irrelevant

irreplaceable [ɪrɪˈpleɪsəbl] adj unersetzlich

irresistible [ɪrɪˈzɪstəbl] adj unwiderstehlich

irrespective of [ɪrɪˈspektɪv ɒv] prep ungeachtet +gen

irresponsible [ɪrɪ'spɒnsəbl] *adj*
verantwortungslos

irretrievable [ɪrɪ'triːvəbl] *adv*
unwiederbringlich; *(loss)* unersetzlich

irritable ['ɪrɪtəbl] *adj* reizbar; **irritate**
['ɪrɪteɪt] *vt (annoy)* ärgern; *(deliberately)*
reizen; **irritation** [ɪrɪ'teɪʃən] *n (anger)*
Ärger *m*; *(Med)* Reizung *f*

IRS *abbr* = **Internal Revenue Service** (US)
Finanzamt *nt*

is [ɪz] *present of* **be** ist

Islam ['ɪzlɑːm] *n* Islam *m*; **Islamic**
[ɪz'læmɪk] *adj* islamisch

island ['aɪlənd] *n* Insel *f*; **Isle** [aɪl] *n* (in
names) **the ~ of Man** die Insel Man; **the
~ of Wight** die Insel Wight; **the British ~s**
die Britischen Inseln

isn't ['ɪznt] *contr of* **is not**

isolate ['aɪsəleɪt] *vt* isolieren; **isolated**
adj (remote) abgelegen; *(cut off)*
abgeschnitten (from *von)*; **an ~ case** ein
Einzelfall; **isolation** [aɪsə'leɪʃən] *n*
Isolierung *f*

Israel ['ɪzreɪl] *n* Israel *nt*; **Israeli** [ɪz'reɪlɪ]
adj israelisch ▷ *n* Israeli *m o f*

issue ['ɪʃuː] *n (matter)* Frage *f*; *(problem)*
Problem *nt*; *(subject)* Thema *nt*; *(of
newspaper etc)* Ausgabe *f*; **that's not the
~** darum geht es nicht ▷ *vt* ausgeben;
(document) ausstellen; *(orders)* erteilen;
(book) herausgeben

⊙ **KEYWORD**

it [ɪt] *pron* **1** *(specific: subject)* er/sie/es;
(: *direct object)* ihn/sie/es; (: *indirect object)*
ihm/ihr/ihm; **about/from/in/of it**
darüber/davon/darin/davon

2 *(impers)* es; **it's raining** es regnet; **it's
Friday tomorrow** morgen ist Freitag;
who is it? — it's me wer ist da? — ich
(bins)

IT *abbr* = **information technology** IT *f*

Italian [ɪ'tæljən] *adj* italienisch ▷ *n*
Italiener(in) *m(f)*; *(language)* Italienisch *nt*

italic [ɪ'tælɪk] *adj* kursiv ▷ *npl* **in ~s** kursiv

Italy ['ɪtəlɪ] *n* Italien *nt*

itch [ɪtʃ] *n* Juckreiz *m*; **I have an ~** mich
juckt es ▷ *vi* jucken; **he is ~ing to ...** es
juckt ihn, zu ...; **itchy** *adj* juckend

it'd ['ɪtd] *contr of* **it would; it had**

item ['aɪtəm] *n (article)* Gegenstand *m*; *(in
catalogue)* Artikel *m*; *(on list, in accounts)*
Posten *m*; *(on agenda)* Punkt *m*; *(in show
programme)* Nummer *f*; *(in news)* Bericht *m*;
(TV: radio) Meldung *f*

itinerary [aɪ'tɪnərərɪ] *n* Reiseroute *f*

it'll ['ɪtl] *contr of* **it will; it shall**

its [ɪts] *pron* sein; *(feminine form)* ihr

it's [ɪts] *contr of* **it is; it has**

itself [ɪt'self] *pron (reflexive)* sich;
(emphatic) **the house ~ is OK** das Haus
selbst o an sich ist in Ordnung; **by ~** allein;
the door closes (by) ~ die Tür schließt
sich von selbst

I've [aɪv] *contr of* **I have**

ivory ['aɪvərɪ] *n* Elfenbein *nt*

ivy ['aɪvɪ] *n* Efeu *m*

j

jab [dʒæb] vt (needle, knife) stechen (into in +akk) ▷ n (fam) Spritze f

jack [dʒæk] n (Auto) Wagenheber m; (Cards) Bube m; **jack in** vt (fam) aufgeben, hinschmeißen; **jack up** vt (car etc) aufbocken

jacket ['dʒækɪt] n Jacke f; (of man's suit) Jackett nt; (of book) Schutzumschlag m; **jacket potato** (pl -es) n (in der Schale) gebackene Kartoffel

jack-knife ['dʒæknaɪf] (pl **jack-knives**) n Klappmesser nt ▷ vi (truck) sich quer stellen

jackpot ['dʒækpɒt] n Jackpot m

jacuzzi® [dʒə'ku:zɪ] n (bath) Whirlpool® m

jail [dʒeɪl] n Gefängnis nt ▷ vt einsperren

jam [dʒæm] n Konfitüre f, Marmelade f; (traffic ~) Stau m ▷ vt (street) verstopfen; (machine) blockieren; **to be ~med** (stuck) klemmen; **to ~ on the brakes** eine Vollbremsung machen

Jamaica [dʒə'meɪkə] n Jamaika nt

jam-packed adj proppenvoll

janitor ['dʒænɪtə*] n (US) Hausmeister(in) m(f)

Jan abbr = **January** Jan

January ['dʒænjʊərɪ] n Januar m

Japan [dʒə'pæn] n Japan nt; **Japanese** [dʒæpə'ni:z] adj japanisch ▷ n (person) Japaner(in) m(f); (language) Japanisch nt

jar [dʒɑ:*] n Glas nt

jaundice ['dʒɔ:ndɪs] n Gelbsucht f

javelin ['dʒævlɪn] n Speer m; (Sport) Speerwerfen nt

jaw [dʒɔ:] n Kiefer m

jazz [dʒæz] n Jazz m

jealous ['dʒeləs] adj eifersüchtig (of auf +akk); **don't make me ~** mach mich nicht neidisch; **jealousy** n Eifersucht f

jeans [dʒi:nz] npl Jeans pl

jeep® [dʒi:p] n Jeep® m

jelly ['dʒelɪ] n Gelee nt; (on meat) Gallert nt; (dessert) Götterspeise f; (US: jam) Marmelade f; **jelly baby** n (sweet) Gummibärchen nt; **jellyfish** n Qualle f

jeopardize ['dʒepədaɪz] vt gefährden

jerk [dʒɜ:k] n Ruck m; (fam: idiot) Trottel m ▷ vt ruckartig bewegen ▷ vi (rope) rucken; (muscles) zucken

Jerusalem [dʒə'ru:sələm] n Jerusalem nt

jet [dʒet] n (of water etc) Strahl m; (nozzle) Düse f; (aircraft) Düsenflugzeug nt; **jet foil** n Tragflächenboot nt; **jetlag** n Jetlag m (Müdigkeit nach langem Flug)

jetty ['dʒetɪ] n Landesteg m; (larger) Landungsbrücke f

Jew [dʒu:] n Jude m, Jüdin f

jewel ['dʒu:əl] n Edelstein m; (esp fig) Juwel nt; **jeweller, jeweler** (US) n Juwelier(in) m(f); **jewellery, jewelery** (US) n Schmuck m

Jewish ['dʒu:ɪʃ] adj jüdisch; **she's ~** sie ist Jüdin

jigsaw (puzzle) ['dʒɪgsɔ:(pʌzl)] n Puzzle nt

jilt [dʒɪlt] vt den Laufpass geben +dat

jingle ['dʒɪŋgl] n (advert) Jingle m; (verse) Reim m

jitters ['dʒɪtəz] npl (fam) **to have the ~** Bammel haben; **jittery** adj (fam) ganz nervös

job [dʒɒb] n (piece of work) Arbeit f; (task) Aufgabe f; (occupation) Stellung f, Job m; **what's your ~?** was machen Sie beruflich?; **it's a good ~ you did that** gut, dass du das gemacht hast; **jobcentre** n Arbeitsvermittlungsstelle f, Arbeitsamt nt; **job-hunting** n **to go ~** auf Arbeitssuche gehen; **jobless** adj

arbeitslos; **job seeker** n
Arbeitssuchende(r) mf; **jobseeker's
allowance** n Arbeitslosengeld nt;
job-sharing n Arbeitsplatzteilung f

jockey ['dʒɒkɪ] n Jockey m

jog [dʒɒg] vt (person) anstoßen ▷ vi (run)
joggen; **jogging** n Jogging nt; **to go
~** joggen gehen

john [dʒɒn] n (US fam) Klo nt

join [dʒɔɪn] vt (put together) verbinden (to
mit); (club etc) beitreten +dat; **to ~ sb** sich
jdm anschließen; (sit with) sich zu jdm
setzen ▷ vi (unite) sich vereinigen; (rivers)
zusammenfließen ▷ n Verbindungsstelle
f; (seam) Naht f; **join in** vi, vt mitmachen
(sth bei etw)

joinery ['dʒɔɪnərɪ] n Schreinerei f

joint [dʒɔɪnt] n (of bones) Gelenk nt; (in pipe
etc) Verbindungsstelle f; (of meat) Braten
m; (of marijuana) Joint m ▷ adj gemeinsam;
joint account n Gemeinschaftskonto nt;
jointly adv gemeinsam

joke [dʒəʊk] n Witz m; (prank) Streich m;
for a ~ zum Spaß; **it's no ~** das ist nicht
zum Lachen ▷ vi Witze machen; **you
must be joking** das ist ja wohl nicht dein
Ernst!

jolly ['dʒɒlɪ] adj lustig, vergnügt

Jordan ['dʒɔːdən] n (country) Jordanien nt;
(river) Jordan m

jot down [dʒɒt daʊn] vt sich notieren;
jotter n Notizbuch nt

journal ['dʒɜːnl] n (diary) Tagebuch nt;
(magazine) Zeitschrift f; **journalism** n
Journalismus m; **journalist** n
Journalist(in) m(f)

journey ['dʒɜːnɪ] n Reise f; (esp on stage,
by car, train) Fahrt f

joy [dʒɔɪ] n Freude f (at über +akk);
joystick n (Inform) Joystick m; (Aviat)
Steuerknüppel m

judge [dʒʌdʒ] n Richter(in) m(f); (Sport)
Punktrichter(in) m(f) ▷ vt beurteilen (by
nach); **as far as I can ~** meinem Urteil
nach ▷ vi urteilen (by nach); **judg(e)ment**
n (Jur) Urteil nt; (opinion) Ansicht f; **an
error of ~** Fehleinschätzung f

judo ['dʒuːdəʊ] n Judo nt

jug [dʒʌg] n Krug m

juggle ['dʒʌgl] vi (lit, fig) jonglieren (with
mit)

juice [dʒuːs] n Saft m; **juicy** adj saftig;
(story, scandal) pikant

July [dʒuːˈlaɪ] n Juli m; see also **September**

jumble ['dʒʌmbl] n Durcheinander nt ▷ vt
to ~ (up) durcheinander werfen; (facts)
durcheinander bringen; **jumble sale** n
(for charity) Wohltätigkeitsbasar m

jumbo ['dʒʌmbəʊ] adj (sausage etc)
Riesen-; **jumbo jet** n Jumbojet m

jump [dʒʌmp] vi springen; (nervously)
zusammenzucken; **to ~ to conclusions**
voreilige Schlüsse ziehen; **to ~ from one
thing to another** dauernd das Thema
wechseln ▷ vt (a. fig: omit) überspringen;
to ~ the lights bei Rot über die Kreuzung
fahren; **to ~ the queue** sich vordrängen
▷ n Sprung m; (for horses) Hindernis nt;
jumper n Pullover m; (US: dress)
Trägerkleid nt; (person, horse) Springer(in)
m(f); **jumper cables** npl (US), **jump leads**
npl (Brit Auto) Starthilfekabel nt

junction ['dʒʌŋkʃən] n (of roads) Kreuzung
f; (Rail) Knotenpunkt m

June [dʒuːn] n Juni m; see also **September**

jungle ['dʒʌŋgl] n Dschungel m

junior ['dʒuːnɪə*] adj (younger) jünger;
(lower position) untergeordnet (to sb jdm)·
▷ n she's two years my ~ sie ist zwei
Jahre jünger als ich; **junior high (school)**
n (US) ≈ Mittelschule f; **junior school** n
(Brit) Grundschule f

junk [dʒʌŋk] n (trash) Plunder m;
junkfood n Nahrungsmittel pl mit
geringem Nährwert, Junkfood nt; **junkie**
n (fam) Junkie m, Fixer(in) m(f); (fig: fan)
Freak m; **junk mail** n Reklame f, (Inform)
Junkmail f; **junk shop** n Trödelladen m

jury ['dʒʊərɪ] n Geschworene pl; (in
competition) Jury f

just [dʒʌst] adj gerecht ▷ adv (recently)
gerade; (exactly) genau; **~ as expected**
genau wie erwartet; **~ as nice** genauso
nett; (barely) **~ in time** gerade noch
rechtzeitig; (immediately) **~ before/after
...** gleich vor/nach ...; (small distance)
~ round the corner gleich um die Ecke; (a
little) **~ over an hour** etwas mehr als eine
Stunde; (only) **the two of us** nur wir
beide; **~ a moment** Moment mal;
(absolutely, simply) **it was ~ fantastic** es
war einfach klasse; **~ about** so etwa;
(more or less) mehr oder weniger; **~ about
ready** fast fertig

justice ['dʒʌstɪs] n Gerechtigkeit f;
justifiable [dʒʌstɪˈfaɪəbl] adj

berechtigt; **justifiably** *adv* zu
Recht; **justify** [ˈdʒʌstɪfaɪ] *vt*
rechtfertigen
jut [dʒʌt] *vi* **to ~ (out)** herausragen
juvenile [ˈdʒuːvənaɪl] *n adj* Jugend-,
jugendlich ▷ *n* Jugendliche(r) *mf*

k

k *abbr* = **thousand; 15k** 15 000

K *abbr* = **kilobyte** KB

kangaroo [kæŋɡəˈruː] *n* Känguru *nt*

karaoke [kærɪˈəʊkɪ] *n* Karaoke *nt*

karate [kəˈrɑːtɪ] *n* Karate *nt*

kart [kɑːt] *n* Gokart *m*

kayak [ˈkaɪæk] *n* Kajak *m o nt*

Kazakhstan [kæzækˈstɑːn] *n* Kasachstan *nt*

kebab [kəˈbæb] *n* (*shish ~*) Schaschlik *nt o m*; (*doner ~*) Kebab *m*

keel [kiːl] *n* (*Naut*) Kiel *m*; **keel over** *vi* (*boat*) kentern; (*person*) umkippen

keen [kiːn] *adj* begeistert (*on* von); (*hardworking*) eifrig; (*mind, wind*) scharf; (*interest, feeling*) stark; **to be ~ on sb** von jdm angetan sein; **she's ~ on riding** sie reitet gern; **to be ~ to do sth** darauf erpicht sein, etw zu tun

keep [kiːp] (**kept, kept**) *vt* (*retain*) behalten; (*secret*) für sich behalten; (*observe*) einhalten; (*promise*) halten; (*run: shop, diary, accounts*) führen; (*animals*) halten; (*support, family etc*) unterhalten, versorgen; (*store*) aufbewahren; **to ~ sb waiting** jdn warten lassen; **to ~ sb from doing sth** jdn davon abhalten, etw zu tun;

to ~ sth clean/secret etw sauber/geheim halten; **'~ clear'** „(bitte) freihalten"; **~ this to yourself** behalten Sie das für sich ▷ *vi* (*food*) sich halten; (*remain, with adj*) bleiben; **~ quiet** sei ruhig!; **~ left** links fahren; **to ~ doing sth** (*repeatedly*) etw immer wieder tun; **~ at it** mach weiter so!; **it ~s happening** es passiert immer wieder ▷ *n* (*livelihood*) Unterhalt *m*; **keep back** *vi* zurückbleiben ▷ *vt* zurückhalten; (*information*) verschweigen (*from sb* jdm); **keep off** *vt* (*person, animal*) fernhalten; **'~ off the grass'** „Betreten des Rasens verboten"; **keep on** *vi* weitermachen; (*walking*) weitergehen; (*in car*) weiterfahren; **to ~ doing sth** (*persistently*) etw immer wieder tun ▷ *vt* (*coat etc*) anbehalten; **keep out** *vt* nicht hereinlassen ▷ *vi* draußen bleiben; **~** (*on sign*) Eintritt verboten; **keep to** *vt* (*road, path*) bleiben auf +*dat*; (*plan etc*) sich halten an +*akk*; **to ~ the point** bei der Sache bleiben; **keep up** *vi* Schritt halten (*with* mit) ▷ *vt* (*maintain*) aufrechterhalten; (*speed*) halten; **to ~ appearances** den Schein wahren; **keep it up!** (*fam*) weiter so!

keeper *n* (*museum etc*) Aufseher(in) *m(f)*; (*goal~*) Torwart *m*; (*zoo~*) Tierpfleger(in) *m(f)*; **keep-fit** *n* Fitnesstraining *nt*; **~ exercises** Gymnastik *f*

kennel [ˈkenl] *n* Hundehütte *f*; **kennels** *n* Hundepension *f*

Kenya [ˈkenjə] *n* Kenia *nt*

kept [kept] *pt, pp of* **keep**

kerb [ˈkɜːb] *n* Randstein *m*

kerosene [ˈkerəsiːn] *n* (*US*) Petroleum *nt*

ketchup [ˈketʃəp] *n* Ket(s)chup *nt o m*

kettle [ˈketl] *n* Kessel *m*

key [kiː] *n* Schlüssel *m*; (*of piano, computer*) Taste *f*; (*Mus*) Tonart *f*; (*for map etc*) Zeichenerklärung *f* ▷ *vt* **to ~ (in)** (*Inform*) eingeben ▷ *adj* entscheidend; **keyboard** *n* (*piano, computer*) Tastatur *f*; **keyhole** *n* Schlüsselloch *nt*; **keypad** *n* (*Inform*) Nummernblock *m*; **keyring** *n* Schlüsselring *m*

kick [kɪk] *n* Tritt *m*; (*Sport*) Stoß *m*; **I get a ~ out of it** (*fam*) es turnt mich an ▷ *vt, vi* treten; **kick out** *vt* (*fam*) rausschmeißen (*of* aus); **kick-off** *n* (*Sport*) Anstoß *m*

kid [kɪd] *n* (*child*) Kind *nt* ▷ *vt* (*tease*) auf den Arm nehmen ▷ *vi* Witze machen;

you're ~ding das ist doch nicht dein Ernst!; no ~ding aber echt!

kidnap ['kɪdnæp] vt entführen; **kidnapper** n Entführer(in) m(f); **kidnapping** n Entführung f

kidney ['kɪdnɪ] n Niere f; **kidney machine** n künstliche Niere

kill [kɪl] vt töten; (esp intentionally) umbringen; (weeds) vernichten; **killer** n Mörder(in) m(f)

kilo ['kiːləʊ] (pl -s) n Kilo nt; **kilobyte** n Kilobyte nt; **kilogramme** n Kilogramm nt; **kilometer** (US), **kilometre** n Kilometer m; ~s per hour Stundenkilometer pl; **kilowatt** n Kilowatt nt

kilt [kɪlt] n Schottenrock m

kind [kaɪnd] adj nett, freundlich (to zu) ▷ n Art f; (of coffee, cheese etc) Sorte f; **what ~ of ...?** was für ein(e) ...?; **this ~ of ...** so ein(e) ...; ~ **of** (+ adj) irgendwie

kindergarten ['kɪndəgɑːtn] n Kindergarten m

kindly ['kaɪndlɪ] adj nett, freundlich ▷ adv liebenswürdigerweise; **kindness** ['kaɪndnəs] n Freundlichkeit f

king [kɪŋ] n König m; **kingdom** n Königreich nt; **kingfisher** n Eisvogel m; **king-size** adj im Großformat; (bed) extra groß

kipper ['kɪpə*] n Räucherhering m

kiss [kɪs] n Kuss m; ~ **of life** Mund-zu-Mund-Beatmung f ▷ vt küssen

kit [kɪt] n (equipment) Ausrüstung f; (fam) Sachen pl; (sports ~) Sportsachen pl; (belongings, clothes) Sachen pl; (for building sth) Bausatz m

kitchen ['kɪtʃɪn] n Küche f; **kitchen foil** n Alufolie f; **kitchen scales** n Küchenwaage f; **kitchen unit** n Küchenschrank m; **kitchenware** n Küchengeschirr nt

kite [kaɪt] n Drachen m

kitten ['kɪtn] n Kätzchen nt

kiwi ['kiːwiː] n (fruit) Kiwi f

km abbr = **kilometres** km

knack [næk] n Dreh m, Trick m; **to get/have got the ~** den Dreh herauskriegen/heraushaben; **knackered** ['nækəd] adj (Brit fam) fix und fertig, kaputt

knee [niː] n Knie nt; **kneecap** n Kniescheibe f; **knee-jerk** adj (reaction) reflexartig; **kneel** [niːl] (knelt o kneeled, knelt o kneeled) vi knien; (action, ~ down) sich hinknien

knelt [nelt] pt, pp of **kneel**

knew [njuː] pt of **know**

knickers ['nɪkəz] npl (Brit) Schlüpfer m

knife [naɪf] (pl knives) n Messer nt

knight [naɪt] n Ritter m; (in chess) Pferd nt, Springer m

knit [nɪt] vt, vi stricken; **knitting** n (piece of work) Strickarbeit f; (activity) Stricken nt; **knitting needle** n Stricknadel f; **knitwear** n Strickwaren pl

knob [nɒb] n (on door) Knauf m; (on radio etc) Knopf m

knock [nɒk] vt (with hammer etc) schlagen; (accidentally) stoßen; **to ~ one's head** sich dat den Kopf anschlagen ▷ vi klopfen (on, at an +akk) ▷ n (blow) Schlag m; (on door) Klopfen nt; **there was a ~ (at the door)** es hat geklopft; **knock down** vt (object) umstoßen; (person) niederschlagen; (with car) anfahren; (building) abreißen; **knock out** vt (stun) bewusstlos schlagen; (boxer) k.o. schlagen; **knock over** vt umstoßen; (with car) anfahren; **knocker** n Türklopfer m; **knockout** n Knockout m, K.o. m

knot [nɒt] n Knoten m

know [nəʊ] (knew, known) vt, vi wissen; (be acquainted with: people, places) kennen; (recognize) erkennen; (language) können; **I'll let you ~** ich sage dir Bescheid; **I ~ some French** ich kann etwas Französisch; **to get to ~ sb** jdn kennen lernen; **to be ~n as** bekannt sein als; **know about** vt Bescheid wissen über +akk; (subject) sich auskennen in +dat; (cars, horses etc) sich auskennen mit; **know of** vt kennen; **not that I ~** nicht dass ich wüsste; **know-all** n (fam) Klugscheißer m; **know-how** n Kenntnis f, Know-how nt; **knowing** adj wissend; (look, smile) vielsagend; **knowledge** ['nɒlɪdʒ] n Wissen nt; (of a subject) Kenntnisse pl; **to (the best of) my ~** meines Wissens

known [nəʊn] pp of **know**

knuckle ['nʌkl] n (Finger)knöchel m; (Gastr) Hachse f; **knuckle down** vi sich an die Arbeit machen

Koran [kɒˈrɑːn] n Koran m

Korea [kəˈrɪə] n Korea nt

Kosovo ['kɒsəvəʊ] n der Kosovo

kph abbr = **kilometres per hour** km/h

Kremlin ['kremlɪn] *n* **the ~** der
Kreml
Kurd [kɛːd] *n* Kurde *m*, Kurdin *f*; **Kurdish**
adj kurdisch
Kuwait [kʊ'weɪt] *n* Kuwait *nt*

L *abbr* (Brit Auto) = **learner**
LA *abbr* = **Los Angeles**
lab [læb] *n* (*fam*) Labor *nt*
label ['leɪbl] *n* Etikett *nt*; (*tied*) Anhänger *m*; (*adhesive*) Aufkleber *m*; (*record ~*) Label *nt* ▷ *vt* etikettieren; (*pej*) abstempeln
laboratory [ləˈbɒrətərɪ] *n* Labor *nt*

Labor Day

Der **Labor Day** ist in den USA und Kanada der Name für den Tag der Arbeit. Er wird dort als gesetzlicher Feiertag am ersten Montag im September begangen.

laborious [ləˈbɔːrɪəs] *adj* mühsam; **labor** (*US*), **labour** ['leɪbə*] *n* Arbeit *f*; (*Med*) Wehen *pl*; **to be in ~** Wehen haben ▷ *adj* (*Pol*) Labour-; **~ Party** Labour Party *f*; **labor union** *n* (*US*) Gewerkschaft *f*; **labourer** *n* Arbeiter(in) *m(f)*
lace [leɪs] *n* (*fabric*) Spitze *f*; (*of shoe*) Schnürsenkel *m* ▷ *vt* **to ~ (up)** zuschnüren; **lace-up** *n* Schnürschuh *m*
lack [læk] *vt, vi* **to be ~ing** fehlen; **sb ~s** *o* **is ~ing in sth** es fehlt jdm an etw *dat*; **we**

~ the time uns fehlt die Zeit ▷ *n* Mangel *m*; **for ~ of** aus Mangel an +*dat*
lacquer ['lækə*] *n* Lack *m*; (*Brit: hair ~*) Haarspray *nt*
lad [læd] *n* junge *m*
ladder ['lædə*] *n* Leiter *f*; (*in tight*) Laufmasche *f*
laddish ['lædɪʃ] *adj* (*Brit*) machohaft
laden ['leɪdn] *adj* beladen (*with* mit)
ladies ['leɪdɪz], **ladies' room** *n* Damentoilette *f*; **lady** ['leɪdɪ] *n* Dame *f*; (*as title*) Lady *f*; **ladybird, ladybug** (*US*) *n* Marienkäfer *m*
lag [læg] *vi* **to ~ (behind)** zurückliegen ▷ *vt* (*pipes*) isolieren
lager ['lɑːɡə*] *n* helles Bier; **~ lout** betrunkener Rowdy
lagging ['læɡɪŋ] *n* Isolierung *f*
laid [leɪd] *pt, pp of* **lay**; **laid-back** *adj* (*fam*) cool, gelassen
lain [leɪn] *pp of* **lie**
lake [leɪk] *n* See *m*; **the Lake District** Seengebiet im Nordwesten Englands
lamb [læm] *n* Lamm *nt*; (*meat*) Lammfleisch *nt*; **lamb chop** *n* Lammkotelett *nt*
lame [leɪm] *adj* lahm; (*excuse*) faul; (*argument*) schwach
lament [ləˈment] *n* Klage *f* ▷ *vt* beklagen
laminated ['læmɪneɪtɪd] *adj* beschichtet
lamp [læmp] *n* Lampe *f*; (*in street*) Laterne *f*; (*in car*) Licht *nt*, Scheinwerfer *m*; **lamppost** *n* Laternenpfahl *m*; **lampshade** *n* Lampenschirm *m*
land [lænd] *n* Land *nt* ▷ *vi* (*from ship*) an Land gehen; (*Aviat*) landen ▷ *vt* (*passengers*) absetzen; (*goods*) abladen; (*plane*) landen; **landing** *n* Landung *f*; (*on stairs*) Treppenabsatz *m*; **landing stage** *n* Landesteg *m*; **landing strip** *n* Landebahn *f*
landlady *n* Hauswirtin *f*, Vermieterin *f*; **landlord** *n* (*of house*) Hauswirt *m*, Vermieter *m*; (*of pub*) Gastwirt *m*; **landmark** *n* Wahrzeichen *nt*; (*event*) Meilenstein *m*; **landowner** *n* Grundbesitzer(in) *m(f)*; **landscape** *n* Landschaft *f*; (*format*) Querformat *nt*; **landslide** *n* (*Geo*) Erdrutsch *m*
lane [leɪn] *n* (*in country*) enge Landstraße, Weg *m*; (*in town*) Gasse *f*; (*of motorway*) Spur *f*; (*Sport*) Bahn *f*; **to get in ~** (*in car*) sich einordnen

language ['læŋgwɪdʒ] n Sprache f; (style) Ausdrucksweise f

lantern ['læntən] n Laterne f

lap [læp] n Schoß m; (in race) Runde f ▷ vt (in race) überholen

lapse [læps] n (mistake) Irrtum m; (moral) Fehltritt m ▷ vi ablaufen

laptop ['læptɒp] n Laptop m

large [lɑːdʒ] adj groß; **by and ~** im Großen und Ganzen; **largely** adv zum größten Teil; **large-scale** adj groß angelegt, Groß-

lark [lɑːk] n (bird) Lerche f

laryngitis [lærɪn'dʒaɪtɪs] n Kehlkopfentzündung f; **larynx** ['lærɪŋks] n Kehlkopf m

laser ['leɪzə*] n Laser m; **laser printer** n Laserdrucker m

lash [læʃ] vt peitschen; **lash out** vi (with fists) um sich schlagen; (spend money) sich in Unkosten stürzen (on mit)

lass [læs] n Mädchen nt

last [lɑːst] adj letzte(r, s); **the ~ but one** der/die/das vorletzte; **~ night** gestern Abend; **~ but not least** nicht zuletzt ▷ adv zuletzt; (last time) das letzte Mal; **at ~** endlich ▷ n (person) Letzte(r) mf; (thing) Letzte(s) nt; **he was the ~ to leave** er ging als Letzter ▷ vi (continue) dauern; (remain in good condition) durchhalten; (remain good) sich halten; (money) ausreichen; **lasting** adj dauerhaft; (impression) nachhaltig; **lastly** adv schließlich; **last-minute** adj in letzter Minute; **last name** n Nachname m

late [leɪt] adj spät; (after proper time) zu spät; (train etc) verspätet; (dead) verstorben; **to be ~** zu spät kommen; (train etc) Verspätung haben ▷ adv spät; (after proper time) zu spät; **late availibility flight** n Last-Minute-Flug m; **lately** adv in letzter Zeit; **late opening** n verlängerte Öffnungszeiten pl; **later** ['leɪtə*] adj, adv später; **see you ~** bis später; **latest** ['leɪtɪst] adj späteste(r, s); (most recent) neueste(r, s) ▷ n **the ~** (news) das Neueste; **at the ~** spätestens

Latin ['lætɪn] n Latein nt ▷ adj lateinisch; **Latin America** n Lateinamerika nt; **Latin-American** adj lateinamerikanisch ▷ n Lateinamerikaner(in) m(f)

latitude ['lætɪtjuːd] n (Geo) Breite f

latter ['lætə*] adj (second of two) letztere(r, s); (last: part, years) letzte(r, s), später

Latvia ['lætvɪə] n Lettland nt

laugh [lɑːf] n Lachen nt; **for a ~** aus Spaß ▷ vi lachen (at, about über +akk); **to ~ at sb** sich über jdn lustig machen; **it's no ~ing matter** es ist nicht zum Lachen; **laughter** ['lɑːftə*] n Gelächter nt

launch [lɔːntʃ] n (launching, of ship) Stapellauf m; (of rocket) Abschuss m; (of product) Markteinführung f; (with hype) Lancierung f; (event) Eröffnungsfeier f ▷ vt (ship) vom Stapel lassen; (rocket) abschießen; (product) einführen; (with hype) lancieren; (project) in Gang setzen

launder ['lɔːndə*] vt waschen und bügeln; (fig: money) waschen; **laundrette** [lɔːn'dret] n (Brit), **laundromat** ['lɔːndrəmæt] n (US) Waschsalon m; **laundry** ['lɔːndrɪ] n (place) Wäscherei f; (clothes) Wäsche f

lavatory ['lævətrɪ] n Toilette f

lavender ['lævɪndə*] n Lavendel m

lavish ['lævɪʃ] adj verschwenderisch; (furnishings etc) üppig; (gift) großzügig

law [lɔː] n (money) Gesetz nt; (system) Recht nt; (for study) Jura; (of sport) Regel f; **against the ~** gesetzwidrig; **law-abiding** adj gesetzestreu; **law court** n Gerichtshof m; **lawful** adj rechtmäßig

lawn [lɔːn] n Rasen m; **lawnmower** n Rasenmäher m

lawsuit ['lɔːsuːt] n Prozess m; **lawyer** ['lɔːjə*] n Rechtsanwalt m, Rechtsanwältin f

laxative ['læksətɪv] n Abführmittel nt

lay [leɪ] pt of **lie** ▷ vt (laid, laid) legen; (table) decken; (vulg) poppen, bumsen; (egg) legen ▷ adj Laien-; **lay down** vt hinlegen; **lay off** vt (workers) (vorübergehend) entlassen; (stop attacking) in Ruhe lassen; **lay on** vt (provide) anbieten; (organize) veranstalten, bereitstellen; **layabout** n Faulenzer(in) m(f); **lay-by** n Parkbucht f; (bigger) Parkplatz m

layer ['leɪə*] n Schicht f

layman ['leɪmən] n Laie m

layout ['leɪaʊt] n Gestaltung f; (of book etc) Lay-out nt

laze [leɪz] vi faulenzen; **laziness** ['leɪzɪnɪs] n Faulheit f; **lazy** ['leɪzɪ] adj faul; (day, time) gemütlich

lb *abbr* = **pound** Pfd.

lead [led] *n* Blei *nt* ▷ *vt*, *vi* [li:d] (**led, led**) führen; (*group etc*) leiten; **to ~ the way** vorangehen; **this is ~ing us nowhere** das bringt uns nicht weiter ▷ [li:d] *n* (*race*) Führung *f*; (*distance, time ahead*) Vorsprung *m* (*over vor +dat*); (*of police*) Spur *f*; (*Theat*) Hauptrolle *f*; (*dog's*) Leine *f*; (*Elec: flex*) Leitung *f*; **lead astray** *vt* irreführen; **lead away** *vt* wegführen; **lead back** *vi* zurückführen; **lead on** *vt* anführen; **lead to** *vt* (*street*) hinführen nach; (*result in*) führen zu; **lead up to** *vt* (*drive*) führen zu

leaded ['ledɪd] *adj* (*petrol*) verbleit

leader ['li:də*] *n* Führer(in) *m(f)*; (*of party*) Vorsitzende(r) *mf*; (*of project, expedition*) Leiter(in) *m(f)*; (*of race*) der/die Erste; (*in league*) Tabellenführer *m*; **leadership** ['li:dəʃɪp] *n* Führung *f*

lead-free ['led'fri:] *adj* (*petrol*) bleifrei

leading ['li:dɪŋ] *adj* führend, wichtig

leaf [li:f] (*pl* **leaves**) *n* Blatt *nt*; **leaflet** ['li:flɪt] *n* Prospekt *m*; (*pamphlet*) Flugblatt *nt*; (*with instructions*) Merkblatt *nt*

league [li:g] *n* Bund *m*; (*Sport*) Liga *f*

leak [li:k] *n* (*gap*) undichte Stelle; (*escape*) Leck *nt*; **to take a ~** (*fam*) pinkeln gehen ▷ *vi* (*pipe etc*) undicht sein; (*liquid etc*) auslaufen; **leaky** *adj* undicht

lean [li:n] *adj* (*meat*) mager; (*face*) schmal; (*person*) drahtig ▷ *vi* (**leant** *o* **leaned, leant** *o* **leaned**) (*not vertical*) sich neigen; (*rest*) **to ~ against sth** sich an etw *akk* lehnen; (*support oneself*) **to ~ on sth** sich auf etw *akk* stützen ⇆ *vt* lehnen (*on, against* an +*akk*); **lean back** *vi* sich zurücklehnen; **lean forward** *vi* sich vorbeugen; **lean over** *vi* sich hinüberbeugen; **lean towards** *vt* tendieren zu

leant [lent] *pt, pp of* **lean**

leap [li:p] *n* Sprung *m* ▷ *vi* (**lept** *o* **leaped, lept** *o* **leaped**) springen; **leap year** *n* Schaltjahr *nt*

learn [lɜ:n] (**learnt** *o* **learned, learnt** *o* **learned**) *vt, vi* lernen; (*find out*) erfahren; **to ~ (how) to swim** schwimmen lernen; **learned** ['lɜ:nɪd] *adj* gelehrt; **learner** *n* Anfänger(in) *m(f)*; (*Brit: driver*) Fahrschüler(in) *m(f)*

learnt [lɜ:nt] *pt, pp of* **learn**

lease [li:s] *n* (*of land, premises etc*) Pacht *f*; (*contract*) Pachtvertrag *m*; (*of house, car etc*) Miete *f*; (*contract*) Mietvertrag *m* ▷ *vt* pachten; (*house, car etc*) mieten; **lease out** *vt* vermieten; **leasing** ['li:sɪŋ] *n* Leasing *nt*

least [li:st] *adj* wenigste(r, s); (*slightest*) geringste(r, s) ▷ *adv* am wenigsten; **~ expensive** billigste(r, s) ▷ *n* **the ~** das Mindeste; **not in the ~** nicht im geringsten; **at ~** wenigstens; (*with number*) mindestens

leather ['leðə*] *n* Leder *nt* ▷ *adj* ledern, Leder-

leave [li:v] *n* (*time off*) Urlaub *m*; **on ~** auf Urlaub; **to take one's ~** Abschied nehmen (*of von*) ▷ *vt* (**left, left**) (*place, person*) verlassen; (*not remove, not change*) lassen; (*~ behind: message, scar etc*) hinterlassen; (*forget*) hinter sich lassen; (*after death*) hinterlassen (*to sb jdm*); (*entrust*) überlassen (*to sb jdm*); **to be left** (*remain*) übrig bleiben; **~ me alone** lass mich in Ruhe!; **don't ~ it to the last minute** warte nicht bis zur letzten Minute ▷ *vi* (*weg*)gehen, (*weg*)fahren; (*on journey*) abreisen; (*bus, train*) abfahren (*for nach*); **leave behind** *vt* zurücklassen; (*scar etc*) hinterlassen; (*forget*) hinter sich lassen; **leave out** *vt* auslassen; (*person*) ausschließen (*of von*)

leaves [li:vz] *pl of* **leaf**

leaving do [li:vɪŋdu:] *n* Abschiedsfeier *f*

Lebanon ['lebənən] *n* **the ~** der Libanon

lecture ['lektʃə*] *n* Vortrag *m*; (*at university*) Vorlesung *f*; **to give a ~** einen Vortrag/eine Vorlesung halten; **lecturer** *n* Dozent(in) *m(f)*; **lecture theatre** *n* Hörsaal *m*

led [led] *pt, pp of* **lead**

LED *abbr* = **light-emitting diode** Leuchtdiode *f*

ledge [ledʒ] *n* Leiste *f*; (*window ~*) Sims *m o nt*

leek [li:k] *n* Lauch *m*

left [left] *pt, pp of* **leave** ▷ *adj* linke(r, s) ▷ *adv* (*position*) links; (*movement*) nach links ▷ *n* (*side*) linke Seite; **the Left** (*Pol*) die Linke; **on/to the ~** links (*of von*); **move/fall to the ~** nach links rücken/fallen; **left-hand** *adj* linke(r, s); **~ bend** Linkskurve *f*; **~ drive** Linkssteuerung *f*; **left-handed** *adj* linkshändig; **left-hand side** *n* linke Seite

left-luggage locker n
Gepäckschließfach nt; **left-luggage office**
n Gepäckaufbewahrung f
left-overs npl Reste pl
left wing n linker Flügel; **left-wing** adj
(Pol) linksgerichtet
leg [leg] n Bein nt; (of meat) Keule f
legacy ['legəsɪ] n Erbe nt, Erbschaft f
legal ['li:gəl] adj Rechts-, rechtlich;
(allowed) legal; (limit, age) gesetzlich; **~ aid**
Rechtshilfe f; **legalize** vt legalisieren;
legally adv legal
legend ['ledʒənd] n Legende f
legible, legibly ['ledʒəbl, -blɪ] adj, adv
leserlich
legislation [ledʒɪs'leɪʃn] n Gesetze pl
legitimate [lɪ'dʒɪtɪmət] adj rechtmäßig,
legitim
legroom ['legrʊm] n Platz m für die Beine
leisure ['leʒə*] n (time) Freizeit f ▷ adj
Freizeit-; **~ centre** Freizeitzentrum nt;
leisurely ['leʒəlɪ] adj gemächlich
lemon ['lemən] n Zitrone f; **lemonade**
[lemə'neɪd] n Limonade f; **lemon curd** n
Brotaufstrich aus Zitronen, Butter, Eiern und
Zucker; **lemon juice** n Zitronensaft m;
lemon sole n Seezunge f
lend [lend] (lent, lent) vt leihen; **to ~ sb**
sth jdm etw leihen; **to (sb) ~ a hand** (jdm)
behilflich sein; **lending library** n
Leihbücherei f
length [leŋθ] n Länge f; **4 metres in ~** 4
Meter lang; **what ~ is it?** wie lange ist es?;
for any ~ of time für längere Zeit; **at**
~ (lengthily) ausführlich; **lengthen**
['leŋθən] vt verlängern; **lengthy** adj sehr
lange; (dragging) langwierig
lenient ['li:nɪənt] adj nachsichtig
lens [lenz] n Linse f; (Foto) Objektiv nt
lent [lent] pt, pp of **lend**
Lent [lent] n Fastenzeit f
lentil ['lentl] n (Bot) Linse f
Leo ['li:əʊ] (pl **-s**) n (Astr) Löwe m
leopard ['lepəd] n Leopard m
lept [lept] pt, pp of **leap**
lesbian ['lezbɪən] adj lesbisch ▷ n Lesbe f
less [les] adj, adv, n weniger; **~ and**
~ immer weniger; (~ often) immer
seltener; **lessen** ['lesn] vi abnehmen,
nachlassen ▷ vt verringern; (pain) lindern;
lesser ['lesə*] adj geringer; (amount)
kleiner
lesson ['lesn] n (at school) Stunde f; (unit

of study) Lektion f; (fig) Lehre f; (Rel) Lesung
f; **~s start at 9** der Unterricht beginnt
um 9
let [let] (**let, let**) vt lassen; (lease)
vermieten; **to ~ sb have sth** jdm etw
geben; **~'s go** gehen wir; **to ~ go (of sth)**
(etw) loslassen; **let down** vt
herunterlassen; (fail to help) im Stich
lassen; (disappoint) enttäuschen; **let in** vt
hereinlassen; **let off** vt (bomb) hochgehen
lassen; (person) laufen lassen; **let out** vt
hinauslassen; (secret) verraten; (scream etc)
ausstoßen; **let up** vi nachlassen; (stop)
aufhören
lethal ['li:θəl] adj tödlich
let's contr = **let us**
letter ['letə*] n (of alphabet) Buchstabe m;
(message) Brief m; (official ~) Schreiben nt;
letter bomb n Briefbombe f; **letterbox** n
Briefkasten m
lettuce ['letɪs] n Kopfsalat m
leukaemia, leukemia (US) [lu:'ki:mɪə] n
Leukämie f
level ['levl] adj (horizontal) waagerecht;
(ground) eben; (two things, two runners) auf
selber Höhe; **to be ~ with sb/sth** mit
jdm/etw auf gleicher Höhe sein; **~ on**
points punktgleich ▷ adv (run etc) auf
gleicher Höhe, gleich auf; **to draw ~** (in
race) gleichziehen (with mit); (in game)
ausgleichen ▷ n (altitude) Höhe f;
(standard) Niveau nt; (amount, degree) Grad
m; **to be on a ~ with** auf gleicher Höhe
sein mit ▷ vt (ground) einebnen; **level**
crossing n (Brit) (schienengleicher)
Bahnübergang m; **level-headed** adj
vernünftig
lever ['li:və*], (US) ['levə*] n Hebel m;
(fig) Druckmittel nt; **lever up** vt
hochstemmen
liability [laɪə'bɪlɪtɪ] n Haftung f; (burden)
Belastung f; (obligation) Verpflichtung f;
liable ['laɪəbl] adj **to be ~ for sth**
(responsible) für etw haften; **~ for tax**
steuerpflichtig
liar ['laɪə*] n Lügner(in) m(f)
Lib Dem [lɪb'dem] abbr = **Liberal**
Democrat
liberal ['lɪbərəl] adj (generous) großzügig;
(broad-minded) liberal; **Liberal Democrat** n
(Brit Pol) Liberaldemokrat(in) m(f) ▷ adj
liberaldemokratisch; **the ~ Party** die
Liberaldemokratische Partei

liberate ['lɪbəreɪt] vt befreien; **liberation**
[lɪbə'reɪʃn] n Befreiung f
Liberia [laɪ'bɪərɪə] n Liberia nt
liberty ['lɪbətɪ] n Freiheit f
Libra ['liːbrə] n (Astr) Waage f
library ['laɪbrərɪ] n Bibliothek f; (lending ~)
Bücherei f
Libya ['lɪbɪə] n Libyen nt
lice [laɪs] pl of **louse**
licence ['laɪsəns] n (permit) Genehmigung
f; (Comm) Lizenz f; (driving ~) Führerschein
m; **license** ['laɪsəns] n (US) see **licence**
▷ vt genehmigen; **licensed** adj
(restaurant etc) mit Schankerlaubnis;
license plate n (US Auto) Nummernschild
nt; **licensing hours** npl Ausschankzeiten
pl
lick [lɪk] vt lecken ▷ n Lecken nt
licorice ['lɪkərɪs] n Lakritze f
lid [lɪd] n Deckel m; (eye~) Lid nt
lie [laɪ] n Lüge f; **~ detector**
Lügendetektor m ▷ vi lügen; **to ~ to sb**
jdn belügen ▷ vi (lay, lain) (rest, be
situated) liegen; (~ down) sich legen; (snow)
liegen bleiben; **to be lying third** an dritter
Stelle liegen; **lie about** vi herumliegen;
lie down vi sich hinlegen
Liechtenstein ['lɪktənstaɪn] n
Liechtenstein nt
lie in [laɪ'ɪn] **to have a ~** ausschlafen
life [laɪf] (pl **lives**) n Leben nt; **to get
~** lebenslänglich bekommen; **there isn't
much ~ here** hier ist nicht viel los; **how
many lives were lost?** wie viele sind ums
Leben gekommen?; **life assurance** n
Lebensversicherung f; **lifebelt** n
Rettungsring m; **lifeboat** n
Rettungsboot nt; **lifeguard** n
Bademeister(in) m(f),
Rettungsschwimmer(in) m(f); **life
insurance** n Lebensversicherung f; **life
jacket** n Schwimmweste f; **lifeless** adj
(dead) leblos; **lifelong** adj lebenslang; **life
preserver** n (US) Rettungsring m;
life-saving adj lebensrettend; **life-size(d)**
adj in Lebensgröße; **life span** n
Lebensspanne f; **life style** n Lebensstil m;
lifetime n Lebenszeit f
lift [lɪft] vt (hoch)heben; (ban)
aufheben ▷ n (Brit: elevator) Aufzug m,
Lift m; **to give sb a ~** jdn im Auto
mitnehmen; **lift up** vt hochheben; **lift-off**
n Start m

ligament ['lɪgəmənt] n Band nt
light [laɪt] (lit o lighted, lit o lighted) vt
beleuchten; (fire, cigarette) anzünden ▷ n
Licht nt; (lamp) Lampe f; **~s** pl (Auto)
Beleuchtung f; (traffic ~s) Ampel f; **in the
~ of** angesichts +gen ▷ adj (bright) hell;
(not heavy, easy) leicht; (punishment) milde;
(taxes) niedrig; **~ blue/green**
hellblau/hellgrün; **light up** vt (illuminate)
beleuchten ▷ vi (a. eyes) aufleuchten
light bulb n Glühbirne f
lighten ['laɪtn] vi hell werden ▷ vt (give
light to) erhellen; (make less heavy) leichter
machen; (fig) erleichtern
lighter ['laɪtə*] n (cigarette ~) Feuerzeug nt
light-hearted adj unbeschwert;
lighthouse n Leuchtturm m; **lighting** n
Beleuchtung f; **lightly** adv leicht; **light
meter** n (Foto) Belichtungsmesser m
lightning ['laɪtnɪŋ] n Blitz m
lightweight adj leicht
like [laɪk] vt mögen, gern haben; **he ~s
swimming** er schwimmt gern; **would you
~ ...?** hätten Sie gern ...?; **I'd ~ to go home**
ich möchte nach Hause (gehen); **I don't
~ the film** der Film gefällt mir nicht ▷ prep
wie; **what's it/he ~?** wie ist es/er?; **he
looks ~ you** er sieht dir ähnlich; **~ that/
this** so; **likeable** ['laɪkəbl] adj
sympathisch
likelihood ['laɪklɪhʊd] n
Wahrscheinlichkeit f; **likely** ['laɪklɪ] adj
wahrscheinlich; **the bus is ~ to be late** der
Bus wird wahrscheinlich Verspätung
haben; **he's not (at all) ~ to come**
(höchst)wahrscheinlich kommt er nicht
like-minded [laɪk'maɪndɪd] adj gleich
gesinnt
likewise ['laɪkwaɪz] adv ebenfalls; **to do
~** das Gleiche tun
liking ['laɪkɪŋ] n (for person) Zuneigung f;
(for type, things) Vorliebe f (for für)
lilac ['laɪlək] n Flieder m ▷ adj
fliederfarben
lily ['lɪlɪ] n Lilie f; **~ of the valley**
Maiglöckchen nt
limb [lɪm] n Glied nt
limbo ['lɪmbəʊ] n **in ~** (plans) auf Eis
gelegt
lime [laɪm] n (tree) Linde f; (fruit) Limone f;
(substance) Kalk m; **lime juice** n
Limonensaft m; **limelight** n (fig)
Rampenlicht nt

limerick ['lɪmərɪk] *n* Limerick *m* (fünfzeiliges komisches Gedicht)

limestone ['laɪmstəʊn] *n* Kalkstein *m*

limit ['lɪmɪt] *n* Grenze *f*; (for pollution etc) Grenzwert *m*; **there's a ~ to that** dem sind Grenzen gesetzt; **to drive over the ~** das Tempolimit überschreiten; **that's the ~** jetzt reicht's!, das ist die Höhe! ▷ *vt* beschränken (to auf +akk); (freedom, spending) einschränken; **limitation** [lɪmɪ'teɪʃən] *n* Beschränkung *f*; (of freedom, spending) Einschränkung *f*; **limited** *adj* begrenzt; **~ liability company** Gesellschaft *f* mit beschränkter Haftung, GmbH *f*; **public ~ company** Aktiengesellschaft *f*

limousine ['lɪməzi:n] *n* Limousine *f*

limp [lɪmp] *vi* hinken ▷ *adj* schlaff

line [laɪn] *n* Linie *f*; (written) Zeile *f*; (rope) Leine *f*; (on face) Falte *f*; (row) Reihe *f*; (US: queue) Schlange *f*; (Rail) Bahnlinie *f*; (between A and B) Strecke *f*; (Tel) Leitung *f*; (range of items) Kollektion *f*; **hold the ~** bleiben Sie am Apparat; **to stand in ~** Schlange stehen; **in ~ with** in Übereinstimmung mit; **something along those ~s** etwas in dieser Art; **drop me a ~** schreib mir ein paar Zeilen; **~s** (Theat) Text *m* ▷ *vt* (clothes) füttern; (streets) säumen; **lined** *adj* (paper) liniert; (face) faltig; **line up** *vi* sich aufstellen; (US: form queue) sich anstellen

linen ['lɪnɪn] *n* Leinen *nt*; (sheets etc) Wäsche *f*

liner ['laɪnə*] *n* Überseedampfer *m*, Passagierschiff *nt*

linesman ['laɪnzmən] (pl -**men**) *n* (Sport) Linienrichter *m*

linger ['lɪŋɡə*] *vi* verweilen; (smell) nicht weggehen

lingerie ['læenʒəri:] *n* Damenunterwäsche *f*

lining ['laɪnɪŋ] *n* (of clothes) Futter *nt*; (brake ~) Bremsbelag *m*

link [lɪŋk] *n* (connection) Verbindung *f*; (of chain) Glied *nt*; (relationship) Beziehung *f* (with zu); (between events) Zusammenhang *m*; (Internet) Link *m* ▷ *vt* verbinden

lion ['laɪən] *n* Löwe *m*; **lioness** *n* Löwin *f*

lip [lɪp] *n* Lippe *f*; **lipstick** *n* Lippenstift *m*

liqueur [lɪ'kjʊə*] *n* Likör *m*

liquid ['lɪkwɪd] *n* Flüssigkeit *f* ▷ *adj* flüssig

liquidate ['lɪkwɪdeɪt] *vt* liquidieren

liquidizer ['lɪkwɪdaɪzə*] *n* Mixer *m*

liquor ['lɪkə*] *n* Spirituosen *pl*

liquorice ['lɪkərɪs] *n* Lakritze *f*

Lisbon ['lɪzbən] *n* Lissabon *nt*

lisp [lɪsp] *vt*, *vi* lispeln

list [lɪst] *n* Liste *f* ▷ *vi* (ship) Schlagseite haben ▷ *vt* auflisten, aufzählen; **~ed building** unter Denkmalschutz stehendes Gebäude

listen ['lɪsn] *vi* zuhören, horchen (for sth auf etw akk); **listen to** *vt* (person) zuhören +dat; (radio) hören; (advice) hören auf; **listener** *n* Zuhörer(in) *m(f)*; (to radio) Hörer(in) *m(f)*

lit [lɪt] *pt*, *pp* of **light**

liter ['li:tə*] *n* (US) Liter *m*

literacy ['lɪtərəsɪ] *n* Fähigkeit *f* zu lesen und zu schreiben; **literal** ['lɪtərəl] *adj* (translation, meaning) wörtlich; (actual) buchstäblich; **literally** *adv* (translate, take sth) wörtlich; (really) buchstäblich, wirklich; **literary** ['lɪtərərɪ] *adj* literarisch; (critic, journal etc) Literatur-; (language) gehoben; **literature** ['lɪtrətʃə*] *n* Literatur *f*; (brochures etc) Informationsmaterial *nt*

Lithuania [lɪθjuː'eɪnjə] *n* Litauen *nt*

litre ['li:tə*] *n* Liter *m*

litter ['lɪtə*] *n* Abfälle *pl*; (of animals) Wurf *m* ▷ *vt* **to be ~ed with** übersät sein mit; **litter bin** *n* Abfalleimer *m*

little ['lɪtl] *adj* (**smaller, smallest**) klein; (in quantity) wenig; **a ~ while ago** vor kurzer Zeit ▷ *adv*, *n* (**fewer, fewest**) wenig; **a ~** ein bisschen, ein wenig; **as ~ as possible** so wenig wie möglich; **for as ~ as £5** ab nur 5 Pfund; **I see very ~ of them** ich sehe sie sehr selten; **~ by ~** nach und nach; **little finger** *n* kleiner Finger

live [laɪv] *adj* lebendig; (Elec) geladen, unter Strom; (TV, Radio: event) live; **~ broadcast** Direktübertragung *f* ▷ [lɪv] *vi* leben; (not die) überleben; (dwell) wohnen; **you ~ and learn** man lernt nie aus ▷ *vt* (life) führen; **to ~ a life of luxury** im Luxus leben; **live on** *vi* weiterleben ▷ *vt* **to ~ sth** von etw leben; (feed) sich von etw ernähren; **to earn enough to ~** genug verdienen, um davon zu leben; **live together** *vi* zusammenleben; **live up to** *vt* (reputation) gerecht werden +dat; (expectations) entsprechen +dat; **live with** *vt* (parents etc) wohnen bei; (partner) zusammenleben mit; (difficulty) **you'll just have to - it** du musst dich eben damit abfinden

liveliness ['laɪvlɪnɪs] n Lebhaftigkeit f; **lively** ['laɪvlɪ] adj lebhaft

liver ['lɪvə*] n Leber f

lives [laɪvz] pl of **life**

livestock ['laɪvstɒk] n Vieh nt

living ['lɪvɪŋ] n Lebensunterhalt m; **what do you do for a ~?** was machen Sie beruflich? ▷ adj lebend; **living room** n Wohnzimmer nt

lizard ['lɪzəd] n Eidechse f

load [ləʊd] n Last f; (cargo) Ladung f; (Tech, fig) Belastung f; **~s of** (fam) massenhaft; **it was a ~ of rubbish** (fam) es war grottenschlecht ▷ vt (vehicle) beladen; (Inform) laden; (gun) einlegen

loaf [ləʊf] (pl **loaves**) n **~ (of bread)** Brot nt; **loaf about** vi faulenzen

loan [ləʊn] n (item leant) Leihgabe f; (Fin) Darlehen nt; **on ~** geliehen ▷ vt leihen (to sb jdm)

loathe [ləʊð] vt verabscheuen

loaves [ləʊvz] pl of **loaf**

lobby ['lɒbɪ] n Vorhalle f; (Pol) Lobby f

lobster ['lɒbstə*] n Hummer m

local ['ləʊkəl] adj (traffic, time etc) Orts-; (radio, news, paper) Lokal-; (government, authority) Kommunal-; (anaesthetic) örtlich; **~ call** (Tel) Ortsgespräch nt; **~ elections** Kommunalwahlen pl; **~ time** Ortszeit f; **~ train** Nahverkehrszug m; **the ~ shops** die Geschäfte am Ort ▷ n (pub) Stammlokal nt; **the ~s** die Ortsansässigen pl; **locally** adv örtlich, am Ort

locate [ləʊ'keɪt] vt (find) ausfindig machen; (position) legen; (establish) errichten; **to be ~d** sich befinden (in, at in +dat); **location** [ləʊ'keɪʃən] n (position) Lage f; (Cine) Drehort m

loch [lɒx] n (Scot) See m

lock [lɒk] n Schloss nt; (Naut) Schleuse f; (of hair) Locke f ▷ vt (door etc) abschließen ▷ vi (door etc) sich abschließen lassen; (wheels) blockieren; **lock in** vt einschließen, einsperren; **lock out** vt aussperren; **lock up** vt (house) abschließen; (person) einsperren

locker ['lɒkə*] n Schließfach nt; **locker room** n (US) Umkleideraum m

locksmith ['lɒksmɪθ] n Schlosser(in) m(f)

locust ['ləʊkəst] n Heuschrecke f

lodge [lɒdʒ] n (small house) Pförtnerhaus nt; (porter's ~) Pförtnerloge f ▷ vi in Untermiete wohnen (with bei); (get stuck) stecken bleiben; **lodger** n Untermieter(in) m(f); **lodging** n Unterkunft f

loft [lɒft] n Dachboden m

log [lɒg] n Klotz m; (Naut) Log nt; **to keep a ~ of sth** über etw Buch führen; **log in** vi (Inform) sich einloggen; **log off** vi (Inform) sich ausloggen; **log on** vi (Inform) sich einloggen; **log out** vi (Inform) sich ausloggen

logic ['lɒdʒɪk] n Logik f; **logical** adj logisch

logo ['ləʊgəʊ] (pl **-s**) n Logo nt

loin [lɔɪn] n Lende f

loiter ['lɔɪtə*] vi sich herumtreiben

lollipop ['lɒlɪpɒp] n Lutscher m; **~ man/lady** (Brit) Schülerlotse m, Schülerlotsin f

lolly ['lɒlɪ] n Lutscher m; (fam: money) Knete f

London ['lʌndən] n London nt; **Londoner** n Londoner(in) m(f)

loneliness ['ləʊnlɪnɪs] n Einsamkeit f; **lonely** ['ləʊnlɪ], (esp US) **lonesome** ['ləʊnsəm] adj einsam

long [lɒŋ] adj lang; (distance) weit; **it's a ~ way** es ist weit (to nach); **for a ~ time** lange; **how ~ is the film?** wie lange dauert der Film?; **in the ~ run** auf die Dauer ▷ adv lange; **not for ~** nicht lange; **~ ago** vor langer Zeit; **before ~** bald; **all day ~** den ganzen Tag; **no ~er** nicht mehr; **as ~ as** solange ▷ vi sich sehnen (for nach); (be waiting) sehnsüchtig warten (for auf); **long-distance call** n Ferngespräch nt; **long drink** n Longdrink m; **long-haul flight** n Langstreckenflug m; **longing** n Sehnsucht f (for nach); **longingly** adv sehnsüchtig; **longitude** ['lɒŋgɪtjuːd] n Länge f; **long jump** n Weitsprung m; **long-life milk** n H-Milch f; **long-range** adj Langstrecken-, Fern-; **~ missile** Langstreckenrakete f; **long-sighted** adj weitsichtig; **long-standing** adj alt, langjährig; **long-term** adj langfristig; (car park, effect etc) Langzeit-;

~ unemployment Langzeitarbeitslosigkeit f; **long wave** n Langwelle f

loo [luː] n (Brit fam) Klo nt

look [lʊk] n Blick m; (appearance) ~(s) pl Aussehen nt; **I'll have a ~** ich schau mal nach; **to have a ~ at sth** sich dat etw ansehen; **can I have a ~?** darf ich mal sehen? ▷ vi schauen, gucken; (with prep) sehen; (search) nachsehen; (appear) aussehen; **(I'm) just ~ing** ich schaue nur; **it ~s like rain** es sieht nach Regen aus ▷ vt **~ what you've done** sieh dir mal an, was du da angestellt hast; (appear) **he ~s his age** man sieht ihm sein Alter an; **to ~ one's best** sehr vorteilhaft aussehen; **look after** vt (care for) sorgen für; (keep an eye on) aufpassen auf +akk; **look at** vt ansehen, anschauen; **look back** vi sich umsehen; (fig) zurückblicken; **look down on** vt (fig) herabsehen auf +akk; **look for** vt suchen; **look forward to** vt sich freuen auf +akk; **look into** vt (investigate) untersuchen; **look out** vi hinaussehen (of the window zum Fenster); (watch out) Ausschau halten (for nach); (be careful) aufpassen, Acht geben (for auf +akk); **~!** Vorsicht!; **look up** vi aufsehen ▷ vt (word etc) nachschlagen; **look up to** vt aufsehen zu

loony [ˈluːnɪ] adj (fam) bekloppt

loop [luːp] n Schleife f

loose [luːs] adj locker; (knot, button) lose; **loosen** vt lockern; (knot) lösen

loot [luːt] n Beute f

lop-sided [ˈlɒpˈsaɪdɪd] adj schief

lord [lɔːd] n (ruler) Herr m; (Brit: title) Lord m; **the Lord** (God) Gott der Herr; **the (House of) Lords** (Brit) das Oberhaus

lorry [ˈlɒrɪ] n (Brit) Lastwagen m

lose [luːz] (lost, lost) vt verlieren; (chance) verpassen; **to ~ weight** abnehmen; **to ~ one's life** umkommen ▷ vi verlieren; (clock, watch) nachgehen; **loser** n Verlierer(in) m(f); **loss** [lɒs] n Verlust m; **lost** [lɒst] pt, pp of **lose**; **we're ~** wir haben uns verlaufen ▷ adj verloren; **lost-and-found** (US), **lost property (office)** n Fundbüro nt

lot [lɒt] n (fam: batch) Menge f, Haufen m, Stoß m; **this is the first ~** das ist die erste Ladung; **a ~** viel(e); **a ~ of money** viel Geld; **~s of people** viele Leute; **the (whole) ~** (people) alle; (parking) **~** (US) Parkplatz m

lotion [ˈləʊʃən] n Lotion f

lottery [ˈlɒtərɪ] n Lotterie f

loud [laʊd] adj laut; (colour) schreiend; **loudspeaker** n Lautsprecher m; (of stereo) Box f

lounge [laʊndʒ] n Wohnzimmer nt; (in hotel) Aufenthaltsraum m; (at airport) Warteraum m ▷ vi sich herumlümmeln

louse [laʊs] (pl **lice**) n Laus f; **lousy** [ˈlaʊzɪ] adj (fam) lausig

lout [laʊt] n Rüpel m

lovable [ˈlʌvəbl] adj liebenswert

love [lʌv] n Liebe f (of zu); (person, address) Liebling m, Schatz m; (Sport) null; **to be in ~** verliebt sein (with sb in jdn); **to fall in ~** sich verlieben (with sb in jdn); **to make ~** (sexually) sich lieben; **to make ~ to** (o with) **sb** mit jdm schlafen; (in letter) **he sends his ~** er lässt grüßen; **give her my ~** grüße sie von mir; **~, Tom** liebe Grüße, Tom ▷ vt (person) lieben; (activity) sehr gerne mögen; **to ~ to do sth** etw für sein Leben gerne tun; **I'd ~ a cup of tea** ich hätte liebend gern eine Tasse Tee; **love affair** n (Liebes)verhältnis nt; **love letter** n Liebesbrief.m; **love life** n Liebesleben nt; **lovely** [ˈlʌvlɪ] adj schön, wunderschön; (charming) reizend; **we had a ~ time** es war sehr schön; **lover** [ˈlʌvə] n Liebhaber(in) m(f); **loving** adj liebevoll

low [ləʊ] adj niedrig; (rank) niedere(r, s); (level, note, neckline) tief; (intelligence, density) gering; (quality, standard) schlecht; (not loud) leise; (depressed) niedergeschlagen; **we're ~ on petrol** wir haben kaum noch Benzin ▷ n (Meteo) Tief nt; **low-calorie** adj kalorienarm; **lowcut** adj (dress) tief ausgeschnitten; **low-emission** adj schadstoffarm; **lower** [ˈləʊə*] adj niedriger; (storey, class etc) untere(r, s) ▷ vt herunterlassen; (eyes, price) senken; (pressure) verringern; **low-fat** adj fettarm; **low tide** [ləʊˈtaɪd] n Ebbe f

loyal [ˈlɔɪəl] adj treu; **loyalty** n Treue f

lozenge [ˈlɒzɪndʒ] n Pastille f

L-Plates

Als **L-Plates** werden in Großbritannien die weißen Schilder mit einem roten „L" bezeichnet, die vorn und hinten an jedem von einem Fahrschüler gesteuerten Fahrzeug

- befestigt werden müssen.
- Fahrschüler müssen einen
- vorläufigen Führerschein
- beantragen und dürfen damit unter
- der Aufsicht eines erfahrenen
- Autofahrers auf allen Straßen außer
- Autobahnen fahren.

Ltd *abbr* = **limited** ≈ GmbH *f*

lubricant ['luːbrɪkənt] *n* Schmiermittel *nt*, Gleitmittel *nt*

luck [lʌk] *n* Glück *nt*; **bad ~** Pech *nt*; **luckily** *adv* glücklicherweise, zum Glück; **lucky** *adj* (*number, day etc*) Glücks-; **to be ~** Glück haben; **~ coincidence** glücklicher Zufall

ludicrous ['luːdɪkrəs] *adj* grotesk

luggage ['lʌgɪdʒ] *n* Gepäck *nt*; **luggage compartment** *n* Gepäckraum *m*; **luggage rack** *n* Gepäcknetz *nt*

lukewarm ['luːkwɔːm] *adj* lauwarm

lullaby ['lʌləbaɪ] *n* Schlaflied *nt*

lumbago [lʌm'beɪgəʊ] *n* Hexenschuss *m*

luminous ['luːmɪnəs] *adj* leuchtend

lump [lʌmp] *n* Klumpen *m*; (*Med*) Schwellung *f*, (*in breast*) Knoten *m*; (*of sugar*) Stück *nt*; **lump sum** *n* Pauschalsumme *f*; **lumpy** *adj* klumpig

lunacy ['luːnəsɪ] *n* Wahnsinn *m*; **lunatic** ['luːnətɪk] *adj* wahnsinnig ▷ *n* Wahnsinnige(r) *mf*

lunch, luncheon [lʌntʃ, -ən] *n* Mittagessen *nt*; **to have ~** zu Mittag essen; **lunch break, lunch hour** *n* Mittagspause *f*; **lunch packet** *n* Lunchpaket *nt*; **lunchtime** *n* Mittagszeit *f*

lung [lʌŋ] *n* Lunge *f*

lurid ['ljʊərɪd] *adj* (*colour*) grell; (*details*) widerlich

lurk [lɜːk] *vi* lauern

lust [lʌst] *n* (sinnliche) Begierde (*for* nach)

luster (*US*), **lustre** ['lʌstə*] *n* Glanz *m*

Luxembourg ['lʌksəmbɜːg] *n* Luxemburg *nt*; **Luxembourger** [lʌksəm'bɜːgə*] *n* Luxemburger(in) *m(f)*

luxurious [lʌg'zjʊərɪəs] *adj* luxuriös, Luxus-; **luxury** ['lʌkʃərɪ] *n* (*a.* luxuries *pl*) Luxus *m*; **~ goods** Luxusgüter *pl*

lynx [lɪŋks] *n* Luchs *m*

lyrics *npl* (*words for song*) Liedtext *m*

m *abbr* = **metre** m

M *abbr* (*street*) = **Motorway** A; (*size*) =
medium M

MA *abbr* = **Master of Arts** Magister Artium
m

ma [maː] *n* (*fam*) Mutti *f*

mac [mæk] *n* (*Brit fam*) Regenmantel *m*

Macedonia [mæfə'dəʊnɪə] *n*
Mazedonien *nt*

machine [mə'ʃiːn] *n* Maschine *f*;
machine gun *n* Maschinengewehr *nt*;
machinery [mə'ʃiːnərɪ] *n* Maschinen *pl*;
(*fig*) Apparat *m*; **machine washable** *adj*
waschmaschinenfest

mackerel ['mækrəl] *n* Makrele *f*

macro ['mækrəʊ] (*pl* **-s**) *n* (*Inform*) Makro
nt

mad [mæd] *adj* wahnsinnig, verrückt;
(*dog*) tollwütig; (*angry*) wütend, sauer (*at*
auf +*akk*); (*fam*) **~ about** (*fond of*) verrückt
nach; **to work like ~** wie verrückt
arbeiten; **are you ~?** spinnst du?

madam ['mædəm] *n* gnädige Frau

mad cow disease [mæd'kaʊdɪ'ziːz] *n*
Rinderwahnsinn *m*; **maddening** *adj* zum
Verrücktwerden

made [meɪd] *pt, pp of* **make**

made-to-measure ['meɪdtə'meʒə*] *adj*
nach Maß; **~ suit** Maßanzug *m*

madly ['mædlɪ] *adv* wie verrückt; (*with*
adj) wahnsinnig; **madman** ['mædmən] (*pl*
-men) *n* Verrückte(r) *m*; **madwoman**
['mædwʊmən] (*pl* **-women**) *n* Verrückte *f*;
madness ['mædnɪs] *n* Wahnsinn *m*

magazine ['mægəziːn] *n* Zeitschrift *f*

maggot ['mægət] *n* Made *f*

magic ['mædʒɪk] *n* Magie *f*; (*activity*)
Zauberei *f*; (*fig: effect*) Zauber *m*; **as if by**
~ wie durch Zauberei ▷ *adj* Zauber-;
(*powers*) magisch; **magician** [mə'dʒɪʃən] *n*
Zauberer *m*, Zaub(r)erin *f*

magnet ['mægnɪt] *n* Magnet *m*;
magnetic [mæg'netɪk] *adj* magnetisch;
magnetism ['mægnɪtɪzəm] *n* (*fig*)
Anziehungskraft *f*

magnificent, magnificently
[mæg'nɪfɪsənt, -lɪ] *adj, adv* herrlich,
großartig

magnify ['mægnɪfaɪ] *vt* vergrößern;
magnifying glass *n* Vergrößerungsglas
nt, Lupe *f*

magpie ['mægpaɪ] *n* Elster *f*

maid [meɪd] *n* Dienstmädchen *nt*;
maiden name *n* Mädchenname *m*;
maiden voyage *n* Jungfernfahrt *f*

mail [meɪl] *n* Post *f*; (*e-mail*) Mail *f* ▷ *vt*
(*post*) aufgeben; (*send*) mit der Post
schicken (*to an* +*akk*); **mailbox** *n* (*US*)
Briefkasten *m*; (*Inform*) Mailbox *f*; **mailing**
list *n* Adressenliste *f*; **mailman** *n* (*pl*
-men) (*US*) Briefträger *m*; **mail order** *n*
Bestellung *f* per Post; **mail order firm** *n*
Versandhaus *nt*; **mailshot** *n* Mailing *nt*

main [meɪn] *adj* Haupt-; **~ course** die
Hauptgericht *nt*; **the ~ thing** die
Hauptsache ▷ *n* (*pipe*) Hauptleitung *f*;
mainframe *n* Großrechner *m*; **mainland**
n Festland *nt*; **mainly** *adv* hauptsächlich;
main road *n* Hauptverkehrsstraße *f*;
main street *n* (*US*) Hauptstraße *f*

maintain [meɪn'teɪn] *vt* (*keep up*)
aufrechterhalten; (*machine, roads*) instand
halten; (*service*) warten; (*claim*)
behaupten; **maintenance** ['meɪntənəns]
n Instandhaltung *f*; (*Tech*) Wartung *f*

maize [meɪz] *n* Mais *m*

majestic [mə'dʒestɪk] *adj* majestätisch;
majesty ['mædʒɪstɪ] *n* Majestät *f*;
his/her Majesty seine/ihre Majestät

major ['meɪdʒə*] adj (bigger) größer; (important) bedeutend; **~ part** Großteil m; (role) wichtige Rolle; **~ road** Hauptverkehrsstraße f; (Mus) **A ~** A-Dur nt ▷ vi (US) **to ~ in** etw als Hauptfach studieren

Majorca [mə'jɔːkə] n Mallorca nt

majority [mə'dʒɒrɪtɪ] n Mehrheit f; **to be in the ~** in der Mehrzahl sein

make [meɪk] n Marke f ▷ vt (**made, made**) machen; (manufacture) herstellen; (clothes) anfertigen; (dress) nähen; (soup) zubereiten; (bread, cake) backen; (tea, coffee) kochen; (speech) halten; (earn) verdienen; (decision) treffen; **it's made of gold** es ist aus Gold; **to ~ sb do sth** jdn dazu bringen, etw zu tun; (force) jdn zwingen, etw zu tun; **she made us wait** sie ließ uns warten; **what ~s you think that?** wie kommen Sie darauf?; **it ~s the room look smaller** es lässt den Raum kleiner wirken; **to ~ (it to) the airport** (reach) den Flughafen erreichen; (in time) es zum Flughafen schaffen; **he never really made it** er hat es nie zu etwas gebracht; **she didn't ~ it through the night** sie hat die Nacht nicht überlebt; (calculate) **I ~ it £5/a quarter to six** nach meiner Rechnung kommt es auf 5 Pfund/nach meiner Uhr ist es dreiviertel sechs; **he's just made for this job** er ist für diese Arbeit wie geschaffen; **make for** vt zusteuern auf +akk; **make of** vt (think of) halten von; **I couldn't ~ anything of it** ich wurde daraus nicht schlau; **make off** vi sich davonmachen (with mit); **make out** vi zurechtkommen ▷ vt (cheque) ausstellen; (list) aufstellen; (understand) verstehen; (discern) ausmachen; **to ~ (that) ...** es so hinstellen, als ob ...; **make up** vt (team etc) bilden; (face) schminken; (invent: story etc) erfinden; **to ~ one's mind** sich entscheiden; **to make it up with sb** sich mit jdm aussöhnen ▷ vi sich versöhnen; **make up for** vt ausgleichen; (time) aufholen

make-believe adj Fantasie-; **makeover** n gründliche Veränderung, Verschönerung f; **maker** n (Comm) Hersteller(in) m(f); **makeshift** adj behelfsmäßig; **make-up** n Make-up nt, Schminke f; **making** ['meɪkɪŋ] n Herstellung f

maladjusted [mælə'dʒʌstɪd] adj verhaltensgestört

malaria [mə'lɛərɪə] n Malaria f

Malaysia [mə'leɪzɪə] n Malaysia nt

male [meɪl] n Mann m; (animal) Männchen nt ▷ adj männlich; **~ chauvinist** Chauvi m, Macho m; **~ nurse** Krankenpfleger m

malfunction [mæl'fʌŋkʃən] vi nicht richtig funktionieren ▷ n Defekt m

malice ['mælɪs] n Bosheit f; **malicious** [mə'lɪʃəs] adj boshaft; (behaviour, action) böswillig; (damage) mutwillig

malignant [mə'lɪgnənt] adj bösartig

mall [mɔːl] n (US) Einkaufszentrum nt

malnutrition [mælnjʊ'trɪʃən] n Unterernährung f

malt [mɔːlt] n Malz nt

Malta ['mɔːltə] n Malta nt; **Maltese** [mɔːl'tiːz] adj maltesisch ▷ n (person) Malteser(in) m(f); (language) Maltesisch nt

maltreat [mæl'triːt] vt schlecht behandeln; (violently) misshandeln

mammal ['mæməl] n Säugetier nt

mammoth ['mæməθ] adj Mammut-, Riesen-

man [mæn] (pl **men**) n (male) Mann m; (human race) der Mensch, die Menschen pl; (in chess) Figur f ▷ vt besetzen

manage ['mænɪdʒ] vi zurechtkommen; **can you ~?** schaffst du es?; **to ~ without sth** ohne etw auskommen, auf etw verzichten können ▷ vt (control) leiten; (musician, sportsman) managen; (cope with) fertig werden mit; (task, portion, climb etc) schaffen; **to ~ to do sth** es schaffen, etw zu tun; **manageable** adj (object) handlich; (task) zu bewältigen; **management** n Leitung f; (directors) Direktion f; (subject) Management nt, Betriebswirtschaft f; **management consultant** n Unternehmensberater(in) m(f); **manager** n Geschäftsführer(in) m(f); (departmental ~) Abteilungsleiter(in) m(f); (of branch, bank) Filialleiter(in) m(f); (of musician, sportsman) Manager(in) m(f); **managing director** n Geschäftsführer(in) m(f)

mane [meɪn] n Mähne f

maneuver (US) see **manoeuvre**

mango ['mæŋgəʊ] (pl **-es**) n Mango f

man-hour n Arbeitsstunde f

manhunt n Fahndung f

mania ['meɪnɪə] n Manie f; **maniac**

['meɪnɪæk] n Wahnsinnige(r) mf; (fan) Fanatiker(in) m(f)

manicure ['mænɪkjʊə*] n Maniküre f

manipulate [mə'nɪpjʊleɪt] vt manipulieren

mankind [mæn'kaɪnd] n Menschheit f

manly ['mænlɪ] adj männlich

man-made ['mænmeɪd] adj (product) künstlich

manner ['mænə*] n Art f; in this ~ auf diese Art und Weise; ~s pl Manieren pl

manoeuvre [mə'nu:və*] n Manöver nt ▷ vt, vi manövrieren

manor ['mænə*] n ~ (house) Herrenhaus nt

manpower ['mænpaʊə*] n Arbeitskräfte pl

mansion ['mænʃən] n Villa f; (of old family) Herrenhaus nt

manslaughter ['mænslɔ:tə*] n Totschlag m

mantelpiece ['mæntlpi:s] n Kaminsims m

manual ['mænjʊəl] adj manuell, Hand- ▷ n Handbuch nt

manufacture [mænjʊ'fæktʃə*] vt herstellen ▷ n Herstellung f; manufacturer n Hersteller m

manure [mə'njʊə*] n Dung m; (esp artificial) Dünger m

many ['menɪ] (more, most) adj, pron viele; ~ times oft; not ~ people nicht viele Leute; too ~ problems zu viele Probleme

map [mæp] n Landkarte f; (of town) Stadtplan m

maple ['meɪpl] n Ahorn m

marathon ['mærəθən] n Marathon m

marble ['mɑ:bl] n Marmor m; (for playing) Murmel f

march [mɑ:tʃ] vi marschieren ▷ n Marsch m; (protest) Demonstration f

March [mɑ:tʃ] n März m; see also September

mare [meə] n Stute f

margarine [mɑ:dʒə'ri:n] n Margarine f

margin ['mɑ:dʒɪn] n Rand m; (extra amount) Spielraum m; (Comm) Gewinnspanne f; marginal adj (difference etc) geringfügig

marijuana [mærjʊ'ɑ:nə] n Marihuana nt

marinade ['mærɪneɪd] n (Gastr)

Marinade f; marinated ['mærɪneɪtd] adj mariniert

marine [mə'ri:n] adj Meeres-

marital ['mærɪtl] adj ehelich; ~ status Familienstand m

maritime ['mærɪtaɪm] adj See-

marjoram ['mɑ:dʒərəm] n Majoran m

mark [mɑ:k] n (spot) Fleck m; (at school) Note f; (sign) Zeichen nt ▷ vt (make ~) Flecken machen auf +akk; (indicate) markieren; (schoolwork) benoten, korrigieren, Flecken machen auf +akk; markedly ['mɑ:kɪdlɪ] adv merklich; (with comp adj) wesentlich; marker n (in book) Lesezeichen nt; (pen) Marker m

market ['mɑ:kɪt] n Markt m; (stock ~) Börse f ▷ vt (Comm: new product) auf den Markt bringen; (goods) vertreiben; marketing n Marketing nt; market leader n Marktführer m; market place n Marktplatz m; market research n Marktforschung f

marmalade ['mɑ:məleɪd] n Orangenmarmelade f

maroon [mə'ru:n] adj rötlich braun

marquee [mɑ:'ki:] n großes Zelt

marriage ['mærɪdʒ] n Ehe f; (wedding) Heirat f (to mit); married ['mærɪd] adj (person) verheiratet

marrow ['mærəʊ] n (bone ~) Knochenmark nt; (vegetable) Kürbis m

marry ['mærɪ] vt heiraten; (join) trauen; (take as husband, wife) heiraten ▷ vi to ~ / to get married heiraten

marsh [mɑ:ʃ] n Marsch f, Sumpf m

marshal ['mɑ:ʃəl] n (at rally etc) Ordner m; (US: police) Bezirkspolizeichef m

martial arts ['mɑ:ʃəl'ɑ:ts] npl Kampfsportarten pl

martyr ['mɑ:tə*] n Märtyrer(in) m(f)

marvel ['mɑ:vəl] n Wunder nt ▷ vi staunen (at über +akk); marvellous, marvelous (US) adj wunderbar

marzipan [mɑ:zɪ'pæn] n Marzipan nt o m

mascara [mæ'skɑ:rə] n Wimperntusche f

mascot ['mæskɒt] n Maskottchen nt

masculine ['mæskjʊlɪn] adj männlich

mashed [mæʃt] adj ~ potatoes pl Kartoffelbrei m, Kartoffelpüree nt

mask [mɑ:sk] n (a. Inform) Maske f ▷ vt (feelings) verbergen

masochist ['mæsəʊkɪst] n Masochist(in) m(f)

mason ['meɪsn] n (stone~) Steinmetz(in) m(f); **masonry** n Mauerwerk nt

mass [mæs] n Masse f; (of people) Menge f; (Rel) Messe f; **~es of** massenhaft

massacre ['mæsəkə*] n Blutbad nt

massage ['mæsɑːʒ] n Massage f ▷ vt massieren

massive ['mæsɪv] adj (powerful) gewaltig; (very large) riesig

mass media ['mæsˈmiːdɪə] npl Massenmedien pl; **mass-produce** vt in Massenproduktion herstellen; **mass production** n Massenproduktion f

master ['mɑːstə*] n Herr m; (of dog) Besitzer m, Herrchen nt; (teacher) Lehrer m; (artist) Meister m ▷ vt meistern; (language etc) beherrschen; **masterly** adj meisterhaft; **masterpiece** n Meisterwerk nt

masturbate ['mæstəbeɪt] vi masturbieren

mat [mæt] n Matte f; (for table) Untersetzer m

match [mætʃ] n Streichholz nt; (Sport) Wettkampf m; (ball games) Spiel nt; (tennis) Match nt ▷ vt (be like, suit) passen zu; (equal) gleichkommen +dat ▷ vi zusammenpassen; **matchbox** n Streichholzschachtel f; **matching** adj (one item) passend; (two items) zusammenpassend

mate [meɪt] n (companion) Kumpel m; (of animal) Weibchen nt/Männchen nt ▷ vi sich paaren

material [mə'tɪərɪəl] n Material nt; (for book etc, cloth) Stoff m; **materialistic** [mətɪərɪə'lɪstɪk] adj materialistisch; **materialize** [mə'tɪərɪəlaɪz] vi zustande kommen; (hope) wahr werden

maternal [mə'tɜːnl] adj mütterlich; **maternity** [mə'tɜːnɪtɪ] adj **~ dress** Umstandskleid nt; **~ leave** Elternzeit f (der Mutter); **~ ward** Entbindungsstation f

math [mæθ] n (US fam) Mathe f; **mathematical** [mæθə'mætɪkəl] adj mathematisch; **mathematics** [mæθə'mætɪks] nsing Mathematik f; **maths** [mæθs] nsing (Brit fam) Mathe f

matinée ['mætɪneɪ] n Nachmittagsvorstellung f

matter ['mætə*] n (substance) Materie f; (affair) Sache f; **a personal ~** eine

persönliche Angelegenheit; **a ~ of taste** eine Frage des Geschmacks; **no ~ how/what** egal wie/was; **what is the ~?** was ist los?; **as a ~ of fact** eigentlich; **a ~ of time** eine Frage der Zeit ▷ vi darauf ankommen, wichtig sein; **it doesn't ~** es macht nichts; **matter-of-fact** adj sachlich, nüchtern

mattress ['mætrəs] n Matratze f

mature [mə'tjʊə*] adj reif ▷ vi reif werden; **maturity** [mə'tjʊərɪtɪ] n Reife f

maximum ['mæksɪməm] adj Höchst-, höchste(r, s); **~ speed** Höchstgeschwindigkeit f ▷ n Maximum nt

may [meɪ] (**might**) vb aux (be possible) können; (have permission) dürfen; **it ~ rain** es könnte regnen; **~ I smoke?** darf ich rauchen?; **it ~ not happen** es passiert vielleicht gar nicht; **we ~ as well go** wir können ruhig gehen

May [meɪ] n Mai m; see also **September**

maybe ['meɪbiː] adv vielleicht

May Day ['meɪdeɪ] n der erste Mai

mayo ['meɪəʊ] (US fam), **mayonnaise** [meɪə'neɪz] n Mayo f, Mayonnaise f, Majonäse f

mayor [mɛə*] n Bürgermeister m

maze [meɪz] n Irrgarten m; (fig) Wirrwarr nt

MB abbr = **megabyte** MB nt

KEYWORD

me [miː] pron **1** (direct) mich; **it's me** ich bins

2 (indirect) mir; **give them to me** gib sie mir

3 (after prep: +acc) mich; (+dat) mir; **with/without me** mit mir/ohne mich

meadow ['medəʊ] n Wiese f

meal [miːl] n Essen nt, Mahlzeit f; **to go out for a ~** essen gehen; **meal pack** n (US) tiefgekühltes Fertiggericht; **meal time** n Essenszeit f

mean [miːn] (**meant, meant**) vt (signify) bedeuten; (have in mind) meinen; (intend) vorhaben; **I ~ it** ich meine das ernst; **what do you ~ (by that)?** was willst du damit sagen?; **to ~ to do sth** etw tun wollen; **it was ~t for you** es war für dich bestimmt (o gedacht); **it was ~t to be a joke** es

sollte ein Witz sein ▷ vi **he ~s well** er
meint es gut ▷ adj (stingy) geizig; (spiteful)
gemein (to zu); **meaning** ['miːnɪŋ] n
Bedeutung f; (of life, poem) Sinn m;
meaningful adj sinnvoll; **meaningless**
adj (text) ohne Sinn

means [miːnz] (pl **means**) n Mittel nt; (pl:
funds) Mittel pl; **by ~ of** durch, mittels; **by
all ~** selbstverständlich; **by no
~** keineswegs; **~ of transport**
Beförderungsmittel

meant [ment] pt, pp of **mean**

meantime [miːnˈtaɪm] adv **in the
~** inzwischen; **meanwhile** [miːnˈwaɪl]
adv inzwischen

measles ['miːzlz] nsing Masern pl;
German ~ Röteln pl

measure ['meʒə*] vt, vi messen ▷ n (unit,
device for measuring) Maß nt; (step)
Maßnahme f; **to take ~s** Maßnahmen
ergreifen; **measurement** n (amount
measured) Maß nt

meat [miːt] n Fleisch nt; **meatball** n
Fleischbällchen nt

mechanic [mɪˈkænɪk] n Mechaniker(in)
m(f); **mechanical** adj mechanisch;
mechanics nsing Mechanik f;
mechanism ['mekənɪzəm] n
Mechanismus m

medal ['medl] n Medaille f; (decoration)
Orden m; **medalist** (US), **medallist**
['medəlɪst] n Medaillengewinner(in) m(f)

media ['miːdɪə] npl Medien pl

median strip ['miːdɪən strɪp] n (US)
Mittelstreifen m

mediate ['miːdɪeɪt] vi vermitteln

medical ['medɪkəl] adj medizinisch;
(treatment etc) ärztlich; **~ student**
Medizinstudent(in) m(f) ▷ n
Untersuchung f; **Medicare** ['medɪkɛə*] n
(US) Krankenkasse f für ältere Leute;
medication [medɪˈkeɪʃən] n
Medikamente pl; **to be on ~** Medikamente
nehmen; **medicinal** [meˈdɪsɪnl] adj Heil-;
~ herbs Heilkräuter pl; **medicine**
['medsɪn] n Arznei f; (science) Medizin f

medieval [medɪˈiːvəl] adj mittelalterlich

mediocre [miːdɪˈəʊkə*] adj mittelmäßig

meditate ['medɪteɪt] vi meditieren; (fig)
nachdenken (on über +akk)

Mediterranean [medɪtəˈreɪnɪən] n (sea)
Mittelmeer nt; (region) Mittelmeerraum m

medium ['miːdɪəm] adj (quality, size)

mittlere(r, s); (steak) halbdurch; **~ (dry)**
(wine) halbtrocken; **~ sized** mittelgroß;
~ wave Mittelwelle f ▷ n (pl **media**)
Medium nt; (means) Mittel nt

meet [miːt] (**met, met**) vt treffen; (by
arrangement) sich treffen mit; (difficulties)
stoßen auf +akk; (get to know) kennen
lernen; (requirement, demand) gerecht
werden +dat; (deadline) einhalten; **pleased
to ~ you** sehr angenehm!; **to ~ sb at the
station** jdn vom Bahnhof abholen ▷ vi
sich treffen; (become acquainted) sich
kennen lernen; **we've met** (before) wir
kennen uns schon; **meet up** vt sich
treffen (with mit); **meet with** vt (group)
zusammenkommen mit; (difficulties,
resistance etc) stoßen auf +akk; **meeting** n
Treffen nt; (business ~) Besprechung f; (of
committee) Sitzung f; (assembly)
Versammlung f; **meeting place, meeting
point** n Treffpunkt m

megabyte ['megabaɪt] n Megabyte nt

melody ['melədɪ] n Melodie f

melon ['melən] n Melone f

melt [melt] vt, vi schmelzen

member ['membə*] n Mitglied nt;
(of tribe, species) Angehörige(r) mf;
Member of Parliament
Parlamentsabgeordnete(r) mf;
membership n Mitgliedschaft f;
membership card n Mitgliedskarte f

memento [məˈmentəʊ] (pl **-es**) n
Andenken nt (of an +akk)

memo ['meməʊ] (pl **-s**) n Mitteilung f,
Memo nt; **memo pad** n Notizblock m

memorable ['memərəbl] adj
unvergesslich; **memorial** [mɪˈmɔːrɪəl] n
Denkmal nt (to für); **memorize**
['meməraɪz] vt sich einprägen,
auswendig lernen; **memory** ['memərɪ] n
Gedächtnis nt; (Inform: of computer)
Speicher m; (sth recalled) Erinnerung f; **in
~ of** zur Erinnerung an +akk

men [men] pl of **man**

menace ['menɪs] n Bedrohung f; (danger)
Gefahr f

mend [mend] vt reparieren; (clothes)
flicken ▷ n **to be on the ~** auf dem Wege
der Besserung sein

meningitis [menɪnˈdʒaɪtɪs] n
Hirnhautentzündung f

menopause ['menəʊpɔːz] n
Wechseljahre pl

mental ['mentl] adj geistig; **~ hospital** psychiatrische Klinik; **mentality** [men'tælɪtɪ] n Mentalität f; **mentally** ['mentəlɪ] adv geistig; **~ handicapped** geistig behindert; **~ ill** geisteskrank

mention ['menʃən] n Erwähnung f ▷ vt erwähnen (to sb jdm gegenüber); **don't ~ it** bitte sehr, gern geschehen

menu ['menju:] n Speisekarte f; (Inform) Menü nt

merchandise ['mɜːtʃəndaɪz] n Handelsware f; **merchant** ['mɜːtʃənt] adj Handels-

merciful ['mɜːsɪfʊl] adj gnädig; **mercifully** adv glücklicherweise

mercury ['mɜːkjʊrɪ] n Quecksilber nt

mercy ['mɜːsɪ] n Gnade f

mere [mɪə*] adj bloß; **merely** ['mɪəlɪ] adv bloß, lediglich

merge [mɜːdʒ] vi verschmelzen; (Auto) sich einfädeln; (Comm) fusionieren; **merger** n (Comm) Fusion f

meringue [məˈræŋ] n Baiser nt

merit ['merɪt] n Verdienst nt; (advantage) Vorzug m

merry ['merɪ] adj fröhlich; (fam: tipsy) angeheitert; **Merry Christmas** Fröhliche Weihnachten!; **merry-go-round** n Karussell nt

mess [mes] n Unordnung f; (muddle) Durcheinander nt; (dirty) Schweinerei f; (trouble) Schwierigkeiten pl; **in a ~** (muddled) durcheinander; (untidy) unordentlich; (fig: person) in der Klemme; **to make a ~ of sth** etw verpfuschen; **to look a ~** unmöglich aussehen; **mess about** vi (tinker with) herummurksen (with an +dat); (play the fool) herumalbern; (do nothing in particular) herumgammeln; **mess up** vt verpfuschen; (make untidy) in Unordnung bringen; (dirty) schmutzig machen

message ['mesɪdʒ] n Mitteilung f, Nachricht f; (meaning) Botschaft f; **can I give him a ~?** kann ich ihm etwas ausrichten?; **please leave a ~** (on answerphones) bitte hinterlassen Sie eine Nachricht; **I get the ~** ich hab's verstanden

messenger ['mesɪndʒə*] n Bote m

messy ['mesɪ] adj (untidy) unordentlich; (situation etc) verfahren

met [met] pt, pp of **meet**

metal ['metl] n Metall nt; **metallic** [mɪ'tælɪk] adj metallisch

meteorology [miːtɪə'rɒlədʒɪ] n Meteorologie f

meter ['miːtə*] n Zähler m; (parking meter) Parkuhr f; (US) see **metre**

method ['meθəd] n Methode f; **methodical** [mɪ'θɒdɪkəl] adj methodisch

meticulous [mɪ'tɪkjʊləs] adj (peinlich) genau

metre ['miːtə*] n Meter m o nt; **metric** ['metrɪk] adj metrisch; **~ system** Dezimalsystem nt

Mexico ['meksɪkəʊ] n Mexiko nt

mice [maɪs] pl of **mouse**

mickey ['mɪkɪ] n **to take the ~ (out of sb)** (fam) (jdn) auf den Arm nehmen

microchip ['maɪkrəʊtʃɪp] n (Inform) Mikrochip m; **microphone** n Mikrofon nt; **microscope** n Mikroskop nt; **microwave (oven)** n Mikrowelle(nherd) f(m)

mid [mɪd] adj **in ~ January** Mitte Januar; **he's in his ~ forties** er ist Mitte vierzig

midday ['mɪddeɪ] n Mittag m; **at ~** mittags

middle ['mɪdl] n Mitte f; (waist) Taille f; **in the ~ of** mitten in +dat; **to be in the ~ of doing sth** gerade dabei sein, etw zu tun ▷ adj mittlere(r, s), Mittel-; **the ~ one** der/die/das Mittlere; **middle-aged** adj mittleren Alters; **Middle Ages** npl **the ~** das Mittelalter; **middle-class** adj mittelständisch; (bourgeois) bürgerlich; **middle classes** npl **the ~** der Mittelstand; **Middle East** n **the ~** der Nahe Osten; **middle name** n zweiter Vorname

Midlands ['mɪdləndz] npl **the ~** Mittelengland nt

midnight ['mɪdnaɪt] n Mitternacht f

midst [mɪdst] n **in the ~ of** mitten in +dat

midsummer ['mɪdsʌmə*] n Hochsommer m; **Midsummer's Day** Sommersonnenwende f

midway [mɪd'weɪ] adv auf halbem Wege; **~ through the film** nach der Hälfte des Films; **midweek** [mɪd'wiːk] adj, adv in der Mitte der Woche

midwife ['mɪdwaɪf] (pl **-wives**) n Hebamme f

midwinter [mɪd'wɪntə*] n tiefster Winter

might [maɪt] pt of **may**; (possibility) könnte; (permission) dürfte; (would) würde;

they ~ still come sie könnten noch
kommen; he ~ have let me know er hätte
mir doch Bescheid sagen können; I
thought she ~ change her mind ich
dachte schon, sie würde sich anders
entscheiden ▷ n Macht f, Kraft f
mighty ['maɪtɪ] adj gewaltig; (powerful)
mächtig
migraine ['miːɡreɪn] n Migräne f
migrant ['maɪɡrənt] n (bird) Zugvogel m;
~ worker Gastarbeiter(in) m(f); migrate
[maɪ'ɡreɪt] vi abwandern; (birds) nach
Süden ziehen
mike [maɪk] n (fam) Mikro nt
Milan [mɪ'læn] n Mailand nt
mild [maɪld] adj mild; (person) sanft;
mildly adv to put it ~ gelinde gesagt;
mildness n Milde f
mile [maɪl] n Meile f (= 1,609 km); for ~s
(and ~s) ≈ kilometerweit; ~s per hour
Meilen pro Stunde; ~s better than
hundertmal besser als; mileage n Meilen
pl, Meilenzahl f; mileometer
[maɪ'lɒmɪtə*] n ≈ Kilometerzähler m;
milestone n (a. fig) Meilenstein m
militant ['mɪlɪtənt] adj militant; military
['mɪlɪtərɪ] adj militär-, militärisch
milk [mɪlk] n Milch f ▷ vt melken; milk
chocolate n Vollmilchschokolade f;
milkman (pl -men) n Milchmann m; milk
shake n Milkshake m, Milchmixgetränk
nt
mill [mɪl] n Mühle f; (factory) Fabrik f
millennium [mɪ'lenɪəm] n Jahrtausend nt
millet ['mɪlɪt] n Hirse f
milligramme ['mɪlɪɡræm] n Milligramm
nt; milliliter (US), millilitre n Milliliter m;
millimeter (US), millimetre n Millimeter
m
million ['mɪljən] n Million f; five ~ fünf
Millionen; ~s of people Millionen von
Menschen; millionaire [mɪljə'nɛə*] n
Millionär(in) m(f)
mime [maɪm] n Pantomime f ▷ vt, vi
mimen; mimic ['mɪmɪk] n Imitator(in)
m(f) ▷ vt, vi nachahmen; mimicry
['mɪmɪkrɪ] n Nachahmung f
mince [mɪns] vt (zer)hacken ▷ n (meat)
Hackfleisch nt; mincemeat n süße
Gebäckfüllung aus Rosinen, Äpfeln, Zucker,
Gewürzen und Talg; mince pie n mit
'mincemeat' gefülltes süßes Weihnachtsgebäck
mind [maɪnd] n (intellect) Verstand m;

(also person) Geist m; out of sight, out of
~ aus den Augen, aus dem Sinn; he is out
of his ~ er ist nicht bei Verstand; to keep
sth in ~ etw im Auge behalten; do you
have sth in ~? denken Sie an etwas
Besonderes?; I've a lot on my ~ mich
beschäftigt so vieles im Moment; to
change one's ~ es sich dat anders
überlegen ▷ vt (look after) aufpassen auf
+akk; (object to) etwas haben gegen;
~ you, ... allerdings ...; I wouldn't ~ ... ich
hätte nichts gegen ...; '~ the step'
„Vorsicht Stufe!" ▷ vi etwas dagegen
haben; do you ~ if I ... macht es Ihnen
etwas aus, wenn ich ...; I don't ~ es ist mir
egal, meinetwegen; never ~ macht nichts
mine [maɪn] pron meine(r, s); this is ~ das
gehört mir; a friend of ~ ein Freund von
mir ▷ n (coalmine) Bergwerk nt; (Mil) Mine
f; miner n Bergarbeiter m
mineral ['mɪnərəl] n Mineral nt; mineral
water n Mineralwasser nt
mingle ['mɪŋɡl] vi sich mischen (with
unter +akk)
miniature ['mɪnɪtʃə*] adj Miniatur-
minibar ['mɪnɪbɑː] n Minibar f; minibus
n Kleinbus m; minicab n Kleintaxi nt
minimal ['mɪnɪml] adj minimal;
minimize ['mɪnɪmaɪz] vt auf ein
Minimum reduzieren; minimum
['mɪnɪməm] n Minimum nt ▷ adj
Mindest-
mining ['maɪnɪŋ] n Bergbau m
miniskirt n Minirock m
minister ['mɪnɪstə*] n (Pol) Minister(in)
m(f); (Rel) Pastor(in) m(f), Pfarrer(in) m(f);
ministry ['mɪnɪstrɪ] n (Pol) Ministerium
nt
minor ['maɪnə*] adj kleiner; (insignificant)
unbedeutend; (operation, offence) harmlos;
~ road Nebenstraße f; (Mus) A ~ a-Moll nt
▷ n (Brit: under 18) Minderjährige(r) mf;
minority [maɪ'nɒrɪtɪ] n Minderheit f
mint [mɪnt] n Minze f; (sweet)
Pfefferminz(bonbon) nt; mint sauce n
Minzsoße f
minus ['maɪnəs] prep minus; (without)
ohne
minute [maɪ'njuːt] adj winzig; in ~ detail
genauestens ▷ ['mɪnɪt] n Minute f; just a
~ Moment mal; any ~ jeden Augenblick;
~s pl (of meeting) Protokoll nt
miracle ['mɪrəkl] n Wunder nt;

miraculous [mɪˈrækjʊləs] *adj* unglaublich

mirage [ˈmɪrɑːʒ] *n* Fata Morgana *f*, Luftspiegelung *f*

mirror [ˈmɪrə*] *n* Spiegel *m*

misbehave [mɪsbɪˈheɪv] *vi* sich schlecht benehmen

miscalculation [ˈmɪskælkjʊˈleɪʃən] *n* Fehlkalkulation *f*; (*misjudgement*) Fehleinschätzung *f*

miscarriage [mɪsˈkærɪdʒ] *n* (*Med*) Fehlgeburt *f*

miscellaneous [mɪsɪˈleɪnɪəs] *adj* verschieden

mischief [ˈmɪstʃɪf] *n* Unfug *m*; **mischievous** [ˈmɪstʃɪvəs] *adj* (*person*) durchtrieben; (*glance*) verschmitzt

misconception [mɪskənˈsepʃən] *n* falsche Vorstellung

misconduct [mɪsˈkɒndʌkt] *n* Vergehen *nt*

miser [ˈmaɪzə*] *n* Geizhals *m*

miserable [ˈmɪzərəbl] *adj* (*person*) todunglücklich; (*conditions, life*) elend; (*pay, weather*) miserabel

miserly [ˈmaɪzəlɪ] *adj* geizig

misery [ˈmɪzərɪ] *n* Elend *nt*; (*suffering*) Qualen *pl*

misfit [ˈmɪsfɪt] *n* Außenseiter(in) *m(f)*

misfortune [mɪsˈfɔːtʃən] *n* Pech *nt*

misguided [mɪsˈgaɪdɪd] *adj* irrig; (*optimism*) unangebracht

misinform [mɪsɪnˈfɔːm] *vt* falsch informieren

misinterpret [mɪsɪnˈtɜːprɪt] *vt* falsch auslegen

misjudge [mɪsˈdʒʌdʒ] *vt* falsch beurteilen

mislay [mɪsˈleɪ] *irr vt* verlegen

mislead [mɪsˈliːd] *irr vt* irreführen; **misleading** *adj* irreführend

misprint [ˈmɪsprɪnt] *n* Druckfehler *m*

mispronounce [mɪsprəˈnaʊns] *vt* falsch aussprechen

miss [mɪs] *vt* (*fail to hit, catch*) verfehlen; (*not notice, hear*) nicht mitbekommen; (*be too late for*) verpassen; (*chance*) versäumen; (*regret the absence of*) vermissen; **I ~ you** du fehlst mir ▷ *vi* nicht treffen; (*shooting*) danebenschießen; (*ball, shot etc*) danebengehen; **miss out** *vt* auslassen ▷ *vi* **to ~ on sth** etw verpassen

Miss [mɪs] *n* (*unmarried woman*) Fräulein *nt*

missile [ˈmɪsaɪl] *n* Geschoss *nt*; (*rocket*) Rakete *f*

missing [ˈmɪsɪŋ] *adj* (*person*) vermisst; (*thing*) fehlend; **to be/go ~** vermisst werden, fehlen

mission [ˈmɪʃən] *n* (*Pol, Mil, Rel*) Auftrag *m*, Mission *f*; **missionary** [ˈmɪʃənrɪ] *n* Missionar(in) *m(f)*

mist [mɪst] *n* (*feiner*) Nebel *m*; (*haze*) Dunst *m*; **mist over, mist up** *vi* sich beschlagen

mistake [mɪsˈteɪk] *n* Fehler *m*; **by ~** aus Versehen ▷ *irr vt* (**mistook, mistaken**) (*misunderstand*) falsch verstehen; (*mix up*) verwechseln (*for* mit); **there's no mistaking ...** ... ist unverkennbar; (*meaning*) ... ist unmissverständlich; **mistaken** *adj* (*idea, identity*) falsch; **to be ~** sich irren, falsch liegen

mistletoe [ˈmɪsltəʊ] *n* Mistel *f*

mistreat [mɪsˈtriːt] *vt* schlecht behandeln

mistress [ˈmɪstrɪs] *n* (*lover*) Geliebte *f*

mistrust [mɪsˈtrʌst] *n* Misstrauen *nt* (*of* gegen) ▷ *vt* misstrauen +*dat*

misty [ˈmɪstɪ] *adj* neblig; (*hazy*) dunstig

misunderstand [mɪsʌndəˈstænd] *irr vt, vi* falsch verstehen; **misunderstanding** *n* Missverständnis *nt*; (*disagreement*) Differenz *f*

mitten [ˈmɪtn] *n* Fausthandschuh *m*

mix [mɪks] *n* (*mixture*) Mischung *f* ▷ *vt* mischen; (*blend*) vermischen (*with* mit); (*drinks, music*) mixen; **to ~ business with pleasure** das Angenehme mit dem Nützlichen verbinden ▷ *vi* (*liquids*) sich vermischen lassen; **mix up** *vt* (*mix*) zusammenmischen; (*confuse*) verwechseln (*with* mit); **mixed** *adj* gemischt; **a ~ bunch** eine bunt gemischte Truppe; **~ grill** Mixedgrill *m*; **~ vegetables** Mischgemüse *nt*; **mixer** *n* (*for food*) Mixer *m*; **mixture** [ˈmɪkstʃə*] *n* Mischung *f*; (*Med*) Saft *m*; **mix-up** *n* Durcheinander *nt*

ml *abbr* = **millilitre** ml

mm *abbr* = **millimetre** mm

moan [məʊn] *n* Stöhnen *nt*; (*complaint*) Gejammer *nt* ▷ *vi* stöhnen; (*complain*) jammern, meckern (*about* über +*akk*)

mobile [ˈməʊbaɪl] *adj* beweglich; (*on wheels*) fahrbar ▷ *n* (*phone*) Handy *nt*; **mobile phone** *n* Mobiltelefon *nt*, Handy *nt*

mobility [məʊˈbɪlɪtɪ] n Beweglichkeit f
mock [mɒk] vt verspotten ▷ adj Schein-;
  mockery n Spott m
mod cons [ˈmɒdˈkɒnz] abbr = **modern
  conveniences** (moderner) Komfort
mode [məʊd] n Art f; (Inform) Modus m
model [ˈmɒdl] n Modell nt; (example)
  Vorbild nt; (fashion ~) Model nt ▷ adj
  (miniature) Modell-; (perfect) Muster- ▷ vt
  (make) formen ▷ vi **she ~s for Versace** sie
  arbeitet als Model bei Versace
modem [ˈməʊdem] n Modem nt
moderate [ˈmɒdərət] adj mäßig; (views,
  politics) gemäßigt; (income, success)
  mittelmäßig ▷ n (Pol) Gemäßigte(r) mf
  ▷ [ˈmɒdəreɪt] vt mäßigen; **moderation**
  [mɒdəˈreɪʃən] n Mäßigung f; **in ~** mit
  Maßen
modern [ˈmɒdən] adj modern; **~ history**
  neuere Geschichte; **~ Greek**
  Neugriechisch nt; **modernize** [ˈmɒdənaɪz]
  vt modernisieren
modest [ˈmɒdɪst] adj bescheiden;
  modesty n Bescheidenheit f
modification [mɒdɪfɪˈkeɪʃən] n
  Abänderung f; **modify** [ˈmɒdɪfaɪ] vt
  abändern
moist [mɔɪst] adj feucht; **moisten**
  [ˈmɔɪsn] vt befeuchten; **moisture**
  [ˈmɔɪstʃə*] n Feuchtigkeit f; **moisturizer**
  n Feuchtigkeitscreme f
molar [ˈməʊlə*] n Backenzahn m
mold [ˈmɒld] (US) see **mould**
mole [məʊl] n (spot) Leberfleck m; (animal)
  Maulwurf m
molecule [ˈmɒlɪkjuːl] n Molekül nt
molest [məʊˈlest] vt belästigen
molt (US) see **moult**
molten [ˈməʊltən] adj geschmolzen
mom [mɒm] n (US) Mutti f
moment [ˈməʊmənt] n Moment m,
  Augenblick m; **just a ~** Moment mall; **at** (o
  for) **the ~** im Augenblick; **in a ~** gleich
momentous [məʊˈmentəs] adj
  bedeutsam
Monaco [ˈmɒnəkəʊ] n Monaco nt
monarchy [ˈmɒnəkɪ] n Monarchie f
monastery [ˈmɒnəstrɪ] n (for monks)
  Kloster nt
Monday [ˈmʌndeɪ] n Montag m; see also
  Tuesday
monetary [ˈmʌnɪtərɪ] adj (reform, policy,
  union) Währungs-; **~ unit** Geldeinheit f

money [ˈmʌnɪ] n Geld nt; **to get one's ~'s
  worth** auf seine Kosten kommen; **money
  order** n Postanweisung f
mongrel [ˈmʌŋgrəl] n
  Promenadenmischung f
monitor [ˈmɒnɪtə*] n (screen) Monitor m
  ▷ vt (progress etc) überwachen;
  (broadcasts) abhören
monk [mʌŋk] n Mönch m
monkey [ˈmʌŋkɪ] n Affe m; **~ business**
  Unfug m
monopolize [məˈnɒpəlaɪz] vt
  monopolisieren; (fig: person, thing) in
  Beschlag nehmen; **monopoly** [məˈnɒpəlɪ]
  n Monopol nt
monotonous [məˈnɒtənəs] adj eintönig,
  monoton
monsoon [mɒnˈsuːn] n Monsun m
monster [ˈmɒnstə*] n (animal, thing)
  Monstrum nt ▷ adj Riesen-; **monstrosity**
  [mɒnˈstrɒsɪtɪ] n Monstrosität f; (thing)
  Ungetüm nt
month [mʌnθ] n Monat m; **monthly** adj
  monatlich; (ticket, salary) Monats- ▷ adv
  monatlich ▷ n (magazine)
  Monats(zeit)schrift f
monty [ˈmɒntɪ] n **to go the full ~** (fam:
  strip) alle Hüllen fallen lassen; (go the whole
  hog) aufs Ganze gehen
monument [ˈmɒnjʊmənt] n Denkmal nt
  (to für); **monumental** [mɒnjʊˈmentl] adj
  (huge) gewaltig
mood [muːd] n (of person) Laune f; (a.
  general) Stimmung f; **to be in a good/bad
  ~** gute/schlechte Laune haben,
  gut/schlecht drauf sein; **to be in the ~ for
  sth** zu etw aufgelegt sein; **I'm not in the
  ~** ich fühle mich nicht danach; **moody** adj
  launisch
moon [muːn] n Mond m; **to be over the
  ~** (fam) überglücklich sein; **moonlight** n
  Mondlicht nt ▷ vi schwarzarbeiten;
  moonlit adj (night, landscape) mondhell
moor [mɔː*] n Moor nt ▷ vt, vi
  festmachen; **moorings** npl Liegeplatz m;
  moorland n Moorland nt, Heideland nt
moose [muːs] (pl -) n Elch m
mop [mɒp] n Mopp m; **mop up** vt
  aufwischen
mope [məʊp] vi Trübsal blasen
moped [ˈməʊped] n (Brit) Moped nt
moral [ˈmɒrəl] adj moralisch; (values)
  sittlich ▷ n Moral f; **~s** pl Moral f; **morale**

[mɔ'ra:l] n Stimmung f, Moral f; **morality** [mə'ræliti] n Moral f, Ethik f
morbid ['mɔ:bid] adj krankhaft

○ KEYWORD

more [mɔ:*] adj (greater in number etc) mehr; (additional) noch mehr; **do you want (some) more tea?** möchten Sie noch etwas Tee?; **I have no** or **I don't have any more money** ich habe kein Geld mehr ▷ pron (greater amount) mehr; (further or additional amount) noch mehr; **is there any more?** gibt es noch mehr?; (left over) ist noch etwas da?; **there's no more** es ist nichts mehr da ▷ adv mehr; **more dangerous/easily** etc **(than)** gefährlicher/einfacher etc (als); **more and more** immer mehr; **more and more excited** immer aufgeregter; **more or less** mehr oder weniger; **more than ever** mehr denn je; **more beautiful than ever** schöner denn je

morgue [mɔ:g] n Leichenschauhaus nt
morning ['mɔ:niŋ] n Morgen m; **in the ~** am Morgen, morgens; (tomorrow) morgen früh; **this ~** heute morgen ▷ adj Morgen-; (early) Früh-; (walk etc) morgendlich; **morning after pill** n die Pille danach; **morning sickness** n Schwangerschaftsübelkeit f
Morocco [mə'rɒkəʊ] n Marokko nt
moron ['mɔ:rɒn] n Idiot(in) m(f)
morphine ['mɔ:fi:n] n Morphium nt
morsel ['mɔ:sl] n Bissen m
mortal ['mɔ:tl] adj sterblich; (wound) tödlich ▷ n Sterbliche(r) mf; **mortality** [mɔ:'tæliti] n (death rate) Sterblichkeitsziffer f; **mortally** adv tödlich
mortgage ['mɔ:gidʒ] n Hypothek f ▷ vt mit einer Hypothek belasten
mortified ['mɔ:tifaid] adj **I was ~** es war mir schrecklich peinlich
mortuary ['mɔ:tjʊəri] n Leichenhalle f
mosaic [məʊ'zeiik] n Mosaik nt
Moscow ['mɒskəʊ] n Moskau nt
Moslem ['mɒzlem] adj, n see **Muslim**
mosque [mɒsk] n Moschee f
mosquito [mɒs'ki:təʊ] n (pl **-es**) n (Stech)mücke f; (tropical) Moskito m; **~ net** Moskitonetz nt

moss [mɒs] n Moos nt
most [məʊst] adj meiste pl, die meisten; **in ~ cases** in den meisten Fällen ▷ adv (with verbs) am meisten; (with adj) ...ste; (with adv) ...sten; (very) äußerst, höchst; **he ate (the) ~** er hat am meisten gegessen; **the ~ beautiful/interesting** der/die/das schönste/interessanteste; **~ interesting** hochinteressant! ▷ n das meiste, der größte Teil; (people) die meisten; **~ of the money/players** das meiste Geld/die meisten Spieler; **for the ~ part** zum größten Teil; **five at the ~** höchstens fünf; **to make the ~ of sth** etw voll ausnützen; **mostly** adv (most of the time) meistens; (mainly) hauptsächlich; (for the most part) größtenteils
MOT abbr = Ministry of Transport; **~ (test)** ≈ TÜV m
motel [məʊ'tel] n Motel nt
moth [mɒθ] n Nachtfalter m; (wool-eating) Motte f; **mothball** n Mottenkugel f
mother ['mʌðə*] n Mutter f ▷ vt bemuttern; **mother-in-law** (pl **mothers-in-law**) n Schwiegermutter f; **mother-to-be** (pl **mothers-to-be**) n werdende Mutter
motif [məʊ'ti:f] n Motiv nt
motion ['məʊʃən] n Bewegung f; (in meeting) Antrag m; **motionless** adj bewegungslos
motivate ['məʊtiveit] vt motivieren; **motive** ['məʊtiv] n Motiv nt
motor ['məʊtə*] n Motor m; (fam: car) Auto nt ▷ adj Motor-; **Motorail train®** n (Brit) Autoreisezug m; **motorbike** n Motorrad nt; **motorboat** n Motorboot nt; **motorcycle** n Motorrad nt; **motor industry** n Automobilindustrie f; **motoring** ['məʊtəriŋ] n Autofahren nt; **~ organization** Automobilklub m; **motorist** ['məʊtərist] n Autofahrer(in) m(f); **motor oil** n Motorenöl nt; **motor racing** n Autorennsport m; **motor scooter** n Motorroller m; **motor show** n Automobilausstellung f; **motor vehicle** n Kraftfahrzeug nt; **motorway** n (Brit) Autobahn f
motto ['mɒtəʊ] (pl **-es**) n Motto nt
mould [məʊld] n Form f; (mildew) Schimmel m ▷ vt (a. fig) formen; **mouldy** ['məʊldi] adj schimmelig
moult [məʊlt] vi sich mausern, haaren

mount [maʊnt] vt (horse) steigen auf +akk; (exhibition etc) organisieren; (painting) mit einem Passepartout versehen ▷ vi **to ~ (up)** (an)steigen ▷ n Passepartout nt

mountain [ˈmaʊntɪn] n Berg m; **mountain bike** n Mountainbike nt; **mountaineer** [maʊntɪˈnɪə*] n Bergsteiger(in) m(f); **mountaineering** [maʊntɪˈnɪərɪŋ] n Bergsteigen nt; **mountainous** adj bergig; **mountainside** n Berghang m

mourn [mɔ:n] vt betrauern ▷ vi trauern (for um); **mourner** n Trauernde(r) mf; **mournful** adj trauervoll; **mourning** n Trauer f; **to be in ~** trauern (for um)

mouse [maʊs] (pl **mice**) n (a. Inform) Maus f; **mouse mat**, **mouse pad** (US) n Mauspad nt; **mouse trap** n Mausefalle f

mousse [mu:s] n (Gastr) Creme f; (styling ~) Schaumfestiger m

moustache [məˈstæʃ] n Schnurrbart m

mouth [maʊθ] n Mund m; (of animal) Maul nt; (of cave) Eingang m; (of bottle etc) Öffnung f; (of river) Mündung f; **to keep one's ~ shut** (fam) den Mund halten; **mouthful** n (of drink) Schluck m; (of food) Bissen m; **mouth organ** n Mundharmonika f; **mouthwash** n Mundwasser nt; **mouthwatering** adj appetitlich, lecker

move [mu:v] n (movement) Bewegung f; (in game) Zug m; (step) Schritt m; (moving house) Umzug m; **to make a ~** (in game) ziehen; (leave) sich auf den Weg machen; **to get a ~ on (with sth)** sich (mit etw) beeilen ▷ vt bewegen; (object) rücken; (car) wegfahren; (transport: goods) befördern; (people) transportieren; (in job) versetzen; (emotionally) bewegen, rühren; **I can't ~ it** (stuck, too heavy) ich bringe es nicht von der Stelle; **to ~ house** umziehen ▷ vi sich bewegen; (change place) gehen; (vehicle, ship) fahren; (move house, town etc) umziehen; (in game) ziehen; **move about** vi sich bewegen; (travel) unterwegs sein; **move away** vi weggehen; (move town) wegziehen; **move in** vi (to house) einziehen; **move off** vi losfahren; **move on** vi weitergehen; (vehicle) weiterfahren; **move out** vi ausziehen; **move up** vi (in queue etc) aufrücken; **movement** n Bewegung f

movie [ˈmu:vɪ] n Film m; **the ~s** (the cinema) das Kino

moving [ˈmu:vɪŋ] adj (emotionally) ergreifend, berührend

mow [məʊ] (**mowed**, **mown** o **mowed**) vt mähen; **mower** n (lawn~) Rasenmäher m

mown [məʊn] pp of **mow**

Mozambique [məʊzæmˈbi:k] n Mosambik nt

MP abbr = **Member of Parliament** Parlamentsabgeordnete(r) mf

mph abbr = **miles per hour** Meilen pro Stunde

MPV abbr = **multi-purpose vehicle** Mehrzweckfahrzeug nt

MP3 n MP3 nt

Mr [ˈmɪstə*] n (form of address) Herr

Mrs [ˈmɪsɪz] n (form of address) Frau

Ms [məz] n (form of address for any woman, married or unmarried) Frau

MS n abbr = **multiple sclerosis** MS f

Mt abbr = **Mount** Berg m

much [mʌtʃ] (**more**, **most**) adj viel; **we haven't got ~ time** wir haben nicht viel Zeit; **how ~ money?** wie viel Geld? ▷ adv viel; (with verb) sehr; **~ better** viel besser; **I like it very ~** es gefällt mir sehr gut; **I don't like it ~** ich mag es nicht besonders; **thank you very ~** danke sehr; **I thought as ~** das habe ich mir gedacht; **~ as I like him** so sehr ich ihn mag; **we don't see them ~** wir sehen sie nicht sehr oft; **~ the same** fast gleich ▷ n viel; **as ~ as you want** so viel du willst; **he's not ~ of a cook** er ist kein großer Koch

muck [mʌk] n (fam) Dreck m; **muck about** vi (fam) herumalbern; **muck up** vt (fam) dreckig machen; (spoil) vermasseln; **mucky** adj dreckig

mucus [ˈmju:kəs] n Schleim m

mud [mʌd] n Schlamm m

muddle [ˈmʌdl] n Durcheinander nt; **to be in a ~** ganz durcheinander sein ▷ vt **to ~ (up)** durcheinander bringen; **muddled** adj konfus

muddy [ˈmʌdɪ] adj schlammig; (shoes) schmutzig; **mudguard** [ˈmʌdgɑ:d] n Schutzblech nt

muesli [ˈmu:zlɪ] n Müsli nt

muffin [ˈmʌfɪn] n Muffin m; (Brit) weiches, flaches Milchbrötchen aus Hefeteig, das meist getoastet und mit Butter gegessen wird

muffle ['mʌfl] vt (sound) dämpfen; **muffler** n (US) Schalldämpfer m

mug [mʌg] n (cup) Becher m; (fam: fool) Trottel m ▷ vt (attack and rob) überfallen; **mugging** n Raubüberfall m

muggy ['mʌgɪ] adj (weather) schwül

mule [mjuːl] n Maulesel m

mull over [mʌl 'əʊvə*] vt nachdenken über +akk

mulled [mʌld] adj ~ **wine** Glühwein m

multicolored (US), **multicoloured** ['mʌltɪˈkʌləd] adj bunt; **multicultural** adj multikulturell; **multi-grade** adj ~ **oil** Mehrbereichsöl nt; **multilingual** adj mehrsprachig; **multinational** n (company) Multi m

multiple ['mʌltɪpl] n Vielfache(s) nt ▷ adj mehrfach; (several) mehrere; **multiple-choice (method)** n Multiple-Choice-Verfahren nt; **multiple sclerosis** ['mʌltɪplskleˈrəʊsɪs] n Multiple Sklerose f

multiplex ['mʌltɪpleks] adj, n ~ **(cinema)** Multiplexkino nt

multiplication [mʌltɪplɪˈkeɪʃən] n Multiplikation f; **multiply** ['mʌltɪplaɪ] vt multiplizieren (by mit) ▷ vi sich vermehren

multi-purpose ['mʌltɪˈpɜːpəs] adj Mehrzweck-; **multistorey (car park)** n Parkhaus nt; **multitasking** n (Inform) Multitasking nt

mum [mʌm] n (fam: mother) Mutti f, Mami f

mumble ['mʌmbl] vt, vi murmeln

mummy ['mʌmɪ] n (dead body) Mumie f; (fam: mother) Mutti f, Mami f

mumps [mʌmps] nsing Mumps m

munch [mʌntʃ] vt, vi mampfen

Munich ['mjuːnɪk] n München nt

municipal [mjuːˈnɪsɪpəl] adj städtisch

mural ['mjʊərəl] n Wandgemälde nt

murder ['mɜːdə*] n Mord m; **the traffic was** ~ der Verkehr war die Hölle ▷ vt ermorden; **murderer** n Mörder(in) m(f)

murky ['mɜːkɪ] adj düster; (water) trüb

murmur ['mɜːmə*] vt, vi murmeln

muscle ['mʌsl] n Muskel m; **muscular** ['mʌskjʊlə*] adj (strong) muskulös; (cramp, pain etc) Muskel-

museum [mjuːˈzɪəm] n Museum nt

mushroom ['mʌʃruːm] n (essbarer) Pilz; (button ~) Champignon m ▷ vi (fig) emporschießen

mushy ['mʌʃɪ] adj breiig; ~ **peas** Erbsenmus nt

music ['mjuːzɪk] n Musik f; (printed) Noten pl; **musical** adj (sound) melodisch; (person) musikalisch; ~ **instrument** Musikinstrument nt ▷ n (show) Musical nt; **musically** adv musikalisch; **musician** [mjuːˈzɪʃən] n Musiker(in) m(f)

Muslim ['mʊzlɪm] adj moslemisch ▷ n Moslem m, Muslime f

mussel ['mʌsl] n Miesmuschel f

must [mʌst] (had to, had to) vb aux (need to) müssen; (in negation) dürfen; **I ~n't forget that** ich darf das nicht vergessen; (certainty) **he ~ be there by now** er ist inzwischen bestimmt schon da; (assumption) **I ~ have lost it** ich habe es wohl verloren; ~ **you?** muss das sein? ▷ n Muss nt

mustache ['mʌstæʃ] n (US) Schnurrbart m

mustard ['mʌstəd] n Senf m; **to cut the ~** es bringen

mustn't ['mʌsnt] contr of **must not**

mute [mjuːt] adj stumm

mutter ['mʌtə*] vt, vi murmeln

mutton ['mʌtn] n Hammelfleisch nt

mutual ['mjuːtjʊəl] adj gegenseitig; **by ~ consent** in gegenseitigem Einvernehmen

my [maɪ] adj mein; **I've hurt ~ leg** ich habe mir das Bein verletzt

Myanmar ['maɪænmaː] n Myanmar nt

myself [maɪˈself] pron (reflexive) mich akk, mir dat; **I've hurt ~** ich habe mich verletzt; **I've bought ~ a flat** ich habe mir eine Wohnung gekauft; **I need it for ~** ich brauche es für mich (selbst); (emphatic) **I did it ~** ich habe es selbst gemacht; **(all) by ~** allein

mysterious [mɪsˈtɪərɪəs] adj geheimnisvoll, mysteriös; (inexplicable) rätselhaft; **mystery** ['mɪstərɪ] n Geheimnis nt; (puzzle) Rätsel nt; **it's a ~ to me** es ist mir schleierhaft; **mystify** ['mɪstɪfaɪ] vt verblüffen

myth [mɪθ] n Mythos m; (fig: untrue story) Märchen nt; **mythical** adj mythisch; (fig: untrue) erfunden; **mythology** [mɪˈθɒlədʒɪ] n Mythologie f

n

N *abbr* = **north** N

nag [næg] *vt, vi* herumnörgeln (*sb* an jdm); **nagging** *n* Nörgelei *f*

nail [neɪl] *n* Nagel *m* ▷ *vt* nageln (*to* an); **nail down** *vt* festnageln; **nailbrush** *n* Nagelbürste *f*; **nail clippers** *npl* Nagelknipser *m*; **nailfile** *n* Nagelfeile *f*; **nail polish** *n* Nagellack *m*; **nail polish remover** *n* Nagellackentferner *m*; **nail scissors** *npl* Nagelschere *f*; **nail varnish** *n* Nagellack *m*

naive [naɪˈiːv] *adj* naiv

naked [ˈneɪkɪd] *adj* nackt

name [neɪm] *n* Name *m*; **his ~ is ...** er heißt ...; **what's your ~?** wie heißen Sie?; (*reputation*) **to have a good/bad ~** einen guten/schlechten Ruf haben ▷ *vt* nennen (*after* nach); (*sth new*) benennen; (*nominate*) ernennen (*as* als/zu); **a boy ~d ...** ein Junge namens ...; **namely** *adv* nämlich; **name plate** *n* Namensschild *nt*

nan bread [ˈnɑːnˈbred] *n* (*warm serviertes*) indisches Fladenbrot

nanny [ˈnænɪ] *n* Kindermädchen *nt*

nap [næp] *n* **to have a ~** ein Nickerchen machen

napkin [ˈnæpkɪn] *n* (*at table*) Serviette *f*

Naples [ˈneɪplz] *n* Neapel *nt*

nappy [ˈnæpɪ] *n* (*Brit*) Windel *f*

narcotic [nɑːˈkɒtɪk] *n* Rauschgift *nt*

narrate [nəˈreɪt] *vt* erzählen; **narration** [nəˈreɪʃən], **narrative** [ˈnærətɪv] *n* Erzählung *f*; **narrator** [nəˈreɪtə*] *n* Erzähler(in) *m(f)*

narrow [ˈnærəʊ] *adj* eng, schmal; (*victory, majority*) knapp; **to have a ~ escape** mit knapper Not davonkommen ▷ *vi* sich verengen; **narrow down** *vt* einschränken (*to sth* auf etw *akk*); **narrow-minded** *adj* engstirnig

nasty [ˈnɑːstɪ] *adj* ekelhaft; (*person*) fies; (*remark*) gehässig; (*accident, wound etc*) schlimm

nation [ˈneɪʃən] *n* Nation *f*; **national** [ˈnæʃənl] *adj* national; **~ anthem** Nationalhymne *f*; **National Health Service** (*Brit*) staatlicher Gesundheitsdienst; **~ insurance** (*Brit*) Sozialversicherung *f*; **~ park** Nationalpark *m*; **~ service** Wehrdienst *m*; **~ socialism** (*Hist*) Nationalsozialismus *m* ▷ *n* Staatsbürger(in) *m(f)*

nationality [næʃˈnælɪtɪ] *n* Staatsangehörigkeit *f*, Nationalität *f*; **nationalize** [ˈnæʃnəlaɪz] *vt* verstaatlichen; **nationwide** *adj, adv* landesweit

National Trust

Der **National Trust** ist ein 1895 gegründeter Natur- und Denkmalschutzverband in Großbritannien, der Gebäude und Gelände von besonderem historischem oder ästhetischem Interesse erhält und der Öffentlichkeit zugänglich macht.

native [ˈneɪtɪv] *adj* einheimisch; (*inborn*) angeboren, natürlich; **Native American** Indianer(in) *m(f)*; **~ country** Heimatland *nt*; **a ~ German** ein gebürtiger Deutscher, eine gebürtige Deutsche; **~ language** Muttersprache *f*; **~ speaker** Muttersprachler(in) *m(f)* ▷ *n* Einheimische(r) *mf*; (*in colonial context*) Eingeborene(r) *mf*

nativity play [nəˈtɪvətɪpleɪ] *n* Krippenspiel *nt*

NATO ['neɪtəʊ] *acr* = **North Atlantic Treaty Organization** Nato *f*

natural ['nætʃrəl] *adj* natürlich; *(law, science, forces etc)* Natur-; *(inborn)* angeboren; **~ gas** Erdgas *nt*; **~ resources** Bodenschätze *pl*; **naturally** *adv* natürlich; *(by nature)* von Natur aus; **it comes ~ to her** es fällt ihr leicht

nature ['neɪtʃə*] *n* Natur *f*; *(type)* Art *f*; **it is not in my ~** es entspricht nicht meiner Art; **by ~** von Natur aus; **nature reserve** *n* Naturschutzgebiet *nt*

naughty ['nɔːtɪ] *adj* *(child)* ungezogen; *(cheeky)* frech

nausea ['nɔːsɪə] *n* Übelkeit *f*

nautical ['nɔːtɪkəl] *adj* nautisch; **~ mile** Seemeile *f*

nave [neɪv] *n* Hauptschiff *nt*

navel ['neɪvəl] *n* Nabel *m*

navigate ['nævɪgeɪt] *vi* navigieren; *(in car)* lotsen, dirigieren; **navigation** [nævɪ'geɪʃən] *n* Navigation *f*; *(in car)* Lotsen *nt*

navy ['neɪvɪ] *n* Marine *f*; **~ blue** Marineblau *nt*

Nazi ['nɑːtsɪ] *n* Nazi *m*

NB *abbr* = **nota bene** NB

NE *abbr* = **northeast** NO

near [nɪə*] *adj* nahe; **my ~est relations** meine nächsten Verwandten; **in the ~ future** in nächster Zukunft; **that was a ~ miss** *(o thing)* das war knapp; *(with price)* **... or ~est offer** Verhandlungsbasis ... ▷ *adv* in der Nähe; **so ~** so nahe; **come ~er** näher kommen; *(event)* näher rücken ▷ *prep* **~ (to)** *(space)* nahe an +*dat*; *(vicinity)* in der Nähe +*gen*; **~ the sea** nahe am Meer; **~ the station** in der Nähe des Bahnhofs, in Bahnhofsnähe; **nearby** *adj* nahe gelegen ▷ *adv* in der Nähe; **nearly** *adv* fast; **nearside** *n* *(Auto)* Beifahrerseite *f*; **near-sighted** *adj* kurzsichtig

neat ['niːt] *adj* ordentlich; *(work, writing)* sauber; *(undiluted)* pur

necessarily [nesə'serɪlɪ] *adv* notwendigerweise; **not ~** nicht unbedingt; **necessary** ['nesəsərɪ] *adj* notwendig, nötig; **it's ~ to ...** man muss ...; **it's not ~ for him to come** er braucht nicht mitzukommen; **necessity** [nɪ'sesɪtɪ] *n* Notwendigkeit *f*; **the bare necessities** das absolut Notwendigste; **there is no**

~ to ... man braucht nicht (zu) ..., man muss nicht ...

neck [nek] *n* Hals *m*; *(size)* Halsweite *f*; **back of the ~** Nacken *m*; **necklace** ['neklɪs] *n* Halskette *f*; **necktie** *n* *(US)* Krawatte *f*

nectarine ['nektərɪn] *n* Nektarine *f*

née [neɪ] *adj* geboren

need [niːd] *n* *(requirement)* Bedürfnis *nt* *(for* für*)*; *(necessity)* Notwendigkeit *f*; *(poverty)* Not *f*; **to be in ~ of sth** etw brauchen; **if ~(s) be** wenn nötig; **there is no ~ to ...** man braucht nicht (zu) ..., man muss nicht ... ▷ *vt* brauchen; **I ~ to speak to you** ich muss mit dir reden; **you ~n't go** du brauchst nicht (zu) gehen, du musst nicht gehen

needle ['niːdl] *n* Nadel *f*

needless, needlessly ['niːdlɪs, -lɪ] *adj, adv* unnötig; **~ to say** selbstverständlich

needy ['niːdɪ] *adj* bedürftig

negative ['negətɪv] *n* *(Ling)* Verneinung *f*; *(Foto)* Negativ *nt* ▷ *adj* negativ; *(answer)* verneinend

neglect [nɪ'glekt] *n* Vernachlässigung *f* ▷ *vt* vernachlässigen; **to ~ to do sth** es versäumen, etw zu tun; **negligence** ['neglɪdʒəns] *n* Nachlässigkeit *f*; **negligent** *adj* nachlässig

negligible ['neglɪdʒəbl] *adj* unbedeutend; *(amount)* geringfügig

negotiate [nɪ'gəʊʃɪeɪt] *vi* verhandeln; **negotiation** [nɪgəʊʃɪ'eɪʃən] *n* Verhandlung *f*

neigh [neɪ] *vi* *(horse)* wiehern

neighbor *(US)*, **neighbour** ['neɪbə*] *n* Nachbar(in) *m(f)*; **neighbo(u)rhood** *n* Nachbarschaft *f*; **neighbo(u)ring** *adj* benachbart

neither ['naɪðə*] *adj, pron* keine(r, s) von beiden; **~ of you/us** keiner von euch/uns beiden ▷ *adv* **~ ... nor ...** weder ... noch ... ▷ *conj* **I'm not going - ~ am I** ich gehe nicht - ich auch nicht

neon ['niːɒn] *n* Neon *nt*; **~ sign** *(advertisement)* Leuchtreklame *f*

nephew ['nefjuː] *n* Neffe *m*

nerd [nɜːv] *n* *(fam)* Schwachkopf *m*; **he's a real computer ~** er ist ein totaler Computerfreak

nerve [nɜːv] *n* Nerv *m*; **he gets on my ~s** er geht mir auf die Nerven; *(courage)* **to keep/lose one's ~** die Nerven behalten/verlieren; (cheek) **to have the ~ to do sth** die Frechheit besitzen, etw zu tun; **nerve-racking** adj nervenaufreibend; **nervous** ['nɜːvəs] adj (apprehensive) ängstlich; (on edge) nervös; **nervous breakdown** n Nervenzusammenbruch m

nest [nest] n Nest nt ▷ vi nisten

net [net] n Netz nt; **the Net** (Internet) das Internet; **on the ~** im Netz ▷ adj (price, weight) Netto-; **~ profit** Reingewinn m; **netball** n Netzball m

Netherlands ['neðələndz] npl **the ~** die Niederlande pl

nettle ['netl] n Nessel f

network ['netwɜːk] n Netz nt; (Tv, Radio) Sendenetz nt; (Inform) Netzwerk nt

neurosis [njʊəˈrəʊsɪs] n Neurose f; **neurotic** [njʊəˈrɒtɪk] adj neurotisch

neuter ['njuːtə*] adj (Bio) geschlechtslos; (Ling) sächlich

neutral ['njuːtrəl] adj neutral ▷ n (gear in car) Leerlauf m

never ['nevə*] adv nie(mals); **~ before** noch nie; **~ mind** macht nichts!; **never-ending** adj endlos; **nevertheless** [nevəðəˈles] adv trotzdem

new [njuː] adj neu; **this is all ~ to me** das ist für mich noch ungewohnt; **newcomer** n Neuankömmling m; (in job, subject) Neuling m

New England [njuːˈɪŋglənd] n Neuengland nt

Newfoundland ['njuːfəndlənd] n Neufundland nt

newly ['njuːlɪ] adv neu; **~ made** (cake) frisch gebacken; **newly-weds** npl Frischvermählte pl; **new moon** n Neumond m

news [njuːz] nsing (item of ~) Nachricht f; (Radio, Tv) Nachrichten pl; **good ~** ein erfreuliche Nachricht; **what's the ~?** was gibt's Neues?; **have you heard the ~?** hast du das Neueste gehört?; **that's ~ to me** das ist mir neu; **newsagent, news dealer** (US) n Zeitungshändler(in) m(f); **news bulletin** n Nachrichtensendung f; **news flash** n Kurzmeldung f; **newsgroup** n (Inform) Diskussionsforum nt, Newsgroup f; **newsletter** n Mitteilungsblatt nt; **newspaper** n Zeitung f

New Year ['njuːˈjɪə*] n das neue Jahr; **Happy ~** (ein) frohes Neues Jahr!; (toast)

Prosit Neujahr!; **~'s Day** Neujahr nt, Neujahrstag m; **~'s Eve** Silvesterabend m; **~'s resolution** guter Vorsatz fürs neue Jahr

New York [njuːˈjɔːk] n New York nt

New Zealand [njuːˈziːlənd] n Neuseeland nt ▷ adj neuseeländisch; **New Zealander** n Neuseeländer(in) m(f)

next [nekst] adj nächste(r, s); **the week after ~** übernächste Woche; **~ time I see him** wenn ich ihn das nächste Mal sehe; **you're ~** du bist jetzt dran ▷ adv als Nächstes; (then) dann, darauf; **~ to** neben +dat; **~ to last** vorletzte(r, s); **~ to impossible** nahezu unmöglich; **the ~ best thing** das Nächstbeste; **~ door** nebenan

NHS abbr = **National Health Service**

Niagara Falls [naɪˈægrəˈfɔːlz] npl Niagarafälle pl

nibble ['nɪbl] vt knabbern an +dat; **nibbles** npl Knabberzeug nt

Nicaragua [nɪkəˈrægjʊə] n Nicaragua nt

nice [naɪs] adj nett, sympathisch; (taste, food, drink) gut; (weather) schön; **~ and ...** schön ...; **be ~ to him** sei nett zu ihm; **have a ~ day** (US) schönen Tag noch!; **nicely** adv nett; (well) gut; **that'll do ~** das genügt vollauf

nick [nɪk] vt (fam: steal) klauen; (capture) schnappen

nickel ['nɪkl] n (Chem) Nickel nt; (US: coin) Nickel m

nickname ['nɪkneɪm] n Spitzname m

nicotine ['nɪkətiːn] n Nikotin nt; **nicotine patch** n Nikotinpflaster nt

niece [niːs] n Nichte f

Nigeria [naɪˈdʒɪərɪə] n Nigeria nt

night [naɪt] n Nacht f; (before bed) Abend m; **good ~** gute Nacht!; **at (o by) ~** nachts; **to have an early ~** früh schlafen gehen; **nightcap** n Schlummertrunk m; **nightclub** n Nachtklub m; **nightdress** n Nachthemd nt; **nightie** ['naɪtɪ] n (fam) Nachthemd nt

nightingale ['naɪtɪŋgeɪl] n Nachtigall f

night life ['naɪtlaɪf] n Nachtleben nt; **nightly** adv (every evening) jeden Abend; (every night) jede Nacht; **nightmare** ['naɪtmɛə*] n Albtraum m; **nighttime** n Nacht f; **at ~** nachts

nil [nɪl] n (Sport) null

Nile [naɪl] n Nil m

nine [naɪn] num neun; **~ times out of ten** so gut wie immer ▷ n (a. bus etc) Neun f;

see also **eight**; **nineteen** [naɪn'tiːn] *num*
neunzehn ▷ *n* (*a. bus etc*) Neunzehn *f*; *see*
also **eight**; **nineteenth** *adj* neunzehnte(r,
s); *see also* **eighth**; **ninetieth** ['naɪntɪəθ]
adj neunzigste(r, s); *see also* **eighth**;
ninety ['naɪntɪ] *num* neunzig ▷ *n*
Neunzig *f*; *see also* **eight**; **ninth** [naɪnθ]
adj neunte(r, s) ▷ *n* (*fraction*) Neuntel *nt*;
see also **eighth**

nipple ['nɪpl] *n* Brustwarze *f*

nitrogen ['naɪtrədʒən] *n* Stickstoff *m*

◯ **KEYWORD**

no [nəʊ] (*pl* **noes** *adv* (*opposite of yes*) nein;
to answer no (*to question*) mit Nein
antworten; (*to request*) Nein *or* nein sagen;
no thank you nein, danke
▷ *adj* (*not any*) kein(e); **I have no
money/time** ich habe kein Geld/keine
Zeit; **"no smoking"** "Rauchen
verboten"
▷ *n* Nein *nt* (*no vote*) Neinstimme *f*

nobility [nəʊ'bɪlɪtɪ] *n* Adel *m*; **noble**
['nəʊbl] *adj* (*rank*) adlig; (*quality*) edel ▷ *n*
Adlige(r) *mf*

nobody ['nəʊbədɪ] *pron* niemand;
(*emphatic*) keiner; **~ knows** keiner weiß es;
~ else sonst niemand, kein anderer ▷ *n*
Niemand *m*

no-claims bonus [nəʊ'kleɪmzbəʊnəs] *n*
Schadenfreiheitsrabatt *m*

nod [nɒd] *vi, vt* nicken; **nod off** *vi*
einnicken

noise [nɔɪz] *n* (*loud*) Lärm *m*; (*sound*)
Geräusch *nt*; **noisy** *adj* laut; (*crowd*)
lärmend

nominate ['nɒmɪneɪt] *vt* (*in election*)
aufstellen; (*appoint*) ernennen

nominative ['nɒmɪnətɪv] *n* (*Ling*)
Nominativ *m*

nominee [nɒmɪ'niː] *n* Kandidat(in) *m(f)*

non- [nɒn] *pref* Nicht-; (*with adj*) nicht-,
un-; **non-alcoholic** *adj* alkoholfrei

none [nʌn] *pron* keine(r, s); **~ of them**
keiner von ihnen; **~ of it is any use** nichts
davon ist brauchbar; **there are ~ left** es
sind keine mehr da; (*with comparative*) **to
be ~ the wiser** auch nicht schlauer sein; **I
was ~ the worse for it** es hat mir nichts
geschadet

nonentity [nɒ'nentɪtɪ] *n* Null *f*

nonetheless [nʌnðə'les] *adv*
nichtsdestoweniger, dennoch

non-event *n* Reinfall *m*; **non-existent**
adj nicht vorhanden; **non-fiction** *n*
Sachbücher *pl*; **non-iron** *adj* bügelfrei;
non-polluting *adj* schadstofffrei;
non-resident *n* **'open to ~s'** „auch für
Nichthotelgäste"; **non-returnable** *adj*
~ bottle Einwegflasche *f*

nonsense ['nɒnsəns] *n* Unsinn *m*; **don't
talk ~** red keinen Unsinn

non-smoker [nɒn'sməʊkə*] *n*
Nichtraucher(in) *m(f)*; **non-smoking** *adj*
Nichtraucher-; **~ area**
Nichtraucherbereich *m*; **non-standard** *adj*
nicht serienmäßig; **nonstop** *adj* (*train*)
durchgehend; (*flight*) Nonstop- ▷ *adv*
(*talk*) ununterbrochen; (*travel*) ohne
Unterbrechung; (*fly*) ohne
Zwischenlandung; **non-violent** *adj*
gewaltfrei

noodles ['nuːdlz] *npl* Nudeln *pl*

noon [nuːn] *n* Mittag *m*; **at ~** um 12 Uhr
mittags

no one ['nəʊwʌn] *pron* niemand;
(*emphatic*) keiner; **~ else** sonst niemand,
kein anderer

nor [nɔː] *conj* **neither ... ~ ...** weder ...
noch ...; **I don't smoke, ~ does he** ich
rauche nicht, er auch nicht

norm [nɔːm] *n* Norm *f*

normal ['nɔːməl] *adj* normal; **to get back
to ~** sich wieder normalisieren; **normally**
adv (*usually*) normalerweise

north [nɔːθ] *n* Norden *m*; **to the ~ of**
nördlich von ▷ *adv* (*go, face*) nach Norden
▷ *adj* Nord-; **~ wind** Nordwind *m*; **North
America** *n* Nordamerika *nt*; **northbound**
adj (in) Richtung Norden; **northeast** *n*
Nordosten *m*; **to the ~ of** nordöstlich von
▷ *adv* (*go, face*) nach Nordosten ▷ *adj*
Nordost-; **northern** ['nɔːðən] *adj*
nördlich; **Northern Ireland** *n* Nordirland *nt*; **North
Pole** *n* Nordpol *m*; **North Sea** *n* Nordsee
f; **northwards** *adv* nach Norden;
northwest *n* Nordwesten *m*; **to the ~ of**
nordwestlich von ▷ *adv* (*go, face*) nach
Nordwesten ▷ *adj* Nordwest-

Norway ['nɔːweɪ] *n* Norwegen *nt*;
Norwegian [nɔː'wiːdʒən] *adj*
norwegisch ▷ *n* (*person*) Norweger(in)
m(f); (*language*) Norwegisch *nt*

nos. *abbr* = **numbers** Nr.

nose [nəʊz] *n* Nase *f*; **nose around** *vi* herumschnüffeln; **nosebleed** *n* Nasenbluten *nt*; **nose-dive** *n* Sturzflug *m*; **to take a ~** abstürzen

nosey ['nəʊzɪ] *see* **nosy**

nostalgia [nɒ'stældʒɪə] *n* Nostalgie *f* (*for* nach); **nostalgic** *adj* nostalgisch

nostril ['nɒstrɪl] *n* Nasenloch *nt*

nosy ['nəʊzɪ] *adj* neugierig

not [nɒt] *adv* nicht; **~ a** kein; **~ one of them** kein einziger von ihnen; **he is ~ an expert** er ist kein Experte; **I told him ~ to (do it)** ich sagte ihm, er solle es nicht tun; **~ at all** überhaupt nicht, keineswegs; (*don't mention it*) gern geschehen; **~ yet** noch nicht

notable ['nəʊtəbl] *adj* bemerkenswert; **note** [nəʊt] *n* (*written*) Notiz *f*; (*short letter*) paar Zeilen *pl*; (*on scrap of paper*) Zettel *m*; (*comment in book etc*) Anmerkung *f*; (*bank~*) Schein *m*; (*Mus: sign*) Note *f*; (*sound*) Ton *m*; **to make a ~ of sth** etw dat etw notieren; **~s** (*of lecture etc*) Aufzeichnungen *pl*; **to take ~s** sich dat Notizen machen (*of über +akk*) ▷ *vt* (*notice*) bemerken (*that* dass); (*write down*) notieren; **notebook** *n* Notizbuch *nt*; (*Inform*) Notebook *nt*; **notepad** *n* Notizblock *m*; **notepaper** *n* Briefpapier *nt*

nothing ['nʌθɪŋ] *n* nichts; **~ but ...** lauter ...; **for ~** umsonst; **he thinks ~ of it** er macht sich nichts daraus

notice ['nəʊtɪs] *n* (*announcement*) Bekanntmachung *f*; (*on ~ board*) Anschlag *m*; (*attention*) Beachtung *f*; (*advance warning*) Ankündigung *f*; (*to leave job, flat etc*) Kündigung *f*; **at short ~** kurzfristig; **until further ~** bis auf weiteres; **to give sb ~** jdm kündigen; **to hand in one's ~** kündigen; **to take (no) ~ of (sth)** etw (nicht) beachten; **take no ~** kümmere dich nicht darum! ▷ *vt* bemerken; **noticeable** *adj* erkennbar; (*visible*) sichtbar; **to be ~** auffallen; **notice board** *n* Anschlagtafel *f*

notification [nəʊtɪfɪ'keɪʃən] *n* Benachrichtigung *f* (*of* von); **notify** ['nəʊtɪfaɪ] *vt* benachrichtigen (*of* von)

notion ['nəʊʃən] *n* Idee *f*

notorious [nəʊ'tɔːrɪəs] *adj* berüchtigt

nought [nɔːt] *n* Null *f*

noun [naʊn] *n* Substantiv *nt*

nourish ['nʌrɪʃ] *vt* nähren; **nourishing** *adj* nahrhaft; **nourishment** *n* Nahrung *f*

novel ['nɒvəl] *n* Roman *m* ▷ *adj* neuartig; **novelist** *n* Schriftsteller(in) *m(f)*; **novelty** *n* Neuheit *f*

November [nəʊ'vembə*] *n* November *m*; *see also* **September**

novice ['nɒvɪs] *n* Neuling *m*

now [naʊ] *adv* (*at the moment*) jetzt; (*introductory phrase*) also; **right ~** jetzt gleich; **just ~** gerade; **by ~** inzwischen; **from ~ on** ab jetzt; **~ and again** (*o then*) ab und zu; **nowadays** *adv* heutzutage

nowhere ['nəʊweə*] *adv* nirgends; **we're getting ~** wir kommen nicht weiter; **~ near** noch lange nicht

nozzle ['nɒzl] *n* Düse *f*

nuclear ['njuːklɪə*] *adj* (*energy etc*) Kern-; **~ power station** Kernkraftwerk *nt*; **nuclear waste** *n* Atommüll *m*

nude [njuːd] *adj* nackt ▷ *n* (*person*) Nackte(r) *mf*; (*painting etc*) Akt *m*

nudge [nʌdʒ] *vt* stupsen; **nudist** ['njuːdɪst] *n* Nudist(in) *m(f)*, FKK-Anhänger(in) *m(f)*; **nudist beach** *n* FKK-Strand *m*

nuisance ['njuːsns] *n* Ärgernis *nt*; (*person*) Plage *f*; **what a ~** wie ärgerlich!

nuke [njuːk] (*US fam*) *n* (*bomb*) Atombombe *f* ▷ *vt* eine Atombombe werfen auf +akk

numb [nʌm] *adj* taub, gefühllos ▷ *vt* betäuben

number ['nʌmbə*] *n* Nummer *f*; (*Math*) Zahl *f*; (*quantity*) (An)zahl *f*; **in small/large ~s** in kleinen/großen Mengen; **a ~ of times** mehrmals ▷ *vt* (*give a number to*) nummerieren; (*count*) zählen (*among* zu); **his days are ~ed** seine Tage sind gezählt; **number plate** *n* (*Brit Auto*) Nummernschild *nt*

numeral ['njuːmərəl] *n* Ziffer *f*; **numerical** [njuː'merɪkəl] *adj* numerisch; (*superiority*) zahlenmäßig; **numerous** ['njuːmərəs] *adj* zahlreich

nun [nʌn] *n* Nonne *f*

Nuremberg ['njʊərəmbɜːg] *n* Nürnberg *nt*

nurse [nɜːs] *n* Krankenschwester *f*; (*male ~*) Krankenpfleger *m* ▷ *vt* (*patient*) pflegen; (*baby*) stillen; **nursery** *n* Kinderzimmer *nt*; (*for plants*) Gärtnerei *f*; (*tree*) Baumschule *f*; **nursery rhyme** *n* Kinderreim *m*; **nursery school** *n* Kindergarten *m*; **~ teacher**

Kindergärtner(in) m(f), Erzieher(in) m(f);
nursing n (profession) Krankenpflege f;
~ home Privatklinik f
nut [nʌt] n Nuss f; (Tech: for bolt) Mutter f;
nutcase n (fam) Spinner(in) m(f);
nutcracker n, **nutcrackers** npl
Nussknacker m
nutmeg ['nʌtmeg] n Muskat m,
Muskatnuss f
nutrient ['njuːtrɪənt] n Nährstoff m
nutrition [njuːˈtrɪʃən] n Ernährung f;
nutritious [njuːˈtrɪʃəs] adj nahrhaft
nuts [nʌts] (fam) adj verrückt; **to be
~ about sth** nach etw verrückt sein ▷ npl
(testicles) Eier pl
nutshell ['nʌtʃel] n Nussschale f; **in a
~** kurz gesagt
nutter ['nʌtə*] n (fam) Spinner(in) m(f);
nutty ['nʌtɪ] adj (fam) verrückt
NW abbr = **northwest** NW
nylon® ['naɪlɒn] n Nylon® nt ▷ adj
Nylon-

O [əʊ] *n* (*Tel*) Null *f*

oak [əʊk] *n* Eiche *f* ▷ *adj* Eichen-

OAP *abbr* = **old-age pensioner** Rentner(in) *m(f)*

oar [ɔː*] *n* Ruder *nt*

oasis [əʊˈeɪsɪs] (*pl* **oases**) *n* Oase *f*

oatcake [ˈəʊtkeɪk] *n* Haferkeks *m*

oath [əʊθ] *n* (*statement*) Eid *m*

oats [əʊts] *npl* Hafer *m*; (*Gastr*) Haferflocken *pl*

obedience [əˈbiːdɪəns] *n* Gehorsam *m*; **obedient** *adj* gehorsam; **obey** [əˈbeɪ] *vt*, *vi* gehorchen +*dat*

object [ˈɒbdʒekt] *n* Gegenstand *m*; (*abstract*) Objekt *nt*; (*purpose*) Ziel *nt* ▷ [əbˈdʒekt] *vi* dagegen sein; (*raise objection*) Einwände erheben (*to* gegen); (*morally*) Anstoß nehmen (*to an* +*dat*); **do you ~ to my smoking?** haben Sie etwas dagegen, wenn ich rauche?; **objection** [əbˈdʒekʃən] *n* Einwand *m*

objective [əbˈdʒektɪv] *n* Ziel *nt* ▷ *adj* objektiv; **objectivity** [ɒbdʒekˈtɪvɪtɪ] *n* Objektivität *f*

obligation [ɒblɪˈɡeɪʃən] *n* (*duty*) Pflicht *f*; (*commitment*) Verpflichtung *f*; **no ~** unverbindlich; **obligatory** [əˈblɪɡətərɪ] *adj* obligatorisch; **oblige** [əˈblaɪdʒ] *vt* **to ~ sb to do sth** jdn (dazu) zwingen, etw zu tun; **he felt ~d to accept the offer** er fühlte sich verpflichtet, das Angebot anzunehmen

oblique [əˈbliːk] *adj* schräg; (*angle*) schief

oblong [ˈɒblɒŋ] *n* Rechteck *nt* ▷ *adj* rechteckig

oboe [ˈəʊbəʊ] *n* Oboe *f*

obscene [əbˈsiːn] *adj* obszön

obscure [əbˈskjʊə*] *adj* unklar; (*unknown*) unbekannt

observant [əbˈzɜːvənt] *adj* aufmerksam; **observation** [ɒbzəˈveɪʃən] *n* (*watching*) Beobachtung *f*; (*remark*) Bemerkung *f*; **observe** [əbˈzɜːv] *vt* (*notice*) bemerken; (*watch*) beobachten; (*customs*) einhalten

obsessed [əbˈsest] *adj* besessen (*with an idea etc* von einem Gedanken etc); **obsession** [əbˈseʃən] *n* Manie *f*

obsolete [ˈɒbsəliːt] *adj* veraltet

obstacle [ˈɒbstəkl] *n* Hindernis *nt* (*to* für); **to be an ~ to sth** einer Sache im Weg stehen

obstinate [ˈɒbstɪnət] *adj* hartnäckig

obstruct [əbˈstrʌkt] *vt* versperren; (*pipe*) verstopfen; (*hinder*) behindern, aufhalten; **obstruction** [əbˈstrʌkʃən] *n* Blockierung *f*; (*of pipe*) Verstopfung *f*; (*obstacle*) Hindernis *nt*

obtain [əbˈteɪn] *vt* erhalten; **obtainable** *adj* erhältlich

obvious [ˈɒbvɪəs] *adj* offensichtlich; **it was ~ to me that ...** es war mir klar, dass ...; **obviously** *adj* offensichtlich

occasion [əˈkeɪʒən] *n* Gelegenheit *f*; (*special event*) (großes) Ereignis; **on the ~ of** anlässlich +*gen*; **special ~** besonderer Anlass; **occasional**, **occasionally** *adj*, *adv* gelegentlich

occupant [ˈɒkjʊpənt] *n* (*of house*) Bewohner(in) *m(f)*; (*of vehicle*) Insasse *m*, Insassin *f*; **occupation** [ɒkjʊˈpeɪʃən] *n* Beruf *m*; (*pastime*) Beschäftigung *f*; (*of country etc*) Besetzung *f*; **occupied** *adj* (*country, seat, toilet*) besetzt; (*person*) beschäftigt; **to keep sb/oneself ~** jdn/sich beschäftigen; **occupy** [ˈɒkjʊpaɪ] *vt* (*country*) besetzen; (*time*) beanspruchen; (*mind, person*) beschäftigen

occur [əˈkɜː*] *vi* vorkommen; **~ to sb** jdm

einfallen; **occurrence** [əˈkʌrəns] n (event) Ereignis nt; (presence) Vorkommen nt

ocean [ˈəʊʃən] n Ozean m; (US: sea) das Meer nt

o'clock [əˈklɒk] adv **5** ~ 5 Uhr; **at 10** ~ um 10 Uhr

octagon [ˈɒktəgən] n Achteck nt

October [ɒkˈtəʊbə*] n Oktober m; see also **September**

octopus [ˈɒktəpəs] n Tintenfisch m

odd [ɒd] adj (strange) sonderbar; (not even) ungerade; (one missing) einzeln; **to be the ~ one out** nicht dazugehören; **~ jobs** Gelegenheitsarbeiten pl; **odds** npl Chancen pl; **against all ~** entgegen allen Erwartungen; **~ and ends** (fam) Kleinkram pl

odometer [əʊˈdɒmətə*] n (US Auto) Meilenzähler m

odor (US), **odour** [ˈəʊdə*] n Geruch m

○ KEYWORD

of [ɒv, əv] prep **1** von +dat = use of gen; **the history of Germany** die Geschichte Deutschlands; **a friend of ours** ein Freund von uns; **a boy of 10** ein 10-jähriger Junge; **that was kind of you** das war sehr freundlich von Ihnen

2 (expressing quantity, amount, dates etc): **a kilo of flour** ein Kilo Mehl; **how much of this do you need?** wie viel brauchen Sie (davon)?; **there were 3 of them** (people) sie waren zu dritt; (objects) es gab 3 (davon); **a cup of tea/vase of flowers** eine Tasse Tee/Vase mit Blumen; **the 5th of July** der 5 Juli

3 (from, out of) aus; **a bridge made of wood** eine Holzbrücke eine Brücke aus Holz

off [ɒf] adv (away) weg, fort; (free) frei; (switch) ausgeschaltet; (milk) sauer; **a mile ~** eine Meile entfernt; **I'll be ~ now** ich gehe jetzt; **to have the day/Monday ~** heute/Montag freihaben; **the lights are ~** die Lichter sind aus; **the concert is ~** das Konzert fällt aus; **I got 10%** ~ ich habe 10% Nachlass bekommen ▷ prep (away from) von; **to jump/fall ~ the roof** vom Dach springen/fallen; **to get ~ the bus** aus dem Bus aussteigen; **he's ~ work/school** er hat frei/schulfrei; **to take £20 ~ the**

price den Preis um 20 Pfund herabsetzen

offence [əˈfens] n (crime) Straftat f; (minor) Vergehen nt; (to feelings) Kränkung f; **to cause/take ~** Anstoß erregen/nehmen; **offend** [əˈfend] vt kränken; (eye, ear) beleidigen; **offender** n Straffällige(r) mf; **offense** (US) see **offence**; **offensive** [əˈfensɪv] adj anstößig; (insulting) beleidigend; (smell) übel, abstoßend ▷ n (Mil) Offensive f

offer [ˈɒfə*] n Angebot nt; **on ~** (Comm) im Angebot ▷ vt anbieten (to sb jdm); (money, a chance etc) bieten

offhand [ɒfˈhænd] adj lässig ▷ adv (say) auf Anhieb

office [ˈɒfɪs] n Büro nt; (position) Amt nt; **doctor's ~** (US) Arztpraxis f; **office block** n Bürogebäude nt; **office hours** npl Dienstzeit f; (notice) Geschäftszeiten pl; **officer** [ˈɒfɪsə*] n (Mil) Offizier(in) m(f); (official) Polizeibeamte(r) m, Polizeibeamtin f; **office worker** [ˈɒfɪswɜ:kə*] n Büroangestellte(r) mf; **official** [əˈfɪʃəl] adj offiziell; (report etc) amtlich; **~ language** Amtssprache f ▷ n Beamte(r) m, Beamtin f, Repräsentant(in) m(f)

off-licence [ˈɒflaɪsəns] n (Brit) Wein- und Spirituosenhandlung f; **off-line** adj (Inform) offline; **off-peak** adj außerhalb der Stoßzeiten; (rate, ticket) verbilligt; **off-putting** adj abstoßend, entmutigend, irritierend; **off-season** adj außerhalb der Saison

offshore [ˈɒfʃɔ:*] adj küstennah, Küsten-; (oil rig) im Meer; **offside** [ˈɒfsaɪd] n (Auto) Fahrerseite f; (Sport) Abseits nt

often [ˈɒfən] adv oft; **every so ~** von Zeit zu Zeit

oil [ɔɪl] n Öl nt ▷ vt ölen; **oil level** n Ölstand m; **oil painting** n Ölgemälde nt; **oil-rig** n (Öl)bohrinsel f; **oil slick** n Ölteppich m; **oil tanker** n Öltanker m; (truck) Tankwagen m; **oily** adj ölig; (skin, hair) fettig

ointment [ˈɔɪntmənt] n Salbe f

OK, okay [əʊˈkeɪ] (fam) okay, in Ordnung; **that's ~ by** (o with) **me** das ist mir recht

old [əʊld] adj alt; **old age** n Alter nt; **~ pension** Rente f; **~ pensioner** Rentner(in) m(f); **old-fashioned** adj altmodisch; **old people's home** n Altersheim nt

olive ['ɒlɪv] n Olive f; **olive oil** n. Olivenöl nt

Olympic [əʊ'lɪmpɪk] adj olympisch; **the ~ Games, the ~s** pl die Olympischen Spiele pl, die Olympiade

omelette ['ɒmlət] n Omelett nt

omission [əʊ'mɪʃən] n Auslassung f; **omit** [əʊ'mɪt] vt auslassen

 KEYWORD

on [ɒn] prep **1** (indicating position) auf +dat; (with vb of motion) auf +acc; (on vertical surface, part of body) an +dat/acc; **it's on the table** es ist auf dem Tisch; **she put the book on the table** sie legte das Buch auf den Tisch; **on the left** links
2 (indicating means, method, condition etc): **on foot** (go, be) zu Fuß; **on the train/plane** (go) mit dem Zug/Flugzeug; (be) im Zug/Flugzeug; **on the telephone/television** am Telefon/im Fernsehen; **to be on drugs** Drogen nehmen; **to be on holiday/business** im Urlaub/auf Geschäftsreise sein
3 (referring to time): **on Friday** (am) Freitag; **on Fridays** freitags; **on June 20th** am 20. Juni; **a week on Friday** Freitag in einer Woche; **on arrival he ...** als er ankam, ... er ...
4 (about, concerning) über +acc
▷ adv **1** (referring to dress) an; **she put her boots/hat on** sie zog ihre Stiefel an/setzte ihren Hut auf
2 (further, continuously) weiter; **to walk on** weitergehen
▷ adj **1** (functioning, in operation: machine, TV, light) an; (: tap) aufgedreht; (: brakes) angezogen; **is the meeting still on?** findet die Versammlung noch statt?; **there's a good film on** es läuft ein guter Film
2: **that's not on!** (inf: of behaviour) das liegt nicht drin!

once [wʌns] adv (one time, in the past) einmal; **at ~** sofort; (at the same time) gleichzeitig; **~ more** noch einmal; **for ~** ausnahmsweise (einmal); **~ in a while** ab und zu mal ▷ conj wenn ... einmal;

~ you've got used to it sobald Sie sich daran gewöhnt haben

oncoming ['ɒnkʌmɪŋ] adj entgegenkommend; **~ traffic** Gegenverkehr m

 KEYWORD

one [wʌn] num eins (with noun, referring back to noun) ein/eine/ein; **it is one** (o'clock) es ist eins es ist ein Uhr; **one hundred and fifty** einhundertfünfzig
▷ adj **1** (sole) einzige(r, s); **the one book which** das einzige Buch, welches
2 (same) derselbe/dieselbe/dasselbe; **they came in the one car** sie kamen alle in dem einen Auto
3 (indef): **one day I discovered ...** eines Tages bemerkte ich ...
▷ pron **1** eine(r, s); **do you have a red one?** haben Sie einen roten/eine rote/ein rotes?; **this one** diese(r, s); **that one** der/die/das; **which one?** welche(r, s)?; **one by one** einzeln
2: **one another** einander; **do you two ever see one another?** seht ihr beide euch manchmal?
3 (impers) man; **one never knows** man kann nie wissen; **to cut one's finger** sich in den Finger schneiden

onion ['ʌnjən] n Zwiebel f

on-line ['ɒnlaɪn] adj (Inform) online; **~ banking** Homebanking nt

only ['əʊnlɪ] adv nur; (with time) erst; **~ yesterday** erst gestern; **he's ~ four** er ist erst vier; **~ just arrived** gerade erst angekommen ▷ adj einzige(r, s); **~ child** Einzelkind nt

o.n.o. abbr = **or nearest offer** VB

onside [ɒn'saɪd] adv (Sport) nicht im Abseits

onto ['ɒntʊ] prep auf +akk; (vertical surface) an +akk; **to be ~ sb** jdm auf die Schliche gekommen sein

onwards ['ɒnwədz] adv voran, vorwärts; **from today ~** von heute an, ab heute

opaque [əʊ'peɪk] adj undurchsichtig

open ['əʊpən] adj offen; **in the ~ air** im Freien; **~ to the public** für die Öffentlichkeit zugänglich; **the shop is ~ all day** das Geschäft hat den ganzen Tag offen ▷ vt öffnen, aufmachen; (*meeting, account, new building*) eröffnen; (*road*) dem Verkehr übergeben ▷ vi (*door, window etc*) aufgehen, sich öffnen; (*shop, bank*) öffnen, aufmachen; (*begin*) anfangen (*with mit*); **open-air** adj Freiluft-; **open day** n Tag m der offenen Tür; **opening** n Öffnung f; (*beginning*) Anfang m; (*official, of exhibition etc*) Eröffnung f; (*opportunity*) Möglichkeit f; ~ **hours** (*o times*) Öffnungszeiten pl; **openly** adv offen; **open-minded** adj aufgeschlossen; **open-plan** adj ~ **office** Großraumbüro nt

opera ['ɒpərə] n Oper f; **opera glasses** npl Opernglas nt; **opera house** n Oper f, Opernhaus nt; **opera singer** n Opernsänger(in) m(f)

operate ['ɒpəreɪt] vt (*machine*) bedienen; (*brakes, lights*) betätigen ▷ vi (*machine*) laufen; (*bus etc*) verkehren (*between zwischen*); **to ~ (on sb)** (*Med*) (jdn) operieren; **operating theatre** n Operationssaal m; **operation** [ɒpə'reɪʃən] n (*of machine*) Bedienung f; (*functioning*) Funktionieren nt; (*Med*) Operation f (*on an +dat*); (*undertaking*) Unternehmen nt; **in ~** (*machine*) in Betrieb; **to have an ~** operiert werden (*for wegen*); **operator** ['ɒpəreɪtə*] n **to phone the ~** die Vermittlung anrufen

opinion [ə'pɪnjən] n Meinung f (*on zu*); **in my ~** meiner Meinung nach

opponent [ə'pəʊnənt] n Gegner(in) m(f)

opportunity [ɒpə'tjuːnɪtɪ] n Gelegenheit f

oppose [ə'pəʊz] vt sich widersetzen +dat; (*idea*) ablehnen; **opposed** adj **to be ~ to** sth gegen etw sein; **as ~ to** im Gegensatz zu; **opposing** adj (*team*) gegnerisch; (*points of view*) entgegengesetzt

opposite ['ɒpəzɪt] adj (*house*) gegenüberliegend; (*direction*) entgegengesetzt; **the ~ sex** das andere Geschlecht ▷ adv gegenüber ▷ prep gegenüber; ~ **me** mir gegenüber ▷ n Gegenteil nt

opposition [ɒpə'zɪʃən] n Widerstand m (*to gegen*); (*Pol*) Opposition f

oppress [ə'pres] vt unterdrücken; **oppressive** adj (*heat*) drückend

opt [ɒpt] vi **to ~ for sth** sich für etw

entscheiden; **to ~ to do sth** sich entscheiden, etw zu tun

optician [ɒp'tɪʃən] n Optiker(in) m(f)

optimist ['ɒptɪmɪst] n Optimist(in) m(f); **optimistic** [ɒptɪ'mɪstɪk] adj optimistisch

optimum ['ɒptɪməm] adj optimal

option ['ɒpʃən] n Möglichkeit f; (*Comm*) Option f; **to have no ~** keine Wahl haben; **optional** adj freiwillig; ~ **extras** (*Auto*) Extras pl

or [ɔː*] conj oder; (*otherwise*) sonst; (*after neg*) noch; **hurry up, ~ (else) we'll be late** beeil dich, sonst kommen wir zu spät

oral ['ɔːrəl] adj mündlich; ~ **sex** Oralverkehr m ▷ n (*exam*) Mündliche(s) nt

orange ['ɒrɪndʒ] n Orange f ▷ adj orangefarben; **orange juice** n Orangensaft m

orbit ['ɔːbɪt] n Umlaufbahn f; **to be out of ~** (*fam*) nicht zu erreichen sein ▷ vt umkreisen

orchard ['ɔːtʃəd] n Obstgarten m

orchestra ['ɔːkɪstrə] n Orchester nt; (*US Theat*) Parkett nt

orchid ['ɔːkɪd] n Orchidee f

ordeal [ɔː'diːl] n Tortur f; (*emotional*) Qual f

order ['ɔːdə*] n (*sequence*) Reihenfolge f; (*good arrangement*) Ordnung f; (*command*) Befehl m; (*Jur*) Anordnung f; (*condition*) Zustand m; (*Comm*) Bestellung f; **out of ~** (*not functioning*) außer Betrieb; (*unsuitable*) nicht angebracht; **in ~** (*items*) richtig geordnet; (*all right*) in Ordnung; **in ~ to do sth** um etw zu tun ▷ vt (*arrange*) ordnen; (*command*) befehlen; **to ~ sb to do sth** jdm befehlen, etw zu tun; (*food, product*) bestellen; **order form** n Bestellschein m

ordinary ['ɔːdnrɪ] adj gewöhnlich, normal; (*average*) durchschnittlich

ore [ɔː*] n Erz nt

organ ['ɔːgən] n (*Mus*) Orgel f; (*Anat*) Organ nt

organic [ɔː'gænɪk] adj organisch; (*farming, vegetables*) Bio-, Öko-; ~ **farmer** Biobauer m, Biobäuerin f; ~ **food** Biokost f

organization [ɔːgənaɪ'zeɪʃən] n Organisation f; (*arrangement*) Ordnung f; **organize** ['ɔːgənaɪz] vt organisieren; **organizer** n (elektronisches) Notizbuch

orgasm ['ɔːgæzəm] n Orgasmus m

orgy ['ɔːdʒɪ] n Orgie f
oriental [ɔːrɪ'entəl] adj orientalisch
orientation ['ɔːrɪenteɪʃən] n
Orientierung f
origin ['ɒrɪdʒɪn] n Ursprung m; (of person)
Herkunft f; **original** [ə'rɪdʒɪnl] adj (first)
ursprünglich; (painting) original; (idea)
originell ▷ n Original nt; **originality**
[ərɪdʒɪ'nælɪtɪ] n Originalität f; **originally**
adv ursprünglich
Orkneys ['ɔːknɪz] npl, **Orkney Islands**
npl Orkneyinseln pl
ornament ['ɔːnəmənt] n
Schmuckgegenstand m; **ornamental**
[ɔːnə'mentl] adj dekorativ
orphan ['ɔːfən] n Waise f, Waisenkind nt;
orphanage ['ɔːfənɪdʒ] n Waisenhaus nt
orthodox ['ɔːθədɒks] adj orthodox
orthopaedic, orthopedic (US)
[ɔːθəʊ'piːdɪk] adj orthopädisch
ostentatious [ɒsten'teɪʃəs] adj protzig
ostrich ['ɒstrɪtʃ] n (Zool) Strauß m
other ['ʌðə*] adj, pron andere(r, s); **any**
~ questions? sonst noch Fragen?; **the**
~ day neulich; **every ~ day** jeden zweiten
Tag; **any person ~ than him** alle außer
ihm; **someone/something or ~** irgend
jemand/irgend etwas; **otherwise** adv
sonst; (differently) anders
OTT adj abbr = **over the top** übertrieben
otter ['ɒtə*] n Otter m
ought [ɔːt] vb aux (obligation) sollte;
(probability) dürfte; (stronger) müsste; **you**
~ to do that Sie sollten das tun; **he ~ to**
win er müsste gewinnen; **that ~ to do** das
müsste (o dürfte) reichen
ounce [aʊns] n Unze f (28,35 g)
our [aʊə*] adj unser; **ours** pron unsere(r,
s); **this is ~** das gehört uns; **a friend of**
~ ein Freund von uns; **ourselves** pron
(reflexive) uns; **we enjoyed ~** wir haben uns
amüsiert; **we've got the house to ~** wir
haben das Haus für uns; (emphatic) **we did**
it ~ wir haben es selbst gemacht; **(all) by**
~ allein
out [aʊt] adv hinaus/heraus; (not indoors)
draußen; (not at home) nicht zu Hause; (not
alight) aus; (unconscious) bewusstlos;
(published) herausgekommen; (results)
bekannt gegeben; **have you been ~ yet?**
waren Sie schon draußen?; **I was ~ when**
they called ich war nicht da, als sie
vorbeikamen; **to be ~ and about**

unterwegs sein; **the sun is ~** die Sonne
scheint; **the fire is ~** das Feuer ist
ausgegangen; (wrong) **the calculation is**
(way) ~ die Kalkulation stimmt (ganz und
gar) nicht; **they're ~ to get him** sie sind
hinter ihm her
outback ['aʊtbæk] n (in Australia) the
~ das Hinterland
outboard ['aʊtbɔːd] adj **~ motor**
Außenbordmotor m
outbreak ['aʊtbreɪk] n Ausbruch m
outburst ['aʊtbɜːst] n Ausbruch m
outcome ['aʊtkʌm] n Ergebnis nt
outcry ['aʊtkraɪ] n (public protest)
Protestwelle f (against gegen)
outdo [aʊt'duː] irr vt übertreffen
outdoor ['aʊtdɔː*] adj Außen-; (Sport) im
Freien; **~ swimming pool** Freibad nt;
outdoors [aʊt'dɔːz] adv draußen, im
Freien
outer ['aʊtə*] adj äußere(r, s); **outer**
space n Weltraum m
outfit ['aʊtfɪt] n Ausrüstung f; (clothes)
Kleidung f
outgoing ['aʊtgəʊɪŋ] adj kontaktfreudig
outgrow [aʊt'grəʊ] irr vt (clothes)
herauswachsen aus
outing ['aʊtɪŋ] n Ausflug m
outlet ['aʊtlet] n Auslass m, Abfluss m;
(US) Steckdose f; (shop) Verkaufsstelle f
outline ['aʊtlaɪn] n Umriss m; (summary)
Abriss m
outlive [aʊt'lɪv] vt überleben
outlook ['aʊtlʊk] n Aussicht(en) f(pl);
(prospects) Aussichten pl; (attitude)
Einstellung f (on zu)
outnumber [aʊt'nʌmbə*] vt
zahlenmäßig überlegen sein +dat; **~ed**
zahlenmäßig unterlegen
out of ['aʊtɒv] prep (motion, motive, origin)
aus; (position, away from) außerhalb +gen;
~ danger/sight/breath außer
Gefahr/Sicht/Atem; **made ~ wood** aus
Holz gemacht; **we are ~ bread** wir haben
kein Brot mehr; **out-of-date** adj veraltet;
out-of-the-way adj abgelegen
outpatient ['aʊtpeɪʃənt] n ambulanter
Patient, ambulante Patientin
output ['aʊtpʊt] n Produktion f; (of
engine) Leistung f; (Inform) Ausgabe f
outrage ['aʊtreɪdʒ] n (great anger)
Empörung f (at über); (wicked deed)
Schandtat f; (crime) Verbrechen nt;

(indecency) Skandal *m*; **outrageous**
[aʊt'reɪdʒəs] *adj* unerhört; *(clothes, behaviour etc)* unmöglich, schrill

outright ['aʊtraɪt] *adv* (killed) sofort ▷ *adj* total; (denial) völlig; (winner) unbestritten

outside [aʊt'saɪd] *n* Außenseite *f*; **on the ~** außen ▷ *adj* äußere(r, s), Außen-; (chance) sehr gering ▷ *adv* außen; **to go ~** nach draußen gehen ▷ *prep* außerhalb +*gen*; **outsider** *n* Außenseiter(in) *m(f)*

outsize ['aʊtsaɪz] *adj* übergroß; (clothes) in Übergröße

outskirts ['aʊtskɜːts] *npl* (of town) Stadtrand *m*

outstanding [aʊt'stændɪŋ] *adj* hervorragend; (debts etc) ausstehend

outward ['aʊtwəd] *adj* äußere(r, s); **~ journey** Hinfahrt *f*; **outwardly** *adv* nach außen hin; **outwards** *adv* nach außen

oval ['əʊvəl] *adj* oval

ovary ['əʊvərɪ] *n* Eierstock *m*

ovation [əʊ'veɪʃən] *n* Ovation *f*, Applaus *m*

oven ['ʌvn] *n* Backofen *m*; **oven glove** *n* Topfhandschuh *m*; **ovenproof** *adj* feuerfest; **oven-ready** *adj* bratfertig

over ['əʊvə*] *prep* (position) über +*dat*; (motion) über +*akk*; **they spent a long time ~ it** sie haben lange dazu gebraucht; **from all ~ England** aus ganz England; **~ £20** mehr als 20 Pfund; **~ the phone/radio** am Telefon/im Radio; **to talk ~ a glass of wine** sich bei einem Glas Wein unterhalten; **~ and above this** darüber hinaus; **~ the summer** während des Sommers ▷ *adv* (across) hinüber/herüber; (finished) vorbei; (match, play etc) zu Ende; (left) übrig; (more) mehr; **~ there/in America** da drüben/drüben in Amerika; **~ to you** Sie sind dran; **it's (all) ~ between us** es ist aus zwischen uns; **~ and ~ again** immer wieder; **to start (all) ~ again** noch einmal von vorn anfangen; **children of 8 and ~** Kinder von 8 Jahren und darüber

over- ['əʊvə*] *pref* über-

overall ['əʊvərɔːl] *n* (Brit) Kittel *m* ▷ *adj* (situation) allgemein; (length) Gesamt-; **~ majority** absolute Mehrheit ▷ *adv* insgesamt; **overalls** *npl* Overall *m*

overboard ['əʊvəbɔːd] *adv* über Bord

overbooked [əʊvə'bʊkt] *adj* überbucht; **overbooking** *n* Überbuchung *f*

overcharge [əʊvə'tʃɑːdʒ] *vt* zu viel verlangen von

overcoat ['əʊvəkəʊt] *n* Wintermantel *m*

overcome [əʊvə'kʌm] *irr vt* überwinden; **~ by sleep/emotion** von Schlaf/Rührung übermannt; **we shall ~** wir werden siegen

overcooked [əʊvə'kʊkt] *adj* zu lange gekocht; (meat) zu lange gebraten

overcrowded [əʊvə'kraʊdɪd] *adj* überfüllt

overdo [əʊvə'duː] *irr vt* übertreiben; **you're ~ing it** du übertreibst es; (doing too much) Sie übernehmen sich; **overdone** *adj* übertrieben; (food) zu lange gekocht; (meat) zu lange gebraten

overdose ['əʊvədəʊs] *n* Überdosis *f*

overdraft ['əʊvədrɑːft] *n* Kontoüberziehung *f*; **overdrawn** [əʊvə'drɔːn] *adj* überzogen

overdue [əʊvə'djuː] *adj* überfällig

overestimate [əʊvər'estɪmeɪt] *vt* überschätzen

overexpose [əʊvərɪks'pəʊz] *vt* (Foto) überbelichten

overflow [əʊvə'fləʊ] *vi* überlaufen

overhead ['əʊvəhed] *adj* (Aviat) **~ locker** Gepäckfach *nt*; **~ projector** Overheadprojektor *m*; **~ railway** Hochbahn *f* ▷ [əʊvə'hed] *adv* oben

overhear [əʊvə'hɪə*] *irr vt* zufällig mit anhören

overheat [əʊvə'hiːt] *vi* (engine) heiß laufen

overjoyed [əʊvə'dʒɔɪd] *adj* überglücklich (at über)

overland ['əʊvəlænd] *adj* Überland- ▷ [əʊvə'lænd] *adv* (travel) über Land

overlap [əʊvə'læp] *vi* (dates etc) sich überschneiden; (objects) sich teilweise decken

overload [əʊvə'ləʊd] *vt* überladen

overlook [əʊvə'lʊk] *vt* (view from above) überblicken; (not notice) übersehen; (pardon) hinwegsehen über +*akk*

overnight [əʊvə'naɪt] *adj* (journey, train) Nacht-; **~ bag** Reisetasche *f*; **~ stay** Übernachtung *f* ▷ *adv* über Nacht

overpass ['əʊvəpɑːs] *n* Überführung *f*

overpay [əʊvə'peɪ] *vt* überbezahlen

overrule [əʊvə'ruːl] *vt* verwerfen; (decision) aufheben

overseas [əʊvəˈsiːz] *adj* Übersee-; (*fam*)
Auslands-; **~ students** Studenten aus
Übersee ▷ *adv* (*go*) nach Übersee; (*live,
work*) in Übersee

oversee [əʊvəˈsiː] *irr vt* beaufsichtigen

overshadow [əʊvəˈʃædəʊ] *vt*
überschatten

overshoot [əʊvəˈʃuːt] *irr vt* (*runway*)
hinausschießen über +*akk*; (*turning*)
vorbeifahren +*dat*

oversight [ˈəʊvəsaɪt] *n* Versehen *nt*

oversimplify [əʊvəˈsɪmplɪfaɪ] *vt* zu sehr
vereinfachen

oversleep [əʊvəˈsliːp] *irr vi* verschlafen

overtake [əʊvəˈteɪk] *irr vt, vi* überholen

overtime [ˈəʊvətaɪm] *n* Überstunden
pl

overturn [əʊvəˈtɜːn] *vt, vi* umkippen

overweight [əʊvəˈweɪt] *adj* **to be
~** Übergewicht haben

overwhelm [əʊvəˈwelm] *vt*
überwältigen; **overwhelming** *adj*
überwältigend

overwork [əʊvəˈwɜːk] *n* Überarbeitung *f*
▷ *vi* sich überarbeiten; **overworked** *adj*
überarbeitet

owe [əʊ] *vt* schulden; **to ~ sth to sb**
(*money*) jdm etw schulden; (*favour etc*) jdm
etw verdanken; **how much do I ~ you?**
was bin ich Ihnen schuldig?; **owing to**
prep wegen +*gen*

owl [aʊl] *n* Eule *f*

own [əʊn] *vt* besitzen ▷ *adj* eigen; **on
one's ~** allein; **he has a flat of his ~** er hat
eine eigene Wohung; **own up** *vi* **to ~ to
sth** etw zugeben; **owner** *n* Besitzer(in)
m(f); (*of business*) Inhaber(in) *m(f)*;
ownership *n* Besitz *m*; **under new
~** unter neuer Leitung

ox [ɒks] (*pl* **oxen**) *n* Ochse *m*; **oxtail**
[ˈɒksteɪl] *n* Ochsenschwanz *m*; **~ soup**
Ochsenschwanzsuppe *f*; **oxygen**
[ˈɒksɪdʒən] *n* Sauerstoff *m*

oyster [ˈɔɪstəʳ] *n* Auster *f*

oz *abbr* = **ounces** Unzen *pl*

Oz [ˈɒz] *n* (*fam*) Australien *nt*

ozone [ˈəʊzəʊn] *n* Ozon *nt*; **~ layer**
Ozonschicht *f*

p *abbr* = **page** S.; *abbr* = **penny, pence**
p.a. *abbr* = **per annum**
pace [peɪs] n (*speed*) Tempo nt; (*step*)
Schritt m; **pacemaker** n (*Med*)
Schrittmacher m
Pacific [pəˈsɪfɪk] n **the ~ (Ocean)** der
Pazifik; **Pacific Standard Time** n
pazifische Zeit
pacifier [ˈpæsɪfaɪə] n (*US: for baby*)
Schnuller m
pack [pæk] n (*of cards*) Spiel nt; (*esp US: of
cigarettes*) Schachtel f; (*gang*) Bande f; (*US:
backpack*) Rucksack m ⊳ vt (*case*) packen;
(*clothes*) einpacken ⊳ vi (*for holiday*)
packen; **pack in** vt (*Brit fam: job*)
hinschmeißen; **package** [ˈpækɪdʒ] n (*a.
Inform, fig*) Paket nt; **package deal** n
Pauschalangebot nt; **package holiday**,
package tour n Pauschalreise f;
packaging n (*material*) Verpackung f;
packed lunch n (*Brit*) Lunchpaket nt;
packet n Päckchen nt; (*of cigarettes*)
Schachtel f
pad [pæd] n (*of paper*) Schreibblock m;
(*padding*) Polster nt; **padded envelope** n
wattierter Umschlag; **padding** n
(*material*) Polsterung f

paddle [ˈpædl] n (*for boat*) Paddel nt ⊳ vi
(*in boat*) paddeln; **paddling pool** n (*Brit*)
Planschbecken nt
padlock [ˈpædlɒk] n Vorhängeschloss nt
page [peɪdʒ] n (*of book etc*) Seite f
pager [ˈpeɪdʒə] n Piepser m
paid [peɪd] pt, pp of **pay** ⊳ adj bezahlt
pain [peɪn] n Schmerz m; **to be in
~** Schmerzen haben; **she's a (real) ~** sie
nervt; **painful** adj (*physically*)
schmerzhaft; (*embarrassing*) peinlich;
painkiller n schmerzstillendes Mittel
painstaking adj sorgfältig
paint [peɪnt] n Farbe f ⊳ vt anstreichen;
(*picture*) malen; **paintbrush** n Pinsel m;
painter n Maler(in) m(f); **painting** n
(*picture*) Bild nt, Gemälde nt
pair [peə] n Paar nt; **a ~ of shoes** ein Paar
Schuhe; **a ~ of scissors** eine Schere; **a ~ of
trousers** eine Hose
pajamas [pəˈdʒɑːməz] npl (*US*)
Schlafanzug m
Pakistan [pɑːkɪˈstɑːn] n Pakistan nt
pal [pæl] n (*fam*) Kumpel m
palace [ˈpæləs] n Palast m
pale [peɪl] adj (*face*) blass, bleich; (*colour*)
hell
palm [pɑːm] n (*of hand*) Handfläche f;
~ (tree) Palme f; **palmtop (computer)** n
Palmtop(computer) m
pamper [ˈpæmpə] vt verhätscheln
pan [pæn] n (*saucepan*) Topf m; (*frying pan*)
Pfanne f; **pancake** [ˈpænkeɪk] n
Pfannkuchen m; **Pancake Day** n (*Brit*)
Fastnachtsdienstag m
panda [ˈpændə] n Panda m
pane [peɪn] n Scheibe f
panel [ˈpænl] n (*of wood*) Tafel f; (*in
discussion*) Diskussionsteilnehmer pl
panic [ˈpænɪk] n Panik f ⊳ vi in Panik
geraten; **panicky** [ˈpænɪkɪ] adj panisch
pansy [ˈpænzɪ] n (*flower*) Stiefmütterchen
nt
panties [ˈpæntɪz] npl (*Damen)slip m
pantomime [ˈpæntəmaɪm] n (*Brit*) um die
Weihnachtszeit aufgeführte Märchenkomödie
pants [pænts] npl Unterhose f; (*esp US:
trousers*) Hose f
pantyhose [ˈpæntɪhəʊz] npl (*US*)
Strumpfhose f; **panty-liner** n Slipeinlage
f
paper [ˈpeɪpə] n Papier nt; (*newspaper*)
Zeitung f; (*exam*) Klausur f; (*for reading at

conference) Referat *nt*; **~s** *pl* (*identity papers*)
Papiere *pl*; **~ bag** Papiertüte *f*; **~ cup**
Pappbecher *m* ▷ *vt* (*wall*) tapezieren;
paperback *n* Taschenbuch *nt*; **paper clip**
n Büroklammer *f*; **paper feed** *n* (*of printer*)
Papiereinzug *m*; **paper round** *n* **to do a**
~ Zeitungen austragen; **paperwork** *n*
Schreibarbeit *f*
parachute ['pærəʃuːt] *n* Fallschirm *m*
▷ *vi* abspringen
paracetamol [pærə'siːtəmɒl] *n* (*tablet*)
Paracetamoltablette *f*
parade [pə'reɪd] *n* (*procession*) Umzug *m*;
(*Mil*) Parade *f* ▷ *vi* vorbeimarschieren
paradise ['pærədaɪs] *n* Paradies *nt*
paragliding ['pærəglaɪdɪŋ] *n*
Gleitschirmfliegen *nt*
paragraph ['pærəɡrɑːf] *n* Absatz *m*
parallel ['pærəlel] *adj* parallel ▷ *n* (*Math*,
fig) Parallele *f*
paralyze ['pærəlaɪz] *vt* lähmen; (*fig*)
lahm legen
paranoid ['pærənɔɪd] *adj* paranoid
paraphrase ['pærəfreɪz] *vt* umschreiben;
(*sth spoken*) anders ausdrücken
parasailing ['pærəseɪlɪŋ] *n* Parasailing *nt*
parasol ['pærəsɒl] *n* Sonnenschirm *m*
parcel ['pɑːsl] *n* Paket *nt*
pardon ['pɑːdn] *n* (*Jur*) Begnadigung *f*;
~ me/I beg your ~ verzeihen Sie bitte;
(*objection*) aber ich bitte Sie; **I beg your ~?/**
~ me? wie bitte?
parent ['peərənt] *n* Elternteil *m*; **~s** *pl*
Eltern *pl*; **~s-in-law** *pl* Schwiegereltern *pl*;
parental [pə'rentl] *adj* elterlich, Eltern-
parish ['pærɪʃ] *n* Gemeinde *f*
park [pɑːk] *n* Park *m* ▷ *vt*, *vi* parken;
parking *n* Parken *nt*; **'no ~'** „Parken
verboten"; **parking brake** *n* (*US*)
Handbremse *f*; **parking disc** *n*
Parkscheibe *f*; **parking fine** *n* Geldbuße *f*
für falsches Parken; **parking lights** *npl*
(*US*) Standlicht *nt*; **parking lot** *n* (*US*)
Parkplatz *m*; **parking meter** *n* Parkuhr *f*;
parking place, **parking space** *n*
Parkplatz *m*; **parking ticket** *n*
Strafzettel *m*
parliament ['pɑːləmənt] *n* Parlament *nt*
parrot ['pærət] *n* Papagei *m*
parsley ['pɑːslɪ] *n* Petersilie *f*
parsnip ['pɑːsnɪp] *n* Pastinake *f*
(*längliches, weißes Wurzelgemüse*)
part [pɑːt] *n* Teil *m*, (*of machine*) Teil *nt*;

(*Theat*) Rolle *f*, (*US: in hair*) Scheitel *m*; **to**
take ~ teilnehmen (*in an +dat*); **for the**
most ~ zum größten Teil ▷ *adj* Teil- ▷ *vt*
(*separate*) trennen; (*hair*) scheiteln ▷ *vi*
(*people*) sich trennen
partial ['pɑːʃəl] *adj* (*incomplete*) teilweise,
Teil-; (*biased*) parteiisch
participant [pɑː'tɪsɪpənt] *n*
Teilnehmer(in) *m(f)*; **participate**
[pɑː'tɪsɪpeɪt] *vi* teilnehmen (*in an +dat*)
particular [pə'tɪkjʊlə*] *adj* (*specific*)
bestimmt; (*exact*) genau; (*fussy*) eigen; **in**
~ insbesondere ▷ *n* **~s** *pl* (*details*)
Einzelheiten *pl*; (*about person*) Personalien
pl; **particularly** *adv* besonders
parting ['pɑːtɪŋ] *n* (*farewell*) Abschied *m*;
(*Brit: in hair*) Scheitel *m*
partly ['pɑːtlɪ] *adv* teilweise
partner ['pɑːtnə*] *n* Partner(in) *m(f)*;
partnership *n* Partnerschaft *f*
partridge ['pɑːtrɪdʒ] *n* Rebhuhn *nt*
part-time ['pɑːt'taɪm] *adj* Teilzeit- ▷ *adv*
to work ~ Teilzeit arbeiten
party ['pɑːtɪ] *n* (*celebration*) Party *f*,
(*Pol*, *Jur*) Partei *f*, (*group*) Gruppe *f* ▷ *vi*
feiern
pass [pɑːs] *vt* (*on foot*) vorbeigehen an
+dat; (*in car etc*) vorbeifahren an *+dat*;
(*time*) verbringen; (*exam*) bestehen; (*law*)
verabschieden; **to ~ sth to sb**, **to ~ sb sth**
jdm etw reichen; **to ~ the ball to sb** jdm
den Ball zuspielen ▷ *vi* (*on foot*)
vorbeigehen; (*in car etc*) vorbeifahren;
(*years*) vergehen; (*in exam*) bestehen ▷ *n*
(*document*) Ausweis *m*; (*Sport*) Pass *m*; **pass**
away *vi* (*die*) verscheiden; **pass by** *vi* (*on*
foot) vorbeigehen; (*in car etc*) vorbeifahren
▷ *vt* (*on foot*) vorbeigehen an *+dat*; (*in car*
etc) vorbeifahren an *+dat*; **pass on** *vt*
weitergeben (*to an +akk*); (*disease*)
übertragen (*to auf +akk*); **pass out** *vi*
(*faint*) ohnmächtig werden; **pass round** *vt*
herumreichen
passage ['pæsɪdʒ] *n* (*corridor*) Gang *m*; (*in*
book, *music*) Passage *f*, **passageway** *n*
Durchgang *m*
passenger ['pæsɪndʒə*] *n* Passagier(in)
m(f); (*on bus*) Fahrgast *m*; (*on train*)
Reisende(r) *mf*; (*in car*) Mitfahrer(in) *m(f)*
passer-by ['pɑːsə'baɪ] (*pl* **passers-by**) *n*
Passant(in) *m(f)*
passion ['pæʃən] *n* Leidenschaft *f*,
passionate ['pæʃənɪt] *adj*

leidenschaftlich; **passion fruit** n
Passionsfrucht

passive ['pæsɪv] adj passiv ▷ n ~ **(voice)**
(Ling) Passiv nt

passport ['pɑːspɔːt] n (Reise)pass m;
passport control n Passkontrolle f

password ['pɑːswɜːd] n (Inform)
Passwort nt

past [pɑːst] n Vergangenheit f ▷ adv (by)
vorbei; **it's five** ~ es ist fünf nach ▷ adj
(years) vergangen; (president etc) ehemalig;
in the ~ two months in den letzten zwei
Monaten ▷ prep (telling time) nach; **it's
half** ~ **10** es ist halb 11; **to go** ~ **sth** an etw
dat vorbeigehen/-fahren

pasta ['pæstə] n Nudeln pl

paste [peɪst] vt (stick) kleben; (Inform)
einfügen ▷ n (glue) Kleister m

pastime ['pɑːstaɪm] n Zeitvertreib m

pastry ['peɪstrɪ] n Teig m; (cake)
Stückchen

pasty ['pæstɪ] n (Brit) Pastete f

patch [pætʃ] n (area) Fleck m; (for mending)
Flicken ▷ vt flicken; **patchy** adj (uneven)
ungleichmäßig

pâté ['pæteɪ] n Pastete f

paternal [pəˈtɜːnl] adj väterlich;
~ **grandmother** Großmutter f
väterlicherseits; **paternity leave**
[pəˈtɜːnɪtɪliːv] n Elternzeit f (des Vaters)

path [pɑːθ] n (a. Inform) Pfad m; (a. fig)
Weg m

pathetic [pəˈθetɪk] adj (bad) kläglich,
erbärmlich; **it's** ~ es ist zum Heulen

patience ['peɪʃəns] n Geduld f; (Brit Cards)
Patience f; **patient** adj geduldig ▷ n
Patient(in) m(f)

patio ['pætɪəʊ] n Terrasse f

patriotic [pætrɪˈɒtɪk] adj patriotisch

patrol car [pəˈtrəʊlkɑː*] n Streifenwagen
m; **patrolman** (pl -**men**) n (US)
Streifenpolizist m

patron ['peɪtrən] n (sponsor) Förderer m,
Förderin f; (in shop) Kunde m, Kundin f

patronize ['pætrənaɪz] vt (treat
condescendingly) von oben herab
behandeln; **patronizing** adj (attitude)
herablassend

pattern ['pætən] n Muster nt

pause [pɔːz] n Pause f ▷ vi (speaker)
innehalten

pavement n (Brit) Bürgersteig m; (US)
Pflaster nt

pay [peɪ] (**paid, paid**) vt bezahlen; **he
paid (me) £20 for it** er hat (mir) 20 Pfund
dafür gezahlt; **to** ~ **attention** Acht geben
(to auf +akk); **to** ~ **sb a visit** jdn besuchen
▷ vi zahlen; (be profitable) sich bezahlt
machen; **to** ~ **for sth** etw bezahlen ▷ n
Bezahlung f, Lohn m; **pay back** vt (money)
zurückzahlen; **pay in** vt (into account)
einzahlen; **payable** adj zahlbar; (due)
fällig; **payday** n Zahltag m; **payee** [peɪˈiː]
n Zahlungsempfänger(in) m(f); **payment**
n Bezahlung f; (money) Zahlung f;
pay-per-view adj- Pay-per-View-; **pay
phone** n Münzfernsprecher m; **pay TV** n
Pay-TV nt

PC abbr = **personal computer** PC
m; abbr = **politically correct** politisch
korrekt

PDA abbr = **personal digital assistant**
PDA m

PE abbr = **physical education** (school)
Sport m

pea [piː] n Erbse f

peace [piːs] n Frieden m; **peaceful** adj
friedlich

peach [piːtʃ] n Pfirsich m

peacock ['piːkɒk] n Pfau m

peak [piːk] n (of mountain) Gipfel m; (fig)
Höhepunkt m; **peak period** n Stoßzeit f;
(season) Hochsaison

peanut ['piːnʌt] n Erdnuss f; **peanut
butter** n Erdnussbutter f

pear [peə*] n Birne f

pearl [pɜːl] n Perle f

pebble ['pebl] n Kiesel m

pecan [prˈkæn] n Pekannuss

peck [pek] vt, vi picken; **peckish** adj (Brit
fam) ein bisschen hungrig

peculiar [prˈkjuːlɪə*] adj (odd) seltsam;
~ **to** charakteristisch für; **peculiarity**
[pɪkjʊlɪˈærɪtɪ] n (singular quality)
Besonderheit f; (strangeness)
Eigenartigkeit f

pedal ['pedl] n Pedal nt

pedestrian [prˈdestrɪən] n Fußgänger(in)
m(f); **pedestrian crossing** n
Fußgängerüberweg m

pee [piː] vi (fam) pinkeln

peel [piːl] n Schale f ▷ vt schälen ▷ vi
(paint etc) abblättern; (skin etc) sich
schälen

peer [pɪə*] n Gleichaltrige(r) mf ▷ vi
starren

peg [peg] n (for coat etc) Haken m; (for tent) Hering m; **(clothes)** ~ (Wäsche)klammer f

pelvis ['pelvɪs] n Becken nt

pen [pen] n (ball-point) Kuli m, Kugelschreiber; (fountain ~) Füller m

penalize ['pi:nəlaɪz] vt (punish) bestrafen; **penalty** ['penltɪ] n (punishment) Strafe f; (in football) Elfmeter m

pence [pens] pl of **penny**

pencil ['pensl] n Bleistift m; **pencil sharpener** n (Bleistift)spitzer m

penetrate ['penɪtreɪt] vt durchdringen; (enter into) eindringen in +akk

penfriend ['penfrend] n Brieffreund(in) m(f)

penguin ['peŋgwɪn] n Pinguin m

penicillin [penɪ'sɪlɪn] n Penizillin nt

peninsula [pɪ'nɪnsjʊlə] n Halbinsel f

penis ['pi:nɪs] n Penis m

penknife ['pennaɪf] (pl **penknives**) n Taschenmesser nt

penny ['penɪ] (pl **pence** o **pennies**) n (Brit) Penny m; (US) Centstück nt

pension ['penʃən] n Rente f; (for civil servants, executives etc) Pension f; **pensioner** n Rentner(in) m(f); **pension plan, pension scheme** n Rentenversicherung f

penultimate [pɪ'nʌltɪmət] adj vorletzte(r, s)

people ['pi:pl] npl (persons) Leute pl; (von Staat) Volk nt; (inhabitants) Bevölkerung f; **people carrier** n Minivan m

pepper ['pepə*] n Pfeffer m; (vegetable) Paprika m; **peppermint** n (sweet) Pfefferminz nt

per [pɜ:*] prep pro; ~ **annum** pro Jahr; ~ **cent** Prozent nt

percentage [pə'sentɪdʒ] n Prozentsatz m

perceptible [pə'septəbl] adj wahrnehmbar

percolator ['pɜ:kəleɪtə*] n Kaffeemaschine f

percussion [pɜ:'kʌʃən] n (Mus) Schlagzeug nt

perfect ['pɜ:fɪkt] adj perfekt; (utter) völlig ▷ [pə'fekt] vt vervollkommnen; **perfectly** adv perfekt; (utterly) völlig

perform [pə'fɔ:m] vt (task) ausführen; (play) aufführen; (Med: operation) durchführen ▷ vi (Theat) auftreten;

performance n (show) Vorstellung f; (efficiency) Leistung f

perfume ['pɜ:fju:m] n Duft m; (substance) Parfüm nt

perhaps [pə'hæps] adv vielleicht

peril ['perɪl] n Gefahr f

period ['pɪərɪəd] n (length of time) Zeit f; (in history) Zeitalter nt; (school) Stunde f; (Med) Periode f; (US: full stop) Punkt m; **for a ~ of three years** für einen Zeitraum von drei Jahren; **periodical** [pɪərɪ'ɒdɪkəl] n Zeitschrift f

peripheral [pə'rɪfərəl] n (Inform) Peripheriegerät nt

perish ['perɪʃ] vi (die) umkommen; (material) verderben

perjury ['pɜ:dʒərɪ] n Meineid m

perm [pɜ:m] n Dauerwelle f

permanent, permanently ['pɜ:mənənt, -lɪ] adj, adv ständig

permission [pə'mɪʃən] n Erlaubnis f; **permit** ['pɜ:mɪt] n Genehmigung f ▷ [pə'mɪt] vt erlauben, zulassen; **to ~ sb to do sth** jdm erlauben, etw zu tun

persecute ['pɜ:sɪkju:t] vt verfolgen

perseverance [pɜ:sɪ'vɪərəns] n Ausdauer f

Persian ['pɜ:ʃən] adj persisch

persist [pə'sɪst] vi (in belief etc) bleiben (in bei); (rain, smell) andauern; **persistent** adj beharrlich

person ['pɜ:sn] n Mensch m; (in official context) Person f; **in ~** persönlich; **personal** adj persönlich; (private) privat; **personality** [pɜ:sə'nælətɪ] n Persönlichkeit f; **personal organizer** n Organizer m; **personal stereo** (pl **-s**) n Walkman® m; **personnel** [pɜ:sə'nel] n Personal nt

perspective [pə'spektɪv] n Perspektive f

perspire [pə'spaɪə*] vi schwitzen

persuade [pə'sweɪd] vt überreden; (convince) überzeugen; **persuasive** [pə'sweɪsɪv] adj überzeugend

perverse [pə'vɜ:s] adj pervers; (obstinate) eigensinnig; **pervert** ['pɜ:vɜ:t] n Perverse(r) mf ▷ [pə'vɜ:t] vt (morally) verderben

pessimist ['pesɪmɪst] n Pessimist(in) m(f); **pessimistic** [pesɪ'mɪstɪk] adj pessimistisch

pest [pest] n (insect) Schädling m; (fig: person) Nervensäge f; (thing) Plage f;

pester ['pestə*] vt plagen; **pesticide** ['pestɪsaɪd] n Schädlingsbekämpf-ungsmittel nt

pet [pet] n (animal) Haustier nt; (person) Liebling m

petal ['petl] n Blütenblatt nt

petition [pə'tɪʃən] n Petition f

petrol ['petrəl] n (Brit) Benzin nt; **petrol pump** n (at garage) Zapfsäule f; **petrol station** n Tankstelle f; **petrol tank** n Benzintank m

pharmacy ['fɑːməsɪ] n (shop) Apotheke f

phase [feɪz] n Phase f

PhD abbr = Doctor of Philosophy Dr. phil; (dissertation) Doktorarbeit f; **to do one's ~** promovieren

pheasant ['feznt] n Fasan m

phenomenon [fɪ'nɒmɪnən] (pl **phenomena**) n Phänomen nt

Philippines ['fɪlɪpiːnz] npl Philippinen pl

philosophical [fɪlə'sɒfɪkəl] adj philosophisch; (fig) gelassen; **philosophy** [fɪ'lɒsəfɪ] n Philosophie f

phone [fəʊn] n Telefon nt ▷ vt, vi anrufen; **phone book** n Telefonbuch nt; **phone bill** n Telefonrechnung f; **phone booth**, **phone box** (Brit) n Telefonzelle f; **phonecall** n Telefonanruf m; **phonecard** n Telefonkarte f; **phone-in** n Rundfunkprogramm, bei dem Hörer anrufen können; **phone number** n Telefonnummer f

photo ['fəʊtəʊ] (pl **-s**) n Foto nt; **photo booth** n Fotoautomat m; **photocopier** ['fəʊtəʊkɒpɪə*] n Kopiergerät nt; **photocopy** ['fəʊtəʊkɒpɪ] n Fotokopie f ▷ vt fotokopieren; **photograph** ['fəʊtəɡrɑːf] n Fotografie f, Aufnahme f ▷ vt fotografieren; **photographer** [fə'tɒɡrəfə*] n Fotograf(in) m(f); **photography** [fə'tɒɡrəfɪ] n Fotografie f

phrase [freɪz] n (expression) Redewendung f, Ausdruck m; **phrase book** n Sprachführer m

physical ['fɪzɪkəl] adj (bodily) körperlich, physisch ▷ n ärztliche Untersuchung; **physically** adv (bodily) körperlich, physisch; **~ handicapped** körperbehindert

physician [fɪ'zɪʃən] n Arzt m, Ärztin f

physics ['fɪzɪks] nsing (=subject) Physik f

physiotherapy [fɪzɪə'θerəpɪ] n Physiotherapie f

physique [fɪ'ziːk] n Körperbau m

piano ['pjɑːnəʊ] (pl **-s**) n Klavier nt

pick [pɪk] vt (flowers, fruit) pflücken; (choose) auswählen; (team) aufstellen; **pick out** vt auswählen; **pick up** vt (lift up) aufheben; (collect) abholen; (learn) lernen

pickle ['pɪkl] n (food) (Mixed) Pickles pl ▷ vt einlegen

pickpocket ['pɪkpɒkɪt] n Taschendieb(in) m(f)

picnic ['pɪknɪk] n Picknick nt

picture ['pɪktʃə*] n Bild nt; **to go to the ~s** (Brit) ins Kino gehen ▷ vt (visualize) sich vorstellen; **picture book** n Bilderbuch nt; **picturesque** [pɪktʃə'resk] adj malerisch

pie [paɪ] n (meat) Pastete f; (fruit) Kuchen m

piece [piːs] n Stück nt; (part) Teil nt; (in chess) Figur f; (in draughts) Stein m; **a ~ of cake** ein Stück Kuchen; **to fall to ~s** auseinanderfallen

pier [pɪə*] n Pier m

pierce [pɪəs] vt durchstechen, durchbohren; (cold, sound) durchdringen; **pierced** adj (part of body) gepierct; **piercing** adj durchdringend

pig [pɪɡ] n Schwein nt

pigeon ['pɪdʒən] n Taube f; **pigeonhole** n (compartment) Ablegefach nt

piggy ['pɪɡɪ] adj (fam) verfressen; **pigheaded** ['pɪɡ'hedɪd] adj dickköpfig; **piglet** ['pɪɡlət] n Ferkel nt; **pigsty** ['pɪɡstaɪ] n Schweinestall m; **pigtail** ['pɪɡteɪl] n Zopf m

pile [paɪl] n (heap) Haufen m; (one on top of another) Stapel m; **pile up** vi (accumulate) sich anhäufen

piles [paɪlz] npl Hämorr(ho)iden pl

pile-up ['paɪlʌp] n (Auto) Massenkarambolage f

pilgrim ['pɪlɡrɪm] n Pilger(in) m(f)

pill [pɪl] n Tablette f; **the ~** die (Antibaby)pille; **to be on the ~** die Pille nehmen

pillar ['pɪlə*] n Pfeiler m

pillow ['pɪləʊ] n (Kopf)kissen nt; **pillowcase** n (Kopf)kissenbezug m

pilot ['paɪlət] n (Aviat) Pilot(in) m(f)

pimple ['pɪmpl] n Pickel m

pin [pɪn] n (for fixing) Nadel f; (in sewing) Stecknadel f; (Tech) Stift m; **I've got ~s and needles in my leg** mein Bein ist mir eingeschlafen ▷ vt (fix with ~) heften (to an +akk)

PIN [pɪn] acr = **personal identification number, PIN (number)** PIN f, Geheimzahl f

pincers ['pɪnsəz] npl (tool) Kneifzange f

pinch [pɪntʃ] n (of salt) Prise f ▷ vt zwicken; (fam: steal) klauen ▷ vi (shoe) drücken

pine [paɪn] n Kiefer f

pineapple ['paɪnæpl] n Ananas f

pink [pɪŋk] adj rosa

pinstripe(d) ['pɪnstraɪp(t)] adj Nadelstreifen-

pint [paɪnt] n Pint nt (Brit: 0,57 l, US: 0,473l); (Brit: glass of beer) Bier nt

pious ['paɪəs] adj fromm

pip [pɪp] n (of fruit) Kern m

pipe [paɪp] n (for smoking) Pfeife f; (for water, gas) Rohrleitung f

pirate ['paɪərɪt] n Pirat(in) m(f); **pirated copy** n Raubkopie f

Pisces ['paɪsiːz] nsing (Astr) Fische pl; **she's a ~** sie ist Fisch

pistachio [pɪˈstɑːʃɪəʊ] (pl -s) n Pistazie f

piste [piːst] n (Ski) Piste f

pistol ['pɪstl] n Pistole f

pit [pɪt] n (hole) Grube f; (coalmine) Zeche f; **the ~s** (in motor racing) die Box; **to be the ~s** (fam) grottenschlecht sein

pitch [pɪtʃ] n (Sport) Spielfeld nt; (Mus: of instrument) Tonlage f; (of voice) Stimmlage f ▷ vt (tent) aufschlagen; (throw) werfen; **pitch-black** adj pechschwarz

pitcher ['pɪtʃə*] n (US: jug) Krug m

pitiful ['pɪtɪful] adj (contemptible) jämmerlich

pitta bread ['pɪtəbred] n Pittabrot nt

pity ['pɪtɪ] n Mitleid nt; **what a ~** wie schade; **it's a ~** es ist schade ▷ vt Mitleid haben mit

pizza ['piːtsə] n Pizza f

place [pleɪs] n m (spot, in text) Stelle f; (town etc) Ort; (house) Haus nt; (position, seat, on course) Platz m; **~ of birth** Geburtsort m; **at my ~** bei mir; **in third ~** auf dem dritten Platz; **to three decimal ~s** bis auf drei Stellen nach dem Komma; **out of ~** nicht an der richtigen Stelle; (fig: remark) unangebracht; **in ~ of** anstelle von; **in the first ~** (firstly) erstens; (immediately) gleich; (in any case) überhaupt ▷ vt (put) stellen, setzen; (lay flat) legen; (advertisement) setzen (in in +akk); (Comm: order) aufgeben; **place mat** n Set nt

plague [pleɪg] n Pest f

plaice [pleɪs] n Scholle f

plain [pleɪn] adj (clear) klar, deutlich; (simple) einfach; (not beautiful) unattraktiv; (yoghurt) Natur-; (Brit: chocolate) (Zart)bitter- ▷ n Ebene f; **plainly** adv (frankly) offen; (simply) einfach; (obviously) eindeutig

plait [plæt] n Zopf m ▷ vt flechten

plan [plæn] n Plan m; (for essay etc) Konzept nt ▷ vt planen; **to ~ to do sth, to ~ on doing sth** vorhaben, etw zu tun ▷ vi planen

plane [pleɪn] n (aircraft) Flugzeug nt; (tool) Hobel m; (Math) Ebene f

planet ['plænɪt] n Planet m

plank [plæŋk] n Brett nt

plant [plɑːnt] n Pflanze f; (equipment) Maschinen pl; (factory) Werk nt ▷ vt (tree etc) pflanzen; **plantation** [plænˈteɪʃən] n Plantage f

plaque [plæk] n Gedenktafel f; (on teeth) Zahnbelag m

plaster ['plɑːstə*] n (Brit Med: sticking plaster) Pflaster nt; (on wall) Verputz m; **to have one's arm in ~** den Arm in Gips haben

plastered ['plɑːstəd] adj (fam) besoffen; **to get (absolutely) ~** sich besaufen

plastic ['plæstɪk] n Kunststoff m; **to pay with ~** mit Kreditkarte bezahlen ▷ adj Plastik-; **plastic bag** n Plastiktüte f, **plastic surgery** n plastische Chirurgie f

plate [pleɪt] n (for food) Teller m; (flat sheet) Platte f; (plaque) Schild nt

platform ['plætfɔːm] n (Rail) Bahnsteig m; (at meeting) Podium nt

platinum ['plætɪnəm] n Platin nt

play [pleɪ] n Spiel nt; (Theat) (Theater)stück nt ▷ vt spielen; (another player or team) spielen gegen; **to ~ the piano** Klavier spielen; **to ~ a part in** (fig) eine Rolle spielen bei ▷ vi spielen; **play at** vt **what are you ~ing at?** was soll das?; **play back** vt abspielen; **play down** vt herunterspielen

playacting n Schauspielerei f; **playback** n Wiedergabe f; **player** n Spieler(in) m(f); **playful** adj (person) verspielt; (remark) scherzhaft; **playground** n Spielplatz m; (in school) Schulhof m; **playgroup** n Spielgruppe f; **playing card** n Spielkarte f; **playing field** n Sportplatz m; **playmate** n Spielkamerad(in) m(f); **playwright** n Dramatiker(in) m(f)

plc abbr = public limited company AG f

plea [pliː] n Bitte f (for um)

plead [pliːd] vi dringend bitten (with sb jdn); (Jur) **to ~ guilty** sich schuldig bekennen

pleasant, pleasantly ['plɛznt, -lɪ] adj, adv angenehm

please [pliːz] adv bitte; **more tea? - yes, ~** noch Tee? - ja, bitte ▷ vt (be agreeable to) gefallen +dat; **~ yourself** wie du willst; **pleased** adj zufrieden; (glad) erfreut; **~ to meet you** freut mich, angenehm; **pleasing** adj erfreulich; **pleasure** ['plɛʒə*] n Vergnügen nt, Freude f; **it's a ~** gern geschehen

pledge [plɛdʒ] n (promise) Versprechen nt ▷ vt (promise) versprechen

plenty ['plɛntɪ] n **~ of** eine Menge, viel(e); **to be ~** genug sein, reichen; **I've got ~** ich habe mehr als genug ▷ adv (US fam) ganz schön

pliable ['plaɪəbl] adj biegsam

pliers ['plaɪəz] npl (Kombi)zange f

plimsolls ['plɪmsəlz] npl (Brit) Turnschuhe pl

plonk [plɒŋk] n (Brit fam: wine) billiger Wein ▷ vt **to ~ sth (down)** etw hinknallen

plot [plɒt] n (of story) Handlung f; (conspiracy) Komplott nt; (of land) Stück nt Land, Grundstück nt ▷ vi ein Komplott schmieden

plough, plow (US) [plaʊ] n Pflug m ▷ vt, vi (Agr) pflügen; **ploughman's lunch** n (Brit) in einer Kneipe serviertes Gericht aus Käse, Brot, Mixed Pickles etc

pluck [plʌk] vt (eyebrows, guitar) zupfen; (chicken) rupfen; **pluck up** vt **to ~ (one's) courage** Mut aufbringen

plug [plʌg] n (for sink, bath) Stöpsel m; (Elec) Stecker m; (Auto) (Zünd)kerze f; (fam: publicity) Schleichwerbung f ▷ vt (fam: advertise) Reklame machen für; **plug in** vt anschließen

plum [plʌm] n Pflaume f ▷ adj (fam: job etc) Super-

plumber ['plʌmə*] n Klempner(in) m(f); **plumbing** ['plʌmɪŋ] n (fittings) Leitungen pl; (craft) Installieren nt

plump [plʌmp] adj rundlich

plunge [plʌndʒ] vt (knife) stoßen; (into water) tauchen ▷ vi stürzen; (into water) tauchen

plural ['plʊərəl] n Plural m

plus [plʌs] prep plus; (as well as) und ▷ adj Plus-; **20 ~** mehr als 20 ▷ n (fig) Plus nt

plywood ['plaɪwʊd] n Sperrholz nt

pm abbr = post meridiem **at 3 ~** um 3 Uhr nachmittags; **at 8 ~** um 8 Uhr abends

pneumonia [njuːˈməʊnɪə] n Lungenentzündung f

poached [pəʊtʃt] adj (egg) pochiert, verloren

PO Box abbr = post office box Postfach nt

pocket ['pɒkɪt] n Tasche f ▷ vt (put in ~) einstecken; **pocketbook** n (US: wallet) Brieftasche f; **pocket calculator** n Taschenrechner m; **pocket money** n Taschengeld nt

poem ['pəʊɪm] n Gedicht nt; **poet** ['pəʊɪt] n Dichter(in) m(f); **poetic** [pəʊˈɛtɪk] adj poetisch; **poetry** ['pəʊɪtrɪ] n (art) Dichtung f; (poems) Gedichte pl

point [pɔɪnt] n Punkt m; (spot) Stelle f; (sharp tip) Spitze f; (moment) Zeitpunkt m; (purpose) Zweck m; (idea) Argument nt; (decimal) Dezimalstelle f; **~s** pl (Rail) Weiche f; **~ of view** Standpunkt m; **three ~ two** drei Komma zwei; **at some ~** irgendwann (mal); **to get to the ~** zur Sache kommen; **there's no ~** es hat keinen Sinn; **I was on the ~ of leaving** ich wollte gerade gehen ▷ vt (gun etc) richten (at auf +akk); **to ~ one's finger at** mit dem Finger zeigen auf +akk ▷ vi (with finger etc) zeigen (at, to auf +akk); **point out** vt (indicate) aufzeigen; (mention) hinweisen auf +akk; **pointed** adj spitz; (question) gezielt; **pointer** n (on dial) Zeiger m; (tip) Hinweis m; **pointless** adj sinnlos

poison ['pɔɪzn] n Gift nt ▷ vt vergiften; **poisonous** adj giftig

poke [pəʊk] vt (with stick, finger) stoßen, stupsen; (put) stecken

Poland ['pəʊlənd] n Polen nt

polar ['pəʊlə*] adj Polar-, polar; **~ bear** Eisbär m

pole [pəʊl] n Stange f; (Geo, Elec) Pol m

Pole [pəʊl] n Pole m, Polin f

pole vault n Stabhochsprung m

police [pə'li:s] n Polizei f; **police car** n
Polizeiwagen m; **policeman** (pl -men) n
Polizist m; **police station** n
(Polizei)wache f; **policewoman** (pl
-women) n Polizistin f

policy ['pɒlɪsɪ] n (plan) Politik f; (principle)
Grundsatz m; (insurance ~)
(Versicherungs)police f

polio ['pəʊlɪəʊ] n Kinderlähmung f

polish ['pɒlɪʃ] n (for furniture) Politur f; (for
floor) Wachs nt; (for shoes) Creme f; (shine)
Glanz m; (fig) Schliff m ▷ vt polieren;
(shoes) putzen; (fig) den letzten Schliff
geben +dat

Polish ['pəʊlɪʃ] adj polnisch ▷ n Polnisch
nt

polite [pə'laɪt] adj höflich; **politeness** n
Höflichkeit f

political, politically [pə'lɪtɪkəl, -ɪ] adj, adv
politisch; **~ly correct** politisch korrekt;
politician [pɒlɪ'tɪʃən] n Politiker(in) m(f);
politics ['pɒlɪtɪks] nsing o pl Politik f

poll [pəʊl] n (election) Wahl f; (opinion ~)
Umfrage f

pollen ['pɒlən] n Pollen m, Blütenstaub m;
pollen count n Pollenflug m

polling station ['pəʊlɪŋsteɪʃən] n
Wahllokal nt

pollute [pə'lu:t] vt verschmutzen;
pollution [pə'lu:ʃən] n Verschmutzung f

pompous ['pɒmpəs] adj aufgeblasen;
(language) geschwollen

pond [pɒnd] n Teich m

ponder ['pɒndə*] vt nachdenken über
+akk

pony ['pəʊnɪ] n Pony nt; **ponytail** n
Pferdeschwanz m

poodle ['pu:dl] n Pudel m

pool [pu:l] n (swimming ~) Schwimmbad
nt; (private) Swimmingpool m; (of spilt
liquid, blood) Lache f; (game) Poolbillard nt
▷ vt (money etc) zusammenlegen

poor [pɔ:*] adj arm; (not good) schlecht
▷ npl **the ~** die Armen pl; **poorly** adv
(badly) schlecht ▷ adj (Brit) krank

pop [pɒp] n (music) Pop m; (noise) Knall m
▷ vt (put) stecken; (balloon) platzen lassen
▷ vi (balloon) platzen; (cork) knallen; **to
~ in** (person) vorbeischauen; **pop concert**
n Popkonzert nt; **popcorn** n Popcorn nt

Pope [pəʊp] n Papst m

pop group ['pɒpgru:p] n Popgruppe f;
pop music n Popmusik f

poppy ['pɒpɪ] n Mohn m

Popsicle® ['pɒpsɪkl] n (US) Eis nt am
Stiel

pop star ['pɒpstɑ:*] n Popstar m

popular ['pɒpjʊlə*] adj (well-liked) beliebt
(with bei); (widespread) weit verbreitet

population [pɒpjʊ'leɪʃən] n Bevölkerung
f; (of town) Einwohner pl

porcelain ['pɔ:slɪn] n Porzellan nt

porch [pɔ:tʃ] n Vorbau m; (US: verandah)
Veranda f

porcupine ['pɔ:kjʊpaɪn] n
Stachelschwein nt

pork [pɔ:k] n Schweinefleisch nt; **pork
chop** n Schweinekotelett; **pork pie** n
Schweinefleischpastete f

porn [pɔ:n] n Porno m; **pornographic**
[pɔ:nə'græfɪk] adj pornografisch;
pornography [pɔ:'nɒgrəfɪ] n
Pornografie f

porridge ['pɒrɪdʒ] n Haferbrei m

port [pɔ:t] n (harbour) Hafen m; (town)
Hafenstadt f; (Naut: left side) Backbord nt;
(wine) Portwein m; (Inform) Anschluss m

portable ['pɔ:təbl] adj tragbar; (radio)
Koffer-

portal ['pɔ:tl] n (Inform) Portal nt

porter ['pɔ:tə*] n Pförtner(in) m(f); (for
luggage) Gepäckträger m

porthole ['pɔ:thəʊl] n Bullauge nt

portion ['pɔ:ʃən] n Teil m; (of food) Portion
f

portrait ['pɔ:trɪt] n Porträt nt

portray [pɔ:'treɪ] vt darstellen

Portugal ['pɔ:tʃʊgl] n Portugal nt;
Portuguese [pɔ:tʃʊ'gi:z] adj
portugiesisch ▷ n Portugiese m,
Portugiesin f; (language) Portugiesisch nt

pose [pəʊz] n Haltung f ▷ vi posieren ▷ vt
(threat, problem) darstellen

posh [pɒʃ] adj (fam) piekfein

position [pə'zɪʃən] n Stellung f; (place)
Position f, Lage f; (job) Stelle f; (opinion)
Standpunkt m; **to be in a ~** in der
Lage sein, etw zu tun; **in third ~** auf
dem dritten Platz ▷ vt aufstellen; (Inform:
cursor) positionieren

positive ['pɒzɪtɪv] adj positiv; (convinced)
sicher; (definite) eindeutig

possess [pə'zes] vt besitzen; **possession**

[pə'zeʃən] n ~(s pl) Besitz m; **possessive** adj (person) Besitz ergreifend

possibility [pɒsə'bɪlɪtɪ] n Möglichkeit f; **possible** ['pɒsəbl] adj möglich; **if ~** wenn möglich; **as big/soon as ~** so groß/bald wie möglich; **possibly** adv (perhaps) vielleicht; **I've done all I ~ can** ich habe mein Möglichstes getan

post [pəʊst] n (mail) Post f; (pole) Pfosten m; (job) Stelle f ▷ vt (letters) aufgeben; **to keep sb ~ed** jdn auf dem Laufenden halten; **postage** ['pəʊstɪdʒ] n Porto nt; **~ and packing** Porto und Verpackung; **postal** adj Post-; (Brit) **~ order** Postanweisung f; **postbox** n Briefkasten m; **postcard** n Postkarte f; **postcode** n (Brit) Postleitzahl f

poster ['pəʊstə*] n Plakat nt, Poster nt

postgraduate [pəʊst'grædjʊɪt] n jmd, der seine Studien nach dem ersten akademischen Grad weiterführt

postman ['pəʊstmən] (pl **-men**) n Briefträger m; **postmark** n Poststempel m

postmortem [pəʊst'mɔːtəm] n Autopsie f

post office ['pəʊstɒfɪs] n Post® f; **post office box** n Postfach nt

postpone [pə'spəʊn] vt verschieben (till auf +akk)

posture ['pɒstʃə*] n Haltung f

pot [pɒt] n Topf m; (tea~, coffee ~) Kanne f; (fam: marijuana) Pot nt ▷ vt (plant) eintopfen

potato [pə'teɪtəʊ] (pl **-es**) n Kartoffel f; **potato chips** (US) npl Kartoffelchips pl; **potato peeler** n Kartoffelschäler m

potent ['pəʊtənt] adj stark

potential [pəʊ'tenʃəl] adj potenziell ▷ n Potenzial nt; **potentially** adv potenziell

pothole ['pɒthəʊl] n Höhle f; (in road) Schlagloch nt

potter about ['pɒtərəbaʊt] vi herumhantieren

pottery ['pɒtərɪ] n (objects) Töpferwaren pl

potty ['pɒtɪ] adj (Brit fam) verrückt ▷ n Töpfchen nt

poultry ['pəʊltrɪ] n Geflügel nt

pounce [paʊns] vi **to ~ on** sich stürzen auf +akk

pound [paʊnd] n (money) Pfund nt; (weight) Pfund nt (0,454 kg); **a ~ of cherries** ein Pfund Kirschen; **ten-~ note** Zehnpfundschein m

pour [pɔː*] vt (liquid) gießen; (rice, sugar etc) schütten; **to ~ sb sth** (drink) jdm etw eingießen; **pouring** adj (rain) strömend

poverty ['pɒvətɪ] n Armut f

powder ['paʊdə*] n Pulver nt; (cosmetic) Puder m; **powdered milk** n Milchpulver nt; **powder room** n Damentoilette f

power ['paʊə*] n Macht f; (ability) Fähigkeit f; (strength) Stärke f; (Elec) Strom m; **to be in ~** an der Macht sein ▷ vt betreiben, antreiben; **power-assisted steering** n Servolenkung f; **power cut** n Stromausfall m; **powerful** adj (politician etc) mächtig; (engine, government) stark; (argument) durchschlagend; **powerless** adj machtlos; **power station** n Kraftwerk nt

p&p abbr = postage and packing

PR abbr = public relations ▷ abbr = proportional representation

practical, practically ['præktɪkəl, -ɪ] adj, adv praktisch; **practice** ['præktɪs] n (training) Übung f; (custom) Gewohnheit f; (doctor's, lawyer's) Praxis f; **in ~** (in reality) in der Praxis; **out of ~** außer Übung; **to put sth into ~** etw in die Praxis umsetzen ▷ vt, vi (US) see **practise**; **practise** ['præktɪs] vt (instrument, movement) üben; (profession) ausüben ▷ vi üben; (doctor, lawyer) praktizieren

Prague [prɑːg] n Prag nt

praise [preɪz] n Lob nt ▷ vt loben

pram [præm] n (Brit) Kinderwagen m

prawn [prɔːn] n Garnele f, Krabbe f; **prawn crackers** npl Krabbenchips pl

pray [preɪ] vi beten; **to ~ for sth** (fig) stark auf etw akk hoffen; **prayer** ['preə*] n Gebet nt

pre- [priː] pref vor-, prä-

preach [priːtʃ] vi predigen

prearrange [priːə'reɪndʒ] vt im Voraus vereinbaren

precaution [prɪ'kɔːʃən] n Vorsichtsmaßnahme f

precede [prɪ'siːd] vt vorausgehen +dat; **preceding** adj vorhergehend

precinct ['priːsɪŋkt] n (Brit: pedestrian ~) Fußgängerzone f; (Brit: shopping ~) Einkaufsviertel nt; (US: district) Bezirk m

precious ['preʃəs] adj kostbar; **~ stone** Edelstein m

précis ['preɪsiː] n Zusammenfassung f
precise, precisely [prɪ'saɪs, -lɪ] adj, adv genau
precondition [priːkən'dɪʃən] n Vorbedingung f
predecessor ['priːdɪsesə*] n Vorgänger(in) m(f)
predicament [prɪ'dɪkəmənt] n missliche Lage
predict [prɪ'dɪkt] vt voraussagen; **predictable** adj vorhersehbar; (person) berechenbar
predominant [prɪ'dɒmɪnənt] adj vorherrschend; **predominantly** adv überwiegend
preface ['prefɪs] n Vorwort nt
prefer [prɪ'fɜː*] vt vorziehen (to dat), lieber mögen (to als); **to ~ to do sth** etw lieber tun; **preferably** ['prefrəblɪ] adv vorzugsweise, am liebsten; **preference** ['prefərəns] n (liking) Vorliebe f; **preferential** [prefə'renʃəl] adj **to get ~ treatment** bevorzugt behandelt werden
prefix ['priːfɪks] n (US Tel) Vorwahl f
pregnancy ['pregnənsɪ] n Schwangerschaft f; **pregnant** ['pregnənt] adj schwanger; **two months ~** im zweiten Monat schwanger
prejudice ['predʒʊdɪs] n Vorurteil nt; **prejudiced** adj (person) voreingenommen
preliminary [prɪ'lɪmɪnərɪ] adj (measures) vorbereitend; (results) vorläufig; (remarks) einleitend
premature ['premətʃʊə*] adj vorzeitig; (hasty) voreilig
premiere ['premɪɛə*] n Premiere f
premises ['premɪsɪz] npl (offices) Räumlichkeiten pl; (of factory, school) Gelände nt
premium-rate ['priːmɪəmreɪt] adj (Tel) zum Höchsttarif
preoccupied [prɪ'ɒkjʊpaɪd] adj **to be ~ with sth** mit etw sehr beschäftigt sein
prepaid [priː'peɪd] adj vorausbezahlt; (envelope) frankiert
preparation [prepə'reɪʃən] n Vorbereitung f; **prepare** [prɪ'pɛə*] vt vorbereiten (for auf +akk); (food) zubereiten; **to be ~d to do sth** bereit sein, etw zu tun ▷ vi sich vorbereiten (for auf +akk)

prerequisite [priː'rekwɪzɪt] n Voraussetzung f
prescribe [prɪ'skraɪb] vt vorschreiben; (Med) verschreiben; **prescription** [prɪ'skrɪpʃən] n Rezept nt
presence ['prezns] n Gegenwart f; **present** ['preznt] adj (in attendance) anwesend (at bei); (current) gegenwärtig; **~ tense** Gegenwart f, Präsens nt ▷ n Gegenwart f; (gift) Geschenk nt; **at ~** zurzeit ▷ [prɪ'zent] vt (TV, Radio) präsentieren; (problem) darstellen; (report etc) vorlegen; **to ~ sb with sth** jdm etw überreichen; **present-day** adj heutig; **presently** adv bald; (at present) zurzeit
preservative [prɪ'zɜː'vətɪv] n Konservierungsmittel nt; **preserve** [prɪ'zɜːv] vt erhalten; (food) einmachen, konservieren
president ['prezɪdənt] n Präsident(in) m(f); **presidential** [prezɪ'denʃəl] adj Präsidenten-; (election) Präsidentschafts-
press [pres] n (newspapers, machine) Presse f ▷ vt (push) drücken; **to ~ a button** auf einen Knopf drücken ▷ vi (push) drücken; **pressing** adj dringend; **press-stud** n Druckknopf m; **press-up** n (Brit) Liegestütz m; **pressure** ['preʃə*] n Druck m; **to be under ~** unter Druck stehen; **to put ~ on sb** jdn unter Druck setzen; **pressure cooker** n Schnellkochtopf m; **pressurize** ['preʃəraɪz] vt (person) unter Druck setzen
presumably [prɪ'zjuː'məblɪ] adv vermutlich; **presume** [prɪ'zjuːm] vt, vi annehmen
presumptuous [prɪ'zʌmptʃʊəs] adj anmaßend
presuppose [priːsə'pəʊz] vt voraussetzen
pretend [prɪ'tend] vt **to ~ that** so tun als ob; **to ~ to do sth** vorgeben, etw zu tun ▷ vi **she's ~ing** sie tut nur so
pretentious [prɪ'tenʃəs] adj anmaßend; (person) wichtigtuerisch
pretty ['prɪtɪ] adj hübsch ▷ adv ziemlich
prevent [prɪ'vent] vt verhindern; **to ~ sb from doing sth** jdn daran hindern, etw zu tun
preview ['priːvjuː] n (Cine) Voraufführung f; (trailer) Vorschau f
previous, previously ['priːvɪəs, -lɪ] adj, adv früher

prey [preɪ] n Beute f
price [praɪs] n Preis m ▷ vt **it's ~d at £10**
es ist mit 10 Pfund ausgezeichnet;
priceless adj unbezahlbar; **price list** n
Preisliste f; **price tag** n Preisschild nt
prick [prɪk] n Stich m; (vulg: penis)
Schwanz m; (vulg: person) Arsch m ▷ vt
stechen in +akk; **to ~ one's finger** sich dat
in den Finger stechen; **prickly** ['prɪklɪ] adj
stachelig
pride [praɪd] n Stolz m; (arrogance)
Hochmut m ▷ vt **to ~ oneself on sth** auf
etw akk stolz sein
priest [priːst] n Priester m
primarily [prɪ'steɪ] adv vorwiegend;
primary ['praɪmərɪ] adj Haupt-;
~ education Grundschulausbildung f;
~ school Grundschule f
prime [praɪm] adj Haupt-; (excellent)
erstklassig ▷ n **in one's ~** in den besten
Jahren; **prime minister** n
Premierminister(in) m(f); **prime time** n
(TV) Hauptsendezeit f
primitive ['prɪmɪtɪv] adj primitiv
primrose ['prɪmrəʊz] n Schlüsselblume f
prince [prɪns] n Prinz m; (ruler) Fürst m;
princess [prɪn'ses] n Prinzessin f; (wife of
ruler) Fürstin f
principal ['prɪnsɪpəl] adj
Haupt-, wichtigste(r, s) ▷ n (school)
Rektor(in) m(f)
principle ['prɪnsəpl] n Prinzip nt; **in ~** im
Prinzip; **on ~** aus Prinzip
print [prɪnt] n (picture) Druck m; (Foto)
Abzug m; (made by feet, fingers) Abdruck m;
out of ~ vergriffen ▷ vt drucken; (photo)
abziehen; (write in block letters) in
Druckschrift schreiben; **print out** vt
(Inform) ausdrucken; **printed matter** n
Drucksache f; **printer** n Drucker m;
printout n (Inform) Ausdruck m
prior ['praɪə*] adj früher; **a
~ engagement** eine vorher getroffene
Verabredung; **~ to sth** vor etw dat; **~ to
going abroad, she had …** bevor sie ins
Ausland ging, hatte sie …
priority [praɪ'ɒrɪtɪ] n (thing having
precedence) Priorität f
prison ['prɪzn] n Gefängnis nt; **prisoner** n
Gefangene(r) mf; **~ of war**
Kriegsgefangene(r) mf
privacy ['prɪvəsɪ] n Privatleben nt;
private ['praɪvɪt] adj privat; (confidential)

vertraulich ▷ n einfacher Soldat; **in
~ privat; privately** adv privat;
(confidentially) vertraulich; **privatize**
['praɪvətaɪz] vt privatisieren
privilege ['prɪvɪlɪdʒ] n Privileg nt;
privileged adj privilegiert
prize [praɪz] n Preis m; **prize money** n
Preisgeld nt; **prizewinner** n Gewinner(in)
m(f); **prizewinning** adj preisgekrönt
pro [prəʊ] (pl **-s**) n (professional) Profi m;
the ~s and cons pl das Für und Wider
pro- [prəʊ] pref pro-
probability [probə'bɪlətɪ] n
Wahrscheinlichkeit f; **probable, probably**
['probəbl, -blɪ] adj, adv wahrscheinlich
probation [prə'beɪʃən] n Probezeit f; (Jur)
Bewährung f
probe [prəʊb] n (investigation)
Untersuchung f ▷ vt untersuchen
problem ['probləm] n Problem nt; **no
~ kein** Problem!
procedure [prə'siːdʒə*] n Verfahren nt
proceed [prə'siːd] vi (continue)
fortfahren; (set about sth) vorgehen ▷ vt
to ~ to do sth anfangen, etw zu tun;
proceedings npl (Jur) Verfahren nt;
proceeds ['prəʊsiːdz] npl Erlös m
process ['prəʊses] n Prozess m, Vorgang
m; (method) Verfahren nt ▷ vt (application
etc) bearbeiten; (food, data) verarbeiten;
(film) entwickeln
procession [prə'seʃən] n Umzug m
processor ['prəʊsesə*] n (Inform)
Prozessor m; (Gastr) Küchenmaschine f
produce ['prodjuːs] n (Agr) Produkte pl,
Erzeugnisse pl ▷ [prə'djuːs] vt
(manufacture) herstellen, produzieren; (on
farm) erzeugen; (film, play, record)
produzieren; (cause) hervorrufen; (evidence,
results) liefern; **producer** n (manufacturer)
Hersteller(in) m(f); (of film, play, record)
Produzent(in) m(f); **product** ['prodʌkt] n
Produkt nt, Erzeugnis nt; **production**
[prə'dʌkʃən] n Produktion f; (Theat)
Inszenierung f; **productive** [prə'dʌktɪv]
adj produktiv; (land) ertragreich
prof [prof] n (fam) Professor(in) m(f)
profession [prə'feʃən] n Beruf m;
professional [prə'feʃənl] n Profi m ▷ adj
beruflich; (expert) fachlich; (sportsman,
actor etc) Berufs-
professor [prə'fesə*] n Professor(in) m(f);
(US: lecturer) Dozent(in) m(f)

proficient [prə'fɪʃənt] *adj* kompetent (*in* in +*dat*)
profile ['prəʊfaɪl] *n* Profil *nt*; **to keep a low ~** sich rar machen
profit ['prɒfɪt] *n* Gewinn *m* ▷ *vi* profitieren (*by, from* von); **profitable** *adj* rentabel
profound [prə'faʊnd] *adj* tief; (*idea, thinker*) tiefgründig; (*knowledge*) profund
program ['prəʊɡræm] *n* (*Inform*) Programm *nt*; (*US*) *see* **programme** ▷ *vt* (*Inform*) programmieren; (*US*) *see* **programme**
programme ['prəʊɡræm] *n* Programm *nt*; (*Tv, Radio*) Sendung *f* ▷ *vt* programmieren; **programmer** *n* Programmierer(in) *m(f)*; **programming** *n* (*Inform*) Programmieren *nt*; **~ language** Programmiersprache *f*
progress ['prəʊɡres] *n* Fortschritt *m*; **to make ~** Fortschritte machen ▷ [prə'ɡres] *vi* (*work, illness etc*) fortschreiten; (*improve*) Fortschritte machen; **progressive** [prə'ɡresɪv] *adj* (*person, policy*) fortschrittlich; **progressively** [prə'ɡresɪvlɪ] *adv* zunehmend
prohibit [prə'hɪbɪt] *vt* verbieten
project ['prɒdʒekt] *n* Projekt *nt*
projector [prə'dʒektə*] *n* Projektor *m*
prolong [prə'lɒŋ] *vt* verlängern
prom [prɒm] *n* (*at seaside*) Promenade *f*; (*Brit: concert*) Konzert *nt* (*bei dem ein Großteil des Publikums im Parkett Stehplätze hat*); (*US: dance*) Ball für die Schüler und Studenten von Highschools oder Colleges
prominent ['prɒmɪnənt] *adj* (*politician, actor etc*) prominent; (*easily seen*) auffallend
promiscuous [prə'mɪskjʊəs] *adj* promisk
promise ['prɒmɪs] *n* Versprechen *nt* ▷ *vt* versprechen; **to ~ sb sth** jdm etw versprechen; **to ~ to do sth** versprechen, etw zu tun ▷ *vi* versprechen; **promising** *adj* viel versprechend
promote [prə'məʊt] *vt* (*in rank*) befördern; (*help on*) fördern; (*Comm*) werben für; **promotion** [prə'məʊʃən] *n* (*in rank*) Beförderung *f*; (*Comm*) Werbung *f* (*of* für)
prompt [prɒmpt] *adj* prompt; (*punctual*) pünktlich ▷ *adv* **at two o'clock ~** Punkt zwei Uhr ▷ *vt* (*Theat: actor*) soufflieren +*dat*

prone [prəʊn] *adj* **to be ~ to sth** zu etw neigen
pronounce [prə'naʊns] *vt* (*word*) aussprechen; **pronounced** *adj* ausgeprägt; **pronunciation** [prənʌnsɪ'eɪʃən] *n* Aussprache *f*
proof [pruːf] *n* Beweis *m*; (*of alcohol*) Alkoholgehalt *m*
prop [prɒp] *n* Stütze *f*; (*Theat*) Requisit *nt* ▷ *vt* **to ~ sth against sth** etw gegen etw lehnen; **prop up** *vt* stützen; (*fig*) unterstützen
proper ['prɒpə*] *adj* richtig; (*morally correct*) anständig
property ['prɒpətɪ] *n* (*possession*) Eigentum *nt*; (*house*) Haus *nt*; (*land*) Grundbesitz *m*; (*characteristic*) Eigenschaft *f*
proportion [prə'pɔːʃən] *n* Verhältnis *nt*; (*share*) Teil *m*; **~s** *pl* (*size*) Proportionen *pl*; **in ~ to** im Verhältnis zu; **proportional** *adj* proportional; **~ representation** Verhältniswahlrecht *nt*
proposal [prə'pəʊzl] *n* Vorschlag *m*; **~ (of marriage)** (Heirats)antrag *m*; **propose** [prə'pəʊz] *vt* vorschlagen ▷ *vi* (*offer marriage*) einen Heiratsantrag machen (*to sb* jdm)
proprietor [prə'praɪətə*] *n* Besitzer(in) *m(f)*; (*of pub, hotel*) Inhaber(in) *m(f)*
prose [prəʊz] *n* Prosa *f*
prosecute ['prɒsɪkjuːt] *vt* verfolgen (*for* wegen)
prospect ['prɒspekt] *n* Aussicht *f*
prosperity [prɒ'sperɪtɪ] *n* Wohlstand *m*; **prosperous** *adj* wohlhabend; (*business*) gut gehend
prostitute ['prɒstɪtjuːt] *n* Prostituierte(r) *mf*
protect [prə'tekt] *vt* schützen (*from, against* vor +*dat*, gegen); **protection** [prə'tekʃən] *n* Schutz *m* (*from, against* vor +*dat*, gegen); **protective** *adj* beschützend; (*clothing etc*) Schutz-
protein ['prəʊtiːn] *n* Protein *nt*, Eiweiß *nt*
protest ['prəʊtest] *n* Protest *m*; (*demonstration*) Protestkundgebung *f* ▷ [prə'test] *vi* protestieren (*against* gegen); (*demonstrate*) demonstrieren
Protestant ['prɒtəstənt] *adj* protestantisch ▷ *n* Protestant(in) *m(f)*
proud, proudly [praʊd, -lɪ] *adj, adv* stolz (*of* auf +*akk*)

prove [pruːv] *vt* beweisen; *(turn out to be)* sich erweisen als

proverb ['prɒvɜːb] *n* Sprichwort *nt*

provide [prə'vaɪd] *vt* zur Verfügung stellen; *(drinks, music etc)* sorgen für; *(person)* versorgen (**with** mit); **provide for** *vt (family etc)* sorgen für; **provided** *conj* ~ **(that)** vorausgesetzt, dass; **provider** *n (Inform)* Provider *m*

provision [prə'vɪʒən] *n (condition)* Bestimmung *f*; ~**s** *pl (food)* Proviant *m*

provisional, provisionally [prə'vɪʒənl, -ɪ] *adj, adv* provisorisch

provoke [prə'vəʊk] *vt* provozieren; *(cause)* hervorrufen

proximity [prɒk'sɪmɪtɪ] *n* Nähe *f*

prudent ['pruːdənt] *adj* klug; *(person)* umsichtig

prudish ['pruːdɪʃ] *adj* prüde

prune [pruːn] *n* Backpflaume *f* ▷ *vt (tree etc)* zurechtstutzen

PS *abbr* = **postscript** PS *nt*

psalm [sɑːm] *n* Psalm *m*

pseudo ['sjuːdəʊ] *adj* pseudo-, Pseudo-; **pseudonym** ['sjuːdənɪm] *n* Pseudonym *nt*

PST *abbr* = **Pacific Standard Time**

psychiatric [saɪkɪ'ætrɪk] *adj* psychiatrisch; *(illness)* psychisch; **psychiatrist** [saɪ'kaɪətrɪst] *n* Psychiater(in) *m(f)*; **psychiatry** [saɪ'kaɪətrɪ] *n* Psychiatrie *f*; **psychic** ['saɪkɪk] *adj* übersinnlich; **I'm not** ~ ich kann keine Gedanken lesen;

psychoanalysis [saɪkəʊə'næləsɪs] *n* Psychoanalyse *f*; **psychoanalyst** [saɪkəʊ'ænəlɪst] *n* Psychoanalytiker(in) *m(f)*; **psychological** [saɪkə'lɒdʒɪkəl] *adj* psychologisch; **psychology** [saɪ'kɒlədʒɪ] *n* Psychologie *f*; **psychopath** ['saɪkəʊpæθ] *n* Psychopath(in) *m(f)*

pt *abbr* = **pint**

pto *abbr* = **please turn over** b.w.

pub [pʌb] *n (Brit)* Kneipe *f*

pub

Ein **pub** ist ein Gasthaus mit einer Lizenz zum Ausschank von alkoholischen Getränken. Ein „Pub" besteht meist aus verschiedenen gemütlichen (**lounge, snug**) oder einfacheren (**public bar**) Räumen, in denen oft auch Spiele wie Darts, Domino und Poolbillard zur Verfügung stehen. In „Pubs" werden vor allem mittags auch Mahlzeiten angeboten (**pub lunch**). „Pubs" sind normalerweise von 11 bis 23 Uhr geöffnet, aber manchmal nachmittags geschlossen.

puberty ['pjuːbətɪ] *n* Pubertät *f*

public ['pʌblɪk] *n* **the (general)** ~ die (breite) Öffentlichkeit; **in** ~ in der Öffentlichkeit ▷ *adj* öffentlich; *(relating to the State)* Staats-; ~ **convenience** *(Brit)* öffentliche Toilette; ~ **holiday** gesetzlicher Feiertag; ~ **opinion** die öffentliche Meinung; ~ **relations** *pl* Öffentlichkeitsarbeit *f*, Public Relations *pl*; ~ **school** *(Brit)* Privatschule *f*, **publication** [pʌblɪ'keɪʃən] *n* Veröffentlichung *f*;

publicity [pʌb'lɪsɪtɪ] *n* Publicity *f*; *(advertisements)* Werbung *f*; **publish** ['pʌblɪʃ] *vt* veröffentlichen; **publisher** *n* Verleger(in) *m(f)*; *(company)* Verlag *m*; **publishing** *n* Verlagswesen *nt*

pub lunch ['pʌb'lʌntʃ] *n (oft einfacheres)* Mittagessen in einer Kneipe

pudding ['pʊdɪŋ] *n (course)* Nachtisch *m*

puddle ['pʌdl] *n* Pfütze *f*

puff [pʌf] *vi (pant)* schnaufen

puffin ['pʌfɪn] *n* Papageientaucher *m*

puff paste *(US)*, **puff pastry** ['pʌf'peɪstrɪ] *n* Blätterteig *m*

pull [pʊl] *n* Ziehen *nt*; **to give sth a** ~ an etw *dat* ziehen ▷ *vt (cart, tooth)* ziehen; *(rope, handle)* ziehen an +*dat*; *(fam: date)* abschleppen; **to** ~ **a muscle** sich *dat* einen Muskel zerren; **to** ~ **sb's leg** jdn auf den Arm nehmen ▷ *vi* ziehen; **pull apart** *vt (separate)* auseinander ziehen; **pull down** *vt (blind)* herunterziehen; *(house)* abreißen; **pull in** *vi* hineinfahren; *(stop)* anhalten; **pull off** *vt (clothes)* ausziehen; *(deal etc)* zuwege bringen; **pull on** *vt (clothes)* anziehen; **pull out** *vi (car from lane)* ausscheren; *(train)* abfahren; *(withdraw)* aussteigen *(of* aus*)* ▷ *vt* herausziehen; *(tooth)* ziehen; *(troops)* abziehen; **pull round, pull through** *vi* durchkommen; **pull up** *vt (raise)* hochziehen; *(chair)* heranziehen ▷ *vi* anhalten

pullover ['pʊləʊvə*] *n* Pullover *m*

pulp [pʌlp] n Brei m; (of fruit) Fruchtfleisch nt

pulpit ['pʊlpɪt] n Kanzel f

pulse [pʌls] n Puls m

pump [pʌmp] n Pumpe f; (in petrol station) Zapfsäule f; **pump up** vt (tyre etc) aufpumpen

pumpkin ['pʌmpkɪn] n Kürbis m

pun [pʌn] n Wortspiel nt

punch [pʌntʃ] n (blow) (Faust)schlag m; (tool) Locher m; (hot drink) Punsch m; (cold drink) Bowle f ▷ vt (strike) schlagen; (ticket, paper) lochen

punctual, punctually ['pʌŋktjʊəl, -ɪ] adj, adv pünktlich

punctuation [pʌŋktjʊ'eɪʃən] n Interpunktion f; **punctuation mark** n Satzzeichen nt

puncture ['pʌŋktʃə*] n (flat tyre) Reifenpanne f

punish ['pʌnɪʃ] vt bestrafen; **punishment** n Strafe f; (action) Bestrafung f

pupil ['pjuːpl] n (school) Schüler(in) m(f)

puppet ['pʌpɪt] n Puppe f; (string ~) Marionette f

puppy ['pʌpɪ] n junger Hund

purchase ['pɜːtʃɪs] n Kauf m ▷ vt kaufen

pure [pjʊə*] adj rein; (clean) sauber; (utter) pur; **purely** ['pjʊəlɪ] adv rein; **purify** ['pjʊərɪfaɪ] vt reinigen; **purity** ['pjʊərɪtɪ] n Reinheit f

purple ['pɜːpl] adj violett

purpose ['pɜːpəs] n Zweck m; (of person) Absicht f; **on ~** absichtlich

purr [pɜː*] vi (cat) schnurren

purse [pɜːs] n Geldbeutel m; (US: handbag) Handtasche f

pursue [pə'sjuː] vt (person, car) verfolgen; (hobby, studies) nachgehen +dat; **pursuit** [pə'sjuːt] n (chase) Verfolgung f; (occupation) Beschäftigung f; (hobby) Hobby nt

pus [pʌs] n Eiter m

push [pʊʃ] n Stoß m ▷ vt (person) stoßen; (car, chair etc) schieben; (button) drücken; (drugs) dealen ▷ vi (in crowd) drängeln; **push in** vi (in queue) sich vordrängeln; **push off** vi (fam: leave) abhauen; **push on** vi (with job) weitermachen; **push up** vt (prices) hochtreiben; **pushchair** n (Brit) Sportwagen m; **pusher** n (of drugs) Dealer(in) m(f); **push-up** n (US)

Liegestütz m; **pushy** adj (fam) aufdringlich, penetrant

put [pʊt] (put, put) vt tun; (upright) stellen; (flat) legen; (express) ausdrücken; (write) schreiben; **he ~ his hand in his pocket** er steckte die Hand in die Tasche; **he ~ his hand on her shoulder** er legte ihr die Hand auf die Schulter; **to ~ money into one's account** Geld auf sein Konto einzahlen; **put aside** vt (money) zurücklegen; **put away** vt (tidy away) wegräumen; **put back** vt zurücklegen; (clock) zurückstellen; **put down** vt (in writing) aufschreiben; (Brit: animal) einschläfern; (rebellion) niederschlagen; **to put the phone down** (den Hörer) auflegen; **to put one's name down for sth** sich für etw eintragen; **put forward** vt (idea) vorbringen; (name) vorschlagen; (clock) vorstellen; **put in** vt (install) einbauen; (submit) einreichen; **put off** vt (switch off) ausschalten; (postpone) verschieben; **to put sb off doing sth** jdn davon abbringen, etw zu tun; **put on** vt (switch on) anmachen; (clothes) anziehen; (hat, glasses) aufsetzen; (make-up, CD) auflegen; (play) aufführen; **to put the kettle on** Wasser aufsetzen; **to put weight on** zunehmen; **put out** vt (hand, foot) ausstrecken; (light, cigarette) ausmachen; **put up** vt (hand) hochheben; (picture) aufhängen; (tent) aufstellen; (building) errichten; (price) erhöhen; (person) unterbringen; **to ~ with** sich abfinden mit; **I won't ~ with it** das lasse ich mir nicht gefallen

putt [pʌt] vt, vi (Sport) putten

puzzle ['pʌzl] n Rätsel nt; (toy) Geduldsspiel nt; (jigsaw) ~ Puzzle nt ▷ vt vor ein Rätsel stellen; **it ~s me** es ist mir ein Rätsel; **puzzling** adj rätselhaft

pyjamas [pɪ'dʒɑːməz] npl Schlafanzug m

pylon ['paɪlən] n Mast m

pyramid ['pɪrəmɪd] n Pyramide f

q

quartet [kwɔː'tet] *n* Quartett *nt*

quay [kiː] *n* Kai *m*

queasy ['kwiːzɪ] *adj* **I feel ~** mir ist übel

queen [kwiːn] *n* Königin *f*; (*in cards, chess*) Dame *f*

queer [kwɪə*] *adj* (*strange*) seltsam, sonderbar; (*pej: homosexual*) schwul ▷ *n* (*pej*) Schwule(r) *m*

quench [kwentʃ] *vt* (*thirst*) löschen

query ['kwɪərɪ] *n* Frage *f* ▷ *vt* in Frage stellen; (*bill*) reklamieren

question ['kwestʃən] *n* Frage *f*; **that's out of the ~** das kommt nicht in Frage ▷ *vt* (*person*) befragen; (*suspect*) verhören; (*express doubt about*) bezweifeln; **questionable** *adj* zweifelhaft; (*improper*) fragwürdig; **question mark** *n* Fragezeichen *nt*; **questionnaire** [kwestʃə'neə*] *n* Fragebogen *m*

queue [kjuː] *n* (*Brit*) Schlange *f*; **to jump the ~** sich vordrängeln ▷ *vi* **to ~ (up)** Schlange stehen

quibble ['kwɪbl] *vi* kleinlich sein; (*argue*) streiten

quiche [kiːʃ] *n* Quiche

quick [kwɪk] *adj* schnell; (*short*) kurz; **be ~ mach schnell!**; **quickly** *adv* schnell

quid [kwɪd] (*pl* **quid**) *n* (*Brit fam*) Pfund *nt*; **20 ~** 20 Pfund

quiet ['kwaɪət] *adj* (*not noisy*) leise; (*peaceful, calm*) still, ruhig; **be ~** sei still!; **to keep ~ about sth** über etw *akk* nichts sagen ▷ *n* Stille *f*, Ruhe *f*; **quiet down** (*US*), **quieten down** ['kwaɪətən'daʊn] *vi* sich beruhigen ▷ *vt* beruhigen; **quietly** *adv* leise; (*calmly*) ruhig

quilt [kwɪlt] *n* (Stepp)decke *f*

quit [kwɪt] (**quit** *o* **quitted**, **quit** *o* **quitted**) *vt* (*leave*) verlassen; (*job*) aufgeben; **to ~ doing sth** aufhören, etw zu tun ▷ *vi* aufhören; (*resign*) kündigen

quite [kwaɪt] *adv* (*fairly*) ziemlich; (*completely*) ganz, völlig; **I don't ~ understand** ich verstehe das nicht ganz; **~ a few** ziemlich viele; **~ so** richtig!

quits [kwɪts] *adj* **to be ~ with sb** mit jdm quitt sein

quiver ['kwɪvə*] *vi* zittern

quiz [kwɪz] *n* (*competition*) Quiz *nt*

quota ['kwəʊtə] *n* Anteil *m*; (*Comm, Pol*) Quote *f*

quack [kwæk] *vi* quaken

quaint [kweɪnt] *adj* (*idea, tradition*) kurios; (*picturesque*) malerisch

qualification [kwɒlɪfɪ'keɪʃən] *n* (*for job*) Qualifikation *f*; (*from school, university*) Abschluss *m*; **qualified** ['kwɒlɪfaɪd] *adj* (*for job*) qualifiziert; **qualify** *vt* (*limit*) einschränken; **to be qualified to do sth** berechtigt sein, etw zu tun ▷ *vi* (*finish training*) seine Ausbildung abschließen; (*Sport*) sich qualifizieren

quality ['kwɒlɪtɪ] *n* Qualität *f*; (*characteristic*) Eigenschaft *f*

quantity ['kwɒntɪtɪ] *n* Menge *f*, Quantität *f*

quarantine ['kwɒrəntiːn] *n* Quarantäne *f*

quarrel ['kwɒrəl] *n* Streit *m* ▷ *vi* sich streiten; **quarrelsome** *adj* streitsüchtig

quarter ['kwɔːtə*] *n* Viertel *nt*; (*of year*) Vierteljahr *nt*; (*US: coin*) Vierteldollar *m*; **a ~ of an hour** eine Viertelstunde; **~ to/past** (*Brit*) (*o* **~ of/after** (*US*)) **three** Viertel vor/nach drei ▷ *vt* vierteln; **quarter final** *n* Viertelfinale *nt*; **quarters** *npl* (*Mil*) Quartier *nt*

quotation [kwəʊˈteɪʃən] *n* Zitat *nt*; (*price*) Kostenvoranschlag *m*; **quotation marks** *npl* Anführungszeichen *pl*; **quote** [kwəʊt] *vt* (*text, author*) zitieren; (*price*) nennen ▷ *n* Zitat *nt*; (*price*) Kostenvoranschlag *m*; **in ~s** in Anführungszeichen

r

rabbi ['ræbaɪ] *n* Rabbiner *m*
rabbit ['ræbɪt] *n* Kaninchen *nt*
rabies ['reɪbiːz] *nsing* Tollwut *f*
raccoon [rə'kuːn] *n* Waschbär *m*
race [reɪs] *n* (*competition*) Rennen *nt*;
(*people*) Rasse *f* ⊳ *vt* um die Wette
laufen/fahren ⊳ *vi* (*rush*) rennen;
racecourse *n* Rennbahn *f*; **racehorse** *n*
Rennpferd *nt*; **racetrack** *n* Rennbahn *f*
racial ['reɪʃəl] *adj* Rassen-;
~ discrimination Rassendiskriminierung *f*
racing ['reɪsɪŋ] *n* (**horse**) **~** Pferderennen
nt; (**motor**) **~** Autorennen *nt*; **racing car** *n*
Rennwagen *m*
racism ['reɪsɪzəm] *n* Rassismus *m*; **racist**
n Rassist(in) *m(f)* ⊳ *adj* rassistisch
rack [ræk] *n* Ständer *m*, Gestell *nt* ⊳ *vt* **to
~ one's brains** sich *dat* den Kopf
zerbrechen
racket ['rækɪt] *n* (*Sport*) Schläger *m*;
(*noise*) Krach *m*
radar ['reɪdɑː*] *n* Radar *nt o m*; **radar trap**
n Radarfalle *f*
radiation [reɪdɪ'eɪʃən] *n* (*radioactive*)
Strahlung *f*
radiator ['reɪdɪeɪtə*] *n* Heizkörper *m*;
(*Auto*) Kühler *m*

radical ['rædɪkəl] *adj* radikal
radio ['reɪdɪəʊ] (*pl* **-s**) *n* Rundfunk *m*,
Radio *nt*
radioactivity [reɪdɪəʊæk'tɪvɪtɪ] *n*
Radioaktivität *f*
radio alarm ['reɪdɪəʊə'lɑːm] *n*
Radiowecker *m*; **radio station** *n*
Rundfunkstation *f*
radiotherapy [reɪdɪəʊ'θerəpɪ] *n*
Strahlenbehandlung *f*
radish ['rædɪʃ] *n* Radieschen *nt*
radius ['reɪdɪəs] *n* Radius *m*; **within a
five-mile ~** im Umkreis von fünf Meilen
(*of* um)
raffle ['ræfl] *n* Tombola *f*; **raffle ticket** *n*
Los *nt*
raft [rɑːft] *n* Floß *nt*
rag [ræg] *n* Lumpen *m*; (*for cleaning*)
Lappen *m*
rage [reɪdʒ] *n* Wut *f*; **to be all the ~** der
letzte Schrei sein ⊳ *vi* toben; (*disease*)
wüten
raid [reɪd] *n* Überfall *m* (*on* auf +*akk*); (*by
police*) Razzia *f* (*on* gegen) ⊳ *vt* (*bank etc*)
überfallen; (*by police*) eine Razzia machen
in +*dat*
rail [reɪl] *n* (*on stairs, balcony etc*) Geländer
nt; (*of ship*) Reling *f*; (*Rail*) Schiene *f*;
railcard *n* (*Brit*) ≈ Bahncard® *f*; **railing** *n*
Geländer *nt*; **~s** *pl* (*fence*) Zaun *m*; **railroad**
n (*US*) Eisenbahn *f*; **railroad station** *n*
(*US*) Bahnhof *m*; **railway** *n* (*Brit*)
Eisenbahn *f*; **railway line** *n* Bahnlinie *f*;
(*track*) Gleis *m*; **railway station** *n*
Bahnhof *m*
rain [reɪn] *n* Regen *m* ⊳ *vi* regnen; **it's
~ing** es regnet; **rainbow** *n* Regenbogen
m; **raincoat** *n* Regenmantel *m*; **rainfall** *n*
Niederschlag *m*; **rainforest** *n* Regenwald
m; **rainy** *adj* regnerisch
raise [reɪz] *n* (*US: of wages/salary*)
Gehalts-/Lohnerhöhung *f* ⊳ *vt* (*lift*)
hochheben; (*increase*) erhöhen; (*family*)
großziehen; (*livestock*) züchten; (*money*)
aufbringen; (*objection*) erheben; **to ~ one's
voice** (*in anger*) laut werden
raisin ['reɪzən] *n* Rosine *f*
rally ['rælɪ] *n* (*Pol*) Kundgebung *f*; (*Auto*)
Rallye *f*; (*Tennis*) Ballwechsel *m*
RAM [ræm] *acr* = **random access
memory** RAM *m*
ramble ['ræmbl] *n* Wanderung *f* ⊳ *vi*
(*walk*) wandern; (*talk*) schwafeln

ramp [ræmp] n Rampe f

ran [ræn] pt of **run**

ranch [rɑ:ntʃ] n Ranch f

rancid [ˈrænsɪd] adj ranzig

random [ˈrændəm] adj willkürlich ▷ n **at ~** (choose) willkürlich; (fire) ziellos

randy [ˈrændɪ] adj (Brit fam) geil, scharf

rang [ræŋ] pt of **ring**

range [reɪndʒ] n (selection) Auswahl f (of an +dat); (Comm) Sortiment nt (of an +dat); (of missile, telescope) Reichweite f; (of mountains) Kette f; **in this price ~** in dieser Preisklasse ▷ vi **to ~ from ... to ...** gehen von ... bis ...; (temperature, sizes, prices) liegen zwischen ... und ...

rank [ræŋk] n (Mil) Rang m; (social position) Stand m ▷ vt einstufen ▷ vi **to ~ among** zählen zu

ransom [ˈrænsəm] n Lösegeld nt

rap [ræp] n (Mus) Rap m

rape [reɪp] n Vergewaltigung f ▷ vt vergewaltigen

rapid, rapidly [ˈræpɪd, -lɪ] adj, adv schnell

rapist [ˈreɪpɪst] n Vergewaltiger m

rare [reə*] adj selten, rar; (especially good) vortrefflich; (steak) blutig; **rarely** adv selten; **rarity** [ˈreərɪtɪ] n Seltenheit f

rash [ræʃ] adj unbesonnen ▷ n (Med) (Haut)ausschlag m

rasher [ˈræʃə*] n **~ (of bacon)** (Speck)scheibe f

raspberry [ˈrɑ:zbərɪ] n Himbeere f

rat [ræt] n Ratte f; (pej: person) Schwein nt

rate [reɪt] n (proportion, frequency) Rate f; (speed) Tempo nt; **~ (of exchange)** (Wechsel)kurs m; **~ of inflation** Inflationsrate f; **~ of interest** Zinssatz m; **at any ~** auf jeden Fall ▷ vt (evaluate) einschätzen (as als)

rather [ˈrɑ:ðə*] adv (in preference) lieber; (fairly) ziemlich; **I'd ~ stay here** ich würde lieber hier bleiben; **I'd ~ not** lieber nicht; **or ~** (more accurately) vielmehr

ratio [ˈreɪʃɪəʊ] (pl **-s**) n Verhältnis nt

rational [ˈræʃənl] adj rational; **rationalize** [ˈræʃnəlaɪz] vt rationalisieren

rattle [ˈrætl] n (toy) Rassel f ▷ vt (keys, coins) klimpern mit; (person) durcheinander bringen ▷ vi (window) klappern; (bottles) klirren; **rattle off** vt herunterrasseln; **rattlesnake** n Klapperschlange f

rave [reɪv] vi (talk wildly) fantasieren; (rage) toben; (enthuse) schwärmen (about von) ▷ n (Brit: event) Raveparty f

raven [ˈreɪvn] n Rabe m

raving [ˈreɪvɪŋ] adv **~ mad** total verrückt

ravishing [ˈrævɪʃɪŋ] adj hinreißend

raw [rɔ:] adj (food) roh; (skin) wund; (climate) rau

ray [reɪ] n (of light) Strahl m; **~ of hope** Hoffnungsschimmer m

razor [ˈreɪzə*] n Rasierapparat m; **razor blade** n Rasierklinge f

Rd n abbr = **road** Str.

re [ri:] prep (Comm) betreffs +gen

RE abbr = **religious education**

reach [ri:tʃ] n **within/out of (sb's) ~** in/außer (jds) Reichweite; **within easy ~ of the shops** nicht weit von den Geschäften ▷ vt (arrive at, contact) erreichen; (come down/up as far as) reichen bis zu; (contact) **can you ~ it?** kommen Sie dran?; **reach for** vt greifen nach; **reach out** vi die Hand ausstrecken; **to ~ for** greifen nach

react [ri:ˈækt] vi reagieren (to auf +akk); **reaction** [ri:ˈækʃən] n Reaktion f (to auf +akk); **reactor** [rɪˈæktə*] n Reaktor m

read [ri:d] (read, read) vt lesen; (meter) ablesen; **to ~ sth to sb** jdm etw vorlesen ▷ vi lesen; **to ~ to sb** jdm etw vorlesen; **it ~s well** es liest sich gut; **it ~s as follows** es lautet folgendermaßen; **read out** vt vorlesen; **read through** vt durchlesen; **read up on** vt nachlesen über +akk; **readable** adj (book) lesenswert; (handwriting) lesbar; **reader** n Leser(in) m(f)

readily [ˈredɪlɪ] adv (willingly) bereitwillig; **~ available** leicht erhältlich

reading [ˈri:dɪŋ] n (action) Lesen nt; (from meter) Zählerstand m; **reading glasses** npl Lesebrille f; **reading lamp** n Leselampe f; **reading list** n Leseliste f; **reading matter** n Lektüre f

readjust [ri:əˈdʒʌst] vt (mechanism etc) neu einstellen ▷ vi sich wieder anpassen (to an +akk)

ready [ˈredɪ] adj fertig, bereit; **to be ~ to do sth** (willing) bereit sein, etw zu tun; **are you ~ to go?** bist du so weit?; **to get sth ~** etw fertig machen; **to get (oneself) ~** sich fertig machen; **ready cash** n

Bargeld *nt*; **ready-made** *adj* (*product*) Fertig-; (*clothes*) Konfektions-; **~ meal** Fertiggericht *nt*

real [rɪəl] *adj* wirklich; (*actual*) eigentlich; (*genuine*) echt; (*idiot etc*) richtig; **for ~** echt; **this time it's for ~** diesmal ist es ernst; **get ~** sei realistisch! ▷ *adv* (*fam, esp US*) echt ▷ *n* **for ~** echt; **this time it's for ~** diesmal ist es ernst; **get ~** sei realistisch!; **real ale** *n* Ale *nt*; **real estate** *n* Immobilien *pl*

realistic, realistically [rɪə'lɪstɪk, -əlɪ] *adj, adv* realistisch; **reality** [riː'ælɪtɪ] *n* Wirklichkeit *f*; **in ~** in Wirklichkeit; **reality TV** *n* Reality-TV *nt*; **realization** [rɪəlaɪ'zeɪʃən] *n* (*awareness*) Erkenntnis *f*; **realize** ['rɪəlaɪz] *vt* (*understand*) begreifen; (*plan, idea*) realisieren; **I ~d (that)** ... mir wurde klar, dass ...

really ['riːəlɪ] *adv* wirklich

real time [rɪəl'taɪm] *n* (*Inform*) **in ~** in Echtzeit

realtor ['rɪəltɔ*] *n* (*US*) Grundstücksmakler(in) *m(f)*

reappear [riː ə'pɪə*] *vi* wieder erscheinen

rear [rɪə*] *adj* hintere(r, s), Hinter- ▷ *n* (*of building, vehicle*) hinterer Teil; **at the ~ of** hinter +*dat*; (*inside*) hinten in +*dat*; **rear light** *n* (*Auto*) Rücklicht *nt*

rearm [riː'ɑːm] *vi* wieder aufrüsten

rearrange [riː ə'reɪndʒ] *vt* (*furniture, system*) umstellen; (*meeting*) verlegen (*for* auf +*akk*)

rear-view mirror ['rɪəvjuː'mɪrə*] *n* Rückspiegel *m*; **rear window** *n* (*Auto*) Heckscheibe *f*

reason ['riːzn] *n* (*cause*) Grund *m* (*for* für); (*ability to think*) Verstand *m*; (*common sense*) Vernunft *f*; **for some ~** aus irgendeinem Grund ▷ *vi* **to ~ with sb** mit jdm vernünftig reden; **reasonable** *adj* (*person, price*) vernünftig; (*offer*) akzeptabel; (*chance*) reell; (*food, weather*) ganz gut; **reasonably** *adv* vernünftig; (*fairly*) ziemlich

reassure [riː ə'ʃʊə*] *vt* beruhigen; **she ~d me that ...** sie versicherte mir, dass ...

rebel ['rebl] *n* Rebell(in) *m(f)* ▷ [rɪ'bel] *vi* rebellieren; **rebellion** [rɪ'belɪən] *n* Aufstand *m*

reboot [riː'buːt] *vt, vi* (*Inform*) rebooten

rebound [rɪ'baʊnd] *vi* (*ball etc*) zurückprallen

rebuild [riː'bɪld] *irr vt* wieder aufbauen

recall [rɪ'kɔːl] *vt* (*remember*) sich erinnern an +*akk*; (*call back*) zurückrufen

recap ['riːkæp] *vt, vi* rekapitulieren

receipt [rɪ'siːt] *n* (*document*) Quittung *f*; (*receiving*) Empfang *m*; **~s** *pl* (*money*) Einnahmen *pl*

receive [rɪ'siːv] *vt* (*news etc*) erhalten, bekommen; (*visitor*) empfangen; **receiver** *n* (*Tel*) Hörer *m*; (*Radio*) Empfänger *m*

recent ['riːsnt] *adj* (*event*) vor kurzem stattgefunden; (*photo*) neueste(r,s); (*invention*) neu; **in ~ years** in den letzten Jahren; **recently** *adv* vor kurzem; (*in the last few days or weeks*) in letzter Zeit

reception [rɪ'sepʃən] *n* Empfang *m*; **receptionist** *n* (*in hotel*) Empfangschef *m*, Empfangsdame *f*; (*woman in firm*) Empfangsdame *f*; (*Med*) Sprechstundenhilfe *f*

recess [rɪ'ses] *n* (*in wall*) Nische *f*; (*US: in school*) Pause *f*

recession [rɪ'seʃən] *n* Rezession *f*

recharge [riː'tʃɑːdʒ] *vt* (*battery*) aufladen; **rechargeable** [riː'tʃɑːdʒəbl] *adj* wieder aufladbar

recipe ['resɪpɪ] *n* Rezept *nt* (*for* für)

recipient [rɪ'sɪpɪənt] *n* Empfänger(in) *m(f)*

reciprocal [rɪ'sɪprəkəl] *adj* gegenseitig

recite [rɪ'saɪt] *vt* vortragen; (*details*) aufzählen

reckless ['rekləs] *adj* leichtsinnig; (*driving*) gefährlich

reckon ['rekən] *vt* (*calculate*) schätzen; (*think*) glauben ▷ *vi* **to ~ with** rechnen mit

reclaim [rɪ'kleɪm] *vt* (*baggage*) abholen; (*expenses, tax*) zurückverlangen

recline [rɪ'klaɪn] *vi* (*person*) sich zurücklehnen; **reclining seat** *n* Liegesitz *m*

recognition [rekəg'nɪʃən] *n* (*acknowledgement*) Anerkennung *f*; **in ~ of** in Anerkennung +*gen*; **recognize** ['rekəgnaɪz] *vt* erkennen; (*approve officially*) anerkennen

recommend [rekə'mend] *vt* empfehlen; **recommendation** [rekəmen'deɪʃən] *n* Empfehlung *f*

reconcile ['rekənsaɪl] *vt* (*people*) versöhnen; (*facts*) (miteinander) vereinbaren

reconsider [riː kən'sɪdə*] *vt* noch einmal

überdenken ▷ vi es sich dat noch einmal überlegen

reconstruct [riːkənˈstrʌkt] vt wieder aufbauen; (crime) rekonstruieren

record [ˈrekɔːd] n (Mus) (Schall)platte f; (best performance) Rekord m; **~s** pl (files) Akten pl; **to keep a ~ of** Buch führen über +akk ▷ adj (time etc) Rekord- ▷ [rɪˈkɔːd] vt (write down) aufzeichnen; (on tape etc) aufnehmen; **~ed message** Ansage f; **recorded delivery** (Brit) **by ~** per Einschreiben

recorder [rɪˈkɔːdə*] n (Mus) Blockflöte f; (cassette) **~** (Kassetten)rekorder m; **recording** [rɪˈkɔːdɪŋ] n (on tape etc) Aufnahme f; **record player** [ˈrekɔːdpleɪə*] n Plattenspieler m

recover [rɪˈkʌvə*] vt (money, item) zurückbekommen; (appetite, strength) wiedergewinnen ▷ vi sich erholen

recreation [rekrɪˈeɪʃən] n Erholung f; **recreational** adj Freizeit-; **~ vehicle** (US) Wohnmobil nt

recruit [rɪˈkruːt] n (Mil) Rekrut(in) m(f); (in firm, organization) neues Mitglied ▷ vt (Mil) rekrutieren; (members) anwerben; (staff) einstellen; **recruitment agency** n Personalagentur f

rectangle [ˈrektæŋgl] n Rechteck nt; **rectangular** [rekˈtæŋgʊlə*] adj rechteckig

rectify [ˈrektɪfaɪ] vt berichtigen

recuperate [rɪˈkuːpəreɪt] vi sich erholen

recyclable [riːˈsaɪkləbl] adj recycelbar, wieder verwertbar; **recycle** [riːˈsaɪkl] vt recyceln, wieder verwerten; **~d paper** Recyclingpapier nt; **recycling** n Recycling nt, Wiederverwertung f

red [red] adj rot ▷ n **in the ~** in den roten Zahlen; **Red Cross** Rotes Kreuz; **red cabbage** n Rotkohl m; **redcurrant** n (rote) Johannisbeere

redeem [rɪˈdiːm] vt (Comm) einlösen

red-handed [redˈhændɪd] adj **to catch sb ~** jdn auf frischer Tat ertappen; **redhead** n Rothaarige(r) mf

redial [riːˈdaɪəl] vt, vi nochmals wählen

redirect [riːdaɪˈrekt] vt (traffic) umleiten; (forward) nachsenden

red light [redˈlaɪt] n (traffic signal) rotes Licht; **to go through the ~** bei Rot über die Ampel fahren; **red meat** n Rind-, Lamm-, Rehfleisch

redo [riːˈduː] irr vt nochmals machen

reduce [rɪˈdjuːs] vt reduzieren (to auf +akk, by um); **reduction** [rɪˈdʌkʃən] n Reduzierung f; (in price) Ermäßigung f

redundant [rɪˈdʌndənt] adj überflüssig; **to be made ~** entlassen werden

red wine [redˈwaɪn] n Rotwein m

reef [riːf] n Riff nt

reel [riːl] n Spule f; (on fishing rod) Rolle f; **reel off** vt herunterrasseln

ref [ref] n (fam: referee) Schiri m

refectory [rɪˈfektərɪ] n (at college) Mensa f

refer [rɪˈfɜː*] vt **to ~ sb to sb/sth** jdn an jdn/etw verweisen; **to ~ sth to sb** (query, problem) etw jdn weiterleiten ▷ vi **to ~ to** (mention, allude to) sich beziehen auf +akk; (book) nachschlagen in +dat

referee [refəˈriː] n Schiedsrichter(in) m(f); (in boxing) Ringrichter m; (Brit: for job) Referenz f

reference [ˈrefrəns] n (allusion) Anspielung f (to auf +akk); (for job) Referenz f; (in book) Verweis m; **~ (number)** (in document) Aktenzeichen nt; **with ~ to** mit Bezug auf +akk; **reference book** n Nachschlagewerk nt

referendum [refəˈrendəm] (pl **referenda**) n Referendum nt

refill [ˈriːfɪl] vt [riːˈfɪl] nachfüllen ▷ n (for ballpoint pen) Ersatzmine f

refine [rɪˈfaɪn] vt (purify) raffinieren; (improve) verfeinern; **refined** adj (genteel) fein

reflect [rɪˈflekt] vt reflektieren; (fig) widerspiegeln ▷ vi nachdenken (on über +akk); **reflection** [rɪˈflekʃən] n (image) Spiegelbild nt; (thought) Überlegung f

reflex [ˈriːfleks] n Reflex m

reform [rɪˈfɔːm] n Reform f ▷ vt reformieren; (person) bessern

refrain [rɪˈfreɪn] vi **to ~ from doing sth** es unterlassen, etw zu tun

refresh [rɪˈfreʃ] vt erfrischen; **refresher course** n Auffrischungskurs m; **refreshing** adj erfrischend; **refreshments** npl Erfrischungen pl

refrigerator [rɪˈfrɪdʒəreɪtə*] n Kühlschrank m

refuel [riːˈfjuːəl] vt, vi auftanken

refuge [ˈrefjuːdʒ] n Zuflucht f (from vor +dat); **to take ~** sich flüchten (from vor +dat, in in +akk); **refugee** [refjʊˈdʒiː] n Flüchtling m

refund ['ri:fʌnd] n (of money)
Rückerstattung f; **to get a ~ (on sth)** sein
Geld (für etw) zurückbekommen
▷ [rɪ'fʌnd] vt zurückerstatten

refusal [rɪ'fju:zəl] n (to do sth) Weigerung
f; **refuse** ['refju:s] n Müll m, Abfall m
▷ [rɪ'fju:z] vt ablehnen; **to ~ sb sth** jdm
etw verweigern; **to ~ to do sth** sich
weigern, etw zu tun ▷ vi sich weigern

regain [rɪ'geɪn] vt wiedergewinnen,
wiedererlangen; **to ~ consciousness**
wieder zu Bewusstsein kommen

regard [rɪ'gɑ:d] n **with ~ to** in Bezug auf
+akk; **in this ~** in dieser Hinsicht; **~s** (at end
of letter) mit freundlichen Grüßen; **give my
~s to ...** viele Grüße an ... +akk ▷ vt **to
~ sb/sth as sth** jdn/etw als etw
betrachten; **as ~s ...** was ... betrifft;
regarding prep bezüglich +gen;
regardless adj **~ of** ohne Rücksicht auf
+akk ▷ adv trotzdem; **to carry on
~** einfach weitermachen

regime [reɪ'ʒi:m] n (Pol) Regime nt

region ['ri:dʒən] n (of country) Region f,
Gebiet nt; **in the ~ of** (about) ungefähr;
regional adj regional

register ['redʒɪstə*] n Register nt; (school)
Namensliste f ▷ vt (with an authority)
registrieren lassen; (birth, death, vehicle)
anmelden ▷ vi (at hotel, for course) sich
anmelden; (at university) sich einschreiben;
registered adj eingetragen; (letter)
eingeschrieben; **by ~ post** per
Einschreiben; **registration** [redʒɪ'streɪʃən]
n (for course) Anmeldung f; (at university)
Einschreibung f; (Auto: number)
(polizeiliches) Kennzeichen; **registration
form** n Anmeldeformular nt;
registration number n (Auto)
(polizeiliches) Kennzeichen; **registry
office** ['redʒɪstrɪɒfɪs] n Standesamt nt

regret [rɪ'gret] n Bedauern nt ▷ vt
bedauern; **regrettable** adj bedauerlich

regular ['regjʊlə*] adj regelmäßig; (size)
normal ▷ n (client) Stammkunde m,
Stammkundin f; (in bar) Stammgast m;
(petrol) Normalbenzin nt; **regularly** adv
regelmäßig

regulate ['regjʊleɪt] vt regulieren; (using
rules) regeln; **regulation** [regjʊ'leɪʃən] n
(rule) Vorschrift f

rehabilitation [ri:əbɪlɪ'teɪʃən] n
Rehabilitation f

rehearsal [rɪ'hɜ:səl] n Probe f; **rehearse**
vt, vi proben

reign [reɪn] n Herrschaft f ▷ vi herrschen
(over über +akk)

reimburse [ri:ɪm'bɜ:s] vt (person)
entschädigen; (expenses) zurückerstatten

reindeer ['reɪndɪə*] n Rentier nt

reinforce [ri:ɪn'fɔ:s] vt verstärken

reinstate [ri:ɪn'steɪt] vt (employee) wieder
einstellen; (passage in text) wieder
aufnehmen

reject ['ri:dʒekt] n (Comm)
Ausschussartikel m ▷ [rɪ'dʒekt] vt
ablehnen; **rejection** [rɪ'dʒekʃən] n
Ablehnung f

relapse [rɪ'læps] n Rückfall m

relate [rɪ'leɪt] vt (story) erzählen; (connect)
in Verbindung bringen (to mit) ▷ vi **to ~ to**
(refer) sich beziehen auf +akk; **related** adj
verwandt (to mit); **relation** [rɪ'leɪʃən] n
(relative) Verwandte(r) mf; (connection)
Beziehung f; **~s** pl (dealings) Beziehungen
pl; **relationship** n (connection) Beziehung
f; (between people) Verhältnis nt

relative ['relətɪv] n Verwandte(r) mf ▷ adj
relativ; **relatively** adv relativ,
verhältnismäßig

relax [rɪ'læks] vi sich entspannen; **~!** reg
dich nicht auf! ▷ vt (grip, conditions)
lockern; **relaxation** [ri:læk'seɪʃən] n
(rest) Entspannung f; **relaxed** adj
entspannt; **relaxing** adj entspannend

release [rɪ'li:s] n (from prison) Entlassung
f, **new/recent ~** (film, CD)
Neuerscheinung f ▷ vt (animal, hostage)
freilassen; (prisoner) entlassen; (handbrake)
lösen; (news) veröffentlichen; (film, CD)
herausbringen

relent [rɪ'lent] vi nachgeben; **relentless**,
relentlessly adj, adv (merciless)
erbarmungslos; (neverending)
unaufhörlich

relevance ['reləvəns] n Relevanz f (to
für); **relevant** adj relevant (to für)

reliable, **reliably** [rɪ'laɪəbl, -blɪ] adj, adv
zuverlässig; **reliant** [rɪ'laɪənt] adj **~ on**
abhängig von

relic ['relɪk] n (from past) Relikt nt

relief [rɪ'li:f] n (from anxiety, pain)
Erleichterung f; (assistance) Hilfe f; **relieve**
[rɪ'li:v] vt (pain) lindern; (boredom)
überwinden; (take over from) ablösen; **I'm
~d** ich bin erleichtert

religion [rɪˈlɪdʒən] n Religion f; **religious** [rɪˈlɪdʒəs] adj religiös

relish [ˈrelɪʃ] n (for food) würzige Soße ▷ vt (enjoy) genießen; **I don't ~ the thought of getting up early** der Gedanke, früh aufzustehen, behagt mir gar nicht

reluctant [rɪˈlʌktənt] adj widerwillig; **to be ~ to do sth** etw nur ungern tun; **reluctantly** adv widerwillig

rely on [rɪˈlaɪ ɒn] vt sich verlassen auf +akk; (depend on) abhängig sein von

remain [rɪˈmeɪn] vi bleiben; (be left over) übrig bleiben; **remainder** n (a. Math) Rest m; **remaining** adj übrig; **remains** npl Überreste pl

remark [rɪˈmɑːk] n Bemerkung f ▷ vt **to ~ that** bemerken, dass ▷ vi **to ~ on sth** über etw akk eine Bemerkung machen; **remarkable, remarkably** adj, adv bemerkenswert

remarry [riˈmærɪ] vi wieder heiraten

remedy [ˈremədɪ] n Mittel nt (for gegen) ▷ vt abhelfen +dat

remember [rɪˈmembə*] vt sich erinnern an +akk; **to ~ to do sth** daran denken, etw zu tun; **I ~ seeing her** ich erinnere mich daran, sie gesehen zu haben; **I must ~ that** das muss ich mir merken ▷ vi sich erinnern

Remembrance Day [rɪˈmembrəns'deɪ] n (Brit) ≈ Volkstrauertag m

Remembrance Day

Remembrance Sunday/Day ist der britische Gedenktag für die Gefallenen der beiden Weltkriege und anderer Kriege. Er fällt auf einen Sonntag vor oder nach dem 11. November (am 11.11.1918 endete der Erste Weltkrieg) und wird mit einer Schweigeminute, Kranzniederlegungen an Kriegerdenkmälern und dem Tragen von Ansteckanadeln in Form einer Mohnblume begangen.

remind [rɪˈmaɪnd] vt **to ~ sb of/about sb/sth** jdn an jdn/etw erinnern; **to ~ sb to do sth** jdn daran erinnern, etw zu tun; **that ~s me** dabei fällt mir ein …; **reminder** n (to pay) Mahnung f

reminisce [remɪˈnɪs] vi in Erinnerungen schwelgen (about an +akk); **reminiscent** [remɪˈnɪsənt] adj **to be ~ of** erinnern an +akk

remittance n Überweisung f (to an +akk)

remnant [ˈremnənt] n Rest m

remote [rɪˈməut] adj (place) abgelegen; (slight) gering ▷ n (Tv) Fernbedienung f; **remote control** n Fernsteuerung f; (device) Fernbedienung f

removal [rɪˈmuːvəl] n Entfernung f; (Brit: move from house) Umzug m; **removal firm** n (Brit) Spedition f; **remove** [rɪˈmuːv] vt entfernen; (lid) abnehmen; (clothes) ausziehen; (doubt, suspicion) zerstreuen

rename [riˈneɪm] vt umbenennen

renew [rɪˈnjuː] vt erneuern; (licence, passport, library book) verlängern lassen

renounce [rɪˈnauns] vt verzichten auf +akk; (faith, opinion) abschwören +dat

renovate [ˈrenəveɪt] vt renovieren

renowned [rɪˈnaund] adj berühmt (for für)

rent [rent] n Miete f; **for ~** (US) zu vermieten ▷ vt (as hirer, tenant) mieten; (as owner) vermieten; **~ed car** Mietwagen m; **rent out** vt vermieten; **rental** n Miete f; (for car, TV etc) Leihgebühr f ▷ adj Miet-

reorganize [riˈɔːgənaɪz] vt umorganisieren

rep [rep] n (Comm) Vertreter(in) m(f)

repair [rɪˈpeə*] n Reparatur f ▷ vt reparieren; (damage) wieder gutmachen; **repair kit** n Flickzeug nt

repay [riˈpeɪ] irr vt (money) zurückzahlen; **to ~ sb for sth** (fig) sich bei jdm für etw revanchieren

repeat [rɪˈpiːt] n (Radio, Tv) Wiederholung f ▷ vt wiederholen; **repetition** [repəˈtɪʃən] n Wiederholung f; **repetitive** [rɪˈpetɪtɪv] adj sich wiederholend

rephrase [riˈfreɪz] vt anders formulieren

replace [rɪˈpleɪs] vt ersetzen (with durch); (put back) zurückstellen, zurücklegen; **replacement** n (thing, person) Ersatz m; (temporarily in job) Vertretung f; **replacement part** n Ersatzteil nt

replay [ˈriːpleɪ] n (action) ~ Wiederholung f ▷ [riːˈpleɪ] vt (game) wiederholen

replica [ˈreplɪkə] n Kopie f

reply [rɪˈplaɪ] n Antwort f ▷ vi antworten; **to ~ to sb/sth** jdm/auf etw *akk* antworten ▷ *vt* **to ~ that** antworten, dass

report [rɪ'pɔːt] *n* Bericht *m*; (*school*) Zeugnis *nt* ▷ *vt* (*tell*) berichten; (*give information against*) melden; (*to police*) anzeigen ▷ *vi* (*present oneself*) sich melden; **to ~ sick** sich krankmelden; **report card** *n* (US: *school*), Zeugnis *nt*; **reporter** *n* Reporter(in) *m(f)*

represent [reprɪ'zent] *vt* darstellen; (*speak for*) vertreten; **representation** [reprɪzen'teɪʃən] *n* (*picture etc*) Darstellung *f*; **representative** [reprɪ'zentətɪv] *n* Vertreter(in) *m(f)*; (US Pol) Abgeordnete(r) *mf* ▷ *adj* repräsentativ (*of* für)

reprimand ['reprɪmɑːnd] *n* Tadel *m* ▷ *vt* tadeln

reprint ['riːprɪnt] *n* Nachdruck *m*

reproduce [riːprə'djuːs] *vt* (*copy*) reproduzieren ▷ *vi* (*Bio*) sich fortpflanzen; **reproduction** [riːprə'dʌkʃən] *n* (*copy*) Reproduktion *f*; (*Bio*) Fortpflanzung *f*

reptile ['reptaɪl] *n* Reptil *nt*

republic [rɪ'pʌblɪk] *n* Republik *f*; **republican** *adj* republikanisch ▷ *n* Republikaner(in) *m(f)*

repulsive [rɪ'pʌlsɪv] *adj* abstoßend

reputable ['repjʊtəbl] *adj* seriös

reputation [repjʊ'teɪʃən] *n* Ruf *m*; **he has a ~ for being difficult** er hat den Ruf, schwierig zu sein

request [rɪ'kwest] *n* Bitte *f* (*for* um); **on ~** auf Wunsch ▷ *vt* bitten um; **to ~ sb to do sth** jdn bitten, etw zu tun

require [rɪ'kwaɪə*] *vt* (*need*) brauchen; (*desire*) verlangen; **what qualifications are ~d?** welche Qualifikationen sind erforderlich?; **required** *adj* erforderlich; **requirement** *n* (*condition*) Anforderung *f*; (*need*) Bedingung *f*

rerun ['riːrʌn] *n* Wiederholung *f*

rescue ['reskjuː] *n* Rettung *f*; **to come to sb's ~** jdm zu Hilfe kommen ▷ *vt* retten; **rescue party** *n* Rettungsmannschaft *f*

research [rɪ'sɜːtʃ] *n* Forschung *f* ▷ *vi* forschen (*into* über +*akk*) ▷ *vt* erforschen; **researcher** *n* Forscher(in) *m(f)*

resemblance [rɪ'zembləns] *n* Ähnlichkeit *f* (*to* mit); **resemble** [rɪ'zembl] *vt* ähneln +*dat*

resent [rɪ'zent] *vt* übel nehmen

reservation [rezə'veɪʃən] *n* (*booking*) Reservierung *f*; (*doubt*) Vorbehalt *m*; **I**

have a ~ (in hotel, restaurant) ich habe reserviert; **reserve** [rɪ'zɜːv] *n* (*store*) Vorrat *m* (*of* an +*dat*); (*manner*) Zurückhaltung *f*; (Sport) Reservespieler(in) *m(f)*; (*game ~*) Naturschutzgebiet *nt* ▷ *vt* (*book in advance*) reservieren; **reserved** *adj* reserviert

reservoir ['rezəvwɑː*] *n* (*for water*) Reservoir *nt*

reside [rɪ'zaɪd] *vi* wohnen; **residence** ['rezɪdəns] *n* Wohnsitz *m*; (*living*) Aufenthalt *m*; **~ permit** *n* Aufenthaltsgenehmigung *f*; **~ hall** Studentenwohnheim *nt*; **resident** ['rezɪdənt] *n* (*in house*) Bewohner(in) *m(f)*; (*in town, area*) Einwohner(in) *m(f)*

resign [rɪ'zaɪn] *vt* (*post*) zurücktreten von; (*job*) kündigen ▷ *vi* (*from post*) zurücktreten; (*from job*) kündigen; **resignation** [rezɪg'neɪʃən] *n* (*from post*) Rücktritt *m*; (*from job*) Kündigung *f*; **resigned** *adj* resigniert; **he is ~ to it** er hat sich damit abgefunden

resist [rɪ'zɪst] *vt* widerstehen +*dat*; **resistance** *n* Widerstand *m* (*to* gegen)

resit [riː'sɪt] (Brit) *irr vt* wiederholen ▷ ['riːsɪt] *n* Wiederholungsprüfung *f*

resolution [rezə'luːʃən] *n* (*intention*) Vorsatz *m*; (*decision*) Beschluss *m*

resolve [rɪ'zɒlv] *vt* (*problem*) lösen

resort [rɪ'zɔːt] *n* (*holiday ~*) Urlaubsort *m*; (*health ~*) Kurort *m*; **as a last ~** als letzter Ausweg ▷ *vi* **to ~ to** greifen zu; (*violence*) anwenden

resources [rɪ'sɔːsɪz] *npl* (*money*) (Geld)mittel *pl*; (*mineral ~*) Bodenschätze *pl*

respect [rɪ'spekt] *n* Respekt *m* (*for* vor +*dat*); (*consideration*) Rücksicht *f* (*for* auf +*akk*); **with ~ to** in Bezug auf +*akk*; **in this ~** in dieser Hinsicht; **in all due ~** bei allem Respekt ▷ *vt* respektieren; **respectable** [rɪ'spektəbl] *adj* (*person, family*) angesehen; (*district*) anständig; (*achievement, result*) beachtlich; **respected** [rɪ'spektɪd] *adj* angesehen

respective [rɪ'spektɪv] *adj* jeweilig; **respectively** *adv* **5% and 10% ~** 5% beziehungsweise 10%

respiratory [rɪ'spɪrətərɪ] *adj* **~ problems** (o **trouble**) Atembeschwerden *pl*

respond [rɪ'spɒnd] *vi* antworten (*to* auf +*akk*); (*react*) reagieren (*to* auf +*akk*); (*to*

treatment) ansprechen (to auf +akk);
response [rɪˈspɒns] n Antwort f;
(reaction) Reaktion f; **in ~ to** als Antwort
auf +akk
responsibility [rɪspɒnsəˈbɪlɪtɪ] n
Verantwortung f; **that's her ~** dafür ist sie
verantwortlich; **responsible** [rɪˈspɒnsəbl]
adj verantwortlich (**for** für); (trustworthy)
verantwortungsbewusst; (job)
verantwortungsvoll
rest [rest] n (relaxation) Ruhe f; (break)
Pause f; (remainder) Rest m; **to have** (or
take) **a ~** sich ausruhen; (break) Pause
machen; **the ~ of the wine/the people**
der Rest des Weins/der Leute ▷ vi (relax)
sich ausruhen; (lean) lehnen (**on, against** an
+dat, gegen)
restaurant [ˈrestərɒnt] n Restaurant nt;
restaurant car n (Brit) Speisewagen m
restful [ˈrestful] adj (holiday etc)
erholsam, ruhig; **restless** [ˈrestləs] adj
unruhig
restore [rɪˈstɔ:*] vt (painting, building)
restaurieren; (order) wiederherstellen;
(give back) zurückgeben
restrain [rɪˈstreɪn] vt (person, feelings)
zurückhalten; **to ~ oneself** sich
beherrschen
restrict [rɪˈstrɪkt] vt beschränken (**to** auf
+akk); **restricted** adj beschränkt;
restriction [rɪˈstrɪkʃən] n Einschränkung
f (**on** +gen)
rest room [ˈrestru:m] n (US) Toilette f
result [rɪˈzʌlt] n Ergebnis nt; (consequence)
Folge f; **as a ~ of** infolge +gen ▷ vi **to ~ in**
führen zu; **to ~ from** sich ergeben aus
resume [rɪˈzjuːm] vt (work, negotiations)
wieder aufnehmen; (journey) fortsetzen
résumé [ˈrezjumeɪ] n Zusammenfassung
f; (US: curriculum vitae) Lebenslauf m
resuscitate [rɪˈsʌsɪteɪt] vt wieder
beleben
retail [ˈriːteɪl] adv im Einzelhandel;
retailer n Einzelhändler(in) m(f)
retain [rɪˈteɪn] vt behalten; (heat) halten
rethink [riːˈθɪŋk] irr vt noch einmal
überdenken
retire [rɪˈtaɪə*] vi (from work) in den
Ruhestand treten; (withdraw) sich
zurückziehen; **retired** adj (person)
pensioniert; **retirement** n (time of life)
Ruhestand m; **retirement age** n
Rentenalter nt

retrace [rɪˈtreɪs] vt zurückverfolgen
retrain [riːˈtreɪn] vi sich umschulen
lassen
retreat [rɪˈtriːt] n (Mil) Rückzug m (**from**
aus); (refuge) Zufluchtsort m ▷ vi (Mil) sich
zurückziehen; (step back) zurückweichen
retrieve [rɪˈtriːv] vt (recover)
wiederbekommen; (rescue) retten; (data)
abrufen
retrospect [ˈretrəʊspekt] n **in
~** rückblickend; **retrospective**
[retrəʊˈspektɪv] adj rückblickend; (pay rise)
rückwirkend
return [rɪˈtɜːn] n (going back) Rückkehr f;
(giving back) Rückgabe f; (profit) Gewinn m;
(Brit: ~ ticket) Rückfahrkarte f; (plane ticket)
Rückflugticket nt; (Tennis) Return m; **in
~ als** Gegenleistung (**for** für); **many happy
~s (of the day)** herzlichen Glückwunsch
zum Geburtstag! ▷ vi (person)
zurückkehren; (doubts, symptoms) wieder
auftreten; **to ~ to school/work** wieder in
die Schule/die Arbeit gehen ▷ vt (give
back) zurückgeben; **I ~ed his call** ich habe
ihn zurückgerufen; **returnable** adj (bottle)
Pfand-; **return flight** n (Brit) Rückflug m;
(both ways) Hin- und Rückflug m; **return
key** n (Inform) Eingabetaste f; **return
ticket** n (Brit) Rückfahrkarte f; (for plane)
Rückflugticket nt
reunification [riːjuːnɪfɪˈkeɪʃən] n
Wiedervereinigung f
reunion [riːˈjuːnjən] n (party) Treffen nt;
reunite [riːjuːˈnaɪt] vt wieder vereinigen
reusable [riːˈjuːzəbl] adj wieder
verwendbar
reveal [rɪˈviːl] vt (make known) enthüllen;
(secret) verraten; (show) zeigen; **revealing**
adj aufschlussreich; (dress) freizügig
revenge [rɪˈvendʒ] n Rache f; (in game)
Revanche f; **to take ~ on sb (for sth)** sich
an jdm (für etw) rächen
revenue [ˈrevənjuː] n Einnahmen pl
reverse [rɪˈvɜːs] n (back) Rückseite f;
(opposite) Gegenteil nt; (Auto) **~ (gear)**
Rückwärtsgang m ▷ adj **in ~ order** in
umgekehrter Reihenfolge ▷ vt (order)
umkehren; (decision) umstoßen; (car)
zurücksetzen; **to ~ the charges** (Brit) ein
R-Gespräch führen ▷ vi (Auto) rückwärts
fahren
review [rɪˈvjuː] n (of book, film etc)
Rezension f; **to be under ~** überprüft

werden ▷ vt (book, film etc) rezensieren; (re-examine) überprüfen

revise [rɪ'vaɪz] vt revidieren; (text) überarbeiten; (Brit: in school) wiederholen ▷ vi (Brit: in school) den Stoff wiederholen; **revision** [rɪ'vɪʒən] n (of text) Überarbeitung f; (Brit: in school) Wiederholung f

revitalize [riː'vaɪtəlaɪz] vt neu beleben

revive [rɪ'vaɪv] vt (person) wieder beleben; (tradition, interest) wieder aufleben lassen ▷ vi (regain consciousness) wieder zu sich kommen

revolt [rɪ'vəʊlt] n Aufstand m; **revolting** adj widerlich

revolution [revə'luːʃən] n (Pol, fig) Revolution f; (turn) Umdrehung f; **revolutionary** adj revolutionär ▷ n Revolutionär(in) m(f)

revolve [rɪ'vɒlv] vi sich drehen (around um); **revolver** n Revolver m; **revolving door** n Drehtür f

reward [rɪ'wɔːd] n Belohnung f ▷ vt belohnen; **rewarding** adj lohnend

rewind [riː'waɪnd] irr vt (tape) zurückspulen

rewrite [riː'raɪt] irr vt (write again; recast) umschreiben

rheumatism ['ruːmətɪzəm] n Rheuma nt

Rhine [raɪn] n Rhein m

rhinoceros [raɪ'nɒsərəs] n Nashorn nt

Rhodes [rəʊdz] n Rhodos nt

rhubarb ['ruːbɑːb] n Rhabarber m

rhyme [raɪm] n Reim m ▷ vi sich reimen (with auf +akk)

rhythm ['rɪðəm] n Rhythmus m

rib [rɪb] n Rippe f

ribbon ['rɪbən] n Band nt

rice [raɪs] n Reis m; **rice pudding** n Milchreis m

rich [rɪtʃ] adj reich; (food) schwer ▷ npl **the ~** die Reichen pl

rickety ['rɪkɪtɪ] adj wackelig

rid [rɪd] (**rid, rid**) vt **to get ~ of sb/sth** jdn/etw loswerden

ridden ['rɪdn] pp of **ride**

riddle ['rɪdl] n Rätsel nt

ride [raɪd] (**rode, ridden**) vt (horse) reiten; (bicycle) fahren ▷ vi (on horse) reiten; (on bike) fahren ▷ n (in vehicle, on bike) Fahrt f; (on horse) (Aus)ritt m; **to go for a ~** (in car, on bike) spazieren fahren; (on horse) reiten gehen; **to take sb for a ~** (fam) jdn

verarschen; **rider** n (on horse) Reiter(in) m(f); (on bike) Fahrer(in) m(f)

ridiculous [rɪ'dɪkjʊləs] adj lächerlich; **don't be ~** red keinen Unsinn!

riding ['raɪdɪŋ] n Reiten nt; **to go ~** reiten gehen ▷ adj Reit-

rifle ['raɪfl] n Gewehr nt

rig [rɪg] n **oil ~** Bohrinsel f ▷ vt (election etc) manipulieren

right [raɪt] adj (correct, just) richtig; (opposite of left) rechte(r, s); (clothes, job etc) passend; **to be ~** (person) Recht haben; (clock) richtig gehen; **that's ~** das stimmt! ▷ n Recht nt (to auf +akk); (side) rechte Seite; **the Right** (Pol) die Rechte; **to take a ~** (Auto) rechts abbiegen; **on the ~** rechts (of von); **to the ~** nach rechts; (on the ~) rechts (of von) ▷ adv (towards the ~) nach rechts; (directly) direkt; (exactly) genau; **to turn ~** (Auto) rechts abbiegen; **~ away** sofort; **~ now** im Moment; (immediately) sofort; **right angle** n rechter Winkel; **right-hand drive** n Rechtssteuerung f ▷ adj rechtsgesteuert; **right-handed** adj **he is ~** er ist Rechtshänder; **right-hand side** n rechte Seite; **on the ~** auf der rechten Seite; **rightly** adv zu Recht; **right of way** n **to have ~** (Auto) Vorfahrt haben; **right wing** n (Pol, Sport) rechter Flügel; **right-wing** adj Rechts-; **~ extremist** Rechtsradikale(r) mf

rigid ['rɪdʒɪd] adj (stiff) starr; (strict) streng

rigorous, rigorously ['rɪgərəs, -lɪ] adj, adv streng

rim [rɪm] n (of cup etc) Rand m; (of wheel) Felge f

rind [raɪnd] n (of cheese) Rinde f; (of bacon) Schwarte f; (of fruit) Schale f

ring [rɪŋ] (**rang, rung**) vt, vi (bell) läuten; (Tel) anrufen ▷ n (on finger, in boxing) Ring m; (circle) Kreis m; (at circus) Manege f; **to give sb a ~** (Tel) jdn anrufen; **ring back** vt, vi zurückrufen; **ring up** vt, vi anrufen

ring binder n Ringbuch nt

ringing tone n (Tel) Rufzeichen nt

ringleader n Anführer(in) m(f)

ring road n (Brit) Umgehungsstraße f

ringtone n Klingelton m

rink [rɪŋk] n (ice ~) Eisbahn f; (for roller-skating) Rollschuhbahn f

rinse [rɪns] vt spülen

riot ['raɪət] n Aufruhr m

rip [rɪp] n Riss m ▷ vt zerreißen; **to ~ sth**

open etw aufreißen ▷ vi reißen; **rip off** vt (fam: person) übers Ohr hauen; **rip up** vt zerreißen

ripe [raɪp] adj (fruit) reif; **ripen** vi reifen

rip-off [ˈrɪpɒf] n **that's a ~** (fam: too expensive) das ist Wucher

rise [raɪz] (**rose, risen**) vi (from sitting, lying) aufstehen; (sun) aufgehen; (prices, temperature) steigen; (ground) ansteigen; (in revolt) sich erheben ▷ n (increase) Anstieg m (in +gen); (pay ~) Gehaltserhöhung f; (to power, fame) Aufstieg m (to zu); (slope) Steigung f; **risen** [ˈrɪzn] pp of **rise**

risk [rɪsk] n Risiko nt ▷ vt riskieren; **to ~ doing sth** es riskieren, etw zu tun; **risky** adj riskant

risotto [rɪˈzɒtəʊ] (pl -s) n Risotto nt

ritual [ˈrɪtjʊəl] n Ritual nt ▷ adj rituell

rival [ˈraɪvəl] n Rivale m, Rivalin f (for um); (Comm) Konkurrent(in) m(f); **rivalry** n Rivalität f; (Comm, Sport) Konkurrenz f

river [ˈrɪvə*] n Fluss m; **the River Thames** (Brit), **the Thames River** (US) die Themse; **riverside** n Flussufer nt ▷ adj am Flussufer

road [rəʊd] n Straße f; (fig) Weg m; **on the ~** (travelling) unterwegs, mit dem Auto/Bus etc fahren; **roadblock** n Straßensperre f; **roadmap** n Straßenkarte f; **road rage** n aggressives Verhalten im Straßenverkehr; **roadside** n **at** (o **by**) **the ~** am Straßenrand; **roadsign** n Verkehrsschild nt; **road tax** n Kraftfahrzeugsteuer f; **roadworks** npl Straßenarbeiten pl; **roadworthy** adj fahrtüchtig

roar [rɔː*] n (of person, lion) Brüllen nt; (von Verkehr) Donnern nt ▷ vi (person, lion) brüllen (with vor +dat)

roast [rəʊst] n Braten m ▷ adj **~ beef** Rinderbraten m; **~ chicken** Brathähnchen nt; **~ pork** Schweinebraten m; **~ potatoes** pl im Backofen gebratene Kartoffeln ▷ vt (meat) braten

rob [rɒb] vt bestehlen; (bank, shop) ausrauben; **robber** n Räuber(in) m(f); **robbery** n Raub m

robe [rəʊb] n (US: dressing gown) Morgenrock m; (of judge, priest etc) Robe f, Talar m

robin [ˈrɒbɪn] n Rotkehlchen nt

robot [ˈrəʊbɒt] n Roboter m

robust [rəʊˈbʌst] adj robust; (defence) stark

rock [rɒk] n (substance) Stein m; (boulder) Felsbrocken m; (Mus) Rock m; **stick of ~** (Brit) Zuckerstange f; **on the ~s** (drink) mit Eis; (marriage) gescheitert ▷ vt, vi (swing) schaukeln; (dance) rocken; **rock climbing** n Klettern nt; **to go ~** klettern gehen

rocket [ˈrɒkɪt] n Rakete f; (in salad) Rucola f

rocking chair [ˈrɒkɪŋtʃɛə*] n Schaukelstuhl m

rocky [ˈrɒkɪ] adj (landscape) felsig; (path) steinig

rod [rɒd] n (bar) Stange f; (fishing ~) Rute f

rode [rəʊd] pt of **ride**

rogue [rəʊg] n Schurke m, Gauner m

role [rəʊl] n Rolle f; **role model** n Vorbild nt

roll [rəʊl] n (of film, paper etc) Rolle f; (bread ~) Brötchen nt ▷ vt (move by ~ing) rollen; (cigarette) drehen ▷ vi (move by ~ing) rollen; (ship) schlingern; (camera) laufen; **roll out** vt (pastry) ausrollen; **roll over** vi (person) sich umdrehen; **roll up** vi (fam: arrive) antanzen ▷ vt (carpet) aufrollen; **to roll one's sleeves up** die Ärmel hochkrempeln

roller n (hair ~) (Locken)wickler m; **Rollerblades®** npl Inlineskates pl; **rollerblading** n Inlineskaten nt; **roller coaster** n Achterbahn f; **roller skates** npl Rollschuhe pl; **roller-skating** n Rollschuhlaufen nt; **rolling pin** n Nudelholz nt; **roll-on (deodorant)** n Deoroller m

ROM [rɒm] acr = **read only memory** ROM m

Roman [ˈrəʊmən] adj römisch ▷ n Römer(in) m(f); **Roman Catholic** adj römisch-katholisch ▷ n Katholik(in) m(f)

romance [rəʊˈmæns] n Romantik f; (love affair) Romanze f

Romania [rəʊˈmeɪnɪə] n Rumänien nt; **Romanian** adj rumänisch ▷ n Rumäne m, Rumänin f; (language) Rumänisch nt

romantic [rəʊˈmæntɪk] adj romantisch

roof [ruːf] n Dach nt; **roof rack** n Dachgepäckträger m

rook [rʊk] n (in chess) Turm m

room [ruːm] n Zimmer nt, Raum m; (large, for gatherings etc) Saal m; (space) Platz m; (fig) Spielraum m; **to make ~ for** Platz

machen für; **roommate** n
Zimmergenosse m, Zimmergenossin f; (US:
sharing apartment) Mitbewohner(in) m(f);
room service n Zimmerservice m; **roomy**
adj geräumig; (*garment*) weit

root [ruːt] n Wurzel f; **root out** vt
(*eradicate*) ausrotten; **root vegetable** n
Wurzelgemüse nt

rope [rəʊp] n Seil nt; **to know the ~s** (*fam*)
sich auskennen

rose [rəʊz] pt of **rise** ▷ n Rose f

rosé [ˈrəʊzeɪ] n Rosé(wein) m

rot [rɒt] vi verfaulen

rota [ˈrəʊtə] n (*Brit*) Dienstplan m

rotate [rəʊˈteɪt] vt (*turn*) rotieren lassen
▷ vi rotieren; **rotation** [rəʊˈteɪʃən] n
(*turning*) Rotation f; **in ~** abwechselnd

rotten [ˈrɒtn] adj (*decayed*) faul; (*mean*)
gemein; (*unpleasant*) scheußlich; (*ill*) elend

rough [rʌf] adj (*not smooth*) rau; (*path*)
uneben; (*coarse, violent*) grob; (*crossing*)
stürmisch; (*without comforts*) hart;
(*unfinished, makeshift*) grob; (*approximate*)
ungefähr; **~ draft** Rohentwurf m; **I have a
~ idea** ich habe eine ungefähre
Vorstellung ▷ adv **to sleep ~** im Freien
schlafen ▷ vt **to ~ it** primitiv leben ▷ n **to
write sth in ~** etw ins Unreine schreiben;
roughly adv grob; (*approximately*)
ungefähr

round [raʊnd] adj rund ▷ adv **all ~** (*on all
sides*) rundherum; **the long way ~** der
längere Weg; **I'll be ~ at 8** ich werde um
acht Uhr da sein; **the other way
~** umgekehrt ▷ prep (*surrounding*) um (...
herum); **~** (*about*) (*approximately*)
ungefähr; **~ the corner** um die Ecke; **to go
~ the world** um die Welt reisen; **she lives
~ here** sie wohnt hier in der Gegend ▷ n
Runde f; (*of bread, toast*) Scheibe f; **it's my
~** (*of drinks*) die Runde geht auf mich ▷ vt
(*corner*) biegen um; **round off** vt
abrunden; **round up** vt (*number, price*)
aufrunden

roundabout n (*Brit Auto*) Kreisverkehr m;
(*Brit: merry-go-round*) Karussell nt ▷ adj
umständlich; **round-the-clock** adj rund
um die Uhr; **round trip** n Rundreise f;
round-trip ticket n (*US*) Rückfahrkarte f;
(*for plane*) Rückflugticket nt

rouse [raʊz] vt (*from sleep*) wecken

route [ruːt] n Route f; (*bus, plane etc
service*) Linie f; (*fig*) Weg m

routine [ruːˈtiːn] n Routine f ▷ adj
Routine-

row [rəʊ] n (*line*) Reihe f; **three times in a
~** dreimal hintereinander ▷ vt, vi (*boat*)
rudern ▷ [raʊ] n (*noise*) Krach m; (*dispute*)
Streit m

rowboat [ˈrəʊbəʊt] n (*US*) Ruderboot nt

row house [ˈrəʊhaʊs] n (*US*) Reihenhaus
nt

rowing [ˈrəʊɪŋ] n Rudern nt; **rowing boat**
n (*Brit*) Ruderboot nt; **rowing machine** n
Rudergerät nt

royal [ˈrɔɪəl] adj königlich; **royalty** n
(*family*) Mitglieder pl der königlichen
Familie; **royalties** pl (*from book, music*)
Tantiemen pl

RSPCA abbr = **Royal Society for the
Prevention of Cruelty to Animals**
britischer Tierschutzverein

RSPCC abbr = **Royal Society for the
Prevention of Cruelty to Children**
britischer Kinderschutzverein

RSVP abbr = **répondez s'il vous plaît** u. A.
w. g.

rub [rʌb] vt reiben; **rub in** vt
einmassieren; **rub out** vt (*with eraser*)
ausradieren

rubber [ˈrʌbə*] n Gummi m; (*Brit: eraser*)
Radiergummi m; (*US fam: contraceptive*)
Gummi m; **rubber band** n Gummiband
nt; **rubber stamp** n Stempel m

rubbish [ˈrʌbɪʃ] n Abfall m; (*nonsense*)
Quatsch m; (*poor-quality thing*) Mist m;
don't talk ~ red keinen Unsinn!; **rubbish
bin** n Mülleimer m; **rubbish dump** n
Müllabladeplatz m

rubble [ˈrʌbl] n Schutt m

ruby [ˈruːbɪ] n (*stone*) Rubin m

rucksack [ˈrʌksæk] n Rucksack m

rude [ruːd] adj (*impolite*) unhöflich;
(*indecent*) unanständig

rug [rʌg] n Teppich m; (*next to bed*)
Bettvorleger m; (*for knees*) Wolldecke f

rugby [ˈrʌgbɪ] n Rugby m

rugged [ˈrʌgɪd] adj (*coastline*) zerklüftet;
(*features*) markant

ruin [ˈruːɪn] n Ruine f; (*financial, social*)
Ruin m ▷ vt ruinieren

rule [ruːl] n Regel f; (*governing*) Herrschaft
f; **as a ~** in der Regel ▷ vt, vi (*govern*)
regieren; (*decide*) entscheiden; **ruler** n
Lineal nt; (*person*) Herrscher(in) m(f)

rum [rʌm] n Rum m

rumble [ˈrʌmbl] vi (stomach) knurren; (train, truck) rumpeln

rummage [ˈrʌmɪdʒ] vi ~ **(around)** herumstöbern

rumor (US), **rumour** [ˈruːmə*] n Gerücht nt

run [rʌn] (**ran, run**) vt (race, distance) laufen; (machine, engine, computer program, water) laufen lassen; (manage) leiten, führen; (car) unterhalten; **I ran her home** ich habe sie nach Hause gefahren ▷ vi laufen; (move quickly) rennen; (bus, train) fahren; (path etc) verlaufen; (machine, engine, computer program) laufen; (flow) fließen; (colours, make-up) verlaufen; **to ~ for President** für die Präsidentschaft kandidieren; **to be ~ning low** knapp werden; **my nose is ~ning** mir läuft die Nase; **it ~s in the family** es liegt in der Familie ▷ n (on foot) Lauf m; (in car) Spazierfahrt f; (series) Reihe f; (sudden demand) Ansturm m (on auf +akk); (in tights) Laufmasche f; (in cricket, baseball) Lauf m; **to go for a ~** laufen gehen; (in car) eine Spazierfahrt machen; **in the long ~** auf die Dauer; **on the ~** auf der Flucht (from vor +dat); **run about** vi herumlaufen; **run away** vi weglaufen; **run down** vt (with car) umfahren; (criticize) heruntermachen; **to be ~** (tired) abgespannt sein; **run into** vt (meet) zufällig treffen; (problem) stoßen auf +akk; **run off** vi weglaufen; **run out** vi (person) hinausrennen; (liquid) auslaufen; (lease, time) ablaufen; (money, supplies) ausgehen; **he ran ~ of money** ihm ging das Geld aus; **run over** vt (with car) überfahren; **run up** vt (debt, bill) machen

rung [rʌŋ] pp of **ring**

runner [ˈrʌnə*] n (athlete) Läufer(in) m(f); **to do a ~** (fam) wegrennen; **runner beans** npl (Brit) Stangenbohnen pl

running [ˈrʌnɪŋ] n (Sport) Laufen nt; (management) Leitung f, Führung f ▷ adj (water) fließend; **~ costs** Betriebskosten pl; (for car) Unterhaltskosten pl; **3 days ~** 3 Tage hintereinander

runny [ˈrʌnɪ] adj (food) flüssig; (nose) laufend

runway [ˈrʌnweɪ] n Start- und Landebahn f

rural [ˈrʊərəl] adj ländlich

rush [rʌʃ] n Eile f; (for tickets etc) Ansturm m (for auf +akk); **to be in a ~** es eilig haben; **there's no ~** es eilt nicht ▷ vt (do too quickly) hastig machen; (meal) hastig essen; **to ~ sb to hospital** jdn auf dem schnellsten Weg ins Krankenhaus bringen; **don't ~ me** dräng mich nicht ▷ vi (hurry) eilen; **don't ~** lass dir Zeit; **rush hour** n Hauptverkehrszeit f

rusk [rʌsk] n Zwieback m

Russia [ˈrʌʃə] n Russland nt; **Russian** adj russisch ▷ n Russe m, Russin f; (language) Russisch nt

rust [rʌst] n Rost m ▷ vi rosten; **rustproof** [ˈrʌstpruːf] adj rostfrei; **rusty** [ˈrʌstɪ] adj rostig

ruthless [ˈruːθləs] adj rücksichtslos; (treatment, criticism) schonungslos

rye [raɪ] n Roggen m; **rye bread** n Roggenbrot nt

S

S *abbr* = **south** S

sabotage [ˈsæbətɑːʒ] *vt* sabotieren

sachet [ˈsæʃeɪ] *n* Päckchen *nt*

sack [sæk] *n* (*bag*) Sack *m*; **to get the ~** (*fam*) rausgeschmissen werden ▷ *vt* (*fam*) rausschmeißen

sacred [ˈseɪkrɪd] *adj* heilig

sacrifice [ˈsækrɪfaɪs] *n* Opfer *nt* ▷ *vt* opfern

sad [sæd] *adj* traurig

saddle [ˈsædl] *n* Sattel *m*

sadistic [səˈdɪstɪk] *adj* sadistisch

sadly [ˈsædlɪ] *adv* (*unfortunately*) leider

safari [səˈfɑːrɪ] *n* Safari *f*

safe [seɪf] *adj* (*free from danger*) sicher; (*out of danger*) in Sicherheit; (*careful*) vorsichtig; **have a ~ journey** gute Fahrt! ▷ *n* Safe *m*; **safeguard** *n* Schutz *m* ▷ *vt* schützen (*against* vor +*dat*); **safely** *adv* sicher; (*arrive*) wohlbehalten; (*drive*) vorsichtig; **safety** *n* Sicherheit *f*; **safety belt** *n* Sicherheitsgurt *m*; **safety pin** *n* Sicherheitsnadel *f*

Sagittarius [sædʒɪˈtɛərɪəs] *n* (*Astr*) Schütze *m*

Sahara [səˈhɑːrə] *n* **the ~** (**Desert**) die (Wüste) Sahara

said [sed] *pt, pp of* **say**

sail [seɪl] *n* Segel *nt*; **to set ~** losfahren (*for* nach) ▷ *vi* (*in yacht*) segeln; (*on ship*) mit dem Schiff fahren; (*ship*) auslaufen (*for* nach) ▷ *vt* (*yacht*) segeln mit; (*ship*) steuern; **sailboat** *n* (*US*) Segelboot *nt*; **sailing** *n* **to go ~** segeln gehen; **sailing boat** *n* (*Brit*) Segelboot *nt*; **sailor** *n* Seemann *m*; (*in navy*) Matrose *m*

saint [seɪnt] *n* Heilige(r) *mf*

sake [seɪk] *n* **for the ~ of** um +*gen* ... willen; **for your ~** deinetwegen, dir zuliebe

salad [ˈsæləd] *n* Salat *m*; **salad cream** *n* (*Brit*) majonäseartige Salatsoße; **salad dressing** *n* Salatsoße *f*

salary [ˈsælərɪ] *n* Gehalt *nt*

sale [seɪl] *n* Verkauf *m*; (*at reduced prices*) Ausverkauf *m*; **the ~s** *pl* (*in summer, winter*) der Schlussverkauf; **for ~** zu verkaufen; **sales clerk** *n* (*US*) Verkäufer(in) *m(f)*; **salesman** (*pl* **-men**) *n* Verkäufer *m*; (*rep*) Vertreter *m*; **sales rep** *n* Vertreter(in) *m(f)*; **sales tax** *n* (*US*) Verkaufssteuer *f*; **saleswoman** (*pl* **-women**) *n* Verkäuferin *f*; (*rep*) Vertreterin *f*

saliva [səˈlaɪvə] *n* Speichel *m*

salmon [ˈsæmən] *n* Lachs *m*

saloon [səˈluːn] *n* (*ship's lounge*) Salon *m*; (*US: bar*) Kneipe *f*

salt [sɔːlt] *n* Salz *nt* ▷ *vt* (*flavour*) salzen; (*roads*) mit Salz streuen; **salt cellar**, **salt shaker** (*US*) *n* Salzstreuer *m*; **salty** *adj* salzig

salvage [ˈsælvɪdʒ] *vt* bergen (*from* aus); (*fig*) retten

same [seɪm] *adj* **the ~** (*similar*) der/die/das gleiche, die gleichen *pl*; (*identical*) der-/die-/dasselbe, dieselben *pl*; **they live in the ~ house** sie wohnen im selben Haus ▷ *pron* **the ~** (*similar*) der/die/das Gleiche, die Gleichen *pl*; (*identical*) der-/die-/dasselbe, dieselben *pl*; **I'll have the ~ again** ich möchte noch mal das Gleiche; **all the ~** trotzdem; **the ~ to you** gleichfalls; **it's all the ~ to me** es ist mir egal ▷ *adv* **the ~** gleich; **they look the ~** sie sehen gleich aus

sample [ˈsɑːmpl] *n* Probe *f*; (*of fabric*) Muster *nt* ▷ *vt* probieren

sanctions [ˈsæŋkʃənz] *npl* (*Pol*) Sanktionen *pl*

sanctuary ['sæŋktjʊərɪ] n (refuge)
Zuflucht f; (for animals) Schutzgebiet nt
sand [sænd] n Sand m
sandal ['sændl] n Sandale f
sandpaper n Sandpapier nt ▷ vt
schmirgeln
sandwich ['sænwɪdʒ] n Sandwich nt
sandy ['sændɪ] adj (full of sand) sandig;
~ **beach** Sandstrand m
sane [seɪn] adj geistig gesund, normal;
(sensible) vernünftig
sang [sæŋ] pt of **sing**
sanitary ['sænɪtərɪ] adj hygienisch;
sanitary napkin (US), **sanitary towel** n
Damenbinde f
sank [sæŋk] pt of **sink**
Santa (Claus) ['sæntə('klɔːz)] n der
Weihnachtsmann
sarcastic [saː'kæstɪk] adj sarkastisch
sardine [saː'diːn] n Sardine f
Sardinia [saː'dɪnɪə] n Sardinien nt
sari [saːrɪ] n Sari m (von indischen Frauen
getragenes Gewand)
sat [sæt] pt, pp of **sit**
Sat abbr = **Saturday** Sa.
satellite ['sætəlaɪt] n Satellit m; **satellite
dish** n Satellitenschüssel f; **satellite TV** n
Satellitenfernsehen nt
satin ['sætɪn] n Satin m
satisfaction [sætɪs'fækʃən] n
(contentment) Zufriedenheit f; **is that to
your ~?** sind Sie damit zufrieden?;
satisfactory [sætɪs'fæktərɪ] adj
zufrieden stellend; **satisfied** ['sætɪsfaɪd]
adj zufrieden (with mit); **satisfy** ['sætɪsfaɪ]
vt zufrieden stellen; (convince)
überzeugen; (conditions) erfüllen; (need,
demand) befriedigen; **satisfying** adj
befriedigend
Saturday ['sætədeɪ] n Samstag m,
Sonnabend m; see also **Tuesday**
sauce [sɔːs] n Soße f; **saucepan** n
Kochtopf m; **saucer** n Untertasse f
saucy ['sɔːsɪ] adj frech
Saudi Arabia ['saʊdɪə'reɪbɪə] n
Saudi-Arabien nt
sauna ['sɔːnə] n Sauna f
sausage ['sɒsɪdʒ] n Wurst f; **sausage roll**
n mit Wurst gefülltes Blätterteigröllchen
savage ['sævɪdʒ] adj (person, attack)
brutal; (animal) wild
save [seɪv] vt (rescue) retten (from vor
+dat); (money, time, electricity etc) sparen;

(strength) schonen; (Inform) speichern; **to
~ sb's life** jdm das Leben retten ▷ vi
sparen ▷ n (in football) Parade f; **save up**
vi sparen (for auf +akk); **saving** n (of
money) Sparen nt; **~s** pl Ersparnisse pl; **~s
account** Sparkonto nt
savory (US), **savoury** ['seɪvərɪ] adj (not
sweet) pikant
saw [sɔː] (**sawed, sawn**) vt, vi sägen ▷ n
(tool) Säge f ▷ pt of **see**; **sawdust** n
Sägemehl nt
saxophone ['sæksəfəʊn] n Saxophon nt
say [seɪ] (**said, said**) vt sagen (to sb jdm);
(prayer) sprechen; **what does the letter ~?**
was steht im Brief?; **the rules ~ that ...** in
den Regeln heißt es, dass ...; **he's said to
be rich** er soll reich sein ▷ n **to have a ~ in
sth** bei etw ein Mitspracherecht haben
▷ adv zum Beispiel; **saying** n Sprichwort
nt
scab [skæb] n (on cut) Schorf m
scaffolding ['skæfəʊldɪŋ] n (Bau)gerüst
nt
scale [skeɪl] n (of map etc) Maßstab m; (on
thermometer etc) Skala f; (of pay)
Tarifsystem nt; (Mus) Tonleiter f; (of fish,
snake) Schuppe f; **to ~** maßstabsgerecht;
on a large/small ~ in großem/kleinem
Umfang; **scales** npl (for weighing) Waage f
scalp [skælp] n Kopfhaut f
scan [skæn] vt (examine) genau prüfen;
(read quickly) überfliegen; (Inform) scannen
▷ n (Med) Ultraschall m; **scan in** vt
(Inform) einscannen
scandal ['skændl] n Skandal m;
scandalous adj skandalös
Scandinavia [skændɪ'neɪvɪə] n
Skandinavien nt; **Scandinavian** adj
skandinavisch ▷ n Skandinavier(in) m(f)
scanner ['skænə*] n Scanner m
scapegoat ['skeɪpgəʊt] n Sündenbock m
scar [skaː*] n Narbe f
scarce ['skeəs] adj selten; (in short supply)
knapp; **scarcely** adv kaum
scare ['skeə*] n (general alarm) Panik f ▷ vt
erschrecken; **to be ~d** Angst haben (of vor
+dat)
scarf [skaːf] n (pl -**scarves**) n Schal m; (on
head) Kopftuch nt
scarlet ['skaːlət] adj scharlachrot; **scarlet
fever** n Scharlach m
scary ['skeərɪ] adj (film, story) gruselig
scatter ['skætə*] vt verstreuen; (seed,

gravel) streuen; (*disperse*) auseinander treiben

scene [si:n] *n* (*location*) Ort *m*; (*division of play*) (*Theat*) Szene *f*; (*view*) Anblick *m*; **to make a ~** eine Szene machen; **scenery** ['si:nərɪ] *n* (*landscape*) Landschaft *f*; (*Theat*) Kulissen *pl*; **scenic** ['si:nɪk] *adj* (*landscape*) malerisch; **~ route** landschaftlich schöne Strecke

scent [sɛnt] *n* (*perfume*) Parfüm *nt*; (*smell*) Duft *m*

sceptical ['skɛptɪkəl] *adj* (*Brit*) skeptisch

schedule ['ʃɛdjuːl, 'skɛdʒʊəl] *n* (*plan*) Programm *nt*; (*of work*) Zeitplan *m*; (*list*) Liste *f*; (*US: of trains, buses, air traffic*) Fahr-, Flugplan *m*; **on ~** planmäßig; **to be behind ~ with sth** mit etw in Verzug sein ▷ *vt* **the meeting is ~d for next Monday** die Besprechung ist für nächsten Montag angesetzt; **scheduled** *adj* (*departure, arrival*) planmäßig; **~ flight** Linienflug *m*

scheme [ski:m] *n* (*plan*) Plan *m*; (*project*) Projekt *nt*; (*dishonest*) Intrige *f* ▷ *vi* intrigieren

schizophrenic [skɪtsə'frɛnɪk] *adj* schizophren

scholar ['skɒlə*] *n* Gelehrte(r) *mf*; **scholarship** *n* (*grant*) Stipendium *nt*

school [sku:l] *n* Schule *f*; (*university department*) Fachbereich *m*; (*US: university*) Universität *f*; **school bag** *n* Schultasche *f*; **schoolbook** *n* Schulbuch *nt*; **schoolboy** *n* Schüler *m*; **school bus** *n* Schulbus *m*; **schoolgirl** *n* Schülerin *f*; **schoolteacher** *n* Lehrer(in) *m(f)*; **schoolwork** *n* Schularbeiten *pl*

sciatica [saɪ'ætɪkə] *n* Ischias *m*

science ['saɪəns] *n* Wissenschaft *f*; (*natural ~*) Naturwissenschaft *f*; **science fiction** *n* Sciencefiction *f*; **scientific** [saɪən'tɪfɪk] *adj* wissenschaftlich; **scientist** ['saɪəntɪst] *n* Wissenschaftler(in) *m(f)*; (*in natural sciences*) Naturwissenschaftler(in) *m(f)*

scissors ['sɪzəz] *npl* Schere *f*

scone [skɒn] *n* *kleines süßes Hefebrötchen mit oder ohne Rosinen, das mit Butter oder Dickrahm und Marmelade gegessen wird*

scoop [sku:p] *n* (*exclusive story*) Exklusivbericht *m*; **a ~ of ice-cream** eine Kugel Eis ▷ *vt* **to ~ (up)** schaufeln

scooter ['sku:tə*] *n* (*Motor*)roller *m*; (*toy*) (Tret)roller *m*

scope [skəʊp] *n* Umfang *m*; (*opportunity*) Möglichkeit *f*

score [skɔ:*] *n* (*Sport*) Spielstand *m*; (*final result*) Spielergebnis *nt*; (*in quiz etc*) Punktestand *m*; (*Mus*) Partitur *f*; **to keep (the) ~** mitzählen ▷ *vt* (*goal*) schießen; (*points*) machen ▷ *vi* (*keep ~*) mitzählen; **scoreboard** *n* Anzeigetafel *f*

scorn [skɔ:n] *n* Verachtung *f*; **scornful** *adj* verächtlich

Scorpio [skɔ:pɪəʊ] (*pl* **-s**) *n* (*Astr*) Skorpion *m*

scorpion ['skɔ:pɪən] *n* Skorpion *m*

Scot [skɒt] *n* Schotte *m*, Schottin *f*;

Scotch [skɒtʃ] *adj* schottisch ▷ *n* (*whisky*) schottischer Whisky, Scotch *m*

Scotch tape® *n* (*US*) Tesafilm® *m*

Scotland ['skɒtlənd] *n* Schottland *nt*; **Scotsman** (*pl* **-men**) *n* Schotte *m*; **Scotswoman** (*pl* **-women**) *n* Schottin *f*; **Scottish** *adj* schottisch

scout [skaʊt] *n* (*boy ~*) Pfadfinder *m*

scowl [skaʊl] *vi* finster blicken

scrambled eggs *npl* Rührei *nt*

scrap [skræp] *n* (*bit*) Stückchen *nt*, Fetzen *m*; (*metal*) Schrott *m* ▷ *vt* (*car*) verschrotten; (*plan*) verwerfen; **scrapbook** *n* Sammelalbum *nt*

scrape [skreɪp] *n* (*scratch*) Kratzer *m* ▷ *vt* (*car*) schrammen; (*wall*) streifen; **to ~ one's knee** sich das Knie schürfen; **scrape through** *vi* (*exam*) mit knapper Not bestehen

scrap heap ['skræphi:p] *n* Schrotthaufen *m*; **scrap metal** *n* Schrott *m*; **scrap paper** *n* Schmierpapier *nt*

scratch ['skrætʃ] *n* (*mark*) Kratzer *m*; **to start from ~** von vorne anfangen ▷ *vt* kratzen; (*car*) zerkratzen; **to ~ one's arm** sich am Arm kratzen ▷ *vi* kratzen; (*~ oneself*) sich kratzen

scream [skri:m] *n* Schrei *m* ▷ *vi* schreien (*with* vor +dat); **to ~ at sb** jdn anschreien

screen [skri:n] *n* (*Tv, Inform*) Bildschirm *m*; (*Cine*) Leinwand *f* ▷ *vt* (*protect*) abschirmen; (*hide*) verdecken; (*film*) zeigen; (*applicants, luggage*) überprüfen; **screenplay** *n* Drehbuch *nt*; **screen saver** *n* (*Inform*) Bildschirmschoner *m*

screw [skru:] *n* Schraube *f* ▷ *vt* (*vulg: have sex with*) poppen; **to ~ sth to sth** etw an etw *akk* schrauben; **to ~ off/on** (*lid*) ab-/aufschrauben; **screw up** *vt* (*paper*) zusammenknüllen; (make a mess of) vermasseln; **screwdriver** n Schraubenzieher m; **screw top** n Schraubverschluss m

scribble ['skrɪbl] vt, vi kritzeln

script [skrɪpt] n (of play) Text m; (of film) Drehbuch nt; (style of writing) Schrift f

scroll down ['skrəʊl'daʊn] vi (Inform) runterscrollen; **scroll up** vi (Inform) raufscrollen; **scroll bar** n (Inform) Scrollbar f

scrub [skrʌb] vt schrubben; **scrubbing brush, scrub brush** (US) n Scheuerbürste f

scruffy ['skrʌfɪ] adj vergammelt

scrupulous, scrupulously ['skruːpjʊləs, -lɪ] adj, adv gewissenhaft; (painstaking) peinlich genau

scuba-diving ['skuːbədaɪvɪŋ] n Sporttauchen nt

sculptor ['skʌlptə*] n Bildhauer(in) m(f); **sculpture** ['skʌlptʃə*] n (Art) Bildhauerei f; (statue) Skulptur f

sea [siː] n Meer nt, See f; **seafood** n Meeresfrüchte pl; **sea front** n Strandpromenade f; **seagull** n Möwe f

seal [siːl] n (animal) Robbe f; (stamp, impression) Siegel nt; (Tech) Verschluss m; (ring etc) Dichtung f ▷ vt versiegeln; (envelope) zukleben

seam [siːm] n Naht f

seaport ['siːpɔːt] n Seehafen m

search [sɜːtʃ] n Suche f (for nach); **to do a ~ for** (Inform) suchen nach; **in ~ of** auf der Suche nach ▷ vi suchen (for nach) ▷ vt durchsuchen; **search engine** n (Inform) Suchmaschine f

seashell ['siːʃel] n Muschel f; **seashore** n Strand m; **seasick** adj seekrank; **seaside** n **at the ~** am Meer; **to go to the ~** ans Meer fahren; **seaside resort** n Seebad nt

season ['siːzn] n Jahreszeit f; (Comm) Saison f; **high/low ~** Hoch-/Nebensaison f ▷ vt (flavour) würzen

seasoning n Gewürz nt

season ticket n (Rail) Zeitkarte f; (Theat) Abonnement nt; (Sport) Dauerkarte f

seat [siːt] n (place) Platz m; (chair) Sitz m; **take a ~** setzen Sie sich ▷ vt **the hall ~s 300** der Saal hat 300 Sitzplätze; **please be ~ed** bitte setzen Sie sich; **to remain ~ed** sitzen bleiben; **seat belt** n Sicherheitsgurt m

sea view ['siːvjuː] n Seeblick m; **seaweed** n Seetang m

secluded [sɪ'kluːdɪd] adj abgelegen

second ['sekənd] adj zweite(r, s); **the ~ of June** der zweite Juni ▷ adv (in ~ position) an zweiter Stelle; (secondly) zweitens; **he came ~** er ist Zweiter geworden ▷ n (of time) Sekunde f; (moment) Augenblick m; **~ (gear)** der zweite Gang; (~ helping) zweite Portion; **just a ~** (einen) Augenblick!; **secondary** adj (less important) zweitrangig; **~ education** höhere Schulbildung f; **~ school** weiterführende Schule; **second-class** adj (ticket) zweiter Klasse; **~ stamp** Briefmarke für nicht bevorzugt beförderte Sendungen ▷ adv (travel) zweiter Klasse; **secondhand** adj, adv gebraucht; (information) aus zweiter Hand; **secondly** adv zweitens; **second-rate** adj (pej) zweitklassig

secret ['siːkrət] n Geheimnis nt ▷ adj geheim; (admirer) heimlich

secretary ['sekrətrɪ] n Sekretär(in) m(f); (minister) Minister(in) m(f); **Secretary of State** n (US) Außenminister(in) m(f)

secretive ['siːkrətɪv] adj (person) geheimnistuerisch; **secretly** ['siːkrətlɪ] adv heimlich

sect [sekt] n Sekte f

section ['sekʃən] n (part) Teil m; (of document) Abschnitt m; (department) Abteilung f

secure [sɪ'kjʊə*] adj (safe) sicher (from vor +dat); (firmly fixed) fest ▷ vt (make firm) befestigen; (window, door) fest verschließen; (obtain) sich sichern; **securely** adv fest; (safely) sicher; **security** [sɪ'kjʊərɪtɪ] n Sicherheit f

sedative ['sedətɪv] n Beruhigungsmittel nt

seduce [sɪ'djuːs] vt verführen; **seductive** [sɪ'dʌktɪv] adj verführerisch; (offer) verlockend

see [siː] (**saw, seen**) vt sehen; (understand) verstehen; (check) nachsehen; (accompany) bringen; (visit) besuchen; (talk to) sprechen; **to ~ the doctor** zum Arzt gehen; **to ~ sb home** jdn nach Hause begleiten; **I saw him swimming** ich habe ihn schwimmen sehen; **~ you** tschüs!; **~ you on Friday** bis Freitag! ▷ vi sehen; (understand) verstehen; (check) nachsehen;

(you) ~ siehst du!; **we'll ~** mal sehen; **see about** vt (attend to) sich kümmern um; **see off** vt (say goodbye to) verabschieden; **see out** vt (show out) zur Tür bringen; **see through** vt **to see sth through** etw zu Ende bringen; **to ~ sb/sth** jdn/etw durchschauen; **see to** vt sich kümmern um; **~ it that ...** sieh zu, dass ...

seed [si:d] n (of plant) Samen m; (in fruit) Kern m; **seedless** adj kernlos

seek [si:k] (**sought, sought**) vt suchen; (fame) streben nach; **to ~ sb's advice** jdn um Rat fragen

seem [si:m] vi scheinen; **he ~s (to be) honest** er scheint ehrlich zu sein; **it ~s to me that ...** es scheint mir, dass ...

seen [si:n] pp of **see**

seesaw ['si:sɔ:] n Wippe f

segment ['segmənt] n Teil m

seize [si:z] vt packen; (confiscate) beschlagnahmen; (opportunity, power) ergreifen

seldom ['seldəm] adv selten

select [sɪ'lekt] adj (exclusive) exklusiv ▷ vt auswählen; **selection** [sɪ'lekʃən] n Auswahl f (of an +dat); **selective** adj (choosy) wählerisch

self [self] (pl **selves**) n Selbst nt, Ich nt; **he's his old ~ again** er ist wieder ganz der Alte; **self-adhesive** adj selbstklebend; **self-assured** n selbstsicher; **self-catering** adj) für Selbstversorger; **self-centred** adj egozentrisch; **self-confidence** n Selbstbewusstsein nt; **self-confident** adj selbstbewusst; **self-conscious** adj befangen, verklemmt; **self-contained** adj (flat) separat; **self-control** n Selbstbeherrschung f; **self-defence** n Selbstverteidigung f; **self-employed** adj selbstständig; **self-evident** adj offensichtlich

selfish, selfishly ['selfɪʃ, -lɪ] adj, adv egoistisch, selbstsüchtig; **selfless, selflessly** adj, adv selbstlos

self-pity [self'pɪtɪ] n Selbstmitleid nt; **self-portrait** n Selbstporträt nt; **self-respect** n Selbstachtung f; **self-service** n Selbstbedienung f ▷ adj Selbstbedienungs-

sell [sel] (**sold, sold**) vt verkaufen; **to ~ sb sth, to ~ sth to sb** jdm etw verkaufen; **do you ~ postcards?** haben Sie Postkarten?

▷ vi (product) sich verkaufen; **sell out** vt **to be sold ~** ausverkauft sein; **sell-by date** n Haltbarkeitsdatum nt

Sellotape® ['seləteɪp] n (Brit) Tesafilm® m

semester [sɪ'mestə*] n Semester nt

semi ['semɪ] n (Brit: house) Doppelhaushälfte f; **semicircle** n Halbkreis m; **semicolon** n Semikolon nt; **semidetached (house)** n (Brit) Doppelhaushälfte f; **semifinal** n Halbfinale nt

seminar ['semɪnɑ:*] n Seminar nt

semiskimmed milk ['semɪskɪmd'mɪlk] n Halbfettmilch f

senate ['senət] n Senat m; **senator** n Senator(in) m(f)

send [send] (**sent, sent**) vt schicken; **to ~ sb sth, to ~ sth to sb** jdm etw schicken; **~ her my best wishes** grüße sie von mir; **send away** vt wegschicken ▷ vi **to ~ for** anfordern; **send back** vt zurückschicken; **send for** vt (person) holen lassen; (by post) anfordern; **send off** vt (by post) abschicken; **send out** vt (invitations etc) verschicken ▷ vi **to ~ for sth** etw holen lassen

sender ['sendə*] n Absender(in) m(f)

senior ['si:nɪə*] adj (older) älter; (high-ranking) höher; (pupils) älter; **he is ~ to me** er ist mir übergeordnet ▷ n **he's eight years my ~** er ist acht Jahre älter als ich; **senior citizen** n Senior(in) m(f)

sensation [sen'seɪʃən] n Gefühl nt; (excitement, person, thing) Sensation f; **sensational** adj sensationell

sense [sens] n (faculty, meaning) Sinn m; (feeling) Gefühl nt; (understanding) Verstand m; **~ of smell/taste** Geruchs-/Geschmackssinn m; **to have a ~ of humour** Humor haben; **to make ~** (sentence etc) einen Sinn ergeben; (be sensible) Sinn machen; **in a ~** gewissermaßen ▷ vt spüren; **senseless** adj (stupid) sinnlos

sensible, sensibly ['sensəbl, -blɪ] adj, adv vernünftig

sensitive ['sensɪtɪv] adj empfindlich (to gegen); (easily hurt) sensibel; (subject) heikel

sensual ['sensjʊəl] adj sinnlich

sensuous ['sensjʊəs] adj sinnlich

sent [sent] pt, pp of **send**

sentence ['sentəns] n (Ling) Satz m; (Jur) Strafe f ▷ vt verurteilen (to zu)

sentiment ['sentɪmənt] n (sentimentality) Sentimentalität f; (opinion) Ansicht f; **sentimental** [sentɪ'mentl] adj sentimental

separate ['seprət] adj getrennt, separat; (individual) einzeln ▷ ['sepəreɪt] vt trennen (from von); **they are ~d** (couple) sie leben getrennt ▷ vi sich trennen; **separately** adv getrennt; (singly) einzeln

September [sep'tembə*] n September m; **in ~** im September; **on the 2nd of ~** am 2. September; **at the beginning/in the middle/at the end of ~** Anfang/Mitte/Ende September; **last/next ~** letzten/nächsten September

septic ['septɪk] adj vereitert

sequel ['si:kwəl] n (to film, book) Fortsetzung f (to von)

sequence ['si:kwəns] n (order) Reihenfolge f

Serb [sɜ:b] n Serbe m, Serbin f; **Serbia** ['sɜ:bjə] n Serbien nt

sergeant ['sɑ:dʒənt] n Polizeimeister(in) m(f); (Mil) Feldwebel(in) m(f)

serial ['sɪərɪəl] n (TV) Serie f; (in newspaper etc) Fortsetzungsroman m ▷ adj (Inform) seriell; **~ number** Seriennummer f

series ['sɪərɪz] nsing Reihe f; (TV, Radio) Serie f

serious ['sɪərɪəs] adj ernst; (injury, illness, mistake) schwer; (discussion) ernsthaft; **are you ~?** ist das dein Ernst?; **seriously** adv ernsthaft; (hurt) schwer; **~?** im Ernst?; **to take sb ~** jdn ernst nehmen

sermon ['sɜ:mən] n (Rel) Predigt f

servant ['sɜ:vənt] n Diener(in) m(f); **serve** [sɜ:v] vt (customer) bedienen; (food) servieren; (one's country etc) dienen +dat; (sentence) verbüßen; **I'm being ~d** ich werde schon bedient; **it ~s him right** es geschieht ihm recht ▷ vi dienen (as als), aufschlagen ▷ n Aufschlag m

server n (Inform) Server m

service ['sɜ:vɪs] n (in shop, hotel) Bedienung f; (activity, amenity) Dienstleistung f; (set of dishes) Service nt; (Auto) Inspektion f; (Tech) Wartung f; (Rel) Gottesdienst m, Aufschlag m; **train/bus ~** Zug-/Busverbindung f; **'~ not included'** „Bedienung nicht inbegriffen" ▷ vt (Auto, Tech) warten;

service area n (on motorway) Raststätte f (mit Tankstelle); **service charge** n Bedienung f; **service provider** n (Inform) Provider m; **service station** n Tankstelle f

serving ['sɜ:vɪŋ] n (portion) Portion f

session ['seʃən] n (of court, assembly) Sitzung f

set [set] (set, set) vt (place) stellen; (lay flat) legen; (arrange) anordnen; (table) decken; (trap, record) aufstellen; (time, price) festsetzen; (watch, alarm) stellen (for auf +akk); **to ~ sb a task** jdm eine Aufgabe stellen; **to ~ free** freilassen; **to ~ a good example** ein gutes Beispiel geben; **the novel is ~ in London** der Roman spielt in London ▷ vi (sun) untergehen; (become hard) fest werden; (bone) zusammenwachsen ▷ n (collection of things) Satz m; (of cutlery, furniture) Garnitur f; (group of people) Kreis m; (Radio, TV) Apparat m, Satz m; (Theat) Bühnenbild nt; (Cine) (Film)kulisse f ▷ adj (agreed, prescribed) festgelegt; (ready) bereit; **~ meal** Menü nt; **set aside** vt (money) beiseite legen; (time) einplanen; **set off** vi aufbrechen (for nach) ▷ vt (alarm) auslösen; (enhance) hervorheben; **set out** vi aufbrechen (for nach) ▷ vt (chairs, chesspieces etc) aufstellen; (state) darlegen; **to ~ to do sth** (intend) beabsichtigen, etw zu tun; **set up** vt (firm, organization) gründen; (stall, tent, camera) aufbauen; (meeting) vereinbaren ▷ vi **to ~ as a doctor** sich als Arzt niederlassen

setback n Rückschlag m

settee [se'ti:] n Sofa nt, Couch f

setting ['setɪŋ] n (of novel, film) Schauplatz m; (surroundings) Umgebung f

settle ['setl] vt (bill, debt) begleichen; (dispute) beilegen; (question) klären; (stomach) beruhigen ▷ vi **to ~ (down)** (feel at home) sich einleben; (calm down) sich beruhigen; **settle in** vi (in place) sich einleben; (in job) sich eingewöhnen; **settle up** vi (be)zahlen; **to ~ with sb** mit jdm abrechnen; **settlement** n (of bill, debt) Begleichung f; (colony) Siedlung f; **to reach a ~** sich einigen

setup ['setʌp] n (organization) Organisation f; (situation) Situation f

seven ['sevn] num sieben ▷ n Sieben f; see also **eight**; **seventeen** ['sevn'ti:n] num

siebzehn ▷ n Siebzehn f; see also **eight**;
seventeenth adj siebzehnte(r, s); see also
eighth; **seventh** ['sevnθ] adj siebte(r, s)
▷ n (fraction) Siebtel nt; see also **eighth**;
seventieth ['sevntɪɪθ] adj siebzigste(r, s);
see also **eighth**; **seventy** ['sevntɪ] num
siebzig; **~-one** einundsiebzig ▷ n Siebzig f;
to be in one's seventies in den Siebzigern
sein; see also **eight**

several ['sevrəl] adj, pron mehrere

severe [sɪ'vɪə*] adj (strict) streng; (serious)
schwer; (pain) stark; (winter) hart;
severely adv (harshly) hart; (seriously)
schwer

sew [səʊ] (**sewed, sewn**) vt, vi nähen

sewage ['suːɪdʒ] n Abwasser nt; **sewer**
['sʊə*] n Abwasserkanal m

sewing ['səʊɪŋ] n Nähen nt; **sewing
machine** n Nähmaschine f

sewn [səʊn] pp of **sew**

sex [seks] n Sex m; (gender) Geschlecht nt;
to have ~ Sex haben (with mit); **sexism**
['seksɪzəm] n Sexismus m; **sexist**
['seksɪst] adj sexistisch ▷ n Sexist(in)
m(f); **sex life** n Sex(ual)leben nt

sexual ['seksjʊəl] adj sexuell;
~ discrimination/harassment sexuelle
Diskriminierung/Belästigung;
~ intercourse Geschlechtsverkehr m;
sexuality [seksjʊ'ælɪtɪ] n Sexualität f;
sexually adv sexuell

sexy ['seksɪ] adj sexy

Seychelles ['seɪʃelz] npl Seychellen pl

shabby ['ʃæbɪ] adj schäbig

shack [ʃæk] n Hütte f

shade [ʃeɪd] n (shadow) Schatten m; (for
lamp) (Lampen)schirm m; (colour) Farbton
m; **~s** (US: sunglasses) Sonnenbrille f ▷ vt
(from sun) abschirmen; (in drawing)
schattieren

shadow ['ʃædəʊ] n Schatten m

shady ['ʃeɪdɪ] adj schattig; (fig)
zwielichtig

shake [ʃeɪk] (**shook, shaken**) vt
schütteln; (shock) erschüttern; **to ~ hands
with sb** jdm die Hand geben; **to ~ one's
head** den Kopf schütteln ▷ vi (tremble)
zittern; (building, ground) schwanken;
shake off vt abschütteln; **shaken** ['ʃeɪkn]
pp of **shake**; **shaky** ['ʃeɪkɪ] adj (trembling)
zittrig; (table, chair, position) wackelig;
(weak) unsicher

shall [ʃæl] (**should**) vb aux werden; (in

questions) sollen; **I ~ do my best** ich werde
mein Bestes tun; **~ I come too?** soll ich
mitkommen?; **where ~ we go?** wo gehen
wir hin?

shallow ['ʃæləʊ] adj (a. fig) seicht; (person)
oberflächlich

shame [ʃeɪm] n (feeling of ~) Scham f;
(disgrace) Schande f; **what a ~** wie schade!;
~ on you schäm dich!; **it's a ~ that ...**
schade, dass ...

shampoo [ʃæm'puː] n Shampoo nt; **to
have a ~ and set** sich die Haare waschen
und legen lassen ▷ vt (hair) waschen;
(carpet) schamponieren

shandy ['ʃændɪ] n Radler m, Alsterwasser
nt

shan't [ʃɑːnt] contr of **shall not**

shape [ʃeɪp] n Form f; (unidentified figure)
Gestalt f; **in the ~ of** in Form +gen; **to be in
good ~** (healthwise) in guter Verfassung
sein; **to take ~** (plan, idea) Gestalt
annehmen ▷ vt (clay, person) formen;
-shaped [ʃeɪpt] suf -förmig;
heart~ herzförmig; **shapeless** adj
formlos

share [ʃɛə*] n Anteil +dat (in, of an m); (Fin)
Aktie f ▷ vt, vi teilen; **shareholder** n
Aktionär(in) m(f)

shark [ʃɑːk] n (Zool) Haifisch m

sharp [ʃɑːp] adj scharf; (pin) spitz; (person)
scharfsinnig; (pain) heftig; (increase, fall)
abrupt; **C/F ~** (Mus) Cis/Dis nt ▷ adv **at 2
o'clock ~** Punkt 2 Uhr; **sharpen** vt (knife)
schärfen; (pencil) spitzen; **sharpener** n
(pencil ~) Spitzer m

shatter ['ʃætə*] vt zerschmettern; (fig)
zerstören ▷ vi zerspringen; **shattered** adj
(exhausted) kaputt

shave [ʃeɪv] (**shaved, shaved o shaven**) vt
rasieren ▷ vi sich rasieren ▷ n Rasur f;
that was a close ~ (fig) das war knapp;
shave off vt **to shave one's beard off**
sich den Bart abrasieren; **shaven** ['ʃeɪvn]
pp of **shave** ▷ adj (head) kahl geschoren;
shaver n (Elec) Rasierapparat m; **shaving
brush** n Rasierpinsel m; **shaving foam** n
Rasierschaum m

shawl [ʃɔːl] n Tuch nt

she [ʃiː] pron sie

shed [ʃed] (**shed, shed**) n Schuppen m
▷ vt (tears, blood) vergießen; (hair, leaves)
verlieren

she'd [ʃiːd] contr of **she had; she would**

sheep [ʃiːp] (pl -) n Schaf nt; **sheepdog** n Schäferhund m; **sheepskin** n Schaffell nt

sheer [ʃɪə*] adj (madness) rein; (steep) steil; (transparent) hauchdünn; **by ~ chance** rein zufällig

sheet [ʃiːt] n (on bed) Betttuch nt; (of paper) Blatt nt; (of metal) Platte f; (of glass) Scheibe f; **a ~ of paper** ein Blatt Papier

shelf [ʃelf] (pl **shelves**) n Bücherbord nt, Regal nt; **shelves** pl (item of furniture) Regal nt

she'll [ʃiːl] contr of **she will; she shall**

shell [ʃel] n (of egg, nut) Schale f; (sea~) Muschel f ▷ vt (peas, nuts) schälen; **shellfish** n (as food) Meeresfrüchte pl

shelter [ˈʃeltə*] n (protection) Schutz m; (accommodation) Unterkunft f; (bus ~) Wartehäuschen nt ▷ vt schützen (from vor +dat) ▷ vi sich unterstellen; **sheltered** adj (spot) geschützt; (life) behütet

shelve [ʃelv] vt (fig) aufschieben; **shelves** pl of **shelf**

shepherd [ˈʃepəd] n Schäfer m; **shepherd's pie** n Hackfleischauflauf mit Decke aus Kartoffelpüree

sherry [ˈʃerɪ] n Sherry m

she's [ʃiːz] contr of **she is; she has**

shield [ʃiːld] n Schild m; (fig) Schutz m ▷ vt schützen (from vor +dat)

shift [ʃɪft] n (change) Veränderung f; (period at work, workers) Schicht f; (on keyboard) Umschalttaste f ▷ vt (furniture etc) verrücken; (stain) entfernen; **to ~ gear(s)** (US Auto) schalten ▷ vi (move) sich bewegen; (move up) rutschen; **shift key** n Umschalttaste f

shin [ʃɪn] n Schienbein nt

shine [ʃaɪn] n (shone, shone) vi (be shiny) glänzen; (sun) scheinen; (lamp) leuchten ▷ vt (polish) polieren ▷ n Glanz m

shingles [ˈʃɪŋglz] nsing (Med) Gürtelrose f

shiny [ˈʃaɪnɪ] adj glänzend

ship [ʃɪp] n Schiff nt ▷ vt (send) versenden; (by ship) verschiffen; **shipment** n (goods) Sendung f; (sent by ship) Ladung f; **shipwreck** n Schiffbruch m; **shipyard** n Werft f

shirt [ʃɜːt] n Hemd nt

shiver [ˈʃɪvə*] vi zittern (with vor +dat)

shock [ʃɒk] n (mental, emotional) Schock m; **to be in ~** unter Schock stehen; **to get a ~** (Elec) einen Schlag bekommen ▷ vt schockieren; **shock absorber** n Stoßdämpfer m; **shocked** adj schockiert (by über +akk); **shocking** adj schockierend; (awful) furchtbar

shoe [ʃuː] n Schuh m; **shoehorn** n Schuhlöffel m; **shoelace** n Schnürsenkel m; **shoe polish** n Schuhcreme f

shone [ʃɒn] pt, pp of **shine**

shook [ʃʊk] pt of **shake**

shoot [ʃuːt] (shot, shot) vt (wound) anschießen; (kill) erschießen; (Cine) drehen; (fam: heroin) drücken ▷ vi (with gun, move quickly) schießen; **to ~ at sb** auf jdn schießen ▷ n (of plant) Trieb m; **shooting** n (exchange of gunfire) Schießerei f; (killing) Erschießung f

shop [ʃɒp] n Geschäft nt, Laden m ▷ vi einkaufen; **shop assistant** n Verkäufer(in) m(f); **shopkeeper** n Geschäftsinhaber(in) m(f); **shoplifting** n Ladendiebstahl m; **shopper** n Käufer(in) m(f); **shopping** n (activity) Einkaufen nt; (goods) Einkäufe pl; **to do the ~** einkaufen; **to go ~** einkaufen gehen; **shopping bag** n Einkaufstasche f; **shopping cart** n (US) Einkaufswagen m; **shopping center** (US), **shopping centre** n Einkaufszentrum nt; **shopping list** n Einkaufszettel m; **shopping trolley** n (Brit) Einkaufswagen m; **shop window** n Schaufenster nt

shore [ʃɔː*] n Ufer nt; **on ~** an Land

short [ʃɔːt] adj kurz; (person) klein; **to be ~ of money** knapp bei Kasse sein; **to be ~ of time** wenig Zeit haben; **~ of breath** kurzatmig; **to cut ~** (holiday) abbrechen; **we are two ~** wir haben zwei zu wenig; **it's ~ for ...** das ist die Kurzform von ... ▷ n (drink, Elec) Kurze(r) m; **shortage** n Knappheit f (of an +dat); **shortbread** n Buttergebäck nt; **short circuit** n Kurzschluss m; **shortcoming** n Unzulänglichkeit f; (of person) Fehler m; **shortcut** n (quicker route) Abkürzung f; (Inform) Shortcut m; **shorten** vt kürzen; (in time) verkürzen; **shorthand** n Stenografie f; **shortlist** n **to be on the ~** in der engeren Wahl sein; **short-lived** adj kurzlebig; **shortly** adv bald; **shorts** npl Shorts pl; **short-sighted** adj (a. fig) kurzsichtig; **short-sleeved** adj kurzärmelig; **short-stay car park** n

Kurzzeitparkplatz m; **short story** n Kurzgeschichte f; **short-term** adj kurzfristig; **short wave** n Kurzwelle f

shot [ʃɒt] pt, pp of **shoot** ▷ n (from gun, in football) Schuss m; (Foto, Cine) Aufnahme f; (injection) Spritze f; (of alcohol) Schuss m

should [ʃʊd] pt of **shall** ▷ vb aux **I ~ go now** ich sollte jetzt gehen; **what ~ I do?** was soll ich tun?; **you ~n't have said that** das hättest du nicht sagen sollen; **that ~ be enough** das müsste reichen

shoulder [ˈʃəʊldə*] n Schulter f

shouldn't [ˈʃʊdnt] contr of **should not**

should've [ˈʃʊdəv] contr of **should have**

shout [ʃaʊt] n Schrei m; (call) Ruf m ▷ vt rufen; (order) brüllen ▷ vi schreien; **to ~ at** anschreien; **to ~ for help** um Hilfe rufen

shove [ʃʌv] vt (person) schubsen; (car, table etc) schieben ▷ vi (in crowd) drängeln

shovel [ˈʃʌvl] n Schaufel f ▷ vt schaufeln

show [ʃəʊ] (showed, shown) vt zeigen; **to ~ sb sth, to ~ sth to sb** jdm etw zeigen; **to ~ sb in** jdn hereinführen; **to ~ sb out** jdn zur Tür bringen ▷ n (Cine, Theat) Vorstellung f; (TV) Show f; (exhibition) Ausstellung f; **show off** vi (pej) angeben; **show round** vt herumführen; **to show sb round the house/the town** jdm das Haus/die Stadt zeigen; **show up** vi (arrive) auftauchen

shower [ˈʃaʊə*] n Dusche f; (rain) Schauer m; **to have** (o **take**) **a ~** duschen ▷ vi (wash) duschen

showing [ˈʃəʊɪŋ] n (Cine) Vorstellung f

shown [ʃəʊn] pp of **show**

showroom [ˈʃəʊruːm] n Ausstellungsraum m

shrank [ʃræŋk] pt of **shrink**

shred [ʃred] n (of paper, fabric) Fetzen m ▷ vt (in shredder) (im Reißwolf) zerkleinern; **shredder** n (for paper) Reißwolf m

shrimp [ʃrɪmp] n Garnele f

shrink [ʃrɪŋk] (shrank, shrunk) vi schrumpfen; (clothes) eingehen

shrivel [ˈʃrɪvl] vi **to ~ (up)** schrumpfen; (skin) runzlig werden; (plant) welken

Shrove Tuesday [ˈʃrəʊvˈtjuːzdeɪ] n Fastnachtsdienstag m

shrub [ʃrʌb] n Busch m, Strauch m

shrug [ʃrʌɡ] vt, vi **to ~ (one's shoulders)** mit den Achseln zucken

shrunk [ʃrʌŋk] pp of **shrink**

shudder [ˈʃʌdə*] vi schaudern; (ground, building) beben

shuffle [ˈʃʌfl] vt, vi mischen

shut [ʃʌt] (shut, shut) vt zumachen, schließen; **~ your mouth** (fam) halt den Mund! ▷ vi schließen ▷ adj geschlossen; **we're ~** wir haben geschlossen; **shut down** vt schließen; (computer) ausschalten ▷ vi schließen; (computer) sich ausschalten; **shut in** vt einschließen; **shut out** vt (lock out) aussperren; **to shut oneself out** sich aussperren; **shut up** vt (lock up) abschließen; (silence) zum Schweigen bringen ▷ vi (keep quiet) den Mund halten; **~!** halt den Mund!; **shutter** n (on window) (Fenster)laden m; **shutter release** n Auslöser m; **shutter speed** n Belichtungszeit f

shuttle bus [ˈʃʌtlbʌs] n Shuttlebus m

shuttlecock [ˈʃʌtlkɒk] n Federball m

shuttle service [ˈʃʌtlsɜːvɪs] n Pendelverkehr m

shy [ʃaɪ] adj schüchtern; (animal) scheu

Siberia [saɪˈbɪərɪə] n Sibirien nt

Sicily [ˈsɪsɪlɪ] n Sizilien nt

sick [sɪk] adj krank; (joke) makaber; **to be ~** (Brit: vomit) sich übergeben; **to be off ~** wegen Krankheit fehlen; **I feel ~** mir ist schlecht; **to be ~ of sb/sth** jdn/etw satt haben; **it makes me ~** (fig) es ekelt mich an; **sickbag** n Spucktüte f; **sick leave** n **to be on ~** krankgeschrieben sein; **sickness** n Krankheit f; (Brit: nausea) Übelkeit f; **sickness benefit** n (Brit) Krankengeld nt

side [saɪd] n Seite f; (of road) Rand m; (of mountain) Hang m; (Sport) Mannschaft f; **by my ~** neben mir; **~ by ~** nebeneinander ▷ adj (door, entrance) Seiten-; **sideboard** n Anrichte f; **sideboards**, **sideburns** (US) npl Koteletten pl; **side dish** n Beilage f; **side effect** n Nebenwirkung f; **sidelight** n (Brit Auto) Parklicht nt; **side order** n Beilage f; **side road** n Nebenstraße f; **side street** n Seitenstraße f; **sidewalk** n (US) Bürgersteig m; **sideways** adv seitwärts

sieve [sɪv] n Sieb nt

sift [sɪft] vt (flour etc) sieben

sigh [saɪ] vi seufzen

sight [saɪt] n (power of seeing) Sehvermögen nt; (view, thing seen) Anblick m; **~s** pl (of city etc) Sehenswürdigkeiten pl;

to have bad ~ schlecht sehen; **to lose** ~ **of** aus den Augen verlieren; **out of** ~ außer Sicht; **sightseeing** n **to go** ~ Sehenswürdigkeiten besichtigen; ~ **tour** Rundfahrt f

sign [saɪn] n Zeichen nt; (notice, road ~) Schild nt ▷ vt unterschreiben ▷ vi unterschreiben; **to** ~ **for sth** den Empfang einer Sache gen bestätigen; **to** ~ **in/out** sich ein-/austragen; **sign on** vi (Brit: register as unemployed) sich arbeitslos melden; **sign up** vi (for course) sich einschreiben; (Mil) sich verpflichten

signal ['sɪɡnl] n Signal nt ▷ vi (car driver) blinken

signature ['sɪɡnətʃə*] n Unterschrift f

significant [sɪɡ'nɪfɪkənt] adj (important) bedeutend, wichtig; (meaning sth) bedeutsam; **significantly** adv (considerably) bedeutend

sign language ['saɪnlæŋɡwɪdʒ] n Zeichensprache f; **signpost** n Wegweiser m

silence ['saɪləns] n Stille f; (of person) Schweigen nt; ~! Ruhe! ▷ vt zum Schweigen bringen; **silent** adj still; (taciturn) schweigsam; **she remained** ~ sie schwieg

silk [sɪlk] n Seide f ▷ adj Seiden-

silly ['sɪlɪ] adj dumm, albern; **don't do anything** ~ mach keine Dummheiten

silver ['sɪlvə*] n Silber nt; (coins) Silbermünzen pl ▷ adj Silber-, silbern; **silver-plated** adj versilbert; **silver wedding** n silberne Hochzeit

similar ['sɪmɪlə*] adj ähnlich (to dat); **similarity** [sɪmɪ'lærɪtɪ] n Ähnlichkeit f (to mit); **similarly** adv (equally) ebenso

simple ['sɪmpl] adj einfach; (unsophisticated) schlicht; **simplify** ['sɪmplɪfaɪ] vt vereinfachen; **simply** adv einfach; (merely) bloß; (dress) schlicht

simulate ['sɪmjʊleɪt] vt simulieren

simultaneous, simultaneously [sɪməl'teɪnɪəs, -lɪ] adj, adv gleichzeitig

sin [sɪn] n Sünde f ▷ vi sündigen

since [sɪns] adv seitdem; (in the meantime) inzwischen ▷ prep seit +dat; **ever** ~ **1995** schon seit 1995 ▷ conj (time) seit, seitdem; (because) da, weil; **ever** ~ **I've known her** seit ich sie kenne; **it's ages** ~ **I've seen him** ich habe ihn seit langem nicht mehr gesehen

sincere [sɪn'sɪə*] adj aufrichtig; **sincerely** adv aufrichtig; **Yours** ~ mit freundlichen Grüßen

sing [sɪŋ] (**sang, sung**) vt, vi singen

Singapore [sɪŋɡə'pɔ:*] n Singapur nt

singer ['sɪŋə*] n Sänger(in) m(f)

single ['sɪŋɡl] adj (one only) einzig; (not double) einfach; (bed, room) Einzel-; (unmarried) ledig; (Brit: ticket) einfach ▷ n (Brit: ticket) einfache Fahrkarte; (Mus) Single f; **a** ~ **to London, please** (Brit Rail) einfach nach London, bitte; **single out** vt (choose) auswählen; **single-handed, single-handedly** adv im Alleingang; **single parent** n Alleinerziehende(r) mf; **single supplement** n (for hotel room) Einzelzimmerzuschlag m

singular ['sɪŋɡjʊlə*] n Singular m

sinister ['sɪnɪstə*] adj unheimlich

sink [sɪŋk] (**sank, sunk**) vt (ship) versenken ▷ vi sinken ▷ n Spülbecken nt; (in bathroom) Waschbecken nt

sip [sɪp] vt nippen an +dat

sir [sɜ:*] n **yes,** ~ ja(, mein Herr); **can I help you,** ~? kann ich Ihnen helfen?; **Sir James** (title) Sir James

sister ['sɪstə*] n Schwester f; (Brit: nurse) Oberschwester f; **sister-in-law** (pl **sisters-in-law**) n Schwägerin f

sit [sɪt] (**sat, sat**) vi (be sitting) sitzen; (~ down) sich setzen; (committee, court) tagen ▷ vt (Brit: exam) machen; **sit down** vi sich hinsetzen; **sit up** vi (from lying position) sich aufsetzen

sitcom ['sɪtkɒm] n Situationskomödie f

site [saɪt] n Platz m; (building ~) Baustelle f; (web~) Site f

sitting ['sɪtɪŋ] n (meeting, for portrait) Sitzung f; **sitting room** n Wohnzimmer nt

situated ['sɪtjʊeɪtɪd] adj **to be** ~ liegen

situation [sɪtjʊ'eɪʃən] n (circumstances) Situation f, Lage f; (job) Stelle f; **'~s vacant/wanted'** (Brit) „Stellenangebote/Stellengesuche"

six [sɪks] num sechs ▷ n Sechs f; see also **eight**; **sixpack** n (of beer etc) Sechserpack nt; **sixteen** ['sɪks'ti:n] num sechzehn ▷ n Sechzehn f; see also **eight**; **sixteenth** adj sechzehnte(r, s); see also **eighth**; **sixth** [sɪksθ] adj sechste(r, s); ~ **form** (Brit) ≈ Oberstufe f ▷ n (fraction) Sechstel nt; see also **eighth**; **sixtieth** ['sɪkstɪɪθ] adj

sechzigste(r, s); *see also* **eighth**; **sixty**
['sıkstı] *num* sechzig; **~-one**
einundsechzig ▷ *n* Sechzig *f*; **to be in
one's sixties** in den Sechzigern sein; *see
also* **eight**

size [saɪz] *n* Größe *f*; **what ~ are you?**
welche Größe haben Sie?; **a ~ too big** eine
Nummer zu groß

sizzle ['sɪzl] *vi* (Gastr) brutzeln

skate [skeɪt] *n* Schlittschuh *m*; (roller ~)
Rollschuh *m* ▷ *vi* Schlittschuh laufen;
(roller-~) Rollschuh laufen; **skateboard** *n*
Skateboard *nt*; **skating** *n* Eislauf *m*;
(roller-~) Rollschuhlauf *m*; **skating rink** *n*
Eisbahn *f*; (for roller-skating) Rollschuhbahn
f

skeleton ['skelıtn] *n* (a. fig) Skelett *nt*

skeptical *n* (US) *see* **sceptical**

sketch [sketʃ] *n* Skizze *f*; (Theat) Sketch *m*
▷ *vt* skizzieren; **sketchbook** *n*
Skizzenbuch *nt*

ski [skiː] *n* Ski *m* ▷ *vi* Ski laufen; **ski boot**
n Skistiefel *m*

skid [skɪd] *vi* (Auto) schleudern

skier ['skiːə*] *n* Skiläufer(in) *m(f)*; **skiing** *n*
Skilaufen *nt*; **to go ~** Ski laufen gehen;
~ holiday Skiurlaub *m*; **skiing instructor**
n Skilehrer(in) *m(f)*

skilful, skilfully ['skɪlful, -fəlı] *adj*, *adv*
geschickt

ski-lift ['skiːlıft] *n* Skilift *m*

skill [skɪl] *n* Geschick *nt*; (acquired
technique) Fertigkeit *f*; **skilled** *adj*
geschickt (at, in in +dat); (worker) Fach-;
(work) fachmännisch

skim [skɪm] *vt* **to ~ (off)** (fat etc)
abschöpfen; **to ~ (through)** (read)
überfliegen; **skimmed milk** *n*
Magermilch *f*

skin [skɪn] *n* Haut *f*; (fur) Fell *nt*; (peel)
Schale *f*; **skin diving** *n* Sporttauchen *nt*;
skinny *adj* dünn

skip [skɪp] *vi* hüpfen; (with rope) Seil
springen ▷ *vt* (miss out) überspringen;
(meal) ausfallen lassen; (school, lesson)
schwänzen

ski pants ['skiːpænts] *npl* Skihose *f*; **ski
pass** *n* Skipass *m*; **ski pole** *n* Skistock *m*;
ski resort *n* Skiort *m*

skirt [skɜːt] *n* Rock *m*

ski run ['skiːrʌn] *n* (Ski)abfahrt *f*; **ski
stick** *n* Skistock *m*; **ski tow** *n* Schlepplift
m

skittle ['skɪtl] *n* Kegel *m*; **~s** (game) Kegeln
nt

skive [skaɪv] *vi* **to ~ (off)** (Brit fam) sich
drücken; (from school) schwänzen; (from
work) blaumachen

skull [skʌl] *n* Schädel *m*

sky [skaɪ] *n* Himmel *m*; **skydiving** *n*
Fallschirmspringen *nt*; **skylight** *n*
Dachfenster *nt*; **skyscraper** *n*
Wolkenkratzer *m*

slam [slæm] *vt* (door) zuschlagen; **slam
on** *vt* **to slam the brakes on** voll auf die
Bremse treten

slander ['slɑːndə*] *n* Verleumdung *f* ▷ *vt*
verleumden

slang [slæŋ] *n* Slang *m*

slap [slæp] *n* Klaps *m*; (across face)
Ohrfeige *f* ▷ *vt* schlagen; **to ~ sb's face**
jdn ohrfeigen

slash [slæʃ] *n* (punctuation mark)
Schrägstrich *m* ▷ *vt* (face, tyre)
aufschlitzen; (prices) stark herabsetzen

slate [sleɪt] *n* (rock) Schiefer *m*; (roof ~)
Schieferplatte *f*

slaughter ['slɔːtə*] *vt* (animals)
schlachten; (people) abschlachten

Slav [slɑːv] *adj* slawisch ▷ *n* Slawe *m*,
Slawin *f*

slave [sleɪv] *n* Sklave *m*, Sklavin *f*; **slave
away** *vi* schuften; **slave-driver** *n* (fam)
Sklaventreiber(in) *m(f)*; **slavery** ['sleɪvərɪ]
n Sklaverei *f*

sleaze [sliːz] *n* (corruption) Korruption *f*;
sleazy *adj* (bar, district) zwielichtig

sledge ['sledʒ] *n* Schlitten *m*

sleep [sliːp] (slept, slept) *vi* schlafen; **to
~ with sb** mit jdm schlafen ▷ *n* Schlaf *m*;
to put to ~ (animal) einschläfern; **sleep in**
vi (lie in) ausschlafen; **sleeper** *n* (Rail:
train) Schlafwagenzug *m*; (carriage)
Schlafwagen *m*; **sleeping bag** *n*
Schlafsack *m*; **sleeping car** *n*
Schlafwagen *m*; **sleeping pill** *n*
Schlaftablette *f*; **sleepless** *adj* schlaflos;
sleepy *adj* schläfrig; (place) verschlafen

sleet [sliːt] *n* Schneeregen *m*

sleeve [sliːv] *n* Ärmel *m*; **sleeveless** *adj*
ärmellos

sleigh [sleɪ] *n* (Pferde)schlitten *m*

slender ['slendə*] *adj* schlank; (fig)
gering

slept [slept] *pt*, *pp of* **sleep**

slice [slaɪs] *n* Scheibe *f*; (of cake, tart, pizza)

Stück nt ▷ vt **to ~ (up)** in Scheiben schneiden; **sliced bread** n geschnittenes Brot
slid [slɪd] pt, pp of **slide**
slide [slaɪd] (**slid, slid**) vt gleiten lassen; (push) schieben ▷ vi gleiten; (slip) rutschen ▷ n (Foto) Dia nt; (in playground) Rutschbahn f; (Brit: for hair) Spange f
slight [slaɪt] adj leicht; (problem, difference) klein; **not in the ~est** nicht im Geringsten; **slightly** adv etwas; (injured) leicht
slim [slɪm] adj (person) schlank; (book) dünn; (chance, hope) gering ▷ vi abnehmen
slime [slaɪm] n Schleim m; **slimy** adj schleimig
sling [slɪŋ] (**slung, slung**) vt werfen ▷ n (for arm) Schlinge f
slip [slɪp] n (mistake) Flüchtigkeitsfehler m; **~ of paper** Zettel m ▷ vt (put) stecken; **to ~ on/off** (garment) an-/ausziehen; **it ~ped my mind** ich habe es vergessen ▷ vi (lose balance) (aus)rutschen; **slip away** vi (leave) sich wegstehlen; **slipper** n Hausschuh m; **slippery** adj (path, road) glatt; (soap, fish) glitschig; **slip-road** n (Brit: onto motorway) Auffahrt f; (off motorway) Ausfahrt f
slit [slɪt] (**slit, slit**) vt aufschlitzen ▷ n Schlitz m
slope [sləʊp] n Neigung f; (side of hill) Hang m ▷ vi (be sloping) schräg sein; **slope down** vi (land, road) abfallen; **sloping** adj (floor, roof) schräg
sloppy ['slɒpɪ] adj (careless) schlampig; (sentimental) rührselig
slot [slɒt] n (opening) Schlitz m; (Inform) Steckplatz m; **we have a ~ free at 2** (free time) um 2 ist noch ein Termin frei; **slot machine** n Automat m; (for gambling) Spielautomat m
Slovak ['sləʊvæk] adj slowakisch ▷ n (person) Slowake m, Slowakin f; (language) Slowakisch nt; **Slovakia** [sləʊ'vækɪə] n Slowakei f
Slovene ['sləʊviːn], **Slovenian** [sləʊ'viːnɪən] adj slowenisch ▷ n (person) Slowene m, Slowenin f; (language) Slowenisch nt; **Slovenia** [sləʊ'viːnɪə] n Slowenien nt
slow [sləʊ] adj langsam; (business) flau; **to be ~** (clock) nachgehen; (stupid)

begriffsstutzig sein; **slow down** vi langsamer werden; (when driving/walking) langsamer fahren/gehen; **slowly** adv langsam; **slow motion** n **in ~** in Zeitlupe
slug [slʌg] n (Zool) Nacktschnecke f
slum [slʌm] n Slum m
slump [slʌmp] n Rückgang m (in an +dat) ▷ vi (onto chair etc) sich fallen lassen; (prices) stürzen
slung [slʌŋ] pt, pp of **sling**
slur [slɜ:*] n (insult) Verleumdung f; **slurred** [slɜ:d] adj undeutlich
slush [slʌʃ] n (snow) Schneematsch m; **slushy** adj matschig; (fig) schmalzig
slut [slʌt] n (pej) Schlampe f
smack [smæk] n Klaps m ▷ vt **to ~ sb** jdm einen Klaps geben ▷ vi **to ~ of** riechen nach
small [smɔ:l] adj klein; **small ads** npl (Brit) Kleinanzeigen pl; **small change** n Kleingeld nt; **small letters** npl **in ~** in Kleinbuchstaben; **smallpox** n Pocken pl; **small print** n **the ~** das Kleingedruckte; **small-scale** adj (map) in kleinem Maßstab; **small talk** n Konversation f, Smalltalk m
smart [smɑ:t] adj (elegant) schick; (clever) clever; **smart card** n Chipkarte f; **smartly** adv (dressed) schick
smash [smæʃ] n (car crash) Zusammenstoß m, Schmetterball m ▷ vt (break) zerschlagen; (fig: record) brechen, deutlich übertreffen ▷ vi (break) zerbrechen; **to ~ into** (car) krachen gegen; **smashing** adj (fam) toll
smear [smɪə*] n (mark) Fleck m; (Med) Abstrich m; (fig) Verleumdung f ▷ vt (spread) schmieren; (make dirty) beschmieren; (fig) verleumden
smell [smel] (**smelt** o **smelled, smelt** o **smelled**) vt riechen ▷ vi riechen (of nach); (unpleasantly) stinken ▷ n Geruch m; (unpleasant) Gestank m; **smelly** adj übel riechend; **smelt** [smelt] pt, pp of **smell**
smile [smaɪl] n Lächeln nt ▷ vi lächeln; **to ~ at sb** jdn anlächeln
smock [smɒk] n Kittel m
smog [smɒg] n Smog m
smoke [sməʊk] n Rauch m ▷ vt rauchen; (food) räuchern ▷ vi rauchen; **smoke alarm** n Rauchmelder m; **smoked** adj (food) geräuchert; **smoke-free** adj (zone, building) rauchfrei; **smoker** n Raucher(in)

m(f); **smoking** n Rauchen nt; **'no ~'** „Rauchen verboten"

smooth [smu:ð] adj glatt; (flight, crossing) ruhig; (movement) geschmeidig; (without problems) reibungslos; (pej: person) aalglatt ▷ vt (hair, dress) glatt streichen; (surface) glätten; **smoothly** adv reibungslos; **to run ~** (engine) ruhig laufen

smudge [smʌdʒ] vt (writing, lipstick) verschmieren

smug [smʌg] adj selbstgefällig

smuggle ['smʌgl] vt schmuggeln; **to ~ in/out** herein-/herausschmuggeln

smutty ['smʌtɪ] adj (obscene) schmutzig

snack [snæk] n Imbiss m; **to have a ~** eine Kleinigkeit essen; **snack bar** n Imbissstube f

snail [sneɪl] n Schnecke f; **snail mail** n (fam) Schneckenpost f

snake [sneɪk] n Schlange f

snap [snæp] n (photo) Schnappschuss m ▷ adj (decision) spontan ▷ vt (break) zerbrechen; (rope) zerreißen ▷ vi (break) brechen; (rope) reißen; (bite) schnappen (at nach); **snap off** vt (break) abbrechen; **snap fastener** n (US) Druckknopf m; **snapshot** n Schnappschuss m

snatch [snætʃ] vt (grab) schnappen

sneak [sni:k] vi (move) schleichen; **sneakers** npl (US) Turnschuhe pl

sneeze [sni:z] vi niesen

sniff [snɪf] vi schniefen; (smell) schnüffeln (at an +dat) ▷ vt schnuppern an +dat; (glue) schnüffeln

snob [snɒb] n Snob m; **snobbish** adj versnobt

snog [snɒg] vi, vt knutschen

snooker ['snu:kə*] n Snooker nt

snoop [snu:p] vi **to ~ (around)** (herum)schnüffeln

snooze [snu:z] n, vi **to (have a) ~** ein Nickerchen machen

snore [snɔ:*] vi schnarchen

snorkel ['snɔ:kl] n Schnorchel m; **snorkelling** n Schnorcheln nt; **to go ~** schnorcheln gehen

snout [snaʊt] n Schnauze f

snow [snəʊ] n Schnee m ▷ vi schneien; **snowball** n Schneeball m; **snowboard** n Snowboard nt; **snowboarding** n Snowboarding nt; **snowdrift** n Schneewehe f; **snowdrop** n Schneeglöckchen nt; **snowflake** n Schneeflocke f; **snowman** (pl -men) n Schneemann m; **snowplough**, **snowplow** (US) n Schneepflug m; **snowstorm** n Schneesturm m; **snowy** adj (region) schneereich; (landscape) verschneit

snug [snʌg] adj (person, place) gemütlich

snuggle up ['snʌglʌp] vi **to ~ to sb** sich an jdn ankuscheln

🔵 **KEYWORD**

so [səʊ] adv **1** (thus) so; (likewise) auch; **so saying he walked away** indem er das sagte, ging er; **if so** wenn ja; **I didn't do it — you did so!** ich hab das nicht gemacht — hast du wohl!; **so do I, so am I** etc ich auch; **so it is!** tatsächlich!; **I hope/think so** hoffentlich/ich glaube schon; **so far** bis jetzt

2 (in comparisons etc: to such a degree) so; **so quickly/big (that)** so schnell/groß, dass; **I'm so glad to see you** ich freue mich so, dich zu sehen

3: **so many** so viele; **so much work** so viel Arbeit; **I love you so much** ich liebe dich so sehr

4 (phrases): **10 or so** etwa 10; **so long!** (inf: goodbye) tschüss!

▷ conj **1** (expressing purpose); **so as to** um ... zu; **so (that)** damit

2 (expressing result) also; **so I was right after all** ich hatte also doch Recht; **so you see ...** wie du siehst ...

soak [səʊk] vt durchnässen; (leave in liquid) einweichen; **I'm ~ed** ich bin durchnässt; **soaking** adj **~ (wet)** durchnässt

soap [səʊp] n Seife f; **soap (opera)** n Seifenoper f; **soap powder** n Waschpulver nt

sob [sɒb] vi schluchzen

sober ['səʊbə*] adj nüchtern; **sober up** vi nüchtern werden

so-called ['səʊ'kɔ:ld] adj so genannt

soccer ['sɒkə*] n Fußball m

sociable ['səʊʃəbl] adj gesellig

social ['səʊʃəl] adj sozial; (sociable) gesellig; **socialist** adj sozialistisch ▷ n Sozialist(in) m(f); **socialize** vi unter die Leute gehen; **social security** n (Brit) Sozialhilfe f; (US) Sozialversicherung f

society [sə'saɪətɪ] n Gesellschaft f; (club) Verein m

sock [sɒk] n Socke f

socket ['sɒkɪt] n (Elec) Steckdose f

soda ['səʊdə] n (~ water) Soda f; (US: pop) Limo f; **soda water** n Sodawasser nt

sofa ['səʊfə] n Sofa nt; **sofa bed** n Schlafcouch f

soft [sɒft] adj weich; (quiet) leise; (lighting) gedämpft; (kind) gutmütig; (weak) nachgiebig; **~ drink** alkoholfreies Getränk; **softly** adv sanft; (quietly) leise; **software** n (Inform) Software f

soil [sɔɪl] n Erde f; (ground) Boden m

solar ['səʊlə*] adj Sonnen-, Solar-

solarium [sə'lɛərɪəm] n Solarium nt

sold [səʊld] pt, pp of **sell**

soldier ['səʊldʒə*] n Soldat(in) m(f)

sole [səʊl] n Sohle f; (fish) Seezunge f ▷ vt besohlen ▷ adj einzig; (owner, responsibility) alleinig; **solely** adv nur

solemn ['sɒləm] adj feierlich; (person) ernst

solicitor [sə'lɪsɪtə*] n (Brit) Rechtsanwalt m, Rechtsanwältin f

solid ['sɒlɪd] adj (hard) fest; (gold, oak etc) massiv; (~ly built) solide; (meal) kräftig; **three hours ~** drei volle Stunden

solitary ['sɒlɪtərɪ] adj einsam; (single) einzeln; **solitude** ['sɒlɪtjuːd] n Einsamkeit f

solo ['səʊləʊ] n (Mus) Solo nt

soluble ['sɒljʊbl] adj löslich; (problem) lösbar; **solution** [sə'luːʃən] n Lösung f (to +gen); **solve** [sɒlv] vt lösen

somber (US), **sombre** ['sɒmbə*] adj düster

🅞 KEYWORD

some [sʌm] adj **1** (a certain amount or number of) einige; (a few) ein paar; (with singular nouns) etwas; **some tea/biscuits** etwas Tee/ein paar Plätzchen; **I've got some money, but not much** ich habe ein bisschen Geld, aber nicht viel

2 (certain: in contrasts) manche(r, s); **some people say that ...** manche Leute sagen, dass ...

3 (unspecified) irgendein(e); **some woman was asking for you** da hat eine Frau nach Ihnen gefragt; **some day** eines Tages;

some day next week irgendwann nächste Woche

▷ pron **1** (a certain number) einige; **have you got some?** haben Sie welche?

2 (a certain amount) etwas; **I've read some of the book** ich habe das Buch teilweise gelesen

▷ adv: **some 10 people** etwa 10 Leute

somebody pron jemand; **~ (or other)** irgendjemand; **~ else** jemand anders; **someday** adv irgendwann; **somehow** adv irgendwie; **someone** pron see **somebody; someplace** adv (US) see **somewhere; something** ['sʌmθɪŋ] pron etwas; **~ (or other)** irgendetwas; **~ else** etwas anderes; **~ nice** etwas Nettes; **would you like ~ to drink?** möchten Sie etwas trinken? ▷ adv: **~ like 20** ungefähr 20; **sometime** adv irgendwann; **sometimes** adv manchmal; **somewhat** adv ein wenig; **somewhere** adv irgendwo; (to a place) irgendwohin; **~ else** irgendwo anders; (to another place) irgendwo anders hin; **~ around 6** ungefähr 6

son [sʌn] n Sohn m

song [sɒŋ] n Lied nt

son-in-law ['sʌnɪnlɔː] (pl **sons-in-law**) n Schwiegersohn m

soon [suːn] adv bald; (early) früh; **too ~** zu früh; **as ~ as I ...** sobald ich ...; **as ~ as possible** so bald wie möglich; **sooner** adv (time) früher; (for preference) lieber

soot [sʊt] n Ruß m

soothe [suːð] vt beruhigen; (pain) lindern

sophisticated [sə'fɪstɪkeɪtɪd] adj (person) kultiviert; (machine) hoch entwickelt; (plan) ausgeklügelt

sophomore ['sɒfəmɔː*] n (US) College-Student(in) m(f) im zweiten Jahr

soppy ['sɒpɪ] adj (fam) rührselig

soprano [sə'prɑːnəʊ] n Sopran m

sore [sɔː*] adj: **to be ~** weh tun; **to have a ~ throat** Halsschmerzen haben ▷ n wunde Stelle

sorrow ['sɒrəʊ] n Kummer m

sorry ['sɒrɪ] adj (sight, figure) traurig; **(I'm) ~** (excusing) Entschuldigung!; **I'm ~** (regretful) es tut mir leid; **~?** wie bitte?; **I feel ~ for him** er tut mir leid

sort [sɔːt] n Art f; **what ~ of film is it?**
was für ein Film ist das?; **a ~ of** eine Art
+gen; **all ~s of things** alles Mögliche ▷ adv
~ of (fam) irgendwie ▷ vt sortieren;
everything's ~ed (dealt with) alles ist
geregelt; **sort out** vt (classify etc)
sortieren; (problems) lösen

sought [sɔːt] pt, pp of **seek**

soul [səʊl] n Seele f; (music) Soul m

sound [saʊnd] adj (healthy) gesund; (safe)
sicher; (sensible) vernünftig; (theory)
stichhaltig; (thrashing) tüchtig ▷ adv **to be
~ asleep** fest schlafen ▷ n (noise)
Geräusch nt; (Mus) Klang m; (TV) Ton m ▷ vt
to ~ the alarm Alarm schlagen; **to ~ one's
horn** hupen ▷ vi (seem) klingen (like wie);
soundcard n (Inform) Soundkarte f;
sound effects npl Klangeffekte pl;
soundproof adj schalldicht; **soundtrack**
n (of film) Filmmusik f, Soundtrack m

soup [suːp] n Suppe f

sour ['saʊə*] adj sauer; (fig) mürrisch

source [sɔːs] n Quelle f; (fig) Ursprung
m

sour cream [saʊə'kriːm] n saure Sahne

south [saʊθ] n Süden m; **to the ~ of**
südlich von ▷ adv (go, face) nach Süden
▷ adj Süd-; **South Africa** n Südafrika nt;
South African adj südafrikanisch ▷ n
Südafrikaner(in) m(f); **South America** . n
Südamerika nt; **South American** adj
südamerikanisch ▷ n Südamerikaner(in)
m(f); **southbound** adj (in) Richtung
Süden; **southern** ['sʌðən] adj
Süd-, südlich; **~ Europe** Südeuropa nt;
southwards ['saʊθwədz] adv nach Süden

souvenir [suːvə'nɪə*] n Andenken nt (of
an +akk)

sow [səʊ] (**sowed, sown** o **sowed**) vt (a.
fig) säen; (field) besäen ▷ [saʊ] n (pig)
Sau f

soya bean ['sɔɪə'biːn] n Sojabohne f

soy sauce ['sɔɪ'sɔːs] n Sojasoße f

spa [spaː] n (place) Kurort m

space [speɪs] n (room) Platz m, Raum m;
(outer ~) Weltraum m; (gap) Zwischenraum
m; (for parking) Lücke f; **space bar** n
Leertaste f; **spacecraft** (pl -) n
Raumschiff nt; **space ship** n Raumschiff
nt; **space shuttle** n Raumfähre f

spacing ['speɪsɪŋ] n (in text)
Zeilenabstand m; **double ~** zweizeiliger
Abstand

spacious ['speɪʃəs] adj geräumig

spade [speɪd] n Spaten m; **~s** Pik nt

spaghetti [spə'getɪ] nsing Spaghetti pl

Spain [speɪn] n Spanien nt

spam [spæm] n (Inform) Spam m

Spaniard ['spænɪəd] n Spanier(in) m(f);
Spanish ['spænɪʃ] adj spanisch ▷ n
(language) Spanisch nt

spanner ['spænə*] n (Brit)
Schraubenschlüssel m

spare [spɛə*] adj (as replacement) Ersatz-;
~ part Ersatzteil n; **~ room** Gästezimmer
nt; **~ time** Freizeit f; **~ tyre** Ersatzreifen m
▷ n (~ part) Ersatzteil nt ▷ vt (lives,
feelings) verschonen; **can you ~ (me) a
moment?** hätten Sie einen Moment Zeit?

spark [spaːk] n Funke m; **sparkle**
['spaːkl] vi funkeln; **sparkling wine** n
Schaumwein m, Sekt m; **spark plug**
['spaːkplʌg] n Zündkerze f

sparrow ['spærəʊ] n Spatz m

sparse [spaːs] adj spärlich; **sparsely** adv
~ populated dünn besiedelt

spasm ['spæzəm] n (Med) Krampf m

spat [spæt] pt, pp of **spit**

speak [spiːk] (**spoke, spoken**) vt
sprechen; **can you ~ French?** sprechen Sie
Französisch?; **to ~ one's mind** seine
Meinung sagen ▷ vi sprechen (to mit, zu);
(make speech) reden; **~ing** (Tel) am Apparat;
so to ~ sozusagen; **~ for yourself** das
meinst auch nur du!; **speak up** vi (louder)
lauter sprechen; **speaker** n Sprecher(in)
m(f); (public ~) Redner(in) m(f); (loud~)
Lautsprecher m

spear [spɪə*] n Speer m

special ['speʃəl] adj besondere(r, s),
speziell ▷ n (on menu) Tagesgericht nt; (Tv,
Radio) Sondersendung f; **special delivery**
n Eilzustellung f; **special effects** npl
Spezialeffekte pl; **specialist** n
Spezialist(in) m(f); (Tech) Fachmann m,
Fachfrau f; (Med) Facharzt m, Fachärztin f;
speciality [speʃi'ælɪtɪ] n Spezialität f;
specialize vi sich spezialisieren (in auf
+akk); **specially** adv besonders;
(specifically) extra; **special offer** n
Sonderangebot nt; **specialty** n (US) see
speciality

species ['spiːʃiːz] nsing Art f

specific [spə'sɪfɪk] adj spezifisch; (precise)
genau; **specify** ['spesɪfaɪ] vt genau
angeben

specimen ['spesɪmən] n (sample) Probe f;
(example) Exemplar nt

specs [speks] npl (fam) Brille f

spectacle ['spektəkl] n Schauspiel nt

spectacles npl Brille f

spectacular [spek'tækjʊlə*] adj
spektakulär

spectator [spek'teɪtə*] n Zuschauer(in)
m(f)

sped [sped] pt, pp of **speed**

speech [spiːtʃ] n (address) Rede f; (faculty)
Sprache f; **to make a ~** eine Rede halten;
speechless adj sprachlos (with vor +dat)

speed [spiːd] (sped o speeded, sped o
speeded) vi rasen; (exceed ~ limit) zu
schnell fahren ▷ n Geschwindigkeit f; (of
film) Lichtempfindlichkeit f; **speed up** vt
beschleunigen ▷ vi schneller
werden/fahren; (drive faster) schneller
fahren; **speedboat** n Rennboot nt; **speed
bump** n Bodenschwelle f; **speed camera**
n Blitzgerät nt; **speed limit** n
Geschwindigkeitsbegrenzung f;
speedometer [spɪ'dɒmɪtə*] n
Tachometer m; **speed trap** n Radarfalle f;
speedy adj schnell

spell [spel] (spelt o spelled, spelt o
spelled) vt buchstabieren; **how do you
~ ...?** wie schreibt man ...? ▷ n (period)
Weile f; (enchantment) Zauber m; **a
cold/hot ~** (weather) ein
Kälteeinbruch/eine Hitzewelle;
spellchecker n (Inform)
Rechtschreibprüfung f; **spelling** n
Rechtschreibung f; (of a word)
Schreibweise f; **~ mistake** Schreibfehler m

spelt [spelt] pt, pp of **spell**

spend [spend] (spent, spent) vt (money)
ausgeben (on für); (time) verbringen;
spending money n Taschengeld nt

spent [spent] pt, pp of **spend**

sperm [spɜːm] n Sperma nt

sphere [sfɪə*] n (globe) Kugel f; (fig)
Sphäre f

spice [spaɪs] n Gewürz nt; (fig) Würze f
▷ vt würzen; **spicy** ['spaɪsɪ] adj würzig;
(fig) pikant

spider ['spaɪdə*] n Spinne f

spike [spaɪk] n (on railing etc) Spitze f; (on
shoe, tyre) Spike m

spill [spɪl] (spilt o spilled, spilt o spilled)
vt verschütten

spin [spɪn] (spun, spun) vi (turn) sich

drehen; (washing) schleudern; **my head is
~ning** mir dreht sich alles ▷ vt (turn)
drehen; (coin) hochwerfen ▷ n (turn)
Drehung f

spinach ['spɪnɪtʃ] n Spinat m

spin-drier ['spɪndraɪə*] n
Wäscheschleuder f; **spin-dry** vt
schleudern

spine [spaɪn] n Rückgrat nt; (of animal,
plant) Stachel m; (of book) Rücken m

spiral ['spaɪrəl] n Spirale f ▷ adj
spiralförmig; **spiral staircase** n
Wendeltreppe f

spire ['spaɪə*] n Turmspitze f

spirit ['spɪrɪt] n (essence, soul) Geist m;
(humour, mood) Stimmung f; (courage) Mut
m; (verve) Elan m; **~s** pl (drinks) Spirituosen
pl

spiritual ['spɪrɪtjʊəl] adj geistig; (Rel)
geistlich

spit [spɪt] (spat, spat) vi spucken ▷ n (for
roasting) (Brat)spieß m; (saliva) Spucke f;
spit out vt ausspucken

spite [spaɪt] n Boshaftigkeit f; **in ~ of**
trotz +gen; **spiteful** adj boshaft

spitting image ['spɪtɪŋ'ɪmɪdʒ] n **he's the
~ of you** er ist dir wie aus dem Gesicht
geschnitten

splash [splæʃ] vt (person, object)
bespritzen ▷ vi (liquid) spritzen; (play in
water) planschen

splendid ['splendɪd] adj herrlich

splinter ['splɪntə*] n Splitter m

split [splɪt] (split, split) vt (stone, wood)
spalten; (share) teilen ▷ vi (stone, wood)
sich spalten; (seam) platzen ▷ n (in stone,
wood) Spalt m; (in clothing) Riss m; (fig)
Spaltung f; **split up** vi (couple) sich
trennen ▷ vt (divide up) aufteilen; **split
ends** npl (Haar)spliss m; **splitting** adj
(headache) rasend

spoil [spɔɪl] (spoiled o spoilt, spoiled o
spoilt) vt verderben; (child) verwöhnen
▷ vi (food) verderben

spoilt [spɔɪlt] pt, pp of **spoil**

spoke [spəʊk] pt of **speak** ▷ n Speiche f

spoken ['spəʊkən] pp of **speak**

spokesperson ['spəʊkspɜːsən] (pl
-people) n Sprecher(in) m(f)

sponge [spʌndʒ] n (for washing)
Schwamm m; **sponge bag** n Kulturbeutel
m; **sponge cake** n Biskuitkuchen m

sponsor ['spɒnsə*] n (of event, programme)

Sponsor(in) m(f) ▷ vt unterstützen; (event, programme) sponsern

spontaneous, spontaneously [spɒn'teɪnɪəs, -lɪ] adj, adv spontan

spool [spu:l] n Spule f

spoon [spu:n] n Löffel m

sport [spɔ:t] n Sport m; **sports car** n Sportwagen m; **sports centre** n Sportzentrum nt; **sports club** n Sportverein m; **sportsman** (pl -**men**) n Sportler m; **sportswear** n Sportkleidung f; **sportswoman** (pl -**women**) n Sportlerin f; **sporty** adj sportlich

spot [spɒt] n (dot) Punkt m; (of paint, blood etc) Fleck m; (place) Stelle f; (pimple) Pickel m; **on the** ~ vor Ort; (at once) auf der Stelle ▷ vt (notice) entdecken; (difference) erkennen; **spotless** adj (clean) blitzsauber; **spotlight** n (lamp) Scheinwerfer m; **spotty** adj (pimply) pickelig

spouse [spaʊs] n Gatte m, Gattin f

spout [spaʊt] n Schnabel m

sprain [spreɪn] n Verstauchung f ▷ vt **to** ~ **one's ankle** sich den Knöchel verstauchen

sprang [spræŋ] pt of **spring**

spray [spreɪ] n (liquid in can) Spray nt o m; (~ (can)) Spraydose f ▷ vt (plant, insects) besprühen; (car) spritzen

spread [spred] (**spread, spread**) vt (open out) ausbreiten; (news, disease) verbreiten; (butter, jam) streichen; (bread, surface) bestreichen ▷ vi (news, disease, fire) sich verbreiten ▷ n (of disease, religion etc) Verbreitung f; (for bread) Aufstrich m; **spreadsheet** n (Inform) Tabellenkalkulation f

spring [sprɪŋ] (**sprang, sprung**) vi (leap) springen ▷ n (season) Frühling m; (coil) Feder f; (water) Quelle f; **springboard** n Sprungbrett nt; **spring onion** n (Brit) Frühlingszwiebel f; **spring roll** n (Brit) Frühlingsrolle f; **springy** adj (mattress) federnd

sprinkle ['sprɪŋkl] vt streuen; (liquid) (be)träufeln; **to** ~ **sth with sth** etw mit etw bestreuen; (with liquid) etw mit etw besprengen; **sprinkler** n (for lawn) Rasensprenger m; (for fire) Sprinkler m

sprint [sprɪnt] vi rennen; (Sport) sprinten

sprout [spraʊt] n (of plant) Trieb m; (from seed) Keim m; (**Brussels**) ~**s** pl Rosenkohl m ▷ vi sprießen

sprung [sprʌŋ] pp of **spring**

spun [spʌn] pt, pp of **spin**

spy [spaɪ] n Spion(in) m(f) ▷ vi spionieren; **to** ~ **on sb** jdm nachspionieren ▷ vt erspähen

squad [skwɒd] n (Sport) Mannschaft f; (police ~) Kommando nt

square [skweə*] n (shape) Quadrat nt; (open space) Platz m; (on chessboard etc) Feld nt ▷ adj (in shape) quadratisch; **2** ~ **metres** 2 Quadratmeter; **2 metres** ~ 2 Meter im Quadrat ▷ vt **3** ~**d** 3 hoch 2; **square root** n Quadratwurzel f

squash [skwɒʃ] n (drink) Fruchtsaftgetränk nt; (Sport) Squash nt; (US: vegetable) Kürbis m ▷ vt zerquetschen

squat [skwɒt] vi (be crouching) hocken; **to** ~ (**down**) sich (hin)hocken

squeak [skwi:k] vi (door, shoes etc) quietschen; (animal) quieken

squeal [skwi:l] vi (person) kreischen (with vor +dat)

squeeze [skwi:z] vt drücken; (orange) auspressen ▷ vi **to** ~ **into the car** sich in den Wagen hineinzwängen; **squeeze up** vi (on bench etc) zusammenrücken

squid [skwɪd] n Tintenfisch m

squint [skwɪnt] vi schielen; (in bright light) blinzeln

squirrel ['skwɪrəl] n Eichhörnchen nt

squirt [skwɜ:t] vt, vi (liquid) spritzen

Sri Lanka [sri:'læŋkə] n Sri Lanka nt

st abbr = **stone** Gewichtseinheit (6,35 kg)

St abbr = **saint** St.; abbr = **street** Str.

stab [stæb] vt (person) einstechen auf +akk; (to death) erstechen; **stabbing** adj (pain) stechend

stabilize ['steɪbəlaɪz] vt stabilisieren ▷ vi sich stabilisieren

stable ['steɪbl] n Stall m ▷ adj stabil

stack [stæk] n (pile) Stapel m ▷ vt **to** ~ (**up**) (auf)stapeln

stadium ['steɪdɪəm] n Stadion nt

staff [stɑ:f] n (personnel) Personal nt, Lehrkräfte pl

stag [stæg] n Hirsch m

stag night n (Brit) Junggesellenabschied m

stage [steɪdʒ] n (Theat) Bühne f; (of project, life etc) Stadium nt; (of journey) Etappe f; **at this** ~ zu diesem Zeitpunkt ▷ vt (Theat) aufführen, inszenieren; (demonstration) veranstalten

stagger ['stægə*] vi wanken ▷ vt (amaze) verblüffen; **staggering** adj (amazing) umwerfend; (amount, price) Schwindel erregend

stagnant ['stægnənt] adj (water) stehend; **stagnate** [stæg'neɪt] vi (fig) stagnieren

stain [steɪn] n Fleck m; **stained-glass window** n Buntglasfenster nt; **stainless steel** n rostfreier Stahl; **stain remover** n Fleck(en)entferner m

stair [steə*] n (Treppen)stufe f; **~s** pl Treppe f; **staircase** n Treppe f

stake [steɪk] n (post) Pfahl m; (in betting) Einsatz m; (Fin) Anteil m (in an +dat); **to be at ~** auf dem Spiel stehen

stale [steɪl] adj (bread) alt; (beer) schal

stalk [stɔːk] n Stiel m ▷ vt (wild animal) sich anpirschen an +akk; (person) nachstellen +dat

stall [stɔːl] n (in market) (Verkaufs)stand m; (in stable) Box f; **~s** pl (Theat) Parkett nt ▷ vt (engine) abwürgen ▷ vi (driver) den Motor abwürgen; (car) stehen bleiben; (delay) Zeit schinden

stamina ['stæmɪnə] n Durchhaltevermögen nt

stammer ['stæmə*] vi, vt stottern

stamp [stæmp] n (postage ~) Briefmarke f; (for document) Stempel m ▷ vt (passport etc) stempeln; (mail) frankieren; **stamped addressed envelope** n frankierter Rückumschlag

stand [stænd] (**stood, stood**) vi stehen; (as candidate) kandidieren ▷ vt (place) stellen; (endure) aushalten; **I can't ~ her** ich kann sie nicht ausstehen ▷ n (stall) Stand m; (seats in stadium) Tribüne f; (for coats, bicycles) Ständer m; (for small objects) Gestell nt; **stand around** vi herumstehen; **stand by** vi (be ready) sich bereithalten; (be inactive) danebenstehen ▷ vt (fig: person) halten zu; (decision, promise) stehen zu; **stand for** vt (represent) stehen für; (tolerate) hinnehmen; **stand in for** vt einspringen für; **stand out** vi (be noticeable) auffallen; **stand up** vi (get up) aufstehen ▷ vt (girlfriend, boyfriend) versetzen; **stand up for** vt sich einsetzen für; **stand up to** vt **to ~ sb** jdm die Stirn bieten

standard ['stændəd] n (norm) Norm f; **~ of living** Lebensstandard m ▷ adj Standard-

standardize ['stændədaɪz] vt vereinheitlichen

stand-by ['stændbaɪ] n (thing in reserve) Reserve f; **on ~** in Bereitschaft ▷ adj (flight, ticket) Standby-; **standing order** n (at bank) Dauerauftrag m; **standpoint** ['stændpɔɪnt] n Standpunkt m; **standstill** ['stændstɪl] n Stillstand m; **to come to a ~** stehen bleiben; (fig) zum Erliegen kommen

stank [stæŋk] pt of **stink**

staple ['steɪpl] n (for paper) Heftklammer f ▷ vt heften (to an +akk); **stapler** n Hefter m

star [stɑː*] n Stern m; (person) Star m ▷ vt **the film ~s Hugh Grant** der Film zeigt Hugh Grant in der Hauptrolle ▷ vi die Hauptrolle spielen

starch [stɑːtʃ] n Stärke f

stare [steə*] vi starren; **to ~ at** anstarren

starfish ['stɑːfɪʃ] n Seestern m

star sign ['stɑːsaɪn] n Sternzeichen nt

start [stɑːt] n (beginning) Anfang m, Beginn m; (Sport) Start m; (lead) Vorsprung m; **from the ~** von Anfang an ▷ vt anfangen; (car, engine) starten; (business, family) gründen; **to ~ to do sth, to ~ doing sth** anfangen, etw zu tun ▷ vi (begin) anfangen; (car) anspringen; (on journey) aufbrechen; (Sport) starten; (jump) zusammenfahren; **~ing from Monday** ab Montag; **start off** vi (discussion, process etc) anfangen, beginnen ▷ vi (begin) anfangen, beginnen; (on journey) aufbrechen; **start over** vi (US) wieder anfangen; **start up** vi (in business) anfangen ▷ vt (car, engine) starten; (business) gründen; **starter** n (Brit: first course) Vorspeise f; (Auto) Anlasser m; **starting point** n (a. fig) Ausgangspunkt m

startle ['stɑːtl] vt erschrecken; **startling** adj überraschend

starve [stɑːv] vi hungern; (to death) verhungern; **I'm ~ing** ich habe einen Riesenhunger

state [steɪt] n (condition) Zustand m; (Pol) Staat m; **~ of health/mind** Gesundheits-/Geisteszustand m; **the (United) States** die (Vereinigten) Staaten

▷ *adj* Staats-; (control, education) staatlich
▷ *vt* erklären; (facts, name etc) angeben;
stated *adj* (fixed) festgesetzt
statement ['steɪtmənt] *n* (official
declaration) Erklärung *f*; (to police) Aussage
f; (from bank) Kontoauszug *m*
state-of-the-art [steɪtəvðɪ:'ɑ:t] *adj*
hochmodern, auf dem neuesten Stand der
Technik
static ['stætɪk] *adj* (unchanging)
konstant
station ['steɪʃən] *n* (for trains, buses)
Bahnhof *m*; (underground ~) Station *f*; (police
~, fire ~) Wache *f*; (TV, Radio) Sender *m* ▷ *vt*
(Mil) stationieren
stationer's ['steɪʃənəz] *n* ~ (shop)
Schreibwarengeschäft *nt*; **stationery** *n*
Schreibwaren *pl*
station wagon ['steɪʃənwægən] *n* (US)
Kombiwagen *m*
statistics [stə'tɪstɪks] *nsing* (science)
Statistik *f*; (figures) Statistiken *pl*
statue ['stætjuː] *n* Statue *f*
status ['steɪtəs] *n* Status *m*; (prestige)
Ansehen *nt*; **status bar** *n* (Inform)
Statuszeile *f*
stay [steɪ] *n* Aufenthalt *m* ▷ *vi* bleiben;
(with friends, in hotel) wohnen (with bei); **to
~ the night** übernachten; **stay away** *vi*
wegbleiben; **to ~ from sb** sich von jdm
fern halten; **stay behind** *vi*
zurückbleiben; (at work) länger bleiben;
stay in *vi* (at home) zu Hause bleiben;
stay out *vi* (not come home) wegbleiben;
stay up *vi* (at night) aufbleiben
steady ['stedɪ] *adj* (speed) gleichmäßig;
(progress, increase) stetig; (job, income,
girlfriend) fest; (worker) zuverlässig; (hand)
ruhig; **they've been going ~ for two
years** sie sind seit zwei Jahren fest
zusammen ▷ *vt* (nerves) beruhigen; **to
~ oneself** Halt finden
steak [steɪk] *n* Steak *nt*; (of fish) Filet *nt*
steal [stiːl] (**stole, stolen**) *vt* stehlen; **to
~ sth from sb** jdm etw stehlen
steam [stiːm] *n* Dampf *m* ▷ *vt* (Gastr)
dämpfen; **steam up** *vi* (window)
beschlagen; **steamer** *n* (Gastr)
Dampfkochtopf *m*; (ship) Dampfer *m*;
steam iron *n* Dampfbügeleisen *nt*
steel [stiːl] *n* Stahl *m* ▷ *adj* Stahl-
steep [stiːp] *adj* steil
steeple ['stiːpl] *n* Kirchturm *m*

steer [stɪə*] *vt*, *vi* steuern; (car, bike etc)
lenken; **steering** *n* (Auto) Lenkung *f*;
steering wheel *n* Steuer *nt*, Lenkrad *nt*
stem [stem] *n* (of plant, glass) Stiel *m*
step [step] *n* Schritt *m*; (stair) Stufe *f*;
(measure) Maßnahme *f*; **~ by ~** Schritt für
Schritt ▷ *vi* treten; **~ this way, please**
hier entlang, bitte; **step down** *vi* (resign)
zurücktreten
stepbrother *n* Stiefbruder *m*; **stepchild**
(*pl* **-children**) *n* Stiefkind *nt*; **stepfather** *n*
Stiefvater *m*
stepladder *n* Trittleiter *f*
stepmother *n* Stiefmutter *f*; **stepsister**
n Stiefschwester *f*
stereo ['sterɪəʊ] (*pl* **-s**) *n* ~ (system)
Stereoanlage *f*
sterile ['steraɪl] *adj* steril; **sterilize**
['sterɪlaɪz] *vt* sterilisieren
sterling ['stɜːlɪŋ] *n* (Fin) das Pfund
Sterling
stern [stɜːn] *adj* streng ▷ *n* Heck *nt*
stew [stjuː] *n* Eintopf *m*
steward ['stjuːəd] *n* (on plane, ship)
Steward *m*; **stewardess** *n* Stewardess *f*
stick [stɪk] (**stuck, stuck**) *vt* (with glue etc)
kleben; (pin etc) stecken; (fam: put) tun ▷ *vi*
(get jammed) klemmen; (hold fast) haften
▷ *n* Stock *m*; (hockey ~) Schläger *m*; (of
chalk) Stück *nt*; (of celery, rhubarb) Stange *f*;
stick out *vi* **to stick one's tongue out
(at sb)** (jdm) die Zunge herausstrecken
▷ *vi* (protrude) vorstehen; (ears) abstehen;
(be noticeable) auffallen; **stick to** *vt* (rules,
plan etc) sich halten an +*akk*; **sticker**
['stɪkə*] *n* Aufkleber *m*; **sticky** ['stɪkɪ] *adj*
klebrig; (weather) schwül; **~ label**
Aufkleber *m*; **~ tape** Klebeband *nt*
stiff [stɪf] *adj* steif
stifle ['staɪfl] *vt* (yawn etc, opposition)
unterdrücken; **stifling** *adj* drückend
still [stɪl] *adj* still; (drink) ohne
Kohlensäure ▷ *adv* (yet, even now) (immer)
noch; (all the same) immerhin; (sit, stand)
still; **he ~ doesn't believe me** er glaubt
mir immer noch nicht; **keep ~** halt still!;
bigger/better ~ noch größer/besser
still life (*pl* **still lives**) *n* Stillleben *nt*
stimulate ['stɪmjʊleɪt] *vt* anregen,
stimulieren; **stimulating** *adj* anregend;
stimulus ['stɪmjʊləs] *n* (incentive) Anreiz
m
sting [stɪŋ] (**stung, stung**) *vt* (wound with

~) stechen ▷ vi (eyes, ointment etc) brennen ▷ n (insect wound) Stich m

stingy ['stɪndʒɪ] adj (fam) geizig

stink [stɪŋk] (**stank, stunk**) vi stinken (of nach) ▷ n Gestank m

stir [stɜ:*] vt (mix) (um)rühren; **stir up** vt (mob) aufhetzen; (memories) wachrufen; **to ~ trouble** Unruhe stiften; **stir-fry** vt (unter Rühren) kurz anbraten

stitch [stɪtʃ] n (in sewing) Stich m; (in knitting) Masche f; **to have a ~** (pain) Seitenstechen haben; **he had to have ~es** er musste genäht werden; **she had her ~es out** ihr wurden die Fäden gezogen; **to be in ~es** (fam) sich kaputtlachen ▷ vt nähen; **stitch up** vt (hole, wound) nähen

stock [stɒk] n (supply) Vorrat m (of an +dat); (of shop) Bestand m; (for soup etc) Brühe f; **~s and shares** pl Aktien und Wertpapiere pl; **to be in/out of ~** vorrätig/nicht vorrätig sein; **to take ~** Inventur machen; (fig) Bilanz ziehen ▷ vt (keep in shop) führen; **stock up** vi sich eindecken (on, with mit)

stockbroker n Börsenmakler(in) m(f)

stock cube n Brühwürfel m

stock exchange n Börse f

stocking ['stɒkɪŋ] n Strumpf m

stock market ['stɒkmɑːkɪt] n Börse f

stole [stəʊl] pt of **steal**; **stolen** ['stəʊlən] pp of **steal**

stomach ['stʌmək] n Magen m; (belly) Bauch m; **on an empty ~** auf leeren Magen; **stomach-ache** n Magenschmerzen pl; **stomach upset** n Magenverstimmung f

stone [stəʊn] n Stein m; (seed) Kern m, Stein m; (weight) britische Gewichtseinheit (6,35 kg) ▷ adj Stein-, aus Stein; **stony** adj (ground) steinig

stood [stʊd] pt, pp of **stand**

stool [stuːl] n Hocker m

stop [stɒp] n Halt m; (for bus, tram, train) Haltestelle f; **to come to a ~** anhalten ▷ vt (vehicle, passer-by) anhalten; (put an end to) ein Ende machen +dat; (cease) aufhören mit; (prevent from happening) verhindern; (bleeding) stillen; (engine, machine) abstellen; (payments) einstellen; (cheque) sperren; **to ~ doing sth** aufhören, etw zu tun; **to ~ sb (from) doing sth** jdn daran hindern, etw zu tun; **~ it** hör auf (damit)! ▷ vi (vehicle) anhalten; (during journey) Halt machen; (pedestrian, clock, heart) stehen bleiben; (rain, noise) aufhören; (stay) bleiben; **stop by** vi vorbeischauen; **stop over** vi Halt machen; (overnight) übernachten; **stopover** n (on journey) Zwischenstation f; **stopper** n Stöpsel m; **stop sign** n Stoppschild nt; **stopwatch** n Stoppuhr f

storage ['stɔːrɪdʒ] n Lagerung f; **store** [stɔː*] n (supply) Vorrat m (of an +dat); (place for storage) Lager nt; (large shop) Kaufhaus nt; (US: shop) Geschäft nt ▷ vt lagern; (Inform) speichern; **storecard** n Kundenkreditkarte f; **storeroom** n Lagerraum m

storey ['stɔːrɪ] n (Brit) Stock m, Stockwerk nt

storm [stɔːm] n Sturm m; (thunder~) Gewitter nt ▷ vt, vi (with movement) stürmen; **stormy** adj stürmisch

story ['stɔːrɪ] n Geschichte f; (plot) Handlung f; (US: of building) Stock m, Stockwerk nt

stout [staʊt] adj (fat) korpulent; (shoes) fest

stove [stəʊv] n Herd m; (for heating) Ofen m

stow [stəʊ] vt verstauen; **stowaway** n blinder Passagier

straight [streɪt] adj (not curved) gerade; (hair) glatt; (honest) ehrlich (with zu); (fam: heterosexual) hetero ▷ adv (directly) direkt; (immediately) sofort; (drink) pur; (think) klar; **~ ahead** geradeaus; **to go ~ on** geradeaus weitergehen/weiterfahren; **straightaway** adv sofort; **straightforward** adj einfach; (person) aufrichtig

strain [streɪn] n Belastung f ▷ vt (eyes) überanstrengen; (rope, relationship) belasten; (vegetables) abgießen; **to ~ a muscle** sich einen Muskel zerren; **strained** adj (laugh, smile) gezwungen; (relations) gespannt; **~ muscle** Muskelzerrung f; **strainer** n Sieb nt

strand [strænd] n (of wool) Faden m; (of hair) Strähne f ▷ vt **to be (left) ~ed** (person) festsitzen

strange [streɪndʒ] adj seltsam; (unfamiliar) fremd; **strangely** adv seltsam; **~ enough** seltsamerweise; **stranger** n Fremde(r) mf; **I'm a ~ here** ich bin hier fremd

strangle ['stræŋgl] vt (kill) erdrosseln

strap [stræp] n Riemen m; (on dress etc) Träger m; (on watch) Band nt ▷ vt (fasten) festschnallen (to an +dat); **strapless** adj trägerlos

strategy ['strætɪdʒɪ] n Strategie f

straw [strɔː] n Stroh nt; (drinking ~) Strohhalm m

strawberry n Erdbeere f

stray [streɪ] n streunendes Tier ▷ adj (cat, dog) streunend ▷ vi streunen

streak ['striːk] n (of colour, dirt) Streifen m; (in hair) Strähne f; (in character) Zug m

stream [striːm] n (flow of liquid) Strom m; (brook) Bach m ▷ vi strömen; **streamer** n (of paper) Luftschlange f

street [striːt] n Straße f; **streetcar** n (US) Straßenbahn f; **street lamp**, **street light** n Straßenlaterne f; **street map** n Stadtplan m

strength [streŋθ] n Kraft f, Stärke f; **strengthen** vt verstärken; (fig) stärken

strenuous ['strenjʊəs] adj anstrengend

stress [stres] n Stress m; (on word) Betonung f; **to be under ~** im Stress sein ▷ vt betonen; (put under ~) stressen; **stressed** adj ~ (out) gestresst

stretch [stretʃ] n (of land) Stück nt; (of road) Strecke f ▷ vt (material, shoes) dehnen; (rope, canvas) spannen; (person in job etc) fordern; **to ~ one's legs** (walk) sich die Beine vertreten ▷ vi (person) sich strecken; (area) sich erstrecken (to bis zu); **stretch out** vt to **stretch one's hand/legs out** die Hand/die Beine ausstrecken, ausstrecken ▷ vi (reach) sich strecken; (lie down) sich ausstrecken; **stretcher** n Tragbahre f

strict, **strictly** [strɪkt, -lɪ] adj, adv (severe(ly)) streng; (exact(ly)) genau

strike [straɪk] (**struck, struck**) vt (match) anzünden; (hit) schlagen; (find) finden; **it struck me as strange** es kam mir seltsam vor ▷ vi (stop work) streiken; (attack) zuschlagen; (clock) schlagen ▷ n (by workers) Streik m; **to be on ~** streiken; **strike up** vt (conversation) anfangen; (friendship) schließen; **striking** adj auffallend; (resemblance) verblüffend

string [strɪŋ] n (for tying) Schnur f; (Mus, Tennis) Saite f; **the ~s** pl (section of orchestra) die Streicher pl

strip [strɪp] n Streifen m; (Brit: of footballer

etc) Trikot nt ▷ vt (undress) ausziehen ▷ vi (undress) sich ausziehen, strippen

stripe [straɪp] n Streifen m; **striped** adj gestreift

stripper ['strɪpə*] n Stripper(in) m(f); (paint ~) Farbentferner m

strip-search ['strɪpsɜːtʃ] n Leibesvisitation f (bei der man sich ausziehen muss)

striptease ['strɪptiːz] n Striptease m

strive [straɪv] (**strove, striven**) vi **to ~ to do sth** bemüht sein, etw zu tun; **to ~ for sth** nach etw streben

stroke [strəʊk] n (Med, Tennis etc) Schlag m; (of pen, brush) Strich m ▷ vt streicheln

stroll [strəʊl] n Spaziergang m ▷ vi spazieren; **stroller** n (US: for baby) Buggy m

strong [strɒŋ] adj stark; (healthy) robust; (wall, table) stabil; (shoes) fest; (influence, chance) groß; **strongly** adv stark; (believe) fest; (constructed) stabil

strove [strəʊv] pt of **strive**

struck [strʌk] pt, pp of **strike**

structural, **structurally** ['strʌktʃərəl, -lɪ] adj strukturell; **structure** ['strʌktʃə*] n Struktur f, (building, bridge) Konstruktion f, Bau m

struggle ['strʌgl] n Kampf m (for um) ▷ vi (fight) kämpfen (for um); (do sth with difficulty) sich abmühen; **to ~ to do sth** sich abmühen, etw zu tun

stub [stʌb] n (of cigarette) Kippe f; (of ticket, cheque) Abschnitt m ▷ vt **to ~ one's toe** sich dat den Zeh stoßen (on an +dat)

stubble ['stʌbl] n Stoppeln pl

stubborn ['stʌbən] adj (person) stur

stuck [stʌk] pt, pp of **stick** ▷ adj **to be ~** (jammed) klemmen; (at a loss) nicht mehr weiterwissen; **to get ~** (car in snow etc) stecken bleiben

student ['stjuːdənt] n Student(in) m(f), Schüler(in) m(f)

studio ['stjuːdɪəʊ] (pl **-s**) n Studio nt

studious ['stjuːdɪəs] adj fleißig

study ['stʌdɪ] n (investigation) Untersuchung f; (studying) Studium nt; (room) Arbeitszimmer nt ▷ vt, vi studieren; **to ~ for an exam** sich auf eine Prüfung vorbereiten

stuff [stʌf] n Zeug nt, Sachen pl ▷ vt (push) stopfen; (Gastr) füllen; **to ~ oneself**

(fam) sich voll stopfen; **stuffing** *n (Gastr)* Füllung *f*

stuffy ['stʌfɪ] *adj (room)* stickig; *(person)* spießig

stumble ['stʌmbl] *vi* stolpern; *(when speaking)* stocken

stun [stʌn] *vt (shock)* fassungslos machen; **I was ~ned** ich war fassungslos *(o* völlig überrascht*)*

stung [stʌŋ] *pt, pp of* **sting**

stunk [stʌŋk] *pp of* **stink**

stunning ['stʌnɪŋ] *adj (marvellous)* fantastisch; *(beautiful)* atemberaubend; *(very surprising, shocking)* überwältigend; unfassbar

stunt [stʌnt] *n (Cine)* Stunt *m*

stupid ['stju:pɪd] *adj* dumm; **stupidity** [stju:'pɪdɪtɪ] *n* Dummheit *f*

sturdy ['stɜ:dɪ] *adj* robust; *(building, car)* stabil

stutter ['stʌtə*] *vi, vt* stottern

stye [staɪ] *n (Med)* Gerstenkorn *nt*

style [staɪl] *n* Stil *m* ▷ *vt (hair)* stylen; **styling mousse** *n* Schaumfestiger *m*; **stylish** ['staɪlɪʃ] *adj* elegant

subconscious [sʌb'kɒnʃəs] *adj* unterbewusst ▷ *n* **the ~** das Unterbewusstsein

subdivide [sʌbdɪ'vaɪd] *vt* unterteilen

subject ['sʌbdʒɪkt] *n (topic)* Thema *nt*; *(in school)* Fach *nt*; *(citizen)* Staatsangehörige(r) *mf*; *(of kingdom)* Untertan(in) *m(f)*; *(Ling)* Subjekt *nt*; **to change the ~** das Thema wechseln ▷ *adj* [səb'dʒekt] **to be ~ to** *(dependent on)* abhängen von; *(under control of)* unterworfen sein +*dat*

subjective [səb'dʒektɪv] *adj* subjektiv

sublet [sʌb'let] *irr vt* untervermieten *(to* an +*akk)*

submarine [sʌbmə'ri:n] *n* U-Boot *nt*

submerge [səb'mɜ:dʒ] *vt (put in water)* eintauchen ▷ *vi* tauchen

submit [səb'mɪt] *vt (application, claim)* einreichen ▷ *vi (surrender)* sich ergeben

subordinate [sə'bɔ:dɪnət] *adj* untergeordnet *(to* +*dat)* ▷ *n* Untergebene(r) *mf*

subscribe [səb'skraɪb] *vi* **to ~ to** *(magazine etc)* abonnieren; **subscription** [səb'skrɪpʃən] *n (to magazine etc)* Abonnement *nt*; *(to club etc)* (Mitglieds)beitrag *m*

subsequent ['sʌbsɪkwənt] *adj* nach(folgend); **subsequently** *adv* später, anschließend

subside [səb'saɪd] *vi (floods)* zurückgehen; *(storm)* sich legen; *(building)* sich senken

substance ['sʌbstəns] *n* Substanz *f*

substantial [səb'stænʃəl] *adj* beträchtlich; *(improvement)* wesentlich; *(meal)* reichhaltig; *(furniture)* solide

substitute ['sʌbstɪtju:t] *n* Ersatz *m*; *(Sport)* Ersatzspieler(in) *m(f)* ▷ *vt* **to ~ A for B** B durch A ersetzen

subtitle ['sʌbtaɪtl] *n* Untertitel *m*

subtle ['sʌtl] *adj (difference, taste)* fein; *(plan)* raffiniert

subtotal ['sʌbtəʊtl] *n* Zwischensumme *f*

subtract [səb'trækt] *vt* abziehen *(from* von*)*

suburb ['sʌbɜ:b] *n* Vorort *m*; **in the ~s** am Stadtrand; **suburban** [sə'bɜ:bən] *adj* vorstädtisch, Vorstadt-

subway ['sʌbweɪ] *n (Brit)* Unterführung *f*; *(US Rail)* U-Bahn *f*

succeed [sək'si:d] *vi* erfolgreich sein; **he ~ed (in doing it)** es gelang ihm(, es zu tun) ▷ *vt* nachfolgen +*dat*; **succeeding** *adj* nachfolgend; **success** [sək'ses] *n* Erfolg *m*; **successful, successfully** *adj, adv* erfolgreich

successive [sək'sesɪv] *adj* aufeinander folgend; **successor** *n* Nachfolger(in) *m(f)*

succulent ['sʌkjʊlənt] *adj* saftig

succumb [sə'kʌm] *vi* erliegen *(to* +*dat)*

such [sʌtʃ] *adj* solche(r, s); **~ a book** so ein Buch, ein solches Buch; **it was ~ a success that ...** es war solch ein Erfolg, dass ...; **~ as** wie ▷ *adv* so; **~ a hot day** so ein heißer Tag ▷ *pron* **as ~** als solche(r, s); **suchlike** *adj* derartig ▷ *pron* dergleichen

suck [sʌk] *vt (toffee etc)* lutschen; *(liquid)* saugen; **it ~s** *(fam)* das ist beschissen

Sudan [su'da:n] *n* **(the) ~** der Sudan

sudden ['sʌdn] *adj* plötzlich; **all of a ~** ganz plötzlich; **suddenly** *adv* plötzlich

sue [su:] *vt* verklagen

suede [sweɪd] *n* Wildleder *nt*

suffer ['sʌfə*] *vt* erleiden ▷ *vi* leiden; **to ~ from** *(Med)* leiden an +*dat*

sufficient, sufficiently [sə'fɪʃənt, -lɪ] *adj, adv* ausreichend

suffocate ['sʌfəkeɪt] *vt, vi* ersticken

sugar ['ʃʊgə*] n Zucker m ▷ vt zuckern;
   sugar bowl n Zuckerdose f; **sugary** adj
   (sweet) süß
suggest [sə'dʒest] vt vorschlagen; (imply)
   andeuten; **I ~ saying nothing** ich schlage
   vor, nichts zu sagen; **suggestion**
   [sə'dʒestʃən] n (proposal) Vorschlag m;
   suggestive adj vielsagend; (sexually)
   anzüglich
suicide ['sʊisaid] n (act) Selbstmord m
suit [suːt] n (man's clothes) Anzug m; (lady's
   clothes) Kostüm nt; (Cards) Farbe f ▷ vt (be
   convenient for) passen +dat; (clothes, colour)
   stehen +dat; (climate, food) bekommen
   +dat; **suitable** adj geeignet (for für);
   suitcase n Koffer m
suite [swiːt] n (of rooms) Suite f; (sofa and
   chairs) Sitzgarnitur f
sulk [sʌlk] vi schmollen; **sulky** adj
   eingeschnappt
sultana [sʌl'tɑːnə] n (raisin) Sultanine f
sum [sʌm] n Summe f; (money a.) Betrag
   m; (calculation) Rechenaufgabe f; **sum up**
   vt, vi (summarize) zusammenfassen
summarize ['sʌməraiz] vt, vi
   zusammenfassen; **summary** n
   Zusammenfassung f
summer ['sʌmə*] n Sommer m; **summer
   camp** n (US) Ferienlager nt; **summer
   holidays** n Sommerferien pl;
   summertime n **in (the) ~** im Sommer
summit ['sʌmit] n (a. Pol) Gipfel m
summon ['sʌmən] vt (doctor, fire brigade
   etc) rufen; (to one's office) zitieren;
   summon up vt (courage, strength)
   zusammennehmen
summons ['sʌmənz] nsing (Jur)
   Vorladung f
sumptuous ['sʌmptjʊəs] adj luxuriös;
   (meal) üppig
sun [sʌn] n Sonne f ▷ vt **to ~ oneself** sich
   sonnen
Sun abbr = **Sunday** So.
sunbathe vi sich sonnen; **sunbathing**
   n Sonnenbaden nt; **sunbed** n
   Sonnenbank f; **sunblock** n Sunblocker m;
   sunburn n Sonnenbrand m; **sunburnt** adj
   to be/get ~ einen Sonnenbrand
   haben/bekommen
sundae ['sʌndei] n Eisbecher m
Sunday ['sʌndi] n Sonntag m; see also
   Tuesday
sung [sʌŋ] pp of **sing**

sunglasses ['sʌnglɑːsiz] npl Sonnenbrille
   f; **sunhat** n Sonnenhut m
sunk [sʌŋk] pp of **sink**
sunlamp ['sʌnlæmp] n Höhensonne f;
   sunlight n Sonnenlicht nt; **sunny** ['sʌni]
   adj sonnig; **sun protection factor** n
   Lichtschutzfaktor m; **sunrise** n
   Sonnenaufgang m; **sunroof** n (Auto)
   Schiebedach nt; **sunscreen** n
   Sonnenschutzmittel nt; **sunset** n
   Sonnenuntergang m; **sunshade** n
   Sonnenschirm m; **sunshine** n
   Sonnenschein m; **sunstroke** n
   Sonnenstich m; **suntan** n
   (Sonnen)bräune f; **to get/have a
   ~** braun werden/sein; **~ lotion** (o **oil**)
   Sonnenöl nt
super ['suːpə*] adj (fam) toll
superb, superbly [suː'pɜːb, -li] adj, adv
   ausgezeichnet
superficial, superficially [suːpə'fiʃəl, -li]
   adj, adv oberflächlich
superfluous [sʊ'pɜːflʊəs] adj überflüssig
superglue ['suːpəgluː] n Sekundenkleber
   m
superior [sʊ'piəriə*] adj (better) besser (to
   als); (higher in rank) höher gestellt (to als),
   höher ▷ n (in rank) Vorgesetzte(r) mf
supermarket ['suːpəmɑːkit] n
   Supermarkt m
supersede [suːpə'siːd] vt ablösen
supersonic [suːpə'sɒnik] adj Überschall-
superstitious [suːpə'stiʃəs] adj
   abergläubisch
superstore ['suːpəstɔː*] n
   Verbrauchermarkt m
supervise ['suːpəvaiz] vt beaufsichtigen;
   supervisor ['suːpəvaizə] n Aufsicht f; (at
   university) Doktorvater m
supper ['sʌpə*] n Abendessen nt;
   (late-night snack) Imbiss
supplement ['sʌplimənt] n (extra
   payment) Zuschlag m; (of newspaper)
   Beilage f ▷ vt ergänzen; **supplementary**
   [sʌpli'mentəri] adj zusätzlich
supplier [sə'plaiə*] n Lieferant(in) m(f);
   supply [sə'plai] vt (deliver) liefern; (drinks,
   music etc) sorgen für; **to ~ sb with sth**
   (provide) jdn mit etw versorgen ▷ n (stock)
   Vorrat m (of an +dat)
support [sə'pɔːt] n Unterstützung f;
   (Tech) Stütze f ▷ vt (hold up) tragen,
   stützen; (provide for) ernähren,

unterhalten; (speak in favour of)
unterstützen; **he ~s Manchester United**
er ist Manchester-United-Fan
suppose [sə'pəʊz] vt (assume) annehmen;
I ~ so ich denke schon; **I ~ not**
wahrscheinlich nicht; **you're not ~d to
smoke here** du darfst hier nicht rauchen;
supposedly [sə'pəʊzɪdlɪ] adv angeblich;
supposing conj angenommen
suppress [sə'pres] vt unterdrücken
surcharge ['sɜ:tʃɑ:dʒ] n Zuschlag m
sure [ʃʊə*] adj sicher; **I'm (not) ~** ich bin
mir (nicht) sicher; **make ~ you lock up**
vergiss nicht abzuschließen ▷ adv **~I** klar!;
~ enough tatsächlich; **surely** adv **~ you
don't mean it?** das ist nicht dein Ernst,
oder?
surf [sɜ:f] n Brandung f ▷ vi (Sport) surfen
▷ vt **to ~ the net** im Internet surfen
surface ['sɜ:fɪs] n Oberfläche f ▷ vi
auftauchen; **surface mail** n **by ~** auf dem
Land-/Seeweg
surfboard ['sɜ:fbɔ:d] n Surfbrett nt;
surfer ['sɜ:fə*] n Surfer(in) m(f);
surfing n Surfen
nt; **to go ~** surfen gehen
surgeon ['sɜ:dʒən] n Chirurg(in) m(f);
surgery ['sɜ:dʒərɪ] n (operation)
Operation f; (room) Praxis f, Sprechzimmer
nt; (consulting time) Sprechstunde f; **to
have ~** operiert werden
surname ['sɜ:neɪm] n Nachname m
surpass [sɜ:'pɑ:s] vt übertreffen
surplus ['sɜ:pləs] n Überschuss m (of an
+dat)
surprise [sə'praɪz] n Überraschung f ▷ vt
überraschen; **surprising** adj
überraschend; **surprisingly** adv
überraschenderweise, erstaunlicherweise
surrender [sə'rendə*] vi sich ergeben (to
+dat) ▷ vt (weapon, passport) abgeben
surround [sə'raʊnd] vt umgeben; (stand
all round) umringen; **surrounding** adj
(countryside) umliegend ▷ n **~s** pl
Umgebung f
survey ['sɜ:veɪ] n (opinion poll) Umfrage
f; (of literature etc) Überblick m (of über
+akk); (of land) Vermessung f ▷ [sɜ:'veɪ] vt
(look out over) überblicken; (land)
vermessen
survive [sə'vaɪv] vt, vi überleben
susceptible [sə'septəbl] adj empfänglich
(to für); (Med) anfällig (to für)
suspect ['sʌspekt] n Verdächtige(r) mf

▷ adj verdächtig ▷ [sə'spekt] vt
verdächtigen (of +gen); (think likely)
vermuten
suspend [sə'spend] vt (from work)
suspendieren; (payment) vorübergehend
einstellen; (player) sperren; (hang up)
aufhängen; **suspender** n (Brit)
Strumpfhalter m; **~s** pl (US: for trousers)
Hosenträger pl
suspense [sə'spens] n Spannung f
suspicious [sə'spɪʃəs] adj misstrauisch (of
sb/sth jdm/etw gegenüber); (causing
suspicion) verdächtig
swallow ['swɒləʊ] n (bird) Schwalbe f
▷ vt, vi schlucken
swam [swæm] pt of **swim**
swamp [swɒmp] n Sumpf m
swan [swɒn] n Schwan m
swap [swɒp] vt, vi tauschen; **to ~ sth for
sth** etw gegen etw eintauschen
sway [sweɪ] vi schwanken
swear [sweə*] (**swore, sworn**) vi (promise)
schwören; (curse) fluchen; **to ~ at sb** jdn
beschimpfen; **swear by** vt (have faith in)
schwören auf +akk; **swearword** n Fluch m
sweat [swet] n Schweiß m ▷ vi
schwitzen; **sweatband** n Schweißband
nt; **sweater** n Pullover m; **sweatshirt** n
Sweatshirt nt; **sweaty** adj verschwitzt
swede [swi:d] n Steckrübe f
Swede [swi:d] n Schwede m, Schwedin f;
Sweden n Schweden nt; **Swedish** adj
schwedisch ▷ n (language) Schwedisch nt
sweep [swi:p] (**swept, swept**) vt, vi (with
brush) kehren, fegen; **sweep up** vt (dirt
etc) zusammenkehren, zusammenfegen
sweet [swi:t] n (Brit: candy) Bonbon nt;
(dessert) Nachtisch m ▷ adj süß; (kind) lieb;
sweet-and-sour adj süßsauer;
sweetcorn n Mais m; **sweeten** vt (tea
etc) süßen; **sweetener** n (substance)
Süßstoff m
swell [swel] (**swelled, swollen** o **swelled**)
vi **to ~ (up)** (an)schwellen ▷ adj (US fam)
toll; **swelling** n (Med) Schwellung f
sweltering ['sweltərɪŋ] adj (heat)
drückend
swept [swept] pt, pp of **sweep**
swift, swiftly [swɪft] adj, adv schnell
swig [swɪg] n (fam) Schluck m
swim [swɪm] (**swam, swum**) vi
schwimmen ▷ n **to go for a
~** schwimmen gehen; **swimmer** n

Schwimmer(in) *m(f)*; **swimming** *n*
Schwimmen *nt*; **to go ~** schwimmen
gehen; **swimming cap** *n* (*Brit*)
Badekappe *f*; **swimming costume** *n* (*Brit*)
Badeanzug *m*; **swimming pool** *n*
Schwimmbad *nt*; (*private, in hotel*)
Swimmingpool *m*; **swimming trunks** *npl*
(*Brit*) Badehose *f*; **swimsuit** *n* Badeanzug
m

swindle ['swɪndl] *vt* betrügen (*out of* um)
swine [swaɪn] *n* (*person*) Schwein *nt*
swing [swɪŋ] (**swung, swung**) *vt, vi*
(*object*) schwingen ▷ *n* (*for child*) Schaukel *f*
swipe [swaɪp] *vt* (*credit card etc*)
durchziehen; (*fam: steal*) klauen; **swipe
card** *n* Magnetkarte *f*
Swiss [swɪs] *adj* schweizerisch ▷ *n*
Schweizer(in) *m(f)*
switch [swɪtʃ] *n* (*Elec*) Schalter *m* ▷ *vt*
(*change*) wechseln; **to ~ sth for sth** etw
gegen etw eintauschen ▷ *vi* (*change*)
wechseln (*to zu*); **switch off** *vt*
abschalten, ausschalten; **switch on** *vt*
anschalten, einschalten; **switchboard** *n*
(*Tel*) Vermittlung *f*
Switzerland ['swɪtsələnd] *n* die Schweiz
swivel ['swɪvl] *vi* sich drehen ▷ *vt*
drehen; **swivel chair** *n* Drehstuhl *m*
swollen ['swəʊlən] *pp of* **swell** ▷ *adj* (*Med*)
geschwollen; (*stomach*) aufgebläht
swop [swɒp] *see* **swap**
sword [sɔːd] *n* Schwert *nt*
swore [swɔː*] *pt of* **swear**
sworn [swɔːn] *pp of* **swear**
swot [swɒt] *vi* (*Brit fam*) büffeln (*for* für)
swum [swʌm] *pp of* **swim**
swung [swʌŋ] *pt, pp of* **swing**
syllable ['sɪləbl] *n* Silbe *f*
syllabus ['sɪləbəs] *n* Lehrplan *m*
symbol ['sɪmbəl] *n* Symbol *nt*; **symbolic**
[sɪmˈbɒlɪk] *adj* symbolisch; **symbolize** *vt*
symbolisieren
symmetrical [sɪˈmetrɪkəl] *adj*
symmetrisch
sympathetic [sɪmpəˈθetɪk] *adj*
mitfühlend; (*understanding*)
verständnisvoll; **sympathize** ['sɪmpəθaɪz]
vi mitfühlen (*with sb* mit jdm); **sympathy**
['sɪmpəθɪ] *n* Mitleid *nt*; (*after death*) Beileid
nt; (*understanding*) Verständnis *nt*
symphony ['sɪmfənɪ] *n* Sinfonie *f*
symptom ['sɪmptəm] *n* (*a. fig*) Symptom
nt

synagogue ['sɪnəgɒg] *n* Synagoge *f*
synonym ['sɪnənɪm] *n* Synonym *nt*;
synonymous [sɪˈnɒnɪməs] *adj* synonym
(*with* mit)
synthetic [sɪnˈθetɪk] *adj* (*material*)
synthetisch
syphilis ['sɪfɪlɪs] *n* Syphilis *f*
Syria ['sɪrɪə] *n* Syrien *nt*
syringe [sɪˈrɪndʒ] *n* Spritze *f*
system ['sɪstəm] *n* System *nt*;
systematic [sɪstəˈmætɪk] *adj*
systematisch; **system disk** *n* (*Inform*)
Systemdiskette *f*; **system(s) software** *n*
(*Inform*) Systemsoftware *f*

tab [tæb] n (for hanging up coat etc) Aufhänger m; (Inform) Tabulator m; **to pick up the ~** (fam) die Rechnung übernehmen

table ['teɪbl] n Tisch m; (list) Tabelle f; **~ of contents** Inhaltsverzeichnis nt; **tablecloth** n Tischdecke f; **tablelamp** n Tischlampe f; **tablemat** n Set nt; **tablespoon** n Servierlöffel m; (in recipes) Esslöffel m

tablet ['tæblət] n (Med) Tablette f

table tennis ['teɪbltɛnɪs] n Tischtennis nt; **table wine** n Tafelwein m

tabloid ['tæblɔɪd] n Boulevardzeitung f

taboo [tə'buː] n Tabu nt ▷ adj tabu

tacit, tacitly ['tæsɪt, -lɪ] adj, adv stillschweigend

tack [tæk] n (small nail) Stift m; (US: thumb~) Reißzwecke f

tackle ['tækl] n (Sport) Angriff m; (equipment) Ausrüstung f ▷ vt (deal with) in Angriff nehmen; (Sport) angreifen; (verbally) zur Rede stellen (about wegen)

tact [tækt] n Takt m; **tactful, tactfully** adj, adv taktvoll; **tactic(s)** ['tæktɪk(s)] n(pl) Taktik f; **tactless, tactlessly** ['tæktləs, -lɪ] adj, adv taktlos

tag [tæg] n (label) Schild nt; (with maker's name) Etikett nt

Tahiti [tɑːˈhiːtɪ] n Tahiti nt

tail [teɪl] n Schwanz m; **heads or ~s?** Kopf oder Zahl?; **tailback** n (Brit) Rückstau m; **taillight** n (Auto) Rücklicht nt

tailor ['teɪlə*] n Schneider(in) m(f)

tailpipe ['teɪlpaɪp] n (US Auto) Auspuffrohr nt

tainted ['teɪntɪd] adj (US: food) verdorben

Taiwan [taɪˈwæn] n Taiwan nt

take [teɪk] (took, taken) vt nehmen; (~ along with one) mitnehmen; (~ to a place) bringen; (subtract) abziehen (from von); (capture: person) fassen; (gain, obtain) bekommen; (Fin, Comm) einnehmen; (train, taxi) nehmen, fahren mit; (trip, walk, holiday, exam, course, photo) machen; (bath) nehmen; (phone call) entgegennehmen; (decision, precautions) treffen; (risk) eingehen; (advice, job) annehmen; (consume) zu sich nehmen; (tablets) nehmen; (heat, pain) ertragen; (react to) aufnehmen; (have room for) Platz haben für; **I'll ~ it** (item in shop) ich nehme es; **how long does it ~?** wie lange dauert es?; **it ~s 4 hours** man braucht 4 Stunden; **do you ~ sugar?** nehmen Sie Zucker?; **I ~ it that ...** ich nehme an, dass ...; **to ~ place** stattfinden; **take after** vt nachschlagen +dat; **take along** vt mitnehmen; **take apart** vt auseinander nehmen; **take away** vt (remove) wegnehmen (from sb jdm); (subtract) abziehen (from von); **take back** vt (return) zurückbringen; (retract) zurücknehmen; (remind) zurückversetzen (to in +akk); **take down** vt (picture, curtains) abnehmen; (write down) aufschreiben; **take in** vt (understand) begreifen; (give accommodation to) aufnehmen; (deceive) hereinlegen; (include) einschließen; (show, film etc) mitnehmen; **take off** vi (plane) starten ▷ vt (clothing) ausziehen; (hat, lid) abnehmen; (deduct) abziehen; (Brit: imitate) nachmachen; **to take a day off** sich einen Tag freinehmen; **take on** vt (undertake) übernehmen; (employ) einstellen; (Sport) antreten gegen; **take out** vt (wallet etc) herausnehmen; (person, dog) ausführen; (insurance) abschließen; (money from bank) abheben; (book from library) ausleihen; **take over** vt übernehmen ▷ vi **he took over (from me)**

er hat mich abgelöst; **take to** vt **I've
taken to her/it** ich mag sie/es; **to ~ doing
sth** (begin) anfangen, etw zu tun; **take up**
vt (carpet) hochnehmen; (space)
einnehmen; (time) in Anspruch nehmen;
(hobby) anfangen mit; (new job) antreten;
(offer) annehmen

takeaway n (Brit: meal) Essen nt zum
Mitnehmen

taken ['teɪkn] pp of **take** ▷ adj (seat)
besetzt; **to be ~ with** angetan sein von

takeoff ['teɪkɒf] n (Aviat) Start m;
(imitation) Nachahmung f; **takeout** (US)
see **takeaway**; **takeover** n (Comm)
Übernahme f ¡

takings ['teɪkɪŋz] npl Einnahmen pl

tale [teɪl] n Geschichte f

talent ['tælənt] n Talent nt; **talented** adj
begabt

talk [tɔ:k] n (conversation) Gespräch nt;
(rumour) Gerede nt; (to audience) Vortrag m
▷ vi sprechen, reden; (have conversation)
sich unterhalten; **to ~ to** (o with) sb
(about sth) mit jdm (über etw akk)
sprechen ▷ vt (language) sprechen;
(nonsense) reden; (politics, business) reden
über +akk; **to ~ sb into doing/out of
doing sth** jdn überreden/jdm ausreden,
etw zu tun; **talk over** vt besprechen

talkative adj gesprächig; **talk show** n
Talkshow f

tall [tɔ:l] adj groß; (building, tree) hoch; **he
is 6ft ~** er ist 1,80m groß

tame [teɪm] adj zahm; (joke, story) fade
▷ vt (animal) zähmen

tampon ['tæmpɒn] n Tampon m

tan [tæn] n (on skin) (Sonnen)bräune f; **to
get/have a ~** braun werden/sein ▷ vi
braun werden

tangerine [tændʒə'ri:n] n Mandarine f

tango ['tæŋɡəʊ] n Tango m

tank [tæŋk] n Tank m; (for fish) Aquarium
nt; (Mil) Panzer m

tanker ['tæŋkə*] n (ship) Tanker m;
(vehicle) Tankwagen m

tanned [tænd] adj (by sun) braun

tantalizing ['tæntəlaɪzɪŋ] adj verlockend

Tanzania [tænzə'nɪə] n Tansania nt

tap [tæp] n (for water) Hahn m ▷ vt, vi
(strike) klopfen; **to ~ sb on the shoulder**
jdm auf die Schulter klopfen; **tap-dance**
vi steppen

tape [teɪp] n (adhesive ~) Klebeband nt; (for

tape recorder) Tonband nt; (cassette)
Kassette f; (video) Video nt ▷ vt (record)
aufnehmen; **tape up** vt (parcel) zukleben;
tape measure n Maßband nt; **tape
recorder** n Tonbandgerät nt

tapestry ['tæpɪstrɪ] n Wandteppich m

tap water ['tæpwɔ:tə*] n
Leitungswasser nt

tar [tɑ:*] n Teer m

target ['tɑ:ɡɪt] n Ziel nt; (board)
Zielscheibe f

tariff ['tærɪf] n (price list) Preisliste f; (tax)
Zoll m

tarmac ['tɑ:mæk] n (Aviat) Rollfeld nt

tart [tɑ:t] n (fruit ~) (Obst)kuchen m;
(small) (Obst)törtchen nt; (fam, pej:
prostitute) Nutte f; (fam: promiscuous person)
Schlampe f

tartan ['tɑ:tən] n Schottenkaro nt;
(material) Schottenstoff m

tartar(e) sauce ['tɑ:tə'sɔ:s] n
Remouladensoße f

task [tɑ:sk] n Aufgabe f; (duty) Pflicht f;
taskbar n (Inform) Taskbar f

Tasmania [tæz'meɪnɪə] n Tasmanien nt

taste [teɪst] n Geschmack m; (sense of ~)
Geschmackssinn m; (small quantity)
Kostprobe f; **it has a strange ~** es
schmeckt komisch ▷ vt schmecken; (try)
probieren ▷ vi (food) schmecken (of nach);
to ~ good/strange gut/komisch
schmecken; **tasteful, tastefully** adj, adv
geschmackvoll; **tasteless, tastelessly**
adj, adv geschmacklos; **tasty** adj
schmackhaft

tattered ['tætəd] adj (clothes) zerlumpt;
(fam: person) angespannt; **I'm absolutely
~** ich bin mit den Nerven am Ende

tattoo [tə'tu:] n (on skin) Tätowierung f

taught [tɔ:t] pt, pp of **teach**

Taurus ['tɔ:rəs] n (Astr) Stier m

tax [tæks] n Steuer f (on auf +akk) ▷ vt
besteuern; **taxable** adj steuerpflichtig;
taxation [tæk'seɪʃən] n Besteuerung f;
tax bracket n Steuerklasse f; **tax disc** n
(Brit Auto) Steuermarke f; **tax-free** adj
steuerfrei

taxi ['tæksɪ] n Taxi nt ▷ vi (plane)
rollen; **taxi driver** n Taxifahrer(in) m(f);
taxi rank (Brit), **taxi stand** n Taxistand
m

tax return ['tæksrɪ'tɜ:n] n
Steuererklärung f

tea [ti:] n Tee m; (afternoon ~) ≈ Kaffee und Kuchen; (meal) frühes Abendessen; **teabag** n Teebeutel m; **tea break** n (Tee)pause f

teach [ti:tʃ] (**taught, taught**) vt (person, subject) unterrichten; **to ~ sb (how) to dance** jdm das Tanzen beibringen ▷ vi unterrichten; **teacher** n Lehrer(in) m(f); **teaching** n (activity) Unterrichten nt; (profession) Lehrberuf m

teacup ['ti:kʌp] n Teetasse f

team [ti:m] n (Sport) Mannschaft f, Team nt; **teamwork** n Teamarbeit f

teapot ['ti:pɒt] n Teekanne f

tear [tɪə*] n (in eye) Träne f

tear [tɛə*] (**tore, torn**) vt zerreißen; **to ~ a muscle** sich einen Muskel zerren ▷ n (in material etc) Riss m; **tear down** vt (building) abreißen; **tear up** vt (paper) zerreißen

tearoom ['ti:rum] n Teestube f, Café, in dem in erster Linie Tee serviert wird

tease [ti:z] vt (person) necken (about wegen)

tea set ['ti:set] n Teeservice nt; **teashop** n Teestube f; **teaspoon** n Teelöffel m; **tea towel** n Geschirrtuch nt

technical ['teknɪkəl] adj technisch; (knowledge, term, dictionary) Fach-; **technically** adv technisch; **technique** [tek'ni:k] n Technik f

techno ['teknəʊ] n Techno f

technological [teknə'lɒdʒɪkəl] adj technologisch; **technology** [tek'nɒlədʒɪ] n Technologie f

tedious ['ti:dɪəs] adj langweilig

teen(age) ['ti:n(eɪdʒ)] adj (fashions etc) Teenager-; **teenager** n Teenager m; **teens** [ti:nz] npl **in one's ~** im Teenageralter

teeth [ti:θ] pl of **tooth**

teetotal ['ti:'təʊtl] adj abstinent

telegraph pole ['teligra:fpəʊl] n (Brit) Telegrafenmast m

telephone ['telifəʊn] n Telefon nt ▷ vi telefonieren ▷ vt anrufen; **telephone banking** n Telefonbanking nt; **telephone book** n Telefonbuch nt; **telephone booth, telephone box** (Brit) n Telefonzelle f; **telephone call** n Telefonanruf m; **telephone directory** n Telefonbuch nt; **telephone number** n Telefonnummer f

telephoto lens ['telifəʊtəʊ'lenz] n Teleobjektiv nt

telescope ['teliskəʊp] n Teleskop nt

televise ['telivaɪz] vt im Fernsehen übertragen; **television** ['telivɪʒən] n Fernsehen nt; **television programme** n Fernsehsendung f; **television set** n Fernsehapparat m

teleworking ['teliwɜ:kɪŋ] n Telearbeit f

tell [tel] (**told, told**) vt (say, inform) sagen (sb sth jdm etw); (story) erzählen; (truth) sagen; (difference) erkennen; (reveal secret) verraten; **to ~ sb about sth** jdm von etw erzählen; **to ~ sth from sth** etw von etw unterscheiden ▷ vi (be sure) wissen; **tell apart** vt unterscheiden; **tell off** vt schimpfen

telling adj aufschlussreich

telly ['teli] n (Brit fam) Glotze f, **on (the) ~** in der Glotze

temp [temp] n Aushilfskraft f ▷ vi als Aushilfskraft arbeiten

temper ['tempə*] n (anger) Wut f; (mood) Laune f; **to lose one's ~** die Beherrschung verlieren; **to have a bad ~** jähzornig sein; **temperamental** [tempərə'mentl] adj (moody) launisch

temperature ['temprɪtʃə*] n Temperatur f; (Med: high ~) Fieber nt; **to have a ~** Fieber haben

temple ['templ] n Tempel m; (Anat) Schläfe f

tempo ['tempəʊ] (pl **-s**) n Tempo nt

temporarily ['tempərərɪlɪ] adv vorübergehend; **temporary** ['tempərərɪ] adj vorübergehend; (road, building) provisorisch

tempt [tempt] vt in Versuchung führen; **I'm ~ed to accept** ich bin versucht anzunehmen; **temptation** [temp'teɪʃən] n Versuchung f; **tempting** adj verlockend

ten [ten] num zehn ▷ n Zehn f; see also **eight**

tenant ['tenənt] n Mieter(in) m(f); (of land) Pächter(in) m(f)

tend [tend] vi **to ~ to do sth** (person) dazu neigen, etw zu tun; **to ~ towards** neigen zu; **tendency** ['tendənsɪ] n Tendenz f; **to have a ~ to do sth** (person) dazu neigen, etw zu tun

tender ['tendə*] adj (loving) zärtlich; (sore) empfindlich; (meat) zart

tendon ['tendən] n Sehne f
Tenerife [tenə'riːf] n Teneriffa nt
tenner ['tenə*] n (Brit fam: note)
Zehnpfundschein m; (amount) zehn Pfund
tennis ['tenɪs] n Tennis nt; **tennis ball** n
Tennisball m; **tennis court** n Tennisplatz
m; **tennis racket** n Tennisschläger m
tenor ['tenə*] n Tenor m
tenpin bowling, tenpins (US)
['tenpɪn'bəʊlɪŋ, 'tenpɪnz] n Bowling nt
tense [tens] adj angespannt; (stretched
tight) gespannt; **tension** ['tenʃən] n
Spannung f; (strain) Anspannung f
tent [tent] n Zelt nt
tenth [tenθ] adj zehnte(r, s) ▷ n (fraction)
Zehntel nt; see also **eighth**
tent peg n ['tentpeg] n Hering m; **tent pole**
n Zeltstange f
term [tɜːm] n (in school, at university)
Trimester nt; (expression) Ausdruck m; **~s** pl
(conditions) Bedingungen pl; **to be on good
~s with sb** mit jdm gut auskommen; **to
come to ~s with sth** sich mit etw
abfinden; **in the long/short
~** langfristig/kurzfristig; **in ~s of ...** was ...
betrifft
terminal ['tɜːmɪnl] n (bus ~ etc)
Endstation f; (Aviat) Terminal m; (Inform)
Terminal nt; (Elec) Pol m ▷ adj (Med)
unheilbar; **terminally** adv (ill) unheilbar
terminate ['tɜːmɪneɪt] vt (contract)
lösen; (pregnancy) abbrechen ▷ vi (train,
bus) enden
terminology [tɜːmɪ'nɒlədʒɪ] n
Terminologie f
terrace ['terəs] n (of houses) Häuserreihe f;
(in garden etc) Terrasse f; **terraced** adj
(garden) terrassenförmig angelegt;
terraced house n (Brit) Reihenhaus nt
terrible ['terəbl] adj schrecklich
terrific [tə'rɪfɪk] adj (very good)
fantastisch
terrify ['terɪfaɪ] vt erschrecken; **to be
terrified** schreckliche Angst haben (of vor
+dat)
territory ['terɪtərɪ] n Gebiet nt
terror ['terə*] n Schrecken m; (Pol) Terror
m; **terrorism** n Terrorismus m; **terrorist**
n Terrorist(in) m(f)
test [test] n Test m, Klassenarbeit f;
(driving ~) Prüfung f; **to put to the ~** auf die
Probe stellen ▷ vt testen, prüfen;
(patience, courage etc) auf die Probe stellen

Testament ['testəmənt] n **the Old/New
~** das Alte/Neue Testament
test-drive ['testdraɪv] vt Probe fahren
testicle ['testɪkl] n Hoden m
testify ['testɪfaɪ] vi (Jur) aussagen
test tube ['testtjuːb] n Reagenzglas nt
tetanus ['tetənəs] n Tetanus m
text [tekst] n Text m; (of document)
Wortlaut m; (sent by mobile phone) SMS f
▷ vt (message) simsen, SMSen; **to ~ sb** jdm
simsen, jdm eine SMS schicken; **I'll ~ it to
you** ich schicke es dir per SMS
textbook n Lehrbuch nt
texting ['tekstɪŋ] n SMS-Messaging nt;
text message n SMS f; **text messaging**
n SMS-Messaging nt
texture ['tekstʃə*] n Beschaffenheit f
Thailand ['taɪlænd] n Thailand nt
Thames [temz] n Themse f
than [ðæn] prep, conj als; **bigger/faster
~ me** größer/schneller als ich; **I'd rather
walk ~ drive** ich gehe lieber zu Fuß als mit
dem Auto
thank [θæŋk] vt danken +dat; **~ you**
danke; **~ you very much** vielen Dank;
thankful adj dankbar; **thankfully** adv
(luckily) zum Glück; **thankless** adj
undankbar; **thanks** npl Dank m; **~ dankel;
~ to** dank +gen

Thanksgiving Day

Thanksgiving (Day) ist ein Feiertag in
den USA, der auf den vierten
Donnerstag im November fällt. Er
soll daran erinnern, wie die
Pilgerväter die gute Ernte im Jahre
1621 feierten. In Kanada gibt es einen
ähnlichen Erntedanktag (, der aber
nichts mit den Pilgervätern zu tun
hat) am zweiten Montag im Oktober.

KEYWORD

that [ðæt, ðət] adj (demonstrative) (pl
those) der/die/das; jene(r, s); **that one** das
da ▷ pron
1 (demonstrative) (pl those) das;
who's/what's that? wer ist da/was ist
das?; **is that you?** bist du das?; **that's
what he said** genau das hat er gesagt;
what happened after that? was
passierte danach?; **that is** das heißt

2 (*relative: subj*) der/die/das die; (: *direct obj*) den/die/das die; (: *indirect obj*) dem/der/dem denen; **all (that) I have** alles, was ich habe

3 (*relative: of time*); **the day (that)** an dem Tag, als; **the winter (that) he came** in dem Winter, in dem er kam
▷ *conj* dass; **he thought that I was ill** er dachte, dass ich krank sei er dachte, ich sei krank
▷ *adv* (*demonstrative*) so; **I can't work that much** ich kann nicht so viel arbeiten

that's [ðæts] *contr of* **that is; that has**
thaw [θɔː] *vi* tauen; (*frozen food*) auftauen
▷ *vt* auftauen lassen

◯ KEYWORD

the [ðiː, ðə] *def art* **1** der/die/das; **to play the piano/violin** Klavier/Geige spielen; **I'm going to the butcher's/the cinema** ich gehe zum Fleischer/ins Kino; **Elizabeth the First** Elisabeth die Erste
2 (*+adj to form noun*) das die; **the rich and the poor** die Reichen und die Armen
3 (*in comparisons*): **the more he works the more he earns** je mehr er arbeitet, desto mehr verdient er

theater (*US*), **theatre** ['θɪətə*] *n* Theater *nt*; (*for lectures etc*) Saal *m*
theft [θeft] *n* Diebstahl *m*
their [ðeə*] *adj* ihr; (*unidentified person*) sein; **they cleaned ~ teeth** sie putzten sich die Zähne; **someone has left ~ umbrella here** jemand hat seinen Schirm hier vergessen; **theirs** ihre(r, s); (*unidentified person*) seine(r, s); **it's ~** es gehört ihnen; **a friend of ~** ein Freund von ihnen; **someone has left ~ here** jemand hat seins hier liegen lassen
them [ðem, ðəm] *pron* (*direct object*) sie; (*indirect object*) ihnen; (*unidentified person*) ihn/ihm, sie/ihr; **do you know ~?** kennst du sie?; **can you help ~?** kannst du ihnen helfen?; **it's ~** sie sind's; **if anyone has a problem you should help ~** wenn jemand ein Problem hat, solltest du ihm helfen
theme [θiːm] *n* Thema *nt*; (*Mus*) Motiv *nt*; **~ park** Themenpark *m*; **~ song** Titelmusik *f*

themselves [ðəm'selvz] *pron* sich; **they hurt ~** sie haben sich verletzt; **they ~ were not there** sie selbst waren nicht da; **they did it ~** sie haben es selbst gemacht; **they are not dangerous in ~** an sich sind sie nicht gefährlich; **(all) by ~** allein
then [ðen] *adv* (*at that time*) damals; (*next*) dann; (*therefore*) also; (*furthermore*) ferner; **from ~ on** von da an; **by ~** bis dahin ▷ *adj* damalig; **our ~ boss** unser damaliger Chef
theoretical, theoretically [θɪə'retɪkəl, -ɪ] *adj*, *adv* theoretisch
theory ['θɪərɪ] *n* Theorie *f*; **in ~** theoretisch
therapy ['θerəpɪ] *n* Therapie *f*

◯ KEYWORD

there [ðeə*] *adv* **1**: **there is, there are** es or da ist/sind; (*there exists/exist also*) es gibt; **there are 3 of them** (*people, things*) es gibt 3 davon; **there has been an accident** da war ein Unfall
2 (*place*) da dort; (*direction*) dahin, dorthin; **put it in/on there** leg es dahinein/dorthinauf
3: **there, there** (*esp to child*) na, na

thermometer [θə'mɒmɪtə*] *n* Thermometer *nt*
Thermos® ['θɜːməs] *n* **~ (flask)** Thermosflasche® *f*
these [ðiːz] *pron, adj* diese; **I don't like ~ apples** ich mag diese Äpfel nicht; **~ are not my books** das sind nicht meine Bücher
thesis ['θiːsɪs] (*pl* **theses**) *n* (*for PhD*) Doktorarbeit *f*
they [ðeɪ] *pron pl* sie; (*people in general*) man; (*unidentified person*) er/sie; **~ are rich** sie sind reich; **~ say that ...** man sagt, dass ...; **if anyone looks at this, ~ will see that ...** wenn sich jemand dies ansieht, wird er erkennen, dass ...
they'd [ðeɪd] *contr of* **they had; they would**
they'll [ðeɪl] *contr of* **they will; they shall**
they've [ðeɪv] *contr of* **they have**
thick [θɪk] *adj* dick; (*fog*) dicht; (*liquid*) dickflüssig; (*fam: stupid*) dumm; **thicken** *vi* (*fog*) dichter werden; (*sauce*) dick werden ▷ *vt* (*sauce*) eindicken

thief [θiːf] (pl **thieves**) n Dieb(in) m(f)
thigh [θaɪ] n Oberschenkel m
thimble ['θɪmbl] n Fingerhut m
thin [θɪn] adj dünn
thing [θɪŋ] n Ding nt; (affair) Sache f; **my ~s** pl meine Sachen pl; **how are ~s?** wie geht's?; **I can't see a ~** ich kann nichts sehen; **he knows a ~ or two about cars** er kennt sich mit Autos aus
think [θɪŋk] (**thought, thought**) vt, vi denken; (believe) meinen; **I ~ so** ich denke schon; **I don't ~ so** ich glaube nicht; **think about** vt denken an +akk; (reflect on) nachdenken über +akk; (have opinion of) halten von; **think of** vt denken an +akk; (devise) sich ausdenken; (have opinion of) halten von; (remember) sich erinnern an +akk; **think over** vt überdenken; **think up** vt sich ausdenken
third [θɜːd] adj dritte(r, s); **the Third World** die Dritte Welt ▷ n (fraction) Drittel nt; **in ~** (gear) im dritten Gang; see also **eighth**; **thirdly** adv drittens; **third-party insurance** n Haftpflichtversicherung f
thirst [θɜːst] n Durst m (for nach); **thirsty** adj **to be ~** Durst haben
thirteen ['θɜːˈtiːn] num dreizehn ▷ n Dreizehn f; see also **eight**; **thirteenth** adj dreizehnte(r, s); see also **eighth**; **thirtieth** ['θɜːtuθ] adj dreißigste(r, s); see also **eighth**; **thirty** ['θɜːtɪ] num dreißig; **~-one** einunddreißig ▷ n Dreißig f; **to be in one's thirties** in den Dreißigern sein; see also **eight**

◯ KEYWORD

this [ðɪs] adj (demonstrative: pl **these**) diese(r, s); **this evening** heute Abend; **this one** diese(r, s) (da)
▷ pron (demonstrative: pl **these**) dies das; **who/what is this?** wer/was ist das?; **this is where I live** hier wohne ich; **this is what he said** das hat er gesagt; **this is Mr Brown** dies ist Mr Brown; (on telephone) hier ist Mr Brown
▷ adv (demonstrative); **this high/long** etc so groß/lang etc

thistle ['θɪsl] n Distel f
thorn [θɔːn] n Dorn m, Stachel m
thorough ['θʌrə] adj gründlich;

thoroughly adv gründlich; (agree etc) völlig
those [ðəʊz] pron die da, jene; **~ who** diejenigen, die ▷ adj die, jene
though [ðəʊ] conj obwohl; **as ~** als ob ▷ adv aber
thought [θɔːt] pt, pp of **think** ▷ n Gedanke m; (thinking) Überlegung f; **thoughtful** adj (kind) rücksichtsvoll; (attentive) aufmerksam; (in Gedanken versunken) nachdenklich; **thoughtless** adj (unkind) rücksichtslos, gedankenlos
thousand ['θaʊzənd] num (one) **~, a ~** tausend; **five ~** fünftausend; **~s of** Tausende von
thrash [θræʃ] vt (hit) verprügeln; (defeat) vernichtend schlagen
thread [θred] n Faden m ▷ vt (needle) einfädeln; (beads) auffädeln
threat [θret] n Drohung f; (danger) Bedrohung f (to für); **threaten** vt bedrohen; **threatening** adj bedrohlich
three [θriː] num drei ▷ n Drei f; see also **eight**; **three-dimensional** adj dreidimensional; **three-piece suit** n Anzug m mit Weste; **three-quarters** npl drei Viertel pl
threshold ['θreʃhəʊld] n Schwelle f
threw [θruː] pt of **throw**
thrifty ['θrɪftɪ] adj sparsam
thrilled [θrɪld] adj **to be ~ (with sth)** sich (über etw akk) riesig freuen; **thriller** n Thriller m; **thrilling** adj aufregend
thrive [θraɪv] vi gedeihen (on bei); (fig, business) florieren
throat [θrəʊt] n Hals m, Kehle f
throbbing ['θrɒbɪŋ] adj (pain, headache) pochend
thrombosis [θrɒmˈbəʊsɪs] n Thrombose f; **deep vein ~** tiefe Venenthrombose f
throne [θrəʊn] n Thron m
through [θruː] prep durch; (time) während +gen; (because of) aus, durch; (US: up to and including) bis; **arranged ~ him** durch ihn arrangiert ▷ adv durch; **to put sb ~** (Tel) jdn verbinden (to mit) ▷ adj (ticket, train) durchgehend; **~ flight** Direktflug m; **to be ~ with sb/sth** mit jdm/etw fertig sein; **throughout** [θruːˈaʊt] prep (place) überall in +dat; (time) während +gen; **~ the night** die ganze Nacht hindurch ▷ adv überall; (time) die ganze Zeit

throw [θrəʊ] (threw, thrown) vt werfen; (rider) abwerfen; (party) geben; to ~ sth to sb, to ~ sb sth jdm etw zuwerfen; I was ~n by his question seine Frage hat mich aus dem Konzept gebracht ▷ n Wurf m; throw away vt wegwerfen; throw in vt (include) dazugeben; throw out vt (unwanted object) wegwerfen; (person) hinauswerfen (of aus); throw up vt, vi (fam: vomit) sich übergeben; throw-in n Einwurf m

thrown [θrəʊn] pp of throw

thru [US] see through

thrush [θrʌʃ] n Drossel f

thrust [θrʌst] (thrust, thrust) vt, vi (push) stoßen

thruway ['θruːweɪ] n (US) Schnellstraße f

thumb [θʌm] n Daumen m ▷ vt to ~ a lift per Anhalter fahren; thumbtack n (US) Reißzwecke f

thunder ['θʌndə*] n Donner m ▷ vi donnern; thunderstorm n Gewitter nt

Thur(s) abbr = Thursday Do.

Thursday ['θɜːzdɪ] n Donnerstag m; see also Tuesday

thus [ðʌs] adv (in this way) so; (therefore) somit, also

thyme [taɪm] n Thymian m

Tibet [tɪ'bet] n Tibet nt

tick [tɪk] n (Brit: mark) Häkchen nt ▷ vt (name) abhaken; (box, answer) ankreuzen ▷ vi (clock) ticken

ticket ['tɪkɪt] n (for train, bus) (Fahr)karte f; (plane ~) Flugschein m, Ticket nt; (for theatre, match, museum etc) (Eintritts)karte f; (price ~) (Preis)schild nt; (raffle ~) Los nt; (for car park) Parkschein m; (for traffic offence) Strafzettel m; ticket collector, ticket inspector (Brit) n Fahrkartenkontrolleur(in) m(f); ticket machine n (for public transport) Fahrscheinautomat m; (in car park) Parkscheinautomat m; ticket office n (Rail) Fahrkartenschalter m; (Theat) Kasse f

tickle ['tɪkl] vt kitzeln; ticklish ['tɪklɪʃ] adj kitzlig

tide [taɪd] n Gezeiten pl; the ~ is in/out es ist Flut/Ebbe

tidy ['taɪdɪ] adj ordentlich ▷ vt aufräumen; tidy up vt, vi aufräumen

tie [taɪ] n (neck~) Krawatte f; (Sport) Unentschieden nt; (bond) Bindung f ▷ vt (attach, do up) binden (to an +akk);

(~ together) zusammenbinden; (knot) machen ▷ vi (Sport) unentschieden spielen; tie down vt festbinden (to an +dat); (fig) binden; tie up vt (dog) anbinden; (parcel) verschnüren; (shoelace) binden; (boat) festmachen; I'm tied up (fig) ich bin beschäftigt

tiger ['taɪgə*] n Tiger m

tight [taɪt] adj (clothes) eng; (knot) fest; (screw, lid) fest sitzend; (control, security measures) streng; (timewise) knapp; (schedule) eng ▷ adv (shut) fest; (pull) stramm; hold ~ festhalten!; sleep ~ schlaf gut!; tighten vt (knot, rope, screw) anziehen; (belt) enger machen; (restrictions, control) verschärfen; tights npl (Brit) Strumpfhose f

tile [taɪl] n (on roof) Dachziegel m; (on wall, floor) Fliese f; tiled adj (roof) Ziegel-; (floor, wall) gefliest

till [tɪl] n Kasse f ▷ prep, conj see until

tilt [tɪlt] vt kippen; (head) neigen ▷ vi sich neigen

time [taɪm] n Zeit f; (occasion) Mal nt; (Mus) Takt m; local ~ Ortszeit; what ~ is it?, what's the ~? wie spät ist es?, wie viel Uhr ist es?; to take one's ~ (over sth) sich (bei etw) Zeit lassen; to have a good ~ Spaß haben; in two weeks' ~ in zwei Wochen; at ~s manchmal; at the same ~ gleichzeitig; all the ~ die ganze Zeit; by the ~ he ... bis er ...; (in past) als er ...; for the ~ being vorläufig; in ~ (not late) rechtzeitig; on ~ pünktlich; the first ~ das erste Mal; this ~ diesmal; five ~s fünfmal; five ~s six fünf mal sechs; four ~s a year viermal im Jahr; three at a ~ drei auf einmal ▷ vt (with stopwatch) stoppen; you ~d that well das hast du gut getimt; time difference n Zeitunterschied m; time limit n Frist f; timer n Timer m; (switch) Schaltuhr f; time-saving adj Zeit sparend; time switch n Schaltuhr f; timetable n (for public transport) Fahrplan m; (school) Stundenplan m; time zone n Zeitzone f

timid ['tɪmɪd] adj ängstlich

timing ['taɪmɪŋ] n (coordination) Timing nt, zeitliche Abstimmung

tin [tɪn] n (metal) Blech nt; (Brit: can) Dose f; tinfoil n Alufolie f; tinned [tɪnd] adj (Brit) aus der Dose; tin opener n (Brit) Dosenöffner m

tinsel ['tɪnsəl] n = Lametta nt

tint [tɪnt] n (Farb)ton m; (in hair) Tönung f; **tinted** adj getönt

tiny ['taɪnɪ] adj winzig

tip [tɪp] n (money) Trinkgeld nt; (hint) Tipp m; (end) Spitze f; (of cigarette) Filter m; (Brit: rubbish ~) Müllkippe f ▷ vt (waiter) Trinkgeld geben +dat; **tip over** vt, vi (overturn) umkippen

tipsy ['tɪpsɪ] adj beschwipst

tiptoe ['tɪptəʊ] n **on ~** auf Zehenspitzen

tire ['taɪə*] n (US) see **tyre** ▷ vt müde machen ▷ vi müde werden; **tired** adj müde; **to be ~ of sb/sth** jdn/etw satt haben; **to be ~ of doing sth** es satt haben, etw zu tun; **tireless, tirelessly** adv unermüdlich; **tiresome** adj lästig; **tiring** adj ermüdend

Tirol ['tɪrəʊl] see **Tyrol**

tissue ['tɪʃuː] n (Anat) Gewebe nt; (paper handkerchief) Tempotaschentuch® nt, Papier(taschen)tuch nt; **tissue paper** n Seidenpapier nt

tit [tɪt] n (bird) Meise f; (fam: breast) Titte f

title ['taɪtl] n Titel m

◯ **KEYWORD**

to [tuː, tə] prep **1** (direction) zu nach; **I go to France/school** ich gehe nach Frankreich/zur Schule; **to the left** nach links

2 (as far as) bis

3 (with expressions of time) vor; **a quarter to 5** Viertel vor 5

4 (for, of) für; **secretary to the director** Sekretärin des Direktors

5 (expressing indirect object): **to give sth to sb** jdm etw geben; **to talk to sb** mit jdm sprechen; **I sold it to a friend** ich habe es einem Freund verkauft

6 (in relation to) zu; **30 miles to the gallon** 30 Meilen pro Gallone

7 (purpose, result) zu; **to my surprise** zu meiner Überraschung

▷ with vb **1** (infin): **to go/eat** gehen/essen; **to want to do sth** etw tun wollen; **to try/start to do sth** versuchen/anfangen, etw zu tun; **he has a lot to lose** er hat viel zu verlieren

2 (with vb omitted): **I don't want to** ich will (es) nicht

3 (purpose, result) um; **I did it to help you** ich tat es, um dir zu helfen

4 (after adj etc): **ready to use** gebrauchsfertig; **too old/young to ...** zu alt/jung, um ... zu ...

▷ adv ; **push/pull the door to** die Tür zuschieben/zuziehen

toad [təʊd] n Kröte f; **toadstool** n Giftpilz m

toast [təʊst] n (bread, drink) Toast m; **a piece (o slice) of ~** eine Scheibe Toast; **to propose a ~ to sb** einen Toast auf jdn ausbringen ▷ vt (bread) toasten; (person) trinken auf +akk; **toaster** n Toaster m

tobacco [tə'bækəʊ] (pl **-es**) n Tabak m; **tobacconist's** [tə'bækənɪsts] n **~ (shop)** Tabakladen m

toboggan [tə'bɒgən] n Schlitten m

today [tə'deɪ] adv heute; **a week ~** heute in einer Woche; **~'s newspaper** die Zeitung von heute

toddler ['tɒdlə*] n Kleinkind nt

toe [təʊ] n Zehe f, Zeh m; **toenail** n Zehennagel m

toffee ['tɒfɪ] n (sweet) Karamellbonbon nt; **toffee apple** n kandierter Apfel

tofu ['təʊfuː] n Tofu m

together [tə'geðə*] adv zusammen; **I tied them ~** ich habe sie zusammengebunden

toilet ['tɔɪlət] n Toilette f; **to go to the ~** auf die Toilette gehen; **toilet bag** n Kulturbeutel m; **toilet paper** n Toilettenpapier nt; **toiletries** ['tɔɪlətrɪz] npl Toilettenartikel pl; **toilet roll** n Rolle f Toilettenpapier

token ['təʊkən] n Marke f; (in casino) Spielmarke f; (voucher, gift ~) Gutschein m; (sign) Zeichen nt

Tokyo ['təʊkjəʊ] n Tokio nt

told [təʊld] pt, pp of **tell**

tolerant ['tɒlərənt] adj tolerant (of gegenüber); **tolerate** ['tɒləreɪt] vt tolerieren; (noise, pain, heat) ertragen

toll [təʊl] n (charge) Gebühr f; **the death ~** die Zahl der Toten; **toll-free** adj, adv (US Tel) gebührenfrei; **toll road** n gebührenpflichtige Straße

tomato [tə'mɑːtəʊ] (pl **-es**) n Tomate f; **tomato juice** n Tomatensaft m; **tomato ketchup** n Tomatenket(s)chup m o nt;

tomato sauce n Tomatensoße f; (Brit: ketchup) Tomatenket(s)chup m o nt

tomb [tuːm] n Grabmal nt; **tombstone** n Grabstein m

tomorrow [təˈmɒrəʊ] adv morgen; ~ **morning** morgen früh; ~ **evening** morgen Abend; **the day after** ~ übermorgen; **a week (from)** ~/~ **week** morgen in einer Woche

ton [tʌn] n (Brit) Tonne f (1016 kg); (US) Tonne f (907 kg); ~**s of books** (fam) eine Menge Bücher

tone [təʊn] n Ton m; **tone down** vt mäßigen; **toner** [ˈtəʊnə*] n (for printer) Toner m; **toner cartridge** n Tonerpatrone f

tongs [tɒŋz] npl Zange f; (curling ~) Lockenstab m

tongue [tʌŋ] n Zunge f

tonic [ˈtɒnɪk] n (Med) Stärkungsmittel nt; ~ **(water)** Tonic nt; **gin and** ~ Gin m Tonic

tonight [təˈnaɪt] adv heute Abend; (during night) heute Nacht

tonsils [ˈtɒnslz] n Mandeln pl; **tonsillitis** [tɒnsɪˈlaɪtɪs] n Mandelentzündung f

too [tuː] adv zu; (also) auch; ~ **fast** zu schnell; ~ **much/many** zu viel/viele; **me** ~ ich auch; **she liked it** ~ ihr gefiel es auch

took [tʊk] pt of **take**

tool [tuːl] n Werkzeug nt; **toolbar** n (Inform) Symbolleiste f; **toolbox** n Werkzeugkasten m

tooth [tuːθ] n (pl teeth) n Zahn m; **toothache** n Zahnschmerzen pl; **toothbrush** n Zahnbürste f; **toothpaste** n Zahnpasta f; **toothpick** n Zahnstocher m

top [tɒp] n (of tower, class, company etc) Spitze f; (of mountain) Gipfel m; (of tree) Krone f; (of street) oberes Ende; (of tube, pen) Kappe f; (of box) Deckel m; (of bikini) Oberteil nt; (sleeveless) Top nt; **at the ~ of the page** oben auf der Seite; **at the ~ of the league** an der Spitze der Liga; **on** ~ oben; **on ~ of** auf +dat; (in addition to) zusätzlich zu; **in ~ (gear)** im höchsten Gang; **over the ~** übertrieben ▷ adj (floor, shelf) oberste(r, s); (price, note) höchste(r, s); (best) Spitzen-; (pupil, school) beste(r, s) ▷ vt (exceed) übersteigen; (be better than) übertreffen; (league) an erster Stelle liegen in +dat; ~**ped with cream** mit Sahne obendrauf; **top up** vt auffüllen; **can I top you up?** darf ich dir nachschenken?

topic [ˈtɒpɪk] n Thema nt; **topical** adj aktuell

topless [ˈtɒpləs] adj, adv oben ohne

topping [ˈtɒpɪŋ] n (on top of pizza, ice-cream etc) Belag m, Garnierung f

top-secret [ˈtɒpˈsiːkrət] adj streng geheim

torch [tɔːtʃ] n (Brit) Taschenlampe f

tore [tɔː*] pt of **tear**

torment [ˈtɔːment] vt quälen

torn [tɔːn] pp of **tear**

tornado [tɔːˈneɪdəʊ] (pl -es) n Tornado m

torrential [təˈrenʃəl] adj (rain) sintflutartig

tortoise [ˈtɔːtəs] n Schildkröte f

torture [ˈtɔːtʃə*] n Folter f; (fig) Qual f ▷ vt foltern

Tory [ˈtɔːrɪ] (Brit) n Tory m, Konservative(r) mf ▷ adj Tory-

toss [tɒs] vt (throw) werfen; (salad) anmachen; **to ~ a coin** eine Münze werfen ▷ vi **I don't give a ~** (fam) es ist mir scheißegal

total [ˈtəʊtl] n (of figures, money) Gesamtsumme f; **a ~ of 30** insgesamt 30; **in ~** insgesamt ▷ adj total; (sum etc) Gesamt- ▷ vt (amount to) sich belaufen auf +akk; **totally** adv total

touch [tʌtʃ] n (act of ~ing) Berührung f; (sense of ~) Tastsinn m; (trace) Spur f; **to be/keep in ~ with sb** mit jdm in Verbindung stehen/bleiben; **to get in ~ with sb** sich mit jdm in Verbindung setzen; **to lose ~ with sb** den Kontakt zu jdm verlieren ▷ vt (feel) berühren; (emotionally) bewegen; **touch on** vt (topic) berühren; **touchdown** n (Aviat) Landung f; (Sport) Touchdown m; **touching** adj (moving) rührend; **touch screen** n Touchscreen m, Berührungsbildschirm m; **touchy** adj empfindlich, zickig

tough [tʌf] adj hart; (meat) zäh; (material) robust; (meat) zäh

tour [tʊə*] n Tour f (of durch); (of town, building) Rundgang m (of durch); (of pop group etc) Tournee f ▷ vt eine Tour/einen Rundgang/eine Tournee machen durch ▷ vi (on holiday) umherreisen; **tour guide** n Reiseleiter(in) m(f)

tourism [ˈtʊərɪzəm] n Tourismus m, Fremdenverkehr m; **tourist** n Tourist(in) m(f); **tourist class** n Touristenklasse f; **tourist guide** n (book) Reiseführer m;

(person) Fremdenführer(in) m(f); **tourist
office** n Fremdenverkehrsamt nt
tournament ['tʊənəmənt] n Tournier
nt
tour operator ['tʊərəpəreɪtə*] n
Reiseveranstalter m
tow [təʊ] vt abschleppen; (caravan,
trailer) ziehen; **tow away** vt
abschleppen
towards [tə'wɔːdz] prep ~ me mir
entgegen, auf mich zu; **we walked ~ the
station** wir gingen in Richtung Bahnhof;
my feelings ~ him meine Gefühle ihm
gegenüber; **she was kind ~ me** sie war
nett zu mir
towel ['taʊəl] n Handtuch nt
tower ['taʊə*] n Turm m; **tower block** n
(Brit) Hochhaus nt
town [taʊn] n Stadt f; **town center** (US),
town centre n Stadtmitte f,
Stadtzentrum nt; **town hall** n Rathaus nt
towrope ['təʊrəʊp] n Abschleppseil nt;
tow truck n (US) Abschleppwagen m
toxic ['tɒksɪk] adj giftig, Gift-
toy [tɔɪ] n Spielzeug nt; **toy with** vt
spielen mit; **toyshop** n
Spielwarengeschäft nt
trace [treɪs] n Spur f; **without ~** spurlos
▷ vt (find) ausfindig machen; **tracing
paper** n Pauspapier nt
track [træk] n (mark) Spur f; (path) Weg m;
(Rail) Gleis nt; (on CD, record) Stück nt; **to
keep/lose ~ of sb/sth** jdn/etw im Auge
behalten/aus den Augen verlieren; **track
down** vt ausfindig machen; **trackball** n
(Inform) Trackball m; **tracksuit** n
Trainingsanzug m
tractor ['træktə*] n Traktor m
trade [treɪd] n (commerce) Handel m;
(business) Geschäft nt; (skilled job)
Handwerk nt ▷ vi handeln (in mit) ▷ vt
(exchange) tauschen (for gegen);
trademark n Warenzeichen nt;
tradesman (pl -men) n (shopkeeper)
Geschäftsmann m; (workman) Handwerker
m; **trade(s) union** n (Brit) Gewerkschaft f
tradition [trə'dɪʃn] n Tradition f;
traditional, traditionally adj, adv
traditionell
traffic ['træfɪk] n Verkehr m; (pej: trading)
Handel m (in mit); **traffic circle** n (US)
Kreisverkehr m; **traffic island** n
Verkehrsinsel f; **traffic jam** n Stau m;

traffic lights npl Verkehrsampel f;
traffic warden n (Brit) ≈ Politesse f
tragedy ['trædʒədɪ] n Tragödie f; **tragic**
['trædʒɪk] adj tragisch
trail [treɪl] n Spur f; (path) Weg m ▷ vt
(follow) verfolgen; (drag) schleppen; (drag
behind) hinter sich herziehen; (Sport)
zurückliegen hinter +dat ▷ vi (hang loosely)
schleifen; (Sport) weit zurückliegen;
trailer n Anhänger m; (Cine) Trailer m
train [treɪn] n (Rail) Zug m ▷ vt (teach)
ausbilden; (Sport) trainieren ▷ vi (Sport)
trainieren; **to ~ as** (o to be) **a teacher** eine
Ausbildung als Lehrer machen; **trained**
adj (person, voice) ausgebildet; **trainee** n
Auszubildende(r) mf; (academic, practical)
Praktikant(in) m(f); **trainer** n (Sport)
Trainer(in) m(f); **~s** (Brit: shoes)
Turnschuhe pl; **training** n Ausbildung f;
(Sport) Training nt; **train station** n
Bahnhof m
tram ['træm] n (Brit) Straßenbahn f
tramp [træmp] n Landstreicher(in) m(f)
▷ vi trotten
tranquillizer ['træŋkwɪlaɪzə*] n
Beruhigungsmittel nt
transaction n (piece of business) Geschäft
nt
transatlantic ['trænzət'læntɪk] adj
transatlantisch; **~ flight** Transatlantikflug
m
transfer ['trænsfə*] n (of money)
Überweisung f; (US: ticket) Umsteigekarte
f ▷ [træns'fɜː*] vt (money) überweisen (to
sb an jdn); (patient) verlegen; (employee)
versetzen; (Sport) transferieren ▷ vi (on
journey) umsteigen; **transferable**
[træns'fɜːrəbl] adj übertragbar
transform [træns'fɔːm] vt umwandeln;
transformation [trænsfə'meɪʃən] n
Umwandlung f
transfusion [træns'fjuːʒən] n
Transfusion f
transistor [træn'zɪstə*] n Transistor m;
~ (radio) Transistorradio nt
transition [træn'zɪʃən] n Übergang m
(from ... to von ... zu)
transit lounge ['trænzɪtlaʊndʒ] n
Transitraum m; **transit passenger** n
Transitreisende(r) mf
translate [trænz'leɪt] vt, vi übersetzen;
translation [trænz'leɪʃən] n Übersetzung

f; **translator** [trænz'leɪtə*] n
Übersetzer(in) m(f)

transmission [trænz'mɪʃən] n (TV, Radio)
Übertragung f; (Auto) Getriebe nt

transparent [træns'pærənt] adj
durchsichtig; (fig) offenkundig

transplant [træns'plɑ:nt] vt
transplantieren ▷ ['trænsplɑ:nt] n
(operation) Transplantation f

transport ['trænspɔ:t] n (of goods, people)
Beförderung f; **public ~** öffentliche
Verkehrsmittel pl ▷ [træns'pɔ:t] vt
befördern, transportieren;
transportation [trænspɔ:'teɪʃən] n see
transport

trap [træp] n Falle f ▷ vt **to be ~ped** (in
snow, job etc) festsitzen

trash [træʃ] n (book, film etc) Schund m;
(US: refuse) Abfall m; **trash can** n (US)
Abfalleimer m; **trashy** adj niveaulos;
(novel) Schund-

traumatic [trɔ:'mætɪk] adj
traumatisch

travel ['trævl] n Reisen nt ▷ vi (journey)
reisen ▷ vt (distance) zurücklegen;
(country) bereisen; **travel agency**, **travel
agent** n (company) Reisebüro nt; (US)
see **traveller**; **traveler's check** (US)
see **traveller's cheque**; **travel insurance**
n Reiseversicherung f; **traveller** n
Reisende(r) mf; **traveller's cheque** n
(Brit) Reisescheck m; **travelsick** adj
reisekrank

tray [treɪ] n Tablett nt; (for mail etc) Ablage
f; (of printer, photocopier) Fach nt

tread [tred] n (on tyre) Profil nt; **tread on**
[tred] (**trod**, **trodden**) vt treten auf +akk

treasure ['treʒə*] n Schatz m ▷ vt
schätzen

treat [tri:t] n besondere Freude; **it's my
~** das geht auf meine Kosten ▷ vt
behandeln; **to ~ sb (to sth)** jdn (zu etw)
einladen; **to ~ oneself to sth** sich etw
leisten; **treatment** ['tri:tmənt] n
Behandlung f

treaty ['tri:tɪ] n Vertrag m

tree [tri:] n Baum m

tremble ['trembl] vi zittern

tremendous [trə'mendəs] adj gewaltig;
(fam: very good) toll

trench [trentʃ] n Graben m

trend [trend] n Tendenz f; (fashion) Mode
f, Trend m; **trendy** adj trendy

trespass ['trespəs] vi **'no ~ing** „Betreten
verboten"

trial ['traɪəl] n (Jur) Prozess m; (test)
Versuch m; **by ~ and error** durch
Ausprobieren; **trial period** n (for employee)
Probezeit f

triangle ['traɪæŋgl] n Dreieck nt; (Mus)
Triangel m; **triangular** [traɪ'æŋgjʊlə*] adj
dreieckig

tribe [traɪb] n Stamm m

trick [trɪk] n Trick m; (mischief) Streich m
▷ vt hereinlegen

tricky ['trɪkɪ] adj (difficult) schwierig;
(situation) verzwickt

trifle ['traɪfl] n Kleinigkeit f, (Brit Gastr)
Trifle nt (Nachspeise aus Biskuit,
Wackelpudding, Obst, Vanillesoße und Sahne)

trigger ['trɪgə*] n (of gun) Abzug m ▷ vt **to
~ (off)** auslösen

trim [trɪm] vt (hair, beard) nachschneiden;
(nails) schneiden; (hedge) stutzen ▷ n **just
a ~, please** nur etwas nachschneiden,
bitte; **trimmings** npl (decorations)
Verzierungen pl; (extras) Zubehör nt;
(Gastr) Beilagen pl

trip [trɪp] n Reise f; (outing) Ausflug m ▷ vi
stolpern (over über +akk)

triple ['trɪpl] adj dreifach ▷ adv **~ the
price** dreimal so teuer ▷ vi sich
verdreifachen; **triplets** ['trɪplɪts] npl
Drillinge pl

tripod ['traɪpɒd] n (Foto) Stativ nt

trite [traɪt] adj banal

triumph ['traɪʌmf] n Triumph m

trivial ['trɪvɪəl] adj trivial

trod [trɒd] pt of **tread**

trodden pp of **tread**

trolley ['trɒlɪ] n (Brit: in shop)
Einkaufswagen m; (for luggage) Kofferkuli
m; (serving ~) Teewagen m

trombone [trɒm'bəʊn] n Posaune f

troops [tru:ps] npl (Mil) Truppen pl

trophy ['trəʊfɪ] n Trophäe f

tropical ['trɒpɪkl] adj tropisch

trouble ['trʌbl] n (problems)
Schwierigkeiten pl; (worry) Sorgen pl;
(effort) Mühe f; (unrest) Unruhen pl;
(Med) Beschwerden pl; **to be in ~** in
Schwierigkeiten sein; **to get into
~ (with authority)** Ärger bekommen; **to
make ~** Schwierigkeiten machen ▷ vt
(worry) beunruhigen; (disturb) stören; **my
back's troubling me** mein Rücken macht

mir zu schaffen; **sorry to ~ you** ich muss dich leider kurz stören; **troubled** adj (worried) beunruhigt; **trouble-free** adj problemlos; **troublemaker** n Unruhestifter(in) m(f); **troublesome** adj lästig

trousers ['traʊzəz] npl Hose f; **trouser suit** n (Brit) Hosenanzug m

trout [traʊt] n Forelle f

truck [trʌk] n Lastwagen m; (Brit Rail) Güterwagen m; **trucker** n (US: driver) Lastwagenfahrer(in) m(f)

true [truː] adj (factually correct) wahr; (genuine) echt; **to come ~** wahr werden

truly ['truːlɪ] adv wirklich; **Yours ~** (in letter) mit freundlichen Grüßen

trump [trʌmp] n (Cards) Trumpf m

trumpet ['trʌmpɪt] n Trompete f

trunk [trʌŋk] n (of tree) Stamm m; (Anat) Rumpf m; (of elephant) Rüssel m; (piece of luggage) Überseekoffer m; (US Auto) Kofferraum m; **trunks** npl (**swimming**) ~ Badehose f

trust [trʌst] n (confidence) Vertrauen nt (in zu) ▷ vt vertrauen +dat; **trusting** adj vertrauensvoll; **trustworthy** adj vertrauenswürdig

truth [truːθ] n Wahrheit f; **truthful** adj ehrlich; (statement) wahrheitsgemäß

try [traɪ] n Versuch m ▷ vt (attempt) versuchen; (~ out) ausprobieren; (sample) probieren; (Jur: person) vor Gericht stellen; (courage, patience) auf die Probe stellen ▷ vi versuchen; (make effort) sich bemühen; **~ and come** versuch zu kommen; **try on** vt (clothes) anprobieren; **try out** vt ausprobieren

T-shirt ['tiːʃɜːt] n T-Shirt nt

tub [tʌb] n (for ice-cream, margarine) Becher m

tube [tjuːb] n (pipe) Rohr nt; (of rubber, plastic) Schlauch m; (for toothpaste, glue etc) Tube f; **the Tube** (in London) die U-Bahn

tube station ['tjuːbsteɪʃən] n U-Bahn-Station f

tuck [tʌk] vt (put) stecken; **tuck in** vt (shirt) in die Hose stecken; (blanket) feststecken; (person) zudecken ▷ vi (eat) zulangen

Tue(s) abbr = Tuesday Di.

Tuesday ['tjuːzdɪ] n Dienstag m; on ~ (am) Dienstag; on ~s dienstags;

this/last/next ~ diesen/letzten/nächsten Dienstag; (on) ~ morning/afternoon/evening (am) Dienstag Morgen/Nachmittag/Abend; every ~ jeden Dienstag; a week on ~/ ~ week Dienstag in einer Woche

tug [tʌg] vt ziehen; **she ~ged his sleeve** sie zog an seinem Ärmel ▷ vi ziehen (at an +dat)

tuition [tjuːˈɪʃən] n Unterricht m; (US: fees) Studiengebühren pl; ~ **fees** pl Studiengebühren pl

tulip ['tjuːlɪp] n Tulpe f

tumble ['tʌmbl] vi (person, prices) fallen; **tumble dryer** n Wäschetrockner m; **tumbler** n (glass) (Becher)glas nt

tummy ['tʌmɪ] n (fam) Bauch m; **tummyache** n (fam) Bauchweh nt

tumor (US), **tumour** ['tjuːmə*] n Tumor m

tuna ['tjuːnə] n Thunfisch m

tune [tjuːn] n Melodie f; **to be in/out of** ~ (instrument) gestimmt/verstimmt sein; (singer) richtig/falsch singen ▷ vt (instrument) stimmen; (radio) einstellen (to auf +akk); **tuner** n (in stereo system) Tuner m

Tunisia [tjuːˈnɪzɪə] n Tunesien nt

tunnel ['tʌnl] n Tunnel m; (under road, railway) Unterführung f

turban ['tɜːbən] n Turban m

turbulence ['tɜːbjʊləns] n (Aviat) Turbulenzen pl; **turbulent** adj stürmisch

Turk [tɜːk] n Türke m, Türkin f

turkey ['tɜːkɪ] n Truthahn m

Turkey ['tɜːkɪ] n die Türkei; **Turkish** adj türkisch ▷ n (language) Türkisch nt

turmoil ['tɜːmɔɪl] n Aufruhr m

turn [tɜːn] n (rotation) Drehung f; (performance) Nummer f; **to make a left** ~ nach links abbiegen; **at the ~ of the century** um die Jahrhundertwende; **it's your** ~ du bist dran; **in** ~, **by ~s** abwechselnd; **to take ~s** sich abwechseln ▷ vt (wheel, key, screw) drehen; (to face other way) umdrehen; (corner) biegen um; (page) umblättern; (transform) verwandeln (into in +akk) ▷ vi (rotate) sich drehen; (to face other way) sich umdrehen; (change direction: driver, car) abbiegen; (become) werden; (weather) umschlagen; **to ~ into sth** (become) sich in etw akk verwandeln; **to** ~ **cold/green** kalt/grün werden; **to** ~ **left/right** links/rechts abbiegen; **turn**

away vt (person) abweisen; **turn back** vt (person) zurückweisen ▷ vi (go back) umkehren; **turn down** vt (refuse) ablehnen; (radio, TV) leiser stellen; (heating) kleiner stellen; **turn off** vi abbiegen ▷ vt (switch off) ausschalten; (tap) zudrehen; (engine, electricity) abstellen; **turn on** vt (switch on) einschalten; (tap) aufdrehen; (engine, electricity) anstellen; (fam: person) anmachen, antörnen; **turn out** vt (light) ausmachen; (pockets) leeren ▷ vi (develop) sich entwickeln; **as it turned out** wie sich herausstellte; **turn over** vt onto other side, umdrehen; (page) umblättern ▷ vi (person) sich umdrehen; (car) sich überschlagen; (TV) umschalten (to auf +akk); **turn round** vt (to face other way) umdrehen ▷ vi (person) sich umdrehen; (go back) umkehren; **turn to** vt sich zuwenden +dat; **turn up** vi (person, lost object) auftauchen ▷ vt (radio, TV) lauter stellen; (heating) höher stellen; **turning** n (in road) Abzweigung f; **turning point** n Wendepunkt m

turnip ['tɜ:nɪp] n Rübe f

turnover ['tɜ:nəʊvə*] n (Fin) Umsatz m

turnpike ['tɜ:npaɪk] n (US) gebührenpflichtige Autobahn

turntable ['tɜ:nteɪbl] n (on record player) Plattenteller m

turn-up ['tɜ:nʌp] n (Brit: on trousers) Aufschlag m

turquoise ['tɜ:kwɔɪz] adj türkis

turtle ['tɜ:tl] n (Brit) Wasserschildkröte f; (US) Schildkröte f

tutor ['tju:tə*] n (private) Privatlehrer(in) m(f); (Brit: at university) Tutor(in) m(f)

tuxedo [tʌk'si:dəʊ] (pl **-s**) n (US) Smoking m

TV ['ti:'vi:] n Fernsehen nt; (~ set) Fernseher m; **to watch ~** fernsehen; **on ~** im Fernsehen ▷ adj Fernseh-; **~ programme** Fernsehsendung f

tweed [twi:d] n Tweed m

tweezers ['twi:zəz] npl Pinzette f

twelfth [twelfθ] adj zwölfte(r, s); see also **eighth**; **twelve** [twelv] num zwölf ▷ n Zwölf f; see also **eight**

twentieth ['twentɪɪθ] adj zwanzigste(r, s); see also **eighth**; **twenty** ['twentɪ] num zwanzig; **--one** einundzwanzig ▷ n

Zwanzig f; **to be in one's twenties** in den Zwanzigern sein; see also **eight**

twice [twaɪs] adv zweimal; **~ as much/many** doppelt so viel/viele

twig [twɪg] n Zweig m

twilight ['twaɪlaɪt] n (in evening) Dämmerung f

twin [twɪn] n Zwilling m ▷ adj (brother etc) Zwillings-; **~ beds** zwei Einzelbetten

twinge [twɪndʒ] n (pain) stechender Schmerz

twinkle ['twɪŋkl] vi funkeln

twin room ['twɪn'ru:m] n Zweibettzimmer nt; **twin town** n Partnerstadt f

twist [twɪst] vt (turn) drehen, winden; (distort) verdrehen; **I've ~ed my ankle** ich bin mit dem Fuß umgeknickt

two [tu:] num zwei; **to break sth in ~** etw in zwei Teile brechen ▷ n Zwei f; **the ~ of them** die beiden; see also **eight**; **two-dimensional** adj zweidimensional; (fig) oberflächlich; **two-faced** adj falsch, heuchlerisch; **two-piece** adj zweiteilig; **two-way** adj **~ traffic** Gegenverkehr

type [taɪp] n (sort) Art f; (typeface) Schrift(art) f; **what ~ of car is it?** was für ein Auto ist das?; **he's not my ~** er ist nicht mein Typ; **typeface** n Schrift(art) f; **typewriter** n Schreibmaschine f

typhoid ['taɪfɔɪd] n Typhus m

typhoon [taɪ'fu:n] n Taifun m

typical ['tɪpɪkəl] adj typisch (of für)

typing error ['taɪpɪŋerə*] n Tippfehler m

tyre [taɪə*] n (Brit) Reifen m; **tyre pressure** n Reifendruck m

Tyrol [tɪ'rəʊl] n **the ~** Tirol nt

U

UFO [ˈjuːfəʊ] *acr* = **unidentified flying object** Ufo *nt*

Uganda [juːˈgændə] *n* Uganda *nt*

ugly [ˈʌglɪ] *adj* hässlich; (*bad*) schlimm

UHT *adj abbr* = **ultra-heat treated ~ milk** H-Milch *f*

UK *abbr* = **United Kingdom**

Ukraine [juːˈkreɪn] *n* **the ~** die Ukraine

ulcer [ˈʌlsə*] *n* Geschwür *nt*

ulterior [ʌlˈtɪərɪə*] *adj* **~ motive** Hintergedanke *m*

ultimate [ˈʌltɪmət] *adj* (*final*) letzte(r, s); (*authority*) höchste(r, s); **ultimately** *adv* letzten Endes; (*eventually*) schließlich; **ultimatum** [ʌltɪˈmeɪtəm] *n* Ultimatum *nt*

ultra- [ˈʌltrə] *pref* ultra-

ultrasound [ˈʌltrəsaʊnd] *n* (*Med*) Ultraschall *m*

umbrella [ʌmˈbrelə] *n* Schirm *m*

umpire [ˈʌmpaɪə*] *n* Schiedsrichter(in) *m(f)*

umpteen [ˈʌmptiːn] *num* (*fam*) zig; **~ times** zigmal

un- [ʌn] *pref* un-

UN *nsing abbr* = **United Nations** UNO *f*

unable [ʌnˈeɪbl] *adj* **to be ~ to do sth** etw nicht tun können

unacceptable [ʌnəˈkseptəbl] *adj* unannehmbar

unaccountably [ʌnəˈkaʊntəblɪ] *adv* unerklärlicherweise

unaccustomed [ʌnəˈkʌstəmd] *adj* **to be ~ to sth** etw nicht gewohnt sein

unanimous, unanimously [juːˈnænɪməs, -lɪ] *adj, adv* einmütig

unattached [ʌnəˈtætʃt] *adj* (*without partner*) ungebunden

unattended [ʌnəˈtendɪd] *adj* (*luggage, car*) unbeaufsichtigt

unauthorized [ʌnˈɔːθəraɪzd] *adj* unbefugt

unavailable [ʌnəˈveɪləbl] *adj* nicht erhältlich; (*person*) nicht erreichbar

unavoidable [ʌnəˈvɔɪdəbl] *adj* unvermeidlich

unaware [ʌnəˈweə*] *adj* **to be ~ of sth** sich einer Sache *dat* nicht bewusst sein; **I was ~ that ...** ich wusste nicht, dass ...

unbalanced [ʌnˈbælənst] *adj* unausgewogen; (*mentally*) gestört

unbearable [ʌnˈbeərəbl] *adj* unerträglich

unbeatable [ʌnˈbiːtəbl] *adj* unschlagbar

unbelievable [ʌnbɪˈliːvəbl] *adj* unglaublich

unblock [ʌnˈblɒk] *vt* (*pipe*) frei machen

unbutton [ʌnˈbʌtn] *vt* aufknöpfen

uncertain [ʌnˈsɜːtən] *adj* unsicher

uncle [ˈʌŋkl] *n* Onkel *m*

uncomfortable [ʌnˈkʌmfətəbl] *adj* unbequem

unconditional [ʌnkənˈdɪʃənl] *adj* bedingungslos

unconscious [ʌnˈkɒnʃəs] *adj* (*Med*) bewusstlos; **to be ~ of sth** sich einer Sache *dat* nicht bewusst sein; **unconsciously** *adv* unbewusst

uncork [ʌnˈkɔːk] *vt* entkorken

uncover [ʌnˈkʌvə*] *vt* aufdecken

undecided [ʌndɪˈsaɪdɪd] *adj* unschlüssig

undeniable [ʌndɪˈnaɪəbl] *adj* unbestreitbar

under [ˈʌndə*] *prep* (*beneath*) unter +*dat*; (*with motion*) unter +*akk*; **children ~ eight** Kinder unter acht; **~ an hour** weniger als eine Stunde ▸ *adv* (*beneath*) unten; (*with motion*) darunter; **children aged eight and ~** Kinder bis zu acht Jahren; **under-age** *adj* minderjährig

undercarriage [ˈʌndəkærɪdʒ] *n* Fahrgestell *nt*

underdog ['ʌndədɒg] n Unterlegene(r)
mf; (outsider) Außenseiter(in) m(f)
underdone [ʌndə'dʌn] adj (Gastr) nicht
gar, durch; (deliberately) nicht
durchgebraten
underestimate [ʌndər'estɪmeɪt] vt
unterschätzen
underexposed [ʌndərɪks'pəʊzd] adj
(Foto) unterbelichtet
undergo [ʌndə'gəʊ] irr vt (experience)
durchmachen; (operation, test) sich
unterziehen +dat
undergraduate [ʌndə'grædjʊət] n
Student(in) m(f)
underground ['ʌndəgraʊnd] adj
unterirdisch ▷ n (Brit Rail) U-Bahn f;
underground station n U-Bahn-Station f
underlie [ʌndə'laɪ] irr vt zugrunde liegen
+dat
underline [ʌndə'laɪn] vt unterstreichen
underlying [ʌndə'laɪɪŋ] adj zugrunde
liegend
underneath [ʌndə'niːθ] prep unter; (with
motion) unter +akk ▷ adv darunter
underpants ['ʌndəpænts] npl Unterhose
f; **undershirt** ['ʌndəʃɜːt] n (US)
Unterhemd nt; **undershorts** ['ʌndəʃɔːts]
npl (US) Unterhose f
understand [ʌndə'stænd] irr vt, vi
verstehen; **I ~ that ...** (been told) ich habe
gehört, dass ...; (sympathize) ich habe
Verständnis dafür, dass ...; **to make
oneself understood** sich verständlich
machen; **understandable** adj
verständlich; **understanding** adj
verständnisvoll
undertake [ʌndə'teɪk] irr vt (task)
übernehmen; **to ~ to do sth** sich
verpflichten, etw zu tun; **undertaker** n
Leichenbestatter(in) m(f); **~'s** (firm)
Bestattungsinstitut nt
underwater [ʌndə'wɔːtə*] adv unter
Wasser ▷ adj Unterwasser-
underwear ['ʌndəweə*] n Unterwäsche f
undesirable [ʌndɪ'zaɪərəbl] adj
unerwünscht
undo [ʌn'duː] irr vt (unfasten) aufmachen;
(work) zunichte machen; (Inform)
rückgängig machen
undoubtedly [ʌn'daʊtɪdlɪ] adv
zweifellos
undress [ʌn'dres] vt ausziehen; **to get
~ed** sich ausziehen ▷ vi sich ausziehen

undue [ʌn'djuː] adj übermäßig
unduly [ʌn'djuːlɪ] adv übermäßig
unearth [ʌn'ɜːθ] vt (dig up) ausgraben;
(find) aufstöbern
unease [ʌn'iːz] n Unbehagen nt; **uneasy**
adj (person) unbehaglich; **I'm ~ about it**
mir ist nicht wohl dabei
unemployed [ʌnɪm'plɔɪd] adj arbeitslos
▷ ▷ npl **the ~** die Arbeitslosen pl;
unemployment [ʌnɪm'plɔɪmənt] n
Arbeitslosigkeit f; **unemployment
benefit** n Arbeitslosengeld nt
unequal [ʌn'iːkwəl] adj ungleich
uneven [ʌn'iːvən] adj (surface, road)
uneben; (contest) ungleich
unexpected [ʌnɪk'spektɪd] adj
unerwartet
unfair [ʌn'feə*] adj unfair
unfamiliar [ʌnfə'mɪljə*] adj **to be ~ with
sb/sth** jdn/etw nicht kennen
unfasten [ʌn'fɑːsn] vt aufmachen
unfit [ʌn'fɪt] adj ungeeignet (for für); (in
bad health) nicht fit
unforeseen [ʌnfɔː'siːn] adj
unvorhergesehen
unforgettable [ʌnfə'getəbl] adj
unvergesslich
unforgivable [ʌnfə'gɪvəbl] adj
unverzeihlich
unfortunate [ʌn'fɔːtʃnət] adj (unlucky)
unglücklich; **it is ~ that ...** es ist
bedauerlich, dass ...; **unfortunately** adv
leider
unfounded [ʌn'faʊndɪd] adj
unbegründet
unhappy [ʌn'hæpɪ] adj (sad) unglücklich,
unzufrieden; **to be ~ with sth** mit etw
unzufrieden sein
unhealthy [ʌn'helθɪ] adj ungesund
unheard-of [ʌn'hɜːdɒv] adj (unknown)
gänzlich unbekannt; (outrageous)
unerhört
unhelpful [ʌn'helpfʊl] adj nicht hilfreich
unhitch [ʌn'hɪtʃ] vt (caravan, trailer)
abkoppeln
unhurt [ʌn'hɜːt] adj unverletzt
uniform ['juːnɪfɔːm] n Uniform f ▷ adj
einheitlich
unify ['juːnɪfaɪ] vt vereinigen
unimportant [ʌnɪm'pɔːtənt] adj
unwichtig
uninhabited [ʌnɪn'hæbɪtɪd] adj
unbewohnt

uninstall [ʌnɪn'stɔ:l] vt (Inform) deinstallieren

unintentional [ʌnɪn'tenʃənl] adj unabsichtlich

union ['ju:njən] n (uniting) Vereinigung f; (alliance) Union f, **Union Jack** n Union Jack m (britische Nationalflagge)

unique [ju:'ni:k] adj einzigartig

unit ['ju:nɪt] n Einheit f; (of system, machine) Teil nt; (in school) Lektion f

unite [ju:'naɪt] vt vereinigen; **the United Kingdom** das Vereinigte Königreich; **the United Nations** pl die Vereinten Nationen pl; **the United States (of America)** pl die Vereinigten Staaten (von Amerika) pl ▷ vi sich vereinigen

universe ['ju:nɪvɜ:s] n Universum nt

university [ju:nɪ'vɜ:sɪtɪ] n Universität f

unkind [ʌn'kaɪnd] adj unfreundlich (to zu)

unknown [ʌn'nəʊn] adj unbekannt (to +dat)

unleaded [ʌn'ledɪd] adj bleifrei

unless [ən'les] conj es sei denn, wenn ... nicht; **don't do it ~ I tell you to** mach das nicht, es sei denn, ich sage es dir; **~ I'm mistaken ...** wenn ich mich nicht irre ...

unlicensed [ʌn'laɪsənst] adj (to sell alcohol) ohne Lizenz

unlike [ʌn'laɪk] prep (in contrast to) im Gegensatz zu; **it's ~ her to be late** es sieht ihr gar nicht ähnlich, zu spät zu kommen; **unlikely** [ʌn'laɪklɪ] adj unwahrscheinlich

unload [ʌn'ləʊd] vt ausladen

unlock [ʌn'lɒk] vt aufschließen

unlucky [ʌn'lʌkɪ] adj unglücklich; **to be ~** Pech haben

unmistakable [ʌnmɪ'steɪkəbl] adj unverkennbar

unnecessary [ʌn'nesəsərɪ] adj unnötig

unobtainable [ʌnəb'teɪnəbl] adj nicht erhältlich

unoccupied [ʌn'ɒkjʊpaɪd] adj (seat) frei; (building, room) leer stehend

unpack [ʌn'pæk] vt, vi auspacken

unpleasant [ʌn'pleznt] adj unangenehm

unplug [ʌn'plʌg] vt **to ~ sth** den Stecker von etw herausziehen

unprecedented [ʌn'presɪdəntɪd] adj beispiellos

unpredictable [ʌnprɪ'dɪktəbl] adj (person, weather) unberechenbar

unreasonable [ʌn'ri:znəbl] adj unvernünftig; (demand) übertrieben

unreliable [ʌnrɪ'laɪəbl] adj unzuverlässig

unsafe [ʌn'seɪf] adj nicht sicher; (dangerous) gefährlich

unscrew [ʌn'skru:] vt abschrauben

unsightly [ʌn'saɪtlɪ] adj unansehnlich

unskilled [ʌn'skɪld] adj (worker) ungelernt

unsuccessful [ʌnsək'sesfʊl] adj erfolglos

unsuitable [ʌn'su:təbl] adj ungeeignet (for für)

until [ən'tɪl] prep bis; **not ~** erst; **from Monday ~ Friday** von Montag bis Freitag; **he didn't come home ~ midnight** er kam erst um Mitternacht nach Hause; **~ then** bis dahin ▷ conj bis; **she won't come ~ you invite her** sie kommt erst, wenn du sie einlädst

unusual, unusually [ʌn'ju:ʒʊəl, -ɪ] adj, adv ungewöhnlich

unwanted [ʌn'wɒntɪd] adj unerwünscht, ungewollt

unwell [ʌn'wel] adj krank; **to feel ~** sich nicht wohl fühlen

unwilling [ʌn'wɪlɪŋ] adj **to be ~ to do sth** nicht bereit sein, etw zu tun

unwind [ʌn'waɪnd] irr vt abwickeln ▷ vi (relax) sich entspannen

unwrap [ʌn'ræp] vt auspacken

unzip [ʌn'zɪp] vt den Reißverschluss aufmachen an +dat; (Inform) entzippen

○ KEYWORD

up [ʌp] prep: **to be up sth** oben auf etw dat sein; **to go up sth** (auf) etw acc hinaufgehen; **go up that road** gehen Sie die Straße hinauf

▷ adv 1 (upwards, higher) oben; **put it up a bit higher** stell es etwas weiter nach oben; **up there** da oben dort oben; **up above** hoch oben

2: **to be up** (out of bed) auf sein (prices, level) gestiegen sein (building, tent) stehen

3: **up to** (as far as) bis; **up to now** bis jetzt

4: **to be up to** (depending on); **it's up to you** das hängt von dir ab; (equal to); **he's not up to it** (job, task etc) er ist dem nicht gewachsen (inf: be doing: showing disapproval, suspicion); **what is he up to?** was führt er im Schilde?; **it's not up to me to decide** die Entscheidung liegt nicht bei mir; **his work is not up to the required standard** seine Arbeit entspricht nicht dem geforderten Niveau

▷ n ; **ups and downs** (in life, career) Höhen und Tiefen pl

upbringing ['ʌpbrɪŋɪŋ] n Erziehung f

update [ʌp'deɪt] n (list etc) Aktualisierung f; (software) Update nt ▷ vt (list etc, person) auf den neuesten Stand bringen, aktualisieren

upgrade [ʌp'greɪd] vt (computer) aufrüsten; **we were ~d** das Hotel hat uns ein besseres Zimmer gegeben

upheaval [ʌp'hiːvəl] n Aufruhr m; (Pol) Umbruch m

uphill [ʌp'hɪl] adv bergauf

upon [ə'pɒn] prep see **on**

upper ['ʌpə*] adj obere(r, s); (arm, deck) Ober-

upright ['ʌpraɪt] adj, adv aufrecht

uprising ['ʌpraɪzɪŋ] n Aufstand m

uproar ['ʌprɔː*] n Aufruhr m

upset [ʌp'set] irr vt (overturn) umkippen; (disturb) aufregen; (sadden) bestürzen; (offend) kränken; (plans) durcheinander bringen ▷ adj (disturbed) aufgeregt; (sad) bestürzt; (offended) gekränkt; **~ stomach** ['ʌpset] Magenverstimmung f

upside down [ʌpsaɪd'daʊn] adv verkehrt herum; (fig) drunter und drüber; **to turn sth ~** (box etc) etw umdrehen/durchwühlen

upstairs [ʌp'steəz] adv oben; (go, take) nach oben

up-to-date ['ʌptə'deɪt] adj modern; (fashion, information) aktuell; **to keep sb ~** jdn auf dem Laufenden halten

upwards ['ʌpwədz] adv nach oben

urban ['ɜːbən] adj städtisch, Stadt-

urge [ɜːdʒ] n Drang m ▷ vt **to ~ sb to do sth** jdn drängen, etw zu tun; **urgent**, **urgently** ['ɜːdʒənt, -lɪ] adj, adv dringend

urine ['jʊərɪn] n Urin m

us [ʌs] pron uns; **do they know ~?** kennen sie uns?; **can he help ~?** kann er uns helfen?; **it's ~** wir sind's; **both of ~** wir beide

US, **USA** nsing abbr = **United States (of America)** USA pl

use [juːs] n (using) Gebrauch m; (for specific purpose) Verwendung f; **to make ~ of** Gebrauch machen von; **in/out of ~** in/außer Gebrauch; **it's no ~ (doing that)** es hat keinen Zweck(, das zu tun); **it's (of) no ~ to me** das kann ich nicht

brauchen ▷ [juːz] vt benutzen, gebrauchen; (for specific purpose) verwenden; (method) anwenden; **use up** vt aufbrauchen

used [juːzd] adj (secondhand) gebraucht ▷ vb aux **to be ~d to sb/sth** an jdn/etw gewöhnt sein; **to get ~d to sb/sth** sich an jdn/etw gewöhnen; **she ~d to live here** sie hat früher mal hier gewohnt; **useful** adj nützlich; **useless** adj nutzlos; (unusable) unbrauchbar; (pointless) zwecklos; **user** ['juːzə*] n Benutzer(in) m(f); **user-friendly** adj benutzerfreundlich

usual ['juːʒəl] adj üblich, gewöhnlich; **as ~** wie üblich; **usually** adv normalerweise

utensil [juː'tensl] n Gerät nt

uterus ['juːtərəs] n Gebärmutter f

utilize ['juːtɪlaɪz] vt verwenden

utmost ['ʌtməʊst] adj äußerst; **to do one's ~** sein Möglichstes tun

utter ['ʌtə*] adj völlig ▷ vt von sich geben; **utterly** adv völlig

U-turn ['juː'tɜːn] n (Auto) Wende f; **to do a ~** wenden; (fig) eine Kehrtwendung machen

V

vacancy ['veɪkənsɪ] n (job) offene Stelle; (room) freies Zimmer; **vacant** ['veɪkənt] adj (room, seat) frei; (post) offen; (building) leer stehend; **vacate** [və'keɪt] vt (room, building) räumen; (seat) frei machen

vacation [və'keɪʃən] n (US) Ferien pl, Urlaub m; (at university) (Semester)ferien pl; **to go on ~** in Urlaub fahren; **~ course** Ferienkurs m

vaccinate ['væksɪneɪt] vt impfen; **vaccination** [væksɪ'neɪʃən] n Impfung f; **~ card** Impfpass m

vacuum ['vækjʊm] n Vakuum nt ▷ vt, vi (staub)saugen; **vacuum cleaner** n Staubsauger m

vagina [və'dʒaɪnə] n Scheide f

vague [veɪg] adj (imprecise) vage; (resemblance) entfernt; **vaguely** adv in etwa, irgendwie

vain [veɪn] adj (attempt) vergeblich; (conceited) eitel; **vainly** adv (in vain) vergeblich

valentine (card) ['væləntaɪn(kɑːd)] n Valentinskarte f; **Valentine's Day** n Valentinstag m

valid ['vælɪd] adj (ticket, passport etc) gültig; (argument) stichhaltig; (claim) berechtigt

valley ['vælɪ] n Tal nt

valuable ['væljʊəbl] adj wertvoll; (time) kostbar; **valuables** npl Wertsachen pl

value ['vælju:] n Wert m ▷ vt (appreciate) schätzen; **value added tax** n Mehrwertsteuer f

valve [vælv] n Ventil nt

van [væn] n (Auto) Lieferwagen m

vanilla [və'nɪlə] n Vanille f

vanish ['vænɪʃ] vi verschwinden

vanity ['vænɪtɪ] n Eitelkeit f; **vanity case** n Schminkkoffer m

vapor (US), **vapour** ['veɪpə*] n (mist) Dunst m; (steam) Dampf m

variable ['vɛərɪəbl] adj (weather, mood) unbeständig; (quality) unterschiedlich; (speed, height) regulierbar; **varied** ['vɛərɪd] adj (interests, selection) vielseitig; (career) bewegt; (work, diet) abwechslungsreich; **variety** [və'raɪətɪ] n (diversity) Abwechslung f; (assortment) Vielfalt f (of an +dat); (type) Art f; **various** ['vɛərɪəs] adj verschieden

varnish ['vɑːnɪʃ] n Lack m ▷ vt lackieren

vary ['vɛərɪ] vt (alter) verändern ▷ vi (be different) unterschiedlich sein; (fluctuate) sich verändern; (prices) schwanken

vase [vɑːz, ç veɪz] (US) n Vase f

vast [vɑːst] adj riesig; (area) weit

VAT abbr = **value added tax** Mehrwertsteuer f, MwSt.

Vatican ['vætɪkən] n **the ~** der Vatikan

VCR abbr = **video cassette recorder** Videorekorder m

VD abbr = **venereal disease**

VDU abbr = **visual display unit**

veal [viːl] n Kalbfleisch nt

vegan ['viːgən] n Veganer(in) m(f)

vegetable ['vedʒtəbl] n Gemüse nt

vegetarian [vedʒɪ'tɛərɪən] n Vegetarier(in) m(f) ▷ adj vegetarisch

vehicle ['viːɪkl] n Fahrzeug nt

veil [veɪl] n Schleier m

vein [veɪn] n Ader f

Velcro® ['velkrəʊ] n Klettband nt

velvet ['velvɪt] n Samt m

vending machine ['vendɪŋməʃiːn] n Automat m

venereal disease [vɪ'nɪərɪəldɪziːz] n Geschlechtskrankheit f

venetian blind [vɪ'niːʃən'blaɪnd] n
Jalousie f

Venezuela [vene'zweɪlə] n Venezuela nt

vengeance ['vendʒəns] n Rache f

Venice ['venɪs] n Venedig nt

venison ['venɪsn] n Rehfleisch nt

vent [vent] n Öffnung f

ventilate ['ventɪleɪt] vt lüften;
ventilation [ventɪ'leɪʃən] n Belüftung f;
ventilator ['ventɪleɪtə*] n (in room)
Ventilator m; **to be on a ~** (Med) künstlich
beatmet werden

venture ['ventʃə*] n (project)
Unternehmung f; (Comm) Unternehmen nt
▷ vi (go) (sich) wagen

venue ['venjuː] n (for concert etc)
Veranstaltungsort m; (Sport)
Austragungsort m

verb [vɜːb] n Verb nt; **verbal** adj
(agreement) mündlich; (skills) sprachlich;
verbally adv mündlich

verdict ['vɜːdɪkt] n Urteil nt

verge [vɜːdʒ] n (of road) (Straßen)rand m;
to be on the ~ of doing sth im Begriff
sein, etw zu tun ▷ vi **to ~ on** grenzen an
+akk

verification [verɪfɪ'keɪʃən] n
(confirmation) Bestätigung f; (check)
Überprüfung f; **verify** ['verɪfaɪ] vt
(confirm) bestätigen; (check) überprüfen

vermin ['vɜːmɪn] npl Schädlinge pl;
(insects) Ungeziefer nt

verruca [ve'ruːkə] n Warze f

versatile ['vɜːsətaɪl] adj vielseitig

verse [vɜːs] n (poetry) Poesie f; (stanza)
Strophe f

version ['vɜːʃən] n Version f

versus ['vɜːsəs] prep gegen; (in contrast
to) im Gegensatz zu

vertical ['vɜːtɪkəl] adj senkrecht,
vertikal

very ['verɪ] adv sehr; **~ much** sehr ▷ adj
the ~ book I need genau das Buch, das ich
brauche; **at that ~ moment** gerade in
dem Augenblick; **at the ~ top** ganz oben;
the ~ best der/die/das Allerbeste

vest [vest] n (Brit) Unterhemd nt; (US:
waistcoat) Weste f

vet [vet] n Tierarzt m, Tierärztin f

veto ['viːtəʊ] n (pl -es) n Veto nt ▷ vt sein
Veto einlegen gegen

VHF abbr = **very high frequency** UKW

via ['vaɪə] prep über +akk

viable ['vaɪəbl] adj (plan) realisierbar;
(company) rentabel

vibrate [vaɪ'breɪt] vi vibrieren; **vibration**
[vaɪ'breɪʃən] n Vibration f

vicar ['vɪkə*] n Pfarrer(in) m(f)

vice [vaɪs] n (evil) Laster nt; (Tech)
Schraubstock m ▷ pref Vize-;
~-chairman stellvertretender
Vorsitzender; **~-president**
Vizepräsident(in) m(f)

vice versa ['vaɪs'vɜːsə] adv umgekehrt

vicinity [vɪ'sɪnɪtɪ] n **in the ~** in der Nähe
(of +gen)

vicious ['vɪʃəs] adj (violent) brutal;
(malicious) gemein; **vicious circle** n
Teufelskreis m

victim ['vɪktɪm] n Opfer nt

Victorian [vɪk'tɔːrɪən] adj viktorianisch

victory ['vɪktərɪ] n Sieg m

video ['vɪdɪəʊ] (pl -s) adj Video- ▷ n Video
nt; (recorder) Videorekorder m ▷ vt (auf
Video) aufnehmen; **video camera** n
Videokamera f; **video cassette** n
Videokassette f; **video clip** n Videoclip m;
video game n Videospiel nt; **video
recorder** n Videorekorder m; **video shop**
n Videothek f; **videotape** n Videoband nt
▷ vt (auf Video) aufnehmen

Vienna [vɪ'enə] n Wien nt

Vietnam [vjet'næm] n Vietnam nt

view [vjuː] n (sight) Blick m (of auf +akk);
(vista) Aussicht f; (opinion) Ansicht f,
Meinung f; **in ~ of** angesichts +gen ▷ vt
(situation, event) betrachten; (house)
besichtigen; **viewer** n (for slides)
Diabetrachter m; (TV) Zuschauer(in) m(f);
viewpoint n (fig) Standpunkt m

vigilant ['vɪdʒɪlənt] adj wachsam

vile [vaɪl] adj abscheulich; (weather, food)
scheußlich

village ['vɪlɪdʒ] n Dorf nt; **villager** n
Dorfbewohner(in) m(f)

villain ['vɪlən] n Schurke m; (in film, story)
Bösewicht m

vine [vaɪn] n (Wein)rebe f

vinegar ['vɪnɪgə*] n Essig m

vineyard ['vɪnjəd] n Weinberg m

vintage ['vɪntɪdʒ] n (of wine) Jahrgang m;
vintage wine n edler Wein

vinyl ['vaɪnɪl] n Vinyl nt

viola [vɪ'əʊlə] n Bratsche f

violate ['vaɪəleɪt] vt (treaty) brechen;
(rights, rule) verletzen

violence ['vaɪələns] n (brutality) Gewalt f;
(of person) Gewalttätigkeit f; **violent** adj
(brutal) brutal; (death) gewaltsam
violet ['vaɪələt] n Veilchen nt
violin [vaɪə'lɪn] n Geige f, Violine f
VIP abbr = **very important person** VIP mf
virgin ['vɜːdʒɪn] n Jungfrau f
Virgo ['vɜːgəʊ] n (Astr) Jungfrau f
virile ['vɪraɪl] adj (man) männlich
virtual ['vɜːtjʊəl] adj (Inform) virtuell;
virtually adv praktisch; **virtual reality** n
virtuelle Realität
virtue ['vɜːtjuː] n Tugend f; **by ~ of**
aufgrund +gen; **virtuous** ['vɜːtjʊəs] adj
tugendhaft
virus ['vaɪrəs] n (Med, Inform) Virus nt
visa ['viːzə] n Visum nt
visibility [vɪzɪ'bɪlɪtɪ] n (Meteo) Sichtweite
f; **good/poor ~** gute/schlechte Sicht;
visible ['vɪzəbl] adj sichtbar; (evident)
sichtlich; **visibly** adv sichtlich
vision ['vɪʒən] n (power of sight)
Sehvermögen nt; (foresight) Weitblick m;
(dream, image) Vision f
visit ['vɪzɪt] n Besuch m; (stay) Aufenthalt
m ▷ vt besuchen; **visiting hours** npl
Besuchszeiten pl; **visitor** n Besucher(in)
m(f); **~s' book** Gästebuch nt; **visitor
centre** n Informationszentrum nt
visor ['vaɪzə*] n (on helmet) Visier nt; (Auto)
Blende f
visual ['vɪzjʊəl] adj Seh-; (image, joke)
visuell; **~ aid** Anschauungsmaterial nt;
~ display unit Monitor m; **visualize** vt
sich vorstelle; **visually** adv visuell;
~ impaired sehbehindert
vital ['vaɪtl] adj (essential) unerlässlich,
wesentlich; (argument, moment)
entscheidend; **vitality** [vaɪ'tælɪtɪ] n
Vitalität f; **vitally** adv äußerst
vitamin ['vɪtəmɪn] n Vitamin nt
vivacious [vɪ'veɪʃəs] adj lebhaft
vivid ['vɪvɪd] adj (description) anschaulich;
(memory) lebhaft; (colour) leuchtend
V-neck ['viːnek] n V-Ausschnitt m
vocabulary [vəʊ'kæbjʊlərɪ] n
Wortschatz m, Vokabular nt
vocal ['vəʊkəl] adj (of the voice) Stimm-;
(group) Gesangs-; (protest, person)
lautstark
vocation [vəʊ'keɪʃən] n Berufung f;
vocational adj Berufs-
vodka ['vɒdkə] n Wodka m

voice [vɔɪs] n Stimme f ▷ vt äußern;
voice mail n Voicemail f
void [vɔɪd] n Leere f ▷ adj (Jur) ungültig;
~ of (ganz) ohne
volcano [vɒl'keɪnəʊ] (pl **-es**) n Vulkan m
volley ['vɒlɪ] n (Tennis) Volley m;
volleyball n Volleyball m
volt [vəʊlt] n Volt nt; **voltage** n
Spannung f
volume ['vɒljuːm] n (of sound) Lautstärke
f; (space occupied by sth) Volumen nt; (size,
amount) Umfang m; (book) Band m;
volume control n Lautstärkeregler m
voluntary, voluntarily ['vɒləntərɪ, -lɪ]
adj, adv freiwillig; (unpaid) ehrenamtlich;
volunteer [vɒlən'tɪə*] n Freiwillige(r) mf
▷ vi sich freiwillig melden ▷ vt **to ~ to do
sth** sich anbieten, etw zu tun
voluptuous [və'lʌptjʊəs] adj sinnlich
vomit ['vɒmɪt] vi sich übergeben
vote [vəʊt] n Stimme f; (ballot) Wahl f;
(result) Abstimmungsergebnis nt; (right to
vote) Wahlrecht nt ▷ vt (elect) wählen;
they ~d him chairman sie wählten ihn
zum Vorsitzenden ▷ vi wählen; **to
~ for/against sth** für/gegen etw
stimmen; **voter** n Wähler(in) m(f)
voucher ['vaʊtʃə*] n Gutschein m
vow [vaʊ] n Gelöbnis nt ▷ vt **to ~ to do
sth** geloben, etw zu tun
vowel ['vaʊəl] n Vokal m
voyage ['vɔɪɪdʒ] n Reise f
vulgar ['vʌlgə*] adj vulgär, ordinär
vulnerable ['vʌlnərəbl] adj verwundbar;
(sensitive) verletzlich
vulture ['vʌltʃə*] n Geier m

W

W *abbr* = **west** W

wade [weɪd] *vi* (*in water*) waten

wafer ['weɪfə*] *n* Waffel *f*; (*Rel*) Hostie *f*; **wafer-thin** *adj* hauchdünn

waffle ['wɒfl] *n* Waffel *f*; (*Brit fam: empty talk*) Geschwafel *nt* ▷ *vi* (*Brit fam*) schwafeln

wag [wæg] *vt* (*tail*) wedeln mit

wage [weɪdʒ] *n* Lohn *m*

waggon (*Brit*), **wagon** ['wægən] *n* (*horse-drawn*) Fuhrwerk *nt*; (*Brit Rail*) Waggon *m*; (*US Auto*) Wagen *m*

waist [weɪst] *n* Taille *f*; **waistcoat** *n* (*Brit*) Weste *f*; **waistline** *n* Taille *f*

wait [weɪt] *n* Wartezeit *f* ▷ *vi* warten (*for* auf +*akk*); **to ~ and see** abwarten; **~ a minute** Moment mal!; **wait up** *vi* aufbleiben

waiter *n* Kellner *m*; **~!** Herr Ober!

waiting *n* 'no ~' „Halteverbot"; **waiting list** *n* Warteliste *f*; **waiting room** *n* (*Med*) Wartezimmer *nt*; (*Rail*) Wartesaal *m*

waitress *n* Kellnerin *f*

wake [weɪk] (**woke** o **waked**, **woken** o **waked**) *vt* wecken ▷ *vi* aufwachen; **wake up** *vt* aufwecken ▷ *vi* aufwachen; **wake-up call** *n* (*Tel*) Weckruf *m*

Wales ['weɪlz] *n* Wales *nt*

walk [wɔ:k] *n* Spaziergang *m*; (*ramble*) Wanderung *f*; (*route*) Weg *m*; **to go for a ~** spazieren gehen; **it's only a five-minute ~** es sind nur fünf Minuten zu Fuß ▷ *vi* gehen; (*stroll*) spazieren gehen; (*ramble*) wandern ▷ *vt* (*dog*) ausführen; **walking** *n* **to go ~** wandern; **walking shoes** *npl* Wanderschuhe *pl*; **walking stick** *n* Spazierstock *m*

Walkman®(*pl* **-s**) *n* Walkman® *m*

wall [wɔ:l] *n* (*inside*) Wand *f*; (*outside*) Mauer *f*

wallet ['wɒlɪt] *n* Brieftasche *f*

wallpaper ['wɔ:lpeɪpə*] *n* Tapete *f*; (*Inform*) Bildschirmhintergrund *m* ▷ *vt* tapezieren

walnut ['wɔ:lnʌt] *n* (*nut*) Walnuss *f*

waltz [wɔ:lts] *n* Walzer *m*

wander ['wɒndə*] *vi* (*person*) herumwandern

want [wɒnt] *n* (*lack*) Mangel *m* (*of* an +*dat*); (*need*) Bedürfnis *nt*; **for ~ of** aus Mangel an +*dat* ▷ *vt* (*desire*) wollen; (*need*) brauchen; **I ~ to stay here** ich will hier bleiben; **he doesn't ~ to** er will nicht

WAP phone ['wæpfəʊn] *n* WAP-Handy *nt*

war [wɔ:*] *n* Krieg *m*

ward [wɔ:d] *n* (*in hospital*) Station *f*; (*child*) Mündel *nt*

warden ['wɔ:dən] *n* Aufseher(in) *m(f)*; (*in youth hostel*) Herbergsvater *m*, Herbergsmutter *f*

wardrobe ['wɔ:drəʊb] *n* Kleiderschrank *m*

warehouse ['wɛəhaʊs] *n* Lagerhaus *nt*

warfare ['wɔ:fɛə*] *n* Krieg *m*; (*techniques*) Kriegsführung *f*

warm [wɔ:m] *adj* warm; (*welcome*) herzlich; **I'm ~** mir ist warm ▷ *vt* wärmen; (*food*) aufwärmen; **warm over** *vt* (*US: food*) aufwärmen; **warm up** *vt* (*food*) aufwärmen; (*room*) erwärmen ▷ *vi* (*food, room*) warm werden; (*Sport*) sich aufwärmen; **warmly** *adv* warm; (*welcome*) herzlich; **warmth** *n* Wärme *f*; (*of welcome*) Herzlichkeit *f*

warn [wɔ:n] *vt* warnen (*of, against* vor +*dat*); **to ~ sb not to do sth** jdn davor warnen, etw zu tun; **warning** *n* Warnung *f*; **warning light** *n* Warnlicht *nt*; **warning triangle** *n* (*Auto*) Warndreieck *nt*

warranty ['wɒrəntɪ] *n* Garantie *f*

wart [wɔ:t] *n* Warze *f*

wary ['wɛərɪ] adj vorsichtig; (*suspicious*) misstrauisch

was [wɒz, wəz] pt of **be**

wash [wɒʃ] n **to have a ~** sich waschen; **it's in the ~** es ist in der Wäsche ▷ vt waschen; (*plates, glasses etc*) abwaschen; **to ~ one's hands** sich dat die Hände waschen; **to ~ the dishes** (das Geschirr) abwaschen ▷ vi (*clean oneself*) sich waschen; **wash off** vt abwaschen; **wash up** vi (*Brit: wash dishes*) abwaschen; (*US: clean oneself*) sich waschen; **washable** adj waschbar; **washbag** n (US) Kulturbeutel m; **washbasin** n Waschbecken nt; **washcloth** n (US) Waschlappen m; **washer** n (*Tech*) Dichtungsring m; (*washing machine*) Waschmaschine f; **washing** n (*laundry*) Wäsche f; **washing machine** n Waschmaschine f; **washing powder** n Waschpulver nt; **washing-up** n (*Brit*) Abwasch m; **to do the ~** abwaschen; **washing-up liquid** n (*Brit*) Spülmittel nt; **washroom** n (US) Toilette f

wasn't ['wɒznt] contr of **was not**

wasp [wɒsp] n Wespe f

waste [weɪst] n (*materials*) Abfall m; (*wasting*) Verschwendung f; **it's a ~ of time** das ist Zeitverschwendung ▷ adj (*superfluous*) überschüssig ▷ vt verschwenden (*on* an +akk); (*opportunity*) vertun; **waste bin** n Abfalleimer m; **wastepaper basket** n Papierkorb m

watch [wɒtʃ] n (*timepiece*) (Armband)uhr f ▷ vt (*observe*) beobachten; (*guard*) aufpassen auf +akk; (*film, play, programme*) sich dat ansehen; **to ~ TV** fernsehen ▷ vi zusehen; (*guard*) Wache halten; **to ~ for sb/sth** nach jdm/etw Ausschau halten; **~ out** pass auf!; **watchdog** n Wachhund m; (*fig*) Aufsichtsbehörde f; **watchful** adj wachsam

water ['wɔːtə*] n Wasser nt; **~s** pl (*territory*) Gewässer pl ▷ vt (*plant*) gießen ▷ vi (*eye*) tränen; **my mouth is ~ing** mir läuft das Wasser im Mund zusammen; **water down** vt verdünnen; **watercolor** (US), **watercolour** n (*painting*) Aquarell nt; (*paint*) Wasserfarbe f; **watercress** n (Brunnen)kresse f; **waterfall** n Wasserfall m; **watering can** n Gießkanne f; **water level** n Wasserstand m; **watermelon** n Wassermelone f; **waterproof** adj

wasserdicht; **water-skiing** n Wasserskilaufen nt; **water sports** npl Wassersport m; **watertight** adj wasserdicht; **water wings** npl Schwimmflügel pl; **watery** adj wässerig

wave [weɪv] n Welle f ▷ vt (*move to and fro*) schwenken; (*hand, flag*) winken mit ▷ vi (*person*) winken; (*flag*) wehen; **wavelength** n Wellenlänge f; **to be on the same ~** (*fig*) die gleiche Wellenlänge haben; **wavy** ['weɪvɪ] adj wellig

wax [wæks] n Wachs nt; (*in ear*) Ohrenschmalz nt

way [weɪ] n Weg m; (*direction*) Richtung f; (*manner*) Art f; **can you tell me the ~ to ...?** wie komme ich (am besten) zu ... ?; **we went the wrong ~** wir sind in die falsche Richtung gefahren/gegangen; **to lose one's ~** sich verirren; **to make ~ for sb/sth** jdm/etw Platz machen; **to get one's own ~** seinen Willen durchsetzen; **'give ~'** (*Auto*) „Vorfahrt achten"; **the other ~ round** andersherum; **one ~ or another** irgendwie; **in a ~** in gewisser Weise; **in the ~** im Weg; **by the ~** übrigens; **'~ in'** „Eingang"; **'~ out'** „Ausgang"; **no ~** (*fam*) kommt nicht infrage!

we [wiː] pron wir

weak [wiːk] adj schwach; **weaken** vt schwächen ▷ vi schwächer werden

wealth [welθ] n Reichtum m; **wealthy** adj reich

weapon ['wepən] n Waffe f

wear [wɛə*] n (*wore, worn*) vt (*have on*) tragen; **what shall I ~?** was soll ich anziehen? ▷ vi (*become worn*) sich abnutzen ▷ n ~ **(and tear)** Abnutzung f; **wear off** vi (*diminish*) nachlassen; **wear out** vt abnutzen; (*person*) erschöpfen ▷ vi sich abnutzen

weary ['wɪərɪ] adj müde

weather ['weðə*] n Wetter nt; **I'm feeling under the ~** ich fühle mich nicht ganz wohl; **weather forecast** n Wettervorhersage f

weave [wiːv] (*wove* o *weaved*, *wóven* o *weaved*) vt (*cloth*) weben; (*basket etc*) flechten

web [web] n (*a. fig*) Netz nt; **the Web** das Web, das Internet; **webcam** ['webkæm] n Webcam f; **web page** n Webseite f; **website** n Website f

we'd [wi:d] *contr* of **we had; we would**
Wed *abbr* = **Wednesday** Mi.
wedding ['wedɪŋ] *n* Hochzeit *f*; **wedding
anniversary** *n* Hochzeitstag *m*; **wedding
dress** *n* Hochzeitskleid *nt*; **wedding ring**
n Ehering *m*
wedding shower *n* (US) Party für die
zukünftige Braut
wedge [wedʒ] *n* (under door etc) Keil *m*; (of
cheese etc) Stück *nt*, Ecke *f*
Wednesday ['wenzdeɪ] *n* Mittwoch *m*;
see also **Tuesday**
wee [wi:] *adj* klein ▷ *vi* (fam) Pipi
machen
weed [wi:d] *n* Unkraut *nt* ▷ *vt* jäten
week [wi:k] *n* Woche *f*; **twice a
~** zweimal in der Woche; **a ~ on
Friday/Friday ~** Freitag in einer Woche; **a
~ last Friday** letzten Freitag vor einer
Woche; **in two ~s' time, in two ~s** in zwei
Wochen; **for ~s** wochenlang; **weekday** *n*
Wochentag *m*; **weekend** *n* Wochenende
nt; **weekly** *adj, adv* wöchentlich;
(magazine) Wochen-
weep [wi:p] (**wept, wept**) *vi* weinen
weigh [weɪ] *vt, vi* wiegen; **it ~s 20 kilos** es
wiegt 20 Kilo; **weigh up** *vt* abwägen;
(person) einschätzen; **weight** [weɪt] *n*
Gewicht *nt*; **to lose/put on
~** abnehmen/zunehmen; **weightlifting** *n*
Gewichtheben *nt*; **weight training** *n*
Krafttraining *nt*; **weighty** *adj* (important)
schwer wiegend
weird [wɪəd] *adj* seltsam; **weirdo**
['wɪədəʊ] *n* Spinner(in) *m(f)*
welcome ['welkəm] *n* Empfang *m* ▷ *adj*
willkommen; (news) angenehm; **~ to
London** willkommen in London! ▷ *vt*
begrüßen; **welcoming** *adj* freundlich
welfare ['welfeə*] *n* Wohl *nt*; (US: social
security) Sozialhilfe *f*; **welfare state** *n*
Wohlfahrtsstaat *m*
well [wel] *n* Brunnen *m* ▷ *adj* (in good
health) gesund; **are you ~?** geht es dir gut?;
to feel ~ sich wohl fühlen; **get ~ soon**
gute Besserung! ▷ *interj* nun; **~, I don't
know** nun, ich weiß nicht ▷ *adv* gut;
~ done gut gemacht!; **it may ~ be** das
kann wohl sein; **as ~** (in addition) auch;
~ over 60 weit über 60
we'll [wi:l] *contr* of **we will; we shall**
well-behaved [welbɪ'heɪvd] *adj* brav;
well-being *n* Wohl *nt*; **well-built** *adj*

(person) gut gebaut; **well-done** *adj* (steak)
durchgebraten; **well-earned** *adj*
wohlverdient
wellingtons ['welɪŋtənz] *npl*
Gummistiefel *pl*
well-known [wel'nəʊn] *adj* bekannt;
well-off *adj* (wealthy) wohlhabend;
well-paid *adj* gut bezahlt
Welsh [welʃ] *adj* walisisch ▷ *n* (language)
Walisisch *nt*; **the ~** *pl* die Waliser *pl*;
Welshman (*pl* **-men**) *n* Waliser *m*;
Welshwoman (*pl* **-women**) *n* Waliserin *f*
went [went] *pt* of **go**
wept [wept] *pt, pp* of **weep**
were [wɜ:] *pt* of **be**
we're [wɪə*] *contr* of **we are**
weren't [wɜ:nt] *contr* of **were not**
west [west] *n* Westen *m*; **the West** (Pol)
der Westen ▷ *adv* (go, face) nach Westen
▷ *adj* West-; **westbound** *adj* (in)
Richtung Westen; **western** *adj*
West-, westlich; **Western Europe**
Westeuropa *nt* ▷ *n* (Cine) Western *m*;
West Germany *n* (the former) ~ (das
ehemalige) Westdeutschland,
Westdeutschland *n*; **westwards**
['westwədz] *adv* nach Westen
wet [wet] (**wet, wet**) *vt* **to ~ oneself** in die
Hose machen ▷ *adj* nass, feucht; '**~ paint**'
„frisch gestrichen"; **wet suit** *n*
Taucheranzug *m*
we've [wi:v] *contr* of **we have**
whale [weɪl] *n* Wal *m*
wharf [wɔ:f] (*pl* **-s** or **wharves**) *n* Kai *m*

◯ KEYWORD

what [wɒt] *adj* **1** (in questions) welche(r, s)
was für ein(e); **what size is it?** welche
Größe ist das?
2 (in exclamations) was für ein(e); **what a
mess!** was für ein Durcheinander!
▷ *pron* (interrogative/relative) was; **what
are you doing?** was machst du gerade?;
what are you talking about? wovon
reden Sie?; **what is it called?** wie heißt
das?; **what about ...?** wie wärs mit ...?; **I
saw what you did** ich habe gesehen, was
du gemacht hast
▷ *excl* (disbelieving) wie was; **what, no
coffee?** wie, kein Kaffee?; **I've crashed the
car — what!** ich hatte einen Autounfall —
was!

what's [wɒts] contr of **what is; what has**

wheat [wi:t] n Weizen m

wheel [wi:l] n Rad nt; (steering wheel) Lenkrad nt ⊳ vt (bicycle, trolley) schieben; **wheelbarrow** n Schubkarren m; **wheelchair** n Rollstuhl m; **wheel clamp** n Parkkralle f

 KEYWORD

when [wɛn] adv wann ⊳ conj **1** (at, during, after the time that) wenn; (in past) als; **she was reading when I came in** sie las, als ich hereinkam; **be careful when you cross the road** seien Sie vorsichtig, wenn Sie über die Straße gehen
2 (on, at which) als; **on the day when I met him** an dem Tag, an dem ich ihn traf
3 (whereas) wo ... doch

where [wɛə*] adv wo; **~ are you going?** wohin gehst du?; **~ are you from?** woher kommst du? ⊳ conj wo; **that's ~ I used to live** da habe ich früher gewohnt; **whereabouts** [wɛərə'baʊts] adv wo ⊳ npl ['wɛərəbaʊts] Aufenthaltsort m; **whereas** [wɛər'æz] conj während, wohingegen; **whereby** adv wodurch; **wherever** [wɛər'ɛvə*] conj wo immer; **~ that may be** wo immer das sein mag; **~ I go** überall, wohin ich gehe
whether ['wɛðə*] conj ob

 KEYWORD

which [wɪtʃ] adj **1** (interrogative: direct, indirect) welche(r, s); **which one?** welche(r, s)?
2: in which case in diesem Fall; **by which time** zu dieser Zeit
⊳ pron **1** (interrogative) welche(r, s); (of people also) wer
2 (relative) der/die/das (referring to people) was; **the apple which you ate/which is on the table** der Apfel, den du gegessen hast/der auf dem Tisch liegt; **he said he saw her, which is true** er sagte, er habe sie gesehen, was auch stimmt

while [waɪl] n **a ~** eine Weile; **for a ~** eine Zeit lang; **a short ~ ago** vor kurzem ⊳ conj während; (although) obwohl

whine [waɪn] vi (person) jammern

whip [wɪp] n Peitsche f ⊳ vt (beat) peitschen; **~ped cream** Schlagsahne f

whirl [wɜːl] vt, vi herumwirbeln; **whirlpool** n (in river, sea) Strudel m; (pool) Whirlpool m

whisk [wɪsk] n Schneebesen m ⊳ vt (cream etc) schlagen

whisker ['wɪskə*] n (of animal) Schnurrhaar nt; **~s** pl (of man) Backenbart m

whisk(e)y ['wɪskɪ] n Whisky m

whisper ['wɪspə*] vi, vt flüstern; **to ~ sth to sb** jdm etw zuflüstern

whistle ['wɪsl] n Pfiff m; (instrument) Pfeife f ⊳ vt, vi pfeifen

white [waɪt] n (of egg) Eiweiß nt; (of eye) Weiße nt ⊳ adj weiß; (with fear) blass; (coffee) mit Milch; **White House** n the **~** das Weiße Haus; **white lie** n Notlüge f; **white meat** n helles Fleisch; **white sauce** n weiße Soße; **white water rafting** n Rafting nt; **white wine** n Weißwein m

Whitsun ['wɪtsn] n Pfingsten nt

 KEYWORD

who [huː] pron **1** (interrogative) wer; (acc) wen; (dat) wem; **who is it?, who's there?** wer ist da?
2 (relative) der/die/das; **the woman/man who spoke to me** die Frau/der Mann, die/der mit mir sprach

whole [həʊl] adj ganz ⊳ n Ganze(s) nt; **the ~ of my family** meine ganze Familie; **on the ~** im Großen und Ganzen; **wholefood** n (Brit) Vollwertkost f; **wholeheartedly** adv voll und ganz; **wholemeal** adj (Brit) Vollkorn-; **wholesale** adv (buy, sell) im Großhandel; **wholesome** adj gesund; **wholewheat** adj Vollkorn-; **wholly** ['həʊlɪ] adv völlig

 KEYWORD

whom [huːm] pron **1** (interrogative: acc) wen; (: dat) wem; **whom did you see?** wen haben Sie gesehen?; **to whom did you give it?** wem haben Sie es gegeben?
2 (relative: acc) den/die/das; (: dat) dem/der/dem; **the man whom I saw/to**

whom I spoke der Mann, den ich sah/mit dem ich sprach

whooping cough ['huːpɪŋkɒf] n Keuchhusten m

whose [huːz] adj (in questions) wessen; (in relative clauses) dessen/deren/dessen, deren pl; **~ bike is that?** wessen Fahrrad ist das? ▷ pron (in questions) wessen; **~ is this?** wem gehört das?

○ KEYWORD

why [waɪ] adv warum weshalb
▷ conj warum weshalb; **that's not why I'm here** ich bin nicht deswegen hier; **that's the reason why** deshalb
▷ excl (expressing surprise, shock) na so was (explaining) also dann; **why, it's you!** na so was, du bist es!

wicked ['wɪkɪd] adj böse; (fam: great) geil
wide [waɪd] adj breit; (skirt, trousers) weit; (selection) groß ▷ adv weit; **wide-angle lens** n Weitwinkelobjektiv nt; **wide-awake** adj hellwach; **widely** adv weit; **~ known** allgemein bekannt; **widen** vt verbreitern; (fig) erweitern; **wide-open** adj weit offen; **widescreen TV** n Breitbildfernseher m; **widespread** adj weit verbreitet
widow ['wɪdəʊ] n Witwe f; **widowed** adj verwitwet; **widower** n Witwer m
width [wɪdθ] n Breite f
wife [waɪf] (pl **wives**) n (Ehe)frau f
wig [wɪg] n Perücke f
wiggle ['wɪgl] vt wackeln mit
wild [waɪld] adj wild; (violent) heftig; (plan, idea) verrückt ▷ n **in the ~** in freier Wildbahn; **wildlife** n Tier- und Pflanzenwelt f; **wildly** adv wild; (enthusiastic, exaggerated) maßlos

○ KEYWORD

will [wɪl] aux vb **1** (forms future tense) werden; **I will finish it tomorrow** ich mache es morgen zu Ende
2 (in conjectures, predictions): **he will or he'll be there by now** er dürfte jetzt da sein; **that will be the postman** das wird der Postbote sein
3 (in commands, requests, offers): **will you be**

quiet! sei endlich still!; **will you help me?** hilfst du mir?; **will you have a cup of tea?** trinken Sie eine Tasse Tee?; **I won't put up with it!** das lasse ich mir nicht gefallen!
▷ vt wollen
▷ n Wille m (Jur) Téstament nt

willow ['wɪləʊ] n Weide f
willpower ['wɪlpaʊə*] n Willenskraft f
wimp [wɪmp] n Weichei nt
win [wɪn] (**won, won**) vt, vi gewinnen ▷ n Sieg m; **win over, win round** vt für sich gewinnen
wind [waɪnd] (**wound, wound**) vt (rope, bandage) wickeln; **wind down** vt (car window) herunterkurbeln; **wind up** vt (clock) aufziehen; (car window) hochkurbeln; (meeting, speech) abschließen; (person) aufziehen, ärgern
wind [wɪnd] n Wind m; (Med) Blähungen pl
wind instrument ['wɪndɪnstrəmənt] n Blasinstrument nt; **windmill** n Windmühle f
window ['wɪndəʊ] n Fenster nt; (counter) Schalter m; **window box** n Blumenkasten m; **windowpane** n Fensterscheibe f; **window-shopping** n **to go ~** einen Schaufensterbummel machen; **windowsill** n Fensterbrett nt
windpipe ['wɪndpaɪp] n Luftröhre f; **windscreen** n (Brit) Windschutzscheibe f; **windscreen wiper** n (Brit) Scheibenwischer m; **windshield** n (US) Windschutzscheibe f; **windshield wiper** n (US) Scheibenwischer m; **windsurfer** n Windsurfer(in) m(f); (board) Surfbrett nt; **windsurfing** n Windsurfen nt
windy ['wɪndɪ] adj windig
wine [waɪn] n Wein m; **wine bar** n Weinlokal nt; **wineglass** n Weinglas nt; **wine list** n Weinkarte f; **wine tasting** n (event) Weinprobe f
wing [wɪŋ] n Flügel m; (Brit Auto) Kotflügel m; **~s** pl (Theat) Kulissen pl
wink [wɪŋk] vi zwinkern; **to ~ at sb** jdm zuzwinkern
winner ['wɪnə*] n Gewinner(in) m(f); (Sport) Sieger(in) m(f); **winning** adj (team, horse etc) siegreich; **~ number** Gewinnzahl f ▷ n **~s** pl Gewinn m
winter ['wɪntə*] n Winter m; **winter sports** npl Wintersport m; **wint(e)ry** ['wɪntrɪ] adj winterlich

wipe [waɪp] vt abwischen; **to ~ one's nose** sich dat die Nase putzen; **to ~ one's feet** (on mat) sich dat die Schuhe abtreten; **wipe off** vt abwischen; **wipe out** vt (destroy) vernichten; (data, debt) löschen; (epidemic etc) ausrotten

wire ['waɪə*] n Draht m; (Elec) Leitung f; (US: telegram) Telegramm nt ▷ vt (plug in) anschließen; (US Tel) telegrafieren (sb sth jdm etw); **wireless** ['waɪələs] adj drahtlos

wisdom ['wɪzdəm] n Weisheit f; **wisdom tooth** n Weisheitszahn m

wise, wisely [waɪz, -lɪ] adj, adv weise

wish [wɪʃ] n Wunsch m (for nach); **with best ~es** (in letter) herzliche Grüße ▷ vt wünschen, wollen; **to ~ sb good luck/Merry Christmas** jdm viel Glück/frohe Weihnachten wünschen; **I ~ I'd never seen him** ich wünschte, ich hätte ihn nie gesehen

witch [wɪtʃ] n Hexe f

🔵 **KEYWORD**

with [wɪð, wɪθ] prep **1** (accompanying, in the company of) mit; **we stayed with friends** wir übernachteten bei Freunden; **I'll be with you in a minute** einen Augenblick ich bin sofort da; **I'm not with you** (I don't understand) das verstehe ich nicht; **to be with it** (inf) (up-to-date) auf dem Laufenden sein (ooo) (alert) (voll) da sein inf
2 (descriptive, indicating manner etc) mit; **the man with the grey hat** der Mann mit dem grauen Hut; **red with anger** rot vor Wut

withdraw [wɪð'drɔ:] irr vt zurückziehen; (money) abheben; (comment) zurücknehmen ▷ vi sich zurückziehen

wither ['wɪðə*] vi (plant) verwelken

withhold [wɪð'həʊld] irr vt vorenthalten (from sb jdm)

within [wɪð'ɪn] prep innerhalb +gen; **~ walking distance** zu Fuß erreichbar

without [wɪð'aʊt] prep ohne; **~ asking** ohne zu fragen

withstand [wɪð'stænd] irr vt standhalten +dat

witness ['wɪtnəs] n Zeuge m, Zeugin f ▷ vt Zeuge sein; **witness box, witness stand** (US) n Zeugenstand m

witty ['wɪtɪ] adj geistreich

wives [waɪvz] pl of **wife**

wobble ['wɒbl] vi wackeln; **wobbly** adj wackelig

wok [wɒk] n Wok m

woke [wəʊk] pt of **wake**

woken ['wəʊkn] pp of **wake**

wolf [wʊlf] (pl **wolves**) n Wolf m

woman ['wʊmən] (pl **women**) n Frau f

womb [wu:m] n Gebärmutter f

women ['wɪmɪn] pl of **woman**

won [wʌn] pt, pp of **win**

wonder ['wʌndə*] n (marvel) Wunder nt; (surprise) Staunen nt ▷ vi, vi (speculate) sich fragen; **I ~ what/if ...** ich frage mich, was/ob ...; **wonderful, wonderfully** adj, adv wunderbar

won't [wəʊnt] contr of **will not**

wood [wʊd] n Holz nt; **~s** Wald m; **wooden** adj Holz-; (fig) hölzern; **woodpecker** n Specht m; **woodwork** n (wooden parts) Holzteile pl; (in school) Werken nt

wool [wʊl] n Wolle f; **woollen, woolen** (US) adj Woll-

word [wɜ:d] n Wort nt; (promise) Ehrenwort nt; **~s** pl (of song) Text m; **to have a ~ with sb** mit jdm sprechen; **in other ~s** mit anderen Worten ▷ vt formulieren; **wording** n Wortlaut m, Formulierung f; **word processing** n Textverarbeitung f; **word processor** n (program) Textverarbeitungsprogramm nt

wore [wɔ:*] pt of **wear**

work [wɜ:k] n Arbeit f; (of art, literature) Werk nt; **~ of art** Kunstwerk nt; **he's at ~** er ist in/auf der Arbeit; **out of ~** arbeitslos ▷ vi arbeiten (at, on an +dat); (machine, plan) funktionieren; (medicine) wirken; (succeed) klappen ▷ vt (machine) bedienen; **work out** vi (plan) klappen; (sum) aufgehen; (person) trainieren ▷ vt (price, speed etc) ausrechnen; (plan) ausarbeiten; **work up** vt **to get worked up** sich aufregen; **workaholic** [wɜ:kə'hɒlɪk] n Arbeitstier nt; **worker** n Arbeiter(in) m(f); **working class** n Arbeiterklasse f; **workman** (pl **-men**) n Handwerker m; **workout** n (Sport) Fitnesstraining nt, Konditionstraining nt; **work permit** n Arbeitserlaubnis f; **workplace** n Arbeitsplatz m; **workshop** n Werkstatt f; (meeting) Workshop m;

work station n (*Inform*) Workstation f
world [wɜːld] n Welt f; **world championship** n Weltmeisterschaft f; **World War** n ~ I/II, the First/Second ~ der Erste/Zweite Weltkrieg; **world-wide** adj, adv weltweit; **World Wide Web** n World Wide Web nt
worm [wɜːm] n Wurm m
worn [wɔːn] pp of **wear** ▷ adj (*clothes*) abgetragen; (*tyre*) abgefahren; **worn-out** adj abgenutzt; (*person*) erschöpft
worried ['wʌrɪd] adj besorgt; **be ~ about** sich dat Sorgen machen um; **worry** ['wʌrɪ] n Sorge f ▷ vt Sorgen machen +dat ▷ vi sich Sorgen machen (*about* um); **don't ~** keine Sorge!; **worrying** adj beunruhigend
worse [wɜːs] adj comparative of **bad**; schlechter; (*pain, mistake etc*) schlimmer ▷ adv comparative of **badly**; schlechter; **worsen** vt verschlechtern ▷ vi sich verschlechtern
worship ['wɜːʃɪp] vt anbeten, anhimmeln
worst [wɜːst] adj superlative of **bad**; schlechteste(r, s); (*pain, mistake etc*) schlimmste(r, s) ▷ adv superlative of **badly**; am schlechtesten ▷ n **the ~ is over** das Schlimmste ist vorbei; **at (the) ~** schlimmstenfalls
worth [wɜːθ] n Wert m; £10 ~ **of food** Essen für 10 Pfund ▷ adj **it is ~ £50** es ist 50 Pfund wert; **~ seeing** sehenswert; **it's ~ it** (*rewarding*) es lohnt sich; **worthless** adj wertlos; **worthwhile** adj lohnend, lohnenswert; **worthy** ['wɜːðɪ] adj (*deserving respect*) würdig; **to be ~ of sth** etw verdienen

⊙ KEYWORD

would [wʊd] aux vb **1** (*conditional tense*): **if you asked him he would do it** wenn du ihn fragtest, würde er es tun; **if you had asked him he would have done it** wenn du ihn gefragt hättest, hätte er es getan
2 (*in offers, invitations, requests*): **would you like a biscuit?** möchten Sie ein Plätzchen?; **would you ask him to come in?** würden Sie ihn bitte hineinbitten?
3 (*in indirect speech*): **I said I would do it** ich sagte, ich würde es tun
4 (*emphatic*): **it WOULD have to snow**

today! es musste ja ausgerechnet heute schneien!
5 (*insistence*): **she wouldn't behave** sie wollte sich partout nicht anständig benehmen
6 (*conjecture*): **it would have been midnight** es mag ungefähr Mitternacht gewesen sein; **it would seem so** es sieht wohl so aus
7 (*indicating habit*): **he would go there on Mondays** er ging jeden Montag dorthin

wouldn't ['wʊdnt] contr of **would not**
would've ['wʊdəv] contr of **would have**
wound [wuːnd] n Wunde f ▷ vt verwunden; (*fig*) verletzen ▷ [waʊnd] pt, pp of **wind**
wove [wəʊv] pt of **weave**
woven ['wəʊvn] pp of **weave**
wrap [ræp] vt (*parcel, present*) einwickeln; **to ~ sth round sth** etw um etw wickeln; **wrap up** vt (*parcel, present*) einwickeln ▷ vi (*dress warmly*) sich warm anziehen; **wrapper** n (*of sweet*) Papier nt; **wrapping paper** n Packpapier nt; (*giftwrap*) Geschenkpapier nt
wreath [riːθ] n Kranz m
wreck [rek] n (*ship, plane, car*) Wrack nt; **a nervous ~** ein Nervenbündel m ▷ vt (*car*) zu Schrott fahren; (*fig*) zerstören; **wreckage** ['rekɪdʒ] n Trümmer pl
wrench [rentʃ] n (*tool*) Schraubenschlüssel m
wrestling ['reslɪŋ] n Ringen nt
wring out ['rɪŋ'aʊt] (**wrung, wrung**) vt auswringen
wrinkle ['rɪŋkl] n Falte f
wrist [rɪst] n Handgelenk nt; **wristwatch** n Armbanduhr f
write [raɪt] (**wrote, written**) vt schreiben; (*cheque*) ausstellen ▷ vi schreiben; **to ~ to sb** jdm schreiben; **write down** vt aufschreiben; **write off** vt (*debt, person*) abschreiben; (*car*) zu Schrott fahren ▷ vi **to ~ off for sth** etw anfordern; **write out** vt (*name etc*) ausschreiben; (*cheque*) ausstellen; **write-protected** adj (*Inform*) schreibgeschützt; **writer** n Verfasser(in) m(f); (*author*) Schriftsteller(in) m(f); **writing** n Schrift f; (*profession*) Schreiben nt; **writing paper** n Schreibpapier nt
written ['rɪtən] pp of **write**

wrong [rɒŋ] *adj* (*incorrect*) falsch; (*morally*)
unrecht; **you're ~** du hast Unrecht;
what's ~ with your leg? was ist mit
deinem Bein los?; **you've got the
~ number** Sie sind falsch verbunden; **I
dialled the ~ number** ich habe mich
verwählt; **don't get me ~** versteh mich
nicht falsch; **to go ~** (*plan*) schief gehen;
wrongly *adv* falsch; (*unjustly*) zu Unrecht
wrote [rəʊt] *pt of* **write**
WWW *abbr* = **World Wide Web** WWW

xenophobia [zenəˈfəʊbɪə] *n*
 Ausländerfeindlichkeit *f*
XL *abbr* = **extra large** XL, übergroß
Xmas [ˈeksməs] *n* Weihnachten *nt*
X-ray [ˈeksreɪ] *n* (*picture*)
 Röntgenaufnahme *f* ▷ *vt* röntgen
xylophone [ˈzaɪləfəʊn] *n* Xylophon *nt*

yacht [jɒt] *n* Jacht *f*; **yachting** *n* Segeln *nt*, **to go ~** segeln gehen

yard [jɑːd] *n* Hof *m*; (US: *garden*) Garten *m*; (*measure*) Yard *nt* (0,91 m)

yawn [jɔːn] *vi* gähnen

yd *abbr* = **yard(s)**

year [jɪə*] *n* Jahr *nt*; **this/last/next ~** dieses/letztes/nächstes Jahr; **he is 28 ~s old** er ist 28 Jahre alt; **~s ago** vor Jahren; **a five-year-old** ein(e) Fünfjährige(r); **yearly** *adj, adv* jährlich

yearn [jɜːn] *vi* sich sehnen (*for* nach +*dat*); **to ~ to do sth** sich danach sehnen, etw zu tun

yeast [jiːst] *n* Hefe *f*

yell [jel] *vi, vt* schreien; **to ~ at sb** jdn anschreien

yellow ['jeləʊ] *adj* gelb; **~ card** (*Sport*) gelbe Karte; **~ fever** Gelbfieber *nt*; **~ line** (*Brit*) = Halteverbot *nt*; **double ~ line** (*Brit*) = absolutes Halteverbot; **the Yellow Pages®** *pl* die Gelben Seiten *pl*

yes [jes] *adv* ja; (*answering negative question*) doch; **to say ~ to sth** ja zu etw sagen ▷ *n* Ja *nt*

yesterday ['jestədeɪ] *adv* gestern; **~ morning/evening** gestern Morgen/

Abend; **the day before ~** vorgestern; **~'s newspaper** die Zeitung von gestern

yet [jet] *adv* (*still*) noch; (*up to now*) bis jetzt; (*in a question: already*) schon; **he hasn't arrived ~** er ist noch nicht gekommen; **have you finished ~?** bist du schon fertig?; **~ again** schon wieder; **as ~** bis jetzt ▷ *conj* doch

yield [jiːld] *n* Ertrag *m* ▷ *vt* (*result, crop*) hervorbringen; (*profit, interest*) bringen ▷ *vi* nachgeben (*to* +*dat*); (*Mil*) sich ergeben (*to* +*dat*); '**~**' (US *Auto*) „Vorfahrt beachten"

yoga ['jəʊɡə] *n* Joga *nt*

yog(h)urt [jɒɡət] *n* Jog(h)urt *m*

yolk [jəʊk] *n* Eigelb *nt*

Yorkshire pudding ['jɔːkʃə'pʊdɪŋ] *n* gebackener Eierteig, der meist zum Roastbeef gegessen wird

 KEYWORD

you [juː] *pron* **1** (*subj, in comparisons: familiar form: sg*) du; (: *pl*) ihr; (*in letters also*) du ihr; (: *polite form*) Sie; **you Germans** ihr Deutschen; **she's younger than you** sie ist jünger als du/Sie

2 (*direct object, after prep +acc: familiar form: sg*) dich; (: *pl*) euch; (*in letters also*) dich euch; (: *polite form*) Sie; **I know you** ich kenne dich/euch/Sie

3 (*indirect object, after prep +dat: familiar form*) (*sg*) dir; (: *pl*) euch; (*in letters also*) dir euch; (: *polite form*) Ihnen; **I gave it to you** ich gab es dir/euch/Ihnen

4 (*impers: one: subj*) man; (: *direct object*) einen; (*indirect object*) einem; **fresh air does you good** frische Luft tut gut

you'd [juːd] *contr of* **you had**; **you would**; **~ better leave** du solltest gehen

you'll [juːl] *contr of* **you will**; **you shall**

young [jʌŋ] *adj* jung ▷ *n* **the ~** *pl* (*~ people*) die jungen Leute *pl*; (*animals*) die Jungen *pl*; **youngster** ['jʌŋstə*] *n* Jugendliche(r) *mf*

your [jɔː*] *adj sing* dein; *polite form* Ihr; *pl* euer; *polite form* Ihr; **have you hurt ~ leg?** hast du dir das Bein verletzt?

you're ['jʊə*] *contr of* **you are**

yours ['jɔːz] *pron sing* deine(r, s); *polite form* Ihre(r, s); *pl* eure(r, s); *polite form* Ihre(r, s); **is this ~?** gehört das dir/Ihnen?; **a**